The Official
SCRABBLE®
Players
Dictionary

ISBN 0-877779-030-1

The name SCRABBLE and the depiction of the game board are registered trademarks of Selchow & Righter Company. Used by permission of trademark owners.

SCRABBLE is a registered trademark of Selchow & Righter Company. Used only to identify the SCRABBLE Brand word game.

All rights reserved. No part of this work covered by the copyright hereon may be reproduced or copied in any form or by any means—graphic, electronic, or mechanical, including photocopying, recording, taping, or information and retrieval systems—without written permission of the publisher.

Made in the United States of America

01PR:SCRABBLE18

MERRIAM-WEBSTER INC., Publishers
SPRINGFIELD, MASSACHUSETTS

Milton Bradley Company
443 Shaker Road
East Longmeadow, MA 01028

The Official SCRABBLE® Players Dictionary
has been endorsed by the
National SCRABBLE® Association.

For information on SCRABBLE® clubs, tournaments, publications and
other activities, contact:

National SCRABBLE® Association
c/o Williams & Company
Box 700
Greenport, NY 11944
(516) 477-0033

PREFACE ● This dictionary has been prepared especially for lovers of SCRABBLE® Brand crossword games and for the National SCRABBLE® Association. It is the voice of authority and is the dictionary of first reference for all official National SCRABBLE® Association crossword game tournaments.

It is important to remember that The Official SCRABBLE® Players Dictionary was edited solely with this limited purpose in mind. It is not intended to serve as a general dictionary of English; thus, such important features of general dictionaries as definitions of multiple senses, pronunciation respellings, etymologies, and usage labels are omitted.

The plan of the dictionary and the policies that governed its editing were developed under the direction of the National SCRABBLE® Association. The finished manuscript was prepared for the typesetter and the dictionary was seen into print by members of the Editorial Department of Merriam-Webster Inc. under the supervision of James G. Lowe, Senior Editor.

The detailed organization and special features of the dictionary are explained in the Introduction which immediately follows. It should be read with care by all who use the dictionary. Now that this work is available, we are confident that it will afford satisfaction and enjoyment to SCRABBLE® Brand crossword game players everywhere.

National SCRABBLE® Association

NTRODUCTION ● **MAIN ENTRIES** ● Main entries are
listed in boldface type and are set flush with the left-hand margin of
each column. Except for an occasional cross-reference (such as
GUNFOUGHT past tense of gunfight), main entries contain from two to
eight letters since words within this range are considered to be most
useful to SCRABBLE® crossword game players. Only words that are
permissible in SCRABBLE® crossword games are included in this
dictionary. Thus, proper names, words requiring hyphens or
apostrophes, words considered foreign, and abbreviations have been
omitted. Because dictionaries have different standards for selecting
entries, several current desk dictionaries were consulted in preparing
the list of main entries for this book in order to insure a wider range of
entries than any single dictionary of that kind offers. Words that
exceed eight letters in length and are not inflected forms of words
entered in this dictionary should be looked up in a desk dictionary
such as Webster's Ninth New Collegiate Dictionary. No attempt was made to
omit obsolete, archaic, slang, or nonstandard words since they are
permitted by the rules of the game. All variant forms of a main entry
are shown at their own alphabetical places and defined in terms of the
principal form.

RUN-ON ENTRIES ● A main entry may be followed by one or
more derivatives in boldface type with a different part-of-speech label.
These are run-on entries. Run-on entries are not defined since their
meanings are readily derivable from the meaning of the root word.

JOYOUS	*adj* joyful **JOYOUSLY** *adv*
KNOW	*v* KNEW, KNOWN, KNOWING, KNOWS to have a true understanding of **KNOWABLE** *adj*

No entry has been run on at another if it would fall alphabetically
more than two places from the entry. **When you do not find a word at
its own place, it is always wise to check several entries above and
below to see if it is run on.**

CROSS-REFERENCES ● A cross-reference is a main entry that
is an inflected form (such as the plural form of a noun, the past tense
form of a verb, or the comparative form of an adjective) of another
word. An inflected form is entered as a main entry only if it undergoes
a spelling change in addition to or instead of suffixation *and* if it falls
alphabetically three or more places away from the root word.

For example, in the entries reproduced below **GAGGED** is a main
entry because it involves a spelling change (the final *-g* of *gag* is
doubled) besides the addition of the *-ed* ending and because it falls

alphabetically three or more places away from the entry **GAG**. On the other hand, *gags* is not a main entry because it involves no spelling change beyond the addition of the ending -*s*. Equally, while **GAGING** is a main entry, *gaged* is not, because, even though it involves a spelling change (the final -*e* of *gage* is dropped) beyond the addition of the -*ed* ending, it would not fall three or more places from **GAGE**.

GAG	*v* GAGGED, GAGGING, GAGS to stop up the mouth
GAGA	*adj* crazy
GAGE	*v* GAGED, GAGING, GAGES to pledge as security
GAGER	*n pl.* -S gauger
GAGGED	past tense of gag
GAGGER	*n pl.* -S one that gags
GAGGING	present participle of gag
GAGGLE	*v* -GLED, -GLING, -GLES to cackle
GAGING	present participle of gage

This policy is intended to make the word desired as easy to find as possible without wasting space. Nevertheless, many inflected forms will appear only at the main entry.

Users of the book should always look at several entries above and below the expected place if they do not find the desired word as a main entry.

Cross-reference entries for present tense third person singular forms of verbs use the abbreviation "sing."

PARTS OF SPEECH ● An italic label indicating a part of speech follows each main entry except cross-references (such as **JOLLIED, JOLLIER, JOLLIES, JOLLIEST**), for which the label is given at the root word. The eight traditional parts of speech are indicated as follows:

n	noun	*pron*	pronoun
v	verb	*prep*	preposition
adj	adjective	*conj*	conjunction
adv	adverb	*interj*	interjection

The label *n/ pl* is given to two kinds of nouns. One is the plural noun that has no singular form.

VIBES   *n/pl* a percussion instrument

The other is the plural noun of which the singular is not entered in this dictionary. Singular forms are omitted if they contain more than eight letters.

ROSTELLA   *n/pl* small, beaklike structures

Rostellum, the singular form, has nine letters and is not entered.

When a word can be used as more than one part of speech, each part of speech is entered separately if the inflected forms are not spelled alike. For example, both the adjective *lazy* and the verb *lazy* are entered because the inflected forms vary.

LAZY   *adj* LAZIER, LAZIEST disinclined to work or exertion

LAZY   *v* LAZIED, LAZYING, LAZIES to move or lie lazily

On the other hand, the verb *suit* is entered while the noun *suit* is not because the inflected form *suits* at the verb is spelled the same as the plural form of the noun. In a dictionary for SCRABBLE® crossword game players, entry of the noun is therefore redundant. Homographs (words spelled alike) which may be used as the same part of speech are treated in the same way. For example, *lepton* is entered as a noun twice because the plurals are spelled differently.

LEPTON   *n* pl. -TA a monetary unit of Greece

LEP   *n* pl. -S an atomic particle . . .

If both plurals were spelled alike, only one *lepton* would be entered in this dictionary. In this way the dictionary includes as many different spellings as possible yet avoids wasting space with repeated entry of words spelled in the same way. The SCRABBLE® crossword game player, after all, needs only one entry to justify his play.

INFLECTED FORMS ●
Inflected forms include the past tense, past participle, present participle, and present tense third person singular of verbs, the plural of nouns, and the comparative and superlative of adjectives and adverbs. They are shown in capital letters immediately following the part-of-speech label. Irregular inflected forms are listed as main entries when they fall three or more alphabetical places away from the root word (see **Cross-References** above). All inflected forms are allowable as entries in SCRABBLE® crossword games.

The principal parts of the majority of verbs are shown as -ED, -ING, -S (or -ES when applicable). This indicates that the past tense and past participle are formed simply by adding -ed to the entry word, that the present participle is formed simply by adding -ing to the entry word, and that the present third person singular is formed simply by adding -s (or -es) to the entry word.

TALK   *v* -ED, -ING, -S to communicate by speaking

When inflection of an entry word involves any spelling change in addition to the suffixal ending (such as the dropping of a final -*e*, the doubling of a final consonant, or the changing of a final -*y* to -*i*-) or when the inflection is irregular, the inflected forms given indicate such changes.

WASTE	*v* WASTED, WASTING, WASTES to use thoughtlessly
DIM	*v* DIMMED, DIMMING, DIMS to make dim
TRY	*v* TRIED, TRYING, TRIES to attempt
RISE	*v* ROSE, RISEN, RISING, RISES to move upward

For verbs of more than one syllable either the last syllable or the last two syllables are shown.

ABDICATE	*v* -CATED, -CATING, -CATES to give up formally
BEGIN	*v* -GAN, -GUN, -GINNING, -GINS to start

The plurals of nouns are preceded by the abbreviation "pl." Most plurals are shown as -S (or -ES when applicable) to indicate that the plural is formed simply by adding the given suffix to the entry word.

VINTNER	*n* pl. -S a wine merchant

When pluralizing a noun involves any spelling change in addition to the suffixal ending (such as the changing of a final -*y* to -*i*- or a final -*f* to -*v*-) or when the plural is irregular, the plural form shown indicates such change.

BEVY	*n* pl. BEVIES a group
LEAF	*n* pl. LEAVES a usually green, flattened organ of vascular plants
CHILD	*n* pl. CHILDREN a young person

In such cases involving polysyllabic nouns at least the last syllable is shown.

SUDATORY	*n* pl. -RIES a hot-air bath for inducing sweating

For the sake of clarity, two groups of nouns that are confusing to many, those ending in -*o* and those ending in -*y*, are always indicated in this dictionary by showing at least the last syllable, even though no spelling change is involved.

RONDO	*n* pl. -DOS a type of musical composition
SAWNEY	*n* pl. -NEYS a foolish person

Variant plurals are shown wherever they add another word permissible in SCRABBLE® crossword games.

GLOSSA   *n* pl. -SAE or -SAS the tongue

Plurals which have the same form as the singular are shown only when they are the only plural for that entry. This is done to show that for the entry in question it is not permissible to add -*s* (or -*es*) to the singular to create a plural.

HAIKU   *n* pl. HAIKU a Japanese poem
CALENDS   *n* pl. CALENDS the first day of
the Roman month

Otherwise, they are omitted and only the plural with the inflection is shown.

DEER   *n* pl. -S a ruminant mammal

The comparative and superlative forms of adjectives and adverbs are shown, when applicable, immediately following the part-of-speech label. Any spelling changes are indicated in the forms shown.

WEAK   *adj* WEAKER, WEAKEST lacking
strength
OFTEN   *adv* -ENER, -ENEST frequently
BALKY   *adj* BALKIER, BALKIEST
stubborn . . .

Not all adjectives or adverbs can be inflected, and only those inflected forms shown are acceptable. None of the adjectives and adverbs listed as run-on entries in this dictionary have inflected forms.

DEFINITIONS ● In most cases, only one very brief definition is given for each main entry since definitions do not play a significant role in the SCRABBLE® crossword game. This definition serves only to orient the player in a general way to a single meaning of the word. It is not intended to have all the precision and detail of a definition in a good general dictionary.

When a word consisting of eight letters or less appears in a definition but is not an entry in this dictionary, it is glossed in parentheses. For example, at the entry for the verb *bomb*, the noun "bombs" is used in the definition and is glossed because the noun *bomb* is not a separate entry.

BOMB   *v* -ED, -ING, -S to attack with
bombs (explosive projectiles)

A main entry that is a variant form of another entry is defined in terms of the most common form, which is entered and defined at its own alphabetical place.

AMPOULE   *n* pl. -S ampule
AMPUL   *n* pl. -S ampule
AMPULE   *n* pl. -S a small glass vial

SCRABBLE® crossword game players in Canada will be pleased to learn that variant forms such as *honour, centre,* and *cheque,* which are often omitted from general dictionaries, have also been included in this book.

LISTS OF UNDEFINED WORDS   ●   Lists of undefined words

appear after the entries of the prefixes **RE-** and **UN-**. These words are not defined because they are self-explanatory: their meanings are simply the sum of a meaning of the prefix combined with a meaning of the root word. All of their inflected forms are given, however.

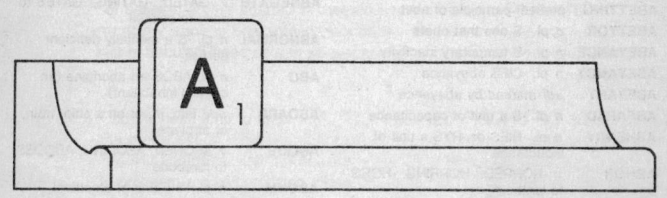

AA	*n* pl. -S rough, cindery lava	**ABATTIS**	*n* pl. -TISES abatis
AAH	*v* -ED, -ING, -S to exclaim in amazement, joy, or surprise	**ABATTOIR**	*n* pl. -S a slaughterhouse
AAL	*n* pl. -S an East Indian shrub	**ABAXIAL**	*adj* situated away from the axis
AALII	*n* pl. -S a tropical tree	**ABAXILE**	*adj* abaxial
AARDVARK	*n* pl. -S an African mammal	**ABBACY**	*n* pl. -CIES the office of an abbot
AARDWOLF	*n* pl. -WOLVES an African mammal	**ABBATIAL**	*adj* pertaining to an abbot
AASVOGEL	*n* pl. -S a vulture	**ABBE**	*n* pl. -S an abbot
ABA	*n* pl. -S a sleeveless garment worn by Arabs	**ABBESS**	*n* pl. -ES the female superior of a convent of nuns
ABACA	*n* pl. -S a Philippine plant	**ABBEY**	*n* pl. -BEYS a monastery or convent
ABACK	*adv* toward the back	**ABBOT**	*n* pl. -S the superior of a monastery
ABACUS	*n* pl. -CI or -CUSES a calculating device	**ABBOTCY**	*n* pl. -CIES abbacy
ABAFT	*adv* toward the stern	**ABDICATE**	*v* -CATED, -CATING, -CATES to give up formally
ABAKA	*n* pl. -S abaca		
ABALONE	*n* pl. -S an edible shellfish	**ABDOMEN**	*n* pl. -MENS or -MINA the body cavity containing the viscera
ABAMP	*n* pl. -S abampere	**ABDUCE**	*v* -DUCED, -DUCING, -DUCES to abduct
ABAMPERE	*n* pl. -S a unit of electric current	**ABDUCENS**	*n* pl. -CENTES a cranial nerve
ABANDON	*v* -ED, -ING, -S to leave or give up completely	**ABDUCENT**	*adj* serving to abduct
ABASE	*v* ABASED, ABASING, ABASES to lower in rank, prestige, or esteem ABASEDLY *adv*	**ABDUCING**	present participle of abduce
		ABDUCT	*v* -ED, -ING, -S to draw away from the original position
ABASER	*n* pl. -S one that abases	**ABDUCTOR**	*n* pl. -ES or -S an abducent muscle
ABASH	*v* -ED, -ING, -ES to make ashamed or embarrassed	**ABEAM**	*adv* at right angles to the keel of a ship
ABASING	present participle of abase	**ABED**	*adv* in bed
ABATE	*v* ABATED, ABATING, ABATES to reduce in degree or intensity ABATABLE *adj*	**ABELE**	*n* pl. -S a Eurasian tree
		ABELMOSK	*n* pl. -S a tropical herb
ABATER	*n* pl. -S one that abates	**ABERRANT**	*n* pl. -S a deviant
ABATIS	*n* pl. -TISES a barrier made of felled trees	**ABET**	*v* ABETTED, ABETTING, ABETS to encourage and support
ABATOR	*n* pl. -S one that unlawfully seizes an inheritance	**ABETMENT**	*n* pl. -S the act of abetting

ABETTAL	n pl. -S abetment
ABETTED	past tense of abet
ABETTER	n pl. -S abettor
ABETTING	present participle of abet
ABETTOR	n pl. -S one that abets
ABEYANCE	n pl. -S temporary inactivity
ABEYANCY	n pl. -CIES abeyance
ABEYANT	adj marked by abeyance
ABFARAD	n pl. -S a unit of capacitance
ABHENRY	n pl. -RIES or -RYS a unit of inductance
ABHOR	v -HORRED, -HORRING, -HORS to loathe
ABHORRER	n pl. -S one that abhors
ABIDANCE	n pl. -S the act of abiding
ABIDE	v ABODE or ABIDED, ABIDING, ABIDES to accept without objection
ABIDER	n pl. -S one that abides
ABIGAIL	n pl. -S a lady's maid
ABILITY	n pl. -TIES the quality of being able to do something
ABIOSIS	n pl. -OSES absence of life **ABIOTIC** adj
ABJECT	adj sunk to a low condition **ABJECTLY** adv
ABJURE	v -JURED, -JURING, -JURES to renounce under oath
ABJURER	n pl. -S one that abjures
ABLATE	v -LATED, -LATING, -LATES to remove by cutting
ABLATION	n pl. -S surgical removal of a bodily part
ABLATIVE	n pl. -S a grammatical case
ABLAUT	n pl. -S a patterned change in root vowels of verb forms
ABLAZE	adj being on fire
ABLE	adj ABLER, ABLEST having sufficient power, skill, or resources
ABLE	n pl. -S a communications code word for the letter A
ABLEGATE	n pl. -S a papal envoy
ABLER	comparative of able
ABLEST	superlative of able
ABLINGS	adv ablins
ABLINS	adv perhaps
ABLOOM	adj blooming
ABLUENT	n pl. -S a cleansing agent
ABLUSH	adj blushing
ABLUTED	adj washed clean
ABLUTION	n pl. -S a washing

ABLY	adv in an able manner
ABMHO	n pl. -MHOS a unit of electrical conductance
ABNEGATE	v -GATED, -GATING, -GATES to deny to oneself
ABNORMAL	n pl. -S a mentally deficient person
ABO	n pl. ABOS an aborigine (an original inhabitant)
ABOARD	adv into, in, or on a ship, train, or airplane
ABODE	v ABODED, ABODING, ABODES to forebode
ABOHM	n pl. -S a unit of electrical resistance
ABOIDEAU	n pl. -DEAUS or -DEAUX a type of dike
ABOIL	adj boiling
ABOITEAU	n pl. -TEAUS or -TEAUX aboideau
ABOLISH	v -ED, -ING, -ES to do away with
ABOLLA	n pl. -LAE a cloak worn in ancient Rome
ABOMA	n pl. -S a South American snake
ABOMASAL	adj pertaining to the abomasum
ABOMASUM	n pl. -SA the fourth stomach of a ruminant
ABOMASUS	n pl. -MASI abomasum
ABOON	adv above
ABORAL	adj situated away from the mouth **ABORALLY** adv
ABORNING	adv while being born
ABORT	v -ED, -ING, -S to bring forth a fetus prematurely
ABORTER	n pl. -S one that aborts
ABORTION	n pl. -S induced expulsion of a nonviable fetus
ABORTIVE	adj failing to succeed
ABOUGHT	past tense of aby and abye
ABOULIA	n pl. -S abulia **ABOULIC** adj
ABOUND	v -ED, -ING, -S to have a large number or amount
ABOUT	adv approximately
ABOVE	n pl. -S something that is above (in a higher place)
ABRADANT	n pl. -S an abrasive
ABRADE	v ABRADED, ABRADING, ABRADES to wear away by friction
ABRADER	n pl. -S a tool for abrading
ABRASION	n pl. -S the act of abrading

ABRASIVE *n* pl. -S an abrading substance

ABREACT *v* -ED, -ING, -S to release repressed emotions by reliving the original traumatic experience

ABREAST *adv* side by side

ABRI *n* pl. -S a bomb shelter

ABRIDGE *v* ABRIDGED, ABRIDGING, ABRIDGES to reduce the length of

ABRIDGER *n* pl. -S one that abridges

ABROACH *adj* astir

ABROAD *adv* out of one's own country

ABROGATE *v* -GATED, -GATING, -GATES to abolish by authoritative action

ABRUPT *adj* -RUPTER, -RUPTEST rudely brief **ABRUPTLY** *adv*

ABSCESS *v* -ED, -ING, -ES to form an abscess (a localized collection of pus surrounded by inflamed tissue)

ABSCISE *v* -SCISED, -SCISING, -SCISES to cut off

ABSCISIN *n* pl. -S a regulatory substance found in plants

ABSCISSA *n* pl. -SAS or -SAE a particular geometric coordinate

ABSCOND *v* -ED, -ING, -S to depart suddenly and secretly

ABSENCE *n* pl. -S the state of being away

ABSENT *v* -ED, -ING, -S to take or keep away

ABSENTEE *n* pl. -S one that is not present

ABSENTER *n* pl. -S one that absents himself

ABSENTLY *adv* in an inattentive manner

ABSINTH *n* pl. -S absinthe

ABSINTHE *n* pl. -S a bitter liqueur

ABSOLUTE *adj* -LUTER, -LUTEST free from restriction

ABSOLUTE *n* pl. -S something that is absolute

ABSOLVE *v* -SOLVED, -SOLVING, -SOLVES to free from the consequences of an action

ABSOLVER *n* pl. -S one that absolves

ABSONANT *adj* unreasonable

ABSORB *v* -ED, -ING, -S to take up or in

ABSORBER *n* pl. -S one that absorbs

ABSTAIN *v* -ED, -ING, -S to refrain voluntarily

ABSTERGE *v* -STERGED, -STERGING, -STERGES to cleanse by wiping

ABSTRACT *adj* -STRACTER, -STRACTEST difficult to understand

ABSTRACT *v* -ED, -ING, -S to take away

ABSTRICT *v* -ED, -ING, -S to form by cutting off

ABSTRUSE *adj* -STRUSER, -STRUSEST difficult to understand

ABSURD *adj* -SURDER, -SURDEST ridiculously incongruous or unreasonable **ABSURDLY** *adv*

ABSURD *n* pl. -S the condition in which man exists in an irrational and meaningless universe

ABUBBLE *adj* bubbling

ABULIA *n* pl. -S loss of will power **ABULIC** *adj*

ABUNDANT *adj* present in great quantity

ABUSE *v* ABUSED, ABUSING, ABUSES to use wrongly or improperly **ABUSABLE** *adj*

ABUSER *n* pl. -S one that abuses

ABUSIVE *adj* characterized by wrong or improper use

ABUT *v* ABUTTED, ABUTTING, ABUTS to touch along a border

ABUTILON *n* pl. -S a flowering plant

ABUTMENT *n* pl. -S something that abuts

ABUTTAL *n* pl. -S an abutment

ABUTTED past tense of abut

ABUTTER *n* pl. -S one that abuts

ABUTTING present participle of abut

ABUZZ *adj* buzzing

ABVOLT *n* pl. -S a unit of electromotive force

ABWATT *n* pl. -S a unit of power

ABY *v* ABOUGHT, ABYING, ABYS to pay the penalty for

ABYE *v* ABOUGHT, ABYING, ABYES to aby

ABYSM *n* pl. -S an abyss

ABYSMAL *adj* immeasurably deep

ABYSS *n* pl. -ES a bottomless chasm **ABYSSAL** *adj*

ACACIA *n* pl. -S a flowering tree or shrub

ACADEME *n* pl. -S a place of instruction

ACADEMIA *n* pl. -S scholastic life or environment

ACADEMIC *n* pl. -S a college student or teacher

ACADEMY *n* pl. -MIES a secondary school

ACAJOU *n* pl. -S a tropical tree

ACALEPH *n* pl. -LEPHAE or -LEPHS a jellyfish

ACALEPHE *n* pl. -S acaleph

ACANTHUS *n* pl. -THI or -THUSES a prickly herb

ACARI pl. of acarus

ACARID *n* pl. -S any of an order of arachnids

ACARIDAN *n* pl. -S acarid

ACARINE *n* pl. -S acarid

ACAROID *adj* resembling an acarid

ACARPOUS *adj* not producing fruit

ACARUS *n* pl. -RI a mite

ACAUDAL *adj* having no tail

ACAUDATE *adj* acaudal

ACAULINE *adj* having no stem

ACAULOSE *adj* acauline

ACAULOUS *adj* acauline

ACCEDE *v* -CEDED, -CEDING, -CEDES to consent

ACCEDER *n* pl. -S one that accedes

ACCENT *v* -ED, -ING, -S to pronounce with prominence

ACCENTOR *n* pl. -S a songbird

ACCEPT *v* -ED, -ING, -S to receive willingly

ACCEPTEE *n* pl. -S one that is accepted

ACCEPTER *n* pl. -S one that accepts

ACCEPTOR *n* pl. -S accepter

ACCESS *v* -ED, -ING, -ES to get at

ACCIDENT *n* pl. -S an unexpected or unintentional occurrence

ACCIDIE *n* pl. -S acedia

ACCLAIM *v* -ED, -ING, -S to shout approval of

ACCOLADE *n* pl. -S an expression of praise

ACCORD *v* -ED, -ING, -S to bring into agreement

ACCORDER *n* pl. -S one that accords

ACCOST *v* -ED, -ING, -S to approach and speak to first

ACCOUNT *v* -ED, -ING, -S to give an explanation

ACCOUTER *v* -ED, -ING, -S to equip

ACCOUTRE *v* -TRED, -TRING, -TRES to accouter

ACCREDIT *v* -ED, -ING, -S to give official authorization to

ACCRETE *v* -CRETED, -CRETING, -CRETES to grow together

ACCRUAL *n* pl. -S the act of accruing

ACCRUE *v* -CRUED, -CRUING, -CRUES to come as an increase or addition

ACCURACY *n* pl. -CIES the quality of being accurate

ACCURATE *adj* free from error

ACCURSED *adj* damnable

ACCURST *adj* accursed

ACCUSAL *n* pl. -S the act of accusing

ACCUSANT *n* pl. -S an accuser

ACCUSE *v* -CUSED, -CUSING, -CUSES to make an assertion against

ACCUSER *n* pl. -S one that accuses

ACCUSTOM *v* -ED, -ING, -S to make familiar

ACE *v* ACED, ACING, ACES to score a point against in a single stroke

ACEDIA *n* pl. -S apathy

ACELDAMA *n* pl. -S a place of bloodshed

ACENTRIC *adj* having no center

ACEQUIA *n* pl. -S an irrigation ditch or canal

ACERATE *adj* acerose

ACERATED *adj* acerose

ACERB *adj* ACERBER, ACERBEST sour

ACERBATE *v* -BATED, -BATING, -BATES to make sour

ACERBIC *adj* acerb

ACERBITY *n* pl. -TIES sourness

ACEROLA *n* pl. -S a West Indian shrub

ACEROSE *adj* needle-shaped

ACEROUS *adj* acerose

ACERVATE *adj* growing in compact clusters

ACERVULI *n/pl* spore-producing organs of certain fungi

ACESCENT *n* pl. -S something that is slightly sour

ACETA pl. of acetum

ACETAL *n* pl. -S a flammable liquid

ACETAMID *n* pl. -S an amide of acetic acid

ACETATE *n* pl. -S a salt of acetic acid **ACETATED** *adj*

ACETIC *adj* pertaining to vinegar

ACETIFY *v* -FIED, -FYING, -FIES to convert into vinegar

ACETONE *n* pl. -S a flammable liquid **ACETONIC** *adj*

ACETOSE *adj* acetous

ACETOUS *adj* tasting like vinegar

ACETOXYL *n* pl. -S a univalent radical

ACETUM *n* pl. -TA vinegar

ACETYL   *n* pl. -S a univalent radical ACETYLIC *adj*

ACHE   *v* ACHED, ACHING, ACHES to suffer a dull, continuous pain

ACHENE   *n* pl. -S a type of fruit ACHENIAL *adj*

ACHIER   comparative of achy

ACHIEST   superlative of achy

ACHIEVE   *v* ACHIEVED, ACHIEVING, ACHIEVES to carry out successfully

ACHIEVER   *n* pl. -S one that achieves

ACHINESS   *n* pl. -ES the state of being achy

ACHING   present participle of ache

ACHINGLY   *adv* in an aching manner

ACHIOTE   *n* pl. -S a yellowish red dye

ACHOO   *interj* ahchoo

ACHROMAT   *n* pl. -S a type of lens

ACHROMIC   *adj* having no color

ACHY   *adj* ACHIER, ACHIEST aching

ACICULA   *n* pl. -LAE or -LAS a needlelike part or process ACICULAR *adj*

ACID   *n* pl. -S a type of chemical compound

ACIDHEAD   *n* pl. -S one who uses LSD

ACIDIC   *adj* sour

ACIDIFY   *v* -FIED, -FYING, -FIES to convert into an acid

ACIDITY   *n* pl. -TIES sourness

ACIDLY   *adv* sourly

ACIDNESS   *n* pl. -ES acidity

ACIDOSIS   *n* pl. -DOSES an abnormal condition of the blood ACIDOTIC *adj*

ACIDY   *adj* sour

ACIERATE   *v* -ATED, -ATING, -ATES to turn into steel

ACIFORM   *adj* needle-shaped

ACING   present participle of ace

ACINUS   *n* pl. -NI a small, saclike division of a gland ACINAR, ACINIC, ACINOSE, ACINOUS *adj*

ACLINIC   *adj* having no inclination

ACME   *n* pl. -S the highest point ACMATIC, ACMIC *adj*

ACNE   *n* pl. -S a skin disease ACNED *adj*

ACNODE   *n* pl. -S an element of a mathematical set that is isolated from the other elements

ACOCK   *adj* cocked

ACOLD   *adj* cold

ACOLYTE   *n* pl. -S an assistant

ACONITE   *n* pl. -S a poisonous herb ACONITIC *adj*

ACONITUM   *n* pl. -S aconite

ACORN   *n* pl. -S the fruit of the oak tree

ACOUSTIC   *n* pl. -S a hearing aid

ACQUAINT   *v* -ED, -ING, -S to cause to know

ACQUEST   *n* pl. -S something acquired

ACQUIRE   *v* -QUIRED, -QUIRING, -QUIRES to come into possession of

ACQUIRER   *n* pl. -S one that acquires

ACQUIT   *v* -QUITTED, -QUITTING, -QUITS to free or clear from a charge of fault or crime

ACRASIN   *n* pl. -S a substance secreted by the cells of a slime mold

ACRE   *n* pl. -S a unit of area

ACREAGE   *n* pl. -S area in acres

ACRED   *adj* owning many acres

ACRID   *adj* -RIDER, -RIDEST sharp and harsh to the taste or smell

ACRIDINE   *n* pl. -S a chemical compound

ACRIDITY   *n* pl. -TIES the state of being acrid

ACRIDLY   *adv* in an acrid manner

ACRIMONY   *n* pl. -NIES sharpness or bitterness of speech or temper

ACROBAT   *n* pl. -S one skilled in feats of agility and balance

ACRODONT   *n* pl. -S an animal having rootless teeth

ACROGEN   *n* pl. -S a plant growing at the apex only

ACROLEIN   *n* pl. -S a flammable liquid

ACROLITH   *n* pl. -S a type of statue

ACROMION   *n* pl. -MIA the outward end of the shoulder blade ACROMIAL *adj*

ACRONIC   *adj* occurring at sunset

ACRONYM   *n* pl. -S a word formed from the initials of a compound term or series of words

ACROSS   *prep* from one side of to the other

ACROSTIC   *n* pl. -S a poem in which certain letters taken in order form a word or phrase

ACROTISM   *n* pl. -S weakness of the pulse ACROTIC *adj*

ACRYLATE   *n* pl. -S an acrylic

ACRYLIC   *n* pl. -S a type of resin

ACT   v -ED, -ING, -S to do something

ACTA   n/pl recorded proceedings

ACTABLE   adj suitable for performance on the stage

ACTIN   n pl. -S a protein in muscle tissue

ACTINAL   adj having tentacles

ACTING   n pl. -S the occupation of an actor

ACTINIA   n pl. -IAE or -IAS a marine animal

ACTINIAN   n pl. -S actinia

ACTINIC   adj pertaining to actinism

ACTINIDE   n pl. -S any of a series of radioactive elements

ACTINISM   n pl. -S the property of radiant energy that effects chemical changes

ACTINIUM   n pl. -S a radioactive element

ACTINOID   n pl. -S an actinide

ACTINON   n pl. -S an isotope of radon

ACTION   n pl. -S the process of acting

ACTIVATE   v -VATED, -VATING, -VATES to set in motion

ACTIVE   n pl. -S a participating member of an organization

ACTIVELY   adv with activity

ACTIVISM   n pl. -S a doctrine that emphasizes direct and decisive action

ACTIVIST   n pl. -S an advocate of activism

ACTIVITY   n pl. -TIES brisk action or movement

ACTOR   n pl. -S a theatrical performer ACTORISH adj

ACTRESS   n pl. -ES a female actor

ACTUAL   adj existing in fact ACTUALLY adv

ACTUARY   n pl. -ARIES a statistician who computes insurance risks and premiums

ACTUATE   v -ATED, -ATING, -ATES to set into action or motion

ACTUATOR   n pl. -S one that actuates

ACUATE   adj sharp

ACUITY   n pl. -ITIES sharpness

ACULEATE   adj having a sting

ACUMEN   n pl. -S mental keenness

ACUTANCE   n pl. -S a measure of photographic clarity

ACUTE   adj ACUTER, ACUTEST marked by sharpness or severity ACUTELY adv

ACUTE   n pl. -S a type of accent mark

ACYCLIC   adj not cyclic

ACYL   n pl. -S a univalent radical

ACYLATE   v -ATED, -ATING, -ATES to introduce acyl into

AD   n pl. -S an advertisement

ADAGE   n pl. -S a traditional saying expressing a common observation ADAGIAL adj

ADAGIO   n pl. -GIOS a musical composition or movement played in a slow tempo

ADAMANCE   n pl. -S adamancy

ADAMANCY   n pl. -CIES unyielding hardness

ADAMANT   n pl. -S an extremely hard substance

ADAMSITE   n pl. -S a lung-irritating gas

ADAPT   v -ED, -ING, -S to make suitable

ADAPTER   n pl. -S one that adapts

ADAPTION   n pl. -S the act of adapting ADAPTIVE adj

ADAPTOR   n pl. -S adapter

ADAXIAL   adj situated on the same side as

ADD   v -ED, -ING, -S to combine or join so as to bring about an increase ADDABLE adj

ADDAX   n pl. -ES a large antelope

ADDEDLY   adv additionally

ADDEND   n pl. -S a number to be added to another

ADDENDUM   n pl. -DA something added or to be added

ADDER   n pl. -S a venomous snake

ADDIBLE   adj capable of being added

ADDICT   v -ED, -ING, -S to devote or surrender to something habitually or compulsively

ADDITION   n pl. -S something added

ADDITIVE   n pl. -S a substance added to another to impart desirable qualities

ADDLE   v -DLED, -DLING, -DLES to confuse

ADDRESS   v -DRESSED or -DREST, -DRESSING, -DRESSES to speak to

ADDUCE   v -DUCED, -DUCING, -DUCES to bring forward as evidence

ADDUCENT   adj serving to adduct

ADDUCER   n pl. -S one that adduces

ADDUCING   present participle of adduce

ADDUCT   v -ED, -ING, -S to draw toward the main axis

ADDUCTOR   n pl. -S an adducent muscle

ADEEM   v -ED, -ING, -S to take away

ADENINE   n pl. -S an alkaloid

ADENITIS   n pl. -TISES inflammation of a lymph node

ADENOID   n pl. -S an enlarged lymphoid growth behind the pharynx

ADENOMA   n pl. -MAS or -MATA a tumor of glandular origin

ADENYL   n pl. -S a univalent radical

ADEPT   adj ADEPTER, ADEPTEST highly skilled **ADEPTLY** adv

ADEPT   n pl. -S an adept person

ADEQUACY   n pl. -CIES the state of being adequate

ADEQUATE   adj sufficient for a specific requirement

ADHERE   v -HERED, -HERING, -HERES to become or remain attached or close to something

ADHEREND   n pl. -S the surface to which an adhesive adheres

ADHERENT   n pl. -S a supporter

ADHERER   n pl. -S one that adheres

ADHERING   present participle of adhere

ADHESION   n pl. -S the act of adhering

ADHESIVE   n pl. -S a substance that causes adhesion

ADHIBIT   v -ED, -ING, -S to take or let in

ADIEU   n pl. ADIEUS or ADIEUX a farewell

ADIOS   interj — used to express farewell

ADIPOSE   n pl. -S animal fat **ADIPIC** adj

ADIPOSIS   n pl. -POSES obesity

ADIPOUS   adj pertaining to adipose

ADIT   n pl. -S an entrance

ADJACENT   adj next to

ADJOIN   v -ED, -ING, -S to lie next to

ADJOINT   n pl. -S a type of mathematical matrix

ADJOURN   v -ED, -ING, -S to suspend until a later time

ADJUDGE   v -JUDGED, -JUDGING, -JUDGES to determine judicially

ADJUNCT   n pl. -S something attached in a subordinate position

ADJURE   v -JURED, -JURING, -JURES to command solemnly

ADJURER   n pl. -S one that adjures

ADJUROR   n pl. -S adjurer

ADJUST   v -ED, -ING, -S to bring to a more satisfactory state

ADJUSTER   n pl. -S one that adjusts

ADJUSTOR   n pl. -S adjuster

ADJUTANT   n pl. -S an assistant

ADJUVANT   n pl. -S an assistant

ADMAN   n pl. -MEN a man employed in the advertising business

ADMASS   adj pertaining to a society strongly influenced by advertising

ADMIRAL   n pl. -S a high-ranking naval officer

ADMIRE   v -MIRED, -MIRING, -MIRES to regard with wonder, pleasure, and approval

ADMIRER   n pl. -S one that admires

ADMIT   v -MITTED, -MITTING, -MITS to allow to enter

ADMITTER   n pl. -S one that admits

ADMIX   v -MIXED or -MIXT, -MIXING, -MIXES to mix

ADMONISH   v -ED, -ING, -ES to reprove mildly or kindly

ADNATE   adj joined to another part or organ

ADNATION   n pl. -S the state of being adnate

ADNEXA   n/pl conjoined anatomical parts **ADNEXAL** adj

ADNOUN   n pl. -S an adjective when used as a noun

ADO   n pl. ADOS bustling excitement

ADOBE   n pl. -S an unburnt, sun-dried brick

ADOPT   v -ED, -ING, -S to take into one's family by legal means

ADOPTEE   n pl. -S one that is adopted

ADOPTER   n pl. -S one that adopts

ADOPTION   n pl. -S the act of adopting **ADOPTIVE** adj

ADORABLE   adj worthy of being adored **ADORABLY** adv

ADORE   v ADORED, ADORING, ADORES to love deeply

ADORER   n pl. -S one that adores

ADORN   v -ED, -ING, -S to add something to for the purpose of making more attractive

ADORNER   n pl. -S one that adorns

ADOWN   adv downward

ADOZE   adj dozing

ADRENAL   n pl. -S an endocrine gland

ADRIFT   adj drifting

ADROIT *adj* ADROITER, ADROITEST skillful **ADROITLY** *adv*

ADSCRIPT *n pl.* -S a distinguishing symbol written after another character

ADSORB *v* -ED, -ING, -S to gather on a surface in a condensed layer

ADULARIA *n pl.* -S a mineral

ADULATE *v* -LATED, -LATING, -LATES to praise excessively

ADULATOR *n pl.* -S one that adulates

ADULT *n pl.* -S a fully developed individual

ADULTERY *n pl.* -TERIES voluntary sexual intercourse between a married person and someone other than his or her spouse

ADULTLY *adv* in a manner typical of an adult

ADUMBRAL *adj* shadowy

ADUNC *adj* bent inward

ADUNCATE *adj* adunc

ADUNCOUS *adj* adunc

ADUST *adj* scorched

ADVANCE *v* -VANCED, -VANCING, -VANCES to move or cause to move ahead

ADVANCER *n pl.* -S one that advances

ADVENT *n pl.* -S arrival

ADVERB *n pl.* -S a word used to modify the meaning of a verb, adjective, or other adverb

ADVERSE *adj* acting in opposition

ADVERT *v* -ED, -ING, -S to call attention

ADVICE *n pl.* -S recommendation regarding a decision or course of conduct

ADVISE *v* -VISED, -VISING, -VISES to give advice to

ADVISEE *n pl.* -S one that is advised

ADVISER *n pl.* -S one that advises

ADVISING present participle of advise

ADVISOR *n pl.* -S adviser

ADVISORY *n pl.* -RIES a report giving information

ADVOCACY *n pl.* -CIES the act of advocating

ADVOCATE *v* -CATED, -CATING, -CATES to speak in favor of

ADVOWSON *n pl.* -S the right of presenting a nominee to a vacant church office

ADYNAMIA *n pl.* -S lack of physical strength **ADYNAMIC** *adj*

ADYTUM *n pl.* -TA an inner sanctuary in an ancient temple

ADZ *n pl.* -ES a cutting tool

ADZE *n pl.* -S adz

AE *adj* one

AECIA pl. of aecium

AECIAL *adj* pertaining to an aecium

AECIDIUM *n pl.* -IA an aecium

AECIUM *n pl.* -IA a spore-producing organ of certain fungi

AEDES *n pl.* AEDES any of a genus of mosquitoes

AEDILE *n pl.* -S a magistrate of ancient Rome

AEDINE *adj* pertaining to an aedes

AEGIS *n pl.* -GISES protection

AENEOUS *adj* having a greenish gold color

AENEUS *adj* aeneous

AEOLIAN *adj* eolian

AEON *n pl.* -S eon

AEONIAN *adj* eonian

AEONIC *adj* eonian

AERATE *v* -ATED, -ATING, -ATES to supply with air

AERATION *n pl.* -S the act of aerating

AERATOR *n pl.* -S one that aerates

AERIAL *n pl.* -S a metallic apparatus for sending and receiving electromagnetic waves

AERIALLY *adv* in a manner pertaining to the air

AERIE *n pl.* -S a bird's nest built high on a mountain or cliff **AERIED** *adj*

AERIER comparative of aery

AERIES pl. of aery

AERIEST superlative of aery

AERIFORM *adj* having the form of air

AERIFY *v* -FIED, -FYING, -FIES to aerate

AERILY *adv* in an aery manner

AERO *adj* pertaining to aircraft

AEROBE *n pl.* -S an organism that requires oxygen to live **AEROBIC** *adj*

AEROBIUM *n pl.* -BIA aerobe

AERODUCT *n pl.* -S a type of jet engine

AERODYNE *n pl.* -S an aircraft that is heavier than air

AEROFOIL *n pl.* -S airfoil

AEROGEL *n pl.* -S a highly porous solid

AEROGRAM *n pl.* -S an airmail letter

AEROLITE *n pl.* -S a meteorite containing more stone than iron

AEROLITH *n pl.* -S aerolite

AEROLOGY *n pl.* -GIES the study of the atmosphere

AERONAUT *n pl.* -S one who operates an airship

AERONOMY *n pl.* -MIES the study of the upper atmosphere

AEROSOL *n pl.* -S a gaseous suspension of fine solid or liquid particles

AEROSTAT *n pl.* -S an aircraft that is lighter than air

AERUGO *n pl.* -GOS a green film that forms on copper

AERY *adj* AERIER, AERIEST airy

AERY *n pl.* AERIES aerie

AESTHETE *n pl.* -S esthete

AESTIVAL *adj* estival

AETHER *n pl.* -S the upper region of the atmosphere **AETHERIC** *adj*

AFAR *n pl.* -S a great distance

AFEARD *adj* afraid

AFEARED *adj* afeard

AFF *adv* off

AFFABLE *adj* easy to talk to **AFFABLY** *adv*

AFFAIR *n pl.* -S anything done or to be done

AFFAIRE *n pl.* -S a brief amorous relationship

AFFECT *v* -ED, -ING, -S to give a false appearance of

AFFECTER *n pl.* -S one that affects

AFFERENT *adj* conducting toward an organ or part

AFFIANCE *v* -ANCED, -ANCING, -ANCES to betroth

AFFIANT *n pl.* -S one who makes a written declaration under oath

AFFICHE *n pl.* -S a poster

AFFINE *n pl.* -S a relative by marriage

AFFINED *adj* closely related

AFFINELY *adv* in the manner of a type of mathematical mapping

AFFINITY *n pl.* -TIES a natural attraction or inclination

AFFIRM *v* -ED, -ING, -S to state positively

AFFIRMER *n pl.* -S one that affirms

AFFIX *v* -ED, -ING, -ES to attach

AFFIXAL *adj* pertaining to a prefix or suffix

AFFIXER *n pl.* -S one that affixes

AFFIXIAL *adj* affixal

AFFLATUS *n pl.* -ES a creative inspiration

AFFLICT *v* -ED, -ING, -S to distress with mental or physical pain

AFFLUENT *n pl.* -S a stream that flows into another

AFFLUX *n pl.* -ES a flowing toward a point

AFFORD *v* -ED, -ING, -S to have sufficient means for

AFFOREST *v* -ED, -ING, -S to convert into forest

AFFRAY *v* -ED, -ING, -S to frighten

AFFRAYER *n pl.* -S one that affrays

AFFRIGHT *v* -ED, -ING, -S to frighten

AFFRONT *v* -ED, -ING, -S to insult openly

AFFUSION *n pl.* -S an act of pouring a liquid on

AFGHAN *n pl.* -S a woolen blanket or shawl

AFGHANI *n pl.* -S a monetary unit of Afghanistan

AFIELD *adv* in the field

AFIRE *adj* being on fire

AFLAME *adj* flaming

AFLOAT *adj* floating

AFLUTTER *adj* nervously excited

AFOOT *adv* on foot

AFORE *adv* before

AFOUL *adj* entangled

AFRAID *adj* filled with apprehension

AFREET *n pl.* -S an evil spirit in Arabic mythology

AFRESH *adv* anew

AFRIT *n pl.* -S afreet

AFT *adv* toward the stern

AFTER *prep* behind in place or order

AFTERS *n/pl* dessert

AFTERTAX *adj* remaining after payment of taxes

AFTMOST *adj* nearest the stern

AFTOSA *n pl.* -S a disease of hoofed mammals

AGA *n pl.* -S a high-ranking Turkish military officer

AGAIN *adv* once more

AGAINST *prep* in opposition to

AGALLOCH *n pl.* -S the fragrant wood of a tropical tree

AGALWOOD n pl. -S agalloch

AGAMA n pl. -S a tropical lizard

AGAMETE n pl. -S an asexual reproductive cell

AGAMIC adj asexual

AGAMOUS adj agamic

AGAPE n pl. -PAE or -PAI the love of God for mankind **AGAPEIC** adj

AGAR n pl. -S a viscous substance obtained from certain seaweeds

AGARIC n pl. -S any of a family of fungi

AGATE n pl. -S a variety of quartz **AGATOID** adj

AGATIZE v -IZED, -IZING, -IZES to cause to resemble agate

AGAVE n pl. -S a tropical plant

AGAZE adj gazing

AGE v AGED, AGING or AGEING, AGES to grow old

AGEDLY adv oldly

AGEDNESS n pl. -ES oldness

AGEE adv to one side

AGEING n pl. -S aging

AGELESS adj never growing old

AGELONG adj lasting for a long time

AGENCY n pl. -CIES an organization that does business for others

AGENDA n pl. -S a list of things to be done

AGENDUM n pl. -S an item on an agenda

AGENE n pl. -S a chemical compound used in bleaching flour

AGENESIA n pl. -S agenesis

AGENESIS n pl. AGENESES absence or imperfect development of a bodily part **AGENETIC** adj

AGENIZE v -NIZED, -NIZING, -NIZES to treat with agene

AGENT n pl. -S one who is authorized to act for another **AGENTIAL** adj

AGENTRY n pl. -RIES the office or duties of an agent

AGER n pl. -S one that ages

AGERATUM n pl. -S a flowering plant

AGGER n pl. -S a mound of earth used as a fortification

AGGIE n pl. -S a type of playing marble

AGGRADE v -GRADED, -GRADING, -GRADES to fill with detrital material

AGGRESS v -ED, -ING, -ES to commit the first act of hostility

AGGRIEVE v -GRIEVED, -GRIEVING, -GRIEVES to distress

AGHA n pl. -S aga

AGHAST adj shocked by something horrible

AGILE adj able to move quickly and easily **AGILELY** adv

AGILITY n pl. -TIES the quality of being agile

AGIN prep against

AGING n pl. -S the process of growing old

AGINNER n pl. -S one that is against change

AGIO n pl. AGIOS a premium paid for the exchange of one currency for another

AGIOTAGE n pl. -S the business of a broker

AGIST v -ED, -ING, -S to feed and take care of for a fee, as livestock

AGITATE v -TATED, -TATING, -TATES to move with a violent, irregular action **AGITABLE** adj

AGITATO adj fast and stirring — used as a musical direction

AGITATOR n pl. -S one that agitates

AGITPROP n pl. -S pro-Communist propaganda

AGLARE adj glaring

AGLEAM adj gleaming

AGLEE adv agley

AGLET n pl. -S a metal sheath at the end of a lace

AGLEY adv awry

AGLIMMER adj glimmering

AGLITTER adj glittering

AGLOW adj glowing

AGLY adv agley

AGLYCON n pl. -S a type of chemical compound

AGLYCONE n pl. -S aglycon

AGMA n pl. -S eng

AGMINATE adj clustered together

AGNAIL n pl. -S a piece of loose skin at the base of a fingernail

AGNATE n pl. -S a relative on the father's side **AGNATIC** adj

AGNATION n pl. -S the relationship of agnates

AGNIZE *v* -NIZED, -NIZING, -NIZES to acknowledge

AGNOMEN *n* pl. -MINA or -MENS an additional name given to an ancient Roman

AGNOSTIC *n* pl. -S one who disclaims any knowledge of God

AGO *adv* in the past

AGOG *adv* in a state of eager curiosity

AGON *n* pl. -S or -ES the dramatic conflict between the main characters in a Greek play

AGONAL *adj* pertaining to agony

AGONE *adv* ago

AGONES a pl. of agon

AGONIC *adj* not forming an angle

AGONIES pl. of agony

AGONISE *v* -NISED, -NISING, -NISES to agonize

AGONIST *n* pl. -S one that is engaged in a struggle

AGONIZE *v* -NIZED, -NIZING, -NIZES to suffer extreme pain

AGONY *n* pl. -NIES extreme pain

AGORA *n* pl. -RAS or -RAE a marketplace in ancient Greece

AGORA *n* pl. AGOROT or AGOROTH a monetary unit of Israel

AGOUTI *n* pl. -S or -ES a burrowing rodent

AGOUTY *n* pl. -TIES agouti

AGRAFE *n* pl. -S agraffe

AGRAFFE *n* pl. -S an ornamental clasp

AGRAPHA *n/pl* the sayings of Jesus not found in the Bible

AGRAPHIA *n* pl. -S a mental disorder marked by inability to write **AGRAPHIC** *adj*

AGRARIAN *n* pl. -S one who favors equal distribution of land

AGREE *v* AGREED, AGREEING, AGREES to have the same opinion

AGRESTAL *adj* growing wild

AGRESTIC *adj* rural

AGRIMONY *n* pl. -NIES a perennial herb

AGROLOGY *n* pl. -GIES the science of soils in relation to crops

AGRONOMY *n* pl. -MIES the application of scientific principles to the cultivation of land

AGROUND *adv* on the ground

AGUE *n* pl. -S a malarial fever **AGUELIKE, AGUISH** *adj* **AGUISHLY** *adv*

AGUEWEED *n* pl. -S a flowering plant

AH *interj* — used to express delight, relief, or contempt

AHA *interj* — used to express surprise, triumph, or derision

AHCHOO *interj* — used to represent the sound of a sneeze

AHEAD *adv* at or to the front

AHEM *interj* — used to attract attention

AHIMSA *n* pl. -S the Hindu principle of nonviolence

AHOLD *n* pl. -S a hold or grasp of something

AHORSE *adv* on a horse

AHOY *interj* — used in hailing a ship or person

AHULL *adj* abandoned and flooded, as a ship

AI *n* pl. -S a three-toed sloth

AIBLINS *adv* ablins

AID *v* -ED, -ING, -S to help

AIDE *n* pl. -S an assistant

AIDER *n* pl. -S one that aids

AIDFUL *adj* helpful

AIDLESS *adj* helpless

AIDMAN *n* pl. -MEN a corpsman

AIGLET *n* pl. -S aglet

AIGRET *n* pl. -S aigrette

AIGRETTE *n* pl. -S a tuft of feathers worn as a head ornament

AIGUILLE *n* pl. -S a sharp, pointed mountain peak

AIKIDO *n* pl. -DOS a Japanese art of self-defense

AIL *v* -ED, -ING, -S to cause pain or discomfort to

AILERON *n* pl. -S a movable control surface on an airplane wing

AILMENT *n* pl. -S a physical or mental disorder

AIM *v* -ED, -ING, -S to direct toward a specified object or goal

AIMER *n* pl. -S one that aims

AIMFUL *adj* full of purpose **AIMFULLY** *adv*

AIMLESS *adj* lacking direction or purpose

AIN *n* pl. -S ayin

AINE *adj* elder or eldest

AINEE *adj* aine

AINSELL n pl. -S own self

AIR v -ED, -ING, -S to expose to the air (the mixture of gases that surrounds the earth)

AIR adv AIRER, AIREST early

AIRBOAT n pl. -S a boat used in swampy areas

AIRBORNE adj flying

AIRBOUND adj stopped up by air

AIRBRUSH v -ED, -ING, -ES to apply in a fine spray by compressed air, as paint

AIRBURST n pl. -S an explosion in the air

AIRBUS n pl. -BUSES or -BUSSES a passenger airplane

AIRCOACH n pl. -ES the cheaper class of accommodations in commercial aircraft

AIRCRAFT n pl. AIRCRAFT any machine or device capable of flying

AIRCREW n pl. -S the crew of an aircraft

AIRDROME n pl. -S an airport

AIRDROP v -DROPPED, -DROPPING, -DROPS to drop from an aircraft

AIRFIELD n pl. -S an airport

AIRFLOW n pl. -S a flow of air

AIRFOIL n pl. -S a part of an aircraft designed to provide lift or control

AIRFRAME n pl. -S the framework and external covering of an airplane

AIRGLOW n pl. -S a glow in the upper atmosphere

AIRHEAD n pl. -S an area in hostile territory secured by paratroops

AIRIER comparative of airy

AIRIEST superlative of airy

AIRILY adv in an airy manner

AIRINESS n pl. -ES the state of being airy

AIRING n pl. -S an exposure to the air

AIRLESS adj having no air

AIRLIFT v -ED, -ING, -S to transport by airplane

AIRLIKE adj resembling air

AIRLINE n pl. -S an air transportation system

AIRLINER n pl. -S a large passenger aircraft

AIRMAIL v -ED, -ING, -S to send mail by airplane

AIRMAN n pl. -MEN an aviator

AIRN n pl. -S iron

AIRPARK n pl. -S a small airport

AIRPLANE n pl. -S a winged aircraft propelled by jet engines or propellers

AIRPORT n pl. -S a tract of land maintained for the landing and takeoff of aircraft

AIRPOST n pl. -S a system of conveying mail by airplane

AIRPROOF v -ED, -ING, -S to make impermeable to air

AIRSCREW n pl. -S an airplane propeller

AIRSHIP n pl. -S a lighter-than-air aircraft having propulsion and steering systems

AIRSICK adj nauseated from flying in an airplane

AIRSPACE n pl. -S the portion of the atmosphere above a particular land area

AIRSPEED n pl. -S the speed of an aircraft with relation to the air

AIRSTRIP n pl. -S a runway

AIRT v -ED, -ING, -S to guide

AIRTH v -ED, -ING, -S to airt

AIRTIGHT adj not allowing air to escape or enter

AIRWARD adv toward the sky

AIRWAVE n pl. -S the medium of radio and television transmission

AIRWAY n pl. -WAYS a passageway in which air circulates

AIRWISE adj skillful in aviation

AIRWOMAN n pl. -WOMEN a female aviator

AIRY adj AIRIER, AIRIEST having the nature of air

AISLE n pl. -S a passageway between sections of seats **AISLED** adj

AIT n pl. -S a small island

AITCH n pl. -ES the letter H

AIVER n pl. -S a draft horse

AJAR adj partly open

AJEE adv agee

AJIVA n pl. -S inanimate matter

AJOWAN n pl. -S the fruit of an Egyptian plant

AKEE n pl. -S a tropical tree

AKELA n pl. -S a leader of a cub scout pack

AKENE n pl. -S achene

AKIMBO adj having hands on hips and elbows bent outward

AKIN adj related by blood

AKVAVIT n pl. -S aquavit

ALA   *n* pl. ALAE a wing or winglike part

ALACK   *interj* — used to express sorrow or regret

ALACRITY   *n* pl. -TIES cheerful promptness

ALAE   pl. of ala

ALAMEDA   *n* pl. -S a shaded walkway

ALAMO   *n* pl. -MOS a softwood tree

ALAMODE   *n* pl. -S a silk fabric

ALAN   *n* pl. -S a large hunting dog

ALAND   *n* pl. -S alan

ALANE   *adj* alone

ALANG   *adv* along

ALANIN   *n* pl. -S alanine

ALANINE   *n* pl. -S an amino acid

ALANT   *n* pl. -S alan

ALANYL   *n* pl. -S a univalent radical

ALAR   *adj* pertaining to wings

ALARM   *v* -ED, -ING, -S to frighten by a sudden revelation of danger

ALARMISM   *n* pl. -S the practice of alarming others needlessly

ALARMIST   *n* pl. -S one who alarms others needlessly

ALARUM   *v* -ED, -ING, -S to alarm

ALARY   *adj* alar

ALAS   *interj* — used to express sorrow or regret

ALASKA   *n* pl. -S a heavy fabric

ALASTOR   *n* pl. -S an avenging deity in Greek tragedy

ALATE   *adj* having wings

ALATED   *adj* alate

ALATION   *n* pl. -S the state of having wings

ALB   *n* pl. -S a long-sleeved vestment

ALBA   *n* pl. -S the white substance of the brain

ALBACORE   *n* pl. -S a marine food fish

ALBATA   *n* pl. -S an alloy of copper, nickel, and zinc

ALBEDO   *n* pl. -DOS the ratio of the light reflected by a planet to that received by it

ALBEIT   *conj* although

ALBICORE   *n* pl. -S albacore

ALBINAL   *adj* albinic

ALBINIC   *adj* pertaining to albinism

ALBINISM   *n* pl. -S the condition of being an albino

ALBINO   *n* pl. -NOS an organism lacking normal pigmentation

ALBITE   *n* pl. -S a mineral **ALBITIC** *adj*

ALBUM   *n* pl. -S a book for preserving photographs or stamps

ALBUMEN   *n* pl. -S the white of an egg

ALBUMIN   *n* pl. -S a simple protein

ALBUMOSE   *n* pl. -S a proteose

ALBURNUM   *n* pl. -S sapwood

ALCADE   *n* pl. -S alcalde

ALCAHEST   *n* pl. -S alkahest

ALCAIC   *n* pl. -S a type of verse form

ALCAIDE   *n* pl. -S the commander of a Spanish fortress

ALCALDE   *n* pl. -S the mayor of a Spanish town

ALCAYDE   *n* pl. -S alcaide

ALCAZAR   *n* pl. -S a Spanish fortress or palace

ALCHEMY   *n* pl. -MIES a medieval form of chemistry **ALCHEMIC** *adj*

ALCHYMY   *n* pl. -MIES alchemy

ALCIDINE   *adj* pertaining to a family of seabirds

ALCOHOL   *n* pl. -S a flammable liquid

ALCOVE   *n* pl. -S a recessed section of a room **ALCOVED** *adj*

ALDEHYDE   *n* pl. -S a type of chemical compound

ALDER   *n* pl. -S a shrub or small tree

ALDERMAN   *n* pl. -MEN a member of a municipal legislative body

ALDOL   *n* pl. -S a chemical compound

ALDOLASE   *n* pl. -S an enzyme

ALDOSE   *n* pl. -S a type of sugar

ALDRIN   *n* pl. -S an insecticide

ALE   *n* pl. -S an alcoholic beverage

ALEATORY   *adj* pertaining to luck

ALEC   *n* pl. -S a herring

ALEE   *adv* toward the side of a vessel sheltered from the wind

ALEF   *n* pl. -S aleph

ALEGAR   *n* pl. -S sour ale

ALEHOUSE   *n* pl. -S a tavern where ale is sold

ALEMBIC   *n* pl. -S an apparatus formerly used in distilling

ALEPH   *n* pl. -S a Hebrew letter

ALERT   *adj* ALERTER, ALERTEST ready for sudden action **ALERTLY** *adv*

ALERT   *v* -ED, -ING, -S to warn

ALEURON n pl. -S aleurone

ALEURONE n pl. -S protein matter found in the seeds of certain plants

ALEVIN n pl. -S a young fish

ALEWIFE n pl. -WIVES a marine fish

ALEXIA n pl. -S a cerebral disorder marked by the loss of the ability to read

ALEXIN n pl. -S a substance in the blood that aids in the destruction of bacteria

ALEXINE n pl. -S alexin

ALFA n pl. -S a communications code word for the letter A

ALFAKI n pl. -S alfaqui

ALFALFA n pl. -S a plant cultivated for use as hay and forage

ALFAQUI n pl. -S a teacher of Muslim law

ALFAQUIN n pl. -S alfaqui

ALFORJA n pl. -S a leather bag

ALFRESCO adv outdoors

ALGA n pl. -GAE or -GAS any of a group of primitive aquatic plants ALGAL adj

ALGAROBA n pl. -S the mesquite

ALGEBRA n pl. -S a branch of mathematics

ALGERINE n pl. -S a woolen fabric

ALGICIDE n pl. -S a substance used to kill algae

ALGID adj cold

ALGIDITY n pl. -TIES coldness

ALGIN n pl. -S a viscous substance obtained from certain algae

ALGINATE n pl. -S a chemical salt

ALGOID adj resembling algae

ALGOLOGY n pl. -GIES the study of algae

ALGOR n pl. -S coldness

ALGORISM n pl. -S the Arabic system of arithmetic notation

ALGUM n pl. -S almug

ALIAS n pl. -ES an assumed name

ALIBI v -BIED, -BIING, -BIES or -BIS to make excuses for oneself

ALIBLE adj nourishing

ALIDAD n pl. -S alidade

ALIDADE n pl. -S a device used in angular measurement

ALIEN v -ED, -ING, -S to transfer to another, as property

ALIENAGE n pl. -S the state of being foreign

ALIENATE v -ATED, -ATING, -ATES to make indifferent or unfriendly

ALIENEE n pl. -S one to whom property is transferred

ALIENER n pl. -S alienor

ALIENISM n pl. -S alienage

ALIENIST n pl. -S a physician who treats mental disorders

ALIENLY adv in a foreign manner

ALIENOR n pl. -S one that transfers property

ALIF n pl. -S an Arabic letter

ALIFORM adj shaped like a wing

ALIGHT v ALIGHTED or ALIT, ALIGHTING, ALIGHTS to come down from something

ALIGN v -ED, -ING, -S to arrange in a straight line

ALIGNER n pl. -S one that aligns

ALIKE adj having close resemblance

ALIMENT v -ED, -ING, -S to nourish

ALIMONY n pl. -NIES an allowance paid to a woman by her divorced husband

ALINE v ALINED, ALINING, ALINES to align

ALINER n pl. -S aligner

ALIPED n pl. -S an animal having a membrane connecting the toes

ALIQUANT adj not dividing evenly into another number

ALIQUOT n pl. -S a number that divides evenly into another

ALIST adj leaning to one side

ALIT a past tense of alight

ALIUNDE adv from a source extrinsic to the matter at hand

ALIVE adj having life

ALIYAH n pl. -S the immigration of Jews to Israel

ALIZARIN n pl. -S a red dye

ALKAHEST n pl. -S the hypothetical universal solvent sought by alchemists

ALKALI n pl. -LIES or -LIS a type of chemical compound ALKALIC adj

ALKALIFY v -FIED, -FYING, -FIES to alkalize

ALKALIN adj alkaline

ALKALINE adj containing an alkali

ALKALISE v -LISED, -LISING, -LISES to alkalize

ALKALIZE *v* -LIZED, -LIZING, -LIZES to convert into an alkali

ALKALOID *n pl.* -S a type of chemical compound

ALKANE *n pl.* -S a type of chemical compound

ALKANET *n pl.* -S a European plant

ALKENE *n pl.* -S a type of chemical compound

ALKINE *n pl.* -S alkyne

ALKOXY *adj* containing a univalent radical composed of alkyl united with oxygen

ALKYD *n pl.* -S a synthetic resin

ALKYL *n pl.* -S a univalent radical **ALKYLIC** *adj*

ALKYLATE *v* -ATED, -ATING, -ATES to combine with alkyl

ALKYNE *n pl.* -S a type of chemical compound

ALL *n pl.* -S everything that one has

ALLANITE *n pl.* -S a mineral

ALLAY *v* -ED, -ING, -S to reduce in intensity or severity

ALLAYER *n pl.* -S one that allays

ALLEGE *v* -LEGED, -LEGING, -LEGES to assert without proof or before proving

ALLEGER *n pl.* -S one that alleges

ALLEGORY *n pl.* -RIES a story presenting a moral principle

ALLEGRO *n pl.* -GROS a musical passage played in rapid tempo

ALLELE *n pl.* -S any of several forms of a gene **ALLELIC** *adj*

ALLELISM *n pl.* -S the state of possessing alleles

ALLELUIA *n pl.* -S a song of praise to God

ALLERGEN *n pl.* -S a substance capable of inducing an allergy

ALLERGIC *adj* pertaining to allergy

ALLERGIN *n pl.* -S allergen

ALLERGY *n pl.* -GIES a state of hypersensitive reaction to certain things

ALLEY *n pl.* -LEYS a narrow passageway

ALLEYWAY *n pl.* -WAYS an alley

ALLHEAL *n pl.* -S a medicinal herb

ALLIABLE *adj* capable of being allied

ALLIANCE *n pl.* -S an association formed to further the common interests of its members

ALLIED past tense of ally

ALLIES present 3d person sing. of ally

ALLIUM *n pl.* -S a bulbous herb

ALLOBAR *n pl.* -S a change in barometric pressure

ALLOCATE *v* -CATED, -CATING, -CATES to set apart for a particular purpose

ALLOD *n pl.* -S allodium

ALLODIUM *n pl.* -DIA land held in absolute ownership **ALLODIAL** *adj*

ALLOGAMY *n pl.* -MIES fertilization of a flower by pollen from another

ALLONGE *n pl.* -S an addition to a document

ALLONYM *n pl.* -S the name of one person assumed by another

ALLOPATH *n pl.* -S one who treats diseases by producing effects incompatible with those of the disease

ALLOT *v* -LOTTED, -LOTTING, -LOTS to give as a share or portion

ALLOTTEE *n pl.* -S one to whom something is allotted

ALLOTTER *n pl.* -S one that allots

ALLOTTING present participle of allot

ALLOTYPE *n pl.* -S a type of antibody

ALLOTYPY *n pl.* -TYPIES the condition of being an allotype

ALLOVER *n pl.* -S a fabric having a pattern extending over the entire surface

ALLOW *v* -ED, -ING, -S to put no obstacle in the way of

ALLOXAN *n pl.* -S a chemical compound

ALLOY *v* -ED, -ING, -S to combine to form an alloy (a homogenous mixture of metals)

ALLSEED *n pl.* -S a plant having many seeds

ALLSPICE *n pl.* -S a tropical tree

ALLUDE *v* -LUDED, -LUDING, -LUDES to make an indirect reference

ALLURE *v* -LURED, -LURING, -LURES to attract with something desirable

ALLURER *n pl.* -S one that allures

ALLUSION *n pl.* -S the act of alluding **ALLUSIVE** *adj*

ALLUVIA a *pl.* of alluvium

ALLUVIAL *n pl.* -S soil composed of alluvium

ALLUVION *n pl.* -S alluvium

ALLUVIUM *n pl.* -VIA or -VIUMS detrital material deposited by running water

ALLY   v -LIED, -LYING, -LIES to unite in a formal relationship

ALLYL   n pl. -S a univalent radical ALLYLIC adj

ALMA   n pl. -S almah

ALMAGEST   n pl. -S a medieval treatise on astrology or alchemy

ALMAH   n pl. -S an Egyptian girl who sings and dances professionally

ALMANAC   n pl. -S an annual publication containing general information

ALME   n pl. -S almah

ALMEH   n pl. -S almah

ALMEMAR   n pl. -S a bema

ALMIGHTY   adj having absolute power over all

ALMNER   n pl. -S almoner

ALMOND   n pl. -S the edible nut of a small tree

ALMONER   n pl. -S one that distributes alms

ALMONRY   n pl. -RIES a place where alms are distributed

ALMOST   adv very nearly

ALMS   n pl. ALMS money or goods given to the poor

ALMSMAN   n pl. -MEN one who receives alms

ALMUCE   n pl. -S a hooded cape

ALMUD   n pl. -S a Spanish unit of capacity

ALMUDE   n pl. -S almud

ALMUG   n pl. -S a precious wood mentioned in the Bible

ALNICO   n pl. -COES a magnetic alloy

ALODIUM   n pl. -DIA allodium ALODIAL adj

ALOE   n pl. -S an African plant ALOETIC adj

ALOFT   adv in or into the air

ALOGICAL   adj being outside the bounds of that to which logic can apply

ALOHA   n pl. -S love — used as a greeting or farewell

ALOIN   n pl. -S a laxative

ALONE   adj apart from others

ALONG   adv onward

ALOOF   adj distant in interest or feeling ALOOFLY adv

ALOPECIA   n pl. -S baldness ALOPECIC adj

ALOUD   adv audibly

ALOW   adv in or to a lower position

ALP   n pl. -S a high mountain

ALPACA   n pl. -S a ruminant mammal

ALPHA   n pl. -S a Greek letter

ALPHABET   v -ED, -ING, -S to arrange in the customary order of the letters of a language

ALPHORN   n pl. -S a wooden horn used by Swiss herdsmen

ALPHOSIS   n pl. -SISES lack of skin pigmentation

ALPHYL   n pl. -S a univalent radical

ALPINE   n pl. -S a plant native to high mountain regions

ALPINELY   adv in a lofty manner

ALPINISM   n pl. -S mountain climbing

ALPINIST   n pl. -S a mountain climber

ALREADY   adv by this time

ALRIGHT   adj satisfactory

ALSIKE   n pl. -S a European clover

ALSO   adv in addition

ALT   n pl. -S a high-pitched musical note

ALTAR   n pl. -S a raised structure used in worship

ALTER   v -ED, -ING, -S to make different

ALTERANT   n pl. -S something that alters

ALTERER   n pl. -S one that alters

ALTHAEA   n pl. -S althea

ALTHEA   n pl. -S a flowering plant

ALTHO   conj although

ALTHORN   n pl. -S a brass wind instrument

ALTHOUGH   conj despite the fact that

ALTITUDE   n pl. -S the vertical elevation of an object above a given level

ALTO   n pl. -TOS a low female singing voice

ALTRUISM   n pl. -S selfless devotion to the welfare of others

ALTRUIST   n pl. -S one that practices altruism

ALUDEL   n pl. -S a pear-shaped vessel

ALULA   n pl. -LAE a tuft of feathers on the first digit of a bird's wing ALULAR adj

ALUM   n pl. -S a chemical compound

ALUMIN   n pl. -S alumina

ALUMINA   n pl. -S an oxide of aluminum

ALUMINE   n pl. -S alumina

ALUMINUM   n pl. -S a metallic element ALUMINIC adj

ALUMNA   n pl. -NAE a female graduate

ALUMNUS   n pl. -NI a male graduate

ALUMROOT   n pl. -S a flowering plant

ALUNITE   n pl. -S a mineral

ALVEOLAR   n pl. -S a sound produced with the tongue touching a place just behind the front teeth

ALVEOLUS   n pl. -LI a small anatomical cavity

ALVINE   adj pertaining to the abdomen and lower intestines

ALWAY   adv always

ALWAYS   adv at all times

ALYSSUM   n pl. -S a flowering plant

AM   present 1st person sing. of be

AMA   n pl. -S amah

AMADAVAT   n pl. -S an Asian songbird

AMADOU   n pl. -S a substance prepared from fungi for use as tinder

AMAH   n pl. -S an Oriental nurse

AMAIN   adv with full strength

AMALGAM   n pl. -S an alloy of mercury with another metal

AMANDINE   adj prepared with almonds

AMANITA   n pl. -S any of a genus of poisonous fungi

AMARANTH   n pl. -S a flowering plant

AMARELLE   n pl. -S a variety of sour cherry

AMARNA   adj pertaining to a certain historical period of ancient Egypt

AMASS   v -ED, -ING, -ES to gather

AMASSER   n pl. -S one that amasses

AMATEUR   n pl. -S one that engages in an activity for pleasure

AMATIVE   adj amorous

AMATOL   n pl. -S a powerful explosive

AMATORY   adj pertaining to sexual love

AMAZE   v AMAZED, AMAZING, AMAZES to overwhelm with surprise or wonder **AMAZEDLY** adv

AMAZON   n pl. -S a tall, powerful woman

AMBAGE   n pl. -S a winding path

AMBARI   n pl. -S ambary

AMBARY   n pl. -RIES an East Indian plant

AMBEER   n pl. -S tobacco juice

AMBER   n pl. -S a fossil resin

AMBEROID   n pl. -S ambroid

AMBERY   n pl. -BERIES ambry

AMBIANCE   n pl. -S ambience

AMBIENCE   n pl. -S the character, mood, or atmosphere of a place or situation

AMBIENT   n pl. -S ambience

AMBIT   n pl. -S the external boundary of something

AMBITION   v -ED, -ING, -S to seek with eagerness

AMBIVERT   n pl. -S a person whose personality type is intermediate between introvert and extravert

AMBLE   v -BLED, -BLING, -BLES to saunter

AMBLER   n pl. -S one that ambles

AMBO   n pl. AMBOS or AMBONES a pulpit in an early Christian church

AMBOINA   n pl. -S amboyna

AMBOYNA   n pl. -S the mottled wood of an Indonesian tree

AMBRIES   pl. of ambry

AMBROID   n pl. -S a synthetic amber

AMBROSIA   n pl. -S the food of the Greek and Roman gods

AMBRY   n pl. -BRIES a recess in a church wall for sacred vessels

AMBSACE   n pl. -S bad luck

AMBULANT   adj ambulating

AMBULATE   v -LATED, -LATING, -LATES to move or walk about

AMBUSH   v -ED, -ING, -ES to attack from a concealed place

AMBUSHER   n pl. -S one that ambushes

AMEBA   n pl. -BAS or -BAE amoeba **AMEBAN, AMEBIC, AMEBOID** adj

AMEBEAN   adj alternately responding

AMEER   n pl. -S amir

AMEERATE   n pl. -S amirate

AMELCORN   n pl. -S a variety of wheat

AMEN   n pl. -S a word used at the end of a prayer to express agreement

AMENABLE   adj capable of being persuaded **AMENABLY** adv

AMEND   v -ED, -ING, -S to improve

AMENDER   n pl. -S one that amends

AMENITY   n pl. -TIES the quality of being pleasant or agreeable

AMENT   n pl. -S a mentally deficient person

AMENTIA   n pl. -S mental deficiency

AMERCE v AMERCED, AMERCING, AMERCES to punish by imposing an arbitrary fine

AMERCER n pl. -S one that amerces

AMESACE n pl. -S ambsace

AMETHYST n pl. -S a variety of quartz

AMI n pl. -S a friend

AMIA n pl. -S a freshwater fish

AMIABLE adj having a pleasant disposition **AMIABLY** adv

AMIANTUS n pl. -ES a variety of asbestos

AMICABLE adj friendly **AMICABLY** adv

AMICE n pl. -S a vestment worn about the neck and shoulders

AMID n pl. -S amide

AMIDASE n pl. -S an enzyme

AMIDE n pl. -S a type of chemical compound **AMIDIC** adj

AMIDIN n pl. -S the soluble matter of starch

AMIDO adj containing an amide united with an acid radical

AMIDOGEN n pl. -S a univalent chemical radical

AMIDOL n pl. -S a chemical compound

AMIDSHIP adv toward the middle of a ship

AMIDST prep in the midst of

AMIE n pl. -S a female friend

AMIGA n pl. -S a female friend

AMIGO n pl. -GOS a friend

AMIN n pl. -S amine

AMINE n pl. -S a type of chemical compound **AMINIC** adj

AMINITY n pl. -TIES the state of being an amine

AMINO adj containing an amine united with a nonacid radical

AMIR n pl. -S a Muslim prince or governor

AMIRATE n pl. -S the rank of an amir

AMISS adj being out of proper order

AMITOSIS n pl. -TOSES a type of cell division **AMITOTIC** adj

AMITROLE n pl. -S an herbicide

AMITY n pl. -TIES friendship

AMMETER n pl. -S an instrument for measuring amperage

AMMINE n pl. -S a type of chemical compound

AMMINO adj pertaining to an ammine

AMMO n pl. -MOS ammunition

AMMOCETE n pl. -S the larva of a lamprey

AMMONAL n pl. -S a powerful explosive

AMMONIA n pl. -S a pungent gas

AMMONIAC n pl. -S a gum resin

AMMONIC adj pertaining to ammonia

AMMONIFY v -FIED, -FYING, -FIES to treat with ammonia

AMMONITE n pl. -S the coiled shell of an extinct mollusk

AMMONIUM n pl. -S a univalent chemical radical

AMMONOID n pl. -S ammonite

AMNESIA n pl. -S loss of memory

AMNESIAC n pl. -S one suffering from amnesia

AMNESIC n pl. -S amnesiac

AMNESTIC adj pertaining to amnesia

AMNESTY v -TIED, -TYING, -TIES to pardon

AMNION n pl. -NIONS or -NIA a membranous sac enclosing an embryo **AMNIC, AMNIONIC, AMNIOTIC** adj

AMNIOTE n pl. -S a vertebrate that develops an amnion during the embryonic stage

AMOEBA n pl. -BAS or -BAE a unicellular microscopic organism **AMOEBAN, AMOEBIC, AMOEBOID** adj

AMOEBEAN adj amebean

AMOK n pl. -S a murderous frenzy

AMOLE n pl. -S a plant root used as a substitute for soap

AMONG prep in the midst of

AMONGST prep among

AMORAL adj lacking a sense of right and wrong **AMORALLY** adv

AMORETTO n pl. -TI or -TOS a cupid

AMORINO n pl. -NI an amoretto

AMORIST n pl. -S a lover

AMOROSO adv tenderly — used as a musical direction

AMOROUS adj pertaining to love

AMORT adj being without life

AMORTISE v -TISED, TISING, TISES to amortize

AMORTIZE v -TIZED, -TIZING, -TIZES to liquidate gradually, as a debt

AMOTION n pl. -S the removal of a corporate officer from his office

AMOUNT v -ED, -ING, -S to combine to yield a sum

AMOUR n pl. -S a love affair

AMP *n* pl. -S ampere

AMPERAGE *n* pl. -S the strength of an electric current expressed in amperes

AMPERE *n* pl. -S a unit of electric current strength

AMPHIBIA *n/pl* organisms adapted for life both on land and in water

AMPHIOXI *n/pl* lancelets

AMPHIPOD *n* pl. -S a small crustacean

AMPHORA *n* pl. -RAE or -RAS a narrow-necked jar used in ancient Greece **AMPHORAL** *adj*

AMPLE *adj* -PLER, -PLEST abundant **AMPLY** *adv*

AMPLIFY *v* -FIED, -FYING, -FIES to make larger or more powerful

AMPOULE *n* pl. -S ampule

AMPUL *n* pl. -S ampule

AMPULE *n* pl. -S a small glass vial

AMPULLA *n* pl. -LAE a globular bottle used in ancient Rome **AMPULLAR** *adj*

AMPUTATE *v* -TATED, -TATING, -TATES to cut off by surgical means

AMPUTEE *n* pl. -S one that has had a limb amputated

AMREETA *n* pl. -S amrita

AMRITA *n* pl. -S a beverage that bestows immortality in Hindu mythology

AMTRAC *n* pl. -S a military vehicle equipped to move on land and water

AMTRACK *n* pl. -S amtrac

AMU *n* pl. -S a unit of mass

AMUCK *n* pl. -S amok

AMULET *n* pl. -S an object worn to protect against evil or injury

AMUSE *v* AMUSED, AMUSING, AMUSES to occupy pleasingly **AMUSABLE** *adj* **AMUSEDLY** *adv*

AMUSER *n* pl. -S one that amuses

AMUSIVE *adj* amusing

AMYGDALA *n* pl. -LAE an almond-shaped anatomical part

AMYGDALE *n* pl. -S amygdule

AMYGDULE *n* pl. -S a small gas bubble in lava

AMYL *n* pl. -S a univalent radical

AMYLASE *n* pl. -S an enzyme

AMYLENE *n* pl. -S a flammable liquid

AMYLIC *adj* pertaining to amyl

AMYLOID *n* pl. -S a hard protein deposit resulting from degeneration of tissue

AMYLOSE *n* pl. -S the relatively soluble component of starch

AMYLUM *n* pl. -S starch

AN *indefinite article* — used before words beginning with a vowel sound

ANA *n* pl. -S a collection of miscellaneous information about a particular subject

ANABAENA *n* pl. -S a freshwater alga

ANABAS *n* pl. -ES a freshwater fish

ANABASIS *n* pl. -ASES a military advance

ANABATIC *adj* pertaining to rising wind currents

ANABLEPS *n* pl. -ES a freshwater fish

ANABOLIC *adj* pertaining to a process by which food is built up into protoplasm

ANACONDA *n* pl. -S a large snake

ANADEM *n* pl. -S a wreath for the head

ANAEMIA *n* pl. -S anemia **ANAEMIC** *adj*

ANAEROBE *n* pl. -S an organism that does not require oxygen to live

ANAGLYPH *n* pl. -S a type of carved ornament

ANAGOGE *n* pl. -S a spiritual interpretation of words **ANAGOGIC** *adj*

ANAGOGY *n* pl. -GIES anagoge

ANAGRAM *v* -GRAMMED, -GRAMMING, -GRAMS to transpose the letters of a word or phrase to form a new one

ANAL *adj* pertaining to the anus

ANALCIME *n* pl. -S analcite

ANALCITE *n* pl. -S a mineral

ANALECTA *n/pl* analects

ANALECTS *n/pl* selections from a literary work or group of works

ANALEMMA *n* pl. -MAS or -MATA a type of graduated scale

ANALGIA *n* pl. -S inability to feel pain

ANALITY *n* pl. -TIES a type of psychological state

ANALLY *adv* at or through the anus

ANALOG *n* pl. -S analogue

ANALOGIC *adj* pertaining to an analogy

ANALOGUE *n* pl. -S something that bears an analogy to something else

ANALOGY *n* pl. -GIES resemblance in some respects between things otherwise unlike

ANALYSE *v* -LYSED, -LYSING, -LYSES to analyze

ANALYSER *n pl.* -S analyzer

ANALYSIS *n pl.* -YSES the separation of a whole into its parts

ANALYST *n pl.* -S one that analyzes

ANALYTIC *adj* pertaining to analysis

ANALYZE *v* -LYZED, -LYZING, -LYZES to subject to analysis

ANALYZER *n pl.* -S one that analyzes

ANANKE *n pl.* -S a compelling necessity in ancient Greek religion

ANAPAEST *n pl.* -S anapest

ANAPEST *n pl.* -S a type of metrical foot

ANAPHASE *n pl.* -S a stage of mitosis

ANAPHORA *n pl.* -S the repetition of a word or phrase at the beginning of several successive verses or sentences

ANARCH *n pl.* -S an advocate of anarchy

ANARCHY *n pl.* -CHIES absence of government **ANARCHIC** *adj*

ANASARCA *n pl.* -S a form of dropsy

ANATASE *n pl.* -S a mineral

ANATHEMA *n pl.* -MAS or -MATA a formal ecclesiastical ban or curse

ANATOMY *n pl.* -MIES the structure of an organism **ANATOMIC** *adj*

ANATOXIN *n pl.* -S a toxoid

ANATTO *n pl.* -TOS annatto

ANCESTOR *n pl.* -S a person from whom one is descended

ANCESTRY *n pl.* -TRIES a line or body of ancestors

ANCHOR *v* -ED, -ING, -S to secure by means of an anchor (a device for holding a floating vessel in place)

ANCHORET *n pl.* -S a recluse

ANCHOVY *n pl.* -VIES a small food fish

ANCHUSA *n pl.* -S a hairy-stemmed plant

ANCHUSIN *n pl.* -S a red dye

ANCIENT *adj* -CIENTER, -CIENTEST of or pertaining to time long past

ANCIENT *n pl.* -S one who lived in ancient times

ANCILLA *n pl.* -LAE or -LAS a helper

ANCON *n pl.* -ES the elbow **ANCONAL, ANCONEAL, ANCONOID** *adj*

ANCONE *n pl.* -S ancon

ANCRESS *n pl.* -ES a female recluse

AND *n pl.* -S an added condition or stipulation

ANDANTE *n pl.* -S a moderately slow musical passage

ANDESITE *n pl.* -S a volcanic rock

ANDESYTE *n pl.* -S andesite

ANDIRON *n pl.* -S a metal support for holding wood in a fireplace

ANDROGEN *n pl.* -S a male sex hormone

ANDROID *n pl.* -S a synthetic man

ANE *n pl.* -S one

ANEAR *v* -ED, -ING, -S to approach

ANECDOTE *n pl.* -DOTES or -DOTA a brief story

ANECHOIC *adj* neither having nor producing echoes

ANELE *v* ANELED, ANELING, ANELES to anoint

ANEMIA *n pl.* -S a disorder of the blood **ANEMIC** *adj*

ANEMONE *n pl.* -S a flowering plant

ANENST *prep* anent

ANENT *prep* in regard to

ANERGIA *n pl.* -S anergy

ANERGY *n pl.* -GIES lack of energy **ANERGIC** *adj*

ANEROID *n pl.* -S a type of barometer

ANESTRUS *n pl.* -TRI a period of sexual dormancy

ANETHOL *n pl.* -S anethole

ANETHOLE *n pl.* -S a chemical compound

ANEURISM *n pl.* -S aneurysm

ANEURYSM *n pl.* -S an abnormal blood-filled dilation of a blood vessel

ANEW *adv* once more

ANGA *n pl.* -S any of the eight practices of yoga

ANGARIA *n pl.* -S angary

ANGARY *n pl.* -RIES the right of a warring state to seize neutral property

ANGEL *n pl.* -S a winged celestial being **ANGELIC** *adj*

ANGELICA *n pl.* -S an aromatic herb

ANGELUS *n pl.* -ES a Roman Catholic prayer

ANGER *v* -ED, -ING, -S to make angry

ANGERLY *adv* in an angry manner

ANGINA *n pl.* -S a disease marked by spasmodic attacks of intense pain **ANGINAL, ANGINOSE, ANGINOUS** *adj*

ANGIOMA *n pl.* -MAS or -MATA a tumor composed of blood or lymph vessels

ANGLE	*v* -GLED, -GLING, -GLES to fish with a hook and line
ANGLEPOD	*n pl.* -S a flowering plant
ANGLER	*n pl.* -S one that angles
ANGLICE	*adv* in readily understood English
ANGLING	*n pl.* -S the sport of fishing
ANGORA	*n pl.* -S the long, silky hair of a domestic goat
ANGRY	*adj* -GRIER, -GRIEST feeling strong displeasure or hostility ANGRILY *adv*
ANGST	*n pl.* -S a feeling of anxiety or dread
ANGSTROM	*n pl.* -S a unit of length
ANGUINE	*adj* resembling a snake
ANGUISH	*v* -ED, -ING, -ES to suffer extreme pain
ANGULAR	*adj* having sharp corners
ANGULATE	*v* -LATED, -LATING, -LATES to make angular
ANGULOSE	*adj* angular
ANGULOUS	*adj* angular
ANHINGA	*n pl.* -S an aquatic bird
ANI	*n pl.* -S a tropical American bird
ANIL	*n pl.* -S a West Indian shrub
ANILE	*adj* resembling an old woman
ANILIN	*n pl.* -S aniline
ANILINE	*n pl.* -S a chemical compound
ANILITY	*n pl.* -TIES the state of being anile
ANIMA	*n pl.* -S the soul
ANIMAL	*n pl.* -S a living organism typically capable of voluntary motion and sensation
ANIMALLY	*adv* physically
ANIMATE	*v* -MATED, -MATING, -MATES to give life to
ANIMATER	*n pl.* -S animator
ANIMATO	*adv* in a lively manner — used as a musical direction
ANIMATOR	*n pl.* -S one that animates
ANIME	*n pl.* -S a resin obtained from a tropical tree
ANIMI	*n pl.* -S anime
ANIMISM	*n pl.* -S the belief that souls may exist apart from bodies
ANIMIST	*n pl.* -S an adherent of animism
ANIMUS	*n pl.* -ES a feeling of hostility
ANION	*n pl.* -S a negatively charged ion ANIONIC *adj*
ANISE	*n pl.* -S a North African plant
ANISEED	*n pl.* -S the seed of the anise used as a flavoring
ANISETTE	*n pl.* -S a liqueur flavored with aniseed
ANISIC	*adj* pertaining to an anise
ANISOLE	*n pl.* -S a chemical compound
ANKERITE	*n pl.* -S a mineral
ANKH	*n pl.* -S an Egyptian symbol of enduring life
ANKLE	*n pl.* -S the joint connecting the foot and the leg
ANKLET	*n pl.* -S an ornament for the ankle
ANKUS	*n pl.* -ES an elephant goad
ANKUSH	*n pl.* -ES ankus
ANKYLOSE	*v* -LOSED, -LOSING, -LOSES to unite or grow together, as the bones of a joint
ANLACE	*n pl.* -S a medieval dagger
ANLAGE	*n pl.* -GEN or -GES the initial cell structure from which an embryonic organ develops
ANLAS	*n pl.* -ES anlace
ANNA	*n pl.* -S a former coin of India and Pakistan
ANNAL	*n pl.* -S a record of a single year
ANNALIST	*n pl.* -S a historian
ANNATES	*n/pl* the first year's revenue of a bishop paid to the pope
ANNATTO	*n pl.* -TOS a yellowish-red dye
ANNEAL	*v* -ED, -ING, -S to toughen
ANNEALER	*n pl.* -S one that anneals
ANNELID	*n pl.* -S any of a phylum of segmented worms
ANNEX	*v* -ED, -ING, -ES to add or attach
ANNEXE	*n pl.* -S something added or attached
ANNOTATE	*v* -TATED, -TATING, -TATES to furnish with critical or explanatory notes
ANNOUNCE	*v* -NOUNCED, -NOUNCING, -NOUNCES to make known publicly
ANNOY	*v* -ED, -ING, -S to be troublesome to
ANNOYER	*n pl.* -S one that annoys
ANNUAL	*n pl.* -S a publication issued once a year
ANNUALLY	*adv* once a year
ANNUITY	*n pl.* -TIES an allowance or income paid at regular intervals

ANNUL *v* -NULLED, -NULLING, -NULS to make or declare void or invalid

ANNULAR *adj* shaped like a ring

ANNULATE *adj* composed of or furnished with rings

ANNULET *n pl.* -S a small ring

ANNULI a *pl.* of annulus

ANNULLED past tense of annul

ANNULLING present participle of annul

ANNULUS *n pl.* -LI or -LUSES a ring or ringlike part ANNULOSE *adj*

ANOA *n pl.* -S a wild ox

ANODE *n pl.* -S a positively charged electrode ANODAL, ANODIC *adj* ANODALLY *adv*

ANODIZE *v* -IZED, -IZING, -IZES to coat with a protective film by chemical means

ANODYNE *n pl.* -S a medicine that relieves pain ANODYNIC *adj*

ANOINT *v* -ED, -ING, -S to apply oil to as a sacred rite

ANOINTER *n pl.* -S one that anoints

ANOLE *n pl.* -S a tropical lizard

ANOLYTE *n pl.* -S the part of an electricity-conducting solution nearest the anode

ANOMALY *n pl.* -LIES a deviation from the common rule, type, or form

ANOMIE *n pl.* -S a collapse of the social structures governing a given society ANOMIC *adj*

ANOMY *n pl.* -MIES anomie

ANON *adv* at another time

ANONYM *n pl.* -S a false or assumed name

ANOOPSIA *n pl.* -S a visual defect

ANOPIA *n pl.* -S anoopsia

ANOPSIA *n pl.* -S anoopsia

ANORAK *n pl.* -S a parka

ANORETIC *adj* lacking appetite

ANOREXIA *n pl.* -S loss of appetite

ANOREXY *n pl.* -OREXIES anorexia

ANORTHIC *adj* denoting a certain type of crystal system

ANOSMIA *n pl.* -S loss of the sense of smell ANOSMIC *adj*

ANOTHER *adj* one more

ANOXEMIA *n pl.* -S a disorder of the blood ANOXEMIC *adj*

ANOXIA *n pl.* -S absence of oxygen ANOXIC *adj*

ANSA *n pl.* -SAE the projecting part of Saturn's rings

ANSATE *adj* having a handle

ANSATED *adj* ansate

ANSERINE *n pl.* -S a chemical compound

ANSEROUS *adj* silly

ANSWER *v* -ED, -ING, -S to say, write, or act in return

ANSWERER *n pl.* -S one that answers

ANT *n pl.* -S a small insect

ANTA *n pl.* -TAE or -TAS a pilaster formed at the termination of a wall

ANTACID *n pl.* -S a substance that neutralizes acid

ANTALGIC *n pl.* -S an anodyne

ANTE *v* ANTED or ANTEED, ANTEING, ANTES to put a fixed stake into the pot before the cards are dealt in poker

ANTEATER *n pl.* -S any of several mammals that feed on ants

ANTECEDE *v* -CEDED, -CEDING, -CEDES to precede

ANTED a past tense of ante

ANTEDATE *v* -DATED, -DATING, -DATES to be of an earlier date than

ANTEFIX *n pl.* -FIXES or -FIXA an upright ornament at the eaves of a tiled roof

ANTELOPE *n pl.* -S a ruminant mammal

ANTENNA *n pl.* -NAE or -NAS a sensory appendage on the head of an insect, myriapod, or crustacean ANTENNAL *adj*

ANTEPAST *n pl.* -S an appetizer

ANTERIOR *adj* situated in or toward the front

ANTEROOM *n pl.* -S a waiting room

ANTETYPE *n pl.* -S an earlier form

ANTEVERT *v* -ED, -ING, -S to displace by tipping forward

ANTHELIA *n/pl* halolike areas seen in the sky opposite the sun

ANTHELIX *n pl.* -LICES the inner curved ridge on the cartilage of the external ear

ANTHEM *v* -ED, -ING, -S to praise in a song

ANTHEMIA *n/pl* decorative floral patterns used in Greek art

ANTHER *n pl.* -S the pollen-bearing part of a stamen ANTHERAL *adj*

ANTHERID *n pl.* -S a male reproductive organ of certain plants

ANTHESIS n pl. -THESES the full bloom of a flower

ANTHILL n pl. -S a mound formed by ants in building their nest

ANTHODIA n/pl flower heads of certain plants

ANTHOID adj resembling a flower

ANTHRAX n pl. -THRACES an infectious disease

ANTI n pl. -S one that is opposed

ANTIAR n pl. -S an arrow poison

ANTIARIN n pl. -S antiar

ANTIBODY n pl. -BODIES a body protein that produces immunity against certain microorganisms or toxins

ANTIC v -TICKED, -TICKING, -TICS to act in a clownish manner

ANTICK v -ED, -ING, -S to antic

ANTICLY adv in a clownish manner

ANTIDOTE n pl. -S a remedy to counteract the effects of a poison

ANTIFAT adj preventing the formation of fat

ANTIGEN n pl. -S a substance that stimulates the production of antibodies

ANTIGENE n pl. -S antigen

ANTIHERO n pl. -ROES a protagonist who is notably lacking in heroic qualities

ANTIKING n pl. -S a usurping king

ANTILOG n pl. -S the number corresponding to a given logarithm

ANTILOGY n pl. -GIES a contradiction in terms or ideas

ANTIMASK n pl. -S a comic performance between the acts of a masque

ANTIMERE n pl. -S a part of an organism symmetrical with a part on the opposite side of the main axis

ANTIMONY n pl. -NIES a metallic element

ANTING n pl. -S the deliberate placing, by certain birds, of living ants among the feathers

ANTINODE n pl. -S a region between adjacent nodes

ANTINOMY n pl. -MIES a contradiction between two seemingly valid principles

ANTIPHON n pl. -S a psalm or hymn sung responsively

ANTIPODE n pl. -S an exact opposite

ANTIPOLE n pl. -S the opposite pole

ANTIPOPE n pl. -S one claiming to be pope in opposition to the one chosen by church law

ANTIPYIC n pl. -S a medicine that prevents the formation of pus

ANTIQUE v -TIQUED, TIQUING, TIQUES to give an appearance of age to

ANTIQUER n pl. -S one that antiques

ANTIRUST n pl. -S something that prevents rust

ANTISERA n/pl serums that contain antibodies

ANTISKID adj designed to prevent skidding

ANTISMOG adj designed to reduce pollutants that cause smog

ANTITANK adj designed to combat tanks

ANTITAX adj opposing taxes

ANTITYPE n pl. -S an opposite type

ANTIWAR adj opposing war

ANTLER n pl. -S the horn of an animal of the deer family ANTLERED adj

ANTLIKE adj resembling an ant

ANTLION n pl. -S a predatory insect

ANTONYM n pl. -S a word opposite in meaning to another

ANTONYMY n pl. -MIES the state of being an antonym

ANTRA pl. of antrum

ANTRAL adj pertaining to an antrum

ANTRE n pl. -S a cave

ANTRORSE adj directed forward or upward

ANTRUM n pl. -TRA a cavity in a bone

ANURAN n pl. -S a frog or toad

ANURESIS n pl. -RESES inability to urinate ANURETIC adj

ANURIA n pl. -S absence of urine ANURIC adj

ANUROUS adj having no tail

ANUS n pl. -ES the excretory opening at the end of the alimentary canal

ANVIL v -VILED, -VILING, -VILS or -VILLED, -VILLING, -VILS to shape on an anvil (a heavy iron block)

ANVILTOP n pl. -S an anvil-shaped cloud mass

ANXIETY n pl. -ETIES painful or apprehensive uneasiness of mind

ANXIOUS adj full of anxiety

ANY adj one, no matter which

ANYBODY *n pl.* -BODIES a person of some importance

ANYHOW *adv* in any way

ANYMORE *adv* at the present time

ANYONE *pron* any person

ANYPLACE *adv* in any place

ANYTHING *n pl.* -S a thing of any kind

ANYTIME *adv* at any time

ANYWAY *adv* in any way

ANYWAYS *adv* anyway

ANYWHERE *n pl.* -S any place

ANYWISE *adv* in any way

AORIST *n pl.* -S a verb tense AORISTIC *adj*

AORTA *n pl.* -TAS or -TAE a main artery AORTAL, AORTIC *adj*

AOUDAD *n pl.* -S a wild sheep

APACE *adv* swiftly

APACHE *n pl.* -S a Parisian gangster

APAGOGE *n pl.* -S establishment of a thesis by showing its contrary to be absurd APAGOGIC *adj*

APANAGE *n pl.* -S appanage

APAREJO *n pl.* -JOS a type of saddle

APART *adv* not together

APATETIC *adj* having coloration serving as natural camouflage

APATHY *n pl.* -THIES lack of emotion

APATITE *n pl.* -S a mineral

APE *v* APED, APING, APES to mimic

APEAK *adv* in a vertical position

APEEK *adv* apeak

APELIKE *adj* resembling an ape (a large, tailless primate)

APER *n pl.* -S one that apes

APERCU *n pl.* -S a brief summary

APERIENT *n pl.* -S a mild laxative

APERITIF *n pl.* -S an alcoholic drink taken before a meal

APERTURE *n pl.* -S an opening

APERY *n pl.* -ERIES the act of aping

APETALY *n pl.* -ALIES the state of having no petals

APEX *n pl.* APEXES or APICES the highest point

APHAGIA *n pl.* -S inability to swallow

APHANITE *n pl.* -S an igneous rock

APHASIA *n pl.* -S loss of the ability to use words

APHASIAC *n pl.* -S one suffering from aphasia

APHASIC *n pl.* -S aphasiac

APHELION *n pl.* -ELIA the point in a planetary orbit farthest from the sun APHELIAN *adj*

APHESIS *n pl.* -ESES the loss of an unstressed vowel from the beginning of a word APHETIC *adj*

APHID *n pl.* -S any of a family of small, soft-bodied insects

APHIDIAN *n pl.* -S an aphid

APHIS *n pl.* APHIDES an aphid

APHOLATE *n pl.* -S a chemical used to control houseflies

APHONIA *n pl.* -S loss of voice

APHONIC *n pl.* -S one affected with aphonia

APHORISE *v* -RISED, -RISING, -RISES to aphorize

APHORISM *n pl.* -S a brief statement of a truth or principle

APHORIST *n pl.* -S one that aphorizes

APHORIZE *v* -RIZED, -RIZING, -RIZES to write or speak in aphorisms

APHOTIC *adj* lacking light

APHTHA *n pl.* -THAE a small blister in the mouth or stomach APHTHOUS *adj*

APHYLLY *n pl.* -LIES the state of being leafless

APIAN *adj* pertaining to bees

APIARIAN *n pl.* -S an apiarist

APIARIST *n pl.* -S a person who raises bees

APIARY *n pl.* -ARIES a place where bees are kept

APICAL *adj* situated at the apex APICALLY *adv*

APICES *a pl.* of apex

APICULUS *n pl.* -LI a sharp point at the end of a leaf

APIECE *adv* for each one

APIMANIA *n pl.* -S an excessive interest in bees

APING present participle of ape

APIOLOGY *n pl.* -GIES the study of bees

APISH *adj* slavishly or foolishly imitative APISHLY *adv*

APLASIA *n pl.* -S defective development of an organ or part

APLASTIC *adj* not plastic

APLENTY *adj* being in sufficient quantity

APLITE *n pl.* -S a fine-grained rock APLITIC *adj*

APLOMB   *n pl.* -S self-confidence

APNEA   *n pl.* -S temporary cessation of respiration **APNEAL, APNEIC** *adj*

APNOEA   *n pl.* -S apnea **APNOEAL, APNOEIC** *adj*

APOCARP   *n pl.* -S a fruit having separated carpels

APOCARPY   *n pl.* -PIES the state of being an apocarp

APOCOPE   *n pl.* -S an omission of the last sound of a word **APOCOPIC** *adj*

APOCRINE   *adj* pertaining to a type of gland

APODAL   *adj* having no feet or footlike appendages

APODOSIS   *n pl.* -OSES the main clause of a conditional sentence

APODOUS   *adj* apodal

APOGAMY   *n pl.* -MIES a form of plant reproduction **APOGAMIC** *adj*

APOGEE   *n pl.* -S the point in the orbit of a celestial body which is farthest from the earth **APOGEAL, APOGEAN, APOGEIC** *adj*

APOLLO   *n pl.* -LOS a handsome young man

APOLOG   *n pl.* -S apologue

APOLOGAL   *adj* pertaining to an apologue

APOLOGIA   *n pl.* -GIAS or -GIAE a formal justification or defense

APOLOGUE   *n pl.* -S an allegory

APOLOGY   *n pl.* -GIES an expression of regret for some error or offense

APOLUNE   *n pl.* -S the point in the orbit of a celestial body which is farthest from the moon

APOMICT   *n pl.* -S an organism produced by apomixis

APOMIXIS   *n pl.* -MIXES a type of reproductive process

APOPHYGE   *n pl.* -S a concave curve in a column

APOPLEXY   *n pl.* -PLEXIES a sudden loss of sensation and muscular control

APORT   *adv* on or toward the left side of a ship

APOSTACY   *n pl.* -CIES apostasy

APOSTASY   *n pl.* -SIES an abandonment of one's faith or principles

APOSTATE   *n pl.* -S one who commits apostasy

APOSTIL   *n pl.* -S a marginal note

APOSTLE   *n pl.* -S a disciple sent forth by Christ to preach the gospel

APOTHECE   *n pl.* -S a spore-producing organ of certain fungi

APOTHEGM   *n pl.* -S a maxim

APOTHEM   *n pl.* -S the perpendicular from the center to any side of a regular polygon

APPAL   *v* -PALLED, -PALLING, -PALS to appall

APPALL   *v* -ED, -ING, -S to fill with horror or dismay

APPANAGE   *n pl.* -S land or revenue granted to a member of a royal family

APPARAT   *n pl.* -S a political organization

APPAREL   *v* -ELED, -ELING, -ELS or -ELLED, -ELLING, -ELS to provide with outer garments

APPARENT   *adj* easily seen

APPEAL   *v* -ED, -ING, -S to make an earnest request

APPEALER   *n pl.* -S one that appeals

APPEAR   *v* -ED, -ING, -S to come into view

APPEASE   *v* -PEASED, -PEASING, -PEASES to bring to a state of peace or contentment

APPEASER   *n pl.* -S one that appeases

APPEL   *n pl.* -S a feint in fencing

APPELLEE   *n pl.* -S the defendant in a type of judicial proceeding

APPELLOR   *n pl.* -S a confessed criminal who accuses an accomplice

APPEND   *v* -ED, -ING, -S to add as a supplement

APPENDIX   *n pl.* -DIXES or -DICES a collection of supplementary material at the end of a book

APPESTAT   *n pl.* -S the mechanism in the central nervous system that regulates appetite

APPETENT   *adj* marked by strong desire

APPETITE   *n pl.* -S a desire for food or drink

APPLAUD   *v* -ED, -ING, -S to express approval by clapping the hands

APPLAUSE   *n pl.* -S the sound made by persons applauding

APPLE   *n pl.* -S an edible fruit

APPLIER   *n pl.* -S one that applies

APPLIQUE   *v* -QUED, -QUEING, -QUES to apply as a decoration to a larger surface

APPLY v -PLIED, -PLYING, -PLIES to bring into contact with something

APPOINT v -ED, -ING, -S to name or assign to a position or office

APPOSE v -POSED, -POSING, -POSES to place side by side

APPOSER n pl. -S one that apposes

APPOSITE adj relevant

APPRAISE v -PRAISED, -PRAISING, -PRAISES to set a value on

APPRISE v -PRISED, -PRISING, -PRISES to notify

APPRISER n pl. -S one that apprises

APPRIZE v -PRIZED, -PRIZING, -PRIZES to appraise

APPRIZER n pl. -S one that apprizes

APPROACH v -ED, -ING, -ES to come near or nearer to

APPROVAL n pl. -S the act of approving

APPROVE v -PROVED, -PROVING, -PROVES to regard favorably

APPROVER n pl. -S one that approves

APPULSE n pl. -S the approach of one moving body toward another

APRAXIA n pl. -S loss of the ability to perform coordinated movements **APRACTIC, APRAXIC** adj

APRICOT n pl. -S an edible fruit

APRON v -ED, -ING, -S to provide with an apron (a garment worn to protect one's clothing)

APROPOS adj relevant

APSE n pl. -S a domed, semicircular projection of a building **APSIDAL** adj

APSIS n pl. -SIDES an apse

APT adj APTER, APTEST suitable

APTERAL adj apterous

APTEROUS adj having no wings

APTERYX n pl. -ES the kiwi

APTITUDE n pl. -S an ability

APTLY adv in an apt manner

APTNESS n pl. -ES the quality of being apt

APYRASE n pl. -S an enzyme

APYRETIC adj having no fever

AQUA n pl. AQUAE or AQUAS water

AQUACADE n pl. -S a swimming and diving exhibition

AQUANAUT n pl. -S a scuba diver trained to live in underwater installations

AQUARIA a pl. of aquarium

AQUARIAL adj pertaining to an aquarium

AQUARIAN n pl. -S a member of the old sects that used water rather than wine in religious ceremonies

AQUARIST n pl. -S one who keeps an aquarium

AQUARIUM n pl. -IUMS or -IA a water-filled enclosure in which aquatic animals are kept

AQUATIC n pl. -S an organism living or growing in or near water

AQUATINT v -ED, -ING, -S to etch, using a certain process

AQUATONE n pl. -S a type of printing process

AQUAVIT n pl. -S a Scandinavian liquor

AQUEDUCT n pl. -S a water conduit

AQUEOUS adj pertaining to water

AQUIFER n pl. -S a water-bearing rock formation

AQUILINE adj curving like an eagle's beak

AQUIVER adj quivering

AR n pl. -S the letter R

ARABESK n pl. -S a design of intertwined floral figures

ARABIZE v -IZED, -IZING, -IZES to cause to acquire Arabic customs

ARABLE n pl. -S land suitable for cultivation

ARACEOUS adj belonging to the arum family of plants

ARACHNID n pl. -S any of a class of segmented invertebrate animals

ARAK n pl. -S arrack

ARANEID n pl. -S a spider

ARAPAIMA n pl. -S a large food fish

ARAROBA n pl. -S a Brazilian tree

ARBALEST n pl. -S a type of crossbow

ARBALIST n pl. -S arbalest

ARBITER n pl. -S one chosen or appointed to judge a disputed issue **ARBITRAL** adj

ARBOR n pl. -S a shady garden shelter

ARBOR n pl. -ES a tree

ARBOREAL adj living in trees

ARBORED adj having trees

ARBORETA n/pl places for the study and exhibition of trees

ARBORIST n pl. -S a tree specialist

ARBORIZE v -IZED, -IZING, -IZES to form many branches

ARBOROUS *adj* pertaining to trees

ARBOUR *n pl.* -S a shady garden shelter **ARBOURED** *adj*

ARBUSCLE *n pl.* -S a dwarf tree

ARBUTE *n pl.* -S an evergreen tree **ARBUTEAN** *adj*

ARBUTUS *n pl.* -ES an evergreen tree

ARC *v* ARCED, ARCING, ARCS or ARCKED, ARCKING, ARCS to move in a curved course

ARCADE *v* -CADED, -CADING, -CADES to provide with an arcade (a series of arches)

ARCADIA *n pl.* -S a region of simple pleasure and quiet

ARCADIAN *n pl.* -S one who lives in an arcadia

ARCADING *n pl.* -S an arcade

ARCANE *adj* mysterious

ARCANUM *n pl.* -NA a mystery

ARCATURE *n pl.* -S a small arcade

ARCH *v* -ED, -ING, -ES to bend like an arch (a curved structure spanning an opening)

ARCHAIC *adj* pertaining to an earlier time

ARCHAISE *v* -ISED, -ISING, -ISES to archaize

ARCHAISM *n pl.* -S an archaic word, idiom, or expression

ARCHAIST *n pl.* -S one that archaizes

ARCHAIZE *v* -IZED, -IZING, -IZES to use archaisms

ARCHDUKE *n pl.* -S an Austrian prince

ARCHER *n pl.* -S one that shoots with a bow and arrow

ARCHERY *n pl.* -CHERIES the sport of shooting with a bow and arrow

ARCHIL *n pl.* -S orchil

ARCHINE *n pl.* -S a Russian unit of linear measure

ARCHING *n pl.* -S a series of arches

ARCHIVE *v* -CHIVED, -CHIVING, -CHIVES to file in an archive (a place where records are kept) **ARCHIVAL** *adj*

ARCHLY *adv* slyly

ARCHNESS *n pl.* -ES slyness

ARCHON *n pl.* -S a magistrate of ancient Athens

ARCHWAY *n pl.* -WAYS a passageway under an arch

ARCIFORM *adj* having the form of an arch

ARCKED a past tense of arc

ARCKING a present participle of arc

ARCO *adv* with the bow — used as a direction to players of stringed instruments

ARCTIC *n pl.* -S a warm, waterproof overshoe

ARCUATE *adj* curved like a bow

ARCUATED *adj* arcuate

ARCUS *n pl.* -ES an arch-shaped cloud

ARDEB *n pl.* -S an Egyptian unit of capacity

ARDENCY *n pl.* -CIES ardor

ARDENT *adj* characterized by intense emotion **ARDENTLY** *adv*

ARDOR *n pl.* -S intensity of emotion

ARDOUR *n pl.* -S ardor

ARDUOUS *adj* involving great labor or hardship

ARE *n pl.* -S a unit of surface measure

AREA *n pl.* AREAE a section of the cerebral cortex having a specific function

AREA *n pl.* -S a particular extent of space or surface **AREAL** *adj* **AREALLY** *adv*

AREAWAY *n pl.* -WAYS a sunken area leading to a basement entrance

ARECA *n pl.* -S a tropical tree

AREIC *adj* pertaining to a region of the earth contributing little surface drainage

ARENA *n pl.* -S an enclosed area for contests

ARENOSE *adj* sandy

ARENOUS *adj* arenose

AREOLA *n pl.* -LAE or -LAS a small space in a network of leaf veins **AREOLAR, AREOLATE** *adj*

AREOLE *n pl.* -S areola

AREOLOGY *n pl.* -GIES the study of the planet Mars

ARETE *n pl.* -S a sharp mountain ridge

ARETHUSA *n pl.* -S a flowering plant

ARF *interj* — used to express the bark of a dog

ARGAL *n pl.* -S argol

ARGALI *n pl.* -S a wild sheep

ARGENT *n pl.* -S silver **ARGENTAL, ARGENTIC** *adj*

ARGENTUM *n pl.* -S silver

ARGIL *n pl.* -S a white clay

ARGINASE *n pl.* -S an enzyme

ARGININE *n pl.* -S an amino acid

ARGLE v -GLED, -GLING, -GLES to argue

ARGOL n pl. -S a crust deposited in wine casks during aging

ARGON n pl. -S a gaseous element

ARGONAUT n pl. -S a marine mollusc

ARGOSY n pl. -SIES a large merchant ship

ARGOT n pl. -S a specialized vocabulary ARGOTIC adj

ARGUABLE adj capable of being argued about ARGUABLY adv

ARGUE v -GUED, -GUING, -GUES to present reasons for or against

ARGUER n pl. -S one that argues

ARGUFIER n pl. -S one that argufies

ARGUFY v -FIED, -FYING, -FIES to argue stubbornly

ARGUING present participle of argue

ARGUMENT n pl. -S a discussion involving differing points of view

ARGUS n pl. -ES an East Indian pheasant

ARGYLE n pl. -S a knitting pattern

ARGYLL n pl. -S argyle

ARHAT n pl. -S a Buddhist who has attained nirvana

ARIA n pl. -S an elaborate melody for a single voice

ARID adj -IDER, -IDEST extremely dry ARIDLY adv

ARIDITY n pl. -TIES the state of being arid

ARIDNESS n pl. -ES aridity

ARIEL n pl. -S an African gazelle

ARIETTA n pl. -S a short aria

ARIETTE n pl. -S arietta

ARIGHT adv rightly; correctly

ARIL n pl. -S an outer covering of certain seeds ARILED, ARILLATE, ARILLOID adj

ARILLODE n pl. -S a type of aril

ARIOSE adj characterized by melody

ARIOSO n pl. -SOS or -SI a musical passage resembling an aria

ARISE v AROSE, ARISEN, ARISING, ARISES to get up

ARISTA n pl. -TAE or -TAS a bristlelike structure or appendage ARISTATE adj

ARK n pl. -S a large boat

ARLES n/pl money paid to bind a bargain

ARM v -ED, -ING, -S to supply with weapons

ARMADA n pl. -S a fleet of warships

ARMAMENT n pl. -S a military force equipped for war

ARMATURE v -TURED, -TURING, -TURES to furnish with armor

ARMBAND n pl. -S a band worn around an arm (an upper appendage of the human body)

ARMCHAIR n pl. -S a chair with armrests

ARMER n pl. -S one that arms

ARMET n pl. -S a medieval helmet

ARMFUL n pl. ARMFULS or ARMSFUL as much as the arm can hold

ARMHOLE n pl. -S an opening for the arm in a garment

ARMIES pl. of army

ARMIGER n pl. -S one who carries the armor of a knight

ARMIGERO n pl. -GEROS armiger

ARMILLA n pl. -LAE or -LAS a thin membrane around the stem of certain fungi

ARMING n pl. -S the act of one that arms

ARMLESS adj having no arms

ARMLET n pl. -S an armband

ARMLIKE adj resembling an arm

ARMLOAD n pl. -S an armful

ARMOIRE n pl. -S a large, ornate cabinet

ARMONICA n pl. -S a type of musical instrument

ARMOR v -ED, -ING, -S to furnish with armor (a defensive covering for the body)

ARMORER n pl. -S one that makes or repairs armor

ARMORIAL n pl. -S a treatise on heraldry

ARMORY n pl. -MORIES a place where weapons are stored

ARMOUR v -ED, -ING, -S to armor

ARMOURER n pl. -S armorer

ARMOURY n pl. -MOURIES armory

ARMPIT n pl. -S the hollow under the arm at the shoulder

ARMREST n pl. -S a support for the arm

ARMSFUL a pl. of armful

ARMURE n pl. -S a woven fabric

ARMY n pl. -MIES a large body of men trained and armed for war

ARMYWORM n pl. -S a destructive moth larva

ARNATTO *n* pl. -TOS annatto

ARNICA *n* pl. -S a perennial herb

ARNOTTO *n* pl. -TOS a tropical tree

AROID *n* pl. -S a flowering plant

AROINT *v* -ED, -ING, -S to drive away

AROMA *n* pl. -S a pleasant odor

AROMATIC *n* pl. -S a fragrant plant or substance

AROSE past tense of arise

AROUND *prep* on all sides of

AROUSAL *n* pl. -S the act of arousing

AROUSE *v* AROUSED, AROUSING, AROUSES to stimulate

AROUSER *n* pl. -S one that arouses

AROYNT *v* -ED, -ING, -S to aroint

ARPEGGIO *n* pl. -GIOS a technique of playing a musical chord

ARPEN *n* pl. -S arpent

ARPENT *n* pl. -S an old French unit of area

ARQUEBUS *n* pl. -ES an early portable firearm

ARRACK *n* pl. -S an Oriental liquor

ARRAIGN *v* -ED, -ING, -S to call before a court of law to answer an indictment

ARRANGE *v* -RANGED, -RANGING, -RANGES to put in definite or proper order

ARRANGER *n* pl. -S one that arranges

ARRANT *adj* outright **ARRANTLY** *adv*

ARRAS *n* pl. ARRAS a tapestry **ARRASED** *adj*

ARRAY *v* -ED, -ING, -S to place in proper or desired order

ARRAYAL *n* pl. -S the act of arraying

ARRAYER *n* pl. -S one that arrays

ARREAR *n* pl. -S an unpaid and overdue debt

ARREST *v* -ED, -ING, -S to seize and hold by legal authority

ARRESTEE *n* pl. -S one that is arrested

ARRESTER *n* pl. -S one that arrests

ARRESTOR *n* pl. -S arrester

ARRHIZAL *adj* rootless

ARRIS *n* pl. -RISES a ridge formed by the meeting of two surfaces

ARRIVAL *n* pl. -S the act of arriving

ARRIVE *v* -RIVED, -RIVING, -RIVES to reach a destination

ARRIVER *n* pl. -S one that arrives

ARROBA *n* pl. -S a Spanish unit of weight

ARROGANT *adj* overly convinced of one's own worth or importance

ARROGATE *v* -GATED, -GATING, -GATES to claim or take without right

ARROW *v* -ED, -ING, -S to indicate the proper position of by means of a linear figure with a wedge-shaped end

ARROWY *adj* moving swiftly

ARROYO *n* pl. -ROYOS a brook or creek

ARSE *n* pl. -S the buttocks — an offensive term

ARSENAL *n* pl. -S a collection or supply of weapons

ARSENATE *n* pl. -S a chemical salt

ARSENIC *n* pl. -S a metallic element

ARSENIDE *n* pl. -S an arsenic compound

ARSENITE *n* pl. -S a chemical salt

ARSENO *adj* containing a certain bivalent chemical radical

ARSENOUS *adj* pertaining to arsenic

ARSHIN *n* pl. -S archine

ARSINE *n* pl. -S a poisonous gas

ARSINO *adj* containing a certain univalent chemical radical

ARSIS *n* pl. ARSES the unaccented part of a musical measure

ARSON *n* pl. -S the malicious or fraudulent burning of property **ARSONOUS** *adj*

ARSONIST *n* pl. -S one that commits arson

ART *n* pl. -S an esthetically pleasing and meaningful arrangement of elements

ARTAL a pl. of rotl

ARTEFACT *n* pl. -S artifact

ARTEL *n* pl. -S a collective farm in Russia

ARTERIAL *n* pl. -S a type of highway

ARTERY *n* pl. -TERIES a vessel that carries blood away from the heart

ARTFUL *adj* crafty **ARTFULLY** *adv*

ARTICLE *v* -CLED, -CLING, -CLES to charge with specific offenses

ARTIER comparative of arty

ARTIEST superlative of arty

ARTIFACT *n* pl. -S an object made by man

ARTIFICE *n* pl. -S a clever stratagem

ARTILY *adv* in an arty manner

ARTINESS *n* pl. -ES the quality of being arty

ARTISAN *n* pl. -S a trained or skilled workman

ARTIST *n* pl. -S one who practices one of the fine arts

ARTISTE *n* pl. -S a skilled public performer

ARTISTIC *adj* characteristic of art

ARTISTRY *n* pl. -RIES artistic quality or workmanship

ARTLESS *adj* lacking cunning or guile

ARTWORK *n* pl. -S illustrative or decorative work in printed matter

ARTY *adj* ARTIER, ARTIEST showily or pretentiously artistic

ARUM *n* pl. -S a flowering plant

ARUSPEX *n* pl. -PICES haruspex

ARVAL *adj* pertaining to plowed land

ARVO *n* pl. -VOS afternoon

ARYL *n* pl. -S a univalent radical

ARYTHMIA *n* pl. -S an irregularity in the rhythm of the heartbeat **ARYTHMIC** *adj*

AS *adv* to the same degree

ASARUM *n* pl. -S a perennial herb

ASBESTOS *n* pl. -ES a mineral **ASBESTIC** *adj*

ASBESTUS *n* pl. -ES asbestos

ASCARID *n* pl. -S a parasitic worm

ASCARIS *n* pl. -RIDES ascarid

ASCEND *v* -ED, -ING, -S to go or move upward

ASCENDER *n* pl. -S one that ascends

ASCENT *n* pl. -S the act of ascending

ASCESIS *n* pl. -CESES the conduct of an ascetic

ASCETIC *n* pl. -S one who practices extreme self-denial for religious reasons

ASCI pl. of ascus

ASCIDIAN *n* pl. -S a small marine animal

ASCIDIUM *n* pl. -DIA a flask-shaped plant appendage

ASCITES *n* pl. ASCITES accumulation of serous fluid in the abdomen **ASCITIC** *adj*

ASCOCARP *n* pl. -S a spore-producing organ of certain fungi

ASCORBIC *adj* relieving scurvy

ASCOT *n* pl. -S a broad neck scarf

ASCRIBE *v* -CRIBED, -CRIBING, -CRIBES to attribute to a specified cause, source, or origin

ASCUS *n* pl. ASCI a spore sac in certain fungi

ASDIC *n* pl. -S sonar

ASEA *adv* at sea

ASEPSIS *n* pl. -SEPSES the condition of being aseptic

ASEPTIC *adj* free from germs

ASEXUAL *adj* occurring or performed without sexual action

ASH *v* -ED, -ING, -ES to convert into ash (the residue of a substance that has been burned)

ASHAMED *adj* feeling shame, guilt, or disgrace

ASHCAN *n* pl. -S a metal receptacle for garbage

ASHEN *adj* consisting of ashes

ASHIER comparative of ashy

ASHIEST superlative of ashy

ASHLAR *v* -ED, -ING, -S to build with squared stones

ASHLER *v* -ED, -ING, -S to ashlar

ASHLESS *adj* having no ashes

ASHMAN *n* pl. -MEN one who collects and removes ashes

ASHORE *adv* toward or on the shore

ASHPLANT *n* pl. -S a walking stick

ASHRAM *n* pl. -S a secluded dwelling of a Hindu sage

ASHTRAY *n* pl. -TRAYS a receptacle for tobacco ashes

ASHY *adj* ASHIER, ASHIEST covered with ashes

ASIDE *n* pl. -S a comment by an actor intended to be heard by the audience but not the other actors

ASININE *adj* obstinately stupid or silly

ASK *v* -ED, -ING, -S to put a question to

ASKANCE *adv* with a side glance

ASKANT *adv* askance

ASKER *n* pl. -S one that asks

ASKESIS *n* pl. ASKESES ascesis

ASKEW *adv* to one side

ASKING *n* pl. -S the act of one who asks

ASLANT *adj* slanting

ASLEEP *adj* sleeping

ASLOPE *adj* sloping

ASOCIAL	adj avoiding the company of others	**ASSAYER**	n pl. -S one that assays
ASP	n pl. -S a venomous snake	**ASSEGAI**	v -GAIED, -GAIING, -GAIS to assagai
ASPECT	n pl. -S appearance of something to the eye or mind	**ASSEMBLE**	v -BLED, -BLING, -BLES to come or bring together
ASPEN	n pl. -S any of several poplars	**ASSEMBLY**	n pl. -BLIES the act of assembling
ASPER	n pl. -S a Turkish money of account	**ASSENT**	v -ED, -ING, -S to express agreement
ASPERATE	v -ATED, -ATING, -ATES to make uneven	**ASSENTER**	n pl. -S one that assents
		ASSENTOR	n pl. -S assenter
ASPERGES	n pl. ASPERGES a Roman Catholic rite	**ASSERT**	v -ED, -ING, -S to state positively
ASPERITY	n pl. -TIES acrimony	**ASSERTER**	n pl. -S one that asserts
ASPERSE	v -PERSED, -PERSING, -PERSES to spread false charges against	**ASSERTOR**	n pl. -S asserter
		ASSESS	v -ED, -ING, -ES to estimate the value of for taxation
ASPERSER	n pl. -S one that asperses	**ASSESSOR**	n pl. -S one that assesses
ASPERSOR	n pl. -S asperser	**ASSET**	n pl. -S a useful quality or thing
ASPHALT	v -ED, -ING, -S to coat with asphalt (a substance used for paving and roofing)	**ASSIGN**	v -ED, -ING, -S to set apart for a particular purpose
ASPHERIC	adj varying slightly from an exactly spherical shape	**ASSIGNAT**	n pl. -S one of the notes issued as currency by the French revolutionary government
ASPHODEL	n pl. -S a flowering plant	**ASSIGNEE**	n pl. -S one to whom property or right is legally transferred
ASPHYXIA	n pl. -S unconsciousness caused by lack of oxygen	
ASPHYXY	n pl. -PHYXIES asphyxia	**ASSIGNER**	n pl. -S one that assigns
ASPIC	n pl. -S the asp	**ASSIGNOR**	n pl. -S one who legally transfers property or right
ASPIRANT	n pl. -S one that aspires	**ASSIST**	v -ED, -ING, -S to give aid or support to
ASPIRATA	n pl. -TAE a type of plosive	
ASPIRATE	v -RATED, -RATING, -RATES to pronounce with an initial release of breath	**ASSISTER**	n pl. -S one that assists
		ASSISTOR	n pl. -S assister
ASPIRE	v -PIRED, -PIRING, -PIRES to have an earnest desire or ambition	**ASSIZE**	n pl. -S a session of a legislative or judicial body
		ASSLIKE	adj resembling an ass
ASPIRER	n pl. -S an aspirant	**ASSOIL**	v -ED, -ING, -S to pardon
ASPIRIN	n pl. -S a pain reliever	**ASSONANT**	n pl. -S a word or syllable that resembles another in sound
ASPIRING	present participle of aspire	
ASPIS	n pl. -PISES aspic	**ASSORT**	v -ED, -ING, -S to distribute into groups according to kind or class
ASPISH	adj resembling an asp	
ASQUINT	adv with a sidelong glance	
ASRAMA	n pl. -S ashram	**ASSORTER**	n pl. -S one that assorts
ASS	n pl. -ES a hoofed mammal	**ASSUAGE**	v -SUAGED, -SUAGING, -SUAGES to make less severe
ASSAGAI	v -GAIED, -GAIING, -GAIS to pierce with a light spear	
		ASSUME	v -SUMED, -SUMING, -SUMES to take on
ASSAI	n pl. -S a tropical tree	
ASSAIL	v -ED, -ING, -S to attack	**ASSUMER**	n pl. -S one that assumes
ASSAILER	n pl. -S one that assails	**ASSURE**	v -SURED, -SURING, -SURES to insure
ASSASSIN	n pl. -S a murderer	
ASSAULT	v -ED, -ING, -S to attack	**ASSURED**	n pl. -S an insured person
ASSAY	v -ED, -ING, -S to attempt	**ASSURER**	n pl. -S one that assures
		ASSURING	present participle of assure

ASSUROR *n* pl. -S assurer

ASSWAGE *v* -SWAGED, -SWAGING, -SWAGES to assuage

ASTASIA *n* pl. -S inability to stand resulting from muscular incoordination

ASTATIC *adj* unstable

ASTATINE *n* pl. -S a radioactive element

ASTER *n* pl. -S a flowering plant

ASTERIA *n* pl. -S a gemstone cut to exhibit asterism

ASTERISK *v* -ED, -ING, -S to mark with an asterisk (a star-shaped printing mark)

ASTERISM *n* pl. -S a property of certain minerals of showing a starlike luminous figure

ASTERN *adv* at or toward the rear of a ship

ASTERNAL *adj* not connected to the sternum

ASTEROID *n* pl. -S a type of celestial body

ASTHENIA *n* pl. -S lack of strength

ASTHENIC *n* pl. -S a slender, lightly muscled person

ASTHENY *n* pl. -NIES asthenia

ASTHMA *n* pl. -S a respiratory disease

ASTIR *adj* moving about

ASTOMOUS *adj* having no stomata

ASTONISH *v* -ED, -ING, -ES to fill with sudden wonder or surprise

ASTONY *v* -TONIED, -TONYING, -TONIES to astonish

ASTOUND *v* -ED, -ING, -S to amaze

ASTRAGAL *n* pl. -S a convex molding

ASTRAL *n* pl. -S a type of oil lamp

ASTRALLY *adv* in a stellar manner

ASTRAY *adv* off the right course

ASTRICT *v* -ED, -ING, -S to restrict

ASTRIDE *adv* with one leg on each side

ASTRINGE *v* -TRINGED, -TRINGING, -TRINGES to bind or draw together

ASTUTE *adj* shrewd **ASTUTELY** *adv*

ASTYLAR *adj* having no columns

ASUNDER *adv* into pieces

ASWARM *adj* swarming

ASWIRL *adj* swirling

ASWOON *adj* swooning

ASYLUM *n* pl. -LUMS or -LA an institution for the care of the mentally ill or aged

ASYNDETA *n/pl* omissions of certain conjunctions

AT *prep* in the position of

ATABAL *n* pl. -S a type of drum

ATAGHAN *n* pl. -S yataghan

ATALAYA *n* pl. -S a watchtower

ATAMAN *n* pl. -S a hetman

ATAMASCO *n* pl. -COS a flowering plant

ATARAXIA *n* pl. -S peace of mind

ATARAXIC *n* pl. -S a tranquilizing drug

ATARAXY *n* pl. -RAXIES ataraxia

ATAVIC *adj* pertaining to a remote ancestor

ATAVISM *n* pl. -S the reappearance of a genetic characteristic after several generations of absence

ATAVIST *n* pl. -S an individual displaying atavism

ATAXIA *n* pl. -S loss of muscular coordination

ATAXIC *n* pl. -S one suffering from ataxia

ATAXY *n* pl. ATAXIES ataxia

ATE *n* pl. -S blind impulse or reckless ambition that drives one to ruin

ATECHNIC *adj* lacking technical knowledge

ATELIC *adj* pertaining to a type of verb form

ATELIER *n* pl. -S a workshop or studio

ATHANASY *n* pl. -SIES immortality

ATHEISM *n* pl. -S the belief that there is no God

ATHEIST *n* pl. -S a believer in atheism

ATHELING *n* pl. -S an Anglo-Saxon prince or nobleman

ATHENEUM *n* pl. -S a literary institution

ATHEROMA *n* pl. -MAS or -MATA a disease of the arteries

ATHIRST *adj* having a strong desire

ATHLETE *n* pl. -S one skilled in feats of physical strength and agility **ATHLETIC** *adj*

ATHODYD *n* pl. -S a type of jet engine

ATHWART *adv* from side to side

ATILT *adj* being in a tilted position

ATINGLE *adj* tingling

ATLAS *n* pl. ATLANTES or ATLASES a male figure used as a supporting column

ATLATL *n* pl. -S a device for throwing a spear or dart

ATMA *n* pl. -S atman

ATMAN n pl. -S the individual soul in Hinduism

ATOLL n pl. -S a ring-shaped coral island

ATOM n pl. -S the smallest unit of an element **ATOMIC, ATOMICAL** adj

ATOMICS n/pl the science dealing with atoms

ATOMIES pl. of atomy

ATOMISE v -ISED, -ISING, -ISES to atomize

ATOMISM n pl. -S the theory that the universe is composed of simple, indivisible, minute particles

ATOMIST n pl. -S an adherent of atomism

ATOMIZE v -IZED, -IZING, -IZES to reduce to a fine spray

ATOMIZER n pl. -S a device for atomizing liquids

ATOMY n pl. -MIES a tiny particle

ATONAL adj lacking tonality **ATONALLY** adv

ATONE v ATONED, ATONING, ATONES to make amends or reparation **ATONABLE** adj

ATONER n pl. -S one that atones

ATONIC n pl. -S an unaccented syllable or word

ATONING present participle of atone

ATONY n pl. -NIES muscular weakness

ATOP adj being on or at the top

ATOPY n pl. -PIES a type of allergy **ATOPIC** adj

ATRAZINE n pl. -S an herbicide

ATREMBLE adj trembling

ATRESIA n pl. -S absence or closure of a natural bodily passage

ATRIA a pl. of atrium

ATRIAL adj pertaining to an atrium

ATRIP adj aweigh

ATRIUM n pl. ATRIA or ATRIUMS the main room of an ancient Roman house

ATROCITY n pl. -TIES a heinous act

ATROPHIA n pl. -S a wasting away of the body or any of its parts **ATROPHIC** adj

ATROPHY v -PHIED, -PHYING, -PHIES to waste away

ATROPIN n pl. -S atropine

ATROPINE n pl. -S a poisonous alkaloid

ATROPISM n pl. -S atropine poisoning

ATTACH v -ED, -ING, -ES to connect as an associated part

ATTACHE n pl. -S a diplomatic official

ATTACHER n pl. -S one that attaches

ATTACK v -ED, -ING, -S to set upon violently

ATTACKER n pl. -S one that attacks

ATTAIN v -ED, -ING, -S to gain or achieve by mental or physical effort

ATTAINER n pl. -S one that attains

ATTAINT v -ED, -ING, -S to disgrace

ATTAR n pl. -S a fragrant oil

ATTEMPER v -ED, -ING, -S to modify the temperature of

ATTEMPT v -ED, -ING, -S to make an effort to do or accomplish

ATTEND v -ED, -ING, -S to be present at

ATTENDEE n pl. -S an attender

ATTENDER n pl. -S one that attends

ATTENT adj heedful

ATTEST v -ED, -ING, -S to affirm to be true or genuine

ATTESTER n pl. -S one that attests

ATTESTOR n pl. -S attester

ATTIC n pl. -S a story or room directly below the roof of a house

ATTICISM n pl. -S a concise and elegant expression

ATTICIST n pl. -S one who uses atticisms

ATTIRE v -TIRED, -TIRING, -TIRES to clothe

ATTITUDE n pl. -S a state of mind with regard to some matter

ATTORN v -ED, -ING, -S to acknowledge a new owner as one's landlord

ATTORNEY n pl. -NEYS a lawyer

ATTRACT v -ED, -ING, -S to cause to approach or adhere

ATTRITE adj attrited

ATTRITED adj worn down by rubbing

ATTUNE v -TUNED, -TUNING, -TUNES to bring into harmony

ATWAIN adv in two

ATWEEN prep between

ATWITTER adj twittering

ATYPIC adj atypical

ATYPICAL adj not typical

AUBADE n pl. -S a morning song

AUBERGE n pl. -S an inn

AUBURN n pl. -S a reddish brown color

AUCTION *v* -ED, -ING, -S to sell publicly to the highest bidder

AUDACITY *n pl.* -TIES boldness

AUDAD *n pl.* -S a aoudad

AUDIBLE *n pl.* -S a type of play in football

AUDIBLY *adv* in a way so as to be heard

AUDIENCE *n pl.* -S a group of listeners or spectators

AUDIENT *n pl.* -S one that hears

AUDILE *n pl.* -S one whose mental imagery is chiefly auditory

AUDING *n pl.* -S the process of hearing, recognizing, and interpreting a spoken language

AUDIO *n pl.* -DIOS sound reception or transmission

AUDIT *v* -ED, -ING, -S to examine with intent to verify

AUDITION *v* -ED, -ING, -S to give a trial performance

AUDITIVE *n pl.* -S an auditory

AUDITOR *n pl.* -S one that audits

AUDITORY *n pl.* -RIES a group of listeners

AUGEND *n pl.* -S a number to which another is to be added

AUGER *n pl.* -S a tool for boring

AUGHT *n pl.* -S a zero

AUGITE *n pl.* -S a mineral AUGITIC *adj*

AUGMENT *v* -ED, -ING, -S to increase

AUGUR *v* -ED, -ING, -S to foretell from omens

AUGURAL *adj* pertaining to augury

AUGURER *n pl.* -S one that augurs

AUGURY *n pl.* -RIES the practice of auguring

AUGUST *adj* -GUSTER, -GUSTEST inspiring reverence or admiration AUGUSTLY *adv*

AUK *n pl.* -S a diving seabird

AUKLET *n pl.* -S a small auk

AULD *adj* AULDER, AULDEST old

AULIC *adj* pertaining to a royal court

AUNT *n pl.* -S the sister of one's father or mother

AUNTHOOD *n pl.* -S the state of being an aunt

AUNTIE *n pl.* -S aunt

AUNTLIKE *adj* resembling an aunt

AUNTLY *adj* -LIER, -LIEST of or suggesting an aunt

AUNTY *n pl.* AUNTIES aunt

AURA *n pl.* -RAS or -RAE an invisible emanation

AURAL *adj* pertaining to the ear AURALLY *adv*

AURAR *pl.* of eyrir

AURATE *adj* having ears

AURATED *adj* aurate

AUREATE *adj* golden

AUREI *pl.* of aureus

AUREOLA *n pl.* -LAS or -LAE a halo

AUREOLE *v* -OLED, -OLING, -OLES to surround with a halo

AURES *pl.* of auris

AUREUS *n pl.* -REI a gold coin of ancient Rome

AURIC *adj* pertaining to gold

AURICLE *n pl.* -S an ear or ear-shaped part AURICLED *adj*

AURICULA *n pl.* -LAS or -LAE an auricle

AURIFORM *adj* ear-shaped

AURIS *n pl.* AURES the ear

AURIST *n pl.* -S a specialist in diseases of the ear

AUROCHS *n pl.* -ES an extinct European ox

AURORA *n pl.* -RAS or -RAE the rising light of the morning AURORAL, AUROREAN *adj*

AUROUS *adj* pertaining to gold

AURUM *n pl.* -S gold

AUSPEX *n pl.* -PICES a soothsayer of ancient Rome

AUSPICE *n pl.* -S a favorable omen

AUSTERE *adj* -TERER, -TEREST grave in disposition or appearance

AUSTRAL *adj* pertaining to the south

AUTACOID *n pl.* -S a hormone

AUTARCHY *n pl.* -CHIES absolute rule or power

AUTARKY *n pl.* -KIES national economic self-sufficiency AUTARKIC, AUTARKIK *adj*

AUTECISM *n pl.* -S the development of the entire life cycle of a parasitic fungus on a single host

AUTHOR *v* -ED, -ING, -S to write

AUTISM *n pl.* -S extreme withdrawal into fantasy AUTISTIC *adj*

AUTO *v* -ED, -ING, -S to ride in an automobile

AUTOBAHN *n pl.* -BAHNS or -BAHNEN a German superhighway

AUTOBUS *n pl.* -BUSES or -BUSSES a bus

AUTOCADE *n pl.* -S a procession of automobiles

AUTOCOID *n pl.* -S autacoid

AUTOCRAT *n pl.* -S an absolute ruler

AUTODYNE *n pl.* -S a type of electrical circuit

AUTOGAMY *n pl.* -MIES fertilization of a flower by its own pollen

AUTOGENY *n pl.* -NIES the production of living organisms from inanimate matter

AUTOGIRO *n pl.* -ROS a type of airplane

AUTOGYRO *n pl.* -ROS autogiro

AUTOLYZE *v* -LYZED, -LYZING, -LYZES to break down tissue by the action of self-contained enzymes

AUTOMATA *n/pl* robots

AUTOMATE *v* -MATED, -MATING, -MATES to convert to a system of automatic control

AUTONOMY *n pl.* -MIES the state of being self-governing

AUTOPSIC *adj* pertaining to an autopsy

AUTOPSY *v* -SIED, -SYING, -SIES to examine a dead body to determine the cause of death

AUTOSOME *n pl.* -S a type of chromosome

AUTOTOMY *n pl.* -MIES the shedding of a damaged body part

AUTOTYPE *n pl.* -S a type of photographic process

AUTOTYPY *n pl.* -TYPIES autotype

AUTUMN *n pl.* -S a season of the year **AUTUMNAL** *adj*

AUTUNITE *n pl.* -S a mineral

AUXESIS *n pl.* AUXESES an increase in cell size without cell division

AUXETIC *n pl.* -S a substance that promotes auxesis

AUXIN *n pl.* -S a substance used to regulate plant growth **AUXINIC** *adj*

AVA *adv* at all

AVAIL *v* -ED, -ING, -S to be of use or advantage to

AVARICE *n pl.* -S greed

AVAST *interj* — used as a command to stop

AVATAR *n pl.* -S the incarnation of a Hindu deity

AVAUNT *interj* — used as an order of dismissal

AVE *n pl.* -S an expression of greeting or farewell

AVELLAN *adj* having the four arms shaped like filberts — used of a heraldic cross

AVELLANE *adj* avellan

AVENGE *v* AVENGED, AVENGING, AVENGES to exact retribution for

AVENGER *n pl.* -S one that avenges

AVENS *n pl.* -ES a perennial herb

AVENTAIL *n pl.* -S ventail

AVENUE *n pl.* -S a wide street

AVER *v* AVERRED, AVERRING, AVERS to declare positively

AVERAGE *v* -AGED, -AGING, -AGES to calculate the arithmetic mean of

AVERMENT *n pl.* -S the act of averring

AVERRED past tense of aver

AVERRING present participle of aver

AVERSE *adj* opposed; reluctant **AVERSELY** *adv*

AVERSION *n pl.* -S a feeling of repugnance **AVERSIVE** *adj*

AVERT *v* -ED, -ING, -S to turn away

AVGAS *n pl.* -GASES or -GASSES gasoline for airplanes

AVIAN *n pl.* -S a bird

AVIANIZE *v* -IZED, -IZING, -IZES to make less severe by repeated culture in a chick embryo, as a virus

AVIARIST *n pl.* -S the keeper of an aviary

AVIARY *n pl.* -ARIES a large enclosure for live birds

AVIATE *v* -ATED, -ATING, -ATES to fly an aircraft

AVIATION *n pl.* -S the act of aviating

AVIATOR *n pl.* -S one that aviates

AVIATRIX *n pl.* -TRICES or -TRIXES a female aviator

AVICULAR *adj* pertaining to birds

AVID *adj* eager

AVIDIN *n pl.* -S a protein found in egg white

AVIDITY *n pl.* -TIES the state of being avid

AVIDLY *adv* in an avid manner

AVIDNESS *n pl.* -ES avidity

AVIFAUNA *n pl.* -NAS or -NAE the bird life of a particular region

AVIGATOR *n pl.* -S one that navigates aircraft

AVION *n pl.* -S an airplane

AVIONICS *n/pl* the science of electronics applied to aviation **AVIONIC** *adj*

AVISO *n* pl. -SOS advice

AVO *n* pl. AVOS a monetary unit of Macao

AVOCADO *n* pl. -DOS or -DOES the edible fruit of a tropical tree

AVOCET *n* pl. -S a shore bird

AVODIRE *n* pl. -S an African tree

AVOID *v* -ED, -ING, -S to keep away from

AVOIDER *n* pl. -S one that avoids

AVOSET *n* pl. -S avocet

AVOUCH *v* -ED, -ING, -ES to affirm

AVOUCHER *n* pl. -S one that avouches

AVOW *v* -ED, -ING, -S to declare openly **AVOWABLE** *adj* **AVOWABLY, AVOWEDLY** *adv*

AVOWAL *n* pl. -S an open declaration

AVOWER *n* pl. -S one that avows

AVULSE *v* AVULSED, AVULSING, AVULSES to tear off forcibly

AVULSION *n* pl. -S the act of avulsing

AW *interj* — used to express protest, disgust, or disbelief

AWA *adv* away

AWAIT *v* -ED, -ING, -S to wait for

AWAITER *n* pl. -S one that awaits

AWAKE *v* AWAKED or AWOKE, AWOKEN, AWAKING, AWAKES to wake up

AWAKEN *v* -ED, -ING, -S to awake

AWAKENER *n* pl. -S one that awakens

AWAKING present participle of awake

AWARD *v* -ED, -ING, -S to grant as due or merited

AWARDEE *n* pl. -S one that is awarded something

AWARDER *n* pl. -S one that awards

AWARE *adj* having perception or knowledge

AWASH *adj* covered with water

AWAY *adv* from a certain place

AWAYNESS *n* pl. -ES the state of being distant

AWE *v* AWED, AWING or AWEING, AWES to inspire with awe (reverential fear)

AWEARY *adj* weary

AWEATHER *adv* toward the windward side of a vessel

AWED past tense of awe

AWEE *adv* awhile

AWEIGH *adj* hanging just clear of the bottom — used of an anchor

AWELESS *adj* lacking awe

AWESOME *adj* inspiring awe

AWFUL *adj* -FULLER, -FULLEST extremely bad or unpleasant **AWFULLY** *adv*

AWHILE *adv* for a short time

AWHIRL *adj* whirling

AWING a present participle of awe

AWKWARD *adj* -WARDER, -WARDEST lacking skill, dexterity, or grace

AWL *n* pl. -S a pointed tool for making small holes

AWLESS *adj* aweless

AWLWORT *n* pl -S an aquatic plant

AWMOUS *n* pl. AWMOUS alms

AWN *n* pl. -S a bristlelike appendage of certain grasses **AWNED, AWNLESS, AWNY** *adj*

AWNING *n* pl. -S a rooflike canvas cover **AWNINGED** *adj*

AWOKE a past tense of awake

AWOKEN a past participle of awake

AWOL *n* pl. -S one who is absent without leave

AWRY *adv* with a turn or twist to one side

AX *v* -ED, -ING, -ES to work on with an ax (a type of cutting tool)

AXAL *adj* axial

AXE *v* AXED, AXING, AXES to ax

AXEL *n* pl. -S a jump in figure skating

AXEMAN *n* pl. -MEN axman

AXENIC *adj* free from germs

AXES pl. of axis

AXIAL *adj* pertaining to or forming an axis **AXIALLY** *adv*

AXIALITY *n* pl. -TIES the state of being axial

AXIL *n* pl. -S the angle between the upper side of a leaf and its supporting stem

AXILE *adj* axial

AXILLA *n* pl. -LAE or -LAS the armpit

AXILLAR *n* pl. -S a feather on the undersurface of a bird's wing

AXILLARY *n* pl. -LARIES an axillar

AXING present participle of axe

AXIOLOGY *n* pl. -GIES the study of values and value judgments

AXIOM *n* pl. -S a self-evident truth

AXIS   n pl. AXES a straight line about which a body rotates AXISED adj

AXIS   n pl. AXISES an Asian deer

AXITE   n pl. -S a fiber of an axon

AXLE   n pl. -S a shaft upon which a wheel revolves AXLED adj

AXLETREE   n pl. -S a type of axle

AXLIKE   adj resembling an ax

AXMAN   n pl. -MEN one who wields an ax

AXOLOTL   n pl. -S a salamander of Mexico and western United States

AXON   n pl. -S the central process of a neuron AXONAL, AXONIC adj

AXONE   n pl. -S axon

AXOPLASM   n pl. -S the protoplasm of an axon

AXSEED   n pl. -S a European herb

AY   n pl. AYS aye

AYAH   n pl. -S a native maid or nurse in India

AYE   n pl. -S an affirmative vote

AYIN   n pl. -S a Hebrew letter

AZALEA   n pl. -S a flowering shrub

AZAN   n pl. -S a Muslim call to prayer

AZIDE   n pl. -S a type of chemical compound AZIDO adj

AZIMUTH   n pl. -S an angle of horizontal deviation

AZINE   n pl. -S a type of chemical compound

AZO   adj containing nitrogen

AZOIC   adj pertaining to geologic periods that precede the appearance of life

AZOLE   n pl. -S a type of chemical compound

AZON   n pl. -S a radio-controlled aerial bomb

AZONAL   adj pertaining to a type of a soil group

AZONIC   adj not restricted to any particular zone

AZOTE   n pl. -S nitrogen AZOTED adj

AZOTEMIA   n pl. -S an excess of nitrogenous substances in the blood AZOTEMIC adj

AZOTH   n pl. -S mercury

AZOTIC   adj pertaining to azote

AZOTISE   v -TISED, -TISING, -TISES to azotize

AZOTIZE   v -TIZED, -TIZING, -TIZES to treat with nitrogen

AZOTURIA   n pl. -S an excess of nitrogenous substances in the urine

AZURE   n pl. -S a blue color

AZURITE   n pl. -S a mineral

AZYGOS   n pl. -ES an azygous anatomical part

AZYGOUS   adj not being one of a pair

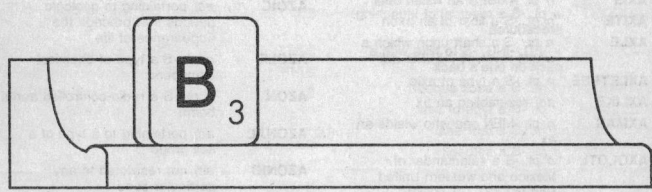

BA   *n* pl. -S the eternal soul, in Egyptian mythology

BAA   *v* -ED, -ING, -S to bleat

BAAL   *n* pl. -S or -IM a false god

BAALISM   *n* pl. -S the worship of a baal

BABA   *n* pl. -S a rum cake

BABASSU   *n* pl. -S a palm tree

BABBITT   *v* -ED, -ING, -S to line with a type of metal

BABBLE   *v* -BLED, -BLING, -BLES to talk idly or excessively

BABBLER   *n* pl. -S one that babbles

BABBLING   *n* pl. -S idle talk

BABBOOL   *n* pl. -S babul

BABE   *n* pl. -S a baby

BABEL   *n* pl. -S confusion

BABESIA   *n* pl. -S a parasitic protozoan

BABICHE   *n* pl. -S rawhide thongs

BABIED   past tense of baby

BABIES   present 3d person sing. of baby

BABIRUSA   *n* pl. -S a wild pig

BABKA   *n* pl. -S a coffee cake

BABOO   *n* pl. -BOOS a Hindu gentleman

BABOOL   *n* pl. -S babul

BABOON   *n* pl. -S a large ape

BABU   *n* pl. -S baboo

BABUL   *n* pl. -S a North African tree

BABUSHKA   *n* pl. -S a woman's scarf

BABY   *v* -BIED, -BYING, -BIES to coddle

BABYHOOD   *n* pl. -S the state of being a baby (an infant)

BABYISH   *adj* resembling a baby

BACCA   *n* pl. -CAE a berry

BACCARA   *n* pl. -S baccarat

BACCARAT   *n* pl. -S a card game

BACCATE   *adj* pulpy like a berry

BACCATED   *adj* baccate

BACCHANT   *n* pl. -S or -ES a carouser

BACCHIC   *adj* riotous

BACCHIUS   *n* pl. -CHII a type of metrical foot

BACH   *v* -ED, -ING, -ES to live as a bachelor

BACHELOR   *n* pl. -S an unmarried man

BACILLAR   *adj* rod-shaped

BACILLUS   *n* pl. -LI any of a class of rod-shaped bacteria

BACK   *v* -ED, -ING, -S to support

BACKACHE   *n* pl. -S a pain in the back

BACKBEND   *n* pl. -S an acrobatic feat

BACKBITE   *v* -BIT, -BITTEN, -BITING, -BITES to slander

BACKBONE   *n* pl. -S the spine

BACKDOOR   *adj* secretive

BACKDROP   *n* pl. -S a stage setting

BACKER   *n* pl. -S a supporter

BACKFILL   *v* -ED, -ING, -S to refill

BACKFIRE   *v* -FIRED, -FIRING, -FIRES to result in undesirable consequences

BACKHAND   *v* -ED, -ING, -S to strike with the back of the hand

BACKHOE   *n* pl. -S an excavating machine

BACKING   *n* pl. -S support

BACKLASH   *v* -ED, -ING, -ES to cause a reaction

BACKLESS   *adj* having no back

BACKLIST   *n* pl. -S a publisher's list of older book titles

BACKLIT   *adj* illuminated from behind

BACKLOG v -LOGGED, -LOGGING, -LOGS to accumulate

BACKMOST adj hindmost

BACKOUT n pl. -S a reversal of launching procedures

BACKPACK v -ED, -ING, -S to hike with a pack on one's back

BACKREST n pl. -S a back support

BACKSAW n pl. -S a type of saw

BACKSEAT n pl. -S a rear seat

BACKSET n pl. -S a setback

BACKSIDE n pl. -S the hind part

BACKSLAP v -SLAPPED, -SLAPPING, -SLAPS to show much approval

BACKSLID past tense of backslide (to revert to sin)

BACKSPIN n pl. -S a backward rotation

BACKSTAY n pl. -STAYS a support for a mast

BACKSTOP v -STOPPED, -STOPPING, -STOPS to bolster

BACKUP n pl. -S a substitute

BACKWARD adv toward the back

BACKWASH v -ED, -ING, -ES to spray water backward

BACKWOOD adj uncouth

BACKYARD n pl. -S an area at the rear of a house

BACON n pl. -S a side of a pig cured and smoked

BACTERIA n/pl microscopic organisms

BACTERIN n pl. -S a vaccine prepared from dead bacteria

BACULINE adj pertaining to a rod

BAD adj WORSE, WORST not good in any way

BAD n pl. -S something that is bad

BADDIE n pl. -S a bad person

BADDY n pl. -DIES baddie

BADE past tense of bid

BADGE v BADGED, BADGING, BADGES to supply with an insignia

BADGER v -ED, -ING, -S to harass

BADGERLY adj bothersome

BADGING present participle of badge

BADINAGE v -NAGED, -NAGING, -NAGES to banter

BADLAND n pl. -S a barren, hilly area

BADLY adv in a bad manner

BADMAN n pl. -MEN an outlaw

BADMOUTH v -ED, -ING, -S to criticize

BADNESS n pl. -ES the state of being bad

BAFF v -ED, -ING, -S to strike under a golf ball

BAFFIES pl. of baffy

BAFFLE v -FLED, -FLING, -FLES to confuse

BAFFLER n pl. -S one that baffles

BAFFY n pl. -FIES a wooden golf club

BAG v BAGGED, BAGGING, BAGS to put into a bag (a flexible container)

BAGASS n pl. -ES bagasse

BAGASSE n pl. -S crushed sugarcane

BAGEL n pl. -S a ring-shaped roll

BAGFUL n pl. BAGFULS or BAGSFUL as much as a bag will hold

BAGGAGE n pl. -S luggage

BAGGED past tense of bag

BAGGIE n pl. -S the stomach

BAGGING n pl. -S material for making bags

BAGGY adj -GIER, -GIEST loose-fitting **BAGGILY** adv

BAGMAN n pl. -MEN a traveling salesman

BAGNIO n pl. -NIOS a brothel

BAGPIPE n pl. -S a wind instrument

BAGPIPER n pl. -S one that plays bagpipes

BAGSFUL a pl. of bagful

BAGUET n pl. -S baguette

BAGUETTE n pl. -S a rectangular gem

BAGWIG n pl. -S a type of wig

BAGWORM n pl. -S the larva of certain moths

BAH interj — an exclamation of disgust

BAHADUR n pl. -S a Hindu title of respect

BAHT n pl. -S a monetary unit of Thailand

BAIDARKA n pl. -S bidarka

BAIL v -ED, -ING, -S to transfer property temporarily **BAILABLE** adj

BAILEE n pl. -S a person to whom property is bailed

BAILER n pl. -S bailor

BAILEY n pl. -LEYS an outer castle wall

BAILIE n pl. -S a Scottish magistrate

BAILIFF n pl. -S a court officer

BAILMENT n pl. -S the act of bailing

BAILOR n pl. -S a person who bails property to another

BAILOUT n pl. -S the act of parachuting from an aircraft

BAILSMAN *n* pl. -MEN one who provides security for another

BAIRN *n* pl. -S a child **BAIRNISH** *adj*

BAIRNLY *adj* -LIER, -LIEST childish

BAIT *v* -ED, -ING, -S to lure

BAITER *n* pl. -S one that baits

BAITH *adj* both

BAIZA *n* pl. -S a monetary unit of Oman

BAIZE *n* pl. -S a green, woolen fabric

BAKE *v* BAKED, BAKING, BAKES to prepare food in an oven

BAKEMEAT *n* pl. -S a pastry

BAKER *n* pl. -S one that bakes

BAKERY *n* pl. -ERIES a place where baked goods are sold

BAKESHOP *n* pl. -S a bakery

BAKING *n* pl. -S a quantity baked

BAKLAVA *n* pl. -S a Turkish pastry

BAKLAWA *n* pl. -S baklava

BAKSHISH *v* -ED, -ING, -ES to give a tip

BAL *n* pl. -S a balmoral

BALANCE *v* -ANCED, -ANCING, -ANCES to weigh

BALANCER *n* pl. -S one that balances

BALAS *n* pl. -ES a red variety of spinel

BALATA *n* pl. -S a tropical tree

BALBOA *n* pl. -S a monetary unit of Panama

BALCONY *n* pl. -NIES an elevated platform

BALD *adj* BALDER, BALDEST lacking hair

BALD *v* -ED, -ING, -S to become bald

BALDHEAD *n* pl. -S a bald person

BALDISH *adj* somewhat bald

BALDLY *adv* in a plain and blunt manner

BALDNESS *n* pl. -ES the state of being bald

BALDPATE *n* pl. -S a baldhead

BALDRIC *n* pl. -S a shoulder belt

BALDRICK *n* pl. -S baldric

BALE *v* BALED, BALING, BALES to form into tightly compressed bundles

BALEEN *n* pl. -S whalebone

BALEFIRE *n* pl. -S a bonfire

BALEFUL *adj* menacing

BALER *n* pl. -S one that bales

BALING present participle of bale

BALISAUR *n* pl. -S a long-tailed badger

BALK *v* -ED, -ING, -S to stop short and refuse to proceed

BALKER *n* pl. -S one that balks

BALKLINE *n* pl. -S the starting line in track events

BALKY *adj* BALKIER, BALKIEST stubborn **BALKILY** *adv*

BALL *v* -ED, -ING, -S to form into a ball (a spherical object)

BALLAD *n* pl. -S a narrative poem or song **BALLADIC** *adj*

BALLADE *n* pl. -S a type of poem

BALLADRY *n* pl. -RIES ballad poetry

BALLAST *v* -ED, -ING, -S to stabilize

BALLER *n* pl. -S one that balls

BALLET *n* pl. -S a classical dance form **BALLETIC** *adj*

BALLISTA *n* pl. -TAE an ancient weapon

BALLON *n* pl. -S lightness of movement

BALLONET *n* pl. -S a small balloon

BALLONNE *n* pl. -S a ballet jump

BALLOON *v* -ED, -ING, -S to swell out

BALLOT *v* -ED, -ING, -S to vote

BALLOTER *n* pl. -S one that ballots

BALLROOM *n* pl. -S a large room for dancing

BALLY *adj* damned

BALLYHOO *v* -ED, -ING, -S to promote by uproar

BALLYRAG *v* -RAGGED, -RAGGING, -RAGS to bullyrag

BALM *n* pl. -S a fragrant resin **BALMLIKE** *adj*

BALMORAL *n* pl. -S a type of shoe

BALMY *adj* BALMIER, BALMIEST mild **BALMILY** *adv*

BALNEAL *adj* pertaining to baths

BALONEY *n* pl. -NEYS bologna

BALSA *n* pl. -S a tropical tree

BALSAM *v* -ED, -ING, -S to anoint with balsam (an aromatic, resinous substance)

BALSAMIC *adj* containing balsam

BALUSTER *n* pl. -S a railing support

BAMBINO *n* pl. -NOS or -NI a baby

BAMBOO *n* pl. -BOOS a tropical grass

BAN *v* BANNED, BANNING, BANS to prohibit

BAN *n* pl. BANI a Rumanian coin

BANAL *adj* ordinary **BANALLY** *adv*

BANALITY *n* pl. -TIES something banal

BANANA *n* pl. -S an edible fruit

BANAUSIC *adj* practical

BANCO *n pl.* -COS a bet in certain gambling games

BAND *v* -ED, -ING, -S to decorate with flexible strips of material

BANDAGE *v* -DAGED, -DAGING, -DAGES to cover a wound with a strip of cloth

BANDAGER *n pl.* -S one that bandages

BANDANA *n pl.* -S bandanna

BANDANNA *n pl.* -S a large, colored handkerchief

BANDBOX *n pl.* -ES a lightweight box

BANDEAU *n pl.* -DEAUX or -DEAUS a headband

BANDER *n pl.* -S one that bands

BANDEROL *n pl.* -S a streamer

BANDIED past tense of bandy

BANDIES present 3d person sing. of bandy

BANDIT *n pl.* -DITS or -DITTI a robber

BANDITRY *n pl.* -TRIES robbery by bandits

BANDOG *n pl.* -S a watchdog

BANDORA *n pl.* -S bandore

BANDORE *n pl.* -S an ancient lute

BANDSMAN *n pl.* -MEN a member of a musical band

BANDY *v* -DIED, -DYING, -DIES to throw to and fro

BANE *v* BANED, BANING, BANES to kill with poison

BANEFUL *adj* poisonous

BANG *v* -ED, -ING, -S to hit sharply

BANGER *n pl.* -S a sausage

BANGKOK *n pl.* -S a straw hat

BANGLE *n pl.* -S a bracelet

BANGTAIL *n pl.* -S a racehorse

BANI pl. of ban

BANIAN *n pl.* -S a Hindu merchant

BANING present participle of bane

BANISH *v* -ED, -ING, -ES to expel

BANISHER *n pl.* -S one that banishes

BANISTER *n pl.* -S a handrail

BANJO *n pl.* -JOS or -JOES a musical instrument

BANJOIST *n pl.* -S one who plays the banjo

BANK *v* -ED, -ING, -S to keep money in a bank (an institution dealing in money matters) **BANKABLE** *adj*

BANKBOOK *n pl.* -S a depositor's book

BANKER *n pl.* -S one who works in a bank

BANKING *n pl.* -S the business of a bank

BANKNOTE *n pl.* -S a promissory note

BANKROLL *v* -ED, -ING, -S to supply the capital for

BANKRUPT *v* -ED, -ING, -S to impoverish

BANKSIA *n* an Australian plant

BANKSIDE *n pl.* -S the slope of a river bank

BANNED past tense of ban

BANNER *n pl.* -S a flag

BANNERET *n pl.* -S a small banner

BANNEROL *n pl.* -S a banderol

BANNET *n pl.* -S a bonnet

BANNING present participle of ban

BANNOCK *n pl.* -S a type of cake

BANNS *n/pl* a marriage notice

BANQUET *v* -ED, -ING, -S to feast

BANSHEE *n pl.* -S a female spirit

BANSHIE *n pl.* -S banshee

BANTAM *n pl.* -S a small fowl

BANTER *v* -ED, -ING, -S to exchange mildly teasing remarks

BANTERER *n pl.* -S one that banters

BANTLING *n pl.* -S a very young child

BANYAN *n pl.* -S an East Indian tree

BANZAI *n pl.* -S a Japanese battle cry

BAOBAB *n pl.* -S a tropical tree

BAPTISE *v* -TISED, -TISING, -TISES to baptize

BAPTISIA *n pl.* -S a flowering plant

BAPTISM *n pl.* -S a Christian ceremony

BAPTIST *n pl.* -S one who baptizes

BAPTIZE *v* -TIZED, -TIZING, -TIZES to administer baptism to

BAPTIZER *n pl.* -S a baptist

BAR *v* BARRED, BARRING, BARS to exclude

BARATHEA *n pl.* -S a silk fabric

BARB *v* -ED, -ING, -S to furnish with a barb (a sharp projection)

BARBAL *adj* pertaining to the beard

BARBARIC *adj* uncivilized

BARBASCO *n pl.* -COS a tropical tree

BARBATE *adj* bearded

BARBE *n pl.* -S a medieval cloth headdress

BARBECUE *v* -CUED, -CUING, -CUES to cook over live coals or an open fire

BARBEL *n* pl. -S an organ of a fish

BARBELL *n* pl. -S an exercise apparatus

BARBER *v* -ED, -ING, -S to cut hair

BARBERRY *n* pl. -RIES a shrub

BARBET *n* pl. -S a tropical bird

BARBETTE *n* pl. -S a platform

BARBICAN *n* pl. -S an outer fortification

BARBICEL *n* pl. -S a part of a feather

BARBITAL *n* pl. -S a sedative

BARBLESS *adj* having no barbs

BARBULE *n* pl. -S a small barb

BARBUT *n* pl. -S a type of helmet

BARBWIRE *n* pl. -S barbed wire

BARD *v* -ED, -ING, -S to armor a horse

BARDE *v* BARDED, BARDING, BARDES to bard

BARDIC *adj* poetic

BARE *adj* BARER, BAREST naked

BARE *v* BARED, BARING, BARES to expose

BAREBACK *adv* without a saddle

BAREFIT *adj* barefoot

BAREFOOT *adj* being without shoes

BAREGE *n* pl. -S a sheer fabric

BAREHEAD *adv* without a hat

BARELY *adv* scarcely

BARENESS *n* pl. -ES the state of being bare

BARER comparative of bare

BARESARK *n* pl. -S an ancient warrior

BAREST superlative of bare

BARF *v* -ED, -ING, -S to vomit

BARFLY *n* pl. -FLIES a drinker who frequents bars

BARGAIN *v* -ED, -ING, -S to discuss terms for selling or buying

BARGE *v* BARGED, BARGING, BARGES to move by barge (a long, large boat)

BARGEE *n* pl. -S a bargeman

BARGEMAN *n* pl. -MEN the master or a crew member of a barge

BARGHEST *n* pl. -S a goblin

BARGING present participle of barge

BARGUEST *n* pl. -S barghest

BARHOP *v* -HOPPED, -HOPPING, -HOPS to visit a number of bars during an evening

BARIC *adj* pertaining to barium

BARILLA *n* pl. -S a chemical compound

BARING present participle of bare

BARITE *n* pl. -S a mineral

BARITONE *n* pl. -S a male singing voice

BARIUM *n* pl. -S a metallic element

BARK *v* -ED, -ING, -S to cry like a dog

BARKEEP *n* pl. -S a bartender

BARKER *n* pl. -S one that barks

BARKLESS *adj* having no bark; unable to bark

BARKY *adj* BARKIER, BARKIEST covered with bark (tough outer covering of a root or stem)

BARLEDUC *n* pl. -S a fruit jam

BARLESS *adj* having no restraints

BARLEY *n* pl. -LEYS a cereal grass

BARLOW *n* pl. -S a jackknife

BARM *n* pl. -S the foam on malt liquors

BARMAID *n* pl. -S a female bartender

BARMAN *n* pl. -MEN a male bartender

BARMIE *adj* barmy

BARMY *adj* BARMIER, BARMIEST full of barm; frothy

BARN *n* pl. -S a large storage building

BARNACLE *n* pl. -S a shellfish

BARNY *adj* BARNIER, BARNIEST resembling a barn in size, shape, or smell

BARNYARD *n* pl. -S a yard near a barn

BAROGRAM *n* pl. -S a barometric reading

BARON *n* pl. -S a lower member of nobility

BARONAGE *n* pl. -S the rank of a baron

BARONESS *n* pl. -ES the wife of a baron

BARONET *n* pl. -S the holder of a rank below that of a baron

BARONG *n* pl. -S a broad knife

BARONIAL *adj* pertaining to a baron

BARONNE *n* pl. -S a baroness

BARONY *n* pl. -ONIES the domain of a baron

BAROQUE *n* pl. -S an ornate object

BAROUCHE *n* pl. -S a type of carriage

BARQUE *n* pl. -S a sailing vessel

BARRABLE *adj* capable of being barred

BARRACK *v* -ED, -ING, -S to shout boisterously

BARRAGE *v* -RAGED, -RAGING, -RAGES to subject to a massive attack

BARRANCA *n* pl. -S a steep ravine

BARRANCO *n* pl. -COS barranca

BARRATER *n* pl. -S barrator

BARRATOR *n* pl. -S one who commits barratry

BARRATRY *n* pl. -TRIES fraud committed by a master or crew of a ship

BARRE *v* BARRED, BARRING, BARRES to play a type of guitar chord

BARRED past tense of bar

BARREL *v* -RELED, -RELING, -RELS or -RELLED, -RELLING, -RELS to move fast

BARREN *adj* -RENER, -RENEST unproductive BARRENLY *adv*

BARREN *n* pl. -S a tract of barren land

BARRET *n* pl. -S a flat cap

BARRETOR *n* pl. -S barrator

BARRETRY *n* pl. -TRIES barratry

BARRETTE *n* pl. -S a hair clip

BARRIER *n* pl. -S an obstacle

BARRING present participle of bar and barre

BARRIO *n* pl. -RIOS a district

BARROOM *n* pl. -S a room where liquor is sold

BARROW *n* pl. -S a type of cart

BARSTOOL *n* pl. -S a stool in a barroom

BARTEND *v* -ED, -ING, -S to tend a barroom

BARTER *v* -ED, -ING, -S to trade

BARTERER *n* pl. -S one that barters

BARTISAN *n* pl. -S bartizan

BARTIZAN *n* pl. -S a small turret

BARWARE *n* pl. -S barroom equipment

BARYE *n* pl. -S a unit of pressure

BARYON *n* pl. -S an atomic particle BARYONIC *adj*

BARYTA *n* pl. -S a compound of barium BARYTIC *adj*

BARYTE *n* pl. -S barite

BARYTONE *n* pl. -S baritone

BASAL *adj* pertaining to the foundation BASALLY *adv*

BASALT *n* pl. -S a volcanic rock BASALTIC *adj*

BASALTES *n* pl. BASALTES unglazed stoneware

BASCULE *n* pl. -S a type of seesaw

BASE *adj* BASER, BASEST morally low

BASE *v* BASED, BASING, BASES to found

BASEBALL *n* pl. -S a type of ball

BASEBORN *adj* of low birth

BASED past tense of base

BASELESS *adj* having no foundation

BASELINE *n* pl. -S a line at either end of a court in certain sports

BASELY *adv* in a base manner

BASEMAN *n* pl. -MEN a certain player in baseball

BASEMENT *n* pl. -S the part of a building below ground level

BASENESS *n* pl. -ES the state of being base

BASENJI *n* pl. -S a barkless dog

BASER comparative of base

BASES pl. of basis

BASEST superlative of base

BASH *v* -ED, -ING, -ES to smash

BASHAW *n* pl. -S a pasha

BASHER *n* pl. -S one that bashes

BASHFUL *adj* shy; timid

BASHLYK *n* pl. -S a cloth hood

BASIC *n* pl. -S a fundamental

BASICITY *n* pl. -TIES the state of being alkaline

BASIDIUM *n* pl. -IA a structure on a fungus BASIDIAL *adj*

BASIFIER *n* pl. -S one that basifies

BASIFY *v* -FIED, -FYING, -FIES to alkalize

BASIL *n* pl. -S an aromatic herb

BASILAR *adj* basal

BASILARY *adj* basilar

BASILIC *adj* pertaining to a basilica

BASILICA *n* pl. -CAS or -CAE an ancient Roman building

BASILISK *n* pl. -S a fabled serpent

BASIN *n* pl. -S an enclosed body of water BASINAL, BASINED *adj*

BASINET *n* pl. -S a medieval helmet

BASING present participle of base

BASION *n* pl. -S a part of the skull

BASIS *n* pl. BASES the foundation of something

BASK *v* -ED, -ING, -S to lie in a pleasant warmth

BASKET *n* pl. -S a wooden container

BASKETRY *n* pl. -RIES basket weaving

BASOPHIL *n* pl. -S a type of cell

BASQUE *n* pl. -S a bodice

BASS *n* pl. -ES an edible fish

BASSET v -SETED, -SETING, -SETS or -SETTED, -SETTING, -SETS to outcrop

BASSI a pl. of basso

BASSINET n pl. -S a basket used as a baby's crib

BASSIST n pl. -S a person who plays a double bass

BASSLY adv in a low-pitched manner

BASSNESS n pl. ·ES the state of being low in pitch

BASSO n pl. -SOS or -SI a low-pitched singer

BASSOON n pl. -S a low-pitched instrument

BASSWOOD n pl. -S a linden tree

BASSY adj low in pitch

BAST n pl. -S a woody fiber

BASTARD n pl. -S an illegitimate child

BASTARDY n pl. -TARDIES the state of being a bastard

BASTE v BASTED, BASTING, BASTES to sew loosely together

BASTER n pl. -S one that bastes

BASTILE n pl. -S bastille

BASTILLE n pl. -S a prison

BASTING n pl. -S the thread used by a baster

BASTION n pl. -S a fortified place

BAT v BATTED, BATTING, BATS to hit a baseball

BATBOY n pl. -BOYS a boy who minds baseball equipment

BATCH v -ED, -ING, -ES to bring together

BATCHER n pl. -S one that batches

BATE v BATED, BATING, BATES to reduce the force of

BATEAU n pl. -TEAUX a flat-bottomed boat

BATFISH n pl. -ES a batlike fish

BATFOWL v -ED, -ING, -S to catch birds at night

BATH n pl. -S a washing

BATHE v BATHED, BATHING, BATHES to wash

BATHER n pl. -S one that bathes

BATHETIC adj trite

BATHING present participle of bathe

BATHLESS adj not having had a bath

BATHOS n pl. -ES triteness

BATHROBE n pl. -S a housecoat

BATHROOM n pl. -S a room in which to bathe

BATHTUB n pl. -S a tub in which to bathe

BATHYAL adj pertaining to deep water

BATIK n pl. -S a dyeing process

BATING present participle of bate

BATISTE n pl. -S a sheer fabric

BATLIKE adj resembling a bat (a flying mammal)

BATMAN n pl. -MEN an orderly

BATON n pl. -S a short rod

BATSMAN n pl. -MEN one who bats

BATT n pl. -S a sheet of cotton

BATTALIA n pl. -S a military unit

BATTEAU n pl. -TEAUX bateau

BATTED past tense of bat

BATTEN v -ED, -ING, -S to fasten with strips of wood

BATTENER n pl. -S one that battens

BATTER v -ED, -ING, -S to beat repeatedly

BATTERIE n pl. -S a ballet movement

BATTERY n pl. -TERIES a device for generating an electric current

BATTIER comparative of batty

BATTIEST superlative of batty

BATTIK n pl. -S batik

BATTING n pl. -S a batt

BATTLE v -TLED, -TLING, -TLES to fight

BATTLER n pl. -S one that battles

BATTU adj pertaining to a ballet movement

BATTUE n pl. -S a type of hunt

BATTY adj -TIER, -TIEST crazy

BATWING adj shaped like a bat's wing

BAUBEE n pl. -S bawbee

BAUBLE n pl. -S a cheap trinket

BAUD n pl. -S a unit of data transmission speed

BAUDEKIN n pl. -S a brocaded fabric

BAUDRONS n pl. -ES a cat

BAULK v -ED, -ING, -S to balk

BAULKY adj BAULKIER, BAULKIEST balky

BAUSOND adj having white marks

BAUXITE n pl. -S an ore of aluminum BAUXITIC adj

BAWBEE n pl. -S a Scottish coin

BAWCOCK n pl. -S a fine fellow

BAWD n pl. -S a madam

BAWDIER comparative of bawdy

BAWDIES pl. of bawdy

BAWDIEST superlative of bawdy

BAWDILY *adv* in a bawdy manner

BAWDRIC *n* pl. -S baldric

BAWDRY *n* pl. -RIES obscenity

BAWDY *adj* BAWDIER, BAWDIEST obscene

BAWDY *n* pl. BAWDIES obscene language

BAWL *v* -ED, -ING, -S to cry loudly

BAWLER *n* pl. -S one that bawls

BAWSUNT *adj* bausond

BAWTIE *n* pl. -S a dog

BAWTY *n* pl. -TIES bawtie

BAY *v* -ED, -ING, -S to howl

BAYADEER *n* pl. -S bayadere

BAYADERE *n* pl. -S a dancing girl

BAYAMO *n* pl. -MOS a strong wind

BAYARD *n* pl. -S a horse

BAYBERRY *n* pl. -RIES a berry tree

BAYONET *v* -NETED, -NETING, -NETS or -NETTED, -NETTING, -NETS to stab with a dagger-like weapon

BAYOU *n* pl. -S a marshy body of water

BAYWOOD *n* pl. -S a coarse mahogany

BAZAAR *n* pl. -S a marketplace

BAZAR *n* pl. -S a bazaar

BAZOOKA *n* pl. -S a small rocket launcher

BDELLIUM *n* pl. -S a gum resin

BE *v* present sing. 1st person AM, 2d ARE or ART, 3d IS, past sing. 1st and 3d persons WAS, 2d WERE or WAST or WERT, past participle BEEN, present participle BEING to have actuality

BEACH *v* -ED, -ING, -ES to drive ashore

BEACHBOY *n* pl. -BOYS a male beach attendant

BEACHY *adj* BEACHIER, BEACHIEST sandy or pebbly

BEACON *v* -ED, -ING, -S to warn or guide

BEAD *v* -ED, -ING, -S to adorn with beads (round pieces of glass)

BEADIER comparative of beady

BEADIEST superlative of beady

BEADILY *adv* in a beady manner

BEADING *n* pl. -S beaded material

BEADLE *n* pl. -S a parish official

BEADLIKE *adj* beady

BEADMAN *n* pl. -MEN beadsman

BEADROLL *n* pl. -S a list of names

BEADSMAN *n* pl. -MEN one who prays for another

BEADWORK *n* pl. -S beading

BEADY *adj* BEADIER, BEADIEST resembling beads

BEAGLE *n* pl. -S a small hound

BEAK *n* pl. -S a bird's bill BEAKED, BEAKLESS, BEAKLIKE *adj*

BEAKER *n* pl. -S a large cup

BEAKY *adj* BEAKIER, BEAKIEST resembling a beak

BEAM *v* -ED, -ING, -S to emit in beams (rays of light)

BEAMIER comparative of beamy

BEAMIEST superlative of beamy

BEAMILY *adv* in a beamy manner

BEAMISH *adj* cheerful

BEAMLESS *adj* having no beam

BEAMLIKE *adj* resembling a beam

BEAMY *adj* BEAMIER, BEAMIEST beaming

BEAN *v* -ED, -ING, -S to hit on the head

BEANBAG *n* pl. -S a small cloth bag

BEANBALL *n* pl. -S a baseball thrown at the head

BEANERY *n* pl. -ERIES a cheap restaurant

BEANIE *n* pl. -S a small cap

BEANLIKE *adj* resembling a bean

BEANO *n* pl. BEANOS a form of bingo

BEANPOLE *n* pl. -S a thin pole

BEAR *v* BORE, BORNE or BORN, BEARING, BEARS to endure BEARABLE *adj* BEARABLY *adv*

BEARCAT *n* pl. -S a small mammal

BEARD *v* -ED, -ING, -S to oppose boldly

BEARER *n* pl. -S one that bears

BEARING *n* pl. -S demeanor

BEARISH *adj* resembling a bear (a large mammal)

BEARLIKE *adj* bearish

BEARSKIN *n* pl. -S the skin of a bear

BEAST *n* pl. -S an animal

BEASTIE *n* pl. -S a tiny animal

BEASTLY *adj* -LIER, -LIEST resembling a beast

BEAT *v* BEAT, BEATEN, BEATING, BEATS to strike repeatedly BEATABLE *adj*

BEATER *n* pl. -S one that beats

BEATIFIC	*adj* blissful
BEATIFY	*v* -FIED, -FYING, -FIES to make happy
BEATING	*n pl.* -S a defeat
BEATLESS	*adj* having no rhythm
BEATNIK	*n pl.* -S a nonconformist
BEAU	*n pl.* BEAUX or BEAUS a boyfriend **BEAUISH** *adj*
BEAUT	*n pl.* -S something beautiful
BEAUTIFY	*v* -FIED, -FYING, -FIES to make beautiful
BEAUTY	*n pl.* -TIES one that is lovely
BEAUX	a *pl.* of beau
BEAVER	*v* -ED, -ING, -S to work hard
BEBEERU	*n pl.* -S a tropical tree
BEBLOOD	*v* -ED, ING, -S to cover with blood
BEBOP	*n pl.* -S a type of jazz
BEBOPPER	*n pl.* -S one that likes bebop
BECALM	*v* -ED, -ING, -S to make calm
BECAME	past tense of become
BECAP	*v* -CAPPED, -CAPPING, -CAPS to put a cap on
BECARPET	*v* -ED, -ING, -S to cover with a carpet
BECAUSE	*conj* for the reason that
BECHALK	*v* -ED, -ING, -S to cover with chalk
BECHAMEL	*n pl.* -S a white sauce
BECHANCE	*v* -CHANCED, -CHANCING, -CHANCES to befall
BECHARM	*v* -ED, -ING, -S to hold under a spell
BECK	*v* -ED, -ING, -S to beckon
BECKET	*n pl.* -S a securing rope
BECKON	*v* -ED, -ING, -S to signal by sign or gesture
BECKONER	*n pl.* -S one that beckons
BECLAMOR	*v* -ED, -ING, -S to clamor loudly
BECLASP	*v* -ED, -ING, -S to embrace
BECLOAK	*v* -ED, -ING, -S to place a cloak on
BECLOG	*v* -CLOGGED, -CLOGGING, -CLOGS to clog thoroughly
BECLOTHE	*v* -CLOTHED, -CLOTHING, -CLOTHES to clothe
BECLOUD	*v* -ED, -ING, -S to make cloudy
BECLOWN	*v* -ED, -ING, -S to cause to appear ridiculous
BECOME	*v* -CAME, -COMING, -COMES to come to be
BECOMING	*n pl.* -S a process of change

BECOWARD	*v* -ED, -ING, -S to accuse of cowardice
BECRAWL	*v* -ED, -ING, -S to crawl over
BECRIME	*v* -CRIMED, -CRIMING, -CRIMES to make guilty of a crime
BECROWD	*v* -ED, -ING, -S to crowd closely
BECRUST	*v* -ED, -ING, -S to cover with a crust
BECUDGEL	*v* -GELLED, -GELLING, -GELS or -GELED, -GELING, -GELS to cudgel thoroughly
BECURSE	*v* -CURSED or -CURST, -CURSING, -CURSES to curse severely
BED	*v* BEDDED, BEDDING, BEDS to provide with a bed (a piece of furniture used for sleeping)
BEDABBLE	*v* -BLED, -BLING, -BLES to soil
BEDAMN	*v* -ED, -ING, -S to swear at
BEDARKEN	*v* -ED, -ING, -S to darken
BEDAUB	*v* -ED, -ING, -S to besmear
BEDAZZLE	*v* -ZLED, -ZLING, -ZLES to confuse
BEDBUG	*n pl.* -S a bloodsucking insect
BEDCHAIR	*n pl.* -S a chair near a bed
BEDCOVER	*n pl.* -S a cover for a bed
BEDDED	past tense of bed
BEDDER	*n pl.* -S one that makes up beds
BEDDING	*n pl.* -S material for making up a bed
BEDEAFEN	*v* -ED, -ING, -S to deafen
BEDECK	*v* -ED, -ING, -S to clothe with finery
BEDEL	*n pl.* -S an English university officer
BEDELL	*n pl.* -S bedel
BEDEMAN	*n pl.* -MEN beadsman
BEDESMAN	*n pl.* -MEN beadsman
BEDEVIL	*v* -ILED, -ILING, -ILS or -ILLED, -ILLING, -ILS to harass
BEDEW	*v* -ED, -ING, -S to wet with dew
BEDFAST	*adj* confined to bed
BEDFRAME	*n pl.* -S the frame of a bed
BEDGOWN	*n pl.* -S a dressing gown
BEDIAPER	*v* -ED, -ING, -S to ornament with a kind of design
BEDIGHT	*v* -ED, -ING, -S to bedeck
BEDIM	*v* -DIMMED, -DIMMING, -DIMS to make dim
BEDIMPLE	*v* -PLED, -PLING, -PLES to dimple

BEDIRTY v -DIRTIED, -DIRTYING, -DIRTIES to make dirty

BEDIZEN v -ED, -ING, -S to dress gaudily

BEDLAM n pl. -S confusion

BEDLAMP n pl. -S a lamp near a bed

BEDLESS adj having no bed

BEDLIKE adj resembling a bed

BEDMAKER n pl. -S one that makes beds

BEDMATE n pl. -S a bed companion

BEDOTTED adj covered with dots

BEDOUIN n pl. -S a nomadic Arab

BEDPAN n pl. -S a toilet pan

BEDPLATE n pl. -S a frame support

BEDPOST n pl. -S a post of a bed

BEDQUILT n pl. -S a quilt for a bed

BEDRAIL n pl. -S a board at the side of a bed

BEDRAPE v -DRAPED, -DRAPING, -DRAPES to drape

BEDRENCH v -ED, -ING, -ES to drench thoroughly

BEDRID adj bedfast

BEDRIVEL v -ELLED, -ELLING, -ELS or -ELED, -ELING, -ELS to cover with saliva

BEDROCK n pl. -S the rock under soil

BEDROLL n pl. -S a portable roll of bedding

BEDROOM n pl. -S a room for sleeping

BEDRUG v -DRUGGED, -DRUGGING, -DRUGS to make sleepy

BEDSIDE n pl. -S the side of a bed

BEDSONIA n pl. -S a virus

BEDSORE n pl. -S a type of sore

BEDSTAND n pl. -S a table next to a bed

BEDSTEAD n pl. -S a support for a bed

BEDSTRAW n pl. -S a woody herb

BEDTICK n pl. -S the cloth case of a mattress

BEDTIME n pl. -S a time for going to bed

BEDUIN n pl. -S bedouin

BEDUMB v -ED, -ING, -S to render speechless

BEDUNCE v -DUNCED, -DUNCING, -DUNCES to make a dunce of

BEDWARD adv toward bed

BEDWARDS adv bedward

BEDWARF v -ED, -ING, -S to cause to appear small by comparison

BEE n pl. -S a winged insect

BEEBEE n pl. -S a pellet

BEEBREAD n pl. -S a pollen mixture

BEECH n pl. -ES a type of tree BEECHEN adj

BEECHNUT n pl. -S the nut of a beech

BEECHY adj BEECHIER, BEECHIEST abounding in beeches

BEEF n pl. BEEFS or BEEVES a steer or cow fattened for food

BEEF v -ED, -ING, -S to add bulk to

BEEFCAKE n pl. -S pictures of male physiques

BEEFIER comparative of beefy

BEEFIEST superlative of beefy

BEEFILY adv in a beefy manner

BEEFLESS adj being without beef

BEEFWOOD n pl. -S a hardwood tree

BEEFY adj BEEFIER, BEEFIEST brawny

BEEHIVE n pl. -S a hive for bees

BEELIKE adj resembling a bee

BEELINE n pl. -S a direct route

BEEN past participle of be

BEEP v -ED, -ING, -S to honk a horn

BEEPER n pl. -S a signaling device

BEER n pl. -S an alcoholic beverage

BEERY adj BEERIER, BEERIEST affected by beer

BEESWAX n pl. -ES a type of wax

BEESWING n pl. -S a crust that forms on old wines

BEET n pl. -S a garden plant

BEETLE v -TLED, -TLING, -TLES to jut out

BEETROOT n pl. -S the root of the beet

BEEVES a pl. of beef

BEFALL v -FELL, -FALLEN, -FALLING, -FALLS to happen to

BEFINGER v -ED, -ING, -S to touch all over

BEFIT v -FITTED, -FITTING, -FITS to be suitable to

BEFLAG v -FLAGGED, -FLAGGING, -FLAGS to deck with flags

BEFLEA v -ED, -ING, -S to infest with fleas

BEFLECK v -ED, -ING, -S to fleck

BEFLOWER v -ED, -ING, -S to cover with flowers

BEFOG v -FOGGED, -FOGGING, -FOGS to envelop in fog

BEFOOL v -ED, -ING, -S to deceive

BEFORE adv previously

BEFOUL v -ED, -ING, -S to foul

BEFOULER n pl. -S one that befouls

BEFRET v -FRETTED, -FRETTING, -FRETS to gnaw

BEFRIEND v -ED, -ING, -S to act as a friend to

BEFRINGE v -FRINGED, -FRINGING, -FRINGES to border with a fringe

BEFUDDLE v -DLED, -DLING, -DLES to confuse

BEG v BEGGED, BEGGING, BEGS to plead

BEGALL v -ED, -ING, -S to make sore by rubbing

BEGAN past tense of begin

BEGAZE v -GAZED, -GAZING, -GAZES to gaze at

BEGET v -GOT or -GAT, -GOTTEN, -GETTING, -GETS to cause to exist

BEGETTER n pl. -S one that begets

BEGGAR v -ED, -ING, -S to impoverish

BEGGARLY adj very poor

BEGGARY n pl. -GARIES extreme poverty

BEGGED past tense of beg

BEGGING present participle of beg

BEGIN v -GAN, -GUN, -GINNING, -GINS to start

BEGINNER n pl. -S one that begins

BEGIRD v -GIRT or -GIRDED, -GIRDING, -GIRDS to surround

BEGIRDLE v -DLED -DLING, -DLES to surround

BEGLAD v -GLADDED, -GLADDING, -GLADS to gladden

BEGLOOM v -ED, -ING, -S to make gloomy

BEGONE interj — used as an order of dismissal

BEGONIA n pl. -S a tropical herb

BEGORAH interj begorra

BEGORRA interj — used as a mild oath

BEGORRAH interj begorra

BEGOT a past tense of beget

BEGOTTEN past participle of beget

BEGRIM v -GRIMMED, -GRIMMING, -GRIMS to begrime

BEGRIME v -GRIMED, -GRIMING, -GRIMES to dirty

BEGROAN v -ED, -ING, -S to groan at

BEGRUDGE v -GRUDGED, -GRUDGING, -GRUDGES to concede reluctantly

BEGUILE v -GUILED, -GUILING, -GUILES to deceive

BEGUILER n pl. -S one that beguiles

BEGUINE n pl. -S a lively dance

BEGULF v -ED, -ING, -S to engulf

BEGUM n pl. -S a Muslim lady of high rank

BEGUN past participle of begin

BEHALF n pl. -HALVES interest, support, or benefit

BEHAVE v -HAVED, -HAVING, -HAVES to act properly

BEHAVER n pl. -S one that behaves

BEHAVIOR n pl. -S demeanor

BEHEAD v -ED, -ING, -S to cut off the head of

BEHELD past tense of behold

BEHEMOTH n pl. -S a large beast

BEHEST n pl. -S a command

BEHIND n pl. -S the buttocks

BEHOLD v -HELD, -HOLDING, -HOLDS to view

BEHOLDEN adj indebted

BEHOLDER n pl. -S one that beholds

BEHOOF n pl. -HOOVES use, advantage, or benefit

BEHOOVE v -HOOVED, -HOOVING, -HOOVES to be proper for

BEHOVE v -HOVED, -HOVING, -HOVES to behoove

BEHOWL v -ED, -ING, -S to howl at

BEIGE n pl. -S a tan color

BEIGY adj of the color beige

BEING n pl. -S something that exists

BEJEWEL v -ELED, -ELING, -ELS or -ELLED, -ELLING, -ELS to adorn with jewels

BEJUMBLE v -BLED, -BLING, -BLES to jumble

BEKISS v -ED, -ING, -ES to cover with kisses

BEKNIGHT v -ED, -ING, -S to raise to knighthood

BEKNOT v -KNOTTED, -KNOTTING, -KNOTS to tie in knots

BEL n pl. -S a unit of power

BELABOR v -ED, -ING, -S to discuss for an absurd amount of time

BELABOUR v -ED, -ING, -S to belabor

BELACED adj adorned with lace

BELADY v -DIED, -DYING, -DIES to apply the title of lady to

BELATED adj late or too late

BELAUD v -ED, -ING, -S to praise

BELAY   v -ED, -ING, -S to fasten a rope

BELCH   v -ED, -ING, -ES to expel gas through the mouth

BELCHER   n pl. -S one that belches

BELDAM   n pl. -S an old woman

BELDAME   n pl. -S beldam

BELEAP   v -LEAPT or -LEAPED, -LEAPING, -LEAPS to leap upon

BELFRY   n pl. -FRIES a bell tower BELFRIED adj

BELGA   n pl. -S a former Belgian monetary unit

BELIE   v -LIED, -LYING, -LIES to misrepresent

BELIEF   n pl. -S acceptance of the truth or actuality of something

BELIER   n pl. -S one that belies

BELIEVE   v -LIEVED, -LIEVING, -LIEVES to accept as true or real

BELIEVER   n pl. -S one that believes

BELIKE   adv perhaps

BELIQUOR   v -ED, -ING, -S to soak with liquor

BELITTLE   v -TLED, -TLING, -TLES to disparage

BELIVE   adv in due time

BELL   v -ED, -ING, -S to provide with a bell (a ringing device)

BELLBIRD   n pl. -S a tropical bird

BELLBOY   n pl. -BOYS a hotel's errand boy

BELLE   n pl. -S an attractive woman

BELLEEK   n pl. -S a very thin translucent porcelain

BELLHOP   n pl. -S a bellboy

BELLIED   past tense of belly

BELLIES   present 3d person sing. of belly

BELLMAN   n pl. -MEN a town crier

BELLOW   v -ED, -ING, -S to shout in a deep voice

BELLOWER   n pl. -S one that bellows

BELLPULL   n pl. -S a cord pulled to ring a bell

BELLWORT   n pl. -S a flowering plant

BELLY   v -LIED, -LYING, -LIES to swell out

BELLYFUL   n pl. -S an excessive amount

BELONG   v -ED, -ING, -S to be a member of

BELOVED   n pl. -S one who is loved

BELOW   n pl. -S something that is beneath

BELT   v -ED, -ING, -S to fasten with a belt (a strap or band worn around the waist)

BELTING   n pl. -S material for belts

BELTLESS   adj having no belt

BELTLINE   n pl. -S the waistline

BELTWAY   n pl. -WAYS a highway around an urban area

BELUGA   n pl. -S a white sturgeon

BELYING   present participle of belie

BEMA   n pl. -MATA or -MAS a platform in a synagogue

BEMADAM   v -ED, -ING, -S to call by the title of madam

BEMADDEN   v -ED, -ING, -S to madden

BEMEAN   v -ED, -ING, -S to debase

BEMINGLE   v -GLED, -GLING, -GLES to mix together

BEMIRE   v -MIRED, -MIRING, -MIRES to soil with mud

BEMIST   v -ED, -ING, -S to envelop in a mist

BEMIX   v -MIXED or -MIXT, -MIXING, -MIXES to mix thoroughly

BEMOAN   v -ED, -ING, -S to lament

BEMOCK   v -ED, -ING, -S to mock

BEMUDDLE   v -DLED, -DLING, -DLES to confuse completely

BEMURMUR   v -ED, -ING, -S to murmur at

BEMUSE   v -MUSED, -MUSING, -MUSES to confuse

BEMUZZLE   v -ZLED, -ZLING, -ZLES to muzzle

BEN   n pl. -S an inner room

BENAME   v -NAMED, -NEMPT or -NEMPTED, -NAMING, -NAMES to name

BENCH   v -ED, -ING, -ES to take a player out of a game

BENCHER   n pl. -S a magistrate

BEND   v BENT or BENDED, BENDING, BENDS to curve BENDABLE adj

BENDAY   v -ED, -ING, -S to reproduce using a certain process

BENDEE   n pl. -S bendy

BENDER   n pl. -S one that bends

BENDWAYS   adv bendwise

BENDWISE   adv diagonally

BENDY   n pl. -DYS okra

BENE   n pl. -S benne

BENEATH   prep under

BENEDICK   n pl. -S benedict

BENEDICT   n pl. -S a newly married man

BENEFIC   adj kindly

BENEFICE   v -FICED, -FICING, -FICES to endow with land

BENEFIT   v -FITED, -FITING, -FITS or -FITTED, -FITTING, -FITS to be helpful or useful to

BENEMPT   a past participle of bename

BENEMPTED a past participle of bename

BENIGN   adj kind **BENIGNLY** adv

BENISON   n pl. -S a blessing

BENJAMIN   n pl. -S benzoin

BENNE   n pl. -S the sesame plant

BENNET   n pl. -S a perennial herb

BENNI   n pl. -S benne

BENNY   n pl. -NIES an amphetamine tablet

BENT   n pl. -S an inclination

BENTHAL   adj benthic

BENTHIC   adj pertaining to oceanic depths

BENTHOS   n pl. -ES benthic sea life

BENTWOOD n pl. -S wood bent for use in furniture

BENUMB   v -ED, -ING, -S to make numb

BENZAL   adj pertaining to a certain chemical group

BENZENE   n pl. -S a volatile liquid

BENZIDIN   n pl. -S a hydrocarbon

BENZIN   n pl. -S benzine

BENZINE   n pl. -S a volatile liquid

BENZOATE n pl. -S a chemical salt

BENZOIN   n pl. -S a gum resin **BENZOIC** adj

BENZOL   n pl. -S a benzene

BENZOLE   n pl. -S benzol

BENZOYL   n pl. -S a univalent chemical radical

BENZYL   n pl. -S a univalent chemical radical **BENZYLIC** adj

BEPAINT   v -ED, -ING, -S to tinge

BEPIMPLE   v -PLED, -PLING, -PLES to cover with pimples

BEQUEATH   v -ED, -ING, -S to grant by testament

BEQUEST   n pl. -S a legacy

BERASCAL   v -ED, -ING, -S to accuse of being a rascal

BERAKE   v -RAKED, -RAKING, -RAKES to rake all over

BERATE   v -RATED, -RATING, -RATES to scold severely

BERBERIN   n pl. -S a medicinal alkaloid

BERCEUSE   n pl. -S a lullaby

BEREAVE   v -REAVED or -REFT, -REAVING, -REAVES to deprive

BEREAVER   n pl. -S one that bereaves

BERET   n pl. -S a soft, flat cap

BERETTA   n pl. -S biretta

BERG   n pl. -S an iceberg

BERGAMOT n pl. -S a citrus tree

BERHYME   v -RHYMED, -RHYMING, -RHYMES to compose in rhyme

BERIBERI   n pl. -S a thiamine deficiency disease

BERIME   v -RIMED, -RIMING, -RIMES to berhyme

BERINGED   adj adorned with rings

BERLIN   n pl. -S a type of carriage

BERLINE   n pl. -S a limousine

BERM   n pl. -S a ledge

BERME   n pl. -S berm

BERNICLE   n pl. -S a wild goose

BEROBED   adj wearing a robe

BEROUGED   adj obviously or thickly rouged

BERRETTA   n pl. -S biretta

BERRY   v -RIED, -RYING, -RIES to produce berries (fleshy fruits)

BERSEEM   n pl. -S a clover

BERSERK   n pl. -S a fierce warrior

BERTH   v -ED, -ING, -S to provide with a mooring

BERTHA   n pl. -S a wide collar

BERYL   n pl. -S a green mineral **BERYLINE** adj

BESCORCH   v -ED, -ING, -ES to scorch

BESCOUR   v -ED, -ING, -S to scour thoroughly

BESCREEN   v -ED, -ING, -S to screen

BESEECH   v -SOUGHT or -SEECHED, -SEECHING, -SEECHES to implore

BESEEM   v -ED, -ING, -S to be suitable

BESET   v -SET, -SETTING, -SETS to assail

BESETTER   n pl. -S one that besets

BESHADOW v -ED, -ING, -S to cast a shadow on

BESHAME   v -SHAMED, -SHAMING, -SHAMES to put to shame

BESHIVER   v -ED, -ING, -S to break into small pieces

BESHOUT   v -ED, -ING, -S to shout at

BESHREW   v -ED, -ING, -S to curse

BESHROUD   v -ED, -ING, -S to cover

BESIDE   prep next to

BESIDES   adv in addition

BESIEGE   v -SIEGED, -SIEGING, -SIEGES to surround

BESIEGER   n pl. -S one that besieges

BESLAVED   adj filled with slaves

BESLIME   v -SLIMED, -SLIMING, -SLIMES to cover with slime

BESMEAR   v -ED, -ING, -S to smear over

BESMILE   v -SMILED, -SMILING, -SMILES to smile on

BESMIRCH   v -ED, -ING, -ES to dirty

BESMOKE   v -SMOKED, -SMOKING, -SMOKES to soil with smoke

BESMOOTH   v -ED, -ING, -S to smooth

BESMUDGE   v -SMUDGED, -SMUDGING, -SMUDGES to smudge

BESMUT   v -SMUTTED, -SMUTTING, -SMUTS to blacken with smut

BESNOW   v -ED, -ING, -S to cover with snow

BESOM   n pl. -S a broom

BESOOTHE   v -SOOTHED, -SOOTHING, -SOOTHES to soothe

BESOT   v -SOTTED, -SOTTING, -SOTS to stupefy

BESOUGHT   a past tense of beseech

BESPEAK   v -SPOKE or -SPAKE, -SPOKEN, -SPEAKING, -SPEAKS to claim in advance

BESPOUSE   v -SPOUSED, -SPOUSING, -SPOUSES to marry

BESPREAD   v -SPREAD, -SPREADING, -SPREADS to spread over

BESPRENT   adj sprinkled over

BEST   v -ED, -ING, -S to outdo

BESTEAD   v -ED, -ING, -S to help

BESTIAL   adj pertaining to beasts

BESTIARY   n pl. -ARIES a collection of animal fables

BESTIR   v -STIRRED, -STIRRING, -STIRS to rouse

BESTOW   v -ED, -ING, -S to present as a gift

BESTOWAL   n pl. -S a gift

BESTREW   v -STREWED, -STREWN, -STREWING, -STREWS to scatter

BESTRIDE   v -STRODE or -STRID, -STRIDDEN, -STRIDING, -STRIDES to straddle

BESTROW   v -STROWED, -STROWN, -STROWING, -STROWS to bestrew

BESTUD   v -STUDDED, -STUDDING, -STUDS to dot

BESWARM   v -ED, -ING, -S to swarm all over

BET   v BET or BETTED, BETTING, BETS to wager

BETA   n pl. -S a Greek letter

BETAINE   n pl. -S an alkaloid

BETAKE   v -TOOK, -TAKEN, -TAKING, -TAKES to cause to go

BETATRON   n pl. -S an electron accelerator

BETATTER   v -ED, -ING, -S to tatter

BETAXED   adj burdened with taxes

BETEL   n pl. -S a climbing plant

BETELNUT   n pl. -S a seed chewed as a stimulant

BETH   n pl. -S a Hebrew letter

BETHANK   v -ED, -ING, -S to thank

BETHEL   n pl. -S a holy place

BETHINK   v -THOUGHT, -THINKING, -THINKS to consider

BETHORN   v -ED, -ING, -S to fill with thorns

BETHUMP   v -ED, -ING, -S to thump soundly

BETIDE   v -TIDED, -TIDING, -TIDES to befall

BETIME   adv betimes

BETIMES   adv soon

BETISE   n pl. -S stupidity

BETOKEN   v -ED, -ING, -S to indicate

BETON   n pl. -S a type of concrete

BETONY   n pl. -NIES a European herb

BETOOK   past tense of betake

BETRAY   v -ED, -ING, -S to aid an enemy of

BETRAYAL   n pl. -S the act of betraying

BETRAYER   n pl. -S one that betrays

BETROTH   v -ED, -ING, -S to engage to marry

BETTA   n pl. -S a freshwater fish

BETTED   a past tense of bet

BETTER   v -ED, -ING, -S to improve

BETTING   present participle of bet

BETTOR   n pl. -S one that bets

BETWEEN   prep in the space that separates

BETWIXT   prep between

BEUNCLED   adj having many uncles

BEVATRON n pl. -S a proton accelerator

BEVEL v -ELED, -ELING, -ELS or -ELLED, -ELLING, -ELS to cut at an angle

BEVELER n pl. -S one that bevels

BEVELLER n pl. -S beveler

BEVELLING a present participle of bevel

BEVERAGE n pl. -S a liquid for drinking

BEVIES pl. of bevy

BEVOMIT v -ED, -ING, -S to vomit all over

BEVOR n pl. -S a piece of armor for the lower face

BEVY n pl. BEVIES a group

BEWAIL v -ED, -ING, -S to lament

BEWAILER n pl. -S one that bewails

BEWARE v -WARED, -WARING, -WARES to be careful

BEWEARY v -WEARIED, -WEARYING, -WEARIES to make weary

BEWEEP v -WEPT, -WEEPING, -WEEPS to lament

BEWIG v -WIGGED, -WIGGING, -WIGS to adorn with a wig

BEWILDER v -ED, -ING, -S to confuse

BEWINGED adj having wings

BEWITCH v -ED, -ING, -ES to affect by witchcraft or magic

BEWORM v -ED, -ING, -S to infest with worms

BEWORRY v -RIED, -RYING, -RIES to worry

BEWRAP v -WRAPPED or -WRAPT, -WRAPPING, -WRAPS to wrap completely

BEWRAY v -ED, -ING, -S to divulge

BEWRAYER n pl. -S one that bewrays

BEY n pl. BEYS a Turkish ruler

BEYLIC n pl. -S the domain of a bey

BEYLIK n pl. -S beylic

BEYOND n pl. -S something that lies farther ahead

BEZANT n pl. -S a coin of ancient Rome

BEZEL n pl. -S a slanted surface

BEZIL n pl. -S bezel

BEZIQUE n pl. -S a card game

BEZOAR n pl. -S a gastric mass

BEZZANT n pl. -S bezant

BHAKTA n pl. -S one who practices bhakti

BHAKTI n pl. -S a selfless devotion to a deity in Hinduism

BHANG n pl. -S the hemp plant

BHEESTIE n pl. -S bheesty

BHEESTY n pl. -TIES a water carrier

BHISTIE n pl. -S bheesty

BHOOT n pl. -S bhut

BHUT n pl. -S a small whirlwind

BI n pl. -S a bisexual

BIACETYL n pl. -S a chemical flavor enhancer

BIALY n pl. -ALYS an onion roll

BIANNUAL adj occurring twice a year

BIAS v -ASED, -ASING, -ASES or -ASSED, -ASSING -ASSES to prejudice BIASEDLY adv

BIASNESS n pl. -ES the state of being slanted

BIATHLON n pl. -S an athletic contest

BIAXAL adj biaxial

BIAXIAL adj having two axes

BIB v BIBBED, BIBBING, BIBS to tipple

BIBASIC adj dibasic

BIBB n pl. -S a mast support

BIBBED past tense of bib

BIBBER n pl. -S a tippler

BIBBERY n pl. -BERIES the act of bibbing

BIBBING present participle of bib

BIBCOCK n pl. -S a type of faucet

BIBELOT n pl. -S a trinket

BIBLE n pl. -S an authoritative publication BIBLICAL adj

BIBLESS adj having no bib (a cloth covering)

BIBLIKE adj resembling a bib

BIBULOUS adj given to drinking

BICARB n pl. -S sodium bicarbonate

BICE n pl. -S a blue or green pigment

BICEPS n pl. -ES an arm muscle

BICHROME adj two-colored

BICKER v -ED, -ING, -S to argue

BICKERER n pl. -S one that bickers

BICOLOR n pl. -S something having two colors

BICOLOUR n pl. -S bicolor

BICONVEX adj convex on both sides

BICORN adj having two horns

BICORNE n pl. -S a type of hat

BICRON n pl. -S one billionth of a meter

BICUSPID n pl. -S a tooth

BICYCLE v -CLED, -CLING, -CLES to ride a bicycle (a two-wheeled vehicle)

BICYCLER   n pl. -S one that bicycles

BICYCLIC   adj having two cycles

BICYCLING   present participle of bicycle

BID   v BADE, BIDDEN, BIDDING, BIDS to make a bid (an offer of a price)

BIDARKA   n pl. -S an Eskimo canoe

BIDARKEE   n pl. -S bidarka

BIDDABLE   adj obedient BIDDABLY adv

BIDDEN   past participle of bid

BIDDER   n pl. -S one that bids

BIDDING   n pl. -S a command

BIDDY   n pl. -DIES a hen

BIDE   v BIDED or BODE, BIDING, BIDES to wait

BIDENTAL   adj having two teeth

BIDER   n pl. -S one that bides

BIDET   n pl. -S a low basin used for washing

BIDING   present participle of bide

BIELD   v -ED, -ING, -S to shelter

BIENNIAL   n pl. -S an event that occurs every two years

BIENNIUM   n pl. -NIA or -NIUMS a period of two years

BIER   n pl. -S a coffin stand

BIFACIAL   adj having two faces

BIFF   v -ED, -ING, -S to hit

BIFFIN   n pl. -S a cooking apple

BIFFY   n pl. -FIES a toilet

BIFID   adj divided into two parts BIFIDLY adv

BIFIDITY   n pl. -TIES the state of being bifid

BIFILAR   adj having two threads

BIFLEX   adj bent in two places

BIFOCAL   n pl. -S a type of lens

BIFOLD   adj twofold

BIFORATE   adj having two perforations

BIFORKED   adj divided into two branches

BIFORM   adj having two forms

BIFORMED   adj biform

BIG   adj BIGGER, BIGGEST of considerable size

BIGAMIES   pl. of bigamy

BIGAMIST   n pl. -S one who commits bigamy

BIGAMOUS   adj guilty of bigamy

BIGAMY   n pl. -MIES the crime of being married to two people simultaneously

BIGAROON   n pl. -S a type of cherry

BIGEMINY   n pl. -NIES the state of having a double pulse

BIGEYE   n pl. -S a marine fish

BIGGER   comparative of big

BIGGEST   superlative of big

BIGGETY   adj biggity

BIGGIE   n pl. -S one that is big

BIGGIN   n pl. -S a house

BIGGING   n pl. -S biggin

BIGGISH   adj somewhat big

BIGGITY   adj conceited

BIGHEAD   n pl. -S a disease of animals

BIGHORN   n pl. -S a wild sheep

BIGHT   v -ED, -ING, -S to fasten with a loop of rope

BIGLY   adv in a big manner

BIGMOUTH   n pl. -S a talkative person

BIGNESS   n pl. -ES the state of being big

BIGNONIA   n pl. -S a climbing plant

BIGOT   n pl. -S a prejudiced person

BIGOTED   adj intolerant

BIGOTRY   n pl. -RIES prejudice

BIGWIG   n pl. -S an important person

BIHOURLY   adj occurring every two hours

BIJOU   n pl. -JOUX or -JOUS a jewel

BIJUGATE   adj two-paired

BIJUGOUS   adj bijugate

BIKE   v BIKED, BIKING, BIKES to bicycle

BIKER   n pl. -S one that bikes

BIKEWAY   n pl. -WAYS a route for bikes

BIKING   present participle of bike

BIKINI   n pl. -S a type of bathing suit BIKINIED adj

BILABIAL   n pl. -S a sound articulated with both lips

BILANDER   n pl. -S a small ship

BILBERRY   n pl. -RIES an edible berry

BILBO   n pl. -BOS or -BOES a finely tempered sword

BILBOA   n pl. -S bilbo

BILE   n pl. -S a fluid secreted by the liver

BILGE   v BILGED, BILGING, BILGES to spring a leak

BILGY   adj BILGIER, BILGIEST smelling like seepage

BILIARY   adj pertaining to bile

BILINEAR   adj pertaining to two lines

BILIOUS   adj pertaining to bile

BILK   v -ED, -ING, -S to cheat

BILKER *n pl.* -S one that bilks

BILL *v* -ED, -ING, -S to present a statement of costs to **BILLABLE** *adj*

BILLBUG *n pl.* -S a weevil

BILLER *n pl.* -S one that bills

BILLET *v* -ED, -ING, -S to lodge soldiers

BILLETER *n pl.* -S one that billets

BILLFISH *n pl.* -ES a fish with long, slender jaws

BILLFOLD *n pl.* -S a wallet

BILLHEAD *n pl.* -S a letterhead

BILLHOOK *n pl.* -S a cutting tool

BILLIARD *n pl.* -S a carom shot in billiards

BILLIE *n pl.* -S a comrade

BILLIES pl. of billy

BILLING *n pl.* -S the relative position in which a performer is listed

BILLION *n pl.* -S a number

BILLON *n pl.* -S an alloy of silver and copper

BILLOW *v* -ED, -ING, -S to swell

BILLOWY *adj* -LOWIER, -LOWIEST swelling; surging

BILLY *n pl.* -LIES a short club

BILLYCAN *n pl.* -S a pot for heating water

BILOBATE *adj* having two lobes

BILOBED *adj* bilobate

BILSTED *n pl.* -S a hardwood tree

BILTONG *n pl.* -S dried and cured meat

BIMA *n pl.* -S bema

BIMAH *n pl.* -S bema

BIMANOUS *adj* two-handed

BIMANUAL *adj* done with two hands

BIMENSAL *adj* occurring every two months

BIMESTER *n pl.* -S a two-month period

BIMETAL *n pl.* -S something composed of two metals

BIMETHYL *n pl.* -S ethane

BIMODAL *adj* having two statistical modes

BIN *v* BINNED, BINNING, BINS to store in a large receptacle

BINAL *adj* twofold

BINARY *n pl.* -RIES a combination of two things

BINATE *adj* growing in pairs **BINATELY** *adv*

BINAURAL *adj* hearing with both ears

BIND *v* BOUND, BINDING, BINDS to tie or secure **BINDABLE** *adj*

BINDER *n pl.* -S one that binds

BINDERY *n pl.* -ERIES a place where books are bound

BINDING *n pl.* -S the cover and fastenings of a book

BINDLE *n pl.* -S a bundle

BINDWEED *n pl.* -S a twining plant

BINE *n pl.* -S a twining plant stem

BINGE *n pl.* -S a drunken carousal

BINGO *n pl.* -GOS a game of chance

BINIT *n pl.* -S a unit of computer information

BINNACLE *n pl.* -S a compass stand

BINNED past tense of bin

BINNING present participle of bin

BINOCLE *n pl.* -S a binocular

BINOMIAL *n pl.* -S an algebraic expression

BINT *n pl.* -S a woman

BIO *n pl.* BIOS a biography

BIOASSAY *v* -ED, -ING, -S to find the strength of a substance

BIOCIDE *n pl.* -S a substance destructive to living organisms **BIOCIDAL** *adj*

BIOCLEAN *adj* free of harmful organisms

BIOCYCLE *n pl.* -S a life-supporting region

BIOGEN *n pl.* -S a hypothetical protein molecule

BIOGENIC *adj* produced by living organisms

BIOGENY *n pl.* -NIES the development of life from preexisting life

BIOHERM *n pl.* -S a mass of marine fossils

BIOLOGIC *n pl.* -S a drug obtained from an organic source

BIOLOGY *n pl.* -GIES the science of life

BIOLYSIS *n pl.* -YSES death **BIOLYTIC** *adj*

BIOMASS *n pl.* -ES an amount of living matter

BIOME *n pl.* -S an ecological community

BIOMETRY *n pl.* -TRIES the statistical study of biological data

BIONICS *n/pl* a science joining biology and electronics **BIONIC** *adj*

BIONOMY *n pl.* -MIES ecology **BIONOMIC** *adj*

BIONT	n pl. -S a living organism **BIONTIC** adj
BIOPLASM	n pl. -S living matter
BIOPSY	n pl. -SIES the examination of tissue **BIOPSIC, BIOPTIC** adj
BIOSCOPE	n pl. -S an early movie projector
BIOSCOPY	n pl. -PIES a type of medical examination
BIOTA	n pl. -S the flora and fauna of a region
BIOTIC	adj pertaining to life
BIOTICAL	adj biotic
BIOTICS	n/pl a life science
BIOTIN	n pl. -S a B vitamin
BIOTITE	n pl. -S a form of mica **BIOTITIC** adj
BIOTOPE	n pl. -S a stable habitat
BIOTRON	n pl. -S a climate control chamber
BIOTYPE	n pl. -S a group of genetically similar organisms **BIOTYPIC** adj
BIOVULAR	adj derived from two ova
BIPACK	n pl. -S a pair of films
BIPAROUS	adj producing offspring in pairs
BIPARTED	adj having two parts
BIPARTY	adj of two parties
BIPED	n pl. -S a two-footed animal **BIPEDAL** adj
BIPHENYL	n pl. -S a hydrocarbon
BIPLANE	n pl. -S a type of airplane
BIPOD	n pl. -S a two-legged support
BIPOLAR	adj having two poles
BIRACIAL	adj including members of two races
BIRADIAL	adj having dual symmetry
BIRAMOSE	adj biramous
BIRAMOUS	adj divided into two branches
BIRCH	v -ED, -ING, -ES to whip
BIRCHEN	adj made of birch wood
BIRD	v -ED, -ING, -S to hunt birds (winged, warm-blooded vertebrates)
BIRDBATH	n pl. -S a bath for birds
BIRDCAGE	n pl. -S a cage for birds
BIRDCALL	n pl. -S the call of a bird
BIRDER	n pl. -S a bird hunter
BIRDFARM	n pl. -S an aircraft carrier
BIRDIE	v BIRDIED, BIRDIEING, BIRDIES to shoot in one stroke under par in golf
BIRDLIKE	adj resembling a bird

BIRDLIME	v -LIMED, -LIMING, -LIMES to trap small birds
BIRDMAN	n pl. -MEN one who keeps birds
BIRDSEED	n pl. -S a mixture of seeds used for feeding birds
BIRDSEYE	n pl. -S a flowering plant
BIREME	n pl. -S an ancient galley
BIRETTA	n pl. -S a cap worn by clergymen
BIRK	n pl. -S a birch tree
BIRKIE	n pl. -S a lively person
BIRL	v -ED, -ING, -S to rotate a floating log
BIRLE	v BIRLED, BIRLING, BIRLES to carouse
BIRLER	n pl. -S one that birls
BIRLING	n pl. -S a lumberjack's game
BIRR	v -ED, -ING, -S to make a whirring noise
BIRRETTA	n pl. -S biretta
BIRSE	n pl. -S a bristle
BIRTH	v -ED, -ING, -S to originate
BIRTHDAY	n pl. -DAYS an anniversary of a birth
BIS	adv twice
BISCUIT	n pl. -S a small cake of shortened bread
BISE	n pl. -S a cold wind
BISECT	v -ED, -ING, -S to cut into two parts
BISECTOR	n pl. -S something that bisects
BISEXUAL	n pl. -S one who is attracted to both sexes
BISHOP	v -ED, -ING, -S to appoint as a bishop (the head of a diocese)
BISK	n pl. -S bisque
BISMUTH	n pl. -S a metallic element
BISNAGA	n pl. -S a type of cactus
BISON	n pl. -S an ox-like animal
BISQUE	n pl. -S a thick soup
BISTATE	adj pertaining to two states
BISTER	n pl. -S a brown pigment **BISTERED** adj
BISTORT	n pl. -S a perennial herb with roots used as astringents
BISTOURY	n pl. -RIES a surgical knife
BISTRE	n pl. -S bister **BISTRED** adj
BISTRO	n pl. -TROS a small tavern **BISTROIC** adj
BIT	v BITTED, BITTING, BITS to restrain

BITABLE	adj capable of being bitten	**BLACK**	v -ED, -ING, -S to make black
BITCH	v -ED, -ING, -ES to complain	**BLACKBOY**	n pl. -BOYS an Australian plant
BITCHERY	n pl. -ERIES bitchy behavior	**BLACKCAP**	n pl. -S a small European bird
BITCHY	adj BITCHIER, BITCHIEST malicious **BITCHILY** adv	**BLACKEN**	v -ED, -ING, -S to make black
		BLACKFIN	n pl. -S a food fish
BITE	v BIT, BITTEN, BITING, BITES to seize with the teeth **BITEABLE** adj	**BLACKFLY**	n pl. -FLIES a biting fly
		BLACKGUM	n pl. -S a tupelo
BITER	n pl. -S one that bites	**BLACKING**	n pl. -S black shoe polish
BITEWING	n pl. -S a dental X-ray film	**BLACKISH**	adj somewhat black
BITING	present participle of bite	**BLACKLEG**	n pl. -S a cattle disease
BITINGLY	adv sarcastically	**BLACKLY**	adv in a black manner
BITSTOCK	n pl. -S a brace on a drill	**BLACKOUT**	n pl. -S a light failure
BITSY	adj tiny	**BLACKTOP**	v -TOPPED, -TOPPING, -TOPS to pave with asphalt
BITT	v -ED, -ING, -S to secure a cable		
		BLADDER	n pl. -S a saclike receptacle **BLADDERY** adj
BITTED	past tense of bit	**BLADE**	n pl. -S a cutting edge **BLADED** adj
BITTEN	a past participle of bite		
BITTER	adj -TERER, -TEREST having a disagreeable taste **BITTERLY** adv	**BLAE**	adj bluish-black
		BLAH	n pl. -S nonsense
		BLAIN	n pl. -S a blister
BITTER	v -ED, -ING, -S to make bitter	**BLAMABLE**	adj being at fault **BLAMABLY** adv
BITTERN	n pl. -S a wading bird		
BITTIER	comparative of bitty	**BLAME**	v BLAMED, BLAMING, BLAMES to find fault with
BITTIEST	superlative of bitty		
BITTING	n pl. -S an indentation in a key	**BLAMEFUL**	adj blamable
BITTOCK	n pl. -S a small amount	**BLAMER**	n pl. -S one that blames
BITTY	adj -TIER, -TIEST fragmented	**BLAMING**	present participle of blame
BITUMEN	n pl. -S an asphalt	**BLANCH**	v -ED, -ING, -ES to whiten
BIVALENT	n pl. -S a pair of chromosomes	**BLANCHER**	n pl. -S a whitener
BIVALVE	n pl. -S a bivalved mollusk	**BLAND**	adj BLANDER, BLANDEST soothing **BLANDLY** adv
BIVALVED	adj having a two-valved shell		
BIVINYL	n pl. -S a flammable gas used in making synthetic rubber	**BLANDISH**	v -ED, -ING, -ES to coax by flattery
		BLANK	adj BLANKER, BLANKEST empty
BIVOUAC	v -OUACKED, -OUACKING, -OUACKS or -OUACS to make a camp		
		BLANK	v -ED, -ING, -S to delete
		BLANKET	v -ED, -ING, -S to cover uniformly
BIWEEKLY	n pl. -LIES a publication issued every two weeks		
		BLANKLY	adv in a blank manner
BIYEARLY	adj occurring every two years	**BLARE**	v BLARED, BLARING, BLARES to sound loudly
BIZARRE	n pl. -S a strangely striped flower		
		BLARNEY	v -NEYED, -NEYING, -NEYS to beguile with flattery
BIZE	n pl. -S bise		
BIZNAGA	n pl. -S bisnaga	**BLASE**	adj indifferent
BIZONE	n pl. -S two combined zones **BIZONAL** adj	**BLAST**	v -ED, -ING, -S to use an explosive
BLAB	v BLABBED, BLABBING, BLABS to talk idly	**BLASTEMA**	n pl. -MAS or -MATA a region of embryonic cells
BLABBER	v -ED, -ING, -S to blab	**BLASTER**	n pl. -S one that blasts
BLABBY	adj talkative	**BLASTIE**	n pl. -S a dwarf
BLACK	adj BLACKER, BLACKEST being of the darkest color	**BLASTIER**	comparative of blasty

BLASTIEST superlative of blasty

BLASTING n pl. -S the act of one that blasts

BLASTOFF n pl. -S the launching of a rocket

BLASTOMA n pl. -MAS or -MATA a type of tumor

BLASTULA n pl. -LAS or -LAE an early embryo

BLASTY adj BLASTIER, BLASTIEST gusty

BLAT v BLATTED, BLATTING, BLATS to bleat

BLATANCY n pl. -CIES something blatant

BLATANT adj obvious

BLATE adj timid

BLATHER v -ED, -ING, -S to talk foolishly

BLATTED past tense of blat

BLATTER v -ED, -ING, -S to chatter

BLATTING present participle of blat

BLAUBOK n pl. -S an extinct antelope

BLAW v BLAWED, BLAWN, BLAWING, BLAWS to blow

BLAZE v BLAZED, BLAZING, BLAZES to burn brightly

BLAZER n pl. -S a lightweight jacket

BLAZON v -ED, -ING, -S to proclaim

BLAZONER n pl. -S one that blazons

BLAZONRY n pl. -RIES a great display

BLEACH v -ED, -ING, -ES to whiten

BLEACHER n pl. -S one that bleaches

BLEAK adj BLEAKER, BLEAKEST dreary

BLEAK n pl. -S a freshwater fish

BLEAKISH adj somewhat bleak

BLEAKLY adv in a bleak manner

BLEAR v -ED, -ING, -S to dim

BLEARY adj BLEARIER, BLEARIEST dimmed BLEARILY adv

BLEAT v -ED, -ING, -S to utter the cry of a sheep

BLEATER n pl. -S one that bleats

BLEB n pl. -S a blister BLEBBY adj

BLEED v BLED, BLEEDING, BLEEDS to lose blood

BLEEDER n pl. -S one that bleeds

BLEEDING n pl. -S the act of losing blood

BLELLUM n pl. -S a babbler

BLEMISH v -ED, -ING, -ES to mar

BLENCH v -ED, -ING, -ES to flinch

BLENCHER n pl. -S one that blenches

BLEND v BLENDED or BLENT, BLENDING, BLENDS to mix smoothly and inseparably together

BLENDE n pl. -S a shiny mineral

BLENDER n pl. -S one that blends

BLENNY n pl. -NIES a marine fish

BLENT a past tense of blend

BLESBOK n pl. -S a large antelope

BLESBUCK n pl. -S blesbok

BLESS v BLESSED or BLEST, BLESSING, BLESSES to sanctify

BLESSED adj -EDER, -EDEST holy

BLESSER n pl. -S one that blesses

BLESSING n pl. -S a prayer

BLEST a past tense of bless

BLET n pl. -S a decay of fruit

BLETHER v -ED, -ING, -S to blather

BLEW past tense of blow

BLIGHT v -ED, -ING, -S to cause decay

BLIGHTER n pl. -S one that blights

BLIGHTY n pl. BLIGHTIES a wound causing one to be sent home to England

BLIMEY interj — used as an expression of surprise

BLIMP n pl. -S a nonrigid aircraft BLIMPISH adj

BLIMY interj blimey

BLIN n pl. BLINI or BLINIS a blintze

BLIND adj BLINDER, BLINDEST sightless

BLIND v -ED, -ING, -S to make sightless

BLINDAGE n pl. -S a protective screen

BLINDER n pl. -S an obstruction to sight

BLINDLY adv in a blind manner

BLINI a pl. of blin

BLINIS a pl. of blin

BLINK v -ED, -ING, -S to open and shut the eyes

BLINKARD n pl. -S one who habitually blinks

BLINKER v -ED, -ING, -S to put blinders on

BLINTZ n pl. -ES blintze

BLINTZE n pl. -S a thin pancake

BLIP v BLIPPED, BLIPPING, BLIPS to remove sound from a videotape

BLISS n pl. -ES happiness BLISSFUL adj

BLISTER v -ED, -ING, -S to cause blisters (skin swellings)

BLISTERY adj having blisters

BLITE n pl. -S an annual herb

BLITHE adj BLITHER, BLITHEST merry BLITHELY adv

BLITHER v -ED, -ING, -S to blather

BLITZ v -ED, -ING, -ES to subject to a sudden attack

BLIZZARD n pl. -S a heavy snowstorm

BLOAT v -ED, -ING, -S to swell

BLOATER n pl. -S a smoked herring

BLOB v BLOBBED, BLOBBING, BLOBS to splotch

BLOC n pl. -S a coalition

BLOCK v -ED, -ING, -S to obstruct

BLOCKADE v -ADED, -ADING, -ADES to block

BLOCKAGE n pl. -S the act of blocking

BLOCKER n pl. -S one that blocks

BLOCKISH adj blocky

BLOCKY adj BLOCKIER, BLOCKIEST short and stout

BLOKE n pl. -S a fellow

BLOND adj BLONDER, BLONDEST light-colored

BLOND n pl. -S a blond person

BLONDE n pl. -S blond

BLONDISH adj somewhat blond

BLOOD v -ED, -ING, -S to stain with blood (the fluid circulated by the heart)

BLOODFIN n pl. -S a freshwater fish

BLOODIED past tense of bloody

BLOODIER comparative of bloody

BLOODIES present 3d person sing. of bloody

BLOODIEST superlative of bloody

BLOODILY adv in a bloody manner

BLOODING n pl. -S a fox hunting ceremony

BLOODRED adj of the color of blood

BLOODY adj BLOODIER, BLOODIEST stained with blood

BLOODY v BLOODIED, BLOODYING, BLOODIES to make bloody

BLOOM v -ED, -ING, -S to bear flowers

BLOOMER n pl. -S a blooming plant

BLOOMERY n pl. -ERIES a furnace for smelting iron

BLOOMY adj BLOOMIER, BLOOMIEST covered with flowers

BLOOP v -ED, -ING, -S to hit a short fly ball

BLOOPER n pl. -S a public blunder

BLOSSOM v -ED, -ING, -S to bloom

BLOSSOMY adj having blossoms

BLOT v BLOTTED, BLOTTING, BLOTS to spot or stain

BLOTCH v -ED, -ING, -ES to mark with large spots

BLOTCHY adj BLOTCHIER, BLOTCHIEST blotched

BLOTLESS adj spotless

BLOTTED past tense of blot

BLOTTER n pl. -S a piece of ink-absorbing paper

BLOTTIER comparative of blotty

BLOTTIEST superlative of blotty

BLOTTING present participle of blot

BLOTTO adj drunk

BLOTTY adj -TIER, -TIEST spotty

BLOUSE v BLOUSED, BLOUSING, BLOUSES to hang loosely

BLOUSON n pl. -S a woman's garment

BLOUSY adj BLOUSIER, BLOUSIEST blowsy BLOUSILY adv

BLOW v BLEW, BLOWN, BLOWING, BLOWS to drive or impel by a current of air

BLOWBACK n pl. -S an escape of gases

BLOWBY n pl. -BYS leakage of exhaust fumes

BLOWER n pl. -S one that blows

BLOWFISH n pl. -ES a marine fish

BLOWFLY n pl. -FLIES a type of fly

BLOWGUN n pl. -S a tube through which darts may be blown

BLOWHARD n pl. -S a braggart

BLOWHOLE n pl. -S an air or gas vent

BLOWIER comparative of blowy

BLOWIEST superlative of blowy

BLOWN past participle of blow

BLOWOFF n pl. -S the expelling of gas

BLOWOUT n pl. -S a sudden rupture

BLOWPIPE n pl. -S a blowgun

BLOWSED adj blowsy

BLOWSY adj -SIER, -SIEST slovenly BLOWSILY adv

BLOWTUBE n pl. -S a blowgun

BLOWUP n pl. -S an explosion

BLOWY adj BLOWIER, BLOWIEST windy

BLOWZED adj blowzy

BLOWZY _adj_ -ZIER, -ZIEST blowsy
BLOWZILY _adv_

BLUBBER _v_ -ED, -ING, -S to weep noisily

BLUBBERY _adj_ fat; swollen

BLUCHER _n_ pl. -S a half boot

BLUDGEON _v_ -ED, -ING, -S to hit with a club

BLUE _adj_ BLUER, BLUEST having the color of the clear sky

BLUE _v_ BLUED, BLUEING or BLUING, BLUES to make blue

BLUEBALL _n_ pl. -S a medicinal herb

BLUEBELL _n_ pl. -S a flowering plant

BLUEBILL _n_ pl. -S the scaup duck

BLUEBIRD _n_ pl. -S a songbird

BLUEBOOK _n_ pl. -S an examination booklet

BLUECAP _n_ pl. -S a flowering plant

BLUECOAT _n_ pl. -S a policeman

BLUED past tense of blue

BLUEFIN _n_ pl. -S a large tuna

BLUEFISH _n_ pl. -ES a marine fish

BLUEGILL _n_ pl. -S an edible sunfish

BLUEGUM _n_ pl. -S a timber tree

BLUEHEAD _n_ pl. -S a marine fish

BLUEING _n_ pl. -S bluing

BLUEISH _adj_ bluish

BLUEJACK _n_ pl. -S an oak tree

BLUEJAY _n_ pl. -JAYS a corvine bird

BLUELINE _n_ pl. -S a line that divides a hockey rink

BLUELY _adv_ in a blue manner

BLUENESS _n_ pl. -ES the state of being blue

BLUENOSE _n_ pl. -S a puritanical person

BLUER comparative of blue

BLUESMAN _n_ pl. -MEN one who plays the blues

BLUEST superlative of blue

BLUESTEM _n_ pl. -S a prairie grass

BLUESY _adj_ resembling the blues (a musical form)

BLUET _n_ pl. -S a meadow flower

BLUEWEED _n_ pl. -S a bristly weed

BLUEWOOD _n_ pl. -S a shrub

BLUEY _n_ pl. BLUEYS a bag of clothing carried in travel

BLUFF _v_ -ED, -ING, -S to mislead

BLUFF _adj_ BLUFFER, BLUFFEST having a broad front **BLUFFLY** _adv_

BLUFFER _n_ pl. -S one that bluffs

BLUING _n_ pl. -S a fabric coloring

BLUISH _adj_ somewhat blue

BLUME _v_ BLUMED, BLUMING, BLUMES to blossom

BLUNDER _v_ -ED, -ING, -S to make a mistake

BLUNGE _v_ BLUNGED, BLUNGING, BLUNGES to mix clay with water

BLUNGER _n_ pl. -S one that blunges

BLUNT _adj_ BLUNTER, BLUNTEST not sharp or pointed **BLUNTLY** _adv_

BLUNT _v_ -ED, -ING, -S to make blunt

BLUR _v_ BLURRED, BLURRING, BLURS to make unclear

BLURB _n_ pl. -S a note on a book jacket

BLURRY _adj_ -RIER, -RIEST unclear **BLURRILY** _adv_

BLURT _v_ -ED, -ING, -S to speak abruptly

BLURTER _n_ pl. -S one that blurts

BLUSH _v_ -ED, -ING, -ES to become red

BLUSHER _n_ pl. -S one that blushes

BLUSHFUL _adj_ of a red color

BLUSTER _v_ -ED, -ING, -S to blow violently

BLUSTERY _adj_ windy

BLYPE _n_ pl. -S a shred

BO _n_ pl. BOS a pal

BOA _n_ pl. -S a large snake

BOAR _n_ pl. -S a male pig

BOARD _v_ -ED, -ING, -S to take meals for a fixed price

BOARDER _n_ pl. -S one that boards

BOARDING _n_ pl. -S a surface of wooden boards

BOARDMAN _n_ pl. -MEN a board member

BOARFISH _n_ pl. -ES a marine fish

BOARISH _adj_ swinish; coarse

BOART _n_ pl. -S bort

BOAST _v_ -ED, -ING, -S to brag

BOASTER _n_ pl. -S one that boasts

BOASTFUL _adj_ given to boasting

BOAT _v_ -ED, -ING, -S to travel by boat (watercraft) **BOATABLE** _adj_

BOATBILL _n_ pl. -S a wading bird

BOATEL _n_ pl. -S a waterside hotel

BOATER _n_ pl. -S one that boats

BOATING _n_ pl. -S the sport of traveling by boat

BOATLOAD _n_ pl. -S the amount that a boat holds

BOATMAN *n pl.* -MEN one who works on boats

BOATSMAN *n pl.* -MEN boatman

BOATYARD *n pl.* -S a marina

BOB *v* BOBBED, BOBBING, BOBS to move up and down

BOBBER *n pl.* -S one that bobs

BOBBERY *n pl.* -BERIES a disturbance

BOBBIES pl. of bobby

BOBBIN *n pl.* -S a thread holder

BOBBINET *n pl.* -S a machine-made net

BOBBING present participle of bob

BOBBLE *v* -BLED, -BLING, -BLES to fumble

BOBBY *n pl.* -BIES a policeman

BOBCAT *n pl.* -S a lynx

BOBECHE *n pl.* -S a glass collar on a candle holder

BOBOLINK *n pl.* -S a songbird

BOBSLED *v* -SLEDDED, -SLEDDING, -SLEDS to ride on a bobsled (a racing sled)

BOBSTAY *n pl.* -STAYS a steadying rope

BOBTAIL *v* -ED, -ING, -S to cut short

BOBWHITE *n pl.* -S a game bird

BOCACCIO *n pl.* -CIOS a rockfish

BOCCE *n pl.* -S boccie

BOCCI *n pl.* -S boccie

BOCCIA *n pl.* -S boccie

BOCCIE *n pl.* -S an Italian bowling game

BOCHE *n pl.* -S a German — an offensive term

BOCK *n pl.* -S a dark beer

BOD *n pl.* -S a body

BODE *v* BODED, BODING, BODES to be an omen of

BODEGA *n pl.* -S a grocery store

BODEMENT *n pl.* -S an omen

BODICE *n pl.* -S a corset

BODIED past tense of body

BODIES present 3d person sing. of body

BODILESS *adj* lacking material form

BODILY *adj* of the body

BODING *n pl.* -S an omen

BODINGLY *adv* ominously

BODKIN *n pl.* -S a sharp instrument

BODY *v* BODIED, BODYING, BODIES to give form to

BODYSURF *v* -ED, -ING, -S to ride a wave without a surfboard

BODYWORK *n pl.* -S a vehicle body

BOEHMITE *n pl.* -S a mineral

BOFF *n pl.* -S a hearty laugh

BOFFIN *n pl.* -S a scientific expert

BOFFO *n pl.* -FOS a boff

BOFFOLA *n pl.* -S a boff

BOG *v* BOGGED, BOGGING, BOGS to impede

BOGAN *n pl.* -S a backwater or tributary

BOGBEAN *n pl.* -S a marsh plant

BOGEY *v* -GEYED, -GEYING, -GEYS to shoot in one stroke over par in golf

BOGEYMAN *n pl.* -MEN a terrifying creature

BOGGED past tense of bog

BOGGIER comparative of boggy

BOGGIEST superlative of boggy

BOGGING present participle of bog

BOGGISH *adj* boggy

BOGGLE *v* -GLED, -GLING, -GLES to hesitate

BOGGLER *n pl.* -S one that causes another to boggle

BOGGY *adj* -GIER, -GIEST marshy

BOGIE *n pl.* -S bogy

BOGIES pl. of bogy

BOGLE *n pl.* -S a bogy

BOGUS *adj* not genuine; fake

BOGWOOD *n pl.* -S preserved tree wood

BOGY *n pl.* -GIES a goblin

BOGYISM *n pl.* -S behavior characteristic of a bogy

BOGYMAN *n pl.* -MEN bogeyman

BOHEA *n pl.* -S a black tea

BOHEMIA *n pl.* -S a community of bohemians

BOHEMIAN *n pl.* -S an unconventional person

BOHUNK *n pl.* -S an unskilled laborer

BOIL *v* -ED, -ING, -S to vaporize liquid BOILABLE *adj*

BOILER *n pl.* -S a vessel for boiling

BOITE *n pl.* -S a nightclub

BOLA *n pl.* -S a throwing weapon

BOLAR *adj* pertaining to bole

BOLAS *n pl.* -ES bola

BOLD *adj* BOLDER, BOLDEST daring BOLDLY *adv*

BOLDFACE *v* -FACED, -FACING, -FACES to print in thick type

BOLDNESS n pl. -ES the quality of being bold

BOLE n pl. -S a fine clay

BOLERO n pl. -ROS a Spanish dance

BOLETE n pl. -S boletus

BOLETUS n pl. -TUSES or -TI a fungus

BOLIDE n pl. -S an exploding meteor

BOLIVAR n pl. -S or -ES a unit of Venezuelan currency

BOLIVIA n pl. -S a soft fabric

BOLL v -ED, -ING, -S to form pods

BOLLARD n pl. -S a thick post on a ship or wharf

BOLLIX v -ED, -ING, -ES to bungle

BOLLOX v -ED, -ING, -ES to bollix

BOLLWORM n pl. -S the larva of a certain moth

BOLO n pl. -LOS a machete

BOLOGNA n pl. -S a seasoned sausage

BOLONEY n pl. -NEYS bologna

BOLSON n pl. -S a flat arid valley

BOLSTER v -ED, -ING, -S to support

BOLT v -ED, -ING, -S to sift

BOLTER n pl. -S a sifting machine

BOLTHEAD n pl. -S a matrass

BOLTONIA n pl. -S a perennial herb

BOLTROPE n pl. -S a rope sewn to a sail

BOLUS n pl. -ES a large pill

BOMB v -ED, -ING, -S to attack with bombs (explosive projectiles)

BOMBARD v -ED, -ING, -S to bomb

BOMBAST n pl. -S pompous language

BOMBE n pl. -S a frozen dessert

BOMBER n pl. -S one that bombs

BOMBLOAD n pl. -S the quantity of bombs being carried

BOMBYCID n pl. -S a moth

BOMBYX n pl. -ES a silkworm

BONACI n pl. -S an edible fish

BONANZA n pl. -S a rich mine

BONBON n pl. -S a sugared candy

BOND v -ED, -ING, -S to join together
BONDABLE adj

BONDAGE n pl. -S slavery

BONDER n pl. -S one that bonds

BONDMAID n pl. -S a female slave

BONDMAN n pl. -MEN a male slave

BONDSMAN n pl. -MEN bondman

BONDUC n pl. -S a prickly seed

BONE v BONED, BONING, BONES to debone

BONEFISH n pl. -ES a slender marine fish

BONEHEAD n pl. -S a stupid person

BONELESS adj having no bones (hard connective tissue)

BONER n pl. -S a blunder

BONESET n pl. -S a perennial herb

BONEY adj BONIER, BONIEST bony

BONEYARD n pl. -S a junkyard

BONFIRE n pl. -S an open fire

BONG v -ED, -ING, -S to make a deep, ringing sound

BONGO n pl. -GOS or -GOES a small drum

BONGOIST n pl. -S a bongo player

BONHOMIE n pl. -S friendliness

BONIER comparative of bony or boney

BONIEST superlative of bony or boney

BONIFACE n pl. -S an innkeeper

BONINESS n pl. -ES the state of being bony

BONING present participle of bone

BONITA n pl. -S bonito

BONITO n pl. -TOS or -TOES a marine food fish

BONKERS adj crazy

BONNE n pl. -S a housemaid

BONNET v -ED, -ING, -S to provide with a bonnet (a type of hat)

BONNIE adj bonny

BONNOCK n pl. -S a bannock

BONNY adj -NIER, -NIEST pretty
BONNILY adv

BONSAI n pl. BONSAI a potted shrub that has been dwarfed

BONSPELL n pl. -S bonspiel

BONSPIEL n pl. -S a curling match or tournament

BONTEBOK n pl. -S an antelope

BONUS n pl. -ES an additional payment

BONY adj BONIER, BONIEST full of bones

BONZE n pl. -S a Buddhist monk

BONZER adj very good

BOO v -ED, -ING, -S to cry "boo"

BOOB n pl. -S a dolt

BOOBOO n pl. -BOOS a mistake

BOOBY n pl. -BIES a dolt

BOODLE v -DLED, -DLING, -DLES to take bribes

BOODLER n pl. -S one that boodles

BOOGER n pl. -S a bogeyman

BOOGIE *n* pl. -S a jazz form

BOOGYMAN *n* pl. -MEN bogeyman

BOOHOO *v* -ED, -ING, -S to weep noisily

BOOK *v* -ED, -ING, -S to engage services

BOOKCASE *n* pl. -S a case which holds books (literary volumes)

BOOKEND *n* pl. -S a support for a row of books

BOOKER *n* pl. -S one that books

BOOKIE *n* pl. -S a bet taker

BOOKING *n* pl. -S an engagement

BOOKISH *adj* pertaining to books

BOOKLET *n* pl. -S a small book

BOOKLORE *n* pl. -S book learning

BOOKMAN *n* pl. -MEN a scholar

BOOKMARK *n* pl. -S a marker for finding a place in a book

BOOKRACK *n* pl. -S a support for an open book

BOOKREST *n* pl. -S a bookrack

BOOKSHOP *n* pl. -S a store where books are sold

BOOKWORM *n* pl. -S an avid book reader

BOOM *v* -ED, -ING, -S to make a deep, resonant sound

BOOMER *n* pl. -S one that booms

BOOMIER comparative of boomy

BOOMIEST superlative of boomy

BOOMKIN *n* pl. -S a bumkin

BOOMLET *n* pl. -S a small increase in prosperity

BOOMTOWN *n* pl. -S a prospering town

BOOMY *adj* BOOMIER, BOOMIEST prospering

BOON *n* pl. -S a timely benefit

BOONIES *n/pl* a backwoods area

BOOR *n* pl. -S a rude person

BOORISH *adj* rude

BOOST *v* -ED, -ING, -S to support

BOOSTER *n* pl. -S one that boosts

BOOT *v* -ED, -ING, -S to provide with boots (protective coverings for the feet)

BOOTEE *n* pl. -S a baby's boot

BOOTERY *n* pl. -ERIES a shoe store

BOOTH *n* pl. -S a small enclosure

BOOTIE *n* pl. -S bootee

BOOTIES pl. of booty

BOOTJACK *n* pl. -S a device for pulling off boots

BOOTLACE *n* pl. -S a shoelace

BOOTLEG *v* -LEGGED, -LEGGING, -LEGS to smuggle

BOOTLESS *adj* useless

BOOTLICK *v* -ED, -ING, -S to flatter servilely

BOOTY *n* pl. -TIES a rich gain or prize

BOOZE *v* BOOZED, BOOZING, BOOZES to drink liquor excessively

BOOZER *n* pl. -S one that boozes

BOOZY *adj* BOOZIER, BOOZIEST drunken **BOOZILY** *adv*

BOP *v* BOPPED, BOPPING, BOPS to hit or strike

BOPPER *n* pl. -S a bebopper

BORA *n* pl. -S a cold wind

BORACES a pl. of borax

BORACIC *adj* boric

BORACITE *n* pl. -S a mineral

BORAGE *n* pl. -S a medicinal herb

BORANE *n* pl. -S a chemical compound

BORATE *n* pl. -S a salt of boric acid **BORATED** *adj*

BORAX *n* pl. -RAXES or -RACES a white crystalline compound

BORAZON *n* pl. -S a hard boron compound

BORDEL *n* pl. -S a brothel

BORDELLO *n* pl. -LOS a brothel

BORDER *v* -ED, -ING, -S to put a border (an edge) on

BORDERER *n* pl. -S one that borders

BORDURE *n* pl. -S a border around a shield

BORE *v* BORED, BORING, BORES to pierce with a rotary tool

BOREAL *adj* pertaining to the north

BORECOLE *n* pl. -S kale

BORED past tense of bore

BOREDOM *n* pl. -S tedium

BORER *n* pl. -S one that bores

BORIC *adj* pertaining to boron

BORIDE *n* pl. -S a boron compound

BORING *n* pl. -S an inner cavity

BORINGLY *adv* tediously

BORN *adj* having particular qualities from birth

BORNE a past participle of bear

BORNEOL *n* pl. -S an alcohol

BORNITE *n* pl. -S an ore of copper

BORON *n* pl. -S a nonmetallic element **BORONIC** *adj*

BOROUGH *n* pl. -S an incorporated town

BORROW *v* -ED, -ING, -S to take on loan

BORROWER *n* pl. -S one that borrows

BORSCH *n* pl. -ES borscht

BORSCHT *n* pl. -S a beet soup

BORSHT *n* pl. -S borscht

BORSTAL *n* pl. -S a reformatory

BORT *n* pl. -S a low-quality diamond **BORTY** *adj*

BORTZ *n* pl. -ES bort

BORZOI *n* pl. -S a Russian hound

BOSCAGE *n* pl. -S a thicket

BOSCHBOK *n* pl. -S bushbuck

BOSH *n* pl. -ES nonsense

BOSHBOK *n* pl. -S bushbuck

BOSHVARK *n* pl. -S a wild hog

BOSK *n* pl. -S a small wooded area

BOSKAGE *n* pl. -S boscage

BOSKER *adj* fine; very good

BOSKET *n* pl. -S a thicket

BOSKY *adj* BOSKIER, BOSKIEST wooded; bushy

BOSOM *v* -ED, -ING, -S to embrace

BOSOMY *adj* swelling outward

BOSON *n* pl. -S an atomic particle

BOSQUE *n* pl. -S bosk

BOSQUET *n* pl. -S bosket

BOSS *v* -ED, -ING, -ES to supervise

BOSSDOM *n* pl. -S the domain of a political boss

BOSSIER comparative of bossy

BOSSIES pl. of bossy

BOSSISM *n* pl. -S control by political bosses

BOSSY *adj* BOSSIER, BOSSIEST domineering **BOSSILY** *adv*

BOSSY *n* pl. BOSSIES a cow

BOSTON *n* pl. -S a card game

BOSUN *n* pl. -S a boatswain

BOT *n* pl. -S the larva of a botfly

BOTANIC *adj* pertaining to botany

BOTANIES pl. of botany

BOTANISE *v* -NISED, -NISING, -NISES to botanize

BOTANIST *n* pl. -S one skilled in botany

BOTANIZE *v* -NIZED, -NIZING, -NIZES to study plants

BOTANY *n* pl. -NIES the science of plants

BOTCH *v* -ED, -ING, -ES to bungle

BOTCHER *n* pl. -S one that botches

BOTCHERY *n* pl. -ERIES something botched

BOTCHY *adj* BOTCHIER, BOTCHIEST badly done **BOTCHILY** *adv*

BOTEL *n* pl. -S boatel

BOTFLY *n* pl. -FLIES a type of fly

BOTH *adj* being the two

BOTHER *v* -ED, -ING, -S to annoy

BOTONEE *adj* having arms ending in a trefoil — used of a heraldic cross

BOTONNEE *adj* botonee

BOTRYOID *adj* resembling a cluster of grapes

BOTRYOSE *adj* botryoid

BOTT *n* pl. -S bot

BOTTLE *v* -TLED, -TLING, -TLES to put into a bottle (a rigid container)

BOTTLER *n* pl. -S one that bottles

BOTTOM *v* -ED, -ING, -S to comprehend

BOTTOMER *n* pl. -S one that bottoms

BOTTOMRY *n* pl. -RIES a maritime contract

BOTULIN *n* pl. -S a nerve poison

BOTULISM *n* pl. -S botulin poisoning

BOUCLE *n* pl. -S a knitted fabric

BOUDOIR *n* pl. -S a woman's bedroom

BOUFFANT *n* pl. -S a woman's hairdo

BOUFFE *n* pl. -S a comic opera

BOUGH *n* pl. -S a tree branch **BOUGHED** *adj*

BOUGHPOT *n* pl. -S a large vase

BOUGHT past tense of buy

BOUGHTEN *adj* purchased

BOUGIE *n* pl. -S a wax candle

BOUILLON *n* pl. -S a clear soup

BOULDER *n* pl. -S a large rock **BOULDERY** *adj*

BOULE *n* pl. -S buhl

BOULLE *n* pl. -S buhl

BOUNCE *v* BOUNCED, BOUNCING, BOUNCES to spring back

BOUNCER *n* pl. -S one that bounces

BOUNCY *adj* BOUNCIER, BOUNCIEST tending to bounce **BOUNCILY** *adv*

BOUND *v* -ED, -ING, -S to leap

BOUNDARY *n* pl. -ARIES a dividing line

BOUNDEN *adj* obliged

BOUNDER *n* pl. -S one that bounds

BOUNTY *n* pl. -TIES a reward
BOUNTIED *adj*

BOUQUET *n* pl. -S a bunch of flowers

BOURBON *n* pl. -S a whiskey

BOURDON *n* pl. -S a part of a bagpipe

BOURG *n* pl. -S a medieval town

BOURGEON *v* -ED, -ING, -S to burgeon

BOURN *n* pl. -S a stream

BOURNE *n* pl. -S bourn

BOURREE *n* pl. -S an old French dance

BOURSE *n* pl. -S a stock exchange

BOURTREE *n* pl. -S a European tree

BOUSE *v* BOUSED, BOUSING, BOUSES to haul by means of a tackle

BOUSOUKI *n* pl. -KIA or -KIS bouzouki

BOUSY *adj* boozy

BOUT *n* pl. -S a contest

BOUTIQUE *n* pl. -S a small shop

BOUZOUKI *n* pl. -KIA or KIS a stringed musical instrument

BOVID *n* pl. -S a bovine

BOVINE *n* pl. -S an ox-like animal

BOVINELY *adv* stolidly

BOVINITY *n* pl. -TIES the state of being a bovine

BOW *v* -ED, -ING, -S to bend forward

BOWEL *v* -ELED, -ELING, -ELS or -ELLED, -ELLING, -ELS to disbowel

BOWER *v* -ED, -ING, -S to embower

BOWERY *n* -ERIES a colonial Dutch farm

BOWFIN *n* pl. -S a freshwater fish

BOWFRONT *adj* having a curved front

BOWHEAD *n* pl. -S an arctic whale

BOWING *n* pl. -S the technique of managing the bow of a stringed instrument

BOWINGLY *adv* in a bowing manner

BOWKNOT *n* pl. -S a type of knot

BOWL *v* -ED, -ING, -S to play at bowling

BOWLDER *n* pl. -S boulder

BOWLEG *n* pl. -S an outwardly curved leg

BOWLER *n* pl. -S one that bowls

BOWLESS *adj* being without an archery bow

BOWLFUL *n* pl. -S as much as a bowl can hold

BOWLIKE *adj* curved

BOWLINE *n* pl. -S a type of knot

BOWLING *n* pl. -S a game in which balls are rolled at objects

BOWLLIKE *adj* concave

BOWMAN *n* pl. -MEN an archer

BOWPOT *n* pl. -S boughpot

BOWSE *v* BOWSED, BOWSING, BOWSES to bouse

BOWSHOT *n* pl. -S the distance an arrow is shot

BOWSPRIT *n* pl. -S a ship's spar

BOWWOW *n* pl. -S the bark of a dog

BOWYER *n* pl. -S a maker of archery bows

BOX *v* -ED, -ING, -ES to put in a box (a rectangular container)

BOXBERRY *n* pl. -RIES an evergreen plant

BOXCAR *n* pl. -S a roofed freight car

BOXER *n* pl. -S one that packs boxes

BOXFISH *n* pl. -ES a marine fish

BOXFUL *n* pl. -S as much as a box can hold

BOXHAUL *v* -ED, -ING, -S to veer a ship around

BOXIER comparative of boxy

BOXIEST superlative of boxy

BOXINESS *n* pl. -ES the state of being boxy

BOXING *n* pl. -S a casing

BOXLIKE *adj* resembling a box

BOXTHORN *n* pl. -S a thorny shrub

BOXWOOD *n* pl. -S an evergreen shrub

BOXY *adj* BOXIER, BOXIEST resembling a box

BOY *n* pl. BOYS a male child

BOYAR *n* pl. -S a former Russian aristocrat

BOYARD *n* pl. -S boyar

BOYARISM *n* pl. -S the rule of boyars

BOYCOTT *v* -ED, -ING, -S to refuse to buy

BOYHOOD *n* pl. -S the state of being a boy

BOYISH *adj* resembling a boy
BOYISHLY *adv*

BOYLA *n* pl. -S a witch doctor

BOYO *n* pl. BOYOS a boy

BOZO *n* pl. -ZOS a fellow

BRA *n* pl. -S a brassiere

BRABBLE *v* -BLED, -BLING, -BLES to quarrel noisily

BRABBLER *n* pl. -S one that brabbles

BRACE *v* BRACED, BRACING, BRACES to support

BRACELET   *n* pl. -S a wrist ornament

BRACER   *n* pl. -S one that braces

BRACERO   *n* pl. -ROS a Mexican laborer

BRACH   *n* pl. -ES a hound bitch

BRACHET   *n* pl. -S a brach

BRACHIAL   *n* pl. -S a part of the arm

BRACHIUM   *n* pl. -IA the upper part of arm

BRACING   *n* pl. -S a brace or reinforcement

BRACKEN   *n* pl. -S a large fern

BRACKET   *v* -ED, -ING, -S to classify

BRACKISH   *adj* salty

BRACT   *n* pl. -S a leaflike plant part **BRACTEAL, BRACTED** *adj*

BRACTLET   *n* pl. -S a small bract

BRAD   *v* BRADDED, BRADDING, BRADS to fasten with thin nails

BRADAWL   *n* pl. -S a type of awl

BRADOON   *n* pl. -S bridoon

BRAE   *n* pl. -S a hillside

BRAG   *adj* BRAGGER, BRAGGEST first-rate

BRAG   *v* BRAGGED, BRAGGING, BRAGS to speak vainly of one's deeds

BRAGGART   *n* pl. -S one who brags

BRAGGER   *n* pl. -S a braggart

BRAGGEST   superlative of brag

BRAGGING   present participle of brag

BRAGGY   *adj* -GIER, -GIEST tending to brag

BRAHMA   *n* pl. -S a large domestic fowl

BRAID   *v* -ED, -ING, -S to weave together

BRAIDER   *n* pl. -S one that braids

BRAIDING   *n* pl. -S something made of braided material

BRAIL   *v* -ED, -ING, -S to haul in a sail

BRAILLE   *v* BRAILLED, BRAILLING, BRAILLES to write in braille (raised writing for the blind)

BRAIN   *v* -ED, -ING, -S to hit on the head

BRAINIER   comparative of brainy

BRAINIEST   superlative of brainy

BRAINILY   *adv* in a brainy manner

BRAINISH   *adj* impetuous

BRAINPAN   *n* pl. -S the skull

BRAINY   *adj* BRAINIER, BRAINIEST smart

BRAISE   *v* BRAISED, BRAISING, BRAISES to cook in fat

BRAIZE   *n* pl. -S a marine fish

BRAKE   *v* BRAKED, BRAKING, BRAKES to slow down or stop

BRAKEAGE   *n* pl. -S the act of braking

BRAKEMAN   *n* pl. -MEN a trainman

BRAKING   present participle of brake

BRAKY   *adj* BRAKIER, BRAKIEST abounding in shrubs or ferns

BRAMBLE   *v* -BLED, -BLING, -BLES to gather berries

BRAMBLY   *adj* -BLIER, -BLIEST prickly

BRAN   *v* BRANNED, BRANNING, BRANS to soak in water mixed with bran (the outer coat of cereals)

BRANCH   *v* -ED, -ING, -ES to form branches (offshoots)

BRANCHIA   *n* pl. -CHIAE a respiratory organ of aquatic animals

BRANCHY   *adj* BRANCHIER, BRANCHIEST having many branches

BRAND   *v* -ED, -ING, -S to mark with a hot iron

BRANDER   *n* pl. -S one that brands

BRANDISH   *v* -ED, -ING, -ES to wave menacingly

BRANDY   *v* -DIED, -DYING, -DIES to mix with brandy (a liquor)

BRANK   *n* pl. -S a device used to restrain the tongue

BRANNED   past tense of bran

BRANNER   *n* pl. -S one that brans

BRANNING   present participle of bran

BRANNY   *adj* -NIER, -NIEST containing bran

BRANT   *n* pl. -S a wild goose

BRANTAIL   *n* pl. -S a singing bird

BRASH   *adj* BRASHER, BRASHEST rash; hasty **BRASHLY** *adv*

BRASH   *n* pl. -ES a mass of fragments

BRASHY   *adj* BRASHIER, BRASHIEST brash

BRASIER   *n* pl. -S brazier

BRASIL   *n* pl. -S brazil

BRASILIN   *n* pl. -S brazilin

BRASS   *n* pl. -ES an alloy of copper and zinc

BRASSAGE   *n* pl. -S a fee for coining money

BRASSARD   *n* pl. -S an insignia

BRASSART   *n* pl. -S brassard

BRASSICA   *n* pl. -S a tall herb

BRASSIE   *n* pl. -S a golf club

BRASSISH   *adj* resembling brass

BRASSY adj BRASSIER, BRASSIEST resembling brass **BRASSILY** adv

BRAT n pl. -S a spoiled child **BRATTISH** adj

BRATTICE v -TICED, -TICING, -TICES to partition

BRATTLE v -TLED, -TLING, -TLES to clatter

BRATTY adj -TIER, -TIEST resembling a brat

BRAUNITE n pl. -S a mineral

BRAVA n pl. -S a shout of approval

BRAVADO n pl. -DOS or -DOES false bravery

BRAVE adj BRAVER, BRAVEST showing courage **BRAVELY** adv

BRAVE v BRAVED, BRAVING, BRAVES to face with courage

BRAVER n pl. -S one that braves

BRAVERY n pl. -ERIES courage

BRAVEST superlative of brave

BRAVING present participle of brave

BRAVO n pl. -VOS or -VOES a hired killer

BRAVO v -ED, -ING, -ES to applaud by shouting "bravo"

BRAVURA n pl. -RAS or -RE fine musical technique

BRAW adj BRAWER, BRAWEST splendid

BRAWL v -ED, -ING, -S to fight

BRAWLER n pl. -S a fighter

BRAWLIE adv splendidly

BRAWLY adj BRAWLIER, BRAWLIEST inclined to brawl

BRAWN n pl. -S muscular strength

BRAWNY adj BRAWNIER, BRAWNIEST muscular **BRAWNILY** adv

BRAWS n/pl fine clothes

BRAXY n pl. BRAXIES a fever of sheep

BRAY v BRAYED, BRAYING, BRAYS to utter a harsh cry

BRAYER n pl. -S a roller used to spread ink

BRAZA n pl. -S a Spanish unit of length

BRAZE v BRAZED, BRAZING, BRAZES to solder together

BRAZEN v -ED, -ING, -S to face boldly

BRAZENLY adv boldly

BRAZER n pl. -S one that brazes

BRAZIER n pl. -S one who works in brass

BRAZIL n pl. -S a dyewood

BRAZILIN n pl. -S a chemical compound

BRAZING present participle of braze

BREACH v -ED, -ING, -ES to break through

BREACHER n pl. -S one that breaches

BREAD v -ED, -ING, -S to cover with bread crumbs

BREADNUT n pl. -S a tropical fruit

BREADTH n pl. -S width

BREAK v BROKE, BROKEN, BREAKING, BREAKS to reduce to fragments

BREAKAGE n pl. -S the act of breaking

BREAKER n pl. -S one that breaks

BREAKING n pl. -S the change of a pure vowel to a diphthong

BREAKOUT n pl. -S an escape

BREAKUP n pl. -S the act of breaking up

BREAM v -ED, -ING, -S to clean a ship's bottom

BREAST v -ED, -ING, -S to confront boldly

BREATH n pl. -S air inhaled and exhaled

BREATHE v BREATHED, BREATHING, BREATHES to inhale and exhale air

BREATHER n pl. -S one that breathes

BREATHY adj BREATHIER, BREATHIEST marked by loud breathing

BRECCIA n pl. -S a type of rock **BRECCIAL** adj

BRECHAM n pl. -S a collar for a horse

BRECHAN n pl. -S brecham

BRED past tense of breed

BREDE n pl. -S a braid

BREE n pl. -S broth

BREECH v -ED, -ING, -ES to clothe with breeches (trousers)

BREED v BRED, BREEDING, BREEDS to cause to give birth

BREEDER n pl. -S one that breeds

BREEDING n pl. -S upbringing

BREEKS n/pl breeches

BREEZE v BREEZED, BREEZING, BREEZES to move swiftly

BREEZY adj BREEZIER, BREEZIEST windy **BREEZILY** adv

BREGMA n pl. -MATA a junction point of the skull **BREGMATE** adj

BRENT n pl. -S brant

BRETHREN a pl. of brother

BREVE n pl. -S a symbol used to indicate a short vowel

BREVET v -VETED, -VETING, -VETS or -VETTED, -VETTING, -VETS to confer an honorary rank upon

BREVETCY n pl. -CIES an honorary rank

BREVIARY n pl. -RIES a prayer book

BREVIER n pl. -S a size of type

BREVITY n pl. -TIES shortness of duration

BREW v -ED, -ING, -S to make beer or the like

BREWAGE n pl. -S a brewed beverage

BREWER n pl. -S one that brews

BREWERY n pl. -ERIES a place for brewing

BREWING n pl. -S a quantity brewed at one time

BREWIS n pl. BREWISES broth

BRIAR n pl. -S brier BRIARY adj

BRIARD n pl. -S a large dog

BRIBE v BRIBED, BRIBING, BRIBES to practice bribery BRIBABLE adj

BRIBER n pl. -S one that bribes

BRIBERY n pl. -ERIES an act of influencing corruptly

BRIBING present participle of bribe

BRICK v -ED, -ING, -S to build with bricks (blocks of clay)

BRICKBAT n pl. -S a piece of brick

BRICKLE adj brittle

BRICKY adj BRICKIER, BRICKIEST made of bricks

BRICOLE n pl. -S a cushion shot in billiards

BRIDAL n pl. -S a wedding

BRIDALLY adv in a manner befitting a bride

BRIDE n pl. -S a woman just married or about to be married

BRIDGE v BRIDGED, BRIDGING, BRIDGES to connect

BRIDGING n pl. -S a bracing

BRIDLE v -DLED, -DLING, -DLES to control with a restraint

BRIDLER n pl. -S one that bridles

BRIDOON n pl. -S a device used to control a horse

BRIE n pl. -S bree

BRIEF adj BRIEFER, BRIEFEST short

BRIEF v -ED, ING, -S to summarize

BRIEFER n pl. -S one that briefs

BRIEFING n pl. -S a short lecture

BRIEFLY adv in a brief manner

BRIER n pl. -S a thorny shrub BRIERY adj

BRIG n pl. -S a two-masted ship

BRIGADE v -GADED, -GADING, -GADES to group together

BRIGAND n pl. -S a bandit

BRIGHT adj BRIGHTER, BRIGHTEST emitting much light BRIGHTLY adv

BRIGHT n pl. -S a light-hued tobacco

BRIGHTEN v -ED, -ING, -S to make bright

BRILL n pl. -S an edible flatfish

BRIM v BRIMMED, BRIMMING, BRIMS to fill to the top

BRIMFUL adj ready to overflow

BRIMFULL adj brimful

BRIMLESS adj having no brim (an upper edge)

BRIMMED past tense of brim

BRIMMER n pl. -S a brimming cup or glass

BRIMMING present participle of brim

BRIN n pl. -S a rib of a fan

BRINDED adj brindled

BRINDLE n pl. -S a brindled color

BRINDLED adj streaked

BRINE v BRINED, BRINING, BRINES to treat with brine (salted water)

BRINER n pl. -S one that brines

BRING v BROUGHT, BRINGING, BRINGS to take with oneself to a place

BRINGER n pl. -S one that brings

BRINIER comparative of briny

BRINIES pl. of briny

BRINIEST superlative of briny

BRINISH adj resembling brine

BRINK n pl. -S an extreme edge

BRINY n pl. BRINIES the sea

BRINY adj BRINIER, BRINIEST salty

BRIO n pl. BRIOS liveliness

BRIOCHE n pl. -S a rich roll

BRIONY n pl. -NIES bryony

BRIQUET v -QUETTED, -QUETTING, -QUETS to mold into small bricks

BRISANCE n pl. -S the shattering effect of an explosive BRISANT adj

BRISK adj BRISKER, BRISKEST lively

BRISK v -ED, -ING, -S to make brisk

BRISKET n pl. -S the breast of an animal

BRISKLY adv in a brisk manner

BRISLING   *n* pl. -S a small herring

BRISTLE   *v* -TLED, -TLING, -TLES to rise stiffly

BRISTLY   *adj* -TLIER, -TLIEST stiffly erect

BRISTOL   *n* pl. -S a smooth cardboard

BRIT   *n* pl. -S a young herring

BRITCHES   *n/pl* breeches; trousers

BRITSKA   *n* pl. -S an open carriage

BRITT   *n* pl. -S brit

BRITTLE   *adj* -TLER, -TLEST likely to break

BRITTLE   *v* -TLED, -TLING, -TLES to become brittle

BRITZKA   *n* pl. -S britska

BRITZSKA   *n* pl. -S britska

BROACH   *v* -ED, -ING, -ES to pierce so as to withdraw a liquid

BROACHER   *n* pl. -S one that broaches

BROAD   *adj* BROADER, BROADEST wide

BROAD   *n* pl. -S an expansion of a river

BROADAX   *n* pl. -ES a broad-edged ax

BROADAXE   *n* pl. -S broadax

BROADEN   *v* -ED, -ING, -S to make broad

BROADISH   *adj* somewhat broad

BROADLY   *adv* in a broad manner

BROCADE   *v* -CADED, -CADING, -CADES to weave with a raised design

BROCATEL   *n* pl. -S a heavy fabric

BROCCOLI   *n* pl. -S a vegetable related to the cabbage

BROCHE   *adj* brocaded

BROCHURE   *n* pl. -S a pamphlet

BROCK   *n* pl. -S a badger

BROCKAGE   *n* pl. -S an imperfectly minted coin

BROCKET   *n* pl. -S a small, red deer

BROCOLI   *n* pl. -S broccoli

BROGAN   *n* pl. -S a heavy shoe

BROGUE   *n* pl. -S an Irish accent

BROGUERY   *n* pl. -ERIES the use of an Irish accent

BROGUISH   *adj* resembling a brogue

BROIDER   *v* -ED, -ING, -S to adorn with needlework

BROIDERY   *n* pl. -DERIES the act of broidering

BROIL   *v* -ED, -ING, -S to cook by direct heat

BROILER   *n* pl. -S a device for broiling

BROKAGE   *n* pl. -S the business of a broker

BROKE   past tense of break

BROKEN   *adj* shattered BROKENLY *adv*

BROKER   *n* pl. -S an agent who buys and sells stocks

BROLLY   *n* pl. -LIES an umbrella

BROMAL   *n* pl. -S a medicinal liquid

BROMATE   *v* -MATED, -MATING, -MATES to combine with bromine

BROME   *n* pl. -S a tall grass

BROMELIN   *n* pl. -S an enzyme

BROMIC   *adj* containing bromine

BROMID   *n* pl. -S bromide

BROMIDE   *n* pl. -S a bromine compound

BROMIDIC   *adj* commonplace; trite

BROMIN   *n* pl. -S bromine

BROMINE   *n* pl. -S a volatile liquid element

BROMISM   *n* pl. -S a diseased condition of the skin

BROMO   *n* pl. -MOS a medicinal compound

BRONC   *n* pl. -S bronco

BRONCHI   pl. of bronchus

BRONCHIA   *n/pl* the main air passages of the lungs

BRONCHO   *n* pl. -CHOS bronco

BRONCHUS   *n* pl. -CHI a tracheal branch

BRONCO   *n* pl. -COS a wild horse

BRONZE   *v* BRONZED, BRONZING, BRONZES to make brown or tan

BRONZER   *n* pl. -S one that bronzes

BRONZING   *n* pl. -S a brownish coloring

BRONZY   *adj* BRONZIER, BRONZIEST of a brownish color

BROO   *n* pl. BROOS a bree

BROOCH   *n* pl. -ES a decorative pin

BROOD   *v* -ED, -ING, -S to ponder gloomily

BROODER   *n* pl. -S one that broods

BROODY   *adj* BROODIER, BROODIEST tending to brood

BROOK   *v* -ED, -ING, -S to tolerate

BROOKITE   *n* pl. -S a mineral

BROOKLET   *n* pl. -S a small brook or creek

BROOM   *v* -ED, -ING, -S to sweep

BROOMY   *adj* BROOMIER, BROOMIEST abounding in broom (a type of shrub)

BROSE   *n* pl. -S a porridge

BROSY   *adj* smeared with brose

BROTH   *n* pl. -S a thin clear soup

BROTHEL   *n* pl. -S a house of prostitution

BROTHER   *n* pl. -S or BRETHREN a male sibling

BROTHER   *v* -ED, -ING, -S to treat like a brother

BROTHY   *adj* resembling broth

BROUGHAM   *n* pl. -S a type of carriage

BROUGHT   past tense of bring

BROUHAHA   *n* pl. -S an uproar

BROW   *n* pl. -S the forehead

BROWBEAT   *v* -BEAT, -BEATEN, -BEATING, -BEATS to intimidate

BROWLESS   *adj* lacking eyebrows

BROWN   *adj* BROWNER, BROWNEST of a dark color

BROWN   *v* -ED, -ING, -S to make brown

BROWNIE   *n* pl. -S a small sprite

BROWNIER   comparative of browny

BROWNIEST superlative of browny

BROWNISH   *adj* somewhat brown

BROWNOUT   *n* pl. -S a power reduction

BROWNY   *adj* BROWNIER, BROWNIEST somewhat brown

BROWSE   *v* BROWSED, BROWSING, BROWSES to look at casually

BROWSER   *n* pl. -S one that browses

BRUCELLA   *n* pl. -LAE or -LAS any of a genus of harmful bacteria

BRUCIN   *n* pl. -S brucine

BRUCINE   *n* pl. -S a poisonous alkaloid

BRUGH   *n* pl. -S a borough

BRUIN   *n* pl. -S a bear

BRUISE   *v* BRUISED, BRUISING, BRUISES to injure without breaking the surface of the skin

BRUISER   *n* pl. -S a big, husky man

BRUIT   *v* -ED, -ING, -S to spread news of

BRUITER   *n* pl. -S one that bruits

BRULOT   *n* pl. -S a biting fly

BRULYIE   *n* pl. -S a noisy quarrel

BRULZIE   *n* pl. -S a brulyie

BRUMAL   *adj* wintry

BRUMBY   *n* pl. -BIES a wild horse

BRUME   *n* pl. -S fog BRUMOUS *adj*

BRUNCH   *v* -ED, -ING, -ES to eat a late morning meal

BRUNET   *n* pl. -S a dark-haired male

BRUNETTE   *n* pl. -S a dark-haired female

BRUNIZEM   *n* pl. -S a prairie soil

BRUNT   *n* pl. -S the main impact

BRUSH   *v* -ED, -ING, -ES to touch lightly

BRUSHER   *n* pl. -S one that brushes

BRUSHIER   comparative of brushy

BRUSHIEST   superlative of brushy

BRUSHOFF   *n* pl. -S an abrupt dismissal

BRUSHUP   *n* pl. -S a quick review

BRUSHY   *adj* BRUSHIER, BRUSHIEST shaggy; rough

BRUSK   *adj* BRUSKER, BRUSKEST brusque

BRUSQUE   *adj* BRUSQUER, BRUSQUEST abrupt in manner

BRUT   *adj* very dry

BRUTAL   *adj* cruel; savage **BRUTALLY** *adv*

BRUTE   *v* BRUTED, BRUTING, BRUTES to shape a diamond by rubbing it with another diamond

BRUTELY   *adv* in a brutal manner

BRUTIFY   *v* -FIED, -FYING, -FIES to make brutal

BRUTING   present participle of brute

BRUTISH   *adj* brutal

BRUTISM   *n* pl. -S the state of being brutal

BRUXISM   *n* pl. -S a nervous grinding of the teeth

BRYOLOGY   *n* pl. -GIES the study of mosses

BRYONY   *n* pl. -NIES a climbing plant

BRYOZOAN   *n* pl. -S a type of small aquatic animal

BUB   *n* pl. -S young fellow

BUBAL   *n* pl. -S a large antelope

BUBALE   *n* pl. -S bubal

BUBALINE   *adj* pertaining to the bubal

BUBALIS   *n* pl. -LISES bubal

BUBBIES   pl. of bubby

BUBBLE   *v* -BLED, -BLING, -BLES to form bubbles (bodies of gas contained within a liquid)

BUBBLER   *n* pl. -S a drinking fountain

BUBBLY   *n* pl. -BLIES champagne

BUBBLY   *adj* -BLIER, -BLIEST full of bubbles

BUBBY   *n* pl. -BIES a breast — an offensive term

BUBINGA   *n* pl. -S an African tree

BUBO   *n* pl. -BOES a swelling of a lymph gland BUBOED *adj*

BUBONIC   *adj* pertaining to a bubo

BUCCAL   *adj* pertaining to the cheek BUCCALLY *adv*

BUCK   *v* -ED, -ING, -S to leap forward and upward suddenly

BUCKAROO n pl. -ROOS a cowboy

BUCKAYRO n pl. -ROS buckaroo

BUCKBEAN n pl. -S a marsh plant

BUCKEEN n pl. -S a poor man who acts as if wealthy

BUCKER n pl. -S a bucking horse

BUCKEROO n pl. -ROOS buckaroo

BUCKET v -ED, -ING, -S to hurry

BUCKEYE n pl. -S a nut-bearing tree

BUCKISH adj foppish

BUCKLE v -LED, -LING, -LES to bend under pressure

BUCKLER v -ED, -ING, -S to shield

BUCKO n pl. BUCKOES a bully

BUCKRA n pl. -S a white man — an offensive term

BUCKRAM v -ED, -ING, -S to stiffen

BUCKSAW n pl. -S a wood-cutting saw

BUCKSHEE n pl. -S something extra obtained free

BUCKSHOT n pl. -S a large lead shot

BUCKSKIN n pl. -S the skin of a male deer

BUCKTAIL n pl. -S a fishing lure

BUCOLIC n pl. -S a pastoral poem

BUD v BUDDED, BUDDING, BUDS to put forth buds (undeveloped plant parts)

BUDDER n pl. -S one that buds

BUDDIES pl. of buddy

BUDDING adj being in an early stage of development

BUDDLE n pl. -S an apparatus on which crushed ore is washed

BUDDLEIA n pl. -S a tropical shrub

BUDDY n pl. -DIES a good friend

BUDGE v BUDGED, BUDGING, BUDGES to move slightly

BUDGER n pl. -S one that budges

BUDGET v -ED, -ING, -S to estimate expenditures

BUDGETER n pl. -S one that budgets

BUDGIE n pl. -S a small parrot

BUDGING present participle of budge

BUDLESS adj being without buds

BUDLIKE adj resembling a bud

BUFF v -ED, -ING, -S to polish BUFFABLE adj

BUFFALO n pl. -LOES or -LOS an ox-like animal

BUFFALO v -ED, -ING, -ES to intimidate

BUFFER v -ED, -ING, -S to cushion

BUFFET v -ED, -ING, -S to hit sharply

BUFFETER n pl. -S one that buffets

BUFFIER comparative of buffy

BUFFIEST superlative of buffy

BUFFO n pl. -FI or -FOS an operatic clown

BUFFOON n pl. -S a clown

BUFFY adj BUFFIER, BUFFIEST of a yellowish-brown color

BUG v BUGGED, BUGGING, BUGS to annoy

BUGABOO n pl. -BOOS a bugbear

BUGBANE n pl. -S a perennial herb

BUGBEAR n pl. -S an object or source of dread

BUGEYE n pl. -S a small boat

BUGGED past tense of bug

BUGGER v -ED, -ING, -S to commit sodomy with — an offensive term

BUGGERY n pl. -GERIES sodomy

BUGGING present participle of bug

BUGGY n pl. -GIES a light carriage

BUGGY adj -GIER, -GIEST infested with bugs

BUGHOUSE n pl. -S an insane asylum

BUGLE v -GLED, -GLING, -GLES to play a bugle (a brass wind instrument)

BUGLER n pl. -S one that plays a bugle

BUGLOSS n pl. -ES a coarse plant

BUGSEED n pl. -S an annual herb

BUGSHA n pl. -S a buqsha

BUHL n pl. -S a style of furniture decoration

BUHLWORK n pl. -S buhl

BUHR n pl. -S a heavy stone

BUILD v BUILT or BUILDED, BUILDING, BUILDS to construct

BUILDER n pl. -S one that builds

BUILDING n pl. -S something that is built

BUILDUP n pl. -S an accumulation

BUILT a past tense of build

BUIRDLY adj burly

BULB n pl. -S an underground bud BULBAR, BULBED adj

BULBEL n pl. -S bulbil

BULBIL n pl. -S a small bulb

BULBOUS adj bulb-shaped; bulging

BULBUL n pl. -S a songbird

BULGE v BULGED, BULGING, BULGES to swell out

BULGER   *n* pl. -S a golf club

BULGUR   *n* pl. -S crushed wheat

BULGY   *adj* BULGIER, BULGIEST bulging

BULIMIA   *n* pl. -S insatiable appetite BULIMIC, BULIMIAC *adj*

BULK   *v* -ED, -ING, -S to gather into a mass

BULKAGE   *n* pl. -S a peristaltic stimulant

BULKHEAD   *n* pl. -S an upright partition in a ship

BULKY   *adj* BULKIER, BULKIEST massive BULKILY *adv*

BULL   *v* -ED, -ING, -S to push ahead

BULLA   *n* pl. -LAE a large blister

BULLACE   *n* pl. -S a purple plum

BULLATE   *adj* having a blistered appearance

BULLBAT   *n* pl. -S a nocturnal bird

BULLDOG   *v* -DOGGED, -DOGGING, -DOGS to throw a steer

BULLDOZE   *v* -DOZED, -DOZING, -DOZES to bully

BULLET   *v* -ED, -ING, -S to move swiftly

BULLETIN   *v* -ED, -ING, -S to issue a news item

BULLFROG   *n* pl. -S a large frog

BULLHEAD   *n* pl. -S a freshwater catfish

BULLHORN   *n* pl. -S an electric megaphone

BULLIED   past tense of bully

BULLIER   comparative of bully

BULLIES   present 3d person sing. of bully

BULLIEST   superlative of bully

BULLION   *n* pl. -S uncoined gold or silver

BULLISH   *adj* stubborn

BULLNECK   *n* pl. -S a thick neck

BULLNOSE   *n* pl. -S a disease of swine

BULLOCK   *n* pl. -S a castrated bull BULLOCKY *adj*

BULLOUS   *adj* resembling bullae

BULLPEN   *n* pl. -S an enclosure for bulls

BULLPOUT   *n* pl. -S a bullhead

BULLRING   *n* pl. -S a bullfight arena

BULLRUSH   *n* pl. -ES bulrush

BULLSHIT   *v* -SHITTED, -SHITTING, -SHITS to mislead — an offensive term

BULLWEED   *n* pl. -S knapweed

BULLWHIP   *v* -WHIPPED, -WHIPPING, -WHIPS to strike with a long whip

BULLY   *v* -LIED, -LYING, -LIES to treat abusively

BULLY   *adj* -LIER, -LIEST wonderful

BULLYBOY   *n* pl. -BOYS a ruffian

BULLYRAG   *v* -RAGGED, -RAGGING, -RAGS to bully

BULRUSH   *n* pl. -ES a tall marsh plant

BULWARK   *v* -ED, -ING, -S to fortify with a defensive wall

BUM   *v* BUMMED, BUMMING, BUMS to live idly

BUMBLE   *v* -BLED, -BLING, -BLES to bungle

BUMBLER   *n* pl. -S one that bumbles

BUMBLING   *n* pl. -S an instance of clumsiness

BUMBOAT   *n* pl. -S a boat used to peddle wares to larger ships

BUMF   *n* pl. -S paperwork

BUMKIN   *n* pl. -S a ship's spar

BUMMED   past tense of bum

BUMMER   *n* pl. -S one that bums

BUMMING   present participle of bum

BUMP   *v* -ED, -ING, -S to knock against

BUMPER   *v* -ED, -ING, -S to fill to the brim

BUMPKIN   *n* pl. -S an unsophisticated rustic

BUMPY   *adj* BUMPIER, BUMPIEST of uneven surface BUMPILY *adv*

BUN   *n* pl. -S a small bread roll

BUNCH   *v* -ED, -ING, -ES to group together

BUNCHY   *adj* BUNCHIER, BUNCHIEST clustered BUNCHILY *adv*

BUNCO   *v* -ED, -ING, -S to swindle

BUNCOMBE   *n* pl. -S nonsense

BUND   *n* pl. -S a political association

BUNDIST   *n* pl. -S a member of a bund

BUNDLE   *v* -DLED, -DLING, -DLES to fasten a group of objects together

BUNDLER   *n* pl. -S one that bundles

BUNDLING   *n* pl. -S a former courtship custom

BUNG   *v* -ED, -ING, -S to plug with a cork or stopper

BUNGALOW   *n* pl. -S a small cottage

BUNGHOLE   *n* pl. -S a hole in a keg or barrel

BUNGLE   *v* -GLED, -GLING, -GLES to work, make, or do clumsily

BUNGLER   *n* pl. -S one that bungles

BUNGLING *n* pl. -S an instance of clumsiness

BUNION *n* pl. -S a painful swelling of the foot

BUNK *v* -ED, -ING, -S to go to bed

BUNKER *v* -ED, -ING, -S to store in a large bin

BUNKMATE *n* pl. -S a person with whom sleeping quarters are shared

BUNKO *v* -ED, -ING, -S to bunco

BUNKUM *n* pl. -S nonsense

BUNN *n* pl. -S bun

BUNNY *n* pl. -NIES a rabbit

BUNT *v* -ED, -ING, -S to butt

BUNTER *n* pl. -S one that bunts

BUNTING *n* pl. -S a fabric used for flags

BUNTLINE *n* pl. -S a rope used to haul up a sail

BUNYA *n* pl. -S an evergreen tree

BUOY *v* -ED, -ING, -S to mark with a buoy (a warning float)

BUOYAGE *n* pl. -S a group of buoys

BUOYANCE *n* pl. -S buoyancy

BUOYANCY *n* pl. -CIES the tendency to float

BUOYANT *adj* having buoyancy

BUQSHA *n* pl. -S a monetary unit of Yemen

BUR *v* BURRED, BURRING, BURS to burr

BURA *n* pl. -S buran

BURAN *n* pl. -S a violent windstorm

BURBLE *v* -BLED, -BLING, -BLES to speak quickly and excitedly

BURBLER *n* pl. -S one that burbles

BURBLY *adj* -BLIER, -BLIEST burbling

BURBOT *n* pl. -S a freshwater fish

BURD *n* pl. -S a maiden

BURDEN *v* -ED, -ING, -S to load heavily

BURDENER *n* pl. -S one that burdens

BURDIE *n* pl. -S burd

BURDOCK *n* pl. -S a coarse weed

BUREAU *n* pl. -REAUS or -REAUX a chest of drawers

BURET *n* pl. -S burette

BURETTE *n* pl. -S a measuring tube

BURG *n* pl. -S a city or town

BURGAGE *n* pl. -S a feudal tenure

BURGEE *n* pl. -S a small flag

BURGEON *v* -ED, -ING, -S to develop rapidly

BURGER *n* pl. -S a hamburger

BURGESS *n* pl. -ES a citizen of an English borough

BURGH *n* pl. -S a Scottish borough **BURGHAL** *adj*

BURGHER *n* pl. -S a citizen of a borough

BURGLAR *n* pl. -S one who commits burglary

BURGLARY *n* pl. -GLARIES a felonious theft

BURGLE *v* -GLED, -GLING, -GLES to commit burglary

BURGONET *n* pl. -S an open helmet

BURGOO *n* pl. -GOOS a thick oatmeal

BURGOUT *n* pl. -S burgoo

BURGRAVE *n* pl. -S a German nobleman

BURGUNDY *n* pl. -DIES a red wine

BURIAL *n* pl. -S the act of burying

BURIED past tense of bury

BURIER *n* pl. -S one that buries

BURIES present 3d person sing. of bury

BURIN *n* pl. -S an engraving tool

BURKE *v* BURKED, BURKING, BURKES to murder by suffocation

BURKER *n* pl. -S one that burkes

BURKITE *n* pl. -S a burker

BURL *v* -ED, -ING, -S to finish cloth by removing lumps

BURLAP *n* pl. -S a coarse fabric

BURLER *n* pl. -S one that burls

BURLESK *n* pl. -S a type of stage show

BURLEY *n* pl. -LEYS a light tobacco

BURLY *adj* -LIER, -LIEST heavy and muscular **BURLILY** *adv*

BURN *v* BURNED or BURNT, BURNING, BURNS to destroy by fire **BURNABLE** *adj*

BURNER *n* pl. -S one that burns

BURNET *n* pl. -S a perennial herb

BURNIE *n* pl. -S a brooklet

BURNING *n* pl. -S the firing of ceramic materials

BURNISH *v* -ED, -ING, -ES to polish

BURNOOSE *n* pl. -S a hooded cloak

BURNOUS *n* pl. -ES burnoose

BURNOUT *n* pl. -S a destructive fire

BURNT a past tense of burn

BURP *v* -ED, -ING, -S to belch

BURR *v* -ED, -ING, -S to remove a rough edge from

BURRED past tense of bur

BURRER   *n* pl. -S one that burrs

BURRIER   comparative of burry

BURRIEST   superlative of burry

BURRING   present participle of bur

BURRO   *n* pl. -ROS a small donkey

BURROW   *v* -ED, -ING, -S to dig a hole or tunnel in the ground

BURROWER   *n* pl. -S one that burrows

BURRY   *adj* -RIER, -RIEST prickly

BURSA   *n* pl. -SAS or -SAE a bodily pouch **BURSAL** *adj*

BURSAR   *n* pl. -S a college treasurer

BURSARY   *n* pl. -RIES a college treasury

BURSATE   *adj* pertaining to a bursa

BURSE   *n* pl. -S a small bag or pouch

BURSEED   *n* pl. -S a coarse weed

BURSITIS   *n* pl. -TISES inflammation of a bursa

BURST   *v* BURST or BURSTED, BURSTING, BURSTS to break open suddenly or violently

BURSTER   *n* pl. -S one that bursts

BURSTONE   *n* pl. -S a heavy stone

BURTHEN   *v* -ED, -ING, -S to burden

BURTON   *n* pl. -S a hoisting tackle

BURWEED   *n* pl. -S a coarse weed

BURY   *v* BURIED, BURYING, BURIES to put in the ground and cover with earth

BUS   *v* BUSED, BUSING, BUSES or BUSSED, BUSSING, BUSSES to transport by bus (a large motor vehicle)

BUSBOY   *n* pl. -BOYS a waiter's assistant

BUSBY   *n* pl. -BIES a tall fur hat

BUSH   *v* -ED, -ING, -ES to cover with bushes (shrubs)

BUSHBUCK   *n* pl. -S a small antelope

BUSHEL   *v* -ELED, -ELING, -ELS or -ELLED, -ELLING, -ELS to mend clothing

BUSHELER   *n* pl. -S one that bushels

BUSHER   *n* pl. -S a minor league baseball player

BUSHFIRE   *n* pl. -S a fire in a wooded area

BUSHGOAT   *n* pl. -S a bushbuck

BUSHIDO   *n* pl. -DOS the code of the samurai

BUSHIER   comparative of bushy

BUSHIEST   superlative of bushy

BUSHILY   *adv* in a bushy manner

BUSHING   *n* pl. -S a lining for a hole

BUSHLAND   *n* pl. -S unsettled forest land

BUSHLESS   *adj* having no bushes

BUSHLIKE   *adj* resembling a bush

BUSHMAN   *n* pl. -MEN a woodsman

BUSHTIT   *n* pl. -S a titmouse

BUSHY   *adj* BUSHIER, BUSHIEST covered with bushes

BUSIED   past tense of busy

BUSIER   comparative of busy

BUSIES   present 3d person sing. of busy

BUSIEST   superlative of busy

BUSILY   *adv* in a busy manner

BUSINESS   *n* pl. -ES an occupation, profession, or trade

BUSING   *n* pl. -S the act of transporting by bus

BUSK   *v* -ED, -ING, -S to prepare

BUSKER   *n* pl. -S a roaming entertainer

BUSKIN   *n* pl. -S a high shoe **BUSKINED** *adj*

BUSMAN   *n* pl. -MEN a bus operator

BUSS   *v* -ED, -ING, -ES to kiss

BUSSED   a past tense of bus

BUSSES   a present 3d person sing. of bus

BUSSING   *n* pl. -S busing

BUST   *v* -ED, -ING, -S to burst

BUSTARD   *n* pl. -S a game bird

BUSTER   *n* pl. -S one that breaks up something

BUSTIC   *n* pl. -S a tropical tree

BUSTLE   *v* -TLED, -TLING, -TLES to move energetically

BUSTY   *adj* BUSTIER, BUSTIEST full-bosomed

BUSULFAN   *n* pl. -S a medicine

BUSY   *adj* BUSIER, BUSIEST occupied

BUSY   *v* BUSIED, BUSYING, BUSIES to make busy

BUSYBODY   *n* pl. -BODIES a nosy person

BUSYNESS   *n* pl. -ES the state of being busy

BUSYWORK   *n* pl. -S active but valueless work

BUT   *n* pl. -S a flatfish

BUTANE   *n* pl. -S a flammable gas

BUTANOL   *n* pl. -S a flammable alcohol

BUTANONE   *n* pl. -S a flammable ketone

BUTCH   *n* pl. -ES a lesbian with mannish traits

BUTCHER v -ED, -ING, -S to slaughter

BUTCHERY n pl. -ERIES wanton or cruel killing

BUTENE n pl. -S butylene

BUTEO n pl. -TEOS a hawk

BUTLER n pl. -S a male servant

BUTLERY n pl. -LERIES a storage room

BUTT v -ED, -ING, -S to hit with the head

BUTTALS n/pl boundary lines

BUTTE n pl. -S an isolated hill

BUTTER v -ED, -ING, -S to spread with butter (a milk product)

BUTTERY adj -TERIER, -TERIEST containing butter

BUTTERY n pl. -TERIES a wine cellar

BUTTIES pl. of butty

BUTTOCK n pl. -S either of the two rounded parts of the rump

BUTTON v -ED, -ING, -S to fasten with a button (a small disk)

BUTTONER n pl. -S one that buttons

BUTTONY adj resembling a button

BUTTRESS v -ED, -ING, -ES to prop up

BUTTY n pl. -TIES a fellow workman

BUTUT n pl. -S a unit of Gambian currency

BUTYL n pl. -S a hydrocarbon radical

BUTYLATE v -ATED, -ATING, -ATES to add a butyl to

BUTYLENE n pl. -S a gaseous hydrocarbon

BUTYRAL n pl. -S a chemical compound

BUTYRATE n pl. -S a chemical salt

BUTYRIC adj derived from butter

BUTYRIN n pl. -S a chemical compound

BUTYROUS adj resembling butter

BUTYRYL n pl. -S a radical of butyric acid

BUXOM adj -OMER, -OMEST healthily plump **BUXOMLY** adv

BUY v BOUGHT, BUYING, BUYS to purchase **BUYABLE** adj

BUYER n pl. -S one that buys

BUZZ v -ED, -ING, -ES to make a vibrating sound

BUZZARD n pl. -S a large bird of prey

BUZZER n pl. -S a signaling device

BUZZWIG n pl. -S a large, thick wig

BUZZWORD n pl. -S a word used to impress someone

BWANA n pl. -S master; boss

BY n pl. BYS a pass in certain card games

BYE n pl. -S a side issue

BYELAW n pl. -S bylaw

BYGONE n pl. -S a past occurrence

BYLAW n pl. -S a secondary law

BYLINE v -LINED, -LINING, -LINES to write under a byline (a line giving the author's name)

BYLINER n pl. -S one that writes under a byline

BYNAME n pl. -S a secondary name

BYPASS v -ED, -ING, -ES to avoid by going around

BYPAST adj past; gone by

BYPATH n pl. -S an indirect road

BYPLAY n pl. -PLAYS secondary action

BYRE n pl. -S a cowshed

BYRL v -ED, -ING, -S to birle

BYRNIE n pl. -S an armored shirt

BYROAD n pl. -S a side road

BYSSUS n pl. BYSSUSES or BYSSI a fine linen

BYSTREET n pl. -S a side street

BYTALK n pl. -S small talk

BYTE n pl. -S a group of adjacent binary digits

BYWAY n pl. -WAYS a side road

BYWORD n pl. -S a well-known saying

BYWORK n pl. -S work done during leisure time

BYZANT n pl. -S bezant

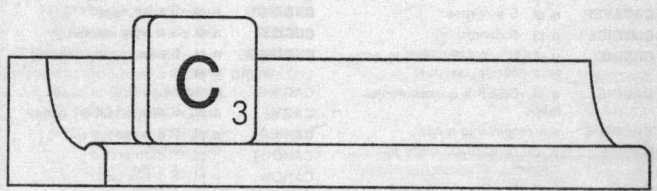

CAB	n pl. -S a taxicab
CABAL	v -BALLED, -BALLING, -BALS to conspire
CABALA	n pl. -S an occult or secret doctrine
CABALISM	n pl. -S adherence to a cabala
CABALIST	n pl. -S one who practices cabalism
CABALLED	past tense of cabal
CABALLING	present participle of cabal
CABANA	n pl. -S a small cabin
CABARET	n pl. -S a music hall
CABBAGE	v -BAGED, -BAGING, -BAGES to steal
CABBALA	n pl. -S cabala
CABBALAH	n pl. -S cabala
CABBIE	n pl. -S cabby
CABBY	n pl. -BIES a driver of a cab
CABER	n pl. -S a heavy pole thrown as a trial of strength
CABESTRO	n pl. -TROS a lasso
CABEZON	n pl. -S a large, edible fish
CABEZONE	n pl. -S cabezon
CABILDO	n pl. -DOS a town council
CABIN	v -ED, -ING, -S to live in a cabin (a roughly built house)
CABINET	n pl. -S a piece of furniture with shelves and drawers
CABLE	v -BLED, -BLING, -BLES to fasten with a cable (a heavy rope)
CABLET	n pl. -S a small cable
CABLEWAY	n pl. -WAYS a suspended cable
CABMAN	n pl. -MEN a driver of a cab
CABOB	n pl. -S kabob
CABOCHED	adj full-faced — used of an animal's head in heraldry

CABOCHON	n pl. -S a precious stone
CABOODLE	n pl. -S a collection
CABOOSE	n pl. -S the last car of a freight train
CABOSHED	adj caboched
CABOTAGE	n pl. -S coastal trade
CABRESTA	n pl. -S cabestro
CABRESTO	n pl. -TOS cabestro
CABRETTA	n pl. -S a soft leather
CABRILLA	n pl. -S a sea bass
CABRIOLE	n pl. -S a curved furniture leg
CABSTAND	n pl. -S a place where cabs await hire
CACAO	n pl. -CAOS a tropical tree
CACHALOT	n pl. -S a large whale
CACHE	v CACHED, CACHING, CACHES to store in a hiding place
CACHEPOT	n pl. -S an ornamental container for a flowerpot
CACHET	n pl. -S an official seal
CACHEXIA	n pl. -S general ill health CACHEXIC adj
CACHEXY	n pl. -CHEXIES cachexia
CACHING	present participle of cache
CACHOU	n pl. -S catechu
CACHUCHA	n pl. -S a Spanish dance
CACIQUE	n pl. -S a tropical oriole
CACKLE	v -LED, -LING, -LES to make the sound of a hen
CACKLER	n pl. -S one that cackles
CACODYL	n pl. -S a poisonous liquid
CACOMIXL	n pl. -S a raccoon-like mammal
CACTUS	n pl. -TI or -TUSES a plant native to arid regions CACTOID adj
CAD	n pl. -S an ungentlemanly man

CADASTER n pl. -S a public record of land ownership

CADASTRE n pl. -S cadaster

CADAVER n pl. -S a corpse

CADDICE n pl. -S caddis

CADDIE v -DIED, -DYING, -DIES to serve as a golfer's assistant

CADDIS n pl. -DISES a coarse woolen fabric

CADDISH adj resembling a cad

CADDY v -DIED, -DYING, -DIES to caddie

CADE n pl. -S a European shrub

CADELLE n pl. -S a small, black beetle

CADENCE v -DENCED, -DENCING, -DENCES to make rhythmic

CADENCY n pl. -CIES a rhythm

CADENT adj having rhythm

CADENZA n pl. -S an elaborate musical passage

CADET n pl. -S a student at a military school

CADGE v CADGED, CADGING, CADGES to get by begging

CADGER n pl. -S one that cadges

CADGY adj cheerful

CADI n pl. -S a Muslim judge

CADMIUM n pl. -S a metallic element CADMIC adj

CADRE n pl. -S a nucleus of trained personnel

CADUCEUS n pl. -CEI a heraldic wand or staff CADUCEAN adj

CADUCITY n pl. -TIES senility

CADUCOUS adj transitory; perishable

CAECUM n pl. -CA cecum CAECAL adj CAECALLY adv

CAEOMA n pl. -S a spore-forming organ of a fungus

CAESIUM n pl. -S cesium

CAESTUS n pl. -ES cestus

CAESURA n pl. -RAS or -RAE a pause in a line of verse CAESURAL, CAESURIC adj

CAFE n pl. -S a restaurant

CAFFEIN n pl. -S caffeine

CAFFEINE n pl. -S a bitter alkaloid used as a stimulant

CAFTAN n pl. -S a full-length tunic

CAGE v CAGED, CAGING, CAGES to confine

CAGELING n pl. -S a caged bird

CAGEY adj CAGIER, CAGIEST shrewd and careful

CAGIER comparative of cagy

CAGIEST superlative of cagy

CAGILY adv in a cagey manner

CAGINESS n pl. -ES the quality of being cagey

CAGING present participle of cage

CAGY adj CAGIER, CAGIEST cagey

CAHIER n pl. -S a notebook

CAHOOT n pl. -S partnership

CAHOW n pl. -S a sea bird

CAID n pl. -S a Muslim leader

CAIMAN n pl. -S a tropical reptile

CAIN n pl. -S kain

CAIQUE n pl. -S a long, narrow rowboat

CAIRD n pl. -S a gypsy

CAIRN n pl. -S a mound of stones set up as a memorial CAIRNED, CAIRNY adj

CAISSON n pl. -S a watertight chamber

CAITIFF n pl. -S a despicable person

CAJAPUT n pl. -S cajeput

CAJEPUT n pl. -S an Australian tree

CAJOLE v -JOLED, -JOLING, -JOLES to persuade by flattery

CAJOLER n pl. -S one that cajoles

CAJOLERY n pl. -ERIES persuasion by flattery

CAJOLING present participle of cajole

CAJON n pl. -ES a steep-sided canyon

CAJUPUT n pl. -S cajeput

CAKE v CAKED, CAKING, CAKES to form into a hardened mass

CAKEWALK v -ED, -ING, -S to step stylishly

CALABASH n pl. -ES a gourd

CALADIUM n pl. -S a tropical plant

CALAMAR n pl. -S calamary

CALAMARY n pl. -MARIES a squid

CALAMI pl. of calamus

CALAMINE v -MINED, -MINING, -MINES to apply an ointment for skin ailments

CALAMINT n pl. -S a perennial herb

CALAMITE n pl. -S an extinct treelike plant

CALAMITY n pl. -TIES a grievous misfortune

CALAMUS n pl. -MI a marsh plant

CALANDO adj gradually diminishing

CALASH n pl. -ES a light carriage

CALATHOS n pl. -THI a fruit basket

CALATHUS n pl. -THI calathos
CALCANEA n/pl calcanei
CALCANEI n/pl bones of the heel
CALCAR n pl. -CARIA an anatomical projection
CALCAR n pl. -S a type of oven
CALCEATE adj wearing shoes
CALCES a pl. of calx
CALCIC adj pertaining to lime or calcium
CALCIFIC adj containing salts of calcium
CALCIFY v -FIED, -FYING, -FIES to harden
CALCINE v -CINED, -CINING, -CINES to reduce to a calx by heat
CALCITE n pl. -S a mineral CALCITIC adj
CALCIUM n pl. -S a metallic element
CALCSPAR n pl. -S a calcite
CALCTUFA n pl. -S a mineral deposit
CALCTUFF n pl. -S calctufa
CALCULUS n pl. -LI or -LUSES a branch of mathematics
CALDERA n pl. -S a large crater
CALDRON n pl. -S a large kettle or boiler
CALECHE n pl. -S a calash
CALENDAL adj pertaining to calends
CALENDAR v -ED, -ING, -S to schedule
CALENDER v -ED, -ING, -S to smooth by pressing between rollers
CALENDS n pl. CALENDS the first day of the Roman month
CALESA n pl. -S a calash
CALF n pl. CALVES or CALFS a young cow or bull CALFLIKE adj
CALFSKIN n pl. -S the skin of a calf
CALIBER n pl. -S the diameter of a gun barrel
CALIBRE n pl. -S caliber CALIBRED adj
CALICES pl. of calix
CALICHE n pl. -S a mineral deposit
CALICLE n pl. -S a cup-shaped, anatomical structure
CALICO n pl. -COES or -COS a cotton fabric
CALIF n pl. -S caliph
CALIFATE n pl. -S the domain of a calif
CALIPASH n pl. -ES an edible part of a turtle
CALIPEE n pl. -S an edible part of a turtle

CALIPER v -ED, -ING, -S to use a type of measuring device
CALIPH n pl. -S a Muslim leader CALIPHAL adj
CALISAYA n pl. -S the medicinal bark of the cinchona
CALIX n pl. -LICES a cup
CALK v -ED, -ING, -S to caulk
CALKER n pl. -S one that calks
CALKIN n pl. -S a gripping projection on a horseshoe
CALL v -ED, -ING, -S to summon CALLABLE adj
CALLA n pl. -S a tropical plant
CALLAN n pl. -S callant
CALLANT n pl. -S a lad
CALLBACK n pl. -S a recall of a defective product
CALLBOY n pl. -BOYS a bellboy
CALLER n pl. -S one that calls
CALLET n pl. -S a prostitute
CALLING n pl. -S a vocation or profession
CALLIOPE n pl. -S a keyboard musical instrument
CALLIPEE n pl. -S calipee
CALLIPER v -ED, -ING, -S to caliper
CALLOSE n pl. -S a part of a plant cell wall
CALLOUS v -ED, -ING, -ES to make or become hard
CALLOW adj -LOWER, -LOWEST immature
CALLUS v -ED, -ING, -ES to form a hard growth
CALM adj CALMER, CALMEST free from agitation CALMLY adv
CALM v -ED, -ING, -S to make calm
CALMNESS n pl. -ES the state of being calm
CALOMEL n pl. -S a chemical compound used as a purgative
CALORIC n pl. -S heat
CALORIE n pl. -S a unit of heat
CALORY n pl. -RIES calorie
CALOTTE n pl. -S a skullcap
CALOYER n pl. -S a monk of the Eastern Church
CALPAC n pl. -S a sheepskin hat
CALPACK n pl. -S calpac

CALQUE *v* CALQUED, CALQUING, CALQUES to model a word's meaning upon that of an analogous word in another language

CALTHROP *n pl.* -S caltrop

CALTRAP *n pl.* -S caltrop

CALTROP *n pl.* -S a spiny plant

CALUMET *n pl.* -S a ceremonial pipe

CALUMNY *n pl.* -NIES a false and malicious accusation

CALUTRON *n pl.* -S a device used for separating isotopes

CALVADOS *n pl.* -ES a dry apple brandy

CALVARIA *n pl.* -S the dome of the skull

CALVARY *n pl.* -RIES a representation of the Crucifixion

CALVE *v* CALVED, CALVING, CALVES to give birth to a calf

CALVES a pl. of calf

CALX *n pl.* -ES or CALCES a mineral residue

CALYCATE *adj* calycine

CALYCEAL *adj* calycine

CALYCES a pl. of calyx

CALYCINE *adj* pertaining to a calyx

CALYCLE *n pl.* -S an outer calyx

CALYCULI *n/pl* small, cup-shaped structures

CALYPSO *n pl.* -SOS or -SOES an improvised song

CALYPTER *n pl.* -S calyptra

CALYPTRA *n pl.* -S a hood-shaped organ of flowers

CALYX *n pl.* -LYXES or -LYCES the outer protective covering of a flower

CAM *n pl.* -S a rotating or sliding piece of machinery

CAMAIL *n pl.* -S a piece of armor for the neck **CAMAILED** *adj*

CAMAS *n pl.* -ES camass

CAMASS *n pl.* -ES a perennial herb

CAMBER *v* -ED, -ING, -S to arch slightly

CAMBIA a pl. of cambium

CAMBIAL *adj* pertaining to cambium

CAMBISM *n pl.* -S the theory and practice of exchange in commerce

CAMBIST *n pl.* -S a dealer in bills of exchange

CAMBIUM *n pl.* -BIUMS or -BIA a layer of plant tissue

CAMBOGIA *n pl.* -S a gum resin

CAMBRIC *n pl.* -S a fine linen

CAME *n pl.* -S a leaden window rod

CAMEL *n pl.* -S a large, humped mammal

CAMELEER *n pl.* -S a camel driver

CAMELIA *n pl.* -S camellia

CAMELLIA *n pl.* -S a tropical shrub

CAMEO *v* -ED, -ING, -S to portray in sharp, delicate relief

CAMERA *n pl.* -ERAS or -ERAE a judge's chamber **CAMERAL** *adj*

CAMION *n pl.* -S a military truck

CAMISA *n pl.* -S a shirt or chemise

CAMISADE *n pl.* -S camisado

CAMISADO *n pl.* -DOS or -DOES an attack made at night

CAMISE *n pl.* -S a loose shirt or gown

CAMISIA *n pl.* -S camise

CAMISOLE *n pl.* -S a brief negligee

CAMLET *n pl.* -S a durable fabric

CAMOMILE *n pl.* -S a medicinal herb

CAMORRA *n pl.* -S an unscrupulous secret society

CAMP *v* -ED, -ING, -S to live in the open

CAMPAGNA *n pl.* -PAGNE a flat, open plain

CAMPAIGN *v* -ED, -ING, -S to conduct a series of operations to reach a specific goal

CAMPER *n pl.* -S one that camps

CAMPFIRE *n pl.* -S an outdoor fire

CAMPHENE *n pl.* -S camphine

CAMPHINE *n pl.* -S an explosive liquid

CAMPHOL *n pl.* -S borneol

CAMPHOR *n pl.* -S a volatile compound

CAMPI pl. of campo

CAMPIER comparative of campy

CAMPIEST superlative of campy

CAMPILY *adv* in a campy manner

CAMPING *n pl.* -S the act of living outdoors

CAMPION *n pl.* -S an herb

CAMPO *n pl.* -PI an open space in a town

CAMPO *n pl.* -POS a level, grassy plain

CAMPONG *n pl.* -S kampong

CAMPOREE *n pl.* -S a gathering of Boy Scouts

CAMPSITE *n pl.* -S an area suitable for camping

CAMPUS *n pl.* -ES the grounds of a school

CAMPY *adj* CAMPIER, CAMPIEST comically exaggerated

CAMSHAFT *n pl.* -S a shaft fitted with cams

CAN *v* CANNED, CANNING, CANS to put in a can (a cylindrical container)

CAN *v* present sing. 2d person CAN or CANST, past sing. 2d person COULD, COULDEST, or COULDST — used as an auxiliary to express ability

CANAILLE *n pl.* -S the common people

CANAKIN *n pl.* -S cannikin

CANAL *v* -NALLED, -NALLING, -NALS or -NALED, -NALING, -NALS to dig an artificial waterway through

CANALISE *v* -ISED, -ISING, -ISES to canalize

CANALIZE *v* -IZED, -IZING, -IZES to canal

CANALLED a past tense of canal

CANALLER *n pl.* -S a freight boat

CANALLING a present participle of canal

CANAPE *n pl.* -S a food served before a meal

CANARD *n pl.* -S a false story

CANARY *n pl.* -NARIES a songbird

CANASTA *n pl.* -S a card game

CANCAN *n pl.* -S a dance marked by high kicking

CANCEL *v* -CELLED, -CELLING, -CELS or -CELED, -CELING, -CELS to annul

CANCELER *n pl.* -S one that cancels

CANCER *n pl.* -S a malignant growth

CANCHA *n pl.* -S a jai alai court

CANCROID *n pl.* -S a skin cancer

CANDELA *n pl.* -S a unit of luminous intensity

CANDENT *adj* glowing

CANDID *adj* -DIDER, -DIDEST frank and sincere

CANDID *n pl.* -S an unposed photograph

CANDIDA *n pl.* -S a parasitic fungus

CANDIDLY *adv* in a candid manner

CANDIED past tense of candy

CANDIES present 3d person sing. of candy

CANDLE *v* -DLED, -DLING, -DLES to examine eggs in front of a light

CANDLER *n pl.* -S one that candles

CANDOR *n pl.* -S frankness; sincerity

CANDOUR *n pl.* -S candor

CANDY *v* -DIED, -DYING, -DIES to coat with sugar

CANE *v* CANED, CANING, CANES to beat with a rod

CANELLA *n pl.* -S a medicinal tree bark

CANER *n pl.* -S one that canes

CANEWARE *n pl.* -S a yellowish stoneware

CANFIELD *n pl.* -S a card game

CANFUL *n pl.* CANFULS or CANSFUL as much as a can holds

CANGUE *n pl.* -S an ancient Chinese punishing device

CANIKIN *n pl.* -S cannikin

CANINE *n pl.* -S a dog

CANING present participle of cane

CANINITY *n pl.* -TIES the state of being a canine

CANISTER *n pl.* -S a small, metal box

CANITIES *n pl.* CANITIES the turning gray of the hair

CANKER *v* -ED, -ING, -S to affect with ulcerous sores

CANNA *n pl.* -S a tropical plant

CANNABIC *adj* pertaining to cannabis

CANNABIN *n pl.* -S a resin extracted from cannabis

CANNABIS *n pl.* -BISES hemp

CANNED past tense of can

CANNEL *n pl.* -S an oily, compact coal

CANNELON *n pl.* -S a stuffed roll

CANNER *n pl.* -S one that cans food

CANNERY *n pl.* -NERIES a place where food is canned

CANNIBAL *n pl.* -S one who eats his own kind

CANNIE *adj* -NIER, -NIEST canny

CANNIER comparative of canny

CANNIEST superlative of canny

CANNIKIN *n pl.* -S a small can or cup

CANNILY *adv* in a canny manner

CANNING *n pl.* -S the business of preserving food in airtight containers

CANNON *v* -ED, -ING, -S to fire a cannon (a heavy firearm)

CANNONRY *n pl.* -RIES artillery

CANNOT the negative form of can

CANNULA *n pl.* -LAS or -LAE a tube inserted into a bodily cavity CANNULAR *adj*

CANNY *adj* -NIER, -NIEST prudent

CANOE v -NOED, -NOEING, -NOES to paddle a canoe (a light, slender boat)

CANOEIST n pl. -S one who canoes

CANON n pl. -S a law decreed by a church council **CANONIC** adj

CANONESS n pl. -ES a woman who lives according to a canon

CANONISE v -ISED, -ISING, -ISES to canonize

CANONIST n pl. -S a specialist in canon law

CANONIZE v -IZED, -IZING, -IZES to declare to be a saint

CANONRY n pl. -RIES a clerical office

CANOPY v -PIED, -PYING, -PIES to cover from above

CANOROUS adj melodic

CANSFUL a pl. of canful

CANSO n pl. -SOS a love song

CANST a present 2d person sing. of can

CANT v -ED, -ING, -S to tilt or slant

CANTALA n pl. -S a tropical plant

CANTATA n pl. -S a vocal composition

CANTDOG n pl. -S a device used to move logs

CANTEEN n pl. -S a small container for carrying water

CANTER v -ED, -ING, -S to ride a horse at a moderate pace

CANTHUS n pl. -THI a corner of the eye **CANTHAL** adj

CANTIC adj slanted

CANTICLE n pl. -S a hymn

CANTINA n pl. -S a saloon

CANTLE n pl. -S the rear part of a saddle

CANTO n pl. -TOS a division of a long poem

CANTON v -ED, -ING, -S to divide into cantons (districts)

CANTONAL adj pertaining to a canton

CANTOR n pl. -S a religious singer

CANTRAIP n pl. -S cantrip

CANTRAP n pl. -S cantrip

CANTRIP n pl. -S a magic spell

CANTUS n pl. CANTUS a style of church music

CANTY adj cheerful

CANULA n pl. -LAS or -LAE cannula

CANULATE v -LATED, -LATING, -LATES to insert a canula into

CANVAS v -ED, -ING, -ES to canvass

CANVASER n pl. -S one that canvases

CANVASS v -ED, -ING, -ES to examine thoroughly

CANYON n pl. -S a deep valley with steep sides

CANZONA n pl. -S canzone

CANZONE n pl. -NI or -NES a form of lyric poetry

CANZONET n pl. -S a short song

CAP v CAPPED, CAPPING, CAPS to provide with a cap (a type of head covering)

CAPABLE adj -BLER, -BLEST having ability **CAPABLY** adv

CAPACITY n pl. -TIES the ability to receive or contain

CAPE n pl. -S a sleeveless garment **CAPED** adj

CAPELAN n pl. -S capelin

CAPELET n pl. -S a small cape

CAPELIN n pl. -S a small, edible fish

CAPER v -ED, -ING, -S to frolic

CAPERER n pl. -S one that capers

CAPESKIN n pl. -S a soft leather

CAPEWORK n pl. -S a bullfighting technique

CAPFUL n pl. -S as much as a cap can hold

CAPH n pl. -S kaph

CAPIAS n pl. -ES a judicial writ

CAPITA pl. of caput

CAPITAL n pl. -S the upper part of a column

CAPITATE adj head-shaped

CAPITOL n pl. -S a building occupied by a state legislature

CAPITULA n/pl flower clusters

CAPLESS adj being without a cap

CAPLIN n pl. -S capelin

CAPMAKER n pl. -S one that makes caps

CAPO n pl. -POS a pitch raising device for fretted instruments

CAPON n pl. -S a gelded rooster

CAPONIER n pl. -S a type of defense

CAPONIZE v -IZED, -IZING, -IZES to geld a rooster

CAPORAL n pl. -S a coarse tobacco

CAPOTE n pl. -S a hooded cloak or overcoat

CAPOUCH n pl. -ES capuche

CAPPED past tense of cap

CAPPER n pl. -S a capmaker

CAPPING	n pl. -S a wax covering in a honeycomb
CAPRIC	adj pertaining to a goat
CAPRICCI	n/pl caprices
CAPRICE	n pl. -S a whim
CAPRIFIG	n pl. -S a European tree
CAPRINE	adj capric
CAPRIOLE	v -OLED, -OLING, -OLES to leap
CAPSICIN	n pl. -S a liquid used as a flavoring
CAPSICUM	n pl. -S a tropical herb
CAPSID	n pl. -S the outer shell of a virus particle CAPSIDAL adj
CAPSIZE	v -SIZED, -SIZING, -SIZES to overturn
CAPSTAN	n pl. -S a machine used to hoist weights
CAPSTONE	n pl. -S the top stone of a structure
CAPSULAR	adj enclosed and compact
CAPSULE	v -SULED, -SULING, -SULES to condense into a brief form
CAPTAIN	v -ED, -ING, -S to lead or command
CAPTAN	n pl. -S a fungicide
CAPTION	v -ED, -ING, -S to provide with a title
CAPTIOUS	adj tending to find fault
CAPTIVE	n pl. -S a prisoner
CAPTOR	n pl. -S one who takes or holds a captive
CAPTURE	v -TURED, -TURING, -TURES to take by force or cunning
CAPTURER	n pl. -S one that captures
CAPUCHE	n pl. -S a hood or cowl CAPUCHED adj
CAPUCHIN	n pl. -S a long-tailed monkey
CAPUT	n pl. CAPITA a head or head-like part
CAPYBARA	n pl. -S a large rodent
CAR	n pl. -S an automobile
CARABAO	n pl. -BAOS a water buffalo
CARABID	n pl. -S a predatory beetle
CARABIN	n pl. -S carbine
CARABINE	n pl. -S carbine
CARACAL	n pl. -S an African lynx
CARACARA	n pl. -S a large hawk
CARACK	n pl. -S carrack
CARACOL	v -COLLED, -COLLING, -COLS to caracole
CARACOLE	v -COLED, -COLING, -COLES to perform a half turn on a horse
CARACUL	n pl. -S karakul
CARAFE	n pl. -S a glass bottle
CARAGANA	n pl. -S an Asian shrub
CARAGEEN	n pl. -S an edible seaweed
CARAMEL	n pl. -S a chewy candy
CARANGID	n pl. -S a marine fish
CARAPACE	n pl. -S a hard, protective outer covering
CARAPAX	n pl. -ES carapace
CARASSOW	n pl. -S curassow
CARAT	n pl. -S a unit of weight for gems
CARATE	n pl. -S a tropical skin disease
CARAVAN	v -VANED, -VANING, -VANS or -VANNED, -VANNING, -VANS to travel in a group
CARAVEL	n pl. -S a small sailing ship
CARAWAY	n pl. -WAYS an herb used in cooking
CARBAMIC	adj pertaining to a type of acid
CARBAMYL	n pl. -S a chemical radical
CARBARN	n pl. -S a garage for buses
CARBARYL	n pl. -S an insecticide
CARBIDE	n pl. -S a carbon compound
CARBINE	n pl. -S a light rifle
CARBINOL	n pl. -S an alcohol
CARBON	n pl. -S a nonmetallic element CARBONIC adj
CARBONYL	n pl. -S a chemical compound
CARBORA	n pl. -S a wood-boring worm
CARBOXYL	n pl. -S a univalent acid radical
CARBOY	n pl. -BOYS a bottle enclosed in a protective basket CARBOYED adj
CARBURET	v -RETED, -RETING, -RETS or -RETTED, -RETTING, -RETS to combine chemically with carbon
CARCAJOU	n pl. -S a carnivorous mammal
CARCANET	n pl. -S a jeweled necklace
CARCASE	n pl. -S carcass
CARCASS	n pl. -ES the body of a dead animal
CARCEL	n pl. -S a unit of illumination
CARD	v -ED, -ING, -S to provide with a card (a stiff piece of paper)
CARDAMOM	n pl. -S a tropical herb
CARDAMON	n pl. -S cardamom
CARDAMUM	n pl. -S cardamom
CARDCASE	n pl. -S a case for holding cards

CARDER n pl. -S one that does carding

CARDIA n pl. -DIAS or -DIAE an opening of the esophagus

CARDIAC n pl. -S a person with a heart disorder

CARDIGAN n pl. -S a type of sweater

CARDINAL n pl. -S a high-ranking official of the Roman Catholic Church

CARDING n pl. -S the process of combing and cleaning cotton fibers; cleaned and combed fibers

CARDIOID n pl. -S a heart-shaped curve

CARDITIS n pl. -TISES inflammation of the heart CARDITIC adj

CARDOON n pl. -S a perennial plant

CARE v CARED, CARING, CARES to be concerned or interested

CAREEN v -ED, -ING, -S to lurch while moving

CAREENER n pl. -S one that careens

CAREER v -ED, -ING, -S to go at full speed

CAREERER n pl. -S one that careers

CAREFREE adj being without worry or anxiety

CAREFUL adj -FULLER, -FULLEST cautious

CARELESS adj inattentive; negligent

CARER n pl. -S one that cares

CARESS v -ED, -ING, -ES to touch lovingly

CARESSER n pl. -S one that caresses

CARET n pl. -S a proofreaders' symbol

CAREWORN adj haggard

CAREX n pl. CARICES a marsh plant

CARFARE n pl. -S payment for a bus or car ride

CARFUL n pl. -S as much as a car can hold

CARGO n pl. -GOS or -GOES conveyed merchandise

CARHOP n pl. -S a waitress at a drive-in restaurant

CARIBE n pl. -S the piranha

CARIBOU n pl. -S a large deer

CARICES pl. of carex

CARIES n pl. CARIES tooth decay CARIED adj

CARILLON v -LONNED, -LONNING, -LONS to play a set of bells

CARINA n pl. -NAS or -NAE a carinate anatomical part CARINAL adj

CARINATE adj shaped like the keel of a ship

CARING present participle of care

CARIOCA n pl. -S a South American dance

CARIOLE n pl. -S a small, open carriage

CARIOUS adj decayed

CARK v -ED, -ING, -S to worry

CARL n pl. -S a peasant

CARLE n pl. -S carl

CARLESS adj being without a car

CARLIN n pl. -S an old woman

CARLINE n pl. -S carling

CARLING n pl. -S a beam supporting a ship's deck

CARLISH adj resembling a carl

CARLOAD n pl. -S as much as a car can hold

CARMAKER n pl. -S an automobile manufacturer

CARMAN n pl. -MEN a streetcar driver

CARMINE n pl. -S a vivid red color

CARN n pl. -S cairn

CARNAGE n pl. -S great and bloody slaughter

CARNAL adj pertaining to bodily appetites CARNALLY adv

CARNAUBA n pl. -S a palm tree

CARNEY n pl. -NEYS carny

CARNIE n pl. -S carny

CARNIES pl. of carny

CARNIFY v -FIED, -FYING, -FIES to form into flesh

CARNIVAL n pl. -S a traveling amusement show

CARNY n pl. -NIES a carnival

CAROACH n pl. -ES caroche

CAROB n pl. -S an evergreen tree

CAROCH n pl. -ES caroche

CAROCHE n pl. -S a stately carriage

CAROL v -OLED, -OLING, -OLS or -OLLED, -OLLING, -OLS to sing joyously

CAROLER n pl. -S one that carols

CAROLI a pl. of carolus

CAROLLED a past tense of carol

CAROLLER n pl. -S caroler

CAROLLING a present participle of carol

CAROLUS n pl. -LUSES or -LI an old English coin

CAROM v -ED, -ING, -S to collide with and rebound

CAROTENE n pl. -S a plant pigment

CAROTID   *n* pl. -S an artery in the neck

CAROTIN   *n* pl. -S carotene

CAROUSAL   *n* pl. -S a boisterous drinking party

CAROUSE   *v* -ROUSED, -ROUSING, -ROUSES to engage in a carousal

CAROUSEL   *n* pl. -S an amusement park ride

CAROUSER   *n* pl. -S one that carouses

CAROUSING present participle of carouse

CARP   *v* -ED, -ING, -S to find fault unreasonably

CARPAL   *n* pl. -S carpale

CARPALE   *n* pl. -LIA a bone of the wrist

CARPEL   *n* pl. -S a simple pistil

CARPER   *n* pl. -S one that carps

CARPET   *v* -ED, -ING, -S to cover a floor with a heavy fabric

CARPI   pl. of carpus

CARPING   *n* pl. -S the act of one who carps

CARPORT   *n* pl. -S a shelter for a car

CARPUS   *n* pl. -PI the wrist

CARRACK   *n* pl. -S a type of merchant ship

CARREL   *n* pl. -S a desk in a library stack for solitary study

CARRELL   *n* pl. -S carrel

CARRIAGE   *n* pl. -S a wheeled, horse-drawn vehicle

CARRIED   past tense of carry

CARRIER   *n* pl. -S one that carries

CARRIES   present 3d person sing. of carry

CARRIOLE   *n* pl. -S cariole

CARRION   *n* pl. -S dead and putrefying flesh

CARRITCH   *n* pl. -ES a religious handbook

CARROCH   *n* pl. -ES caroche

CARROM   *v* -ED, -ING, -S to carom

CARROT   *n* pl. -S an edible orange root

CARROTIN   *n* pl. -S carotene

CARROTY   *adj* -ROTIER, -ROTIEST resembling a carrot in color

CARRY   *v* -RIED, -RYING, -RIES to convey from one place to another

CARRYALL   *n* pl. -S a light covered carriage

CARRYON   *n* pl. -S a small piece of luggage

CARRYOUT   *n* pl. -S a take-out order of food

CARSE   *n* pl. -S low, fertile land along a river

CARSICK   *adj* nauseated from riding in a car

CART   *v* -ED, -ING, -S to convey in a cart (a two-wheeled vehicle) **CARTABLE** *adj*

CARTAGE   *n* pl. -S the act of carting

CARTE   *n* pl. -S a menu

CARTEL   *n* pl. -S a business organization

CARTER   *n* pl. -S one that carts

CARTLOAD   *n* pl. -S as much as a cart can hold

CARTON   *v* -ED, -ING, -S to pack in a cardboard box

CARTOON   *v* -ED, -ING, -S to sketch a humorous representation of

CARTOP   *adj* able to fit on top of a car

CARTOUCH   *n* pl. -ES a scroll-like tablet

CARUNCLE   *n* pl. -S a fleshy outgrowth

CARVE   *v* CARVED, CARVING, CARVES to form by cutting

CARVEL   *n* pl. -S caravel

CARVEN   *adj* carved

CARVER   *n* pl. -S one that carves

CARVING   *n* pl. -S a carved figure or design

CARYATID   *n* pl. -S or -ES a sculptured female figure used as a column

CARYOTIN   *n* pl. -S karyotin

CASA   *n* pl. -S a dwelling

CASABA   *n* pl. -S a variety of melon

CASAVA   *n* pl. -S cassava

CASCABEL   *n* pl. -S the rear part of a cannon

CASCABLE   *n* pl. -S cascabel

CASCADE   *v* -CADED, -CADING, -CADES to fall like a waterfall

CASCARA   *n* pl. -S a medicinal tree bark

CASE   *v* CASED, CASING, CASES to put in a case (a container or receptacle)

CASEASE   *n* pl. -S an enzyme

CASEATE   *v* -ATED, -ATING, -ATES to become cheesy

CASEBOOK   *n* pl. -S a law textbook

CASED   past tense of case

CASEFY   *v* -FIED, -FYING, -FIES to caseate

CASEIN   *n* pl. -S a milk protein **CASEIC** *adj*

CASEMATE   *n* pl. -S a bombproof shelter

CASEMENT   *n* pl. -S a type of window

CASEOSE   n pl. -S a proteose

CASEOUS   adj cheesy

CASERN   n pl. -S a barracks for soldiers

CASERNE   n pl. -S casern

CASETTE   n pl. -S cassette

CASEWORK   n pl. -S a form of social work

CASEWORM   n pl. -S an insect larva

CASH   v -ED, -ING, -ES to convert into cash (ready money) CASHABLE adj

CASHAW   n pl. -S cushaw

CASHBOOK   n pl. -S a book of monetary records

CASHBOX   n pl. -ES a container for money

CASHEW   n pl. -S a nut-bearing tree

CASHIER   v -ED, -ING, -S to dismiss in disgrace

CASHLESS   adj having no cash

CASHMERE   n pl. -S a fine wool

CASHOO   n pl. -SHOOS catechu

CASIMERE   n pl. -S a woolen fabric

CASIMIRE   n pl. -S casimere

CASING   n pl. -S a protective outer covering

CASINO   n pl. -NOS a gambling room

CASK   v -ED, -ING, -S to store in a cask (a strong barrel)

CASKET   v -ED, -ING, -S to place in a burial case

CASKY   adj resembling a cask

CASQUE   n pl. -S a helmet CASQUED adj

CASSABA   n pl. -S casaba

CASSAVA   n pl. -S a tropical plant

CASSETTE   n pl. -S a small case containing audiotape or videotape

CASSIA   n pl. -S a variety of cinnamon

CASSINO   n pl. -NOS a card game

CASSIS   n pl. -SISES a European bush

CASSOCK   n pl. -S a long garment worn by clergymen

CAST   v CAST, CASTING, CASTS to throw with force

CASTANET   n pl. -S a rhythm instrument

CASTAWAY   n pl. -WAYS an outcast

CASTE   n pl. -S a system of distinct social classes

CASTEISM   n pl. -S the use of a caste system

CASTER   n pl. -S a small, swiveling wheel

CASTING   n pl. -S something made in a mold

CASTLE   v -TLED, -TLING, -TLES to make a certain move in chess

CASTOFF   n pl. -S a discarded person or thing

CASTOR   n pl. -S caster

CASTRATE   v -TRATED, -TRATING, -TRATES to remove the testes of

CASTRATO   n pl. -TI a singer castrated in boyhood

CASUAL   n pl. -S one who works occasionally

CASUALLY   adv informally

CASUALTY   n pl. -TIES a victim of war or disaster

CASUIST   n pl. -S one who resolves ethical problems

CASUS   n pl. CASUS a legal occurrence or event

CAT   v CATTED, CATTING, CATS to hoist an anchor to the cathead

CATACOMB   n pl. -S an underground cemetery

CATALASE   n pl. -S an enzyme

CATALO   n pl. -LOS or -LOES a hybrid between a buffalo and a cow

CATALOG   v -ED, -ING, -S to classify information descriptively

CATALPA   n pl. -S a tree

CATALYST   n pl. -S a substance that accelerates a chemical reaction

CATALYZE   v -LYZED, -LYZING, -LYZES to act as a catalyst

CATAMITE   n pl. -S a boy used in sodomy

CATAPULT   v -ED, -ING, -S to hurl through the air

CATARACT   n pl. -S a tremendous waterfall

CATARRH   n pl. -S inflammation of a mucous membrane

CATBIRD   n pl. -S a songbird

CATBOAT   n pl. -S a small sailboat

CATBRIER   n pl. -S a thorny vine

CATCALL   v -ED, -ING, -S to deride by making shrill sounds

CATCH   v CAUGHT, CATCHING, CATCHES to capture after pursuit

CATCHALL   n pl. -S a container for odds and ends

CATCHER   n pl. -S one that catches

CATCHFLY   n pl. -FLIES an insect-catching plant

CATCHUP *n* pl. -S ketchup

CATCHY *adj* CATCHIER, CATCHIEST pleasing and easily remembered

CATE *n* pl. -S a choice food

CATECHIN *n* pl. -S a chemical used in dyeing

CATECHOL *n* pl. -S a chemical used in photography

CATECHU *n* pl. -S a resin used in tanning

CATEGORY *n* pl. -RIES a division in any system of classification

CATENA *n* pl. -NAS or -NAE a closely linked series

CATENARY *n* pl. -NARIES a mathematical curve

CATENATE *v* -NATED, -NATING, -NATES to link together

CATENOID *n* pl. -S a geometric surface

CATER *v* -ED, -ING, -S to provide food and service for

CATERAN *n* pl. -S a brigand

CATERER *n* pl. -S one that caters

CATERESS *n* pl. -ES a woman who caters

CATFACE *n* pl. -S a deformity of fruit

CATFALL *n* pl. -S an anchor line

CATFISH *n* pl. -ES a scaleless, large-headed fish

CATGUT *n* pl. -S a strong cord

CATHEAD *n* pl. -S a beam projecting from a ship's bow

CATHECT *v* -ED, -ING, -S to invest with psychic energy

CATHEDRA *n* pl. -DRAS or -DRAE a bishop's throne

CATHETER *n* pl. -S a medical instrument

CATHEXIS *n* pl. -THEXES the concentration of psychic energy on a person or idea

CATHODE *n* pl. -S a negatively charged electrode **CATHODIC** *adj*

CATHOLIC *adj* universal

CATHOUSE *n* pl. -S a brothel

CATION *n* pl. -S a positively charged ion **CATIONIC** *adj*

CATKIN *n* pl. -S a flower cluster

CATLIKE *adj* resembling a cat; stealthy; silent

CATLIN *n* pl. -S catling

CATLING *n* pl. -S a surgical knife

CATMINT *n* pl. -S catnip

CATNAP *v* -NAPPED, -NAPPING, -NAPS to doze

CATNAPER *n* pl. -S one that steals cats

CATNIP *n* pl. -S an aromatic herb

CATSPAW *n* pl. -S a light wind

CATSUP *n* pl. -S ketchup

CATTAIL *n* pl. -S a marsh plant

CATTALO *n* pl. -LOS or -LOES catalo

CATTED past tense of cat

CATTIE *n* pl. -S an Asian unit of weight

CATTIER comparative of catty

CATTIEST superlative of catty

CATTILY *adv* in a catty manner

CATTING present participle of cat

CATTISH *adj* catty

CATTLE *n/pl* domesticated bovines

CATTLEYA *n* pl. -S a tropical orchid

CATTY *adj* -TIER, -TIEST catlike; spiteful

CATWALK *n* pl. -S a narrow walkway

CAUCUS *v* -CUSED, -CUSING, -CUSES or -CUSSED, -CUSSING, -CUSSES to hold a political meeting

CAUDAD *adv* toward the tail

CAUDAL *adj* taillike **CAUDALLY** *adv*

CAUDATE *adj* having a tail

CAUDATED *adj* caudate

CAUDEX *n* pl. -DICES or -DEXES the woody base of some plants

CAUDILLO *n* pl. -LLOS a military dictator

CAUDLE *n* pl. -S a warm beverage

CAUGHT past tense of catch

CAUL *n* pl. -S a fetal membrane

CAULD *n* pl. -S cold

CAULDRON *n* pl. -S caldron

CAULES pl. of caulis

CAULICLE *n* pl. -S a small stem

CAULINE *adj* pertaining to a stem

CAULIS *n* pl. -LES a plant stem

CAULK *v* -ED, -ING, -S to make the seams of a ship watertight

CAULKER *n* pl. -S one that caulks

CAULKING *n* pl. -S the material used to caulk

CAUSABLE *adj* capable of being caused

CAUSAL *n* pl. -S a word expressing cause or reason

CAUSALLY *adv* by way of causing

CAUSE *v* CAUSED, CAUSING, CAUSES to bring about

CAUSER *n* pl. -S one that causes

CAUSERIE *n* pl. -S an informal conversation

CAUSEWAY v -ED, -ING, -S to build a raised roadway over

CAUSEY n pl. -SEYS a paved road

CAUSING present participle of cause

CAUSTIC n pl. -S a corrosive substance

CAUTERY n pl. -TERIES something used to destroy tissue

CAUTION v -ED, -ING, -S to warn

CAUTIOUS adj exercising prudence to avoid danger

CAVALERO n pl. -ROS a horseman

CAVALIER v -ED, -ING, -S to behave haughtily

CAVALLA n pl. -S a large food fish

CAVALLY n pl. -LIES cavalla

CAVALRY n pl. -RIES a mobile army unit

CAVATINA n pl. -NAS or -NE a simple song

CAVE v CAVED, CAVING, CAVES to hollow out

CAVEAT n pl. -S a legal warning

CAVEATOR n pl. -S one that files a caveat

CAVED past tense of cave

CAVEFISH n pl. -ES a sightless fish

CAVELIKE adj resembling a cave (an underground chamber)

CAVEMAN n pl. -MEN a cave dweller

CAVER n pl. -S one that caves

CAVERN v -ED, -ING, -S to hollow out

CAVETTO n pl. -TOS or -TI a concave molding

CAVIAR n pl. -S the roe of sturgeon

CAVIARE n pl. -S caviar

CAVICORN adj having hollow horns

CAVIE n pl. -S a hencoop

CAVIES pl. of cavy

CAVIL v -ILED, -ILING, -ILS or -ILLED, -ILLING, -ILS to carp

CAVILER n pl. -S one that cavils

CAVILLER n pl. -S caviler

CAVILLING a present participle of cavil

CAVING present participle of cave

CAVITARY adj pertaining to the formation of cavities in tissue

CAVITATE v -TATED, -TATING, -TATES to form cavities

CAVITY n pl. -TIES an unfilled space within a mass CAVITIED adj

CAVORT v -ED, -ING, -S to frolic

CAVORTER n pl. -S one that cavorts

CAVY n pl. -VIES a short-tailed rodent

CAW v -ED, -ING, -S to utter the sound of a crow

CAY n pl. CAYS a small, low island

CAYENNE n pl. -S a hot seasoning CAYENNED adj

CAYMAN n pl. -S caiman

CAYUSE n pl. -S an Indian pony

CAZIQUE n pl. -S cacique

CEASE v CEASED, CEASING, CEASES to stop

CEBID n pl. -S ceboid

CEBOID n pl. -S one of a family of monkeys

CECUM n pl. CECA a bodily cavity with one opening CECAL adj CECALLY adv

CEDAR n pl. -S an evergreen tree CEDARN adj

CEDE v CEDED, CEDING, CEDES to yield

CEDER n pl. -S one that cedes

CEDI n pl. -S a monetary unit of Ghana

CEDILLA n pl. -S a pronunciation mark

CEDING present participle of cede

CEDULA n pl. -S a Philippine tax

CEE n pl. -S the letter C

CEIBA n pl. -S a tropical tree

CEIL v -ED, -ING, -S to furnish with a ceiling

CEILER n pl. -S one that ceils

CEILING n pl. -S the overhead lining of a room

CEINTURE n pl. -S a belt for the waist

CELADON n pl. -S a pale green color

CELEB n pl. -S a celebrity; a famous person

CELERIAC n pl. -S a variety of celery

CELERITY n pl. -TIES swiftness

CELERY n pl. -ERIES a plant with edible stalks

CELESTA n pl. -S a keyboard instrument

CELESTE n pl. -S celesta

CELIAC adj pertaining to the abdomen

CELIBACY n pl. -CIES abstention from sexual intercourse

CELIBATE n pl. -S one who lives a life of celibacy

CELL v -ED, -ING, -S to store in a honeycomb

CELLA n pl. -LAE the interior of an ancient temple

CELLAR v -ED, ING, -S to store in an underground room

CELLARER n pl. -S the steward of a monastery

CELLARET n pl. -S a cabinet for wine bottles

CELLIST n pl. -S one who plays the cello

CELLO n pl. -LOS or -LI a stringed musical instrument

CELLULAR adj pertaining to a cell (a basic unit of life)

CELLULE n pl. -S a small cell

CELOM n pl. -LOMS or -LOMATA coelom

CELT n pl. -S a primitive ax

CEMBALO n pl. -LI or -LOS a harpsichord

CEMENT v -ED, -ING, -S to bind firmly

CEMENTER n pl. -S one that cements

CEMENTUM n pl. -TA the hard tissue covering the roots of the teeth

CEMETERY n pl. -TERIES a burial ground

CENACLE n pl. -S a small dining room

CENOBITE n pl. -S a member of a religious order

CENOTAPH n pl. -S an empty tomb

CENOTE n pl. -S a sinkhole in limestone

CENSE v CENSED, CENSING, CENSES to perfume with incense

CENSER n pl. -S a vessel for burning incense

CENSOR v -ED, -ING, -S to delete an objectionable word or passage

CENSUAL adj pertaining to the act of censusing

CENSURE v -SURED, -SURING, -SURES to criticize severely

CENSURER n pl. -S one that censures

CENSUS v -ED, -ING, -ES to take an official count of

CENT n pl. -S the 100th part of a dollar

CENTAL n pl. -S a unit of weight

CENTARE n pl. -S a measure of land area

CENTAUR n pl. -S a mythological creature

CENTAURY n pl. -RIES a medicinal herb

CENTAVO n pl. -VOS a coin of various Spanish-American nations

CENTER v -ED, -ING, -S to place at the center (the midpoint)

CENTESIS n pl. -TESES a surgical puncture

CENTIARE n pl. -S centare

CENTILE n pl. -S a value of a statistical variable

CENTIME n pl. -S the 100th part of a franc

CENTIMO n pl. -MOS any of various small coins

CENTNER n pl. -S a unit of weight

CENTO n pl. -TONES or -TOS a literary work made up of parts from other works

CENTRA a pl. of centrum

CENTRAL n pl. -S a telephone exchange

CENTRAL adj -TRALER, -TRALEST situated at, in, or near the center

CENTRE v -TRED, -TRING, -TRES to center

CENTRIC adj situated at the center

CENTRING n pl. -S a temporary framework for an arch

CENTRISM n pl. -S moderate political philosophy

CENTRIST n pl. -S an advocate of centrism

CENTROID n pl. -S the center of mass of an object

CENTRUM n pl. -TRUMS or -TRA the body of a vertebra

CENTUM n pl. -S one hundred

CENTUPLE v -PLED, -PLING, -PLES to increase a hundredfold

CENTURY n pl. -RIES a period of 100 years

CEORL n pl. -S a freeman of low birth **CEORLISH** adj

CEPHALAD adv toward the head

CEPHALIC adj pertaining to the head

CEPHALIN n pl. -S a bodily chemical

CERAMAL n pl. -S a heat-resistant alloy

CERAMIC n pl. -S an item made of baked clay

CERAMIST n pl. -S one who makes ceramics

CERASTES n pl. CERASTES a venomous snake

CERATE n pl. -S a medicated ointment

CERATED adj covered with wax

CERATIN n pl. -S keratin

CERATOID adj hornlike

CERCARIA n pl. -IAE or -IAS a parasitic worm

CERCIS n pl. -CISES a shrub

CERCUS n pl. CERCI a sensory appendage of an insect

CERE   v CERED, CERING, CERES to wrap in a waxy cloth

CEREAL   n pl. -S a food made from grain

CEREBRAL   n pl. -S a kind of consonant

CEREBRUM   n pl. -BRUMS or -BRA a part of the brain CEREBRIC adj

CERED   past tense of cere

CEREMENT   n pl. -S a waxy cloth

CEREMONY   n pl. -NIES a formal observance

CEREUS   n pl. -ES a tall cactus

CERIA   n pl. -S a chemical compound

CERIC   adj containing cerium

CERING   present participle of cere

CERIPH   n pl. -S serif

CERISE   n pl. -S a red color

CERITE   n pl. -S a mineral

CERIUM   n pl. -S a metallic element

CERMET   n pl. -S ceramal

CERNUOUS   adj drooping or nodding

CERO   n pl. CEROS a large food fish

CEROTIC   adj pertaining to beeswax

CEROTYPE   n pl. -S a process of engraving using wax

CEROUS   adj pertaining to cerium

CERTAIN   adj -TAINER, -TAINEST absolutely confident

CERTES   adv in truth

CERTIFY   v -FIED, -FYING, -FIES to confirm

CERULEAN   n pl. -S a blue color

CERUMEN   n pl. -S a waxy secretion of the ear

CERUSE   n pl. -S a lead compound

CERUSITE   n pl. -S a lead ore

CERVELAT   n pl. -S a smoked sausage

CERVICAL   adj pertaining to the cervix

CERVINE   adj pertaining to deer

CERVIX   n pl. -VICES or -VIXES the neck

CESAREAN   n pl. -S a method of child delivery

CESARIAN   n pl. -S cesarean

CESIUM   n pl. -S a metallic element

CESS   v -ED, -ING, -ES to tax or assess

CESSION   n pl. -S the act of ceding

CESSPIT   n pl. -S a cesspool

CESSPOOL   n pl. -S a covered well or pit for sewage

CESTA   n pl. -S a basket used in jai alai

CESTI   pl. of cestus

CESTODE   n pl. -S a tapeworm

CESTOID   n pl. -S cestode

CESTOS   n pl. -TOI cestus

CESTUS   n pl. -TI a belt or girdle

CESTUS   n pl. -ES a hand covering for ancient Roman boxers

CESURA   n pl. -RAS or -RAE caesura

CETACEAN   n pl. -S an aquatic mammal

CETANE   n pl. -S a diesel fuel

CETE   n pl. -S a group of badgers

CETOLOGY   n pl. -GIES the study of whales

CHABOUK   n pl. -S a type of whip

CHABUK   n pl. -S chabouk

CHACMA   n pl. -S a large baboon

CHACONNE   n pl. -S an ancient dance

CHAD   n pl. -S a scrap of paper CHADLESS adj

CHADARIM   a pl. of cheder

CHAETA   n pl. -TAE a bristle or seta CHAETAL adj

CHAFE   v CHAFED, CHAFING, CHAFES to warm by rubbing

CHAFER   n pl. -S a large beetle

CHAFF   v -ED, -ING, -S to poke fun at

CHAFFER   v -ED, -ING, -S to bargain or haggle

CHAFFY   adj CHAFFIER, CHAFFIEST worthless

CHAFING   present participle of chafe

CHAGRIN   v -GRINED, -GRINING, -GRINS or -GRINNED, -GRINNING, -GRINS to humiliate

CHAIN   v -ED, -ING, -S to bind with a chain (a series of connected rings)

CHAINE   n pl. -S a series of ballet turns

CHAINMAN   n pl. -MEN a surveyor's assistant who uses a measuring chain

CHAIR   v -ED, -ING, -S to install in office

CHAIRMAN   n pl. -MEN the presiding officer of a meeting

CHAIRMAN   v -MANED, -MANING, -MANS or -MANNED, -MANNING, -MANS to act as chairman of a meeting

CHAISE   n pl. -S a light carriage

CHALAH   n pl. -LAHS, -LOTH or -LOT challah

CHALAZA   n pl. -ZAS or -ZAE a band of tissue in an egg CHALAZAL adj

CHALCID   n pl. -S a tiny fly

CHALDRON   n pl. -S a unit of dry measure

CHALEH *n pl.* -S challah

CHALET *n pl.* -S a Swiss cottage

CHALICE *n pl.* -S a drinking cup
CHALICED *adj*

CHALK *v* -ED, -ING, -S to mark with
chalk (a soft limestone)

CHALKY *adj* CHALKIER, CHALKIEST
resembling chalk

CHALLAH *n pl.* -LAHS, -LOTH, or -LOT a
kind of bread

CHALLIE *n pl.* -S challis

CHALLIES *pl. of* chally

CHALLIS *n pl.* -LISES a light fabric

CHALLOT *a pl. of* challah

CHALLOTH *a pl. of* challah

CHALLY *n pl.* -LIES challis

CHALONE *n pl.* -S a hormone

CHALOT *a pl. of* chalah

CHALOTH *a pl. of* chalah

CHALUTZ *n pl.* -LUTZIM halutz

CHAM *n pl.* -S a khan

CHAMADE *n pl.* -S a signal made with a
drum

CHAMBER *v* -ED, -ING, -S to put in a
chamber (a room)

CHAMBRAY *n pl.* -BRAYS a fine fabric

CHAMFER *v* -ED, -ING, -S to groove

CHAMFRON *n pl.* -S armor for a horse's
head

CHAMISE *n pl.* -S chamiso

CHAMISO *n pl.* -SOS a flowering shrub

CHAMMY *v* -MIED, -MYING, -MIES to
chamois

CHAMOIS *n pl.* -OIX a soft leather

CHAMOIS *v* -ED, -ING, -ES to prepare
leather like chamois

CHAMP *v* -ED, -ING, -S to chew noisily

CHAMPAC *n pl.* -S champak

CHAMPAK *n pl.* -S an East Indian tree

CHAMPER *n pl.* -S one that champs

CHAMPION *v* -ED, -ING, -S to defend or
support

CHAMPY *adj* broken up by the trampling
of beasts

CHANCE *v* CHANCED, CHANCING,
CHANCES to risk

CHANCEL *n pl.* -S an area around a
church altar

CHANCERY *n pl.* -CERIES a court of public
record

CHANCIER *comparative of* chancy

CHANCIEST *superlative of* chancy

CHANCILY *adv* in a chancy manner

CHANCING *present participle of* chance

CHANCRE *n pl.* -S a hard-based sore

CHANCY *adj* CHANCIER, CHANCIEST
risky

CHANDLER *n pl.* -S a dealer in provisions

CHANFRON *n pl.* -S chamfron

CHANG *n pl.* -S a cattie

CHANGE *v* CHANGED, CHANGING,
CHANGES to make different

CHANGER *n pl.* -S one that changes

CHANNEL *v* -NELED, -NELING, -NELS or
-NELLED, -NELLING, -NELS to
direct along some desired
course

CHANSON *n pl.* -S a song

CHANT *v* -ED, -ING, -S to sing

CHANTAGE *n pl.* -S blackmail

CHANTER *n pl.* -S one that chants

CHANTEY *n pl.* -TEYS a sailor's song

CHANTIES *pl. of* chanty

CHANTOR *n pl.* -S chanter

CHANTRY *n pl.* -TRIES an endowment
given to a church

CHANTY *n pl.* -TIES chantey

CHAOS *n pl.* -ES a state of total
disorder; a confused mass
CHAOTIC *adj*

CHAP *v* CHAPPED or CHAPT,
CHAPPING, CHAPS to split,
crack, or redden

CHAPBOOK *n pl.* -S a small book of popular
tales

CHAPE *n pl.* -S a part of a scabbard

CHAPEAU *n pl.* -PEAUX or -PEAUS a hat

CHAPEL *n pl.* -S a place of worship

CHAPERON *v* -ED, -ING, -S to accompany

CHAPITER *n pl.* -S the capital of a column

CHAPLAIN *n pl.* -S a clergyman attached
to a chapel

CHAPLET *n pl.* -S a wreath for the head

CHAPMAN *n pl.* -MEN a peddler

CHAPPED *a past tense of* chap

CHAPPING *present participle of* chap

CHAPT *a past tense of* chap

CHAPTER *v* -ED, -ING, -S to divide a book
into main sections

CHAQUETA *n pl.* -S a jacket worn by
cowboys

CHAR *v* CHARRED, CHARRING,
CHARS to burn slightly

CHARACID *n pl.* -S characin

CHARACIN n pl. -S a tropical fish

CHARADE n pl. -S a word represented by pantomime

CHARAS n pl. -ES hashish

CHARCOAL v -ED, -ING, -S to blacken with charcoal (a dark, porous carbon)

CHARD n pl. -S a variety of beet

CHARE v CHARED, CHARING, CHARES to do small jobs

CHARGE v CHARGED, CHARGING, CHARGES to accuse formally

CHARGER n pl. -S one that charges

CHARIER comparative of chary

CHARIEST superlative of chary

CHARILY adv in a chary manner

CHARING present participle of chare

CHARIOT v -ED, -ING, -S to ride in a type of cart

CHARISM n pl. -S charisma

CHARISMA n pl. -MATA a special magnetic appeal

CHARITY n pl. -TIES something given to the needy

CHARK v -ED, -ING, -S to char

CHARKA n pl. -S charkha

CHARKHA n pl. -S a spinning wheel

CHARLADY n pl. -DIES a cleaning woman

CHARLOCK n pl. -S a troublesome weed

CHARM v -ED, -ING, -S to attract irresistibly

CHARMER n pl. -S one that charms

CHARMING adj -INGER, -INGEST pleasing

CHARNEL n pl. -S a room where corpses are placed

CHARPAI n pl. -S charpoy

CHARPOY n pl. -POYS a bed used in India

CHARQUI n pl. -S a type of meat CHARQUID adj

CHARR n pl. -S a small-scaled trout

CHARRED past tense of char

CHARRIER comparative of charry

CHARRIEST superlative of charry

CHARRING present participle of char

CHARRO n pl. -ROS a cowboy

CHARRY adj -RIER, -RIEST resembling charcoal

CHART v -ED, -ING, -S to map out

CHARTER v -ED, -ING, -S to lease or hire

CHARTIST n pl. -S a stock market specialist

CHARY adj CHARIER, CHARIEST cautious

CHASE v CHASED, CHASING, CHASES to pursue

CHASER n pl. -S one that chases

CHASING n pl. -S a design engraved on metal

CHASM n pl. -S a deep cleft in the earth CHASMAL, CHASMED, CHASMIC, CHASMY adj

CHASSE v CHASSED, CHASSEING, CHASSES to perform a dance movement

CHASSEUR n pl. -S a cavalry soldier

CHASSIS n pl. CHASSIS the frame of a car

CHASTE adj CHASTER, CHASTEST morally pure CHASTELY adv

CHASTEN v -ED, -ING, -S to chastise

CHASTISE v -TISED, -TISING, -TISES to discipline by punishment

CHASTITY n pl. -TIES moral purity

CHASUBLE n pl. -S a sleeveless vestment

CHAT v CHATTED, CHATTING, CHATS to converse informally

CHATEAU n pl. -TEAUX or -TEAUS a large country house

CHATTEL n pl. -S a slave

CHATTER v -ED, -ING, -S to talk rapidly and trivially CHATTERY adj

CHATTING present participle of chat

CHATTY adj -TIER, -TIEST talkative CHATTILY adv

CHAUFER n pl. -S chauffer

CHAUFFER n pl. -S a small furnace

CHAUNT v -ED, -ING, -S to chant

CHAUNTER n pl. -S one that chaunts

CHAUSSES n/pl medieval armor

CHAW v -ED, -ING, -S to chew

CHAWER n pl. -S one that chaws

CHAYOTE n pl. -S a tropical vine

CHAZAN n pl. -ZANS or -ZANIM a cantor

CHAZZEN n pl. -ZENS or -ZENIM chazan

CHEAP adj CHEAPER, CHEAPEST inexpensive

CHEAP n pl. -S a market

CHEAPEN v -ED, -ING, -S to make cheap

CHEAPIE n pl. -S one that is cheap

CHEAPISH adj somewhat cheap

CHEAPLY adv in a cheap manner

CHEAT v -ED, -ING, -S to defraud

CHEATER n pl. -S one that cheats

CHEBEC n pl. -S a small bird

CHECHAKO n pl. -KOS a newcomer

CHECK v -ED, -ING, -S to inspect

CHECKER v -ED, -ING, -S to mark with squares

CHECKOFF n pl. -S a method of collecting union dues

CHECKOUT n pl. -S a test of a machine

CHECKROW v -ED, -ING, -S to plant in rows which divide the land into squares

CHECKUP n pl. -S an examination

CHEDDAR n pl. -S a type of cheese

CHEDDITE n pl. -S chedite

CHEDER n pl. CHADARIM or CHEDERS heder

CHEDITE n pl. -S an explosive

CHEEK v -ED, -ING, -S to speak impudently to

CHEEKFUL n pl. -S the amount held in one's cheek

CHEEKY adj CHEEKIER, CHEEKIEST impudent CHEEKILY adv

CHEEP v -ED, -ING, -S to chirp

CHEEPER n pl. -S one that cheeps

CHEER v -ED, -ING, -S to applaud with shouts of approval

CHEERER n pl. -S one that cheers

CHEERFUL adj -FULLER, -FULLEST full of spirits

CHEERIER comparative of cheery

CHEERIEST superlative of cheery

CHEERILY adv in a cheery manner

CHEERIO n pl. -IOS a greeting

CHEERO n pl. CHEEROS cheerio

CHEERY adj CHEERIER, CHEERIEST cheerful

CHEESE v CHEESED, CHEESING, CHEESES to stop

CHEESY adj CHEESIER, CHEESIEST resembling cheese (a food made from milk curds) CHEESILY adv

CHEETAH n pl. -S a swift-running wildcat

CHEF n pl. -S a chief cook

CHEFDOM n pl. -S the status or function of a chef

CHEGOE n pl. -S a chigoe

CHELA n pl. -LAE a pincerlike claw

CHELA n pl. -S a pupil of a guru

CHELATE v -LATED, -LATING, -LATES to subject a compound to combination with a metal ion

CHELATOR n pl. -S one that chelates

CHELOID n pl. -S keloid

CHEMIC n pl. -S a chemist

CHEMICAL n pl. -S a substance obtained by a process of chemistry (the science of the various properties and transformations of substances)

CHEMISE n pl. -S a loose dress

CHEMISM n pl. -S chemical attraction

CHEMIST n pl. -S one versed in chemistry

CHEMURGY n pl. -GIES a branch of applied chemistry

CHENILLE n pl. -S a soft fabric

CHENOPOD n pl. -S a flowering plant

CHEQUE n pl. -S a written order directing a bank to pay money

CHEQUER v -ED, -ING, -S to checker

CHERISH v -ED, -ING, -ES to hold dear

CHEROOT n pl. -S a square-cut cigar

CHERRY n pl. -RIES a fruit

CHERT n pl. -S a compact rock

CHERTY adj CHERTIER, CHERTIEST resembling chert

CHERUB n pl. -UBS or -UBIM an angel CHERUBIC adj

CHERVIL n pl. -S an aromatic herb

CHESS n pl. -ES a weed

CHESSMAN n pl. -MEN one of the pieces used in chess (a board game for two players)

CHEST n pl. -S a part of the body CHESTED adj

CHESTFUL n pl. -S as much as a chest or box can hold

CHESTNUT n pl. -S an edible nut

CHESTY adj CHESTIER, CHESTIEST proud

CHETAH n pl. -S cheetah

CHETH n pl. -S heth

CHEVALET n pl. -S a part of a stringed instrument

CHEVERON n pl. -S chevron

CHEVIED past tense of chevy

CHEVIES present 3d person sing. of chevy

CHEVIOT n pl. -S a coarse fabric

CHEVRON n pl. -S a V-shaped pattern

CHEVY v CHEVIED, CHEVYING, CHEVIES to chase about

CHEW	v -ED, -ING, -S to crush or grind with the teeth CHEWABLE adj	CHIGOE	n pl. -S a tropical flea
		CHILD	n pl. CHILDREN a young person
CHEWER	n pl. -S one that chews	CHILDBED	n pl. -S the state of a woman giving birth
CHEWINK	n pl. -S a common finch		
CHEWY	adj CHEWIER, CHEWIEST not easily chewed	CHILDE	n pl. -S a youth of noble birth
		CHILDING	adj pregnant
CHEZ	prep at the home of	CHILDISH	adj resembling a child
CHI	n pl. -S a Greek letter	CHILDLY	adj -LIER, -LIEST resembling a child
CHIA	n pl. -S a Mexican herb		
CHIAO	n pl. CHIAO a monetary unit of China	CHILDREN	pl. of child
		CHILE	n pl. -S chili
CHIASM	n pl. -S chiasma	CHILI	n pl. -ES a hot pepper
CHIASMA	n pl. -MATA or -MAS an anatomical junction CHIASMAL, CHIASMIC adj	CHILIAD	n pl. -S a group of one thousand
		CHILIASM	n pl. -S a religious doctrine
CHIASMUS	n pl. -MI a reversal of word order between parallel phrases CHIASTIC adj	CHILIAST	n pl. -S a supporter of chiliasm
		CHILL	v -ED, -ING, -S to make cold
		CHILL	adj CHILLER, CHILLEST cool
CHIAUS	n pl. -ES a Turkish messenger	CHILLER	n pl. -S one that chills
CHIBOUK	n pl. -S a tobacco pipe	CHILLI	n pl. -ES chili
CHIC	n pl. -S elegance	CHILLUM	n pl. -S a part of a water pipe
CHICANE	v -CANED, -CANING, -CANES to trick	CHILLY	adj CHILLIER, CHILLIEST cool CHILLILY adv
CHICANER	n pl. -S one that chicanes		
CHICCORY	n pl. -RIES chicory	CHILOPOD	n pl. -S a multi-legged insect
CHICHI	n pl. -S elaborate ornamentation	CHIMAERA	n pl. -S a marine fish
		CHIMAR	n pl. -S chimere
CHICK	n pl. -S a young bird	CHIMB	n pl. -S the rim of a cask
CHICKEN	v -ED, -ING, -S to lose one's nerve	CHIMBLEY	n pl. -BLEYS chimley
		CHIMBLY	n pl. -BLIES chimley
CHICKPEA	n pl. -S an Asian herb	CHIME	v CHIMED, CHIMING, CHIMES to ring harmoniously
CHICLE	n pl. -S a tree gum		
CHICLY	adv in an elegant manner	CHIMER	n pl. -S one that chimes
CHICNESS	n pl. -ES elegance	CHIMERA	n pl. -S an imaginary monster
CHICO	n pl. -COS a prickly shrub	CHIMERE	n pl. -S a bishop's robe
CHICORY	n pl. -RIES a perennial herb	CHIMERIC	adj imaginary; unreal
CHIDE	v CHIDED or CHID, CHIDDEN, CHIDING, CHIDES to scold	CHIMING	present participle of chime
		CHIMLA	n pl. -S chimley
CHIDER	n pl. -S one that chides	CHIMLEY	n pl. -LEYS a chimney
CHIEF	adj CHIEFER, CHIEFEST highest in authority	CHIMNEY	n pl. -NEYS a flue
		CHIMP	n pl. -S a chimpanzee
CHIEF	n pl. -S the person highest in authority	CHIN	v CHINNED, CHINNING, CHINS to hold with the chin (the lower part of the face)
CHIEFDOM	n pl. -S the domain of a chief		
CHIEFLY	adv above all	CHINA	n pl. -S fine porcelain ware
CHIEL	n pl. -S chield	CHINBONE	n pl. -S the lower jaw
CHIELD	n pl. -S a young man	CHINCH	n pl. -ES a bedbug
CHIFFON	n pl. -S a sheer fabric	CHINCHY	adj CHINCHIER, CHINCHIEST stingy
CHIGETAI	n pl. -S a wild ass		
CHIGGER	n pl. -S a parasitic mite	CHINE	v CHINED, CHINING, CHINES to cut through the backbone of
CHIGNON	n pl. -S a woman's hairdo		

CHINK v -ED, -ING, -S to fill cracks or fissures in

CHINKY adj CHINKIER, CHINKIEST full of cracks

CHINLESS adj lacking a chin

CHINNED past tense of chin

CHINNING present participle of chin

CHINO n pl. -NOS a strong fabric

CHINONE n pl. -S quinone

CHINOOK n pl. -S a warm wind

CHINTS n pl. -ES chintz

CHINTZ n pl. -ES a cotton fabric

CHINTZY adj CHINTZIER, CHINTZIEST gaudy; cheap

CHIP v CHIPPED, CHIPPING, CHIPS to break a small piece from

CHIPMUCK n pl. -S a chipmunk

CHIPMUNK n pl. -S a small rodent

CHIPPED past tense of chip

CHIPPER v -ED, -ING, -S to chirp

CHIPPIE n pl. -S chippy

CHIPPING present participle of chip

CHIPPY n pl. -PIES a prostitute

CHIRK v -ED, -ING, -S to make a shrill noise

CHIRK adj CHIRKER, CHIRKEST cheerful

CHIRM v -ED, -ING, -S to chirp

CHIRO n pl. -ROS a marine fish

CHIRP v -ED, -ING, -S to utter a short, shrill sound

CHIRPER n pl. -S one that chirps

CHIRPY adj CHIRPIER, CHIRPIEST cheerful CHIRPILY adv

CHIRR v -ED, -ING, -S to make a harsh, vibrant sound

CHIRRE v CHIRRED, CHIRRING, CHIRRES to chirr

CHIRRUP v -ED, -ING, -S to chirp repeatedly CHIRRUPY adj

CHISEL v -ELED, -ELING, -ELS or -ELLED, -ELLING, -ELS to use a chisel (a cutting tool)

CHISELER n pl. -S one that chisels

CHIT n pl. -S a short letter

CHITAL n pl. CHITAL an Asian deer

CHITCHAT v -CHATTED, -CHATTING, -CHATS to indulge in small talk

CHITIN n pl. -S the main component of insect shells

CHITLIN n pl. -S chitling

CHITLING n pl. -S a part of the small intestine of swine

CHITON n pl. -S a tunic worn in ancient Greece

CHITTER v -ED, -ING, -S to twitter

CHITTY n pl. -TIES a chit

CHIVALRY n pl. -RIES knightly behavior and skill

CHIVAREE v -REED, -REEING, -REES to perform a mock serenade

CHIVARI v -ED, -ING, -ES to chivaree

CHIVE n pl. -S an herb used as a seasoning

CHIVVY v -VIED, -VYING, -VIES to chevy

CHIVY v CHIVIED, CHIVYING, CHIVIES to chevy

CHLAMYS n pl. -MYSES or -MYDES a garment worn in ancient Greece

CHLORAL n pl. -S a chemical compound

CHLORATE n pl. -S a chemical salt

CHLORDAN n pl. -S a toxic compound of chlorine

CHLORIC adj pertaining to chlorine

CHLORID n pl. -S chloride

CHLORIDE n pl. -S a chlorine compound

CHLORIN n pl. -S chlorine

CHLORINE n pl. -S a gaseous element

CHLORITE n pl. -S a mineral group

CHLOROUS adj pertaining to chlorine

CHOCK v -ED, -ING, -S to secure with a wedge of wood or metal

CHOICE n pl. -S one that is chosen

CHOICE adj CHOICER, CHOICEST of fine quality CHOICELY adv

CHOIR v -ED, -ING, -S to sing in unison

CHOIRBOY n pl. -BOYS a boy who sings in a body of church singers

CHOKE v CHOKED, CHOKING, CHOKES to impede the breathing of

CHOKER n pl. -S one that chokes

CHOKEY adj CHOKIER, CHOKIEST choky

CHOKING present participle of choke

CHOKY adj CHOKIER, CHOKIEST tending to cause choking

CHOLATE n pl. -S a chemical salt

CHOLER n pl. -S anger

CHOLERA n pl. -S an acute disease

CHOLERIC adj bad-tempered

CHOLINE n pl. -S a B vitamin

CHOLLA n pl. -S a treelike cactus

CHOMP v -ED, -ING, -S to champ

CHON n pl. CHON a monetary unit of South Korea

CHOOSE v CHOSE, CHOSEN, CHOOSING, CHOOSES to take by preference

CHOOSER n pl. -S one that chooses

CHOOSEY adj CHOOSIER, CHOOSIEST choosy

CHOOSING present participle of choose

CHOOSY adj CHOOSIER, CHOOSIEST hard to please

CHOP v CHOPPED, CHOPPING, CHOPS to sever with a sharp tool

CHOPIN n pl. -S chopine

CHOPINE n pl. -S a type of shoe

CHOPPED past tense of chop

CHOPPER n pl. -S one that chops

CHOPPING present participle of chop

CHOPPY adj CHOPPIER, CHOPPIEST full of short, rough waves CHOPPILY adv

CHORAGUS n pl. -GI or -GUSES the leader of a chorus or choir CHORAGIC adj

CHORAL n pl. -S chorale

CHORALE n pl. -S a hymn that is sung in unison

CHORALLY adv harmoniously

CHORD v -ED, -ING, -S to play a chord (a combination of three or more musical tones)

CHORDAL adj pertaining to a chord

CHORDATE n pl. -S any of a large phylum of animals

CHORE v CHORED, CHORING, CHORES to do small jobs

CHOREA n pl. -S a nervous disorder CHOREAL, CHOREIC adj

CHOREGUS n pl. -GI or -GUSES choragus

CHOREMAN n pl. -MEN a menial worker

CHOREOID adj resembling chorea

CHORIAL adj pertaining to the chorion

CHORIAMB n pl. -S a type of metrical foot

CHORIC adj pertaining to a chorus

CHORINE n pl. -S a chorus girl

CHORING present participle of chore

CHORIOID n pl. -S choroid

CHORION n pl. -S an embryonic membrane

CHORIZO n pl. -ZOS a highly seasoned sausage

CHOROID n pl. -S a membrane of the eye

CHORTLE v -TLED, -TLING, -TLES to chuckle with glee

CHORTLER n pl. -S one that chortles

CHORUS v -RUSED, -RUSING, -RUSES or -RUSSED, -RUSSING, -RUSSES to sing in unison

CHOSE n pl. -S an item of personal property

CHOSEN past participle of choose

CHOTT n pl. -S a saline lake

CHOUGH n pl. -S a crow-like bird

CHOUSE v CHOUSED, CHOUSING, CHOUSES to swindle

CHOUSER n pl. -S one that chouses

CHOUSH n pl. -ES chiaus

CHOUSING present participle of chouse

CHOW v -ED, -ING, -S to eat

CHOWCHOW n pl. -S a relish of mixed pickles in mustard

CHOWDER v -ED, -ING, -S to make a thick soup of

CHOWSE v CHOWSED, CHOWSING, CHOWSES to chouse

CHOWTIME n pl. -S mealtime

CHRESARD n pl. -S the available water of the soil

CHRISM n pl. -S a consecrated oil CHRISMAL adj

CHRISMON n pl. -MA or -MONS a Christian monogram

CHRISOM n pl. -S chrism

CHRISTEN v -ED, -ING, -S to baptize

CHRISTIE n -S christy

CHRISTY n pl. -TIES a skiing turn

CHROMA n pl. -S the purity of a color

CHROMATE n pl. -S a chemical salt

CHROME v CHROMED, CHROMING, CHROMES to plate with chromium

CHROMIC adj pertaining to chromium

CHROMIDE n pl. -S a tropical fish

CHROMING present participle of chrome

CHROMITE n pl. -S a chromium ore

CHROMIUM n pl. -S a metallic element

CHROMIZE v -MIZED, -MIZING, MIZES to chrome

CHROMO n pl. -MOS a type of color picture

CHROMOUS adj pertaining to chromium

CHROMYL *adj* containing chromium

CHRONAXY *n* pl. -AXIES the time required to excite a nerve cell electrically

CHRONIC *n* pl. -S one that suffers from a long-lasting disease

CHRONON *n* pl. -S a hypothetical unit of time

CHTHONIC *adj* pertaining to the gods of the underworld

CHUB *n* pl. -S a freshwater fish

CHUBASCO *n* pl. -COS a violent thunderstorm

CHUBBY *adj* -BIER, -BIEST plump **CHUBBILY** *adv*

CHUCK *v* -ED, -ING, -S to throw

CHUCKIES pl. of chucky

CHUCKLE *v* -LED, -LING, -LES to laugh quietly

CHUCKLER *n* pl. -S one that chuckles

CHUCKY *n* pl. CHUCKIES a little chick

CHUDDAH *n* pl. -S chuddar

CHUDDAR *n* pl. -S a large, square shawl

CHUDDER *n* pl. -S chuddar

CHUFA *n* pl. -S a European sedge

CHUFF *adj* CHUFFER, CHUFFEST gruff

CHUFF *v* -ED, -ING, -S to chug

CHUFFY *adj* -FIER, -FIEST plump

CHUG *v* CHUGGED, CHUGGING, CHUGS to move with a dull explosive sound

CHUGGER *n* pl. -S one that chugs

CHUKAR *n* pl. -S a game bird

CHUKKA *n* pl. -S a type of boot

CHUKKAR *n* pl. -S chukker

CHUKKER *n* pl. -S a period of play in polo

CHUM *v* CHUMMED, CHUMMING, CHUMS to be close friends with someone

CHUMMY *adj* -MIER, -MIEST friendly **CHUMMILY** *adv*

CHUMP *v* -ED, -ING, -S to munch

CHUMSHIP *n* pl. -S friendship

CHUNK *v* -ED, -ING, -S to make a dull explosive sound

CHUNKY *adj* CHUNKIER, CHUNKIEST stocky **CHUNKILY** *adv*

CHUNTER *v* -ED, -ING, -S to mutter

CHURCH *v* -ED, -ING, -ES to bring to church (a building for Christian worship)

CHURCHLY *adj* -LIER, -LIEST pertaining to a church

CHURCHY *adj* CHURCHIER, CHURCHIEST churchly

CHURL *n* pl. -S a rude person **CHURLISH** *adj*

CHURN *v* -ED, -ING, -S to stir briskly in order to make butter

CHURNER *n* pl. -S one that churns

CHURNING *n* pl. -S the butter churned at one time

CHURR *v* -ED, -ING, -S to make a vibrant sound

CHUTE *v* CHUTED, CHUTING, CHUTES to convey by chute (a vertical passage)

CHUTIST *n* pl. -S a parachutist

CHUTNEE *n* pl. -S chutney

CHUTNEY *n* pl. -NEYS a sweet and sour sauce

CHUTZPA *n* pl. -S chutzpah

CHUTZPAH *n* pl. -S supreme self-confidence

CHYLE *n* pl. -S a digestive fluid **CHYLOUS** *adj*

CHYME *n* pl. -S semi-digested food

CHYMIC *n* pl. -S chemic

CHYMIST *n* pl. -S chemist

CHYMOSIN *n* pl. -S rennin

CHYMOUS *adj* pertaining to chyme

CIAO *interj* —used as an expression of greeting and farewell

CIBOL *n* pl. -S a variety of onion

CIBORIUM *n* pl. -RIA a vessel for holding holy bread

CIBOULE *n* pl. -S cibol

CICADA *n* pl. -DAS or -DAE a winged insect

CICALA *n* pl. -LAS or -LE cicada

CICATRIX *n* pl. -TRICES scar tissue

CICELY *n* pl. -LIES a fragrant herb

CICERO *n* pl. -ROS a unit of measure in printing

CICERONE *n* pl. -NES or -NI a tour guide

CICHLID *n* pl. -LIDS or -LIDAE a tropical fish

CICISBEO *n* pl. -BEI a lover of a married woman

CICOREE *n* pl. -S a perennial herb

CIDER *n* pl. -S the juice pressed from apples

CIGAR *n* pl. -S a roll of tobacco leaf for smoking

CIGARET *n* pl. -S a narrow roll of finely cut tobacco for smoking

CILANTRO n pl. -TROS an herb used in cooking

CILIA pl. of cilium

CILIARY adj pertaining to cilia

CILIATE n pl. -S one of a class of ciliated protozoans

CILIATED adj having cilia

CILICE n pl. -S a coarse cloth

CILIUM n pl. CILIA a short, hairlike projection

CIMEX n pl. -MICES a bedbug

CINCH v -ED, -ING, -ES to girth

CINCHONA n pl. -S a Peruvian tree

CINCTURE v -TURED, -TURING, -TURES to gird or encircle

CINDER v -ED, -ING, -S to reduce to cinders (ashes))

CINDERY adj containing cinders

CINE n pl. -S a motion picture

CINEAST n pl. -S a devotee of motion pictures

CINEASTE n pl. -S cineast

CINEMA n pl. -S a motion-picture theater

CINEOL n pl. -S a liquid used as an antiseptic

CINEOLE n pl. -S cineol

CINERARY adj used for cremated ashes

CINERIN n pl. -S a compound used in insecticides

CINGULUM n pl. -LA an anatomical band or girdle

CINNABAR n pl. -S the principal ore of mercury

CINNAMON n pl. -S spice obtained from tree bark CINNAMIC adj

CINNAMYL n pl. -S a chemical used to make soap

CINQUAIN n pl. -S a stanza of five lines

CINQUE n pl. -S the number five

CION n pl. -S a cutting from a plant or tree

CIPHER v -ED, -ING, -S to solve problems in arithmetic

CIPHONY n pl. -NIES the electronic scrambling of voice transmissions

CIPOLIN n pl. -S a type of marble

CIRCA prep about; around

CIRCLE v -CLED, -CLING, -CLES to move or revolve around

CIRCLER n pl. -S one that circles

CIRCLET n pl. -S a small ring or ring-shaped object

CIRCLING present participle of circle

CIRCUIT v -ED, -ING, -S to move around

CIRCUITY n pl. -ITIES lack of straightforwardness

CIRCULAR n pl. -S a leaflet intended for wide distribution

CIRCUS n pl. -ES a public entertainment CIRCUSY adj

CIRQUE n pl. -S a deep, steep-walled basin

CIRRATE adj having cirri

CIRRI pl. of cirrus

CIRRIPED n pl. -S any of an order of crustaceans

CIRROSE adj cirrous

CIRROUS adj having cirri

CIRRUS n pl. -RI a tendril or similar part

CIRSOID adj varicose

CISCO n pl. -COS or -COES a freshwater fish

CISLUNAR adj situated between the earth and the moon

CISSOID n pl. -S a type of geometric curve

CIST n pl. -S a prehistoric stone coffin

CISTERN n pl. -S a water tank

CISTERNA n pl. -NAE a fluid-containing sac

CISTRON n pl. -S a segment of DNA

CITABLE adj citeable

CITADEL n pl. -S a fortress or stronghold

CITATION n pl. -S the act of citing CITATORY adj

CITE v CITED, CITING, CITES to quote as an authority or example

CITEABLE adj suitable for citation

CITER n pl. -S one that cites

CITHARA n pl. -S an ancient stringed instrument

CITHER n pl. -S cittern

CITHERN n pl. -S cittern

CITHREN n pl. -S cittern

CITIED adj having cities

CITIES pl. of city

CITIFY v -FIED, -FYING, -FIES to urbanize

CITING present participle of cite

CITIZEN n pl. -S a resident of a city or town

CITOLA   n pl. -S a cittern

CITOLE   n pl. -S citola

CITRAL   n pl. -S a lemon flavoring

CITRATE   n pl. -S a salt of citric acid
CITRATED adj

CITREOUS   adj having a lemonlike color

CITRIC   adj derived from citrus fruits

CITRIN   n pl. -S a citric vitamin

CITRINE   n pl. -S a variety of quartz

CITRON   n pl. -S a lemonlike fruit

CITROUS   adj pertaining to a citrus tree

CITRUS   n pl. -ES any of a genus of
tropical, fruit-bearing trees

CITTERN   n pl. -S a pear-shaped guitar

CITY   n pl. CITIES a large town

CITYFIED   adj having the customs and
manners of city people

CITYWARD   adv toward the city

CIVET   n pl. -S a catlike mammal

CIVIC   adj pertaining to a city

CIVICISM   n pl. -S a system of
government based upon
individual rights

CIVICS   n/pl the science of civic affairs

CIVIE   n pl. -S civvy

CIVIL   adj pertaining to citizens

CIVILIAN   n pl. -S a nonmilitary person

CIVILISE   v -LISED, -LISING, -LISES to
civilize

CIVILITY   n pl. -TIES courtesy; politeness

CIVILIZE   v -LIZED, -LIZING, -LIZES to
bring out of savagery

CIVILLY   adv politely

CIVISM   n pl. -S good citizenship

CIVVY   n pl. -VIES a civilian

CLABBER   v -ED, -ING, -S to curdle

CLACH   n pl. -S clachan

CLACHAN   n pl. -S a hamlet

CLACK   v -ED, -ING, -S to make an
abrupt, dry sound

CLACKER   n pl. -S one that clacks

CLAD   v CLAD, CLADDING, CLADS to
coat one metal over another

CLADDING   n pl. -S something that overlays

CLADODE   n pl. -S a leaflike part of a
stem

CLAG   v CLAGGED, CLAGGING,
CLAGS to clog

CLAIM   v -ED, -ING, -S to demand as
one's due

CLAIMANT   n pl. -S one that asserts a right
or title

CLAIMER   n pl. -S one that claims

CLAM   v CLAMMED, CLAMMING,
CLAMS to dig for clams (bivalve
mollusks)

CLAMANT   adj noisy

CLAMBAKE   n pl. -S a beach picnic

CLAMBER   v -ED, -ING, -S to climb
awkwardly

CLAMMED   past tense of clam

CLAMMING   present participle of clam

CLAMMY   adj CLAMMIER, CLAMMIEST
cold and damp CLAMMILY adv

CLAMOR   v -ED, -ING, -S to make loud
outcries

CLAMORER   n pl. -S one that clamors

CLAMOUR   v -ED, -ING, -S to clamor

CLAMP   v -ED, -ING, -S to fasten with a
clamp (a securing device)

CLAMPER   n pl. -S a device worn on
shoes to prevent slipping on ice

CLAMWORM   n pl. -S a marine worm

CLAN   n pl. -S a united group of
families

CLANG   v -ED, -ING, -S to ring loudly

CLANGOR   v -ED, -ING, -S to clang
repeatedly

CLANGOUR   v -ED, -ING, -S to clangor

CLANK   v -ED, -ING, -S to make a
sharp, metallic sound

CLANNISH   adj characteristic of a clan

CLANSMAN   n pl. -MEN a member of a clan

CLAP   v CLAPPED or CLAPT,
CLAPPING, CLAPS to strike one
palm against the other

CLAPPER   n pl. -S one that claps

CLAPTRAP   n pl. -S pretentious language

CLAQUE   n pl. -S a group of hired
applauders

CLAQUER   n pl. -S claqueur

CLAQUEUR   n pl. -S a member of a claque

CLARENCE   n pl. -S a closed carriage

CLARET   n pl. -S a dry red wine

CLARIES   pl. of clary

CLARIFY   v -FIED, -FYING, -FIES to make
clear

CLARINET   n pl. -S a woodwind instrument

CLARION   v -ED, -ING, -S to proclaim by
blowing a medieval trumpet

CLARITY   n pl. -TIES the state of being
clear

CLARKIA   n pl. -S an annual herb

CLARO   n pl. -ROS or -ROES a mild
cigar

CLARY n pl. CLARIES an aromatic herb

CLASH v -ED, -ING, -ES to conflict or disagree

CLASHER n pl. -S one that clashes

CLASP v CLASPED or CLASPT, CLASPING, CLASPS to embrace tightly

CLASPER n pl. -S one that clasps

CLASS v -ED, -ING, -ES to classify

CLASSER n pl. -S one that classes

CLASSES pl. of classis

CLASSIC n pl. -S a work of enduring excellence

CLASSIER comparative of classy

CLASSIEST superlative of classy

CLASSIFY v -FIED, -FYING, -FIES to arrange according to characteristics

CLASSIS n pl. CLASSES a governing body in certain churches

CLASSY adj CLASSIER, CLASSIEST stylish; elegant CLASSILY adv

CLAST n pl. -S a fragment of rock

CLASTIC n pl. -S a rock made up of other rocks

CLATTER v -ED, -ING, -S to move with a rattling noise

CLATTERY adj having a rattling noise

CLAUCHT a past tense of cleek

CLAUGHT v -ED, -ING, -S to clutch

CLAUSE n pl. -S a distinct part of a composition CLAUSAL adj

CLAVATE adj shaped like a club

CLAVE a past tense of cleave

CLAVER v -ED, -ING, -S to gossip

CLAVICLE n pl. -S a bone of the shoulder

CLAVIER n pl. -S a keyboard instrument

CLAW v -ED, -ING, -S to scratch with claws (sharp, curved toenails)

CLAWER n pl. -S one that claws

CLAWLESS adj having no claws

CLAXON n pl. -S klaxon

CLAY v -ED, -ING, -S to treat with clay (a fine-grained, earthy material)

CLAYBANK n pl. -S a yellow-brown color

CLAYEY adj CLAYIER, CLAYIEST resembling clay

CLAYISH adj resembling or containing clay

CLAYLIKE adj resembling clay

CLAYMORE n pl. -S a type of sword

CLAYPAN n pl. -S a shallow natural depression

CLAYWARE n pl. -S pottery

CLEAN adj CLEANER, CLEANEST free from dirt or stain

CLEAN v -ED, -ING, -S to rid of dirt or stain

CLEANER n pl. -S one that cleans

CLEANLY adj -LIER, -LIEST habitually clean

CLEANSE v CLEANSED, CLEANSING, CLEANSES to clean

CLEANSER n pl. -S one that cleanses

CLEANUP n pl. -S an act of cleaning

CLEAR adj CLEARER, CLEAREST clean and pure

CLEAR v -ED, -ING, -S to remove obstructions

CLEARER n pl. -S one that clears

CLEARING n pl. -S an open space

CLEARLY adv in a clear manner

CLEAT v -ED, -ING, -S to strengthen with a strip of wood or iron

CLEAVAGE n pl. -S the act of cleaving

CLEAVE v CLEAVED, CLEFT, CLOVE or CLAVE, CLOVEN, CLEAVING, CLEAVES to split or divide

CLEAVER n pl. -S a heavy knife

CLEEK v CLAUCHT or CLEEKED, CLEEKING, CLEEKS to clutch

CLEF n pl. -S a musical symbol

CLEFT n pl. -S a space or opening made by cleavage

CLEMATIS n pl. -TISES a flowering vine

CLEMENCY n pl. -CIES mercy

CLEMENT adj merciful

CLENCH v -ED, -ING, -ES to grasp firmly

CLEOME n pl. -S a tropical plant

CLEPE v CLEPED or CLEPT, CLEPING, CLEPES to call by name

CLERGY n pl. -GIES the body of men ordained for religious service

CLERIC n pl. -S a member of the clergy

CLERICAL n pl. -S a cleric

CLERID n pl. -S a predatory beetle

CLERIHEW n pl. -S a humorous poem

CLERISY n pl. -SIES the well-educated class

CLERK v -ED, -ING, -S to serve as a clerk (an office worker)

CLERKDOM n pl. -S the status or function of a clerk

CLERKISH *adj* resembling or suitable to a clerk

CLERKLY *adj* -LIER, -LIEST pertaining to a clerk

CLEVEITE *n pl.* -S a radioactive mineral

CLEVER *adj* -ERER, -EREST mentally keen **CLEVERLY** *adv*

CLEVIS *n pl.* -ISES a metal fastening device

CLEW *v* -ED, -ING, -S to roll into a ball

CLICHE *n pl.* -S a trite expression **CLICHED** *adj*

CLICK *v* -ED, -ING, -S to make a short, sharp sound

CLICKER *n pl.* -S one that clicks

CLIENT *n pl.* -S a customer **CLIENTAL** *adj*

CLIFF *n pl.* -S a high, steep face of rock

CLIFFY *adj* CLIFFIER, CLIFFIEST abounding in cliffs

CLIFT *n pl.* -S cliff

CLIMATE *n pl.* -S the weather conditions characteristic of an area **CLIMATAL, CLIMATIC** *adj*

CLIMAX *v* -ED, -ING, -ES to reach a high or dramatic point

CLIMB *v* CLIMBED or CLOMB, CLIMBING, CLIMBS to ascend

CLIMBER *n pl.* -S one that climbs

CLIME *n pl.* -S climate

CLINAL *adj* pertaining to a cline

CLINALLY *adv* in a clinal manner

CLINCH *v* -ED, -INGS, -ES to settle a matter decisively

CLINCHER *n pl.* -S a decisive fact or remark

CLINE *n pl.* -S a series of changes within a species

CLING *v* CLUNG, CLINGING, CLINGS to adhere closely

CLING *v* -ED, -ING, -S to make a high-pitched ringing sound

CLINGER *n pl.* -S one that clings

CLINGY *adj* CLINGIER, CLINGIEST adhesive

CLINIC *n pl.* -S a medical facility **CLINICAL** *adj*

CLINK *v* -ED, -ING, -S to make a soft, sharp, ringing sound

CLINKER *v* -ED, -ING, -S to form fused residue in burning

CLIP *v* CLIPPED, CLIPT, CLIPPING, CLIPS to trim by cutting

CLIPPER *n pl.* -S one that clips

CLIPPING *n pl.* -S something that is clipped out or off

CLIPT a past participle of clip

CLIQUE *v* CLIQUED, CLIQUING, CLIQUES to form a clique (an exclusive group of persons)

CLIQUEY *adj* CLIQUIER, CLIQUIEST inclined to form cliques

CLIQUISH *adj* cliquey

CLIQUY *adj* CLIQUIER, CLIQUIEST cliquey

CLITELLA *n/pl* regions in the body walls of certain annelids

CLITORIS *n pl.* -RISES a sex organ **CLITORAL, CLITORIC** *adj*

CLIVERS *n pl.* CLIVERS an annual herb

CLOACA *n pl.* -ACAE a sewer **CLOACAL** *adj*

CLOAK *v* -ED, -ING, -S to conceal

CLOBBER *v* -ED, -ING, -S to trounce

CLOCHE *n pl.* -S a bell-shaped hat

CLOCK *v* -ED, -ING, -S to time with a stopwatch

CLOCKER *n pl.* -S one that clocks

CLOD *n pl.* -S a dolt **CLODDISH** *adj*

CLODDY *adj* -DIER, -DIEST lumpy

CLODPATE *n pl.* -S a stupid person

CLODPOLE *n pl.* -S clodpate

CLODPOLL *n pl.* -S clodpate

CLOG *v* CLOGGED, CLOGGING, CLOGS to block up or obstruct

CLOGGY *adj* -GIER, -GIEST clogging or able to clog

CLOISTER *v* -ED, -ING, -S to seclude

CLOMB a past tense of climb

CLOMP *v* -ED, -ING, -S to walk heavily and clumsily

CLON *n pl.* -S a group of asexually derived organisms **CLONAL** *adj* **CLONALLY** *adv*

CLONE *v* CLONED, CLONING, CLONES to reproduce by asexual means

CLONIC *adj* pertaining to clonus

CLONISM *n pl.* -S the condition of having clonus

CLONK *v* -ED, -ING, -S to make a dull thumping sound

CLONUS *n pl.* -ES a form of muscular spasm

CLOOT *n pl.* -S a cloven hoof

CLOP *v* CLOPPED, CLOPPING, CLOPS to make the sound of a hoof striking pavement

CLOSE *adj* CLOSER, CLOSEST near CLOSELY *adv*

CLOSE *v* CLOSED, CLOSING, CLOSES to block against entry or passage CLOSABLE *adj*

CLOSEOUT *n pl.* -S a clearance sale

CLOSER *n pl.* -S one that closes

CLOSEST superlative of close

CLOSET *v* -ED, -ING, -S to enclose in a private room

CLOSING *n pl.* -S a concluding part

CLOSURE *v* -SURED, -SURING, -SURES to cloture

CLOT *v* CLOTTED, CLOTTING, CLOTS to form into a clot (a thick mass)

CLOTH *n pl.* -S fabric

CLOTHE *v* CLOTHED or CLAD, CLOTHING, CLOTHES to provide with clothing

CLOTHIER *n pl.* -S one who makes or sells clothing

CLOTHING *n pl.* -S wearing apparel

CLOTTED past tense of clot

CLOTTING present participle of clot

CLOTTY *adj* tending to clot

CLOTURE *v* -TURED, -TURING, -TURES to end a debate by calling for a vote

CLOUD *v* -ED, -ING, -S to cover with clouds (masses of visible vapor)

CLOUDLET *n pl.* -S a small cloud

CLOUDY *adj* CLOUDIER, CLOUDIEST overcast with clouds CLOUDILY *adv*

CLOUGH *n pl.* -S a ravine

CLOUR *v* -ED, -ING, -S to knock or bump

CLOUT *v* -ED, -ING, -S to hit with the hand

CLOUTER *n pl.* -S one that clouts

CLOVE *n pl.* -S a spice

CLOVEN *adj* split; divided

CLOVER *n pl.* -S a plant

CLOWDER *n pl.* -S a group of cats

CLOWN *v* -ED, -ING, -S to act like a clown (a humorous performer)

CLOWNERY *n pl.* -ERIES clownish behavior

CLOWNISH *adj* resembling or befitting a clown

CLOY *v* -ED, -ING, -S to gratify beyond desire

CLOZE *adj* pertaining to a type of reading comprehension test

CLUB *v* CLUBBED, CLUBBING, CLUBS to form a club (an organized group of persons)

CLUBABLE *adj* sociable

CLUBBER *n pl.* -S a member of a club

CLUBBING present participle of club

CLUBBY *adj* -BIER, -BIEST characteristic of a club

CLUBFOOT *n pl.* -FEET a deformed foot

CLUBHAND *n pl.* -S a deformed hand

CLUBHAUL *v* -ED, -ING, -S to put a vessel about

CLUBMAN *n pl.* -MEN a male member of a club

CLUBROOT *n pl.* -S a plant disease

CLUCK *v* -ED, -ING, -S to make the sound of a hen

CLUE *v* CLUED, CLUEING or CLUING, CLUES to give guiding information

CLUMBER *n pl.* -S a stocky spaniel

CLUMP *v* -ED, -ING, -S to form into a thick mass

CLUMPISH *adj* resembling a clump (a thick mass)

CLUMPY *adj* CLUMPIER, CLUMPIEST lumpy

CLUMSY *adj* -SIER, -SIEST awkward CLUMSILY *adv*

CLUNG past tense of cling

CLUNK *v* -ED, -ING, -S to thump

CLUNKER *n pl.* -S a jalopy

CLUPEID *n pl.* -S a fish of the herring family

CLUPEOID *n pl.* -S a clupeid

CLUSTER *v* -ED, -ING, -S to form into a cluster (a group of similar objects)

CLUSTERY *adj* pertaining to a cluster

CLUTCH *v* -ED, -ING, -ES to grasp and hold tightly

CLUTCHY *adj* tending to clutch

CLUTTER *v* -ED, -ING, -S to pile in a disorderly state

CLYPEUS *n pl.* CLYPEI a shield-like structure CLYPEAL, CLYPEATE *adj*

CLYSTER *n pl.* -S an enema

COACH *v* -ED, -ING, -ES to tutor or train

COACHER *n pl.* -S one that coaches

COACHMAN *n pl.* -MEN one who drives a coach or carriage

COACT *v* -ED, -ING, -S to act together

COACTION *n* pl. -S joint action

COACTIVE *adj* mutually active

COADMIRE *v* -MIRED, -MIRING, -MIRES to admire together

COADMIT *v* -MITTED, -MITTING, -MITS to admit several things equally

COAEVAL *n* pl. -S coeval

COAGENCY *n* pl. -CIES a joint agency

COAGENT *n* pl. -S a person, force, or other agent working together with another

COAGULUM *n* pl. -LA or -LUMS a clot

COAL *v* -ED, -ING, -S to supply with coal (a carbon fuel)

COALA *n* pl. -S koala

COALBIN *n* pl. -S a bin for storing coal

COALBOX *n* pl. -ES a box for storing coal

COALER *n* pl. -S one that supplies coal

COALESCE *v* -ALESCED, -ALESCING, -ALESCES to blend

COALFISH *n* pl. -ES a blackish fish

COALHOLE *n* pl. -S a compartment for storing coal

COALIFY *v* -FIED, -FYING, -FIES to convert into coal

COALLESS *adj* lacking coal

COALPIT *n* pl. -S a pit from which coal is obtained

COALSACK *n* pl. -S a dark region of the Milky Way

COALSHED *n* pl. -S a shed for storing coal

COALYARD *n* pl. -S a yard for storing coal

COAMING *n* pl. -S a raised border

COANNEX *v* -ED, -ING, -ES to annex jointly

COAPPEAR *v* -ED, -ING, -S to appear together or at the same time

COAPT *v* -ED, -ING, -S to fit together and make fast

COARSE *adj* COARSER, COARSEST rough COARSELY *adv*

COARSEN *v* -ED, -ING, -S to make coarse

COASSIST *v* -ED, -ING, -S to assist jointly

COASSUME *v* -SUMED, -SUMING, -SUMES to assume together

COAST *v* -ED, -ING, -S to slide down a hill

COASTAL *adj* pertaining to or located near a seashore

COASTER *n* pl. -S a sled

COASTING *n* pl. -S coastal trade

COAT *v* -ED, -ING, -S to cover with a coat (an outer garment)

COATEE *n* pl. -S a small coat

COATER *n* pl. -S one that coats

COATI *n* pl. -S a tropical mammal

COATING *n* pl. -S a covering layer

COATLESS *adj* lacking a coat

COATRACK *n* pl. -S a rack or stand for coats

COATROOM *n* pl. -S a room for storing coats

COATTAIL *n* pl. -S the back lower portion of a coat

COATTEND *v* -ED, -ING, -S to attend together

COATTEST *v* -ED, -ING, -S to attest jointly

COAUTHOR *v* -ED, -ING, -S to write together

COAX *v* -ED, -ING, -ES to cajole

COAXAL *adj* coaxial

COAXER *n* pl. -S one that coaxes

COAXIAL *adj* having a common axis

COB *n* pl. -S a corncob

COBALT *n* pl. -S a metallic element COBALTIC *adj*

COBB *n* pl. -S a sea gull

COBBER *n* pl. -S a comrade

COBBIER comparative of cobby

COBBIEST superlative of cobby

COBBLE *v* -BLED, -BLING, -BLES to mend

COBBLER *n* pl. -S a mender of shoes

COBBY *adj* -BIER, -BIEST stocky

COBIA *n* pl. -S a large game fish

COBLE *n* pl. -S a small fishing boat

COBNUT *n* pl. -S an edible nut

COBRA *n* pl. -S a venomous snake

COBWEB *v* -WEBBED, -WEBBING, -WEBS to cover with cobwebs (spider webs)

COBWEBBY *adj* -BIER, -BIEST covered with cobwebs

COCA *n* pl. -S a South American shrub

COCAIN *n* pl. -S cocaine

COCAINE *n* pl. -S a narcotic alkaloid

COCCAL *adj* pertaining to a coccus

COCCI pl. of coccus

COCCIC *adj* coccal

COCCID *n* pl. -S an insect

COCCIDIA *n/pl* parasitic protozoans

COCCOID *n* pl. -S a spherical cell or body

COCCUS *n* pl. COCCI a spherical bacterium COCCOUS *adj*

COCCYX n pl. -CYGES or -CYXES a bone of the spine

COCHAIR v -ED, -ING, -S to serve jointly as chairman of

COCHIN n pl. -S a large domestic chicken

COCHLEA n pl. -CHLEAE or -CHLEAS a part of the ear **COCHLEAR** adj

COCINERA n pl. -S a cook

COCK v -ED, -ING, -S to tilt to one side

COCKADE n pl. -S an ornament worn on a hat **COCKADED** adj

COCKATOO n pl. -TOOS a parrot

COCKBILL v -ED, -ING, -S to raise the yardarm on a ship

COCKBOAT n pl. -S a small boat

COCKCROW n pl. -S daybreak

COCKER v -ED, -ING, -S to pamper

COCKEREL n pl. -S a young rooster

COCKEYE n pl. -S a squinting eye **COCKEYED** adj

COCKIER comparative of cocky

COCKIEST superlative of cocky

COCKILY adv in a cocky manner

COCKISH adj cocky

COCKLE v -LED, -LING, -LES to wrinkle or pucker

COCKLIKE adj resembling a rooster

COCKLOFT n pl. -S a small attic

COCKNEY n pl. -NEYS a resident of the East End of London

COCKPIT n pl. -S a pilot's compartment in certain airplanes

COCKSHUT n pl. -S the close of day

COCKSHY n pl. -SHIES a target in a throwing contest

COCKSPUR n pl. -S a thorny plant

COCKSURE adj certain

COCKTAIL v -ED, -ING, -S to drink alcoholic beverages

COCKUP n pl. -S a turned-up part of something

COCKY adj COCKIER, COCKIEST arrogantly self-confident

COCO n pl. -COS a tall palm tree

COCOA n pl. -S chocolate

COCOANUT n pl. -S coconut

COCOBOLA n pl. -S cocobolo

COCOBOLO n pl. -LOS a tropical tree

COCOMAT n pl. -S a matting made from coir

COCONUT n pl. -S the fruit of the coco

COCOON v -ED, -ING, -S to wrap or envelop tightly

COCOTTE n pl. -S a prostitute

COCREATE v -ATED, -ATING, -ATES to create together

COD n pl. -S a marine food fish

CODA n pl. -S a passage at the end of a musical composition

CODABLE adj capable of being coded

CODDER n pl. -S a cod fisherman

CODDLE v -DLED, -DLING, -DLES to pamper

CODDLER n pl. -S one that coddles

CODE v CODED, CODING, CODES to convert into symbols

CODEBTOR n pl. -S one that shares a debt

CODEIA n pl. -S codeine

CODEIN n pl. -S codeine

CODEINA n pl. -S codeine

CODEINE n pl. -S a narcotic alkaloid

CODELESS adj being without a set of laws

CODEN n pl. -S a coding classification

CODER n pl. -S one that codes

CODERIVE v -RIVED, -RIVING, -RIVES to derive jointly

CODEX n pl. -DICES an ancient manuscript

CODFISH n pl. -ES the cod

CODGER n pl. -S an old man

CODICES pl. of codex

CODICIL n pl. -S a supplement to a will

CODIFIER n pl. -S one that codifies

CODIFY v -FIED, -FYING, -FIES to arrange or systematize

CODING present participle of code

CODLIN n pl. -S codling

CODLING n pl. -S an unripe apple

CODON n pl. -S a triplet of nucleotides (basic components of DNA)

CODPIECE n pl. -S a cover for the crotch in men's breeches

COED n pl. -S a female student

COEDITOR n pl. -S one who edits with another person

COEFFECT n pl. -S an accompanying effect

COELIAC adj celiac

COELOM n pl. -LOMS or -LOMATA a body cavity in some animals **COELOMIC** adj

COELOME n pl. -S coelom

COEMBODY v -BODIED, -BODYING, -BODIES to embody jointly

COEMPLOY v -ED, -ING, -S to employ together

COEMPT v -ED, -ING, -S to buy up the entire supply of a product

COENACT v -ED, -ING, -S to enact jointly or at the same time

COENAMOR v -ED, -ING, -S to inflame with mutual love

COENDURE v -DURED, -DURING, -DURES to endure together

COENURE n pl. -S coenurus

COENURUS n pl. -RI a tapeworm larva

COENZYME n pl. -S a substance necessary for the functioning of certain enzymes

COEQUAL n pl. -S one who is equal with another

COEQUATE v -QUATED, -QUATING, -QUATES to equate with something else

COERCE v -ERCED, -ERCING, -ERCES to compel by force or threat

COERCER n pl. -S one that coerces

COERCION n pl. -S the act of coercing

COERCIVE adj serving to coerce

COERECT v -ED, -ING, -S to erect together

COEVAL n pl. -S one of the same era or period as another

COEVALLY adv contemporarily

COEXERT v -ED, -ING, -S to exert jointly

COEXIST v -ED, -ING, -S to exist together

COEXTEND v -ED, -ING, -S to extend through the same space or time as another

COFACTOR n pl. -S a coenzyme

COFF v COFT, COFFING, COFFS to buy

COFFEE n pl. -S an aromatic, mildly stimulating beverage

COFFER v -ED, -ING, -S to put in a strongbox

COFFIN v -ED, -ING, -S to put in a coffin (a burial case)

COFFING present participle of coff

COFFLE v -FLED, -FLING, -FLES to chain slaves together

COFFRET n pl. -S a small strongbox

COFT past tense of coff

COG v COGGED, COGGING, COGS to cheat at dice

COGENCY n pl. -CIES the state of being cogent

COGENT adj convincing **COGENTLY** adv

COGGED past tense of cog

COGGING present participle of cog

COGITATE v -TATED, -TATING, -TATES to ponder

COGITO n pl. -TOS a philosophical principle

COGNAC n pl. -S a brandy

COGNATE n pl. -S one that is related to another

COGNISE v -NISED, -NISING, -NISES to cognize

COGNIZE v -NIZED, -NIZING, -NIZES to become aware of in one's mind

COGNIZER n pl. -S one that cognizes

COGNOMEN n pl. -MENS or -MINA a family name

COGNOVIT n pl. -S a written admission of liability

COGON n pl. -S a tall tropical grass

COGWAY n pl. -WAYS a railway operating on steep slopes

COGWHEEL n pl. -S a toothed wheel

COHABIT v -ED, -ING, -S to live together as man and wife while unmarried

COHEIR n pl. -S a joint heir

COHERE v -HERED, -HERING, -HERES to stick together

COHERENT adj sticking together

COHERER n pl. -S a device used to detect radio waves

COHERING present participle of cohere

COHESION n pl. -S the act or state of cohering **COHESIVE** adj

COHO n pl. -HOS a small salmon

COHOBATE v -BATED, -BATING, -BATES to distill again

COHOG n pl. -S a quahog

COHORT n pl. -S a companion or associate

COHOSH n pl. -ES a medicinal plant

COHUNE n pl. -S a palm tree

COIF v -ED, -ING -S to style the hair

COIFFE v COIFFED, COIFFING, COIFFES to coif

COIFFEUR n pl. -S a male hairdresser

COIFFURE v -FURED, -FURING, -FURES to coif

COIGN v -ED, -ING, -S to quoin

COIGNE   v COIGNED, COIGNING, COIGNES to quoin

COIL   v -ED, -ING, -S to wind in even rings

COILER   n pl. -S one that coils

COIN   v -ED, -ING, -S to make coins (metal currency) COINABLE adj

COINAGE   n pl. -S the act of making coins

COINCIDE   v -CIDED, -CIDING, -CIDES to be in the same place

COINER   n pl. -S one that coins

COINFER   v -FERRED, -FERRING, -FERS to infer jointly

COINHERE   v -HERED, -HERING, -HERES to inhere jointly

COINMATE   n pl. -S a fellow inmate

COINSURE   v -SURED, -SURING, -SURES to insure with another

COINTER   v -TERRED, -TERRING, -TERS to bury together

COIR   n pl. -S a fiber obtained from coconut husks

COISTREL   n pl. -S a knave

COISTRIL   n pl. -S coistrel

COITION   n pl. -S coitus

COITUS   n pl. -ES sexual intercourse COITAL adj COITALLY adv

COKE   v COKED, COKING, COKES to change into a carbon fuel

COL   n pl. -S a depression between two mountains

COLA   n pl. -S a carbonated beverage

COLANDER   n pl. -S a kitchen utensil for draining off liquids

COLD   adj COLDER, COLDEST having little or no warmth

COLD   n pl. -S the relative lack of heat; a chill

COLDISH   adj somewhat cold

COLDLY   adv in a cold manner

COLDNESS   n pl. -ES the state of being cold

COLE   n pl. -S a plant of the cabbage family

COLESEED   n pl. -S colza

COLESLAW   n pl. -S a salad made of shredded raw cabbage

COLESSEE   n pl. -S a joint lessee

COLESSOR   n pl. -S a joint lessor

COLEUS   n pl. -ES a tropical plant

COLEWORT   n pl. -S cole

COLIC   n pl. -S acute abdominal pain

COLICIN   n pl. -S an antibacterial substance

COLICINE   n pl. -S colicin

COLICKY   adj pertaining to or associated with colic

COLIES   pl. of coly

COLIFORM   n pl. -S a bacillus of the colon

COLIN   n pl. -S the bobwhite

COLINEAR   adj lying in the same straight line

COLISEUM   n pl. -S a large structure for public entertainment

COLISTIN   n pl. -S an antibiotic

COLITIS   n pl. -TISES inflammation of the colon COLITIC adj

COLLAGE   n pl. -S a kind of artistic composition

COLLAGEN   n pl. -S a protein

COLLAPSE   v -LAPSED, -LAPSING, -LAPSES to crumble suddenly

COLLAR   v -ED, -ING, -S to provide with a collar (something worn around the neck)

COLLARD   n pl. -S a variety of kale

COLLARET   n pl. -S a small collar

COLLATE   v -LATED, -LATING, -LATES to compare critically

COLLATOR   n pl. -S one that collates

COLLECT   v -ED, -ING, -S to bring together in a group

COLLEEN   n pl. -S an Irish girl

COLLEGE   n pl. -S a school of higher learning

COLLEGER   n pl. -S a student supported by funds from his college

COLLEGIA   n/pl soviet executive councils

COLLET   v -ED, -ING, -S to set a gem in a rim or ring

COLLIDE   v -LIDED, -LIDING, -LIDES to come together with violent impact

COLLIE   n pl. -S a large dog

COLLIED   past tense of colly

COLLIER   n pl. -S a coal miner

COLLIERY   n pl. -LIERIES a coal mine

COLLIES   present 3d person sing. of colly

COLLINS   n pl. -ES an alcoholic beverage

COLLOGUE   v -LOGUED, -LOGUING, -LOGUES to conspire

COLLOID   n pl. -S a type of chemical suspension

COLLOP   n pl. -S a small portion of meat

COLLOQUY n pl. -QUIES a conversation

COLLUDE v -LUDED, -LUDING, -LUDES to conspire

COLLUDER n pl. -S one that colludes

COLLUVIA n/pl rock debris

COLLY v -LIED, -LYING, -LIES to blacken with coal dust

COLLYRIA n/pl medicinal lotions

COLOCATE v -CATED, -CATING, -CATES to place two or more housing units in close proximity

COLOG n pl. -S the logarithm of the reciprocal of a number

COLOGNE n pl. -S a scented liquid **COLOGNED** adj

COLON n pl. -S a section of the large intestine

COLON n pl. -ES a monetary unit of Costa Rica

COLONEL n pl. -S a military officer

COLONI pl. of colonus

COLONIAL n pl. -S a citizen of a colony

COLONIC adj pertaining to the colon

COLONIES pl. of colony

COLONISE v -NISED, -NISING, -NISES to colonize

COLONIST n pl. -S one who settles a colony

COLONIZE v -NIZED, -NIZING, -NIZES to establish a colony

COLONUS n pl. -NI a freeborn serf

COLONY n pl. -NIES a group of emigrants living in a new land

COLOPHON n pl. -S an inscription placed at the end of a book

COLOR v -ED, -ING, -S to give color (a visual attribute of objects) to

COLORADO adj of medium strength and color — used of cigars

COLORANT n pl. -S a pigment or dye

COLORED n pl. -S a nonwhite person

COLORER n pl. -S one that colors

COLORFUL adj full of color

COLORING n pl. -S appearance in regard to color

COLORISM n pl. -S coloring

COLORIST n pl. -S a person skilled in the use of color

COLOSSAL adj gigantic

COLOSSUS n pl. -LOSSI or -LOSSUSES a gigantic statue

COLOTOMY n pl. -MIES a surgical incision of the colon

COLOUR v -ED, -ING, -S to color

COLOURER n pl. -S colorer

COLPITIS n pl. -TISES a vaginal inflammation

COLT n pl. -S a young male horse **COLTISH** adj

COLTER n pl. -S a blade on a plow

COLUBRID n pl. -S any of a large family of snakes

COLUGO n pl. -GOS a small mammal

COLUMBIC adj pertaining to niobium

COLUMEL n pl. -S a small column-like anatomical part

COLUMN n pl. -S a vertical cylindrical support **COLUMNAL, COLUM-NAR, COLUMNED** adj

COLURE n pl. -S an astronomical circle

COLY n pl. COLIES an African bird

COLZA n pl. -S a plant of the cabbage family

COMA n pl. -S a condition of prolonged unconsciousness

COMA n pl. -MAE a tuft of silky hairs

COMAKER n pl. -S one who assumes financial responsibility for another's default

COMAL adj comose

COMATE n pl. -S a companion

COMATIC adj having blurred vision as a result of coma

COMATIK n pl. -S komatik

COMATOSE adj affected with coma

COMATULA n pl. -LAE a marine animal

COMB v -ED, -ING, -S to arrange or clean with a comb (a toothed instrument)

COMBAT v -BATED, -BATING, -BATS or -BATTED, -BATTING, -BATS to fight against

COMBATER n pl. -S one that combats

COMBE n pl. -S a narrow valley

COMBER n pl. -S one that combs

COMBINE v -BINED, -BINING, -BINES to blend

COMBINER n pl. -S one that combines

COMBINGS n/pl hair removed by a comb

COMBINING present participle of combine

COMBLIKE adj resembling a comb

COMBO n pl. -BOS a small jazz band

COMBUST v -ED, -ING, -S to burn

COME v CAME, COMING, COMES or COMETH to move toward something or someone

COMEBACK *n* pl. -S a return to former prosperity

COMEDIAN *n* pl. -S a humorous entertainer

COMEDIC *adj* pertaining to comedy

COMEDIES pl. of comedy

COMEDO *n* pl. -DOS or -DONES a skin blemish

COMEDOWN *n* pl. -S a drop in status

COMEDY *n* pl. -DIES a humorous play, movie, or other work

COMELY *adj* -LIER, -LIEST pleasing to look at COMELILY *adv*

COMER *n* pl. -S one showing great promise

COMET *n* pl. -S a celestial body COMETARY *adj*

COMETH a present 3d person sing. of come

COMETHER *n* pl. -S an affair or matter

COMETIC *adj* pertaining to a comet

COMFIER comparative of comfy

COMFIEST superlative of comfy

COMFIT *n* pl. -S a candy

COMFORT *v* -ED, -ING, -S to soothe in time of grief

COMFREY *n* pl. -FREYS a coarse herb

COMFY *adj* -FIER, -FIEST comfortable

COMIC *n* pl. -S a comedian

COMICAL *adj* funny

COMING *n* pl. -S arrival

COMITIA *n* pl. COMITIA a public assembly in ancient Rome COMITIAL *adj*

COMITY *n* pl. -TIES civility

COMMA *n* pl. -MAS or -MATA a fragment of a few words or feet in ancient prosody

COMMAND *v* -ED, -ING, -S to direct with authority

COMMANDO *n* pl. -DOES or -DOS a military unit

COMMATA a pl. of comma

COMMENCE *v* -MENCED, -MENCING, -MENCES to begin

COMMEND *v* -ED, -ING, -S to praise

COMMENT *v* -ED, -ING, -S to remark

COMMERCE *v* -MERCED, -MERCING, -MERCES to commune

COMMIE *n* pl. -S a Communist

COMMIES pl. of commy

COMMIT *v* -MITTED, -MITTING, -MITS to do, perform, or perpetrate

COMMIX *v* -MIXED or -MIXT, -MIXING, -MIXES to mix together

COMMODE *n* pl. -S a cabinet

COMMON *adj* -MONER, -MONEST ordinary

COMMON *n* pl. -S a tract of publicly used land

COMMONER *n* pl. -S one of the common people

COMMONLY *adv* in a common manner

COMMOVE *v* -MOVED, -MOVING, -MOVES to move violently

COMMUNAL *adj* belonging to a community; public

COMMUNE *v* -MUNED, -MUNING, -MUNES to converse intimately

COMMUTE *v* -MUTED, -MUTING, -MUTES to exchange

COMMUTER *n* pl. -S one that commutes

COMMY *n* pl. -MIES commie

COMOSE *adj* bearing a tuft of silky hairs

COMOUS *adj* comose

COMP *v* -ED, -ING, -S to play a jazz accompaniment

COMPACT *adj* -PACTER, -PACTEST closely and firmly united

COMPACT *v* -ED, -ING, -S to pack closely together

COMPADRE *n* pl. -S a close friend

COMPANY *v* -NIED, -NYING, -NIES to associate with

COMPARE *v* -PARED, -PARING, -PARES to represent as similar

COMPARER *n* pl. -S one that compares

COMPART *v* -ED, -ING, -S to divide into parts

COMPASS *v* -ED, -ING, -ES to go around

COMPEER *v* -ED, -ING, -S to equal or match

COMPEL *v* -PELLED, -PELLING, -PELS to urge forcefully

COMPEND *n* pl. -S a brief summary

COMPERE *v* -PERED, -PERING, -PERES to act as master of ceremonies

COMPETE *v* -PETED, -PETING, -PETES to vie

COMPILE *v* -PILED, -PILING, -PILES to collect into a volume

COMPILER *n* pl. -S one that compiles

COMPLAIN *v* -ED, -ING, -S to express discontent

COMPLEAT *adj* highly skilled

COMPLECT *v* -ED, -ING, -S to weave together

COMPLETE *adj* -PLETER, -PLETEST having all necessary parts

COMPLETE *v* -PLETED, -PLETING, -PLETES to bring to an end

COMPLEX *adj* -PLEXER, -PLEXEST complicated

COMPLEX *v* -ED, -ING, -ES to make complex

COMPLICE *n pl.* -S an associate

COMPLIED past tense of comply

COMPLIER *n pl.* -S one that complies

COMPLIES present 3d person sing. of comply

COMPLIN *n pl.* -S compline

COMPLINE *n pl.* -S the last liturgical prayer of the day

COMPLOT *v* -PLOTTED, -PLOTTING, -PLOTS to conspire

COMPLY *v* -PLIED, -PLYING, -PLIES to obey

COMPO *n pl.* -POS a mixed substance

COMPONE *adj* compony

COMPONY *adj* composed of squares of alternating colors

COMPORT *v* -ED, -ING -S to conduct oneself in a certain way

COMPOSE *v* -POSED, -POSING, -POSES to form the substance of

COMPOSER *n pl.* -S one that writes music

COMPOST *v* -ED, -ING, -S to fertilize

COMPOTE *n pl.* -S fruit stewed in syrup

COMPOUND *v* -ED, -ING, -S to add to

COMPRESS *v* -ED, -ING, -ES to compact

COMPRISE *v* -PRISED, -PRISING, -PRISES to include or contain

COMPRIZE *v* -PRIZED, -PRIZING, -PRIZES to comprise

COMPT *v* -ED, -ING, -S to count

COMPUTE *v* -PUTED, -PUTING, -PUTES to determine by mathematical means

COMPUTER *n pl.* -S a machine that computes automatically

COMRADE *n pl.* -S a close friend

COMTE *n pl.* -S a French nobleman

CON *v* CONNED, CONNING, CONS to study carefully

CONATION *n pl.* -S the inclination to act purposefully CONATIVE *adj*

CONATUS *n pl.* CONATUS an effort

CONCAVE *v* -CAVED, -CAVING, -CAVES to make concave (curving inward)

CONCEAL *v* -ED, -ING, -S to keep from sight or discovery

CONCEDE *v* -CEDED, -CEDING, -CEDES to acknowledge as true

CONCEDER *n pl.* -S one that concedes

CONCEIT *v* -ED, -ING, -S to imagine

CONCEIVE *v* -CEIVED, -CEIVING, -CEIVES to understand

CONCENT *n pl.* -S harmony

CONCEPT *n pl.* -S a general idea

CONCERN *v* -ED, -ING, -S to be of interest to

CONCERT *v* -ED, -ING, -S to plan

CONCERTO *n pl.* -TOS or -TI a musical composition

CONCH *n pl.* -S or -ES a marine mollusk

CONCHA *n pl.* -CHAE an anatomical shell-like structure CONCHAL *adj*

CONCHOID *n pl.* -S a type of geometric curve

CONCHY *n pl.* -CHIES a conscientious objector

CONCISE *adj* -CISER, -CISEST succinct

CONCLAVE *n pl.* -S a secret meeting

CONCLUDE *v* -CLUDED, -CLUDING, -CLUDES to finish

CONCOCT *v* -ED, -ING, -S to prepare by combining ingredients

CONCORD *n pl.* -S a state of agreement

CONCRETE *v* -CRETED, -CRETING, -CRETES to solidify

CONCUR *v* -CURRED, -CURRING, -CURS to agree

CONCUSS *v* -ED, -ING, -ES to injure the brain by a violent blow

CONDEMN *v* -ED, -ING, -S to criticize severely

CONDENSE *v* -DENSED, -DENSING, -DENSES to compress

CONDIGN *adj* deserved; appropriate

CONDOLE *v* -DOLED, -DOLING, -DOLES to mourn

CONDOLER *n pl.* -S one that condoles

CONDOM *n pl.* -S a prophylactic

CONDONE *v* -DONED, -DONING, -DONES to forgive or overlook

CONDONER *n pl.* -S one that condones

CONDOR *n pl.* -S or -ES a coin of Chile

CONDUCE *v* -DUCED, -DUCING, -DUCES to contribute to a result

CONDUCER *n pl.* -S one that conduces

CONDUCT *v* -ED, -ING, -S to lead or guide

CONDUIT *n pl.* -S a channel or pipe for conveying fluids

CONDYLE *n* pl. -S a protuberance on a bone **CONDYLAR** *adj*

CONE *v* CONED, CONING, CONES to shape like a cone (a geometric solid)

CONELRAD *n* pl. -S a system of defense in the event of air attack

CONENOSE *n* pl. -S a bloodsucking insect

CONEPATE *n* pl. -S a skunk

CONEPATL *n* pl. -S conepate

CONEY *n* pl. -NEYS cony

CONFAB *v* -FABBED, -FABBING, FABS to chat

CONFECT *v* -ED, -ING, -S to prepare from various ingredients

CONFER *v* -FERRED, -FERRING, -FERS to bestow

CONFEREE *n* pl. -S one upon whom something is conferred

CONFERVA *n* pl. -VAE or -VAS a freshwater alga

CONFESS *v* -ED, -ING, -ES to acknowledge or disclose

CONFETTO *n* pl. -TI a bonbon

CONFIDE *v* -FIDED, -FIDING, -FIDES to reveal in trust or confidence

CONFIDER *n* pl. -S one that confides

CONFINE *v* -FINED, -FINING, -FINES to shut within an enclosure

CONFINER *n* pl. -S one that confines

CONFIRM *v* -ED, -ING, -S to assure the validity of

CONFLATE *v* -FLATED, -FLATING, -FLATES to blend

CONFLICT *v* -ED, -ING, -S to come into opposition

CONFLUX *n* pl. -ES a flowing together of streams

CONFOCAL *adj* having the same focus or foci

CONFORM *v* -ED, -ING, -S to become the same or similar

CONFOUND *v* -ED, -ING, -S to confuse

CONFRERE *n* pl. -S a colleague

CONFRONT *v* -ED, -ING, -S to face defiantly

CONFUSE *v* -FUSED, -FUSING, -FUSES to mix up mentally

CONFUTE *v* -FUTED, -FUTING, -FUTES to disprove

CONFUTER *n* pl. -S one that confutes

CONGA *v* -ED, -ING, -S to perform a Latin American dance

CONGE *n* pl. -S permission to depart

CONGEAL *v* -ED, -ING, -S to change from a fluid to a solid

CONGEE *v* -GEED, -GEEING, -GEES to bow politely

CONGENER *n* pl. -S one of the same kind or class

CONGER *n* pl. -S a marine eel

CONGEST *v* -ED, -ING, -S to fill to excess

CONGIUS *n* pl. -GII an ancient unit of measure

CONGLOBE *v* -GLOBED, -GLOBING, -GLOBES to become a globule

CONGO *n* pl. -GOS congou

CONGO *n* pl. -GOES an eellike amphibian

CONGOU *n* pl. -S a Chinese tea

CONGRESS *v* -ED, -ING, -ES to assemble together

CONI pl. of conus

CONIC *n* pl. -S a geometric curve

CONICAL *adj* shaped like a cone

CONICITY *n* pl. -TIES the state of being conical

CONIDIUM *n* pl. -NIDIA a fungus spore **CONIDIAL, CONIDIAN** *adj*

CONIES pl. of cony

CONIFER *n* pl. -S an evergreen tree

CONIINE *n* pl. -S a poisonous alkaloid

CONIN *n* pl. -S coniine

CONINE *n* pl. -S coniine

CONING present participle of cone

CONIUM *n* pl. -S a poisonous herb

CONJOIN *v* -ED, -ING, -S to join together **CONJOINT** *adj*

CONJUGAL *adj* pertaining to marriage

CONJUNCT *n* pl. -S one that is joined with another

CONJURE *v* -JURED, -JURING, -JURES to summon a spirit

CONJURER *n* pl. -S a sorcerer

CONJUROR *n* pl. -S conjurer

CONK *v* -ED, -ING, -S to hit on the head

CONKER *n* pl. -S a chestnut used in a British game

CONKY *adj* full of a tree fungus

CONN *v* -ED, -ING, -S to direct the steering of a ship

CONNATE *adj* innate

CONNECT *v* -ED, -ING, -S to join together

CONNED past tense of con

CONNER *n* pl. -S one that cons

CONNING present participle of con

CONNIVE v -NIVED, -NIVING, -NIVES to feign ignorance of wrongdoing

CONNIVER n pl. -S one that connives

CONNOTE v -NOTED, -NOTING, -NOTES to imply another meaning besides the literal one

CONODONT n pl. -S a fossil

CONOID n pl. -S a geometric solid CONOIDAL adj

CONQUER v -ED, -ING, -S to overcome by force

CONQUEST n pl. -S the act of conquering

CONQUIAN n pl. -S a card game

CONSENT v -ED, -ING, -S to permit or approve

CONSERVE v -SERVED, -SERVING, -SERVES to protect from loss or depletion

CONSIDER v -ED, -ING, -S to think about

CONSIGN v -ED, -ING, -S to give over to another's care

CONSIST v -ED, -ING, -S to be made up or composed

CONSOL n pl. -S a government bond

CONSOLE v -SOLED, -SOLING, -SOLES to comfort

CONSOLER n pl. -S one that consoles

CONSOMME n pl. -S a clear soup

CONSORT v -ED, -ING, -S to keep company

CONSPIRE v -SPIRED, -SPIRING, -SPIRES to plan secretly with another

CONSTANT n pl. -S something that does not vary

CONSTRUE v -STRUED, -STRUING, -STRUES to interpret

CONSUL n pl. -S an official serving abroad CONSULAR adj

CONSULT v -ED, -ING, -S to ask an opinion of

CONSUME v -SUMED, -SUMING, -SUMES to use up

CONSUMER n pl. -S one that consumes

CONTACT v -ED, -ING, -S to communicate with

CONTAGIA n/pl causative agents of infectious diseases

CONTAIN v -ED, -ING, -S to hold within

CONTE n pl. -S a short story

CONTEMN v -ED, -ING, -S to scorn

CONTEMPT n pl. -S the feeling of one who views something as mean, vile, or worthless

CONTEND v -ED, -ING, -S to vie

CONTENT v -ED, -ING, -S to satisfy

CONTEST v -ED, -ING, -S to compete for

CONTEXT n pl. -S the part of a discourse in which a particular word or phrase appears

CONTINUA n/pl mathematical sets

CONTINUE v -UED, -UING, -UES to go on with

CONTINUO n pl. -UOS a type of instrumental part

CONTO n pl. -TOS a Portuguese money of account

CONTORT v -ED, -ING, -S to twist out of shape

CONTOUR v -ED, -ING, -S to make the outline of

CONTRA prep against

CONTRACT v -ED, -ING, -S to decrease in size or volume

CONTRAIL n pl. -S a visible trail of water vapor from an aircraft

CONTRARY n pl. -TRARIES an opposite

CONTRAST v -ED, -ING, -S to place in opposition to set off differences

CONTRITE adj deeply sorry for one's sins

CONTRIVE v -TRIVED, -TRIVING, -TRIVES to devise

CONTROL v -TROLLED, -TROLLING, -TROLS to exercise authority over

CONTUSE v -TUSED, -TUSING, -TUSES to bruise

CONUS n pl. CONI an anatomical part in mammals

CONVECT v -ED, -ING, -S to transfer heat by a process of circulation

CONVENE v -VENED, -VENING, -VENES to assemble

CONVENER n pl. -S one that convenes

CONVENT v -ED, -ING, -S to convene

CONVERGE v -VERGED, -VERGING, -VERGES to come together

CONVERSE v -VERSED, -VERSING, -VERSES to speak together

CONVERT v -ED, -ING, -S to change into another form

CONVEX n pl. -ES a surface or body that is convex (curving outward)

CONVEXLY adv in a convex manner

CONVEY v -ED, -ING, -S to transport

CONVEYER n pl. -S one that conveys

CONVEYOR n pl. -S conveyer

CONVICT v -ED, -ING, -S to prove guilty

CONVINCE v -VINCED, -VINCING, -VINCES to cause to believe something

CONVOKE v -VOKED, -VOKING, -VOKES to cause to assemble

CONVOKER n pl. -S one that convokes

CONVOLVE v -VOLVED, -VOLVING, -VOLVES to roll together

CONVOY v -ED, -ING, -S to escort

CONVULSE v -VULSED, -VULSING, -VULSES to shake violently

CONY n pl. CONIES a rabbit

COO v COOED, COOING, COOS to make the sound of a dove

COOCH n pl. -ES a sinuous dance

COOEE v COOEED, COOEEING, COOEES to cry out shrilly

COOER n pl. -S one that coos

COOEY v -EYED, -EYING, -EYS to cooee

COOF n pl. -S a dolt

COOINGLY adv in the manner of cooing doves; affectionately

COOK v -ED, -ING, -S to prepare food by heating COOKABLE adj

COOKBOOK n pl. -S a book of recipes

COOKER n pl. -S one that cooks

COOKERY n pl. -ERIES the art of cooking

COOKEY n pl. -EYS cookie

COOKIE n pl. -S a small, flat cake

COOKIES pl. of cooky

COOKING n pl. -S the act of one that cooks

COOKLESS adj having no person that cooks

COOKOUT n pl. -S a meal eaten and prepared outdoors

COOKSHOP n pl. -S a shop that sells cooked food

COOKWARE n pl. -S utensils used in cooking

COOKY n pl. COOKIES cookie

COOL adj COOLER, COOLEST moderately cold

COOL v -ED, -ING, -S to make less warm

COOLANT n pl. -S a fluid used to cool engines

COOLER n pl. -S something that cools

COOLIE n pl. -S an Oriental laborer

COOLIES pl. of cooly

COOLISH adj somewhat cool

COOLLY adv in a cool manner

COOLNESS n pl. -ES the state of being cool

COOLY n pl. COOLIES coolie

COOMB n pl. -S combe

COOMBE n pl. -S combe

COON n pl. -S a raccoon

COONCAN n pl. -S conquian

COONSKIN n pl. -S the pelt of a raccoon

COONTIE n pl. -S a tropical plant

COOP v -ED, -ING, -S to confine

COOPER v -ED, -ING, -S to make or mend barrels

COOPERY n pl. -ERIES the trade of coopering

COOPT v -ED, -ING, -S to elect or appoint

COOPTION n pl. -S the act of coopting

COOT n pl. -S an aquatic bird

COOTIE n pl. -S a body louse

COP v COPPED, COPPING, COPS to steal

COPAIBA n pl. -S a resin

COPAL n pl. -S a resin

COPALM n pl. -S a hardwood tree

COPARENT n pl. -S a fellow parent

COPASTOR n pl. -S one that shares the duties of a pastor

COPATRON n pl. -S a fellow patron

COPE v COPED, COPING, COPES to contend or strive

COPECK n pl. -S kopeck

COPEMATE n pl. -S an antagonist

COPEN n pl. -S a blue color

COPEPOD n pl. -S a minute crustacean

COPER n pl. -S a horse dealer

COPIED past tense of copy

COPIER n pl. -S one that copies

COPIES present 3d person sing. of copy

COPIHUE n -pl. -S a climbing vine

COPILOT n pl. -S a pilot who assists the pilot in command

COPING n pl. -S the top part of a wall

COPIOUS adj abundant

COPLANAR adj lying in the same plane

COPLOT v -PLOTTED, -PLOTTING, -PLOTS to plot together

COPPED past tense of cop

COPPER v -ED, -ING, -S to cover with copper (a metallic element)

COPPERAH n pl. -S copra

COPPERAS n pl. -ES a compound used in making inks

COPPERY adj resembling copper

COPPICE n pl. -S a thicket COPPICED adj

COPPING present participle of cop

COPPRA n pl. -S copra

COPRA n pl. -S dried coconut meat

COPRAH n pl. -S copra

COPREMIA n pl. -S a form of blood poisoning COPREMIC adj

COPSE n pl. -S a coppice

COPTER n pl. -S a helicopter

COPULA n pl. -LAS or -LAE something that links COPULAR adj

COPULATE v -LATED, -LATING, -LATES to engage in coitus

COPY v COPIED, COPYING, COPIES to imitate

COPYBOOK n pl. -S a book used in teaching penmanship

COPYBOY n pl. -BOYS an office boy

COPYCAT v -CATTED, -CATTING, -CATS to imitate

COPYDESK n pl. -S an editor's desk in a newspaper office

COPYHOLD n pl. -S a type of ownership of land

COPYIST n pl. -S an imitator

COQUET v -QUETTED, -QUETTING, -QUETS to flirt

COQUETRY n pl. -TRIES flirtatious behavior

COQUETTE v -QUETTED, -QUETTING, -QUETTES to coquet

COQUILLE n pl. -S a cooking utensil

COQUINA n pl. -S a small marine clam

COQUITO n pl. -TOS a palm tree

CORACLE n pl. -S a small boat

CORACOID n pl. -S a bone of the shoulder girdle

CORAL n pl. -S a mass of marine animal skeletons

CORANTO n pl. -TOS or -TOES courante

CORBAN n pl. -S an offering to God

CORBEIL n pl. -S a sculptured fruit basket

CORBEL v -BELED, -BELING, -BELS or -BELLED, -BELLING, -BELS to provide a wall with a bracket

CORBIE n pl. -S a raven or crow

CORBINA n pl. -S a food and game fish

CORBY n pl. CORBIES corbie

CORD v -ED, -ING, -S to fasten with a cord (a thin rope)

CORDAGE n pl. -S the amount of wood in an area

CORDATE adj heart-shaped

CORDER n pl. -S one that cords

CORDIAL n pl. -S a liqueur

CORDITE n pl. -S an explosive powder

CORDLESS adj having no cord

CORDLIKE adj resembling a cord

CORDOBA n pl. -S a monetary unit of Nicaragua

CORDON v -ED, -ING, -S to form a barrier around

CORDOVAN n pl. -S a fine leather

CORDUROY v -ED, -ING, -S to build a type of road

CORDWAIN n pl. -S cordovan

CORDWOOD n pl. -S wood used for fuel

CORE v CORED, CORING, CORES to remove the core (the central part) of

COREDEEM v -ED, -ING, -S to redeem jointly

COREIGN n pl. -S a joint reign

CORELATE v -LATED, -LATING, -LATES to place into mutual or reciprocal relation

CORELESS adj having no core

COREMIUM n pl. -MIA an organ of certain fungi

CORER n pl. -S a utensil for coring apples

CORF n pl. CORVES a wagon used in a mine

CORGI n pl. -S a short-legged dog

CORING present participle of core

CORIUM n pl. -RIA a skin layer

CORK v -ED, -ING, -S to stop up

CORKAGE n pl. -S a charge for wine in a restaurant

CORKER n pl. -S one that corks

CORKIER comparative of corky

CORKIEST superlative of corky

CORKLIKE adj resembling cork (a porous tree bark)

CORKWOOD n pl. -S a small tree

CORKY adj CORKIER, CORKIEST corklike

CORM n pl. -S a stem of certain plants CORMOID, CORMOUS, CORMLIKE adj

CORMEL n pl. -S a small corm

CORN	v -ED, -ING, -S to preserve with salt	**CORONET**	n pl. -S a small crown
CORNBALL	n pl. -S a hick	**COROTATE**	v -TATED, -TATING, -TATES to rotate together
CORNCAKE	n pl. -S a cake made of cornmeal	**CORPORA**	pl. of corpus
CORNCOB	n pl. -S the woody core of an ear of corn	**CORPORAL**	n pl. -S a military rank
CORNCRIB	n pl. -S a building in which corn is stored	**CORPS**	n pl. CORPS a military unit
CORNEA	n pl. -S a part of the eye **CORNEAL** adj	**CORPSE**	n pl. -S a dead body
		CORPSMAN	n pl. -MEN an enlisted man trained to give minor medical treatment
CORNEL	n pl. -S a hardwood tree or shrub	**CORPUS**	n pl. -PORA a human or animal body
CORNEOUS	adj of a hornlike texture		
CORNER	v -ED, -ING, -S to gain control of	**CORRADE**	v -RADED, -RADING, -RADES to erode
CORNET	n pl. -S a trumpetlike instrument	**CORRAL**	v -RALLED, -RALLING, -RALS to place livestock in an enclosure
CORNETCY	n -CIES a rank in the British cavalry	**CORRECT**	v -ED, -ING, -S to make free from error
CORNFED	adj fed on corn	**CORRECT**	adj -RECTER, -RECTEST free from error
CORNHUSK	n pl. -S the husk covering an ear of corn	**CORRIDA**	n pl. -S a bullfight
CORNICE	v -NICED, -NICING, -NICES to decorate with a molding	**CORRIDOR**	n pl. -S a narrow hallway
CORNICHE	n pl. -S a road built along a cliff	**CORRIE**	n pl. -S a cirque
CORNICLE	n pl. -S a part of an aphid	**CORRIVAL**	n pl. -S a rival or opponent
CORNIER	comparative of corny	**CORRODE**	v -RODED, -RODING, -RODES to eat away gradually
CORNIEST	superlative of corny		
CORNILY	adv in a corny manner	**CORRODY**	n pl. -DIES corody
CORNMEAL	n pl. -S meal made from corn	**CORRUPT**	adj -RUPTER, -RUPTEST dishonest and venal
CORNU	n pl. -NUA a hornlike bone formation **CORNUAL** adj	**CORRUPT**	v -ED, -ING, -S to subvert the honesty or integrity of
CORNUS	n pl. -ES a cornel	**CORSAC**	n pl. -S an Asian fox
CORNUTE	adj horn-shaped	**CORSAGE**	n pl. -S a small bouquet of flowers
CORNUTED	adj cornute		
CORNUTO	n pl. -TOS the husband of an unfaithful wife	**CORSAIR**	n pl. -S a pirate
		CORSE	n pl. -S a corpse
CORNY	adj CORNIER, CORNIEST trite	**CORSELET**	n pl. -S a piece of body armor
CORODY	n pl. -DIES an allowance of food or clothes	**CORSET**	v -ED, -ING, -S to fit with a corset (a supporting undergarment)
COROLLA	n pl. -S a protective covering of a flower		
		CORSLET	n pl. -S corselet
CORONA	n pl. -NAS or -NAE a luminous circle around a celestial body	**CORTEGE**	n pl. -S a retinue
		CORTEX	n pl. -TICES or -TEXES the outer layer of an organ **CORTICAL** adj
CORONACH	n pl. -S a dirge		
CORONAL	n pl. -S a wreath worn on the head	**CORTIN**	n pl. -S a hormone
CORONARY	n pl. -NARIES an artery supplying blood to the heart	**CORTISOL**	n pl. -S a hormone
		CORUNDUM	n pl. -S a hard mineral
CORONEL	n pl. -S coronal	**CORVEE**	n pl. -S an obligation to perform feudal service
CORONER	n pl. -S an officer who investigates questionable deaths		
		CORVES	pl. of corf
		CORVET	n pl. -S corvette

CORVETTE n pl. -S a swift warship

CORVINA n pl. -S corbina

CORVINE adj pertaining or belonging to the crow family of birds

CORYMB n pl. -S a flower cluster **CORYMBED** adj

CORYPHEE n pl. -S a ballet dancer

CORYZA n pl. -S a head cold **CORYZAL** adj

COS n pl. -ES a variety of lettuce

COSEC n pl. -S cosecant

COSECANT n pl. -S a trigonometric function of an angle

COSET n pl. -S a mathematical subset

COSEY n pl. -SEYS a cozy

COSH v -ED, -ING, -ES to bludgeon

COSHER v -ED, -ING, -S to coddle

COSIE n pl. -S a cozy

COSIER comparative of cosy

COSIES pl. of cosy

COSIEST superlative of cosy

COSIGN v -ED, -ING, -S to sign jointly

COSIGNER n pl. -S one that cosigns

COSILY adv in a cosy manner

COSINE n pl. -S a trigonometric function of an angle

COSINESS n pl. -ES coziness

COSMETIC n pl. -S a beauty preparation

COSMIC adj pertaining to the cosmos

COSMICAL adj cosmic

COSMISM n pl. -S a philosophical theory

COSMIST n pl. -S a supporter of cosmism

COSMOS n pl. -ES the universe regarded as an orderly system

COSS n pl. COSS kos

COSSACK n pl. -S a Russian cavalryman

COSSET v -ED, -ING, -S to fondle

COST v COST or COSTED, COSTING, COSTS to estimate a price for production of

COSTA n pl. -TAE a rib **COSTAL** adj

COSTAR v -STARRED, -STARRING, -STARS to star with another actor

COSTARD n pl. -S a large cooking apple

COSTATE adj having a rib or ribs

COSTER n pl. -S a hawker of fruit or vegetables

COSTIVE adj constipated

COSTLESS adj free of charge

COSTLY adj -LIER, -LIEST expensive

COSTMARY n pl. -MARIES an herb used in salads

COSTREL n pl. -S a flask

COSTUME v -TUMED, -TUMING, -TUMES to supply with a costume (a style of dress)

COSTUMER n pl. -S one that costumes

COSTUMEY adj of or pertaining to a costume

COSTUMING present participle of costume

COSY adj COSIER, COSIEST cozy

COSY n pl. COSIES a cozy

COT n pl. -S a light, narrow bed

COTAN n pl. -S a trigonometric function of an angle

COTE v COTED, COTING, COTES to pass by

COTEAU n pl. -TEAUX the higher ground of a region

COTENANT n pl. -S one who is a tenant with another in the same place

COTERIE n pl. -S a clique

COTHURN n pl. -S a buskin worn by ancient Roman actors

COTHURNI n/pl cothurns

COTIDAL adj indicating coincidence of the tides

COTILLON n pl. -S a ballroom dance

COTING present participle of cote

COTQUEAN n pl. -S a vulgar woman

COTTA n pl. -TAE or -TAS a short surplice

COTTAGE n pl. -S a small house **COTTAGEY** adj

COTTAGER n pl. -S one that lives in a cottage

COTTAR n pl. -S cotter

COTTER n pl. -S a tenant farmer

COTTIER n pl. -S cotter

COTTON v -ED, -ING, -S to take a liking

COTTONY adj resembling cotton (a soft, fibrous material)

COTYLOID adj cup-shaped

COTYPE n pl. -S a taxonomic type

COUCH v -ED, -ING, -ES to put into words

COUCHANT adj lying down

COUCHER n pl. -S one that couches

COUCHING n pl. -S a form of embroidery

COUDE adj pertaining to a type of telescope

COUGAR n pl. -S a mountain lion

COUGH v -ED, -ING, -S to expel air from the lungs noisily

COUGHER n pl. -S one that coughs

COULD past tense of can

COULDEST a past 2d person sing. of can

COULDST a past 2d person sing. of can

COULEE n pl. -S a small ravine

COULISSE n pl. -S a side scene of a theatre stage

COULOIR n pl. -S a deep gorge or gully

COULOMB n pl. -S an electrical measure

COULTER n pl. -S colter

COUMARIN n pl. -S a chemical compound COUMARIC adj

COUMAROU n pl. -S the seed of a tropical tree

COUNCIL n pl. -S a group of persons appointed for a certain function

COUNSEL v -SELED, -SELING, -SELS or -SELLED, -SELLING, -SELS to advise

COUNT v -ED, -ING, -S to list or mention the units of one by one to ascertain the total

COUNTER v -ED, -ING, -S to oppose

COUNTESS n pl. -ES a noblewoman

COUNTIAN n pl. -S a resident of a county

COUNTRY n pl. -TRIES the territory of a nation

COUNTY n pl. -TIES an administrative division of a state

COUP v -ED, -ING, -S to overturn

COUPE n pl. -S an automobile with two doors

COUPLE v -PLED, -PLING, -PLES to unite in pairs

COUPLER n pl. -S one that couples

COUPLET n pl. -S a pair of successive lines of verse

COUPLING n pl. -S a joining device

COUPON n pl. -S a certificate entitling the holder to certain benefits

COURAGE n pl. -S the quality that enables one to face danger fearlessly; spirit

COURANT n pl. -S courante

COURANTE n pl. -S an old, lively dance

COURANTO n pl. -TOS or -TOES courante

COURIER n pl. -S a messenger

COURLAN n pl. -S a wading bird

COURSE v COURSED, COURSING, COURSES to cause hounds to chase game

COURSER n pl. -S one that courses

COURSING n pl. -S the pursuit of game by hounds

COURT v -ED, -ING, -S to woo

COURTESY v -SIED, -SYING, -SIES to curtsy

COURTIER n pl. -S one who attends a royal court

COURTLY adj -LIER, -LIEST stately

COUSCOUS n pl. -ES a North African cereal

COUSIN n pl. -S a child of one's aunt or uncle COUSINLY adj

COUSINRY n pl. -RIES cousins collectively

COUTEAU n pl. -TEAUX a knife

COUTER n pl. -S a piece of armor for the elbow

COUTH adj COUTHER, COUTHEST sophisticated

COUTH n pl. -S refinement

COUTHIE adj COUTHIER, COUTHIEST friendly

COUTURE n pl. -S the business of dressmaking

COUVADE n pl. -S a primitive birth ritual

COVALENT adj sharing electron pairs

COVE v COVED, COVING, COVES to curve over or inward

COVEN n pl. -S a group of thirteen witches

COVENANT v -ED, -ING, -S to enter into a binding agreement

COVER v -ED, -ING, -S to place something over or upon

COVERAGE n pl. -S the extent to which something is covered

COVERALL n pl. -S a one-piece work garment

COVERER n pl. -S one that covers

COVERING n pl. -S something that covers

COVERLET n pl. -S a bed covering

COVERLID n pl. -S a coverlet

COVERT n pl. -S a hiding place

COVERTLY adv secretly

COVET v -ED, -ING, -S to desire greatly

COVETER n pl. -S one that covets

COVETOUS adj excessively desirous

COVEY n pl. -EYS a flock of birds

COVING n pl. -S a concave molding

COW n pl. -S or KINE a farm animal

COW v -ED, -ING, -S to intimidate

COWAGE n pl. -S a tropical vine

COWARD n pl. -S one who lacks courage

COWARDLY _adj_ lacking courage

COWBANE _n pl._ -S a poisonous plant

COWBELL _n pl._ -S a bell around a cow's neck

COWBERRY _n pl._ -RIES a pasture shrub

COWBIND _n pl._ -S a species of bryony

COWBIRD _n pl._ -S a blackbird

COWBOY _n pl._ -BOYS a ranch worker

COWEDLY _adv_ in a cowed manner

COWER _v_ -ED, -ING, -S to cringe

COWFISH _n pl._ -ES an aquatic mammal

COWGIRL _n pl._ -S a female ranch worker

COWHAGE _n pl._ -S cowage

COWHAND _n pl._ -S a cowboy

COWHERB _n pl._ -S an annual herb

COWHERD _n pl._ -S one who tends cattle

COWHIDE _v_ -HIDED, -HIDING, -HIDES to flog with a leather whip

COWIER comparative of cowy

COWIEST superlative of cowy

COWINNER _n pl._ -S one of two or more winners

COWL _v_ -ED, -ING, -S to cover with a hood

COWLICK _n pl._ -S a lock of unruly hair

COWLING _n pl._ -S a covering for an aircraft engine

COWMAN _n pl._ -MEN one who owns cattle

COWORKER _n pl._ -S a fellow worker

COWPAT _n pl._ -S a dropping of cow dung

COWPEA _n pl._ -S a black-eyed pea

COWPOKE _n pl._ -S a cowboy

COWPOX _n pl._ -ES a cattle disease

COWRIE _n pl._ -S cowry

COWRY _n pl._ -RIES a glossy seashell

COWSHED _n pl._ -S a shelter for cows

COWSKIN _n pl._ -S the hide of a cow

COWSLIP _n pl._ -S a flowering plant

COWY _adj_ COWIER, COWIEST suggestive of a cow

COX _v_ -ED, -ING, -ES to coxswain

COXA _n pl._ -COXAE the hip or hip joint. COXAL _adj_

COXALGIA _n pl._ -S pain in the hip COXALGIC _adj_

COXALGY _n pl._ -GIES coxalgia

COXCOMB _n pl._ -S a conceited dandy

COXSWAIN _v_ -ED, -ING, -S to steer a racing rowboat

COY _adj_ COYER, COYEST shy

COY _v_ -ED, -ING, -S to caress

COYISH _adj_ somewhat coy

COYLY _adv_ in a coy manner

COYNESS _n pl._ -ES the state of being coy

COYOTE _n pl._ -S a small wolf

COYPOU _n pl._ -S a coypu

COYPU _n pl._ -S an aquatic rodent

COZ _n pl._ -COZES or COZZES a cousin

COZEN _v_ -ED, -ING, -S to deceive

COZENAGE _n pl._ -S the practice of cozening

COZENER _n pl._ -S one that cozens

COZEY _n pl._ -ZEYS a cozy

COZIE _n pl._ -S a cozy

COZIER comparative of cozy

COZIES pl. of cozy

COZIEST superlative of cozy

COZINESS _n pl._ -ES the state of being cozy

COZY _adj_ COZIER, COZIEST snug and comfortable COZILY _adv_

COZY _n pl._ -ZIES a covering for a teapot

COZZES pl. of coz

CRAAL _v_ -ED, -ING, -S to kraal

CRAB _v_ CRABBED, CRABBING, CRABS to complain

CRABBER _n pl._ -S one that crabs

CRABBY _adj_ -BIER, -BIEST grumpy

CRABWISE _adv_ sideways

CRACK _v_ -ED, -ING, -S to break without dividing into parts

CRACKER _n pl._ -S a thin, crisp biscuit

CRACKING _n pl._ -S a chemical process

CRACKLE _v_ -LED, -LING, -ES to make a succession of snapping sounds

CRACKLY _adj_ -LIER, -LIEST brittle

CRACKNEL _n pl._ -S a hard, crisp biscuit

CRACKPOT _n pl._ -S an eccentric person

CRACKUP _n pl._ -S a collision

CRACKY _interj_ — used to express surprise

CRADLE _v_ -DLED, -DLING, -DLES to nurture during infancy

CRADLER _n pl._ -S one that cradles

CRAFT _v_ -ED, -ING, -S to make by hand

CRAFTY _adj_ CRAFTIER, CRAFTIEST skillful in deceiving CRAFTILY _adv_

CRAG _n pl._ -S a rough rock CRAGGED _adj_

CRAGGY *adj* -GIER, -GIEST full of crags **CRAGGILY** *adv*

CRAGSMAN *n pl.* -MEN one who climbs crags

CRAKE *n pl.* -S a small, harsh-voiced bird

CRAM *v* CRAMMED, CRAMMING, CRAMS to fill or pack tightly

CRAMBE *n pl.* -S an annual herb

CRAMBO *n pl.* -BOS or -BOES a word game

CRAMMED past tense of cram

CRAMMER *n pl.* -S one that crams

CRAMMING present participle of cram

CRAMOISY *n pl.* -SIES crimson cloth

CRAMP *v* -ED, -ING, -S to restrain or confine

CRAMPIT *n pl.* -S a piece of equipment used in curling

CRAMPON *n pl.* -S a device for raising heavy objects

CRAMPOON *n pl.* -S crampon

CRANCH *v* -ED, -ING, -ES to craunch

CRANE *v* CRANED, CRANING, CRANES to stretch out one's neck

CRANIA a *pl.* of cranium

CRANIAL *adj* pertaining to the skull

CRANIATE *n pl.* -S one that has a skull

CRANING present participle of crane

CRANIUM *n pl.* -NIUMS or -NIA the skull

CRANK *v* -ED, -ING, -S to start manually

CRANK *adj* CRANKER, CRANKEST lively

CRANKIER comparative of cranky

CRANKIEST superlative of cranky

CRANKILY *adv* in a cranky manner

CRANKLE *v* -KLED, -KLING, -KLES to crinkle

CRANKLY *adv* in a crank manner

CRANKOUS *adj* cranky

CRANKPIN *n pl.* -S the handle of a crank

CRANKY *adj* CRANKIER, CRANKIEST grumpy

CRANNIED *adj* having crannies

CRANNIES *pl.* of cranny

CRANNOG *n pl.* -S an artificial island

CRANNOGE *n pl.* -S crannog

CRANNY *n pl.* -NIES a crevice **CRANNIED** *adj*

CRAP *v* CRAPPED, CRAPPING, CRAPS to defecate — an offensive term

CRAPE *v* CRAPED, CRAPING, CRAPES to crepe

CRAPPER *n pl.* -S a toilet — an offensive term

CRAPPIE *n pl.* -S an edible fish

CRAPPING present participle of crap

CRAPPY *adj* -PIER, -PIEST markedly inferior in quality

CRASES *pl.* of crasis

CRASH *v* -ED, -ING, -ES to collide noisily

CRASHER *n pl.* -S one that crashes

CRASIS *n pl.* CRASES a vowel contraction

CRASS *adj* CRASSER, CRASSEST grossly vulgar or stupid **CRASSLY** *adv*

CRATCH *n pl.* -ES a manger

CRATE *v* CRATED, CRATING, CRATES to put in a packing box

CRATER *v* -ED, -ING, -S to form cavities in a surface

CRATON *n pl.* -S a part of the earth's crust **CRATONIC** *adj*

CRAUNCH *v* -ED, -ING, -ES to crunch

CRAVAT *n pl.* -S a necktie

CRAVE *v* CRAVED, CRAVING, CRAVES to desire greatly

CRAVEN *v* -ED, -ING, -S to make cowardly

CRAVENLY *adv* in a cowardly manner

CRAVER *n pl.* -S one that craves

CRAVING *n pl.* -S a great desire

CRAW *n pl.* -S the stomach of an animal

CRAWDAD *n pl.* -S a crayfish

CRAWFISH *v* -ED, -ING, -ES to back out or retreat

CRAWL *v* -ED, -ING, -S to move with the body on or near the ground

CRAWLER *n pl.* -S one that crawls

CRAWLWAY *n pl.* -WAYS a small, low tunnel

CRAWLY *adj* CRAWLIER, CRAWLIEST creepy

CRAYFISH *n pl.* -ES a crustacean

CRAYON *v* -ED, -ING, -S to use a drawing implement

CRAZE *v* CRAZED, CRAZING, CRAZES to make insane

CRAZY	adj -ZIER, -ZIEST insane CRAZILY adv
CREAK	v -ED, -ING, -S to squeak
CREAKY	adj CREAKIER, CREAKIEST creaking CREAKILY adv
CREAM	v -ED, -ING, -S to form cream (a part of milk)
CREAMER	n pl. -S a cream pitcher
CREAMERY	n pl. -ERIES a dairy
CREAMY	adj CREAMIER, CREAMIEST rich in cream CREAMILY adv
CREASE	v CREASED, CREASING, CREASES to make a fold or wrinkle in
CREASER	n pl. -S one that creases
CREASY	adj CREASIER, CREASIEST having folds or wrinkles
CREATE	v -ATED, -ATING, -ATES to cause to exist
CREATIN	n pl. -S creatine
CREATINE	n pl. -S a chemical compound
CREATION	n pl. -S something created
CREATIVE	adj having the ability to create
CREATOR	n pl. -S one that creates
CREATURE	n pl. -S a living being
CRECHE	n pl. -S a day nursery
CREDAL	adj pertaining to a creed
CREDENCE	n pl. -S belief
CREDENDA	n/pl articles of faith
CREDENT	adj believing
CREDENZA	n pl. -S a piece of furniture
CREDIBLE	adj believable CREDIBLY adv
CREDIT	v -ED, -ING, -S to accept as true
CREDITOR	n pl. -S one to whom money is owed
CREDO	n pl. -DOS a creed
CREED	n pl. -S a statement of belief CREEDAL adj
CREEK	n pl. -S a watercourse smaller than a river
CREEL	n pl. -S a fish basket
CREEP	v CREPT, CREEPING, CREEPS to crawl
CREEPAGE	n pl. -S gradual movement
CREEPER	n pl. -S one that creeps
CREEPIE	n pl. -S a low stool
CREEPY	adj CREEPIER, CREEPIEST repugnant CREEPILY adv
CREESE	n pl. -S kris
CREESH	v -ED, -ING, -ES to grease

CREMAINS	n/pl the ashes of a cremated body
CREMATE	v -MATED, -MATING, -MATES to reduce to ashes by burning
CREMATOR	n pl. -S one that cremates
CREME	n pl. -S cream
CRENATE	adj having an edge with rounded projections
CRENATED	adj crenate
CRENEL	v -ELED, -ELING, -ELS or -ELLED, -ELLING, -ELS to provide with crenelles
CRENELLE	n pl. -S a rounded projection
CREODONT	n pl. -S an extinct carnivore
CREOLE	n pl. -S a type of mixed language
CREOSOL	n pl. -S a chemical compound
CREOSOTE	v -SOTED, -SOTING, -SOTES to treat with a wood preservative
CREPE	v CREPED, CREPING, CREPES to frizz the hair
CREPEY	adj CREPIER, CREPIEST crinkly
CREPT	past tense of creep
CREPY	adj CREPIER, CREPIEST crepey
CRESCENT	n pl. -S the figure of the moon in its first or last quarter
CRESCIVE	adj increasing
CRESOL	n pl. -S a chemical disinfectant
CRESS	n pl. -ES a plant used in salads
CRESSET	n pl. -S a metal cup for burning oil
CREST	v -ED, -ING, -S to reach a crest (a peak)
CRESTAL	adj pertaining to a crest
CRESTING	n pl. -S a decorative coping
CRESYL	n pl. -S tolyl
CRESYLIC	adj pertaining to cresol
CRETIC	n pl. -S a type of metrical foot
CRETIN	n pl. -S an idiot
CRETONNE	n pl. -S a heavy fabric
CREVALLE	n pl. -S a food and game fish
CREVASSE	v -VASSED, -VASSING, -VASSES to fissure
CREVICE	n pl. -S a cleft CREVICED adj
CREW	v -ED, -ING, -S to serve aboard a ship
CREWEL	n pl. -S a woolen yarn
CREWLESS	adj being without any crewmen
CREWMAN	n pl. -MEN one who serves on a ship
CRIB	v CRIBBED, CRIBBING, CRIBS to confine closely

CRIBBAGE *n pl.* -S a card game

CRIBBER *n pl.* -S one that cribs

CRIBBING *n pl.* -S a supporting framework

CRIBBLED *adj* covered with dots

CRIBROUS *adj* pierced with small holes

CRIBWORK *n pl.* -S a framework of logs

CRICETID *n pl.* -S a small rodent

CRICK *v* -ED, -ING, -S to cause a spasm of the neck

CRICKET *v* -ED, -ING, -S to play cricket (a ball game)

CRICOID *n pl.* -S a cartilage of the larynx

CRIED past tense of cry

CRIER *n pl.* -S one that cries

CRIES present 3d person sing. of cry

CRIME *n pl.* -S a violation of the law

CRIMINAL *n pl.* -S one who has committed a crime

CRIMMER *n pl.* -S krimmer

CRIMP *v* -ED, -ING, -S to pleat

CRIMPER *n pl.* -S one that crimps

CRIMPLE *v* -PLED, -PLING, -PLES to wrinkle

CRIMPY *adj* CRIMPIER, CRIMPIEST wavy

CRIMSON *v* -ED, -ING, -S to make crimson (a red color)

CRINGE *v* CRINGED, CRINGING, CRINGES to shrink in fear

CRINGER *n pl.* -S one that cringes

CRINGLE *n pl.* -S a small loop of rope

CRINITE *n pl.* -S a fossil crinoid

CRINKLE *v* -KLED, -KLING, -KLES to wrinkle

CRINKLY *adj* -KLIER, -KLIEST crinkled

CRINOID *n pl.* -S a marine animal

CRINUM *n pl.* -S a tropical herb

CRIOLLO *n pl.* -LLOS a person of Spanish ancestry

CRIPPLE *v* -PLED, -PLING, -PLES to disable or impair

CRIPPLER *n pl.* -S one that cripples

CRIS *n pl.* -ES kris

CRISIS *n pl.* CRISES a crucial turning point **CRISIC** *adj*

CRISP *adj* CRISPER, CRISPEST brittle

CRISP *v* -ED, -ING, -S to make crisp

CRISPATE *adj* curled

CRISPEN *v* -ED, -ING, -S to make crisp

CRISPER *n pl.* -S one that crisps

CRISPLY *adv* in a crisp manner

CRISPY *adj* CRISPIER, CRISPIEST crisp **CRISPILY** *adv*

CRISSUM *n pl.* CRISSA a region of feathers on a bird **CRISSAL** *adj*

CRISTA *n pl.* -TAE a part of a cell

CRISTATE *adj* having a projection on the head

CRITERIA *n/pl* standards of judgment

CRITIC *n pl.* -S one who judges the merits of something **CRITICAL** *adj*

CRITIQUE *v* -TIQUED, -TIQUING, -TIQUES to judge as a critic

CRITTER *n pl.* -S a creature

CRITTUR *n pl.* -S critter

CROAK *v* -ED, -ING, -S to utter a low, hoarse sound

CROAKER *n pl.* -S one that croaks

CROAKY *adj* CROAKIER, CROAKIEST low and hoarse **CROAKILY** *adv*

CROCEIN *n pl.* -S a red dye

CROCEINE *n pl.* -S crocein

CROCHET *v* -ED, -ING, -S to do a type of needlework

CROCI a pl. of crocus

CROCINE *adj* pertaining to the crocus

CROCK *v* -ED, -ING, -S to stain or soil

CROCKERY *n pl.* -ERIES pottery

CROCKET *n pl.* -S an architectural ornament

CROCOITE *n pl.* -S a mineral

CROCUS *n pl.* -CUSES or -CI a flowering plant

CROFT *n pl.* -S a small tenant farm

CROFTER *n pl.* -S a tenant farmer

CROJIK *n pl.* -S a triangular sail

CROMLECH *n pl.* -S a dolmen

CRONE *n pl.* -S a withered old woman

CRONY *n pl.* CRONIES a close friend

CRONYISM *n pl.* -S a kind of political favoritism

CROOK *v* -ED, -ING, -S to bend

CROOKED *adj* -EDER, -EDEST dishonest

CROON *v* -ED, -ING, -S to sing softly

CROONER *n pl.* -S one that croons

CROP *v* CROPPED, CROPPING, CROPS to cut off short

CROPLAND *n pl.* -S farmland

CROPLESS *adj* being without crops (agricultural produce)

CROPPED past tense of crop

CROPPER *n* pl. -S one that crops

CROPPING present participle of crop

CROQUET *v* -ED, -ING, -S to drive a ball away in a certain game

CROQUIS *n* pl. CROQUIS a sketch

CRORE *n* pl. -S a monetary unit of India

CROSIER *n* pl. -S a bishop's staff

CROSS *v* -ED, -ING, -ES to intersect

CROSS *adj* CROSSER, CROSSEST ill-tempered **CROSSLY** *adv*

CROSSARM *n* pl. -S a horizontal bar

CROSSBAR *v* -BARRED, BARRING, -BARS to fasten with crossarms

CROSSBOW *n* pl. -S a kind of weapon

CROSSCUT *v* -CUT, -CUTTING, -CUTS to cut across

CROSSE *n* pl. -S a lacrosse stick

CROSSER *n* pl. -S one that crosses

CROSSING *n* pl. -S an intersection

CROSSLET *n* pl. -S a heraldic symbol

CROSSTIE *n* pl. -S a transverse beam

CROSSWAY *n* pl. -S a road that crosses another road

CROTCH *n* pl. -ES an angle formed by two diverging parts **CROTCHED** *adj*

CROTCHET *n* pl. -S a small hook

CROTON *n* pl. -S a tropical plant

CROUCH *v* -ED, -ING, -ES to stoop

CROUP *n* pl. -S a disease of the throat

CROUPE *n* pl. -S the rump of certain animals

CROUPIER *n* pl. -S an attendant in a casino

CROUPOUS *adj* pertaining to croup

CROUPY *adj* CROUPIER, CROUPIEST affected with croup **CROUPILY** *adv*

CROUSE *adj* lively **CROUSELY** *adv*

CROUTON *n* pl. -S a small cube of toasted bread

CROW *v* -ED, -ING, -S to boast

CROWBAR *n* pl. -S a steel bar used as a lever

CROWD *v* -ED, -ING, -S to press into an insufficient space

CROWDER *n* pl. -S one that crowds

CROWDIE *n* pl. -S crowdy

CROWDY *n* pl. -DIES porridge

CROWER *n* pl. -S one that crows

CROWFOOT *n* pl. -FOOTS or -FEET a flowering plant

CROWN *v* -ED, -ING, -S to supply with a crown (a royal headpiece)

CROWNER *n* pl. -S a coroner

CROWNET *n* pl. -S a coronet

CROWSTEP *n* pl. -S a step on top of a wall

CROZE *n* pl. -S a tool used in barrel-making

CROZER *n* pl. -S a croze

CROZIER *n* pl. -S crosier

CRUCES a pl. of crux

CRUCIAL *adj* of supreme importance

CRUCIAN *n* pl. -S a European fish

CRUCIATE *adj* cross-shaped

CRUCIBLE *n* pl. -S a heat-resistant vessel

CRUCIFER *n* pl. -S one who carries a cross

CRUCIFIX *n* pl. -ES a cross bearing an image of Christ

CRUCIFY *v* -FIED, -FYING, -FIES to put to death on a cross

CRUD *v* CRUDDED, CRUDDING, CRUDS to curd

CRUDDY *adj* trashy

CRUDE *adj* CRUDER, CRUDEST unrefined **CRUDELY** *adv*

CRUDE *n* pl. -S unrefined petroleum

CRUDITY *n* pl. -TIES the state of being crude

CRUEL *adj* CRUELER, CRUELEST or CRUELLER, CRUELLEST indifferent to the pain of others **CRUELLY** *adv*

CRUELTY *n* pl. -TIES a cruel act

CRUET *n* pl. -S a glass bottle

CRUISE *v* CRUISED, CRUISING, CRUISES to sail about touching at several ports

CRUISER *n* pl. -S a boat that cruises

CRULLER *n* pl. -S a small sweet cake

CRUMB *v* -ED, -ING, -S to break into crumbs (small pieces)

CRUMBER *n* pl. -S one that crumbs

CRUMBIER comparative of crumby

CRUMBIEST superlative of crumby

CRUMBLE *v* -BLED, -BLING, -BLES to break into small pieces

CRUMBLY *adj* -BLIER, -BLIEST easily crumbled

CRUMBY *adj* CRUMBIER, CRUMBIEST full of crumbs

CRUMMIE *n* pl. -S a cow with crooked horns

CRUMMY *adj* -MIER, -MIEST of little or no value

CRUMP v -ED, -ING, -S to crunch

CRUMPET n pl. -S a small cake cooked on a grille

CRUMPLE v -PLED, -PLING, -PLES to wrinkle

CRUMPLY adj full of wrinkles

CRUNCH v -ED, -ING, -ES to chew with a crackling sound

CRUNCHER n pl. -S one that crunches

CRUNCHY adj CRUNCHIER, CRUNCHIEST crisp

CRUNODE n pl. -S a point at which a curve crosses itself. CRUNODAL adj

CRUOR n pl. -S clotted blood

CRUPPER n pl. -S the rump of a horse

CRURAL adj pertaining to the thigh or leg

CRUS n pl. CRURA a part of the leg

CRUSADE v -SADED, -SADING, -SADES to engage in a holy war

CRUSADER n pl. -S one that crusades

CRUSADO n pl. -DOES or -DOS a Portuguese coin

CRUSE n pl. -S a small bottle

CRUSET n pl. -S a melting pot

CRUSH v -ED, -ING, -ES to press or squeeze out of shape

CRUSHER n pl. -S one that crushes

CRUSILY adj covered with crosslets

CRUST v -ED, -ING, -S to form a crust (an outer surface)

CRUSTAL adj pertaining to the crust of the earth

CRUSTOSE adj forming a thin, brittle crust

CRUSTY adj CRUSTIER, CRUSTIEST surly CRUSTILY adv

CRUTCH v -ED, -ING, -ES to prop up or support

CRUX n pl. CRUXES or CRUCES a basic or decisive point

CRUZADO n pl. -DOES or -DOS crusado

CRUZEIRO n pl. -ROS a monetary unit of Brazil

CRWTH n pl. -S an ancient stringed musical instrument

CRY v CRIED, CRYING, CRIES to weep CRYINGLY adv

CRYBABY n pl. -BIES a person who cries easily

CRYOGEN n pl. -S a substance for producing low temperatures

CRYOGENY n pl. -NIES a branch of physics

CRYOLITE n pl. -S a mineral

CRYONICS n/pl the practice of freezing dead bodies for future revival CRYONIC adj

CRYOSTAT n pl. -S a refrigerating device

CRYOTRON n pl. -S an electronic device

CRYPT n pl. -S a burial vault CRYPTAL adj

CRYPTIC adj mysterious

CRYPTO n pl. -TOS one who belongs secretly to a group

CRYSTAL n pl. -S a transparent mineral

CTENIDIA n/pl comblike anatomical structures

CTENOID adj comblike

CUB n pl. -S the young of certain animals

CUBAGE n pl. -S cubature

CUBATURE n pl. -S cubical content

CUBBISH adj resembling a cub

CUBBY n pl. -BIES a small, enclosed space

CUBE v CUBED, CUBING, CUBES to form into a cube (a regular solid)

CUBEB n pl. -S a woody vine

CUBER n pl. -S a device that cubes meat

CUBIC n pl. -S a mathematical equation or expression

CUBICAL adj shaped like a cube

CUBICITY n pl. -TIES the state of being cubical

CUBICLE n pl. -S a small chamber

CUBICLY adv in the form of a cube

CUBICULA n/pl burial chambers

CUBIFORM adj shaped like a cube

CUBING present participle of cube

CUBISM n pl. -S a style of art CUBISTIC adj

CUBIST n pl. -S an adherent of cubism

CUBIT n pl. -S an ancient measure of length CUBITAL adj

CUBOID n pl. -S a bone of the foot CUBOIDAL adj

CUCKOLD v -ED, -ING, -S to make a cuckold (a cornuto) of

CUCKOO v -ED, -ING, -S to repeat monotonously

CUCUMBER n pl. -S a garden vegetable

CUCURBIT n pl. -S a gourd

CUD n pl. -S a portion of food to be chewed again

CUDBEAR n pl. -S a red dye

CUDDIE n pl. -S cuddy

CUDDIES pl. of cuddy

CUDDLE v -DLED, -DLING, -DLES to hug tenderly

CUDDLY adj -DLIER, -DLIEST fit for cuddling

CUDDY n pl. -DIES a donkey

CUDGEL v -ELED, -ELING, -ELS or -ELLED, -ELLING, -ELS to beat with a heavy club

CUDGELER n pl. -S one that cudgels

CUDWEED n pl. -S a perennial herb

CUE v CUED, CUING or CUEING, CUES to give a signal to an actor

CUESTA n pl. -S a type of land elevation

CUFF v -ED, -ING, -S to furnish with a cuff (a part of a sleeve)

CUFFLESS adj having no cuff

CUIF n pl. -S coof

CUING a present participle of cue

CUIRASS v -ED, -ING, -ES to cover with a type of armor

CUISH n pl. -ES cuisse

CUISINE n pl. -S a style of cooking

CUISSE n pl. -S a piece of armor for the thigh

CUITTLE v -TLED, -TLING, -TLES to coax

CUKE n pl. -S a cucumber

CULCH n pl. -ES an oyster bed

CULET n pl. -S a piece of armor for the lower back

CULEX n pl. CULICES a mosquito

CULICID n pl. -S a culicine

CULICINE n pl. -S a mosquito

CULINARY adj pertaining to cookery

CULL v -ED, -ING, -S to select from others

CULLAY n pl. -LAYS quillai

CULLER n pl. -S one that culls

CULLET n pl. -S broken glass gathered for remelting

CULLIED past tense of cully

CULLIES present 3d person sing. of cully

CULLION n pl. -S a vile fellow

CULLIS n pl. -LISES a gutter in a roof

CULLY v CULLIED, -LYING, -LIES to trick

CULM v -ED, -ING, -S to form a hollow stem

CULOTTE n pl. -S a divided skirt

CULPA n pl. -PAE negligence for which one is liable

CULPABLE adj deserving blame or censure CULPABLY adv

CULPRIT n pl. -S one that is guilty

CULT n pl. -S a religious society CULTIC adj

CULTCH n pl. -ES culch

CULTI a pl. of cultus

CULTIGEN n pl. -S a cultivar

CULTISM n pl. -S devotion to a cult

CULTIST n pl. -S a member of a cult

CULTIVAR n pl. -S a variety of plant originating under cultivation

CULTRATE adj sharp-edged and pointed

CULTURAL adj produced by breeding

CULTURE v -TURED, -TURING, -TURES to make fit for raising crops

CULTUS n pl. -TUSES or -TI a cult

CULVER n pl. -S a pigeon

CULVERIN n pl. -S a medieval musket

CULVERT n pl. -S a conduit

CUM prep together with

CUMARIN n pl. -S coumarin

CUMBER v -ED, -ING, -S to hinder

CUMBERER n pl. -S one that cumbers

CUMBROUS adj unwieldy

CUMIN n pl. -S a plant used in cooking

CUMMER n pl. -S a godmother

CUMMIN n pl. -S cumin

CUMQUAT n pl. -S kumquat

CUMSHAW n pl. -S a gift

CUMULATE v -LATED, -LATING, -LATES to heap

CUMULUS n pl. -LI a type of cloud CUMULOUS adj

CUNDUM n pl. -S condom

CUNEAL adj cuneate

CUNEATE adj wedge-shaped; triangular

CUNEATED adj cuneate

CUNEATIC adj cuneate

CUNIFORM n pl. -S wedge-shaped writing characters

CUNNER n pl. -S a marine fish

CUNNING adj -NINGER, -NINGEST crafty

CUNNING n pl. -S skill in deception

CUNT n pl. -S the female pudendum — an offensive term

CUP v CUPPED, CUPPING, CUPS to place in a cup (a small, open container)

CUPBOARD n pl. -S a cabinet

CUPCAKE n pl. -S a small cake

CUPEL v -PELED, -PELING, -PELS or -PELLED, -PELLING, -PELS to refine gold or silver in a cuplike vessel

CUPELER n pl. -S cupeller

CUPELLER n pl. -S one that cupels

CUPFUL n pl. CUPFULS or CUPSFUL as much as a cup can hold

CUPID n pl. -S a naked, winged representation of the Roman god of love

CUPIDITY n pl. -TIES greed; lust

CUPLIKE adj resembling a cup

CUPOLA v -ED, -ING, -S to shape like a dome

CUPPA n pl. -S a cup of tea

CUPPED past tense of cup

CUPPER n pl. -S one that performs cupping

CUPPING n pl. -S an archaic medical process

CUPPY adj -PIER, -PIEST cuplike

CUPREOUS adj containing copper

CUPRIC adj containing copper

CUPRITE n pl. -S an ore of copper

CUPROUS adj containing copper

CUPRUM n pl. -S copper

CUPSFUL a pl. of cupful

CUPULA n pl. -LAE a cup-shaped anatomical structure

CUPULAR adj cupulate

CUPULATE adj cup-shaped

CUPULE n pl. -S a cup-shaped anatomical structure

CUR n pl. -S a mongrel dog

CURABLE adj capable of being cured **CURABLY** adv

CURACAO n pl. -S a type of liqueur

CURACOA n pl. -S curacao

CURACY n pl. -CIES the office of a curate

CURAGH n pl. -S currach

CURARA n pl. -S curare

CURARE n pl. -S an arrow poison

CURARI n pl. -S curare

CURARINE n pl. -S a poisonous alkaloid

CURARIZE v -RIZED, -RIZING, -RIZES to poison with curare

CURASSOW n pl. -S a turkey-like bird

CURATE n pl. -S a clergyman in charge of a parish

CURATIVE n pl. -S something that cures

CURATOR n pl. -S a museum manager

CURB v -ED, -ING, -S to restrain **CURBABLE** adj

CURBER n pl. -S one that curbs

CURBING n pl. -S a concrete border along a street

CURCH n pl. -ES a kerchief

CURCULIO n pl. -LIOS a weevil

CURCUMA n pl. -S a tropical plant

CURD v -ED, -ING, -S to curdle

CURDIER comparative of curdy

CURDIEST superlative of curdy

CURDLE v -DLED, -DLING, -DLES to congeal

CURDLER n pl. -S one that curdles

CURDY adj CURDIER, CURDIEST curdled

CURE v CURED, CURING, CURES to restore to health

CURELESS adj not curable

CURER n pl. -S one that cures

CURET n pl. -S a surgical instrument

CURETTE v -RETTED, -RETTING, -RETTES to treat with a curet

CURF n pl. -S an incision made by a cutting tool

CURFEW n pl. -S a regulation concerning the hours which one may keep

CURIA n pl. -RIAE a court of justice **CURIAL** adj

CURIE n pl. -S a unit of radioactivity

CURING present participle of cure

CURIO n pl. -RIOS an unusual art object

CURIOSA n/pl pornographic books

CURIOUS adj -OUSER, -OUSEST eager for information

CURITE n pl. -S a radioactive mineral

CURIUM n pl. -S a radioactive element

CURL v -ED, -ING, -S to form into ringlets

CURLER n pl. -S one that curls

CURLEW n pl. -S a shore bird

CURLICUE v -CUED, -CUING, -CUES to decorate with curlicues (fancy spiral figures)

CURLING n pl. -S a game played on ice

CURLY adj CURLIER, CURLIEST tending to curl **CURLILY** adv

CURLYCUE	*n* pl. -S curlicue
CURN	*n* pl. -S grain
CURR	*v* -ED, -ING, -S to purr
CURRACH	*n* pl. -S a coracle
CURRAGH	*n* pl. -S a currach
CURRAN	*n* pl. -S curn
CURRANT	*n* pl. -S an edible berry
CURRENCY	*n* pl. -CIES money
CURRENT	*n* pl. -S a continuous flow
CURRICLE	*n* pl. -S a light carriage
CURRIE	*v* -RIED, -RYING, -RIES to prepare food a certain way
CURRIED	past tense of curry
CURRIER	*n* pl. -S one that curries leather
CURRIERY	*n* pl. -ERIES the shop of a currier
CURRISH	*adj* resembling a cur
CURRY	*v* -RIED, -RYING, -RIES to prepare leather for use or sale
CURRYING	present participle of currie
CURSE	*v* CURSED or CURST, CURSING, CURSES to wish evil upon
CURSED	*adj* CURSEDER, CURSEDEST wicked **CURSEDLY** *adv*
CURSER	*n* pl. -S one that curses
CURSING	present participle of curse
CURSIVE	*n* pl. -S a style of print
CURSORY	*adj* hasty and superficial
CURST	a past tense of curse
CURT	*adj* CURTER, CURTEST abrupt
CURTAIL	*v* -ED, -ING, -S to cut short
CURTAIN	*v* -ED, -ING, -S to provide with a hanging piece of fabric
CURTAL	*n* pl. -S an animal with a clipped tail
CURTALAX	*n* pl. -ES a cutlass
CURTATE	*adj* shortened
CURTESY	*n* pl. -SIES a type of legal tenure
CURTLY	*adv* in a curt manner
CURTNESS	*n* pl. -ES the quality of being curt
CURTSEY	*v* -ED, -ING, -S to curtsy
CURTSY	*v* -SIED, -SYING, -SIES to bow politely
CURULE	*adj* of the highest rank
CURVE	*v* CURVED, CURVING, CURVES to deviate from straightness
CURVET	*v* -VETED, -VETING, -VETS or -VETTED, -VETTING, -VETS to prance

CURVEY	*adj* CURVIER, CURVIEST curvy
CURVING	present participle of curve
CURVY	*adj* CURVIER, CURVIEST curved
CUSCUS	*n* pl. -ES an arboreal mammal
CUSEC	*n* pl. -S a volumetric unit of flow of liquids
CUSHAT	*n* pl. -S a pigeon
CUSHAW	*n* pl. -S a variety of squash
CUSHIER	comparative of cushy
CUSHIEST	superlative of cushy
CUSHILY	*adv* in a cushy manner
CUSHION	*v* -ED, -ING, -S to pad with soft material
CUSHIONY	*adj* soft
CUSHY	*adj* CUSHIER, CUSHIEST easy
CUSK	*n* pl. -S a marine food fish
CUSP	*n* pl. -S a pointed end **CUSPATE, CUSPATED, CUSPED** *adj*
CUSPID	*n* pl. -S a pointed tooth
CUSPIDAL	*adj* having a cusp
CUSPIDOR	*n* pl. -S a spittoon
CUSPIS	*n* pl. -PIDES a cusp
CUSS	*v* -ED, -ING, -ES to curse
CUSSEDLY	*adv* in a cranky manner
CUSSER	*n* pl. -S one that cusses
CUSSO	*n* pl. -SOS an Ethiopian tree
CUSSWORD	*n* pl. -S a profane or obscene word
CUSTARD	*n* pl. -S a dessert
CUSTODES	pl. of custos
CUSTODY	*n* pl. -DIES guardianship
CUSTOM	*n* pl. -S a habitual practice
CUSTOMER	*n* pl. -S one who buys something
CUSTOS	*n* pl. -TODES a guardian or keeper
CUSTUMAL	*n* pl. -S a written record of laws and customs
CUT	*v* CUT, CUTTING, CUTS to divide into parts with a sharp-edged instrument
CUTAWAY	*n* pl. -AWAYS a type of coat
CUTBACK	*n* pl. -S a reduction
CUTCH	*n* pl. -ES catechu
CUTCHERY	*n* pl. -CHERIES a judicial office in India
CUTDOWN	*n* pl. -S a reduction
CUTE	*adj* CUTER, CUTEST pleasingly attractive **CUTELY** *adv*

CUTENESS n pl. -ES the quality of being cute

CUTES a pl. of cutis

CUTEST superlative of cute

CUTESY adj -SIER, -SIEST self-consciously cute

CUTEY n pl. -TEYS cutie

CUTGRASS n pl. -ES a swamp grass

CUTICLE n pl. -S the epidermis

CUTICULA n pl. -LAE the outer hard covering of an insect

CUTIE n pl. -S a cute person

CUTIN n pl. -S a waxy substance found on plants

CUTINISE v -ISED, -ISING, -ISES to cutinize

CUTINIZE v -IZED, -IZING, -IZES to become coated with cutin

CUTIS n pl. -TES or -TISES the corium

CUTLAS n pl. -ES cutlass

CUTLASS n pl. -ES a short sword

CUTLER n pl. -S one who sells and repairs cutting tools

CUTLERY n pl. -LERIES the occupation of a cutler

CUTLET n pl. -S a slice of meat

CUTLINE n pl. -S a caption

CUTOFF n pl. -S the point at which something terminates

CUTOUT n pl. -S something cut out

CUTOVER adj cleared of trees

CUTPURSE n pl. -S a pickpocket

CUTTABLE adj capable of being cut

CUTTAGE n pl. -S a means of plant propagation

CUTTER n pl. -S one that cuts

CUTTING n pl. -S a section cut from a plant

CUTTLE v -TLED, -TLING, -TLES to fold cloth in a particular fashion

CUTTY n pl. -TIES a thickset girl

CUTUP n pl. -S a mischievous person

CUTWATER n pl. -S the front part of a ship's prow

CUTWORK n pl. -S a type of embroidery

CUTWORM n pl. -S a caterpillar

CUVETTE n pl. -S a small tube or vessel

CWM n pl. -S a cirque

CYAN n pl. -S a blue color

CYANAMID n pl. -S a chemical compound

CYANATE n pl. -S a chemical salt

CYANIC adj blue or bluish

CYANID n pl. -S a compound of cyanogen

CYANIDE v -NIDED, -NIDING, -NIDES to treat an ore with cyanid

CYANIN n pl. -S cyanine

CYANINE n pl. -S a blue dye

CYANITE n pl. -S a mineral **CYANITIC** adj

CYANO adj pertaining to cyanogen

CYANOGEN n pl. -S a reactive compound of carbon and nitrogen

CYANOSIS n pl. -NOSES bluish discoloration of the skin **CYANOSED, CYANOTIC** adj

CYBORG n pl. -S a human linked to a mechanical device for life support

CYCAD n pl. -S a tropical plant

CYCAS n pl. -ES a tropical plant

CYCASIN n pl. -S a sugar derivative

CYCLAMEN n pl. -S a flowering plant

CYCLASE n pl. -S an enzyme

CYCLE v -CLED, -CLING, -CLES to ride a bicycle

CYCLECAR n pl. -S a type of motor vehicle

CYCLER n pl. -S a cyclist

CYCLIC adj moving in complete circles **CYCLICLY** adv

CYCLICAL adj cyclic

CYCLING n pl. -S the act of riding a bicycle

CYCLIST n pl. -S one who rides a bicycle

CYCLITOL n pl. -S a chemical compound

CYCLIZE v -CLIZED, -CLIZING, -CLIZES to form one or more rings in a chemical compound

CYCLO n pl. -CLOS a three-wheeled motor vehicle

CYCLOID n pl. -S a geometric curve

CYCLONE n pl. -S a rotating system of winds **CYCLONAL, CYCLONIC** adj

CYCLOPS n pl. CYCLOPS a freshwater animal

CYCLOSIS n pl. -CLOSES the circulation of protoplasm within a cell

CYDER n pl. -S cider

CYESIS n pl. CYESES pregnancy

CYGNET n pl. -S a young swan

CYLINDER v -ED, -ING, -S to furnish with a cylinder (a chamber in an engine)

CYLIX n pl. CYLICES kylix

CYMA n pl. -MAS or -MAE a curved molding

CYMAR n pl. -S simar

CYMATIUM n pl. -TIA a cyma

CYMBAL n pl. -S a percussion instrument

CYMBALER n pl. -S one that plays the cymbals

CYMBLING n pl. -S cymling

CYME n pl. -S a flower cluster

CYMENE n pl. -S a hydrocarbon

CYMLIN n pl. -S cymling

CYMLING n pl. -S a variety of squash

CYMOGENE n pl. -S a volatile compound

CYMOID adj resembling a cyma

CYMOL n pl. -S cymene

CYMOSE adj resembling a cyme
CYMOSELY adv

CYMOUS adj cymose

CYNIC n pl. -S a cynical person

CYNICAL adj distrusting the motives of others

CYNICISM n pl. -S cynical quality

CYNOSURE n pl. -S a center of attraction

CYPHER v -ED, -ING, -S to cipher

CYPRES n pl. -ES a legal doctrine

CYPRESS n pl. -ES a thin fabric

CYPRIAN n pl. -S a prostitute

CYPRINID n pl. -S a small freshwater fish

CYPRUS n pl. -ES cypress

CYPSELA n pl. -LAE an achene in certain plants

CYST n pl. -S a sac

CYSTEIN n pl. -S cysteine

CYSTEINE n pl. -S an amino acid

CYSTIC adj pertaining to a cyst

CYSTINE n pl. -S an amino acid

CYSTITIS n pl. -TITIDES inflammation of the urinary bladder

CYSTOID n pl. -S a cyst-like structure

CYTASTER n pl. -S a structure formed in a cell during mitosis

CYTIDINE n pl. -S a compound containing cytosine

CYTOGENY n pl. -NIES the formation of cells

CYTOLOGY n pl. -GIES a study of cells

CYTON n pl. -S the body of a nerve cell

CYTOSINE n pl. -S a component of DNA and RNA

CZAR n pl. -S an emperor or king

CZARDAS n pl. CZARDAS a Hungarian dance

CZARDOM n pl. -S the domain of a czar

CZAREVNA n pl. -S the daughter of a czar

CZARINA n pl. -S the wife of a czar

CZARISM n pl. -S autocratic government

CZARIST n pl. -S a supporter of czarism

CZARITZA n pl. -S a czarina

DA	*prep* of; from — used in names	**DAFT**	*adj* DAFTER, DAFTEST insane **DAFTLY** *adv*
DAB	*v* DABBED, DABBING, DABS to touch lightly	**DAFTNESS**	*n* pl. -ES the quality of being daft
DABBER	*n* pl. -S one that dabs	**DAG**	*n* pl. -S a hanging end or shred
DABBLE	*v* -BLED, -BLING, -BLES to splash	**DAGGER**	*v* -ED, -ING, -S to stab with a small knife
DABBLER	*n* pl. -S one that dabbles	**DAGGLE**	*v* -GLED, -GLING, -GLES to drag in mud
DABBLING	*n* pl. -S a superficial interest		
DABCHICK	*n* pl. -S a small grebe	**DAGLOCK**	*n* pl. -S a dirty or tangled lock of wool
DABSTER	*n* pl. -S a bungler		
DACE	*n* pl. -S a freshwater fish	**DAGO**	*n* pl. -GOS or -GOES an Italian or Spaniard — an offensive term
DACHA	*n* pl. -S a Russian cottage		
DACKER	*v* -ED, -ING, -S to waver		
DACOIT	*n* pl. -S a bandit in India	**DAGOBA**	*n* pl. -S a Buddhist shrine
DACOITY	*n* pl. -COITIES robbery by dacoits	**DAH**	*n* pl. -S a dash in Morse code
		DAHABEAH	*n* pl. -S a large passenger boat
DACTYL	*n* pl. -S a type of metrical foot	**DAHABIAH**	*n* pl. -S dahabeah
DACTYLIC	*n* pl. -S a verse consisting of dactyls	**DAHABIEH**	*n* pl. -S dahabeah
		DAHABIYA	*n* pl. -S dahabeah
DACTYLUS	*n* pl. -LI a leg joint of certain insects	**DAHLIA**	*n* pl. -S a flowering plant
		DAHOON	*n* pl. -S an evergreen tree
DAD	*n* pl. -S father	**DAIKER**	*v* -ED, -ING, -S to dacker
DADA	*n* pl. -S an artistic and literary movement	**DAILY**	*n* pl. -LIES a newspaper published every weekday
DADAISM	*n* pl. -S the dada movement	**DAIMEN**	*adj* occasional
DADAIST	*n* pl. -S a follower of dadaism	**DAIMIO**	*n* pl. -MIOS a former Japanese nobleman
DADDLE	*v* -DLED, -DLING, -DLES to diddle		
		DAIMON	*n* pl. -S or -ES an attendant spirit **DAIMONIC** *adj*
DADDY	*n* pl. -DIES father		
DADO	*v* -ED, -ING, -ES or -S to set into a groove	**DAIMYO**	*n* pl. -MYOS daimio
		DAINTY	*n* pl. -TIES something delicious
DAEDAL	*adj* skillful	**DAINTY**	*adj* -TIER, -TIEST delicately pretty **DAINTILY** *adv*
DAEMON	*n* pl. -S demon **DAEMONIC** *adj*		
DAFF	*v* -ED, -ING, -S to thrust aside	**DAIQUIRI**	*n* pl. -S a cocktail
DAFFODIL	*n* pl. -S a flowering plant	**DAIRY**	*n* pl. DAIRIES an establishment dealing in milk products
DAFFY	*adj* -FIER, -FIEST silly		

DAIRYING   *n* pl. -S the business of a dairy

DAIRYMAN   *n* pl. -MEN a man who works in or owns a dairy

DAIS   *n* pl. -ISES a raised platform

DAISHIKI   *n* pl. -S dashiki

DAISY   *n* pl. -SIES a flowering plant **DAISIED** *adj*

DAK   *n* pl. -S transportation by relays of men and horses

DAKERHEN   *n* pl. -S a European bird

DAKOIT   *n* pl. -S dacoit

DAKOITY   *n* pl. -TIES dacoity

DALAPON   *n* pl. -S an herbicide used on unwanted grasses

DALASI   *n* pl. DALASI a unit of Gambian currency

DALE   *n* pl. -S a valley

DALESMAN   *n* pl. -MEN one living in a dale

DALETH   *n* pl. -S a Hebrew letter

DALLES   *n/pl* rapids

DALLIER   *n* pl. -S one that dallies

DALLY   *v* -LIED, -LYING, -LIES to waste time

DALMATIC   *n* pl. -S a wide-sleeved vestment

DALTONIC   *adj* pertaining to a form of color blindness

DAM   *v* DAMMED, DAMMING, DAMS to build a barrier to obstruct the flow of water

DAMAGE   *v* -AGED, -AGING, -AGES to injure

DAMAGER   *n* pl. -S one that damages

DAMAN   *n* pl. -S a small mammal

DAMAR   *n* pl. -S dammar

DAMASK   *v* -ED, -ING, -S to weave with elaborate design

DAME   *n* pl. -S a matron

DAMEWORT   *n* pl. -S a flowering plant

DAMMAR   *n* pl. -S a hard resin

DAMMED   past tense of dam

DAMMER   *n* pl. -S dammar

DAMMING   present participle of dam

DAMN   *v* -ED, -ING, -S to curse

DAMNABLE   *adj* detestable **DAMNABLY** *adv*

DAMNDEST   *n* pl. -S utmost

DAMNED   *adj* DAMNEDER, DAMNEDEST or DAMNDEST damnable

DAMNER   *n* pl. -S one that damns

DAMNIFY   *v* -FIED, -FYING, -FIES to cause loss or damage to

DAMOSEL   *n* pl. -S damsel

DAMOZEL   *n* pl. -S damsel

DAMP   *adj* DAMPER, DAMPEST moist

DAMP   *v* -ED, -ING, -S to moisten

DAMPEN   *v* -ED, -ING, -S to moisten

DAMPENER   *n* pl. -S one that dampens

DAMPER   *n* pl. -S one that damps

DAMPISH   *adj* somewhat damp

DAMPLY   *adv* in a damp manner

DAMPNESS   *n* pl. -ES the state of being damp

DAMSEL   *n* pl. -S a maiden

DAMSON   *n* pl. -S a small purple plum

DANCE   *v* DANCED, DANCING, DANCES to move rhythmically to music

DANCER   *n* pl. -S one that dances

DANDER   *v* -ED, -ING, -S to stroll

DANDIER   comparative of dandy

DANDIES   pl. of dandy

DANDIEST   superlative of dandy

DANDIFY   *v* -FIED, -FYING, -FIES to cause to resemble a dandy

DANDILY   *adv* in a dandy manner

DANDLE   *v* -DLED, -DLING, -DLES to fondle

DANDLER   *n* pl. -S one that dandles

DANDRIFF   *n* pl. -S dandruff

DANDRUFF   *n* pl. -S a scurf that forms on the scalp

DANDY   *adj* -DIER, -DIEST fine

DANDY   *n* pl. -DIES a man who is overly concerned about his appearance

DANDYISH   *adj* suggestive of a dandy

DANDYISM   *n* pl. -S the style or conduct of a dandy

DANEGELD   *n* pl. -S an annual tax in medieval England

DANEWEED   *n* pl. -S a danewort

DANEWORT   *n* pl. -S a flowering plant

DANG   *v* -ED, -ING, -S to damn

DANGER   *v* -ED, -ING, -S to endanger

DANGLE   *v* -GLED, -GLING, -GLES to hang loosely

DANGLER   *n* pl. -S one that dangles

DANIO   *n* pl. -NIOS an aquarium fish

DANK   *adj* DANKER, DANKEST unpleasantly damp **DANKLY** *adv*

DANKNESS   *n* pl. -ES the state of being dank

DANSEUR   *n* pl. -S a male ballet dancer

DANSEUSE   *n* pl. -S a female ballet dancer

DAP   v DAPPED, DAPPING, DAPS to dip lightly or quickly into water

DAPHNE   n pl. -S a flowering shrub

DAPHNIA   n pl. -S a minute crustacean

DAPPED   past tense of dap

DAPPER   adj -PERER, -PEREST looking neat and trim DAPPERLY adv

DAPPING   present participle of dap

DAPPLE   v -PLED, -PLING, -PLES to mark with spots

DARB   n pl. -S something considered extraordinary

DARBIES   n/pl handcuffs

DARE   v DARED or DURST, DARING, DARES to have the necessary courage

DAREFUL   adj brave

DARER   n pl. -S one that dares

DARESAY   v to venture to say — DARESAY is the only form of this verb; it is not conjugated

DARIC   n pl. -S an ancient Persian coin

DARING   n pl. -S bravery

DARINGLY   adv in a brave manner

DARIOLE   n pl. -S a type of pastry filled with cream, custard, or jelly

DARK   adj DARKER, DARKEST having little or no light

DARK   v -ED, -ING, -S to darken

DARKEN   v -ED, -ING, -S to make dark

DARKENER   n pl. -S one that darkens

DARKEY   n pl. -EYS darky — an offensive term

DARKIE   n pl. -S darky — an offensive term

DARKIES   pl. of darky — an offensive term

DARKISH   adj somewhat dark

DARKLE   v -KLED, -KLING, -KLES to become dark

DARKLY   adv -LIER, -LIEST in a dark manner

DARKNESS   n pl. -ES the state of being dark

DARKROOM   n pl. -S a room in which film is processed

DARKSOME   adj dark

DARKY   n pl. DARKIES a black person — an offensive term

DARLING   n pl. -S a much-loved person

DARN   v -ED, -ING, -S to mend with interlacing stitches

DARNDEST   n pl. -S damndest

DARNED   adj DARNEDER, DARNEDEST or DARNDEST damned

DARNEL   n pl. -S an annual grass

DARNER   n pl. -S one that darns

DARNING   n pl. -S things to be darned

DART   v -ED, -ING, -S to move suddenly or swiftly

DARTER   n pl. -S one that darts

DARTLE   v -TLED, -TLING, -TLES to dart repeatedly

DASH   v -ED, -ING, -ES to strike violently

DASHEEN   n pl. -S a tropical plant

DASHER   n pl. -S one that dashes

DASHIER   comparative of dashy

DASHIEST   superlative of dashy

DASHIKI   n pl. -S an African tunic

DASHPOT   n pl. -S a shock absorber

DASHY   adj DASHIER, DASHIEST stylish

DASSIE   n pl. -S a hyrax

DASTARD   n pl. -S a base coward

DASYURE   n pl. -S a flesh-eating mammal

DATA   a pl. of datum

DATABLE   adj capable of being dated

DATARY   n pl. -RIES a cardinal in the Roman Catholic Church

DATCHA   n pl. -S dacha

DATE   v DATED, DATING, DATES to determine or record the date of DATEABLE adj

DATEDLY   adv in an old-fashioned manner

DATELESS   adj having no date

DATELINE   v -LINED, -LINING, -LINES to provide a news story with its date and place of origin

DATER   n pl. -S one that dates

DATING   present participle of date

DATIVE   n pl. -S a grammatical case DATIVAL adj DATIVELY adv

DATO   n pl. -TOS datto

DATTO   n pl. -TOS a Philippine tribal chief

DATUM   n pl. -TA or -TUMS something used as a basis for calculating

DATURA   n pl. -S a flowering plant DATURIC adj

DAUB   v -ED, -ING, -S to smear

DAUBE   n pl. -S a braised meat stew

DAUBER   n pl. -S one that daubs

DAUBERY   n pl. -ERIES a bad or inexpert painting

DAUBRY   n pl. -RIES daubery

DAUBY *adj* DAUBIER, DAUBIEST smeary

DAUGHTER *n* pl. -S a female child

DAUNDER *v* -ED, -ING, -S to dander

DAUNT *v* -ED, -ING, -S to intimidate

DAUNTER *n* pl. -S one that daunts

DAUPHIN *n* pl. -S the eldest son of a French king

DAUPHINE *n* pl. -S the wife of a dauphin

DAUT *v* -ED, -ING, -S to fondle

DAUTIE *n* pl. -S a small pet

DAVEN *v* -ED, -ING, -S to utter Jewish prayers

DAVIT *n* pl. -S a hoisting device on a ship

DAVY *n* pl. -VIES a safety lamp

DAW *v* DAWED, DAWEN, DAWING, DAWS to dawn

DAWDLE *v* -DLED, -DLING, -DLES to waste time

DAWDLER *n* pl. -S one that dawdles

DAWEN past participle of daw

DAWK *n* pl. -S dak

DAWN *v* -ED, -ING, -S to begin to grow light in the morning

DAWNLIKE *adj* suggestive of daybreak

DAWT *v* -ED, -ING, -S to daut

DAWTIE *n* pl. -S dautie

DAY *n* pl. DAYS the time between sunrise and sunset

DAYBED *n* pl. -S a couch that can be converted into a bed

DAYBOOK *n* pl. -S a diary

DAYBREAK *n* pl. -S the first appearance of light in the morning

DAYDREAM *v* -DREAMED or -DREAMT, -DREAMING, -DREAMS to fantasize

DAYFLY *n* pl. -FLIES a mayfly

DAYGLOW *n* pl. -S airglow seen during the day

DAYLIGHT *v* -LIGHTED or -LIT, -LIGHTING, -LIGHTS to illuminate with the light of day

DAYLILY *n* pl. -LILIES a flowering plant

DAYLONG *adj* lasting all day

DAYMARE *n* pl. -S a nightmarish fantasy experienced while awake

DAYROOM *n* pl. -S a room for reading and recreation

DAYSIDE *n* pl. -S the sun side of a planet or the moon

DAYSMAN *n* pl. -MEN an arbiter

DAYSTAR *n* pl. -S a planet visible in the east just before sunrise

DAYTIME *n* pl. -S day

DAZE *v* DAZED, DAZING, DAZES to stun DAZEDLY *adv*

DAZZLE *v* -ZLED, -ZLING, -ZLES to blind by bright light

DAZZLER *n* pl. -S one that dazzles

DE *prep* of; from — used in names and phrases

DEACON *v* -ED, -ING, -S to read a hymn aloud

DEACONRY *n* pl. -RIES a clerical office

DEAD *adj* DEADER, DEADEST deprived of life

DEAD *n* pl. -S the period of greatest intensity

DEADBEAT *n* pl. -S a loafer

DEADEN *v* -ED, -ING, -S to diminish the sensitivity or vigor of

DEADENER *n* pl. -S one that deadens

DEADEYE *n* pl. -S an expert marksman

DEADFALL *n* pl. -S a type of animal trap

DEADHEAD *v* -ED, -ING, -S to travel without freight

DEADLIER comparative of deadly

DEADLIEST superlative of deadly

DEADLINE *n* pl. -S a time limit

DEADLOCK *v* -ED, -ING, -S to come to a standstill

DEADLY *adj* -LIER, -LIEST fatal

DEADNESS *n* pl. -ES the state of being dead

DEADPAN *v* -PANNED, -PANNING, -PANS to act without emotion

DEADWOOD *n* pl. -S a reinforcement in a ship's keel

DEAERATE *v* -ATED, -ATING, -ATES to remove air or gas from

DEAF *adj* DEAFER, DEAFEST lacking the sense of hearing

DEAFEN *v* -ED, -ING, -S to make deaf

DEAFISH *adj* somewhat deaf

DEAFLY *adv* in a deaf manner

DEAFNESS *n* pl. -ES the state of being deaf

DEAIR *v* -ED, -ING, -S to remove air from

DEAL *v* DEALT, DEALING, DEALS to trade or do business

DEALATE *n* pl. -S an insect divested of its wings DEALATED *adj*

DEALER *n* pl. -S one that deals

DEALFISH n pl. -ES a marine fish

DEALING n pl. -S a business transaction

DEALT past tense of deal

DEAN v -ED, -ING, -S to serve as dean (the head of a faculty)

DEANERY n pl. -ERIES the office of a dean

DEANSHIP n pl. -S deanery

DEAR adj DEARER, DEAREST greatly loved

DEAR n pl. -S a loved one

DEARIE n pl. -S deary

DEARIES pl. of deary

DEARLY adv in a dear manner

DEARNESS n pl. -ES the state of being dear

DEARTH n pl. -S scarcity

DEARY n pl. DEARIES darling

DEASH v -ED, -ING, -ES to remove ash from

DEASIL adv clockwise

DEATH n pl. -S the end of life

DEATHBED n pl. -S the bed on which a person dies

DEATHCUP n pl. -S a poisonous mushroom

DEATHFUL adj fatal

DEATHLY adj fatal

DEATHY adj deathly

DEAVE v DEAVED, DEAVING, DEAVES to deafen

DEB n pl. -S a debutante

DEBACLE n pl. -S a sudden collapse

DEBAR v -BARRED, -BARRING, -BARS to exclude

DEBARK v -ED, -ING, -S to unload from a ship

DEBASE v -BASED, -BASING, -BASES to lower in character, quality, or value

DEBASER n pl. -S one that debases

DEBATE v -BATED, -BATING, -BATES to argue about

DEBATER n pl. -S one that debates

DEBAUCH v -ED, -ING, -ES to corrupt

DEBILITY n pl. -TIES weakness

DEBIT v -ED, -ING, -S to charge with a debt

DEBONAIR adj suave

DEBONE v -BONED, -BONING, -BONES to remove the bones from

DEBONER n pl. -S a bone remover

DEBOUCH v -ED, -ING, -ES to march into the open

DEBOUCHE n pl. -S an opening for the passage of troops

DEBRIEF v -ED, -ING, -S to question after a mission

DEBRIS n pl. DEBRIS fragments or scattered remains

DEBRUISE v -BRUISED, -BRUISING, -BRUISES to cross a coat of arms

DEBT n pl. -S something that is owed **DEBTLESS** adj

DEBTOR n pl. -S one who owes something to another

DEBUG v -BUGGED, -BUGGING, -BUGS to remove insects from

DEBUNK v -ED, -ING, -S to expose the sham or falseness of

DEBUNKER n pl. -S one that debunks

DEBUT v -ED, -ING, -S to make one's first public appearance

DEBUTANT n pl. -S one who is debuting

DEBYE n pl. -S a unit of measure for electric dipole moments

DECADE n pl. -S a period of ten years **DECADAL** adj

DECADENT n pl. -S one in a state of mental or moral decay

DECAGON n pl. -S a ten-sided polygon

DECAGRAM n pl. -S dekagram

DECAL n pl. -S a picture or design made to be transferred from specially prepared paper

DECAMP v -ED, -ING, -S to depart from a camping ground

DECANAL adj pertaining to a dean

DECANE n pl. -S a hydrocarbon

DECANT v -ED, -ING, -S to pour from one container into another

DECANTER n pl. -S a decorative bottle

DECAPOD n pl. -S a ten-legged crustacean

DECARE n pl. -S dekare

DECAY v -ED, -ING, -S to decompose

DECAYER n pl. -S one that decays

DECEASE v -CEASED, -CEASING, -CEASES to die

DECEDENT n pl. -S a deceased person

DECEIT n pl. -S the act of deceiving

DECEIVE v -CEIVED, -CEIVING, -CEIVES to mislead by falsehood

DECEIVER n pl. -S one that deceives

DECEMVIR *n pl.* -VIRS or -VIRI one of a body of ten Roman magistrates

DECENARY *n pl.* -RIES a tithing

DECENCY *n pl.* -CIES the state of being decent

DECENNIA *n/pl* decades

DECENT *adj* -CENTER, -CENTEST conforming to recognized standards of propriety
DECENTLY *adv*

DECENTER *v* -ED, -ING, -S to put out of center

DECENTRE *v* -TRED, -TRING, -TRES to decenter

DECERN *v* -ED, -ING, -S to decree by judicial sentence

DECIARE *n pl.* -S a metric unit of area

DECIBEL *n pl.* -S a unit of sound intensity

DECIDE *v* -CIDED, -CIDING, -CIDES to make a choice or judgment

DECIDER *n pl.* -S one that decides

DECIDUA *n pl.* -UAS or -UAE a mucous membrane of the uterus
DECIDUAL *adj*

DECIGRAM *n pl.* -S one tenth of a gram

DECILE *n pl.* -S a statistical interval

DECIMAL *n pl.* -S a fraction whose denominator is some power of ten

DECIMATE *v* -MATED, -MATING, -MATES to destroy a large part of

DECIPHER *v* -ED, -ING, -S to determine the meaning of

DECISION *n pl.* -S the act of deciding

DECISIVE *adj* conclusive

DECK *v* -ED, -ING, -S to adorn

DECKEL *n pl.* -S deckle

DECKER *n pl.* -S something having a specified number of levels, floors, or layers

DECKHAND *n pl.* -S a seaman who performs manual duties

DECKING *n pl.* -S material for a ship's deck

DECKLE *n pl.* -S a frame used in making paper by hand

DECLAIM *v* -ED, -ING, -S to speak formally

DECLARE *v* -CLARED, -CLARING, -CLARES to make known clearly

DECLARER *n pl.* -S one that declares

DECLASS *v* -ED, -ING, -ES to lower in status

DECLASSE *adj* lowered in status

DECLINE *v* -CLINED, -CLINING, -CLINES to refuse

DECLINER *n pl.* -S one that declines

DECOCT *v* -ED, -ING, -S to extract the flavor of by boiling

DECODE *v* -CODED, -CODING, -CODES to convert a coded message into plain language

DECODER *n pl.* -S one that decodes

DECOLOR *v* -ED, -ING, -S to deprive of color

DECOLOUR *v* -ED, -ING, -S to decolor

DECOR *n pl.* -S style or mode of decoration

DECORATE *v* -RATED, -RATING, -RATES to adorn

DECOROUS *adj* proper

DECORUM *n pl.* -S conformity to social conventions

DECOY *v* -ED, -ING, -S to lure into a trap

DECOYER *n pl.* -S one that decoys

DECREASE *v* -CREASED, -CREASING, -CREASES to diminish

DECREE *v* -CREED, -CREEING, -CREES to order or establish by law or edict

DECREER *n pl.* -S one that decrees

DECREPIT *adj* worn out by long use

DECRETAL *n pl.* -S a papal edict

DECRIAL *n pl.* -S the act of decrying

DECRIED past tense of decry

DECRIER *n pl.* -S one that decries

DECROWN *v* -ED, -ING, -S to deprive of a crown; depose

DECRY *v* -CRIED, -CRYING, -CRIES to denounce

DECRYPT *v* -ED, -ING, -S to decode

DECUMAN *adj* extremely large

DECUPLE *v* -PLED, -PLING, -PLES to increase tenfold

DECURION *n pl.* -S a commander of a decury

DECURVE *v* -CURVED, -CURVING, -CURVES to curve downward

DECURY *n pl.* -RIES a group of ten soldiers in ancient Rome

DEDAL *adj* daedal

DEDANS *n pl.* DEDANS a gallery for tennis spectators

DEDICATE *v* -CATED, -CATING, -CATES to set apart for some special use

DEDUCE v -DUCED, -DUCING, -DUCES to infer

DEDUCT v -ED, -ING, -S to subtract

DEE n pl. -S the letter D

DEED v -ED, -ING, -S to transfer by deed (a legal document)

DEEDLESS adj being without deeds

DEEDY adj DEEDIER, DEEDIEST industrious

DEEJAY n pl. -JAYS a disc jockey

DEEM v -ED, -ING, -S to hold as an opinion

DEEMSTER n pl. -S a judicial officer of the Isle of Man

DEEP adj DEEPER, DEEPEST extending far down from a surface

DEEP n pl. -S a place or thing of great depth

DEEPEN v -ED, -ING, -S to make deep

DEEPENER n pl. -S one that deepens

DEEPLY adv at or to a great depth

DEEPNESS n pl. -ES the quality of being deep

DEER n pl. -S a ruminant mammal

DEERFLY n pl. -FLIES a bloodsucking fly

DEERSKIN n pl. -S the skin of a deer

DEERWEED n pl. -S a bushlike herb

DEERYARD n pl. -S an area where deer herd in winter

DEEWAN n pl. -S dewan

DEFACE v -FACED, -FACING, -FACES to mar the appearance of

DEFACER n pl. -S one that defaces

DEFAME v -FAMED, -FAMING, -FAMES to attack the good name of

DEFAMER n pl. -S one that defames

DEFAT v -FATTED, -FATTING, -FATS to remove fat from

DEFAULT v -ED, -ING, -S to fail to do something required

DEFEAT v -ED, -ING, -S to win victory over

DEFEATER n pl. -S one that defeats

DEFECATE v -CATED, -CATING, -CATES to discharge feces

DEFECT v -ED, -ING, -S to desert an allegiance

DEFECTOR n pl. -S one that defects

DEFENCE n pl. -S something that defends

DEFEND v -ED, -ING, -S to protect

DEFENDER n pl. -S one that defends

DEFENSE v -FENSED, -FENSING, -FENSES to guard against a specific attack

DEFER v -FERRED, -FERRING, -FERS to postpone

DEFERENT n pl. -S an imaginary circle around the earth

DEFERRAL n pl. -S the act of deferring

DEFERRED past tense of defer

DEFERRER n pl. -S one that defers

DEFERRING present participle of defer

DEFI n pl. -S a challenge

DEFIANCE n pl. -S bold opposition

DEFIANT adj showing defiance

DEFICIT n pl. -S a shortage

DEFIED past tense of defy

DEFIER n pl. -S one that defies

DEFIES present 3d person sing. of defy

DEFILADE v -LADED, -LADING, -LADES to shield from enemy fire

DEFILE v -FILED, -FILING, -FILES to make dirty

DEFILER n pl. -S one that defiles

DEFINE v -FINED, -FINING, -FINES to state the meaning of

DEFINER n pl. -S one that defines

DEFINITE adj known for certain

DEFLATE v -FLATED, -FLATING, -FLATES to release the air or gas from

DEFLATOR n pl. -S one that deflates

DEFLEA v -ED, -ING, -S to rid of fleas

DEFLECT v -ED, -ING, -S to turn aside

DEFLEXED adj bent downward

DEFLOWER v -ED, -ING, -S to deprive of flowers

DEFOAM v -ED, -ING, -S to remove foam from

DEFOAMER n pl. -S one that defoams

DEFOG v -FOGGED, -FOGGING, -FOGS to remove fog from

DEFOGGER n pl. -S one that defogs

DEFORCE v -FORCED, -FORCING, -FORCES to withhold by force

DEFOREST v -ED, -ING, -S to clear of forests

DEFORM v -ED, -ING, -S to spoil the form of

DEFORMER n pl. -S one that deforms

DEFRAUD v -ED, -ING, -S to swindle

DEFRAY v -ED, -ING, -S to pay

DEFRAYAL n pl. -S the act of defraying

DEFRAYER *n* pl. -S one that defrays

DEFROCK *v* -ED, -ING, -S to unfrock

DEFROST *v* -ED, -ING, -S to remove frost from

DEFT *adj* DEFTER, DEFTEST skillful **DEFTLY** *adv*

DEFTNESS *n* pl. -ES the quality of being deft

DEFUNCT *adj* deceased

DEFUSE *v* -FUSED, -FUSING, -FUSES to remove the fuse from

DEFUZE *v* -FUZED, -FUZING, -FUZES to defuse

DEFY *v* -FIED, -FYING, -FIES to resist openly and boldly

DEGAGE *adj* free and relaxed in manner

DEGAME *n* pl. -S a tropical tree

DEGAMI *n* pl. -S degame

DEGAS *v* -GASSED, -GASSING, -GASSES or -GASES to remove gas from

DEGASSER *n* pl. -S one that degasses

DEGAUSS *v* -ED, -ING, -ES to demagnetize

DEGERM *v* -ED, -ING, -S to remove germs from

DEGLAZE *v* -GLAZED, -GLAZING, -GLAZES to remove the glaze from

DEGRADE *v* -GRADED, -GRADING, -GRADES to debase

DEGRADER *n* pl. -S one that degrades

DEGREASE *v* -GREASED, -GREASING, -GREASES to remove the grease from

DEGREE *n* pl. -S one of a series of stages **DEGREED** *adj*

DEGUM *v* -GUMMED, -GUMMING, -GUMS to free from gum

DEGUST *v* -ED, -ING, -S to taste with pleasure

DEHISCE *v* -HISCED, -HISCING, -HISCES to split open

DEHORN *v* -ED, -ING, -S to deprive of horns

DEHORNER *n* pl. -S one that dehorns

DEHORT *v* -ED, -ING, -S to try to dissuade

DEI *prep* of; from — used in names

DEICE *v* -ICED, -ICING, -ICES to free from ice

DEICER *n* pl. -S one that deices

DEICIDE *n* pl. -S the killing of a god **DEICIDAL** *adj*

DEICTIC *adj* proving directly

DEIFIC *adj* godlike

DEIFICAL *adj* deific

DEIFIED past tense of deify

DEIFIER *n* pl. -S one that deifies

DEIFORM *adj* having the form of a god

DEIFY *v* -FIED, -FYING, -FIES to make a god of

DEIGN *v* -ED, -ING, -S to lower oneself to do something

DEIL *n* pl. -S the devil

DEIONIZE *v* -IZED, -IZING, -IZES to remove ions from

DEISM *n* pl. -S a religious philosophy

DEIST *n* pl. -S an adherent of deism **DEISTIC** *adj*

DEITY *n* pl. -TIES a god or goddess

DEJECT *v* -ED, -ING, -S to depress

DEJECTA *n/pl* excrements

DEJEUNER *n* pl. -S a late breakfast

DEKAGRAM *n* pl. -S a measure equal to ten grams

DEKARE *n* pl. -S a measure equal to ten ares

DEKE *v* DEKED, DEKING, DEKES to feint in hockey

DEL *n* pl. -S an operator in differential calculus

DELAINE *n* pl. -S a wool fabric

DELATE *v* -LATED, -LATING, -LATES to accuse

DELATION *n* pl. -S the act of delating

DELATOR *n* pl. -S one that delates

DELAY *v* -ED, -ING, -S to put off to a later time

DELAYER *n* pl. -S one that delays

DELE *v* DELED, DELEING, DELES to delete

DELEAD *v* -ED, -ING, -S to remove lead from

DELEGACY *n* pl. -CIES the act of delegating

DELEGATE *v* -GATED, -GATING, -GATES to appoint as one's representative

DELETE *v* -LETED, -LETING, -LETES to remove written or printed matter

DELETION *n* pl. -S the act of deleting

DELF *n* pl. -S delft

DELFT *n* pl. -S an earthenware

DELI *n* pl. DELIS a delicatessen

DELICACY *n* pl. -CIES a choice food

DELICATE *n* pl. -S a delicacy

DELICT n pl. -S an offense against civil law

DELIGHT v -ED, -ING, -S to give great pleasure to

DELIME v -LIMED, -LIMING, -LIMES to free from lime

DELIMIT v -ED, -ING, -S to mark the boundaries of

DELIRIUM n pl. -IUMS or -IA wild excitement

DELIST v -ED, -ING, -S to remove from a list

DELIVER v -ED, -ING, -S to take to the intended recipient

DELIVERY n pl. -ERIES the act of delivering

DELL n pl. -S a small, wooded valley

DELLY n pl. DELLIES deli

DELOUSE v -LOUSED, -LOUSING, -LOUSES to remove lice from

DELTA n pl. -S an alluvial deposit at the mouth of a river DELTAIC, DELTIC adj

DELTOID n pl. -S a shoulder muscle

DELUDE v -LUDED, -LUDING, -LUDES to mislead the mind or judgment of

DELUDER n pl. -S one that deludes

DELUGE v -UGED, -UGING, -UGES to flood

DELUSION n pl. -S the act of deluding

DELUSIVE adj tending to delude

DELUSORY adj delusive

DELUSTER v -ED, -ING, -S to lessen the sheen of

DELUXE adj of special elegance or luxury

DELVE v DELVED, DELVING, DELVES to search in depth

DELVER n pl. -S one that delves

DEMAGOG n pl. -S an unethical leader

DEMAGOGY n pl. -GOGIES the rule of a demagog

DEMAND v -ED, -ING, -S to ask for with authority

DEMANDER n pl. -S one that demands

DEMARCHE n pl. -S a procedure

DEMARK v -ED, -ING, -S to delimit

DEMAST v -ED, -ING, -S to strip masts from

DEME n pl. -S a Greek district

DEMEAN v -ED, -ING, -S to conduct oneself in a particular manner

DEMEANOR n pl. -S the manner in which one conducts oneself

DEMENT v -ED, -ING, -S to make insane

DEMENTIA n pl. -S mental illness

DEMERIT v -ED, -ING, -S to lower in rank or status

DEMESNE n pl. -S the legal possession of land as one's own

DEMIES pl. of demy

DEMIGOD n pl. -S a lesser god

DEMIJOHN n pl. -S a narrow-necked jug

DEMILUNE n pl. -S a half-moon

DEMIREP n pl. -S a prostitute

DEMISE v -MISED, -MISING, -MISES to bequeath

DEMIT v -MITTED, -MITTING, -MITS to resign

DEMIURGE n pl. -S a magistrate of ancient Greece

DEMIVOLT n pl. -S a half turn made by a horse

DEMO n pl. DEMOS a demonstration

DEMOB v -MOBBED, -MOBBING, -MOBS to discharge from military service

DEMOCRAT n pl. -S one who believes in political and social equality

DEMODE adj demoded

DEMODED adj out-of-date

DEMOLISH v -ED, -ING, -ES to destroy

DEMON n pl. -S an evil spirit

DEMONESS n pl. -ES a female demon

DEMONIAC n pl. -S one regarded as possessed by a demon

DEMONIAN adj demonic

DEMONIC adj characteristic of a demon

DEMONISE v -ISED, -ISING, -ISES to demonize

DEMONISM n pl. -S belief in demons

DEMONIST n pl. -S one who believes in demons

DEMONIZE v -IZED, -IZING, -IZES to make a demon of

DEMOS n pl. -ES the people of an ancient Greek state

DEMOTE v -MOTED, -MOTING, -MOTES to lower in rank or grade

DEMOTIC adj pertaining to a simplified form of ancient Egyptian writing

DEMOTICS n/pl the study of people in society

DEMOTING present participle of demote

DEMOTION n pl. -S the act of demoting

DEMOTIST n pl. -S a student of demotic writings

DEMOUNT v -ED, -ING, -S to remove from a mounting

DEMPSTER n pl. -S a deemster

DEMUR v -MURRED, -MURRING, -MURS to object

DEMURE adj -MURER, -MUREST shy and modest **DEMURELY** adv

DEMURRAL n pl. -S the act of demurring

DEMURRED past tense of demur

DEMURRER n pl. -S one that demurs

DEMURRING present participle of demur

DEMY n pl. -MIES a size of paper

DEN v DENNED, DENNING, DENS to live in a lair

DENARIUS n pl. DENARII a coin of ancient Rome

DENARY adj containing ten

DENATURE v -TURED, -TURING, -TURES to deprive of natural qualities

DENAZIFY v -FIED, -FYING, -FIES to rid of Nazism

DENDRITE n pl. -S a branched part of a nerve cell

DENDROID adj shaped like a tree

DENDRON n pl. -S a dendrite

DENE n pl. -S a valley

DENGUE n pl. -S a tropical disease

DENIABLE adj capable of being denied **DENIABLY** adv

DENIAL n pl. -S the act of denying

DENIED past tense of deny

DENIER n pl. -S one that denies

DENIES present 3d person sing. of deny

DENIM n pl. -S a durable fabric

DENIZEN v -ED, -ING, -S to make a citizen of

DENNED past tense of den

DENNING present participle of den

DENOTE v -NOTED, -NOTING, -NOTES to indicate **DENOTIVE** adj

DENOUNCE v -NOUNCED, -NOUNCING, -NOUNCES to condemn openly

DENSE adj DENSER, DENSEST compact **DENSELY** adv

DENSIFY v -FIED, -FYING, -FIES to make denser

DENSITY n pl. -TIES the state of being dense

DENT v -ED, -ING, -S to make a depression in

DENTAL n pl. -S a dentally produced sound

DENTALIA n/pl mollusks with long, tapering shells

DENTALLY adv with the tip of the tongue against the upper front teeth

DENTATE adj having teeth

DENTATED adj dentate

DENTICLE n pl. -S a small tooth

DENTIL n pl. -S a small rectangular block

DENTIN n pl. -S the hard substance forming the body of a tooth **DENTINAL** adj

DENTINE n pl. -S dentin

DENTIST n pl. -S one who treats the teeth

DENTOID adj resembling a tooth

DENTURE n pl. -S a set of teeth **DENTURAL** adj

DENUDATE v -DATED, -DATING, -DATES to denude

DENUDE v -NUDED, -NUDING, -NUDES to strip of all covering

DENUDER n pl. -S one that denudes

DENY v -NIED, -NYING, -NIES to declare to be untrue

DEODAND n pl. -S property forfeited to the crown under a former English law

DEODAR n pl. -S an East Indian cedar

DEODARA n pl. -S deodar

DEPAINT v -ED, -ING, -S to depict

DEPART v -ED, -ING, -S to go away

DEPEND v -ED, -ING, -S to rely

DEPERM v -ED, -ING, -S to demagnetize

DEPICT v -ED, -ING, -S to portray

DEPICTER n pl. -S one that depicts

DEPICTOR n pl. -S depicter

DEPILATE v -LATED, -LATING, -LATES to remove hair from

DEPLANE v -PLANED, -PLANING, -PLANES to get off an airplane

DEPLETE v -PLETED, -PLETING, -PLETES to lessen or exhaust the supply of

DEPLORE v -PLORED, -PLORING, -PLORES to regret strongly

DEPLORER n pl. -S one that deplores

DEPLOY v -ED, -ING, -S to position troops for battle

DEPLUME v -PLUMED, -PLUMING, -PLUMES to deprive of feathers

DEPOLISH v -ED, -ING, -ES to remove the gloss or polish of

DEPONE v -PONED, -PONING, -PONES to testify under oath

DEPONENT n pl. -S one that depones

DEPORT v -ED, -ING, -S to expel from a country

DEPORTEE n pl. -S one who is deported

DEPOSAL n pl. -S the act of deposing

DEPOSE v -POSED, -POSING, -POSES to remove from office

DEPOSER n pl. -S one that deposes

DEPOSIT v -ED, -ING, -S to place

DEPOT n pl. -S a railroad or bus station

DEPRAVE v -PRAVED, -PRAVING, -PRAVES to corrupt in morals

DEPRAVER n pl. -S one that depraves

DEPRESS v -ED, -ING, -ES to make sad

DEPRIVAL n pl. -S the act of depriving

DEPRIVE v -PRIVED, -PRIVING, -PRIVES to take something away from

DEPRIVER n pl. -S one that deprives

DEPSIDE n pl. -S an aromatic compound

DEPTH n pl. -S deepness

DEPURATE v -RATED, -RATING, -RATES to free from impurities

DEPUTE v -PUTED, -PUTING, -PUTES to delegate

DEPUTIZE v -TIZED, -TIZING, -TIZES to appoint as a deputy

DEPUTY n pl. -TIES one appointed to act for another

DERAIGN v -ED, -ING, -S to dispute a claim

DERAIL v -ED, -ING, -S to run off the rails of a track

DERANGE v -RANGED, -RANGING, -RANGES to disorder

DERAT v -RATTED, -RATTING, -RATS to rid of rats

DERAY n pl. -RAYS disorderly revelry

DERBY n pl. -BIES a type of hat

DERE adj dire

DERELICT n pl. -S something abandoned

DERIDE v -RIDED, -RIDING, -RIDES to ridicule

DERIDER n pl. -S one that derides

DERINGER n pl. -S a short-barreled pistol

DERISION n pl. -S the act of deriding

DERISIVE adj expressing derision

DERISORY adj derisive

DERIVATE n pl. -S something derived

DERIVE v -RIVED, -RIVING, -RIVES to obtain or receive from a source

DERIVER n pl. -S one that derives

DERM n pl. -S derma

DERMA n pl. -S a layer of the skin **DERMAL** adj

DERMIS n pl. -MISES derma **DERMIC** adj

DERMOID adj resembling skin

DERNIER adj last

DEROGATE v -GATED, -GATING, -GATES to detract

DERRICK n pl. -S a hoisting apparatus

DERRIERE n pl. -S the buttocks

DERRIS n pl. -RISES a climbing plant

DERRY n pl. -RIES a meaningless word used as part of a chorus in old songs

DERVISH n pl. -ES a member of a Muslim religious order

DES prep of the — used in names

DESALT v -ED, -ING, -S to remove the salt from

DESALTER n pl. -S one that desalts

DESAND v -ED, -ING, -S to remove sand from

DESCANT v -ED, -ING, -S to sing

DESCEND v -ED, -ING, -S to come or go down

DESCENT n pl. -S the act of descending

DESCRIBE v -SCRIBED, -SCRIBING, -SCRIBES to give a verbal account of

DESCRIER n pl. -S one that descries

DESCRY v -SCRIED, -SCRYING, -SCRIES to discern

DESELECT v -ED, -ING, -S to dismiss from a training program

DESERT v -ED, -ING, -S to abandon

DESERTER n pl. -S one that deserts

DESERTIC adj arid and barren

DESERVE v -SERVED, -SERVING, -SERVES to be entitled to or worthy of

DESERVER n pl. -S one that deserves

DESEX v -ED, -ING, -ES to castrate or spay

DESIGN v -ED, -ING, -S to conceive and plan out

DESIGNEE n pl. -S one who is designated

DESIGNER n pl. -S one that designs

DESILVER v -ED, -ING, -S to remove the silver from

DESINENT adj terminating

DESIRE v -SIRED, -SIRING, -SIRES to wish for

DESIRER n pl. -S one that desires

DESIROUS adj desiring

DESIST v -ED, -ING, -S to cease doing something

DESK n pl. -S a writing table

DESKMAN n pl. -MEN one who works at a desk

DESMAN n pl. -S an aquatic mammal

DESMID n pl. -S a freshwater alga

DESMOID n pl. -S a very hard tumor

DESOLATE v -LATED, -LATING, -LATES to lay waste

DESORB v -ED, -ING, -S to remove by the reverse of absorption

DESPAIR v -ED, -ING, -S to lose all hope

DESPATCH v -ED, -ING, -ES to dispatch

DESPISE v -SPISED, -SPISING, -SPISES to loathe

DESPISER n pl. -S one that despises

DESPITE v -SPITED, -SPITING, -SPITES to treat with contempt

DESPOIL v -ED, -ING, -S to plunder

DESPOND v -ED, -ING, -S to lose spirit or hope

DESPOT n pl. -S a tyrant **DESPOTIC** adj

DESSERT n pl. -S something served as the last course of a meal

DESTAIN v -ED, -ING, -S to remove stain from

DESTINE v -TINED, -TINING, -TINES to determine beforehand

DESTINY n pl. -NIES the fate or fortune to which one is destined

DESTRIER n pl. -S a war horse

DESTROY v -ED, -ING, -S to damage beyond repair or renewal

DESTRUCT v -ED, -ING, -S to destroy

DESUGAR v -ED, -ING, -S to remove sugar from

DESULFUR v -ED, -ING, -S to free from sulfur

DETACH v -ED, -ING, -ES to unfasten and separate

DETACHER n pl. -S one that detaches

DETAIL v -ED, -ING, -S to report with complete particulars

DETAILER n pl. -S one that details

DETAIN v -ED, -ING, -S to hold in custody

DETAINEE n pl. -S one who is detained

DETAINER n pl. -S the unlawful withholding of another's property

DETECT v -ED, -ING, -S to discover or perceive

DETECTER n pl. -S detector

DETECTOR n pl. -S one that detects

DETENT n pl. -S a mechanical device that either stops or releases a movement

DETENTE n pl. -S an easing of international tension

DETER v -TERRED, -TERRING, -TERS to stop from proceeding

DETERGE v -TERGED, -TERGING, -TERGES to cleanse

DETERGER n pl. -S one that deterges

DETERRED past tense of deter

DETERRER n pl. -S one that deters

DETERRING present participle of deter

DETEST v -ED, -ING, -S to dislike intensely

DETESTER n pl. -S one that detests

DETHRONE v -THRONED, -THRONING, -THRONES to remove from a throne

DETICK v -ED, -ING, -S to remove ticks from

DETICKER n pl. -S one that deticks

DETINUE n pl. -S an action to recover property wrongfully detained

DETONATE v -NATED, -NATING, -NATES to cause to explode

DETOUR v -ED, -ING, -S to take an indirect route

DETOXIFY v -FIED, -FYING, -FIES to remove a toxin from

DETRACT v -ED, -ING, -S to take away

DETRAIN v -ED, -ING, -S to get off a railroad train

DETRITUS n pl. DETRITUS particles of rock **DETRITAL** adj

DETRUDE v -TRUDED, -TRUDING, -TRUDES to thrust out

DEUCE v DEUCED, DEUCING, DEUCES to bring a tennis score to a tie

DEUCEDLY adv extremely

DEUTERIC adj pertaining to heavy hydrogen

DEUTERON n pl. -S an atomic particle

DEUTZIA n pl. -S an ornamental shrub

DEV n pl. -S deva

DEVA n pl. -S a Hindu god

DEVALUE v -UED, -UING, -UES to lessen the worth of

DEVEIN v -ED, -ING, -S to remove the dorsal vein from

DEVEL v -ED, -ING, -S to strike forcibly

DEVELOP v -ED, -ING, -S to bring to a more advanced or effective state

DEVELOPE v -OPED, -OPING, -OPES to develop

DEVEST v -ED, -ING, -S to divest

DEVIANCE n pl. -S the behavior of a deviant

DEVIANCY n pl. -CIES deviance

DEVIANT n pl. -S one that deviates from a norm

DEVIATE v -ATED, -ATING, -ATES to turn aside from a course or norm

DEVIATOR n pl. -S one that deviates

DEVICE n pl. -S something devised or constructed for a specific purpose

DEVIL v -ILED, -ILING, -ILS or -ILLED, -ILLING, -ILS to prepare food with pungent seasoning

DEVILISH adj fiendish

DEVILKIN n pl. -S a small demon

DEVILLED a past tense of devil

DEVILLING a present participle of devil

DEVILRY n pl. -RIES deviltry

DEVILTRY n pl. -TRIES mischief

DEVIOUS adj indirect

DEVISAL n pl. -S the act of devising

DEVISE v -VISED, -VISING, -VISES to form in the mind

DEVISEE n pl. -S one to whom a will is made

DEVISER n pl. -S one that devises

DEVISING present participle of devise

DEVISOR n pl. -S one who makes a will

DEVOICE v -VOICED, -VOICING, -VOICES to unvoice

DEVOID adj completely lacking

DEVOIR n pl. -S an act of civility or respect

DEVOLVE v -VOLVED, -VOLVING, -VOLVES to transfer from one person to another

DEVON n pl. -S one of a breed of small, hardy cattle

DEVOTE v -VOTED, -VOTING, -VOTES to give oneself wholly to

DEVOTEE n pl. -S an ardent follower or supporter

DEVOTION n pl. -S the act of devoting

DEVOUR v -ED, -ING, -S to eat up voraciously

DEVOURER n pl. -S one that devours

DEVOUT adj pious DEVOUTLY adv

DEW v -ED, -ING, -S to wet with dew (condensed moisture)

DEWAN n pl. -S an official in India

DEWATER v -ED, -ING, -S to remove water from

DEWAX v -ED, -ING, -ES to remove wax from

DEWBERRY n pl. -RIES an edible berry

DEWCLAW n pl. -S a vestigial toe

DEWDROP n pl. -S a drop of dew

DEWFALL n pl. -S the formation of dew

DEWIER comparative of dewy

DEWIEST superlative of dewy

DEWILY adv in a dewy manner

DEWINESS n pl. -ES the state of being dewy

DEWLAP n pl. -S a fold of loose skin under the neck

DEWLESS adj having no dew

DEWOOL v -ED, -ING, -S to remove the wool from

DEWORM v -ED, -ING, -S to rid of worms

DEWY adj DEWIER, DEWIEST moist with dew

DEX n pl. -ES a sulfate used as a central nervous system stimulant

DEXIES n/pl tablets of dex

DEXTER adj situated on the right

DEXTRAL adj pertaining to the right

DEXTRAN n pl. -S a substance used as a plasma substitute

DEXTRIN n pl. -S a substance used as an adhesive

DEXTRINE n pl. -S dextrin

DEXTRO adj turning to the right

DEXTROSE n pl. -S a form of glucose

DEXTROUS adj adroit

DEY n pl. DEYS a former North African ruler

DEZINC v -ZINCKED, -ZINCKING, -ZINCS or -ZINCED, -ZINCING, -ZINCS to remove zinc from

DHAK n pl. -S an Asian tree

DHARMA n pl. -S conformity to Hindu law DHARMIC adj

DHARNA n pl. -S a form of protest in India

DHOLE n pl. -S a wild dog of India

DHOOLY   n pl. -LIES dooly

DHOORA   n pl. -S durra

DHOOTI   n pl. -S dhoti

DHOOTIE   n pl. -S dhoti

DHOTI   n pl. -S a loincloth worn by Hindu men

DHOURRA   n pl. -S durra

DHOW   n pl. -S an Arabian sailing vessel

DHURNA   n pl. -S dharna

DHUTI   n pl. -S dhoti

DIABASE   n pl. -S an igneous rock DIABASIC adj

DIABETES   n pl. DIABETES a metabolic disorder

DIABETIC   n pl. -S one who has diabetes

DIABLERY   n pl. -RIES sorcery

DIABOLIC   adj devilish

DIABOLO   n pl. -LOS a game requiring manual dexterity

DIACETYL   n pl. -S biacetyl

DIACID   n pl. -S a type of acid DIACIDIC adj

DIACONAL   adj pertaining to a deacon

DIADEM   v -ED, -ING, -S to adorn with a crown

DIAGNOSE   v -NOSED, -NOSING, -NOSES to recognize a disease by its signs and symptoms

DIAGONAL   n pl. -S an oblique line

DIAGRAM   v -GRAMED, -GRAMING, -GRAMS or -GRAMMED, -GRAMMING, -GRAMS to illustrate by a diagram (a graphic design)

DIAGRAPH   n pl. -S a drawing device

DIAL   v DIALED, DIALING, DIALS or DIALLED, DIALLING, DIALS to manipulate a calibrated disk

DIALECT   n pl. -S a regional variety of a language

DIALER   n pl. -S one that dials

DIALING   n pl. -S the measurement of time by sundials

DIALIST   n pl. -S a dialer

DIALLAGE   n pl. -S a mineral

DIALLED   a past tense of dial

DIALLEL   adj pertaining to a genetic crossing

DIALLER   n pl. -S dialer

DIALLING   n pl. -S dialing

DIALLIST   n pl. -S dialist

DIALOG   v -ED, -ING, -S to dialogue

DIALOGER   n pl. -S one that dialogs

DIALOGIC   adj conversational

DIALOGUE   v -LOGUED, -LOGUING, -LOGUES to carry on a conversation

DIALYSE   v -LYSED, -LYSING, -LYSES to dialyze

DIALYSER   n pl. -S dialyzer

DIALYSIS   n pl. -YSES the separation of substances in a solution by diffusion through a membrane

DIALYTIC   adj pertaining to dialysis

DIALYZE   v -LYZED, -LYZING, -LYZES to subject to dialysis

DIALYZER   n pl. -S an apparatus used for dialysis

DIAMETER   n pl. -S a straight line passing through the center of a circle and ending at the periphery

DIAMIDE   n pl. -S a chemical compound

DIAMIN   n pl. -S diamine

DIAMINE   n pl. -S a chemical compound

DIAMOND   v -ED, -ING, -S to adorn with diamonds (precious gems)

DIANTHUS   n pl. -ES an ornamental herb

DIAPASON   n pl. -S a burst of harmonious sound

DIAPAUSE   v -PAUSED, -PAUSING, -PAUSES to undergo dormancy

DIAPER   v -ED, -ING, -S to put a diaper (a baby's breechcloth) on

DIAPHONE   n pl. -S a low-pitched foghorn

DIAPHONY   n pl. -NIES organum

DIAPIR   n pl. -S a bend in a layer of rock DIAPIRIC adj

DIAPSID   adj pertaining to a type of reptile

DIARCHY   n pl. -CHIES a government with two rulers DIARCHIC adj

DIARIES   pl. of diary

DIARIST   n pl. -S one who keeps a diary

DIARRHEA   n pl. -S an intestinal disorder

DIARY   n pl. -RIES a personal journal

DIASPORA   n pl. -S migration

DIASPORE   n pl. -S a mineral

DIASTASE   n pl. -S an enzyme

DIASTEMA   n pl. -MATA a space between teeth

DIASTER   n pl. -S a stage in mitosis DIASTRAL adj

DIASTOLE   n pl. -S the normal rhythmical dilation of the heart

DIATOM   n pl. -S any of a class of algae

DIATOMIC *adj* composed of two atoms

DIATONIC *adj* pertaining to a type of musical scale

DIATRIBE *n pl.* -S a bitter and abusive criticism

DIAZEPAM *n pl.* -S a tranquilizer

DIAZIN *n pl.* -S diazine

DIAZINE *n pl.* -S a chemical compound

DIAZO *adj* containing a certain chemical group

DIAZOLE *n pl.* -S a chemical compound

DIB *v* DIBBED, DIBBING, DIBS to fish by letting the bait bob lightly on the water

DIBASIC *adj* having two replaceable hydrogen atoms

DIBBER *n pl.* -S a planting implement

DIBBING present participle of dib

DIBBLE *v* -BLED, -BLING, -BLES to dib

DIBBLER *n pl.* -S one that dibbles

DIBBUK *n pl.* -BUKS or -BUKIM dybbuk

DICAST *n pl.* -S a judge of ancient Athens **DICASTIC** *adj*

DICE *v* DICED, DICING, DICES to cut into small cubes

DICENTRA *n pl.* -S a perennial herb

DICER *n pl.* -S a device that dices food

DICEY *adj* DICIER, DICIEST dangerous

DICHASIA *n/pl* flower clusters

DICHOTIC *adj* affecting the two ears differently

DICHROIC *adj* having two colors

DICIER comparative of dicey

DICIEST superlative of dicey

DICING present participle of dice

DICK *n pl.* -S a detective

DICKENS *n pl.* -ES devil

DICKER *v* -ED, -ING, -S to bargain

DICKEY *n pl.* -EYS a blouse front

DICKIE *n pl.* -S dickey

DICKY *n pl.* DICKIES dickey

DICLINY *n pl.* -NIES the state of having stamens and pistils in separate flowers

DICOT *n pl.* -S a plant with two seed leaves

DICOTYL *n pl.* -S dicot

DICROTAL *adj* dicrotic

DICROTIC *adj* having a double pulse beat

DICTA a *pl.* of dictum

DICTATE *v* -TATED, -TATING, -TATES to read aloud for recording

DICTATOR *n pl.* -S one that dictates

DICTION *n pl.* -S choice and use of words in speech or writing

DICTUM *n pl.* -TA or -TUMS an authoritative statement

DICYCLIC *adj* having two maxima of population each year

DICYCLY *n pl.* -CLIES the state of being dicyclic

DID a past tense of do

DIDACT *n pl.* -S a didactic person

DIDACTIC *adj* instructive

DIDACTYL *adj* having two digits at the end of each limb

DIDAPPER *n pl.* -S a dabchick

DIDDLE *v* -DLED, -DLING, -DLES to swindle

DIDDLER *n pl.* -S one that diddles

DIDIES *pl.* of didy

DIDO *n pl.* -DOS or -DOES a mischievous act

DIDST a past tense of do

DIDY *n pl.* -DIES a diaper

DIDYMIUM *n pl.* -S a mixture of rare-earth elements

DIDYMOUS *adj* occurring in pairs

DIDYNAMY *n pl.* -MIES the state of having four stamens in pairs of unequal length

DIE *v* DIED, DYING, DIES to cease living

DIE *v* DIED, DIEING, DIES to cut with a die (a device for shaping material)

DIEBACK *n pl.* -S a gradual dying of plant shoots

DIECIOUS *adj* dioicous

DIED past tense of die

DIEHARD *n pl.* -S a stubborn person

DIEL *adj* involving a full day

DIELDRIN *n pl.* -S an insecticide

DIEMAKER *n pl.* -S one that makes dies

DIENE *n pl.* -S a chemical compound

DIERESIS *n pl.* DIERESES the separation of two vowels into two syllables **DIERETIC** *adj*

DIES present 3d person sing. of die

DIESEL *n pl.* -S a type of engine

DIESIS *n pl.* DIESES a reference mark in printing

DIESTER	*n pl.* -S a type of chemical compound
DIESTOCK	*n pl.* -S a frame for holding dies
DIESTRUM	*n pl.* -S diestrus
DIESTRUS	*n pl.* -ES a period of sexual inactivity
DIET	*v* -ED, -ING, -S to regulate one's daily sustenance
DIETARY	*n pl.* -ETARIES a system of dieting
DIETER	*n pl.* -S one that diets
DIETETIC	*adj* pertaining to diet
DIFFER	*v* -ED, -ING, -S to be unlike
DIFFRACT	*v* -ED, -ING, -S to separate into parts
DIFFUSE	*v* -FUSED, -FUSING, -FUSES to spread widely or thinly
DIFFUSER	*n pl.* -S one that diffuses
DIFFUSOR	*n pl.* -S diffuser
DIG	*v* DUG or DIGGED, DIGGING, DIGS to break up, turn over, or remove earth
DIGAMIST	*n pl.* -S one who practices digamy
DIGAMMA	*n pl.* -S a Greek letter
DIGAMY	*n pl.* -MIES a second legal marriage **DIGAMOUS** *adj*
DIGEST	*v* -ED, -ING, -S to render food usable for the body
DIGESTER	*n pl.* -S an apparatus in which substances are softened or decomposed
DIGESTOR	*n pl.* -S digester
DIGGED	a past tense of dig
DIGGER	*n pl.* -S one that digs
DIGGING	present participle of dig
DIGGINGS	*n/pl* an excavation site
DIGHT	*v* -ED, -ING, -S to adorn
DIGIT	*n pl.* -S a finger or toe
DIGITAL	*n pl.* -S a piano key
DIGITATE	*adj* having digits
DIGITIZE	*v* -TIZED, -TIZING, -TIZES to put data into digital notation
DIGLOT	*n pl.* -S a bilingual book or edition
DIGNIFY	*v* -FIED, -FYING, -FIES to add dignity to
DIGNITY	*n pl.* -TIES stateliness and nobility of manner
DIGOXIN	*n pl.* -S a poisonous steroid
DIGRAPH	*n pl.* -S a pair of letters representing a single speech sound
DIGRESS	*v* -ED, -ING, -ES to stray from the main topic
DIHEDRAL	*n pl.* -S a dihedron
DIHEDRON	*n pl.* -S a figure formed by two intersecting planes
DIHYBRID	*n pl.* -S an offspring of parents differing in two pairs of genes
DIHYDRIC	*adj* containing two hydroxyl radicals
DIKDIK	*n pl.* -S a small antelope
DIKE	*v* DIKED, DIKING, DIKES to furnish with an embankment
DIKER	*n pl.* -S one that dikes
DIKTAT	*n pl.* -S a harsh settlement imposed on a defeated nation
DILATANT	*n pl.* -S a dilator
DILATATE	*adj* dilated
DILATE	*v* -LATED, -LATING, -LATES to make wider or larger
DILATER	*n pl.* -S dilator
DILATION	*n pl.* -S the act of dilating
DILATIVE	*adj* tending to dilate
DILATOR	*n pl.* -S one that dilates
DILATORY	*adj* tending to delay
DILDO	*n pl.* -DOS an object used as a penis substitute
DILDOE	*n pl.* -S dildo
DILEMMA	*n pl.* -S a perplexing situation **DILEMMIC** *adj*
DILIGENT	*adj* persevering
DILL	*n pl.* -S an annual herb
DILLY	*n pl.* DILLIES something remarkable
DILUENT	*n pl.* -S a diluting substance
DILUTE	*v* -LUTED, -LUTING, -LUTES to thin or reduce the concentration of
DILUTER	*n pl.* -S one that dilutes
DILUTION	*n pl.* -S the act of diluting
DILUTIVE	*adj* tending to dilute
DILUTOR	*n pl.* -S diluter
DILUVIA	a pl. of diluvium
DILUVIAL	*adj* pertaining to a flood
DILUVIAN	*adj* diluvial
DILUVION	*n pl.* -S diluvium
DILUVIUM	*n pl.* -VIA or -VIUMS coarse rock material deposited by glaciers
DIM	*adj* DIMMER, DIMMEST obscure
DIM	*v* DIMMED, DIMMING, DIMS to make dim

DIME n pl. -S a coin of the United States

DIMER n pl. -S a molecule composed of two identical molecules

DIMERIC adj dimerous

DIMERISM n pl. -S the state of being dimerous

DIMERIZE v -IZED, -IZING, -IZES to form a dimer

DIMEROUS adj composed of two parts

DIMETER n pl. -S a verse of two metrical feet

DIMETHYL n pl. -S ethane

DIMETRIC adj pertaining to a type of crystal system

DIMINISH v -ED, -ING, -ES to lessen

DIMITY n pl. -TIES a cotton fabric

DIMLY adv in a dim manner

DIMMABLE adj capable of being dimmed

DIMMED past tense of dim

DIMMER n pl. -S a device for varying the intensity of illumination

DIMMEST superlative of dim

DIMMING present participle of dim

DIMNESS n pl. -ES the state of being dim

DIMORPH n pl. -S either of two distinct forms

DIMOUT n pl. -S a condition of partial darkness

DIMPLE v -PLED, -PLING, -PLES to mark with indentations

DIMPLY adj -PLIER, -PLIEST dimpled

DIMWIT n pl. -S a dunce

DIN v DINNED, DINNING, DINS to make a loud noise

DINAR n pl. -S an ancient gold coin of Muslim areas

DINDLE v -DLED, -DLING, -DLES to tingle

DINE v DINED, DINING, DINES to eat dinner

DINER n pl. -S one that dines

DINERIC adj pertaining to the interface between two immiscible liquids

DINERO n pl. -ROS a former silver coin of Peru

DINETTE n pl. -S a small dining room

DING v -ED, -ING, -S to ring

DINGBAT n pl. -S a typographical ornament

DINGDONG v -ED, -ING, -S to make a ringing sound

DINGEY n pl. -GEYS dinghy

DINGHY n pl. -GHIES a small boat

DINGIER comparative of dingy

DINGIEST superlative of dingy

DINGILY adv in a dingy manner

DINGLE n pl. -S a dell

DINGO n pl. -GOES a wild dog of Australia

DINGUS n pl. -ES a gadget or object whose name is unknown or forgotten

DINGY n pl. -GIES dinghy

DINGY adj DINGIER, DINGIEST grimy

DINING present participle of dine

DINK v -ED, -ING, -S to adorn

DINKEY n pl. -KEYS a small locomotive

DINKIER comparative of dinky

DINKIES pl. of dinky

DINKIEST superlative of dinky

DINKLY adv neatly

DINKUM adj genuine

DINKY n pl. -KIES dinkey

DINKY adj -KIER, -KIEST small

DINNED past tense of din

DINNER n pl. -S the main meal of the day

DINNING present participle of din

DINOSAUR n pl. -S one of a group of extinct reptiles

DINT v -ED, -ING, -S to dent

DIOBOL n pl. -S a coin of ancient Greece

DIOBOLON n pl. -S diobol

DIOCESAN n pl. -S a bishop

DIOCESE n pl. -S an ecclesiastical district

DIODE n pl. -S a type of electron tube

DIOECISM n pl. -S the state of being dioicous

DIOICOUS adj unisexual

DIOL n pl. -S a chemical compound

DIOLEFIN n pl. -S a hydrocarbon

DIOPSIDE n pl. -S a mineral

DIOPTASE n pl. -S a mineral

DIOPTER n pl. -S a measure of refractive power DIOPTRAL adj

DIOPTRE n pl. -S diopter

DIOPTRIC adj aiding the vision by refraction

DIORAMA n pl. -S a three-dimensional exhibit DIORAMIC adj

DIORITE n pl. -S an igneous rock DIORITIC adj

DIOXANE *n* pl. -S a flammable liquid

DIOXID *n* pl. -S dioxide

DIOXIDE *n* pl. -S a type of oxide

DIP *v* DIPPED or DIPT, DIPPING, DIPS to immerse briefly into a liquid

DIPHASE *adj* having two phases

DIPHASIC *adj* diphase

DIPHENYL *n* pl. -S biphenyl

DIPLEGIA *n* pl. -S paralysis of the same part on both sides of the body

DIPLEX *adj* pertaining to the simultaneous transmission or reception of two radio signals

DIPLOE *n* pl. -S a bony tissue of the cranium **DIPLOIC** *adj*

DIPLOID *n* pl. -S a cell having the basic chromosome number doubled

DIPLOIDY *n* pl. -DIES the condition of being a diploid

DIPLOMA *n* pl. -MAS or -MATA a certificate of an academic degree

DIPLOMA *v* -ED, -ING, -S to furnish with a diploma

DIPLOMAT *n* pl. -S a governmental official

DIPLONT *n* pl. -S an organism having a particular chromosomal structure

DIPLOPIA *n* pl. -S double vision **DIPLOPIC** *adj*

DIPLOPOD *n* pl. -S a multi-legged insect

DIPLOSIS *n* pl. -LOSES a method of chromosome formation

DIPNOAN *n* pl. -S a lungfish

DIPODY *n* pl. -DIES a dimeter **DIPODIC** *adj*

DIPOLE *n* pl. -S a pair of equal and opposite electric charges **DIPOLAR** *adj*

DIPPABLE *adj* capable of being dipped

DIPPED a past tense of dip

DIPPER *n* pl. -S one that dips

DIPPING present participle of dip

DIPPY *adj* -PIER, -PIEST foolish

DIPSAS *n* pl. DIPSADES a fabled serpent

DIPSTICK *n* pl. -S a measuring rod

DIPT a past tense of dip

DIPTERA pl. of dipteron

DIPTERAL *adj* having two rows or columns

DIPTERAN *n* pl. -S a two-winged fly

DIPTERON *n* pl. -TERA dipteran

DIPTYCA *n* pl. -S diptych

DIPTYCH *n* pl. -S an ancient writing tablet

DIQUAT *n* pl. -S an herbicide

DIRDUM *n* pl. -S blame

DIRE *adj* DIRER, DIREST disastrous

DIRECT *v* -ED, -ING, -S to control or conduct the affairs of

DIRECT *adj* -RECTER, -RECTEST straightforward **DIRECTLY** *adv*

DIRECTOR *n* pl. -S one that directs

DIREFUL *adj* dreadful

DIRELY *adv* in a dire manner

DIRENESS *n* pl. -ES the state of being dire

DIRER comparative of dire

DIREST superlative of dire

DIRGE *n* pl. -S a funeral song **DIRGEFUL** *adj*

DIRHAM *n* pl. -S a monetary unit of Morocco

DIRIMENT *adj* nullifying

DIRK *v* -ED, -ING, -S to stab with a small knife

DIRL *v* -ED, -ING, -S to tremble

DIRNDL *n* pl. -S a woman's dress

DIRT *n* pl. -S earth or soil

DIRTY *adj* DIRTIER, DIRTIEST unclean **DIRTILY** *adv*

DIRTY *v* DIRTIED, DIRTYING, DIRTIES to make dirty

DISABLE *v* -ABLED, -ABLING, -ABLES to render incapable or unable

DISABUSE *v* -ABUSED, -ABUSING, -ABUSES to free from false or mistaken ideas

DISAGREE *v* -AGREED, -AGREEING, -AGREES to differ in opinion

DISALLOW *v* -ED, -ING, -S to refuse to allow

DISANNUL *v* -NULLED, -NULLING, -NULS to annul

DISARM *v* -ED, -ING, -S to deprive of weapons

DISARMER *n* pl. -S one that disarms

DISARRAY *v* -ED, -ING, -S to disorder

DISASTER *n* pl. -S a calamity

DISAVOW *v* -ED, -ING, -S to disclaim responsibility for

DISBAND *v* -ED, -ING, -S to break up

DISBAR *v* -BARRED, -BARRING, -BARS to expel from the legal profession

DISBOSOM *v* -ED, -ING, -S to confess

DISBOUND *adj* not having a binding

DISBOWEL *v* -ELED, -ELING, -ELS or -ELLED, -ELLING, -ELS to remove the intestines of

DISBUD *v* -BUDDED, -BUDDING, -BUDS to remove buds from

DISBURSE *v* -BURSED, -BURSING, -BURSES to pay out

DISC *v* -ED, -ING, -S to disk

DISCANT *v* -ED, -ING, -S to descant

DISCARD *v* -ED, -ING, -S to throw away

DISCASE *v* -CASED, -CASING, -CASES to remove the case of

DISCEPT *v* -ED, -ING, -S to debate

DISCERN *v* -ED, -ING, -S to perceive

DISCI a pl. of discus

DISCIPLE *v* -PLED, -PLING, -PLES to cause to become a follower

DISCLAIM *v* -ED, -ING, -S to renounce any claim to or connection with

DISCLIKE *adj* disklike

DISCLOSE *v* -CLOSED, -CLOSING, -CLOSES to reveal

DISCO *n* pl. -COS a discotheque

DISCOID *n* pl. -S a disk

DISCOLOR *v* -ED, -ING, -S to alter the color of

DISCORD *v* -ED, -ING, -S to disagree

DISCOUNT *v* -ED, -ING, -S to reduce the price of

DISCOVER *v* -ED, -ING, -S to gain sight or knowledge of

DISCREET *adj* -CREETER, -CREETEST tactful

DISCRETE *adj* separate

DISCROWN *v* -ED, -ING, -S to deprive of a crown

DISCUS *n* pl. -CUSES or -CI a disk hurled in athletic competition

DISCUSS *v* -ED, -ING, -ES to talk over or write about

DISDAIN *v* -ED, -ING, -S to scorn

DISEASE *v* -EASED, -EASING, -EASES to make unhealthy

DISENDOW *v* -ED, -ING, -S to deprive of endowment

DISEUSE *n* pl. -S a female entertainer

DISFAVOR *v* -ED, -ING, -S to regard with disapproval

DISFROCK *v* -ED, -ING, -S to unfrock

DISGORGE *v* -GORGED, -GORGING, -GORGES to vomit

DISGRACE *v* -GRACED, -GRACING, -GRACES to bring shame or discredit upon

DISGUISE *v* -GUISED, -GUISING, -GUISES to alter the appearance of

DISGUST *v* -ED, -ING, -S to cause nausea or loathing in

DISH *v* -ED, -ING, -ES to put into a dish (a concave vessel)

DISHELM *v* -ED, -ING, -S to deprive of a helmet

DISHERIT *v* -ED, -ING, -S to deprive of an inheritance

DISHEVEL *v* -ELED, -ELING, -ELS or -ELLED, -ELLING, -ELS to make messy

DISHFUL *n* pl. -S as much as a dish can hold

DISHIER comparative of dishy

DISHIEST superlative of dishy

DISHLIKE *adj* resembling a dish

DISHONOR *v* -ED, -ING, -S to deprive of honor

DISHPAN *n* pl. -S a pan for washing dishes

DISHRAG *n* pl. -S a cloth for washing dishes

DISHWARE *n* pl. -S tableware used in serving food

DISHY *adj* DISHIER, DISHIEST attractive

DISINTER *v* -TERRED, -TERRING, -TERS to exhume

DISJECT *v* -ED, -ING, -S to disperse

DISJOIN *v* -ED, -ING, -S to separate

DISJOINT *v* -ED, -ING, -S to put out of order

DISJUNCT *n* pl. -S an alternative in a logical disjunction

DISK *v* -ED, -ING, -S to break up land with a type of farm implement

DISKLIKE *adj* resembling a disk (a flat, circular plate)

DISLIKE *v* -LIKED, -LIKING, -LIKES to regard with aversion

DISLIKER *n* pl. -S one that dislikes

DISLIMN *v* -ED, -ING, -S to make dim

DISLODGE *v* -LODGED, -LODGING, -LODGES to remove from a firm position

DISLOYAL *adj* not loyal

DISMAL *n* pl. -S a track of swampy land

DISMAL *adj* -MALER, -MALEST cheerless and depressing **DISMALLY** *adv*

DISMAST *v* -ED, -ING, -S to remove the mast of

DISMAY *v* -ED, -ING, -S to deprive of courage or resolution

DISME *n pl.* -S a former coin of the United States

DISMISS *v* -ED, -ING, -ES to permit or cause to leave

DISMOUNT *v* -ED, -ING, -S to get down from an elevated position

DISOBEY *v* -ED, -ING, -S to fail to obey

DISOMIC *adj* having a number of chromosomes duplicated

DISORDER *v* -ED, -ING, -S to put out of order

DISOWN *v* -ED, -ING, -S to deny the ownership of

DISPART *v* -ED, -ING, -S to separate

DISPATCH *v* -ED, -ING, -ES to send off with speed

DISPEL *v* -PELLED, -PELLING, -PELS to drive off in various directions

DISPEND *v* -ED, -ING, -S to squander

DISPENSE *v* -PENSED, -PENSING, -PENSES to distribute

DISPERSE *v* -PERSED, -PERSING, -PERSES to scatter

DISPIRIT *v* -ED, -ING, -S to lower in spirit

DISPLACE *v* -PLACED, -PLACING, -PLACES to remove from the usual or proper place

DISPLANT *v* -ED, -ING, -S to dislodge

DISPLAY *v* -ED, -ING, -S to make evident or obvious

DISPLODE *v* -PLODED, -PLODING, -PLODES to explode

DISPLUME *v* -PLUMED, -PLUMING, -PLUMES to deplume

DISPORT *v* -ED, -ING, -S to amuse oneself

DISPOSAL *n pl.* -S the act of disposing

DISPOSE *v* -POSED, -POSING, -POSES to put in place

DISPOSER *n pl.* -S one that disposes

DISPREAD *v* -SPREAD, -SPREADING, -SPREADS to spread out

DISPRIZE *v* -PRIZED, -PRIZING, -PRIZES to disdain

DISPROOF *n pl.* -S the act of disproving

DISPROVE *v* -PROVED, -PROVEN, -PROVING, -PROVES to refute

DISPUTE *v* -PUTED, -PUTING, -PUTES to argue about

DISPUTER *n pl.* -S one that disputes

DISQUIET *v* -ED, -ING, -S to deprive of quiet, rest, or peace

DISRATE *v* -RATED, -RATING, -RATES to lower in rating or rank

DISROBE *v* -ROBED, -ROBING, -ROBES to undress

DISROBER *n pl.* -S one that disrobes

DISROOT *v* -ED, -ING, -S to uproot

DISRUPT *v* -ED, -ING, -S to throw into confusion

DISSAVE *v* -SAVED, -SAVING, -SAVES to use savings for current expenses

DISSEAT *v* -ED, -ING, -S to unseat

DISSECT *v* -ED, -ING, -S to cut apart for scientific examination

DISSEISE *v* -SEISED, -SEISING, -SEISES to deprive

DISSEIZE *v* -SEIZED, -SEIZING, -SEIZES to disseise

DISSENT *v* -ED, -ING, -S to disagree

DISSERT *v* -ED, -ING, -S to discuss in a learned or formal manner

DISSERVE *v* -SERVED, -SERVING, -SERVES to treat badly

DISSEVER *v* -ED, -ING, -S to sever

DISSOLVE *v* -SOLVED, -SOLVING, -SOLVES to make into a solution

DISSUADE *v* -SUADED, -SUADING, -SUADES to persuade not to do something

DISTAFF *n pl.* -TAFFS or -TAVES a type of staff

DISTAIN *v* -ED, -ING, -S to stain

DISTAL *adj* located far from the point of origin **DISTALLY** *adv*

DISTANCE *v* -TANCED, -TANCING, -TANCES to leave behind

DISTANT *adj* far off or apart

DISTASTE *v* -TASTED, -TASTING, -TASTES to dislike

DISTAVES *a pl.* of distaff

DISTEND *v* -ED, -ING, -S to swell

DISTENT *adj* distended

DISTICH *n pl.* -S a couplet

DISTIL *v* -TILLED, -TILLING, -TILS to distill

DISTILL *v* -ED, -ING, -S to extract by vaporization and condensation

DISTINCT *adj* -TINCTER, -TINCTEST clearly different

DISTOME *n* pl. -S a parasitic flatworm

DISTORT *v* -ED, -ING, -S to twist or bend out of shape

DISTRACT *v* -ED, -ING, -S to divert the attention of

DISTRAIN *v* -ED, -ING, -S to seize and hold property as security

DISTRAIT *adj* absentminded

DISTRESS *v* -ED, -ING, -ES to cause anxiety or suffering to

DISTRICT *v* -ED, -ING, -S to divide into localities

DISTRUST *v* -ED, -ING, -S to have no trust in

DISTURB *v* -ED, -ING, -S to interrupt the quiet, rest, or peace of

DISULFID *n* pl. -S a chemical compound

DISUNION *n* pl. -S the state of being disunited

DISUNITE *v* -UNITED, -UNITING, -UNITES to separate

DISUNITY *n* pl. -TIES lack of unity

DISUSE *v* -USED, -USING, -USES to stop using

DISVALUE *v* -UED, -UING, -UES to treat as of little value

DISYOKE *v* -YOKED, -YOKING, -YOKES to free from a yoke

DIT *n* pl. -S a dot in Morse code

DITA *n* pl. -S a Philippine tree

DITCH *v* -ED, -ING, -ES to dig a long, narrow excavation in the ground

DITCHER *n* pl. -S one that ditches

DITE *n* pl. -S a small amount

DITHEISM *n* pl. -S belief in two coequal gods

DITHEIST *n* pl. -S an adherent of ditheism

DITHER *v* -ED, -ING, -S to act nervously or indecisively

DITHERY *adj* nervously excited

DITHIOL *adj* containing two chemical groups both of which include sulfur and hydrogen

DITTANY *n* pl. -NIES a perennial herb

DITTO *v* -ED, -ING, -S to repeat

DITTY *n* pl. -TIES a short, simple song

DIURESIS *n* pl. DIURESES excessive discharge of urine

DIURETIC *n* pl. -S a drug which increases urinary discharge

DIURNAL *n* pl. -S a diary

DIURON *n* pl. -S an herbicide

DIVA *n* pl. -S a distinguished female operatic singer

DIVAGATE *v* -GATED, -GATING, -GATES to wander

DIVALENT *adj* having a valence of two

DIVAN *n* pl. -S a sofa or couch

DIVE *v* DIVED or DOVE, DIVING, DIVES to plunge headfirst into water

DIVER *n* pl. -S one that dives

DIVERGE *v* -VERGED, -VERGING, -VERGES to move in different directions from a common point

DIVERSE *adj* different

DIVERT *v* -ED, -ING, -S to turn aside

DIVERTER *n* pl. -S one that diverts

DIVEST *v* -ED, -ING, -S to strip or deprive of anything

DIVIDE *v* -VIDED, -VIDING, -VIDES to separate into parts, areas, or groups

DIVIDEND *n* pl. -S a quantity to be divided

DIVIDER *n* pl. -S one that divides

DIVIDING present participle of divide

DIVIDUAL *adj* capable of being divided

DIVINE *v* -VINED, -VINING, -VINES to foretell by occult means

DIVINE *adj* -VINER, -VINEST pertaining to or characteristic of a god **DIVINELY** *adv*

DIVINER *n* pl. -S one that divines

DIVING present participle of dive

DIVINING present participle of divine

DIVINISE *v* -NISED, -NISING, -NISES to divinize

DIVINITY *n* pl. -TIES the state of being divine

DIVINIZE *v* -NIZED, -NIZING, -NIZES to make divine

DIVISION *n* pl. -S the act of dividing

DIVISIVE *adj* causing disunity or dissension

DIVISOR *n* pl. -S a number by which a dividend is divided

DIVORCE *v* -VORCED, -VORCING, -VORCES to terminate the marriage contract between

DIVORCEE *n* pl. -S a divorced woman

DIVORCER *n* pl. -S one that divorces

DIVORCING present participle of divorce

DIVOT *n* pl. -S a piece of turf

DIVULGE *v* -VULGED, -VULGING, -VULGES to reveal

DIVULGER n pl. -S one that divulges

DIVVY v -VIED, -VYING, -VIES to divide

DIWAN n pl. -S dewan

DIXIT n pl. -S a statement

DIZEN v -ED, -ING, -S to dress in fine clothes

DIZYGOUS adj developed from two fertilized ova

DIZZY adj -ZIER, -ZIEST having a sensation of whirling **DIZZILY** adv

DIZZY v -ZIED, -ZYING, -ZIES to make dizzy

DJEBEL n pl. -S jebel

DJELLABA n pl. -S a long hooded garment

DJIN n pl. -S jinni

DJINN n pl. -S jinni

DJINNI n pl. DJINN jinni

DJINNY n pl. DJINN jinni

DO v DID or DIDST, DONE, DOING, present sing. 2d person DO, DOEST or DOST, 3d person DOES, DOETH or DOTH to begin and carry through to completion

DO n pl. DOS the first tone of the diatonic musical scale

DOABLE adj able to be done

DOAT v -ED, -ING, -S to dote

DOBBER n pl. -S a float for a fishing line

DOBBIN n pl. -S a farm horse

DOBBY n pl. -BIES a fool

DOBIE n pl. -S adobe

DOBIES pl. of doby

DOBLA n pl. -S a former gold coin of Spain

DOBLON n pl. -S or -ES a former gold coin of Spain and Spanish America

DOBRA n pl. -S a former gold coin of Portugal

DOBSON n pl. -S an aquatic insect larva

DOBY n pl. -BIES dobie

DOC n pl. -S doctor

DOCENT n pl. -S a college or university lecturer

DOCETIC adj pertaining to a religious doctrine

DOCILE adj easily trained **DOCILELY** adv

DOCILITY n pl. -TIES the quality of being docile

DOCK v -ED, -ING, -S to bring into a dock (a wharf)

DOCKAGE n pl. -S a charge for the use of a dock

DOCKER n pl. -S a dock worker

DOCKET v -ED, -ING, -S to supply with an identifying statement

DOCKHAND n pl. -S a docker

DOCKLAND n pl. -S the part of a port occupied by docks

DOCKSIDE n pl. -S the area adjacent to a dock

DOCKYARD n pl. -S a shipyard

DOCTOR v -ED, -ING, -S to treat medically

DOCTORAL adj pertaining to a doctor

DOCTRINE n pl. -S a belief or set of beliefs taught or advocated

DOCUMENT v -ED, -ING, -S to support by conclusive information or evidence

DODDER v -ED, -ING, -S to totter

DODDERER n pl. -S one that dodders

DODDERY adj feeble

DODGE v DODGED, DODGING, DODGES to evade

DODGER n pl. -S one that dodges

DODGERY n pl. -ERIES evasion

DODGING present participle of dodge

DODGY adj DODGIER, DODGIEST evasive

DODO n pl. -DOES or -DOS an extinct flightless bird

DODOISM n pl. -S a stupid remark

DOE n pl. -S a female deer

DOER n pl. -S one that does something

DOES a present 3d person sing. of do

DOESKIN n pl. -S the skin of a doe

DOEST a present 2d person sing. of do

DOETH a present 3d person sing. of do

DOFF v -ED, -ING, -S to take off

DOFFER n pl. -S one that doffs

DOG v DOGGED, DOGGING, DOGS to follow after like a dog (a domesticated, carnivorous mammal)

DOGBANE n pl. -S a perennial herb

DOGBERRY n pl. -RIES a wild berry

DOGCART n pl. -S a one-horse carriage

DOGDOM n pl. -S the world of dogs

DOGE n pl. -S the chief magistrate in the former republics of Venice and Genoa

DOGEDOM *n* pl. -S the domain of a doge

DOGESHIP *n* pl. -S the office of a doge

DOGEY *n* pl. -GEYS dogie

DOGFACE *n* pl. -S a soldier in the U.S. Army

DOGFIGHT *v* -FOUGHT, -FIGHTING, -FIGHTS to engage in an aerial battle

DOGFISH *n* pl. -ES a small shark

DOGGED past tense of dog

DOGGEDLY *adv* stubbornly

DOGGER *n* pl. -S a fishing vessel

DOGGEREL *n* pl. -S trivial, awkwardly written verse

DOGGERY *n* pl. -GERIES surly behavior

DOGGIE *n* pl. -S doggy

DOGGIER comparative of doggy

DOGGIES pl. of doggy

DOGGIEST superlative of doggy

DOGGING present participle of dog

DOGGISH *adj* doglike

DOGGO *adv* in hiding

DOGGONE *v* -GONED, -GONING, -GONES to damn

DOGGONE *adj* -GONER, -GONEST damned

DOGGONED *adj* -GONEDER, -GONEDEST damned

DOGGONING present participle of doggone

DOGGREL *n* pl. -S doggerel

DOGGY *n* pl. -GIES a small dog

DOGGY *adj* -GIER, -GIEST resembling or suggestive of a dog

DOGHOUSE *n* pl. -S a shelter for a dog

DOGIE *n* pl. -S a stray calf

DOGIES pl. of dogy

DOGLEG *v* -LEGGED, -LEGGING, -LEGS to move along a bent course

DOGLIKE *adj* resembling a dog

DOGMA *n* pl. -MAS or -MATA a principle or belief put forth as authoritative **DOGMATIC** *adj*

DOGNAP *v* -NAPED, -NAPING, -NAPS or -NAPPED, -NAPPING, -NAPS to steal a dog

DOGNAPER *n* pl. -S one that dognaps

DOGSBODY *n* pl. -BODIES a menial worker

DOGSLED *n* pl. -S a sled drawn by dogs

DOGTOOTH *n* pl. -TEETH a cuspid

DOGTROT *v* -TROTTED, -TROTTING, -TROTS to move at a steady trot

DOGVANE *n* pl. -S a small vane

DOGWATCH *n* pl. -ES a short period of watch duty on a ship

DOGWOOD *n* pl. -S a tree

DOGY *n* pl. -GIES dogie

DOILED *adj* dazed

DOILY *n* pl. -LIES a small napkin

DOING *n* pl. -S an action

DOIT *n* pl. -S a former Dutch coin

DOITED *adj* old and feeble

DOJO *n* pl. -JOS a school that teaches judo or karate

DOL *n* pl. -S a unit of pain intensity

DOLCE *n* pl. -CI a soft-toned organ stop

DOLDRUMS *n/pl* a state of inactivity or stagnation

DOLE *v* DOLED, DOLING, DOLES to distribute in small portions

DOLEFUL *adj* -FULLER, -FULLEST mournful

DOLERITE *n* pl. -S a variety of basalt

DOLESOME *adj* doleful

DOLING present participle of dole

DOLL *v* -ED, -ING, -S to dress stylishly

DOLLAR *n* pl. -S a monetary unit of the United States

DOLLIED past tense of dolly

DOLLIES present 3d person sing. of dolly

DOLLISH *adj* pretty

DOLLOP *n* pl. -S a serving

DOLLY *v* -LIED, -LYING, -LIES to move on a wheeled platform

DOLMAN *n* pl. -S a Turkish robe

DOLMEN *n* pl. -S a prehistoric monument

DOLOMITE *n* pl. -S a mineral

DOLOR *n* pl. -S grief

DOLOROSO *adj* having a mournful musical quality

DOLOROUS *adj* mournful

DOLOUR *n* pl. -S dolor

DOLPHIN *n* pl. -S a marine mammal

DOLT *n* pl. -S a stupid person **DOLTISH** *adj*

DOM *n* pl. -S a title given to certain monks

DOMAIN *n* pl. -S an area of control

DOMAL *adj* domical

DOME *v* DOMED, DOMING, DOMES to cover with a dome (a rounded roof)

DOMELIKE *adj* resembling a dome

DOMESDAY *n* pl. -DAYS doomsday

DOMESTIC *n* pl. -S a household servant

DOMIC *adj* domical

DOMICAL *adj* shaped like a dome

DOMICIL *v* -ED, -ING, -S to domicile

DOMICILE *v* -CILED, -CILING, -CILES to establish in a residence

DOMINANT *n* pl. -S a controlling genetic character

DOMINATE *v* -NATED, -NATING, -NATES to control

DOMINE *n* pl. -S master

DOMINEER *v* -ED, -ING, -S to tyrannize

DOMING present participle of dome

DOMINICK *n* pl. -S one of an American breed of chickens

DOMINIE *n* pl. -S a clergyman

DOMINION *n* pl. -S supreme authority

DOMINIUM *n* pl. -S the right of ownership and control of property

DOMINO *n* pl. -NOES or -NOS a small mask

DON *v* DONNED, DONNING, DONS to put on

DONA *n* pl. -S a Spanish lady

DONATE *v* -NATED, -NATING, -NATES to contribute

DONATION *n* pl. -S something donated

DONATIVE *n* pl. -S a donation

DONATOR *n* pl. -S a donor

DONE past participle of do

DONEE *n* pl. -S a recipient of a gift

DONENESS *n* pl. -ES the state of being cooked enough

DONG *n* pl. -S a deep sound like that of a large bell

DONGOLA *n* pl. -S a type of leather

DONJON *n* pl. -S the main tower of a castle

DONKEY *n* pl. -KEYS the domestic ass

DONNA *n* pl. DONNAS or DONNE an Italian lady

DONNED past tense of don

DONNEE *n* pl. -S the set of assumptions upon which a story proceeds

DONNERD *adj* donnered

DONNERED *adj* dazed

DONNERT *adj* donnered

DONNING present participle of don

DONNISH *adj* scholarly

DONOR *n* pl. -S one that donates

DONSIE *adj* unlucky

DONSY *adj* donsie

DONUT *n* pl. -S doughnut

DONZEL *n* pl. -S a young squire

DOODAD *n* pl. -S a dingus

DOODLE *v* -DLED, -DLING, -DLES to draw or scribble aimlessly

DOODLER *n* pl. -S one that doodles

DOOLEE *n* pl. -S a stretcher for the sick or wounded

DOOLIE *n* pl. -S doolee

DOOLY *n* pl. -LIES doolee

DOOM *v* -ED, -ING, -S to destine to an unhappy fate

DOOMFUL *adj* ominous

DOOMSDAY *n* pl. -DAYS judgment day

DOOMSTER *n* pl. -S a judge

DOOR *n* pl. -S a movable barrier for opening and closing an entranceway

DOORBELL *n* pl. -S a bell at a door

DOORJAMB *n* pl. -S a vertical piece at the side of a doorway

DOORKNOB *n* pl. -S a handle for opening a door

DOORLESS *adj* having no door

DOORMAN *n* pl. -MEN the door attendant of a building

DOORMAT *n* pl. -S a mat placed in front of a door

DOORNAIL *n* pl. -S a large-headed nail

DOORPOST *n* pl. -S a doorjamb

DOORSILL *n* pl. -S the sill of a door

DOORSTEP *n* pl. -S a step leading to a door

DOORSTOP *n* pl. -S a wedge for holding a door open

DOORWAY *n* pl. -WAYS the entranceway to a room or building

DOORYARD *n* pl. -S a yard in front of a house

DOOZER *n* pl. -S an extraordinary one of its kind

DOOZY *n* pl. -ZIES doozer

DOPA *n* pl. -S an amino acid

DOPAMINE *n* pl. -S a form of dopa

DOPANT *n* pl. -S an impurity added to a pure substance

DOPE *v* DOPED, DOPING, DOPES to give a narcotic to

DOPER *n* pl. -S one that dopes

DOPESTER *n* pl. -S a forecaster of the outcome of sports events or other contests

DOPEY *adj* DOPIER, DOPIEST lethargic; stupid

DOPIER comparative of dopy

DOPIEST superlative of dopy

DOPINESS *n* pl. -ES the state of being dopey

DOPING present participle of dope

DOPY *adj* DOPIER, DOPIEST dopey

DOR *n* pl. -S a black European beetle

DORADO *n* pl. -DOS a marine fish

DORBUG *n* pl. -S a dor

DORHAWK *n* pl. -S a nocturnal bird

DORIES pl. of dory

DORM *n* pl. -S a dormitory

DORMANCY *n* pl. -CIES the state of being dormant

DORMANT *adj* lying asleep

DORMER *n* pl. -S a type of window

DORMICE pl. of dormouse

DORMIE *adj* being ahead by as many holes in golf as remain to be played

DORMIENT *adj* dormant

DORMIN *n* pl. -S a plant hormone

DORMOUSE *n* pl. -MICE a small rodent

DORMY *adj* dormie

DORNECK *n* pl. -S dornick

DORNICK *n* pl. -S a heavy linen fabric

DORNOCK *n* pl. -S dornick

DORP *n* pl. -S a village

DORPER *n* pl. -S one of a breed of mutton-producing sheep

DORR *n* pl. -S a dor

DORSA pl. of dorsum

DORSAD *adv* dorsally

DORSAL *n* pl. -S a dorsally located anatomical part

DORSALLY *adv* toward the back

DORSER *n* pl. -S dosser

DORSUM *n* pl. -SA the back

DORTY *adj* sullen

DORY *n* pl. -RIES a flat-bottomed boat

DOSAGE *n* pl. -S the amount of medicine to be given

DOSE *v* DOSED, DOSING, DOSES to give a specified quantity of medicine to

DOSER *n* pl. -S one that doses

DOSS *v* -ED, -ING, -ES to sleep in any convenient place

DOSSAL *n* pl. -S an ornamental cloth hung behind an altar

DOSSEL *n* pl. -S dossal

DOSSER *n* pl. -S a basket carried on the back

DOSSERET *n* pl. -S a block resting on the capital of a column

DOSSIER *n* pl. -S a file of papers on a single subject

DOSSIL *n* pl. -S a cloth roll for wiping ink

DOST a present 2d person sing. of do

DOT *v* DOTTED, DOTTING, DOTS to cover with dots (tiny round marks)

DOTAGE *n* pl. -S a state of senility

DOTAL *adj* pertaining to a dowry

DOTARD *n* pl. -S a senile person **DOTARDLY** *adj*

DOTATION *n* pl. -S an endowment

DOTE *v* DOTED, DOTING, DOTES to show excessive affection

DOTER *n* pl. -S one that dotes

DOTH a present 3d person sing. of do

DOTIER comparative of doty

DOTIEST superlative of doty

DOTING present participle of dote

DOTINGLY *adv* in an excessively affectionate manner

DOTTED past tense of dot

DOTTEL *n* pl. -S dottle

DOTTER *n* pl. -S one that dots

DOTTEREL *n* pl. -S a shore bird

DOTTIER comparative of dotty

DOTTIEST superlative of dotty

DOTTILY *adv* in a dotty manner

DOTTING present participle of dot

DOTTLE *n* pl. -S a mass of half-burnt pipe tobacco

DOTTREL *n* pl. -S dotterel

DOTTY *adj* -TIER, -TIEST crazy

DOTY *adj* DOTIER, DOTIEST stained by decay

DOUBLE *v* -BLED, -BLING, -BLES to make twice as great

DOUBLER *n* pl. -S one that doubles

DOUBLET *n* pl. -S a close-fitting jacket

DOUBLING present participle of double

DOUBLOON *n* pl. -S a former Spanish gold coin

DOUBLURE *n* pl. -S the lining of a book cover

DOUBLY *adv* to twice the degree

DOUBT *v* -ED, -ING, -S to be uncertain about

DOUBTER *n* pl. -S one that doubts

DOUBTFUL *adj* uncertain

DOUCE *adj* sedate **DOUCELY** *adv*

DOUCEUR *n* pl. -S a gratuity

DOUCHE *v* DOUCHED, DOUCHING, DOUCHES to cleanse with a jet of water

DOUGH *n* pl. -S a flour mixture

DOUGHBOY *n* pl. -BOYS an infantryman

DOUGHIER comparative of doughy

DOUGHIEST superlative of doughy

DOUGHNUT *n* pl. -S a ring-shaped cake

DOUGHT a past tense of dow

DOUGHTY *adj* -TIER, -TIEST courageous

DOUGHY *adj* DOUGHIER, DOUGHIEST resembling dough

DOUMA *n* pl. -S duma

DOUR *adj* DOURER, DOUREST sullen

DOURA *n* pl. -S durra

DOURAH *n* pl. -S durra

DOURINE *n* pl. -S a disease of horses

DOURLY *adv* in a dour manner

DOURNESS *n* pl. -ES the state of being dour

DOUSE *v* DOUSED, DOUSING, DOUSES to plunge into water

DOUSER *n* pl. -S one that douses

DOUZEPER *n* pl. -S one of twelve legendary knights

DOVE *n* pl. -S a bird of the pigeon family

DOVECOT *n* pl. -S dovecote

DOVECOTE *n* pl. -S a roost for domesticated pigeons

DOVEKEY *n* pl. -KEYS dovekie

DOVEKIE *n* pl. -S a seabird

DOVELIKE *adj* resembling or suggestive of a dove

DOVEN *v* -ED, -ING, -S to daven

DOVETAIL *v* -ED, -ING, -S to fit together closely

DOVISH *adj* not warlike

DOW *v* DOWED or DOUGHT, DOWING, DOWS to prosper

DOWABLE *adj* entitled to an endowment

DOWAGER *n* pl. -S a dignified elderly woman

DOWDY *adj* DOWDIER, DOWDIEST lacking in stylishness or neatness **DOWDILY** *adv* **DOWDYISH** *adj*

DOWDY *n* pl. DOWDIES a dowdy woman

DOWEL *v* -ELED, -ELING, -ELS or -ELLED, -ELLING, -ELS to fasten with wooden pins

DOWER *v* -ED, -ING, -S to provide with a dowry

DOWERY *n* pl. -ERIES dowry

DOWIE *adj* dreary

DOWN *v* -ED, -ING, -S to cause to fall

DOWNBEAT *n* pl. -S the first beat of a musical measure

DOWNCAST *n* pl. -S an overthrow or ruin

DOWNCOME *n* pl. -S downfall

DOWNER *n* pl. -S a depressant drug

DOWNFALL *n* pl. -S a sudden fall

DOWNHAUL *n* pl. -S a rope for hauling down sails

DOWNHILL *n* pl. -S a downward slope

DOWNIER comparative of downy

DOWNIEST superlative of downy

DOWNPLAY *v* -ED, -ING, -S to de-emphasize

DOWNPOUR *n* pl. -S a heavy rain

DOWNTIME *n* pl. -S the time when a machine or factory is inactive

DOWNTOWN *n* pl. -S the business district of a city

DOWNTROD *adj* oppressed

DOWNTURN *n* pl. -S a downward turn

DOWNWARD *adv* from a higher to a lower place

DOWNWIND *adv* in the direction that the wind blows

DOWNY *adj* DOWNIER, DOWNIEST soft

DOWRY *n* pl. -RIES the money or property a wife brings to her husband at marriage

DOWSABEL *n* pl. -S a sweetheart

DOWSE *v* DOWSED, DOWSING, DOWSES to search for underground water with a divining rod

DOWSER *n* pl. -S one that dowses

DOXIE *n* pl. -S doxy

DOXOLOGY *n* pl. -GIES a hymn or verse of praise to God

DOXY *n* pl. DOXIES a doctrine

DOYEN *n* pl. -S the senior member of a group

DOYENNE n pl. -S a female doyen

DOYLEY n pl. -LEYS doily

DOYLY n pl. -LIES doily

DOZE v DOZED, DOZING, DOZES to sleep lightly

DOZEN v -ED, -ING, -S to stun

DOZENTH n pl. -S twelfth

DOZER n pl. -S one that dozes

DOZILY adv in a dozy manner

DOZINESS n pl. -ES the state of being dozy

DOZING present participle of doze

DOZY adj DOZIER, DOZIEST drowsy

DRAB adj DRABBER, DRABBEST cheerless

DRAB v DRABBED, DRABBING, DRABS to consort with prostitutes

DRABBET n pl. -S a coarse linen fabric

DRABBLE v -BLED, -BLING, -BLES to draggle

DRABLY adv in a drab manner

DRABNESS n pl. -ES the quality of being drab

DRACAENA n pl. -S a tropical plant

DRACHM n pl. -S a unit of weight

DRACHMA n pl. -MAS, -MAE or -MAI a Greek coin

DRACONIC adj pertaining to a dragon

DRAFF n pl. -S the damp remains of malt after brewing

DRAFFISH adj draffy

DRAFFY adj DRAFFIER, DRAFFIEST worthless

DRAFT v -ED, -ING, -S to conscript for military service

DRAFTEE n pl. -S one that is drafted

DRAFTER n pl. -S one that drafts

DRAFTING n pl. -S mechanical drawing

DRAFTY adj DRAFTIER, DRAFTIEST having or exposed to currents of air **DRAFTILY** adv

DRAG v DRAGGED, DRAGGING, DRAGS to pull along the ground

DRAGEE n pl. -S a sugarcoated candy

DRAGGER n pl. -S one that drags

DRAGGIER comparative of draggy

DRAGGIEST superlative of draggy

DRAGGING present participle of drag

DRAGGLE v -GLED, -GLING, -GLES to make wet and dirty

DRAGGY adj -GIER, -GIEST sluggish

DRAGLINE n pl. -S a line used for dragging

DRAGNET n pl. -S a net for trawling

DRAGOMAN n pl. -MANS or -MEN an interpreter in Near Eastern countries

DRAGON n pl. -S a mythical, serpentlike monster

DRAGONET n pl. -S a marine fish

DRAGOON v -ED, -ING, -S to harass by the use of troops

DRAGROPE n pl. -S a rope used for dragging

DRAGSTER n pl. -S a vehicle used in drag racing

DRAIL n pl. -S a heavy fishhook

DRAIN v -ED, -ING, -S to draw off a liquid

DRAINAGE n pl. -S the act of draining

DRAINER n pl. -S one that drains

DRAKE n pl. -S a male duck

DRAM v DRAMMED, DRAMMING, DRAMS to tipple

DRAMA n pl. -S a composition written for theatrical performance

DRAMATIC adj pertaining to drama

DRAMMED past tense of dram

DRAMMING present participle of dram

DRAMMOCK n pl. -S raw oatmeal mixed with cold water

DRAMSHOP n pl. -S a barroom

DRANK past tense of drink

DRAPE v DRAPED, DRAPING, DRAPES to arrange in graceful folds **DRAPABLE** adj

DRAPER n pl. -S a dealer in cloth

DRAPERY n pl. -ERIES cloth arranged in graceful folds

DRAPING present participle of drape

DRASTIC adj extremely severe

DRAT v DRATTED, DRATTING, DRATS to damn

DRAUGHT v -ED, -ING, -S to draft

DRAUGHTY adj DRAUGHTIER, DRAUGHTIEST drafty

DRAVE a past tense of drive

DRAW v DREW, DRAWN, DRAWING, DRAWS to move by pulling **DRAWABLE** adj

DRAWBACK n pl. -S a hindrance

DRAWBAR n pl. -S a railroad coupler

DRAWBORE n pl. -S a hole for joining a mortise and tenon

DRAWDOWN n pl. -S a lowering of a water level

DRAWEE n pl. -S the person on whom a bill of exchange is drawn

DRAWER n pl. -S one that draws

DRAWING n pl. -S a portrayal in lines of a form or figure

DRAWL v -ED, -ING, -S to speak slowly with vowels greatly prolonged

DRAWLER n pl. -S one that drawls

DRAWLY adj DRAWLIER, DRAWLIEST marked by drawling

DRAWN past participle of draw

DRAWTUBE n pl. -S a tube that slides within another tube

DRAY v -ED, -ING, -S to transport by dray (a low, strong cart)

DRAYAGE n pl. -S transportation by dray

DRAYMAN n pl. -MEN one who drives a dray

DREAD v -ED, -ING, -S to fear greatly

DREADFUL n pl. -S a publication containing sensational material

DREAM v DREAMED or DREAMT, DREAMING, DREAMS to have a dream (a series of images occurring during sleep)

DREAMER n pl. -S one that dreams

DREAMFUL adj dreamy

DREAMT a past tense of dream

DREAMY adj DREAMIER, DREAMIEST full of dreams DREAMILY adv

DREAR adj dreary

DREARY adj DREARIEST, DREARIER dismal DREARILY adv

DREARY n pl. DREARIES a dismal person

DRECK n pl. -S rubbish

DREDGE v DREDGED, DREDGING, DREDGES to clear with a scooping device

DREDGER n pl. -S one that dredges

DREDGING n pl. -S matter that is dredged up

DREE v DREED, DREEING, DREES to suffer

DREG n pl. -S the sediment of liquors DREGGISH adj

DREGGY adj -GIER, -GIEST full of dregs

DREICH adj dreary

DREIDEL n pl. -S a spinning toy

DREIDL n pl. -S dreidel

DREIGH adj dreich

DREK n pl. -S dreck

DRENCH v -ED, -ING, -ES to wet thoroughly

DRENCHER n pl. -S one that drenches

DRESS v DRESSED or DREST, DRESSING, DRESSES to put clothes on

DRESSAGE n pl. -S the training of a horse in obedience and deportment

DRESSER n pl. -S one that dresses

DRESSING n pl. -S material applied to cover a wound

DRESSY adj DRESSIER, DRESSIEST stylish DRESSILY adv

DREST a past tense of dress

DREW past tense of draw

DRIB v DRIBBED, DRIBBING, DRIBS to drip

DRIBBLE v -BLED, -BLING, -BLES to drivel

DRIBBLER n pl. -S one that dribbles

DRIBBLET n pl. -S driblet

DRIBBLING present participle of dribble

DRIBLET n pl. -S a small drop of liquid

DRIED past tense of dry

DRIER n pl. -S one that dries

DRIES present 3d person sing. of dry

DRIEST a superlative of dry

DRIFT v -ED, -ING, -S to move along in a current

DRIFTAGE n pl. -S the act of drifting

DRIFTER n pl. -S one that drifts

DRIFTPIN n pl. -S a metal rod for securing timbers

DRIFTY adj DRIFTIER, DRIFTIEST full of drifts (masses of wind-driven snow)

DRILL v -ED, -ING, -S to bore a hole in

DRILLER n pl. -S one that drills

DRILLING n pl. -S a heavy twilled cotton fabric

DRILY adv dryly

DRINK v DRANK, DRUNK, DRINKING, DRINKS to swallow liquid

DRINKER n pl. -S one that drinks

DRIP v DRIPPED or DRIPT, DRIPPING, DRIPS to fall in drops

DRIPLESS adj designed not to drip

DRIPPER n pl. -S something from which a liquid drips

DRIPPING n pl. -S juice drawn from meat during cooking

DRIPPY *adj* -PIER, -PIEST very wet

DRIPT a past tense of drip

DRIVE *v* DROVE or DRAVE, DRIVEN, DRIVING, DRIVES to urge or propel forward **DRIVABLE** *adj*

DRIVEL *v* -ELED, -ELING, -ELS or -ELLED, -ELLING, -ELS to let saliva flow from the mouth

DRIVELER *n pl.* -S one that drivels

DRIVEN past participle of drive

DRIVER *n pl.* -S one that drives

DRIVEWAY *n pl.* -WAYS a private road providing access to a building

DRIVING present participle of drive

DRIZZLE *v* -ZLED, -ZLING, -ZLES to rain lightly

DRIZZLY *adj* -ZLIER, -ZLIEST characterized by light rain

DROGUE *n pl.* -S a canvas bag dragged behind a ship to reduce drifting

DROIT *n pl.* -S a legal right

DROLL *adj* DROLLER, DROLLEST comical

DROLL *v* -ED, -ING, -S to jest

DROLLERY *n pl.* -ERIES something droll

DROLLY *adv* in a droll manner

DROMON *n pl.* -S dromond

DROMOND *n pl.* -S a large fast-sailing medieval galley

DRONE *v* DRONED, DRONING, DRONES to make a continuous low sound

DRONER *n pl.* -S one that drones

DRONGO *n pl.* -GOS a tropical bird

DRONING present participle of drone

DRONISH *adj* habitually lazy

DROOL *v* -ED, -ING, -S to drivel

DROOP *v* -ED, -ING, -S to hang downward

DROOPY *adj* DROOPIER, DROOPIEST drooping **DROOPILY** *adv*

DROP *v* DROPPED or DROPT, DROPPING, DROPS to fall in drops (globules)

DROPHEAD *n pl.* -S a convertible car

DROPKICK *n pl.* -S a type of kick in football

DROPLET *n pl.* -S a tiny drop

DROPOUT *n pl.* -S one who quits school prematurely

DROPPED past tense of drop

DROPPER *n pl.* -S a tube for dispensing liquid in drops

DROPPING *n pl.* -S something that has been dropped

DROPSHOT *n pl.* -S a type of shot in tennis

DROPSY *n pl.* -SIES an excessive accumulation of serous fluid **DROPSIED** *adj*

DROPT a past tense of drop

DROPWORT *n pl.* -S a perennial herb

DROSERA *n pl.* -S a sundew

DROSHKY *n pl.* -KIES an open carriage

DROSKY *n pl.* -KIES droshky

DROSS *n pl.* -ES waste matter

DROSSY *adj* DROSSIER, DROSSIEST worthless

DROUGHT *n pl.* -S a dry period

DROUGHTY *adj* DROUGHTIER, DROUGHTIEST dry

DROUK *v* -ED, -ING, -S to drench

DROUTH *n pl.* -S drought

DROUTHY *adj* DROUTHIER, DROUTHIEST droughty

DROVE *v* DROVED, DROVING, DROVES to drive cattle or sheep

DROVER *n pl.* -S a driver of cattle or sheep

DROWN *v* -ED, -ING, -S to suffocate in water

DROWND *v* -ED, -ING, -S to drown

DROWNER *n pl.* -S one that drowns

DROWSE *v* DROWSED, DROWSING, DROWSES to doze

DROWSY *adj* DROWSIER, DROWSIEST sleepy **DROWSILY** *adv*

DRUB *v* DRUBBED, DRUBBING, DRUBS to beat severely

DRUBBER *n pl.* -S one that drubs

DRUBBING *n pl.* -S a severe beating

DRUDGE *v* DRUDGED, DRUDGING, DRUDGES to do hard, menial, or tedious work

DRUDGER *n pl.* -S one that drudges

DRUDGERY *n pl.* -ERIES hard, menial, or tedious work

DRUDGING present participle of drudge

DRUG *v* DRUGGED, DRUGGING, DRUGS to affect with a medicinal substance

DRUGGET *n pl.* -S a coarse woolen fabric

DRUGGIST *n pl.* -S a pharmacist

DRUID *n pl.* -S one of an ancient Celtic order of priests **DRUIDIC** *adj*

DRUIDESS *n pl.* -ES a female druid

DRUIDISM *n* pl. -S the religious system of the druids

DRUM *v* DRUMMED, DRUMMING, DRUMS to beat a drum (a percussion instrument)

DRUMBEAT *n* pl. -S the sound of a drum

DRUMBLE *v* -BLED, -BLING, -BLES to move slowly

DRUMFIRE *n* pl. -S heavy, continuous gunfire

DRUMFISH *n* pl. -ES a fish that makes a drumming sound

DRUMHEAD *n* pl. -S the material stretched over the end of a drum

DRUMLIER comparative of drumly

DRUMLIEST superlative of drumly

DRUMLIKE *adj* resembling the head of a drum

DRUMLIN *n* pl. -S a long hill of glacial drift

DRUMLY *adj* -LIER, -LIEST dark and gloomy

DRUMMED past tense of drum

DRUMMER *n* pl. -S one that drums

DRUMMING present participle of drum

DRUMROLL *n* pl. -S a roll played on a drum

DRUNK *adj* DRUNKER, DRUNKEST intoxicated

DRUNK *n* pl. -S a drunken person

DRUNKARD *n* pl. -S one who is habitually drunk

DRUNKEN *adj* drunk

DRUPE *n* pl. -S a fleshy fruit

DRUPELET *n* pl. -S a small drupe

DRUSE *n* pl. -S a crust of small crystals lining a rock cavity

DRUTHERS *n/pl* one's preference

DRY *adj* DRIER, DRIEST or DRYER, DRYEST having no moisture

DRY *v* DRIED, DRYING, DRIES to make dry **DRYABLE** *adj*

DRY *n* pl. DRYS a prohibitionist

DRYAD *n* pl. -S or -ES a nymph of the woods **DRYADIC** *adj*

DRYER *n* pl. -S drier

DRYLOT *n* pl. -S an enclosure for livestock

DRYLY *adv* in a dry manner

DRYNESS *n* pl. -ES the state of being dry

DRYPOINT *n* pl. -S a method of engraving

DUAD *n* pl. -S a pair

DUAL *n* pl. -S a linguistic form

DUALISM *n* pl. -S a philosophical theory

DUALIST *n* pl. -S an adherent of dualism

DUALITY *n* pl. -TIES the state of being twofold

DUALIZE *v* -IZED, -IZING, -IZES to make twofold

DUALLY *adv* in two ways

DUB *v* DUBBED, DUBBING, DUBS to confer knighthood on

DUBBER *n* pl. -S one that dubs

DUBBIN *n* pl. -S material for softening and waterproofing leather

DUBBING *n* pl. -S dubbin

DUBIETY *n* pl. -ETIES the state of being dubious

DUBIOUS *adj* doubtful

DUBONNET *n* pl. -S a red color

DUC *n* pl. -S a duke

DUCAL *adj* pertaining to a duke **DUCALLY** *adv*

DUCAT *n* pl. -S any of several gold coins formerly used in Europe

DUCE *n* pl. DUCES or DUCI a leader

DUCHESS *n* pl. -ES the wife or widow of a duke

DUCHY *n* pl. DUCHIES the domain of a duke

DUCI a pl. of duce

DUCK *v* -ED, -ING, -S to lower quickly

DUCKBILL *n* pl. -S a platypus

DUCKER *n* pl. -S one that ducks

DUCKIE *adj* ducky

DUCKIER comparative of ducky

DUCKIES pl. of ducky

DUCKIEST superlative of ducky

DUCKLING *n* pl. -S a young duck

DUCKPIN *n* pl. -S a type of bowling pin

DUCKTAIL *n* pl. -S a style of haircut

DUCKWEED *n* pl. -S an aquatic plant

DUCKY *adj* DUCKIER, DUCKIEST excellent

DUCKY *n* pl. DUCKIES a darling

DUCT *v* -ED, -ING, -S to convey through a duct (a tubular passage)

DUCTILE *adj* easily molded or shaped

DUCTING *n* pl. -S a system of ducts

DUCTLESS *adj* being without a duct

DUCTULE *n* pl. -S a small duct

DUD *n* pl. -S a bomb that fails to explode

DUDDIE *adj* ragged

DUDDY *adj* duddie

DUDE n pl. -S a dandy

DUDEEN n pl. -S a short tobacco pipe

DUDGEON n pl. -S a feeling of resentment

DUDISH adj resembling a dude

DUDISHLY adv in the manner of a dude

DUE n pl. -S something that is owed

DUECENTO n pl. -TOS the thirteenth century

DUEL v DUELED, DUELING, DUELS or DUELLED, DUELLING, DUELS to fight formally

DUELER n pl. -S one that duels

DUELIST n pl. -S a dueler

DUELLED a past tense of duel

DUELLER n pl. -S dueler

DUELLI a pl. of duello

DUELLING a present participle of duel

DUELLIST n pl. -S duelist

DUELLO n pl. -LOS or -LI the art of dueling; a duel

DUENDE n pl. -S charisma

DUENESS n pl. -ES the state of being owed

DUENNA n pl. -S a governess

DUET v DUETTED, DUETTING, DUETS to perform a duet (a musical composition for two)

DUETTIST n pl. -S a participant in a duet

DUFF n pl. -S a thick pudding

DUFFEL n pl. -S a coarse woolen fabric

DUFFER n pl. -S a clumsy person

DUFFLE n pl. -S duffel

DUG n pl. -S the teat or udder of a female mammal

DUGONG n pl. -S an aquatic mammal

DUGOUT n pl. -S a canoe made by hollowing out a log

DUI a pl. of duo

DUIKER n pl. -S a small antelope

DUIT n pl. -S doit

DUKE n pl. -S a high-ranking nobleman

DUKEDOM n pl. -S a duchy

DULCET n pl. -S a soft-toned organ stop

DULCETLY adv melodiously

DULCIANA n pl. -S a soft-toned organ stop

DULCIFY v -FIED, -FYING, -FIES to sweeten

DULCIMER n pl. -S a stringed instrument

DULCINEA n pl. -S a sweetheart

DULIA n pl. -S veneration of saints

DULL adj DULLER, DULLEST mentally slow

DULL v -ED, -ING, -S to make less sharp

DULLARD n pl. -S a dolt

DULLISH adj somewhat dull

DULLNESS n pl. -ES the state of being dull

DULLY adv in a dull manner

DULNESS n pl. -ES dullness

DULSE n pl. -S an edible seaweed

DULY adv rightfully

DUMA n pl. -S a Russian council

DUMB adj DUMBER, DUMBEST incapable of speech DUMBLY adv

DUMB v -ED, -ING, -S to make silent

DUMBBELL n pl. -S a weight lifted for muscular exercise

DUMBNESS n pl. -ES the state of being dumb

DUMDUM n pl. -S a type of bullet

DUMFOUND v -ED, -ING, -S to astonish

DUMKA n pl. -KY a Slavic folk ballad

DUMMKOPF n pl. -S a dolt

DUMMY v -MIED, -MYING, -MIES to make a representation of

DUMP v -ED, -ING, -S to let fall heavily

DUMPCART n pl. -S a type of cart

DUMPER n pl. -S one that dumps

DUMPIER comparative of dumpy

DUMPIEST superlative of dumpy

DUMPILY adv in a dumpy manner

DUMPING n pl. -S the selling of large quantities of goods at below the market price

DUMPISH adj sad

DUMPLING n pl. -S a ball of dough cooked with stew or soup

DUMPY adj DUMPIER, DUMPIEST short and thick

DUN v DUNNED, DUNNING, DUNS to make demands upon for payment of a debt

DUN adj DUNNER, DUNNEST of a dull brown color

DUNCE n pl. -S a stupid person DUNCICAL, DUNCISH adj

DUNCH n pl. -ES a push

DUNE n pl. -S a hill of sand DUNELIKE adj

DUNELAND n pl. -S an area having many dunes

DUNG v -ED, -ING, -S to fertilize with manure

DUNGAREE n pl. -S a coarse cotton fabric

DUNGEON n pl. -S an underground prison

DUNGHILL n pl. -S a heap of manure

DUNGY adj DUNGIER, DUNGIEST filthy

DUNITE n pl. -S an igneous rock **DUNITIC** adj

DUNK v -ED, -ING, -S to dip into liquid

DUNKER n pl. -S one that dunks

DUNLIN n pl. -S a wading bird

DUNNAGE n pl. -S packing material used to protect cargo

DUNNED past tense of dun

DUNNER comparative of dun

DUNNESS n pl. -ES the state of being dun

DUNNEST superlative of dun

DUNNING present participle of dun

DUNNITE n pl. -S an explosive

DUNT v -ED, -ING, -S to strike with a heavy blow

DUO n pl. DUOS or DUI an instrumental duet

DUODENUM n pl. -DENA or -DENUMS the first portion of the small intestine **DUODENAL** adj

DUOLOG n pl. -S duologue

DUOLOGUE n pl. -S a conversation between two persons

DUOMO n pl. -MOS or -MI a cathedral

DUOPOLY n pl. -LIES the market condition existing when there are two sellers only

DUOPSONY n pl. -NIES the market condition existing when there are two buyers only

DUOTONE n pl. -S an illustration in two tones

DUP v DUPPED, DUPPING, DUPS to open

DUPE v DUPED, DUPING, DUPES to deceive **DUPABLE** adj

DUPER n pl. -S one that dupes

DUPERY n pl. -ERIES the act of duping

DUPING present participle of dupe

DUPLE adj having two parts or elements

DUPLEX v -ED, -ING, -ES to make duple

DUPLEXER n pl. -S an electronic switching device

DUPPED past tense of dup

DUPPING present participle of dup

DURA n pl. -S durra

DURABLE adj able to withstand wear or decay **DURABLY** adv

DURABLES n/pl durable goods

DURAL adj of the dura mater (a brain membrane)

DURAMEN n pl. -S the central wood of a tree

DURANCE n pl. -S restraint by or as if by physical force

DURATION n pl. -S continuance in time

DURATIVE n pl. -S a type of verb

DURBAR n pl. -S the court of a native ruler in India

DURE v DURED, DURING, DURES to endure

DURESS n pl. -ES compulsion by threat

DURIAN n pl. -S an East Indian tree

DURING prep throughout the duration of

DURION n pl. -S durian

DURMAST n pl. -S a European oak

DURN v -ED, -ING, -S to damn

DURNED adj DURNEDER, DURNEDEST or DURNDEST damned

DURO n pl. -ROS a Spanish silver dollar

DUROC n pl. -S a large red hog

DURR n pl. -S durra

DURRA n pl. -S a cereal grain

DURST a past tense of dare

DURUM n pl. -S a kind of wheat

DUSK v -ED, -ING, -S to become dark

DUSKISH adj dusky

DUSKY adj DUSKIER, DUSKIEST somewhat dark **DUSKILY** adv

DUST v -ED, -ING, -S to make free of dust (minute particles of matter)

DUSTBIN n pl. -S a trash can

DUSTER n pl. -S one that dusts

DUSTHEAP n pl. -S a pile of trash

DUSTIER comparative of dusty

DUSTIEST superlative of dusty

DUSTILY adv in a dusty manner

DUSTLESS adj being without dust

DUSTLIKE adj resembling dust

DUSTMAN n pl. -MEN a trashman

DUSTPAN n pl. -S a pan for holding swept dust

DUSTRAG n pl. -S a rag used for dusting

DUSTUP n pl. -S an argument

DUSTY adj DUSTIER, DUSTIEST full of dust

DUTCH	*adv* with each person paying for himself	**DYER**	*n pl.* -S one that dyes
DUTCHMAN	*n pl.* -MEN something used to hide structural defects	**DYESTUFF**	*n pl.* -S a material yielding or used as a dye
DUTEOUS	*adj* dutiful	**DYEWEED**	*n pl.* -S a shrub that yields a yellow dye
DUTIABLE	*adj* subject to import tax		
DUTIFUL	*adj* obedient	**DYEWOOD**	*n pl.* -S a wood used as a dyestuff
DUTY	*n pl.* -TIES a moral or legal obligation	**DYING**	*n pl.* -S a passing out of existence
DUUMVIR	*n pl.* -VIRS or -VIRI a magistrate of ancient Rome	**DYKE**	*v* DYKED, DYKING, DYKES to dike
DUVETINE	*n pl.* -S duvetyn	**DYNAMIC**	*n pl.* -S a physical force
DUVETYN	*n pl.* -S a soft fabric	**DYNAMISM**	*n pl.* -S a theory that explains the universe in terms of force or energy
DUVETYNE	*n pl.* -S duvetyn		
DWARF	*adj* DWARFER, DWARFEST extremely small	**DYNAMIST**	*n pl.* -S an adherent of dynamism
DWARF	*n pl.* DWARFS or DWARVES an extremely small person	**DYNAMITE**	*v* -MITED, -MITING, -MITES to blow up with a powerful explosive
DWARF	*v* -ED, -ING, -S to cause to appear small	**DYNAMO**	*n pl.* -MOS a generator
DWARFISH	*adj* resembling a dwarf	**DYNAST**	*n pl.* -S a ruler
DWARFISM	*n pl.* -S a condition of stunted growth	**DYNASTY**	*n pl.* -TIES a succession of rulers from the same line of descent DYNASTIC *adj*
DWARVES	a pl. of dwarf		
DWELL	*v* DWELT or DWELLED, DWELLING, DWELLS to reside	**DYNATRON**	*n pl.* -S a type of electron tube
		DYNE	*n pl.* -S a unit of force
DWELLER	*n pl.* -S one that dwells	**DYNODE**	*n pl.* -S a type of electrode
DWELLING	*n pl.* -S a place of residence	**DYSGENIC**	*adj* causing the deterioration of hereditary qualities
DWELT	a past tense of dwell		
DWINDLE	*v* -DLED, -DLING, -DLES to decrease steadily	**DYSLEXIA**	*n pl.* -S impairment of the ability to read DYSLEXIC *adj*
DWINE	*v* DWINED, DWINING, DWINES to pine or waste away	**DYSPEPSY**	*n pl.* -SIES indigestion
		DYSPNEA	*n pl.* -S labored breathing DYSPNEAL, DYSPNEIC *adj*
DYABLE	*adj* dyeable		
DYAD	*n pl.* -S a pair of units	**DYSPNOEA**	*n pl.* -S dyspnea DYSPNOIC *adj*
DYADIC	*n pl.* -S a sum of mathematical dyads		
		DYSTAXIA	*n pl.* -S a form of muscular tremor
DYARCHY	*n pl.* -CHIES diarchy DYARCHIC *adj*		
		DYSTOCIA	*n pl.* -S difficult labor and delivery in childbirth
DYBBUK	*n pl.* -BUKS or -BUKIM a wandering soul in Jewish folklore		
		DYSTONIA	*n pl.* -S a condition of disordered tonicity of muscle tissue
DYE	*v* DYED, DYEING, DYES to treat with a dye (a coloring material or matter)		
		DYSTOPIA	*n pl.* -S a wretched place
DYEABLE	*adj* capable of being dyed	**DYSURIA**	*n pl.* -S painful urination DYSURIC *adj*
DYEING	*n pl.* -S something colored with a dye		
		DYVOUR	*n pl.* -S one who is bankrupt

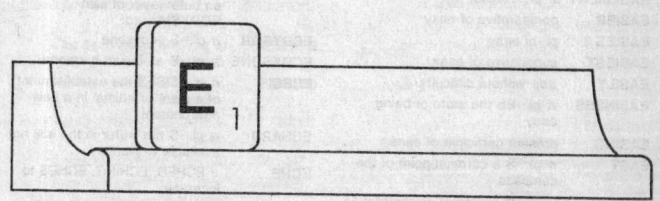

EACH	*adj* being one of two or more distinct individuals	**EARN**	*v* -ED, -ING, -S to gain or deserve for one's labor or service
EAGER	*adj* -GERER, -GEREST impatiently longing **EAGERLY** *adv*	**EARNER**	*n pl.* -S one that earns
EAGER	*n pl.* -S eagre	**EARNEST**	*n pl.* -S a down payment
EAGLE	*n pl.* -S a large bird of prey	**EARNINGS**	*n/pl* something earned
EAGLET	*n pl.* -S a young eagle	**EARPHONE**	*n pl.* -S a listening device worn over the ear
EAGRE	*n pl.* -S a tidal flood		
EANLING	*n pl.* -S yeanling	**EARPIECE**	*n pl.* -S an earphone
EAR	*n pl.* -S the organ of hearing	**EARPLUG**	*n pl.* -S a plug for the ear
EARACHE	*n pl.* -S a pain in the ear	**EARRING**	*n pl.* -S an ornament for the earlobe
EARDROP	*n pl.* -S an earring		
EARDRUM	*n pl.* -S the tympanic membrane	**EARSHOT**	*n pl.* -S the range within which sound can be heard
		EARSTONE	*n pl.* -S an otolith
EARED	*adj* having ears	**EARTH**	*v* -ED, -ING, -S to cover with earth (soil)
EARFLAP	*n pl.* -S a part of a cap designed to cover the ears		
		EARTHEN	*adj* made of earth
EARFUL	*n pl.* -S a flow of information	**EARTHIER**	comparative of earthy
EARING	*n pl.* -S a line on a ship	**EARTHIEST**	superlative of earthy
EARL	*n pl.* -S a British nobleman	**EARTHILY**	*adv* in an earthy manner
EARLAP	*n pl.* -S an earflap	**EARTHLY**	*adj* -LIER, -LIEST worldly
EARLDOM	*n pl.* -S the rank of an earl	**EARTHMAN**	*n pl.* -MEN a person from the planet earth
EARLESS	*adj* lacking ears		
EARLIER	comparative of early	**EARTHNUT**	*n pl.* -S a European herb
EARLIEST	superlative of early	**EARTHPEA**	*n pl.* -S a twining plant
EARLOBE	*n pl.* -S a part of the ear	**EARTHSET**	*n pl.* -S the setting of the earth as seen from the moon
EARLOCK	*n pl.* -S a curl of hair by the ear		
EARLSHIP	*n pl.* -S earldom	**EARTHY**	*adj* EARTHIER, EARTHIEST composed of, resembling, or suggestive of earth
EARLY	*adv* -LIER, -LIEST near the beginning of a period of time or a series of events		
		EARWAX	*n pl.* -ES cerumen
EARMARK	*v* -ED, -ING, -S to designate for a specific use	**EARWIG**	*v* -WIGGED, -WIGGING, -WIGS to insinuate against in secret
		EARWORM	*n pl.* -S a bollworm
EARMUFF	*n pl.* -S one of a pair of ear coverings	**EASE**	*v* EASED, EASING, EASES to give rest of relief to

EASEFUL *adj* restful

EASEL *n* pl. -S a three-legged frame

EASEMENT *n* pl. -S relief

EASIER comparative of easy

EASIES pl. of easy

EASIEST superlative of easy

EASILY *adv* without difficulty

EASINESS *n* pl. -ES the state of being easy

EASING present participle of ease

EAST *n* pl. -S a cardinal point of the compass

EASTER *n* pl. -S a wind or storm from the east

EASTERLY *n* pl. -LIES a wind from the east

EASTERN *adj* being to, toward, or in the east

EASTING *n* pl. -S a movement toward the east

EASTWARD *n* pl. -S a direction toward the east

EASY *adj* EASIER, EASIEST not difficult

EASY *n* pl. EASIES a communications code word for the letter E

EAT *v* ATE or ET, EATEN, EATING, EATS to consume food

EATABLE *n* pl. -S an edible

EATER *n* pl. -S one that eats

EATERY *n* pl. -ERIES a lunchroom

EATH *adj* easy

EATING *n* pl. -S the act of consuming food

EAU *n* pl. EAUX water

EAVE *n* pl. -S the lower projecting edge of a roof EAVED *adj*

EBB *v* -ED, -ING, -S to recede

EBBET *n* pl. -S a common green newt

EBON *n* pl. -S ebony

EBONIES pl. of ebony

EBONISE *v* -ISED, -ISING, -ISES to ebonize

EBONITE *n* pl. -S a hard rubber

EBONIZE *v* -IZED, -IZING, -IZES to stain black in imitation of ebony

EBONY *n* pl. -NIES a hard, heavy wood

ECARTE *n* pl. -S a card game

ECAUDATE *adj* having no tail

ECBOLIC *n* pl. -S a type of drug

ECCLESIA *n* pl. -SIAE an assembly in ancient Greece

ECCRINE *adj* producing secretions externally

ECDYSIS *n* pl. -DYSES the shedding of an outer layer of skin ECDYSIAL *adj*

ECDYSON *n* pl. -S ecdysone

ECDYSONE *n* pl. -S an insect hormone

ECESIS *n* pl. -SISES the establishment of a plant or animal in a new environment

ECHARD *n* pl. -S the water in the soil not available to plants

ECHE *v* ECHED, ECHING, ECHES to increase

ECHELON *v* -ED, -ING, -S to group in a particular formation

ECHIDNA *n* pl. -NAS or -NAE a spiny anteater

ECHINATE *adj* spiny

ECHING present participle of eche

ECHINOID *n* pl. -S a spiny marine animal

ECHINUS *n* pl. -NI echinoid

ECHO *v* -ED, -ING, -ES to produce an echo (a repetition of sound by reflection of sound waves)

ECHOER *n* pl. -S one that echoes

ECHOEY *adj* full of echoes

ECHOIC *adj* resembling an echo

ECHOISM *n* pl. -S the formation of words in imitation of sounds

ECHOLESS *adj* producing no echo

ECLAIR *n* pl. -S a type of pastry

ECLAT *n* pl. -S brilliance

ECLECTIC *n* pl. -S one who draws his beliefs from various sources

ECLIPSE *v* ECLIPSED, ECLIPSING, ECLIPSES to obscure

ECLIPSIS *n* pl. -SES or -SISES an ellipsis

ECLIPTIC *n* pl. -S an astronomical plane

ECLOGITE *n* pl. -S a type of rock

ECLOGUE *n* pl. -S a pastoral poem

ECLOSION *n* pl. -S the emergence of an insect larva from an egg

ECOLE *n* pl. -S a French school

ECOLOGY *n* pl. -GIES an environmental science ECOLOGIC *adj*

ECONOMIC *adj* pertaining to financial matters

ECONOMY *n* pl. -MIES thrift

ECOTONE *n* pl. -S a type of ecological zone ECOTONAL *adj*

ECOTYPE *n* pl. -S a subspecies adapted to specific environmental conditions ECOTYPIC *adj*

ECRASEUR *n pl.* -S a surgical instrument

ECRU *n pl.* -S a yellowish brown color

ECSTASY *n pl.* -SIES a state of exaltation

ECSTATIC *n pl.* -S one that is subject to ecstasies

ECTASIS *n pl.* -TASES the lengthening of a usually short syllable **ECTATIC** *adj*

ECTHYMA *n pl.* -MATA a virus disease

ECTODERM *n pl.* -S the outermost germ layer of an embryo

ECTOMERE *n pl.* -S a cell that develops into ectoderm

ECTOPIA *n pl.* -S congenital displacement of parts or organs **ECTOPIC** *adj*

ECTOSARC *n pl.* -S the outermost layer of protoplasm of certain protozoans

ECTOZOAN *n pl.* -S ectozoon

ECTOZOON *n pl.* -ZOA a parasite on the body of an animal

ECTYPE *n pl.* -S a copy **ECTYPAL** *adj*

ECU *n pl.* -S an old French coin

ECUMENIC *adj* universal

ECZEMA *n pl.* -S a skin disease

EDACIOUS *adj* voracious

EDACITY *n pl.* -TIES gluttony

EDAPHIC *adj* pertaining to the soil

EDDO *n pl.* -DOES a tropical plant

EDDY *v* -DIED, -DYING, -DIES to move against the main current

EDEMA *n pl.* -MAS or -MATA an excessive accumulation of serous fluid

EDENTATE *n pl.* -S a toothless mammal

EDGE *v* EDGED, EDGING, EDGES to provide with an edge (a bounding or dividing line)

EDGELESS *adj* lacking an edge

EDGER *n pl.* -S a tool used to trim a lawn's edge

EDGEWAYS *adv* edgewise

EDGEWISE *adv* sideways

EDGIER comparative of edgy

EDGIEST superlative of edgy

EDGILY *adv* in an edgy manner

EDGINESS *n pl.* -ES the state of being edgy

EDGING *n pl.* -S something that forms or serves as an edge

EDGY *adj* EDGIER, EDGIEST tense, nervous, or irritable

EDH *n pl.* -S an Old English letter

EDIBLE *n pl.* -S something fit to be eaten

EDICT *n pl.* -S an authoritative order having the force of law **EDICTAL** *adj*

EDIFICE *n pl.* -S a building

EDIFIER *n pl.* -S one that edifies

EDIFY *v* -FIED, -FYING, -FIES to enlighten

EDILE *n pl.* -S aedile

EDIT *v* -ED, -ING, -S to correct and prepare for publication **EDITABLE** *adj*

EDITION *n pl.* -S a particular series of printed material

EDITOR *n pl.* -S one that edits

EDITRESS *n pl.* -ES a female editor

EDUCABLE *n pl.* -S a mildly retarded person

EDUCATE *v* -CATED, -CATING, -CATES to teach

EDUCATOR *n pl.* -S one that educates

EDUCE *v* EDUCED, EDUCING, EDUCES to draw forth or bring out **EDUCIBLE** *adj*

EDUCT *n pl.* -S something educed

EDUCTION *n pl.* -S the act of educing **EDUCTIVE** *adj*

EDUCTOR *n pl.* -S one that educes

EEL *n pl.* -S a snakelike fish

EELGRASS *n pl.* -ES an aquatic plant

EELIER comparative of eely

EELIEST superlative of eely

EELLIKE *adj* resembling an eel

EELPOUT *n pl.* -S a marine fish

EELWORM *n pl.* -S a small roundworm

EELY *adj* EELIER, EELIEST resembling an eel

EERIE *adj* -RIER, -RIEST weird **EERILY** *adv*

EERINESS *n pl.* -ES the state of being eerie

EERY *adj* -RIER, -RIEST eerie

EF *n pl.* -S the letter F

EFF *n pl.* -S ef

EFFABLE *adj* capable of being uttered or expressed

EFFACE *v* -FACED, -FACING, -FACES to rub or wipe out

EFFACER *n pl.* -S one that effaces

EFFECT *v* -ED, -ING, -S to bring about

EFFECTER *n pl.* -S effector

EFFECTOR   *n* pl. -S a bodily organ that responds to a nerve impulse

EFFENDI   *n* pl. -S a Turkish title of respect

EFFERENT   *n* pl. -S an organ or part conveying nervous impulses to an effector

EFFETE   *adj* exhausted of vigor or energy **EFFETELY** *adv*

EFFICACY   *n* pl. -CIES effectiveness

EFFIGY   *n* pl. -GIES a likeness or representation

EFFLUENT   *n* pl. -S an outflow

EFFLUVIA   *n/pl* byproducts in the form of waste

EFFLUX   *n* pl. -ES an outflow

EFFORT   *n* pl. -S a deliberate exertion

EFFULGE   *v* -FULGED, -FULGING, -FULGES to shine forth

EFFUSE   *v* -FUSED, -FUSING, -FUSES to pour forth

EFFUSION   *n* pl. -S an outpouring of emotion

EFFUSIVE   *adj* pouring forth

EFT   *n* pl. -S a newt

EFTSOON   *adv* soon afterward

EFTSOONS   *adv* eftsoon

EGAD   *interj* — used as a mild oath

EGADS   *interj* egad

EGAL   *adj* equal

EGALITE   *n* pl. -S equality

EGER   *n* pl. -S eagre

EGEST   *v* -ED, -ING, -S to discharge from the body

EGESTA   *n/pl* egested matter

EGESTION   *n* pl. -S the act of egesting **EGESTIVE** *adj*

EGG   *v* -ED, -ING, -S to incite or urge

EGGAR   *n* pl. -S egger

EGGCUP   *n* pl. -S a cup from which an egg is eaten

EGGER   *n* pl. -S a kind of moth

EGGHEAD   *n* pl. -S an intellectual

EGGNOG   *n* pl. -S a beverage

EGGPLANT   *n* pl. -S a perennial herb yielding edible fruit

EGGSHELL   *n* pl. -S the hard exterior of a bird's egg

EGIS   *n* pl. EGISES aegis

EGLATERE   *n* pl. -S a wild rose

EGO   *n* pl. EGOS the conscious self

EGOISM   *n* pl. -S extreme devotion to self-interest

EGOIST   *n* pl. -S one who practices egoism **EGOISTIC** *adj*

EGOMANIA   *n* pl. -S extreme egotism

EGOTISM   *n* pl. -S self-conceit

EGOTIST   *n* pl. -S a conceited person

EGRESS   *v* -ED, -ING, -ES to go out

EGRET   *n* pl. -S a wading bird

EH   *interj* — used to express doubt or surprise

EIDE   pl. of eidos

EIDER   *n* pl. -S a large sea duck

EIDETIC   *adj* pertaining to vivid recall

EIDOLON   *n* pl. -LONS or -LA a phantom

EIDOS   *n* pl. EIDE an essence

EIGHT   *n* pl. -S a number

EIGHTEEN   *n* pl. -S a number

EIGHTH   *n* pl. -S one of eight equal parts

EIGHTHLY   *adv* in the eighth place

EIGHTVO   *n* pl. -VOS octavo

EIGHTY   *n* pl. EIGHTIES a number

EIKON   *n* pl. -S or -ES icon

EINKORN   *n* pl. -S a variety of wheat

EIRENIC   *adj* irenic

EITHER   *adj* being one or the other

EJECT   *v* -ED, -ING, -S to throw out forcibly

EJECTA   *n/pl* ejected material

EJECTION   *n* pl. -S the act of ejecting

EJECTIVE   *n* pl. -S a sound produced with air compressed above the closed glottis

EJECTOR   *n* pl. -S one that ejects

EKE   *v* EKED, EKING, EKES to supplement with great effort

EKISTICS   *n/pl* a science dealing with human habitats **EKISTIC** *adj*

EKTEXINE   *n* pl. -S an outer layer of the exine

EL   *n* pl. -S an elevated railroad or train

ELAIN   *n* pl. -S olein

ELAN   *n* pl. -S enthusiasm

ELAND   *n* pl. -S a large antelope

ELAPHINE   *adj* pertaining to a genus of deer

ELAPID   *n* pl. -S a venomous snake

ELAPINE   *adj* pertaining to a family of snakes

ELAPSE   *v* ELAPSED, ELAPSING, ELAPSES to pass away

ELASTASE   *n* pl. -S an enzyme

ELASTIC   *n* pl. -S a stretchable material

ELASTIN   *n* pl. -S a bodily protein

ELATE   *v* ELATED, ELATING, ELATES to raise the spirits of **ELATEDLY** *adv*

ELATER   *n* pl. -S a click beetle

ELATERID   *n* pl. -S an elater

ELATERIN   *n* pl. -S a chemical compound

ELATING   present participle of elate

ELATION   *n* pl. -S a feeling of great joy

ELATIVE   *n* pl. -S an adjectival form in some languages

ELBOW   *v* -ED, -ING, -S to jostle

ELD   *n* pl. -S old age

ELDER   *n* pl. -S an older person

ELDERLY   *adj* rather old

ELDEST   *adj* oldest

ELDRICH   *adj* eldritch

ELDRITCH   *adj* weird

ELECT   *v* -ED, -ING, -S to select by vote for an office

ELECTION   *n* pl. -S the act of electing

ELECTIVE   *n* pl. -S an optional course of study

ELECTOR   *n* pl. -S one that elects

ELECTRET   *n* pl. -S a type of nonconductor

ELECTRIC   *n* pl. -S something run by electricity

ELECTRO   *v* -ED, -ING, -S to make a metallic copy of a page of type for printing

ELECTRON   *n* pl. -S an atomic particle

ELECTRUM   *n* pl. -S an alloy of gold and silver

ELEGANCE   *n* pl. -S tasteful opulence

ELEGANCY   *n* pl. -CIES elegance

ELEGANT   *adj* tastefully opulent

ELEGIAC   *n* pl. -S a type of verse

ELEGIES   pl. of elegy

ELEGISE   *v* -GISED, -GISING, -GISES to elegize

ELEGIST   *n* pl. -S one that writes elegies

ELEGIT   *n* pl. -S a type of judicial writ

ELEGIZE   *v* -GIZED, -GIZING, -GIZES to write an elegy

ELEGY   *n* pl. -GIES a mournful poem for one who is dead

ELEMENT   *n* pl. -S any of a class of substances that cannot be separated into simpler substances by chemical means

ELEMI   *n* pl. -S a fragrant resin

ELENCHUS   *n* pl. -CHI a logical refutation **ELENCHIC, ELENCTIC** *adj*

ELEPHANT   *n* pl. -S a large mammal

ELEVATE   *v* -VATED, -VATING, -VATES to raise

ELEVATOR   *n* pl. -S one that elevates

ELEVEN   *n* pl. -S a number

ELEVENTH   *n* pl. -S one of eleven equal parts

ELEVON   *n* pl. -S a type of airplane control surface

ELF   *n* pl. ELVES a small, often mischievous fairy

ELFIN   *n* pl. -S an elf

ELFISH   *adj* resembling an elf **ELFISHLY** *adv*

ELFLOCK   *n* pl. -S a lock of tangled hair

ELHI   *adj* pertaining to school grades 1 through 12

ELICIT   *v* -ED, -ING, -S to educe

ELICITOR   *n* pl. -S one that elicits

ELIDE   *v* ELIDED, ELIDING, ELIDES to omit **ELIDIBLE** *adj*

ELIGIBLE   *n* pl. -S one that is qualified to be chosen

ELIGIBLY   *adv* in a qualified manner

ELISION   *n* pl. -S the act of eliding

ELITE   *n* pl. -S a socially superior group

ELITISM   *n* pl. -S belief in rule by an elite

ELITIST   *n* pl. -S an adherent of elitism

ELIXIR   *n* pl. -S a medicinal beverage

ELK   *n* pl. -S a large deer

ELKHOUND   *n* pl. -S a hunting dog

ELL   *n* pl. -S the letter L

ELLIPSE   *n* pl. -S a type of plane curve

ELLIPSIS   *n* pl. -LIPSES an omission of a word or words in a sentence

ELLIPTIC   *adj* having the shape of an ellipse

ELM   *n* pl. -S a deciduous tree

ELMY   *adj* -MIER, -MIEST abounding in elms

ELODEA   *n* pl. -S an aquatic herb

ELOIGN   *v* -ED, -ING, -S to remove to a distant place

ELOIGNER   *n* pl. -S one that eloigns

ELOIN   *v* -ED, -ING, -S to eloign

ELOINER   *n* pl. -S one that eloins

ELONGATE   *v* -GATED, -GATING, -GATES to lengthen

ELOPE   *v* ELOPED, ELOPING, ELOPES to run off secretly to be married

ELOPER	n pl. -S one that elopes
ELOQUENT	adj fluent and convincing in speech
ELSE	adv in a different place, time, or way
ELUANT	n pl. -S a solvent
ELUATE	n pl. -S the material obtained by eluting
ELUDE	v ELUDED, ELUDING, ELUDES to evade
ELUDER	n pl. -S one that eludes
ELUENT	n pl. -S eluant
ELUSION	n pl. -S the act of eluding
ELUSIVE	adj tending to elude
ELUSORY	adj elusive
ELUTE	v ELUTED, ELUTING, ELUTES to remove by means of a solvent
ELUTION	n pl. -S the act of eluting
ELUVIA	a pl. of eluvium
ELUVIAL	adj pertaining to an eluvium
ELUVIATE	v -ATED, -ATING, -ATES to undergo a transfer of materials in the soil
ELUVIUM	n pl. -VIA or -VIUMS a soil deposit
ELVER	n pl. -S a young eel
ELVES	pl. of elf
ELVISH	adj elfish ELVISHLY adv
ELYSIAN	adj delightful
ELYTRON	n pl. -TRA a hardened forewing of certain insects ELYTROID, ELYTROUS adj
ELYTRUM	n pl. -TRA elytron
EM	n pl. -S the letter M
EMACIATE	v -ATED, -ATING, -ATES to make thin
EMANATE	v -NATED, -NATING, -NATES to send forth
EMANATOR	n pl. -S one that emanates
EMBALM	v -ED, -ING, -S to treat so as to protect from decay
EMBALMER	n pl. -S one that embalms
EMBANK	v -ED, -ING, -S to confine or protect with a raised structure
EMBAR	v -BARRED, -BARRING, -BARS to imprison
EMBARGO	v -ED, -ING, -ES to restrain trade by a governmental order
EMBARK	v -ED, -ING, -S to make a start
EMBARRED	past tense of embar
EMBARRING	present participle of embar

EMBASSY	n pl. -SIES the headquarters of an ambassador
EMBATTLE	v -TLED, -TLING, -TLES to prepare for battle
EMBAY	v -ED, -ING, -S to enclose in a bay
EMBED	v -BEDDED, -BEDDING, -BEDS to fix firmly into a surrounding mass
EMBER	n pl. -S a glowing fragment from a fire
EMBEZZLE	v -ZLED, -ZLING, -ZLES to appropriate fraudulently to one's own use
EMBITTER	v -ED, -ING, -S to make bitter
EMBLAZE	v -BLAZED, -BLAZING, -BLAZES to set on fire
EMBLAZER	n pl. -S one that emblazes
EMBLAZON	v -ED, -ING, -S to decorate with brilliant colors
EMBLEM	v -ED, -ING, -S to represent with an emblem (a graphical symbol)
EMBODIER	n pl. -S one that embodies
EMBODY	v -BODIED, -BODYING, -BODIES to provide with a body
EMBOLDEN	v -ED, -ING, -S to instill with courage
EMBOLI	pl. of embolus
EMBOLIES	pl. of emboly
EMBOLISM	n pl. -S the obstruction of a blood vessel by an embolus EMBOLIC adj
EMBOLUS	n pl. -LI an abnormal particle circulating in the blood
EMBOLY	n pl. -LIES a phase of embryonic growth
EMBORDER	v -ED, -ING, -S to provide with a border
EMBOSK	v -ED, -ING, -S to conceal with foliage
EMBOSOM	v -ED, -ING, -S to embrace
EMBOSS	v -ED, -ING, -ES to decorate with raised designs
EMBOSSER	n pl. -S one that embosses
EMBOW	v -ED, -ING, -S to arch
EMBOWEL	v -ELED, -ELING, -ELS or -ELLED, -ELLING, -ELS to disbowel
EMBOWER	v -ED, -ING, -S to surround with foliage
EMBRACE	v -BRACED, -BRACING, -BRACES to hug
EMBRACER	n pl. -S one that embraces

EMBROIL	v -ED, -ING, -S to involve in conflict	**EMIR**	n pl. -S an Arab chieftain or prince
EMBROWN	v -ED, -ING, -S to make brown	**EMIRATE**	n pl. -S the rank of an emir
EMBRUE	v -BRUED, -BRUING, -BRUES to imbrue	**EMISSARY**	n pl. -SARIES a person sent on a mission
EMBRUTE	v -BRUTED, -BRUTING, -BRUTES to imbrute	**EMISSION**	n pl. -S the act of emitting **EMISSIVE** adj
EMBRYO	n pl. -BRYOS an organism in its early stages of development **EMBRYOID** adj	**EMIT**	v EMITTED, EMITTING, EMITS to send forth
EMBRYON	n pl. -S an embryo	**EMITTER**	n pl. -S one that emits
EMCEE	v -CEED, -CEEING, -CEES to serve as master of ceremonies	**EMMER**	n pl. -S a type of wheat
		EMMET	n pl. -S an ant
EME	n pl. -S an uncle	**EMODIN**	n pl. -S a chemical compound
EMEER	n pl. -S emir	**EMOTE**	v EMOTED, EMOTING, EMOTES to express emotion in an exaggerated manner
EMEERATE	n pl. -S emirate		
EMEND	v -ED, -ING, -S to correct	**EMOTER**	n pl. -S one that emotes
EMENDATE	v -DATED, -DATING, -DATES to emend	**EMOTION**	n pl. -S an affective state of consciousness
EMENDER	n pl. -S one that emends	**EMOTIVE**	adj pertaining to emotion
EMERALD	n pl. -S a green gem	**EMPALE**	v -PALED, -PALING, -PALES to impale
EMERGE	v EMERGED, EMERGING, EMERGES to come out into view	**EMPALER**	n pl. -S one that empales
		EMPANEL	v -ELED, -ELING, -ELS or -ELLED, -ELLING, -ELS to impanel
EMERGENT	n pl. -S a type of aquatic plant		
EMERITA	adj retired but retaining an honorary title — used of a woman	**EMPATHY**	n pl. -THIES imaginative identification with another's thoughts and feelings **EMPATHIC** adj
EMERITUS	n pl. -ITI a retired person who retains an honorary title		
		EMPEROR	n pl. -S the ruler of an empire
EMEROD	n pl. -S a tumor	**EMPERY**	n pl. -PERIES absolute dominion
EMEROID	n pl. -S emerod		
EMERSED	adj standing out of water	**EMPHASIS**	n pl. -PHASES special significance imparted to something
EMERSION	n pl. -S the act of emerging		
EMERY	n pl. -ERIES a granular corundum	**EMPHATIC**	adj strongly expressive
		EMPIRE	n pl. -S a major political unit
EMESIS	n pl. EMESES the act of vomiting	**EMPIRIC**	n pl. -S one who relies on practical experience
EMETIC	n pl. -S a substance which induces vomiting	**EMPLACE**	v -PLACED, -PLACING, -PLACES to position
EMETIN	n pl. -S emetine	**EMPLANE**	v -PLANED, -PLANING, -PLANES to enplane
EMETINE	n pl. -S an alkaloid		
EMEU	n pl. -S an emu	**EMPLOY**	v -ED, -ING, -S to hire
EMEUTE	n pl. -S a riot	**EMPLOYE**	n pl. -S employee
EMIGRANT	n pl. -S one that emigrates	**EMPLOYEE**	n pl. -S a person who is employed
EMIGRATE	v -GRATED, -GRATING, -GRATES to leave one country or region to settle in another	**EMPLOYER**	n pl. -S one that employs
		EMPOISON	v -ED, -ING, -S to embitter
EMIGRE	n pl. -S an emigrant	**EMPORIUM**	n pl. -RIUMS or -RIA a trading or market center
EMINENCE	n pl. -S high station or rank		
EMINENCY	n pl. -CIES eminence	**EMPOWER**	v -ED, -ING, -S to give legal power to
EMINENT	adj of high station or rank		

EMPRESS *n* pl. -ES a female ruler of an empire

EMPRISE *n* pl. -S an adventurous undertaking

EMPRIZE *n* pl. -S emprise

EMPTIED past tense of empty

EMPTIER *n* pl. -S one that empties

EMPTIES present 3d person sing. of empty

EMPTIEST superlative of empty

EMPTILY *adv* in an empty manner

EMPTINGS *n/pl* emptins

EMPTINS *n/pl* a liquid leavening

EMPTY *adj* -TIER, -TIEST containing nothing

EMPTY *v* -TIED, -TYING, -TIES to remove the contents of

EMPURPLE *v* -PLED, -PLING, -PLES to tinge with purple

EMPYEMA *n* pl. -EMATA or -EMAS a collection of pus in a body cavity **EMPYEMIC** *adj*

EMPYREAL *adj* pertaining to the sky

EMPYREAN *n* pl. -S the highest heaven

EMU *n* pl. -S a large, flightless bird

EMULATE *v* -LATED, -LATING, -LATES to try to equal or surpass

EMULATOR *n* pl. -S one that emulates

EMULOUS *adj* eager to equal or surpass another

EMULSIFY *v* -FIED, -FYING, -FIES to make into an emulsion

EMULSION *n* pl. -S a type of liquid mixture **EMULSIVE** *adj*

EMULSOID *n* pl. -S a liquid dispersed in another liquid

EMYD *n* pl. -S a freshwater tortoise

EMYDE *n* pl. -S emyd

EN *n* pl. -S the letter N

ENABLE *v* -BLED, -BLING, -BLES to make possible

ENABLER *n* pl. -S one that enables

ENACT *v* -ED, -ING, -S to make into a law

ENACTIVE *adj* having the power to enact

ENACTOR *n* pl. -S one that enacts

ENACTORY *adj* pertaining to the enactment of law

ENAMEL *v* -ELED, -ELING, -ELS or -ELLED, -ELLING, -ELS to cover with a hard, glossy surface

ENAMELER *n* pl. -S one that enamels

ENAMINE *n* pl. -S a type of amine

ENAMOR *v* -ED, -ING, -S to inspire with love

ENAMOUR *v* -ED, -ING, -S to enamor

ENATE *n* pl. -S a relative on the mother's side **ENATIC** *adj*

ENATION *n* pl. -S an outgrowth from the surface of an organ

ENCAENIA *n/pl* annual university ceremonies

ENCAGE *v* -CAGED, -CAGING, -CAGES to confine in a cage

ENCAMP *v* -ED, -ING, -S to set up a camp

ENCASE *v* -CASED, -CASING, -CASES to enclose in a case

ENCASH *v* -ED, -ING, -ES to cash

ENCEINTE *n* pl. -S an encircling fortification

ENCHAIN *v* -ED, -ING, -S to bind with chains

ENCHANT *v* -ED, -ING, -S to delight

ENCHASE *v* -CHASED, -CHASING, -CHASES to place in an ornamental setting

ENCHASER *n* pl. -S one that enchases

ENCHORIC *adj* belonging to a particular country

ENCINA *n* pl. -S an evergreen oak **ENCINAL** *adj*

ENCIPHER *v* -ED, -ING, -S to write in characters of hidden meaning

ENCIRCLE *v* -CLED, -CLING, -CLES to form a circle around

ENCLASP *v* -ED, -ING, -S to embrace

ENCLAVE *n* pl. -S a territorial unit enclosed within foreign territory

ENCLITIC *n* pl. -S a word pronounced as part of the preceding word

ENCLOSE *v* -CLOSED, -CLOSING, -CLOSES to close in on all sides

ENCLOSER *n* pl. -S one that encloses

ENCODE *v* -CODED, -CODING, -CODES to put into code

ENCODER *n* pl. -S one that encodes

ENCOMIUM *n* pl. -MIUMS or -MIA a eulogy

ENCORE *v* -CORED, -CORING, -CORES to call for the reappearance of a performer

ENCROACH *v* -ED, -ING, -ES to advance beyond the proper limits

ENCRUST *v* -ED, -ING, -S to cover with a crust

ENCRYPT *v* -ED, -ING, -S to encipher

ENCUMBER *v* -ED, -ING, -S to hinder in action or movement

ENCYCLIC *n* pl. -S a letter addressed by the pope to the bishops of the world

ENCYST *v* -ED, -ING, -S to enclose in a cyst

END *v* -ED, -ING, -S to terminate

ENDAMAGE *v* -AGED, -AGING, -AGES to damage

ENDAMEBA *n* pl. -BAS or -BAE a parasitic ameba

ENDANGER *v* -ED, -ING, -S to imperil

ENDARCH *adj* formed from the center outward

ENDARCHY *n* pl. -CHIES the condition of being endarch

ENDBRAIN *n* pl. -S a part of the brain

ENDEAR *v* -ED, -ING, -S to make dear or beloved

ENDEAVOR *v* -ED, -ING, -S to make an effort

ENDEMIAL *adj* peculiar to a country or people

ENDEMIC *n* pl. -S an endemial disease

ENDEMISM *n* pl. -S the state of being endemial

ENDER *n* pl. -S one that ends something

ENDERMIC *adj* acting by absorption through the skin

ENDEXINE *n* pl. -S an inner layer of the exine

ENDING *n* pl. -S a termination

ENDITE *v* -DITED, -DITING, -DITES to indite

ENDIVE *n* pl. -S an herb cultivated as a salad plant

ENDLEAF *n* pl. -LEAVES an endpaper

ENDLESS *adj* enduring forever

ENDLONG *adv* lengthwise

ENDMOST *adj* farthest

ENDOCARP *n* pl. -S the inner layer of a pericarp

ENDODERM *n* pl. -S the innermost germ layer of an embryo

ENDOGAMY *n* pl. -MIES marriage within a particular group

ENDOGEN *n* pl. -S a type of plant

ENDOGENY *n* pl. -NIES growth from within

ENDOPOD *n* pl. -S a branch of a crustacean limb

ENDORSE *v* -DORSED, -DORSING, -DORSES to sign the back of a negotiable document

ENDORSEE *n* pl. -S one to whom a document is transferred by endorsement

ENDORSER *n* pl. -S one that endorses

ENDORSING present participle of endorse

ENDORSOR *n* pl. -S endorser

ENDOSARC *n* pl. -S a portion of a cell

ENDOSMOS *n* pl. -ES a form of osmosis

ENDOSOME *n* pl. -S a cellular particle

ENDOSTEA *n/pl* bone membranes

ENDOW *v* -ED, -ING, -S to provide with something

ENDOWER *n* pl. -S one that endows

ENDOZOIC *adj* involving passage through an animal

ENDPAPER *n* pl. -S a sheet of paper used in bookbinding

ENDPLATE *n* pl. -S a type of nerve terminal

ENDRIN *n* pl. -S an insecticide

ENDUE *v* -DUED, -DUING, -DUES to provide with some quality or gift

ENDURE *v* -DURED, -DURING, -DURES to last

ENDURO *n* pl. -DUROS a long race

ENDWAYS *adv* endwise

ENDWISE *adv* lengthwise

ENEMA *n* pl. -MAS or -MATA a liquid injected into the rectum

ENEMY *n* pl. -MIES one that is antagonistic toward another

ENERGID *n* pl. -S a nucleus and the body of cytoplasm with which it interacts

ENERGIES pl. of energy

ENERGISE *v* -GISED, -GISING, -GISES to energize

ENERGIZE *v* -GIZED, -GIZING, -GIZES to give energy to

ENERGY *n* -GIES the capacity for vigorous activity

ENERVATE *v* -VATED, -VATING, -VATES to deprive of strength or vitality

ENFACE *v* -FACED, -FACING, -FACES to write on the front of

ENFEEBLE *v* -BLED, -BLING, -BLES to make feeble

ENFEOFF *v* -ED, -ING, -S to invest with a feudal estate

ENFETTER *v* -ED, -ING, -S to enchain

ENFEVER *v* -ED, -ING, -S to fever

ENFILADE *v* -LADED, -LADING, -LADES to direct heavy gunfire along the length of

ENFIN *adv* finally

ENFLAME *v* -FLAMED, -FLAMING, -FLAMES to inflame

ENFOLD *v* -ED, -ING, -S to envelop

ENFOLDER *n pl.* -S one that enfolds

ENFORCE *v* -FORCED, -FORCING, -FORCES to compel obedience to

ENFORCER *n pl.* -S one that enforces

ENFRAME *v* -FRAMED, -FRAMING, -FRAMES to frame

ENG *n pl.* -S a phonetic symbol

ENGAGE *v* -GAGED, -GAGING, -GAGES to employ

ENGAGER *n pl.* -S one that engages

ENGENDER *v* -ED, -ING, -S to bring into existence

ENGILD *v* -ED, -ING, -S to brighten

ENGINE *v* -GINED, -GINING, -GINES to equip with machinery

ENGINEER *v* -ED, -ING, -S to carry through or manage by contrivance

ENGINERY *n pl.* -RIES machinery

ENGINING present participle of engine

ENGINOUS *adj* ingenious

ENGIRD *v* -GIRT or -GIRDED, -GIRDING, -GIRDS to gird

ENGIRDLE *v* -DLED, -DLING, -DLES to engird

ENGLISH *v* -ED, -ING, -ES to cause a billiard ball to spin around its vertical axis

ENGLUT *v* -GLUTTED, -GLUTTING, -GLUTS to gulp down

ENGORGE *v* -GORGED, -GORGING, -GORGES to fill with blood

ENGRAFT *v* -ED, -ING, -S to graft for propagation

ENGRAIL *v* -ED, -ING, -S to ornament the edge of with curved indentations

ENGRAIN *v* -ED, -ING, -S to ingrain

ENGRAM *n pl.* -S the durable mark caused by a stimulus upon protoplasm

ENGRAMME *n pl.* -S engram

ENGRAVE *v* -GRAVED, -GRAVING, -GRAVES to form by incision

ENGRAVER *n pl.* -S one that engraves

ENGROSS *v* -ED, -ING, -ES to occupy completely

ENGULF *v* -ED, -ING, -S to surround completely

ENHALO *v* -ED, -ING, -ES or -S to surround with a halo

ENHANCE *v* -HANCED, -HANCING, -HANCES to raise to a higher degree

ENHANCER *n pl.* -S one that enhances

ENIGMA *n pl.* -MAS or -MATA something that is hard to understand or explain

ENISLE *v* -ISLED, -ISLING, -ISLES to isolate

ENJAMBED *adj* marked by the continuation of a sentence from one line of a poem to the next

ENJOIN *v* -ED, -ING, -S to command

ENJOINER *n pl.* -S one that enjoins

ENJOY *v* -ED, -ING, -S to receive pleasure from

ENJOYER *n pl.* -S one that enjoys

ENKINDLE *v* -DLED, -DLING, -DLES to set on fire

ENLACE *v* -LACED, -LACING, -LACES to bind with laces

ENLARGE *v* -LARGED, -LARGING, -LARGES to make or become larger

ENLARGER *n pl.* -S a device used to enlarge photographs

ENLIST *v* -ED, -ING, -S to engage for military service

ENLISTEE *n pl.* -S one that is enlisted

ENLISTER *n pl.* -S one that enlists

ENLIVEN *v* -ED, -ING, -S to make lively

ENMESH *v* -ED, -ING, -ES to ensnare or entangle in a net

ENMITY *n pl.* -TIES hostility

ENNEAD *n pl.* -S a group of nine
ENNEADIC *adj*

ENNEAGON *n pl.* -S a nonagon

ENNOBLE *v* -BLED, -BLING, -BLES to make noble

ENNOBLER *n pl.* -S one that ennobles

ENNUI *n pl.* -S a feeling of weariness and discontent

ENNUYE *adj* oppressed with ennui

ENNUYEE *adj* ennuye

ENOL *n pl.* -S a chemical compound
ENOLIC *adj*

ENOLASE *n pl.* -S an enzyme

ENOLOGY *n pl.* -GIES oenology

ENORM *adj* enormous

ENORMITY *n pl.* -TIES a grave offense against decency

ENORMOUS *adj* huge

ENOSIS _n_ pl. -SISES union

ENOUGH _n_ pl. -S a sufficient supply

ENOUNCE _v_ ENOUNCED, ENOUNCING, ENOUNCES to announce

ENOW _n_ pl. -S enough

ENPLANE _v_ -PLANED, -PLANING, -PLANES to board an airplane

ENQUIRE _v_ -QUIRED, -QUIRING, -QUIRES to inquire

ENQUIRY _n_ pl. -RIES inquiry

ENRAGE _v_ -RAGED, -RAGING, -RAGES to make very angry

ENRAPT _adj_ rapt

ENRAVISH _v_ -ED, -ING, -ES to delight greatly

ENRICH _v_ -ED, -ING, -ES to add desirable elements to

ENRICHER _n_ pl. -S one that enriches

ENROBE _v_ -ROBED, -ROBING, -ROBES to dress

ENROBER _n_ pl. -S one that enrobes

ENROL _v_ -ROLLED, -ROLLING, -ROLS to enroll

ENROLL _v_ -ED, -ING, -S to enter the name of in a register, record, or roll

ENROLLEE _n_ pl. -S one that is enrolled

ENROLLER _n_ pl. -S one that enrolls

ENROLLING present participle of enrol

ENROOT _v_ -ED, -ING, -S to implant

ENS _n_ pl. ENTIA an entity

ENSAMPLE _n_ pl. -S an example

ENSCONCE _v_ -SCONCED, -SCONCING, -SCONCES to settle securely or comfortably

ENSCROLL _v_ -ED, -ING, -S to write on a scroll

ENSEMBLE _n_ pl. -S a group of complementary parts

ENSERF _v_ -ED, -ING, -S to make a serf of

ENSHEATH _v_ -ED, -ING, -S to enclose in a sheath

ENSHRINE _v_ -SHRINED, -SHRINING, -SHRINES to place in a shrine

ENSHROUD _v_ -ED, -ING, -S to conceal

ENSIFORM _adj_ sword-shaped

ENSIGN _n_ pl. -S a navy officer

ENSIGNCY _n_ pl. -CIES the rank of an ensign

ENSILAGE _v_ -LAGED, -LAGING, -LAGES to ensile

ENSILE _v_ -SILED, -SILING, -SILES to store in a silo

ENSKY _v_ -SKIED or -SKYED, -SKYING, -SKIES to raise to the skies

ENSLAVE _v_ -SLAVED, -SLAVING, -SLAVES to make a slave of

ENSLAVER _n_ pl. -S one that enslaves

ENSNARE _v_ -SNARED, -SNARING, -SNARES to trap

ENSNARER _n_ pl. -S one that ensnares

ENSNARL _v_ -ED, -ING, -S to tangle

ENSORCEL _v_ -ED, -ING, -S to bewitch

ENSOUL _v_ -ED, -ING, -S to endow with a soul

ENSPHERE _v_ -SPHERED, -SPHERING, -SPHERES to enclose in a sphere

ENSUE _v_ -SUED, -SUING, -SUES to occur afterward or as a result

ENSURE _v_ -SURED, -SURING, -SURES to make certain

ENSURER _n_ pl. -S one that ensures

ENSWATHE _v_ -SWATHED, -SWATHING, -SWATHES to swathe

ENTAIL _v_ -ED, -ING, -S to restrict the inheritance of to a specified line of heirs

ENTAILER _n_ pl. -S one that entails

ENTAMEBA _n_ pl. -BAE or -BAS endameba

ENTANGLE _v_ -TANGLED, -TANGLING, -TANGLES to tangle

ENTASIA _n_ pl. -S spasmodic contraction of a muscle

ENTASIS _n_ pl. -TASES a slight convexity in a column **ENTASTIC** _adj_

ENTELLUS _n_ pl. -ES a hanuman

ENTENTE _n_ pl. -S an agreement between nations

ENTER _v_ -ED, -ING, -S to come or go into

ENTERA a pl. of enteron

ENTERAL _adj_ enteric

ENTERER _n_ pl. -S one that enters

ENTERIC _adj_ pertaining to the enteron

ENTERON _n_ pl. -TERONS or -TERA the alimentary canal

ENTHALPY _n_ pl. -PIES a thermodynamic measure

ENTHETIC _adj_ introduced from outside

ENTHRAL _v_ -THRALLED, -THRALLING, -THRALS to enthrall

ENTHRALL _v_ -ED, -ING, -S to charm

ENTHRONE _v_ -THRONED, -THRONING, -THRONES to place on a throne

ENTHUSE _v_ -THUSED, -THUSING, -THUSES to show enthusiasm

ENTIA pl. of ens

ENTICE v -TICED, -TICING, -TICES to allure

ENTICER n pl. -S one that entices

ENTIRE n pl. -S the whole of something

ENTIRELY adv completely

ENTIRETY n pl. -TIES completeness

ENTITLE v -TLED, -TLING, -TLES to give a title to

ENTITY n pl. -TIES something that has a real existence

ENTODERM n pl. -S endoderm

ENTOIL v -ED, -ING, -S to entrap

ENTOMB v -ED, -ING, -S to place in a tomb

ENTOPIC adj situated in the normal place

ENTOZOA a pl. of entozoan and pl. of entozoon

ENTOZOAL adj entozoic

ENTOZOAN n pl. -ZOANS or -ZOA an entozoic parasite

ENTOZOIC adj living within an animal

ENTOZOON n pl. -ZOA entozoan

ENTRAILS n/pl the internal organs

ENTRAIN v -ED, -ING, -S to board a train

ENTRANCE v -TRANCED, -TRANCING, -TRANCES to fill with delight or wonder

ENTRANT n pl. -S one that enters

ENTRAP v -TRAPPED, -TRAPPING, -TRAPS to trap

ENTREAT v -ED, -ING, -S to ask for earnestly

ENTREATY n pl. -TREATIES an earnest request

ENTREE n pl. -S the principal dish of a meal

ENTRENCH v -ED, -ING, -ES to establish firmly

ENTREPOT n pl. -S a warehouse

ENTRESOL n pl. -S a mezzanine

ENTRIES pl. of entry

ENTROPY n pl. -PIES a thermodynamic measure

ENTRUST v -ED, -ING, -S to give over for safekeeping

ENTRY n pl. -TRIES a place of entrance

ENTRYWAY n pl. -WAYS a passage serving as an entrance

ENTWINE v -TWINED, -TWINING, -TWINES to twine around

ENTWIST v -ED, -ING, -S to twist together

ENURE v -URED, -URING, -URES to inure

ENURESIS n pl. -SISES involuntary urination **ENURETIC** adj

ENVELOP v -ED, -ING, -S to cover completely

ENVELOPE n pl. -S a paper container

ENVENOM v -ED, -ING, -S to put venom into

ENVIABLE adj desirable **ENVIABLY** adv

ENVIED past tense of envy

ENVIER n pl. -S one that envies

ENVIES present 3d person sing. of envy

ENVIOUS adj resentful and desirous of another's possessions or qualities

ENVIRON v -ED, -ING, -S to encircle

ENVISAGE v -AGED, -AGING, -AGES to form a mental image of

ENVISION v -ED, -ING, -S to envisage

ENVOI n pl. -S the closing of a poem or prose work

ENVOY n pl. -VOYS a representative

ENVY v -VIED, -VYING, -VIES to be envious of

ENWHEEL v -ED, -ING, -S to encircle

ENWIND v -WOUND, -WINDING, -WINDS to wind around

ENWOMB v -ED, -ING, -S to enclose as if in a womb

ENWRAP v -WRAPPED, -WRAPPING, -WRAPS to envelop

ENZOOTIC n pl. -S a type of animal disease

ENZYM n pl. -S enzyme

ENZYME n pl. -S a complex protein **ENZYMIC** adj

EOBIONT n pl. -S a type of basic organism

EOHIPPUS n pl. -ES an extinct horse

EOLIAN adj pertaining to the wind

EOLIPILE n pl. -S a type of engine

EOLITH n pl. -S a prehistoric stone tool **EOLITHIC** adj

EOLOPILE n pl. -S eolipile

EON n pl. -S an indefinitely long period of time

EONIAN adj everlasting

EONISM n pl. -S adoption of the dress and mannerisms of the opposite sex

EOSIN n pl. -S a red dye **EOSINIC** adj

EOSINE   *n* pl. -S eosin

EPACT   *n* pl. -S the difference between the lengths of the solar and lunar years

EPARCH   *n* pl. -S the head of an eparchy

EPARCHY   *n* pl. -CHIES a district of modern Greece

EPAULET   *n* pl. -S a shoulder ornament

EPEE   *n* pl. -S a type of sword

EPEEIST   *n* pl. -S one who fences with an epee

EPEIRIC   *adj* pertaining to vertical movement of the earth's crust

EPERGNE   *n* pl. -S an ornamental dish

EPHA   *n* pl. -S ephah

EPHAH   *n* pl. -S a Hebrew unit of dry measure

EPHEBE   *n* pl. -S ephebus EPHEBIC *adj*

EPHEBOS   *n* pl. -BOI ephebus

EPHEBUS   *n* pl. -BI a young man of ancient Greece

EPHEDRA   *n* pl. -S a desert shrub

EPHEDRIN   *n* pl. -S an alkaloid used to treat allergies

EPHEMERA   *n* pl. -ERAS or -ERAE something of very short life or duration

EPHOD   *n* pl. -S an ancient Hebrew vestment

EPHOR   *n* pl. -ORS or -ORI a magistrate of ancient Greece EPHORAL *adj*

EPHORATE   *n* pl. -S the office of ephor

EPIBLAST   *n* pl. -S the ectoderm

EPIBOLY   *n* pl. -LIES the growth of one part around another EPIBOLIC *adj*

EPIC   *n* pl. -S a long narrative poem EPICAL *adj* EPICALLY *adv*

EPICALYX   *n* pl. -LYXES or -LYCES a set of bracts close to and resembling a calyx

EPICARP   *n* pl. -S the outer layer of a pericarp

EPICEDIA   *n/pl* funeral songs

EPICENE   *n* pl. -S one having both male and female characteristics

EPICLIKE   *adj* resembling an epic

EPICOTYL   *n* pl. -S a part of a plant embryo

EPICURE   *n* pl. -S a gourmet

EPICYCLE   *n* pl. -S a circle that rolls on the circumference of another circle

EPIDEMIC   *n* pl. -S a rapid spread of a disease

EPIDERM   *n* pl. -S the outer layer of skin

EPIDOTE   *n* pl. -S a mineral EPIDOTIC *adj*

EPIDURAL   *adj* situated on the membrane that encloses the brain

EPIFAUNA   *n* pl. -FAUNAE or -FAUNAS fauna living on a hard sea floor

EPIFOCAL   *adj* pertaining to the point of origin of an earthquake

EPIGEAL   *adj* epigeous

EPIGEAN   *adj* epigeous

EPIGENE   *adj* occurring near the surface of the earth

EPIGENIC   *adj* pertaining to change in the mineral character of a rock

EPIGEOUS   *adj* growing on or close to the ground

EPIGON   *n* pl. -S epigone

EPIGONE   *n* pl. -S an inferior imitator EPIGONIC *adj*

EPIGONUS   *n* pl. -NI epigone

EPIGRAM   *n* pl. -S a brief, witty remark

EPIGRAPH   *n* pl. -S an engraved inscription

EPIGYNY   *n* pl. -NIES the state of having floral organs near the top of the ovary

EPILEPSY   *n* pl. -SIES a disorder of the nervous system

EPILOG   *n* pl. -S a concluding section

EPILOGUE   *v* -LOGUED, -LOGUING, -LOGUES to provide with a concluding section

EPIMER   *n* pl. -S a type of sugar compound EPIMERIC *adj*

EPIMERE   *n* pl. -S a part of an embryo

EPIMYSIA   *n/pl* muscle sheaths

EPINAOS   *n* pl. -NAOI a rear vestibule

EPINASTY   *n* pl. -TIES a downward bending of plant parts

EPIPHANY   *n* pl. -NIES an appearance of a deity

EPIPHYTE   *n* pl. -S a plant growing upon another plant

EPISCIA   *n* pl. -S a tropical herb

EPISCOPE   *n* pl. -S a type of projector

EPISODE   *n* pl. -S an incident in the course of a continuous experience EPISODIC *adj*

EPISOME   *n* pl. -S a genetic determinant EPISOMAL *adj*

EPISTASY   *n* pl. -SIES a suppression of genetic effect

EPISTLE *n* pl. -S a long or formal letter

EPISTLER *n* pl. -S one that writes epistles

EPISTYLE *n* pl. -S a part of a classical building

EPITAPH *n* pl. -S an inscription on a tomb

EPITASIS *n* pl. -ASES the main part of a classical drama

EPITAXY *n* pl. -TAXIES a type of crystalline growth

EPITHET *n* pl. -S a term used to characterize a person or thing

EPITOME *n* pl. -S a typical or ideal example **EPITOMIC** *adj*

EPIZOA pl. of epizoon

EPIZOIC *adj* living on the body of an animal

EPIZOISM *n* pl. -S the state of being epizoic

EPIZOITE *n* pl. -S an epizoic organism

EPIZOON *n* pl. -ZOA an epizoic parasite

EPIZOOTY *n* pl. -TIES a type of animal disease

EPOCH *n* pl. -S a particular period of time **EPOCHAL** *adj*

EPODE *n* pl. -S a type of poem

EPONYM *n* pl. -S the person for whom something is named **EPONYMIC** *adj*

EPONYMY *n* pl. -MIES the derivation of an eponymic name

EPOPEE *n* pl. -S an epic poem

EPOPOEIA *n* pl. -S epopee

EPOS *n* pl. -ES an epic poem

EPOXIDE *n* pl. -S an epoxy compound

EPOXY *v* EPOXIED or EPOXYED, EPOXYING, EPOXIES to glue with epoxy (a type of resin)

EPSILON *n* pl. -S a Greek letter

EQUABLE *adj* not changing or varying greatly **EQUABLY** *adv*

EQUAL *adj* having the same capability, quantity, or effect as another

EQUAL *v* EQUALED, EQUALING, EQUALS or EQUALLED, EQUALLING, EQUALS to be equal to

EQUALISE *v* -ISED, -ISING, -ISES to equalize

EQUALITY *n* pl. -TIES the state of being equal

EQUALIZE *v* -IZED, -IZING, -IZES to make equal

EQUALLED a past tense of equal

EQUALLING a past participle of equal

EQUALLY *adv* in an equal manner

EQUATE *v* EQUATED, EQUATING, EQUATES to make equal

EQUATION *n* pl. -S the act of equating

EQUATOR *n* pl. -S the great circle of the earth

EQUERRY *n* pl. -RIES an officer in charge of the care of horses

EQUINE *n* pl. -S a horse

EQUINELY *adv* in a horselike manner

EQUINITY *n* pl. -TIES the state of being like a horse

EQUINOX *n* pl. -ES a point on the celestial sphere

EQUIP *v* EQUIPPED, EQUIPPING, EQUIPS to provide with whatever is needed

EQUIPAGE *n* pl. -S a carriage

EQUIPPER *n* pl. -S one that equips

EQUIPPING present participle of equip

EQUISETA *n/pl* rushlike plants

EQUITANT *adj* overlapping

EQUITES *n/pl* a privileged military class of ancient Rome

EQUITY *n* pl. -TIES fairness or impartiality

EQUIVOKE *n* pl. -S a play on words

ER *interj* — used to express hesitation

ERA *n* pl. -S an epoch

ERADIATE *v* -ATED, -ATING, -ATES to radiate

ERASE *v* ERASED, ERASING, ERASES to rub or scrape out **ERASABLE** *adj*

ERASER *n* pl. -S one that erases

ERASION *n* pl. -S the act of erasing

ERASURE *n* pl. -S erasion

ERBIUM *n* pl. -S a metallic element

ERE *prep* previous to; before

ERECT *v* -ED, -ING, -S to build

ERECTER *n* pl. -S erector

ERECTILE *adj* capable of being raised upright

ERECTION *n* pl. -S the act of erecting

ERECTIVE *adj* tending to erect

ERECTLY *adv* in an upright manner

ERECTOR *n* pl. -S one that erects

ERELONG *adv* soon

EREMITE *n* pl. -S a hermit **EREMITIC** *adj*

EREMURUS *n* pl. -URI a perennial herb

ERENOW *adv* before this time

EREPSIN *n pl.* -S a mixture of enzymes in the small intestine

ERETHISM *n pl.* -S abnormal irritability **ERETHIC** *adj*

EREWHILE *adv* some time ago

ERG *n pl.* -S a unit of work or energy

ERGASTIC *adj* constituting the nonliving by-products of protoplasmic activity

ERGATE *n pl.* -S a worker ant

ERGO *conj* therefore

ERGODIC *adj* pertaining to the probability that any state will recur

ERGOT *n pl.* -S a fungus **ERGOTIC** *adj*

ERGOTISM *n pl.* -S poisoning produced by eating ergot-infected grain

ERICA *n pl.* -S a shrub of the heath family

ERICOID *adj* resembling heath

ERIGERON *n pl.* -S an herb

ERINGO *n pl.* -GOES or -GOS eryngo

ERISTIC *n pl.* -S an expert in debate

ERLKING *n pl.* -S an evil spirit of Germanic folklore

ERMINE *n pl.* -S the fur of certain weasels **ERMINED** *adj*

ERN *n pl.* -S erne

ERNE *n pl.* -S a sea eagle

ERODE *v* ERODED, ERODING, ERODES to wear away by constant friction

ERODENT *adj* erosive

ERODIBLE *adj* erosible

ERODING present participle of erode

EROGENIC *adj* arousing sexual desire

EROS *n pl.* -ES sexual desire

EROSE *adj* uneven **EROSELY** *adv*

EROSIBLE *adj* capable of being eroded

EROSION *n pl.* -S the act of eroding

EROSIVE *adj* causing erosion

EROTIC *n pl.* -S an amatory poem **EROTICAL** *adj*

EROTICA *n/pl* literature or art dealing with sexual love

EROTISM *n pl.* -S sexual excitement

ERR *v* -ED, -ING, -S to make a mistake

ERRANCY *n pl.* -CIES an instance of erring

ERRAND *n pl.* -S a short trip made for a particular purpose

ERRANT *n pl.* -S a wanderer

ERRANTLY *adv* in a wandering manner

ERRANTRY *n pl.* -RIES the state of wandering

ERRATA *n pl.* -S a list of printing errors

ERRATIC *n pl.* -S an eccentric person

ERRATUM *n pl.* -TA a printing error

ERRHINE *n pl.* -S a substance that promotes nasal discharge

ERRINGLY *adv* in a mistaken manner

ERROR *n pl.* -S a mistake

ERS *n pl.* -ES ervil

ERSATZ *n pl.* -ES a substitute

ERST *adv* formerly

ERUCT *v* -ED, -ING, -S to belch

ERUCTATE *v* -TATED, -TATING, -TATES to eruct

ERUDITE *adj* scholarly

ERUGO *n pl.* -GOS aerugo

ERUMPENT *adj* bursting forth

ERUPT *v* -ED, -ING, -S to burst forth

ERUPTION *n pl.* -S the act of erupting

ERUPTIVE *n pl.* -S a type of rock

ERVIL *n pl.* -S a European vetch

ERYNGO *n pl.* -GOES or -GOS a medicinal herb

ERYTHEMA *n pl.* -S a redness of the skin

ERYTHRON *n pl.* -S a bodily organ consisting of the red blood cells

ES *n pl.* ESES ess

ESCALADE *v* -LADED, -LADING, -LADES to enter by means of ladders

ESCALATE *v* -LATED, -LATING, -LATES to increase

ESCALLOP *v* -ED, -ING, -S to scallop

ESCALOP *v* -ED, -ING, -S to escallop

ESCAPADE *n pl.* -S a reckless adventure

ESCAPE *v* -CAPED, -CAPING, -CAPES to get away

ESCAPEE *n pl.* -S one that has escaped

ESCAPER *n pl.* -S one that escapes

ESCAPING present participle of escape

ESCAPISM *n pl.* -S the avoidance of reality by diversion of the mind

ESCAPIST *n pl.* -S one given to escapism

ESCAR *n pl.* -S esker

ESCARGOT *n pl.* -S an edible snail

ESCAROLE *n pl.* -S a variety of endive

ESCARP *v* -ED, -ING, -S to cause to slope steeply

ESCHALOT *n pl.* -S a shallot

ESCHAR   n pl. -S a hard, dry scab

ESCHEAT   v -ED, -ING, -S to confiscate

ESCHEW   v -ED, -ING, -S to avoid

ESCHEWAL   n pl. -S the act of eschewing

ESCOLAR   n pl. -S a food fish

ESCORT   v -ED, -ING, -S to accompany

ESCOT   v -ED, -ING, -S to provide support for

ESCROW   v -ED, -ING, -S to place in the custody of a third party

ESCUAGE   n pl. -S scutage

ESCUDO   n pl. -DOS a monetary unit of Portugal

ESCULENT   n pl. -S something that is edible

ESERINE   n pl. -S a toxic alkaloid

ESKAR   n pl. -S esker

ESKER   n pl. -S a narrow ridge of gravel and sand

ESOPHAGI   n/pl tubes connecting the mouth to the stomach

ESOTERIC   adj designed for a select few

ESPALIER   v -ED, -ING, -S to furnish with a trellis

ESPANOL   n pl. -ES a native of Spain

ESPARTO   n pl. -TOS a perennial grass

ESPECIAL   adj special

ESPIAL   n pl. -S the act of espying

ESPIED   past tense of espy

ESPIEGLE   adj playful

ESPIES   present 3d person sing. of espy

ESPOUSAL   n pl. -S a marriage ceremony

ESPOUSE   v -POUSED, -POUSING, -POUSES to marry

ESPOUSER   n pl. -S one that espouses

ESPRESSO   n pl. -SOS a strong coffee

ESPRIT   n pl. -S spirit

ESPY   v -PIED, -PYING, -PIES to catch sight of

ESQUIRE   v -QUIRED, -QUIRING, -QUIRES to escort

ESS   n pl. -ES the letter S

ESSAY   v -ED, -ING, -S to try

ESSAYER   n pl. -S one that essays

ESSAYIST   n pl. -S a writer of essays (prose compositions)

ESSENCE   n pl. -S a fundamental nature or quality

ESSOIN   n pl. -S an excuse

ESSONITE   n pl. -S a variety of garnet

ESTANCIA   n pl. -S a cattle ranch

ESTATE   v -TATED, -TATING, -TATES to provide with landed property

ESTEEM   v -ED, -ING, -S to have a high opinion of

ESTER   n pl. -S a type of chemical compound

ESTERASE   n pl. -S a type of enzyme

ESTERIFY   v -FIED, -FYING, -FIES to convert into an ester

ESTHESIA   n pl. -S the ability to receive sensation

ESTHESIS   n pl. -THESISES or -THESES esthesia

ESTHETE   n pl. -S an esthetic person

ESTHETIC   adj keenly appreciative of the beautiful

ESTIMATE   v -MATED, -MATING, -MATES to make an approximate judgment of

ESTIVAL   adj pertaining to summer

ESTIVATE   v -VATED, -VATING, -VATES to spend the summer

ESTOP   v -TOPPED, -TOPPING, -TOPS to impede by estoppel

ESTOPPEL   n pl. -S a legal restraint preventing a person from contradicting his own previous statement

ESTOVERS   n/pl necessities allowed by law

ESTRAGON   n pl. -S tarragon

ESTRAL   adj estrous

ESTRANGE   v -TRANGED, -TRANGING, -TRANGES to alienate

ESTRAY   v -ED, -ING, -S to stray

ESTREAT   v -ED, -ING, -S to copy from court records for use in prosecution

ESTRIN   n pl. -S estrone

ESTRIOL   n pl. -S an estrogen

ESTROGEN   n pl. -S any of a group of female hormones promoting or producing estrus

ESTRONE   n pl. -S an estrogen

ESTROUS   adj pertaining to estrus

ESTRUAL   adj estrous

ESTRUM   n pl. -S estrus

ESTRUS   n pl. -ES the period of heat in female mammals

ESTUARY   n pl. -ARIES an inlet of the sea at a river's lower end

ESURIENT   adj greedy

ET   a past tense of eat

ETA   n pl. -S a Greek letter

ETAGERE   n pl. -S an ornamental stand

ETAMIN *n pl.* -S etamine

ETAMINE *n pl.* -S a loosely woven fabric

ETAPE *n pl.* -S a warehouse

ETATISM *n pl.* -S state socialism **ETATIST** *adj*

ETCETERA *n pl.* -S a number of additional items

ETCH *v* -ED, -ING, -ES to engrave with acid

ETCHER *n pl.* -S one that etches

ETCHING *n pl.* -S an etched design

ETERNAL *n pl.* -S something lasting forever

ETERNE *adj* everlasting

ETERNISE *v* -NISED, -NISING, -NISES to eternize

ETERNITY *n pl.* -TIES infinite time

ETERNIZE *v* -NIZED, -NIZING, -NIZES to make everlasting

ETESIAN *n pl.* -S an annually recurring wind

ETH *n pl.* -S edh

ETHANE *n pl.* -S a gaseous hydrocarbon

ETHANOL *n pl.* -S an alcohol

ETHENE *n pl.* -S ethylene

ETHER *n pl.* -S a volatile liquid used as an anesthetic **ETHERIC** *adj*

ETHEREAL *adj* airy

ETHERIFY *v* -FIED, -FYING, -FIES to convert into ether

ETHERISH *adj* resembling ether

ETHERIZE *v* -IZED, -IZING, -IZES to treat with ether

ETHIC *n pl.* -S a body of moral principles

ETHICAL *n pl.* -S a drug sold by prescription only

ETHICIAN *n pl.* -S an ethicist

ETHICIST *n pl.* -S a specialist in ethics

ETHICIZE *v* -CIZED, -CIZING, -CIZES to make ethical

ETHINYL *n pl.* -S ethynyl

ETHION *n pl.* -S a pesticide

ETHMOID *n pl.* -S a bone of the nasal cavity

ETHNARCH *n pl.* -S the ruler of a people or province

ETHNIC *n pl.* -S a member of a particular ethnos **ETHNICAL** *adj*

ETHNOS *n pl.* -ES a group of people who share a common and distinctive culture

ETHOLOGY *n pl.* -GIES the study of animal behavior

ETHOS *n pl.* -ES the fundamental character of a culture

ETHOXY *adj* pertaining to ethoxyl

ETHOXYL *n pl.* -S a univalent chemical radical

ETHYL *n pl.* -S a univalent chemical radical

ETHYLATE *v* -ATED, -ATING, -ATES to introduce the ethyl group into

ETHYLENE *n pl.* -S a flammable gas

ETHYLIC *adj* pertaining to ethyl

ETHYNE *n pl.* -S a flammable gas

ETHYNYL *n pl.* -S a univalent chemical radical

ETIOLATE *v* -LATED, -LATING, -LATES to whiten

ETIOLOGY *n pl.* -GIES the study of the causes of diseases

ETNA *n pl.* -S a container for heating liquids

ETOILE *n pl.* -S a star

ETUDE *n pl.* -S a piece of music for the practice of a point of technique

ETUI *n pl.* -S a case for holding small articles

ETWEE *n pl.* -S etui

ETYMON *n pl.* -MA or -MONS the earliest known form of a word

EUCAINE *n pl.* -S an anesthetic

EUCALYPT *n pl.* -S an evergreen tree

EUCHARIS *n pl.* -RISES a flowering plant

EUCHRE *v* -CHRED, -CHRING, -CHRES to prevent from winning three tricks in euchre (a card game)

EUCLASE *n pl.* -S a mineral

EUCRITE *n pl.* -S a type of meteorite **EUCRITIC** *adj*

EUDAEMON *n pl.* -S eudemon

EUDEMON *n pl.* -S a good spirit

EUGENICS *n/pl* the science of hereditary improvement **EUGENIC** *adj*

EUGENIST *n pl.* -S a student of eugenics

EUGENOL *n pl.* -S an aromatic liquid

EUGLENA *n pl.* -S a freshwater protozoan

EULACHAN *n pl.* -S eulachon

EULACHON *n pl.* -S a marine food fish

EULOGIA *n pl.* -GIAE holy bread

EULOGIA *n pl.* -S a blessing

EULOGISE *v* -GISED, -GISING, -GISES to eulogize

EULOGIST n pl. -S one that eulogizes

EULOGIUM n pl. -GIA or -GIUMS a eulogy

EULOGIZE v -GIZED, -GIZING, -GIZES to praise highly

EULOGY n pl. -GIES a formal expression of high praise

EUNUCH n pl. -S a castrated man

EUONYMUS n pl. -ES any of a genus of shrubs or small trees

EUPATRID n pl. -RIDS or -RIDAE an aristocrat of ancient Athens

EUPEPSIA n pl. -S good digestion **EUPEPTIC** adj

EUPEPSY n pl. -SIES eupepsia

EUPHENIC adj dealing with biological improvement

EUPHONY n pl. -NIES pleasant sound **EUPHONIC** adj

EUPHORIA n pl. -S a feeling of well-being **EUPHORIC** adj

EUPHOTIC adj pertaining to the upper layer of a body of water

EUPHRASY n pl. -SIES an annual herb

EUPHROE n pl. -S a device used to adjust a shipboard awning

EUPHUISM n pl. -S an artificially elegant style of speech or writing

EUPHUIST n pl. -S one given to euphuism

EUPLOID n pl. -S a cell having three or more identical genomes

EUPLOIDY n pl. -DIES the state of being a euploid

EUPNEA n pl. -S normal breathing **EUPNEIC** adj

EUPNOEA n pl. -S eupnea **EUPNOEIC** adj

EUREKA interj — used to express triumph upon discovering something

EURIPUS n pl. -PI a swift sea channel

EURO n pl. EUROS a large kangaroo

EUROPIUM n pl. -S a metallic element

EURYTHMY n pl. -MIES harmony of movement or structure

EUSTACY n pl. -CIES a worldwide change in sea level **EUSTATIC** adj

EUSTELE n pl. -S a plant part

EUTAXY n pl. -TAXIES good order

EUTECTIC n pl. -S an alloy that has the lowest possible melting point

EUTROPHY n pl. -PHIES healthful nutrition

EUXENITE n pl. -S a mineral

EVACUANT n pl. -S a cathartic medicine

EVACUATE v -ATED, -ATING, -ATES to remove from a dangerous area

EVACUEE n pl. -S one that is evacuated

EVADE v EVADED, EVADING, EVADES to escape or avoid by cleverness or deceit **EVADABLE, EVADIBLE** adj

EVADER n pl. -S one that evades

EVALUATE v -ATED, -ATING, -ATES to determine the value of

EVANESCE v -NESCED, -NESCING, -NESCES to fade away

EVANGEL n pl. -S a preacher of the gospel

EVANISH v -ED, -ING, -ES to vanish

EVASION n pl. -S the act of evading

EVASIVE adj tending to evade

EVE n pl. -S evening

EVECTION n pl. -S irregularity in the moon's motion

EVEN adj EVENER, EVENEST flat and smooth

EVEN v -ED, -ING, -S to make even

EVENER n pl. -S one that evens

EVENFALL n pl. -S twilight

EVENING n pl. -S the latter part of the day and early part of the night

EVENLY adv in an even manner

EVENNESS n pl. -ES the state of being even

EVENSONG n pl. -S an evening prayer service

EVENT n pl. -S something that occurs

EVENTFUL adj momentous

EVENTIDE n pl. -S evening

EVENTUAL adj occurring at a later time

EVER adv at all times

EVERMORE adv forever

EVERSION n pl -S the act of everting

EVERT v -ED, -ING, -S to turn outward or inside out

EVERTOR n pl. -S a muscle that turns a part outward

EVERY adj each without exception

EVERYDAY adj ordinary

EVERYMAN n pl. -MEN the typical or ordinary man

EVERYONE pron every person

EVERYWAY adv in every way

EVICT v -ED, -ING, -S to expel by legal process

EVICTEE n pl. -S one that is evicted

EVICTION n pl. -S the act of evicting

EVICTOR n pl. -S one that evicts

EVIDENCE	v -DENCED, -DENCING, -DENCES to indicate clearly		**EXAMINING**	present participle of examine
EVIDENT	adj clear to the vision or understanding		**EXAMPLE**	v -PLED, -PLING, -PLES to show by representation
EVIL	adj EVILER, EVILEST or EVILLER, EVILLEST morally bad		**EXANTHEM**	n pl. -S a skin eruption
EVIL	n pl. -S something that is evil		**EXARCH**	n pl. -S the ruler of a province in the Byzantine Empire EXARCHAL adj
EVILDOER	n pl. -S one that does evil			
EVILLER	a comparative of evil		**EXARCHY**	n pl. -CHIES the domain of an exarch
EVILLEST	a superlative of evil			
EVILLY	adv in an evil manner		**EXCAVATE**	v -VATED, -VATING, -VATES to dig out
EVILNESS	n pl. -ES the quality of being evil			
			EXCEED	v -ED, -ING, -S to go beyond
EVINCE	v EVINCED, EVINCING, EVINCES to show clearly EVINCIVE adj		**EXCEEDER**	n pl. -S one that exceeds
			EXCEL	v -CELLED, -CELLING, -CELS to surpass others
EVITE	v EVITED, EVITING, EVITES to avoid EVITABLE adj		**EXCEPT**	v -ED, -ING, -S to leave out
			EXCERPT	v -ED, -ING, -S to pick out a passage from for quoting
EVOCABLE	adj capable of being evoked			
EVOCATOR	n pl. -S one that evokes		**EXCESS**	n pl. -ES an overabundance
EVOKE	v EVOKED, EVOKING, EVOKES to call forth		**EXCHANGE**	v -CHANGED, -CHANGING, -CHANGES to give and receive reciprocally
EVOKER	n pl. -S an evocator			
EVOLUTE	n pl. -S a type of geometric curve		**EXCIDE**	v -CIDED, -CIDING, -CIDES to excise
EVOLVE	v EVOLVED, EVOLVING, EVOLVES to develop		**EXCIPLE**	n pl. -S a rim around the hymenium of various lichens
EVOLVER	n pl. -S one that evolves		**EXCISE**	v -CISED, -CISING, -CISES to remove by cutting out
EVONYMUS	n pl. -ES euonymus			
EVULSION	n pl. -S the act of pulling out		**EXCISION**	n pl. -S the act of excising
EVZONE	n pl. -S a Greek soldier		**EXCITANT**	n pl. -S a stimulant
EWE	n pl. -S a female sheep		**EXCITE**	v -CITED, -CITING, -CITES to arouse the emotions of
EWER	n pl. -S a large pitcher			
EX	n pl. -ES the letter X		**EXCITER**	n pl. -S one that excites
EXACT	adj -ACTER, -ACTEST precise		**EXCITON**	n pl. -S an energy level of a crystal
EXACT	v -ED, -ING, -S to force the payment or yielding of		**EXCITOR**	n pl. -S exciter
EXACTA	n pl. -S a type of horse racing bet		**EXCLAIM**	v -ED, -ING, -S to cry out suddenly
			EXCLAVE	n pl. -S a portion of a country which is isolated in foreign territory
EXACTER	n pl. -S one that exacts			
EXACTION	n pl. -S the act of exacting			
EXACTLY	adv in an exact manner		**EXCLUDE**	v -CLUDED, -CLUDING, -CLUDES to shut out
EXACTOR	n pl. -S exacter			
EXALT	v -ED, -ING, -S to raise		**EXCLUDER**	n pl. -S one that excludes
EXALTER	n pl. -S one that exalts		**EXCRETA**	n/pl excreted matter EXCRETAL adj
EXAM	n pl. -S an examination			
EXAMEN	n pl. -S a critical study		**EXCRETE**	v -CRETED, -CRETING, -CRETES to separate and eliminate from an organic body
EXAMINE	v -INED, -INING, -INES to inspect			
			EXCRETER	n pl. -S one that excretes
EXAMINEE	n pl. -S one that is taking an examination		**EXCUSE**	v -CUSED, -CUSING, -CUSES to apologize for
			EXCUSER	n pl. -S one that excuses
EXAMINER	n pl. -S one that examines		**EXEC**	n pl. -S an executive officer

EXECRATE v -CRATED, -CRATING, -CRATES to curse

EXECUTE v -CUTED, -CUTING, -CUTES to carry out

EXECUTER n pl. -S executor

EXECUTOR n pl. -S one that executes

EXEDRA n pl. -DRAE a curved outdoor bench

EXEGESIS n pl. -GESES critical explanation or analysis **EXEGETIC** adj

EXEGETE n pl. -S one skilled in exegesis

EXEMPLAR n pl. -S one that is worthy of being copied

EXEMPLUM n pl. -PLA an example

EXEMPT v -ED, -ING, -S to free from an obligation required of others

EXEQUY n pl. -QUIES a funeral procession **EXEQUIAL** adj

EXERCISE v -CISED, -CISING, -CISES to make use of

EXERGUE n pl. -S a space on a coin **EXERGUAL** adj

EXERT v -ED, -ING, -S to put into action

EXERTION n pl. -S the act of exerting

EXERTIVE adj tending to exert

EXHALANT n pl. -S something that exhales

EXHALE v -HALED, -HALING, -HALES to expel air or vapor

EXHALENT n pl. -S exhalant

EXHAUST v -ED, -ING, -S to use up

EXHIBIT v -ED, -ING, -S to present for public viewing

EXHORT v -ED, -ING, -S to advise urgently

EXHORTER n pl. -S one that exhorts

EXHUME v -HUMED, -HUMING, -HUMES to dig out of the earth

EXHUMER n pl. -S one that exhumes

EXIGENCE n pl. -S exigency

EXIGENCY n pl. -CIES urgency

EXIGENT adj urgent

EXIGIBLE adj liable to be demanded

EXIGUITY n pl. -ITIES the state of being exiguous

EXIGUOUS adj meager

EXILE v -ILED, -ILING, -ILES to banish from one's own country

EXILIAN adj exilic

EXILIC adj pertaining to exile (banishment from one's own country)

EXIMIOUS adj excellent

EXINE n pl. -S the outer layer of certain spores

EXIST v -ED, -ING, -S to be

EXISTENT n pl. -S something that exists

EXIT v -ED, -ING, -S to go out

EXOCARP n pl. -S the epicarp

EXOCRINE n pl. -S an external secretion

EXODERM n pl. -S the ectoderm

EXODOS n pl. -DOI a concluding dramatic scene

EXODUS n pl. -ES a movement away

EXOERGIC adj releasing energy

EXOGAMY n pl. -MIES marriage outside of a particular group **EXOGAMIC** adj

EXOGEN n pl. -S a type of plant

EXORABLE adj persuadable

EXORCISE v -CISED, -CISING, -CISES to free of an evil spirit

EXORCISM n pl. -S the act of exorcising

EXORCIST n pl. -S one who practices exorcism

EXORCIZE v -CIZED, -CIZING, -CIZES to exorcise

EXORDIUM n pl. -DIUMS or -DIA a beginning **EXORDIAL** adj

EXOSMOSE n pl. -S a form of osmosis **EXOSMIC** adj

EXOSPORE n pl. -S the outer coat of a spore

EXOTERIC adj suitable for the public

EXOTIC n pl. -S something from another part of the world

EXOTICA n/pl things excitingly different or unusual

EXOTISM n pl. -S an exotic

EXOTOXIN n pl. -S an excreted toxin **EXOTOXIC** adj

EXPAND v -ED, -ING, -S to increase in size or volume

EXPANDER n pl. -S one that expands

EXPANSE n pl. -S a wide, continuous area

EXPECT v -ED, -ING, -S to anticipate

EXPEDITE v -DITED, -DITING, -DITES to speed up the progress of

EXPEL v -PELLED, -PELLING, -PELS to force out

EXPELLEE n pl. -S a deportee

EXPELLER n pl. -S one that expels

EXPELLING present participle of expel

EXPEND v -ED, -ING, -S to use up

EXPENDER   *n* pl. -S one that expends

EXPENSE   *v* -PENSED, -PENSING, -PENSES to charge with costs

EXPERT   *v* -ED, -ING, -S to serve as an authority

EXPERTLY   *adv* skillfully

EXPIABLE   *adj* capable of being expiated

EXPIATE   *v* -ATED, ATING, -ATES to atone for

EXPIATOR   *n* pl. -S one that expiates

EXPIRE   *v* -PIRED, -PIRING, -PIRES to come to an end

EXPIRER   *n* pl. -S one that expires

EXPIRY   *n* pl. -RIES a termination

EXPLAIN   *v* -ED, -ING, -S to make plain or understandable

EXPLANT   *v* -ED, -ING, -S to remove from the natural site of growth and place in a medium

EXPLICIT   *n* pl. -S a statement formerly used at the close of a book

EXPLODE   *v* -PLODED, -PLODING, -PLODES to blow up

EXPLODER   *n* pl. -S one that explodes

EXPLOIT   *v* -ED, -ING, -S to take advantage of

EXPLORE   *v* -PLORED, -PLORING, -PLORES to travel through for the purpose of discovery

EXPLORER   *n* pl. -S one that explores

EXPO   *n* pl. -POS a public exhibition

EXPONENT   *n* pl. -S one who expounds

EXPORT   *v* -ED, -ING, -S to send to other countries for commercial purposes

EXPORTER   *n* pl. -S one that exports

EXPOSAL   *n* pl. -S an exposure

EXPOSE   *v* -POSED, -POSING, -POSES to lay open to view

EXPOSER   *n* pl. -S one that exposes

EXPOSIT   *v* -ED, -ING, -S to expound

EXPOSURE   *n* pl. -S the act of exposing

EXPOUND   *v* -ED, -ING, -S to explain in detail

EXPRESS   *v* -ED, -ING, -ES to set forth in words

EXPULSE   *v* -PULSED, -PULSING, -PULSES to expel

EXPUNGE   *v* -PUNGED, PUNGING, -PUNGES to delete

EXPUNGER   *n* pl. -S one that expunges

EXSCIND   *v* -ED, -ING, -S to cut out

EXSECANT   *n* pl. -S a trigonometric function of an angle

EXSECT   *v* -ED, -ING, -S to cut out

EXSERT   *v* -ED, -ING, -S to thrust out

EXTANT   *adj* still in existence

EXTEND   *v* -ED, -ING, -S to stretch out to full length

EXTENDER   *n* pl. -S a substance added to another substance

EXTENSOR   *n* pl. -S a muscle that extends a limb

EXTENT   *n* pl. -S the range over which something extends

EXTERIOR   *n* pl. -S a part or surface that is outside

EXTERN   *n* pl. -S a nonresident of an institution

EXTERNAL   *n* pl. -S an exterior

EXTERNE   *n* pl. -S extern

EXTINCT   *v* -ED, -ING, -S to extinguish

EXTOL   *v* -TOLLED, -TOLLING, -TOLS to praise highly

EXTOLL   *v* -ED, -ING, -S to extol

EXTOLLER   *n* pl. -S one that extols

EXTOLLING   present participle of extol

EXTORT   *v* -ED, -ING, -S to obtain from a person by violence or intimidation

EXTORTER   *n* pl. -S one that extorts

EXTRA   *n* pl. -S something additional

EXTRACT   *v* -ED, -ING, -S to pull or draw out

EXTRADOS   *n* pl. -ES the outer curve of an arch

EXTREMA   pl. of extremum

EXTREME   *adj* -TREMER, -TREMEST existing in a very high degree

EXTREME   *n* pl. -S the highest degree

EXTREMUM   *n* pl. -MA a maximum or a minimum of a mathematical function

EXTRORSE   *adj* facing outward

EXTRUDE   *v* -TRUDED, -TRUDING, -TRUDES to force, thrust, or push out

EXTRUDER   *n* pl. -S one that extrudes

EXUDATE   *n* pl. -S an exuded substance

EXUDE   *v* -UDED, -UDING, -UDES to ooze forth

EXULT   *v* -ED, -ING, -S to rejoice greatly

EXULTANT   *adj* exulting

EXURB   *n* pl. -S a residential area lying beyond the suburbs of a city
EXURBAN *adj*

EXURBIA	n pl. -S an exurb	**EYEN**	a pl. of eye
EXUVIATE	v -ATED, -ATING, -ATES to molt	**EYEPIECE**	n pl. -S the lens or lens group nearest the eye in an optical instrument
EXUVIUM	n pl. -VIAE or -VIA the molted covering of an animal **EXUVIAL** adj		
		EYEPOINT	n pl. -S the point at which an eye is placed in using an optical instrument
EYAS	n pl. -ES a young hawk		
EYE	v EYED, EYING or EYEING, EYES to watch closely **EYEABLE** adj	**EYER**	n pl. -S one that eyes
		EYESHADE	n pl. -S a visor for shading the eyes
EYE	n pl. EYES, EYEN or EYNE the organ of sight	**EYESHOT**	n pl. -S the range of vision
EYEBALL	v -ED, -ING, -S to eye	**EYESIGHT**	n pl. -S the ability to see
EYEBEAM	n pl. -S a glance	**EYESOME**	adj pleasant to look at
EYEBOLT	n pl. -S a type of bolt or screw	**EYESORE**	n pl. -S something offensive to the sight
EYEBROW	n pl. -S the ridge over the eye		
EYECUP	n pl. -S a cup used for applying lotions to the eyes	**EYESPOT**	n pl. -S a simple visual organ of lower animals
		EYESTALK	n pl. -S a stalklike structure with an eye at its tip
EYED	past tense of eye		
EYEDNESS	n pl. -ES preference for the use of one eye over the other	**EYESTONE**	n pl. -S a disk used to remove foreign matter from the eye
EYEFUL	n pl. -S a complete view	**EYETOOTH**	n pl. -TEETH a cuspid
EYEGLASS	n pl. -ES a lens used to aid vision	**EYEWASH**	n pl. -ES an eye lotion
		EYEWATER	n pl. -S an eyewash
EYEHOLE	n pl. -S a small opening	**EYEWINK**	n pl. -S a wink of the eye
EYEHOOK	n pl. -S a type of hook	**EYING**	a present participle of eye
EYELASH	n pl. -ES a hair growing on the edge of an eyelid	**EYNE**	a pl. of eye
EYELESS	adj lacking eyes	**EYRA**	n pl. -S a wild cat of tropical America
EYELET	v -LETTED, -LETTING, -LETS to make a small hole in		
		EYRE	n pl. -S a journey
EYELID	n pl. -S the lid of skin that can be closed over an eyeball	**EYRIE**	n pl. -S aerie
		EYRIR	n pl. AURAR a monetary unit of Iceland
EYELIKE	adj resembling an eye		
EYELINER	n pl. -S makeup for the eyes	**EYRY**	n pl. -RIES aerie

FA	*n pl.* -S the fourth tone of the diatonic musical scale		**FACILITY**	*n pl.* -TIES the quality of being facile
FABLE	*v* -BLED, -BLING, -BLES to compose or tell fictitious tales		**FACING**	*n pl.* -S a lining at the edge of a garment
FABLER	*n pl.* -S one that fables		**FACT**	*n pl.* -S something known with certainty **FACTFUL** *adj*
FABLIAU	*n pl.* -AUX a short metrical tale popular in medieval France		**FACTION**	*n pl.* -S a clique within a larger group
FABLING	present participle of fable		**FACTIOUS**	*adj* promoting dissension
FABRIC	*n pl.* -S a woven, felted, or knitted material		**FACTOR**	*v* -ED, -ING, -S to express as a product of two or more quantities
FABULAR	*adj* legendary			
FABULIST	*n pl.* -S a liar		**FACTORY**	*n pl.* -RIES a building or group of buildings in which goods are manufactured
FABULOUS	*adj* almost unbelievable			
FACADE	*n pl.* -S the front of a building			
FACE	*v* FACED, FACING, FACES to oppose or meet defiantly **FACEABLE** *adj*		**FACTOTUM**	*n pl.* -S a person employed to do many kinds of work
			FACTUAL	*adj* pertaining to facts
FACEDOWN	*adv* with the front part down		**FACTURE**	*n pl.* -S the act of making something
FACELESS	*adj* lacking personal distinction or identity		**FACULA**	*n pl.* -LAE an unusually bright spot on the sun's surface **FACULAR** *adj*
FACER	*n pl.* -S one that faces			
FACET	*v* -ETED, -ETING, -ETS or -ETTED, -ETTING, -ETS to cut small plane surfaces on			
			FACULTY	*n pl.* -TIES an inherent power or ability
FACETE	*adj* witty **FACETELY** *adv*		**FAD**	*n pl.* -S a practice or interest that enjoys brief popularity
FACETIAE	*n/pl* witty sayings or writings			
FACETTED	past tense of facet		**FADABLE**	*adj* capable of fading
FACETTING	present participle of facet		**FADDIER**	comparative of faddy
FACEUP	*adv* with the front part up		**FADDIEST**	superlative of faddy
FACIA	*n pl.* -S fascia		**FADDISH**	*adj* inclined to take up fads
FACIAL	*n pl.* -S a treatment for the face		**FADDISM**	*n pl.* -S inclination to take up fads
FACIALLY	*adv* with respect to the face			
FACIEND	*n pl.* -S a number to be multiplied by another		**FADDIST**	*n pl.* -S a faddish person
FACIES	*n pl.* FACIES general appearance		**FADDY**	*adj* -DIER, -DIEST faddish
FACILE	*adj* easily achieved or performed **FACILELY** *adv*		**FADE**	*v* FADED, FADING, FADES to lose color or brightness **FADEDLY** *adv*

FADEAWAY *n pl.* -AWAYS a type of pitch in baseball

FADELESS *adj* not fading

FADER *n pl.* -S one that fades

FADGE *v* FADGED, FADGING, FADGES to succeed

FADING *n pl.* -S an Irish dance

FADO *n pl.* -DOS a Portuguese folk song

FAECES *n/pl* feces FAECAL *adj*

FAENA *n pl.* -S a series of passes made by a matador in a bullfight

FAERIE *n pl.* -S a fairy

FAERY *n pl.* -ERIES faerie

FAG *v* FAGGED, FAGGING, FAGS to make weary by hard work

FAGGOT *v* -ED, -ING, -S to fagot

FAGIN *n pl.* -S a person who instructs others in crime

FAGOT *v* -ED, -ING, -S to bind together into a bundle

FAGOTER *n pl.* -S one that fagots

FAGOTING *n pl.* -S a type of embroidery

FAHLBAND *n pl.* -S a band or stratum of rock impregnated with metallic sulfides

FAIENCE *n pl.* -S a variety of glazed pottery

FAIL *v* -ED, -ING, -S to be unsuccessful in an attempt

FAILING *n pl.* -S a minor fault or weakness

FAILLE *n pl.* -S a woven fabric

FAILURE *n pl.* -S the act of failing

FAIN *adj* FAINER, FAINEST glad

FAINEANT *n pl.* -S a lazy person

FAINT *v* -ED, -ING, -S to lose consciousness

FAINT *adj* FAINTER, FAINTEST lacking strength or vigor

FAINTER *n pl.* -S one that faints

FAINTISH *adj* somewhat faint

FAINTLY *adv* in a faint manner

FAIR *adj* FAIRER, FAIREST free from bias, dishonesty, or injustice

FAIR *v* -ED, -ING, -S to make smooth

FAIRIES pl. of fairy

FAIRING *n pl.* -S a structure on an aircraft serving to reduce drag

FAIRISH *adj* moderately good

FAIRLEAD *n pl.* -S a device used to hold a ship's rigging in place

FAIRLY *adv* in a fair manner

FAIRNESS *n pl.* -ES the quality of being fair

FAIRWAY *n pl.* -WAYS the mowed part of a golf course between tee and green

FAIRY *n pl.* FAIRIES an imaginary supernatural being

FAIRYISM *n pl.* -S the quality of being like a fairy

FAITH *v* -ED, -ING, -S to believe or trust

FAITHFUL *n pl.* -S a loyal follower or member

FAITOUR *n pl.* -S an impostor

FAKE *v* FAKED, FAKING, FAKES to contrive and present as genuine

FAKEER *n pl.* -S fakir

FAKER *n pl.* -S one that fakes

FAKERY *n pl.* -ERIES the practice of faking

FAKING present participle of fake

FAKIR *n pl.* -S a Hindu ascetic

FALBALA *n pl.* -S a trimming for a woman's garment

FALCATE *adj* curved and tapering to a point

FALCATED *adj* falcate

FALCHION *n pl.* -S a broad-bladed sword

FALCON *n pl.* -S a bird of prey

FALCONER *n pl.* -S one that hunts with hawks

FALCONET *n pl.* -S a small falcon

FALCONRY *n pl.* -RIES the sport of hunting with falcons

FALDERAL *n pl.* -S nonsense

FALDEROL *n pl.* -S falderal

FALL *v* FELL, FALLEN, FALLING, FALLS to descend under the force of gravity

FALLACY *n pl.* -CIES a false idea

FALLAL *n pl.* -S a showy article of dress

FALLBACK *n pl.* -S an act of retreating

FALLEN past participle of fall

FALLER *n pl.* -S one that falls

FALLFISH *n pl.* -ES a freshwater fish

FALLIBLE *adj* capable of erring **FALLIBLY** *adv*

FALLOFF *n pl.* -S a decline in quantity or quality

FALLOUT *n pl.* -S radioactive debris resulting from a nuclear explosion

FALLOW   v -ED, -ING, -S to plow and leave unseeded

FALSE   adj FALSER, FALSEST contrary to truth or fact **FALSELY** adv

FALSETTO   n pl. -TOS an artificially high voice

FALSIE   n pl. -S a pad worn within a brassiere

FALSIFY   v -FIED, -FYING, -FIES to represent falsely

FALSITY   n pl. -TIES something false

FALTBOAT   n pl. -S a collapsible boat resembling a kayak

FALTER   v -ED, -ING, -S to hesitate

FALTERER   n pl. -S one that falters

FAME   v FAMED, FAMING, FAMES to make famous

FAMELESS   adj not famous

FAMILIAL   adj pertaining to a family

FAMILIAR   n pl. -S a close friend or associate

FAMILY   n pl. -LIES a group of persons related by blood or marriage

FAMINE   n pl. -S a widespread scarcity of food

FAMING   present participle of fame

FAMISH   v -ED, -ING, -ES to suffer extreme hunger

FAMOUS   adj well-known **FAMOUSLY** adv

FAMULUS   n pl. -LI a servant or attendant

FAN   v FANNED, FANNING, FANS to cool or refresh with a fan (a device for putting air into motion)

FANATIC   n pl. -S a zealot

FANCIED   past tense of fancy

FANCIER   n pl. -S one that has a special liking for something

FANCIES   present 3d person sing. of fancy

FANCIFUL   adj unrealistic

FANCY   adj -CIER, -CIEST ornamental **FANCILY** adv

FANCY   v -CIED, -CYING, -CIES to take a liking to

FANDANGO   n pl. -GOS a lively Spanish dance

FANDOM   n pl. -S an aggregate of enthusiastic devotees

FANE   n pl. -S a temple

FANEGA   n pl. -S a Spanish unit of dry measure

FANEGADA   n pl. -S a Spanish unit of area

FANFARE   n pl. -S a short, lively musical flourish

FANFARON   n pl. -S a braggart

FANFOLD   n pl. -S a type of writing pad or tablet

FANG   n pl. -S a long, pointed tooth **FANGED, FANGLESS, FANGLIKE** adj

FANGA   n pl. -S fanega

FANION   n pl. -S a small flag

FANJET   n pl. -S a type of jet engine

FANLIGHT   n pl. -S a type of window

FANLIKE   adj resembling a fan

FANNED   past tase of fan

FANNER   n pl. -S one that fans

FANNING   present participle of fan

FANNY   n pl. -NIES the buttocks

FANO   n pl. FANOS a fanon

FANON   n pl. -S a cape worn by the pope

FANTAIL   n pl. -S a fan-shaped tail or end

FANTASIA   n pl. -S a free-form musical composition

FANTASIE   n pl. -S a fantasia

FANTASIED   past tense of fantasy

FANTASIES   present 3d person sing. of fantasy

FANTASM   n pl. -S phantasm

FANTAST   n pl. -S an impractical person

FANTASY   v -SIED, -SYING, -SIES to imagine

FANTOD   n pl. -S an emotional outburst

FANTOM   n pl. -S phantom

FANUM   n pl. -S fanon

FANWISE   adj spread out like an open fan

FANWORT   n pl. -S an aquatic plant

FAQIR   n pl. -S fakir

FAQUIR   n pl. -S fakir

FAR   adv FARTHER, FARTHEST or FURTHER, FURTHEST at or to a great distance

FARAD   n pl. -S a unit of electrical capacitance

FARADAIC   adj faradic

FARADAY   n pl. -DAYS a unit of electricity

FARADIC   adj pertaining to a type of electric current

FARADISE   v -DISED, -DISING, -DISES to faradize

FARADISM   n pl. -S the use of faradic current for therapeutic purposes

FARADIZE *v* -DIZED, -DIZING, -DIZES to treat by faradism

FARAWAY *adj* distant

FARCE *v* FARCED, FARCING, FARCES to fill out with witty material

FARCER *n* pl. -S farcer

FARCEUR *n* pl. -S a joker

FARCI *adj* stuffed with finely chopped meat

FARCICAL *adj* absurd

FARCIE *adj* farci

FARCING present participle of farce

FARCY *n* pl. -CIES a disease of horses

FARD *v* -ED, -ING, -S to apply cosmetics to

FARDEL *n* pl. -S a bundle

FARE *v* FARED, FARING, FARES to get along

FARER *n* pl. -S a traveler

FAREWELL *v* -ED, -ING, -S to say goodby

FARFAL *n* pl. -S farfel

FARFEL *n* pl. -S noodles in the form of small pellets or granules

FARINA *n* pl. -S a fine meal made from cereal grain

FARING present participle of fare

FARINHA *n* pl. -S a meal made from the root of the cassava

FARINOSE *adj* resembling farina

FARL *n* pl. -S a thin oatmeal cake

FARLE *n* pl. -S farl

FARM *v* -ED, -ING, -S to manage and cultivate as a farm (a tract of land devoted to agriculture) FARMABLE *adj*

FARMER *n* pl. -S one that farms

FARMHAND *n* pl. -S a farm laborer

FARMING *n* pl. -S the business of operating a farm

FARMLAND *n* pl. -S cultivated land

FARMYARD *n* pl. -S an area surrounded by farm buildings

FARNESOL *n* pl. -S an alcohol used in perfumes

FARNESS *n* pl. -ES the state of being far off or apart

FARO *n* pl. FAROS a card game

FAROUCHE *adj* sullenly shy

FARRAGO *n* pl. -GOES a confused mixture

FARRIER *n* pl. -S one that shoes horses

FARRIERY *n* pl. -ERIES the trade of a farrier

FARROW *v* -ED, -ING, -S to give birth to a litter of pigs

FART *v* -ED, -ING, -S to expel gas through the anus — an offensive term

FARTHER a comparative of far

FARTHEST a superlative of far

FARTHING *n* pl. -S a former British coin

FASCES *n* pl. FASCES an ancient Roman symbol of power

FASCIA *n* pl. -CIAE or -CIAS a broad and distinct band of color FASCIAL, FASCIATE *adj*

FASCICLE *n* pl. -S a small bundle

FASCINE *n* pl. -S a bundle of sticks used in building fortifications

FASCISM *n* pl. -S an oppressive political system

FASCIST *n* pl. -S an advocate of fascism

FASH *v* -ED, -ING, -ES to annoy

FASHION *v* -ED, -ING, -S to give a particular shape or form to

FASHIOUS *adj* annoying

FAST *adj* FASTER, FASTEST moving or able to move quickly

FAST *v* -ED, -ING, -S to abstain from eating

FASTBACK *n* pl. -S a type of automobile roof

FASTBALL *n* pl. -S a type of pitch in baseball

FASTEN *v* -ED, -ING, -S to secure

FASTENER *n* pl. -S one that fastens

FASTING *n* pl. -S abstention from eating

FASTNESS *n* pl. -ES the quality of being fast

FASTUOUS *adj* arrogant

FAT *adj* FATTER, FATTEST having an abundance of flesh

FAT *v* FATTED, FATTING, FATS to make fat

FATAL *adj* causing or capable of causing death

FATALISM *n* pl. -S the doctrine that all events are predetermined

FATALIST *n* pl. -S a believer in fatalism

FATALITY *n* pl. -TIES a death resulting from an unexpected occurrence

FATALLY *adv* in a fatal manner

FATBACK *n* pl. -S a marine fish

FATBIRD *n* pl. -S a wading bird

FATE *v* FATED, FATING, FATES to destine

FATEFUL	*adj* decisively important	FAUN	*n pl.* -S a woodland deity of Roman mythology **FAUNLIKE** *adj*
FATHEAD	*n pl.* -S a dolt		
FATHER	*v* -ED, -ING, -S to cause to exist	FAUNA	*n pl.* -NAS or -NAE the animal life of a particular region **FAUNAL** *adj* **FAUNALLY** *adv*
FATHERLY	*adj* paternal		
FATHOM	*v* -ED, -ING, -S to understand	FAUTEUIL	*n pl.* -S an armchair
FATIDIC	*adj* pertaining to prophecy	FAUVE	*n pl.* -S a fauvist
FATIGUE	*v* -TIGUED, -TIGUING, -TIGUES to weary	FAUVISM	*n pl.* -S a movement in painting
		FAUVIST	*n pl.* -S an advocate of fauvism
FATING	present participle of fate	FAVELA	*n pl.* -S a slum area
FATLESS	*adj* having no fat	FAVONIAN	*adj* pertaining to the west wind
FATLIKE	*adj* resembling fat	FAVOR	*v* -ED, -ING, -S to regard with approval
FATLING	*n pl.* -S a young animal fattened for slaughter		
		FAVORER	*n pl.* -S one that favors
FATLY	*adv* in the manner of one that is fat	FAVORITE	*n pl.* -S a person or thing preferred above all others
FATNESS	*n pl.* -ES the state of being fat	FAVOUR	*v* -ED, -ING, -S to favor
FATSO	*n pl.* -SOES or -SOS a fat person	FAVOURER	*n pl.* -S favorer
		FAVUS	*n pl.* -ES a skin disease
FATSTOCK	*n pl.* -S livestock that is fat and ready for market	FAWN	*v* -ED, -ING, -S to seek notice or favor by servile demeanor
FATTED	past tense of fat		
FATTEN	*v* -ED, -ING, -S to make fat	FAWNER	*n pl.* -S one that fawns
FATTENER	*n pl.* -S one that fattens	FAWNLIKE	*adj* resembling a young deer
FATTER	comparative of fat	FAWNY	*adj* FAWNIER, FAWNIEST of a yellowish-brown color
FATTEST	superlative of fat		
FATTIER	comparative of fatty	FAX	*v* -ED, -ING, -ES to reproduce by electronic means
FATTIES	pl. of fatty		
FATTIEST	superlative of fatty	FAY	*v* -ED, -ING, -S to join closely
FATTILY	*adv* in a fatty manner	FAYALITE	*n pl.* -S a mineral
FATTING	present participle of fat	FAZE	*v* FAZED, FAZING, FAZES to disturb the composure of
FATTISH	*adj* somewhat fat		
FATTY	*adj* -TIER, -TIEST greasy; oily	FAZENDA	*n pl.* -S a Brazilian plantation
FATTY	*n pl.* -TIES one that is fat	FEAL	*adj* loyal
FATUITY	*n pl.* -ITIES something foolish or stupid	FEALTY	*n pl.* -TIES loyalty
		FEAR	*v* -ED, -ING, -S to be afraid of
FATUOUS	*adj* smugly stupid	FEARER	*n pl.* -S one that fears
FAUBOURG	*n pl.* -S a suburb	FEARFUL	*adj* -FULLER, -FULLEST afraid
FAUCAL	*n pl.* -S a sound produced in the fauces	FEARLESS	*adj* unafraid
		FEARSOME	*adj* frightening
FAUCES	*n/pl* the passage from the mouth to the pharynx	FEASANCE	*n pl.* -S the performance of a condition, obligation, or duty
FAUCET	*n pl.* -S a device for controlling the flow of liquid from a pipe	FEASE	*v* FEASED, FEASING, FEASES to faze
FAUCIAL	*adj* pertaining to the fauces	FEASIBLE	*adj* capable of being done **FEASIBLY** *adv*
FAUGH	*interj* — used to express disgust		
		FEAST	*v* -ED, -ING, -S to eat sumptuously
FAULD	*n pl.* -S a piece of armor below the breastplate		
		FEASTER	*n pl.* -S one that feasts
FAULT	*v* -ED, -ING, -S to criticize	FEASTFUL	*adj* festive
FAULTY	*adj* FAULTIER, FAULTIEST imperfect **FAULTILY** *adv*	FEAT	*n pl.* -S a notable act or achievement

FEAT	*adj* FEATER, FEATEST skillful	**FEELING**	*n* pl. -S the function or power of perceiving by touch
FEATHER	*v* -ED, -ING, -S to cover with feathers (horny structures that form the principal covering of birds)	**FEET**	pl. of foot **FEETLESS** *adj*
		FEEZE	*v* FEEZED, FEEZING, FEEZES to faze
FEATHERY	*adj* -ERIER, -ERIEST resembling feathers	**FEIGN**	*v* -ED, -ING, -S to pretend
FEATLY	*adj* -LIER, -LIEST graceful	**FEIGNER**	*n* pl. -S one that feigns
FEATURE	*v* -TURED, -TURING, -TURES to give special prominence to	**FEINT**	*v* -ED, -ING, -S to make a deceptive movement
FEAZE	*v* FEAZED, FEAZING, FEAZES to faze	**FEIRIE**	*adj* nimble
		FEIST	*n* pl. -S a small dog of mixed breed
FEBRIFIC	*adj* feverish	**FEISTY**	*adj* FEISTIER, FEISTIEST full of nervous energy
FEBRILE	*adj* feverish	**FELDSPAR**	*n* pl. -S a mineral
FECAL	*adj* pertaining to feces	**FELICITY**	*n* pl. -TIES happiness
FECES	*n/pl* bodily waste discharged through the anus	**FELID**	*n* pl. -S a feline
		FELINE	*n* pl. -S an animal of the cat family
FECIAL	*n* pl. -S fetial	**FELINELY**	*adv* in a catlike manner
FECK	*n* pl. -S value	**FELINITY**	*n* pl. -TIES the quality of being catlike
FECKLESS	*adj* worthless		
FECKLY	*adv* almost	**FELL**	*v* -ED, -ING, -S to cause to fall
FECULA	*n* pl. -LAE fecal matter	**FELL**	*adj* FELLER, FELLEST cruel
FECULENT	*adj* foul with impurities	**FELLA**	*n* pl. -S a man or boy
FECUND	*adj* fruitful	**FELLABLE**	*adj* capable of being felled
FED	*n* pl. -S a federal agent	**FELLAH**	*n* pl. -LAHS, -LAHIN, or -LAHEEN a peasant or laborer in Arab countries
FEDAYEE	*n* pl. -YEEN an Arab commando		
FEDERACY	*n* pl. -CIES an alliance	**FELLATIO**	*n* pl. -TIOS oral stimulation of the penis
FEDERAL	*n* pl. -S a supporter of a type of central government		
		FELLER	*n* pl. -S one that fells
FEDERATE	*v* -ATED, -ATING, -ATES to unite in an alliance	**FELLIES**	pl. of felly
		FELLNESS	*n* pl. -ES extreme cruelty
FEDORA	*n* pl. -S a type of hat	**FELLOE**	*n* pl. -S the rim of a wheel
FEE	*v* FEED, FEEING, FEES to pay a fee (a fixed charge) to	**FELLOW**	*v* -ED, -ING, -S to produce an equal to
FEEBLE	*adj* -BLER, -BLEST weak **FEEBLY** *adv*	**FELLOWLY**	*adj* friendly
		FELLY	*n* pl. -LIES a felloe
FEEBLISH	*adj* somewhat feeble	**FELON**	*n* pl. -S a person who has committed a felony
FEED	*v* FED, FEEDING, FEEDS to give food to **FEEDABLE** *adj*		
		FELONRY	*n* pl. -RIES the whole class of felons
FEEDBACK	*n* pl. -S the return of a portion of the output to the input		
		FELONY	*n* pl. -NIES a grave crime
FEEDBAG	*n* pl. -S a bag for feeding horses	**FELSITE**	*n* pl. -S an igneous rock **FELSITIC** *adj*
FEEDBOX	*n* pl. -ES a box for animal feed		
FEEDER	*n* pl. -S one that feeds	**FELSPAR**	*n* pl. -S feldspar
FEEDLOT	*n* pl. -S a plot of land on which livestock is fattened	**FELSTONE**	*n* pl. -S felsite
		FELT	*v* -ED, -ING, -S to mat together
FEEL	*v* FELT, FEELING, FEELS to perceive through the sense of touch	**FELTING**	*n* pl. -S felted material
		FELUCCA	*n* pl. -S a swift sailing vessel
FEELER	*n* pl. -S a tactile organ	**FELWORT**	*n* pl. -S a flowering plant
FEELESS	*adj* requiring no fee		

FEMALE   *n* pl. -S an individual that bears young or produces ova

FEME   *n* pl. -S a wife

FEMINACY   *n* pl. -CIES the state of being a female

FEMINIE   *n/pl* women collectively

FEMININE   *n* pl. -S a word or form having feminine gender

FEMINISE   *v* -NISED, -NISING, -NISES to feminize

FEMINISM   *n* pl. -S a doctrine advocating rights for women equal to those of men

FEMINIST   *n* pl. -S a supporter of feminism

FEMINITY   *n* pl. -TIES the quality of being womanly

FEMINIZE   *v* -NIZED, -NIZING, -NIZES to make womanly

FEMME   *n* pl. -S a woman

FEMORAL   *adj* pertaining to the femur

FEMUR   *n* pl. -MURS or -MORA a bone of the leg

FEN   *n* pl. -S a marsh

FENAGLE   *v* -GLED, -GLING, -GLES to finagle

FENCE   *v* FENCED, FENCING, FENCES to practice the art of fencing

FENCER   *n* pl. -S one that fences

FENCIBLE   *n* pl. -S a soldier enlisted for home service only

FENCING   *n* pl. -S the art of using a sword in attack and defense

FEND   *v* -ED, -ING, -S to ward off

FENDER   *n* pl. -S a metal guard over the wheel of a motor vehicle **FENDERED** *adj*

FENESTRA   *n* pl. -TRAE a small anatomical opening

FENNEC   *n* pl. -S an African fox

FENNEL   *n* pl. -S a perennial herb

FENNY   *adj* marshy

FEOD   *n* pl. -S a fief

FEODARY   *n* pl. -RIES a vassal

FEOFF   *v* -ED, -ING, -S to grant a fief to

FEOFFEE   *n* pl. -S one to whom a fief is granted

FEOFFER   *n* pl. -S one that grants a fief to another

FEOFFOR   *n* pl. -S feoffer

FER   *prep* for

FERACITY   *n* pl. -TIES the state of being fruitful

FERAL   *adj* wild

FERBAM   *n* pl. -S a fungicide

FERE   *n* pl. -S a companion

FERETORY   *n* pl. -RIES a receptacle in which sacred relics are kept

FERIA   *n* pl. -RIAS or -RIAE a weekday of a church calendar on which no feast is celebrated **FERIAL** *adj*

FERINE   *adj* feral

FERITY   *n* pl. -TIES wildness

FERLIE   *n* pl. -S a strange sight

FERLY   *n* pl. -LIES ferlie

FERMATA   *n* pl. -TAS or -TE the sustaining of a musical note, chord, or rest beyond its written time value

FERMENT   *v* -ED, -ING, -S to undergo a type of chemical reaction

FERMI   *n* pl. -S a unit of length

FERMION   *n* pl. -S a type of atomic particle

FERMIUM   *n* pl. -S a radioactive element

FERN   *n* pl. -S a flowerless vascular plant **FERNLESS, FERNLIKE** *adj*

FERNERY   *n* pl. -ERIES a place in which ferns are grown

FERNY   *adj* FERNIER, FERNIEST abounding in ferns

FEROCITY   *n* pl. -TIES fierceness

FERRATE   *n* pl. -S a chemical salt

FERREL   *v* -RELED, -RELING, -RELS or -RELLED, -RELLING, -RELS ferrule

FERREOUS   *adj* containing iron

FERRET   *v* -ED, -ING, -S to search out by careful investigation

FERRETER   *n* pl. -S one that ferrets

FERRETY   *adj* suggestive of a ferret (a polecat)

FERRIAGE   *n* pl. -S transportation by ferry

FERRIC   *adj* pertaining to iron

FERRIED   past tense of ferry

FERRIES   present 3d person sing. of ferry

FERRITE   *n* pl. -S a magnetic substance **FERRITIC** *adj*

FERRITIN   *n* pl. -S a protein that contains iron

FERROUS   *adj* pertaining to iron

FERRULE   *v* -RULED, -RULING, -RULES to furnish with a metal ring or cap to prevent splitting

FERRUM   *n* pl. -S iron

FERRY v -RIED, -RYING, -RIES to transport by ferry (a type of boat)

FERRYMAN n pl. -MEN one who operates a ferry

FERTILE adj capable of reproducing

FERULA n pl. -LAE or -LAS a flat piece of wood

FERULE v -ULED, -ULING, -ULES to ferrule

FERVENCY n pl. -CIES fervor

FERVENT adj marked by fervor

FERVID adj fervent **FERVIDLY** adv

FERVOR n pl. -S great warmth or intensity

FERVOUR n pl. -S fervor

FESCUE n pl. -S a perennial grass

FESS v -ED, -ING, -ES to confess

FESSE n pl. -S a horizontal band across the middle of a heraldic shield

FESSWISE adv horizontally

FESTAL adj festive **FESTALLY** adv

FESTER v -ED, -ING, -S to generate pus

FESTIVAL n pl. -S a day or time of celebration

FESTIVE adj of or befitting a festival

FESTOON v -ED, -ING, -S to hang decorative chains or strips on

FET v FETTED, FETTING, FETS to fetch

FETA n pl. -S a Greek cheese

FETAL adj pertaining to a fetus

FETATION n pl. -S the development of a fetus

FETCH v -ED, -ING, -ES to go after and bring back

FETCHER n pl. -S one that fetches

FETE v FETED, FETING, FETES to honor with a celebration

FETERITA n pl. -S a cereal grass

FETIAL n pl. -S a priest of ancient Rome

FETIALIS n pl. -LES fetial

FETICH n pl. -ES fetish

FETICIDE n pl. -S the killing of a fetus

FETID adj having an offensive odor **FETIDLY** adv

FETING present participle of fete

FETISH n pl. -ES an object believed to have magical power

FETLOCK n pl. -S a joint of a horse's leg

FETOLOGY n pl. -GIES the branch of medicine dealing with the fetus

FETOR n pl. -S an offensive odor

FETTED past tense of fet

FETTER v -ED, -ING, -S to shackle

FETTERER n pl. -S one that fetters

FETTING present participle of fet

FETTLE v -TLED, -TLING, -TLES to cover the hearth of with fettling

FETTLING n pl. -S loose material thrown on the hearth of a furnace to protect it

FETUS n pl. -ES the unborn organism carried within the womb in the later stages of its development

FEU v -ED, -ING, -S to grant land to under Scottish feudal law

FEUAR n pl. -S one granted land under Scottish feudal law

FEUD v -ED, -ING, -S to engage in a feud (a bitter, continuous hostility)

FEUDAL adj pertaining to a political and economic system of medieval Europe **FEUDALLY** adv

FEUDARY n pl. -RIES a vassal

FEUDIST n pl. -S one that feuds

FEVER v -ED, -ING, -S to affect with fever (abnormal elevation of the body temperature)

FEVERFEW n pl. -S a perennial herb

FEVERISH adj having a fever

FEVEROUS adj feverish

FEW adj FEWER, FEWEST amounting to or consisting of a small number

FEWNESS n pl. -ES the state of being few

FEWTRILS n/pl things of little value

FEY adj FEYER, FEYEST crazy

FEYNESS n pl. -ES the state of being fey

FEZ n pl. FEZZES or FEZES a brimless cap worn by men in the Near East **FEZZED** adj

FIACRE n pl. -S a small carriage

FIANCE n pl. -S a man engaged to be married

FIANCEE n pl. -S a woman engaged to be married

FIAR n pl. -S the holder of a type of absolute ownership of land under Scottish law

FIASCO n pl. -COES or -CHI a wine bottle

FIASCO n pl. -COES or -COS a complete failure

FIAT   *n pl.* -S an authoritative order

FIB   *v* FIBBED, FIBBING, FIBS to tell a trivial lie

FIBBER   *n pl.* -S one that fibs

FIBER   *n pl.* -S a thread or threadlike object or structure FIBERED *adj*

FIBERIZE   *v* -IZED, -IZING, -IZES to break into fibers

FIBRE   *n pl.* -S fiber

FIBRIL   *n pl.* -S a small fiber

FIBRILLA   *n pl.* -LAE a fibril

FIBRIN   *n pl.* -S an insoluble protein

FIBROID   *n pl.* -S a fibroma

FIBROIN   *n pl.* -S an insoluble protein

FIBROMA   *n pl.* -MAS or -MATA a benign tumor composed of fibrous tissue

FIBROSIS   *n pl.* -BROSES the development of excess fibrous tissue in a bodily organ FIBROTIC *adj*

FIBROUS   *adj* containing, consisting of, or resembling fibers

FIBULA   *n pl.* -LAE or -LAS a bone of the leg FIBULAR *adj*

FICE   *n pl.* -S a feist

FICHE   *n pl.* -S a sheet of microfilm

FICHU   *n pl.* -S a woman's scarf

FICIN   *n pl.* -S an enzyme

FICKLE   *adj* -LER, -LEST not constant or loyal

FICO   *n pl.* -COES something of little worth

FICTILE   *adj* moldable

FICTION   *n pl.* -S a literary work whose content is produced by the imagination

FICTIVE   *adj* imaginary

FID   *n pl.* -S a square bar used as a support for a topmast

FIDDLE   *v* -DLED, -DLING, -DLES to play a violin

FIDDLER   *n pl.* -S one that fiddles

FIDEISM   *n pl.* -S reliance on faith rather than reason

FIDEIST   *n pl.* -S a believer in fideism

FIDELITY   *n pl.* -TIES loyalty

FIDGE   *v* FIDGED, FIDGING, FIDGES to fidget

FIDGET   *v* -ED, -ING, -S to move nervously or restlessly

FIDGETER   *n pl.* -S one that fidgets

FIDGETY   *adj* nervously restless

FIDGING   present participle of fidge

FIDO   *n pl.* -DOS a defective coin

FIDUCIAL   *adj* based on faith or trust

FIE   *interj* — used to express disapproval

FIEF   *n pl.* -S a feudal estate

FIEFDOM   *n pl.* -S a fief

FIELD   *v* -ED, -ING, -S to play as a fielder

FIELDER   *n pl.* -S one that catches or picks up a ball in play

FIEND   *n pl.* -S a demon

FIENDISH   *adj* extremely wicked or cruel

FIERCE   *adj* FIERCER, FIERCEST violently hostile or aggressive FIERCELY *adv*

FIERY   *adj* -ERIER, -ERIEST intensely hot FIERILY *adv*

FIESTA   *n pl.* -S a festival

FIFE   *v* FIFED, FIFING, FIFES to play a fife (a high-pitched flute)

FIFER   *n pl.* -S one that plays a fife

FIFTEEN   *n pl.* -S a number

FIFTH   *n pl.* -S one of five equal parts

FIFTHLY   *adv* in the fifth place

FIFTIETH   *n pl.* -S one of fifty equal parts

FIFTY   *n pl.* -TIES a number

FIG   *v* FIGGED, FIGGING, FIGS to adorn

FIGEATER   *n pl.* -S a large beetle

FIGHT   *v* FOUGHT, FIGHTING, FIGHTS to attempt to defeat an adversary

FIGHTER   *n pl.* -S one that fights

FIGHTING   *n pl.* -S the act of one that fights

FIGMENT   *n pl.* -S a product of mental invention

FIGULINE   *n pl.* -S a piece of pottery

FIGURAL   *adj* consisting of human or animal forms

FIGURANT   *n pl.* -S a ballet dancer who dances only in groups

FIGURATE   *adj* having a definite shape

FIGURE   *v* -URED, -URING, -URES to compute

FIGURER   *n pl.* -S one that figures

FIGURINE   *n pl.* -S a small statue

FIGURING   present participle of figure

FIGWORT   *n pl.* -S a flowering plant

FIL   *n pl.* -S a coin of Iraq and Jordan

FILA pl. of filum

FILAGREE v -GREED, -GREEING, -GREES to filigree

FILAMENT n pl. -S a very thin thread or threadlike structure

FILAR adj pertaining to a thread

FILAREE n pl. -S a European weed

FILARIA n pl. -IAE a parasitic worm FILARIAL, FILARIAN adj

FILARIID n pl. -S filaria

FILATURE n pl. -S the reeling of silk from cocoons

FILBERT n pl. -S the edible nut of a European shrub

FILCH v -ED, -ING, -ES to steal

FILCHER n pl. -S one that filches

FILE v FILED, FILING, FILES to remove with a file (an abrading tool)

FILEFISH n pl. -ES a marine fish

FILEMOT adj of a brownish yellow color

FILER n pl. -S one that files

FILET v -ED, -ING, -S to fillet

FILIAL adj pertaining to a son or daughter FILIALLY adv

FILIATE v -ATED, -ATING, -ATES to bring into close association

FILIBEG n pl. -S a pleated skirt worn by Scottish Highlanders

FILICIDE n pl. -S the killing of one's child

FILIFORM adj shaped like a filament

FILIGREE v -GREED, -GREEING, -GREES to adorn with intricate ornamental work

FILING n pl. -S a particle removed by a file

FILISTER n pl. -S a groove on a window frame

FILL v -ED, -ING, -S to put as much as can be held into

FILLE n pl. -S a girl

FILLER n pl. -S one that fills

FILLET v -ED, -ING, -S to cut boneless slices from

FILLIES pl. of filly

FILLING n pl. -S that which is used to fill something

FILLIP v -ED, -ING, -S to strike sharply

FILLY n pl. -LIES a young female horse

FILM v -ED, -ING, -S to cover with a film (a thin layer or coating)

FILMCARD n pl. -S a fiche

FILMDOM n pl. -S the motion-picture industry

FILMGOER n pl. -S one that goes to see motion pictures

FILMIC adj pertaining to motion pictures

FILMIER comparative of filmy

FILMIEST superlative of filmy

FILMILY adv in a filmy manner

FILMLAND n pl. -S filmdom

FILMSET v -SET, -SETTING, -SETS to photoset

FILMY adj FILMIER, FILMIEST resembling or covered with film; hazy

FILOSE adj resembling a thread

FILTER v -ED, -ING, -S to pass through a filter (a device for removing suspended matter)

FILTERER n pl. -S one that filters

FILTH n pl. -S foul or dirty matter

FILTHY adj FILTHIER, FILTHIEST offensively dirty FILTHILY adv

FILTRATE v -TRATED, -TRATING, -TRATES to filter

FILUM n pl. -LA a threadlike anatomical structure

FIMBLE n pl. -S the male hemp plant

FIMBRIA n pl. -BRIAE a fringe or fringe-like structure FIMBRIAL adj

FIN v FINNED, FINNING, FINS to equip with fins (external paddle-like structures)

FINABLE adj subject to the payment of a fine

FINAGLE v -GLED, -GLING, -GLES to obtain by trickery

FINAGLER n pl. -S one that finagles

FINAL n pl. -S the last examination of an academic course

FINALE n pl. -S a close or termination of something

FINALIS n pl. -LES a type of tone in medieval music

FINALISM n pl. -S the doctrine that all events are determined by ultimate purposes

FINALIST n pl. -S a contestant who reaches the last part of a competition

FINALITY n pl. -TIES the state of being conclusive

FINALIZE v -IZED, -IZING, -IZES to put into finished form

FINALLY adv at the end

FINANCE · *v* -NANCED, -NANCING, -NANCES to supply the money for

FINBACK · *n pl.* -S the rorqual

FINCH · *n pl.* -ES a small bird

FIND · *v* FOUND, FINDING, FINDS to come upon after a search

FINDER · *n pl.* -S one that finds

FINDING · *n pl.* -S something that is found

FINE · *adj* FINER, FINEST of excellent quality

FINE · *v* FINED, FINING, FINES to subject to a fine (a monetary penalty)

FINEABLE · *adj* finable

FINELY · *adv* in a fine manner

FINENESS · *n pl.* -ES the quality of being fine

FINER · comparative of fine

FINERY · *n pl.* -ERIES elaborate adornment

FINESPUN · *adj* developed with extreme care

FINESSE · *v* -NESSED, -NESSING, -NESSES to bring about by adroit maneuvering

FINEST · superlative of fine

FINFISH · *n pl.* -ES a true fish

FINFOOT · *n pl.* -S an aquatic bird

FINGER · *v* -ED, -ING, -S to touch with the fingers (the terminating members of the hand)

FINGERER · *n pl.* -S one that fingers

FINIAL · *n pl.* -S a crowning ornament FINIALED *adj*

FINICAL · *adj* finicky

FINICKIN · *adj* finicky

FINICKY · *adj* -ICKIER, -ICKIEST difficult to please

FINIKIN · *adj* finicky

FINIKING · *adj* finicky

FINING · *n pl.* -S the clarifying of wines

FINIS · *n pl.* -NISES the end

FINISH · *v* -ED, -ING, -ES to bring to an end

FINISHER · *n pl.* -S one that finishes

FINITE · *n pl.* -S something that is finite (having definite limits)

FINITELY · *adv* to a finite extent

FINITUDE · *n pl.* -S the state of being finite

FINK · *v* -ED, -ING, -S to inform to the police

FINLESS · *adj* having no fins

FINLIKE · *adj* resembling a fin

FINMARK · *n pl.* -S a monetary unit of Finland

FINNED · past tense of fin

FINNIER · comparative of finny

FINNIEST · superlative of finny

FINNING · present participle of fin

FINNICKY · *adj* -NICKIER, -NICKIEST finicky

FINNMARK · *n pl.* -S finmark

FINNY · *adj* -NIER, -NIEST having or characterized by fins

FINOCHIO · *n pl.* -CHIOS a perennial herb

FIORD · *n pl.* -S fjord

FIPPLE · *n pl.* -S a plug of wood at the mouth of certain wind instruments

FIQUE · *n pl.* -S a tropical plant

FIR · *n pl.* -S an evergreen tree

FIRE · *v* FIRED, FIRING, FIRES to project by discharging from a gun

FIREARM · *n pl.* -S a weapon from which a shot is discharged by gunpowder

FIREBALL · *n pl.* -S a luminous meteor

FIREBIRD · *n pl.* -S a brightly colored bird

FIREBOAT · *n pl.* -S a boat equipped with fire-fighting apparatus

FIREBOMB · *v* -ED, -ING, -S to attack with incendiary bombs

FIREBOX · *n pl.* -ES a chamber in which fuel is burned

FIREBRAT · *n pl.* -S a small, wingless insect

FIREBUG · *n pl.* -S an arsonist

FIRECLAY · *n pl.* -CLAYS a heat-resistant clay

FIRED · past tense of fire

FIREDAMP · *n pl.* -S a combustible gas

FIREDOG · *n pl.* -S an andiron

FIREFANG · *v* -ED, -ING, -S to decompose by oxidation

FIREFLY · *n pl.* -FLIES a luminous insect

FIREHALL · *n pl.* -S a fire station

FIRELESS · *adj* having no fire

FIRELOCK · *n pl.* -S a type of gun

FIREMAN · *n pl.* -MEN a man employed to extinguish fires

FIREPAN · *n pl.* -S an open pan for holding live coals

FIREPINK · *n pl.* -S a flowering plant

FIREPLUG · *n pl.* -S a hydrant

FIRER · *n pl.* -S one that fires

FIREROOM n pl. -S a room containing a ship's boilers

FIRESIDE n pl. -S the area immediately surrounding a fireplace

FIRETRAP n pl. -S a building that is likely to catch on fire

FIREWEED n pl. -S a perennial herb

FIREWOOD n pl. -S wood used as fuel

FIREWORK n pl. -S a device for producing a striking display of light or a loud noise

FIREWORM n pl. -S a glowworm

FIRING n pl. -S the process of maturing ceramic products by heat

FIRKIN n pl. -S a British unit of capacity

FIRM adj FIRMER, FIRMEST unyielding to pressure

FIRM v -ED, -ING, -S to make firm

FIRMAN n pl. -S an edict issued by a Middle Eastern sovereign

FIRMER n pl. -S a woodworking tool

FIRMLY adv in a firm manner

FIRMNESS n pl. -ES the state of being firm

FIRN n pl. -S neve

FIRRY adj abounding in firs

FIRST n pl. -S something that precedes all others

FIRSTLY adv before all others

FIRTH n pl. -S an inlet of the sea

FISC n pl. -S a state or royal treasury

FISCAL n pl. -S a public prosecutor

FISCALLY adv with regard to financial matters

FISH v -ED, -ING, -ES to catch or try to catch fish (cold-blooded aquatic vertebrates)

FISHABLE adj suitable for fishing

FISHBOLT n pl. -S a type of bolt

FISHBONE n pl. -S a bone of a fish

FISHBOWL n pl. -S a bowl in which live fish are kept

FISHER n pl. -S one that fishes

FISHERY n pl. -ERIES a place for catching fish

FISHEYE n pl. -S a suspicious stare

FISHGIG n pl. -S a pronged implement for spearing fish

FISHHOOK n pl. -S a barbed hook for catching fish

FISHIER comparative of fishy

FISHIEST superlative of fishy

FISHILY adv in a fishy manner

FISHING n pl. -S the occupation or pastime of catching fish

FISHLESS adj having no fish

FISHLIKE adj resembling a fish

FISHLINE n pl. -S a line used in fishing

FISHMEAL n pl. -S ground dried fish

FISHNET n pl. -S a net for catching fish

FISHPOLE n pl. -S a fishing rod

FISHPOND n pl. -S a pond abounding in edible fish

FISHTAIL v -ED, -ING, -S to have the rear end of a moving vehicle slide from side to side

FISHWAY n pl. -WAYS a device for enabling fish to pass around a dam

FISHWIFE n pl. -WIVES a woman who sells fish

FISHY adj FISHIER, FISHIEST of or resembling fish

FISSATE adj deeply split

FISSILE adj capable of being split

FISSION v -ED, -ING, -S to split into parts

FISSIPED n pl. -S a mammal that has separated toes

FISSURE v -SURED, -SURING, -SURES to split

FIST v -ED, -ING, -S to strike with the fist (the hand closed tightly)

FISTFUL n pl. -S a handful

FISTIC adj pertaining to pugilism

FISTNOTE n pl. -S a part of a text to which attention is drawn by an index mark

FISTULA n pl. -LAE or -LAS a duct formed by the imperfect closing of a wound FISTULAR adj

FIT adj FITTER, FITTEST healthy

FIT v FITTED, FITTING, FITS to bring to a required form and size

FITCH n pl. -ES a polecat

FITCHEE adj fitchy

FITCHET n pl. -S a fitch

FITCHEW n pl. -S a fitch

FITCHY adj having the arms ending in a point — used of a heraldic cross

FITFUL adj recurring irregularly FITFULLY adv

FITLY adv in a fit manner

FITMENT *n* pl. -S equipment

FITNESS *n* pl. -ES the state of being fit

FITTABLE *adj* capable of being fitted

FITTED past tense of fit

FITTER *n* pl. -S one that fits

FITTEST superlative of fit

FITTING *n* pl. -S a small often standardized accessory part

FIVE *n* pl. -S a number

FIVEFOLD *adj* five times as great

FIVEPINS *n/pl* a bowling game

FIVER *n* pl. -S a five-dollar bill

FIX *v* FIXED or FIXT, FIXING, FIXES to repair FIXABLE *adj*

FIXATE *v* -ATED, -ATING, -ATES to make stable or stationary

FIXATIF *n* pl. -S fixative

FIXATION *n* pl. -S the act of fixating

FIXATIVE *n* pl. -S a substance for preserving paintings or drawings

FIXEDLY *adv* firmly

FIXER *n* pl. -S one that fixes

FIXINGS *n/pl* accompaniments to the main dish of a meal

FIXITY *n* pl. -TIES stability

FIXT a past tense of fix

FIXTURE *n* pl. -S a permanent part or appendage of a house

FIXURE *n* pl. -S firmness

FIZ *n* pl. FIZZES a hissing or sputtering sound

FIZGIG *n* pl. -S fishgig

FIZZ *v* -ED, -ING, -ES to make a hissing or sputtering sound

FIZZER *n* pl. -S one that fizzes

FIZZES pl. of fiz

FIZZLE *v* -ZLED, -ZLING, -ZLES to fizz

FIZZY *adj* FIZZIER, FIZZIEST fizzing

FJELD *n* pl. -S a high, barren plateau

FJORD *n* pl. -S a narrow inlet of the sea between steep cliffs

FLAB *n* pl. -S flabby body tissue

FLABBY *adj* -BIER, -BIEST flaccid FLABBILY *adv*

FLABELLA *n/pl* fan-shaped anatomical structures

FLACCID *adj* lacking firmness

FLACK *n* pl. -S a press agent

FLACON *n* pl. -S a small stoppered bottle

FLAG *v* FLAGGED, FLAGGING, FLAGS to mark with a flag (a piece of cloth used as a symbol)

FLAGELLA *n/pl* long, slender plant shoots

FLAGGER *n* pl. -S one that flags

FLAGGING *n* pl. -S a type of pavement

FLAGGY *adj* -GIER, -GIEST drooping

FLAGLESS *adj* having no flag

FLAGMAN *n* pl. -MEN one who carries a flag

FLAGON *n* pl. -S a large bulging bottle

FLAGPOLE *n* pl. -S a pole on which a flag is displayed

FLAGRANT *adj* extremely or deliberately conspicuous

FLAGSHIP *n* pl. -S a ship bearing the flag of a fleet

FLAIL *v* -ED, -ING, -S to swing freely

FLAIR *n* pl. -S a natural aptitude

FLAK *n* pl. FLAK antiaircraft fire

FLAKE *v* FLAKED, FLAKING, FLAKES to peel off in flakes (flat, thin pieces)

FLAKER *n* pl. -S one that flakes

FLAKY *adj* FLAKIER, FLAKIEST resembling flakes FLAKILY *adv*

FLAM *v* FLAMMED, FLAMMING FLAMS to deceive

FLAMBE *v* -BEED, -BEING, -BES to douse with a liqueur and ignite

FLAMBEAU *n* pl. -BEAUX or -BEAUS a flaming torch

FLAMBEE *adj* flaming

FLAME *v* FLAMED, FLAMING, FLAMES to burn brightly

FLAMEN *n* pl. -MENS or -MINES a priest of ancient Rome

FLAMENCO *n* pl. -COS a strongly rhythmic style of dancing

FLAMEOUT *n* pl. -S a failure of a jet engine in flight

FLAMER *n* pl. -S one that flames

FLAMIER comparative of flamy

FLAMIEST superlative of flamy

FLAMINES a pl. of flamen

FLAMING present participle of flame

FLAMINGO *n* pl. -GOS or -GOES a wading bird

FLAMMED past tense of flam

FLAMMING present participle of flam

FLAMY *adj* FLAMIER, FLAMIEST flaming

FLAN *n* pl. -S or -ES a type of custard

FLANCARD *n* pl. -S a piece of armor for the side of a horse

FLANERIE *n* pl. -S idleness

FLANEUR *n* pl. -S an idler

FLANGE *v* FLANGED, FLANGING, FLANGES to provide with a protecting rim

FLANGER *n* pl. -S one that flanges

FLANK *v* -ED, -ING, -S to be located at the side of

FLANKER *n* pl. -S one that flanks

FLANNEL *v* -NELED, -NELING, -NELS or -NELLED, -NELLING, -NELS to cover with flannel (a soft fabric)

FLAP *v* FLAPPED, FLAPPING, FLAPS to wave up and down

FLAPJACK *n* pl. -S a pancake

FLAPLESS *adj* having no flap (a flat appendage)

FLAPPED past tense of flap

FLAPPER *n* pl. -S one that flaps

FLAPPING present participle of flap

FLAPPY *adj* -PIER, -PIEST flapping

FLARE *v* FLARED, FLARING, FLARES to burn with a bright, wavering light

FLASH *v* -ED, -ING, -ES to send forth a sudden burst of light

FLASHER *n* pl. -S one that flashes

FLASHGUN *n* pl. -S a photographic apparatus

FLASHING *n* pl. -S sheet metal used in waterproofing a roof

FLASHY *adj* FLASHIER, FLASHIEST gaudy FLASHILY *adv*

FLASK *n* pl. -S a narrow-necked container

FLASKET *n* pl. -S a small flask

FLAT *adj* FLATTER, FLATTEST having a smooth or even surface

FLAT *v* FLATTED, FLATTING, FLATS to flatten

FLATBED *n* pl. -S a type of truck or trailer

FLATBOAT *n* pl. -S a flat-bottomed boat

FLATCAP *n* pl. -S a type of hat

FLATCAR *n* pl. -S a railroad car without sides or roof

FLATFISH *n* pl. -ES any of an order of marine fishes

FLATFOOT *n* pl. -FEET a foot condition

FLATFOOT *v* -ED, -ING, -S to walk with a dragging gait

FLATHEAD *n* pl. -S a marine food fish

FLATIRON *n* pl. -S a device for pressing clothes

FLATLAND *n* pl. -S land lacking significant variation in elevation

FLATLET *n* pl. -S a type of apartment

FLATLING *adv* with a flat side or edge

FLATLY *adv* in a flat manner

FLATNESS *n* pl. -ES the state of being flat

FLATTED past tense of flat

FLATTEN *v* -ED, -ING, -S to make or become flat

FLATTER *v* -ED, -ING, -S to praise excessively

FLATTERY *n* pl. -TERIES the act of flattering

FLATTEST superlative of flat

FLATTING present participle of flat

FLATTISH *adj* somewhat flat

FLATTOP *n* pl. -S an aircraft carrier

FLATUS *n* pl. -ES intestinal gas

FLATWARE *n* pl. -S tableware that is fairly flat

FLATWASH *n* pl. -ES flatwork

FLATWAYS *adv* flatwise

FLATWISE *adv* with the flat side in a particular position

FLATWORK *n* pl. -S laundry that can be ironed mechanically

FLATWORM *n* pl. -S a flat-bodied worm

FLAUNT *v* -ED, -ING, -S to exhibit in a gaudy manner

FLAUNTER *n* pl. -S one that flaunts

FLAUNTY *adj* FLAUNTIER, FLAUNTIEST gaudy

FLAUTIST *n* pl. -S flutist

FLAVIN *n* pl. -S a yellow pigment

FLAVINE *n* pl. -S flavin

FLAVONE *n* pl. -S a chemical compound

FLAVONOL *n* pl. -S a derivative of flavone

FLAVOR *v* -ED, -ING, -S to give flavor (distinctive taste) to

FLAVORER *n* pl. -S one that flavors

FLAVORY *adj* full of flavor

FLAVOUR *v* -ED, -ING, -S to flavor

FLAVOURY *adj* flavory

FLAW *v* -ED, -ING, -S to produce a flaw (an imperfection) in

FLAWLESS *adj* having no flaw

FLAWY	*adj* FLAWIER, FLAWIEST full of flaws
FLAX	*n pl.* -ES an annual herb
FLAXEN	*adj* of a pale yellow color
FLAXSEED	*n pl.* -S the seed of flax
FLAXY	*adj* FLAXIER, FLAXIEST flaxen
FLAY	*v* -ED, -ING, -S to strip off the skin of
FLAYER	*n pl.* -S one that flays
FLEA	*n pl.* -S a parasitic insect
FLEABAG	*n pl.* -S an inferior hotel
FLEABANE	*n pl.* -S a flowering plant
FLEABITE	*n pl.* -S the bite of a flea
FLEAM	*n pl.* -S a surgical instrument
FLEAWORT	*n pl.* -S a European herb
FLECHE	*n pl.* -S a steeple
FLECK	*v* -ED, -ING, -S to mark with flecks (tiny streaks or spots)
FLECKY	*adj* flecked
FLECTION	*n pl.* -S the act of bending
FLED	past tense of flee
FLEDGE	*v* FLEDGED, FLEDGING, FLEDGES to furnish with feathers
FLEDGY	*adj* FLEDGIER, FLEDGIEST covered with feathers
FLEE	*v* FLED, FLEEING, FLEES to run away
FLEECE	*v* FLEECED, FLEECING, FLEECES to remove the coat of wool from
FLEECER	*n pl.* -S one that fleeces
FLEECH	*v* -ED, -ING, -ES to coax
FLEECING	present participle of fleece
FLEECY	*adj* FLEECIER, FLEECIEST woolly FLEECILY *adv*
FLEER	*v* -ED, -ING, -S to deride
FLEET	*adj* FLEETER, FLEETEST swift FLEETLY *adv*
FLEET	*v* -ED, -ING, -S to move swiftly
FLEISHIG	*adj* made of meat or meat products
FLEMISH	*v* -ED, -ING, -ES to coil rope in a certain manner
FLENCH	*v* -ED, -ING, -ES to flense
FLENSE	*v* FLENSED, FLENSING, FLENSES to strip the blubber or skin from
FLENSER	*n pl.* -S one that flenses
FLESH	*v* -ED, -ING, -ES to plunge into the flesh (soft body tissue)
FLESHER	*n pl.* -S one that removes flesh from animal hides
FLESHIER	comparative of fleshy
FLESHIEST	superlative of fleshy
FLESHING	*n pl.* -S the distribution of the lean and fat on an animal
FLESHLY	*adj* -LIER, -LIEST pertaining to the body
FLESHPOT	*n pl.* -S a pot for cooking meat
FLESHY	*adj* FLESHIER, FLESHIEST having much flesh
FLETCH	*v* -ED, -ING, -ES to fledge
FLETCHER	*n pl.* -S one that makes arrows
FLEURY	*adj* having the arms terminating in three leaves — used of a heraldic cross
FLEW	*n pl.* -S a fishing net
FLEX	*v* -ED, -ING, -ES to bend
FLEXIBLE	*adj* capable of being bent FLEXIBLY *adv*
FLEXILE	*adj* flexible
FLEXION	*n pl.* -S flection
FLEXOR	*n pl.* -S a muscle that serves to bend a bodily part
FLEXUOSE	*adj* flexuous
FLEXUOUS	*adj* winding
FLEXURE	*n pl.* -S the act of bending FLEXURAL *adj*
FLEY	*v* -ED, -ING, -S to frighten
FLIC	*n pl.* -S a Parisian policeman
FLICHTER	*v* -ED, -ING, -S to flicker
FLICK	*v* -ED, -ING, -S to strike with a quick, light blow
FLICKER	*v* -ED, -ING, -S to move waveringly
FLICKERY	*adj* flickering
FLIED	a past tense of fly
FLIER	*n pl.* -S one that flies
FLIES	present 3d person sing. of fly
FLIEST	superlative of fly
FLIGHT	*v* -ED, -ING, -S to fly in a flock
FLIGHTY	*adj* FLIGHTIER, FLIGHTIEST fickle
FLIMFLAM	*v* -FLAMMED, -FLAMMING, -FLAMS to swindle
FLIMSY	*adj* -SIER, -SIEST lacking solidity or strength FLIMSILY *adv*
FLIMSY	*n pl.* -SIES a thin paper
FLINCH	*v* -ED, -ING, -ES to shrink back involuntarily
FLINCHER	*n pl.* -S one that flinches

FLINDER n pl. -S a small fragment

FLING v FLUNG, FLINGING, FLINGS to throw with force

FLINGER n pl. -S one that flings

FLINT v -ED, -ING, -S to provide with flint (a spark-producing rock)

FLINTY adj FLINTIER, FLINTIEST resembling flint **FLINTILY** adv

FLIP v FLIPPED, FLIPPING, FLIPS to throw with a brisk motion

FLIP adj FLIPPER, FLIPPEST flippant

FLIPPANT adj impudent

FLIPPED past tense of flip

FLIPPER n pl. -S a broad, flat limb adapted for swimming

FLIPPEST superlative of flip

FLIPPING present participle of flip

FLIRT v -ED, -ING, -S to behave amorously without serious intent

FLIRTER n pl. -S one that flirts

FLIRTY adj FLIRTIER, FLIRTIEST given to flirting

FLIT v FLITTED, FLITTING, FLITS to move lightly and swiftly

FLITCH v -ED, -ING, -ES to cut into strips

FLITE v FLITED, FLITING, FLITES to quarrel

FLITTED past tense of flit

FLITTER v -ED, -ING, -S to flutter

FLITTING present participle of flit

FLIVVER n pl. -S an old, battered car

FLOAT v -ED, -ING, -S to rest or remain on the surface of a liquid

FLOATAGE n pl. -S flotage

FLOATER n pl. -S one that floats

FLOATY adj FLOATIER, FLOATIEST tending to float

FLOC v FLOCCED, FLOCCING, FLOCS to aggregate into floccules

FLOCCI pl. of floccus

FLOCCOSE adj having woolly tufts

FLOCCULE n pl. -S a tuft-like mass

FLOCCULI n/pl small, loosely aggregated masses

FLOCCUS n pl. FLOCCI a floccule

FLOCK v -ED, -ING, -S to gather or move in a crowd

FLOCKING n pl. -S a velvety design in short fibers on cloth or paper

FLOCKY adj FLOCKIER, FLOCKIEST woolly

FLOE n pl. -S a large mass of floating ice

FLOG v FLOGGED, FLOGGING, FLOGS to beat with a whip or rod

FLOGGER n pl. -S one that flogs

FLOGGING n pl. -S a whipping

FLONG n pl. -S a sheet of a certain type of paper

FLOOD v -ED, -ING, -S to inundate

FLOODER n pl. -S one that floods

FLOODLIT adj illuminated by floodlights

FLOODWAY n pl. -WAYS an overflow channel

FLOOEY adj awry

FLOOR v -ED, -ING, -S to provide with a floor (the level base of a room)

FLOORAGE n pl. -S floor space

FLOORER n pl. -S one that floors

FLOORING n pl. -S a floor

FLOOSY n pl. -SIES floozy

FLOOZIE n pl. -S floozy

FLOOZY n pl. -ZIES a prostitute

FLOP v FLOPPED, FLOPPING, FLOPS to fall heavily and noisily

FLOPOVER n pl. -S a defect in television reception

FLOPPER n pl. -S one that flops

FLOPPING present participle of flop

FLOPPY adj -PIER, -PIEST soft and flexible **FLOPPILY** adv

FLORA n pl. -RAS or -RAE the plant life of a particular region

FLORAL adj pertaining to flowers **FLORALLY** adv

FLORENCE n pl. -S florin

FLORET n pl. -S a small flower

FLORID adj ruddy **FLORIDLY** adv

FLORIGEN n pl. -S a plant hormone

FLORIN n pl. -S a former gold coin of Europe

FLORIST n pl. -S a grower or seller of flowers

FLORUIT n pl. -S a period of flourishing

FLOSS n pl. -ES a soft, light fiber

FLOSSIE n pl. -S a floozy

FLOSSY adj FLOSSIER, FLOSSIEST resembling floss

FLOTA n pl. -S a fleet of Spanish ships

FLOTAGE   n pl. -S the act of floating

FLOTILLA   n pl. -S a fleet of ships

FLOTSAM   n pl. -S floating wreckage of a ship or its cargo

FLOUNCE   v FLOUNCED, FLOUNCING, FLOUNCES to move with exaggerated motions

FLOUNCY   adj FLOUNCIER, FLOUNCIEST flouncing

FLOUNDER   v -ED, -ING, -S to struggle clumsily

FLOUR   v -ED, -ING, -S to cover with flour (a finely ground meal of grain)

FLOURISH   v -ED, -ING, -ES to thrive

FLOURY   adj resembling flour

FLOUT   v -ED, -ING, -S to treat with contempt

FLOUTER   n pl. -S one that flouts

FLOW   v -ED, -ING, -S to move steadily and smoothly along

FLOWAGE   n pl. -S the act of flowing

FLOWER   v -ED, -ING, -S to put forth flowers (reproductive structures of seed-bearing plants)

FLOWERER   n pl. -S a plant that flowers at a certain time

FLOWERET   n pl. -S a floret

FLOWERY   adj -ERIER, -ERIEST abounding in flowers

FLOWN   a past participle of fly

FLU   n pl. -S a virus disease

FLUB   v FLUBBED, FLUBBING, FLUBS to bungle

FLUBDUB   n pl. -S pretentious nonsense

FLUE   n pl. -S an enclosed passageway for directing a current **FLUED** adj

FLUENCY   n pl. -CIES the quality of being fluent

FLUENT   adj spoken or written with effortless ease **FLUENTLY** adv

FLUERICS   n/pl fluidics **FLUERIC** adj

FLUFF   v -ED, -ING, -S to make fluffy

FLUFFY   adj FLUFFIER, FLUFFIEST light and soft **FLUFFILY** adv

FLUID   n pl. -S a substance that tends to flow **FLUIDAL** adj

FLUIDICS   n/pl a branch of mechanical engineering **FLUIDIC** adj

FLUIDISE   v -ISED, -ISING, -ISES to fluidize

FLUIDITY   n pl. -TIES the quality of being able to flow

FLUIDIZE   v -IZED, -IZING, -IZES to cause to flow like a fluid

FLUIDLY   adv with fluidity

FLUIDRAM   n pl. -S a unit of liquid capacity

FLUKE   v FLUKED, FLUKING, FLUKES to obtain by chance

FLUKEY   adj FLUKIER, FLUKIEST fluky

FLUKY   adj FLUKIER, FLUKIEST happening by or depending on chance

FLUME   v FLUMED, FLUMING, FLUMES to convey by means of an artificial water channel

FLUMMERY   n pl. -MERIES a sweet dessert

FLUMMOX   v -ED, -ING, -ES to confuse

FLUMP   v -ED, -ING, -S to fall heavily

FLUNG   past tense of fling

FLUNK   v -ED, -ING, -S to fail an examination or course

FLUNKER   n pl. -S one that flunks

FLUNKEY   n pl. -KEYS flunky

FLUNKY   n pl. -KIES a servile follower

FLUOR   n pl. -S fluorite **FLUORIC** adj

FLUORENE   n pl. -S a chemical compound

FLUORID   n pl. -S fluoride

FLUORIDE   n pl. -S a compound of fluorine

FLUORIN   n pl. -S fluorine

FLUORINE   n pl. -S a gaseous element

FLUORITE   n pl. -S a mineral

FLURRY   v -RIED, -RYING, -RIES to confuse

FLUSH   adj FLUSHER, FLUSHEST ruddy

FLUSH   v -ED, -ING, -ES to blush

FLUSHER   n pl. -S one that flushes

FLUSTER   v -ED, -ING, -S to put into a state of nervous confusion

FLUTE   v FLUTED, FLUTING, FLUTES to play on a flute (a woodwind instrument)

FLUTER   n pl. -S a flutist

FLUTIER   comparative of fluty

FLUTIEST   superlative of fluty

FLUTING   n pl. -S a series of parallel grooves

FLUTIST   n pl. -S one who plays the flute

FLUTTER   v -ED, -ING, -S to wave rapidly and irregularly

FLUTTERY   adj marked by fluttering

FLUTY   adj FLUTIER, FLUTIEST resembling a flute in sound

FLUVIAL   adj pertaining to a river

FLUX · v -ED, -ING, -ES to melt

FLUXION · n pl. -S the act of flowing

FLUYT · n pl. -S a type of ship

FLY · v FLEW, FLOWN, FLYING, FLIES to move through the air

FLY · v FLIED, FLYING, FLIES to hit a ball high into the air in baseball

FLY · adj FLIER, FLIEST clever

FLYABLE · adj suitable for flying

FLYAWAY · n pl. -AWAYS one that is elusive

FLYBELT · n pl. -S an area infested with tsetse flies

FLYBLOW · v -BLEW, -BLOWN, -BLOWING, -BLOWS to taint

FLYBOAT · n pl. -S a small, fast boat

FLYBY · n pl. -BYS a flight of aircraft close to a specified place

FLYER · n pl. -S flier

FLYING · n pl. -S the operation of an aircraft

FLYLEAF · n pl. -LEAVES a blank leaf at the beginning or end of a book

FLYMAN · n pl. -MEN a stage worker in a theater

FLYOVER · n pl. -S a flight of aircraft over a specific location

FLYPAPER · n pl. -S paper designed to catch or kill flies

FLYPAST · n pl. -S a flyby

FLYSCH · n pl. -ES a sandstone deposit

FLYSPECK · v -ED, -ING, -S to mark with minute spots

FLYTE · v FLYTED, FLYTING, FLYTES to flite

FLYTIER · n pl. -S a maker of fishing flies

FLYTING · n pl. -S a dispute in verse form

FLYTRAP · n pl. -S a trap for catching flies

FLYWAY · n pl. -WAYS an established air route of migratory birds

FLYWHEEL · n pl. -S a heavy disk used in machinery

FOAL · v -ED, -ING, -S to give birth to a horse

FOAM · v -ED, -ING, -S to form foam (a light, bubbly, gas and liquid mass)

FOAMER · n pl. -S one that foams

FOAMIER · comparative of foamy

FOAMIEST · superlative of foamy

FOAMILY · adv in a foamy manner

FOAMLESS · adj being without foam

FOAMLIKE · adj resembling foam

FOAMY · adj FOAMIER, FOAMIEST covered with foam

FOB · v FOBBED, FOBBING, FOBS to deceive

FOCAL · adj pertaining to a focus

FOCALISE · v -ISED, -ISING, -ISES to focalize

FOCALIZE · v -IZED, -IZING, -IZES to focus

FOCALLY · adv with regard to focus

FOCUS · n pl. -CUSES or -CI a point at which rays converge or from which they diverge

FOCUS · v -CUSED, -CUSING, -CUSES or -CUSSED, -CUSSING, -CUSSES to bring to a focus

FOCUSER · n pl. -S one that focuses

FODDER · v -ED, -ING, -S to feed with coarse food

FODGEL · adj plump

FOE · n pl. -S an enemy

FOEHN · n pl. -S a warm, dry wind

FOEMAN · n pl. -MEN an enemy in war

FOETAL · adj fetal

FOETID · adj fetid

FOETOR · n pl. -S fetor

FOETUS · n pl. -ES fetus

FOG · v FOGGED, FOGGING, FOGS, to cover with fog (condensed water vapor near the earth's surface)

FOGBOUND · adj surrounded by fog

FOGBOW · n pl. -S a nebulous arc of light sometimes seen in a fog

FOGDOG · n pl. -S a fogbow

FOGEY · n pl. -GEYS fogy

FOGFRUIT · n pl. -S a flowering plant

FOGGAGE · n pl. -S a second growth of grass

FOGGED · past tense of fog

FOGGER · n pl. -S one that fogs

FOGGING · present participle of fog

FOGGY · adj -GIER, -GIEST filled with fog FOGGILY adv

FOGHORN · n pl. -S a horn sounded in a fog to give warning

FOGIE · n pl. -S fogy

FOGLESS · adj having no fog

FOGY · n pl. -GIES an old-fashioned person FOGYISH adj

FOGYISM · n pl. -S old-fashioned behavior

FOH · interj faugh

FOHN · n pl. -S foehn

FOIBLE *n* pl. -S a minor weakness

FOIL *v* -ED, -ING, -S to prevent the success of **FOILABLE** *adj*

FOILSMAN *n* pl. -MEN a fencer

FOIN *v* -ED, -ING, -S to thrust with a pointed weapon

FOISON *n* pl. -S strength

FOIST *v* -ED, -ING, -S to force upon slyly

FOLACIN *n* pl. -S a B vitamin

FOLATE *n* pl. -S folacin

FOLD *v* -ED, -ING, -S to lay one part over another part of **FOLDABLE** *adj*

FOLDAWAY *adj* designed to fold out of the way

FOLDBOAT *n* pl. -S a faltboat

FOLDER *n* pl. -S one that folds

FOLDEROL *n* pl. -S a falderal

FOLDOUT *n* pl. -S a gatefold

FOLIA a pl. of folium

FOLIAGE *n* pl. -S the growth of leaves of a plant **FOLIAGED** *adj*

FOLIAR *adj* pertaining to a leaf

FOLIATE *v* -ATED, -ATING, -ATES to hammer into thin plates

FOLIO *v* -ED, -ING, -S to number the pages of

FOLIOSE *adj* having leaves

FOLIOUS *adj* foliose

FOLIUM *n* pl. -LIA or -LIUMS a thin layer

FOLK *n* pl. -S a people or tribe

FOLKISH *adj* characteristic of the common people

FOLKLIKE *adj* folkish

FOLKLORE *n* pl. -S the lore of a people

FOLKMOOT *n* pl. -S a general assembly of the people in early England

FOLKMOT *n* pl. -S folkmoot

FOLKMOTE *n* pl. -S folkmoot

FOLKSY *adj* FOLKSIER, FOLKSIEST friendly **FOLKSILY** *adv*

FOLKTALE *n* pl. -S a tale forming part of the oral tradition of a people

FOLKWAY *n* pl. -WAYS a traditional custom of a people

FOLLICLE *n* pl. -S a small bodily cavity

FOLLIES pl. of folly

FOLLIS *n* pl. -LES a coin of ancient Rome

FOLLOW *v* -ED, -ING, -S to come or go after

FOLLOWER *n* pl. -S one that follows

FOLLY *n* pl. -LIES a foolish idea or action

FOMENT *v* -ED, -ING, -S to promote the development of

FOMENTER *n* pl. -S one that foments

FON *n* pl. -S foehn

FOND *adj* FONDER, FONDEST having an affection

FOND *v* -ED, -ING, -S to display affection

FONDANT *n* pl. -S a soft, creamy candy

FONDLE *v* -DLED, -DLING, -DLES to caress

FONDLER *n* pl. -S one that fondles

FONDLING *n* pl. -S one that is fondled

FONDLY *adv* in a fond manner

FONDNESS *n* pl. -ES affection

FONDU *n* pl. -S fondue

FONDUE *n* pl. -S a dish of melted cheese

FONT *n* pl. -S a receptacle for the water used in baptism **FONTAL** *adj*

FONTANEL *n* pl. -S a space in the fetal and infantile skull

FONTINA *n* pl. -S an Italian cheese

FOOD *n* pl. -S a substance taken into the body to maintain life and growth **FOODLESS** *adj*

FOOFARAW *n* pl. -S excessive ornamentation

FOOL *v* -ED, -ING, -S to deceive

FOOLERY *n* pl. -ERIES foolish behavior or speech

FOOLFISH *n* pl. -ES a marine fish

FOOLISH *adj* -ISHER, -ISHEST lacking good sense or judgment

FOOLSCAP *n* pl. -S a paper size

FOOT *n* pl. FEET the terminal part of the leg on which the body stands and moves

FOOT *v* -ED, -ING, -S to walk

FOOTAGE *n* pl. -S a length or quantity expressed in feet

FOOTBALL *n* pl. -S a type of ball

FOOTBATH *n* pl. -S a bath for the feet

FOOTBOY *n* pl. -BOYS a serving boy

FOOTER *n* pl. -S one that walks

FOOTFALL *n* pl. -S the sound of a footstep

FOOTGEAR *n* pl. -S footwear

FOOTHILL *n* pl. -S a low hill at the foot of higher hills

FOOTHOLD *n* pl. -S a secure support for the feet

FOOTIER comparative of footy

FOOTIEST superlative of footy

FOOTING *n* pl. -S a foothold

FOOTLE *v* -TLED, -TLING, -TLES to waste time

FOOTLER *n* pl. -S one that footles

FOOTLESS *adj* having no feet

FOOTLIKE *adj* resembling a foot

FOOTLING present participle of footle

FOOTMAN *n* pl. -MEN a male servant

FOOTMARK *n* pl. -S a mark left by the foot on a surface

FOOTNOTE *v* -NOTED, -NOTING, -NOTES to furnish with explanatory notes

FOOTPACE *n* pl. -S a walking pace

FOOTPAD *n* pl. -S one who robs a pedestrian

FOOTPATH *n* pl. -S a path for pedestrians

FOOTRACE *n* pl. -S a race run on foot

FOOTREST *n* pl. -S a support for the feet

FOOTROPE *n* pl. -S a rope used in sailing

FOOTSIE *n* pl. -S a flirting game played with the feet

FOOTSLOG *v* -SLOGGED, -SLOGGING, -SLOGS to march through mud

FOOTSORE *adj* having sore or tired feet

FOOTSTEP *n* pl. -S a step with the foot

FOOTWALL *n* pl. -S the layer of rock beneath a vein of ore

FOOTWAY *n* pl. -WAYS a footpath

FOOTWEAR *n* pl. -S wearing apparel for the feet

FOOTWORK *n* pl. -S the use of the feet

FOOTWORN *adj* footsore

FOOTY *adj* -TIER, -TIEST paltry

FOOZLE *v* -ZLED, -ZLING, -ZLES to bungle

FOOZLER *n* pl. -S one that foozles

FOP *v* FOPPED, FOPPING, FOPS to deceive

FOPPERY *n* pl. -PERIES foppish behavior

FOPPISH *adj* characteristic of a dandy

FOR *prep* directed or sent to

FORA a pl. of forum

FORAGE *v* -AGED, -AGING, -AGES to search about

FORAGER *n* pl. -S one that forages

FORAM *n* pl. -S a marine rhizopod

FORAMEN *n* pl. -MINA or -MENS a small anatomical opening

FORAY *v* -ED, -ING, -S to raid

FORAYER *n* pl. -S one that forays

FORB *n* pl. -S an herb other than grass

FORBAD a past tense of forbid

FORBADE a past tense of forbid

FORBEAR *v* -BORE, -BORNE, -BEARING, -BEARS to refrain from

FORBID *v* -BADE or -BAD, -BIDDEN, -BIDDING, -BIDS to command not to do something

FORBIDAL *n* pl. -S the act of forbidding

FORBODE *v* -BODED, -BODING, -BODES to forebode

FORBORE past tense of forbear

FORBORNE past participle of forbear

FORBY *prep* close by

FORBYE *prep* forby

FORCE *v* FORCED, FORCING, FORCES to overcome resistance by the exertion of strength **FORCEDLY** *adv*

FORCEFUL *adj* strong

FORCEPS *n* pl. -CIPES an instrument for seizing and holding objects

FORCER *n* pl. -S one that forces

FORCIBLE *adj* effected by force **FORCIBLY** *adv*

FORCING present participle of force

FORCIPES pl. of forceps

FORD *v* -ED, -ING, -S to cross by wading **FORDABLE** *adj*

FORDLESS *adj* unable to be forded

FORDO *v* -DID, -DONE, -DOING, -DOES to destroy

FORE *n* pl. -S the front part of something

FOREARM *v* -ED, -ING, -S to arm in advance

FOREBAY *n* pl. -BAYS a reservoir from which water is taken to run equipment

FOREBEAR *n* pl. -S an ancestor

FOREBODE *v* -BODED, -BODING, -BODES to indicate in advance

FOREBODY *n* pl. -BODIES the forward part of a ship

FOREBOOM *n* pl. -S the boom of a ship's foremast

FOREBY *prep* forby

FOREBYE *prep* forby

FORECAST *v* -ED, -ING, -S to estimate or calculate in advance

FOREDATE v -DATED, -DATING, -DATES to antedate

FOREDECK n pl. -S the forward part of a ship's deck

FOREDO v -DID, -DONE, -DOING, -DOES to fordo

FOREDOOM v -ED, -ING, -S to doom in advance

FOREFACE n pl. -S the front part of the head of a quadruped

FOREFEEL v -FELT, -FEELING, -FEELS to have a premonition of

FOREFEND v -ED, -ING, -S to forfend

FOREFOOT n pl. -FEET one of the front feet of an animal

FOREGO v -WENT, -GONE, -GOING, -GOES to go before

FOREGOER n pl. -S one that foregoes

FOREGUT n pl. -S the front part of the embryonic alimentary canal

FOREHAND n pl. -S a type of tennis stroke

FOREHEAD n pl. -S the part of the face above the eyes

FOREHOOF n pl. -HOOFS or -HOOVES the hoof of a forefoot

FOREIGN adj situated outside a place or country

FOREKNOW v -KNEW, -KNOWN, -KNOWING, -KNOWS to know in advance

FORELADY n pl. -DIES a woman who supervises workers

FORELAND n pl. -S a projecting mass of land

FORELEG n pl. -S one of the front legs of an animal

FORELIMB n pl. -S a foreleg

FORELOCK n pl. -S a lock of hair growing over the forehead

FOREMAN n pl. -MEN a man who supervises workers

FOREMAST n pl. -S the forward mast of a ship

FOREMILK n pl. -S the milk secreted immediately after childbirth

FOREMOST adj first in position

FORENAME n pl. -S a first name

FORENOON n pl. -S the period of daylight before noon

FORENSIC n pl -S an argumentative exercise

FOREPART n pl. -S the front part

FOREPAST adj already in the past

FOREPAW n pl. -S the paw of a foreleg

FOREPEAK n pl. -S the forward part of a ship's hold

FOREPLAY n pl. -PLAYS erotic stimulation preceding sexual intercourse

FORERANK n pl. -S the first rank

FORERUN v -RAN, -RUNNING, -RUNS to run in advance of

FORESAID adj previously said

FORESAIL n pl. -S the lowest sail on a foremast

FORESEE v -SAW, -SEEN, -SEEING, -SEES to see in advance

FORESEER n pl. -S one that foresees

FORESHOW v -SHOWED, -SHOWN, -SHOWING, -SHOWS to show in advance

FORESIDE n pl. -S the front side

FORESKIN n pl. -S the prepuce

FOREST v -ED, -ING, -S to convert into a forest (a densely wooded area)

FORESTAL adj of or pertaining to a forest

FORESTAY n pl. -STAYS a wire or rope used to support a foremast

FORESTER n pl. -S one skilled in forestry

FORESTRY n pl. -RIES the science of planting and managing forests

FORETELL v -TOLD, -TELLING, -TELLS to tell of or about in advance

FORETIME n pl. -S the past

FORETOP n pl. -S a forelock

FOREVER n pl. -S an indefinite length of time

FOREWARN v -ED, -ING, -S to warn in advance

FOREWENT past tense of forego

FOREWING n pl. -S an anterior wing of an insect

FOREWORD n pl. -S an introductory statement

FOREWORN adj forworn

FOREYARD n pl. -S the lowest yard on a foremast

FORFEIT v -ED, -ING, -S to lose as a penalty

FORFEND v -ED, -ING, -S to protect

FORGAT a past tense of forget

FORGAVE past tense of forgive

FORGE v FORGED, FORGING, FORGES to fashion or reproduce for fraudulent purposes

FORGER n pl. -S one that forges

FORGERY n pl. -ERIES the act of forging

FORGET v -GOT or -GAT, -GOTTEN, -GETTING, -GETS to fail to remember

FORGING n pl. -S a forgery

FORGIVE v -GAVE, -GIVEN, -GIVING, -GIVES to pardon

FORGIVER n pl. -S one that forgives

FORGO v -WENT, -GONE, -GOING, -GOES to refrain from

FORGOER n pl. -S one that forgoes

FORGOT a past tense of forget

FORGOTTEN past participle of forget

FORINT n pl. -S a monetary unit of Hungary

FORJUDGE v -JUDGED, -JUDGING, -JUDGES to deprive by judgment of a court

FORK v -ED, -ING, -S to work with a fork (a pronged implement) **FORKEDLY** adv

FORKER n pl. -S one that forks

FORKFUL n pl. FORKFULS or FORKSFUL as much as a fork will hold

FORKIER comparative of forky

FORKIEST superlative of forky

FORKLESS adj having no fork

FORKLIFT n pl. -S a machine for lifting and carrying loads

FORKLIKE adj resembling a fork

FORKSFUL a pl. of forkful

FORKY adj FORKIER, FORKIEST resembling a fork

FORLORN adj -LORNER, -LORNEST dreary

FORM v -ED, -ING, -S to produce **FORMABLE** adj

FORMAL n pl. -S a social event that requires evening dress

FORMALIN n pl. -S an aqueous solution of formaldehyde

FORMALLY adv in a prescribed or customary manner

FORMANT n pl. -S a characteristic component of the quality of a speech sound

FORMAT v -MATTED, -MATTING, -MATS to produce in a specified style

FORMATE n pl. -S a chemical salt

FORME n pl. -S an assemblage of printing type secured in a metal frame

FORMEE adj having the arms narrow at the center and expanding toward the ends — used of a heraldic cross

FORMER n pl. -S one that forms

FORMERLY adv previously

FORMFUL adj exhibiting good form

FORMIC adj pertaining to ants

FORMLESS adj lacking structure

FORMOL n pl. -S formalin

FORMULA n pl. -LAS or -LAE an exact method for doing something

FORMYL n pl. -S a univalent chemical radical

FORNIX n pl. -NICES an arched anatomical structure **FORNICAL** adj

FORRADER adv further ahead

FORRIT adv toward the front

FORSAKE v -SOOK, -SAKEN, -SAKING, -SAKES to quit or leave entirely

FORSAKER n pl. -S one that forsakes

FORSOOTH adv in truth

FORSPENT adj worn out

FORSWEAR v -SWORE, -SWORN, -SWEARING, -SWEARS to deny under oath

FORT n pl. -S a fortified enclosure or structure

FORTE n pl. -S a strong point

FORTH adv onward in time, place, or order

FORTIES pl. of forty

FORTIETH n pl. -S one of forty equal parts

FORTIFY v -FIED, -FYING, -FIES to strengthen against attack

FORTIS n pl. -TES a consonant pronounced with relatively strong release of breath

FORTRESS v -ED, -ING, -ES to fortify

FORTUITY n pl. -ITIES an accidental occurrence

FORTUNE v -TUNED, -TUNING, -TUNES to endow with wealth

FORTY n pl. -TIES a number

FORUM n pl. -RUMS or -RA a public meeting place

FORWARD adj -WARDER, -WARDEST being at or near a point in advance

FORWARD v -ED, -ING, -S to help onward

FORWENT past tense of forgo

FORWHY adv for what reason

FORWORN	adj worn out	FOWL	v -ED, -ING, -S to hunt birds
FORZANDO	n pl. -DOS sforzato	FOWLER	n pl. -S one that fowls
FOSS	n pl. -ES fosse	FOWLING	n pl. -S the hunting of birds
FOSSA	n pl. -SAE an anatomical depression FOSSATE adj	FOWLPOX	n pl. -ES a virus disease of poultry
FOSSE	n pl. -S a ditch	FOX	v -ED, -ING, -ES to outwit
FOSSETTE	n pl. -S a small fossa	FOXFIRE	n pl. -S a glow produced by certain fungi on decaying wood
FOSSICK	v -ED, -ING, -S to search for gold	FOXFISH	n pl. -ES a large shark
FOSSIL	n pl. -S the remains of an animal or plant preserved in the earth's crust	FOXGLOVE	n pl. -S a flowering plant
		FOXHOLE	n pl. -S a small pit used for cover in a battle area
FOSTER	v -ED, -ING, -S to promote the growth of	FOXHOUND	n pl. -S a hunting dog
FOSTERER	n pl. -S one that fosters	FOXIER	comparative of foxy
FOU	adj drunk	FOXIEST	superlative of foxy
FOUGHT	past tense of fight	FOXILY	adv in a foxy manner
FOUGHTEN	adj exhausted especially from fighting	FOXINESS	n pl. -ES the state of being foxy
FOUL	adj FOULER, FOULEST offensive to the senses	FOXING	n pl. -S a piece of material used to cover the upper portion of a shoe
FOUL	v -ED, -ING, -S to make foul	FOXLIKE	adj resembling a fox (a carnivorous mammal)
FOULARD	n pl. -S a soft fabric		
FOULING	n pl. -S a deposit or crust	FOXSKIN	n pl. -S the skin of a fox
FOULLY	adv in a foul manner	FOXTAIL	n pl. -S the tail of a fox
FOULNESS	n pl. -ES the state of being foul	FOXY	adj FOXIER, FOXIEST crafty
FOUND	v -ED, -ING, -S to establish	FOY	n pl. FOYS a farewell feast or gift
FOUNDER	v -ED, -ING, -S to become disabled	FOYER	n pl. -S an entrance room or hall
FOUNDRY	n pl. -RIES an establishment in which metal is cast	FOZINESS	n pl. -ES the state of being fozy
FOUNT	n pl. -S a fountain	FOZY	adj -ZIER, -ZIEST too ripe
FOUNTAIN	v -ED, -ING, -S to flow like a fountain (a spring of water)	FRACAS	n pl. -ES a brawl
FOUR	n pl. -S a number	FRACTED	adj broken
FOURCHEE	adj having the end of each arm forked — used of a heraldic cross	FRACTION	v -ED, -ING, -S to divide into portions
		FRACTUR	n pl. -S fraktur
FOURFOLD	adj four times as great	FRACTURE	v -TURED, -TURING, -TURES to break
FOURGON	n pl. -S a wagon for carrying baggage	FRAE	prep from
FOURSOME	n pl. -S a group of four	FRAENUM	n pl. -NA or -NUMS frenum
FOURTEEN	n pl. -S a number	FRAG	v FRAGGED, FRAGGING, FRAGS to injure with a type of grenade
FOURTH	n pl. -S one of four equal parts		
FOURTHLY	adv in the fourth place		
FOVEA	n pl. -VEAE a shallow anatomical depression FOVEAL, FOVEATE, FOVEATED adj	FRAGGING	n pl. -S the act of one that frags
		FRAGILE	adj easily broken or damaged
FOVEOLA	n pl. -LAE or -LAS a small fovea FOVEOLAR adj	FRAGMENT	v -ED, -ING, -S to break into pieces
		FRAGRANT	adj having a pleasant odor
FOVEOLE	n pl. -S a foveola	FRAIL	adj FRAILER, FRAILEST fragile FRAILLY adv
FOVEOLET	n pl. -S a foveola		

FRAIL	n pl. -S a basket for holding dried fruits	**FREE**	adj FREER, FREEST not subject to restriction or control
FRAILTY	n pl. -TIES a weakness of character	**FREE**	v FREED, FREEING, FREES to make free
FRAISE	n pl. -S a barrier of pointed stakes	**FREEBEE**	n pl. -S freebie
FRAKTUR	n pl. -S a style of type	**FREEBIE**	n pl. -S something given or received without charge
FRAME	v FRAMED, FRAMING, FRAMES to construct by putting together the various parts FRAMABLE adj	**FREEBOOT**	v -ED, -ING, -S to plunder
		FREEBORN	adj born free
		FREED	past tense of free
FRAMER	n pl. -S one that frames	**FREEDMAN**	n pl. -MEN a man who has been freed from slavery
FRANC	n pl. -S a monetary unit of France	**FREEDOM**	n pl. -S the state of being free
FRANCIUM	n pl. -S a radioactive element	**FREEFORM**	adj having a free flowing design or shape
FRANK	adj FRANKER, FRANKEST honest and unreserved in speech	**FREEHAND**	adj drawn by hand without mechanical aids
FRANK	v -ED, -ING, -S to mark (a piece of mail) for free delivery	**FREEHOLD**	n pl. -S a form of tenure of real property
FRANKER	n pl. -S one that franks	**FREELOAD**	v -ED, -ING, -S to live at the expense of others
FRANKEST	superlative of frank	**FREELY**	adv in a free manner
FRANKLIN	n pl. -S a medieval English landowner	**FREEMAN**	n pl. -MEN one who is free
FRANKLY	adv in a frank manner	**FREENESS**	n pl. -ES freedom
FRANTIC	adj wildly excited	**FREER**	n pl. -S one that frees
FRAP	v FRAPPED, FRAPPING, FRAPS to bind firmly	**FREESIA**	n pl. -S an African herb
		FREEST	superlative of free
FRAPPE	n pl. -S a partly frozen drink	**FREEWAY**	n pl. -WAYS an express highway
FRAT	n pl. -S a college fraternity		
FRATER	n pl. -S a comrade	**FREEWILL**	adj voluntary
FRAUD	n pl. -S trickery	**FREEZE**	v FROZE, FROZEN, FREEZING, FREEZES to become hardened into a solid body by loss of heat
FRAUGHT	v -ED, -ING, -S to load down		
FRAULEIN	n pl. -S a German governess	**FREEZER**	n pl. -S an apparatus for freezing food
FRAY	v -ED, -ING, -S to wear off by rubbing		
FRAYING	n pl. -S something worn off by rubbing	**FREIGHT**	v -ED, -ING, -S to load with goods for transportation
FRAZZLE	v -ZLED, -ZLING, -ZLES to fray	**FREMD**	adj strange
FREAK	v -ED, -ING, -S to streak with color	**FREMITUS**	n pl. -ES a palpable vibration
		FRENA	a pl. of frenum
FREAKIER	comparative of freaky	**FRENCH**	v -ED, -ING, -ES to cut into thin strips before cooking
FREAKIEST	superlative of freaky		
FREAKILY	adv in a ?eaky manner	**FRENETIC**	n pl. -S a frantic person
FREAKISH	adj unusual	**FRENULUM**	n pl. -LA a frenum
FREAKOUT	n pl. -S an event marked by wild excitement	**FRENUM**	n pl. -NA or -NUMS a connecting fold of membrane
FREAKY	adj FREAKIER, FREAKIEST freakish	**FRENZILY**	adv in a frantic manner
		FRENZY	v -ZIED, -ZYING, -ZIES to make frantic
FRECKLE	v -LED, -LING, -LES to mark with freckles (small, brownish spots)	**FREQUENT**	adj -QUENTER, -QUENTEST occurring again and again
FRECKLY	adj -LIER, -LIEST marked with freckles	**FREQUENT**	v -ED, -ING, -S to be in or at often

FRERE   *n* pl. -S brother

FRESCO   *v* -ED, -ING, -ES or -S to paint on a surface of plaster

FRESCOER   *n* pl. -S one that frescoes

FRESH   *adj* FRESHER, FRESHEST new

FRESH   *v* -ED, -ING, -ES to freshen

FRESHEN   *v* -ED, -ING, -S to make or become fresh

FRESHET   *n* pl. -S a sudden overflow of a stream

FRESHLY   *adv* in a fresh manner

FRESHMAN   *n* pl. -MEN a first-year student

FRESNEL   *n* pl. -S a unit of frequency

FRET   *v* FRETTED, FRETTING, FRETS to worry

FRETFUL   *adj* inclined to fret

FRETLESS   *adj* having no fretwork

FRETSAW   *n* pl. -S a narrow-bladed saw

FRETSOME   *adj* fretful

FRETTED   past tense of fret

FRETTING   present participle of fret

FRETTY   *adj* -TIER, -TIEST fretful

FRETWORK   *n* pl. -S ornamental work consisting of interlacing parts

FRIABLE   *adj* easily crumbled

FRIAR   *n* pl. -S a member of a religious order FRIARLY *adj*

FRIARY   *n* pl. -ARIES a monastery of friars

FRIBBLE   *v* -BLED, -BLING, -BLES to act foolishly

FRIBBLER   *n* pl. -S one that fribbles

FRICANDO   *n* pl. -DOES a roasted loin of veal

FRICTION   *n* pl. -S the rubbing of one body against another

FRIDGE   *n* pl. -S a refrigerator

FRIED   past tense of fry

FRIEND   *v* -ED, -ING, -S to enter into a warm association with

FRIENDLY   *adj* -LIER, -LIEST inclined to approve, help, or support

FRIENDLY   *n* pl. -LIES one who is friendly

FRIER   *n* pl. -S fryer

FRIES   present 3d person sing. of fry

FRIEZE   *n* pl. -S a coarse woolen fabric

FRIG   *v* FRIGGED, FRIGGING, FRIGS to copulate — an offensive term

FRIGATE   *n* pl. -S a sailing vessel

FRIGHT   *v* -ED, -ING, -S to frighten

FRIGHTEN   *v* -ED, -ING, -S to make afraid

FRIGID   *adj* very cold FRIGIDLY *adv*

FRIJOL   *n* pl. -ES a bean used as food

FRIJOLE   *n* pl. -S frijol

FRILL   *v* -ED, -ING, -S to provide with a frill (an ornamental ruffled edge)

FRILLER   *n* pl. -S one that frills

FRILLING   *n* pl. -S an arrangement of frills

FRILLY   *adj* FRILLIER, FRILLIEST having frills

FRINGE   *v* FRINGED, FRINGING, FRINGES to provide with a fringe (an ornamental border)

FRINGY   *adj* FRINGIER, FRINGIEST resembling a fringe

FRIPPERY   *n* pl. -PERIES excessive ornamentation

FRISE   *n* pl. -S frieze

FRISETTE   *n* pl. -S frizette

FRISEUR   *n* pl. -S a hairdresser

FRISK   *v* -ED, -ING, -S to move or leap about playfully

FRISKER   *n* pl. -S one that frisks

FRISKET   *n* pl. -S a frame used to protect paper in a printing press

FRISKY   *adj* FRISKIER, FRISKIEST lively and playful FRISKILY *adv*

FRISSON   *n* pl. -S a shudder

FRIT   *v* FRITTED, FRITTING, FRITS to fuse into a vitreous substance

FRITH   *n* pl. -S firth

FRITT   *v* -ED, -ING, -S to frit

FRITTED   past tense of frit

FRITTER   *v* -ED, -ING, -S to squander little by little

FRITTING   present participle of frit

FRIVOL   *v* -OLED, -OLING, -OLS or -OLLED, -OLLING, -OLS to behave playfully

FRIVOLER   *n* pl. -S one that frivols

FRIZ   *n* pl. -ES a tight curl

FRIZ   *v* -ED, -ING, -ES to frizz

FRIZER   *n* pl. -S frizzer

FRIZETTE   *n* pl. -S a frizzed fringe of hair

FRIZZ   *n* pl. -ES friz

FRIZZ   *v* -ED, -ING, -ES to form into small, tight curls

FRIZZER   *n* pl. -S one that frizzes

FRIZZIER   comparative of frizzy

FRIZZIEST   superlative of frizzy

FRIZZILY   *adv* in a frizzy manner

FRIZZLE   *v* -ZLED, -ZLING, -ZLES to frizz

FRIZZLER   *n* pl. -S one that frizzles

FRIZZLY   *adj* -ZLIER, -ZLIEST frizzy

FRIZZY   *adj* FRIZZIER, FRIZZIEST tightly curled

FRO   *adv* away

FROCK   *v* -ED, -ING, -S to clothe in a long, loose outer garment

FROE   *n* pl. -S a cleaving tool

FROG   *v* FROGGED, FROGGING, FROGS to hunt frogs (web-footed, tailless amphibians)

FROGEYE   *n* pl. -S a plant disease **FROGEYED** *adj*

FROGFISH   *n* pl. -ES a marine fish

FROGGED   past tense of frog

FROGGING   present participle of frog

FROGGY   *adj* -GIER, -GIEST abounding in frogs

FROGLIKE   *adj* resembling a frog

FROGMAN   *n* pl. -MEN a person equipped for extended periods of underwater swimming

FROLIC   *v* -ICKED, -ICKING, -ICS to play and run about merrily **FROLICKY** *adj*

FROM   *prep* starting at

FROMAGE   *n* pl. -S cheese

FROMENTY   *n* pl. -TIES frumenty

FROND   *n* pl. -S a type of leaf **FRONDED, FRONDOSE** *adj*

FRONDEUR   *n* pl. -S a rebel

FRONS   *n* pl. FRONTES the upper anterior portion of an insect's head

FRONT   *v* -ED, -ING, -S to provide with a front (a forward part)

FRONT   *adj* FRONTER articulated at the front of the oral passage

FRONTAGE   *n* pl. -S the front of a building or lot

FRONTAL   *n* pl. -S a bone of the skull

FRONTES   pl. of frons

FRONTIER   *n* pl. -S a border between two countries

FRONTLET   *n* pl. -S a decorative band worn across the forehead

FRONTON   *n* pl. -S a jai alai arena

FRORE   *adj* frozen

FROSH   *n* pl. FROSH a freshman

FROST   *v* -ED, -ING, -S to cover with frost (a deposit of minute ice crystals)

FROSTBIT   *adj* injured by extreme cold

FROSTED   *n* pl. -S a type of milk shake

FROSTING   *n* pl. -S icing

FROSTY   *adj* FROSTIER, FROSTIEST covered with frost **FROSTILY** *adv*

FROTH   *v* -ED, -ING, -S to foam

FROTHY   *adj* FROTHIER, FROTHIEST foamy **FROTHILY** *adv*

FROTTAGE   *n* pl. -S masturbation by rubbing against another person

FROTTEUR   *n* pl. -S one who practices frottage

FROUFROU   *n* pl. -S a rustling sound

FROUNCE   *v* FROUNCED, FROUNCING, FROUNCES to pleat

FROUZY   *adj* -ZIER, -ZIEST frowzy

FROW   *n* pl. -S froe

FROWARD   *adj* disobedient

FROWN   *v* -ED, -ING, -S to contract the brow in displeasure

FROWNER   *n* pl. -S one that frowns

FROWSTY   *adj* -TIER, -TIEST musty

FROWSY   *adj* -SIER, -SIEST frowzy

FROWZY   *adj* -ZIER, -ZIEST unkempt **FROWZILY** *adv*

FROZE   past tense of freeze

FROZEN   *adj* very cold **FROZENLY** *adv*

FRUCTIFY   *v* -FIED, -FYING, -FIES to bear fruit

FRUCTOSE   *n* pl. -S a sugar found in various fruits

FRUG   *v* FRUGGED, FRUGGING, FRUGS to perform a type of vigorous dance

FRUGAL   *adj* thrifty **FRUGALLY** *adv*

FRUIT   *v* -ED, -ING, -S to bear fruit (usually edible reproductive bodies of a seed plant)

FRUITAGE   *n* pl. -S the process of bearing fruit

FRUITER   *n* pl. -S one that grows or sells fruit

FRUITFUL   *adj* -FULLER, -FULLEST producing abundantly

FRUITIER   comparative of fruity

FRUITIEST   superlative of fruity

FRUITION   *n* pl. -S the accomplishment of something desired

FRUITLET   *n* pl. -S a small fruit

FRUITY   *adj* FRUITIER, FRUITIEST suggestive of fruit

FRUMENTY   *n* pl. -TIES a dish of wheat boiled in milk and sweetened with sugar

FRUMP   n pl. -S a dowdy woman **FRUMPISH** adj

FRUMPY   adj FRUMPIER, FRUMPIEST dowdy **FRUMPILY** adv

FRUSTA   a pl. of frustum

FRUSTULE   n pl. -S the shell of a diatom

FRUSTUM   n pl. -TA or -TUMS a part of a conical solid

FRY   v FRIED, FRYING, FRIES to cook over direct heat in hot fat or oil

FRYER   n pl. -S one that fries

FRYPAN   n pl. -S a pan for frying food

FUB   v FUBBED, FUBBING, FUBS to fob

FUBSY   adj FUBSIER, FUBSIEST chubby and somewhat squat

FUCHSIA   n pl. -S a flowering shrub

FUCHSIN   n pl. -S a red dye

FUCHSINE   n pl. -S fuchsin

FUCI   a pl. of fucus

FUCK   v -ED, -ING, -S to copulate — an offensive term

FUCOID   n pl. -S a brown seaweed **FUCOIDAL** adj

FUCOSE   n pl. -S a type of sugar

FUCOUS   adj of or pertaining to fucoids

FUCUS   n pl. -CI or -CUSES any of a genus of brown algae

FUD   n pl. -S an old-fashioned person

FUDDLE   v -DLED, -DLING, -DLES to confuse

FUDGE   v FUDGED, FUDGING, FUDGES to falsify

FUEHRER   n pl. -S fuhrer

FUEL   v -ELED, -ELING, -ELS or -ELLED, -ELLING, -ELS to provide with fuel (material used to produce energy)

FUELER   n pl. -S one that fuels

FUELLER   n pl. -S fueler

FUELLING   a present participle of fuel

FUG   v FUGGED, FUGGING, FUGS to make stuffy and odorous

FUGACITY   n pl. -TIES lack of enduring qualities

FUGAL   adj being in the style of a fugue **FUGALLY** adv

FUGATO   n pl. -TOS a fugal composition

FUGGED   past tense of fug

FUGGING   present participle of fug

FUGGY   adj -GIER, -GIEST stuffy and odorous

FUGIO   n pl. -GIOS a former coin of the United States

FUGITIVE   n pl. -S one who flees

FUGLE   v -GLED, -GLING, -GLES to lead

FUGLEMAN   n pl. -MEN a leader

FUGUE   v FUGUED, FUGUING, FUGUES to compose a fugue (a type of musical composition)

FUGUIST   n pl. -S one who composes fugues

FUHRER   n pl. -S a leader

FUJI   n pl. -S a silk fabric

FULCRUM   n pl. -CRUMS or -CRA a support for a lever

FULFIL   v -FILLED, -FILLING, -FILS to fulfill

FULFILL   v -ED, -ING, -S to bring about the accomplishment of

FULGENT   adj shining brightly

FULGID   adj fulgent

FULHAM   n pl. -S a loaded die

FULL   adj FULLER, FULLEST filled completely

FULL   v -ED, -ING, -S to shrink and thicken, as cloth

FULLAM   n pl. -S fulham

FULLBACK   n pl. -S an offensive back in football

FULLER   v -ED, -ING, -S to groove with a type of hammer

FULLERY   n pl. -ERIES a place for fulling cloth

FULLFACE   n pl. -S a heavy-faced type

FULLNESS   n pl. -ES the state of being full

FULLY   adv in a full manner

FULMAR   n pl. -S an arctic seabird

FULMINE   v -MINED, -MINING, -MINES to explode loudly

FULMINIC   adj highly explosive

FULNESS   n pl. -ES fullness

FULSOME   adj repulsive

FULVOUS   adj of a brownish yellow color

FUMARASE   n pl. -S an enzyme

FUMARATE   n pl. -S a chemical salt

FUMARIC   adj pertaining to a certain acid

FUMAROLE   n pl. -S a hole from which volcanic vapors issue

FUMATORY   n pl. -RIES a fumigation chamber

FUMBLE   v -BLED, -BLING, -BLES to handle clumsily

FUMBLER   n pl. -S one that fumbles

FUME v FUMED, FUMING, FUMES to give off fumes (gaseous exhalations)

FUMELESS adj having no fumes

FUMELIKE adj resembling fumes

FUMER n pl. -S one that fumes

FUMET n pl. -S the odor of meat while cooking

FUMETTE n pl. -S fumet

FUMIER comparative of fumy

FUMIEST superlative of fumy

FUMIGANT n pl. -S a substance used in fumigating

FUMIGATE v -GATED, -GATING, -GATES to subject to fumes in order to destroy pests

FUMING present participle of fume

FUMITORY n pl. -RIES a climbing plant

FUMULUS n pl. -LI a thin cloud

FUMY adj FUMIER, FUMIEST producing or full of fumes

FUN v FUNNED, FUNNING, FUNS to act playfully

FUNCTION v -ED, -ING, -S to be in action

FUNCTOR n pl. -S one that functions

FUND v -ED, -ING, -S to provide money for

FUNDUS n pl. -DI the inner basal surface of a bodily organ FUNDIC adj

FUNERAL n pl. -S a ceremony held for a dead person

FUNERARY adj pertaining to a funeral

FUNEREAL adj funerary

FUNEST adj portending death or evil

FUNFAIR n pl. -S an amusement park

FUNGAL n pl. -S a fungus

FUNGI a pl. of fungus

FUNGIBLE n pl. -S something that may be exchanged for an equivalent unit of the same class

FUNGIC adj fungous

FUNGO n pl. -GOES a fly ball hit to a fielder for practice in baseball

FUNGOID n pl. -S a growth resembling a fungus

FUNGOUS adj pertaining to a fungus

FUNGUS n pl. -GI or -GUSES any of a major group of lower plants

FUNICLE n pl. -S a cordlike anatomical structure

FUNICULI n/pl funicles

FUNK v -ED, -ING, -S to shrink back in fear

FUNKER n pl. -S one that funks

FUNKIA n pl. -S a flowering plant

FUNKY adj FUNKIER, FUNKIEST having an offensive odor

FUNNED past tense of fun

FUNNEL v -NELED, -NELING, -NELS or -NELLED, -NELLING, -NELS to pass through a funnel (a cone-shaped utensil)

FUNNING present participle of fun

FUNNY adj -NIER, -NIEST causing laughter or amusement FUNNILY adv

FUNNY n pl. -NIES a comic strip

FUNNYMAN n pl. -MEN a comedian

FUR v FURRED, FURRING, FURS to cover with fur (a dressed animal pelt)

FURAN n pl. -S a flammable liquid

FURANE n pl. -S furan

FURANOSE n pl. -S a type of sugar

FURBELOW v -ED, -ING, -S to decorate with ruffles

FURBISH v -ED, -ING, -ES to polish

FURCATE v -CATED, -CATING, -CATES to divide into branches

FURCRAEA n pl. -S a tropical plant

FURCULA n pl. -LAE a forked bone FURCULAR adj

FURCULUM n pl. -LA a furcula

FURFUR n pl. -ES dandruff

FURFURAL n pl. -S a chemical compound

FURFURAN n pl. -S furan

FURIBUND adj furious

FURIES pl. of fury

FURIOSO adv with great force — used as a musical direction

FURIOUS adj extremely angry

FURL v -ED, -ING, -S to roll up FURLABLE adj

FURLER n pl. -S one that furls

FURLESS adj having no fur

FURLONG n pl. -S a unit of distance

FURLOUGH v -ED, -ING, -S to grant a leave of absence to

FURMENTY n pl. -TIES frumenty

FURMETY n pl. -TIES frumenty

FURMITY n pl. -TIES frumenty

FURNACE v -NACED, -NACING, -NACES to subject to heat

FURNISH v -ED, -ING, -ES to equip

FUROR n pl. -S an uproar

FURORE n pl. -S furor

FURRED past tense of fur

FURRIER n pl. -S one that deals in furs

FURRIERY n pl. -ERIES the business of a furrier

FURRIEST superlative of furry

FURRILY adv in a furry manner

FURRINER n pl. -S a foreigner

FURRING n pl. -S a trimming or lining of fur

FURROW v -ED, -ING, -S to make furrows (narrow depressions) in

FURROWER n pl. -S one that furrows

FURROWY adj marked by furrows

FURRY adj -RIER, -RIEST covered with fur

FURTHER v -ED, -ING, -S to help forward

FURTHEST a superlative of far

FURTIVE adj stealthy

FURUNCLE n pl. -S a painful swelling of the skin

FURY n pl. -RIES violent anger

FURZE n pl. -S a spiny shrub

FURZY adj FURZIER, FURZIEST abounding in furze

FUSAIN n pl. -S a fine charcoal used in drawing

FUSCOUS adj of a dusky color

FUSE v FUSED, FUSING, FUSES to equip with a fuse (a detonating device)

FUSEE n pl. -S a large-headed friction match

FUSEL n pl. -S an oily liquid

FUSELAGE n pl. -S the body of an airplane

FUSELESS adj lacking a fuse

FUSIBLE adj capable of being melted FUSIBLY adv

FUSIFORM adj tapering toward each end

FUSIL n pl. -S a type of musket

FUSILE adj formed by melting

FUSILEER n pl. -S fusilier

FUSILIER n pl. -S a soldier armed with a fusil

FUSING present participle of fuse

FUSION n pl. -S the act of melting together

FUSS v -ED, -ING, -ES to be overly concerned with small details

FUSSER n pl. -S one that fusses

FUSSPOT n pl. -S a fusser

FUSSY adj FUSSIER, FUSSIEST overly concerned with small details FUSSILY adv

FUSTIAN n pl. -S a cotton fabric

FUSTIC n pl. -S a tropical tree

FUSTY adj -TIER, -TIEST musty FUSTILY adv

FUTHARC n pl. -S futhark

FUTHARK n pl. -S an ancient alphabet

FUTHORC n pl. -S futhark

FUTHORK n pl. -S futhark

FUTILE adj having no useful result FUTILELY adv

FUTILITY n pl. -TIES the quality of being futile

FUTTOCK n pl. -S a curved timber in the frame of a wooden ship

FUTURE n pl. -S the time yet to come FUTURAL adj

FUTURISM n pl. -S an artistic and literary movement

FUTURIST n pl. -S an advocate of futurism

FUTURITY n pl. -TIES the future

FUZE v FUZED, FUZING, FUZES to fuse

FUZEE n pl. -S fusee

FUZIL n pl. -S fusil

FUZING present participle of fuze

FUZZ v -ED, -ING, -ES to become fuzzy

FUZZY adj FUZZIER, FUZZIEST blurry FUZZILY adv

FYCE n pl. -S feist

FYKE n pl. -S a bag-shaped fishnet

FYLFOT n pl. -S a swastika

FYTTE n pl. -S a division of a poem or song

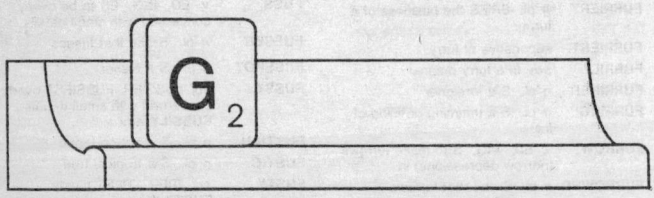

GAB	v GABBED, GABBING, GABS to chatter	**GADID**	n pl. -S gadoid
		GADOID	n pl. -S a type of fish
GABBARD	n pl. -S a barge	**GADROON**	n pl. -S a band of fluted or reeded molding
GABBART	n pl. -S gabbard		
GABBED	past tense of gab	**GADWALL**	n pl. -S a wild duck
GABBER	n pl. -S one that gabs	**GADZOOKS**	interj — used as a mild oath
GABBING	present participle of gab	**GAE**	v GAED, GANE or GAEN, GAUN, GAES to go
GABBLE	v -BLED, -BLING, -BLES to jabber		
		GAFF	v -ED, -ING, -S to catch a fish with a sharp hook
GABBLER	n pl. -S one that gabbles		
GABBRO	n pl. -BROS a type of rock GABBROIC, GABBROID adj	**GAFFE**	n pl. -S a social blunder
		GAFFER	n pl. -S an old man
GABBY	adj -BIER, -BIEST talkative	**GAG**	v GAGGED, GAGGING, GAGS to stop up the mouth
GABELLE	n pl. -S a tax on salt GABELLED adj		
		GAGA	adj crazy
GABFEST	n pl. -S an informal gathering for general talk	**GAGE**	v GAGED, GAGING, GAGES to pledge as security
GABIES	pl. of gaby	**GAGER**	n pl. -S gauger
GABION	n pl. -S a type of basket	**GAGGED**	past tense of gag
GABLE	v -BLED, -BLING, -BLES to form a triangular section of a wall	**GAGGER**	n pl. -S one that gags
		GAGGING	present participle of gag
GABOON	n pl. -S a spittoon	**GAGGLE**	v -GLED, -GLING, -GLES to cackle
GABY	n pl. -BIES a dolt		
GAD	v GADDED, GADDING, GADS to roam about restlessly	**GAGING**	present participle of gage
		GAGMAN	n pl. -MEN one who writes jokes
GADABOUT	n pl. -S one that gads about		
GADARENE	adj headlong	**GAGSTER**	n pl. -S a gagman
GADDED	past tense of gad	**GAHNITE**	n pl. -S a mineral
GADDER	n pl. -S one that gads about	**GAIETY**	n pl. -ETIES festive activity
GADDI	n pl. -S a hassock	**GAILY**	adv in a gay manner
GADDING	present participle of gad	**GAIN**	v -ED, -ING, -S to acquire GAINABLE adj
GADFLY	n pl. -FLIES a biting fly		
GADGET	n pl. -S a mechanical device GADGETY adj	**GAINER**	n pl. -S one that gains
		GAINFUL	adj profitable
GADGETRY	n pl. -RIES the devising or constructing of gadgets	**GAINLESS**	adj profitless
		GAINLY	adj -LIER, -LIEST graceful
GADI	n pl. -S gaddi		

GAINSAY v -SAID, -SAYING, -SAYS to deny

GAINST prep against

GAIT v -ED, -ING, -S to train a horse to move in a particular way

GAITER n pl. -S a covering for the lower leg

GAL n pl. -S a girl

GALA n pl. -S a celebration

GALACTIC adj pertaining to a galaxy

GALAGO n pl. -GOS a small primate

GALAH n pl. -S a cockatoo

GALANGAL n pl. -S a medicinal plant

GALATEA n pl. -S a strong cotton fabric

GALAVANT v -ED, -ING, -S to gad about

GALAX n pl. -ES an evergreen herb

GALAXY n pl. -AXIES a large system of celestial bodies

GALBANUM n pl. -S a gum resin

GALE n pl. -S a strong wind

GALEA n pl. -LEAE or -LEAS a helmet-shaped anatomical part **GALEATE, GALEATED** adj

GALENA n pl. -S the principal ore of lead **GALENIC** adj

GALENITE n pl. -S galena

GALERE n pl. -S a group of people having a common quality

GALILEE n pl. -S a type of porch

GALIOT n pl. -S a galliot

GALIPOT n pl. -S a type of turpentine

GALIVANT v -ED, -ING, -S to gad about

GALL v -ED, -ING, -S to vex or irritate

GALLANT v -ED, -ING, -S to court a woman

GALLATE n pl. -S a chemical salt

GALLEASS n pl. -ES a large war galley

GALLEIN n pl. -S a green dye

GALLEON n pl. -S a large sailing vessel

GALLERY v -LERIED, -LERYING, -LERIES to provide with a long covered area

GALLETA n pl. -S a perennial grass

GALLEY n pl. -LEYS a long, low medieval ship

GALLFLY n pl. -FLIES a small insect

GALLIARD n pl. -S a lively dance

GALLIASS n pl. -ES galleass

GALLIC adj containing gallium

GALLICAN adj pertaining to a French religious movement

GALLIED past tense of gally

GALLIES present 3d person sing. of gally

GALLIOT n pl. -S a small galley

GALLIPOT n pl. -S a small earthen jar

GALLIUM n pl. -S a metallic element

GALLNUT n pl. -S an abnormal swelling of plant tissue

GALLON n pl. -S a unit of liquid measure

GALLOON n pl. -S an ornamental braid

GALLOOT n pl. -S galoot

GALLOP v -ED, -ING, -S to ride a horse at full speed

GALLOPER n pl. -S one that gallops

GALLOUS adj containing gallium

GALLOWS n pl. -ES a structure used for hanging a condemned person

GALLUS n pl. -ES a suspender for trousers **GALLUSED** adj

GALLY v -LIED, -LYING, -LIES to frighten

GALOOT n pl. -S an awkward or uncouth person

GALOP n pl. -S a lively dance

GALOPADE n pl. -S a galop

GALORE n pl. -S abundance

GALOSH n pl. -ES an overshoe **GALOSHED** adj

GALOSHE n pl. -S galosh

GALUMPH v -ED, -ING, -S to move clumsily

GALVANIC adj pertaining to a direct electric current

GALYAC n pl. -S galyak

GALYAK n pl. -S a fur made from lambskin

GAM v GAMMED, GAMMING, GAMS to visit socially

GAMASHES n/pl boots worn by horseback riders

GAMB n pl. -S a leg

GAMBA n pl. -S a bass viol

GAMBADE n pl. -S a gambado

GAMBADO n pl. -DOES or -DOS a leap made by a horse

GAMBE n pl. -S gamb

GAMBESON n pl. -S a medieval coat

GAMBIA n pl. -S gambier

GAMBIER n pl. -S an extract obtained from an Asian vine

GAMBIR n pl. -S gambier

GAMBIT n pl. -S a type of chess opening

GAMBLE	v -BLED, -BLING, -BLES to play a game of chance for money or valuables
GAMBLER	n pl. -S one that gambles
GAMBOGE	n pl. -S a gum resin
GAMBOL	v -BOLED, -BOLING, -BOLS or -BOLLED, -BOLLING, -BOLS to leap about playfully
GAMBREL	n pl. -S a part of a horse's leg
GAMBUSIA	n pl. -S a small fish
GAME	adj GAMER, GAMEST plucky
GAME	v GAMED, GAMING, GAMES to gamble
GAMECOCK	n pl. -S a rooster trained for fighting
GAMELAN	n pl. -S a type of orchestra
GAMELIKE	adj similar to a game (a contest governed by a set of rules)
GAMELY	adv in a game manner
GAMENESS	n pl. -ES the quality of being game
GAMER	comparative of game
GAMESOME	adj playful
GAMEST	superlative of game
GAMESTER	n pl. -S a gambler
GAMETE	n pl. -S a mature reproductive cell GAMETIC adj
GAMEY	adj GAMIER, GAMIEST gamy
GAMIC	adj requiring fertilization
GAMIER	comparative of gamy
GAMIEST	superlative of gamy
GAMILY	adv in a game manner
GAMIN	n pl. -S an urchin
GAMINE	n pl. -S a tomboy
GAMINESS	n pl. -ES the quality of being gamy
GAMING	n pl. -S the practice of gambling
GAMMA	n pl. -S a Greek letter
GAMMADIA	n/pl Greek ornamental designs
GAMMED	past tense of gam
GAMMER	n pl. -S an old woman
GAMMING	present participle of gam
GAMMON	v -ED, -ING, -S to mislead by deceptive talk
GAMMONER	n pl. -S one that gammons
GAMODEME	n pl. -S a somewhat isolated breeding community of organisms
GAMP	n pl. -S a large umbrella
GAMUT	n pl. -S an entire range
GAMY	adj GAMIER, GAMIEST plucky

GAN	past tense of gin
GANDER	v -ED, -ING, -S to wander
GANE	past participle of gae
GANEF	n pl. -S a thief
GANEV	n pl. -S ganef
GANG	v -ED, -ING, -S to form into a gang (a group)
GANGER	n pl. -S a foreman of a gang of laborers
GANGLAND	n pl. -S the criminal underworld
GANGLIA	a pl. of ganglion
GANGLIAL	adj gangliar
GANGLIAR	adj pertaining to a ganglion
GANGLIER	comparative of gangly
GANGLIEST	superlative of gangly
GANGLING	adj awkwardly tall and lanky
GANGLION	n pl. -GLIA or -GLIONS a group of nerve cells
GANGLY	adj -GLIER, -GLIEST gangling
GANGPLOW	n pl. -S an agricultural implement
GANGREL	n pl. -S a vagabond
GANGRENE	v -GRENED, -GRENING, -GRENES to suffer the loss of tissue in part of the body
GANGSTER	n pl. -S a member of a criminal gang
GANGUE	n pl. -S the worthless rock in which valuable minerals are found
GANGWAY	n pl. -WAYS a passageway
GANISTER	n pl. -S a type of rock
GANJA	n pl. -S cannabis used for smoking
GANNET	n pl. -S a large seabird
GANOF	n pl. -S ganef
GANOID	n pl. -S a type of fish
GANTLET	v -ED, -ING, -S to overlap railroad tracks
GANTLINE	n pl. -S a rope on a ship
GANTLOPE	n pl. -S a former military punishment
GANTRY	n pl. -TRIES a structure for supporting railroad signals
GANYMEDE	n pl. -S a youth who serves liquors
GAOL	v -ED, -ING, -S to jail
GAOLER	n pl. -S jailer
GAP	v GAPPED, GAPPING, GAPS to make an opening in
GAPE	v GAPED, GAPING, GAPES to stare with open mouth

GAPER	*n pl.* -S one that gapes
GAPESEED	*n pl.* -S something that causes wonder
GAPEWORM	*n pl.* -S a worm that causes a disease of young birds
GAPING	present participle of gape
GAPINGLY	*adv* in a gaping manner
GAPOSIS	*n pl.* -SISES a gap in a row of buttons or snaps
GAPPED	past tense of gap
GAPPING	present participle of gap
GAPPY	*adj* -PIER, -PIEST having openings
GAPY	*adj* infested with gapeworms
GAR	*v* GARRED, GARRING, GARS to cause or compel
GARAGE	*v* -RAGED, -RAGING, -RAGES to put in a garage (a car shelter)
GARB	*v* -ED, -ING, -S to clothe
GARBAGE	*n pl.* -S food waste
GARBANZO	*n pl.* -ZOS a chickpea
GARBLE	*v* -BLED, -BLING, -BLES to distort the meaning of
GARBLER	*n pl.* -S one that garbles
GARBLESS	*adj* being without clothing
GARBOARD	*n pl.* -S a plank on a ship's bottom
GARBOIL	*n pl.* -S turmoil
GARCON	*n pl.* -S a waiter
GARDANT	*adj* turned directly toward the observer — used of a heraldic animal
GARDEN	*v* -ED, -ING, -S to cultivate a plot of ground
GARDENER	*n pl.* -S one that gardens
GARDENIA	*n pl.* -S a tropical shrub or tree
GARDYLOO	*interj* — used as a warning cry
GARFISH	*n pl.* -ES a freshwater fish
GARGANEY	*n pl.* -NEYS a small duck
GARGET	*n pl.* -S mastitis of domestic animals **GARGETY** *adj*
GARGLE	*v* -GLED, -GLING, -GLES to rinse the mouth or throat
GARGLER	*n pl.* -S one that gargles
GARGOYLE	*n pl.* -S an ornamental figure
GARISH	*adj* gaudy **GARISHLY** *adv*
GARLAND	*v* -ED, -ING, -S to deck with wreaths of flowers
GARLIC	*n pl.* -S an herb used in cooking **GARLICKY** *adj*
GARMENT	*v* -ED, -ING, -S to clothe

GARNER	*v* -ED, -ING, -S to gather and store
GARNET	*n pl.* -S a mineral
GARNISH	*v* -ED, -ING, -ES to decorate
GAROTE	*v* -ROTED, -ROTING, -ROTES to garrote
GAROTTE	*v* -ROTTED, -ROTTING, -ROTTES to garrote
GAROTTER	*n pl.* -S one that garottes
GARPIKE	*n pl.* -S a garfish
GARRED	past tense of gar
GARRET	*n pl.* -S an attic
GARRING	present participle of gar
GARRISON	*v* -ED, -ING, -S to assign to a military post
GARRON	*n pl.* -S a small, sturdy horse
GARROTE	*v* -ROTED, -ROTING, -ROTES to execute by strangling
GARROTER	*n pl.* -S one that garrotes
GARROTTE	*v* -ROTTED, -ROTTING, -ROTTES to garrote
GARTER	*v* -ED, -ING, -S to fasten with an elastic band
GARTH	*n pl.* -S a yard or garden
GARVEY	*n pl.* -VEYS a small scow
GAS	*v* GASSED, GASSING, GASES or GASSES to supply with gas (a substance capable of indefinite expansion)
GASALIER	*n pl.* -S gaselier
GASBAG	*n pl.* -S a bag for holding gas
GASCON	*n pl.* -S a boaster
GASELIER	*n pl.* -S a gaslight chandelier
GASEOUS	*adj* pertaining to gas
GASH	*v* -ED, -ING, -ES to make a long deep cut in
GASH	*adj* GASHER, GASHEST knowing
GASHOUSE	*n pl.* -S a gasworks
GASIFIED	past tense of gasify
GASIFIER	*n pl.* -S one that gasifies
GASIFORM	*adj* having the form of gas
GASIFY	*v* -IFIED, -IFYING, -IFIES to convert into gas
GASKET	*n pl.* -S packing for making something fluid-tight
GASKIN	*n pl.* -S a part of a horse's leg
GASKING	*n pl.* -S a gasket
GASLESS	*adj* having no gas
GASLIGHT	*n pl.* -S light made by burning gas
GASLIT	*adj* illuminated by gaslight

GASMAN *n pl.* -MEN an employee of a gas company

GASOGENE *n pl.* -S gazogene

GASOLENE *n pl.* -S gasoline

GASOLIER *n pl.* -S gaselier

GASOLINE *n pl.* -S a liquid fuel

GASP *v* -ED, -ING, -S to breathe convulsively

GASPER *n pl.* -S a cigarette

GASSED past tense of gas

GASSER *n pl.* -S one that gasses

GASSES a present 3d person sing. of gas

GASSING *n pl.* -S a poisoning by noxious gas

GASSY *adj* -SIER, -SIEST containing gas

GAST *v* -ED, -ING, -S to scare

GASTIGHT *adj* not allowing gas to escape or enter

GASTNESS *n pl.* -ES fright

GASTRAEA *n pl.* -S a type of metazoan

GASTRAL *adj* pertaining to the stomach

GASTREA *n pl.* -S gastraea

GASTRIC *adj* pertaining to the stomach

GASTRIN *n pl.* -S a hormone

GASTRULA *n pl.* -LAS or -LAE a metazoan embryo

GASWORKS *n pl.* GASWORKS a factory where gas is produced

GAT *n pl.* -S a pistol

GATE *v* GATED, GATING, GATES to supply with a gate (a movable barrier)

GATEFOLD *n pl.* -S a folded insert in a book or magazine

GATELESS *adj* lacking a gate

GATELIKE *adj* resembling a gate

GATEMAN *n pl.* -MEN a person in charge of a gate

GATEPOST *n pl.* -S a post from which a gate is hung

GATEWAY *n pl.* -WAYS a passage that may be closed by a gate

GATHER *v* -ED, -ING, -S to bring together into one place or group

GATHERER *n pl.* -S one that gathers

GATING present participle of gate

GAUCHE *adj* GAUCHER, GAUCHEST lacking social grace **GAUCHELY** *adv*

GAUCHO *n pl.* -CHOS a cowboy of the South American pampas

GAUD *n pl.* -S a showy ornament

GAUDERY *n pl.* -ERIES finery

GAUDY *adj* GAUDIER, GAUDIEST tastelessly showy **GAUDILY** *adv*

GAUDY *n pl.* -DIES a festival

GAUFFER *v* -ED, -ING, -S to goffer

GAUGE *v* GAUGED, GAUGING, GAUGES to measure precisely

GAUGER *n pl.* -S one that gauges

GAULT *n pl.* -S a heavy, thick clay soil

GAUM *v* -ED, -ING, -S to smear

GAUN present participle of gae

GAUNT *adj* GAUNTER, GAUNTEST emaciated **GAUNTLY** *adv*

GAUNTLET *v* -ED, -ING, -S to gantlet

GAUNTRY *n pl.* -TRIES gantry

GAUR *n pl.* -S a wild ox

GAUSS *n pl.* -ES a unit of magnetic induction

GAUZE *n pl.* -S a transparent fabric

GAUZY *adj* GAUZIER, GAUZIEST resembling gauze **GAUZILY** *adv*

GAVAGE *n pl.* -S introduction of material into the stomach by a tube

GAVE past tense of give

GAVEL *v* -ELED, -ELING, -ELS or -ELLED, -ELLING, -ELS to signal for attention or order by use of a gavel (a small mallet)

GAVELOCK *n pl.* -S a crowbar

GAVIAL *n pl.* -S a large reptile

GAVOT *n pl.* -S a French dance

GAVOTTE *v* -VOTTED, -VOTTING, -VOTTES to dance a gavot

GAWK *v* -ED, -ING, -S to stare stupidly

GAWKER *n pl.* -S one that gawks

GAWKIER comparative of gawky

GAWKIES pl. of gawky

GAWKISH *adj* gawky

GAWKY *adj* GAWKIER, GAWKIEST awkward **GAWKILY** *adv*

GAWKY *n pl.* GAWKIES an awkward person

GAWSIE *adj* well-fed and healthy looking

GAWSY *adj* gawsie

GAY *adj* GAYER, GAYEST merry

GAY *n pl.* GAYS a homosexual

GAYAL *n pl.* -S a domesticated ox

GAYETY *n pl.* -ETIES gaiety

GAYLY *adv* in a gay manner

GAYNESS *n pl.* -ES gaiety

GAYWINGS *n pl.* GAYWINGS a perennial herb

GAZABO *n pl.* -BOS or -BOES a fellow

GAZE *v* GAZED, GAZING, GAZES to look intently

GAZEBO *n pl.* -BOS or -BOES a roofed structure open on the sides

GAZELLE *n pl.* -S a small antelope

GAZER *n pl.* -S one that gazes

GAZETTE *v* -ZETTED, -ZETTING, -ZETTES to announce in an official journal

GAZING present participle of gaze

GAZOGENE *n pl.* -S an apparatus for carbonating liquids

GAZPACHO *n pl.* -CHOS a cold, spicy soup

GEAR *v* -ED, -ING, -S to provide with gears (toothed machine parts)

GEARBOX *n pl.* -ES an automotive transmission

GEARCASE *n pl.* -S a casing for gears

GEARING *n pl.* -S a system of gears

GEARLESS *adj* being without gears

GECK *v* -ED, -ING, -S to mock

GECKO *n pl.* GECKOS or GECKOES a small lizard

GED *n pl.* -S a food fish

GEE *v* GEED, GEEING, GEES to turn to the right

GEEGAW *n pl.* -S gewgaw

GEEK *n pl.* -S a carnival performer

GEEPOUND *n pl.* -S a unit of mass

GEESE *pl.* of goose

GEEST *n pl.* -S old alluvial matter

GEEZER *n pl.* -S an eccentric man

GEISHA *n pl.* -S a Japanese girl trained to entertain

GEL *v* GELLED, GELLING, GELS to become like jelly GELABLE *adj*

GELADA *n pl.* -S a baboon

GELANT *n pl.* -S gellant

GELATE *v* -ATED, -ATING, -ATES to gel

GELATIN *n pl.* -S a glutinous substance

GELATINE *n pl.* -S gelatin

GELATION *n pl.* -S the process of gelling

GELD *v* -ED, -ING, -S to castrate

GELDER *n pl.* -S one that gelds

GELDING *n pl.* -S a castrated animal

GELEE *n pl.* -S a cosmetic gel

GELID *adj* icy GELIDLY *adv*

GELIDITY *n pl.* -TIES iciness

GELLANT *n pl.* -S a substance used to produce gelling

GELLED past tense of gel

GELLING present participle of gel

GELSEMIA *n/pl* medicinal plant roots

GELT *n pl.* -S money

GEM *v* GEMMED, GEMMING, GEMS to adorn with gems (precious stones)

GEMINAL *adj* of or pertaining to two substituents on the same atom

GEMINATE *v* -NATED, -NATING, -NATES to arrange in pairs

GEMLIKE *adj* resembling a gem

GEMMA *n pl.* -MAE an asexual reproductive structure

GEMMATE *v* -MATED, -MATING, -MATES to produce gemmae

GEMMED past tense of gem

GEMMIER comparative of gemmy

GEMMIEST superlative of gemmy

GEMMILY *adv* in a manner suggesting a gem

GEMMING present participle of gem

GEMMULE *n pl.* -S a small gemma

GEMMY *adj* -MIER, -MIEST resembling a gem

GEMOLOGY *n pl.* -GIES the science of gems

GEMOT *n pl.* -S a public meeting in Anglo-Saxon England

GEMOTE *n pl.* -S gemot

GEMSBOK *n pl.* -S a large antelope

GEMSBUCK *n pl.* -S gemsbok

GEMSTONE *n pl.* -S a precious stone

GENDARME *n pl.* -S a policeman

GENDER *v* -ED, -ING, -S to engender

GENE *n pl.* -S a hereditary unit

GENERA *a pl.* of genus

GENERAL *n pl.* -S a military officer

GENERATE *v* -ATED, -ATING, -ATES to bring into existence

GENERIC *n pl.* -S a type of drug

GENEROUS *adj* willing to give

GENESIS *n pl.* GENESES an origin

GENET *n pl.* -S a carnivorous mammal

GENETIC *adj* pertaining to genetics

GENETICS *n/pl* the science of heredity

GENETTE *n pl.* -S genet

GENEVA *n pl.* -S a liquor

GENIAL *adj* having a pleasant or friendly manner GENIALLY *adv*

GENIC	adj pertaining to genes	**GEOID**	n pl. -S a hypothetical surface of the earth **GEOIDAL** adj
GENIE	n pl. -S jinni		
GENII	a pl. of genius	**GEOLOGER**	n pl. -S a specialist in geology
GENIP	n pl. -S a tropical tree	**GEOLOGY**	n pl. -GIES the science that deals with the origin and structure of the earth **GEOLOGIC** adj
GENIPAP	n pl. -S a tropical tree		
GENITAL	adj pertaining to reproduction		
GENITALS	n/pl the sexual organs		
GENITIVE	n pl. -S a grammatical case	**GEOMANCY**	n pl. -CIES a method of foretelling the future by geographical features
GENITOR	n pl. -S a male parent		
GENITURE	n pl. -S birth	**GEOMETER**	n pl. -S a specialist in geometry
GENIUS	n pl. GENIUSES or GENII an exceptional natural aptitude	**GEOMETRY**	n pl. -TRIES a branch of mathematics
GENOA	n pl. -S a triangular sail	**GEOPHAGY**	n pl. -GIES the practice of eating earthy substances
GENOCIDE	n pl. -S the deliberate extermination of a national or racial group		
		GEOPHONE	n pl. -S a device that detects vibrations in the earth
GENOM	n pl. -S genome		
GENOME	n pl. -S a haploid set of chromosomes **GENOMIC** adj	**GEOPHYTE**	n pl. -S a plant having underground buds
		GEOPONIC	adj pertaining to farming
GENOTYPE	n pl. -S the genetic constitution of an organism	**GEORGIC**	n pl. -S a poem about farming
GENRE	n pl. -S a type or kind	**GEOTAXIS**	n pl. -TAXES the movement of an organism in response to gravity
GENRO	n pl. -ROS a group of elder statesmen in Japan		
GENS	n pl. GENTES a type of clan	**GERAH**	n pl. -S a Hebrew unit of weight
GENSENG	n pl. -S ginseng	**GERANIAL**	n pl. -S citral
GENT	n pl. -S a gentleman	**GERANIOL**	n pl. -S an alcohol used in perfumes
GENTEEL	adj -TEELER, -TEELEST well-bred or refined		
		GERANIUM	n pl. -S a flowering plant
GENTES	pl. of gens	**GERARDIA**	n pl. -S an herb
GENTIAN	n pl. -S a flowering plant	**GERBERA**	n pl. -S an herb
GENTIL	adj kind	**GERBIL**	n pl. -S a burrowing rodent
GENTILE	n pl. -S a non-Jewish person	**GERBILLE**	n pl. -S gerbil
GENTLE	adj -TLER, -TLEST mild **GENTLY** adv	**GERENT**	n pl. -S a ruler or manager
		GERENUK	n pl. -S a long-necked antelope
GENTLE	v -TLED, -TLING, -TLES to tame	**GERM**	n pl. -S a microorganism that causes disease
GENTRICE	n pl. -S good breeding		
GENTRY	n pl. -TRIES people of high social class	**GERMAN**	n pl. -S an elaborate dance
		GERMANE	adj relevant
GENU	n pl. GENUA the knee	**GERMANIC**	adj containing germanium (a metallic element)
GENUINE	adj authentic		
GENUS	n pl. GENERA or GENUSES a kind, sort, or class	**GERMEN**	n pl. -MENS or -MINA something that serves as an origin
GEODE	n pl. -S a type of rock		
GEODESIC	n pl. -S a geometric line	**GERMFREE**	adj free from germs
GEODESY	n pl. -SIES geographical surveying	**GERMIER**	comparative of germy
		GERMIEST	superlative of germy
		GERMINA	a pl. of germen
GEODETIC	adj pertaining to geodesy	**GERMINAL**	adj being in the earliest stage of development
GEODIC	adj of or pertaining to a geode		
GEODUCK	n pl. -S a large, edible clam	**GERMY**	adj GERMIER, GERMIEST full of germs
GEOGNOSY	n pl. -SIES a branch of geology	**GERONTIC**	adj pertaining to old age

GERUND n pl. -S a verbal noun

GESSO n pl. -SOES a plaster mixture

GEST n pl. -S a feat

GESTALT n pl. -STALTS or -STALTEN a unified whole

GESTAPO n pl. -POS a secret-police organization

GESTATE v -TATED, -TATING, -TATES to carry in the uterus during pregnancy

GESTE n pl. -S gest

GESTIC adj pertaining to bodily motion

GESTICAL adj gestic

GESTURAL adj pertaining to or consisting of gestures (expressive bodily motions)

GESTURE v -TURED, -TURING, -TURES to express by bodily motion

GESTURER n pl. -S one that gestures

GET v GOT, GOTTEN, GETTING, GETS to obtain or acquire **GETABLE, GETTABLE** adj

GETAWAY n pl. -AWAYS an escape

GETTER v -ED, -ING, -S to purify with a chemically active substance

GETTING present participle of get

GETUP n pl. -S a costume

GEUM n pl. -S a perennial herb

GEWGAW n pl. -S a showy trinket

GEY adv very

GEYSER n pl. -S a spring that ejects jets of hot water and steam

GHARRI n pl. -S gharry

GHARRY n pl. -RIES a carriage used in India

GHAST adj ghastly

GHASTFUL adj frightful

GHASTLY adj -LIER, -LIEST terrifying

GHAT n pl. -S a passage leading down to a river

GHAUT n pl. -S ghat

GHAZI n pl. -S or -ES a Muslim war hero

GHEE n pl. -S a kind of liquid butter made in India

GHERAO v -ED, -ING, -ES to coerce by physical means

GHERKIN n pl. -S a small cucumber

GHETTO v -ED, -ING, -S or -ES to isolate in a slum

GHI n pl. -S ghee

GHIBLI n pl. -S a hot desert wind

GHILLIE n pl. -S a type of shoe

GHOST v -ED, -ING, -S to haunt

GHOSTLY adj -LIER, -LIEST spectral

GHOSTY adj GHOSTIER, GHOSTIEST ghostly

GHOUL n pl. -S a demon **GHOULISH** adj

GHYLL n pl. -S a ravine

GIANT n pl. -S a person or thing of great size

GIANTESS n pl. -ES a female giant

GIANTISM n pl. -S the condition of being a giant

GIAOUR n pl. -S a non-Muslim

GIB v GIBBED, GIBBING, GIBS to fasten with a wedge of wood or metal

GIBBER v -ED, -ING, -S to jabber

GIBBET v -BETED, -BETING, -BETS or -BETTED, -BETTING, -BETS to execute by hanging

GIBBING present participle of gib

GIBBON n pl. -S an arboreal ape

GIBBOSE adj gibbous

GIBBOUS adj irregularly rounded

GIBBSITE n pl. -S a mineral

GIBE v GIBED, GIBING, GIBES to jeer **GIBINGLY** adv

GIBER n pl. -S one that gibes

GIBLET n pl. -S an edible part of a fowl

GID n pl. -S a disease of sheep

GIDDAP interj — used as a command to a horse to go faster

GIDDY adj -DIER, -DIEST dizzy **GIDDILY** adv

GIDDY v -DIED, -DYING, -DIES to make giddy

GIE v GIED, GIEN, GIEING, GIES to give

GIFT v -ED, -ING, -S to present with a gift (something given without charge)

GIFTEDLY adv in a talented manner

GIFTLESS adj being without a gift

GIG v GIGGED, GIGGING, GIGS to catch fish with a pronged spear

GIGA n pl. GIGHE a gigue

GIGABIT n pl. -S a unit of information

GIGANTIC adj huge

GIGAS adj pertaining to variations in plant development

GIGATON n pl. -S a unit of weight

GIGAWATT n pl. -S a unit of power

GIGGED past tense of gig

GIGGING   present participle of gig

GIGGLE   v -GLED, -GLING, -GLES to laugh in a silly manner

GIGGLER   n pl. -S one that giggles

GIGGLY   adj -GLIER, -GLIEST tending to giggle

GIGHE   pl. of giga

GIGLET   n pl. -S a playful girl

GIGLOT   n pl. -S giglet

GIGOLO   n pl. -LOS a man supported financially by a woman

GIGOT   n pl. -S a leg of lamb

GIGUE   n pl. -S a lively dance

GILBERT   n pl. -S a unit of magnetomotive force

GILD   v GILDED or GILT, GILDING, GILDS to cover with a thin layer of gold

GILDER   n pl. -S one that gilds

GILDHALL   n pl. -S a town hall

GILDING   n pl. -S the application of gilt

GILL   v -ED, -ING, -S to catch fish with a type of net

GILLER   n pl. -S one that gills

GILLIE   n pl. -S a ghillie

GILLNET   v -NETTED, -NETTING, -NETS to gill

GILLY   v -LIED, -LYING, -LIES to transport on a type of wagon

GILT   n pl. -S the gold with which something is gilded

GILTHEAD   n pl. -S a marine fish

GIMBAL   v -BALED, -BALING, -BALS or -BALLED, -BALLING, -BALS to support on a set of rings

GIMCRACK   n pl. -S a gewgaw

GIMEL   n pl. -S a Hebrew letter

GIMLET   n -ED, -ING, -S to pierce with a boring tool

GIMMAL   n pl. -S a pair of interlocked rings

GIMMICK   v -ED, -ING, -S to provide with a gimmick (a novel or tricky feature)

GIMMICKY   adj having or being like a gimmick

GIMP   v -ED, -ING, -S to limp

GIMPY   adj GIMPIER, GIMPIEST limping

GIN   v GINNED, GINNING, GINS to remove seeds from cotton

GIN   v GAN, GUNNEN, GINNING, GINS to begin

GINGAL   n pl. -S jingal

GINGALL   n pl. -S jingal

GINGELEY   n pl. -LEYS gingelly

GINGELI   n pl. -S gingelly

GINGELLY   n pl. -LIES the sesame seed or its oil

GINGELY   n pl. -LIES gingelly

GINGER   v -ED, -ING, -S to flavor with ginger (a pungent spice)

GINGERLY   adv in a careful manner

GINGERY   adj having the characteristics of ginger

GINGHAM   n pl. -S a cotton fabric

GINGILI   n pl. -LIS gingelly

GINGIVA   n pl. -VAE the fleshy tissue that surrounds the teeth GINGIVAL adj

GINGKO   n pl. -KOES ginkgo

GINK   n pl. -S a fellow

GINKGO   n pl. -GOES an ornamental tree

GINNED   past tense of gin

GINNER   n pl. -S one that gins cotton

GINNING   n pl. -S cotton as it comes from a gin

GINNY   adj GINNIER, GINNIEST affected with gin (a strong liquor)

GINSENG   n pl. -S a perennial herb

GIP   v GIPPED, GIPPING, GIPS to gyp

GIPON   n pl. -S jupon

GIPPER   n pl. -S one that gips

GIPPING   present participle of gip

GIPSY   v -SIED, -SYING, -SIES to gypsy

GIRAFFE   n pl. -S a long-necked mammal

GIRASOL   n pl. -S a variety of opal

GIRASOLE   n pl. -S girasol

GIRD   v GIRDED or GIRT, GIRDING, GIRDS to surround

GIRDER   n pl. -S a horizontal support

GIRDLE   v -DLED, -DLING, -DLES to encircle with a belt

GIRDLER   n pl. -S one that girdles

GIRL   n pl. -S a female child

GIRLHOOD   n pl. -S the state of being a girl

GIRLIE   n pl. -S a girl

GIRLISH   adj of, pertaining to, or having the characteristics of a girl

GIRLY   adj featuring scantily clothed women

GIRN   v -ED, -ING, -S to snarl

GIRO   n pl. -ROS an autogiro

GIRON	n pl. -S gyron
GIROSOL	n pl. -S girasol
GIRSH	n pl. -ES qursh
GIRT	v -ED, -ING, -S to gird
GIRTH	v -ED, -ING, -S to encircle
GISARME	n pl. -S a medieval weapon
GISMO	n pl. -MOS a gadget
GIST	n pl. -S the main point of a matter
GIT	interj — used as an order of dismissal
GITANO	n pl. -NOS a Spanish gypsy
GITTERN	n pl. -S a medieval guitar
GIVE	v GAVE, GIVEN, GIVING, GIVES to transfer freely to another's possession GIVEABLE adj
GIVEAWAY	n pl. -AWAYS something given away free of charge
GIVEN	n pl. -S something assigned as a basis for a calculation
GIVER	n pl. -S one that gives
GIVING	present participle of give
GIZMO	n pl. -MOS gismo
GIZZARD	n pl. -S a digestive organ
GJETOST	n pl. -S a hard brown cheese
GLABELLA	n pl. -BELLAE the smooth area between the eyebrows
GLABRATE	adj glabrous
GLABROUS	adj smooth
GLACE	v -CEED, -CEING, -CES to cover with icing
GLACIAL	adj of or pertaining to glaciers
GLACIATE	v -ATED, -ATING, -ATES to cover with glaciers
GLACIER	n pl. -S a huge mass of ice
GLACIS	n pl. -CISES a slope
GLAD	adj GLADDER, GLADDEST feeling pleasure
GLAD	v GLADDED, GLADDING, GLADS to gladden
GLADDEN	v -ED, -ING, -S to make glad
GLADDER	comparative of glad
GLADDEST	superlative of glad
GLADDING	present participle of glad
GLADE	n pl. -S an open space in a forest
GLADIATE	adj shaped like a sword
GLADIER	comparative of glady
GLADIEST	superlative of glady
GLADIOLA	n pl. -S a flowering plant
GLADIOLI	n/pl segments of the sternum
GLADLY	adv -LIER, -LIEST in a glad manner
GLADNESS	n pl. -ES the state of being glad
GLADSOME	adj -SOMER, -SOMEST glad
GLADY	adj GLADIER, GLADIEST having glades
GLAIKET	adj glaikit
GLAIKIT	adj foolish
GLAIR	v -ED, -ING, -S to coat with egg white
GLAIRE	v GLAIRED, GLAIRING, GLAIRES to glair
GLAIRY	adj GLAIRIER, GLAIRIEST resembling egg white
GLAIVE	n pl. -S a sword GLAIVED adj
GLAMOR	n pl. -S alluring attractiveness
GLAMOUR	v -ED, -ING, -S to bewitch
GLANCE	v GLANCED, GLANCING, GLANCES to look quickly
GLAND	n pl. -S a secreting organ
GLANDERS	n/pl a disease of horses
GLANDULE	n pl. -S a small gland
GLANS	n pl. GLANDES the tip of the penis or clitoris
GLARE	v GLARED, GLARING, GLARES to shine with a harshly brilliant light
GLARY	adj GLARIER, GLARIEST glaring
GLASS	v -ED, -ING, -ES to encase in glass (a transparent substance)
GLASSFUL	n pl. -FULS as much as a drinking glass will hold
GLASSIE	n pl. -S a type of playing marble
GLASSIER	comparative of glassy
GLASSIEST	superlative of glassy
GLASSILY	adv in a glassy manner
GLASSINE	n pl. -S a type of paper
GLASSMAN	n pl. -MEN a glazier
GLASSY	adj GLASSIER, GLASSIEST resembling glass
GLAUCOMA	n pl. -S a disease of the eye
GLAUCOUS	adj bluish green
GLAZE	v GLAZED, GLAZING, GLAZES to fit windows with glass panes
GLAZER	n pl. -S a glazier
GLAZIER	n pl. -S one that glazes
GLAZIERY	n pl. -ZIERIES the work of a glazier
GLAZING	n pl. -S glaziery

GLAZY   *adj* GLAZIER, GLAZIEST covered with a smooth, glossy coating

GLEAM   *v* -ED, -ING, -S to shine with a soft radiance

GLEAMY   *adj* GLEAMIER, GLEAMIEST gleaming

GLEAN   *v* -ED, -ING, -S to gather little by little

GLEANER   *n pl.* -S one that gleans

GLEANING   *n pl.* -S something that is gleaned

GLEBA   *n pl.* -BAE a spore-bearing mass of some fungi

GLEBE   *n pl.* -S the soil or earth

GLED   *n pl.* -S a glede

GLEDE   *n pl.* -S a bird of prey

GLEE   *n pl.* -S an unaccompanied song

GLEED   *n pl.* -S a glowing coal

GLEEFUL   *adj* merry

GLEEK   *v* -ED, -ING, -S to gibe

GLEEMAN   *n pl.* -MEN a minstrel

GLEESOME   *adj* gleeful

GLEET   *v* -ED, -ING, -S to discharge mucus from the urethra

GLEETY   *adj* GLEETIER, GLEETIEST resembling mucus

GLEG   *adj* alert GLEGLY *adv*

GLEGNESS   *n pl.* -ES alertness

GLEN   *n pl.* -S a small valley GLENLIKE *adj*

GLENOID   *adj* having the shallow or slightly cupped form of a bone socket

GLEY   *n pl.* GLEYS a soil layer

GLIADIN   *n pl.* -S a simple protein

GLIADINE   *n pl.* -S gliadin

GLIAL   *adj* pertaining to the supporting tissue of the central nervous system

GLIB   *adj* GLIBBER, GLIBBEST fluent GLIBLY *adv*

GLIBNESS   *n pl.* -ES the quality of being glib

GLIDE   *v* GLIDED, GLIDING, GLIDES to move effortlessly

GLIDER   *n pl.* -S a type of aircraft

GLIFF   *n pl.* -S a brief moment

GLIM   *n pl.* -S a light or lamp

GLIME   *v* GLIMED, GLIMING, GLIMES to glance slyly

GLIMMER   *v* -ED, -ING, -S to shine faintly or unsteadily

GLIMPSE   *v* GLIMPSED, GLIMPSING, GLIMPSES to see for an instant

GLIMPSER   *n pl.* -S one that glimpses

GLINT   *v* -ED, -ING, -S to glitter

GLIOMA   *n pl.* -MAS or -MATA a type of tumor

GLISSADE   *v* -SADED, -SADING, -SADES to perform a gliding dance step

GLISTEN   *v* -ED, -ING, -S to shine by reflection

GLISTER   *v* -ED, -ING, -S to glisten

GLITCH   *n pl.* -ES a malfunction

GLITTER   *v* -ED, -ING, -S to sparkle

GLITTERY   *adj* glittering

GLOAM   *n pl.* -S twilight

GLOAMING   *n pl.* -S twilight

GLOAT   *v* -ED, -ING, -S to regard with great or excessive satisfaction

GLOATER   *n pl.* -S one that gloats

GLOB   *n pl.* -S a rounded mass

GLOBAL   *adj* spherical GLOBALLY *adv*

GLOBATE   *adj* spherical

GLOBATED   *adj* spherical

GLOBE   *v* GLOBED, GLOBING, GLOBES to form into a perfectly round body

GLOBIN   *n pl.* -S a simple protein

GLOBOID   *n pl.* -S a spheroid

GLOBOSE   *adj* spherical

GLOBOUS   *adj* spherical

GLOBULAR   *adj* spherical

GLOBULE   *n pl.* -S a small spherical mass

GLOBULIN   *n pl.* -S a simple protein

GLOCHID   *n pl.* -S a barbed hair on some plants

GLOGG   *n pl.* -S an alcoholic beverage

GLOM   *v* GLOMMED, GLOMMING, GLOMS to steal

GLOMUS   *n pl.* -MERA a type of vascular tuft

GLOOM   *v* -ED, -ING, -S to become dark

GLOOMFUL   *adj* gloomy

GLOOMING   *n pl.* -S gloaming

GLOOMY   *adj* GLOOMIER, GLOOMIEST dismally dark GLOOMILY *adv*

GLOP   *n pl.* -S a messy mass or mixture

GLORIA   *n pl.* -S a halo

GLORIED   past tense of glory

GLORIES present 3d person sing. of glory

GLORIFY v -FIED, -FYING, -FIES to bestow honor or praise on

GLORIOLE n pl. -S a halo

GLORIOUS adj magnificent

GLORY v -RIED, -RYING, -RIES to rejoice proudly

GLOSS v -ED, -ING, -ES to make lustrous

GLOSSA n pl. -SAE or -SAS the tongue **GLOSSAL** adj

GLOSSARY n pl. -RIES a list of terms and their definitions

GLOSSEME n pl. -S the smallest linguistic unit that signals a meaning

GLOSSER n pl. -S one that glosses

GLOSSIES pl. of glossy

GLOSSINA n pl. -S a tsetse fly

GLOSSY adj GLOSSIER, GLOSSIEST lustrous **GLOSSILY** adv

GLOSSY n pl. GLOSSIES a type of photograph

GLOST n pl. -S pottery that has been coated with a glassy surface

GLOTTIS n pl. -TISES or -TIDES the opening between the vocal cords **GLOTTAL, GLOTTIC** adj

GLOUT v -ED, -ING, -S to scowl

GLOVE v GLOVED, GLOVING, GLOVES to furnish with gloves (hand coverings)

GLOVER n pl. -S a maker or seller of gloves

GLOW v -ED, -ING, -S to emit light and heat

GLOWER v -ED, -ING, -S to scowl

GLOWFLY n pl. -FLIES a firefly

GLOWWORM n pl. -S a luminous insect

GLOXINIA n pl. -S a tropical plant

GLOZE v GLOZED, GLOZING, GLOZES to explain away

GLUCAGON n pl. -S a hormone

GLUCINUM n pl. -S a metallic element **GLUCINIC** adj

GLUCOSE n pl. -S a sugar **GLUCOSIC** adj

GLUE v GLUED, GLUING or GLUEING, GLUES to fasten with glue (an adhesive substance)

GLUELIKE adj resembling glue

GLUER n pl. -S one that glues

GLUEY adj GLUIER, GLUIEST resembling glue **GLUILY** adv

GLUING present participle of glue

GLUM adj GLUMMER, GLUMMEST being in low spirits **GLUMLY** adv

GLUME n pl. -S a bract on grassy plants

GLUMNESS n pl. -ES the state of being glum

GLUMPY adj GLUMPIER, GLUMPIEST glum **GLUMPILY** adv

GLUNCH v -ED, -ING, -ES to frown

GLUT v GLUTTED, GLUTTING, GLUTS to feed or fill to excess

GLUTEAL adj of or pertaining to the buttock muscles

GLUTEI pl. of gluteus

GLUTELIN n pl. -S a plant protein

GLUTEN n pl. -S a tough elastic plant protein substance

GLUTEUS n pl. -TEI a buttock muscle

GLUTTED past tense of glut

GLUTTING present participle of glut

GLUTTON n pl. -S a person who eats to excess

GLUTTONY n pl. -TONIES excessive eating

GLYCAN n pl. -S a carbohydrate

GLYCERIN n pl. -S a glycerol **GLYCERIC** adj

GLYCEROL n pl. -S a syrupy alcohol

GLYCERYL n pl. -S a radical derived from glycerol

GLYCIN n pl. -S a compound used in photography

GLYCINE n pl. -S an amino acid

GLYCOGEN n pl. -S a carbohydrate

GLYCOL n pl. -S an alcohol **GLYCOLIC** adj

GLYCONIC n pl. -S a type of verse line

GLYCOSYL n pl. -S a radical derived from glucose

GLYCYL n pl. -S a radical derived from glycine

GLYPH n pl. -S an ornamental groove **GLYPHIC** adj

GLYPTIC n pl. -S the art or process of engraving on gems

GNAR v GNARRED, GNARRING, GNARS to snarl

GNARL v -ED, -ING, -S to twist into a state of deformity

GNARLY adj GNARLIER, GNARLIEST gnarled

GNARR v -ED, -ING, -S to gnar

GNARRED	past tense of gnar		GOATFISH	n pl. -ES a tropical fish
GNARRING	present participle of gnar		GOATHERD	n pl. -S one who tends goats
GNASH	v -ED, -ING, -ES to grind the teeth together		GOATISH	adj resembling a goat
			GOATLIKE	adj goatish
GNAT	n pl. -S a small winged insect		GOATSKIN	n pl. -S the hide of a goat
GNATHAL	adj gnathic		GOB	v GOBBED, GOBBING, GOBS to fill a mine pit with waste material
GNATHIC	adj of or pertaining to the jaw			
GNATHION	n pl. -S the tip of the chin			
GNATHITE	n pl. -S a jawlike appendage of an insect		GOBAN	n pl. -S gobang
			GOBANG	n pl. -S a Japanese game
GNATLIKE	adj resembling a gnat		GOBBED	past tense of gob
GNATTY	adj -TIER, -TIEST infested with gnats		GOBBET	n pl. -S a piece of raw meat
			GOBBING	present participle of gob
GNAW	v GNAWED, GNAWN, GNAWING, GNAWS to wear away by persistent biting GNAWABLE adj		GOBBLE	v -BLED, -BLING, -BLES to eat hastily
			GOBBLER	n pl. -S a male turkey
			GOBIES	pl. of goby
GNAWER	n pl. -S one that gnaws		GOBIOID	n pl. -S a fish of the goby family
GNAWING	n pl. -S a persistent dull pain			
GNAWN	a past participle of gnaw		GOBLET	n pl. -S a drinking vessel
GNEISS	n pl. -ES a type of rock GNEISSIC adj		GOBLIN	n pl. -S an evil or mischievous creature
			GOBO	n pl. -BOS or -BOES a device used to shield a microphone from extraneous sounds
GNOCCHI	n/pl dumplings made of pasta			
GNOME	n pl. -S a dwarf			
GNOMIC	adj resembling or containing aphorisms			
			GOBONEE	adj gobony
GNOMICAL	adj gnomic		GOBONY	adj compony
GNOMISH	adj resembling a gnome		GOBY	n pl. GOBIES a small fish
GNOMIST	n pl. -S a writer of aphorisms		GOD	v GODDED, GODDING, GODS to treat as a god (a supernatural being)
GNOMON	n pl. -S a part of a sundial GNOMONIC adj			
GNOSIS	n pl. GNOSES mystical knowledge		GODCHILD	n pl. -CHILDREN one whom a person sponsors at baptism
GNOSTIC	adj possessing knowledge		GODDAM	v -DAMMED, -DAMMING, -DAMS goddamn
GNU	n pl. -S a large antelope			
GO	v WENT, GONE, GOING, GOES to move along		GODDAMN	v -ED, -ING, -S to damn
			GODDED	past tense of god
GOA	n pl. -S an Asian gazelle		GODDESS	n pl. -ES a female god
GOAD	v -ED, -ING, -S to drive animals with a goad (a pointed stick)		GODDING	present participle of god
			GODHEAD	n pl. -S godhood
GOADLIKE	adj resembling a goad		GODHOOD	n pl. -S the state of being a god
GOAL	v -ED, -ING, -S to score a goal (a point-scoring play in some games)			
			GODLESS	adj worshiping no god
			GODLIER	comparative of godly
GOALIE	n pl. -S a player who defends against goals		GODLIEST	superlative of godly
			GODLIKE	adj divine
GOALLESS	adj having no goal		GODLING	n pl. -S a lesser god
GOALPOST	n pl. -S a post that marks a boundary of the scoring area in some games		GODLY	adj -LIER, -LIEST pious GODLILY adv
			GODOWN	n pl. -S an oriental warehouse
GOAT	n pl. -S a horned mammal		GODROON	n pl. -S gadroon
GOATEE	n pl. -S a small pointed beard GOATEED adj		GODSEND	n pl. -S an unexpected boon

GODSHIP *n* pl. -S the rank of a god

GODSON *n* pl. -S a male godchild

GODWIT *n* pl. -S a wading bird

GOER *n* pl. -S one that goes

GOETHITE *n* pl. -S an ore of iron

GOFFER *v* -ED, -ING, -S to press ridges or pleats into

GOGGLE *v* -GLED, -GLING, -GLES to stare with wide eyes

GOGGLER *n* pl. -S one that goggles

GOGGLY *adj* -GLIER, -GLIEST wide-eyed

GOGLET *n* pl. -S a long-necked jar

GOGO *n* pl. -GOS a discotheque

GOING *n* pl. -S an advance toward an objective

GOITER *n* pl. -S an enlargement of the thyroid gland GOITROUS *adj*

GOITRE *n* pl. -S goiter

GOLCONDA *n* pl. -S a source of great wealth

GOLD *n* pl. -S a precious metallic element

GOLD *adj* GOLDER, GOLDEST golden

GOLDARN *n* pl. -S an expression of anger

GOLDBUG *n* pl. -S a gold beetle

GOLDEN *adj* -ENER, -ENEST of the color of gold GOLDENLY *adv*

GOLDEYE *n* pl. -S a freshwater fish

GOLDFISH *n* pl. -ES a freshwater fish

GOLDURN *n* pl. -S goldarn

GOLEM *n* pl. -S a legendary creature

GOLF *v* -ED, -ING, -S to play golf (a type of ball game)

GOLFER *n* pl. -S one that golfs

GOLFING *n* pl. -S the game of golf

GOLGOTHA *n* pl. -S a place of burial

GOLIARD *n* pl. -S a wandering student

GOLLIWOG *n* pl. -S a grotesque doll

GOLLY *interj* — used as a mild oath

GOLOSH *n* pl. -ES a galosh

GOMBO *n* pl. -BOS gumbo

GOMBROON *n* pl. -S a kind of Persian pottery

GOMERAL *n* pl. -S a fool

GOMEREL *n* pl. -S gomeral

GOMERIL *n* pl. -S gomeral

GOMUTI *n* pl. -S a palm tree

GONAD *n* pl. -S a sex gland GONADAL, GONADIAL, GONADIC *adj*

GONDOLA *n* pl. -S a long, narrow boat

GONE *adj* departed

GONENESS *n* pl. -ES a state of exhaustion

GONER *n* pl. -S one who is in a hopeless situation

GONFALON *n* pl. -S a banner

GONFANON *n* pl. -S gonfalon

GONG *v* -ED, -ING, -S to make the sound of a gong (a disk-shaped percussion instrument)

GONGLIKE *adj* resembling a gong

GONIA pl. of gonion and of gonium

GONIDIUM *n* pl. -IA an asexual reproductive cell GONIDIAL, GONIDIC *adj*

GONIF *n* pl. -S ganef

GONION *n* pl. -NIA a part of the lower jaw

GONIUM *n* pl. -NIA an immature reproductive cell

GONOCYTE *n* pl. -S a cell that produces gametes

GONOF *n* pl. -S ganef

GONOPH *n* pl. -S ganef

GONOPORE *n* pl. -S a genital pore

GOO *n* pl. GOOS a sticky or viscid substance

GOOBER *n* pl. -S a peanut

GOOD *adj* BETTER, BEST having positive or desirable qualities

GOOD *n* pl. -S something that is good

GOODBY *n* pl. -BYS goodbye

GOODBYE *n* pl. -S a concluding remark or gesture at parting

GOODIES pl. of goody

GOODISH *adj* somewhat good

GOODLY *adj* -LIER, -LIEST of pleasing appearance

GOODMAN *n* pl. -MEN the master of a household

GOODNESS *n* pl. -ES the state of being good

GOODWIFE *n* pl. -WIVES the mistress of a household

GOODWILL *n* pl. -S an attitude of friendliness

GOODY *n* pl. GOODIES a desirable food

GOOEY *adj* GOOIER, GOOIEST sticky or viscid

GOOF *v* -ED, -ING, -S to blunder

GOOFBALL *n* pl. -S a sleeping pill

GOOFY *adj* GOOFIER, GOOFIEST silly GOOFILY *adv*

GOOGLY n pl. -GLIES a type of bowled ball in cricket

GOOGOL n pl. -S an enormous number

GOOIER comparative of gooey

GOOIEST superlative of gooey

GOOK n pl. -S goo **GOOKY** adj

GOON n pl. -S a hired thug

GOONEY n pl. -NEYS an albatross

GOONIE n pl. -S gooney

GOONY n pl. -NIES gooney

GOOP n pl. -S a boor

GOORAL n pl. -S a goral

GOOSE n pl. GEESE a swimming bird

GOOSE v GOOSED, GOOSING, GOOSES to poke between the buttocks

GOOSEY adj GOOSIER, GOOSIEST goosy

GOOSY adj GOOSIER, GOOSIEST resembling a goose

GOPHER n pl. -S a burrowing rodent

GOR interj — used as a mild oath

GORAL n pl. -S a goat antelope

GORBELLY n pl. -LIES a potbelly

GORBLIMY interj blimey

GORCOCK n pl. -S the male red grouse

GORE v GORED, GORING, GORES to pierce with a horn or tusk

GORGE v GORGED, GORGING, GORGES to stuff with food **GORGEDLY** adv

GORGEOUS adj beautiful

GORGER n pl. -S one that gorges

GORGERIN n pl. -S a part of a column

GORGET n pl. -S a piece of armor for the throat **GORGETED** adj

GORGING present participle of gorge

GORGON n pl. -S an ugly woman

GORHEN n pl. -S the female red grouse

GORIER comparative of gory

GORIEST superlative of gory

GORILLA n pl. -S a large ape

GORILY adv in a gory manner

GORINESS n pl. -ES the state of being gory

GORING present participle of gore

GORMAND n pl. -S a gourmand

GORSE n pl. -S furze

GORSY adj GORSIER, GORSIEST abounding in gorse

GORY adj GORIER, GORIEST bloody

GOSH interj — used as an exclamation of surprise

GOSHAWK n pl. -S a large hawk

GOSLING n pl. -S a young goose

GOSPEL n pl. -S the message concerning Christ, the kingdom of God, and salvation

GOSPELER n pl. -S one that teaches the gospel

GOSPORT n pl. -S a communication device in an airplane

GOSSAMER n pl. -S a fine film of cobwebs

GOSSAN n pl. -S a type of decomposed rock

GOSSIP v -SIPED, -SIPING, -SIPS or -SIPPED, -SIPPING, -SIPS to talk idly about the affairs of others

GOSSIPER n pl. -S one that gossips

GOSSIPRY n pl. -RIES the practice of gossiping

GOSSIPY adj inclined to gossip

GOSSOON n pl. -S a boy

GOSSYPOL n pl. -S a toxic pigment

GOT past tense of get

GOTHIC n pl. -S a style of printing

GOTHITE n pl. -S goethite

GOTTEN past participle of get

GOUACHE n pl. -S a method of painting

GOUGE v GOUGED, GOUGING, GOUGES to cut or scoop out

GOUGER n pl. -S one that gouges

GOULASH n pl. -ES a beef stew

GOURAMI n pl. -S a food fish

GOURD n pl. -S a hard-shelled fruit

GOURDE n pl. -S a monetary unit of Haiti

GOURMAND n pl. -S one who loves to eat

GOURMET n pl. -S a connoisseur of fine food and drink

GOUT n pl. -S a metabolic disease

GOUTY adj GOUTIER, GOUTIEST affected with gout **GOUTILY** adv

GOVERN v -ED, -ING, -S to rule or direct

GOVERNOR n pl. -S one that governs

GOWAN n pl. -S a daisy **GOWANED, GOWANY** adj

GOWD n pl. -S gold

GOWK n pl. -S a fool

GOWN v -ED, -ING, -S to dress in a gown (a long, loose outer garment)

GOWNSMAN n pl. -MEN a professional or academic person

GOX n pl. -ES gaseous oxygen

GOY n pl. GOYIM or GOYS a non-Jewish person **GOYISH** adj

GRAAL n pl. -S grail

GRAB v GRABBED, GRABBING, GRABS to grasp suddenly

GRABBER n pl. -S one that grabs

GRABBIER comparative of grabby

GRABBIEST superlative of grabby

GRABBING present participle of grab

GRABBLE v -BLED, -BLING, -BLES to grope

GRABBLER n pl. -S one that grabbles

GRABBY adj -BIER, -BIEST tending to grab

GRABEN n pl. -S a depression of the earth's crust

GRACE v GRACED, GRACING, GRACES to give beauty to

GRACEFUL adj -FULLER, -FULLEST having beauty of form or movement

GRACILE adj gracefully slender

GRACILIS n pl. -LES a thigh muscle

GRACING present participle of grace

GRACIOSO n pl. -SOS a clown in Spanish comedy

GRACIOUS adj marked by kindness and courtesy

GRACKLE n pl. -S a blackbird

GRAD n pl. -S a graduate

GRADATE v -DATED, -DATING, -DATES to change by degrees

GRADE v GRADED, GRADING, GRADES to arrange in steps or degrees **GRADABLE** adj

GRADER n pl. -S one that grades

GRADIENT n pl. -S a rate of inclination

GRADIN n pl. -S gradine

GRADINE n pl. -S one of a series of steps

GRADING present participle of grade

GRADUAL n pl. -S a hymn sung in alternate parts

GRADUAND n pl. -S one who is about to graduate

GRADUATE v -ATED, -ATING, -ATES to receive an academic degree or diploma

GRADUS n pl. -ES a dictionary of prosody

GRAECIZE v -CIZED, -CIZING, -CIZES to grecize

GRAFFITO n pl. -TI an inscription or drawing made on a rock or wall

GRAFT v -ED, -ING, -S to unite with a growing plant by insertion

GRAFTAGE n pl. -S the process of grafting

GRAFTER n pl. -S one that grafts

GRAHAM adj made of whole wheat flour

GRAIL n pl. -S the cup used by Christ at the Last Supper

GRAIN v -ED, -ING, -S to form into small particles

GRAINER n pl. -S one that grains

GRAINY adj GRAINIER, GRAINIEST granular

GRAM pl. -S a unit of mass and weight

GRAMA n pl. -S a pasture grass

GRAMARY n pl. -RIES gramarye

GRAMARYE n pl. -S occult learning; magic

GRAMERCY n pl. -CIES an expression of gratitude

GRAMMAR n pl. -S the study of the formal features of a language

GRAMME n pl. -S gram

GRAMP n pl. -S grandfather

GRAMPUS n pl. -ES a marine mammal

GRANA pl. of granum

GRANARY n pl. -RIES a storehouse for grain

GRAND adj GRANDER, GRANDEST large and impressive

GRAND n pl. -S a type of piano

GRANDAD n pl. -S granddad

GRANDAM n pl. -S a grandmother

GRANDAME n pl. -S grandam

GRANDDAD n pl. -S a grandfather

GRANDEE n pl. -S man of high social position

GRANDEUR n pl. -S the state of being grand

GRANDLY adv in a grand manner

GRANDMA n pl. -S a grandmother

GRANDPA n pl. -S a grandfather

GRANDSIR n pl. -S a grandfather

GRANDSON n pl. -S a son of one's son or daughter

GRANGE n pl. -S a farm

GRANGER n pl. -S a farmer

GRANITE n pl. -S a type of rock **GRANITIC** adj

GRANNIE *n* pl. -S granny

GRANNY *n* pl. -NIES a grandmother

GRANT *v* -ED, -ING, -S to bestow upon

GRANTEE *n* pl. -S one to whom something is granted

GRANTER *n* pl. -S one that grants

GRANTOR *n* pl. -S granter

GRANULAR *adj* composed of granules

GRANULE *n* pl. -S a small particle

GRANUM *n* pl. GRANA a part of a plant chloroplast

GRAPE *n* pl. -S an edible berry

GRAPERY *n* pl. -ERIES a vinery

GRAPH *v* -ED, -ING, -S to represent by means of a diagram

GRAPHEME *n* pl. -S a unit of a writing system

GRAPHIC *n* pl. -S a product of the art of representation

GRAPHITE *n* pl. -S a variety of carbon

GRAPIER comparative of grapy

GRAPIEST superlative of grapy

GRAPLIN *n* pl. -S a grapnel

GRAPLINE *n* pl. -S graplin

GRAPNEL *n* pl. -S a type of anchor

GRAPPA *n* pl. -S an Italian brandy

GRAPPLE *v* -PLED, -PLING, -PLES to struggle or contend

GRAPPLER *n* pl. -S one that grapples

GRAPY *adj* GRAPIER, GRAPIEST resembling grapes

GRASP *v* -ED, -ING, -S to seize firmly with the hand

GRASPER *n* pl. -S one that grasps

GRASS *v* -ED, -ING, -ES to cover with grass (herbaceous plants)

GRASSY *adj* GRASSIER, GRASSIEST of, resembling, or pertaining to grass GRASSILY *adv*

GRAT past tense of greet (to weep)

GRATE *v* GRATED, GRATING, GRATES to reduce to shreds by rubbing

GRATEFUL *adj* -FULLER, -FULLEST deeply thankful

GRATER *n* pl. -S one that grates

GRATIFY *v* -FIED, -FYING, -FIES to satisfy

GRATIN *n* pl. -S a type of food crust

GRATING *n* pl. -S a network of bars covering an opening

GRATIS *adj* free of charge

GRATUITY *n* pl. -ITIES a gift of money

GRAUPEL *n* pl. -S precipitation consisting of granular snow pellets

GRAVAMEN *n* pl. -MENS or -MINA the most serious part of an accusation

GRAVE *adj* GRAVER, GRAVEST extremely serious

GRAVE *v* GRAVED, GRAVEN, GRAVING, GRAVES to engrave

GRAVEL *v* -ELED, -ELING, -ELS or -ELLED, -ELLING, -ELS to pave with gravel (a mixture of rock fragments)

GRAVELLY *adj* containing gravel

GRAVELY *adv* in a grave manner

GRAVEN past participle of grave

GRAVER *n* pl. -S an engraver

GRAVEST superlative of grave

GRAVID *adj* pregnant GRAVIDLY *adv*

GRAVIDA *n* pl. -DAS or -DAE a pregnant woman

GRAVIES pl. of gravy

GRAVING present participle of grave

GRAVITON *n* pl. -S a hypothetical particle

GRAVITY *n* pl. -TIES the force of attraction toward the earth's center

GRAVURE *n* pl. -S a printing process

GRAVY *n* pl. -VIES a sauce of the fat and juices from cooked meat

GRAY *adj* GRAYER, GRAYEST of a color between white and black

GRAY *v* -ED, -ING, -S to make gray

GRAYBACK *n* pl. -S a gray bird

GRAYFISH *n* pl. -ES a dogfish

GRAYISH *adj* somewhat gray

GRAYLAG *n* pl. -S a wild goose

GRAYLING *n* pl. -S a food fish

GRAYLY *adv* in a gray manner

GRAYNESS *n* pl. -ES the state of being gray

GRAYOUT *n* pl. -S a temporary blurring of vision

GRAZE *v* GRAZED, GRAZING, GRAZES to feed on growing grass GRAZABLE *adj*

GRAZER *n* pl. -S one that grazes

GRAZIER *n* pl. -S one that grazes cattle

GRAZING *n* pl. -S land used for the feeding of animals

GRAZIOSO *adj* graceful in style

GREASE *v* GREASED, GREASING, GREASES to smear with grease (a lubricating substance)

GREASER	n pl. -S one that greases
GREASY	adj GREASIER, GREASIEST containing or resembling grease **GREASILY** adv
GREAT	adj GREATER, GREATEST large
GREAT	n pl. -S a distinguished or outstanding person
GREATEN	v -ED, -ING, -S to make greater
GREATLY	adv in a great manner
GREAVE	n pl. -S a piece of armor for the leg **GREAVED** adj
GREBE	n pl. -S a diving bird
GRECIZE	v -CIZED, -CIZING, -CIZES to provide with a Greek style
GREE	v GREED, GREEING, GREES to agree
GREED	n pl. -S excessive desire for gain or wealth
GREEDY	adj GREEDIER, GREEDIEST marked by greed **GREEDILY** adv
GREEGREE	n pl. -S grigri
GREEK	n pl. GREEK something unintelligible
GREEN	adj GREENER, GREENEST of the color of growing foliage
GREEN	v -ED, -ING, -S to become green
GREENBUG	n pl. -S a green aphid
GREENERY	n pl. -ERIES green vegetation
GREENFLY	n pl. -FLIES a green aphid
GREENIER	comparative of greeny
GREENIEST	superlative of greeny
GREENING	n pl. -S a variety of apple
GREENISH	adj somewhat green
GREENLET	n pl. -S a vireo
GREENLY	adv in a green manner
GREENTH	n pl. -S verdure
GREENY	adj GREENIER, GREENIEST somewhat green
GREET	v -ED, -ING, -S to address in a friendly and courteous way
GREET	v GRAT, GRUTTEN, GREETING, GREETS to weep
GREETER	n pl. -S one that greets
GREETING	n pl. -S a salutation
GREGO	n pl. -GOS a hooded coat
GREIGE	n pl. -S fabric in an unfinished state
GREISEN	n pl. -S a type of rock
GREMIAL	n pl. -S a lap cloth used by a bishop during a service
GREMLIN	n pl. -S a mischievous creature
GREMMIE	n pl. -S an inexperienced surfer
GREMMY	n pl. -MIES gremmie
GRENADE	n pl. -S an explosive device
GREW	past tense of grow
GREWSOME	adj -SOMER, -SOMEST gruesome
GREY	adj GREYER, GREYEST gray
GREY	v -ED, -ING, -S to gray
GREYHEN	n pl. -S the female black grouse
GREYISH	adj grayish
GREYLAG	n pl. -S graylag
GREYLY	adv grayly
GREYNESS	n pl. -ES grayness
GRIBBLE	n pl. -S a marine isopod
GRID	n pl. -S a grating
GRIDDLE	v -DLED, -DLING, -DLES to cook on a flat pan
GRIDE	v GRIDED, GRIDING, GRIDES to scrape harshly
GRIDIRON	n pl. -S a grate for broiling food
GRIEF	n pl. -S intense mental distress
GRIEVANT	n pl. -S one that submits a complaint for arbitration
GRIEVE	v GRIEVED, GRIEVING, GRIEVES to feel grief
GRIEVER	n pl. -S one that grieves
GRIEVOUS	adj causing grief
GRIFF	n pl. -S griffe
GRIFFE	n pl. -S the offspring of a black person and a mulatto
GRIFFIN	n pl. -S a mythological creature
GRIFFON	n pl. -S griffin
GRIFT	v -ED, -ING, -S to swindle
GRIFTER	n pl. -S a swindler
GRIG	n pl. -S a lively person
GRIGRI	n pl. -S a fetish or amulet
GRILL	v -ED, -ING, -S to broil on a gridiron
GRILLADE	n pl. -S a dish of grilled meat
GRILLAGE	n pl. -S a framework of timber
GRILLE	n pl. -S a grating
GRILLER	n pl. -S one that grills
GRILSE	n pl. -S a young salmon
GRIM	adj GRIMMER, GRIMMEST stern and unrelenting
GRIMACE	v -MACED, -MACING, -MACES to contort the facial features
GRIMACER	n pl. -S one that grimaces

GRIME	v GRIMED, GRIMING, GRIMES to make dirty
GRIMIER	comparative of grimy
GRIMIEST	superlative of grimy
GRIMILY	adv in a grimy manner
GRIMING	present participle of grime
GRIMLY	adv in a grim manner
GRIMMER	comparative of grim
GRIMMEST	superlative of grim
GRIMNESS	n pl. -ES the quality of being grim
GRIMY	adj GRIMIER, GRIMIEST dirty
GRIN	v GRINNED, GRINNING, GRINS to smile broadly
GRIND	v GROUND or GRINDED, GRINDING, GRINDS to wear, smooth, or sharpen by friction
GRINDER	n pl. -S one that grinds
GRINDERY	n pl. -ERIES a place where tools are ground
GRINGO	n pl. -GOS a foreigner in Latin America — an offensive term
GRINNED	past tense of grin
GRINNER	n pl. -S one that grins
GRINNING	present participle of grin
GRIP	v GRIPPED or GRIPT, GRIPPING, GRIPS to grasp
GRIPE	v GRIPED, GRIPING, GRIPES to grasp
GRIPER	n pl. -S one that gripes
GRIPEY	adj GRIPIER, GRIPIEST gripy
GRIPIER	comparative of gripy
GRIPIEST	superlative of gripy
GRIPING	present participle of gripe
GRIPPE	n pl. -S a virus disease
GRIPPED	a past tense of grip
GRIPPER	n pl. -S one that grips
GRIPPIER	comparative of grippy
GRIPPIEST	superlative of grippy
GRIPPING	present participle of grip
GRIPPLE	adj greedy
GRIPPY	adj GRIPPIER, GRIPPIEST affected with the grippe
GRIPSACK	n pl. -S a valise
GRIPT	a past tense of grip
GRIPY	adj GRIPIER, GRIPIEST causing sharp pains in the bowels
GRISEOUS	adj grayish
GRISETTE	n pl. -S a young French working-class girl
GRISKIN	n pl. -S the lean part of a loin of pork
GRISLY	adj -LIER, -LIEST horrifying
GRISON	n pl. -S a carnivorous mammal
GRIST	n pl. -S grain for grinding
GRISTLE	n pl. -S the tough part of meat
GRISTLY	adj -TLIER, -TLIEST containing gristle
GRIT	v GRITTED, GRITTING, GRITS to press the teeth together
GRITH	n pl. -S sanctuary for a limited period of time
GRITTY	adj -TIER, -TIEST plucky GRITTILY adv
GRIVET	n pl. -S a small monkey
GRIZZLE	v -ZLED, -ZLING, -ZLES to complain
GRIZZLER	n pl. -S one that grizzles
GRIZZLY	adj -ZLIER, -ZLIEST grayish
GRIZZLY	n pl. -ZLIES a large bear
GROAN	v -ED, -ING, -S to utter a low, mournful sound
GROANER	n pl. -S one that groans
GROAT	n pl. -S an old English coin
GROCER	n pl. -S a dealer in foodstuffs and household supplies
GROCERY	n pl. -CERIES a grocer's store
GROG	n pl. -S a mixture of liquor and water
GROGGERY	n pl. -GERIES a barroom
GROGGY	adj -GIER, -GIEST dazed GROGGILY adv
GROGRAM	n pl. -S a coarse silk fabric
GROGSHOP	n pl. -S a groggery
GROIN	v -ED, -ING, -S to build with intersecting arches
GROMMET	n pl. -S a reinforcing ring of metal
GROMWELL	n pl. -S an herb
GROOM	v -ED, -ING, -S to clean and care for
GROOMER	n pl. -S one that grooms
GROOVE	v GROOVED, GROOVING, GROOVES to form a groove (a long, narrow depression)
GROOVER	n pl. -S one that grooves
GROOVY	adj GROOVIER, GROOVIEST marvelous
GROPE	v GROPED, GROPING, GROPES to feel about with the hands
GROPER	n pl. -S one that gropes
GROSBEAK	n pl. -S a finch
GROSCHEN	n pl. GROSCHEN an Austrian coin

GROSS	*adj* GROSSER, GROSSEST flagrant
GROSS	*v* -ED, -ING, -ES to earn exclusive of deductions
GROSSER	*n pl.* -S a product yielding a large volume of business
GROSSLY	*adv* in a gross manner
GROSZ	*n pl.* GROSZY a Polish coin
GROT	*n pl.* -S a grotto
GROTTO	*n pl.* -TOES or -TOS a cave
GROUCH	*v* -ED, -ING, -ES to complain
GROUCHY	*adj* GROUCHIER, GROUCHIEST ill-tempered
GROUND	*v* -ED, -ING, -S to place on a foundation
GROUNDER	*n pl.* -S a type of batted baseball
GROUP	*v* -ED, -ING, -S to arrange in a group (an assemblage of persons or things)
GROUPER	*n pl.* -S a food fish
GROUPIE	*n pl.* -S a female follower of rock groups
GROUPING	*n pl.* -S a set of objects
GROUPOID	*n pl.* -S a type of mathematical set
GROUSE	*v* GROUSED, GROUSING, GROUSES to complain
GROUSER	*n pl.* -S one that grouses
GROUT	*v* -ED, -ING, -S to fill with a thin mortar
GROUTER	*n pl.* -S one that grouts
GROUTY	*adj* GROUTIER, GROUTIEST surly
GROVE	*n pl.* -S a small forested area GROVED *adj*
GROVEL	*v* -ELED, -ELING, -ELS or -ELLED, -ELLING, -ELS to crawl in an abject manner
GROVELER	*n pl.* -S one that grovels
GROW	*v* GREW, GROWN, GROWING, GROWS to cultivate GROWABLE *adj*
GROWER	*n pl.* -S one that grows
GROWL	*v* -ED, -ING, -S to utter a deep, harsh sound
GROWLER	*n pl.* -S one that growls
GROWLY	*adj* GROWLIER, GROWLIEST deep and harsh in speech
GROWN	*adj* mature
GROWNUP	*n pl.* -S a mature person
GROWTH	*n pl.* -S development
GROYNE	*n pl.* -S a structure built to protect a shore from erosion

GRUB	*v* GRUBBED, GRUBBING, GRUBS to dig
GRUBBER	*n pl.* -S one that grubs
GRUBBY	*adj* -BIER, -BIEST dirty GRUBBILY *adv*
GRUBWORM	*n pl.* -S the larva of some insects
GRUDGE	*v* GRUDGED, GRUDGING, GRUDGES to be unwilling to give or admit
GRUDGER	*n pl.* -S one that grudges
GRUEL	*v* -ELED, -ELING, -ELS or -ELLED, -ELLING, -ELS to disable by hard work
GRUELER	*n pl.* -S one that gruels
GRUELING	*n pl.* -S an exhausting experience
GRUELLED	a past tense of gruel
GRUELLER	*n pl.* -S grueler
GRUELLING	*n pl.* -S grueling
GRUESOME	*adj* -SOMER, -SOMEST repugnant
GRUFF	*adj* GRUFFER, GRUFFEST low and harsh in speech
GRUFF	*v* -ED, -ING, -S to utter in a gruff voice
GRUFFIER	comparative of gruffy
GRUFFIEST	superlative of gruffy
GRUFFILY	*adv* in a gruffy manner
GRUFFISH	*adj* somewhat gruff
GRUFFLY	*adv* in a gruff manner
GRUFFY	*adj* GRUFFIER, GRUFFIEST gruff
GRUGRU	*n pl.* -S a palm tree
GRUM	*adj* GRUMMER, GRUMMEST morose
GRUMBLE	*v* -BLED, -BLING, -BLES to mutter in discontent GRUMBLY *adj*
GRUMBLER	*n pl.* -S one that grumbles
GRUME	*n pl.* -S a thick, viscid substance
GRUMMER	comparative of grum
GRUMMEST	superlative of grum
GRUMMET	*n pl.* -S grommet
GRUMOSE	*adj* grumous
GRUMOUS	*adj* consisting of clustered grains
GRUMP	*v* -ED, -ING, -S to complain
GRUMPHIE	*n pl.* -S a pig
GRUMPHY	*n pl.* GRUMPHIES grumphie
GRUMPISH	*adj* grumpy

GRUMPY *adj* GRUMPIER, GRUMPIEST ill-tempered **GRUMPILY** *adv*

GRUNION *n pl.* -S a small food fish

GRUNT *v* -ED, -ING, -S to utter a deep, guttural sound

GRUNTER *n pl.* -S one that grunts

GRUNTLE *v* -TLED, -TLING, -TLES to put in a good humor

GRUSHIE *adj* thriving

GRUTCH *v* -ED, -ING, -ES to grudge

GRUTTEN past participle of greet (to weep)

GRYPHON *n pl.* -S griffin

GUACHARO *n pl.* -ROS or -ROES a tropical bird

GUACO *n pl.* -COS a tropical plant

GUAIAC *n pl.* -S guaiacum

GUAIACOL *n pl.* -S a chemical compound

GUAIACUM *n pl.* -S a medicinal resin

GUAIOCUM *n pl.* -S guaiacum

GUAN *n pl.* -S a large bird

GUANACO *n pl.* -COS a South American mammal

GUANASE *n pl.* -S an enzyme

GUANIDIN *n pl.* -S a chemical compound

GUANIN *n pl.* -S guanine

GUANINE *n pl.* -S a chemical compound

GUANO *n pl.* -NOS the accumulated excrement of sea birds

GUAR *n pl.* -S a drought-tolerant legume

GUARANI *n pl.* -NIS or -NIES a monetary unit of Paraguay

GUARANTY *v* -TIED, -TYING, -TIES to assume responsibility for the quality of

GUARD *v* -ED, -ING, -S to protect

GUARDANT *n pl.* -S a guardian

GUARDER *n pl.* -S one that guards

GUARDIAN *n pl.* -S one that guards

GUAVA *n pl.* -S a tropical shrub

GUAYULE *n pl.* -S a shrub that is a source of rubber

GUCK *n pl.* -S a messy substance

GUDE *n pl.* -S good

GUDGEON *v* -ED, -ING, -S to dupe

GUENON *n pl.* -S a long-tailed monkey

GUERDON *v* -ED, -ING, -S to reward

GUERILLA *n pl.* -S a member of a small independent band of soldiers

GUERNSEY *n pl.* -SEYS a woolen shirt

GUESS *v* -ED, -ING, -ES to form an opinion from little or no evidence

GUESSER *n pl.* -S one that guesses

GUEST *v* -ED, -ING, -S to appear as a visitor

GUFF *n pl.* -S foolish talk

GUFFAW *v* -ED, -ING, -S to laugh loudly

GUGGLE *v* -GLED, -GLING, GLES to gurgle

GUGLET *n pl.* -S goglet

GUID *n pl.* -S good

GUIDANCE *n pl.* -S advice

GUIDE *v* GUIDED, GUIDING, GUIDES to show the way to **GUIDABLE** *adj*

GUIDER *n pl.* -S one that guides

GUIDON *n pl.* -S a small flag

GUILD *n pl.* -S an association of people of the same trade

GUILDER *n pl.* -S a monetary unit of the Netherlands

GUILE *v* GUILED, GUILING, GUILES to beguile

GUILEFUL *adj* cunning

GUILT *n pl.* -S the fact of having committed an offense

GUILTY *adj* GUILTIER, GUILTIEST worthy of blame for an offense **GUILTILY** *adv*

GUIMPE *n pl.* -S a short blouse

GUINEA *n pl.* -S a former British coin

GUIPURE *n pl.* -S a type of lace

GUIRO *n pl.* -ROS a percussion instrument

GUISARD *n pl.* -S a masker

GUISE *v* GUISED, GUISING, GUISES to disguise

GUITAR *n pl.* -S a stringed musical instrument

GUL *n pl.* -S a design in oriental carpets

GULAR *adj* of or pertaining to the throat

GULCH *n pl.* -ES a deep, narrow ravine

GULDEN *n pl.* -S a guilder

GULES *n pl.* GULES the color red

GULF *v* -ED, -ING, -S to swallow up

GULFIER comparative of gulfy

GULFIEST superlative of gulfy

GULFLIKE *adj* resembling a deep chasm

GULFWEED *n pl.* -S a brownish seaweed

GULFY *adj* GULFIER, GULFIEST full of whirlpools

GULL v -ED, -ING, -S to deceive

GULLABLE adj gullible **GULLABLY** adv

GULLET n pl. -S the throat

GULLEY n pl. -LEYS a ravine

GULLIBLE adj easily deceived **GULLIBLY** adv

GULLY v -LIED, -LYING, -LIES to form ravines by the action of water

GULOSITY n pl. -TIES gluttony

GULP v -ED, -ING, -S to swallow rapidly

GULPER n pl. -S one that gulps

GULPY adj **GULPIER, GULPIEST** marked by gulping

GUM v **GUMMED, GUMMING, GUMS** to smear, seal, or clog with gum (a sticky, viscid substance)

GUMBO n pl. -BOS the okra plant

GUMBOIL n pl. -S an abscess in the gum

GUMBOTIL n pl. -S a sticky clay

GUMDROP n pl. -S a chewy candy

GUMLESS adj having no gum

GUMLIKE adj resembling gum

GUMMA n pl. -MAS or -MATA a soft tumor

GUMMED past tense of gum

GUMMER n pl. -S one that gums

GUMMIER comparative of gummy

GUMMIEST superlative of gummy

GUMMING present participle of gum

GUMMITE n pl. -S a mixture of various minerals

GUMMOSE adj gummy

GUMMOSIS n pl. -MOSES a disease of plants

GUMMOUS adj gummy

GUMMY adj -MIER, -MIEST resembling gum

GUMPTION n pl. -S shrewdness

GUMSHOE v -SHOED, -SHOEING, -SHOES to investigate stealthily

GUMTREE n pl. -S a tree that yields gum

GUMWEED n pl. -S a plant covered with a gummy substance

GUMWOOD n pl. -S the wood of a gumtree

GUN v **GUNNED, GUNNING, GUNS** to shoot with a gun (a portable firearm)

GUNBOAT n pl. -S an armed vessel

GUNDOG n pl. -S a hunting dog

GUNFIGHT v -FOUGHT, -FIGHTING, -FIGHTS to fight with guns

GUNFIRE n pl. -S the firing of guns

GUNFLINT n pl. -S the flint in a flintlock

GUNFOUGHT past tense of gunfight

GUNK n pl. -S filthy, sticky, or greasy matter

GUNLESS adj having no gun

GUNLOCK n pl. -S the mechanism which ignites the charge of a gun

GUNMAN n pl. -MEN one who is armed with a gun

GUNMETAL n pl. -S a dark gray color

GUNNED past tense of gun

GUNNEL n pl. -S a marine fish

GUNNEN past participle of gin

GUNNER n pl. -S one that operates a gun

GUNNERY n pl. -NERIES the use of guns

GUNNING n pl. -S the sport of hunting with a gun

GUNNY n pl. -NIES a coarse fabric

GUNPAPER n pl. -S a type of explosive paper

GUNPLAY n pl. -PLAYS the shooting of guns

GUNPOINT n pl. -S the point or aim of a gun

GUNROOM n pl. -S a room on a British warship

GUNSEL n pl. -S a gunman

GUNSHIP n pl. -S an armed helicopter

GUNSHOT n pl. -S a projectile fired from a gun

GUNSMITH n pl. -S one who makes or repairs firearms

GUNSTOCK n pl. -S the rear wooden part of a rifle

GUNWALE n pl. -S the upper edge of a ship's side

GUPPY n pl. -PIES a small, tropical fish

GURGE v **GURGED, GURGING, GURGES** to swirl

GURGLE v -GLED, -GLING, -GLES to flow unevenly

GURGLET n pl. -S goglet

GURNARD n pl. -S a marine fish

GURNET n pl. -S a gurnard

GURNEY n pl. -NEYS a wheeled cot

GURRY n pl. -RIES fish offal

GURSH n pl. -ES qursh

GURU n pl. -S a Hindu spiritual teacher

GURUSHIP n pl. -S the office of a guru

GUSH   v -ED, -ING, -ES to flow forth forcefully

GUSHER   n pl. -S a gushing oil well

GUSHY   adj GUSHIER, GUSHIEST overly sentimental **GUSHILY** adv

GUSSET   v -ED, -ING, -S to furnish with a reinforcing piece of material

GUST   v -ED, -ING, -S to blow in gusts (sudden blasts of wind)

GUSTABLE   n pl. -S a savory food

GUSTIER   comparative of gusty

GUSTIEST   superlative of gusty

GUSTILY   adv in a gusty manner

GUSTLESS   adj having no gusts

GUSTO   n pl. -TOES vigorous enjoyment

GUSTY   adj GUSTIER, GUSTIEST blowing in gusts

GUT   v GUTTED, GUTTING, GUTS to remove the guts (intestines) of

GUTLESS   adj lacking courage

GUTLIKE   adj resembling guts

GUTSY   adj GUTSIER, GUTSIEST brave

GUTTA   n pl. -TAE a drop of liquid

GUTTATE   adj resembling a drop

GUTTATED   adj guttate

GUTTED   past tense of gut

GUTTER   v -ED, -ING, -S to form channels for draining off water

GUTTERY   adj marked by extreme vulgarity or indecency

GUTTIER   comparative of gutty

GUTTIEST   superlative of gutty

GUTTING   present participle of gut

GUTTLE   v -TLED, -TLING, -TLES to eat rapidly

GUTTLER   n pl. -S one that guttles

GUTTURAL   n pl. -S a throaty sound

GUTTY   adj -TIER, -TIEST marked by courage

GUY   v -ED, -ING, -S to ridicule

GUYOT   n pl. -S a flat-topped seamount

GUZZLE   v -ZLED, -ZLING, -ZLES to drink rapidly

GUZZLER   n pl. -S one that guzzles

GWEDUC   n pl. -S geoduck

GWEDUCK   n pl. -S geoduck

GYBE   v GYBED, GYBING, GYBES to shift from side to side while sailing

GYM   n pl. -S a room for athletic activities

GYMKHANA   n pl. -S an athletic meet

GYMNASIA   n/pl gyms

GYMNAST   n pl. -S one who is skilled in physical exercises

GYNAECEA   n/pl gynecia

GYNAECIA   n/pl gynecia

GYNANDRY   n pl. -DRIES the condition of having both male and female sexual organs

GYNARCHY   n pl. -CHIES government by women

GYNECIA   pl. of gynecium

GYNECIC   adj pertaining to women

GYNECIUM   n pl. -CIA the pistil of a flower

GYNECOID   adj resembling a woman

GYNIATRY   n pl. -TRIES the treatment of women's diseases

GYNOECIA   n/pl gynecia

GYP   v GYPPED, GYPPING, GYPS to swindle

GYPPER   n pl. -S one that gyps

GYPSEIAN   adj of or pertaining to gypsies

GYPSEOUS   adj containing gypsum

GYPSUM   n pl. -S a mineral

GYPSY   v -SIED, -SYING, -SIES to live like a gypsy (a wanderer)

GYPSYDOM   n pl. -S the realm of gypsies

GYPSYISH   adj resembling a gypsy

GYPSYISM   n pl. -S the mode of life of gypsies

GYRAL   adj gyratory **GYRALLY** adv

GYRATE   v -RATED, -RATING, -RATES to revolve or rotate

GYRATION   n pl. -S the act of gyrating

GYRATOR   n pl. -S one that gyrates

GYRATORY   adj moving in a circle or spiral

GYRE   v GYRED, GYRING, GYRES to move in a circle or spiral

GYRENE   n pl. -S a marine

GYRI   pl. of gyrus

GYRING   present participle of gyre

GYRO   n pl. -ROS a gyroscope

GYROIDAL   adj spiral in arrangement

GYRON   n pl. -S a heraldic design

GYROSE   adj marked with wavy lines

GYROSTAT   n pl. -S a type of stabilizing device

GYRUS   n pl. -RI a ridge in the brain

GYVE   v GYVED, GYVING, GYVES to shackle

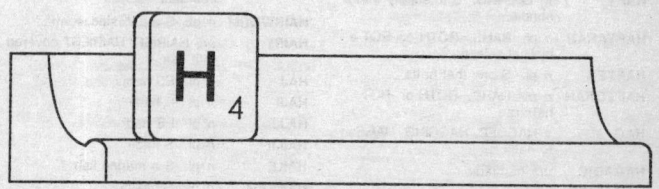

HA	*n* pl. -S a sound of surprise	**HACKNEY**	*v* -NEYED, -NEYING, -NEYS to make common
HAAF	*n* pl. -S a deep-sea fishing ground	**HACKSAW**	*n* pl. -S a type of saw
HAAR	*n* pl. -S a fog	**HACKWORK**	*n* pl. -S artistic work done according to formula
HABANERA	*n* pl. -S a Cuban dance	**HAD**	a past tense of have
HABDALAH	*n* pl. -S a Jewish ceremony	**HADAL**	*adj* pertaining to deep parts of the ocean
HABILE	*adj* skillful	**HADARIM**	a pl. of heder
HABIT	*v* -ED, -ING, -S to clothe or dress	**HADDEST**	a past 2d person sing. of have
HABITAN	*n* pl. -S a French settler	**HADDOCK**	*n* pl. -S a food fish
HABITANT	*n* pl. -S an inhabitant	**HADE**	*v* HADED, HADING, HADES to incline
HABITAT	*n* pl. -S the natural environment of an organism	**HADJ**	*n* pl. -ES a pilgrimage to Mecca
HABITUAL	*adj* occurring frequently or constantly	**HADJEE**	*n* pl. -S hadji
HABITUDE	*n* pl. -S a usual course of action	**HADJI**	*n* pl. -S one who has made a hadj
HABITUE	*n* pl. -S a frequent customer	**HADRON**	*n* pl. -S an elementary particle **HADRONIC** *adj*
HABITUS	*n* pl. HABITUS bodily build and constitution	**HADST**	a past 2d person sing. of have
HABU	*n* pl. -S a poisonous snake	**HAE**	*v* HAED, HAEN, HAEING, HAES to have
HACEK	*n* pl. -S a mark placed over a letter to modify it	**HAEM**	*n* pl. -S heme
HACHURE	*v* -CHURED, -CHURING, -CHURES to make a hatching on a map	**HAEMAL**	*adj* hemal
		HAEMATAL	*adj* hemal
HACIENDA	*n* pl. -S an estate	**HAEMATIC**	*n* pl. -S hematic
HACK	*v* -ED, -ING, -S to cut or chop roughly	**HAEMATIN**	*n* pl. -S hematin
		HAEMIC	*adj* hemic
HACKBUT	*n* pl. -S a type of gun	**HAEMIN**	*n* pl. -S hemin
HACKEE	*n* pl. -S a chipmunk	**HAEMOID**	*adj* hemoid
HACKER	*n* pl. -S one that hacks	**HAEN**	past participle of hae
HACKIE	*n* pl. -S a taxicab driver	**HAERES**	*n* pl. -REDES heres
HACKLE	*v* -LED, -LING, -LES to hack	**HAET**	*n* pl. -S a small amount
HACKLER	*n* pl. -S one that hackles	**HAFFET**	*n* pl. -S the cheekbone and temple
HACKLY	*adj* -LIER, -LIEST jagged		
HACKMAN	*n* pl. -MEN a hackie	**HAFFIT**	*n* pl. -S haffet

HAFIZ *n* pl. HAFIS a Muslim who knows the Koran by heart

HAFNIUM *n* pl. -S a metallic element

HAFT *v* -ED, -ING, -S to supply with a handle

HAFTARAH *n* pl. -RAHS, -ROTH or -ROT a biblical selection

HAFTER *n* pl. -S one that hafts

HAFTORAH *n* pl. -RAHS, -ROTH or -ROT haftarah

HAG *v* HAGGED, HAGGING, HAGS to hack

HAGADIC *adj* haggadic

HAGADIST *n* pl. -S a haggadic scholar

HAGBERRY *n* pl. -RIES a small cherry

HAGBORN *adj* born of a witch

HAGBUSH *n* pl. -ES a large tree

HAGBUT *n* pl. -S hackbut

HAGDON *n* pl. -S a seabird

HAGFISH *n* pl. -ES an eellike fish

HAGGADIC *adj* pertaining to the story of Exodus

HAGGARD *n* pl. -S an adult hawk

HAGGED past tense of hag

HAGGING present participle of hag

HAGGIS *n* pl. -GISES a Scottish dish

HAGGISH *adj* resembling a hag

HAGGLE *v* -GLED, -GLING, -GLES to bargain

HAGGLER *n* pl. -S one that haggles

HAGRIDE *v* -RODE, -RIDDEN, -RIDING, -RIDES to harass

HAH *n* pl. -S ha

HAIK *n* pl. HAIKS or HAIKA an outer garment worn by Arabs

HAIKU *n* pl. HAIKU a Japanese poem

HAIL *v* -ED, -ING, -S to welcome

HAILER *n* pl. -S one that hails

HAIR *n* pl. -S a threadlike growth

HAIRBALL *n* pl. -S a ball of hair

HAIRBAND *n* pl. -S a headband

HAIRCAP *n* pl. -S a hat

HAIRCUT *n* pl. -S a cutting of the hair

HAIRDO *n* pl. -DOS a style of wearing the hair

HAIRED *adj* having hair

HAIRIER comparative of hairy

HAIRIEST superlative of hairy

HAIRLESS *adj* having no hair

HAIRLIKE *adj* resembling a hair

HAIRLINE *n* pl. -S a very thin line

HAIRLOCK *n* pl. -S a lock of hair

HAIRPIN *n* pl. -S a hair fastener

HAIRWORK *n* pl. -S the making of articles from hair

HAIRWORM *n* pl. -S a parasitic worm

HAIRY *adj* HAIRIER, HAIRIEST covered with hair

HAJ *n* pl. -ES hadj

HAJI *n* pl. -S hadji

HAJJ *n* pl. -ES hadj

HAJJI *n* pl. -S hadji

HAKE *n* pl. -S a marine fish

HAKEEM *n* pl. -S hakim

HAKIM *n* pl. -S a Muslim physician

HALAKAH *n* pl. -KOTH or -KAHS the legal part of the Talmud

HALAKIC *adj* pertaining to the halakah

HALAKIST *n* pl. -S a halakic writer

HALAKOTH a pl. of halakah

HALALA *n* pl. -S a Saudi Arabian coin

HALALAH *n* pl. -S halala

HALATION *n* pl. -S a blurring of light in photographs

HALAVAH *n* pl. -S halvah

HALBERD *n* pl. -S an axlike weapon of the 15th and 16th centuries

HALBERT *n* pl. -S halberd

HALCYON *n* pl. -S a mythical bird

HALE *adj* HALER, HALEST healthy

HALE *v* HALED, HALING, HALES to compel to go

HALENESS *n* pl. -ES the state of being hale

HALER *n* pl. -LERS or -LERU a Czechoslovakian coin

HALEST superlative of hale

HALF *n* pl. HALVES one of two equal parts

HALFBACK *n* pl. -S a football player

HALFBEAK *n* pl. -S a marine fish

HALFLIFE *n* pl. -LIVES a measure of radioactive decay

HALFNESS *n* pl. -ES the state of being half

HALFTIME *n* pl. -S an intermission in a football game

HALFTONE *n* pl. -S a shade between light and dark

HALFWAY *adj* being in the middle

HALIBUT *n* pl. -S a flatfish

HALID *n* pl. -S halide

HALIDE *n* pl. -S a chemical compound

HALIDOM   *n* pl. -S something holy

HALIDOME   *n* pl. -S halidom

HALING   present participle of hale

HALITE   *n* pl. -S a mineral

HALITUS   *n* pl. -ES an exhalation

HALL   *n* pl. -S a large room for assembly

HALLAH   *n* pl. -LAHS, -LOTH or -LOT challah

HALLEL   *n* pl. -S a chant of praise

HALLIARD   *n* pl. -S halyard

HALLMARK   *v* -ED, -ING, -S to mark with an official stamp

HALLO   *v* -ED, -ING, -S or -ES to shout

HALLOA   *v* -ED, -ING, -S to hallo

HALLOO   *v* -ED, -ING, -S to hallo

HALLOT   a pl. of hallah

HALLOTH   a pl. of hallah

HALLOW   *v* -ED, -ING, -S to make holy

HALLOWER   *n* pl. -S one that hallows

HALLUX   *n* pl. -LUCES the big toe

HALLWAY   *n* pl. -WAYS a hall

HALM   *n* pl. -S haulm

HALO   *v* -ED, -ING, -ES or -S to form a halo (a ring of light)

HALOGEN   *n* pl. -S a nonmetallic element

HALOID   *n* pl. -S a chemical salt

HALOLIKE   *adj* resembling a halo

HALT   *v* -ED, -ING, -S to stop

HALTER   *v* -ED, -ING, -S to put restraint upon

HALTERE   *n* pl. -S a pair of wings of an insect

HALTLESS   *adj* not hesitant

HALUTZ   *n* pl. -LUTZIM an Israeli farmer

HALVA   *n* pl. -S halvah

HALVAH   *n* pl. -S a Turkish confection

HALVE   *v* HALVED, HALVING, HALVES to divide into two equal parts

HALVERS   *n* pl. HALVERS half shares

HALVES   pl. of half

HALYARD   *n* pl. -S a line used to hoist a sail

HAM   *v* HAMMED, HAMMING, HAMS to overact

HAMAL   *n* pl. -S a porter in eastern countries

HAMARTIA   *n* pl. -S a defect of character

HAMATE   *n* pl. -S a wrist bone

HAMAUL   *n* pl. -S hamal

HAMBURG   *n* pl. -S a patty of ground beef

HAME   *n* pl. -S a part of a horse collar

HAMLET   *n* pl. -S a small town

HAMMAL   *n* pl. -S hamal

HAMMED   past tense of ham

HAMMER   *v* -ED, -ING, -S to strike repeatedly

HAMMERER   *n* pl. -S one that hammers

HAMMIER   comparative of hammy

HAMMIEST   superlative of hammy

HAMMILY   *adv* in a hammy manner

HAMMING   present participle of ham

HAMMOCK   *n* pl. -S a hanging cot

HAMMY   *adj* -MIER, -MIEST overly theatrical

HAMPER   *v* -ED, -ING, -S to hinder

HAMPERER   *n* pl. -S one that hampers

HAMSTER   *n* pl. -S a burrowing rodent

HAMULUS   *n* pl. -LI a small hook
HAMULAR, HAMULATE,
HAMULOSE, HAMULOUS *adj*

HAMZA   *n* pl. -S an Arabic diacritical mark

HAMZAH   *n* pl. -S hamza

HANAPER   *n* pl. -S a wicker receptacle

HANCE   *n* pl. -S a side of an arch

HAND   *v* -ED, -ING, -S to present with the hand (the end of the forearm)

HANDBAG   *n* pl. -S a small carrying bag

HANDBALL   *n* pl. -S a small rubber ball

HANDBILL   *n* pl. -S a circular

HANDBOOK   *n* pl. -S a manual

HANDCAR   *n* pl. -S a hand-operated railroad car

HANDCART   *n* pl. -S a cart pushed by hand

HANDCUFF   *v* -ED, -ING, -S to fetter with restraining cuffs

HANDFAST   *v* -ED, -ING, -S to grip securely

HANDFUL   *n* pl. HANDFULS or HANDSFUL as much as the hand can hold

HANDGRIP   *n* pl. -S a grip by the hand or hands

HANDGUN   *n* pl. -S a small firearm

HANDHOLD   *n* pl. -S a handgrip

HANDICAP   *v* -CAPPED, -CAPPING, -CAPS to hinder

HANDIER   comparative of handy

HANDIEST   superlative of handy

HANDILY   *adv* in a handy manner

HANDLE   *v* -DLED, -DLING, -DLES to touch with the hands

HANDLER   *n* pl. -S one that handles

HANDLESS *adj* having no hands

HANDLIKE *adj* resembling a hand

HANDLING *n* pl. -S the manner in which something is handled

HANDLIST *n* pl. -S a reference list

HANDLOOM *n* pl. -S a manually operated loom

HANDMADE *adj* made by hand

HANDMAID *n* pl. -S a female servant

HANDOFF *n* pl. -S a play in football

HANDOUT *n* pl. -S something given out free

HANDPICK *v* -ED, -ING, -S to choose carefully

HANDRAIL *n* pl. -S a railing used for support

HANDSAW *n* pl. -S a saw used manually

HANDSEL *v* -SELED, -SELING, -SELS or -SELLED, -SELLING, -SELS to give a gift to

HANDSET *n* pl. -S a type of telephone

HANDSEWN *adj* sewn by hand

HANDSFUL a pl. of handful

HANDSOME *adj* -SOMER, -SOMEST attractive

HANDWORK *n* pl. -S manual labor

HANDWRIT *adj* written by hand

HANDY *adj* HANDIER, HANDIEST convenient for handling

HANDYMAN *n* pl. -MEN a man who does odd jobs

HANG *v* HUNG or HANGED, HANGING, HANGS to attach from above only **HANGABLE** *adj*

HANGAR *v* -ED, -ING, -S to place in an aircraft shelter

HANGBIRD *n* pl. -S a type of bird

HANGDOG *n* pl. -S a sneaky person

HANGER *n* pl. -S one that hangs

HANGFIRE *n* pl. -S a delay in detonation

HANGING *n* pl. -S an execution by strangling with a suspended noose

HANGMAN *n* pl. -MEN an executioner

HANGNAIL *n* pl. -S an agnail

HANGNEST *n* pl. -S a hangbird

HANGOUT *n* pl. -S a place often visited

HANGOVER *n* pl. -S the physical effects following a drinking binge

HANGTAG *n* pl. -S a type of tag used commercially

HANGUP *n* pl. -S an inhibition or obsession

HANK *v* -ED, -ING, -S to fasten a sail

HANKER *v* -ED, -ING, -S to long for

HANKERER *n* pl. -S one that hankers

HANKIE *n* pl. -S hanky

HANKY *n* pl. -KIES a handkerchief

HANSE *n* pl. -S a guild of merchants

HANSEL *v* -SELED, -SELING, -SELS or -SELLED, -SELLING, -SELS to handsel

HANSOM *n* pl. -S a light carriage

HANT *v* -ED, -ING, -S to haunt

HANTLE *n* pl. -S a large amount

HANUMAN *n* pl. -S an East Indian monkey

HAOLE *n* pl. -S one who is not a native Hawaiian

HAP *v* HAPPED, HAPPING, HAPS to happen

HAPAX *n* pl. -ES a word that occurs only once

HAPLESS *adj* luckless

HAPLITE *n* pl. -S aplite

HAPLOID *n* pl. -S a cell having only one set of chromosomes

HAPLOIDY *n* pl. -DIES the state of being a haploid

HAPLONT *n* pl. -S an organism having a particular chromosomal structure

HAPLOPIA *n* pl. -S normal vision

HAPLOSIS *n* pl. -LOSES the halving of the chromosome number

HAPLY *adv* by chance

HAPPED past tense of hap

HAPPEN *v* -ED, -ING, -S to occur

HAPPING present participle of hap

HAPPY *adj* -PIER, -PIEST marked by joy **HAPPILY** *adv*

HAPTEN *n* pl. -S a substance similar to an antigen **HAPTENIC** *adj*

HAPTENE *n* pl. -S hapten

HAPTIC *adj* pertaining to the sense of touch

HAPTICAL *adj* haptic

HARANGUE *v* -RANGUED, -RANGUING, -RANGUES to deliver a tirade to

HARASS *v* -ED, -ING, ES to bother persistently

HARASSER *n* pl. -S one that harasses

HARBOR *v* -ED, -ING, -S to shelter

HARBORER *n* pl. -S one that harbors

HARBOUR *v* -ED, -ING, -S to harbor

HARD *adj* HARDER, HARDEST firm and unyielding

HARDBACK *n* pl. -S a hardcover book

HARDBALL *n* pl. -S baseball

HARDBOOT *n* pl. -S a horseman

HARDCASE *adj* tough

HARDCORE *adj* unyielding

HARDEN *v* -ED, -ING, -S to make hard

HARDENER *n* pl. -S one that hardens

HARDHACK *n* pl. -S a woody plant

HARDHAT *n* pl. -S a conservative

HARDHEAD *n* pl. -S a practical person

HARDIER comparative of hardy

HARDIES pl. of hardy

HARDIEST superlative of hardy

HARDILY *adv* in a hardy manner

HARDLY *adv* scarcely

HARDNESS *n* pl. -ES the state of being hard

HARDPAN *n* pl. -S a layer of hard subsoil

HARDS *n/pl* the coarse refuse of flax

HARDSET *adj* rigid

HARDSHIP *n* pl. -S a difficult, painful condition

HARDTACK *n* pl. -S a hard biscuit

HARDTOP *n* pl. -S a type of car

HARDWARE *n* pl. -S metal goods

HARDWOOD *n* pl. -S the hard, compact wood of various trees

HARDY *adj* -DIER, -DIEST very sturdy

HARDY *n* pl. -DIES a blacksmith's chisel

HARE *v* HARED, HARING, HARES to run

HAREBELL *n* pl. -S a perennial herb

HAREEM *n* pl. -S harem

HARELIKE *adj* resembling a hare (a long-eared mammal)

HARELIP *n* pl. -S a deformity of the upper lip

HAREM *n* pl. -S the section of a Muslim household reserved for women

HARIANA *n* pl. -S a breed of cattle

HARICOT *n* pl. -S the seed of various string beans

HARIJAN *n* pl. -S an outcaste in India

HARING present participle of hare

HARK *v* -ED, -ING, -S to listen to

HARKEN *v* -ED, -ING, -S to hearken

HARKENER *n* pl. -S one that harkens

HARL *n* pl. -S a herl

HARLOT *n* pl. -S a prostitute

HARLOTRY *n* pl. -RIES prostitution

HARM *v* -ED, -ING, -S to injure

HARMER *n* pl. -S one that harms

HARMFUL *adj* capable of harming

HARMIN *n* pl. -S harmine

HARMINE *n* pl. -S an alkaloid used as a stimulant

HARMLESS *adj* not harmful

HARMONIC *n* pl. -S an overtone

HARMONY *n* pl. -NIES agreement

HARNESS *v* -ED, -ING, -ES to put tackle on a draft animal

HARP *v* -ED, -ING, -S to play on a harp (a type of stringed musical instrument)

HARPER *n* pl. -S a harpist

HARPIES pl. of harpy

HARPIN *n* pl. -S harping

HARPING *n* pl. -S a wooden plank used in shipbuilding

HARPIST *n* pl. -S one that plays the harp

HARPOON *v* -ED, -ING, -S to strike with a harpoon

HARPY *n* pl. -PIES a shrewish person

HARRIDAN *n* pl. -S a haggard woman

HARRIED past tense of harry

HARRIER *n* pl. -S a hunting dog

HARRIES present 3d person sing. of harry

HARROW *v* -ED, -ING, -S to break up and level soil

HARROWER *n* pl. -S one that harrows

HARRUMPH *v* -ED, -ING, -S to make a guttural sound

HARRY *v* -RIED, -RYING, -RIES to pillage

HARSH *adj* HARSHER, HARSHEST severe

HARSHEN *v* -ED, -ING, -S to make harsh

HARSHLY *adv* in a harsh manner

HARSLET *n* pl. -S haslet

HART *n* pl. -S a male deer

HARTAL *n* pl. -S a stoppage of work

HARUSPEX *n* pl. -PICES a soothsayer of ancient Rome

HARVEST *v* -ED, -ING, -S to gather a crop

HAS a present 3d person sing. of have

HASH *v* -ED, -ING, -ES to mince

HASHEESH *n* pl. -ES hashish

HASHISH *n* pl. -ES a mild narcotic

HASLET *n* pl. -S the edible viscera of an animal

HASP	v -ED, -ING, -S to fasten with a clasp	**HATRED**	n pl. -S intense dislike or aversion
HASSEL	n pl. -S an argument	**HATSFUL**	a pl. of hatful
HASSLE	v -SLED, -SLING, -SLES to argue	**HATTED**	past tense of hat
HASSOCK	n pl. -S a footstool	**HATTER**	n pl. -S a hatmaker
HAST	a present 2d person sing. of have	**HATTERIA**	n pl. -S a reptile
HASTATE	adj triangular	**HATTING**	present participle of hat
HASTE	v HASTED, HASTING, HASTES to hasten	**HAUBERK**	n pl. -S a coat of armor
		HAUGH	n pl. -S a low-lying meadow
HASTEFUL	adj hasty	**HAUGHTY**	adj -TIER, -TIEST arrogant
HASTEN	v -ED, -ING, -S to hurry	**HAUL**	v -ED, -ING, -S to pull with force
HASTENER	n pl. -S one that hastens		
HASTING	present participle of haste	**HAULAGE**	n pl. -S the act of hauling
HASTY	adj HASTIER, HASTIEST speedy **HASTILY** adv	**HAULER**	n pl. -S one that hauls
		HAULIER	n pl. -S hauler
HAT	v HATTED, HATTING, HATS to provide with a hat (a covering for the head)	**HAULM**	n pl. -S a plant stem
		HAULMY	adj HAULMIER, HAULMIEST having haulms
HATABLE	adj hateable	**HAULYARD**	n pl. -S halyard
HATBAND	n pl. -S a band worn on a hat	**HAUNCH**	n pl. -ES the hindquarter **HAUNCHED** adj
HATBOX	n pl. -ES a box for a hat		
HATCH	v -ED, -ING, -ES to bring forth young from an egg	**HAUNT**	v -ED, -ING, -S to visit frequently
		HAUNTER	n pl. -S one that haunts
HATCHECK	adj pertaining to the checking of hats	**HAUSEN**	n pl. -S a Russian sturgeon
HATCHEL	v -ELED, -ELING, -ELS or -ELLED, -ELLING, -ELS to separate flax fibers with a comb	**HAUSFRAU**	n pl. -FRAUS or -FRAUEN a housewife
		HAUTBOIS	n pl. HAUTBOIS hautboy
HATCHER	n pl. -S one that hatches	**HAUTBOY**	n pl. -BOYS an oboe
HATCHERY	n pl. -ERIES a place for hatching eggs	**HAUTEUR**	n pl. -S haughty manner or spirit
HATCHET	n pl. -S a small ax	**HAVDALAH**	n pl. -S habdalah
HATCHING	n pl. -S a series of lines used to show shading	**HAVE**	v past 2d person sing. HAD, HADDEST or HADST, present participle HAVING, present 2d person sing. HAVE or HAST, 3d person sing. HAS or HATH to be in possession of
HATCHWAY	n pl. -WAYS an opening in the deck of a ship		
HATE	v HATED, HATING, HATES to despise		
		HAVE	n pl. -S a wealthy person
HATEABLE	adj meriting hatred	**HAVELOCK**	n pl. -S a covering for a cap
HATEFUL	adj detestable	**HAVEN**	v -ED, -ING, -S to shelter
HATER	n pl. -S one that hates	**HAVER**	v -ED, -ING, -S to hem and haw
HATFUL	n pl. HATSFUL or HATFULS as much as a hat can hold	**HAVEREL**	n pl. -S a fool
		HAVIOR	n pl. -S behavior
HATH	a present 3d person sing. of have	**HAVIOUR**	n pl. -S havior
HATING	present participle of hate	**HAVOC**	v -OCKED, -OCKING, -OCS to destroy
HATLESS	adj lacking a hat		
HATLIKE	adj resembling a hat	**HAVOCKER**	n pl. -S one that havocs
HATMAKER	n pl. -S one that makes hats	**HAW**	v -ED, -ING, -S to turn left
HATPIN	n pl. -S a pin for securing a hat	**HAWFINCH**	n pl. -ES a Eurasian finch
HATRACK	n pl. -S a rack for hats	**HAWK**	v -ED, -ING, -S to peddle
		HAWKBILL	n pl. -S a sea turtle

HAWKER *n* pl. -S one that hawks

HAWKEY *n* pl. -EYS a hawkie

HAWKIE *n* pl. -S a white-faced cow

HAWKING *n* pl. -S falconry

HAWKISH *adj* warlike

HAWKLIKE *adj* resembling a hawk (a bird of prey)

HAWKMOTH *n* pl. -S a large moth

HAWKNOSE *n* pl. -S a large, curved nose

HAWKSHAW *n* pl. -S a detective

HAWKWEED *n* pl. -S a weedlike herb

HAWSE *n* pl. -S a part of a ship's bow

HAWSER *n* pl. -S a mooring rope

HAWTHORN *n* pl. -S a thorny shrub

HAY *v* -ED, -ING, -S to convert into hay (grass, cut and dried for fodder)

HAYCOCK *n* pl. -S a pile of hay

HAYER *n* pl. -S one that hays

HAYFORK *n* pl. -S a tool for pitching hay

HAYING *n* pl. -S the season for harvesting hay

HAYLAGE *n* pl. -S a type of hay

HAYLOFT *n* pl. -S a loft for hay storage

HAYMAKER *n* pl. -S one that makes hay

HAYMOW *n* pl. -S a hayloft

HAYRACK *n* pl. -S a frame used in hauling hay

HAYRICK *n* pl. -S a haystack

HAYRIDE *n* pl. -S a wagon ride

HAYSEED *n* pl. -S a bumpkin

HAYSTACK *n* pl. -S a pile of hay

HAYWARD *n* pl. -S an officer who tends cattle

HAYWIRE *n* pl. -S wire used in baling hay

HAZAN *n* pl. -ZANIM or -ZANS a cantor

HAZARD *v* -ED, -ING, -S to venture

HAZE *v* HAZED, HAZING, HAZES to subject to a humiliating initiation

HAZEL *n* pl. -S a shrub

HAZELLY *adj* yellowish brown

HAZELNUT *n* pl. -S an edible nut

HAZER *n* pl. -S one that hazes

HAZIER comparative of hazy

HAZIEST superlative of hazy

HAZILY *adv* in a hazy manner

HAZINESS *n* pl. -ES the state of being hazy

HAZING *n* pl. -S an attempt to embarrass or ridicule

HAZY *adj* HAZIER, HAZIEST unclear

HAZZAN *n* pl. HAZZANIM or HAZZANS hazan

HE *n* pl. -S a male person

HEAD *v* -ED, -ING, -S to be chief of

HEADACHE *n* pl. -S a pain inside the head

HEADACHY *adj* -ACHIER, -ACHIEST having a headache

HEADBAND *n* pl. -S a band worn on the head

HEADER *n* pl. -S a grain harvester

HEADGATE *n* pl. -S a gate to control the flow of water

HEADGEAR *n* pl. -S a covering for the head

HEADHUNT *v* -ED, -ING, -S to seek out, decapitate, and preserve the heads of enemies

HEADIER comparative of heady

HEADIEST superlative of heady

HEADILY *adv* in a heady manner

HEADING *n* pl. -S a title

HEADLAMP *n* pl. -S a light on the front of a car

HEADLAND *n* pl. -S a cliff

HEADLESS *adj* lacking a head

HEADLINE *v* -LINED, -LINING, -LINES to provide with a title

HEADLOCK *n* pl. -S a wrestling hold

HEADLONG *adj* rash; impetuous

HEADMAN *n* pl. -MEN a foreman

HEADMOST *adj* foremost

HEADNOTE *n* pl. -S a prefixed note

HEADPIN *n* pl. -S a bowling pin

HEADRACE *n* pl. -S a water channel

HEADREST *n* pl. -S a support for the head

HEADROOM *n* pl. -S clear vertical space

HEADSAIL *n* pl. -S a type of sail

HEADSET *n* pl. -S a pair of earphones

HEADSHIP *n* pl. -S the position of a leader

HEADSMAN *n* pl. -MEN an executioner

HEADSTAY *n* pl. -STAYS a support for a ship's foremast

HEADWAY *n* pl. -WAYS forward movement

HEADWIND *n* pl. -S an oncoming wind

HEADWORD *n* pl. -S a word put at the beginning

HEADWORK *n* pl. -S mental work

HEADY *adj* HEADIER, HEADIEST intoxicating

HEAL *v* -ED, -ING, -S to make sound or whole **HEALABLE** *adj*

HEALER *n* pl. -S one that heals

HEALTH n pl. -S the physical condition of an organism

HEALTHY adj HEALTHIER, HEALTHIEST having good health

HEAP v -ED, -ING, -S to pile up

HEAR v HEARD, HEARING, HEARS to perceive by the ear **HEARABLE** adj

HEARER n pl. -S one that hears

HEARING n pl. -S a preliminary examination

HEARKEN v -ED, -ING, -S to listen to

HEARSAY n pl. -SAYS secondhand information

HEARSE v HEARSED, HEARSING, HEARSES to transport in a hearse (a vehicle for conveying corpses)

HEART v -ED, -ING, -S to hearten

HEARTEN v -ED, -ING, -S to give courage to

HEARTH n pl. -S the floor of a fireplace

HEARTY adj HEARTIER, HEARTIEST very friendly **HEARTILY** adv

HEARTY n pl. HEARTIES a comrade

HEAT v HEATED or HET, HEATING, HEATS to make hot **HEATABLE** adj

HEATEDLY adv in an inflamed or excited manner

HEATER n pl. -S an apparatus for heating

HEATH n pl. -S an evergreen shrub

HEATHEN n pl. -S an uncivilized person

HEATHER n pl. -S an evergreen shrub **HEATHERY** adj

HEATHY adj HEATHIER, HEATHIEST abounding in heath

HEATLESS adj having no warmth

HEAUME n pl. -S a medieval helmet

HEAVE v HEAVED or HOVE, HEAVING, HEAVES to lift forcefully

HEAVEN n pl. -S the sky

HEAVENLY adj -LIER, -LIEST full of beauty and peace

HEAVER n pl. -S one that heaves

HEAVIER comparative of heavy

HEAVIES pl. of heavy

HEAVING present participle of heave

HEAVY adj HEAVIER, HEAVIEST having much weight **HEAVILY** adv

HEAVY n pl. HEAVIES a villain

HEAVYSET adj solidly built; stocky

HEBDOMAD n pl. -S the number seven

HEBETATE v -TATED, -TATING, -TATES to make dull

HEBETIC adj pertaining to puberty

HEBETUDE n pl. -S mental dullness

HEBRAIZE v -IZED, -IZING, -IZES to make Hebrew

HECATOMB n pl. -S a great sacrifice or slaughter

HECK n pl. -S hell

HECKLE v -LED, -LING, -LES to harass a speaker

HECKLER n pl. -S one that heckles

HECTARE n pl. -S a unit of area

HECTIC adj filled with turmoil . **HECTICLY** adv

HECTICAL adj hectic

HECTOR v -ED, -ING, -S to bully

HEDDLE n pl. -S a part of a loom

HEDER n pl. HEDERS or HADARIM a Jewish school

HEDGE v HEDGED, HEDGING, HEDGES to surround with a hedge

HEDGER n pl. -S one that hedges

HEDGEHOG n pl. -S a small mammal

HEDGEHOP v -HOPPED, -HOPPING, -HOPS to fly near the ground

HEDGEPIG n pl. -S a hedgehog

HEDGEROW n pl. -S a row of bushes

HEDGING present participle of hedge

HEDGY adj HEDGIER, HEDGIEST abounding in hedges

HEDONIC adj pertaining to pleasure

HEDONICS n/pl a branch of psychology

HEDONISM n pl. -S the pursuit of pleasure

HEDONIST n pl. -S a follower of hedonism

HEED v -ED, -ING, -S to pay attention to

HEEDER n pl. -S one that heeds

HEEDFUL adj paying close attention

HEEDLESS adj paying little or no attention

HEEHAW v -ED, -ING, -S to guffaw

HEEL v -ED, -ING, -S to supply with a heel (the raised part of a shoe)

HEELBALL n pl. -S a composition used for polishing

HEELER n pl. -S one that puts heels on shoes

HEELING n pl. -S the act of inclining laterally

HEELLESS adj lacking heels

HEELPOST *n* pl. -S a post fitted to the end of something

HEELTAP *n* pl. -S material put on the heel of a shoe

HEEZE *v* HEEZED, HEEZING, HEEZES to hoist

HEFT *v* -ED, -ING, -S to lift up

HEFTER *n* pl. -S one that hefts

HEFTY *adj* HEFTIER, HEFTIEST heavy HEFTILY *adv*

HEGARI *n* pl. -S a grain

HEGEMONY *n* pl. -NIES great authority

HEGIRA *n* pl. -S an exodus

HEGUMEN *n* pl. -S the head of a monastery

HEGUMENE *n* pl. -S the head of a nunnery

HEGUMENY *n* pl. -NIES the office of a hegumen

HEIFER *n* pl. -S a young cow

HEIGH *interj* — used to attract attention

HEIGHT *n* pl. -S the highest point

HEIGHTEN *v* -ED, -ING, -S to raise

HEIGHTH *n* pl. -S height

HEIL *v* -ED, -ING, -S to salute

HEINIE *n* pl. -S the buttocks

HEINOUS *adj* very wicked

HEIR *v* -ED, -ING, -S to inherit

HEIRDOM *n* pl. -S heirship

HEIRESS *n* pl. -ES a female inheritor

HEIRLESS *adj* having no inheritors

HEIRLOOM *n* pl. -S an inherited possession

HEIRSHIP *n* pl. -S the right to inheritance

HEIST *v* -ED, -ING, -S to steal

HEISTER *n* pl. -S one that heists

HEJIRA *n* pl. -S hegira

HEKTARE *n* pl. -S hectare

HELD past tense of hold

HELIAC *adj* heliacal

HELIACAL *adj* pertaining to the sun

HELIAST *n* pl. -S an Athenian judge

HELICAL *adj* shaped like a helix

HELICES a pl. of helix

HELICITY *n* pl. -TIES a component of a particle's spin

HELICOID *n* pl. -S a type of geometrical surface

HELICON *n* pl. -S a large bass tuba

HELICOPT *v* -ED, -ING, -S to travel by helicopter

HELIO *n* pl. -LIOS a signaling mirror

HELIPAD *n* pl. -S a heliport

HELIPORT *n* pl. -S an airport for helicopters

HELISTOP *n* pl. -S a heliport

HELIUM *n* pl. -S a gaseous element

HELIX *n* pl. -LIXES or -LICES something spiral in form

HELL *v* -ED, -ING, -S to behave raucously

HELLBENT *adj* stubbornly determined

HELLBOX *n* pl. -ES a printer's receptacle

HELLCAT *n* pl. -S a shrewish person

HELLER *n* pl. -S a hellion

HELLERI *n* pl. -ES a tropical fish

HELLERY *n* pl. -LERIES rough play

HELLFIRE *n* pl. -S the torment of hell

HELLHOLE *n* pl. -S a horrible place

HELLION *n* pl. -S a troublesome person

HELLISH *adj* horrible

HELLKITE *n* pl. -S a cruel person

HELLO *v* -ED, -ING, -ES or -S to greet

HELLUVA *adj* disagreeable

HELM *v* -ED, -ING, -S to steer a ship

HELMET *v* -ED, -ING, -S to supply with a helmet (a protective covering for the head)

HELMINTH *n* pl. -S a worm

HELMLESS *adj* lacking a helm (a steering system)

HELMSMAN *n* pl. -MEN one that steers a ship

HELOT *n* pl. -S a slave or serf

HELOTAGE *n* pl. -S helotism

HELOTISM *n* pl. -S slavery or serfdom

HELOTRY *n* pl. -RIES helotism

HELP *v* HELPED or HOLP, HOLPEN, HELPING, HELPS to give assistance to HELPABLE *adj*

HELPER *n* pl. -S one that helps

HELPFUL *adj* being of service or assistance

HELPING *n* pl. -S a portion of food

HELPLESS *adj* defenseless

HELPMATE *n* pl. -S a helpful companion

HELPMEET *n* pl. -S a helpmate

HELVE *v* HELVED, HELVING, HELVES to provide with a handle

HEM *v* HEMMED, HEMMING, HEMS to provide with an edge

HEMAGOG *n* pl. -S an agent that promotes blood flow

HEMAL *adj* pertaining to the blood

HEMATAL *adj* hemal

HEMATEIN *n* pl. -S a chemical compound

HEMATIC *n* pl. -S a medicine for a blood disease

HEMATIN *n* pl. -S heme

HEMATINE *n* pl. -S hematin

HEMATITE *n* pl. -S an ore of iron

HEMATOID *adj* resembling blood

HEMATOMA *n* pl. -MAS or -MATA a swelling filled with blood

HEME *n* pl. -S a component of hemoglobin

HEMIC *adj* hemal

HEMIN *n* pl. -S a chloride of heme

HEMIOLA *n* pl. -S a rhythmic alteration in music

HEMIPTER *n* pl. -S an insect

HEMLINE *n* pl. -S the bottom edge of a garment

HEMLOCK *n* pl. -S a poisonous herb

HEMMED past tense of hem

HEMMER *n* pl. -S one that hems

HEMMING present participle of hem

HEMOCOEL *n* pl. -S a body cavity

HEMOCYTE *n* pl. -S a blood cell

HEMOID *adj* hemal

HEMOLYZE *v* -LYZED, -LYZING, -LYZES to break down red blood cells

HEMOSTAT *n* pl. -S an instrument for reducing bleeding

HEMP *n* pl. -S a tall herb

HEMPEN *adj* made of hemp

HEMPIE *adj* HEMPIER, HEMPIEST hempy

HEMPIER comparative of hempy

HEMPIEST superlative of hempy

HEMPLIKE *adj* resembling hemp

HEMPSEED *n* pl. -S the seed of hemp

HEMPWEED *n* pl. -S a climbing plant

HEMPY *adj* HEMPIER, HEMPIEST mischievous

HEN *n* pl. -S a female chicken

HENBANE *n* pl. -S a poisonous herb

HENBIT *n* pl. -S a perennial herb

HENCE *adv* consequently

HENCHMAN *n* pl. -MEN an unscrupulous supporter

HENCOOP *n* pl. -S a cage for hens

HENEQUEN *n* pl. -S a fiber used to make ropes

HENEQUIN *n* pl. -S henequen

HENHOUSE *n* pl. -S a shelter for poultry

HENIQUEN *n* pl. -S henequen

HENLIKE *adj* resembling a hen

HENNA *v* -ED, -ING, -S to dye with a reddish coloring

HENNERY *n* pl. -NERIES a poultry farm

HENPECK *v* -ED, -ING, -S to dominate by nagging

HENRY *n* pl. -RIES or -RYS a unit of inductance

HENT *v* -ED, -ING, -S to grasp

HEP *adj* hip

HEPARIN *n* pl. -S a biochemical

HEPATIC *n* pl. -S a drug acting on the liver

HEPATICA *n* pl. -CAS or -CAE a perennial herb

HEPATIZE *v* -TIZED, -TIZING, -TIZES to convert tissue into a firm mass

HEPATOMA *n* pl. -MAS or -MATA a tumor of the liver

HEPCAT *n* pl. -S a jazz enthusiast

HEPTAD *n* pl. -S a group of seven

HEPTAGON *n* pl. -S a seven-sided polygon

HEPTANE *n* pl. -S a hydrocarbon used as a solvent

HEPTARCH *n* pl. -S one of a group of seven rulers

HEPTOSE *n* pl. -S a chemical compound

HER *pron* the objective or possessive case of the pronoun she

HERALD *v* -ED, -ING, -S to proclaim

HERALDIC *adj* pertaining to heraldry

HERALDRY *n* pl. -RIES the art or science of armorial bearings

HERB *n* pl. -S a flowering plant with a nonwoody stem

HERBAGE *n* pl. -S nonwoody plant life

HERBAL *n* pl. -S a book about herbs and plants

HERBARIA *n/pl* collections of dried plants

HERBIER comparative of herby

HERBIEST superlative of herby

HERBLESS *adj* lacking herbs

HERBLIKE *adj* resembling an herb

HERBY *adj* HERBIER, HERBIEST abounding in herbs

HERCULES *n* pl. -LESES any man of great size and strength

HERD *v* -ED, -ING, -S to bring together in a herd (a group of animals)

HERDER n pl. -S one who tends a herd

HERDIC n pl. -S a type of carriage

HERDLIKE adj resembling a herd

HERDMAN n pl. -MEN herdsman

HERDSMAN n pl. -MEN a herder

HERE n pl. -S this place

HEREAT adv at this time

HEREAWAY adv in this vicinity

HEREBY adv by this means

HEREDES pl. of heres

HEREDITY n pl. -TIES the genetic transmission of characteristics

HEREIN adv in this

HEREINTO adv into this place

HEREOF adv of this

HEREON adv on this

HERES n pl. HEREDES an heir

HERESY n pl. -SIES a belief contrary to a church doctrine

HERETIC n pl. -S one that upholds heresy

HERETO adv to this matter

HERETRIX n pl. -TRIXES or -TRICES heritrix

HEREUNTO adv hereto

HEREUPON adv immediately following this

HEREWITH adv along with this

HERIOT n pl. -S a feudal tribute or payment

HERITAGE n pl. -S something that is inherited

HERITOR n pl. -S one that inherits

HERITRIX n pl. -TRIXES or -TRICES a female heritor

HERL n pl. -S a feathered fishing lure

HERM n pl. -S a type of statue

HERMA n pl. -MAE or -MAI a herm **HERMAEAN** adj

HERMETIC adj airtight

HERMIT n pl. -S a recluse **HERMITIC** adj

HERMITRY n pl. -RIES the state of being a hermit

HERN n pl. -S a heron

HERNIA n pl. -NIAS or -NIAE the protrusion of an organ through its surrounding wall **HERNIAL** adj

HERNIATE v -ATED, -ATING, -ATES to protrude through an abnormal bodily opening

HERO n pl. -ROES or -ROS one who shows great courage

HEROIC n pl. -S an epic verse

HEROICAL adj courageous; noble

HEROIN n pl. -S an addictive narcotic

HEROINE n pl. -S a brave woman

HEROISM n pl. -S heroic behavior

HEROIZE v -IZED, -IZING, -IZES to make heroic

HERON n pl. -S a wading bird

HERONRY n pl. -RIES a place where herons breed

HERPES n pl. -PESES a skin infection **HERPETIC** adj

HERRING n pl. -S a food fish

HERRY v -RIED, -RYING, -RIES to harry

HERS pron the possessive case of the pronoun she

HERSELF pron a form of the 3d person sing. feminine pronoun

HERTZ n pl. -ES a unit of frequency

HESITANT adj tending to hesitate

HESITATE v -TATED, -TATING, -TATES to hold back in uncertainty

HESSIAN n pl. -S a coarse cloth

HESSITE n pl. -S a mineral

HEST n pl. -S a command

HET a past tense of heat

HETAERA n pl. -RAE or -RAS a concubine **HETAERIC** adj

HETAIRA n pl. -RAI or -RAS hetaera

HETERO n pl. -EROS a heterosexual

HETH n pl. -S a Hebrew letter

HETMAN n pl. -S a cossack leader

HEUCH n pl. -S heugh

HEUGH n pl. -S a steep cliff

HEW v HEWED, HEWN, HEWING, HEWS to cut with an ax **HEWABLE** adj

HEWER n pl. -S one that hews

HEX v -ED, -ING, -ES to cast an evil spell upon

HEXAD n pl. -S a group of six **HEXADIC** adj

HEXADE n pl. -S hexad

HEXAGON n pl. -S a polygon having six sides

HEXAGRAM n pl. -S a six-pointed star

HEXAMINE n pl. -S a chemical compound

HEXANE n pl. -S a volatile liquid

HEXAPLA n pl. -S an edition in which six texts are set in parallel columns **HEXAPLAR** adj

HEXAPOD *n pl.* -S a six-legged insect

HEXAPODY *n pl.* -DIES a line of verse with six feet

HEXARCHY *n pl.* -CHIES a group of six separate states

HEXER *n pl.* -S one that hexes

HEXEREI *n pl.* -S witchcraft

HEXONE *n pl.* -S a hydrocarbon solvent

HEXOSAN *n pl.* -S a carbohydrate

HEXOSE *n pl.* -S a simple sugar

HEXYL *n pl.* -S a hydrocarbon radical

HEY *interj* — used to attract attention

HEYDAY *n pl.* -DAYS the period of one's greatest success

HEYDEY *n pl.* -DEYS heyday

HI *interj* — used as a greeting

HIATUS *n pl.* -ES a gap or missing section HIATAL *adj*

HIBACHI *n pl.* -S a cooking device

HIBERNAL *adj* pertaining to winter

HIBISCUS *n pl.* -ES a tropical plant

HIC *interj* — used to represent a hiccup

HICCOUGH *v* -ED, -ING, -S to hiccup

HICCUP *v* -CUPED, -CUPING, -CUPS or -CUPPED, -CUPPING, -CUPS to make a peculiar-sounding, spasmodic inhalation

HICK *n pl.* -S a rural person

HICKEY *n pl.* -EYS a gadget

HICKORY *n pl.* -RIES a hardwood tree

HID a past tense of hide

HIDABLE *adj* able to be hidden

HIDALGO *n pl.* -GOS a minor Spanish nobleman

HIDDEN *adj* concealed; obscure HIDDENLY *adv*

HIDE *v* HID, HIDDEN, HIDING, HIDES to conceal

HIDE *v* HIDED, HIDING, HIDES to flog

HIDEAWAY *n pl.* -AWAYS a hideout

HIDELESS *adj* lacking a skin

HIDEOUS *adj* very ugly

HIDEOUT *n pl.* -S a place of refuge

HIDER *n pl.* -S one that hides

HIDING *n pl.* -S a beating

HIDROSIS *n pl.* -DROSES abnormal perspiration HIDROTIC *adj*

HIE *v* HIED, HIEING or HYING, HIES to hurry

HIEMAL *adj* pertaining to winter

HIERARCH *n pl.* -S a religious leader

HIERATIC *adj* pertaining to priests

HIGGLE *v* -GLED, -GLING, -GLES to haggle

HIGGLER *n pl.* -S one that higgles

HIGH *adj* HIGHER, HIGHEST reaching far upward

HIGH *n pl.* -S a high level

HIGHBALL *v* -ED, -ING, -S to go at full speed

HIGHBORN *adj* of noble birth

HIGHBOY *n pl.* -BOYS a tall chest of drawers

HIGHBRED *adj* highborn

HIGHBROW *n pl.* -S a person who has superior tastes

HIGHBUSH *adj* forming a tall bush

HIGHJACK *v* -ED, -ING, -S to hijack

HIGHLAND *n pl.* -S an elevated region

HIGHLY *adv* to a high degree

HIGHNESS *n pl.* -ES the state of being high

HIGHROAD *n pl.* -S a highway

HIGHT *v* -ED, -ING, -S to command

HIGHTAIL *v* -ED, -ING, -S to retreat rapidly

HIGHTH *n pl.* -S height

HIGHWAY *n pl.* -WAYS a main road

HIJACK *v* -ED, -ING, -S to seize a vehicle while in transit

HIJACKER *n pl.* -S one that hijacks

HIJINKS *n/pl* mischievous fun

HIKE *v* HIKED, HIKING, HIKES to walk a long distance

HIKER *n pl.* -S one that hikes

HILA *pl.* of hilum

HILAR *adj* pertaining to a hilum

HILARITY *n pl.* -TIES noisy merriment

HILDING *n pl.* -S a vile person

HILI *pl.* of hilus

HILL *v* -ED, -ING, -S to form into a hill (a rounded elevation)

HILLER *n pl.* -S one that hills

HILLIER comparative of hilly

HILLIEST superlative of hilly

HILLO *v* -ED, -ING, -S or -ES to hallo

HILLOA *v* -ED, -ING, -S to hallo

HILLOCK *n pl.* -S a small hill HILLOCKY *adj*

HILLSIDE *n pl.* -S the side of a hill

HILLTOP *n pl.* -S the top of a hill

HILLY	*adj* HILLIER, HILLIEST abounding in hills		**HIPSHOT**	*adj* lame; awkward
HILT	*v* -ED, -ING, -S to provide with a hilt (a handle for a weapon)		**HIPSTER**	*n pl.* -S one that is hip
			HIRABLE	*adj* available for hire
HILTLESS	*adj* having no hilt		**HIRAGANA**	*n pl.* -S a Japanese cursive script
HILUM	*n pl.* HILA a small opening in a bodily organ		**HIRCINE**	*adj* pertaining to a goat
HILUS	*n pl.* HILI hilum		**HIRE**	*v* HIRED, HIRING, HIRES to engage the services of for payment HIREABLE *adj*
HIM	*pron* the objective case of the pronoun he		
HIMATION	*n pl.* -MATIA or -MATIONS a loose outer garment		**HIRELING**	*n pl.* -S one that works for money only
HIMSELF	*pron* a form of the 3d person sing. masculine pronoun		**HIRER**	*n pl.* -S one that hires
			HIRING	present participle of hire
HIN	*n pl.* -S a Hebrew unit of liquid measure		**HIRPLE**	*v* -PLED, -PLING, -PLES to limp
HIND	*n pl.* -S a female red deer		**HIRSEL**	*v* -SELED, -SELING, -SELS or -SELLED, -SELLING, -SELS to herd sheep
HINDER	*v* -ED, -ING, -S to impede		
HINDERER	*n pl.* -S one that hinders		**HIRSLE**	*v* -SLED, -SLING, -SLES to slide along
HINDGUT	*n pl.* -S the rear part of the alimentary canal		
HINDMOST	*adj* farthest to the rear		**HIRSUTE**	*adj* hairy
HINGE	*v* HINGED, HINGING, HINGES to attach a jointed device		**HIRUDIN**	*n pl.* -S an anticoagulant
			HIS	*pron* the possessive form of the pronoun he
HINGER	*n pl.* -S one that hinges		**HISN**	*pron* his
HINNY	*v* -NIED, -NYING, -NIES to whinny		**HISPID**	*adj* covered with stiff hairs
HINT	*v* -ED, -ING, -S to suggest indirectly		**HISS**	*v* -ED, -ING, -ES to make a sibilant sound
HINTER	*n pl.* -S one that hints		**HISSELF**	*pron* himself
HIP	*v* HIPPED, HIPPING, HIPS to build a type of roof		**HISSER**	*n pl.* -S one that hisses
			HISSING	*n pl.* -S an object of scorn
HIP	*adj* HIPPER, HIPPEST aware of the most current styles and trends		**HIST**	*v* -ED, -ING, -S to hoist
			HISTAMIN	*n pl.* -S an amine released in allergic reactions
HIPBONE	*n pl.* -S a pelvic bone		**HISTIDIN**	*n pl.* -S an amino acid
HIPLESS	*adj* lacking a hip (the pelvic joint)		**HISTOGEN**	*n pl.* -S interior plant tissue
HIPLIKE	*adj* suggestive of a hip		**HISTOID**	*adj* pertaining to connective tissue
HIPNESS	*n pl.* -ES the state of being hip		
HIPPARCH	*n pl.* -S a cavalry commander in ancient Greece		**HISTONE**	*n pl.* -S a simple protein
			HISTORIC	*adj* important in history
HIPPED	past tense of hip		**HISTORY**	*n pl.* -RIES a chronological record of past events
HIPPER	comparative of hip		
HIPPEST	superlative of hip		**HIT**	*v* HIT, HITTING, HITS to strike forcibly
HIPPIE	*n pl.* -S a nonconformist		**HITCH**	*v* -ED, -ING, -ES to fasten with a knot or hook
HIPPIER	comparative of hippy		
HIPPIEST	superlative of hippy		**HITCHER**	*n pl.* -S one that hitches
HIPPING	present participle of hip		**HITHER**	*adv* toward this place
HIPPISH	*adj* depressed; sad		**HITHERTO**	*adv* up to now
HIPPO	*n pl.* -POS a hippopotamus		**HITLESS**	*adj* being without a hit
HIPPY	*adj* -PIER, -PIEST having big hips		**HITTER**	*n pl.* -S one that hits
			HITTING	present participle of hit

HIVE   v HIVED, HIVING, HIVES to cause to enter a hive (a bee's nest)

HIVELESS   adj lacking a hive

HO   interj — used to express surprise

HOACTZIN   n pl. -S or -ES hoatzin

HOAGIE   n pl. -S a long sandwich

HOAGY   n pl. -GIES hoagie

HOAR   n pl. -S a white coating

HOARD   v -ED, -ING, -S to gather and store away

HOARDER   n pl. -S one that hoards

HOARDING   n pl. -S something hoarded

HOARIER   comparative of hoary

HOARIEST   superlative of hoary

HOARILY   adv in a hoary manner

HOARSE   adj HOARSER, HOARSEST low and rough in sound **HOARSELY** adv

HOARSEN   v -ED, -ING, -S to make hoarse

HOARY   adj HOARIER, HOARIEST white with age

HOATZIN   n pl. -S or -ES a tropical bird

HOAX   v -ED, -ING, -ES to deceive

HOAXER   n pl. -S one that hoaxes

HOB   v HOBBED, HOBBING, HOBS to furnish with hobnails

HOBBIES   pl. of hobby

HOBBLE   v -BLED, -BLING, -BLES to limp

HOBBLER   n pl. -S one that hobbles

HOBBY   n pl. -BIES a recreational pastime

HOBBYIST   n pl. -S one that pursues a hobby

HOBLIKE   adj suggestive of an elf

HOBNAIL   n pl. -S a short nail with a thick head

HOBNOB   v -NOBBED, -NOBBING, -NOBS to associate in a friendly way

HOBO   v -ED, -ING, -S or -ES to live like a hobo (a vagrant or tramp)

HOBOISM   n pl. -S the state of being a hobo

HOCK   v -ED, -ING, -S to pawn

HOCKER   n pl. -S one that hocks

HOCKEY   n pl. -EYS a game played on ice

HOCKSHOP   n pl. -S a pawnshop

HOCUS   v -CUSED, -CUSING, -CUSES or -CUSSED, -CUSSING, -CUSSES to deceive or cheat

HOD   n pl. -S a portable trough

HODAD   n pl. -S a nonsurfer

HODADDY   n pl. -DIES hodad

HODDEN   n pl. -S a coarse cloth

HODDIN   n pl. -S hodden

HOE   v HOED, HOEING, HOES to use a hoe (a gardening tool)

HOECAKE   n pl. -S a cornmeal cake

HOEDOWN   n pl. -S a square dance

HOELIKE   adj resembling a hoe

HOER   n pl. -S one that hoes

HOG   v HOGGED, HOGGING, HOGS to take more than one's share

HOGAN   n pl. -S a Navaho Indian dwelling

HOGBACK   n pl. -S a sharp ridge

HOGFISH   n pl. -ES a tropical fish

HOGG   n pl. -S a young sheep

HOGGED   past tense of hog

HOGGER   n pl. -S one that hogs

HOGGING   present participle of hog

HOGGISH   adj coarsely selfish

HOGLIKE   adj hoggish

HOGMANAY   n pl. -NAYS a Scottish celebration

HOGMANE   n pl. -S hogmanay

HOGMENAY   n pl. -NAYS hogmanay

HOGNOSE   n pl. -S a nonvenomous snake

HOGNUT   n pl. -S a hickory nut

HOGSHEAD   n pl. -S a large cask

HOGTIE   v -TIED, -TIEING or -TYING, -TIES to tie together the legs of

HOGWASH   n pl. -ES meaningless talk

HOGWEED   n pl. -S a coarse plant

HOICK   v -ED, -ING, -S to change directions abruptly

HOIDEN   v -ED, -ING, -S to hoyden

HOISE   v HOISED, HOISING, HOISES to hoist

HOIST   v -ED, -ING, -S to haul up by some mechanical means

HOISTER   n pl. -S one that hoists

HOKE   v HOKED, HOKING, HOKES to give false value to

HOKEY   adj false; contrived

HOKKU   n pl. HOKKU haiku

HOKUM   n pl. -S nonsense

HOKYPOKY   n pl. -KIES trickery

HOLARD   n pl. -S the total quantity of water in the soil

HOLD   v HELD, HOLDEN, HOLDING, HOLDS to maintain possession of **HOLDABLE** adj

HOLDALL *n* pl. -S a carrying case

HOLDBACK *n* pl. -S a restraining device

HOLDEN a past participle of hold

HOLDER *n* pl. -S one that holds

HOLDFAST *n* pl. -S a fastening device

HOLDING *n* pl. -S something held

HOLDOUT *n* pl. -S one who delays signing a contract

HOLDOVER *n* pl. -S something left over

HOLDUP *n* pl. -S a delay

HOLE *v* HOLED, HOLING, HOLES to make a hole (a cavity in a solid)

HOLELESS *adj* lacking a hole

HOLEY *adj* full of holes

HOLIBUT *n* pl. -S halibut

HOLIDAY *v* -ED, -ING, -S to take a vacation

HOLIER comparative of holy

HOLIES pl. of holy

HOLIEST superlative of holy

HOLILY *adv* in a holy manner

HOLINESS *n* pl. -ES the state of being holy

HOLING present participle of hole

HOLISM *n* pl. -S a philosophical theory

HOLIST *n* pl. -S one who adheres to the theory of holism **HOLISTIC** *adj*

HOLK *v* -ED, -ING, -S to howk

HOLLA *v* -ED, -ING, -S to hallo

HOLLAND *n* pl. -S a cotton fabric

HOLLER *v* -ED, -ING, -S to yell

HOLLO *v* -ED, -ING, -S or -ES to hallo

HOLLOA *v* -ED, -ING, -S to hallo

HOLLOO *v* -ED, -ING, -S to hallo

HOLLOW *adj* -LOWER, -LOWEST not solid **HOLLOWLY** *adv*

HOLLOW *v* -ED, -ING, -S to make hollow

HOLLY *n* pl. -LIES a tree

HOLM *n* pl. -S an island in a river

HOLMIUM *n* pl. -S a metallic element **HOLMIC** *adj*

HOLOGRAM *n* pl. -S a three-dimensional photograph

HOLOGYNY *n* pl. -NIES a trait transmitted solely in the female line

HOLOTYPE *n* pl. -S an animal or plant specimen

HOLOZOIC *adj* eating solid foods

HOLP a past tense of help

HOLPEN a past participle of help

HOLSTEIN *n* pl. -S a breed of cattle

HOLSTER *n* pl. -S a case for a pistol

HOLT *n* pl. -S a grove

HOLY *adj* -LIER, -LIEST having a divine nature or origin

HOLY *n* pl. -LIES a holy place

HOLYDAY *n* pl. -DAYS a religious holiday

HOLYTIDE *n* pl. -S a time of religious observance

HOMAGE *v* -AGED, -AGING, -AGES to pay tribute to

HOMAGER *n* pl. -S a feudal vassal

HOMBRE *n* pl. -S a fellow

HOMBURG *n* pl. -S a felt hat

HOME *v* HOMED, HOMING, HOMES to return to one's home (place of residence)

HOMEBODY *n* pl. -BODIES one who likes to stay at home

HOMEBRED *n* pl. -S a native athlete

HOMED past tense of home

HOMELAND *n* pl. -S one's native land

HOMELESS *adj* lacking a home

HOMELIKE *adj* suggestive of a home; comfortably familiar

HOMELY *adj* -LIER, -LIEST unattractive

HOMEMADE *adj* made at home

HOMER *v* -ED, -ING, -S to hit a home run

HOMEROOM *n* pl. -S the classroom where pupils report before classes begin

HOMESICK *adj* longing for home

HOMESITE *n* pl. -S a location for a house

HOMESPUN *n* pl. -S a loosely woven fabric

HOMETOWN *n* pl. -S the town of one's birth or residence

HOMEWARD *adv* toward home

HOMEWORK *n* pl. -S work done at home

HOMEY *adj* HOMIER, HOMIEST homelike

HOMICIDE *n* pl. -S the killing of one person by another

HOMIER comparative of homy

HOMIEST superlative of homy

HOMILIST *n* pl. -S one that delivers a homily

HOMILY *n* pl. -LIES a sermon

HOMINESS *n* pl. -ES the quality of being homey

HOMING present participle of home

HOMINIAN *n* pl. -S a hominid

HOMINID *n* pl. -S a manlike creature

HOMINIES pl. of hominy

HOMININE adj characteristic of man

HOMINOID n pl. -S a manlike animal

HOMINY n pl. -NIES hulled, dried corn

HOMMOCK n pl. -S a ridge in an ice field

HOMO n pl. -MOS a homosexual — an offensive term

HOMOGAMY n pl. -MIES the bearing of sexually similar flowers

HOMOGENY n pl. -NIES correspondence in form or structure

HOMOGONY n pl. -NIES the condition of having flowers with uniform stamens and pistils

HOMOLOG n pl. -S something that exhibits homology

HOMOLOGY n pl. -GIES similarity in structure

HOMONYM n pl. -S a namesake

HOMONYMY n pl. -MIES the condition of having the same name

HOMY adj HOMIER, HOMIEST homey

HONAN n pl. -S a fine silk

HONCHO n pl. -CHOS a chief

HONDA n pl. -S a part of a lariat

HONE v HONED, HONING, HONES to sharpen

HONER n pl. -S one that hones

HONEST adj -ESTER, -ESTEST truthful
HONESTLY adv

HONESTY n pl. -TIES the quality of being honest

HONEWORT n pl. -S a perennial herb

HONEY v -EYED or -IED, -EYING, -EYS to sweeten with honey (a sweet, viscid fluid)

HONEYBEE n pl. -S a type of bee

HONEYBUN n pl. -S a sweetheart

HONEYDEW n pl. -S a sweet fluid

HONEYFUL adj containing much honey

HONG n pl. -S a Chinese factory

HONIED a past tense of honey

HONING present participle of hone

HONK v -ED, -ING, -S to emit a cry like that of a goose

HONKER n pl. -S one that honks

HONKEY n pl. -KEYS honkie — an offensive term

HONKIE n pl. -S a white man — an offensive term

HONKY n pl. -KIES honkie — an offensive term

HONOR v -ED, -ING, -S to treat with respect

HONORAND n pl. -S an honoree

HONORARY n pl. -ARIES an honor society

HONOREE n pl. -S one that receives an honor

HONORER n pl. -S one that honors

HONOUR v -ED, -ING, -S to honor

HONOURER n pl. -S honorer

HOOCH n pl. -ES cheap whiskey

HOOD v -ED, -ING, -S to furnish with a hood (a covering for the head)

HOODIE n pl. -S a gray crow of Europe

HOODLESS adj lacking a hood

HOODLIKE adj resembling a hood

HOODLUM n pl. -S a thug

HOODOO v -ED, -ING, -S to bring bad luck to

HOODWINK v -ED, -ING, -S to trick

HOOEY n pl. -EYS something false or nonsensical

HOOF v -ED, -ING, -S to dance

HOOF n pl. HOOVES or HOOFS the hard covering on the feet of certain animals

HOOFBEAT n pl. -S the sound of hooves striking the ground

HOOFER n pl. -S a professional dancer

HOOFLESS adj lacking hooves

HOOFLIKE adj resembling a hoof

HOOK v -ED, -ING, -S to catch with a hook (a bent piece of metal)

HOOKA n pl. -S hookah

HOOKAH n pl. -S a water pipe

HOOKED past tense of hook

HOOKER n pl. -S a prostitute

HOOKEY n pl. -EYS hooky

HOOKIER comparative of hooky

HOOKIES pl. of hooky

HOOKIEST superlative of hooky

HOOKLESS adj lacking a hook

HOOKLET n pl. -S a small hook

HOOKLIKE adj resembling a hook

HOOKNOSE n pl. -S an aquiline nose

HOOKUP n pl. -S an electrical assemblage

HOOKWORM n pl. -S a parasitic worm

HOOKY n pl. HOOKIES truancy

HOOKY adj HOOKIER, HOOKIEST full of hooks

HOOLIE adj easy; slow

HOOLIGAN n pl. -S a hoodlum

HOOLY adj hoolie

HOOP   v -ED, -ING, -S to fasten with a hoop (a circular band of metal)

HOOPER   n pl. -S one that hoops

HOOPLA   n pl. -S commotion

HOOPLESS   adj lacking a hoop

HOOPLIKE   adj suggestive of a hoop

HOOPOE   n pl. -S a European bird

HOOPOO   n pl. -POOS hoopoe

HOOPSTER   n pl. -S a basketball player

HOORAH   v -ED, -ING, -S to hurrah

HOORAY   v -ED, -ING, -S to hurrah

HOOSEGOW   n pl. -S a jail

HOOSGOW   n pl. -S hoosegow

HOOT   v -ED, -ING, -S to cry like an owl

HOOTCH   n pl. -ES hooch

HOOTER   n pl. -S one that hoots

HOOVES   a pl. of hoof

HOP   v HOPPED, HOPPING, HOPS to move by jumping on one foot

HOPE   v HOPED, HOPING, HOPES to have a desire or expectation

HOPEFUL   n pl. -S one that seems promising

HOPELESS   adj despairing

HOPER   n pl. -S one that hopes

HOPHEAD   n pl. -S a drug addict

HOPING   present participle of hope

HOPLITE   n pl. -S a foot soldier of ancient Greece HOPLITIC adj

HOPPED   past tense of hop

HOPPER   n pl. -S one that hops

HOPPING   present participle of hop

HOPPLE   v -PLED, -PLING, -PLES to hobble

HOPSACK   n pl. -S a coarse fabric

HOPTOAD   n pl. -S a toad

HORA   n pl. -S an Israeli dance

HORAH   n pl. -S hora

HORAL   adj hourly

HORARY   adj hourly

HORDE   v HORDED, HORDING, HORDES to gather in a large group

HORDEIN   n pl. -S a simple protein

HORIZON   n pl. -S the line where the sky seems to meet the earth

HORMONE   n pl. -S a secretion of the endocrine organs HORMONAL, HORMONIC adj

HORN   v -ED, -ING, -S to form a horn (a hard, bonelike projection of the head)

HORNBEAM   n pl. -S a small tree

HORNBILL   n pl. -S a large-billed bird

HORNBOOK   n pl. -S a primer

HORNET   n pl. -S a stinging insect

HORNFELS   n pl. HORNFELS a silicate rock

HORNIER   comparative of horny

HORNIEST   superlative of horny

HORNILY   adv in a horny manner

HORNITO   n pl. -TOS a mound of volcanic matter

HORNLESS   adj lacking a horn

HORNLIKE   adj resembling a horn

HORNPIPE   n pl. -S a musical instrument

HORNPOUT   n pl. -S a catfish

HORNTAIL   n pl. -S a wasplike insect

HORNWORM   n pl. -S the larva of a hawkmoth

HORNWORT   n pl. -S an aquatic herb

HORNY   adj HORNIER, HORNIEST hornlike in hardness

HOROLOGE   n pl. -S a timepiece

HOROLOGY   n pl. -GIES the science of measuring time

HORRENT   adj bristling; standing erect

HORRIBLE   n pl. -S something that causes horror

HORRIBLY   adv dreadfully

HORRID   adj repulsive HORRIDLY adv

HORRIFIC   adj causing horror

HORRIFY   v -FIED, -FYING, -FIES to cause to feel horror

HORROR   n pl. -S a feeling of intense fear or repugnance

HORSE   v HORSED, HORSING, HORSES to provide with a horse (a large, hoofed mammal)

HORSECAR   n pl. -S a streetcar drawn by a horse

HORSEFLY   n pl. -FLIES a large fly

HORSEMAN   n pl. -MEN one who rides a horse

HORSEY   adj HORSIER, HORSIEST horsy

HORSIER   comparative of horsy

HORSIEST   superlative of horsy

HORSILY   adv in a horsy manner

HORSING   present participle of horse

HORST   n pl. -S a portion of the earth's crust

HORSTE   n pl. -S horst

HORSY   adj HORSIER, HORSIEST resembling a horse

HOSANNA   v -ED, -ING, -S to praise

HOSE   v HOSED, HOSING, HOSES to spray with water

HOSE   n pl. HOSEN stockings or socks

HOSEL   n pl. -S a part of a golf club

HOSIER   n pl. -S one that makes hose

HOSIERY   n pl. -SIERIES hose

HOSING   present participle of hose

HOSPICE   n pl. -S a shelter

HOSPITAL   n pl. -S a medical institution

HOSPITIA   n/pl places of shelter

HOSPODAR   n pl. -S a governor of a region under Turkish rule

HOST   v -ED, -ING, -S to entertain socially

HOSTAGE   n pl. -S a person held as security

HOSTEL   v -ED, -ING, -S to stay at inns overnight while traveling

HOSTELER   n pl. -S an innkeeper

HOSTELRY   n pl. -RIES an inn

HOSTESS   v -ED, -ING, -ES to act as a hostess (a woman who entertains socially)

HOSTILE   n pl. -S an unfriendly person

HOSTLER   n pl. -S a person who tends horses or mules

HOSTLY   adj pertaining to one who hosts

HOT   adj HOTTER, HOTTEST having a high temperature

HOT   v HOTTED, HOTTING, HOTS to heat

HOTBED   n pl. -S a bed of rich soil

HOTBLOOD   n pl. -S a thoroughbred horse

HOTBOX   n pl. -ES an overheated bearing of a railroad car

HOTCAKE   n pl. -S a pancake

HOTCH   v -ED, -ING, -ES to wiggle

HOTCHPOT   n pl. -S the combining of properties in order to divide them equally among heirs

HOTDOG   v -DOGGED, -DOGGING, -DOGS to perform in a showy manner

HOTEL   n pl. -S a public lodging

HOTELIER   n pl. -S a hotel manager

HOTELMAN   n pl. -MEN a hotelier

HOTFOOT   v -FOOTED, -FOOTING, -FOOTS to hurry

HOTHEAD   n pl. -S a quick-tempered person

HOTHOUSE   n pl. -S a heated greenhouse

HOTLY   adv in a hot manner

HOTNESS   n pl. -ES the state of being hot

HOTPRESS   v -ED, -ING, -ES to subject to heat and pressure

HOTROD   n pl. -S a car modified for high speeds

HOTSHOT   n pl. -S a showily skillful person

HOTSPUR   n pl. -S a hothead

HOTTED   past tense of hot

HOTTER   comparative of hot

HOTTEST   superlative of hot

HOTTING   present participle of hot

HOTTISH   adj somewhat hot

HOUDAH   n pl. -S howdah

HOUND   v -ED, -ING, -S to pursue relentlessly

HOUNDER   n pl. -S one that hounds

HOUR   n pl. -S a period of sixty minutes

HOURI   n pl. -S a beautiful maiden in Muslim belief

HOURLY   adj occurring every hour

HOUSE   v HOUSED, HOUSING, HOUSES to lodge in a house (a building in which people live)

HOUSEBOY   n pl. -BOYS a male servant

HOUSEFLY   n pl. -FLIES a common fly

HOUSEFUL   n pl. -S as much as a house will hold

HOUSEL   v -SELED, -SELING, -SELS or -SELLED, -SELLING, -SELS to administer the Eucharist to

HOUSEMAN   n pl. -MEN a male servant

HOUSER   n pl. -S one who organizes housing projects

HOUSETOP   n pl. -S the roof of a house

HOUSING   n pl. -S any dwelling place

HOVE   a past tense of heave

HOVEL   v -ELED, -ELING, -ELS or -ELLED, -ELLING, -ELS to live in a small, miserable dwelling

HOVER   v -ED, -ING, -S to hang suspended in the air

HOVERER   n pl. -S something that hovers

HOW   n pl. -S a method of doing something

HOWBEIT   adv nevertheless

HOWDAH   n pl. -S a seat on an elephant or camel for riders

HOWDIE   n pl. -S a midwife

HOWDY   n pl. -DIES howdie

HOWE   n pl. -S a valley

HOWEVER   adv nevertheless

HOWF   n pl. -S a place frequently visited

HOWFF   n pl. -S howf

HOWITZER   n pl. -S a short cannon

HOWK   v -ED, -ING, -S to dig

HOWL   v -ED, -ING, -S to cry like a dog

HOWLER   n pl. -S one that howls

HOWLET   n pl. -S an owl

HOY   n pl. HOYS a heavy barge or scow

HOYDEN   v -ED, -ING, -S to act like a tomboy

HOYLE   n pl. -S a rule book

HUARACHE   n pl. -S a flat-heeled sandal

HUARACHO   n pl. -CHOS huarache

HUB   n pl. -S the center of a wheel

HUBBUB   n pl. -S an uproar

HUBBY   n pl. -BIES a husband

HUBCAP   n pl. -S a covering for the hub of a wheel

HUBRIS   n pl. -BRISES arrogance

HUCK   n pl. -S a durable fabric

HUCKLE   n pl. -S the hip

HUCKSTER   v -ED, -ING, -S to peddle

HUDDLE   v -DLED, -DLING, -DLES to crowd together

HUDDLER   n pl. -S one that huddles

HUE   n pl. -S color HUED, HUELESS adj

HUFF   v -ED, -ING, -S to breathe heavily

HUFFISH   adj sulky

HUFFY   adj HUFFIER, HUFFIEST easily offended HUFFILY adv

HUG   v HUGGED, HUGGING, HUGS to clasp tightly in the arms

HUGE   adj HUGER, HUGEST very large HUGELY adv

HUGENESS   n pl. -ES the quality of being huge

HUGEOUS   adj huge

HUGER   comparative of huge

HUGEST   superlative of huge

HUGGABLE   adj cuddlesome

HUGGED   past tense of hug

HUGGER   n pl. -S one that hugs

HUGGING   present participle of hug

HUH   interj — used to express surprise

HUIC   interj — used to encourage hunting hounds

HULA   n pl. -S a Hawaiian dance

HULK   v -ED, -ING, -S to appear impressively large

HULKY   adj HULKIER, HULKIEST massive

HULL   v -ED, -ING, -S to remove the shell from a seed

HULLER   n pl. -S one that hulls

HULLO   v -ED, -ING, -S or -ES to hallo

HULLOA   v -S to hallo

HUM   v HUMMED, HUMMING, HUMS to sing without opening the lips or saying words

HUMAN   n pl. -S a person

HUMANE   adj -MANER, -MANEST compassionate HUMANELY adv

HUMANISE   v -ISED, -ISING, -ISES to humanize

HUMANISM   n pl. -S the quality of being human

HUMANIST   n pl. -S one who studies human nature

HUMANITY   n pl. -TIES the human race

HUMANIZE   v -IZED, -IZING, -IZES to make human

HUMANLY   adv in a human manner

HUMANOID   n pl. -S something having human form

HUMATE   n pl. -S a chemical salt

HUMBLE   adj -BLER, -BLEST modest

HUMBLE   v -BLED, -BLING, -BLES to reduce the pride of

HUMBLER   n pl. -S one that humbles

HUMBLEST   superlative of humble

HUMBLING   present participle of humble

HUMBLY   adv in a humble manner

HUMBUG   v -BUGGED, -BUGGING, -BUGS to deceive

HUMDRUM   n pl. -S a dull, boring person

HUMERAL   n pl. -S a bone of the shoulder

HUMERUS   n pl. -MERI the large bone of the upper arm

HUMIC   adj derived from humus

HUMID   adj having much humidity

HUMIDIFY   v -FIED, -FYING, -FIES to make humid

HUMIDITY   n pl. -TIES moisture of the air

HUMIDLY   adv in a humid manner

HUMIDOR   n pl. -S a cigar case

HUMIFIED   adj converted into humus

HUMILITY   n pl. -TIES the quality of being humble

HUMMABLE	*adj* capable of being hummed	**HURLER**	*n pl.* -S one that hurls
HUMMED	past tense of hum	**HURLEY**	*n pl.* -LEYS hurling
HUMMER	*n pl.* -S one that hums	**HURLING**	*n pl.* -S an Irish game
HUMMING	present participle of hum	**HURLY**	*n pl.* -LIES commotion
HUMMOCK	*n pl.* -S a small hill **HUMMOCKY** *adj*	**HURRAH**	*v* -ED, -ING, -S to cheer
HUMOR	*v* -ED, -ING, -S to indulge	**HURRAY**	*v* -ED, -ING, -S to hurrah
HUMORAL	*adj* pertaining to bodily fluids	**HURRIER**	*n pl.* -S one that hurries
HUMORFUL	*adj* humorous	**HURRY**	*v* -RIED, -RYING, -RIES to move swiftly
HUMORIST	*n pl.* -S a humorous writer or entertainer	**HURT**	*v* HURT, HURTING, HURTS to injure
HUMOROUS	*adj* funny; witty	**HURTER**	*n pl.* -S one that hurts
HUMOUR	*v* -ED, -ING, -S to humor	**HURTFUL**	*adj* causing injury
HUMP	*v* -ED, -ING, -S to arch into a hump (a rounded protuberance)	**HURTLE**	*v* -TLED, -TLING, -TLES to rush violently
HUMPBACK	*n pl.* -S a humped back	**HURTLESS**	*adj* harmless
HUMPH	*v* -ED, -ING, -S to utter a grunt	**HUSBAND**	*v* -ED, -ING, -S to spend wisely
HUMPLESS	*adj* lacking a hump	**HUSH**	*v* -ED, -ING, -ES to quiet **HUSHEDLY** *adv*
HUMPY	*adj* HUMPIER, HUMPIEST full of humps	**HUSHABY**	*v* go to sleep — used imperatively to soothe a child
HUMUS	*n pl.* -ES decomposed organic matter	**HUSHFUL**	*adj* quiet
HUN	*n pl.* -S a barbarous, destructive person	**HUSK**	*v* -ED, -ING, -S to remove the husk (the outer covering) from
HUNCH	*v* -ED, -ING, -ES to arch forward	**HUSKER**	*n pl.* -S one that husks
HUNDRED	*n pl.* -S a number	**HUSKIER**	comparative of husky
HUNG	a past tense of hang	**HUSKIES**	pl. of husky
HUNGER	*v* -ED, -ING, -S to crave	**HUSKIEST**	superlative of husky
HUNGRY	*adj* -GRIER, -GRIEST wanting food **HUNGRILY** *adv*	**HUSKILY**	*adv* in a husky manner
HUNK	*n pl.* -S a large piece	**HUSKING**	*n pl.* -S a gathering of families to husk corn
HUNKER	*v* -ED, -ING, -S to squat	**HUSKLIKE**	*adj* resembling a husk
HUNKY	*n pl.* -KIES an unskilled laborer	**HUSKY**	*adj* -KIER, -KIEST hoarse
HUNNISH	*adj* resembling a hun	**HUSKY**	*n pl.* -KIES an Eskimo dog
HUNT	*v* -ED, -ING, -S to pursue for food or sport **HUNTABLE** *adj* **HUNTEDLY** *adv*	**HUSSAR**	*n pl.* -S a cavalry soldier
		HUSSY	*n pl.* -SIES a lewd woman
		HUSTINGS	*n pl.* HUSTINGS a British court
HUNTER	*n pl.* -S one that hunts	**HUSTLE**	*v* -TLED, -TLING, -TLES to hurry
HUNTING	*n pl.* -S an instance of searching	**HUSTLER**	*n pl.* -S one that hustles
HUNTRESS	*n pl.* -ES a female hunter	**HUSWIFE**	*n pl.* -WIFES or -WIVES a sewing kit
HUNTSMAN	*n pl.* -MEN a hunter		
HUP	*interj* — used to mark a marching cadence	**HUT**	*v* HUTTED, HUTTING, HUTS to live in a hut (a simple shelter)
HURDIES	*n/pl* the buttocks	**HUTCH**	*v* -ED, -ING, -ES to store away
HURDLE	*v* -DLED, -DLING, -DLES to jump over	**HUTLIKE**	*adj* resembling a hut
		HUTMENT	*n pl.* -S a group of huts
HURDLER	*n pl.* -S one that hurdles	**HUTTED**	past tense of hut
HURDS	*n/pl* hards	**HUTTING**	present participle of hut
HURL	*v* -ED, -ING, -S to throw with great force	**HUTZPA**	*n pl.* -S chutzpah
		HUTZPAH	*n pl.* -S chutzpah

HUZZA   v -ED, -ING, -S to cheer
HUZZAH   v -ED, -ING, -S to huzza
HWAN   n pl. HWAN a monetary unit of South Korea
HYACINTH   n pl. -S a flowering plant
HYAENA   n pl. -S hyena **HYAENIC** adj
HYALIN   n pl. -S hyaline
HYALINE   n pl. -S a transparent substance
HYALITE   n pl. -S a colorless opal
HYALOGEN   n pl. -S a substance found in animal cells
HYALOID   n pl. -S a membrane of the eye
HYBRID   n pl. -S the offspring of genetically dissimilar parents
HYBRIS   n pl. -BRISES hubris
HYDATID   n pl. -S a cyst caused by a tapeworm
HYDRA   n pl. -DRAS or -DRAE a freshwater polyp
HYDRACID   n pl. -S an acid
HYDRAGOG   n pl. -S a purgative causing watery discharges
HYDRANT   n pl. -S an outlet from a water main
HYDRANTH   n pl. -S the oral opening of a hydra
HYDRASE   n pl. -S an enzyme
HYDRATE   v -DRATED, -DRATING, -DRATES to combine with water
HYDRATOR   n pl. -S one that hydrates
HYDRIA   n pl. -DRIAE a water jar
HYDRIC   adj pertaining to moisture
HYDRID   n pl. -S hydride
HYDRIDE   n pl. -S a chemical compound
HYDRO   n pl. -DROS electricity produced by waterpower
HYDROGEL   n pl. -S a colloid
HYDROGEN   n pl. -S a gaseous element
HYDROID   n pl. -S a polyp
HYDROMEL   n pl. -S a mixture of honey and water
HYDRONIC   adj pertaining to heating and cooling by water
HYDROPIC   adj affected with hydropsy
HYDROPS   n pl. -ES hydropsy
HYDROPSY   n pl. -SIES dropsy
HYDROSOL   n pl. -S an aqueous solution of a colloid
HYDROUS   adj containing water
HYDROXY   adj containing hydroxyl

HYDROXYL   n pl. -S the radical or group containing oxygen and hydrogen
HYENA   n pl. -S a wolflike mammal **HYENIC, HYENINE, HYENOID** adj
HYETAL   adj pertaining to rain
HYGEIST   n pl. -S an expert in hygiene
HYGIEIST   n pl. -S hygeist
HYGIENE   n pl. -S the science of health **HYGIENIC** adj
HYING   present participle of hie
HYLA   n pl. -S a tree frog
HYLOZOIC   adj pertaining to the doctrine that life and matter are inseparable
HYMEN   n pl. -S a vaginal membrane **HYMENAL** adj
HYMENEAL   n pl. -S a wedding song or poem
HYMENIUM   n pl. -NIA or -NIUMS a layer in certain fungi **HYMENIAL** adj
HYMN   v -ED, -ING, -S to sing a hymn (a song of praise to God)
HYMNAL   n pl. -S a book of hymns
HYMNARY   n pl. -RIES a hymnal
HYMNBOOK   n pl. -S a hymnal
HYMNIST   n pl. -S one who composes hymns
HYMNLESS   adj lacking a hymn
HYMNLIKE   adj resembling a hymn
HYMNODY   n pl. -DIES the singing of hymns
HYOID   n pl. -S a bone of the tongue **HYOIDAL, HYOIDEAN** adj
HYOSCINE   n pl. -S a sedative
HYP   n pl. -S hypochondria
HYPE   n pl. -S a deception
HYPERGOL   n pl. -S a rocket fuel
HYPERON   n pl. -S an atomic particle
HYPEROPE   n pl. -S a farsighted person
HYPHA   n pl. -PHAE a threadlike element of a fungus **HYPHAL** adj
HYPHEMIA   n pl. -S deficiency of blood
HYPHEN   v -ED, -ING, -S to connect words or syllables with a hyphen (a mark of punctuation)
HYPNIC   adj pertaining to sleep
HYPNOID   adj pertaining to hypnosis or sleep
HYPNOSIS   n pl. -NOSES an artificially induced state resembling sleep

HYPNOTIC   *n* pl. -S a sleep-inducing drug

HYPO   *v* -ED, -ING, -S to inject with a hypodermic needle

HYPOACID   *adj* having a lower than normal degree of acidity

HYPODERM   *n* pl. -S a skin layer

HYPOGEA   pl. of hypogeum

HYPOGEAL   *adj* underground

HYPOGEAN   *adj* hypogeal

HYPOGENE   *adj* formed underground

HYPOGEUM   *n* pl. -GEA an underground chamber

HYPOGYNY   *n* pl. -NIES the condition of having flowers with organs situated below the ovary

HYPONEA   *n* pl. -S hyponoia

HYPONOIA   *n* pl. -S dulled mental activity

HYPOPNEA   *n* pl. -S abnormally shallow breathing

HYPOPYON   *n* pl. -S an accumulation of pus in the eye

HYPOTHEC   *n* pl. -S a type of mortgage

HYPOXIA   *n* pl. -S a deficiency of oxygen in body tissue **HYPOXIC** *adj*

HYRACOID   *n* pl. -S a hyrax

HYRAX   *n* pl. -RAXES or -RACES a small, harelike mammal

HYSON   *n* pl. -S a Chinese tea

HYSSOP   *n* pl. -S a medicinal herb

HYSTERIA   *n* pl. -S uncontrollable excitement or fear

HYSTERIC   *n* pl. -S one who is subject to fits of hysteria

HYTE   *adj* insane

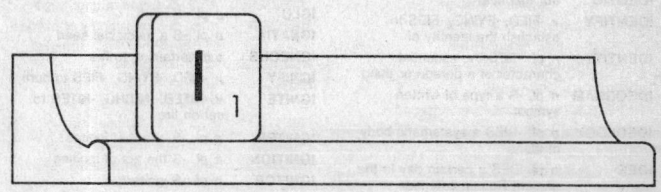

IAMB	n pl. -S a type of metrical foot
IAMBIC	n pl. -S an iamb
IAMBUS	n pl. -BUSES or -BI an iamb
IATRIC	adj pertaining to medicine
IATRICAL	adj iatric
IBEX	n pl. IBEXES or IBICES a wild goat
IBIDEM	adv in the same place
IBIS	n pl. IBISES a wading bird
ICE	v ICED, ICING, ICES to cover with ice (frozen water)
ICEBERG	n pl. -S a large floating body of ice
ICEBLINK	n pl. -S a glare over an ice field
ICEBOAT	n pl. -S a vehicle that sails on ice
ICEBOUND	adj surrounded by ice
ICEBOX	n pl. -ES a cabinet for cooling food
ICECAP	n pl. -S a covering of ice and snow
ICED	past tense of ice
ICEFALL	n pl. -S a kind of frozen waterfall
ICEHOUSE	n pl. -S a building for storing ice
ICEKHANA	n pl. -S an automotive event held on a frozen lake
ICELESS	adj having no ice
ICELIKE	adj resembling ice
ICEMAN	n pl. -MEN a man who supplies ice
ICH	n pl. ICHS a disease of certain fishes
ICHNITE	n pl. -S a fossil footprint
ICHOR	n pl. -S a watery discharge from a wound ICHOROUS adj
ICHTHYIC	adj pertaining to fishes

ICICLE	n pl. -S a hanging spike of ice ICICLED adj
ICIER	comparative of icy
ICIEST	superlative of icy
ICILY	adv in an icy manner
ICINESS	n pl. -ES the state of being icy
ICING	n pl. -S a sweet mixture for covering cakes
ICKER	n pl. -S a head of grain
ICKY	adj ICKIER, ICKIEST repulsive
ICON	n pl. -S or -ES a representation ICONIC, ICONICAL adj
ICTERIC	n pl. -S a remedy for icterus
ICTERUS	n pl. -ES a diseased condition of the liver
ICTUS	n pl. -ES a recurring stress or beat in a poetical form ICTIC adj
ICY	adj ICIER, ICIEST covered with ice
ID	n pl. -S a part of the psyche
IDEA	n pl. -S a conception existing in the mind IDEALESS adj
IDEAL	n pl. -S a standard of perfection
IDEALISE	v -ISED, -ISING, -ISES to idealize
IDEALISM	n pl. -S the pursuit of noble goals
IDEALIST	n pl. -S an adherent of idealism
IDEALITY	n pl. -TIES the state of being perfect; something idealized
IDEALIZE	v -IZED, -IZING, -IZES to regard as perfect
IDEALLY	adv perfectly
IDEALOGY	n pl. -GIES ideology
IDEATE	v -ATED, -ATING, -ATES to form an idea

IDEATION	*n pl.* -S the act of ideating
IDEATIVE	*adj* pertaining to ideation
IDEM	*adj* the same
IDENTIC	*adj* identical
IDENTIFY	*v* -FIED, -FYING, -FIES to establish the identity of
IDENTITY	*n pl.* -TIES the essential character of a person or thing
IDEOGRAM	*n pl.* -S a type of written symbol
IDEOLOGY	*n pl.* -GIES a systematic body of ideas
IDES	*n pl.* IDES a certain day in the ancient Roman calendar
IDIOCY	*n pl.* -CIES the condition of being an idiot
IDIOLECT	*n pl.* -S one's speech pattern
IDIOM	*n pl.* -S an expression peculiar to a language
IDIOT	*n pl.* -S a mentally deficient person **IDIOTIC** *adj*
IDIOTISM	*n pl.* -S idiocy
IDLE	*adj* IDLER, IDLEST inactive
IDLE	*v* IDLED, IDLING, IDLES to pass time idly
IDLENESS	*n pl.* -ES the state of being idle
IDLER	*n pl.* -S one that idles
IDLESSE	*n pl.* -S idleness
IDLEST	superlative of idle
IDLING	present participle of idle
IDLY	*adv* in an idle manner
IDOCRASE	*n pl.* -S a mineral
IDOL	*n pl.* -S an object of worship
IDOLATER	*n pl.* -S one that worships idols
IDOLATRY	*n pl.* -TRIES the worship of idols
IDOLISE	*v* -ISED, -ISING, -ISES to idolize
IDOLISER	*n pl.* -S one that idolises
IDOLISM	*n pl.* -S idolatry
IDOLIZE	*v* -IZED, -IZING, -IZES to worship
IDOLIZER	*n pl.* -S one that idolizes
IDONEITY	*n pl.* -TIES the state of being idoneous
IDONEOUS	*adj* suitable
IDYL	*n pl.* -S a poem or prose work depicting scenes of rural simplicity
IDYLIST	*n pl.* -S a writer of idyls
IDYLL	*n pl.* -S idyl **IDYLLIC** *adj*
IDYLLIST	*n pl.* -S idylist
IF	*n pl.* -S a possibility

IFFINESS	*n pl.* -ES the state of being iffy
IFFY	*adj* IFFIER, IFFIEST full of uncertainty
IGLOO	*n pl.* -LOOS an Eskimo dwelling
IGLU	*n pl.* -S igloo
IGNATIA	*n pl.* -S a medicinal seed
IGNEOUS	*adj* pertaining to fire
IGNIFY	*v* -FIED, -FYING, -FIES to burn
IGNITE	*v* -NITED, -NITING, -NITES to set on fire
IGNITER	*n pl.* -S one that ignites
IGNITION	*n pl.* -S the act of igniting
IGNITOR	*n pl.* -S igniter
IGNITRON	*n pl.* -S a type of rectifier tube
IGNOBLE	*adj* of low character **IGNOBLY** *adv*
IGNOMINY	*n pl.* -NIES disgrace or dishonor
IGNORANT	*adj* having no knowledge
IGNORE	*v* -NORED, -NORING, -NORES to refuse to notice
IGNORER	*n pl.* -S one that ignores
IGUANA	*n pl.* -S a tropical lizard
IGUANIAN	*n pl.* -S a lizard related to the iguana
IHRAM	*n pl.* -S the garb worn by Muslim pilgrims
IKEBANA	*n pl.* -S the Japanese art of flower arranging
IKON	*n pl.* -S icon
ILEA	pl. of ileum
ILEAC	*adj* pertaining to the ileum
ILEAL	*adj* ileac
ILEITIS	*n pl.* ILEITIDES inflammation of the ileum
ILEUM	*n pl.* ILEA a part of the small intestine
ILEUS	*n pl.* -ES intestinal obstruction
ILEX	*n pl.* -ES a holly
ILIA	pl. of ilium
ILIAC	*adj* pertaining to the ilium
ILIAD	*n pl.* -S a long poem
ILIAL	*adj* iliac
ILIUM	*n pl.* ILIA a bone of the pelvis
ILK	*n pl.* -S a class or kind
ILKA	*adj* each
ILL	*n pl.* -S an evil
ILLATION	*n pl.* -S the act of inferring
ILLATIVE	*n pl.* -S a word or phrase introducing an inference
ILLEGAL	*adj* prohibited by law

ILLICIT	*adj* not permitted
ILLINIUM	*n* pl. -S a radioactive element
ILLIQUID	*adj* not readily convertible into cash
ILLITE	*n* pl. -S a group of minerals **ILLITIC** *adj*
ILLNESS	*n* pl. -ES sickness
ILLOGIC	*n* pl. -S absence of logic
ILLUME	*v* -LUMED, -LUMING, -LUMES to illuminate
ILLUMINE	*v* -MINED, -MINING, -MINES to illuminate
ILLUSION	*n* pl. -S a false perception
ILLUSIVE	*adj* illusory
ILLUSORY	*adj* based on illusion
ILLUVIUM	*n* pl. -VIA or -VIUMS a type of material accumulated in soil **ILLUVIAL** *adj*
ILLY	*adv* badly
ILMENITE	*n* pl. -S a mineral
IMAGE	*v* -AGED, -AGING, -AGES to imagine
IMAGERY	*n* pl. -ERIES mental pictures
IMAGINAL	*adj* pertaining to an imago
IMAGINE	*v* -INED, -INING, -INES to form a mental picture of
IMAGINER	*n* pl. -S one that imagines
IMAGING	present participle of image
IMAGINING	present participle of imagine
IMAGISM	*n* pl. -S a movement in poetry
IMAGIST	*n* pl. -S an adherent of imagism
IMAGO	*n* pl. -GOES an adult insect
IMAM	*n* pl. -S a Muslim priest
IMAMATE	*n* pl. -S the office of an imam
IMARET	*n* pl. -S a Turkish inn
IMAUM	*n* pl. -S imam
IMBALM	*v* -ED, -ING, -S to embalm
IMBALMER	*n* pl. -S embalmer
IMBARK	*v* -ED, -ING, -S to embark
IMBECILE	*n* pl. -S a mentally deficient person
IMBED	*v* -BEDDED, -BEDDING, -BEDS to embed
IMBIBE	*v* -BIBED, -BIBING, -BIBES to drink
IMBIBER	*n* pl. -S one that imbibes
IMBITTER	*v* -ED, -ING, -S to embitter
IMBLAZE	*v* -BLAZED, -BLAZING, -BLAZES to emblaze
IMBODY	*v* -BODIED, -BODYING, -BODIES to embody
IMBOLDEN	*v* -ED, -ING, -S to embolden

IMBOSOM	*v* -ED, -ING, -S to embosom
IMBOWER	*v* -ED, -ING, -S to embower
IMBROWN	*v* -ED, -ING, -S to embrown
IMBRUE	*v* -BRUED, -BRUING, -BRUES to stain
IMBRUTE	*v* -BRUTED, -BRUTING, -BRUTES to make brutal
IMBUE	*v* -BUED, -BUING, -BUES to make thoroughly wet
IMID	*n* pl. -S imide
IMIDE	*n* pl. -S a chemical compound **IMIDIC** *adj*
IMIDO	*adj* containing an imide
IMINE	*n* pl. -S a chemical compound
IMINO	*adj* containing an imine
IMITABLE	*adj* capable of being imitated
IMITATE	*v* -TATED, -TATING, -TATES to behave in the same way as
IMITATOR	*n* pl. -S one that imitates
IMMANE	*adj* great in size
IMMANENT	*adj* existing within
IMMATURE	*n* pl. -S an individual that is not fully grown or developed
IMMENSE	*adj* -MENSER, -MENSEST great in size
IMMERGE	*v* -MERGED, -MERGING, -MERGES to immerse
IMMERSE	*v* -MERSED, -MERSING, -MERSES to plunge into a liquid
IMMESH	*v* -ED, -ING, -ES to enmesh
IMMIES	pl. of immy
IMMINENT	*adj* ready to take place
IMMINGLE	*v* -GLED, -GLING, -GLES to blend
IMMIX	*v* -ED, -ING, -ES to mix in
IMMOBILE	*adj* incapable of being moved
IMMODEST	*adj* not modest
IMMOLATE	*v* -LATED, -LATING, -LATES to kill as a sacrifice
IMMORAL	*adj* contrary to established morality
IMMORTAL	*n* pl. -S one who is not subject to death
IMMOTILE	*adj* lacking mobility
IMMUNE	*n* pl. -S one who is protected from a disease
IMMUNISE	*v* -NISED, -NISING, -NISES to immunize
IMMUNITY	*n* pl. -TIES the state of being protected from a disease
IMMUNIZE	*v* -NIZED, -NIZING, -NIZES to protect from a disease

IMMURE   v -MURED, -MURING, -MURES to imprison

IMMY   n pl. -MIES a type of playing marble

IMP   v -ED, -ING, -S to graft feathers onto a bird's wing

IMPACT   v -ED, -ING, -S to pack firmly together

IMPACTER   n pl. -S one that impacts

IMPACTOR   n pl. -S impacter

IMPAINT   v -ED, -ING, -S to paint or depict

IMPAIR   v -ED, -ING, -S to make worse

IMPAIRER   n pl. -S one that impairs

IMPALA   n pl. -S an African antelope

IMPALE   v -PALED, -PALING, -PALES to pierce with a pointed object

IMPALER   n pl. -S one that impales

IMPANEL   v -ELED, -ELING, -ELS or -ELLED, -ELLING, -ELS to enter on a list for jury duty

IMPARITY   n pl. -TIES lack of equality

IMPARK   v -ED, -ING, -S to confine in a park

IMPART   v -ED, -ING, -S to make known

IMPARTER   n pl. -S one that imparts

IMPASSE   n pl. -S a road or passage having no exit

IMPASTE   v -PASTED, -PASTING, -PASTES to make into a paste

IMPASTO   n pl. -TOS a painting technique

IMPAVID   adj brave

IMPAWN   v -ED, -ING, -S to pawn

IMPEACH   v -ED, -ING, -ES to charge with misconduct in office

IMPEARL   v -ED, -ING, -S to make pearly

IMPEDE   v -PEDED, -PEDING, -PEDES to obstruct the progress of

IMPEDER   n pl. -S one that impedes

IMPEL   v -PELLED, -PELLING, -PELS to force into action

IMPELLER   n pl. -S one that impels

IMPELLOR   n pl. -S impeller

IMPEND   v -ED, -ING, -S to be imminent

IMPERIA   a pl. of imperium

IMPERIAL   n pl. -S an emperor or empress

IMPERIL   v -ILED, -ILING, -ILS or -ILLED, -ILLING, -ILS to place in jeopardy

IMPERIUM   n pl. -RIUMS or -RIA absolute power

IMPETIGO   n pl. -GOS a skin disease

IMPETUS   n pl. -ES an impelling force

IMPHEE   n pl. -S an African grass

IMPI   n pl. -S a body of warriors

IMPIETY   n pl. -TIES lack of piety

IMPING   n pl. -S the process of grafting

IMPINGE   v -PINGED, -PINGING, -PINGES to collide

IMPINGER   n pl. -S one that impinges

IMPIOUS   adj not pious

IMPISH   adj mischievous **IMPISHLY** adv

IMPLANT   v -ED, -ING, -S to set securely

IMPLEAD   v -ED, -ING, -S to sue in a court of law

IMPLEDGE   v -PLEDGED, -PLEDGING, -PLEDGES to pawn

IMPLICIT   adj implied

IMPLIED   past tense of imply

IMPLIES   present 3d person sing. of imply

IMPLODE   v -PLODED, -PLODING, -PLODES to collapse inward

IMPLORE   v -PLORED, -PLORING, -PLORES to beg for urgently

IMPLORER   n pl. -S one that implores

IMPLY   v -PLIED, -PLYING, -PLIES to indicate or suggest indirectly

IMPOLICY   n pl. -CIES an unwise course of action

IMPOLITE   adj not polite

IMPONE   v -PONED, -PONING, -PONES to wager

IMPOROUS   adj extremely dense

IMPORT   v -ED, -ING, -S to bring into a country from abroad

IMPORTER   n pl. -S one that imports

IMPOSE   v -POSED, -POSING, -POSES to establish as compulsory

IMPOSER   n pl. -S one that imposes

IMPOST   v -ED, -ING, -S to determine customs duties

IMPOSTER   n pl. -S impostor

IMPOSTOR   n pl. -S one that poses as another for deceptive purposes

IMPOTENT   n pl. -S one that is powerless

IMPOUND   v -ED, -ING, -S to seize and retain in legal custody

IMPOWER   v -ED, -ING, -S to empower

IMPREGN   v -ED, -ING, -S to make pregnant

IMPRESA   n pl. -S a type of emblem

IMPRESE   n pl. -S impresa

IMPRESS   v -ED, -ING, -ES to affect strongly

IMPREST	n pl. -S a loan or advance of money
IMPRIMIS	adv in the first place
IMPRINT	v -ED, -ING, -S to produce a mark by pressure
IMPRISON	v -ED, -ING, -S to confine
IMPROPER	adj not proper
IMPROVE	v -PROVED, -PROVING, -PROVES to make better
IMPROVER	n pl. -S one that improves
IMPUDENT	adj offensively bold or disrespectful
IMPUGN	v -ED, -ING, -S to make insinuations against
IMPUGNER	n pl. -S one that impugns
IMPULSE	v -PULSED, -PULSING, -PULSES to give impetus to
IMPUNITY	n pl. -TIES exemption from penalty
IMPURE	adj not pure IMPURELY adv
IMPURITY	n pl. -TIES something that is impure
IMPUTE	v -PUTED, -PUTING, -PUTES to credit to a person or a cause
IMPUTER	n pl. -S one that imputes
IN	v INNED, INNING, INS to harvest
INACTION	n pl. -S lack of action
INACTIVE	adj not active
INANE	adj INANER, INANEST nonsensical INANELY adv
INANE	n pl. -S empty space
INANITY	n pl. -TIES something that is inane
INAPT	adj not apt INAPTLY adv
INARABLE	adj not arable
INARCH	v -ED, -ING, -ES to graft with in a certain way
INARM	v -ED, -ING, -S to encircle with the arms
INBEING	n pl. -S the state of being inherent
INBOARD	n pl. -S a type of boat motor
INBORN	adj existing in one from birth
INBOUND	adj approaching a destination
INBOUNDS	adj being within certain boundaries
INBREED	v -BRED, -BREEDING, -BREEDS to breed closely related stock
INBUILT	adj forming an integral part of a structure
INBURST	n pl. -S the act of bursting inward

INBY	adv inward
INBYE	adv inby
INCAGE	v -CAGED, -CAGING, -CAGES to encage
INCASE	v -CASED, -CASING, -CASES to encase
INCENSE	v -CENSED, -CENSING, -CENSES to make angry
INCEPT	v -ED, -ING, -S to take in
INCEPTOR	n pl. -S one that incepts
INCEST	n pl. -S sexual intercourse between closely related persons
INCH	v -ED, -ING, -ES to move very slowly
INCHMEAL	adv little by little
INCHOATE	adj being in an early stage
INCHWORM	n pl. -S a type of worm
INCIDENT	n pl. -S an event
INCIPIT	n pl. -S the opening words of a text
INCISE	v -CISED, -CISING, -CISES to cut into
INCISION	n pl. -S the act of incising
INCISIVE	adj penetrating
INCISOR	n pl. -S a cutting tooth
INCISORY	adj adapted for cutting
INCISURE	n pl. -S a notch or cleft of a body part
INCITANT	n pl. -S something that incites
INCITE	v -CITED, -CITING, -CITES to arouse to action
INCITER	n pl. -S one that incites
INCIVIL	adj discourteous
INCLASP	v -ED, -ING, -S to enclasp
INCLINE	v -CLINED, -CLINING, -CLINES to slant
INCLINER	n pl. -S one that inclines
INCLIP	v -CLIPPED, -CLIPPING, -CLIPS to clasp
INCLOSE	v -CLOSED, -CLOSING, -CLOSES to enclose
INCLOSER	n pl. -S one that incloses
INCLUDE	v -CLUDED, -CLUDING, -CLUDES to have as a part
INCOG	n pl. -S a disguised person
INCOME	n pl. -S a sum of money earned regularly
INCOMER	n pl. -S one that comes in
INCOMING	n pl. -S an arrival
INCONNU	n pl. -S a large food fish
INCONY	adj pretty

INCORPSE v -CORPSED, -CORPSING, -CORPSES to become combined with

INCREASE v -CREASED, -CREASING, -CREASES to make or become greater

INCREATE adj not created

INCROSS n pl. -ES an individual produced by inbreeding

INCRUST v -ED, -ING, -S to encrust

INCUBATE v -BATED, -BATING, -BATES to warm eggs for hatching

INCUBUS n pl. -BI or -BUSES a demon

INCUDAL adj pertaining to the incus

INCUDATE adj incudal

INCUDES pl. of incus

INCULT adj uncultivated

INCUMBER v -ED, -ING, -S to encumber

INCUR v -CURRED, -CURRING, -CURS to bring upon oneself

INCURVE v -CURVED, -CURVING, -CURVES to curve inward

INCUS n pl. INCUDES a bone in the middle ear

INCUSE v -CUSED, -CUSING, -CUSES to mark by stamping

INDABA n pl. -S a meeting of South African tribes

INDAGATE v -GATED, -GATING, -GATES to investigate

INDAMIN n pl. -S indamine

INDAMINE n pl. -S a chemical compound

INDEBTED adj beholden

INDECENT adj -CENTER, -CENTEST not decent

INDEED adv in truth

INDENE n pl. -S a hydrocarbon

INDENT v -ED, -ING, -S to cut or tear irregularly

INDENTER n pl. -S one that indents

INDENTOR n pl. -S indenter

INDEVOUT adj not devout

INDEX n pl. INDEXES or INDICES a type of reference guide at the end of a book

INDEX v -ED, -ING, -ES to provide with an index

INDEXER n pl. -S one that indexes

INDICAN n pl. -S a chemical compound

INDICANT n pl. -S something that indicates

INDICATE v -CATED, -CATING, -CATES to point out

INDICES a pl. of index

INDICIA n pl. -S a distinctive mark

INDICIUM n pl. -S an indicia

INDICT v -ED, -ING, -S to charge with a crime

INDICTEE n pl. -S one that is indicted

INDICTER n pl. -S one that indicts

INDICTOR n pl. -S indicter

INDIGEN n pl. -S indigene

INDIGENE n pl. -S a native

INDIGENT n pl. -S a needy person

INDIGN adj disgraceful **INDIGNLY** adv

INDIGO n pl. -GOS or -GOES a blue dye

INDIGOID n pl. -S a blue dye

INDIRECT adj not direct

INDITE v -DITED, -DITING, -DITES to write or compose

INDITER n pl. -S one that indites

INDIUM n pl. -S a metallic element

INDOCILE adj not docile

INDOL n pl. -S indole

INDOLE n pl. -S a chemical compound

INDOLENT adj lazy

INDOOR adj pertaining to the interior of a building

INDOORS adv in or into a house

INDORSE v -DORSED, -DORSING, -DORSES to endorse

INDORSEE n pl. -S endorsee

INDORSER n pl. -S endorser

INDORSING present participle of indorse

INDORSOR n pl. -S endorsor

INDOW v -ED, -ING, -S to endow

INDOXYL n -S a chemical compound

INDRAFT n pl. -S an inward flow or current

INDRAWN adj drawn in

INDRI n pl. -S a short-tailed lemur

INDUCE v -DUCED, -DUCING, -DUCES to influence into doing something

INDUCER n pl. -S one that induces

INDUCT v -ED, -ING, -S to bring into military service

INDUCTEE n pl. -S one that is inducted

INDUCTOR n pl. -S one that inducts

INDUE v -DUED, -DUING, -DUES to endue

INDULGE v -DULGED, -DULGING, -DULGES to yield to the desire of

INDULGER *n pl.* -S one that indulges

INDULIN *n pl.* -S induline

INDULINE *n pl.* -S a blue dye

INDULT *n pl.* -S a privilege granted by the pope

INDURATE *v* -RATED, -RATING, -RATES to make hard

INDUSIUM *n pl.* -SIA an enclosing membrane **INDUSIAL** *adj*

INDUSTRY *n pl.* -TRIES a group of productive enterprises

INDWELL *v* -DWELT, -DWELLING, -DWELLS to live within

INEARTH *v* -ED, -ING, -S to bury

INEDIBLE *adj* not fit to be eaten

INEDITA *n/pl* unpublished literary works

INEDITED *adj* not published

INEPT *adj* not suitable **INEPTLY** *adv*

INEQUITY *n pl.* -TIES unfairness

INERRANT *adj* free from error

INERT *n pl.* -S something that lacks active properties

INERTIA *n pl.* -TIAS or -TIAE the tendency of a body to resist acceleration **INERTIAL** *adj*

INERTLY *adv* inactively

INEXACT *adj* not exact

INEXPERT *n pl.* -S a novice

INFAMOUS *adj* having a vile reputation

INFAMY *n pl.* -MIES the state of being infamous

INFANCY *n pl.* -CIES the state of being an infant

INFANT *n pl.* -S a child in the earliest stages of life

INFANTA *n pl.* -S a daughter of a Spanish or Portuguese monarch

INFANTE *n pl.* -S a younger son of a Spanish or Portuguese monarch

INFANTRY *n pl.* -TRIES a branch of the army composed of foot soldiers

INFARCT *n pl.* -S an area of dead or dying tissue

INFARE *n pl.* -S a reception for newlyweds

INFAUNA *n pl.* -NAS or -NAE fauna living on a soft sea floor **INFAUNAL** *adj*

INFECT *v* -ED, -ING, -S to contaminate with disease-producing germs

INFECTER *n pl.* -S one that infects

INFECTOR *n pl.* -S infecter

INFECUND *adj* barren

INFEOFF *v* -ED, -ING, -S to enfeoff

INFER *v* -FERRED, -FERRING, -FERS to reach or derive by reasoning

INFERIOR *n pl.* -S one of lesser rank

INFERNAL *adj* pertaining to hell

INFERNO *n pl.* -NOS a place that resembles or suggests hell

INFERRED past tense of infer

INFERRER *n pl.* -S one that infers

INFERRING present participle of infer

INFEST *v* -ED, -ING, -S to overrun in large numbers

INFESTER *n pl.* -S one that infests

INFIDEL *n pl.* -S one who has no religious faith

INFIELD *n pl.* -S a part of a baseball field

INFINITE *n pl.* -S something that has no limits

INFINITY *n pl.* -TIES the state of having no limits

INFIRM *v* -ED, -ING, -S to weaken or destroy the validity of

INFIRMLY *adv* in a feeble manner

INFIX *v* -ED, -ING, -ES to implant

INFIXION *n pl.* -S the act of infixing

INFLAME *v* -FLAMED, -FLAMING, -FLAMES to set on fire

INFLAMER *n pl.* -S one that inflames

INFLATE *v* -FLATED, -FLATING, -FLATES to cause to expand by filling with gas or air

INFLATER *n pl.* -S one that inflates

INFLATOR *n pl.* -S inflater

INFLECT *v* -ED, -ING, -S to bend

INFLEXED *adj* bent inward

INFLICT *v* -ED, -ING, -S to cause to be endured; impose

INFLIGHT *adj* done during an air voyage

INFLOW *n pl.* -S the act of flowing in

INFLUENT *n pl.* -S a tributary

INFLUX *n pl.* -ES a flowing in

INFO *n pl.* -FOS information

INFOLD *v* -ED, -ING, -S to fold inward

INFOLDER *n pl.* -S one that infolds

INFORM *v* -ED, -ING, -S to supply with information

INFORMAL *adj* marked by the absence of formality or ceremony

INFORMER *n pl.* -S one that informs

INFRA *adv* below

INFRACT *v* -ED, -ING, -S to break a legal rule

INFRARED *n* pl. -S a part of the invisible spectrum

INFRINGE *v* -FRINGED, -FRINGING, -FRINGES to violate an oath or a law

INFRUGAL *adj* not frugal

INFUSE *v* -FUSED, -FUSING, -FUSES to permeate with something

INFUSER *n* pl. -S one that infuses

INFUSION *n* pl. -S the act of infusing

INFUSIVE *adj* capable of infusing

INGATE *n* pl. -S a channel by which molten metal enters a mold

INGATHER *v* -ED, -ING, -S to gather in

INGENUE *n* pl. -S a naive young woman

INGEST *v* -ED, -ING, -S to take into the body

INGESTA *n/pl* ingested material

INGLE *n* pl. -S a fire

INGOING *adj* entering

INGOT *v* -ED, -ING, -S to shape into a convenient form for storage

INGRAFT *v* -ED, -ING, -S to engraft

INGRAIN *v* -ED, -ING, -S to impress firmly on the mind

INGRATE *n* pl. -S an ungrateful person

INGRESS *n* pl. -ES the act of entering

INGROUP *n* pl. -S a group united by common interests

INGROWN *adj* grown into the flesh

INGROWTH *n* pl. -S growth inward

INGUINAL *adj* pertaining to the groin

INGULF *v* -ED, -ING, -S to engulf

INHABIT *v* -ED, -ING, -S to live in

INHALANT *n* pl. -S something that is inhaled

INHALE *v* -HALED, -HALING, -HALES to take into the lungs

INHALER *n* pl. -S one that inhales

INHAUL *n* pl. -S a line for bringing in a sail

INHAULER *n* pl. -S an inhaul

INHERE *v* -HERED, -HERING, -HERES to be inherent

INHERENT *adj* existing in something as an essential characteristic

INHERIT *v* -ED, -ING, -S to receive by legal succession

INHESION *n* pl. -S the state of inhering

INHIBIT *v* -ED, -ING, -S to restrain or hold back

INHUMAN *adj* lacking desirable human qualities

INHUMANE *adj* not humane

INHUME *v* -HUMED, -HUMING, -HUMES to bury

INHUMER *n* pl. -S one that inhumes

INIMICAL *adj* unfriendly

INION *n* pl. INIA a part of the skull

INIQUITY *n* pl. -TIES a gross injustice

INITIAL *v* -TIALED, -TIALING, -TIALS or -TIALLED, -TIALLING, -TIALS to mark with the first letters of one's name

INITIATE *v* -ATED, -ATING, -ATES to originate

INJECT *v* -ED, -ING, -S to force a fluid into

INJECTOR *n* pl. -S one that injects

INJURE *v* -JURED, -JURING, -JURES to do or cause injury to

INJURER *n* pl. -S one that injures

INJURY *n* pl. -RIES harm inflicted or suffered

INK *v* -ED, -ING, -S to mark with ink (a colored fluid used for writing)

INKBERRY *n* pl. -RIES a small shrub

INKBLOT *n* pl. -S a blotted pattern of spilled ink

INKER *n* pl. -S one that inks

INKHORN *n* pl. -S a small container for ink

INKIER comparative of inky

INKIEST superlative of inky

INKINESS *n* pl. -ES the state of being inky

INKLE *n* pl. -S a tape used for trimming

INKLESS *adj* being without ink

INKLIKE *adj* resembling ink

INKLING *n* pl. -S a slight suggestion

INKPOT *n* pl. -S an inkwell

INKSTAND *n* pl. -S an inkwell

INKWELL *n* pl. -S a small container for ink

INKWOOD *n* pl. -S an evergreen tree

INKY *adj* INKIER, INKIEST resembling ink

INLACE *v* -LACED, -LACING, -LACES to enlace

INLAID past tense of inlay

INLAND *n* pl. -S the interior of a region

INLANDER *n* pl. -S one living in the interior of a region

INLAY *v* -LAID, -LAYING, -LAYS to set into a surface

INLAYER   n pl. -S one that inlays

INLET   v -LET, -LETTING, -LETS to insert

INLIER   n pl. -S a type of rock formation

INLY   adv inwardly

INMATE   n pl. -S one who is confined to an institution

INMESH   v -ED, -ING, -ES to enmesh

INMOST   adj farthest within

INN   v -ED, -ING, -S to put up at an inn (a public lodging house)

INNARDS   n/pl the internal organs

INNATE   adj inborn **INNATELY** adv

INNED   past tense of in

INNER   n pl. -S something that is within

INNERLY   adv inwardly

INNERVE   v -NERVED, -NERVING, -NERVES to stimulate

INNING   n pl. -S a division of a baseball game

INNLESS   adj having no inns

INNOCENT   adj -CENTER, -CENTEST free from guilt or sin

INNOCENT   n pl. -S an innocent person

INNOVATE   v -VATED, -VATING, -VATES to introduce something new

INNUENDO   v -ED, -ING, -S or -ES to make a derogatory implication

INOCULUM   n pl. -LA or -LUMS the material used in an inoculation

INOSITE   n pl. -S inositol

INOSITOL   n pl. -S an alcohol found in plant and animal tissue

INPHASE   adj having matching electrical phases

INPOUR   v -ED, -ING, -S to pour in

INPUT   v -PUTTED, -PUTTING, -PUTS to enter data into a computer

INQUEST   n pl. -S a legal inquiry

INQUIET   v -ED, -ING, -S to disturb

INQUIRE   v -QUIRED, -QUIRING, -QUIRES to ask about

INQUIRER   n pl. -S one that inquires

INQUIRY   n pl. -RIES a question

INROAD   n pl. -S a hostile invasion

INRUSH   n pl. -ES a rushing in

INSANE   adj -SANER, -SANEST mentally unsound **INSANELY** adv

INSANITY   n pl. -TIES the state of being insane; something utterly foolish

INSCRIBE   v -SCRIBED, -SCRIBING, -SCRIBES to write or engrave as a lasting record

INSCROLL   v -ED, -ING, -S to enscroll

INSCULP   v -ED, -ING, -S to engrave

INSEAM   n pl. -S an inner seam

INSECT   n pl. -S any of a class of small invertebrate animals

INSECTAN   adj pertaining to insects

INSECURE   adj unsafe

INSERT   v -ED, -ING, -S to put in

INSERTER   n pl. -S one that inserts

INSET   v -SETTED, -SETTING, -SETS to insert

INSETTER   n pl. -S one that inserts

INSHEATH   v -ED, -ING, -S to ensheath

INSHORE   adj near the shore

INSHRINE   v -SHRINED, -SHRINING, -SHRINES to enshrine

INSIDE   n pl. -S something that lies within

INSIDER   n pl. -S an accepted member of a clique

INSIGHT   n pl. -S a perception of the inner nature of things

INSIGNE   n pl. INSIGNIA an insignia

INSIGNIA   n pl. -S an emblem of authority or honor

INSIPID   adj dull and uninteresting

INSIST   v -ED, -ING, -S to be resolute on some matter

INSISTER   n pl. -S one that insists

INSNARE   v -SNARED, -SNARING, -SNARES to ensnare

INSNARER   n pl. -S ensnarer

INSOFAR   adv to such an extent

INSOLATE   v -LATED, -LATING, -LATES to expose to sunlight

INSOLE   n pl. -S the inner sole of a boot or shoe

INSOLENT   n pl. -S an extremely rude person

INSOMNIA   n pl. -S chronic inability to sleep

INSOMUCH   adv to such a degree

INSOUL   v -ED, -ING, -S to ensoul

INSPAN   v -SPANNED, -SPANNING, -SPANS to harness or yoke to a vehicle

INSPECT   v -ED, -ING, -S to look carefully at or over

INSPHERE   v -SPHERED, -SPHERING, -SPHERES to ensphere

INSPIRE	v -SPIRED, -SPIRING, -SPIRES to animate the mind or emotions of
INSPIRER	n pl. -S one that inspires
INSPIRIT	v -ED, -ING, -S to fill with spirit or life
INSTABLE	adj unstable
INSTAL	v -STALLED, -STALLING, -STALS to install
INSTALL	v -ED, -ING, -S to place in position for use
INSTANCE	v -STANCED, -STANCING, -STANCES to cite as an example
INSTANCY	n pl. -CIES urgency
INSTANT	n pl. -S a very short time
INSTAR	v -STARRED, -STARRING, -STARS to adorn with stars
INSTATE	v -STATED, -STATING, -STATES to place in office
INSTEAD	adv as a substitute or equivalent
INSTEP	n pl. -S a part of the foot
INSTIL	v -STILLED, -STILLING, -STILS to instill
INSTILL	v -ED, -ING, -S to infuse slowly
INSTINCT	n pl. -S an inborn behavioral pattern
INSTROKE	n pl. -S an inward stroke
INSTRUCT	v -ED, -ING, -S to supply with knowledge
INSULANT	n pl. -S an insulating material
INSULAR	n pl. -S an islander
INSULATE	v -LATED, -LATING, -LATES to separate with nonconducting material
INSULIN	n pl. -S a hormone
INSULT	v -ED, -ING, -S to treat offensively
INSULTER	n pl. -S one that insults
INSURANT	n pl. -S one who is insured
INSURE	v -SURED, -SURING, -SURES to guarantee against loss
INSURED	n pl. -S one who is insured
INSURER	n pl. -S one that insures
INSURING	present participle of insure
INSWATHE	v -SWATHED, -SWATHING, -SWATHES to enswathe
INSWEPT	adj narrowed in front
INTACT	adj not damaged in any way
INTAGLIO	n pl. -GLIOS or -GLI an incised or sunken design
INTAKE	n pl. -S the act of taking in

INTARSIA	n pl. -S a decorative technique
INTEGER	n pl. -S a whole number
INTEGRAL	n pl. -S a total unit
INTEND	v -ED, -ING, -S to have as a specific aim or purpose
INTENDED	n pl. -S one's spouse to-be
INTENDER	n pl. -S one that intends
INTENSE	adj -TENSER, -TENSEST existing in an extreme degree
INTENT	n pl. -S a purpose
INTENTLY	adv in an unwavering manner
INTER	v -TERRED, -TERRING, -TERS to bury
INTERACT	v -ED, -ING, -S to act on each other
INTERCOM	n pl. -S a type of communication system
INTERCUT	v -CUT, -CUTTING, -CUTS to alternate camera shots
INTEREST	v -ED, -ING, -S to engage the attention of
INTERIM	n pl. -S an interval
INTERIOR	n pl. -S the inside
INTERLAP	v -LAPPED, -LAPPING, -LAPS to lap one over another
INTERLAY	v -LAID, -LAYING, -LAYS to place between
INTERMIT	v -MITTED, -MITTING, -MITS to stop temporarily
INTERMIX	v -ED, -ING, -ES to mix together
INTERN	v -ED, -ING, -S to confine during a war
INTERNAL	n pl. -S an inner attribute
INTERNE	n pl. -S a recent medical school graduate on a hospital staff
INTERNEE	n pl. -S one who has been interned
INTERRED	past tense of inter
INTERREX	n pl. -REGES a type of sovereign
INTERRING	present participle of inter
INTERSEX	n pl. -ES a person having characteristics of both sexes
INTERTIE	n pl. -S a type of electrical connection
INTERVAL	n pl. -S a space of time between periods or events
INTERWAR	adj happening between wars
INTHRAL	v -THRALLED, -THRALLING, -THRALS to enthrall
INTHRALL	v -ED, -ING, -S to enthrall

INTHRONE v -THRONED, -THRONING, -THRONES to enthrone

INTIMA n pl. -MAE or -MAS the innermost layer of an organ **INTIMAL** adj

INTIMACY n pl. -CIES the state of being closely associated

INTIMATE v -MATED, -MATING, -MATES to make known indirectly

INTIME adj cozy

INTINE n pl. -S the inner wall of a spore

INTITLE v -TLED, -TLING, -TLES to entitle

INTITULE v -ULED, -ULING, -ULES to entitle

INTO prep to the inside of

INTOMB v -ED, -ING, -S to entomb

INTONATE v -NATED, -NATING, -NATES to intone

INTONE v -TONED, -TONING, -TONES to speak in a singing voice

INTONER n pl. -S one that intones

INTORT v -ED, -ING, -S to twist inward

INTOWN adj located in the center of a city

INTRADOS n pl. -ES the inner curve of an arch

INTRANT n pl. -S an entrant

INTREAT v -ED, -ING, -S to entreat

INTRENCH v -ED, -ING, -ES to entrench

INTREPID adj fearless

INTRIGUE v -TRIGUED, -TRIGUING, -TRIGUES to arouse the curiosity of

INTRO n pl. -TROS an introduction

INTROFY v -FIED, -FYING, -FIES to increase the wetting properties of

INTROIT n pl. -S music sung at the beginning of a worship service

INTROMIT v -MITTED, -MITTING, -MITS to put in

INTRORSE adj facing inward

INTRUDE v -TRUDED, -TRUDING, -TRUDES to thrust or force oneself in

INTRUDER n pl. -S one that intrudes

INTRUST v -ED, -ING, -S to entrust

INTUBATE v -BATED, -BATING, -BATES to insert a tube into

INTUIT v -ED, -ING, -S to know without conscious reasoning

INTURN n pl. -S a turning inward **INTURNED** adj

INTWINE v -TWINED, -TWINING, -TWINES to entwine

INTWIST v -ED, -ING, -S to entwist

INULASE n pl. -S an enzyme

INULIN n pl. -S a chemical compound

INUNDANT adj inundating

INUNDATE v -DATED, -DATING, -DATES to overwhelm with water

INURBANE adj not urbane

INURE v -URED, -URING, -URES to accustom to accept something undesirable

INURN v -ED, -ING, -S to put in an urn

INUTILE adj useless

INVADE v -VADED, -VADING, -VADES to enter for conquest or plunder

INVADER n pl. -S one that invades

INVALID v -ED, -ING, -S to disable physically

INVAR n pl. -S a steel alloy

INVASION n pl. -S the act of invading **INVASIVE** adj

INVECTED adj edged by convex curves

INVEIGH v -ED, -ING, -S to protest angrily

INVEIGLE v -GLED, -GLING, -GLES to induce by guile or flattery

INVENT v -ED, -ING, -S to devise originally

INVENTER n pl. -S inventor

INVENTOR n pl. -S one that invents

INVERITY n pl. -TIES lack of truth

INVERSE n pl. -S something that is opposite

INVERT v -ED, -ING, -S to turn upside down

INVERTER n pl. -S one that inverts

INVERTOR n pl. -S a type of electrical device

INVEST v -ED, -ING, -S to commit something of value for future profit

INVESTOR n pl. -S one that invests

INVIABLE adj not viable **INVIABLY** adv

INVIRILE adj not virile

INVISCID adj not viscid

INVITAL adj not vital

INVITE v -VITED, -VITING, -VITES to request the presence of

INVITEE n pl. -S one that is invited

INVITER	*n* pl. -S one that invites
INVITING	present participle of invite
INVOCATE	*v* -CATED, -CATING, -CATES to invoke
INVOICE	*v* -VOICED, -VOICING, -VOICES to bill
INVOKE	*v* -VOKED, -VOKING, -VOKES to appeal to for aid
INVOKER	*n* pl. -S one that invokes
INVOLUTE	*v* -LUTED, -LUTING, -LUTES to roll or curl up
INVOLVE	*v* -VOLVED, -VOLVING, -VOLVES to contain or include as a part
INVOLVER	*n* pl. -S one that involves
INWALL	*v* -ED, -ING, -S to surround with a wall
INWARD	*adv* toward the inside
INWARDLY	*adv* on the inside
INWARDS	*adv* inward
INWEAVE	*v* -WOVE or -WEAVED, -WOVEN, -WEAVING, -WEAVES to weave together
INWIND	*v* -WOUND, -WINDING, -WINDS to enwind
INWRAP	*v* -WRAPPED, -WRAPPING, -WRAPS to enwrap
IODATE	*v* -DATED, -DATING, -DATES to iodize
IODATION	*n* pl. -S the act of iodating
IODIC	*adj* pertaining to iodine
IODID	*n* pl. -S iodide
IODIDE	*n* pl. -S a compound of iodine
IODIN	*n* pl. -S iodine
IODINATE	*v* -ATED, -ATING, -ATES to iodize
IODINE	*n* pl. -S a nonmetallic element
IODISM	*n* pl. -S iodine poisoning
IODIZE	*v* -DIZED, -DIZING, -DIZES to treat with iodine
IODIZER	*n* pl. -S one that iodizes
IODOFORM	*n* pl. -S an iodine compound
IODOL	*n* pl. -S an iodine compound
IODOPHOR	*n* pl. -S an iodine compound
IODOPSIN	*n* pl. -S a pigment in the retina
IODOUS	*adj* pertaining to iodine
IOLITE	*n* pl. -S a mineral
ION	*n* pl. -S an electrically charged atom
IONIC	*n* pl. -S a style of type
IONICITY	*n* pl. -TIES the state of existing as or like an ion

IONISE	*v* -ISED, -ISING, -ISES to ionize
IONIUM	*n* pl. -S an isotope of thorium
IONIZE	*v* -IZED, -IZING, -IZES to convert into ions
IONIZER	*n* pl. -S one that ionizes
IONOMER	*n* pl. -S a type of plastic
IONONE	*n* pl. -S a chemical compound
IOTA	*n* pl. -S a Greek letter
IOTACISM	*n* pl. -S excessive use of the letter iota
IPECAC	*n* pl. -S a medicinal plant
IPOMOEA	*n* pl. -S a flowering plant
IRACUND	*adj* easily angered
IRADE	*n* pl. -S a decree of a Muslim ruler
IRATE	*adj* IRATER, IRATEST angry IRATELY *adv*
IRE	*v* IRED, IRING, IRES to anger
IREFUL	*adj* angry IREFULLY *adv*
IRELESS	*adj* not angry
IRENIC	*adj* peaceful in purpose
IRENICAL	*adj* irenic
IRENICS	*n/pl* a branch of theology
IRIDES	a pl. of iris
IRIDIC	*adj* pertaining to iridium
IRIDIUM	*n* pl. -S a metallic element
IRING	present participle of ire
IRIS	*n* pl. IRISES or IRIDES a part of the eye
IRIS	*v* -ED, -ING, -ES to give the form of a rainbow to
IRITIS	*n* pl. -TISES inflammation of the iris IRITIC *adj*
IRK	*v* -ED, -ING, -S to annoy or weary
IRKSOME	*adj* tending to irk
IRON	*v* -ED, -ING, -S to furnish with iron (a metallic element)
IRONBARK	*n* pl. -S a timber tree
IRONCLAD	*n* pl. -S an armored warship
IRONE	*n* pl. -S an aromatic oil
IRONER	*n* pl. -S a machine for pressing clothes
IRONIC	*adj* pertaining to irony
IRONICAL	*adj* ironic
IRONIES	pl. of irony
IRONING	*n* pl. -S clothes pressed or to be pressed
IRONIST	*n* pl. -S one who uses irony
IRONLIKE	*adj* resembling iron
IRONNESS	*n* pl. -ES the state of being iron

IRONSIDE *n pl.* -S a man of great strength

IRONWARE *n pl.* -S articles made of iron

IRONWEED *n pl.* -S a shrub

IRONWOOD *n pl.* -S a hardwood tree

IRONWORK *n pl.* -S objects made of iron

IRONY *n pl.* -NIES the use of words to express the opposite of what is literally said

IRREAL *adj* not real

IRRIGATE *v* -GATED, -GATING, -GATES to supply with water by artificial means

IRRITANT *n pl.* -S something that irritates

IRRITATE *v* -TATED, -TATING, -TATES to excite to impatience or anger

IRRUPT *v* -ED, -ING, -S to rush in forcibly

IS present 3d person sing. of be

ISAGOGE *n pl.* -S a type of introduction to a branch of study

ISAGOGIC *n pl.* -S a branch of theology

ISARITHM *n pl.* -S an isopleth

ISATIN *n pl.* -S a chemical compound **ISATINIC** *adj*

ISATINE *n pl.* -S isatin

ISBA *n pl.* -S a Russian log hut

ISCHEMIA *n pl.* -S a type of anemia **ISCHEMIC** *adj*

ISCHIUM *n pl.* -CHIA a pelvic bone **ISCHIAL** *adj*

ISLAND *v* -ED, -ING, -S to make into an island (a land area entirely surrounded by water)

ISLANDER *n pl.* -S one that lives on an island

ISLE *v* ISLED, ISLING, ISLES to place on an isle (a small island)

ISLELESS *adj* lacking an isle

ISLET *n pl.* -S a small island

ISLING present participle of isle

ISM *n pl.* -S a distinctive theory or doctrine

ISOBAR *n pl.* -S a type of atom **ISOBARIC** *adj*

ISOBARE *n pl.* -S isobar

ISOBATH *n pl.* -S a line on a map connecting points of equal water depth

ISOCHEIM *n pl.* -S a type of isotherm

ISOCHIME *n pl.* -S isocheim

ISOCHOR *n pl.* -S isochore

ISOCHORE *n pl.* -S a curve used to show a relationship between pressure and temperature

ISOCHRON *n pl.* -S a line on a chart connecting points representing the same time

ISOCLINE *n pl.* -S a type of rock formation

ISOCRACY *n pl.* -CIES a form of government

ISODOSE *adj* pertaining to zones that receive equal doses of radiation

ISOGAMY *n pl.* -MIES the fusion of two similar gametes

ISOGENIC *adj* genetically similar

ISOGENY *n pl.* -NIES the state of being of similar origin

ISOGLOSS *n pl.* -ES a line on a map between linguistically varied areas

ISOGON *n pl.* -S a polygon having equal angles

ISOGONAL *n pl.* -S isogone

ISOGONE *n pl.* -S a line on a map used to show characteristics of the earth's magnetic field

ISOGONIC *n pl.* -S isogone

ISOGONY *n pl.* -NIES an equivalent relative growth of parts

ISOGRAM *n pl.* -S a line on a map connecting points of equal value

ISOGRAPH *n pl.* -S a line on a map indicating areas that are linguistically similar

ISOGRIV *n pl.* -S a line drawn on a map such that all points have equal grid variation

ISOHEL *n pl.* -S a line on a map connecting points receiving equal sunshine

ISOHYET *n pl.* -S a line on a map connecting points having equal rainfall

ISOLABLE *adj* capable of being isolated

ISOLATE *v* -LATED, -LATING, -LATES to set apart from others

ISOLATOR *n pl.* -S one that isolates

ISOLEAD *n pl.* -S a line on a ballistic graph

ISOLINE *n pl.* -S an isogram

ISOLOG *n pl.* -S isologue

ISOLOGUE *n pl.* -S a type of chemical compound

ISOMER *n pl.* -S a type of chemical compound **ISOMERIC** *adj*

ISOMETRY *n pl.* -TRIES equality of measure

ISOMORPH *n pl.* -S something similar to something else in form

ISONOMY	*n* pl. -MIES equality of civil rights **ISONOMIC** *adj*
ISOPHOTE	*n* pl. -S a curve on a chart joining points of equal light intensity
ISOPLETH	*n* pl. -S a type of isogram
ISOPOD	*n* pl. -S a kind of crustacean
ISOPODAN	*n* pl. -S an isopod
ISOPRENE	*n* pl. -S a volatile liquid
ISOSPIN	*n* pl. -S a type of quantum number
ISOSPORY	*n* pl. -RIES the condition of producing sexual or asexual spores of but one kind
ISOSTASY	*n* pl. -SIES the state of balance in the earth's crust
ISOTACH	*n* pl. -S a line on a map connecting points of equal wind velocity
ISOTHERE	*n* pl. -S a type of isotherm
ISOTHERM	*n* pl. -S a line on a map connecting points of equal mean temperature
ISOTONE	*n* pl. -S a type of atom
ISOTONIC	*adj* of equal tension
ISOTOPE	*n* pl. -S a form of an element **ISOTOPIC** *adj*
ISOTOPY	*n* pl. -PIES the state of being an isotope
ISOTROPY	*n* pl. -PIES the state of being identical in all directions
ISOTYPE	*n* pl. -S a type of diagram **ISOTYPIC** *adj*
ISOZYME	*n* pl. -S a type of enzyme **ISOZYMIC** *adj*
ISSEI	*n* pl. -S a Japanese immigrant to the United States
ISSUABLE	*adj* authorized for issuing **ISSUABLY** *adv*
ISSUANCE	*n* pl. -S the act of issuing
ISSUANT	*adj* coming forth
ISSUE	*v* -SUED, -SUING, -SUES to come forth
ISSUER	*n* pl. -S one that issues
ISTHMI	a pl. of isthmus

ISTHMIAN	*n* pl. -S a native of an isthmus
ISTHMIC	*adj* pertaining to an isthmus
ISTHMOID	*adj* isthmic
ISTHMUS	*n* pl. -MUSES or -MI a strip of land connecting two larger land masses
ISTLE	*n* pl. -S a strong fiber
IT	*pron* the 3d person sing. neuter pronoun
ITALIC	*n* pl. -S a style of print
ITCH	*v* -ED, -ING, -ES to have an uneasy or tingling skin sensation
ITCHING	*n* pl. -S an uneasy or tingling skin sensation
ITCHY	*adj* ITCHIER, ITCHIEST causing an itching sensation
ITEM	*v* -ED, -ING, -S to itemize
ITEMIZE	*v* -IZED, -IZING, -IZES to set down the particulars of
ITEMIZER	*n* pl. -S one that itemizes
ITERANCE	*n* pl. -S repetition
ITERANT	*adj* repeating
ITERATE	*v* -ATED, -ATING, -ATES to repeat
ITERUM	*adv* again; once more
ITHER	*adj* other
ITS	*pron* the possessive form of the pronoun it
ITSELF	*pron* a reflexive form of the pronoun it
IVIED	*adj* covered with ivy
IVORY	*n* pl. -RIES a hard white substance found in elephant tusks
IVY	*n* pl. IVIES a climbing vine **IVYLIKE** *adj*
IWIS	*adv* certainly
IXIA	*n* pl. -S a flowering plant
IXODID	*n* pl. -S a bloodsucking insect
IXTLE	*n* pl. -S istle
IZAR	*n* pl. -S an outer garment worn by Muslim women
IZZARD	*n* pl. -S the letter Z

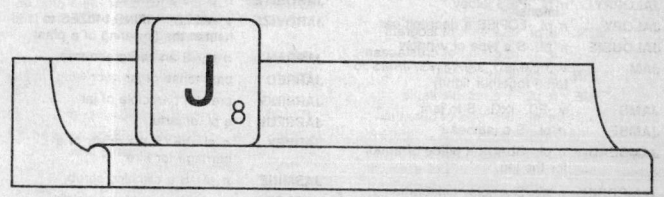

JAB   v JABBED, JABBING, JABS to poke sharply

JABBER   v -ED, -ING, -S to talk rapidly

JABBERER   n pl. -S one that jabbers

JABBING   present participle of jab

JABIRU   n pl. -S a wading bird

JABOT   n pl. -S a decoration on a shirt

JACAL   n pl. -ES or -S a hut

JACAMAR   n pl. -S a tropical bird

JACANA   n pl. -S a wading bird

JACINTH   n pl. -S a variety of zircon

JACINTHE   n pl. -S an orange color

JACK   v -ED, -ING, -S to raise with a type of lever

JACKAL   n pl. -S a doglike mammal

JACKAROO   n pl. -ROOS jackeroo

JACKASS   n pl. -ES a male donkey

JACKBOOT   n pl. -S a heavy boot

JACKDAW   n pl. -S a crowlike bird

JACKER   n pl. -S one that jacks

JACKEROO   n pl. -ROOS an inexperienced ranch hand

JACKET   v -ED, -ING, -S to provide with a jacket (a short coat)

JACKFISH   n pl. -ES a food fish

JACKIES   pl. of jacky

JACKLEG   n pl. -S an unskilled worker

JACKPOT   n pl. -S a top prize or reward

JACKSTAY   n pl. -STAYS a rope on a ship

JACKY   n pl. JACKIES a sailor

JACOBIN   n pl. -S a pigeon

JACOBUS   n pl. -ES an old English coin

JACONET   n pl. -S a cotton cloth

JACQUARD   n pl. -S a fabric of intricate weave

JACULATE   v -LATED, -LATING, -LATES to throw

JADE   v JADED, JADING, JADES to weary **JADEDLY** adv

JADEITE   n pl. -S a mineral **JADITIC** adj

JADISH   adj worn-out **JADISHLY** adv

JAEGER   n pl. -S a hunter

JAG   v JAGGED, JAGGING, JAGS to cut unevenly

JAGER   n pl. -S jaeger

JAGG   v -ED, -ING, -S to jag

JAGGARY   n pl. -RIES jaggery

JAGGED   adj -GEDER, -GEDEST having a sharply uneven edge or surface **JAGGEDLY** adv

JAGGER   n pl. -S one that jags

JAGGERY   n pl. -GERIES a coarse, dark sugar

JAGGHERY   n pl. -GHERIES jaggery

JAGGING   present participle of jag

JAGGY   adj -GIER, -GIEST jagged

JAGLESS   adj smooth and even

JAGRA   n pl. -S jaggery

JAGUAR   n pl. -S a large feline animal

JAIL   v -ED, -ING, -S to put in jail (a place of confinement)

JAILBAIT   n pl. JAILBAIT a girl under the age of consent with whom sexual intercourse constitutes statutory rape

JAILBIRD   n pl. -S a prisoner

JAILER   n pl. -S a keeper of a jail

JAILOR   n pl. -S jailer

JAKE   adj all right; fine

JAKES   n/pl an outhouse

JALAP   n pl. -S a Mexican plant **JALAPIC** adj

JALAPIN n pl. -S a medicinal substance contained in jalap

JALOP n pl. -S jalap

JALOPPY n pl. -PIES jalopy

JALOPY n pl. -LOPIES a decrepit car

JALOUSIE n pl. -S a type of window

JAM v JAMMED, JAMMING, JAMS to force together tightly

JAMB v -ED, -ING, -S to jam

JAMBE n pl. -S a jambeau

JAMBEAU n pl. -BEAUX a piece of armor for the leg

JAMBOREE n pl. -S a noisy celebration

JAMMED past tense of jam

JAMMER n pl. -S one that jams

JAMMING present participle of jam

JANE n pl. -S a girl or woman

JANGLE v -GLED, -GLING, -GLES to make a harsh, metallic sound

JANGLER n pl. -S one that jangles

JANIFORM adj hypocritical

JANISARY n pl. -SARIES janizary

JANITOR n pl. -S a maintenance man

JANIZARY n pl. -ZARIES a Turkish soldier

JANTY adj jaunty

JAPAN v -PANNED, -PANNING, -PANS to coat with a glossy, black lacquer

JAPANIZE v -NIZED, -NIZING, -NIZES to make Japanese

JAPANNER n pl. -S one that japans

JAPANNING present participle of japan

JAPE v JAPED, JAPING, JAPES to mock

JAPER n pl. -S one that japes

JAPERY n pl. -ERIES mockery

JAPING present participle of jape

JAPINGLY adv in a japing manner

JAPONICA n pl. -S an Asian shrub

JAR v JARRED, JARRING, JARS to cause to shake

JARFUL n pl. JARFULS or JARSFUL the quantity held by a jar (a cylindrical container)

JARGON v -ED, -ING, -S to speak or write an obscure and often pretentious kind of language

JARGONEL n pl. -S a variety of pear

JARGOON n pl. -S a variety of zircon

JARINA n pl. -S the hard seed of a palm tree

JARL n pl. -S a Scandinavian nobleman

JARLDOM n pl. -S the domain of a jarl

JAROSITE n pl. -S a mineral

JAROVIZE v -VIZED, -VIZING, -VIZES to hasten the flowering of a plant

JARRAH n pl. -S an evergreen tree

JARRED past tense of jar

JARRING present participle of jar

JARSFUL a pl. of jarful

JARVEY n pl. -VEYS the driver of a carriage for hire

JASMINE n pl. -S a climbing shrub

JASPER n pl. -S a variety of quartz JASPERY adj

JASSID n pl. -S any of a family of plant pests

JATO n pl. -TOS a takeoff aided by jet propulsion

JAUK v -ED, -ING, -S to dawdle

JAUNCE v JAUNCED, JAUNCING, JAUNCES to prance

JAUNDICE v -DICED, -DICING, -DICES to prejudice unfavorably

JAUNT v -ED, -ING, -S to make a pleasure trip

JAUNTY adj -TIER, -TIEST having a lively and self-confident manner JAUNTILY adv

JAUP v -ED, -ING, -S to splash

JAVA n pl. -S coffee

JAVELIN v -ED, -ING, -S to pierce with a javelin (a light spear)

JAVELINA n pl. -S a peccary

JAW v -ED, -ING, -S to jabber

JAWAN n pl. -S a soldier of India

JAWBONE v -BONED, -BONING, -BONES to attempt to convince

JAWLIKE adj resembling the jaw (the framework of the mouth)

JAWLINE n pl. -S the outline of the lower jaw

JAY n pl. JAYS a corvine bird

JAYBIRD n pl. -S a jay

JAYGEE n pl. -S a military officer

JAYVEE n pl. -S a junior varsity player

JAYWALK v -ED, -ING, -S to cross a street recklessly

JAZZ v -ED, -ING, -ES to enliven

JAZZER n pl. -S one that jazzes

JAZZMAN n pl. -MEN a type of musician

JAZZY adj JAZZIER, JAZZIEST lively JAZZILY adv

JEALOUS *adj* resentful of another's advantages

JEALOUSY *n pl.* -SIES a jealous feeling

JEAN *n pl.* -S a durable cotton fabric

JEBEL *n pl.* -S a mountain

JEE *v* JEED, JEEING, JEES to gee

JEEP *n pl.* -S a type of motor vehicle

JEEPERS *interj* — used as a mild oath

JEER *v* -ED, -ING, -S to mock

JEERER *n pl.* -S one that jeers

JEEZ *interj* — used as a mild oath

JEFE *n pl.* -S a chief

JEHAD *n pl.* -S a jihad

JEHU *n pl.* -S a fast driver

JEJUNA pl. of jejunum

JEJUNAL *adj* pertaining to the jejunum

JEJUNE *adj* uninteresting; childish **JEJUNELY** *adv*

JEJUNITY *n pl.* -TIES something that is jejune

JEJUNUM *n pl.* -NA a part of the small intestine

JELL *v* -ED, -ING, -S to congeal

JELLIFY *v* -FIED, -FYING, -FIES to jelly

JELLY *v* -LIED, -LYING, -LIES to make into a jelly (a soft, semisolid substance)

JELUTONG *n pl.* -S a tropical tree

JEMADAR *n pl.* -S an officer in the army of India

JEMIDAR *n pl.* -S jemadar

JEMMY *v* -MIED, -MYING, -MIES to jimmy

JENNET *n pl.* -S a small horse

JENNY *n pl.* -NIES a female donkey

JEOPARD *v* -ED, -ING, -S to imperil

JEOPARDY *n pl.* -DIES risk of loss or injury

JERBOA *n pl.* -S a small rodent

JEREED *n pl.* -S a wooden javelin

JEREMIAD *n pl.* -S a tale of woe

JERID *n pl.* -S jereed

JERK *v* -ED, -ING, -S to move with a sharp, sudden motion

JERKER *n pl.* -S one that jerks

JERKIES pl. of jerky

JERKIN *n pl.* -S a sleeveless jacket

JERKY *adj* JERKIER, JERKIEST characterized by jerking movements **JERKILY** *adv*

JERKY *n pl.* -KIES dried meat

JEROBOAM *n pl.* -S a wine bottle

JERREED *n pl.* -S jereed

JERRICAN *n pl.* -S jerrycan

JERRID *n pl.* -S jereed

JERRY *n pl.* -RIES a German soldier

JERRYCAN *n pl.* -S a fuel container

JERSEY *n pl.* -SEYS a close-fitting knitted shirt **JERSEYED** *adj*

JESS *v* -ED, -ING, -ES to fasten straps around the legs of a hawk

JESSANT *adj* shooting forth

JESSE *v* JESSED, JESSING, JESSES to jess

JEST *v* -ED, -ING, -S to joke

JESTER *n pl.* -S one that jests

JESTFUL *adj* tending to jest

JESTING *n pl.* -S the act of one who jests

JESUIT *n pl.* -S a scheming person — an offensive term **JESUITIC** *adj*

JESUITRY *n pl.* -RIES an unethical principle or practice — an offensive term

JET *v* JETTED, JETTING, JETS to spurt forth in a stream

JETBEAD *n pl.* -S an ornamental shrub

JETE *n pl.* -S a ballet leap

JETLINER *n pl.* -S a type of aircraft

JETON *n pl.* -S jetton

JETPORT *n pl.* -S a type of airport

JETSAM *n pl.* -S goods cast overboard

JETSOM *n pl.* -S jetsam

JETTED past tense of jet

JETTIED past tense of jetty

JETTIES present 3d person sing. of jetty

JETTING present participle of jet

JETTISON *v* -ED, -ING, -S to cast overboard

JETTON *n pl.* -S a piece used in counting

JETTY *v* -TIED, -TYING, -TIES to jut

JEU *n pl.* JEUX a game

JEW *v* -ED, -ING, -S to bargain with — an offensive term

JEWEL *v* -ELED, -ELING, -ELS or -ELLED, -ELLING, -ELS to adorn or equip with jewels (precious stones)

JEWELER *n pl.* -S a dealer or maker of jewelry

JEWELLER *n pl.* -S jeweler

JEWELLING a present participle of jewel

JEWELRY n pl. -RIES an article or articles for personal adornment

JEWFISH n pl. -ES a large marine fish

JEZAIL n pl. -S a type of firearm

JEZEBEL n pl. -S a scheming, wicked woman

JIB v JIBBED, JIBBING, JIBS to refuse to proceed further

JIBB v -ED, -ING, -S to shift from side to side while sailing

JIBBER n pl. -S a horse that jibs

JIBBING present participle of jib

JIBBOOM n pl. -S a ship's spar

JIBE v JIBED, JIBING, JIBES to gibe **JIBINGLY** adv

JIBER n pl. -S one that jibes

JIFF n pl. -S jiffy

JIFFY n pl. -FIES a short time

JIG v JIGGED, JIGGING, JIGS to bob

JIGABOO n pl. -BOOS a black person — an offensive term

JIGGER n pl. -S a small whiskey glass

JIGGERED adj damned

JIGGING present participle of jig

JIGGLE v -GLED, -GLING, -GLES to shake lightly

JIGGLY adj -GLIER, -GLIEST unsteady

JIGSAW v -SAWED, -SAWN, -SAWING, -SAWS to cut with a type of saw

JIHAD n pl. -S a Muslim holy war

JILL n pl. -S a unit of liquid measure

JILLION n pl. -S a very large number

JILT v -ED, -ING, -S to reject a lover

JILTER n pl. -S one that jilts

JIMINY interj — used to express surprise

JIMJAMS n/pl violent delirium

JIMMINY interj jiminy

JIMMY v -MIED, -MYING, -MIES to pry open with a crowbar

JIMP adj JIMPER, JIMPEST natty **JIMPLY** adv

JIMPY adj jimp

JIN n pl. -S jinn

JINGAL n pl. -S a heavy musket

JINGALL n pl. -S jingal

JINGKO n pl. -KOES ginkgo

JINGLE v -GLED, -GLING, -GLES to make a tinkling sound

JINGLER n pl. -S one that jingles

JINGLY adj -GLIER, -GLIEST jingling

JINGO n pl. -GOES a zealous patriot **JINGOISH** adj

JINGOISM n pl. -S the spirit or policy of jingoes

JINGOIST n pl. -S a jingo

JINK v -ED, -ING, -S to move quickly out of the way

JINKER n pl. -S one that jinks

JINN n pl. -S a supernatural being in Muslim mythology

JINNEE n pl. JINN jinn

JINNI n pl. JINN jinn

JINX v -ED, -ING, -ES to bring bad luck to

JIPIJAPA n pl. -S a tropical plant

JITNEY n pl. -NEYS a small bus

JITTER v -ED, -ING, -S to fidget

JITTERY adj extremely nervous

JIUJITSU n pl. -S jujitsu

JIUJUTSU n pl. -S jujitsu

JIVE v JIVED, JIVING, JIVES to play jazz or swing music

JNANA n pl. -S knowledge acquired through meditation

JO n pl. JOES a sweetheart

JOANNES n pl. JOANNES johannes

JOB v JOBBED, JOBBING, JOBS to work by the piece

JOBBER n pl. -S a pieceworker

JOBBERY n pl. -BERIES corruption in public office

JOBBING present participle of job

JOBLESS adj having no job

JOCK n pl. -S an athletic supporter

JOCKEY v -EYED, -EYING, -EYS to maneuver for an advantage

JOCKO n pl. JOCKOS a monkey

JOCOSE adj humorous **JOCOSELY** adv

JOCOSITY n pl. -TIES the state of being jocose

JOCULAR adj given to joking

JOCUND adj cheerful **JOCUNDLY** adv

JODHPUR n pl. -S a type of boot

JOE n pl. -S a fellow

JOEY n pl. -EYS a young kangaroo

JOG v JOGGED, JOGGING, JOGS to run at a slow, steady pace

JOGGER n pl. -S one that jogs

JOGGLE v -GLED, -GLING, -GLES to shake slightly

JOGGLER   n pl. -S one that joggles

JOHANNES   n pl. JOHANNES a Portuguese coin

JOHN   n pl. -S a toilet

JOHNBOAT   n pl. -S a narrow square-ended boat

JOHNNY   n pl. -NIES a sleeveless hospital gown

JOIN   v -ED, -ING, -S to unite JOINABLE adj

JOINDER   n pl. -S a joining of parties in a lawsuit

JOINER   n pl. -S a carpenter

JOINERY   n pl. -ERIES the trade of a joiner

JOINING   n pl. -S a juncture

JOINT   v -ED, -ING, -S to fit together by means of a junction

JOINTER   n pl. -S one that joints

JOINTLY   adv together

JOINTURE   v -TURED, -TURING, -TURES to set aside property as an inheritance

JOIST   v -ED, -ING, -S to support with horizontal beams

JOJOBA   n pl. -S a small tree

JOKE   v JOKED, JOKING, JOKES to say something amusing

JOKER   n pl. -S one that jokes

JOKESTER   n pl. -S a practical joker

JOKING   present participle of joke

JOKINGLY   adv in a joking manner

JOLE   n pl. -S jowl

JOLLIED   past tense of jolly

JOLLIER   comparative of jolly

JOLLIES   present 3d person sing. of jolly

JOLLIEST   superlative of jolly

JOLLIFY   v -FIED, -FYING, -FIES to make jolly

JOLLITY   n pl. -TIES mirth

JOLLY   adj -LIER, -LIEST cheerful JOLLILY adv

JOLLY   v -LIED, -LYING, -LIES to put in a good humor for one's own purposes

JOLT   v -ED, -ING, -S to jar or shake roughly

JOLTER   n pl. -S one that jolts

JOLTY   adj JOLTIER, JOLTIEST marked by a jolting motion JOLTILY adv

JONGLEUR   n pl. -S a minstrel

JONQUIL   n pl. -S a perennial herb

JORAM   n pl. -S jorum

JORDAN   n pl. -S a type of container

JORUM   n pl. -S a large drinking bowl

JOSEPH   n pl. -S a woman's long cloak

JOSH   v -ED, -ING, -ES to tease

JOSHER   n pl. -S one that joshes

JOSS   n pl. -ES a Chinese idol

JOSTLE   v -TLED, -TLING, -TLES to bump or push roughly

JOSTLER   n pl. -S one that jostles

JOT   v JOTTED, JOTTING, JOTS to write down quickly

JOTA   n pl. -S a Spanish dance

JOTTING   n pl. -S a brief note

JOTTY   adj written down quickly

JOUK   v -ED, -ING, -S to dodge

JOULE   n pl. -S a unit of energy

JOUNCE   v JOUNCED, JOUNCING, JOUNCES to move roughly up and down

JOUNCY   adj JOUNCIER, JOUNCIEST marked by a jouncing motion

JOURNAL   n pl. -S a record of daily events

JOURNEY   v -ED, -ING, -S to travel

JOUST   v -ED, -ING, -S to engage in personal combat

JOUSTER   n pl. -S one that jousts

JOVIAL   adj good-humored JOVIALLY adv

JOVIALTY   n pl. -TIES the quality or state of being jovial

JOW   v -ED, -ING, -S to toll

JOWL   n pl. -S the fleshy part under the lower jaw JOWLED adj

JOWLY   adj JOWLIER, JOWLIEST having prominent jowls

JOY   v -ED, -ING, -S to rejoice

JOYANCE   n pl. -S gladness

JOYFUL   adj -FULLER, -FULLEST happy JOYFULLY adv

JOYLESS   adj being without gladness

JOYOUS   adj joyful JOYOUSLY adv

JOYPOP   v -POPPED, -POPPING, -POPS to use habit-forming drugs occasionally

JOYRIDE   n pl. -S a ride taken for pleasure

JOYRIDER   n pl. -S one that takes a joyride

JOYSTICK   n pl. -S the control stick in an airplane

JUBA   n pl. -S a lively dance

JUBBAH   n pl. -S a loose outer garment

JUBE   n pl. -S a platform in a church

JUBHAH n pl. -S jubbah

JUBILANT adj exultant

JUBILATE v -LATED, -LATING, -LATES to exult

JUBILE n pl. -S jubilee

JUBILEE n pl. -S a celebration

JUDAS n pl. -ES a peephole

JUDDER v -ED, -ING, -S to vibrate

JUDGE v JUDGED, JUDGING, JUDGES to decide on critically

JUDGER n pl. -S one that judges

JUDGMENT n pl. -S an authoritative opinion

JUDICIAL adj pertaining to courts of law

JUDO n pl. -DOS a form of jujitsu

JUDOIST n pl. -S one skilled in judo

JUDOKA n pl. -S a judoist

JUG v JUGGED, JUGGING, JUGS to put into a jug (a large, deep container with a narrow mouth and a handle)

JUGA a pl. of jugum

JUGAL adj pertaining to the cheek or cheekbone

JUGATE adj occurring in pairs

JUGFUL n pl. JUGFULS or JUGSFUL as much as a jug will hold

JUGGED past tense of jug

JUGGING present participle of jug

JUGGLE v -GLED, -GLING, -GLES to perform feats of manual dexterity

JUGGLER n pl. -S one that juggles

JUGGLERY n pl. -GLERIES the art of a juggler

JUGGLING n pl. -S jugglery

JUGHEAD n pl. -S a dolt

JUGSFUL a pl. of jugful

JUGULA pl. of jugulum

JUGULAR n pl. -S a vein of the neck

JUGULATE v -LATED, -LATING, -LATES to suppress a disease by extreme measures

JUGULUM n pl. -LA a part of a bird's neck

JUGUM n pl. -GA or -GUMS a pair of the opposite leaflets of a pinnate leaf

JUICE v JUICED, JUICING, JUICES to extract the juice (the liquid part of a fruit or vegetable) from

JUICER n pl. -S a juice extractor

JUICY adj JUICIER, JUICIEST full of juice JUICILY adv

JUJITSU n pl. -S a Japanese art of self-defense

JUJU n pl. -S an object regarded as having magical power

JUJUBE n pl. -S a fruit-flavored candy

JUJUISM n pl. -S the system of beliefs connected with jujus

JUJUIST n pl. -S a follower of jujuism

JUJUTSU n pl. -S jujitsu

JUKE v JUKED, JUKING, JUKES to fake out of position

JUKEBOX n pl. -ES a coin-operated phonograph

JULEP n pl. -S a sweet drink

JULIENNE n pl. -S a clear soup

JUMBLE v -BLED, -BLING, -BLES to mix in a disordered manner

JUMBLER n pl. -S one that jumbles

JUMBO n pl. -BOS a very large specimen of its kind

JUMBUCK n pl. -S a sheep

JUMP v -ED, -ING, -S to spring off the ground

JUMPER n pl. -S one that jumps

JUMPOFF n pl. -S a starting point

JUMPY adj JUMPIER, JUMPIEST nervous JUMPILY adv

JUN n pl. JUN a coin of North Korea

JUNCO n pl. -COS or -COES a small finch

JUNCTION n pl. -S a place where things join

JUNCTURE n pl. -S the act of joining

JUNGLE n pl. -S land covered with dense tropical vegetation

JUNGLY adj -GLIER, -GLIEST resembling a jungle

JUNIOR n pl. -S a person who is younger than another

JUNIPER n pl. -S an evergreen tree

JUNK v -ED, -ING, -S to discard as trash

JUNKER n pl. -S something ready for junking

JUNKET v -ED, -ING, -S to banquet

JUNKETER n pl. -S one that junkets

JUNKIE n pl. -S a drug addict

JUNKMAN n pl. -MEN one who buys and sells junk

JUNKY adj JUNKIER, JUNKIEST worthless

JUNKYARD n pl. -S a place where junk is stored

JUNTA   n pl. -S a political or governmental council

JUNTO   n pl. -TOS a political faction

JUPE   n pl. -S a woman's jacket

JUPON   n pl. -S a tunic

JURA   pl. of jus

JURAL   adj pertaining to law **JURALLY** adv

JURANT   n pl. -S one that takes an oath

JURAT   n pl. -S a statement on an affidavit

JURATORY   adj pertaining to an oath

JUREL   n pl. -S a food fish

JURIDIC   adj pertaining to the law

JURIES   pl. of jury

JURIST   n pl. -S one versed in the law **JURISTIC** adj

JUROR   n pl. -S a member of a jury

JURY   n pl. -RIES a group of persons sworn to render a verdict

JURYMAN   n pl. -MEN a juror

JUS   n pl. JURA a legal right

JUSSIVE   n pl. -S a word used to express command

JUST   v -ED, -ING, -S to joust

JUST   adj JUSTER, JUSTEST acting in conformity with what is morally good

JUSTER   n pl. -S jouster

JUSTICE   n pl. -S a judge

JUSTIFY   v -FIED, -FYING, -FIES to show to be just, right, or valid

JUSTLE   v -TLED, -TLING, -TLES to jostle

JUSTLY   adv in a just manner

JUSTNESS   n pl. -ES the quality of being just

JUT   v JUTTED, JUTTING, JUTS to protrude

JUTE   n pl. -S a strong, coarse fiber

JUTTY   v -TIED, -TYING, -TIES to jut

JUVENAL   n pl. -S a young bird's plumage

JUVENILE   n pl. -S a young person

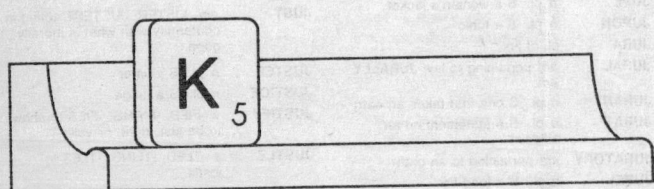

KA *n* pl. -S the spiritual self of a human being in Egyptian religion

KAAS *n* pl. KAAS kas

KAB *n* pl. -S an ancient Hebrew unit of measure

KABAB *n* pl. -S kabob

KABAKA *n* pl. -S a Ugandan emperor

KABALA *n* pl. -S cabala

KABAR *n* pl. -S caber

KABAYA *n* pl. -S a cotton jacket

KABBALA *n* pl. -S cabala

KABBALAH *n* pl. -S cabala

KABELJOU *n* pl. -S a large food fish

KABIKI *n* pl. -S a tropical tree

KABOB *n* pl. -S cubes of meat cooked on a skewer

KABUKI *n* pl. -S a form of Japanese theater

KACHINA *n* pl. -S an ancestral spirit

KADDISH *n* pl. -DISHIM a Jewish prayer

KADI *n* pl. -S a cadi

KAE *n* pl. -S a bird resembling a crow

KAFFIR *n* pl. -S kafir

KAFFIYEH *n* pl. -S a large, square kerchief

KAFIR *n* pl. -S a cereal grass

KAFTAN *n* pl. -S a caftan

KAGU *n* pl. -S a flightless bird

KAHUNA *n* pl. -S a medicine man

KAIAK *n* pl. -S kayak

KAIF *n* pl. -S kef

KAIL *n* pl. -S kale

KAILYARD *n* pl. -S kaleyard

KAIN *n* pl. -S a tax paid in produce or livestock

KAINIT *n* pl. -S kainite

KAINITE *n* pl. -S a mineral salt

KAISER *n* pl. -S an emperor

KAISERIN *n* pl. -S a kaiser's wife

KAJEPUT *n* pl. -S cajuput

KAKA *n* pl. -S a parrot

KAKAPO *n* pl. -POS a flightless parrot

KAKEMONO *n* pl. -NOS a Japanese scroll

KAKI *n* pl. -S a Japanese tree

KALAM *n* pl. -S a type of Muslim theology

KALE *n* pl. -S a variety of cabbage

KALENDS *n* pl. KALENDS calends

KALEWIFE *n* pl. -WIVES a female vegetable vendor

KALEYARD *n* pl. -S a kitchen garden

KALIAN *n* pl. -S a hookah

KALIF *n* pl. -S caliph

KALIFATE *n* pl. -S califate

KALIMBA *n* pl. -S an African musical instrument

KALIPH *n* pl. -S caliph

KALIUM *n* pl. -S potassium

KALLIDIN *n* pl. -S a hormone

KALMIA *n* pl. -S an evergreen shrub

KALONG *n* pl. -S a fruit-eating bat

KALPA *n* pl. -S a period of time in Hindu religion

KALPAK *n* pl. -S calpac

KALYPTRA *n* pl. -S a thin veil

KAMAAINA *n* pl. -S a longtime resident of Hawaii

KAMACITE *n* pl. -S an alloy of nickel and iron

KAMALA *n* pl. -S an Asian tree

KAME *n pl.* -S a mound of detrital material

KAMI *n pl.* KAMI a sacred power or force

KAMIK *n pl.* -S a type of boot

KAMIKAZE *n pl.* -S a plane to be flown in a suicide crash on a target

KAMPONG *n pl.* -S a small village

KAMSEEN *n pl.* -S khamsin

KAMSIN *n pl.* -S khamsin

KANA *n pl.* -S the Japanese syllabic script

KANE *n pl.* -S kain

KANGAROO *n pl.* -ROOS an Australian mammal

KANJI *n pl.* -S a system of Japanese writing

KANTAR *n pl.* -S a unit of weight

KANTELE *n pl.* -S a type of harp

KAOLIANG *n pl.* -S an Asian sorghum

KAOLIN *n pl.* -S a fine white clay KAOLINIC *adj*

KAOLINE *n pl.* -S kaolin

KAON *n pl.* -S a type of meson

KAPA *n pl.* -S a coarse cloth

KAPH *n pl.* -S a Hebrew letter

KAPOK *n pl.* -S a mass of silky fibers

KAPPA *n pl.* -S a Greek letter

KAPUT *adj* ruined

KAPUTT *adj* kaput

KARAKUL *n pl.* -S an Asian sheep

KARAT *n pl.* -S a unit of quality for gold

KARATE *n pl.* -S a Japanese art of self-defense

KARMA *n pl.* -S the force generated by a person's actions KARMIC *adj*

KARN *n pl.* -S a cairn

KAROO *n pl.* -ROOS karroo

KAROSS *n pl.* -ES an African garment

KARROO *n pl.* -ROOS a dry plateau

KARST *n pl.* -S a limestone region KARSTIC *adj*

KART *n pl.* -S a small motor vehicle

KARTING *n pl.* -S the sport of racing karts

KARYOTIN *n pl.* -S the nuclear material of a cell

KAS *n pl.* KAS a large cupboard

KASHA *n pl.* -S a cooked cereal

KASHER *v* -ED, -ING, -S to kosher

KASHMIR *n pl.* -S cashmere

KASHRUT *n pl.* -S kashruth

KASHRUTH *n pl.* -S the Jewish dietary laws

KAT *n pl.* -S an evergreen shrub

KATAKANA *n pl.* -S a Japanese syllabic symbol

KATHODE *n pl.* -S cathode KATHODAL, KATHODIC *adj*

KATION *n pl.* -S cation

KATYDID *n pl.* -S a grasshopper

KAURI *n pl.* -S a timber tree

KAURY *n pl.* -RIES kauri

KAVA *n pl.* -S a tropical shrub

KAVASS *n pl.* -ES a Turkish policeman

KAY *n pl.* KAYS the letter K

KAYAK *n pl.* -S an Eskimo canoe

KAYAKER *n pl.* -S one that rides in a kayak

KAYLES *n/pl* a British game

KAYO *v* -ED, -ING, -S or -ES to knock out

KAZOO *n pl.* -ZOOS a toy musical instrument

KEA *n pl.* -S a parrot

KEBAB *n pl.* -S kabob

KEBAR *n pl.* -S caber

KEBBIE *n pl.* -S a rough walking stick

KEBBOCK *n pl.* -S kebbuck

KEBBUCK *n pl.* -S a whole cheese

KEBLAH *n pl.* -S kiblah

KEBOB *n pl.* -S kabob

KECK *v* -ED, -ING, -S to retch

KECKLE *v* -LED, -LING, -LES to wind with rope to prevent chafing

KEDDAH *n pl.* -S an enclosure for elephants

KEDGE *v* KEDGED, KEDGING, KEDGES to move a vessel with the use of an anchor

KEDGEREE *n pl.* -S a food in India

KEEF *n pl.* -S kef

KEEK *v* -ED, -ING, -S to peep

KEEL *v* -ED, -ING, -S to capsize

KEELAGE *n pl.* -S the amount paid to keep a boat in a harbor

KEELBOAT *n pl.* -S a freight boat

KEELHALE *v* -HALED, -HALING, -HALES to keelhaul

KEELHAUL *v* -ED, -ING, -S to rebuke severely

KEELLESS *adj* having no keel (the main structural part of a ship)

KEELSON *n pl.* -S a beam in a ship

KEEN	adj KEENER, KEENEST enthusiastic	**KENO**	n pl. -NOS a game of chance
KEEN	v -ED, -ING, -S to wail loudly over the dead	**KENOSIS**	n pl. -SISES the incarnation of Christ **KENOTIC** adj
KEENER	n pl. -S one that keens	**KENOTRON**	n pl. -S a type of diode
KEENLY	adv in a keen manner	**KENT**	a past tense of ken
KEENNESS	n pl. -ES sharpness	**KEP**	v KEPPED, KEPPEN or KIPPEN, KEPPING, KEPS to catch
KEEP	v KEPT, KEEPING, KEEPS to continue to possess **KEEPABLE** adj	**KEPHALIN**	n pl. -S cephalin
KEEPER	n pl. -S one that keeps	**KEPI**	n pl. -S a type of cap
KEEPING	n pl. -S custody	**KEPPED**	past tense of kep
KEEPSAKE	n pl. -S a memento	**KEPPEN**	a past participle of kep
KEESHOND	n pl. -HONDS or -HONDEN a small, heavy-coated dog	**KEPPING**	present participle of kep
KEESTER	n pl. -S keister	**KEPT**	past tense of keep
KEET	n pl. -S a young guinea fowl	**KERAMIC**	n pl. -S ceramic
KEEVE	n pl. -S a tub or vat	**KERATIN**	n pl. -S a fibrous protein
KEF	n pl. -S hemp smoked to produce euphoria	**KERATOID**	adj horny
KEFIR	n pl. -S a fermented beverage made from cow's milk	**KERATOMA**	n pl. -MAS or -MATA a skin disease
		KERATOSE	adj of or resembling horny tissue
KEG	n pl. -S a small barrel	**KERB**	v -ED, -ING, -S to provide with curbing
KEGELER	n pl. -S kegler		
KEGLER	n pl. -S a bowler	**KERCHIEF**	n pl. -CHIEFS or -CHIEVES a cloth worn as a head covering
KEGLING	n pl. -S bowling		
KEIR	n pl. -S kier	**KERCHOO**	interj ahchoo
KEISTER	n pl. -S the buttocks	**KERF**	v -ED, -ING, -S to make an incision with a cutting tool
KEITLOA	n pl. -S a rhinoceros		
KELOID	n pl. -S a scar caused by excessive growth of fibrous tissue **KELOIDAL** adj	**KERMES**	n pl. KERMES a red dye
		KERMESS	n pl. -ES kermis
		KERMIS	n pl. -MISES a festival
KELP	v -ED, -ING, -S to burn a type of seaweed	**KERN**	v -ED, -ING, -S to be formed with a projecting typeface
		KERNE	n pl. -S a medieval foot soldier
KELPIE	n pl. -S a water sprite	**KERNEL**	v -NELED, -NELING, -NELS or -NELLED, -NELLING, -NELS to envelop as a kernel (the inner part of a nut)
KELPY	n pl. -PIES kelpie		
KELSON	n pl. -S keelson		
KELTER	n pl. -S kilter		
KELVIN	n pl. -S a unit of temperature	**KERNITE**	n pl. -S a mineral
KEMP	n pl. -S a champion	**KEROGEN**	n pl. -S a substance found in shale
KEMPT	adj neatly kept		
KEN	v KENNED or KENT, KENNING, KENS to know	**KEROSENE**	n pl. -S a fuel oil
		KEROSINE	n pl. -S kerosene
KENAF	n pl. -S an East Indian plant	**KERPLUNK**	adv with a muffled sound
KENCH	n pl. -ES a bin for salting fish	**KERRIA**	n pl. -S a Chinese shrub
KENDO	n pl. -DOS a Japanese sport	**KERRY**	n pl. -RIES one of an Irish breed of cattle
KENNED	a past tense of ken		
KENNEL	v -NELED, -NELING, -NELS or -NELLED, -NELLING, -NELS to keep in a shelter for dogs	**KERSEY**	n pl. -SEYS a woolen cloth
		KERYGMA	n pl. -MATA the preaching of the gospel
		KESTREL	n pl. -S a small falcon
KENNING	n pl. -S a metaphorical compound word or phrase	**KETCH**	n pl. -ES a sailing vessel
		KETCHUP	n pl. -S a spicy tomato sauce

KETENE *n pl.* -S a toxic gas

KETO *adj* of or pertaining to ketone

KETONE *n pl.* -S a type of chemical compound **KETONIC** *adj*

KETOSE *n pl.* -S a simple sugar

KETOSIS *n pl.* -TOSES a buildup of ketones in the body **KETOTIC** *adj*

KETTLE *n pl.* -S a vessel for boiling liquids

KEVEL *n pl.* -S a belaying cleat or peg

KEVIL *n pl.* -S kevel

KEX *n pl.* -ES a dry, hollow stalk

KEY *v* -ED, -ING, -S to provide with a key (a device used to turn the bolt in a lock)

KEYBOARD *v* -ED, -ING, -S to operate a machine by means of a keyset

KEYHOLE *n pl.* -S a hole for a key

KEYLESS *adj* being without a key

KEYNOTE *v* -NOTED, -NOTING, -NOTES to deliver the main speech at a function

KEYNOTER *n pl.* -S one that keynotes

KEYPUNCH *v* -ED, -ING, -ES to perforate with a machine

KEYSET *n pl.* -S a system of finger levers

KEYSTER *n pl.* -S keister

KEYSTONE *n pl.* -S the central stone of an arch

KEYWAY *n pl.* -WAYS a slot for a key

KEYWORD *n pl.* -S a significant word

KHADDAR *n pl.* -S a cotton cloth

KHADI *n pl.* -S khaddar

KHAKI *n pl.* -S a durable cloth

KHALIF *n pl.* -S caliph

KHALIFA *n pl.* -S caliph

KHAMSEEN *n pl.* -S khamsin

KHAMSIN *n pl.* -S a hot, dry wind

KHAN *n pl.* -S an Asian ruler

KHANATE *n pl.* -S the domain of a khan

KHAT *n pl.* -S kat

KHAZEN *n pl.* -ZENS or -ZENIM hazzan

KHEDA *n pl.* -S keddah

KHEDAH *n pl.* -S keddah

KHEDIVE *n pl.* -S a Turkish viceroy **KHEDIVAL** *adj*

KHI *n pl.* -S chi

KHIRKAH *n pl.* -S a patchwork garment

KIANG *n pl.* -S a wild ass

KIAUGH *n pl.* -S trouble; worry

KIBBLE *v* -BLED, -BLING, -BLES to grind coarsely

KIBBUTZ *n pl.* -BUTZIM a collective farm in Israel

KIBE *n pl.* -S a sore caused by exposure to cold

KIBITZ *v* -ED, -ING, -ES to meddle

KIBITZER *n pl.* -S one that kibitzes

KIBLA *n pl.* -S kiblah

KIBLAH *n pl.* -S the direction toward which Muslims face while praying

KIBOSH *v* -ED, -ING, -ES to stop

KICK *v* -ED, -ING, -S to strike out with the foot or feet

KICKBACK *n pl.* -S a strong reaction

KICKER *n pl.* -S one that kicks

KICKOFF *n pl.* -S the kick that begins play in football

KICKSHAW *n pl.* -S a trifle or trinket

KICKUP *n pl.* -S a noisy argument

KID *v* KIDDED, KIDDING, KIDS to tease

KIDDER *n pl.* -S one that kids

KIDDIE *n pl.* -S a small child

KIDDIES *pl.* of kiddy

KIDDING present participle of kid

KIDDISH *adj* childish

KIDDO *n pl.* -DOS or -DOES — used as a form of familiar address

KIDDUSH *n pl.* -ES a Jewish prayer

KIDDY *n pl.* -DIES kiddie

KIDLIKE *adj* resembling a child

KIDNAP *v* -NAPED, -NAPING, -NAPS or -NAPPED, -NAPPING, -NAPS to take a person by force and often for ransom

KIDNAPER *n pl.* -S one that kidnaps

KIDNAPPER *n pl.* -S kidnaper

KIDNAPPING present participle of kidnap

KIDNEY *n pl.* -NEYS a bodily organ

KIDSKIN *n pl.* -S a type of leather

KIEF *n pl.* -S kef

KIELBASA *n pl.* -BASAS or -BASY a smoked sausage

KIER *n pl.* -S a vat for boiling and dyeing fabrics

KIESTER *n pl.* -S keister

KIF *n pl.* -S kef

KIKE *n pl.* -S a Jew — an offensive term

KILIM *n pl.* -S an oriental tapestry

KILL   v -ED, -ING, -S to cause to die

KILLDEE   n pl. -S killdeer

KILLDEER   n pl. -S a wading bird

KILLER   n pl. -S one that kills

KILLICK   n pl. -S a small anchor

KILLING   n pl. -S a sudden notable success

KILLJOY   n pl. -JOYS one who spoils the fun of others

KILLOCK   n pl. -S killick

KILN   v -ED, -ING, -S to bake in a type of oven

KILO   n pl. KILOS a kilogram or kilometer

KILOBAR   n pl. -S a unit of atmospheric pressure

KILOBIT   n pl. -S a unit of computer information

KILOGRAM   n pl. -S a unit of mass and weight

KILOMOLE   n pl. -S one thousand moles

KILORAD   n pl. -S a unit of nuclear radiation

KILOTON   n pl. -S a unit of weight

KILOVOLT   n pl. -S a unit of electromotive force

KILOWATT   n pl. -S a unit of power

KILT   v -ED, -ING, -S to make creases or pleats in

KILTER   n pl. -S good condition

KILTIE   n pl. -S one who wears a kilt (a type of skirt)

KILTING   n pl. -S an arrangement of kilt pleats

KILTY   n pl. KILTIES kiltie

KIMONO   n pl. -NOS a loose robe **KIMONOED** adj

KIN   n pl. -S a group of persons of common ancestry

KINASE   n pl. -S an enzyme

KIND   adj KINDER, KINDEST having a gentle, giving nature

KIND   n pl. -S a class of similar or related objects or individuals

KINDLE   v -DLED, -DLING, -DLES to cause to burn

KINDLER   n pl. -S one that kindles

KINDLESS   adj lacking kindness

KINDLING   n pl. -S material that is easily ignited

KINDLY   adj -LIER, -LIEST kind

KINDNESS   n pl. -ES the quality of being kind

KINDRED   n pl. -S a natural grouping

KINE   n pl. -S a type of television tube

KINEMA   n pl. -S cinema

KINESICS   n/pl the study of body motion in relation to communication

KINESIS   n pl. -NESES a type of movement

KINETIC   adj pertaining to motion

KINETICS   n/pl a branch of science dealing with motion

KINETIN   n pl. -S a substance that increases plant growth

KINFOLK   n/pl relatives

KINFOLKS   n/pl kinfolk

KING   v -ED, -ING, -S to reign as king (a male monarch)

KINGBIRD   n pl. -S an American bird

KINGBOLT   n pl. -S a kingpin

KINGCUP   n pl. -S a marsh plant

KINGDOM   n pl. -S the area ruled by a king

KINGFISH   n pl. -ES a marine food fish

KINGHOOD   n pl. -S the office of a king

KINGLESS   adj having no king

KINGLET   n pl. -S a king who rules over a small area

KINGLIKE   adj resembling a king

KINGLY   adj -LIER, -LIEST of or befitting a king

KINGPIN   n pl. -S a central bolt connecting an axle to a vehicle

KINGPOST   n pl. -S a supporting structure of a roof

KINGSHIP   n pl. -S the power or position of a king

KINGSIDE   n pl. -S a part of a chessboard

KINGWOOD   n pl. -S a hardwood tree

KININ   n pl. -S a hormone

KINK   v -ED, -ING, -S to form a tight curl or bend in

KINKAJOU   n pl. -S an arboreal mammal

KINKY   adj KINKIER, KINKIEST tightly curled **KINKILY** adv

KINO   n pl. -NOS a gum resin

KINSFOLK   n/pl kinfolk

KINSHIP   n pl. -S relationship

KINSMAN   n pl. -MEN a male relative

KIOSK   n pl. -S an open booth

KIP   v KIPPED, KIPPING, KIPS to sleep

KIPPEN   a past participle of kep

KIPPER *v* -ED, -ING, -S to cure fish by salting and smoking

KIPPING present participle of kip

KIPSKIN *n pl.* -S an animal hide that has not been tanned

KIRIGAMI *n pl.* -S the Japanese art of folding paper

KIRK *n pl.* -S a church

KIRKMAN *n pl.* -MEN a member of a church

KIRMESS *n pl.* -ES kermis

KIRN *v* -ED, -ING, -S to churn

KIRSCH *n pl.* -ES a kind of brandy

KIRTLE *n pl.* -S a man's tunic or coat **KIRTLED** *adj*

KISHKA *n pl.* -S kishke

KISHKE *n pl.* -S a sausage

KISMAT *n pl.* -S kismet

KISMET *n pl.* -S destiny **KISMETIC** *adj*

KISS *v* -ED, -ING, -ES to touch with the lips as a sign of affection **KISSABLE** *adj* **KISSABLY** *adv*

KISSER *n pl.* -S one that kisses

KIST *n pl.* -S a chest, box, or coffin

KISTFUL *n pl.* -S as much as a kist can hold

KIT *v* -KITTED, KITTING, KITS to equip

KITCHEN *n pl.* -S a room where food is cooked

KITE *v* -KITED, KITING, KITES to obtain money or credit fraudulently

KITER *n pl.* -S one that kites

KITH *n pl.* -S one's friends and neighbors

KITHARA *n pl.* -S cithara

KITHE *v* KITHED, KITHING, KITHES to make known

KITING present participle of kite

KITLING *n pl.* -S a young animal

KITSCH *n pl.* -ES faddish art or literature **KITSCHY** *adj*

KITTED past tense of kit

KITTEL *n pl.* KITTEL a Jewish ceremonial robe

KITTEN *v* -ED, -ING, -S to bear kittens (young cats)

KITTIES pl. of kitty

KITTING present participle of kit

KITTLE *v* -TLED, -TLING, -TLES to tickle

KITTLE *adj* -TLER, -TLEST ticklish

KITTY *n pl.* -TIES a kitten or cat

KIVA *n pl.* -S an underground ceremonial chamber

KIWI *n pl.* -S a flightless bird

KLATCH *n pl.* -ES a social gathering

KLATSCH *n pl.* -ES klatch

KLAVERN *n pl.* -S a local branch of the Ku Klux Klan

KLAXON *n pl.* -S a low-pitched horn

KLEAGLE *n pl.* -S an official in the Ku Klux Klan

KLEPHT *n pl.* -S a Greek guerrilla **KLEPHTIC** *adj*

KLONG *n pl.* -S a canal

KLOOF *n pl.* -S a ravine

KLUDGE *n pl.* -S a system composed of ill-fitting components

KLUTZ *n pl.* -ES a clumsy person

KLUTZY *adj* KLUTZIER, KLUTZIEST clumsy

KLYSTRON *n pl.* -S a type of electron tube

KNACK *v* -ED, -ING, -S to strike sharply

KNACKER *n pl.* -S one that buys old livestock

KNACKERY *n pl.* -ERIES the place of business of a knacker

KNAP *v* KNAPPED, KNAPPING, KNAPS to strike sharply

KNAPPER *n pl.* -S one that knaps

KNAPSACK *n pl.* -S a bag carried on the back

KNAPWEED *n pl.* -S a meadow plant

KNAR *n pl.* -S a bump on a tree **KNARRED, KNARRY** *adj*

KNAVE *n pl.* -S a dishonest person **KNAVISH** *adj*

KNAVERY *n pl.* -ERIES trickery

KNAWEL *n pl.* -S a Eurasian plant

KNEAD *v* -ED, -ING, -S to work into a uniform mixture with the hands

KNEADER *n pl.* -S one that kneads

KNEE *v* KNEED, KNEEING, KNEES to strike with the knee (a joint of the leg)

KNEECAP *n pl.* -S a bone at the front of the knee

KNEEHOLE *n pl.* -S a space for the knees

KNEEL *v* KNELT or KNEELED, KNEELING, KNEELS to rest on the knees

KNEELER *n pl.* -S one that kneels

KNEEPAD *n pl.* -S a covering for a knee

KNEEPAN *n pl.* -S the kneecap

KNELL *v* -ED, -ING, -S to sound a bell

KNELT a past tense of kneel

KNEW past tense of know

KNICKERS n/pl loose-fitting pants gathered at the knee

KNIFE n pl. KNIVES a sharp-edged instrument used for cutting

KNIFE v KNIFED, KNIFING, KNIFES to cut with a knife

KNIFER n pl. -S one that knifes

KNIGHT v -ED, -ING, -S to make a knight (a medieval gentleman-soldier) of

KNIGHTLY adj of or befitting a knight

KNISH n pl. -ES dough stuffed with filling and fried

KNIT v KNITTED, KNITTING, KNITS to make a fabric or garment by joining loops of yarn

KNITTER n pl. -S one that knits

KNITTING n pl. -S work done by a knitter

KNITWEAR n pl. -S knitted clothing

KNIVES pl. of knife

KNOB n pl. -S a rounded protuberance KNOBBED, KNOBLIKE adj

KNOBBY adj -BIER, -BIEST full of knobs

KNOCK v -ED, -ING, -S to strike sharply

KNOCKER n pl. -S one that knocks

KNOCKOFF n pl. -S a copy that sells for less than the original

KNOCKOUT n pl. -S a blow that induces unconsciousness

KNOLL v -ED, -ING, -S to knell

KNOLLER n pl. -S one that knolls

KNOLLY adj hilly

KNOP n pl. -S a knob KNOPPED adj

KNOSP n pl. -S a knob

KNOT v KNOTTED, KNOTTING, KNOTS to tie in a knot (a closed loop)

KNOTHOLE n pl. -S a hole in a plank

KNOTLESS adj having no knots

KNOTLIKE adj resembling a knot

KNOTTER n pl. -S one that knots

KNOTTY adj -TIER, -TIEST full of knots KNOTTILY adv

KNOTWEED n pl. -S a common weed

KNOUT v -ED, -ING, -S to flog with a leather whip

KNOW v KNEW, KNOWN, KNOWING, KNOWS to have a true understanding of KNOWABLE adj

KNOWER n pl. -S one that knows

KNOWING adj -INGER, -INGEST astute

KNOWING n pl. -S knowledge

KNOWN n pl. -S a mathematical quanity whose value is given

KNUCKLE v -LED, -LING, -LES to hit with the knuckles (the joints of the fingers)

KNUCKLER n pl. -S a type of baseball pitch

KNUCKLY adj -LIER, -LIEST having prominent knuckles

KNUR n pl. -S a bump on a tree

KNURL v -ED, -ING, -S to make grooves or ridges in

KNURLY adj KNURLIER, KNURLIEST gnarly

KOA n pl. -S a timber tree

KOALA n pl. -S an Australian mammal

KOAN n pl. -S a paradox meditated on by Buddhist monks

KOBOLD n pl. -S an elf

KOEL n pl. -S an Australian bird

KOHL n pl. -S a type of eye makeup

KOHLRABI n pl. -ES a variety of cabbage

KOINE n pl. -S a type of dialect

KOKANEE n pl. -S a food fish

KOLA n pl. -S cola

KOLACKY n pl. KOLACKY a kind of pastry

KOLHOZ n pl. -HOZY or -HOZES kolkhoz

KOLINSKI n pl. -ES kolinsky

KOLINSKY n pl. -SKIES an Asian mink

KOLKHOS n pl. -KHOSY or -KHOSES kolkhoz

KOLKHOZ n pl. -KHOZY or -KHOZES a collective farm in Russia

KOLKOZ n pl. -KOZY or -KOZES kolkhoz

KOLO n pl. -LOS a European folk dance

KOMATIK n pl. -S an Eskimo sledge

KOMONDOR n pl. -DORS, -DOROK, or -DOROCK a large, shaggy-coated dog

KOODOO n pl. -DOOS kudu

KOOK n pl. -S an eccentric person

KOOKIE adj KOOKIER, KOOKIEST kooky

KOOKY adj KOOKIER, KOOKIEST eccentric

KOP n pl. -S a hill

KOPECK n pl. -S a Russian coin

KOPEK n pl. -S kopeck

KOPH n pl. -S a Hebrew letter

KOPJE n pl. -S a small hill

KOPPA n pl. -S a Greek letter

KOPPIE	*n* pl. -S kopje	**KRULLER**	*n* pl. -S cruller
KOR	*n* pl. -S a Hebrew unit of measure	**KRYOLITE**	*n* pl. -S cryolite
		KRYOLITH	*n* pl. -S cryolite
KORUNA	*n* pl. KORUNAS, KORUNY, or KORUN a monetary unit of Czechoslovakia	**KRYPTON**	*n* pl. -S a gaseous element
		KUCHEN	*n* pl. KUCHEN a coffee cake
KOS	*n* pl. KOS a land measure in India	**KUDO**	*n* pl. -DOS award; honor
		KUDU	*n* pl. -S a large antelope
KOSHER	*v* -ED, -ING, -S to make fit to be eaten according to Jewish dietary laws	**KUDZU**	*n* pl. -S an Asian vine
		KUE	*n* pl. -S the letter Q
		KULAK	*n* pl. -LAKS or -LAKI a rich Russian peasant
KOSS	*n* pl. KOSS kos		
KOTO	*n* pl. -TOS a musical instrument	**KULTUR**	*n* pl. -S culture; civilization
KOTOW	*v* -ED, -ING, -S to kowtow	**KUMISS**	*n* pl. -ES koumiss
KOTOWER	*n* pl. -S one that kotows	**KUMMEL**	*n* pl. -S a type of liqueur
KOUMIS	*n* pl. -MISES koumiss	**KUMQUAT**	*n* pl. -S a citrus fruit
KOUMISS	*n* pl. -ES a beverage made from camel's milk	**KUMYS**	*n* pl. -ES koumiss
		KUNZITE	*n* pl. -S a mineral
KOUMYS	*n* pl. -ES koumiss	**KURBASH**	*v* -ED, -ING, -ES to flog with a leather whip
KOUMYSS	*n* pl. -ES koumiss		
KOUSSO	*n* pl. -SOS cusso	**KURGAN**	*n* pl. -S a mound of earth over a grave
KOWTOW	*v* -ED, -ING, -S to behave in a servile manner		
		KURTA	*n* pl. -S a shirt worn in India
KOWTOWER	*n* pl. -S one that kowtows	**KURTOSIS**	*n* pl. -SISES the relative degree of curvature in a statistical curve
KRAAL	*v* -ED, -ING, -S to pen in a type of enclosure		
KRAFT	*n* pl. -S a strong paper	**KURU**	*n* pl. -S a disease of the nervous system
KRAIT	*n* pl. -S a venomous snake		
KRAKEN	*n* pl. -S a legendary sea monster	**KUSSO**	*n* pl. -SOS cusso
		KVAS	*n* pl. -ES kvass
KRATER	*n* pl. -S a type of vase	**KVASS**	*n* pl. -ES a Russian beer
KRAUT	*n* pl. -S sauerkraut	**KVETCH**	*v* -ED, -ING, -ES to complain
KREMLIN	*n* pl. -S a Russian citadel	**KWACHA**	*n* pl. KWACHA a monetary unit of Zambia
KREUTZER	*n* pl. -S an Austrian coin		
KREUZER	*n* pl. -S kreutzer	**KYACK**	*n* pl. -S a packsack
KRILL	*n* pl. -S an aggregate of small marine crustaceans	**KYANISE**	*v* -ISED, -ISING, -ISES to kyanize
		KYANITE	*n* pl. -S cyanite
KRIMMER	*n* pl. -S a kind of fur	**KYANIZE**	*v* -IZED, -IZING, -IZES to treat wood with a type of preservative
KRIS	*n* pl. -ES a short sword		
KRONA	*n* pl. KRONUR a monetary unit of Iceland		
		KYAR	*n* pl. -S coir
KRONA	*n* pl. KRONOR a monetary unit of Sweden	**KYAT**	*n* pl. -S a monetary unit of Burma
KRONE	*n* pl. KRONER a monetary unit of Denmark	**KYLIX**	*n* pl. -LIKES a drinking vessel
		KYMOGRAM	*n* pl. -S a record of fluid pressure
KRONE	*n* pl. KRONEN a former monetary unit of Austria		
		KYPHOSIS	*n* pl. -PHOSES abnormal curvature of the spine **KYPHOTIC** *adj*
KRONOR	pl. of krona		
KRONUR	pl. of krona		
KROON	*n* pl. KROONS or KROONI a former monetary unit of Estonia	**KYRIE**	*n* pl. -S a religious petition for mercy
KRUBI	*n* pl. -S a tropical plant	**KYTE**	*n* pl. -S the stomach
KRUBUT	*n* pl. -S krubi	**KYTHE**	*v* KYTHED, KYTHING, KYTHES to kithe

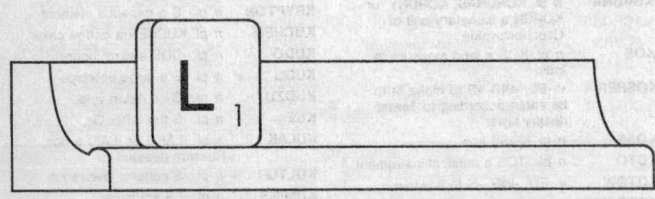

LA	*n* pl. -S the sixth tone of the diatonic musical scale
LAAGER	*v* -ED, -ING, -S to form a defensive encampment
LAB	*n* pl. -S a laboratory
LABARUM	*n* pl. -RA or -RUMS an ecclesiastical banner
LABDANUM	*n* pl. -S a fragrant resin
LABEL	*v* -BELED, -BELING, -BELS or -BELLED, -BELLING, -BELS to describe or designate
LABELER	*n* pl. -S one that labels
LABELLA	pl. of labellum
LABELLED	a past tense of label
LABELLER	*n* pl. -S labeler
LABELLING	a present participle of label
LABELLUM	*n* pl. -LA the lower petal of an orchid
LABIA	pl. of labium
LABIAL	*n* pl. -S a labially produced sound
LABIALLY	*adv* by means of the lips
LABIATE	*n* pl. -S a labiated plant
LABIATED	*adj* having corollas that are divided into two liplike parts
LABILE	*adj* likely to change
LABILITY	*n* pl. -TIES the state of being labile
LABIUM	*n* pl. -BIA a fold of the vulva
LABOR	*v* -ED, -ING, -S to work
LABORER	*n* pl. -S one that labors
LABORITE	*n* pl. -S a supporter of labor interests
LABOUR	*v* -ED, -ING, -S to labor
LABOURER	*n* pl. -S laborer
LABRA	a pl. of labrum
LABRET	*n* pl. -S an ornament worn in a perforation of the lip
LABROID	*n* pl. -S a marine fish
LABRUM	*n* pl. -BRA or -BRUMS a lip or liplike structure
LABURNUM	*n* pl. -S an ornamental tree
LAC	*n* pl. -S a resinous substance secreted by certain insects
LACE	*v* LACED, LACING, LACES to fasten by means of a lace (a cord for drawing together two edges)
LACELESS	*adj* lacking lace
LACELIKE	*adj* resembling lace
LACER	*n* pl. -S one that laces
LACERATE	*v* -ATED, -ATING, -ATES to tear roughly
LACERTID	*n* pl. -S a type of lizard
LACEWING	*n* pl. -S a winged insect
LACEWOOD	*n* pl. -S an Australian tree
LACEWORK	*n* pl. -S a delicate openwork fabric
LACEY	*adj* LACIER, LACIEST lacy
LACHES	*n* pl. LACHES undue delay in asserting a legal right
LACIER	comparative of lace
LACIEST	superlative of lace
LACILY	*adv* in a lacy manner
LACINESS	*n* pl. -ES the quality of being lacy
LACING	*n* pl. -S a contrasting marginal band of color
LACK	*v* -ED, -ING, -S to be without
LACKADAY	*interj* — used to express regret
LACKER	*v* -ED, -ING, -S to lacquer
LACKEY	*v* -ED, -ING, -S to act in a servile manner
LACONIC	*adj* using a minimum of words
LACONISM	*n* pl. -S brevity of expression

LACQUER v -ED, -ING, -S to coat with a glossy substance

LACQUEY v -ED, -ING, -S to lackey

LACRIMAL n pl. -S a type of vase

LACROSSE n pl. -S a type of ball game

LACTAM n pl. -S a chemical compound

LACTARY adj pertaining to milk

LACTASE n pl. -S an enzyme

LACTATE v -TATED, -TATING, -TATES to secrete milk

LACTEAL n pl. -S a lymphatic vessel

LACTEAN adj lacteous

LACTEOUS adj resembling milk

LACTIC adj derived from milk

LACTONE n pl. -S any of a group of esters **LACTONIC** adj

LACTOSE n pl. -S a lactic sugar

LACUNA n pl. -NAE or -NAS an empty space or missing part **LACUNAL, LACUNARY, LACUNATE** adj

LACUNAR n pl. -NARS or -NARIA a ceiling with recessed panels

LACUNE n pl. -S lacuna

LACUNOSE adj marked by shallow depressions

LACY adj LACIER, LACIEST resembling lacework

LAD n pl. -S a boy or youth

LADANUM n pl. -S labdanum

LADDER v -ED, -ING, -S to cause a run in a stocking

LADDIE n pl. -S a lad

LADE v LADED, LADEN, LADING, LADES to load with a cargo

LADEN v -ED, -ING, -S to lade

LADER n pl. -S one that lades

LADIES pl. of lady

LADING n pl. -S cargo; freight

LADINO n pl. -NOS a fast-growing clover

LADLE v -DLED, -DLING, -DLES to lift out with a ladle (a type of spoon)

LADLEFUL n pl. -S as much as a ladle will hold

LADLER n pl. -S one that ladles

LADRON n pl. -S a ladrone

LADRONE n pl. -S a thief

LADY n pl. -DIES a woman of refinement and gentle manners

LADYBIRD n pl. -S a ladybug

LADYBUG n pl. -S a small beetle

LADYFISH n pl. -ES a bonefish

LADYHOOD n pl. -S the state of being a lady

LADYISH adj somewhat ladylike

LADYKIN n pl. -S a small lady

LADYLIKE adj resembling or suitable to a lady

LADYLOVE n pl. -S a sweetheart

LADYPALM n pl. -S a palm tree

LADYSHIP n pl. -S the condition of being a lady

LAEVO adj levo

LAG v LAGGED, LAGGING, LAGS to stay or fall behind

LAGAN n pl. -S goods thrown into the sea with a buoy attached to enable recovery

LAGEND n pl. -S lagan

LAGER v -ED, -ING, -S to laager

LAGGARD n pl. -S one that lags

LAGGED past tense of lag

LAGGER n pl. -S a laggard

LAGGING n pl. -S an insulating material

LAGNAPPE n pl. -S a small gift given to a customer with his purchase

LAGOON n pl. -S a shallow body of water **LAGOONAL** adj

LAGUNA n pl. -S lagoon

LAGUNE n pl. -S lagoon

LAIC n pl. -S a layman **LAICAL** adj **LAICALLY** adv

LAICH n pl. -S laigh

LAICISE v -ICISED, -ICISING, -ICISES to laicize

LAICISM n pl. -S a political system free from clerical control

LAICIZE v -ICIZED, -ICIZING, -ICIZES to free from clerical control

LAID a past tense of lay

LAIGH n pl. -S a lowland

LAIN past participle of lie

LAIR v -ED, -ING, -S to live in a lair (a wild animal's resting or dwelling place)

LAIRD n pl. -S the owner of a landed estate **LAIRDLY** adj

LAITANCE n pl. -S a milky deposit on the surface of fresh concrete

LAITH adj loath **LAITHLY** adv

LAITY n pl. -ITIES the nonclerical membership of a religious faith

LAKE n pl. -S a sizable inland body of water

LAKED *adj* subjected to the process of laking

LAKEPORT *n* pl. -S a city located on the shore of a lake

LAKER *n* pl. -S a lake fish

LAKESIDE *n* pl. -S the land along the edge of a lake

LAKH *n* pl. -S the sum of one hundred thousand

LAKING *n* pl. -S the reddening of blood plasma by the release of hemoglobin from the red corpuscles

LAKY *adj* LAKIER, LAKIEST of the color of blood

LALL *v* -ED, -ING, -S to articulate the letter *r* as *l*

LALLAN *n* pl. -S a lowland

LALLAND *n* pl. -S a lowland

LALLYGAG *v* -GAGGED, -GAGGING, -GAGS to dawdle

LAM *v* LAMMED, LAMMING, LAMS to flee hastily

LAMA *n* pl. -S a Buddhist monk

LAMASERY *n* pl. -SERIES a monastery of lamas

LAMB *v* -ED, -ING, -S to give birth to a lamb (a young sheep)

LAMBAST *v* -ED, -ING, -S to lambaste

LAMBASTE *v* -BASTED, -BASTING, -BASTES to beat severely

LAMBDA *n* pl. -S a Greek letter LAMBDOID *adj*

LAMBENCY *n* pl. -CIES the quality or an instance of being lambent

LAMBENT *adj* flickering lightly and gently over a surface

LAMBER *n* pl. -S a ewe that is lambing

LAMBERT *n* pl. -S a unit of brightness

LAMBIE *n* pl. -S a lambkin

LAMBKILL *n* pl. -S an evergreen shrub

LAMBKIN *n* pl. -S a small lamb

LAMBLIKE *adj* resembling a lamb

LAMBSKIN *n* pl. -S the skin of a lamb

LAME *adj* LAMER, LAMEST physically disabled

LAME *v* LAMED, LAMING, LAMES to make lame

LAMED *n* pl. -S a Hebrew letter

LAMEDH *n* pl. -S lamed

LAMELLA *n* pl. -LAE or -LAS a thin plate, scale, or membrane LAMELLAR *adj*

LAMELY *adv* in a lame manner

LAMENESS *n* pl. -ES the state of being lame

LAMENT *v* -ED, -ING, -S to express sorrow or regret for

LAMENTER *n* pl. -S one that laments

LAMER comparative of lame

LAMEST superlative of lame

LAMIA *n* pl. -MIAS or -MIAE a female demon

LAMINA *n* pl. -NAE or -NAS a thin plate, scale, or layer LAMINAL, LAMINAR, LAMINARY *adj*

LAMINATE *v* -NATED, -NATING, -NATES to compress into a thin plate

LAMING present participle of lame

LAMINOSE *adj* composed of laminae

LAMINOUS *adj* laminose

LAMISTER *n* pl. -S lamster

LAMMED past tense of lam

LAMMING present participle of lam

LAMP *v* -ED, -ING, -S to look at

LAMPAD *n* pl. -S a candlestick

LAMPAS *n* pl. -ES inflammation of the roof of a horse's mouth

LAMPERS *n* pl. -ES lampas

LAMPION *n* pl. -S a type of light-generating device

LAMPOON *v* -ED, -ING, -S to ridicule in a satirical composition

LAMPPOST *n* pl. -S a post supporting a streetlight

LAMPREY *n* pl. -PREYS an eellike fish

LAMPYRID *n* pl. -S any of a family of beetles

LAMSTER *n* pl. -S a fugitive

LANAI *n* pl. -S a veranda

LANATE *adj* covered with wool

LANATED *adj* lanate

LANCE *v* LANCED, LANCING, LANCES to pierce with a lance (a spearlike weapon)

LANCELET *n* pl. -S a small marine organism

LANCER *n* pl. -S a cavalryman armed with a lance

LANCET *n* pl. -S a narrow, pointed arch LANCETED *adj*

LANCIERS *n* pl. LANCIERS a French dance

LANCING present participle of lance

LAND *v* -ED, -ING, -S to set down upon land (solid ground)

LANDAU *n* pl. -S a type of carriage

LANDER *n* pl. -S one that lands

LANDFALL *n* pl. -S a sighting or approach to land

LANDFILL *n* pl. -S a system of waste disposal

LANDFORM *n* pl. -S a natural feature of the earth's surface

LANDING *n* pl. -S a place for discharging or taking on passengers or cargo

LANDLADY *n* pl. -DIES a female landlord

LANDLER *n* pl. -S a slow Austrian dance

LANDLESS *adj* owning no land

LANDLORD *n* pl. -S one who owns and rents out real estate

LANDMAN *n* pl. -MEN one who lives and works on land

LANDMARK *n* pl. -S an object that marks a boundary line

LANDMASS *n* pl. -ES a large area of land

LANDMEN pl. of landman

LANDSIDE *n* pl. -S a part of a plow

LANDSKIP *n* pl. -S landscape

LANDSLEIT pl. of landsman

LANDSLID past tense of landslide (to win an election by an overwhelming majority)

LANDSLIP *n* pl. -S the fall of a mass of earth

LANDSMAN *n* pl. LANDSLEIT a fellow Jew coming from one's own section of Eastern Europe

LANDSMAN *n* pl. -MEN landman

LANDWARD *adv* toward the land

LANE *n* pl. -S a narrow passageway

LANELY *adj* lonely

LANG *adj* long

LANGLAUF *n* pl. -S a cross-country ski run

LANGLEY *n* pl. -LEYS a unit of illumination

LANGRAGE *n* pl. -S a shot formerly used in naval warfare

LANGREL *n* pl. -S langrage

LANGSHAN *n* pl. -S any of a breed of large domestic fowl

LANGSYNE *n* pl. -S time long past

LANGUAGE *n* pl. -S a body of words and systems serving as a means of communication

LANGUE *n* pl. -S a type of language

LANGUET *n* pl. -S a tonguelike part

LANGUID *adj* lacking in vigor or vitality

LANGUISH *v* -ED, -ING, -ES to lose vigor or vitality

LANGUOR *n* pl. -S the state of being languid

LANGUR *n* pl. -S an Asian monkey

LANIARD *n* pl. -S lanyard

LANIARY *n* pl. -ARIES a cuspid

LANITAL *n* pl. -S a woollike fiber

LANK *adj* LANKER, LANKEST long and slender **LANKLY** *adv*

LANKNESS *n* pl. -ES the state of being lank

LANKY *adj* LANKIER, LANKIEST ungracefully tall and thin **LANKILY** *adv*

LANNER *n* pl. -S a falcon of Europe and Asia

LANNERET *n* pl. -S a male lanner

LANOLIN *n* pl. -S a fatty substance obtained from wool

LANOLINE *n* pl. -S lanolin

LANOSE *adj* lanate

LANOSITY *n* pl. -TIES the state of being lanose

LANTANA *n* pl. -S a tropical shrub

LANTERN *n* pl. -S a protective case for a light

LANTHORN *n* pl. -S a lantern

LANUGO *n* pl. -GOS fine, soft hair

LANYARD *n* pl. -S a fastening rope on a ship

LAP *v* LAPPED, LAPPING, LAPS to fold over or around something

LAPBOARD *n* pl. -S a flat board used as a table or desk

LAPDOG *n* pl. -S a small dog

LAPEL *n* pl. -S an extension of the collar of a garment **LAPELLED** *adj*

LAPFUL *n* pl. -S as much as the lap can hold

LAPIDARY *n* pl. -DARIES one who works with precious stones

LAPIDATE *v* -DATED, -DATING, -DATES to hurl stones at

LAPIDES pl. of lapis

LAPIDIFY *v* -FIED, -FYING, -FIES to turn to stone

LAPIDIST *n* pl. -S a lapidary

LAPILLUS *n* pl. -LI a small fragment of lava

LAPIN *n* pl. -S a rabbit

LAPIS *n* pl. LAPIDES a stone

LAPIS *n* pl. -PISES a mineral

LAPPED past tense of lap

LAPPER *v* -ED, -ING, -S to lopper

LAPPET n pl. -S a decorative flap on a garment **LAPPETED** adj

LAPPING present participle of lap

LAPSE v LAPSED, LAPSING, LAPSES to fall from a previous standard **LAPSABLE, LAPSIBLE** adj

LAPSER n pl. -S one that lapses

LAPSUS n pl. LAPSUS a mistake

LAPWING n pl. -S a shore bird

LAR n pl. -ES or -S a tutelary god or spirit of an ancient Roman household

LARBOARD n pl. -S the left-hand side of a ship

LARCENER n pl. -S one that commits larceny

LARCENY n pl. -NIES the felonious taking and removal of another's personal goods

LARCH n pl. -ES a coniferous tree

LARD v -ED, -ING, -S to coat with lard (the melted fat of hogs)

LARDER n pl. -S a place where food is stored

LARDIER comparative of lardy

LARDIEST superlative of lardy

LARDLIKE adj resembling lard

LARDON n pl. -S a thin slice of bacon or pork

LARDOON n pl. -S lardon

LARDY adj LARDIER, LARDIEST resembling lard

LARES a pl. of lar

LARGE adj LARGER, LARGEST of considerable size or quantity **LARGELY** adv

LARGE n pl. -S generosity

LARGESS n pl. -ES generosity

LARGESSE n pl. -S largess

LARGISH adj somewhat large

LARGO n pl. -GOS a slow musical movement

LARIAT v -ED, -ING, -S to lasso

LARINE adj resembling a gull

LARK v -ED, -ING, -S to behave playfully

LARKER n pl. -S one that larks

LARKIER comparative of larky

LARKIEST superlative of larky

LARKSOME adj playful

LARKSPUR n pl. -S a flowering plant

LARKY adj LARKIER, LARKIEST playful

LARRIGAN n pl. -S a type of moccasin

LARRIKIN n pl. -S a rowdy

LARRUP v -ED, -ING, -S to beat or thrash

LARRUPER n pl. -S one that larrups

LARUM n pl. -S an alarm

LARVA n pl. -VAE or -VAS the immature form of various insects and animals when newly hatched **LARVAL** adj

LARYNX n pl. LARYNGES or LARYNXES an organ of the respiratory tract **LARYNGAL** adj

LASAGNA n pl. -S an Italian baked dish

LASAGNE n pl. -S lasagna

LASCAR n pl. -S an East Indian sailor

LASE v LASED, LASING, LASES to function as a laser

LASER n pl. -S a device that amplifies light waves

LASH v -ED, -ING, -ES to strike with a whip

LASHER n pl. -S one that lashes

LASHING n pl. -S a flogging

LASHINS n/pl an abundance

LASHKAR n pl. -S lascar

LASING present participle of lase

LASS n pl. -ES a young woman

LASSIE n pl. -S a lass

LASSO v -ED, -ING, -S or -ES to catch with a lasso (a long rope with a running noose)

LASSOER n pl. -S one that lassos

LAST v -ED, -ING, -S to continue in existence

LASTER n pl. -S one that lasts

LASTING n pl. -S a durable fabric

LASTLY adv in conclusion

LAT n pl. LATS or LATI a former monetary unit of Latvia

LATAKIA n pl. -S a variety of Turkish tobacco

LATCH v -ED, -ING, -ES to close with a type of fastening device

LATCHET n pl. -S a thong used to fasten a shoe

LATCHKEY n pl. -KEYS a key for opening a latched door

LATE adj LATER, LATEST coming or occurring after the expected time

LATED adj belated

LATEEN n pl. -S a sailing vessel

LATEENER n pl. -S a lateen

LATELY *adv* not long ago

LATEN *v* -ED, -ING, -S to become late

LATENCY *n* pl. -CIES the state of being present but not manifest

LATENESS *n* pl. -ES the state of being late

LATENT *n* pl. -S a barely visible fingerprint that can be developed for study

LATENTLY *adv* dormantly

LATER comparative of late

LATERAD *adv* toward the side

LATERAL *v* -ED, -ING, -S to throw a sideward pass in football

LATERITE *n* pl. -S a type of soil

LATEST *n* pl. -S the most recent development

LATEWOOD *n* pl. -S a part of an annual ring of wood

LATEX *n* pl. LATICES or LATEXES a milky liquid of certain plants

LATH *v* -ED, -ING, -S to cover with laths (thin strips of wood)

LATHE *v* LATHED, LATHING, LATHES to cut or shape on a type of machine

LATHER *v* -ED, -ING, -S to cover with lather (a light foam)

LATHERER *n* pl. -S one that lathers

LATHERY *adj* covered with lather

LATHIER comparative of lathy

LATHIEST superlative of lathy

LATHING *n* pl. -S work made of or using laths

LATHWORK *n* pl. -S lathing

LATHY *adj* LATHIER, LATHIEST long and slender

LATI a pl. of lat

LATICES a pl. of latex

LATIGO *n* pl. -GOS or -GOES a strap used to fasten a saddle

LATINITY *n* pl. -TIES a manner of writing or speaking Latin

LATINIZE *v* -IZED, -IZING, -IZES to translate into Latin

LATISH *adj* somewhat late

LATITUDE *n* pl. -S freedom from narrow restrictions

LATOSOL *n* pl. -S a tropical soil

LATRIA *n* pl. -S the supreme worship given to God only, in Roman Catholicism

LATRINE *n* pl. -S a type of toilet

LATTEN *n* pl. -S a brass-like alloy

LATTER *adj* being the second mentioned of two

LATTERLY *adv* lately

LATTICE *v* -TICED, -TICING, -TICES to form a structure consisting of interlaced strips of material

LATTIN *n* pl. -S latten

LAUAN *n* pl. -S a Philippine timber

LAUD *v* -ED, -ING, -S to praise

LAUDABLE *adj* worthy of praise LAUDABLY *adv*

LAUDANUM *n* pl. -S a type of opium preparation

LAUDATOR *n* pl. -S a lauder

LAUDER *n* pl. -S one that lauds

LAUGH *v* -ED, -ING, -S to express emotion, typically mirth, by a series of inarticulate sounds

LAUGHER *n* pl. -S one that laughs

LAUGHING *n* pl. -S laughter

LAUGHTER *n* pl. -S the act or sound of one that laughs

LAUNCE *n* pl. -S a marine fish

LAUNCH *v* -ED, -ING, -ES to set in motion

LAUNCHER *n* pl. -S a launching device

LAUNDER *v* -ED, -ING, -S to wash clothes

LAUNDRY *n* pl. -DRIES a collection of clothes to be washed

LAURA *n* pl. -RAS or -RAE a type of monastery

LAUREATE *v* -ATED, -ATING, -ATES to laurel

LAUREL *v* -RELED, -RELING, -RELS or -RELLED, -RELLING, -RELS to crown with a wreath of evergreen leaves

LAUWINE *n* pl. -S an avalanche

LAVA *n* pl. -S molten rock that issues from a volcano

LAVABO *n* pl. -BOES or -BOS a ceremonial washing in certain Christian churches

LAVAGE *n* pl. -S a washing

LAVALAVA *n* pl. -S a Polynesian garment

LAVALIER *n* pl. -S a pendant worn on a chain around the neck

LAVALIKE *adj* resembling lava

LAVATION *n* pl. -S the act of washing

LAVATORY *n* pl. -RIES a room equipped with washing and toilet facilities

LAVE *v* LAVED, LAVING, LAVES to wash

LAVEER v -ED, -ING, -S to sail against the wind

LAVENDER v -ED, -ING, -S to sprinkle with a type of perfume

LAVER n pl. -S a vessel used for ancient Hebrew ceremonial washings

LAVEROCK n pl. -S a songbird

LAVING present participle of lave

LAVISH adj -ISHER, -ISHEST expending or giving in great amounts **LAVISHLY** adv

LAVISH v -ED, -ING, -ES to expend or give in great amounts

LAVISHER n pl. -S one that lavishes

LAVROCK n pl. -S laverock

LAW v -ED, -ING, -S to take a complaint to court for settlement

LAWFUL adj allowed by law (the body of rules governing the affairs of a community) **LAWFULLY** adv

LAWGIVER n pl. -S one who institutes a legal system

LAWINE n pl. -S lauwine

LAWING n pl. -S a bill for food or drink in a tavern

LAWLESS adj having no system of laws

LAWLIKE adj being like the law

LAWMAKER n pl. -S a legislator

LAWMAN n pl. -MEN a law-enforcement officer

LAWN n pl. -S an area of grass-covered land **LAWNY** adj

LAWSUIT n pl. -S a legal action

LAWYER n pl. -S a member of the legal profession **LAWYERLY** adj

LAX adj LAXER, LAXEST not strict or stringent

LAXATION n pl. -S the act of relaxing

LAXATIVE n pl. -S a drug that stimulates evacuation of the bowels

LAXITY n pl. -ITIES the state of being lax

LAXLY adv in a lax manner

LAXNESS n pl. -ES laxity

LAY v LAID or LAYED, LAYING, LAYS to deposit as a wager

LAYABOUT n pl. -S a lazy person

LAYAWAY n pl. -AWAYS an item that has been reserved with a down payment

LAYER v -ED, -ING, -S to form a layer (a single thickness, coating, or covering)

LAYERAGE n pl. -S a method of plant propagation

LAYERING n pl. -S layerage

LAYETTE n pl. -S an outfit of clothing and equipment for a newborn child

LAYMAN n pl. -MEN a member of the laity

LAYOFF n pl. -S the suspension or dismissal of employees

LAYOUT n pl. -S an arrangement or plan

LAYOVER n pl. -S a stopover

LAYWOMAN n pl. -WOMEN a female member of the laity

LAZAR n pl. -S a beggar afflicted with a loathsome disease

LAZARET n pl. -S a hospital treating contagious diseases

LAZE v LAZED, LAZING, LAZES to pass time lazily

LAZIED past tense of lazy

LAZIER comparative of lazy

LAZIES present 3d person sing. of lazy

LAZIEST superlative of lazy

LAZILY adv in a lazy manner

LAZINESS n pl. -ES the state of being lazy

LAZING present participle of laze

LAZULI n pl. -S a mineral

LAZULITE n pl. -S a mineral

LAZURITE n pl. -S a mineral

LAZY adj LAZIER, LAZIEST disinclined to work or exertion

LAZY v LAZIED, LAZYING, LAZIES to move or lie lazily

LAZYISH adj somewhat lazy

LEA n pl. -S a meadow

LEACH v -ED, -ING, -ES to subject to the filtering action of a liquid

LEACHATE n pl. -S a solution obtained by leaching

LEACHER n pl. -S one that leaches

LEACHY adj LEACHIER, LEACHIEST porous

LEAD v LED, LEADING, LEADS to show the way to by going in advance

LEAD v -ED, -ING, -S to cover with lead (a heavy metallic element)

LEADEN adj oppressively heavy **LEADENLY** adv

LEADER n pl. -S one that leads or guides

LEADIER comparative of leady

LEADIEST superlative of leady

LEADING *n* pl. -S a covering or border of lead

LEADLESS *adj* having no lead

LEADOFF *n* pl. -S an opening play or move

LEADSMAN *n* pl. -MEN a seaman who measures the depth of water

LEADWORK *n* pl. -S something made of lead

LEADWORT *n* pl. -S a tropical plant

LEADY *adj* LEADIER, LEADIEST resembling lead

LEAF *n* pl. LEAVES a usually green, flattened organ of vascular plants

LEAF *v* -ED, -ING, -S to turn pages rapidly

LEAFAGE *n* pl. -S foliage

LEAFIER comparative of leafy

LEAFIEST superlative of leafy

LEAFLESS *adj* having no leaves

LEAFLET *n* pl. -S a small printed sheet of paper

LEAFLIKE *adj* resembling a leaf

LEAFWORM *n* pl. -S a moth larva that feeds on leaves

LEAFY *adj* LEAFIER, LEAFIEST covered with leaves

LEAGUE *v* LEAGUED, LEAGUING, LEAGUES to come together for a common purpose

LEAGUER *v* -ED, -ING, -S to besiege

LEAK *v* -ED, -ING, -S to permit the escape of something through a breach or flaw

LEAKAGE *n* pl. -S the act or an instance of leaking

LEAKER *n* pl. -S one that leaks

LEAKLESS *adj* designed not to leak

LEAKY *adj* LEAKIER, LEAKIEST tending to leak LEAKILY *adv*

LEAL *adj* loyal LEALLY *adv*

LEALTY *n* pl. -TIES loyalty

LEAN *v* LEANED or LEANT, LEANING, LEANS to deviate from a vertical position

LEAN *adj* LEANER, LEANEST having little fat LEANLY *adv*

LEANING *n* pl. -S a tendency

LEANNESS *n* pl. -ES the state of being lean

LEANT a past tense of lean

LEAP *v* LEAPED or LEAPT, LEAPING, LEAPS to spring off the ground

LEAPER *n* pl. -S one that leaps

LEAPFROG *v* -FROGGED, -FROGGING, -FROGS to jump over with the legs wide apart

LEAPT a past tense of leap

LEAR *n* pl. -S learning

LEARIER comparative of leary

LEARIEST superlative of leary

LEARN *v* LEARNED or LEARNT, LEARNING, LEARNS to gain knowledge by experience, instruction, or study

LEARNER *n* pl. -S one that learns

LEARNING *n* pl. -S acquired knowledge

LEARNT a past tense of learn

LEARY *adj* LEARIER, LEARIEST leery

LEASE *v* LEASED, LEASING, LEASES to grant temporary use of in exchange for rent LEASABLE *adj*

LEASER *n* pl. -S one that leases

LEASH *v* -ED, -ING, -ES to restrain an animal with a line or thong

LEASING *n* pl. -S a falsehood

LEAST *n* pl. -S something that is smallest in size or degree

LEATHER *v* -ED, -ING, -S to cover with leather (the dressed or tanned hide of an animal)

LEATHERN *adj* made of leather

LEATHERY *adj* resembling leather

LEAVE *v* LEFT, LEAVING, LEAVES to go away from

LEAVED *adj* having a leaf or leaves

LEAVEN *v* -ED, -ING, -S to produce fermentation in

LEAVER *n* pl. -S one that leaves

LEAVES pl. of leaf

LEAVING *n* pl. -S a leftover

LEAVY *adj* LEAVIER, LEAVIEST leafy

LEBEN *n* pl. -S a type of liquid food

LECH *n* pl. -ES letch

LECHAYIM *n* pl. -S lehayim

LECHER *v* -ED, -ING, -S to engage in lechery

LECHERY *n* pl. -ERIES excessive sexual indulgence

LECITHIN *n* pl. -S any of a group of fatty substances found in plant and animal tissues

LECTERN *n* pl. -S a reading desk

LECTION *n* pl. -S a portion of sacred writing read in a church service

LECTOR *n pl.* -S a low-ranking church officer

LECTURE *v* -TURED, -TURING, -TURES to expound on a specific subject

LECTURER *n pl.* -S one that lectures

LECYTHUS *n pl.* -THI lekythos

LED past tense of lead

LEDGE *n pl.* -S a narrow, shelflike projection

LEDGER *n pl.* -S an account book of final entry

LEDGY *adj* LEDGIER, LEDGIEST abounding in ledges

LEE *n pl.* -S shelter from the wind

LEEBOARD *n pl.* -S a board attached to a sailing vessel to prevent leeway

LEECH *v* -ED, -ING, -ES to cling to and feed upon or drain

LEEK *n pl.* -S an herb used in cookery

LEER *v* -ED, -ING, -S to look with a sideways glance

LEERY *adj* LEERIER, LEERIEST suspicious LEERILY *adv*

LEET *n pl.* -S a former English court for petty offenses

LEEWARD *n pl.* -S the direction toward which the wind is blowing

LEEWAY *n pl.* -WAYS the lateral drift of a ship

LEFT *adj* LEFTER, LEFTEST pertaining to the side of the body to the north when one faces east

LEFT *n pl.* -S the left side or hand

LEFTISM *n pl.* -S a liberal political philosophy

LEFTIST *n pl.* -S an advocate of leftism

LEFTOVER *n pl.* -S an unused or unconsumed portion

LEFTWARD *adv* toward the left

LEFTWING *adj* favoring leftism

LEFTY *n pl.* LEFTIES a left-handed person

LEG *v* LEGGED, LEGGING, LEGS to move with the legs (appendages that serve as a means of support and locomotion)

LEGACY *n pl.* -CIES something bequeathed

LEGAL *n pl.* -S an authorized investment that may be made by investors such as savings banks

LEGALESE *n pl.* -S the specialized language of lawyers

LEGALISE *v* -ISED, -ISING, -ISES to legalize

LEGALISM *n pl.* -S strict conformity to the law

LEGALIST *n pl.* -S an adherent of legalism

LEGALITY *n pl.* -TIES the condition of being lawful

LEGALIZE *v* -IZED, -IZING, -IZES to make lawful

LEGALLY *adv* in a lawful manner

LEGATE *v* -GATED, -GATING, -GATES to bequeath

LEGATEE *n pl.* -S the inheritor of a legacy

LEGATINE *adj* pertaining to an official envoy

LEGATING present participle of legate

LEGATION *n pl.* -S the sending of an official envoy

LEGATO *n pl.* -TOS a smooth and flowing musical style

LEGATOR *n pl.* -S one that legates

LEGEND *n pl.* -S an unverified story from earlier times

LEGENDRY *n pl.* -RIES a collection of legends

LEGER *n pl.* -S fishing bait made to lie on the bottom

LEGERITY *n pl.* -TIES quickness of the mind or body

LEGES *pl.* of lex

LEGGED past tense of leg

LEGGIER comparative of leggy

LEGGIEST superlative of leggy

LEGGIN *n pl.* -S legging

LEGGING *n pl.* -S a covering for the leg

LEGGY *adj* -GIER, -GIEST having long legs

LEGHORN *n pl.* -S a smooth, plaited straw

LEGIBLE *adj* capable of being read LEGIBLY *adv*

LEGION *n pl.* -S a large military force

LEGIST *n pl.* -S one learned or skilled in the law

LEGIT *n pl.* -S legitimate drama

LEGLESS *adj* having no legs

LEGLIKE *adj* resembling a leg

LEGMAN *n pl.* -MEN a newspaperman assigned to gather information

LEGROOM *n pl.* -S space in which to extend the legs

LEGUME *n pl.* -S a type of plant

LEGUMIN *n pl.* -S a plant protein

LEGWORK *n pl.* -S work that involves extensive walking

LEHAYIM *n pl.* -S a traditional Jewish toast

LEHR *n pl.* -S a type of oven

LEHUA *n pl.* -S a tropical tree

LEI *n pl.* -S a wreath of flowers

LEISTER *v* -ED, -ING, -S to spear with a three-pronged fishing implement

LEISURE *n pl.* -S freedom from the demands of work or duty
LEISURED *adj*

LEK *n pl.* -S a monetary unit of Albania

LEKYTHOS *n pl.* -THOI an oil jar used in ancient Greece

LEKYTHUS *n pl.* -THI lekythos

LEMAN *n pl.* -S a lover

LEMMA *n pl.* -MAS or -MATA a type of proposition in logic

LEMMING *n pl.* -S a mouselike rodent

LEMNISCI *n/pl* bands of nerve fibers

LEMON *n pl.* -S a citrus fruit
LEMONISH, LEMONY *adj*

LEMONADE *n pl.* -S a beverage

LEMPIRA *n pl.* -S a monetary unit of Honduras

LEMUR *n pl.* -S an arboreal mammal related to the monkeys

LEMURES *n/pl* the ghosts of the dead in ancient Roman religion

LEMUROID *n pl.* -S a lemur

LEND *v* LENT, LENDING, LENDS to give the temporary use of

LENDER *n pl.* -S one that lends

LENES *pl.* of lenis

LENGTH *n pl.* -S the longer or longest dimension of an object

LENGTHEN *v* -ED, -ING, -S to make or become longer

LENGTHY *adj* LENGTHIER, LENGTHIEST very long

LENIENCE *n pl.* -S leniency

LENIENCY *n pl.* -CIES the quality of being lenient

LENIENT *adj* gently tolerant

LENIS *n pl.* LENES a speech sound pronounced with little or no aspiration

LENITIVE *n pl.* -S a soothing medicine

LENITY *n pl.* -TIES leniency

LENO *n pl.* -NOS a style of weaving

LENS *n pl.* -ES a piece of transparent material used in changing the convergence of light rays
LENSED, LENSLESS *adj*

LENSE *n pl.* -S lens

LENT past tense of lend

LENTANDO *adv* becoming slower — used as a musical direction

LENTEN *adj* meager

LENTIC *adj* pertaining to still water

LENTICEL *n pl.* -S a mass of cells on a plant stem

LENTIGO *n pl.* -TIGINES a freckle

LENTIL *n pl.* -S a Eurasian annual plant

LENTISK *n pl.* -S an evergreen tree

LENTO *n pl.* -TOS a slow musical movement

LENTOID *adj* lens-shaped

LEONE *n pl.* -S a monetary unit of Sierra Leone

LEONINE *adj* pertaining to a lion

LEOPARD *n pl.* -S a large, carnivorous feline mammal

LEOTARD *n pl.* -S a close-fitting garment

LEPER *n pl.* -S one affected with leprosy

LEPIDOTE *adj* covered with small scales

LEPORID *n pl.* -S a gnawing mammal

LEPORINE *adj* resembling a rabbit or hare

LEPROSE *adj* leprous

LEPROSY *n pl.* -SIES a chronic disease characterized by skin lesions and deformities

LEPROTIC *adj* leprous

LEPROUS *adj* affected with leprosy

LEPTON *n pl.* -TA a monetary unit of Greece

LEPTON *n pl.* -S an atomic particle
LEPTONIC *adj*

LESBIAN *n pl.* -S a female homosexual

LESION *n pl.* -S an abnormal change in the structure of an organ or tissue

LESS *adj* LESSER, LEAST not as great in quantity or degree

LESSEE *n pl.* -S one to whom a lease is granted

LESSEN *v* -ED, -ING, -S to make or become less

LESSER *adj* not as large or important

LESSON *v* -ED, -ING, -S to instruct

LESSOR *n pl.* -S one that grants a lease

LEST *conj* for fear that

LET *v* LETTED, LETTING, LETS to hinder

LETCH *n* pl. -ES a strong sexual craving

LETDOWN *n* pl. -S a decrease

LETHAL *n* pl. -S a death-causing genetic defect

LETHALLY *adv* in a deadly manner

LETHARGY *n* pl. -GIES drowsiness; sluggishness

LETHE *n* pl. -S forgetfulness **LETHEAN** *adj*

LETTED past tense of let

LETTER *v* -ED, -ING, -S to mark with letters (written symbols representing speech sounds)

LETTERER *n* pl. -S one that letters

LETTING present participle of let

LETTUCE *n* pl. -S an herb cultivated as a salad plant

LETUP *n* pl. -S a lessening or relaxation

LEU *n* pl. LEI a monetary unit of Rumania

LEUCEMIA *n* pl. -S leukemia **LEUCEMIC** *adj*

LEUCIN *n* pl. -S leucine

LEUCINE *n* pl. -S an amino acid

LEUCITE *n* pl. -S a mineral **LEUCITIC** *adj*

LEUCOMA *n* pl. -S leukoma

LEUD *n* pl. -S or -ES a feudal vassal

LEUKEMIA *n* pl. -S a disease of the blood-forming organs

LEUKEMIC *n* pl. -S one affected with leukemia

LEUKOMA *n* pl. -S an opacity of the cornea

LEUKON *n* pl. -S a bodily organ consisting of the white blood cells

LEUKOSIS *n* pl. -KOSES leukemia **LEUKOTIC** *adj*

LEV *n* pl. LEVA a monetary unit of Bulgaria

LEVANT *v* -ED, -ING, -S to avoid a debt

LEVANTER *n* pl. -S an easterly Mediterranean wind

LEVATOR *n* pl. -ES or -S a muscle that raises an organ or part

LEVEE *v* LEVEED, LEVEEING, LEVEES to provide with an embankment

LEVEL *v* -ELED, -ELING, -ELS or -ELLED, -ELLING, -ELS to make even

LEVELER *n* pl. -S one that levels

LEVELLER *n* pl. -S leveler

LEVELLING present participle of level

LEVELLY *adv* in an even manner

LEVER *v* -ED, -ING, -S to move with a lever (a rigid body used to lift weight)

LEVERAGE *v* -AGED, -AGING, -AGES to provide with a type of economic advantage

LEVERET *n* pl. -S a young hare

LEVIABLE *adj* liable to be levied

LEVIED past tense of levy

LEVIER *n* pl. -S one that levies

LEVIES present 3d person sing. of levy

LEVIGATE *v* -GATED, -GATING, -GATES to reduce to a fine powder

LEVIN *n* pl. -S lightning

LEVIRATE *n* pl. -S the custom of marrying the widow of one's brother

LEVITATE *v* -TATED, -TATING, -TATES to rise and float in the air

LEVITY *n* pl. -TIES conduct characterized by a lack of seriousness

LEVO *adj* turning toward the left

LEVOGYRE *adj* turning toward the left

LEVULIN *n* pl. -S a chemical compound

LEVULOSE *n* pl. -S a very sweet sugar

LEVY *v* LEVIED, LEVYING, LEVIES to impose or collect by legal authority

LEWD *adj* LEWDER, LEWDEST obscene **LEWDLY** *adv*

LEWDNESS *n* pl. -ES the state of being lewd

LEWIS *n* pl. -ISES a hoisting device

LEWISITE *n* pl. -S a vesicant liquid

LEWISSON *n* pl. -S a lewis

LEX *n* pl. LEGES law

LEXICAL *adj* pertaining to the words of a language

LEXICON *n* pl. -CA or -CONS a dictionary

LEY *n* pl. LEYS lea

LI *n* pl. -S a Chinese unit of distance

LIABLE *adj* subject or susceptible to something possible or likely

LIAISE *v* LIAISED, LIAISING, LIAISES to establish liaison

LIAISON *n* pl. -S a means for maintaining communication

LIANA *n* pl. -S a tropical vine

LIANE   n pl. -S liana

LIANG   n pl. -S a Chinese unit of weight

LIANOID   adj pertaining to a liana

LIAR   n pl. -S one that speaks falsely

LIARD   n pl. -S a former silver coin of France

LIB   n pl. -S liberation

LIBATION   n pl. -S a ceremonial pouring of a liquid

LIBBER   n pl. -S one that supports a liberation movement

LIBECCIO   n pl. -CIOS a southwest wind

LIBEL   v -BELED, -BELING, -BELS or -BELLED, -BELLING, -BELS to make or publish a defamatory statement about

LIBELANT   n pl. -S a plaintiff in a type of lawsuit

LIBELEE   n pl. -S a defendant in a type of lawsuit

LIBELER   n pl. -S one that libels

LIBELIST   n pl. -S a libeler

LIBELLED   a past tense of libel

LIBELLEE   n pl. -S libelee

LIBELLER   n pl. -S libeler

LIBELLING   a present participle of libel

LIBELOUS   adj defamatory

LIBER   n pl. LIBRI or LIBERS a book of public records

LIBERAL   n pl. -S a person favorable to progress or reform

LIBERATE   v -ATED, -ATING, -ATES to set free

LIBERTY   n pl. -TIES the state of being free

LIBIDO   n pl. -DOS the energy derived from instinctual biological drives

LIBRA   n pl. -BRAE an ancient Roman unit of weight

LIBRA   n pl. -S a former gold coin of Peru

LIBRARY   n pl. -BRARIES a place where literary materials are kept for reading and reference

LIBRATE   v -BRATED, -BRATING, -BRATES to move from side to side

LIBRETTO   n pl. -TOS or -TI the text of an opera

LIBRI   a pl. of liber

LICE   pl. of louse

LICENCE   v -CENCED, -CENCING, -CENCES to license

LICENCEE   n pl. -S licensee

LICENCER   n pl. -S licenser

LICENSE   v -CENSED, -CENSING, -CENSES to issue or grant authoritative permission to

LICENSEE   n pl. -S one that is licensed

LICENSER   n pl. -S one that licenses

LICENSOR   n pl. -S licenser

LICHEE   n pl. -S litchi

LICHEN   v -ED, -ING, -S to cover with lichens (flowerless plants)

LICHENIN   n pl. -S a chemical compound

LICHI   n pl. -S litchi

LICHT   v -ED, -ING, -S to light

LICHTLY   adv lightly

LICIT   adj lawful LICITLY adv

LICK   v -ED, -ING, -S to pass the tongue over the surface of

LICKER   n pl. -S one that licks

LICKING   n pl. -S a thrashing or beating

LICKSPIT   n pl. -S a fawning person

LICORICE   n pl. -S a perennial herb

LICTOR   n pl. -S a magistrate's attendant in ancient Rome

LID   v LIDDED, LIDDING, LIDS to provide with a lid (a movable cover)

LIDAR   n pl. -S an electronic locating device

LIDLESS   adj having no lid

LIDO   n pl. -DOS a fashionable beach resort

LIE   v LIED, LYING, LIES to speak falsely

LIE   v LAY, LAIN, LYING, LIES to be in or get into a horizontal position

LIED   n pl. LIEDER a German song

LIEF   adj LIEFER, LIEFEST willing LIEFLY adv

LIEGE   n pl. -S a feudal lord

LIEGEMAN   n pl. -MEN a feudal vassal

LIEN   n pl. -S a legal right to hold or sell a debtor's property

LIENABLE   adj capable of being subjected to a lien

LIENAL   adj pertaining to the spleen

LIENTERY   n pl. -TERIES a form of diarrhea

LIER   n pl. -S one that lies or reclines

LIERNE   n pl. -S a connecting part in Gothic vaulting

LIEU *n* pl. -S place; stead

LIEVE *adv* LIEVER, LIEVEST gladly

LIFE *n* pl. LIVES the quality that distinguishes animals and plants from inanimate matter

LIFEBOAT *n* pl. -S a small rescue boat

LIFEFUL *adj* full of life

LIFELESS *adj* having no life

LIFELIKE *adj* resembling a living thing

LIFELINE *n* pl. -S a rope used to aid a person in distress

LIFELONG *adj* lasting for a lifetime

LIFER *n* pl. -S a prisoner serving a life sentence

LIFETIME *n* pl. -S the period of living existence

LIFEWAY *n* pl. -WAYS a way of living

LIFEWORK *n* pl. -S the major work of one's lifetime

LIFT *v* -ED, -ING, -S to move to a higher position LIFTABLE *adj*

LIFTER *n* pl. -S one that lifts

LIFTMAN *n* pl. -MEN an elevator operator

LIFTOFF *n* pl. -S the vertical takeoff of a rocket

LIGAMENT *n* pl. -S a band of firm, fibrous tissue

LIGAN *n* pl. -S lagan

LIGAND *n* pl. -S a type of ion or molecule

LIGASE *n* pl. -S an enzyme

LIGATE *v* -GATED, -GATING, -GATES to bind

LIGATION *n* pl. -S the act of ligating LIGATIVE *adj*

LIGATURE *v* -TURED, -TURING, -TURES to ligate

LIGHT *adj* LIGHTER, LIGHTEST having little weight

LIGHT *v* LIGHTED or LIT, LIGHTING, LIGHTS to illuminate

LIGHTEN *v* -ED, -ING, -S to reduce the weight of

LIGHTER *v* -ED, -ING, -S to convey in a type of barge

LIGHTFUL *adj* brightly illuminated

LIGHTING *n* pl. -S illumination

LIGHTISH *adj* somewhat light

LIGHTLY *adv* to a moderate degree

LIGNEOUS *adj* of or resembling wood

LIGNIFY *v* -FIED, -FYING, -FIES to convert into wood

LIGNIN *n* pl. -S an essential part of woody tissue

LIGNITE *n* pl. -S a type of coal LIGNITIC *adj*

LIGROIN *n* pl. -S a flammable liquid

LIGROINE *n* pl. -S ligroin

LIGULA *n* pl. -LAE or -LAS a strap-shaped organ or part LIGULAR, LIGULATE, LIGULOID *adj*

LIGULE *n* pl. -S a strap-shaped plant part

LIGURE *n* pl. -S a precious stone

LIKABLE *adj* pleasant

LIKE *v* LIKED, LIKING, LIKES to find pleasant

LIKE *adj* LIKER, LIKEST possessing the same or almost the same characteristics

LIKEABLE *adj* likable

LIKED past tense of like

LIKELY *adj* -LIER, -LIEST probable

LIKEN *v* -ED, -ING, -S to represent as similar

LIKENESS *n* pl. -ES a pictorial representation

LIKER *n* pl. -S one that likes

LIKEST superlative of like

LIKEWISE *adv* in a similar manner

LIKING *n* pl. -S a feeling of attraction or affection

LIKUTA *n* pl. MAKUTA a monetary unit of Zaire

LILAC *n* pl. -S a flowering shrub

LILIED *adj* covered with lilies

LILLIPUT *n* pl. -S a very small person

LILT *v* -ED, -ING, -S to sing or speak rhythmically

LILY *n* pl. LILIES a flowering plant LILYLIKE *adj*

LIMA *n* pl. -S the edible seed of a tropical American plant

LIMACINE *adj* resembling a type of mollusk

LIMACON *n* pl. -S a type of geometric curve

LIMAN *n* pl. -S a lagoon

LIMB *v* -ED, -ING, -S to cut off the arms or legs of

LIMBA *n* pl. -S an African tree

LIMBATE *adj* having an edge of a different color

LIMBECK *n* pl. -S alembic

LIMBER *adj* -BERER, -BEREST flexible LIMBERLY *adv*

LIMBER	v -ED, -ING, -S to make flexible	**LIMPER**	n pl. -S one that limps
LIMBI	a pl. of limbus	**LIMPET**	n pl. -S a type of mollusk
LIMBIC	adj pertaining to a system of the brain	**LIMPID**	adj transparent **LIMPIDLY** adv
LIMBIER	comparative of limby	**LIMPKIN**	n pl. -S a wading bird
LIMBIEST	superlative of limby	**LIMPLY**	adv in a limp manner
LIMBLESS	adj having no arms or legs	**LIMPNESS**	n pl. -ES the state of being limp
LIMBO	n pl. -BOS a condition of oblivion or neglect	**LIMPSY**	adj lacking strength or vigor
LIMBUS	n pl. -BUSES or -BI a distinctive border	**LIMULOID**	n pl. -S a horseshoe crab
		LIMULUS	n pl. -LI a horseshoe crab
LIMBY	adj LIMBIER, LIMBIEST having many large branches	**LIMY**	adj LIMIER, LIMIEST resembling or containing lime
		LIN	n pl. -S linn
LIME	v LIMED, LIMING, LIMES to treat with lime (a calcium compound)	**LINABLE**	adj lineable
		LINAC	n pl. -S a device for imparting high velocities to charged particles
LIMEADE	n pl. -S a beverage		
LIMEKILN	n pl. -S a furnace in which shells are burned to produce lime	**LINAGE**	n pl. -S the number of lines of printed material
		LINALOL	n pl. -S linalool
LIMELESS	adj having no lime	**LINALOOL**	n pl. -S a fragrant alcohol
LIMEN	n pl. -MENS or -MINA a sensory threshold	**LINCHPIN**	n pl. -S a locking pin inserted in the end of a shaft
LIMERICK	n pl. -S a humorous verse	**LINDANE**	n pl. -S an insecticide
LIMES	n pl. LIMITES a fortified boundary	**LINDEN**	n pl. -S a tall forest tree
		LINDY	n pl. -DIES a lively dance
LIMEY	n pl. -EYS a British sailor	**LINE**	v LINED, LINING, LINES to mark with lines (slender, continuous marks)
LIMIER	comparative of limy		
LIMIEST	superlative of limy		
LIMINA	a pl. of limen	**LINEABLE**	adj lying in a straight line
LIMINAL	adj pertaining to the limen	**LINEAGE**	n pl. -S direct descent from an ancestor
LIMINESS	n pl. -ES the state of being limy		
LIMING	present participle of lime	**LINEAL**	adj being directly descended from an ancestor **LINEALLY** adv
LIMIT	v -ED, -ING, -S to restrict		
LIMITARY	adj limiting		
LIMITED	n pl. -S a train or bus making few stops	**LINEAR**	adj of or resembling a straight line **LINEARLY** adv
LIMITER	n pl. -S one that limits	**LINEATE**	adj marked with lines
LIMITES	pl. of limes	**LINEATED**	adj lineate
LIMMER	n pl. -S a scoundrel	**LINEBRED**	adj produced by interbreeding within a particular line of descent
LIMN	v -ED, -ING, -S to depict by painting or drawing		
		LINECUT	n pl. -S a type of printing plate
LIMNER	n pl. -S one that limns	**LINED**	past tense of line
LIMNETIC	adj pertaining to the open water of a lake or pond	**LINELESS**	adj having no lines
		LINELIKE	adj resembling a line
LIMNIC	adj limnetic	**LINEMAN**	n pl. -MEN one who installs or repairs telephone wires
LIMO	n pl. LIMOS a limousine		
LIMONENE	n pl. -S a chemical compound	**LINEN**	n pl. -S a fabric woven from the fibers of flax **LINENY** adj
LIMONITE	n pl. -S a major ore of iron		
LIMP	v -ED, -ING, -S to walk lamely	**LINER**	n pl. -S a commercial ship or airplane
LIMP	adj LIMPER, LIMPEST lacking rigidity		
		LINESMAN	n pl. -MEN a football official

LINEUP *n pl.* -S a row of persons

LINEY *adj* LINIER, LINIEST liny

LING *n pl.* -S a heath plant

LINGA *n pl.* -S lingam

LINGAM *n pl.* -S a Hindu phallic symbol

LINGCOD *n pl.* -S a marine food fish

LINGER *v* -ED, -ING, -S to delay leaving

LINGERER *n pl.* -S one that lingers

LINGERIE *n pl.* -S women's underwear

LINGIER comparative of lingy

LINGIEST superlative of lingy

LINGO *n pl.* -GOES strange or incomprehensible language

LINGUA *n pl.* -GUAE the tongue or a tonguelike part

LINGUAL *n pl.* -S a sound articulated with the tongue

LINGUINE *n pl.* -S linguini

LINGUINI *n pl.* -S a type of pasta

LINGUIST *n pl.* -S a person skilled in several languages

LINGY *adj* LINGIER, LINGIEST covered with heaths

LINIER comparative of liny

LINIEST superlative of liny

LINIMENT *n pl.* -S a medicinal liquid

LININ *n pl.* -S a substance in the nucleus of a cell

LINING *n pl.* -S an inner layer

LINK *v* -ED, -ING, -S to connect LINKABLE *adj*

LINKAGE *n pl.* -S the act of linking

LINKBOY *n pl.* -BOYS a man or boy hired to carry a torch to light the way along dark streets

LINKER *n pl.* -S one that links

LINKMAN *n pl.* -MEN a linkboy

LINKSMAN *n pl.* -MEN a golfer

LINKUP *n pl.* -S something that serves as a linking device

LINKWORK *n pl.* -S something composed of interlocking rings

LINKY *adj* full of interlocking rings

LINN *n pl.* -S a waterfall

LINNET *n pl.* -S a European songbird

LINO *n pl.* -NOS linoleum

LINOCUT *n pl.* -S a print made from a design cut into linoleum

LINOLEUM *n pl.* -S a durable material used as a floor covering

LINSANG *n pl.* -S a carnivorous mammal

LINSEED *n pl.* -S flaxseed

LINSEY *n pl.* -SEYS a coarse fabric

LINSTOCK *n pl.* -S a stick having one end divided to hold a match

LINT *n pl.* -S an accumulation of bits of fiber

LINTEL *n pl.* -S a horizontal supporting beam

LINTER *n pl.* -S a machine for removing fibers from cotton seeds

LINTIER comparative of linty

LINTIEST superlative of linty

LINTLESS *adj* free from lint

LINTOL *n pl.* -S lintel

LINTY *adj* LINTIER, LINTIEST covered with lint

LINUM *n pl.* -S a plant of the flax family

LINY *adj* LINIER, LINIEST resembling a line

LION *n pl.* -S a large, carnivorous feline mammal

LIONESS *n pl.* -ES a female lion

LIONFISH *n pl.* -ES a tropical fish

LIONISE *v* -ISED, -ISING, -ISES to lionize

LIONISER *n pl.* -S one that lionises

LIONIZE *v* -IZED, -IZING, -IZES to treat or regard as a celebrity

LIONIZER *n pl.* -S one that lionizes

LIONLIKE *adj* resembling a lion

LIP *v* LIPPED, LIPPING, LIPS to touch with the lips (the folds of flesh around the mouth)

LIPASE *n pl.* -S an enzyme

LIPID *n pl.* -S any of a class of fatty substances LIPIDIC *adj*

LIPIDE *n pl.* -S lipid

LIPIN *n pl.* -S a lipid

LIPLESS *adj* having no lips

LIPLIKE *adj* resembling a lip

LIPOCYTE *n pl.* -S a fat-producing cell

LIPOID *n pl.* -S a lipid LIPOIDAL *adj*

LIPOMA *n pl.* -MAS or -MATA a tumor of fatty tissue

LIPPED past tense of lip

LIPPEN *v* -ED, -ING, -S to trust

LIPPER *v* -ED, -ING, -S to ripple

LIPPING *n pl.* -S a liplike outgrowth of bone

LIPPY *adj* -PIER, -PIEST impudent

LIPSTICK *n pl.* -S a cosmetic used to color the lips

LIQUATE v -QUATED, -QUATING, -QUATES to purify metal by heating

LIQUEFY v -FIED, -FYING, -FIES to make or become liquid

LIQUEUR n pl. -S a sweetened alcoholic beverage

LIQUID n pl. -S a substance that flows freely

LIQUIDLY adv in a free-flowing manner

LIQUIFY v -FIED, -FYING, -FIES to liquefy

LIQUOR v -ED, -ING, -S to intoxicate with liquor (an alcoholic beverage)

LIRA n pl. LIRE or LIRAS a monetary unit of Italy

LIRA n pl. LIROTH or LIROT a monetary unit of Israel

LIRIPIPE n pl. -S a long scarf

LISLE n pl. -S a fine, tightly twisted cotton thread

LISP v -ED, -ING -S to pronounce the letters s and z imperfectly

LISPER n pl. -S one that lisps

LISSOM adj lissome LISSOMLY adv

LISSOME adj lithe

LIST v -ED, -ING, -S to write down in a particular order LISTABLE adj

LISTEL n pl. -S a narrow molding

LISTEN v -ED, -ING, -S to make conscious use of the sense of hearing

LISTENER n pl. -S one that listens

LISTER n pl. -S a type of plow

LISTING n pl. -S something that is listed

LISTLESS adj languid

LIT n pl. -S the litas

LITANY n pl. -NIES a ceremonial form of prayer

LITAS n pl. LITAI or LITU a former monetary unit of Lithuania

LITCHI n pl. -S the edible fruit of a Chinese tree

LITER n pl. -S a unit of capacity

LITERACY n pl. -CIES the ability to read and write

LITERAL n pl. -S a small error in printing or writing

LITERARY adj of, pertaining to, or having the characteristics of books and writings

LITERATE n pl. -S one who can read and write

LITERATI n/pl scholars collectively

LITHARGE n pl. -S a monoxide of lead

LITHE adj LITHER, LITHEST bending easily LITHELY adv

LITHEMIA n pl. -S an excess of uric acid in the blood LITHEMIC adj

LITHIA n pl. -S an oxide of lithium

LITHIC adj pertaining to lithium

LITHIUM n pl. -S a metallic element

LITHO n pl. LITHOS a type of print

LITHOID adj resembling stone

LITHOSOL n pl. -S a type of soil

LITIGANT n pl. -S one who is engaged in a lawsuit

LITIGATE v -GATED, -GATING, -GATES to subject to legal proceedings

LITMUS n pl. -ES a blue coloring matter

LITORAL adj pertaining to a coastal region

LITOTES n pl. LITOTES a figure of speech in which an assertion is made by the negation of its opposite

LITRE n pl. -S liter

LITTEN adj lighted

LITTER v -ED, -ING, -S to scatter rubbish about

LITTERER n pl. -S one that litters

LITTERY adj covered with rubbish

LITTLE adj -TLER, -TLEST small

LITTLE n pl. -S a small amount

LITTLISH adj somewhat little

LITTORAL n pl. -S a coastal region

LITU a pl. of litas

LITURGY n pl. -GIES a prescribed system of public worship LITURGIC adj

LIVABLE adj suitable for living in

LIVE v LIVED, LIVING, LIVES to function as an animal or plant

LIVE adj LIVER, LIVEST having life

LIVEABLE adj livable

LIVELONG adj long in passing

LIVELY adj -LIER, -LIEST full of energy LIVELILY adv

LIVEN v -ED, -ING, -S to make lively

LIVENER n pl. -S one that livens

LIVENESS n pl. -ES the state of being live

LIVER n pl. -S a secreting organ

LIVERIED adj wearing a livery

LIVERISH *adj* having a liver disorder

LIVERY *n* pl. -ERIES a uniform worn by servants

LIVES pl. of life

LIVEST superlative of live

LIVETRAP *v* -TRAPPED, -TRAPPING, -TRAPS to capture in a type of animal trap

LIVID *adj* having the skin abnormally discolored **LIVIDLY** *adv*

LIVIDITY *n* pl. -TIES the state of being livid

LIVIER *n* pl. -S livyer

LIVING *n* pl. -S a means of subsistence

LIVINGLY *adv* realistically

LIVRE *n* pl. -S a former monetary unit of France

LIVYER *n* pl. -S a permanent resident of Newfoundland

LIXIVIUM *n* pl. -IA or -IUMS a solution obtained by leaching **LIXIVIAL** *adj*

LIZARD *n* pl. -S any of a suborder of reptiles

LLAMA *n* pl. -S a ruminant mammal

LLANO *n* pl. -NOS an open, grassy plain

LO *interj* — used to attract attention or to express surprise

LOACH *n* pl. -ES a freshwater fish

LOAD *v* -ED, -ING, -S to place in or on a means of conveyance

LOADER *n* pl. -S one that loads

LOADING *n* pl. -S a burden

LOADSTAR *n* pl. -S lodestar

LOAF *n* pl. LOAVES a shaped mass of bread

LOAF *v* -ED, -ING, -S to pass time idly

LOAFER *n* pl. -S one that loafs

LOAM *v* -ED, -ING, -S to cover with loam (a type of soil)

LOAMLESS *adj* having no loam

LOAMY *adj* LOAMIER, LOAMIEST resembling loam

LOAN *v* -ED, -ING, -S to lend **LOANABLE** *adj*

LOANER *n* pl. -S one that loans

LOANING *n* pl. -S a lane

LOANWORD *n* pl. -S a word taken from another language

LOATH *adj* unwilling

LOATHE *v* LOATHED, LOATHING, LOATHES to detest greatly

LOATHER *n* pl. -S one that loathes

LOATHFUL *adj* repulsive

LOATHING *n* pl. -S extreme dislike

LOATHLY *adj* repulsive

LOAVES pl. of loaf

LOB *v* LOBBED, LOBBING, LOBS to throw or hit in a high arc

LOBAR *adj* pertaining to a lobe

LOBATE *adj* having lobes **LOBATELY** *adv*

LOBATED *adj* lobate

LOBATION *n* pl. -S the formation of lobes

LOBBED past tense of lob

LOBBING present participle of lob

LOBBY *v* -BIED, -BYING, -BIES to attempt to influence legislators

LOBBYER *n* pl. -S a lobbyist

LOBBYGOW *n* pl. -S an errand boy

LOBBYISM *n* pl. -S the practice of lobbying

LOBBYIST *n* pl. -S one who lobbies

LOBE *n* pl. -S a rounded, projecting anatomical part **LOBED** *adj*

LOBEFIN *n* pl. -S a bony fish

LOBELIA *n* pl. -S a flowering plant

LOBELINE *n* pl. -S a poisonous alkaloid

LOBLOLLY *n* pl. -LIES a pine tree

LOBO *n* pl. -BOS the timber wolf

LOBOTOMY *n* pl. -MIES a type of surgical operation

LOBSTER *n* pl. -S an edible marine crustacean

LOBSTICK *n* pl. -S a tree with its lower branches trimmed

LOBULE *n* pl. -S a small lobe **LOBULAR, LOBULATE, LOBULOSE** *adj*

LOBWORM *n* pl. -S a lugworm

LOCA a pl. of locus

LOCAL *n* pl. -S a train or bus making all stops

LOCALE *n* pl. -S a locality

LOCALISE *v* -ISED, -ISING, -ISES to localize

LOCALISM *n* pl. -S a custom or mannerism peculiar to a locality

LOCALIST *n* pl. -S one who is strongly concerned with the matters of a locality

LOCALITE *n* pl. -S a resident of a locality

LOCALITY *n* pl. -TIES an area or neighborhood

LOCALIZE v -IZED, -IZING, -IZES to confine to a particular area

LOCALLY adv in a particular area

LOCATE v -CATED, -CATING, -CATES to determine the position of

LOCATER n pl. -S one that locates

LOCATION n pl. -S the place where something is at a given moment

LOCATIVE n pl. -S a type of grammatical case

LOCATOR n pl. -S locater

LOCH n pl. -S a lake

LOCHIA n pl. LOCHIA a vaginal discharge following childbirth **LOCHIAL** adj

LOCI a pl. of locus

LOCK v -ED, -ING, -S to secure by means of a mechanical fastening device **LOCKABLE** adj

LOCKAGE n pl. -S a toll on a ship passing through a canal

LOCKBOX n pl. -ES a box that locks

LOCKER n pl. -S an enclosure that may be locked

LOCKET n pl. -S a small ornamental case

LOCKJAW n pl. -S a form of tetanus

LOCKNUT n pl. -S a nut which keeps another from loosening

LOCKOUT n pl. -S a closing of a business to coerce employees to agree to terms

LOCKRAM n pl. -S a coarse, linen fabric

LOCKSTEP n pl. -S a mode of marching in close file

LOCKUP n pl. -S a jail

LOCO n pl. -COS or -COES locoweed

LOCO v -ED, -ING, -S to poison with locoweed

LOCOFOCO n pl. -COS a type of friction match

LOCOISM n pl. -S a disease of livestock

LOCOMOTE v -MOTED, -MOTING, -MOTES to move about

LOCOWEED n pl. -S a plant that causes poisoning when eaten by livestock

LOCULAR adj having or divided into loculi

LOCULATE adj locular

LOCULE n pl. -S loculus **LOCULED** adj

LOCULUS n pl. -LI a small, cell-like chamber

LOCUM n pl. -S a temporary substitute

LOCUS n pl. LOCI or LOCA a place

LOCUST n pl. -S a migratory grasshopper

LOCUSTA n pl. -TAE a spikelet **LOCUSTAL** adj

LOCUTION n pl. -S a particular form of expression

LOCUTORY n pl. -RIES a room in a monastery

LODE n pl. -S a deposit of ore

LODEN n pl. -S a thick, woolen fabric

LODESTAR n pl. -S a star used as a point of reference

LODGE v LODGED, LODGING, LODGES to furnish with temporary quarters

LODGER n pl. -S one that resides in rented quarters

LODGING n pl. -S a temporary place to live

LODGMENT n pl. -S a lodging

LODICULE n pl. -S a scale at the base of the ovary of a grass

LOESS n pl. -ES a soil deposit **LOESSAL, LOESSIAL** adj

LOFT v -ED, -ING, -S to store in a loft (an upper room)

LOFTER n pl. -S a type of golf club

LOFTILY adv in a lofty manner

LOFTLESS adj having no loft

LOFTY adj LOFTIER, LOFTIEST extending high in the air

LOG v LOGGED, LOGGING, LOGS to cut down trees for timber

LOGAN n pl. -S a stone balanced to permit easy movement

LOGBOOK n pl. -S a record book of a ship or aircraft

LOGE n pl. -S a small compartment

LOGGATS n/pl loggets

LOGGED past tense of log

LOGGER n pl. -S one that logs

LOGGETS n/pl an old English throwing game

LOGGIA n pl. -GIAS or -GIE an open gallery

LOGGING n pl. -S the business of cutting down trees for timber

LOGGY adj -GIER, -GIEST logy

LOGIA a pl. of logion

LOGIC n pl. -S the science of reasoning

LOGICAL adj pertaining to logic

LOGICIAN *n pl.* -S one who is skilled in logic

LOGICISE *v* -CISED, -CISING, -CISES to logicize

LOGICIZE *v* -CIZED, -CIZING, -CIZES to reason

LOGIER comparative of logy

LOGIEST superlative of logy

LOGILY *adv* in a logy manner

LOGINESS *n pl.* -ES the state of being logy

LOGION *n pl.* -GIA or -GIONS a saying attributed to Jesus

LOGISTIC *n pl.* -S symbolic logic

LOGJAM *n pl.* -S a tangled mass of logs

LOGO *n pl.* LOGOS an identifying symbol

LOGOGRAM *n pl.* -S a symbol used to represent an entire word

LOGOMACH *n pl.* -S one given to arguing about words

LOGOS *n pl.* LOGOI the rational principle that governs the universe in ancient Greek philosophy

LOGOTYPE *n pl.* -S a piece of type bearing a syllable, word, or words

LOGOTYPY *n pl.* -TYPIES the use of logotypes

LOGROLL *v* -ED, -ING, -S to obtain passage of by exchanging political favors

LOGWAY *n pl.* -WAYS a ramp used in logging

LOGWOOD *n pl.* -S a tropical tree

LOGY *adj* -GIER, -GIEST sluggish

LOIN *n pl.* -S a part of the side and back between the ribs and the hipbone

LOITER *v* -ED, -ING, -S to stand idly about

LOITERER *n pl.* -S one that loiters

LOLL *v* -ED, -ING, -S to lounge

LOLLER *n pl.* -S one that lolls

LOLLIPOP *n pl.* -S a piece of candy on the end of a stick

LOLLOP *v* -ED, -ING, -S to loll

LOLLY *n pl.* -LIES a lollipop

LOLLYGAG *v* -GAGGED, -GAGGING, -GAGS to lallygag

LOLLYPOP *n pl.* -S lollipop

LOMENT *n pl.* -S a type of plant pod

LOMENTUM *n pl.* -TA or -TUMS loment

LONE *adj* having no companions

LONELY *adj* -LIER, -LIEST sad from lack of companionship **LONELILY** *adv*

LONENESS *n pl.* -ES the state of being lone

LONER *n pl.* -S one that avoids others

LONESOME *n pl.* -S self

LONG *adj* LONGER, LONGEST extending for a considerable distance

LONG *v* -ED, -ING, -S to desire strongly

LONGAN *n pl.* -S the edible fruit of a Chinese tree

LONGBOAT *n pl.* -S the largest boat carried by a sailing vessel

LONGBOW *n pl.* -S a type of archery bow

LONGE *v* LONGED, LONGEING, LONGES to guide a horse by means of a long rope

LONGER *n pl.* -S one that longs

LONGERON *n pl.* -S a longitudinal support of an airplane

LONGHAIR *n pl.* -S an intellectual

LONGHAND *n pl.* -S ordinary handwriting

LONGHEAD *n pl.* -S a person having a long skull

LONGHORN *n pl.* -S one of a breed of long-horned cattle

LONGING *n pl.* -S a strong desire

LONGISH *adj* somewhat long

LONGLEAF *n pl.* -LEAVES an evergreen tree

LONGLINE *n pl.* -S a type of fishing line

LONGLY *adv* for a considerable distance

LONGNESS *n pl.* -ES the state of being long

LONGSHIP *n pl.* -S a medieval ship

LONGSOME *adj* tediously long

LONGSPUR *n pl.* -S a long-clawed finch

LONGTIME *adj* of long duration

LONGUEUR *n pl.* -S a dull and tedious section

LONGWAYS *adv* longwise

LONGWISE *adv* lengthwise

LOO *v* -ED, -ING, -S to subject to a forfeit at loo (a card game)

LOOBY *n pl.* -BIES a large, awkward person

LOOEY *n pl.* -EYS looie

LOOF *n pl.* -S the palm of the hand

LOOFA *n pl.* -S loofah

LOOFAH *n pl.* -S a tropical vine

LOOIE *n* pl. -S a lieutenant of the armed forces

LOOK *v* -ED, -ING, -S to use one's eyes in seeing

LOOKDOWN *n* pl. -S a marine fish

LOOKER *n* pl. -S one that looks

LOOKOUT *n* pl. -S one engaged in keeping watch

LOOKUP *n* pl. -S the process of looking something up

LOOM *v* -ED, -ING, -S to appear in an enlarged and indistinct form

LOON *n* pl. -S a diving waterfowl

LOONEY *adj* -NIER, -NIEST loony

LOONY *adj* -NIER, -NIEST crazy

LOONY *n* pl. -NIES a loony person

LOOP *v* -ED, -ING, -S to form loops (circular or oval openings)

LOOPER *n* pl. -S one that loops

LOOPHOLE *v* -HOLED, -HOLING, -HOLES to make small openings in

LOOPY *adj* LOOPIER, LOOPIEST full of loops

LOOSE *adj* LOOSER, LOOSEST not firm, taut, or rigid **LOOSELY** *adv*

LOOSE *v* LOOSED, LOOSING, LOOSES to set free

LOOSEN *v* -ED, -ING, -S to make looser

LOOSENER *n* pl. -S one that loosens

LOOSED past tense of loose

LOOSER comparative of loose

LOOSEST superlative of loose

LOOSING present participle of loose

LOOT *v* -ED, -ING, -S to plunder

LOOTER *n* pl. -S one that loots

LOP *v* LOPPED, LOPPING, LOPS to cut off branches or twigs from

LOPE *v* LOPED, LOPING, LOPES to run with a steady, easy gait

LOPER *n* pl. -S one that lopes

LOPPED past tense of lop

LOPPER *v* -ED, -ING, -S to curdle

LOPPING present participle of lop

LOPPY *adj* -PIER, -PIEST hanging limply

LOPSIDED *adj* leaning to one side

LOPSTICK *n* pl. -S lobstick

LOQUAT *n* pl. -S a small evergreen tree

LORAL *adj* pertaining to the space between the eye and bill of a bird

LORAN *n* pl. -S a type of navigational system

LORD *v* -ED, -ING, -S to invest with the power of a lord (a person having dominion over others)

LORDING *n* pl. -S a lordling

LORDLESS *adj* having no lord

LORDLIER comparative of lordly

LORDLIEST superlative of lordly

LORDLIKE *adj* lordly

LORDLING *n* pl. -S a young or unimportant lord

LORDLY *adj* -LIER, -LIEST of or befitting a lord

LORDOMA *n* pl. -S lordosis

LORDOSIS *n* pl. -DOSES a curvature of the spinal column **LORDOTIC** *adj*

LORDSHIP *n* pl. -S the power of a lord

LORE *n* pl. -S traditional knowledge or belief

LOREAL *adj* loral

LORGNON *n* pl. -S a pair of eyeglasses with a handle

LORICA *n* pl. -CAE a protective covering or shell

LORICATE *n* pl. -S an animal having a lorica

LORIKEET *n* pl. -S a small parrot

LORIMER *n* pl. -S a maker of implements for harnesses and saddles

LORINER *n* pl. -S lorimer

LORIS *n* pl. -RISES an Asian lemur

LORN *adj* abandoned

LORNNESS *n* pl. -ES the state of being lorn

LORRY *n* pl. -RIES a type of wagon or truck

LORY *n* pl. -RIES a small parrot

LOSE *v* LOST, LOSING, LOSES to come to be without and be unable to find **LOSABLE** *adj*

LOSEL *n* pl. -S a worthless person

LOSER *n* pl. -S one that loses

LOSING *n* pl. -S a loss

LOSINGLY *adv* in a manner characterized by defeat

LOSS *n* pl. -ES the act of one that loses

LOSSY *adj* causing dissipation of electrical energy

LOST *adj* not to be found or recovered

LOSTNESS *n* pl. -ES the state of being lost

LOT	v LOTTED, LOTTING, LOTS to distribute proportionately
LOTA	n pl. -S lotah
LOTAH	n pl. -S a small water vessel used in India
LOTH	adj loath
LOTHARIO	n pl. -IOS a seducer of women
LOTHSOME	adj repulsive
LOTIC	adj pertaining to moving water
LOTION	n pl. -S a liquid preparation for external application
LOTOS	n pl. -ES lotus
LOTTED	past tense of lot
LOTTERY	n pl. -TERIES a type of gambling game
LOTTING	present participle of lot
LOTTO	n pl. -TOS a game of chance
LOTUS	n pl. -ES an aquatic plant
LOUD	adj LOUDER, LOUDEST strongly audible
LOUDEN	v -ED, -ING, -S to make or become louder
LOUDISH	adj somewhat loud
LOUDLY	adv -LIER, -LIEST in a loud manner
LOUDNESS	n pl. -ES the quality of being loud
LOUGH	n pl. -S a lake
LOUIE	n pl. -S looie
LOUIS	n pl. LOUIS a former gold coin of France
LOUNGE	v LOUNGED, LOUNGING, LOUNGES to recline or lean in a relaxed, lazy manner
LOUNGER	n pl. -S one that lounges
LOUNGY	adj suitable for lounging
LOUP	v LOUPED, LOUPEN, LOUPING, LOUPS to leap
LOUPE	n pl. -S a small magnifying glass
LOUR	v -ED, -ING, -S to lower
LOURY	adj lowery
LOUSE	n pl. LICE a parasitic insect
LOUSE	v LOUSED, LOUSING, LOUSES to spoil or bungle
LOUSY	adj LOUSIER, LOUSIEST mean or contemptible LOUSILY adv
LOUT	v -ED, -ING, -S to bow in respect
LOUTISH	adj clumsy
LOUVER	n pl. -S a type of window LOUVERED adj
LOUVRE	n pl. -S louver

LOVABLE	adj having qualities that attract love LOVABLY adv
LOVAGE	n pl. -S a perennial herb
LOVE	v LOVED, LOVING, LOVES to feel great affection for
LOVEABLE	adj lovable LOVEABLY adv
LOVEBIRD	n pl. -S a small parrot
LOVED	past tense of love
LOVELESS	adj feeling no love
LOVELIER	comparative of lovely
LOVELIES	pl. of lovely
LOVELIEST	superlative of lovely
LOVELILY	adv in a lovely manner
LOVELOCK	n pl. -S a lock of hair hanging separately
LOVELORN	adj not loved
LOVELY	adj -LIER, -LIEST beautiful
LOVELY	n pl. -LIES a beautiful woman
LOVER	n pl. -S one that loves another LOVERLY adj
LOVESICK	adj languishing with love
LOVESOME	adj lovely
LOVEVINE	n pl. -S a twining herb
LOVING	adj affectionate
LOVINGLY	adv in a loving manner
LOW	adj LOWER, LOWEST having relatively little upward extension
LOW	v -ED, -ING, -S to utter the sound characteristic of cattle
LOWBORN	adj of humble birth
LOWBOY	n pl. -BOYS a low chest of drawers
LOWBRED	adj lowborn
LOWBROW	n pl. -S an uncultivated person
LOWDOWN	n pl. -S the whole truth
LOWE	v LOWED, LOWING, LOWES to blaze
LOWER	v -ED, -ING, -S to appear dark and threatening
LOWERY	adj dark and threatening
LOWING	n pl. -S the sound characteristic of cattle
LOWISH	adj somewhat low
LOWLAND	n pl. -S an area of land lying lower than the adjacent country
LOWLIFE	n pl. -S a despicable person
LOWLY	adj -LIER, -LIEST low in position or rank
LOWN	adj peaceful
LOWNESS	n pl. -ES the state of being low
LOWSE	adj loose

LOX   v -ED, -ING, -ES to supply with lox (liquid oxygen)

LOYAL   adj -ALER, -ALEST faithful to one's allegiance

LOYALISM   n pl. -S loyalty

LOYALIST   n pl. -S one who is loyal

LOYALLY   adv in a loyal manner

LOYALTY   n pl. -TIES the state of being loyal

LOZENGE   n pl. -S a small, often medicated candy

LUAU   n pl. -S a Hawaiian feast

LUBBER   n pl. -S a clumsy person **LUBBERLY** adj

LUBE   n pl. -S a lubricant

LUBRIC   adj slippery

LUCARNE   n pl. -S a type of window

LUCE   n pl. -S a freshwater fish

LUCENCE   n pl. -S lucency

LUCENCY   n pl. -CIES the quality of being lucent

LUCENT   adj giving off light **LUCENTLY** adv

LUCERN   n pl. -S lucerne

LUCERNE   n pl. -S alfalfa

LUCES   a pl. of lux

LUCID   adj easily understood **LUCIDLY** adv

LUCIDITY   n pl. -TIES the quality of being lucid

LUCIFER   n pl. -S a friction match

LUCK   v -ED, -ING, -S to succeed by chance or good fortune

LUCKIE   n pl. -S an old woman

LUCKLESS   adj unlucky

LUCKY   adj LUCKIER, LUCKIEST having good fortune **LUCKILY** adv

LUCRE   n pl. -S monetary gain

LUCULENT   adj lucid

LUES   n pl. LUES syphilis

LUETIC   n pl. -S one infected with syphilis

LUFF   v -ED, -ING, -S to steer a sailing vessel nearer into the wind

LUFFA   n pl. -S loofah

LUG   v LUGGED, LUGGING, LUGS to carry or pull with effort

LUGE   n pl. -S a small sled

LUGGAGE   n pl. -S articles containing a traveler's belongings

LUGGED   past tense of lug

LUGGER   n pl. -S a small sailing vessel

LUGGIE   n pl. -S a small wooden dish or pail

LUGGING   present participle of lug

LUGSAIL   n pl. -S a type of sail

LUGWORM   n pl. -S a burrowing marine worm

LUKEWARM   adj moderately warm

LULL   v -ED, -ING, -S to cause to sleep or rest

LULLABY   v -BIED, -BYING, -BIES to lull with a soothing song

LULU   n pl. -S something remarkable

LUM   n pl. -S a chimney

LUMBAGO   n pl. -GOS pain in the lower back

LUMBAR   n pl. -S an anatomical part situated near the loins

LUMBER   v -ED, -ING, -S to cut down and prepare timber for market

LUMBERER   n pl. -S one that lumbers

LUMEN   n pl. -MENS or -MINA the inner passage of a tubular organ **LUMENAL, LUMINAL** adj

LUMINARY   n pl. -NARIES a body that gives light

LUMINIST   n pl. -S a painter who uses the effects of light

LUMINOUS   adj giving off light

LUMMOX   n pl. -ES a clumsy person

LUMP   v -ED, -ING, -S to make into lumps (shapeless masses)

LUMPEN   n pl. -S an uprooted individual

LUMPER   n pl. -S a laborer employed to load and unload ships

LUMPFISH   n pl. -ES a marine fish

LUMPISH   adj stupid

LUMPY   adj LUMPIER, LUMPIEST full of lumps **LUMPILY** adv

LUNA   n pl. -S an alchemical designation for silver

LUNACY   n pl. -CIES insanity

LUNAR   n pl. -S an observation of the moon taken for navigational purposes

LUNARIAN   n pl. -S a supposed inhabitant of the moon

LUNATE   adj crescent-shaped **LUNATELY** adv

LUNATED   adj lunate

LUNATIC   n pl. -S an insane person

LUNATION   n pl. -S the interval between two successive new moons

LUNCH   v -ED, -ING, -ES to eat a noonday meal

LUNCHEON   n pl. -S a noonday meal

LUNCHER   n pl. -S one that lunches

LUNE   n pl. -S a crescent-shaped figure

LUNET   n pl. -S lunette

LUNETTE   n pl. -S a crescent-shaped object

LUNG   n pl. -S a respiratory organ

LUNGAN   n pl. -S longan

LUNGE   v LUNGED, LUNGING, LUNGES to make a forceful forward movement

LUNGEE   n pl. -S lungi

LUNGER   n pl. -S one that lunges

LUNGFISH   n pl. -ES a type of fish

LUNGI   n pl. -S a loincloth worn by men in India

LUNGING   present participle of lunge

LUNGWORM   n pl. -S a parasitic worm

LUNGWORT   n pl. -S a European herb

LUNGYI   n pl. -S lungi

LUNIER   comparative of luny

LUNIES   pl. of luny

LUNIEST   superlative of luny

LUNK   n pl. -S a lunkhead

LUNKER   n pl. -S a large game fish

LUNKHEAD   n pl. -S a stupid person

LUNT   v -ED, -ING, -S to emit smoke

LUNULA   n pl. -LAE a small crescent-shaped structure LUNULAR, LUNULATE adj

LUNULE   n pl. -S lunula

LUNY   adj -NIER, -NIEST loony

LUNY   n pl. -NIES a loony

LUPANAR   n pl. -S a brothel

LUPIN   n pl. -S lupine

LUPINE   n pl. -S a flowering plant

LUPOUS   adj pertaining to lupus

LUPULIN   n pl. -S a medicinal powder obtained from the hop plant

LUPUS   n pl. -ES a skin disease

LURCH   v -ED, -ING, -ES to sway abruptly

LURCHER   n pl. -S one that lurks or prowls

LURDAN   n pl. -S a lazy or stupid person

LURDANE   n pl. -S lurdan

LURE   v LURED, LURING, LURES to attract with something desirable

LURER   n pl. -S one that lures

LURID   adj causing shock or horror LURIDLY adv

LURING   present participle of lure

LURK   v -ED, -ING, -S to wait in concealment

LURKER   n pl. -S one that lurks

LUSCIOUS   adj having a very pleasing taste or smell

LUSH   adj LUSHER, LUSHEST abounding in vegetation LUSHLY adv

LUSH   v -ED, -ING, -ES to drink to excess

LUSHNESS   n pl. -ES the state of being lush

LUST   v -ED, -ING, -S to have an intense desire

LUSTER   v -ED, -ING -S to make or become lustrous

LUSTFUL   adj marked by excessive sexual desire

LUSTIER   comparative of lusty

LUSTIEST   superlative of lusty

LUSTILY   adv in a lusty manner

LUSTRA   a pl. of lustrum

LUSTRAL   adj pertaining to a lustrum

LUSTRATE   v -TRATED, -TRATING, -TRATES to purify ceremonially

LUSTRE   v -TRED, -TRING, -TRES to luster

LUSTRING   n pl. -S a glossy silk fabric

LUSTROUS   adj reflecting light evenly and efficiently

LUSTRUM   n pl. -TRUMS or -TRA a ceremonial purification of the population in ancient Rome

LUSTY   adj LUSTIER, LUSTIEST full of vigor

LUSUS   n pl. -ES an abnormality

LUTANIST   n pl. -S one who plays the lute

LUTE   v LUTED, LUTING, LUTES to play a lute (a stringed musical instrument)

LUTEA   pl. of luteum

LUTEAL   adj pertaining to the luteum

LUTECIUM   n pl. -S lutetium

LUTED   past tense of lute

LUTEIN   n pl. -S a yellow pigment

LUTENIST   n pl. -S lutanist

LUTEOLIN   n pl. -S a yellow pigment

LUTEOUS   adj light to moderate greenish yellow in color

LUTETIUM   n pl. -S a metallic element

LUTEUM   n pl. -TEA a hormone-secreting body

LUTHERN n pl. -S a type of window

LUTING n pl. -S a substance used as a sealant

LUTIST n pl. -S a lutanist

LUX n pl. LUXES or LUCES a unit of illumination

LUXATE v -ATED, -ATING, -ATES to put out of joint

LUXATION n pl. -S the act of luxating

LUXE n pl. -S luxury

LUXURY n pl. -RIES free indulgence in that which affords pleasure or comfort

LYARD adj streaked with gray

LYART adj lyard

LYASE n pl. -S an enzyme

LYCEA a pl. of lyceum

LYCEE n pl. -S a French secondary school

LYCEUM n pl. -CEUMS or -CEA a hall for public lectures or discussions

LYCHEE n pl. -S litchi

LYCHNIS n pl. -NISES a flowering plant

LYCOPENE n pl. -S a red pigment

LYCOPOD n pl. -S an evergreen plant

LYDDITE n pl. -S an explosive

LYE n pl. -S a solution used in making soap

LYING n pl. -S the act of telling lies

LYINGLY adv falsely

LYMPH n pl. -S a body fluid containing white blood cells **LYMPHOID** adj

LYMPHOMA n pl. -MAS or -MATA a type of tumor

LYNCEAN adj of or resembling a lynx

LYNCH v -ED, -ING, -ES to put to death without legal sanction

LYNCHER n pl. -S one that lynches

LYNCHING n pl. -S the act of one who lynches

LYNX n pl. -ES a short-tailed wildcat

LYOPHILE adj pertaining to a type of colloid

LYRATE adj having the shape of a lyre **LYRATELY** adv

LYRATED adj lyrate

LYRE n pl. -S an ancient harp-like instrument

LYREBIRD n pl. -S an Australian bird

LYRIC n pl. -S a lyrical poem

LYRICAL adj having the form of a song

LYRICISE v -CISED, -CISING, -CISES to lyricize

LYRICISM n pl. -S the quality of being lyrical

LYRICIST n pl. -S one who writes the words for songs

LYRICIZE v -CIZED, -CIZING, -CIZES to write lyrically

LYRIFORM adj lyrate

LYRISM n pl. -S lyricism

LYRIST n pl. -S one who plays the lyre

LYSATE n pl. -S a product of lysis

LYSE v LYSED, LYSING, LYSES to cause to undergo lysis

LYSIN n pl. -S a substance capable of disintegrating blood cells or bacteria

LYSINE n pl. -S an amino acid

LYSING present participle of lyse

LYSIS n pl. LYSES the disintegration of cells by lysins

LYSOGEN n pl. -S a type of antigen

LYSOGENY n pl. -NIES the state of being like a lysogen

LYSOSOME n pl. -S a saclike part of a cell

LYSOZYME n pl. -S an enzyme

LYSSA n pl. -S rabies

LYTIC adj pertaining to lysis

LYTTA n pl. -TAE or -TAS a fibrous band in the tongue of certain carnivorous mammals

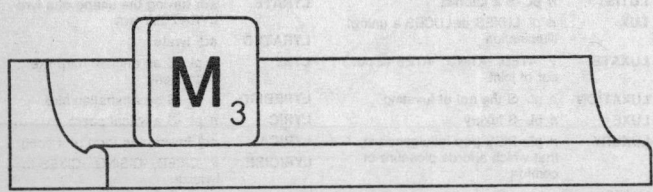

MA	*n pl.* -S mother	**MACKEREL**	*n pl.* -S a marine food fish
MAAR	*n pl.* -S a volcanic crater	**MACKINAW**	*n pl.* -S a woolen fabric
MAC	*n pl.* -S a raincoat	**MACKLE**	*v* -LED, -LING, -LES to blur in printing
MACABER	*adj* macabre		
MACABRE	*adj* gruesome	**MACLE**	*n pl.* -S a spot or discoloration in a mineral **MACLED** *adj*
MACACO	*n pl.* -COS a lemur		
MACADAM	*n pl.* -S a type of pavement	**MACRAME**	*n pl.* -S a trimming of knotted thread or cord
MACAQUE	*n pl.* -S a short-tailed monkey		
MACARONI	*n pl.* -NIS or -NIES a tubular pasta	**MACRO**	*n pl.* -ROS a type of computer instruction
MACAROON	*n pl.* -S a type of cookie	**MACRON**	*n pl.* -S a symbol placed over a vowel to show that it has a long sound
MACAW	*n pl.* -S a large parrot		
MACCABAW	*n pl.* -S maccaboy		
MACCABOY	*n pl.* -BOYS a type of snuff	**MACRURAL**	*adj* pertaining to macruran
MACCHIA	*n pl.* -CHIE a dense growth of small trees and shrubs	**MACRURAN**	*n pl.* -S any of a suborder of crustaceans
		MACULA	*n pl.* -LAE or -LAS a spot **MACULAR** *adj*
MACCOBOY	*n pl.* -BOYS maccaboy		
MACE	*v* MACED, MACING, MACES to attack with a clublike weapon	**MACULATE**	*v* -LATED, -LATING, -LATES to mark with spots
MACER	*n pl.* -S an official who carries a ceremonial staff	**MACULE**	*v* -ULED, -ULING, -ULES to mackle
MACERATE	*v* -ATED, -ATING, -ATES to soften by soaking in liquid	**MAD**	*adj* MADDER, MADDEST insane
MACH	*n pl.* -S a number indicating the ratio of the speed of a body to the speed of sound	**MAD**	*v* MADDED, MADDING, MADS to madden
		MADAM	*n pl.* -S a woman who manages a brothel
MACHETE	*n pl.* -S a large, heavy knife	**MADAME**	*n pl.* -S madam
MACHINE	*v* -CHINED, -CHINING, -CHINES to process by machine (a mechanical device)	**MADAME**	*n pl.* MESDAMES the French title of respect for a married woman
MACHISMO	*n pl.* -MOS strong masculinity	**MADCAP**	*n pl.* -S an impulsive person
MACHO	*n pl.* -CHOS a person who exhibits machismo	**MADDED**	past tense of mad
MACHREE	*n pl.* -S dear	**MADDEN**	*v* -ED, -ING, -S to make or become mad
MACHZOR	*n pl.* -ZORIM or -ZORS mahzor	**MADDER**	*n pl.* -S a perennial herb
MACING	present participle of mace	**MADDEST**	superlative of mad
MACK	*n pl.* -S mac	**MADDING**	present participle of mad

MADDISH   *adj* somewhat mad

MADE   past tense of make

MADEIRA   *n* pl. -S a white wine

MADHOUSE   *n* pl. -S an insane asylum

MADLY   *adv* in a mad manner

MADMAN   *n* pl. -MEN a man who is insane

MADNESS   *n* pl. -ES the state of being mad

MADONNA   *n* pl. -S a former Italian title of respect for a woman

MADRAS   *n* pl. -ES a cotton fabric

MADRE   *n* pl. -S mother

MADRIGAL   *n* pl. -S a short lyric poem

MADRONA   *n* pl. -S an evergreen tree

MADRONE   *n* pl. -S madrona

MADRONO   *n* pl. -NOS madrona

MADURO   *n* pl. -ROS a dark-colored, relatively strong cigar

MADWOMAN   *n* pl. -WOMEN a woman who is insane

MADWORT   *n* pl. -S a flowering plant

MADZOON   *n* pl. -S matzoon

MAE   *n* pl. -S more

MAENAD   *n* pl. -S or -ES a female participant in ancient Greek orgies MAENADIC *adj*

MAESTOSO   *n* pl. -SOS a stately musical passage

MAESTRO   *n* pl. -STROS or -STRI a master of an art

MAFFIA   *n* pl. -S mafia

MAFFICK   *v* -ED, -ING, -S to celebrate boisterously

MAFIA   *n* pl. -S a secret organization operating in opposition to legal authority

MAFIC   *adj* pertaining to minerals rich in magnesium and iron

MAFIOSO   *n* pl. -SI a member of the mafia

MAFTIR   *n* pl. -S the concluding section of a parashah

MAG   *n* pl. -S a magazine

MAGAZINE   *n* pl. -S a type of periodical publication

MAGDALEN   *n* pl. -S a reformed prostitute

MAGE   *n* pl. -S a magician

MAGENTA   *n* pl. -S a red dye

MAGGOT   *n* pl. -S the legless larva of certain insects MAGGOTY *adj*

MAGI   pl. of magus

MAGIC   *v* -ICKED, -ICKING, -ICS to affect by magic (sorcery)

MAGICAL   *adj* resembling magic

MAGICIAN   *n* pl. -S one skilled in magic

MAGICKED   past tense of magic

MAGICKING   present participle of magic

MAGILP   *n* pl. -S megilp

MAGISTER   *n* pl. -S a master or teacher

MAGMA   *n* pl. -MAS or -MATA the molten matter from which igneous rock is formed MAGMATIC *adj*

MAGNATE   *n* pl. -S a powerful or influential person

MAGNESIA   *n* pl. -S a medicinal compound MAGNESIC *adj*

MAGNET   *n* pl. -S a body that possesses the property of attracting iron

MAGNETIC   *n* pl. -S a magnet

MAGNETO   *n* pl. -TOS a type of electric generator

MAGNETON   *n* pl. -S a unit of magnetic moment

MAGNIFIC   *adj* magnificent

MAGNIFY   *v* -FIED, -FYING, -FIES to increase the perceived size of

MAGNOLIA   *n* pl. -S a flowering shrub or tree

MAGNUM   *n* pl. -S a large wine bottle

MAGOT   *n* pl. -S a tailless ape

MAGPIE   *n* pl. -S a corvine bird

MAGUEY   *n* pl. -GUEYS a tropical plant

MAGUS   *n* pl. -GI a magician

MAHARAJA   *n* pl. -S a king or prince in India

MAHARANI   *n* pl. -S the wife of a maharaja

MAHATMA   *n* pl. -S a Hindu sage

MAHJONG   *n* pl. -S a game of Chinese origin

MAHJONGG   *n* pl. -S mahjong

MAHOE   *n* pl. -S a tropical tree

MAHOGANY   *n* pl. -NIES a tropical tree

MAHONIA   *n* pl. -S a flowering shrub

MAHOUT   *n* pl. -S the keeper and driver of an elephant

MAHUANG   *n* pl. -S an Asian plant

MAHZOR   *n* pl. -ZORIM or -ZORS a Jewish prayer book

MAID   *n* pl. -S a maiden MAIDISH *adj*

MAIDEN   *n* pl. -S a young unmarried woman MAIDENLY *adj*

MAIDHOOD   *n* pl. -S the state of being a maiden

MAIEUTIC   *adj* pertaining to a method of eliciting knowledge

MAIGRE   *adj* containing neither flesh nor its juices

MAIHEM n pl. -S mayhem

MAIL v -ED,- ING, -S to send by a governmental postal system **MAILABLE** adj

MAILBAG n pl. -S a bag for carrying mail (postal material)

MAILBOX n pl. -ES a box for depositing mail

MAILE n pl. -S a Pacific island vine

MAILER n pl. -S one that mails

MAILING n pl. -S a rented farm

MAILL n pl. -S a payment

MAILLESS adj having no armor

MAILLOT n pl. -S a woman's one-piece bathing suit

MAILMAN n pl. -MEN a man who carries and delivers mail

MAIM v -ED, -ING, -S to injure so as to cause lasting damage

MAIMER n pl. -S one that maims

MAIN n pl. -S the principal part

MAINLAND n pl. -S a principal land mass

MAINLINE v -LINED, -LINING, -LINES to inject a narcotic into a major vein

MAINLY adv for the most part

MAINMAST n pl. -S the principal mast of a vessel

MAINSAIL n pl. -S the principal sail of a vessel

MAINSTAY n pl. -STAYS a principal support

MAINTAIN v -ED, -ING, -S to keep in proper condition

MAINTOP n pl. -S a platform at the head of a mainmast

MAIOLICA n pl. -S majolica

MAIR n pl. -S more

MAIST n pl. -S most

MAIZE n pl. -S an American cereal grass

MAJAGUA n pl. -S a tropical tree

MAJESTIC adj having majesty

MAJESTY n pl. -TIES regal dignity

MAJOLICA n pl. -S a type of pottery

MAJOR v -ED, -ING, -S to pursue a specific principal course of study

MAJORITY n pl. -TIES the greater number or part

MAKAR n pl. -S a poet

MAKE v MADE, MAKING, MAKES to cause to exist **MAKABLE**, **MAKEABLE** adj

MAKEBATE n pl. -S one that encourages quarrels

MAKEFAST n pl. -S an object to which a boat is tied

MAKER n pl. -S one that makes

MAKEUP n pl. -S the way in which the parts or ingredients of something are put together

MAKIMONO n pl. -NOS a Japanese ornamental scroll

MAKING n pl. -S material from which something can be developed

MAKO n pl. -KOS a large shark

MAKUTA pl. of likuta

MALADY n pl. -DIES an illness

MALAISE n pl. -S a feeling of vague discomfort

MALAMUTE n pl. -S an Alaskan sled dog

MALAPERT n pl. -S an impudent person

MALAPROP n pl. -S a humorous misuse of a word

MALAR n pl. -S the cheekbone

MALARIA n pl. -S an infectious disease **MALARIAL, MALARIAN** adj

MALARKEY n pl. -KEYS nonsense

MALARKY n pl. -KIES malarkey

MALAROMA n pl. -S a malodor

MALATE n pl. -S a chemical salt

MALE n pl. -S an individual that begets young by fertilizing the female

MALEATE n pl. -S a chemical salt

MALEDICT v -ED, -ING, -S to curse

MALEFIC adj producing or causing evil

MALEMIUT n pl. -S malamute

MALEMUTE n pl. -S malamute

MALENESS n pl. -ES the quality of being a male

MALFED adj badly fed

MALGRE prep in spite of

MALIC adj pertaining to apples

MALICE n pl. -S a desire to injure another

MALIGN v -ED, -ING, -S to speak evil of

MALIGNER n pl. -S one that maligns

MALIGNLY adv in an evil manner

MALIHINI n pl. -S a newcomer to Hawaii

MALINE n pl. -S a delicate net used for veils

MALINGER v -ED, -ING, -S to feign illness in order to avoid duty or work

MALISON n pl. -S a curse

MALKIN *n pl.* -S an untidy woman

MALL *v* -ED, -ING -S to maul

MALLARD *n pl.* -S a wild duck

MALLEE *n pl.* -S an evergreen tree

MALLEI *pl. of* malleus

MALLEOLI *n/pl* bony protuberances of the ankle

MALLET *n pl.* -S a type of hammer

MALLEUS *n pl.* -LEI a bone of the middle ear

MALLOW *n pl.* -S a flowering plant

MALM *n pl.* -S a soft, friable limestone

MALMSEY *n pl.* -SEYS a white wine

MALMY *adj* MALMIER, MALMIEST resembling malm

MALODOR *n pl.* -S an offensive odor

MALPOSED *adj* being in the wrong position

MALT *v* -ED, -ING, -S to treat or combine with malt (germinated grain)

MALTASE *n pl.* -S an enzyme

MALTED *n pl.* -S a sweet beverage

MALTHA *n pl.* -S a natural tar

MALTIER *comparative of* malty

MALTIEST *superlative of* malty

MALTOL *n pl.* -S a chemical compound

MALTOSE *n pl.* -S a type of sugar

MALTREAT *v* -ED, -ING, -S to treat badly

MALTSTER *n pl.* -S one that makes malt

MALTY *adj* MALTIER, MALTIEST resembling malt

MALVASIA *n pl.* -S malmsey

MAMA *n pl.* -S mother

MAMBA *n pl.* -S a venomous snake

MAMBO *v* -ED, -ING, -ES or -S to perform a ballroom dance

MAMELUKE *n pl.* -S a slave in Muslim countries

MAMEY *n pl.* -MEYS or -MEYES a tropical tree

MAMIE *n pl.* -S mamey

MAMLUK *n pl.* -S mameluke

MAMMA *n pl.* -S mama

MAMMA *n pl.* -MAE a milk-secreting organ

MAMMAL *n pl.* -S any of a class of warm-blooded vertebrates

MAMMARY *adj* pertaining to the mammae

MAMMATE *adj* having mammae

MAMMATUS *n pl.* -TI a type of cloud

MAMMEE *n pl.* -S mamey

MAMMER *v* -ED, -ING, -S to hesitate

MAMMET *n pl.* -S maumet

MAMMEY *n pl.* -MEYS mamey

MAMMIE *n pl.* -S mammy

MAMMIES *pl. of* mammy

MAMMILLA *n pl.* -LAE a nipple

MAMMITIS *n pl.* -MITIDES mastitis

MAMMOCK *v* -ED, -ING, -S to shred

MAMMON *n pl.* -S material wealth

MAMMOTH *n pl.* -S an extinct elephant

MAMMY *n pl.* -MIES mother

MAN *n pl.* MEN an adult human male

MAN *v* MANNED, MANNING, MANS to supply with men

MANA *n pl.* -S a supernatural force in certain Pacific island religions

MANACLE *v* -CLED, -CLING, -CLES to handcuff

MANAGE *v* -AGED, -AGING, -AGES to control or direct

MANAGER *n pl.* -S one that manages

MANAKIN *n pl.* -S a tropical bird

MANANA *n pl.* -S tomorrow

MANATEE *n pl.* -S an aquatic mammal **MANATOID** *adj*

MANCHE *n pl.* -S a heraldic design

MANCHET *n pl.* -S a small loaf of fine white bread

MANCIPLE *n pl.* -S an officer authorized to purchase provisions

MANDALA *n pl.* -S a Hindu or Buddhist graphic symbol of the universe **MANDALIC** *adj*

MANDAMUS *v* -ED, -ING, -ES to command by means of writ issued by a superior court

MANDARIN *n pl.* -S a citrus fruit

MANDATE *v* -DATED, -DATING, -DATES to authorize or decree

MANDATOR *n pl.* -S one that mandates

MANDIBLE *n pl.* -S the bone of the lower jaw

MANDIOCA *n pl.* -S manioc

MANDOLA *n pl.* -S an ancient lute

MANDOLIN *n pl.* -S a stringed musical instrument

MANDRAKE *n pl.* -S a European herb

MANDREL *n pl.* -S a shaft on which a tool is mounted

MANDRIL *n pl.* -S mandrel

MANDRILL *n pl.* -S a large baboon

MANE n pl. -S the long hair growing on and about the neck of some animals **MANED, MANELESS** adj

MANEGE n pl. -S the art of training and riding horses

MANEUVER v -ED, -ING, -S to change the position of for a specific purpose

MANFUL adj courageous **MANFULLY** adv

MANGABEY n pl. -BEYS a long-tailed monkey

MANGABY n pl. -BIES mangabey

MANGANIC adj containing manganese (a metallic element)

MANGE n pl. -S a skin disease of domestic animals

MANGEL n pl. -S a variety of beet

MANGER n pl. -S a trough or box from which horses or cattle eat

MANGEY adj MANGIER, MANGIEST mangy

MANGIER comparative of mangy

MANGIEST superlative of mangy

MANGILY adv in a mangy manner

MANGLE v -GLED, -GLING, -GLES to cut, slash, or crush so as to disfigure

MANGLER n pl. -S one that mangles

MANGO n pl. -GOES or -GOS an edible tropical fruit

MANGOLD n pl. -S mangel

MANGONEL n pl. -S a medieval military device for hurling stones

MANGROVE n pl. -S a tropical tree or shrub

MANGY adj MANGIER, MANGIEST affected with mange

MANHOLE n pl. -S a hole providing entrance to an underground or enclosed structure

MANHOOD n pl. -S the state of being a man

MANHUNT n pl. -S an intensive search for a person

MANIA n pl. -S an excessive interest or enthusiasm

MANIAC n pl. -S an insane person **MANIACAL** adj

MANIC n pl. -S one that is affected with mania

MANICURE v -CURED, -CURING, -CURES to trim and polish the fingernails of

MANIFEST v -ED, -ING, -S to show clearly

MANIFOLD v -ED, -ING, -S to make several copies of

MANIHOT n pl. -S a tropical plant

MANIKIN n pl. -S an anatomical model of the human body

MANILA n pl. -S a strong paper

MANILLA n pl. -S manila

MANILLE n pl. -S the second highest trump in certain card games

MANIOC n pl. -S a tropical plant

MANIOCA n pl. -S manioc

MANIPLE n pl. -S a silk band worn on the left arm as a vestment

MANITO n pl. -TOS manitou

MANITOU n pl. -S an Algonquian Indian deity

MANITU n pl. -S manitou

MANKIND n pl. MANKIND the human race

MANLESS adj destitute of men

MANLIKE adj resembling a man

MANLY adj -LIER, -LIEST having the qualities of a man **MANLILY** adv

MANMADE adj made by man

MANNA n pl. -S divinely supplied food

MANNAN n pl. -S a type of sugar

MANNED past tense of man

MANNER n pl. -S a way of acting **MANNERED** adj

MANNERLY adj polite

MANNIKIN n pl. -S manikin

MANNING present participle of man

MANNISH adj resembling or characteristic of a man

MANNITE n pl. -S mannitol **MANNITIC** adj

MANNITOL n pl. -S an alcohol

MANNOSE n pl. -S a type of sugar

MANO n pl. -NOS a stone used for grinding foods

MANOR n pl. -S a landed estate or territorial unit **MANORIAL** adj

MANPACK adj designed to be carried by one person

MANPOWER n pl. -S the number of men available for service

MANQUE adj frustrated in the fulfillment of one's aspirations

MANROPE n pl. -S a rope used as a handrail

MANSARD n pl. -S a type of roof

MANSE n pl. -S a clergyman's house

MANSION n pl. -S a large, impressive house

MANTA *n pl.* -S a cotton fabric

MANTEAU *n pl.* -TEAUS or -TEAUX a loose cloak

MANTEL *n pl.* -S a shelf above a fireplace

MANTELET *n pl.* -S a mobile screen used to protect soldiers

MANTES a pl. of mantis

MANTIC *adj* having powers of prophecy

MANTID *n pl.* -S mantis

MANTILLA *n pl.* -S a woman's scarf

MANTIS *n pl.* -TISES or -TES a predatory insect

MANTISSA *n pl.* -S the decimal part of a logarithm

MANTLE *v* -TLED, -TLING, -TLES to cloak

MANTLET *n pl.* -S mantelet

MANTLING *n pl.* -S an ornamental cloth

MANTRA *n pl.* -S a mystical formula of prayer or incantation in Hinduism

MANTRAP *n pl.* -S a trap for catching men

MANTUA *n pl.* -S a woman's gown

MANUAL *n pl.* -S a small reference book

MANUALLY *adv* by means of the hands

MANUARY *adj* involving the hands

MANUBRIA *n/pl* handle-shaped anatomical parts

MANUMIT *v* -MITTED, -MITTING, -MITS to free from slavery

MANURE *v* -NURED, -NURING, -NURES to fertilize with manure (animal excrement)

MANURER *n pl.* -S one that manures

MANURIAL *adj* of or pertaining to manure

MANURING present participle of manure

MANUS *n pl.* MANUS the end of the forelimb in vertebrates

MANWARD *adv* toward man

MANWARDS *adv* manward

MANWISE *adv* in a manner characteristic of man

MANY *adj* MORE, MOST consisting of or amounting to a large number

MANYFOLD *adv* by many times

MAP *v* MAPPED, MAPPING, MAPS to delineate on a map (a representation of a region)

MAPLE *n pl.* -S a hardwood tree

MAPMAKER *n pl.* -S one that makes maps

MAPPABLE *adj* capable of being mapped

MAPPED past tense of map

MAPPER *n pl.* -S one that maps

MAPPING *n pl.* -S a mathematical correspondence

MAQUETTE *n pl.* -S a small preliminary model

MAQUI *n pl.* -S maquis

MAQUIS *n pl.* MAQUIS a thick underbrush

MAR *v* MARRED, MARRING, MARS to detract from the perfection or wholeness of

MARABOU *n pl.* -S an African stork

MARABOUT *n pl.* -S a marabou

MARACA *n pl.* -S a percussion instrument

MARANTA *n pl.* -S a tropical plant

MARASCA *n pl.* -S a wild cherry

MARASMUS *n pl.* -ES a wasting away of the body **MARASMIC** *adj*

MARATHON *n pl.* -S a long-distance race

MARAUD *v* -ED, -ING, -S to rove in search of booty

MARAUDER *n pl.* -S one that marauds

MARAVEDI *n pl.* -S a former coin of Spain

MARBLE *v* -BLED, -BLING, -BLES to give a mottled appearance to

MARBLER *n pl.* -S one that marbles

MARBLING *n pl.* -S an intermixture of fat and lean in meat

MARBLY *adj* -BLIER, -BLIEST mottled

MARC *n pl.* -S the residue remaining after a fruit has been pressed

MARCEL *v* -CELLED, -CELLING, -CELS to make a deep, soft wave in the hair

MARCH *v* -ED, -ING, -ES to walk in a formal military manner

MARCHEN *n pl.* MARCHEN a folktale

MARCHER *n pl.* -S one that marches

MARCHESA *n pl.* -CHESE the wife or widow of a marchese

MARCHESE *n p.* -CHESI an Italian nobleman

MARE *n pl.* -S a mature female horse

MARE *n pl.* -RIA a dark area on the surface of the moon or Mars

MAREMMA *n pl.* -REMME a marshy coastal region

MARGARIC *adj* pearly

MARGARIN *n pl.* -S a butter substitute

MARGAY *n pl.* -GAYS a small American wildcat

MARGE *n pl.* -S a margin

MARGENT *v* -ED, -ING, -S to margin

MARGIN *v* -ED, -ING, -S to provide with a margin (a border)

MARGINAL *adj* of or pertaining to a margin

MARGRAVE *n* pl. -S the military governor of a medieval German border province

MARIA pl. of mare

MARIACHI *n* pl. -S a Mexican musical band

MARIGOLD *n* pl. -S a flowering plant

MARIMBA *n* pl. -S a percussion instrument

MARINA *n* pl. -S a docking area for small boats

MARINADE *v* -NADED, -NADING, -NADES to marinate

MARINARA *n* pl. -S a seasoned tomato sauce

MARINATE *v* -NATED, -NATING, -NATES to soak in a seasoned liquid before cooking

MARINE *n* pl. -S a soldier trained for service at sea and on land

MARINER *n* pl. -S a sailor

MARIPOSA *n* pl. -S a flowering plant

MARISH *n* pl. -ES a marsh

MARITAL *adj* pertaining to marriage

MARITIME *adj* pertaining to navigation or commerce on the sea

MARJORAM *n* pl. -S fragrant herb

MARK *v* -ED, -ING, -S to make a visible impression on

MARKDOWN *n* pl. -S a reduction in price

MARKEDLY *adv* in an evident manner

MARKER *n* pl. -S one that marks

MARKET *v* -ED, -ING, -S to offer for sale

MARKETER *n* pl. -S one that markets

MARKHOOR *n* pl. -S markhor

MARKHOR *n* pl. -S a wild goat

MARKING *n* pl. -S a pattern of marks

MARKKA *n* pl. -KAA or -KAS a monetary unit of Finland

MARKSMAN *n* pl. -MEN a person skillful at hitting a target

MARKUP *n* pl. -S an increase in price

MARL *v* -ED, -ING, -S to fertilize with marl (an earthy deposit containing lime, clay, and sand)

MARLIER comparative of marly

MARLIEST superlative of marly

MARLIN *n* pl. -S a marine game fish

MARLINE *n* pl. -S a rope used on a ship

MARLING *n* pl. -S marline

MARLITE *n* pl. -S a type of marl
MARLITIC *adj*

MARLY *adj* MARLIER, MARLIEST abounding with marl

MARMITE *n* pl. -S a large soup kettle

MARMOSET *n* pl. -S a small monkey

MARMOT *n* pl. -S a burrowing rodent

MAROON *v* -ED, -ING, -S to abandon in an isolated place

MARPLOT *n* pl. -S one that ruins a plan by meddling

MARQUE *n* pl. -S reprisal

MARQUEE *n* pl. -S a rooflike structure projecting over an entrance

MARQUESS *n* pl. -ES marquis

MARQUIS *n* pl. -ES a European nobleman

MARQUISE *n* pl. -S the wife or widow of a marquis

MARRAM *n* pl. -S a beach grass

MARRED past tense of mar

MARRER *n* pl. -S one that mars

MARRIAGE *n* pl. -S the legal union of a man and woman

MARRIED *n* pl. -S one who has entered into marriage

MARRIER *n* pl. -S one that marries

MARRIES present 3d person sing. of marry

MARRING present participle of mar

MARRON *n* pl. -S a variety of chestnut

MARROW *v* -ED, -ING, -S to marry

MARROWY *adj* pithy

MARRY *v* -RIED, -RYING, -RIES to enter into marriage

MARSE *n* pl. -S master

MARSH *n* pl. -ES a tract of low, wet land

MARSHAL *v* -ED, -ING, -S to put in proper order

MARSHALL *v* -ED, -ING, -S to marshal

MARSHY *adj* MARSHIER, MARSHIEST resembling a marsh

MARSUPIA *n/pl* abdominal pouches of certain mammals

MART *v* -ED, -ING, -S to market

MARTAGON *n* pl. -S a flowering plant

MARTELLO *n* pl. -LOS a circular fort

MARTEN *n* pl. -S a carnivorous mammal

MARTIAL *adj* pertaining to war

MARTIAN *n* pl. -S a supposed inhabitant of the planet Mars

MARTIN *n* pl. -S a small bird

MARTINET *n* pl. -S one who demands rigid adherence to rules

MARTINI *n* pl. -S an alcoholic beverage

MARTLET *n* pl. -S a martin

MARTYR *v* -ED, -ING, -S to put to death for adhering to a belief

MARTYRLY *adj* resembling a martyr

MARTYRY *n* pl. -TYRIES a shrine erected in honor of a martyred person

MARVEL *v* -VELED, -VELING, -VELS or -VELLED, -VELLING, -VELS to be filled with wonder or astonishment

MARZIPAN *n* pl. -S an almond candy

MASCARA *n* pl. -S a cosmetic for coloring the eyelashes and eyebrows

MASCON *n* pl. -S a concentration of dense mass beneath the moon's surface

MASCOT *n* pl. -S a person, animal, or object believed to bring good luck

MASER *n* pl. -S a device for amplifying electrical impulses

MASH *v* -ED, -ING, -ES to reduce to a pulpy mass

MASHER *n* pl. -S one that mashes

MASHIE *n* pl. -S a golf club

MASHY *n* pl. MASHIES mashie

MASJID *n* pl. -S a mosque

MASK *v* -ED, -ING, -S to cover with a mask (a covering used to disguise the face) **MASKABLE** *adj*

MASKEG *n* pl. -S muskeg

MASKER *n* pl. -S one that wears a mask

MASKING *n* pl. -S a piece of scenery used to conceal parts of a stage from the audience

MASKLIKE *adj* suggestive of a mask

MASON *v* -ED, -ING, -S to build with stone or brick

MASONIC *adj* pertaining to masonry

MASONRY *n* pl. -RIES a structure built of stone or brick

MASQUE *n* pl. -S a dramatic entertain-ment formerly popular in England

MASQUER *n* pl. -S masker

MASS *v* -ED, -ING, -ES to assemble in a mass (a body of coherent matter)

MASSA *n* pl. -S master

MASSACRE *v* -CRED, -CRING, -CRES to kill indiscriminately

MASSAGE *v* -SAGED, -SAGING, -SAGES to manipulate parts of the body for remedial or hygienic purposes

MASSAGER *n* pl. -S one that massages

MASSE *n* pl. -S a type of shot in billiards

MASSEDLY *adv* in a massed manner

MASSETER *n* pl. -S a muscle that raises the lower jaw

MASSEUR *n* pl. -S a man who massages

MASSEUSE *n* pl. -S a woman who massages

MASSICOT *n* pl. -S a yellow pigment

MASSIER comparative of massy

MASSIEST superlative of massy

MASSIF *n* pl. -S a principal mountain mass

MASSIVE *adj* of considerable size

MASSLESS *adj* having no mass

MASSY *adj* MASSIER, MASSIEST massive

MAST *v* -ED, -ING, -S to provide with a mast (a long pole on a ship that supports the sails and rigging)

MASTABA *n* pl. -S an ancient Egyptian tomb

MASTABAH *n* pl. -S mastaba

MASTER *v* -ED, -ING, -S to become skilled in

MASTERLY *adj* very skillful

MASTERY *n* pl. -TERIES superior knowledge or skill

MASTHEAD *v* -ED, -ING, -S to raise to the top of a mast

MASTIC *n* pl. -S an aromatic resin

MASTICHE *n* pl. -S mastic

MASTIFF *n* pl. -S a large, short-haired dog

MASTITIS *n* pl. -TITIDES inflammation of the breast **MASTITIC** *adj*

MASTIX *n* pl. -ES mastic

MASTLESS *adj* having no mast

MASTLIKE *adj* resembling a mast

MASTODON *n* pl. -S an extinct elephant-like mammal

MASTOID *n* pl. -S the rear portion of the temporal bone

MASURIUM *n* pl. -S a metallic element

MAT *v* MATTED, MATTING, MATS to pack down so as to form a dense mass

MATADOR *n* pl. -S the bullfighter who kills the bull in a bullfight

MATCH *v* -ED, -ING, -ES to set in competition or opposition

MATCHBOX *n* pl. -ES a small box

MATCHER *n* pl. -S one that matches

MATE *v* MATED, MATING, MATES to join as mates (partners in a union)

MATELESS *adj* having no mate

MATELOTE *n* pl. -S a fish stew

MATER *n* pl. -TERS or -TRES mother

MATERIAL *n* pl. -S the substance of which anything is or may be composed

MATERIEL *n* pl. -S the aggregate of equipment and supplies used by an organization

MATERNAL *adj* pertaining to a mother

MATESHIP *n* pl. -S the state of being a mate

MATEY *n* pl. -EYS a friend

MATH *n* pl. -S mathematics

MATILDA *n* pl. -S a hobo's bundle

MATIN *n* pl. -S a morning song, as of birds

MATINAL *adj* pertaining to the morning

MATINEE *n* pl. -S a daytime performance

MATINESS *n* pl. -ES friendliness

MATING *n* pl. -S the period during which a seasonal-breeding animal can mate

MATLESS *adj* having no mats (small floor coverings)

MATRASS *n* pl. -ES a long-necked glass vessel

MATRES a pl. of mater

MATRIX *n* pl. -TRICES or -TRIXES something within which something else originates or develops

MATRON *n* pl. -S a married woman of established social position **MATRONAL, MATRONLY** *adj*

MATT *v* -ED, -ING, -S to matte

MATTE *v* MATTED, MATTING, MATTES to produce a dull finish on

MATTED past tense of mat, matt, and matte

MATTEDLY *adv* in a tangled manner

MATTER *v* -ED, -ING, -S to be of importance

MATTERY *adj* producing pus

MATTIN *n* pl. -S matin

MATTING *n* pl. -S a woven fabric used as a floor covering

MATTOCK *n* pl. -S a digging tool

MATTOID *n* pl. -S a mentally unbalanced person

MATTRASS *n* pl. -ES matrass

MATTRESS *n* pl. -ES a large pad filled with resilient material used on or as a bed

MATURATE *v* -RATED, -RATING, -RATES to mature

MATURE *adj* -TURER, -TUREST fully developed **MATURELY** *adv*

MATURE *v* -TURED, -TURING, -TURES to make or become mature

MATURITY *n* pl. -TIES the state of being mature

MATZA *n* pl. -S matzo

MATZAH *n* pl. -S matzo

MATZO *n* pl. -ZOS, -ZOT, or -ZOTH an unleavened bread

MATZOH *n* pl. -S matzo

MATZOON *n* pl. -S a food made from milk

MATZOT a pl. of matzo

MATZOTH a pl. of matzo

MAUDLIN *adj* excessively emotional

MAUGER *prep* maugre

MAUGRE *prep* in spite of

MAUL *v* -ED, -ING, -S to injure by beating

MAULER *n* pl. -S one that mauls

MAUMET *n* pl. -S an idol

MAUMETRY *n* pl. -RIES idolatry

MAUN *v* must — MAUN is the only form of this verb; it cannot be conjugated

MAUND *n* pl. -S an Asian unit of weight

MAUNDER *v* -ED, -ING, -S to talk incoherently

MAUNDY *n* pl. -DIES the religious ceremony of washing the feet of the poor

MAUSOLEA *n/pl* large, stately tombs

MAUT *n* pl. -S malt

MAUVE *n* pl. -S a purple color

MAVEN *n* pl. -S a mavin

MAVERICK *n* pl. -S an unbranded range animal

MAVIE *n* pl. -S a mavis

MAVIN *n* pl. -S an expert

MAVIS *n* pl. -VISES a songbird

MAW *v* MAWED, MAWN, MAWING, MAWS to mow

MAWKISH *adj* offensively sentimental

MAXI *n* pl. **-S** a long skirt or coat

MAXICOAT *n* pl. **-S** a long coat

MAXILLA *n* pl. **-LAE** or **-LAS** the upper jaw or jawbone

MAXIM *n* pl. **-S** a brief statement of a general truth or principle

MAXIMA a pl. of maximum

MAXIMAL *n* pl. **-S** an element of a mathematical set that is followed by no other

MAXIMIN *n* pl. **-S** the maximum of a set of minima

MAXIMISE *v* **-MISED, -MISING, -MISES** to maximize

MAXIMITE *n* pl. **-S** a powerful explosive

MAXIMIZE *v* **-MIZED, -MIZING, -MIZES** to make as great as possible

MAXIMUM *n* pl. **-MUMS** or **-MA** the greatest possible amount, quantity, or degree

MAXIXE *n* pl. **-S** a Brazilian dance

MAXWELL *n* pl. **-S** a unit of magnetic flux

MAY *v* present 2d person sing. **MAY, MAYEST,** or **MAYST,** past tense **MIGHT** — used as an auxiliary to express permission

MAY *v* **-ED, -ING, -S** to gather flowers in the spring

MAYA *n* pl. **-S** the power to produce illusions, in Hindu philosophy **MAYAN** *adj*

MAYAPPLE *n* pl. **-S** a perennial herb

MAYBE *adv* possibly

MAYBUSH *n* pl. **-ES** a flowering shrub

MAYDAY *n* pl. **-DAYS** a radio distress call

MAYEST a present 2d person sing. of may

MAYFLY *n* pl. **-FLIES** a winged insect

MAYHAP *adv* maybe

MAYHEM *n* pl. **-S** the offense of willfully maiming a person

MAYING *n* pl. **-S** the gathering of spring flowers

MAYOR *n* pl. **-S** the chief executive official of a city or borough **MAYORAL** *adj*

MAYORESS *n* pl. **-ES** a female mayor

MAYPOLE *n* pl. **-S** a decorated pole used in a spring celebration

MAYPOP *n* pl. **-S** a flowering vine

MAYST a present 2d person sing. of may

MAYVIN *n* pl. **-S** mavin

MAYWEED *n* pl. **-S** a malodorous weed

MAZAEDIA *n/pl* spore-producing organs of certain lichens

MAZARD *n* pl. **-S** the head or face

MAZE *v* **MAZED, MAZING, MAZES** to bewilder **MAZEDLY** *adv*

MAZELIKE *adj* mazy

MAZER *n* pl. **-S** a large drinking bowl

MAZIER comparative of mazy

MAZIEST superlative of mazy

MAZILY *adv* in a mazy manner

MAZINESS *n* pl. **-ES** the quality of being mazy

MAZING present participle of maze

MAZOURKA *n* pl. **-S** mazurka

MAZUMA *n* pl. **-S** money

MAZURKA *n* pl. **-S** a Polish dance

MAZY *adj* **MAZIER, MAZIEST** full of confusing turns and passages

MAZZARD *n* pl. **-S** a wild cherry

MBIRA *n* pl. **-S** an African musical instrument

ME *pron* the objective case of the pronoun I

MEAD *n* pl. **-S** an alcoholic beverage

MEADOW *n* pl. **-S** a tract of grassland **MEADOWY** *adj*

MEAGER *adj* deficient in quantity or quality **MEAGERLY** *adv*

MEAGRE *adj* meager **MEAGRELY** *adv*

MEAL *n* pl. **-S** the food served and eaten in one sitting

MEALIE *n* pl. **-S** an ear of corn

MEALIER comparative of mealy

MEALIEST superlative of mealy

MEALLESS *adj* lacking a meal

MEALTIME *n* pl. **-S** the usual time for a meal

MEALWORM *n* pl. **-S** the destructive larva of certain beetles

MEALY *adj* **MEALIER, MEALIEST** soft, dry, and friable

MEALYBUG *n* pl. **-S** a destructive insect

MEAN *v* **MEANT, MEANING, MEANS** to intend

MEAN *adj* **MEANER, MEANEST** inferior in grade, quality, or character

MEANDER *v* **-ED, -ING, -S** to wander

MEANER *n* pl. **-S** one that means

MEANEST superlative of mean

MEANIE *n* pl. **-S** a nasty person

MEANIES pl. of meany

MEANING n pl. -S something that one intends to convey by language

MEANLY adv in a mean manner

MEANNESS n pl. -ES the state of being mean

MEANT past tense of mean

MEANTIME n pl. -S the intervening time

MEANY n pl. MEANIES meanie

MEASLE n pl. -S a tapeworm larva MEASLED adj

MEASLY adj -SLIER, -SLIEST meager

MEASURE v -SURED, -SURING, -SURES to ascertain the dimensions, quantity, or capacity of

MEASURER n pl. -S one that measures

MEAT n pl. -S animal flesh used as food

MEATAL adj pertaining to a meatus

MEATBALL n pl. -S a small ball of chopped meat

MEATHEAD n pl. -S a dolt

MEATIER comparative of meaty

MEATIEST superlative of meaty

MEATILY adv in a meaty manner

MEATLESS adj having no meat

MEATMAN n pl. -MEN a vendor of meat

MEATUS n pl. -ES a natural body passage

MEATY adj MEATIER, MEATIEST full of meat

MECCA n pl. -S a place visited by many people

MECHANIC n pl. -S a person who works with machines

MECONIUM n pl. -S the first fecal excretion of a newborn child

MEDAKA n pl. -S a Japanese fish

MEDAL v -ALED, -ALING, -ALS or -ALLED, -ALLING, -ALS to honor with a medal (a commemorative piece of metal)

MEDALIST n pl. -S a person to whom a medal has been awarded

MEDALLIC adj of or pertaining to a medal

MEDALLING a present participle of medal

MEDDLE v -DLED, -DLING, -DLES to interest oneself in what is not one's concern

MEDDLER n pl. -S one that meddles

MEDIA n pl. -DIAE the middle layer of a blood or lymph vessel

MEDIA n pl. -S a channel of communication

MEDIACY n pl. -CIES the act of mediating

MEDIAD adv toward the middle of a body or part

MEDIAL n pl. -S a sound, syllable, or letter in the middle of a word

MEDIALLY adv in a central manner

MEDIAN n pl. -S a central part

MEDIANLY adv medially

MEDIANT n pl. -S a type of musical tone

MEDIATE v -ATED, -ATING, -ATES to act between disputing parties in order to bring about a settlement

MEDIATOR n pl. -S one that mediates

MEDIC n pl. -S one engaged in medical work

MEDICAID n pl. -S a type of governmental health program

MEDICAL n pl. -S a physical examination

MEDICARE n pl. -S a type of governmental health program

MEDICATE v -CATED, -CATING, -CATES to treat with medicine

MEDICINE v -CINED, -CINING, -CINES to administer medicine (a substance used in the treatment of disease) to

MEDICK n pl. -S a flowering plant

MEDICO n pl. -COS a doctor or medical student

MEDIEVAL n pl. -S a person belonging to the Middle Ages

MEDII pl. of medius

MEDIOCRE adj neither good nor bad

MEDITATE v -TATED, -TATING, -TATES to ponder

MEDIUM n pl. -DIA or -DIUMS a surrounding environment in which something functions and thrives

MEDIUS n pl. -DII the middle finger

MEDLAR n pl. -S a Eurasian tree

MEDLEY n pl. -LEYS a mixture

MEDULLA n pl. -LAS or -LAE the central tissue in the stems of certain plants MEDULLAR adj

MEDUSA n pl. -SAE or -SAS a jellyfish

MEDUSAN n pl. -S medusa

MEDUSOID n pl. -S medusa

MEED n pl. -S a deserved reward

MEEK adj MEEKER, MEEKEST lacking in spirit and courage MEEKLY adv

MEEKNESS n pl. -ES the quality of being meek

MEET v MET, MEETING, MEETS to come into the company or presence of

MEETER n pl. -S one that meets

MEETING n pl. -S an assembly for a common purpose

MEETLY adv suitably

MEETNESS n pl. -ES suitability

MEGABAR n pl. -S a unit of pressure

MEGABIT n pl. -S a unit of computer information

MEGABUCK n pl. -S one million dollars

MEGADYNE n pl. -S a unit of force

MEGALITH n pl. -S a huge stone used in prehistoric monuments

MEGAPOD adj having large feet

MEGAPODE n pl. -S a large-footed bird

MEGASS n pl. -ES a bagasse

MEGASSE n pl. -S megass

MEGATON n pl. -S a unit of explosive force

MEGAVOLT n pl. -S a unit of electromotive force

MEGAWATT n pl. -S a unit of power

MEGILLAH n pl. -S a long, involved story

MEGILP n pl. -S a substance with which pigments are mixed in painting

MEGILPH n pl. -S megilp

MEGOHM n pl. -S a unit of electrical resistance

MEGRIM n pl. -S a migraine

MEIKLE adj large

MEINIE n pl. -S meiny

MEINY n pl. -NIES a retinue

MEIOSIS n pl. -OSES a type of cell division MEIOTIC adj

MEL n pl. -S honey

MELAMINE n pl. -S a chemical compound

MELANGE n pl. -S a mixture

MELANIAN adj pertaining to dark pigmentation

MELANIC n pl. -S one who is affected with melanism

MELANIN n pl. -S a dark pigment

MELANISM n pl. -S abnormally dark pigmentation of the skin

MELANIST n pl. -S a melanic

MELANITE n pl. -S a black variety of garnet

MELANIZE v -NIZED, -NIZING, -NIZES to make dark

MELANOID n pl. -S a dark pigment

MELANOMA n pl. -MAS or -MATA a darkly pigmented tumor

MELANOUS adj having dark skin and hair

MELD v -ED, -ING, -S to blend

MELDER n pl. -S the amount of grain ground at one time

MELEE n pl. -S a confused struggle

MELIC adj pertaining to song

MELILITE n pl. -S a mineral group

MELILOT n pl. -S a flowering plant

MELINITE n pl. -S a powerful explosive

MELISMA n pl. -MAS or -MATA melodic embellishment

MELL v -ED, -ING, -S to mix

MELLIFIC adj producing honey

MELLOW adj -LOWER, -LOWEST soft and full-flavored from ripeness MELLOWLY adv

MELLOW v -ED, -ING, -S to make or become mellow

MELODEON n pl. -S a musical instrument

MELODIA n pl. -S a type of organ stop

MELODIC adj pertaining to melody

MELODIES pl. of melody

MELODISE v -DISED, -DISING, -DISES to melodize

MELODIST n pl. -S a composer of melodies

MELODIZE v -DIZED, -DIZING, -DIZES to compose a melody

MELODY n pl. -DIES an agreeable succession of musical sounds

MELOID n pl. -S a type of beetle

MELON n pl. -S any of various gourds

MELT v -ED, -ING, -S to change from a solid to a liquid state by heat MELTABLE adj

MELTAGE n pl. -S the process of melting

MELTER n pl. -S one that melts

MELTON n pl. -S a heavy woolen fabric

MEM n pl. -S a Hebrew letter

MEMBER n pl. -S a distinct part of a whole MEMBERED adj

MEMBRANE n pl. -S a thin, pliable layer of tissue

MEMENTO n pl. -TOS or -TOES something that serves as a reminder of the past

MEMO n pl. MEMOS a note designating something to be remembered

MEMOIR n pl. -S a biography

MEMORIAL *n* pl. -S something that serves as a remembrance of a person or event

MEMORIZE *v* -RIZED, -RIZING, -RIZES to commit to memory

MEMORY *n* pl. -RIES the mental faculty of retaining and recalling past experience

MEMSAHIB *n* pl. -S a European woman living in colonial India

MEN pl. of man

MENACE *v* -ACED, -ACING, -ACES to theaten

MENACER *n* pl. -S one that menaces

MENAD *n* pl. -S maenad

MENAGE *n* pl. -S a household

MENARCHE *n* pl. -S the first occurrence of menstruation

MEND *v* -ED, -ING, -S to repair **MENDABLE** *adj*

MENDER *n* pl. -S one that mends

MENDIGO *n* pl. -GOS a freshwater fish

MENDING *n* pl. -S an accumulation of articles to be mended

MENFOLK *n/pl* the men of a family or community

MENFOLKS *n/pl* menfolk

MENHADEN *n* pl. -S a marine fish

MENHIR *n* pl. -S a prehistoric monument

MENIAL *n* pl. -S a domestic servant

MENIALLY *adv* in a servile manner

MENINX *n* pl. -NINGES any of the membranes enclosing the brain and spinal cord

MENISCUS *n* pl. -CI or -CUSES a crescent-shaped body **MENISCAL** *adj*

MENO *adv* less — used as a musical direction

MENOLOGY *n* pl. -GIES an ecclesiastical calendar

MENORAH *n* pl. -S a candleholder used in Jewish worship

MENSA *n* pl. -SAS or -SAE the grinding surface of a tooth

MENSAL *adj* pertaining to or used at the table

MENSCH *n* pl. MENSCHES or MENSCHEN an admirable person

MENSE *v* MENSED, MENSING, MENSES to do honor to

MENSEFUL *adj* proper

MENSTRUA *n/pl* solvents

MENSURAL *adj* pertaining to measure

MENSWEAR *n* pl. -S clothing for men

MENTA pl. of mentum

MENTAL *adj* pertaining to the mind **MENTALLY** *adv*

MENTHENE *n* pl. -S a liquid hydrocarbon

MENTHOL *n* pl. -S an alcohol

MENTION *v* -ED, -ING, -S to refer to in a casual manner

MENTOR *n* pl. -S a wise and trusted teacher

MENTUM *n* pl. -TA the chin

MENU *n* pl. -S a list of the dishes available in a restaurant

MEOW *v* -ED, -ING, -S to make the crying sound of a cat

MEPHITIS *n* pl. -TISES an offensive odor **MEPHITIC** *adj*

MERCAPTO *adj* containing a particular chemical group

MERCER *n* pl. -S a dealer in textiles

MERCERY *n* pl. -CERIES a mercer's shop

MERCHANT *v* -ED, -ING, -S to buy and sell goods for profit

MERCIES pl. of mercy

MERCIFUL *adj* full of mercy

MERCURY *n* pl. -RIES a metallic element **MERCURIC** *adj*

MERCY *n* pl. -CIES compassion shown to an offender or enemy

MERE *n* pl. -S a pond or lake

MERE *adj* MERER, MEREST being nothing more than **MERELY** *adv*

MERENGUE *n* pl. -S a ballroom dance

MERGE *v* MERGED, MERGING, MERGES to combine

MERGENCE *n* pl. -S the act of merging

MERGER *n* pl. -S the union of two or more businesses into a single enterprise

MERGING present participle of merge

MERIDIAN *n* pl. -S a circle around the earth passing through both poles

MERINGUE *n* pl. -S a topping for pastries

MERINO *n* pl. -NOS a fine wool

MERISIS *n* pl. -MERISES growth

MERISTEM *n* pl. -S formative plant tissue

MERISTIC *adj* made up of segments

MERIT *v* -ED, -ING, -S to earn

MERK *n* pl. -S a former coin of Scotland

MERL *n* pl. -S merle

MERLE   *n pl.* -S a blackbird

MERLIN   *n pl.* -S a European falcon

MERLON   *n pl.* -S the solid part of an indented parapet

MERMAID   *n pl.* -S a legendary marine creature

MERMAN   *n pl.* -MEN a legendary marine creature

MEROPIA   *n pl.* -S partial blindness **MEROPIC** *adj*

MERRY   *adj* -RIER, -RIEST cheerful **MERRILY** *adv*

MESA   *n pl.* -S a land formation having a flat top and steep sides

MESALLY   *adv* medially

MESARCH   *adj* originating in a mesic habitat

MESCAL   *n pl.* -S a cactus

MESDAMES pl. of madame

MESEEMS   *v* past tense MESEEMED it seems to me — MESEEMS is an impersonal verb and is used only in the 3d person sing.

MESH   *v* -ED, -ING, -ES to entangle

MESHWORK *n pl.* -S a network

MESHY   *adj* MESHIER, MESHIEST netty

MESIAL   *adj* situated in the middle **MESIALLY** *adv*

MESIAN   *adj* mesial

MESIC   *adj* characterized by a medium supply of moisture

MESMERIC *adj* pertaining to hypnotism

MESNALTY *n pl.* -TIES a type of feudal estate

MESNE   *adj* being between two extremes

MESOCARP *n pl.* -S the middle layer of a pericarp

MESODERM *n pl.* -S the middle germ layer of an embryo

MESOGLEA *n pl.* -S a gelatinous material in sponges

MESOMERE *n pl.* -S an embryonic segment

MESON   *n pl.* -S an atomic particle **MESONIC** *adj*

MESOPHYL *n pl.* -S the soft tissue of a leaf

MESOSOME *n pl.* -S a specialized cellular part

MESOTRON *n pl.* -S a meson

MESQUIT   *n pl.* -S mesquite

MESQUITE *n pl.* -S a spiny tree or shrub

MESS   *v* -ED, -ING, -ES to make dirty or untidy

MESSAGE   *n pl.* -S an oral, written, or signaled communication

MESSAN   *n pl.* -S a lapdog

MESSIAH   *n pl.* -S an expected liberator

MESSIER comparative of messy

MESSIEST superlative of messy

MESSIEURS pl. of monsieur

MESSILY   *adv* in a messy manner

MESSMAN   *n pl.* -MEN a serviceman who works in a dining facility

MESSMATE *n pl.* -S a person with whom one eats regularly

MESSUAGE *n pl.* -S a dwelling house with its adjacent buildings and land

MESSY   *adj* MESSIER, MESSIEST dirty or untidy

MESTEE   *n pl.* -S mustee

MESTESO   *n pl.* -SOS or -SOES mestizo

MESTINO   *n pl.* -NOS or -NOES mestizo

MESTIZA   *n pl.* -S a female mestizo

MESTIZO   *n pl.* -ZOS or -ZOES a person of mixed ancestry

MET   past tense of meet

META   *adj* pertaining to positions in a benzene ring separated by one carbon atom

METAGE   *n pl.* -S an official measurement of weight or contents

METAL   *v* -ALED, -ALING, -ALS or -ALLED, -ALLING, -ALS to cover with metal (any of various ductile, fusible, and lustrous substances)

METALISE *v* -ISED, -ISING, -ISES to metalize

METALIST *n pl.* -S one who works with metals

METALIZE *v* -IZED, -IZING, -IZES to treat with metal

METALLED past tense of metal

METALLIC *adj* pertaining to or containing a metal

METALLING a present participle of metal

METAMER   *n pl.* -S a type of chemical compound

METAMERE *n pl.* -S a somite

METAPHOR *n pl.* -S a type of figure of speech

METATE   *n pl.* -S a stone used for grinding grains

METAZOAN *n pl.* -S any of a major division of multicellular animals **METAZOAL, METAZOIC** *adj*

METAZOON *n* pl. -ZOA a metazoan

METE *v* METED, METING, METES to distribute by measure

METEOR *n* pl. -S a small celestial body that enters the earth's atmosphere **METEORIC** *adj*

METEPA *n* pl. -S a chemical compound

METER *v* -ED, -ING, -S to measure by mechanical means

METERAGE *n* pl. -S the process of metering

METHADON *n* pl. -S a narcotic drug

METHANE *n* pl. -S a flammable gas

METHANOL *n* pl. -S a toxic alcohol

METHINKS *v* past tense METHOUGHT it seems to me — METHINKS is an impersonal verb and is used only in the 3d person sing.

METHOD *n* pl. -S a means of procedure

METHODIC *adj* systematic

METHOUGHT past tense of methinks

METHOXY *adj* containing a certain chemical group

METHOXYL *adj* methoxy

METHYL *n* pl. -S a univalent radical **METHYLIC** *adj*

METHYLAL *n* pl. -S a flammable liquid

METIER *n* pl. -S a vocation

METING present participle of mete

METIS *n* pl. METIS a person of mixed ancestry

METISSE *n* pl. -S a female metis

METONYM *n* pl. -S a word used in metonymy

METONYMY *n* pl. -MIES a type of figure of speech

METOPE *n* pl. -PES or -PAE a space between two triglyphs

METOPIC *adj* pertaining to the forehead

METOPON *n* pl. -S a narcotic drug

METRE *v* -TRED, -TRING, -TRES to meter

METRIC *n* pl. -S a standard of measurement

METRICAL *adj* pertaining to or composed in a system of arranged and measured rhythm

METRIFY *v* -FIED, -FYING, -FIES to compose in metrical form

METRING present participle of metre

METRIST *n* pl. -S one who metrifies

METRITIS *n* pl. -TISES inflammation of the uterus

METRO *n* pl. -ROS a subway

METTLE *n* pl. -S quality of character **METTLED** *adj*

METUMP *n* pl. -S a tumpline

MEUNIERE *adj* cooked in browned butter

MEW *v* -ED, -ING, -S to confine

MEWL *v* -ED, -ING, -S to whimper

MEWLER *n* pl. -S one that mewls

MEZCAL *n* pl. -S mescal

MEZEREON *n* pl. -S a flowering shrub

MEZEREUM *n* pl. -S mezereon

MEZQUIT *n* pl. -S mesquite

MEZQUITE *n* pl. -S mesquite

MEZUZA *n* pl. -S mezuzah

MEZUZAH *n* pl. -ZAHS, -ZOT, or -ZOTH a Judaic scroll

MEZZO *n* pl. -ZOS a female voice of a full, deep quality

MHO *n* pl. MHOS a unit of electrical conductance

MI *n* pl. -S the third tone of the diatonic musical scale

MIAOU *v* -ED, -ING, -S to meow

MIAOW *v* -ED, -ING, -S to meow

MIASM *n* pl. -S miasma

MIASMA *n* pl. -MAS or -MATA a noxious vapor **MIASMAL, MIASMIC** *adj*

MIAUL *v* -ED, -ING, -S to meow

MIB *n* pl. -S a type of playing marble

MICA *n* pl. -S a mineral

MICAWBER *n* pl. -S a person who remains hopeful despite adversity

MICE pl. of mouse

MICELL *n* pl. -S micelle

MICELLA *n* pl. -LAE micelle

MICELLE *n* pl. -S a coherent strand or structure in a fiber **MICELLAR** *adj*

MICK *n* pl. -S an Irishman — an offensive term

MICKEY *n* pl. -EYS a drugged drink

MICKLE *adj* -LER, -LEST large

MICKLE *n* pl. -S a large amount

MICRA a pl. of micron

MICRIFY *v* -FIED, -FYING, -FIES to make small

MICRO *adj* very small

MICROBAR *n* pl. -S a unit of atmospheric pressure

MICROBE *n* pl. -S a minute life form **MICROBIC** *adj*

MICROBUS n pl. -BUSES or -BUSSES a small bus

MICROHM n pl. -S a unit of electrical resistance

MICROLUX n pl. -LUXES or -LUCES a unit of illumination

MICROMHO n pl. -S a unit of electrical conductance

MICRON n pl. -CRONS or -CRA a unit of length

MICRURGY n pl. -GIES the use of minute tools under high magnification

MID n pl. -S the middle

MIDAIR n pl. -S a region in the middle of the air

MIDBRAIN n pl. -S the middle region of the brain

MIDDAY n pl. -DAYS the middle of the day

MIDDEN n pl. -S a dunghill

MIDDIES pl. of middy

MIDDLE v -DLED, -DLING, -DLES to place in the middle (the area or point equidistant from extremes or limits)

MIDDLER n pl. -S a student in an intermediate grade

MIDDLING n pl. -S a cut of pork

MIDDY n pl. -DIES a loosely fitting blouse

MIDFIELD n pl. -S the middle portion of a playing field

MIDGE n pl. -S a small winged insect

MIDGET n pl. -S a very small person

MIDGUT n pl. -S the middle part of the embryonic digestive tract

MIDI n pl. -S a skirt or coat that extends to the middle of the calf

MIDIRON n pl. -S a golf club

MIDLAND n pl. -S the middle part of a country

MIDLEG n pl. -S the middle of the leg

MIDLINE n pl. -S a median line

MIDMONTH n pl. -S the middle of the month

MIDMOST n pl. -S a part exactly in the middle

MIDNIGHT n pl. -S the middle of the night

MIDNOON n pl. -S midday

MIDPOINT n pl. -S a point at the middle

MIDRANGE n pl. -S the middle of a range

MIDRASH n pl. -RASHIM an early Jewish interpretation of a biblical text

MIDRIB n pl. -S the central vein of a leaf

MIDRIFF n pl. -S the middle part of the body

MIDSHIP adj pertaining to the middle of a ship

MIDSHIPS adv toward the middle of a ship

MIDSPACE n pl. -S the middle of a space

MIDST n pl. -S the middle

MIDSTORY n pl. -RIES the middle of a story

MIDTERM n pl. -S an examination given in the middle of an academic semester

MIDTOWN n pl. -S the central part of a city

MIDWATCH n pl. -ES a watch on a ship between midnight and 4 A.M.

MIDWAY n pl. -WAYS an avenue at a fair or carnival for concessions and amusements

MIDWEEK n pl. -S the middle of the week

MIDWIFE v -WIFED, -WIFING, -WIFES or -WIVED, -WIVING, -WIVES to assist a woman in childbirth

MIDYEAR n pl. -S the middle of the year

MIEN n pl. -S demeanor

MIFF v -ED, -ING, -S to annoy

MIFFY adj MIFFIER, MIFFIEST easily annoyed

MIG n pl. -S a type of playing marble

MIGG n pl. -S mig

MIGGLE n pl. -S a mig

MIGHT n pl. -S strength

MIGHTY adj MIGHTIER, MIGHTIEST strong MIGHTILY adv

MIGNON n pl. -S a cut of beef

MIGNONNE adj daintily small

MIGRAINE n pl. -S a severe headache

MIGRANT n pl. -S one that migrates

MIGRATE v -GRATED, -GRATING, -GRATES to move from one region to another

MIGRATOR n pl. -S a migrant

MIJNHEER n pl. -S mynheer

MIKADO n pl. -DOS an emperor of Japan

MIKE n pl. -S a microphone

MIKRON n pl. -KRONS or -KRA micron

MIKVAH n pl. -VAHS or -VOTH a place for ritual bathing by Orthodox Jews

MIKVEH n pl. -S mikvah

MIL n pl. -S a unit of length

MILADI n pl. -S milady

MILADY n pl. -DIES an English gentlewoman

MILAGE n pl. -S mileage

MILCH adj giving milk

MILCHIG adj made of or derived from milk

MILD adj MILDER, MILDEST not harsh or rough **MILDLY** adv

MILDEN v -ED, -ING, -S to make or become mild

MILDEW v -ED, -ING, -S to affect with mildew (a whitish growth produced by fungi)

MILDEWY adj affected with or resembling mildew

MILDNESS n pl. -ES the quality of being mild

MILE n pl. -S a unit of distance

MILEAGE n pl. -S total distance expressed in miles

MILEPOST n pl. -S a post indicating distance in miles

MILER n pl. -S one that runs a mile race

MILESIMO n pl. -MOS a monetary unit of Chile

MILFOIL n pl. -S a perennial herb

MILIA pl. of milium

MILIARIA n pl. -S a skin disease

MILIARY adj made up of many small projections

MILIEU n pl. -LIEUS or -LIEUX environment

MILITANT n pl. -S a person who is aggressively engaged in a cause

MILITARY n pl. -TARIES armed forces

MILITATE v -TATED, -TATING, -TATES to have influence or effect

MILITIA n pl. -S a citizen army

MILIUM n pl. -IA a small, whitish lump in the skin

MILK v -ED, -ING, -S to draw milk (a whitish, nutritious liquid) from the udder of

MILKER n pl. -S one that milks

MILKFISH n pl. -ES a marine food fish

MILKIER comparative of milky

MILKIEST superlative of milky

MILKILY adv in a milky manner

MILKMAID n pl. -S a woman who milks cows

MILKMAN n pl. -MEN a man who sells or delivers milk

MILKSOP n pl. -S an effeminate man

MILKWEED n pl. -S a plant that secretes a milky juice

MILKWOOD n pl. -S a tropical tree

MILKWORT n pl. -S a flowering plant

MILKY adj MILKIER, MILKIEST resembling or suggestive of milk

MILL v -ED, -ING, -S to grind by mechanical means **MILLABLE** adj

MILLAGE n pl. -S a type of monetary rate

MILLDAM n pl. -S a dam built to form a millpond

MILLE n pl. -S a thousand

MILLEPED n pl. -S milliped

MILLER n pl. -S one that mills

MILLET n pl. -S a cereal grass

MILLIARD n pl. -S a billion

MILLIARE n pl. -S a unit of area

MILLIARY adj marking the distance of a Roman mile

MILLIBAR n pl. -S a unit of atmospheric pressure

MILLIEME n pl. -S a coin of Egypt and Libya

MILLIER n pl. -S a unit of weight

MILLIGAL n pl. -S a unit of acceleration

MILLILUX n pl. -LUXES or -LUCES a unit of illumination

MILLIME n pl. -S a coin of Tunisia

MILLIMHO n pl. -MHOS a unit of electrical conductance

MILLINE n pl. -S a unit of advertising space

MILLINER n pl. -S one who makes or sells women's hats

MILLING n pl. -S a corrugated edge on a coin

MILLIOHM n pl. -S a unit of electrical resistance

MILLION n pl. -S a number

MILLIPED n pl. -S a multi-legged arthropod

MILLIREM n pl. -S a quantity of ionizing radiation

MILLPOND n pl. -S a pond for supplying water to run a mill wheel (a type of waterwheel)

MILLRACE n pl. -S the current of water that drives a mill wheel

MILLRUN n pl. -S a millrace

MILLWORK n pl. -S woodwork produced by milling

MILO n pl. -LOS a cereal grass

MILORD n pl. -S an English gentleman

MILPA n pl. -S a field that is cleared from a jungle for farming purposes

MILREIS n pl. MILREIS a former monetary unit of Portugal

MILT v -ED, -ING, -S to impregnate with milt (fish sperm)

MILTER n pl. -S a male fish at breeding time

MILTY adj MILTIER, MILTIEST full of milt

MIM adj primly demure

MIMBAR n pl. -S a pulpit in a mosque

MIME v MIMED, MIMING, MIMES to mimic

MIMER n pl. -S one that mimes

MIMESIS n pl. -SISES mimicry **MIMETIC** adj

MIMETITE n pl. -S an ore of lead

MIMIC v -ICKED, -ICKING, -ICS to imitate closely

MIMICAL adj of the nature of mimicry

MIMICKER n pl. -S one that mimics

MIMICKING present participle of mimic

MIMICRY n pl. -RIES an instance of mimicking

MIMING present participle of mime

MIMOSA n pl. -S a tropical plant

MINA n pl. -NAS or -NAE an ancient unit of weight and value

MINABLE adj capable of being mined

MINACITY n pl. -TIES the state of being threatening

MINARET n pl. -S a slender tower attached to a mosque

MINATORY adj threatening

MINCE v MINCED, MINCING, MINCES to cut into very small pieces

MINCER n pl. -S one that minces

MINCY adj MINCIER, MINCIEST affectedly dainty

MIND v -ED, -ING, -S to heed

MINDER n pl. -S one that minds

MINDFUL adj heedful

MINDLESS adj lacking intelligence

MINE v MINED, MINING, MINES to dig into for valuable materials

MINEABLE adj minable

MINER n pl. -S one that mines

MINERAL n pl. -S a naturally occurring inorganic substance having a characteristic set of physical properties

MINGIER comparative of mingy

MINGIEST superlative of mingy

MINGLE v -GLED, -GLING, -GLES to mix together

MINGLER n pl. -S one that mingles

MINGY adj -GIER, -GIEST mean and stingy

MINI n pl. -S something distinctively smaller than others of its kind

MINIBIKE n pl. -S a small motorcycle

MINIBUS n pl. -BUSES or -BUSSES a small bus

MINICAB n pl. -S a small taxicab

MINICAR n pl. -S a small automobile

MINIFY v -FIED, -FYING, -FIES to make small or smaller

MINIKIN n pl. -S a small or dainty creature

MINIM n pl. -S a unit of liquid measure

MINIMA a pl. of minimum

MINIMAL n pl. -S an element of a mathematical set that precedes all others

MINIMAX n pl. -ES the minimum of a set of maxima

MINIMISE v -MISED, -MISING, -MISES to minimize

MINIMIZE v -MIZED, -MIZING, -MIZES to make as small as possible

MINIMUM n pl. -MUMS or -MA the least possible amount, quantity, or degree

MINING n pl. -S the process or business of working mines (excavations in the earth)

MINION n pl. -S a servile follower

MINISH v -ED, -ING, -ES to diminish

MINISTER v -ED, -ING, -S to give aid or service

MINISTRY n pl. -TRIES the act of ministering

MINIUM n pl. -S a red pigment

MINIVER n pl. -S a white fur

MINK n pl. -S a carnivorous mammal

MINNOW n pl. -S a small fish

MINNY n pl. -NIES minnow

MINOR v -ED, -ING, -S to pursue a specific subordinate course of study

MINORCA *n pl.* -S any of a breed of large domestic fowls

MINORITY *n pl.* -TIES the smaller number or part

MINSTER *n pl.* -S a large or important church

MINSTREL *n pl.* -S a medieval musician

MINT *v* -ED, -ING, -S to produce by stamping metal, as coins

MINTAGE *n pl.* -S the act of minting

MINTER *n pl.* -S one that mints

MINTY *adj* MINTIER, MINTIEST having the flavor mint (an aromatic herb)

MINUEND *n pl.* -S a number from which another is to be subtracted

MINUET *n pl.* -S a slow, stately dance

MINUS *n pl.* -ES a negative quantity

MINUTE *v* -UTED, -UTING, -UTES to make a brief note of

MINUTE *adj* -NUTER, -NUTEST very small **MINUTELY** *adv*

MINUTIA *n pl.* -TIAE a small detail **MINUTIAL** *adj*

MINUTING present participle of minute

MINX *n pl.* -ES a pert girl **MINXISH** *adj*

MINYAN *n pl.* -YANS or -YANIM the minimum number required to be present for the conduct of a Jewish service

MIOSIS *n pl.* -OSES excessive contraction of the pupil of the eye

MIOTIC *n pl.* -S an agent that causes miosis

MIQUELET *n pl.* -S a former Spanish or French soldier

MIR *n pl.* MIRS or MIRI a Russian peasant commune

MIRACLE *n pl.* -S an event ascribed to supernatural or divine origin

MIRADOR *n pl.* -S an architectural feature designed to afford an extensive view

MIRAGE *n pl.* -S a type of optical illusion

MIRE *v* MIRED, MIRING, MIRES to cause to stick in swampy ground

MIREX *n pl.* -ES an insecticide

MIRI *a pl.* of mir

MIRIER comparative of miry

MIRIEST superlative of miry

MIRINESS *n pl.* -ES the state of being miry

MIRING present participle of mire

MIRK *adj* MIRKER, MIRKEST murk

MIRK *n pl.* -S murk

MIRKY *adj* MIRKIER, MIRKIEST murky **MIRKILY** *adv*

MIRROR *v* -ED, -ING, -S to reflect an image of

MIRTH *n pl.* -S spirited gaiety **MIRTHFUL** *adj*

MIRY *adj* MIRIER, MIRIEST swampy

MIRZA *n pl.* -S a Persian title of honor

MISACT *v* -ED, -ING, -S to act badly

MISADAPT *v* -ED, -ING, -S to adapt wrongly

MISADD *v* -ED, -ING, -S to add incorrectly

MISAGENT *n pl.* -S a bad agent

MISAIM *v* -ED, -ING, -S to aim badly

MISALLY *v* -LIED, -LYING, -LIES to ally badly

MISALTER *v* -ED, -ING, -S to alter wrongly

MISAPPLY *v* -PLIED, -PLYING, -PLIES to apply wrongly

MISASSAY *v* -ED, -ING, -S to attempt unsuccessfully

MISATE past tense of miseat

MISATONE *v* -ATONED, -ATONING, -ATONES to atone wrongly

MISAVER *v* -AVERRED, -AVERRING, -AVERS to speak erroneously

MISAWARD *v* -ED, -ING, -S to award wrongly

MISBEGIN *v* -GAN, -GUN, -GINNING, -GINS to begin wrongly

MISBEGOT *adj* born out of wedlock

MISBIAS *v* -ASED, -ASING, -ASES or -ASSED, -ASSING, -ASSES to bias wrongly

MISBILL *v* -ED, -ING, -S to bill wrongly

MISBIND *v* -BOUND, -BINDING, -BINDS to bind imperfectly

MISBRAND *v* -ED, -ING, -S to brand incorrectly

MISBUILD *v* -BUILT, -BUILDING, -BUILDS to build imperfectly

MISCALL *v* -ED, -ING, -S to call by a wrong name

MISCARRY *v* -RIED, -RYING, -RIES to be unsuccessful

MISCAST *v* -CAST, -CASTING, -CASTS to cast in an unsuitable role

MISCHIEF *n pl.* -S action that causes irritation, harm, or trouble

MISCIBLE *adj* capable of being mixed

MISCITE v -CITED, -CITING, -CITES to misquote

MISCLAIM v -ED, -ING, -S to claim wrongfully

MISCLASS v -ED, -ING, -ES to put in the wrong class

MISCOIN v -ED, -ING, -S to coin improperly

MISCOLOR v -ED, -ING, -S to color incorrectly

MISCOOK v -ED, -ING, -S to cook badly

MISCOPY v -COPIED, -COPYING, -COPIES to copy incorrectly

MISCOUNT v -ED, -ING, -S to count incorrectly

MISCUE v -CUED, -CUING, -CUES to make a faulty stroke in billiards

MISCUT v -CUT, -CUTTING, -CUTS to cut incorrectly

MISDATE v -DATED, -DATING, -DATES to date incorrectly

MISDEAL v -DEALT, -DEALING, -DEALS to deal cards incorrectly

MISDEED n pl. -S an evil act

MISDEEM v -ED, -ING, -S to judge unfavorably

MISDO v -DID, -DONE, -DOING, -DOES to do wrongly

MISDOER n pl. -S one that misdoes

MISDOING n pl. -S an instance of doing wrong

MISDONE past participle of misdo

MISDOUBT v -ED, -ING, -S to doubt

MISDRAW v -DREW, -DRAWN, -DRAWING, -DRAWS to draw incorrectly

MISDRIVE v -DROVE, -DRIVEN, -DRIVING, -DRIVES to drive wrongly or improperly

MISE n pl. -S an agreement or settlement

MISEASE n pl. -S discomfort

MISEAT v -ATE, -EATEN, -EATING, -EATS to eat improperly

MISEDIT v -ED, -ING, -S to edit incorrectly

MISENROL v -ROLLED, -ROLLING, -ROLS to misenroll

MISENROLL v -ED, -ING, -S to enroll improperly

MISENTER v -ED, -ING, -S to enter erroneously

MISENTRY n pl. -TRIES an erroneous entry

MISER n pl. -S one who hoards money greedily

MISERERE n pl. -S a part of a church seat

MISERLY adj characteristic of a miser

MISERY n pl. -ERIES a state of great suffering

MISEVENT n pl. -S a mishap

MISFAITH n pl. -S lack of faith; disbelief

MISFIELD v -ED, -ING, -S to field badly

MISFILE v -FILED, -FILING, -FILES to file in the wrong place

MISFIRE v -FIRED, -FIRING, -FIRES to fail to fire

MISFIT v -FITTED, -FITTING, -FITS to fit badly

MISFORM v -ED, -ING, -S to misshape

MISFRAME v -FRAMED, -FRAMING, -FRAMES to frame badly

MISGAUGE v -GAUGED, -GAUGING, -GAUGES to gauge wrongly or inaccurately

MISGIVE v -GAVE, -GIVEN, -GIVING, -GIVES to make doubtful or fearful

MISGRAFT v -ED, -ING, -S to graft wrongly

MISGROW v -GREW, -GROWN, -GROWING, -GROWS to grow abnormally

MISGUESS v -ED, -ING, -ES to guess wrongly

MISGUIDE v -GUIDED, -GUIDING, -GUIDES to guide wrongly

MISHAP n pl. -S an unfortunate accident

MISHEAR v -HEARD, -HEARING, -HEARS to hear incorrectly

MISHIT v -HIT, -HITTING, -HITS to hit poorly

MISHMASH n pl. -ES a confused mixture

MISHMOSH n pl. -ES mishmash

MISINFER v -FERRED, -FERRING, -FERS to infer wrongly

MISINTER v -TERRED, -TERRING, -TERS to inter improperly

MISJOIN v -ED, -ING, -S to join improperly

MISJUDGE v -JUDGED, -JUDGING, -JUDGES to judge wrongly

MISKAL n pl. -S an Oriental unit of weight

MISKEEP v -KEPT, -KEEPING, -KEEPS to keep wrongly

MISKNOW v -KNEW, -KNOWN, -KNOWING, -KNOWS to fail to understand or recognize

MISLABEL v -BELED, -BELING, -BELS or -BELLED, -BELLING, -BELS to label incorrectly or falsely

MISLABOR v -ED, -ING, -S to labor badly

MISLAIN past participle of mislie

MISLAY v -LAID, -LAYING, -LAYS to put in a forgotten place

MISLAYER n pl. -S one that mislays

MISLEAD v -LED, -LEADING, -LEADS to lead astray

MISLEARN v -LEARNED or -LEARNT, -LEARNING, -LEARNS to learn wrongly

MISLIE v -LAY, -LAIN, -LYING, -LIES to lie in a wrong position

MISLIGHT v -LIGHTED or -LIT, -LIGHTING, -LIGHTS to lead astray by its light

MISLIKE v -LIKED, -LIKING, -LIKES to dislike

MISLIKER n pl. -S one that mislikes

MISLIT a past tense of mislight

MISLIVE v -LIVED, -LIVING, -LIVES to live a bad life

MISLODGE v -LODGED, -LODGING, -LODGES to lodge in a wrong place

MISLYING present participle of mislie

MISMARK v -ED, -ING, -S to mark wrongly

MISMATCH v -ED, -ING, -ES to match badly

MISMATE v -MATED, -MATING, -MATES to mate unsuitably

MISMEET v -MET, -MEETING, -MEETS to meet under unfortunate circumstances

MISMOVE v -MOVED, -MOVING, -MOVES to move wrongly

MISNAME v -NAMED, -NAMING, -NAMES to call by a wrong name

MISNOMER n pl. -S a name wrongly used

MISO n pl. -SOS a type of food paste

MISOGAMY n pl. -MIES a hatred of marriage

MISOGYNY n pl. -NIES a hatred of women

MISOLOGY n pl. -GIES a hatred of debate or reasoning

MISPAGE v -PAGED, -PAGING, -PAGES to page incorrectly

MISPAINT v -ED, -ING, -S to paint wrongly

MISPARSE v -PARSED, -PARSING, -PARSES to parse incorrectly

MISPART v -ED, -ING, -S to part badly

MISPATCH v -ED, -ING, -ES to patch badly

MISPEN v -PENNED, -PENNING, -PENS to write incorrectly

MISPLACE v -PLACED, -PLACING, -PLACES to put in a wrong place

MISPLANT v -ED, -ING, -S to plant wrongly

MISPLAY v -ED, -ING, -S to make a bad play in a game

MISPLEAD v -PLEADED or -PLED, -PLEADING, -PLEADS to plead wrongly or falsely

MISPOINT v -ED, -ING, -S to point improperly

MISPOISE v -POISED, -POISING, -POISES to poise incorrectly

MISPRINT v -ED, -ING, -S to print incorrectly

MISPRIZE v -PRIZED, -PRIZING, -PRIZES to despise

MISQUOTE v -QUOTED, -QUOTING, -QUOTES to quote incorrectly

MISRAISE v -RAISED, -RAISING, -RAISES to raise wrongly

MISRATE v -RATED, -RATING, -RATES to rate incorrectly

MISREAD v -READ, -READING, -READS to read incorrectly

MISREFER v -FERRED, -FERRING, -FERS to refer incorrectly

MISRELY v -LIED, -LYING, -LIES to rely wrongly

MISRULE v -RULED, -RULING, -RULES to rule unwisely or unjustly

MISS v -ED, -ING, -ES to fail to make contact with

MISSAL n pl. -S a prayer book

MISSAY v -SAID, -SAYING, -SAYS to say incorrectly

MISSEAT v -ED, -ING, -S to seat wrongly

MISSEL n pl. -S a European thrush

MISSEND v -SENT, -SENDING, -SENDS to send incorrectly

MISSENSE n pl. -S a form of genetic mutation

MISSHAPE v -SHAPED, -SHAPEN, -SHAPING, -SHAPES to shape badly

MISSHOD adj improperly shod

MISSIES pl. of missy

MISSILE n pl. -S an object or weapon that is thrown or projected

MISSILRY n pl. -RIES the science of designing and operating guided missiles

MISSION v -ED, -ING, -S to send to perform a specific task

MISSIS n pl. -SISES a wife

MISSIVE n pl. -S a written communication

MISSORT _v_ -ED, -ING, -S to sort badly or improperly

MISSOUND _v_ -ED, -ING, -S to sound wrongly

MISSOUT _n pl._ -S a losing throw of dice

MISSPACE _v_ -SPACED, -SPACING, -SPACES to space incorrectly

MISSPEAK _v_ -SPOKE, -SPOKEN, -SPEAKING, -SPEAKS to speak incorrectly

MISSPELL _v_ -SPELLED or -SPELT, -SPELLING, -SPELLS to spell incorrectly

MISSPEND _v_ -SPENT, -SPENDING, -SPENDS to spend wrongly

MISSPOKE past tense of misspeak

MISSPOKEN past participle of misspeak

MISSTART _v_ -ED, -ING, -S to start off badly

MISSTATE _v_ -STATED, -STATING, -STATES to state wrongly

MISSTEER _v_ -ED, -ING, -S to steer wrongly

MISSTEP _n pl._ -S a false step

MISSTOP _v_ -STOPPED, -STOPPING, -STOPS to stop wrongly

MISSTYLE _v_ -STYLED, -STYLING, -STYLES to style or call wrongly

MISSUIT _v_ -ED, -ING, -S to suit badly

MISSUS _n pl._ -ES missis

MISSY _n pl._ MISSIES a young girl

MIST _v_ -ED, -ING, -S to become blurry

MISTAKE _v_ -TOOK or -TEUK, -TAKEN, -TAKING, -TAKES to interpret wrongly

MISTAKER _n pl._ -S one that mistakes

MISTBOW _n pl._ -S a fogbow

MISTEACH _v_ -TAUGHT, -TEACHING, -TEACHES to teach wrongly or badly

MISTEND _v_ -ED, -ING, -S to tend to improperly

MISTER _n pl._ -S sir

MISTERM _v_ -ED, -ING, -S to call by a wrong name

MISTEUK a past tense of mistake

MISTHINK _v_ -THOUGHT, -THINKING, -THINKS to think wrongly

MISTHROW _v_ -THREW, -THROWN, -THROWING, -THROWS to throw errantly

MISTIER comparative of misty

MISTIEST superlative of misty

MISTILY _adv_ in a misty manner

MISTIME _v_ -TIMED, -TIMING, -TIMES to time wrongly

MISTITLE _v_ -TLED, -TLING, -TLES to call by a wrong title

MISTOOK a past tense of mistake

MISTOUCH _v_ -ED, -ING, -ES to touch improperly

MISTRACE _v_ -TRACED, -TRACING, -TRACES to trace wrongly

MISTRAL _n pl._ -S a cold, dry wind

MISTREAT _v_ -ED, -ING, -S to treat badly

MISTRESS _n pl._ -ES a woman in a position of authority

MISTRIAL _n pl._ -S a trial made invalid because of some error in procedure

MISTRUST _v_ -ED, -ING, -S to distrust

MISTRYST _v_ -ED, -ING, -S to fail to keep an appointment with

MISTUNE _v_ -TUNED, -TUNING, -TUNES to tune incorrectly

MISTUTOR _v_ -ED, -ING, -S to instruct or bring up badly

MISTY _adj_ MISTIER, MISTIEST blurry

MISTYPE _v_ -TYPED, -TYPING, -TYPES to type incorrectly

MISUNION _n pl._ -S a bad union

MISUSAGE _n pl._ -S incorrect use

MISUSE _v_ -USED, -USING, -USES to use incorrectly

MISUSER _n pl._ -S one that misuses

MISVALUE _v_ -UED, -UING, -UES to value incorrectly

MISWORD _v_ -ED, -ING, -S to word wrongly

MISWRITE _v_ -WROTE or -WRIT, -WRITTEN, -WRITING, -WRITES to write incorrectly

MISYOKE _v_ -YOKED, -YOKING, -YOKES to yoke improperly

MITE _n pl._ -S a small arachnid

MITER _v_ -ED, -ING, -S to raise to the rank of a bishop

MITERER _n pl._ -S one that miters

MITHER _n pl._ -S mother

MITICIDE _n pl._ -S a substance used to kill mites

MITIER comparative of mity

MITIEST superlative of mity

MITIGATE _v_ -GATED, -GATING, -GATES to make less severe

MITIS _n pl._ -TISES a type of wrought iron

MITOGEN _n pl._ -S a substance that induces mitosis

MITOSIS *n pl.* -TOSES a type of cell division MITOTIC *adj*

MITRAL *adj* pertaining to a valve of the heart

MITRE *v* -TRED, -TRING, -TRES to miter

MITSVAH *n pl.* -VAHS or -VOTH mitzvah

MITT *n pl.* -S a type of baseball glove

MITTEN *n pl.* -S a type of covering for the hand

MITTIMUS *n pl.* -ES a warrant committing a person to prison

MITY *adj* MITIER, MITIEST infested with mites

MITZVAH *n pl.* -VAHS or -VOTH a commandment of Jewish law

MIX *v* MIXED or MIXT, MIXING, MIXES to put together into one mass MIXABLE, MIXIBLE *adj*

MIXER *n pl.* -S one that mixes

MIXOLOGY *n pl.* -GIES the art of making mixed drinks

MIXT a past tense of mix

MIXTURE *n pl.* -S something produced by mixing

MIXUP *n pl.* -S a state of confusion

MIZEN *n pl.* -S mizzen

MIZZEN *n pl.* -S a type of sail

MIZZLE *v* -ZLED, -ZLING, -ZLES to rain in fine droplets

MIZZLY *adj* characterized by a fine rain

MNEMONIC *n pl.* -S a device to assist the memory

MOA *n pl.* -S an extinct flightless bird

MOAN *v* -ED, -ING, -S to utter a low, mournful sound

MOANFUL *adj* moaning

MOAT *v* -ED, -ING, -S to surround with a moat (a water-filled trench)

MOATLIKE *adj* suggestive of a moat

MOB *v* MOBBED, MOBBING, MOBS to crowd about

MOBBER *n pl.* -S one that mobs

MOBBISH *adj* characteristic of a mob (a disorderly crowd of people)

MOBCAP *n pl.* -S a woman's cap

MOBILE *n pl.* -S a form of sculpture

MOBILISE *v* -LISED, -LISING, -LISES to mobilize

MOBILITY *n pl.* -TIES the ability to move

MOBILIZE *v* -LIZED, -LIZING, -LIZES to put into movement

MOBOCRAT *n pl.* -S a supporter of mob rule

MOBSTER *n pl.* -S a gangster

MOCCASIN *n pl.* -S a type of shoe

MOCHA *n pl.* -S a choice, pungent coffee

MOCHILA *n pl.* -S a leather covering for a saddle

MOCK *v* -ED, -ING, -S to ridicule MOCKABLE *adj*

MOCKER *n pl.* -S one that mocks

MOCKERY *n pl.* -ERIES the act of mocking

MOCKUP *n pl.* -S a full-sized model

MOD *n pl.* -S one who wears boldly stylish clothes

MODAL *adj* pertaining to a mode MODALLY *adv*

MODALITY *n pl.* -TIES the state of being modal

MODE *n pl.* -S a method of doing or acting

MODEL *v* -ELED, -ELING, -ELS or -ELLED, -ELLING, -ELS to plan or form after a pattern

MODELER *n pl.* -S one that models

MODELING *n pl.* -S the treatment of volume in sculpture

MODELLED a past tense of model

MODELLER *n pl.* -S modeler

MODELLING a present participle of model

MODERATE *v* -ATED, -ATING, -ATES to make less extreme

MODERATO *n pl.* -TOS a musical passage played at a medium tempo

MODERN *adj* -ERNER, -ERNEST pertaining to present or recent time MODERNLY *adv*

MODERN *n pl.* -S a person of modern times or views

MODEST *adj* -ESTER, -ESTEST having a moderate regard for oneself MODESTLY *adv*

MODESTY *n pl.* -TIES the quality of being modest

MODI *pl.* of modus

MODICUM *n pl.* -CA or -CUMS a small amount

MODIFIER *n pl.* -S one that modifies

MODIFY *v* -FIED, -FYING, -FIES to change in form or character

MODIOLUS *n pl.* -LI a bony shaft of the inner ear

MODISH *adj* stylish MODISHLY *adv*

MODISTE *n pl.* -S a dealer in stylish women's clothing

MODULAR *adj* pertaining to a module

MODULATE *v* -LATED, -LATING, -LATES to adjust to a certain proportion

MODULE *n* pl. -S a standard of measurement

MODULO *adv* with respect to a modulus

MODULUS *n* pl. -LI a number that produces the same remainder when divided into each of two numbers

MODUS *n* pl. -DI a mode

MOFETTE *n* pl. -S a noxious emanation from a fissure in the earth

MOFFETTE *n* pl. -S mofette

MOG *v* MOGGED, MOGGING, MOGS to move away

MOGUL *n* pl. -S an important person

MOHAIR *n* pl. -S the long, silky hair of the Angora goat

MOHEL *n* pl. -HALIM or -HELS a person who performs Jewish ritual circumcisions

MOHUR *n* pl. -S a former gold coin of India

MOIDORE *n* pl. -S a former gold coin of Portugal

MOIETY *n* pl. -ETIES a half

MOIL *v* -ED, -ING, -S to work hard

MOILER *n* pl. -S one that moils

MOIRA *n* pl. -RAI fate or destiny, in ancient Greek religion

MOIRE *n* pl. -S a fabric having a wavy pattern

MOIST *adj* MOISTER, MOISTEST slightly wet

MOISTEN *v* -ED, -ING, -S to make or become moist

MOISTFUL *adj* moist

MOISTLY *adv* in a moist manner

MOISTURE *n* pl. -S condensed or diffused liquid

MOJARRA *n* pl. -S a marine fish

MOKE *n* pl. -S a donkey

MOL *n* pl. -S mole

MOLA *n* pl. -S a marine fish

MOLAL *adj* pertaining to a mole

MOLALITY *n* pl. -TIES the number of moles of solute per liter of solvent

MOLAR *n* pl. -S a grinding tooth

MOLARITY *n* pl. -TIES the number of moles of solute per liter of solution

MOLASSES *n* pl. -LASSESES a thick syrup

MOLD *v* -ED, -ING, -S to work into a particular shape **MOLDABLE** *adj*

MOLDER *v* -ED, -ING, -S to turn to dust by natural decay

MOLDIER comparative of moldy

MOLDIEST superlative of moldy

MOLDING *n* pl. -S a long, narrow strip used to decorate a surface

MOLDWARP *n* pl. -S a burrowing mammal

MOLDY *adj* MOLDIER, MOLDIEST musty

MOLE *n* pl. -S the quantity of a compound that has a weight equal to the compound's molecular weight

MOLECULE *n* pl. -S the smallest physical unit of an element

MOLEHILL *n* pl. -S a small mold of earth

MOLESKIN *n* pl. -S a cotton fabric

MOLEST *v* -ED, -ING, -S to disturb or annoy

MOLESTER *n* pl. -S one that molests

MOLIES pl. of moly

MOLINE *adj* having arms forked and curved at the ends — used of a heraldic cross

MOLL *n* pl. -S a gangster's girl friend

MOLLAH *n* pl. -S mullah

MOLLIE *n* pl. -S a tropical fish

MOLLIES pl. of molly

MOLLIFY *v* -FIED, -FYING, -FIES to soothe

MOLLUSC *n* pl. -S mollusk

MOLLUSK *n* pl. -S any of a phylum of soft-bodied invertebrates

MOLLY *n* pl. -LIES mollie

MOLOCH *n* pl. -S a spiny lizard

MOLT *v* -ED, -ING, -S to cast off an outer covering

MOLTEN *adj* made liquid by heat **MOLTENLY** *adv*

MOLTER *n* pl. -S one that molts

MOLTO *adv* very — used in musical directions

MOLY *n* pl. -LIES a wild garlic

MOLYBDIC *adj* pertaining to a certain metallic element

MOM *n* pl. -S mother

MOME *n* pl. -S a fool

MOMENT *n* pl. -S a brief period of time

MOMENTA a pl. of momentum

MOMENTLY *adv* from moment to moment

MOMENTO n pl. -TOS or -TOES memento

MOMENTUM n pl. -TA or -TUMS force of movement

MOMI a pl. of momus

MOMISM n pl. -S an excessive dependence on mothers

MOMMA n pl. -S mother

MOMMY n pl. -MIES mother

MOMUS n pl. -MUSES or -MI a carping person

MON n pl. MEN man

MONACHAL adj pertaining to monks

MONACID n pl. -S monoacid

MONAD n pl. -S a single-celled organism **MONADAL**, **MONADIC** adj

MONADES pl. of monas

MONADISM n pl. -S a philosophical doctrine

MONANDRY n pl. -DRIES the condition of having one husband at a time

MONARCH n pl. -S an absolute ruler

MONARCHY n pl. -CHIES rule by a monarch

MONARDA n pl. -S an aromatic herb

MONAS n pl. MONADES a monad

MONASTIC n pl. -S a monk

MONAURAL adj pertaining to sound transmission, recording, or reproduction involving a single transmission path

MONAXIAL adj having one axis

MONAZITE n pl. -S a mineral

MONDE n pl. -S the world

MONDO n pl. -DOS a rapid question and answer technique employed in Zen Buddhism

MONECIAN adj having both male and female sex organs in the same individual

MONETARY adj pertaining to money

MONETISE v -TISED, -TISING, -TISES to monetize

MONETIZE v -TIZED, -TIZING, -TIZES to coin into money

MONEY n pl. MONEYS or MONIES an official medium of exchange and measure of value

MONEYBAG n pl. -S a bag for holding money

MONEYED adj having much money

MONEYER n pl. -S one that coins money

MONGEESE a pl. of mongoose

MONGER v -ED, -ING, -S to peddle

MONGO n pl. -GOS mungo

MONGOE n pl. -S mungo

MONGOL n pl. -S a person affected with a form of mental deficiency

MONGOOSE n pl. -GOOSES or -GEESE a carnivorous mammal

MONGREL n pl. -S an animal or plant of mixed breed

MONGST prep amongst

MONICKER n pl. -S moniker

MONIE adj many

MONIED adj moneyed

MONIES a pl. of money

MONIKER n pl. -S a name

MONISH v -ED, -ING, -ES to warn

MONISM n pl. -S a philosophical theory

MONIST n pl. -S an adherent of monism **MONISTIC** adj

MONITION n pl. -S a warning

MONITIVE adj giving warning

MONITOR v -ED, -ING, -S to keep track of

MONITORY n pl. -RIES a letter of warning

MONK n pl. -S a man who is a member of a secluded religious order

MONKERY n pl. -ERIES the mode of life of monks

MONKEY v -ED, -ING, -S to mimic

MONKFISH n pl. -ES a marine fish

MONKHOOD n pl. -S the state of being a monk

MONKISH adj pertaining to monks

MONO n pl. MONOS an infectious disease

MONOACID n pl. -S a type of acid

MONOCARP n pl. -S a plant that yields fruit only once before dying

MONOCLE n pl. -S an eyeglass for one eye **MONOCLED** adj

MONOCOT n pl. -S a type of seed plant

MONOCRAT n pl. -S an autocrat

MONOCYTE n pl. -S a type of white blood cell

MONODIST n pl. -S one who writes monodies

MONODY n pl. -DIES an elegy performed by one person **MONODIC** adj

MONOECY n pl. -CIES the condition of being monecian

MONOFIL n pl. -S a single filament of synthetic fiber

MONOFUEL n pl. -S a type of rocket propellant

MONOGAMY n pl. -MIES marriage with one person at a time

MONOGENY n pl. -NIES asexual reproduction

MONOGERM adj being a fruit that produces a single plant

MONOGRAM v -GRAMED, -GRAMING, -GRAMS or -GRAMMED, -GRAMMING, -GRAMS to mark with a design of one's initials

MONOGYNY n pl. -NIES the condition of having one wife at a time

MONOLITH n pl. -S a large block of stone

MONOLOG n pl. -S a lengthy speech by one person

MONOLOGY n pl. -GIES the act of uttering a monolog

MONOMER n pl. -S a type of chemical compound

MONOMIAL n pl. -S an algebraic expression consisting of a single term

MONOPODE n pl. -S a creature having one foot

MONOPODY n pl. -DIES a measure consisting of a single metrical foot

MONOPOLE n pl. -S a type of radio antenna

MONOPOLY n pl. -LIES exclusive control of a commodity or service in a particular market

MONORAIL n pl. -S a single rail serving as a track for a wheeled vehicle

MONOSOME n pl. -S a type of chromosome

MONOTINT n pl. -S a painting done in different shades of one color

MONOTONE n pl. -S a vocal utterance in one unvaried tone

MONOTONY n pl. -NIES tedious sameness

MONOTYPE n pl. -S the only representative of its group

MONOXIDE n pl. -S a type of oxide

MONS n pl. MONTES a protuberance of the body

MONSIEUR n pl. MESSIEURS a French title of courtesy for a man

MONSOON n pl. -S a seasonal wind

MONSTER n pl. -S a strange or terrifying creature

MONTAGE v -TAGED, -TAGING, -TAGES to combine into a composite picture

MONTANE n pl. -S the lower vegetation belt of a mountain

MONTE n pl. -S a card game

MONTEITH n pl. -S a large punch bowl

MONTERO n pl. -ROS a type of cap

MONTES pl. of mons

MONTH n pl. -S a period of approximately 30 days

MONTHLY n pl. -LIES a publication issued once a month

MONUMENT n pl. -S a structure built as a memorial

MONURON n pl. -S an herbicide

MONY adj many

MOO v -ED, -ING, -S to make the deep, moaning sound of a cow

MOOCH v -ED, -ING, -ES to obtain without paying

MOOCHER n pl. -S one that mooches

MOOD n pl. -S a person's emotional state at a particular moment

MOODY adj MOODIER, MOODIEST given to changing moods MOODILY adv

MOOL n pl. -S soft soil

MOOLA n pl. -S moolah

MOOLAH n pl. -S money

MOOLEY n pl. -EYS muley

MOON v -ED, -ING, -S to spend time idly

MOONBEAM n pl. -S a ray of light from the moon (the earth's natural satellite)

MOONBOW n pl. -S a rainbow formed by light from the moon

MOONCALF n pl. -CALVES a foolish person

MOONEYE n pl. -S a freshwater fish

MOONFISH n pl. -ES a marine fish

MOONIER comparative of moony

MOONIEST superlative of moony

MOONILY adv in a moony manner

MOONISH adj fickle

MOONLESS adj lacking the light of the moon

MOONLET n pl. -S a small satellite

MOONLIKE adj resembling the moon

MOONLIT adj lighted by the moon

MOONRISE n pl. -S the rising of the moon above the horizon

MOONSAIL n pl. -S a light, square sail

MOONSEED n pl. -S a climbing plant

MOONSET n pl. -S the setting of the moon below the horizon

MOONSHOT n pl. -S the launching of a spacecraft to the moon

MOONWARD *adv* toward the moon

MOONWORT *n* pl. -S a flowering plant

MOONY *adj* MOONIER, MOONIEST resembling the moon

MOOR *v* -ED, -ING, -S to secure a vessel by means of cables

MOORAGE *n* pl. -S the act of mooring

MOORFOWL *n* pl. -S a game bird

MOORHEN *n* pl. -S an aquatic bird

MOORIER comparative of moory

MOORIEST superlative of moory

MOORING *n* pl. -S a place where a vessel may be moored

MOORISH *adj* marshy

MOORLAND *n* pl. -S a tract of marshy land

MOORWORT *n* pl. -S a marsh plant

MOORY *adj* MOORIER, MOORIEST marshy

MOOSE *n* pl. MOOSE a ruminant mammal

MOOT *v* -ED, -ING, -S to bring up for discussion

MOOTER *n* pl. -S one that moots

MOP *v* MOPPED, MOPPING, MOPS to wipe with a mop (an implement for cleaning floors)

MOPBOARD *n* pl. -S a board at the base of a wall

MOPE *v* MOPED, MOPING, MOPES to act in a dejected or gloomy manner

MOPED *n* pl. -S a type of motorbike

MOPER *n* pl. -S one that mopes

MOPING present participle of mope

MOPINGLY *adv* in a moping manner

MOPISH *adj* given to moping **MOPISHLY** *adv*

MOPOKE *n* pl. -S an Australian bird

MOPPED past tense of mop

MOPPER *n* pl. -S one that mops

MOPPET *n* pl. -S a child

MOPPING present participle of mop

MOQUETTE *n* pl. -S a woolen fabric

MOR *n* pl. -S a forest humus

MORA *n* pl. -RAE or -RAS a unit of metrical time in prosody

MORAINE *n* pl. -S an accumulation of debris deposited by a glacier **MORAINAL, MORAINIC** *adj*

MORAL *adj* pertaining to principles of right and wrong **MORALLY** *adv*

MORALE *n* pl. -S the state of the spirits of an individual or group

MORALISE *v* -ISED, -ISING, -ISES to moralize

MORALISM *n* pl. -S the practice of moralizing

MORALIST *n* pl. -S a teacher of morality

MORALITY *n* pl. -TIES conformity to the rules of right conduct

MORALIZE *v* -IZED, -IZING, -IZES to explain in a moral sense

MORALS *n/pl* rules of conduct with respect to right and wrong

MORASS *n* pl. -ES a marsh **MORASSY** *adj*

MORATORY *adj* authorizing delay of payment

MORAY *n* pl. -RAYS a tropical eel

MORBID *adj* gruesome **MORBIDLY** *adv*

MORBIFIC *adj* causing disease

MORBILLI *n/pl* a virus disease

MORCEAU *n* pl. -CEAUX a short literary or musical composition

MORDANCY *n* pl. -CIES a sarcastic quality

MORDANT *v* -ED, -ING, -S to treat with a caustic substance

MORDENT *n* pl. -S a melodic embellishment

MORE *n* pl. -S a greater amount

MOREEN *n* pl. -S a heavy fabric

MOREL *n* pl. -S an edible mushroom

MORELLE *n* pl. -S a flowering plant

MORELLO *n* pl. -LOS a variety of sour cherry

MOREOVER *adv* in addition

MORESQUE *n* pl. -S an ancient decorative style

MORGEN *n* pl. -S a Dutch unit of land area

MORGUE *n* pl. -S a place where dead bodies are kept for identification

MORIBUND *adj* being about to die

MORION *n* pl. -S a type of helmet

MORN *n* pl. -S morning

MORNING *n* pl. -S the early part of the day

MOROCCO *n* pl. -COS a soft leather

MORON *n* pl. -S a mentally deficient person **MORONIC** *adj*

MORONISM *n* pl. -S the condition of being a moron

MORONITY *n* pl. -TIES moronism

MOROSE *adj* sullen **MOROSELY** *adv*

MOROSITY *n* pl. -TIES the state of being morose

MORPH *n* pl. -S a type of phoneme

MORPHEME *n* pl. -S a linguistic unit

MORPHIA *n* pl. -S morphine

MORPHIC *adj* pertaining to form

MORPHIN *n* pl. -S morphine

MORPHINE *n* pl. -S a narcotic alkaloid

MORPHO *n* pl. -PHOS a tropical butterfly

MORRION *n* pl. -S morion

MORRIS *n* pl. -RISES an English folk dance

MORRO *n* pl. -ROS a rounded elevation

MORROW *n* pl. -S the next day

MORSEL *v* -SELED, -SELING, -SELS or -SELLED, -SELLING, -SELS to divide into small pieces

MORT *n* pl. -S a note sounded on a hunting horn to announce the killing of an animal

MORTAL *n* pl. -S a human being

MORTALLY *adv* fatally

MORTAR *v* -ED, -ING, -S to secure with mortar (a type of cement)

MORTARY *adj* containing or resembling mortar

MORTGAGE *v* -GAGED, -GAGING, -GAGES to pledge to a creditor as security

MORTICE *v* -TICED, -TICING, -TICES to mortise

MORTIFY *v* -FIED, -FYING, -FIES to humiliate

MORTISE *v* -TISED, -TISING, -TISES to join or fasten securely

MORTISER *n* pl. -S one that mortises

MORTMAIN *n* pl. -S perpetual ownership of land

MORTUARY *n* pl. -ARIES a place where dead bodies are kept until burial

MORULA *n* pl. -LAE or -LAS an embryonic mass of cells **MORULAR** *adj*

MOSAIC *v* -ICKED, -ICKING, -ICS to form into a mosaic (a type of inlaid surface decoration)

MOSCHATE *adj* musky

MOSEY *v* -ED, -ING, -S to saunter

MOSHAV *n* pl. -SHAVIM a cooperative settlement of small farms in Israel

MOSK *n* pl. -S mosque

MOSQUE *n* pl. -S a Muslim house of worship

MOSQUITO *n* pl. -TOES or -TOS a winged insect

MOSS *v* -ED, -ING, -ES to cover with moss (a growth of small, leafy-stemmed plants)

MOSSBACK *n* pl. -S a large, old fish

MOSSER *n* pl. -S one that gathers or works with moss

MOSSIER comparative of mossy

MOSSIEST superlative of mossy

MOSSLIKE *adj* resembling moss

MOSSO *adv* rapidly — used as a musical direction

MOSSY *adj* MOSSIER, MOSSIEST covered with moss

MOST *n* pl. -S the greatest amount

MOSTE past tense of mote

MOSTLY *adv* mainly

MOT *n* pl. -S a witty saying

MOTE *v* past tense MOSTE may

MOTE *n* pl. -S a small particle

MOTEL *n* pl. -S a roadside hotel

MOTET *n* pl. -S a type of choral composition

MOTEY *adj* full of motes

MOTH *n* pl. -S a winged insect

MOTHBALL *v* -ED, -ING, -S to put into storage

MOTHER *v* -ED, -ING, -S to give birth to

MOTHERLY *adj* maternal

MOTHERY *adj* slimy

MOTHY *adj* MOTHIER, MOTHIEST full of moths

MOTIF *n* pl. -S a recurring thematic element in an artistic work

MOTILE *n* pl. -S one whose mental imagery consists chiefly of inner feelings of action

MOTILITY *n* pl. -TIES the ability to move

MOTION *v* -ED, -ING, -S to signal by a bodily movement

MOTIONAL *adj* pertaining to movement

MOTIONER *n* pl. -S one that motions

MOTIVATE *v* -VATED, -VATING, -VATES to provide with an incentive

MOTIVE *v* -TIVED, -TIVING, -TIVES to motivate

MOTIVIC *adj* pertaining to a musical motif

MOTIVITY *n* pl. -TIES the ability to move

MOTLEY *adj* -LEYER, -LEYEST or -LIER, -LIEST composed of diverse elements

MOTLEY *n* pl. -LEYS a garment of various colors

MOTMOT *n pl.* -S a tropical bird

MOTOR *v* -ED, -ING, -S to travel by automobile

MOTORBUS *n pl.* -BUSES or -BUSSES a bus

MOTORCAR *n pl.* -S an automobile

MOTORIC *adj* pertaining to muscular movement

MOTORING *n pl.* -S the recreation of traveling by automobile

MOTORISE *v* -ISED, -ISING, -ISES to motorize

MOTORIST *n pl.* -S one who travels by automobile

MOTORIZE *v* -IZED, -IZING, -IZES to equip with motor vehicles

MOTORMAN *n pl.* -MEN one who operates an electric streetcar or subway train

MOTORWAY *n pl.* -WAYS a type of highway

MOTT *n pl.* -S motte

MOTTE *n pl.* -S a small growth of trees on a prairie

MOTTLE *v* -TLED, -TLING, -TLES to mark with spots or streaks of different colors

MOTTLER *n pl.* -S one that mottles

MOTTO *n pl.* -TOES or -TOS a short expression of a guiding principle

MOUCH *v* -ED, -ING, -ES to mooch

MOUCHOIR *n pl.* -S a small handkerchief

MOUE *n pl.* -S a pouting grimace

MOUFFLON *n pl.* -S moufion

MOUFLON *n pl.* -S a wild sheep

MOUILLE *adj* pronounced with the front of the tongue against the palate

MOUJIK *n pl.* -S muzhik

MOULAGE *n pl.* -S the making of a cast or mold of a mark for use in a criminal investigation

MOULD *v* -ED, -ING, -S to mold

MOULDER *v* -ED, -ING, -S to molder

MOULDING *n pl.* -S molding

MOULDY *adj* MOULDIER, MOULDIEST moldy

MOULIN *n pl.* -S a vertical cavity in a glacier

MOULT *v* -ED, -ING, -S to molt

MOULTER *n pl.* -S molter

MOUND *v* -ED, -ING, -S to pile

MOUNT *v* -ED, -ING, -S to get up on

MOUNTAIN *n pl.* -S a large, natural elevation of the earth's surface

MOUNTER *n pl.* -S one that mounts

MOUNTING *n pl.* -S something that provides a backing or appropriate setting for something else

MOURN *v* -ED, -ING, -S to feel or express grief or sorrow

MOURNER *n pl.* -S one that mourns

MOURNFUL *adj* -FULLER, -FULLEST expressing grief or sorrow

MOURNING *n pl.* -S an outward sign of grief

MOUSE *n pl.* MICE a small rodent

MOUSE *v* MOUSED, MOUSING, MOUSES to catch mice

MOUSER *n pl.* -S an animal that catches mice

MOUSEY *adj* MOUSIER, MOUSIEST mousy

MOUSIER comparative of mousy

MOUSIEST superlative of mousy

MOUSILY *adv* in a mousy manner

MOUSING *n pl.* -S a wrapping around the shank end of a hook

MOUSSAKA *n pl.* -S a Middle Eastern dish of meat and eggplant

MOUSSE *n pl.* -S a chilled dessert

MOUSY *adj* MOUSIER, MOUSIEST resembling a mouse

MOUTH *v* -ED, -ING, -S to put into the mouth

MOUTHER *n pl.* -S a speaker

MOUTHFUL *n pl.* -S as much as the mouth can hold

MOUTHY *adj* MOUTHIER, MOUTHIEST very talkative **MOUTHILY** *adv*

MOUTON *n pl.* -S sheepskin processed to resemble seal or beaver

MOVABLE *n pl.* -S something that can be moved

MOVABLY *adv* so as to be capable of being moved

MOVE *v* MOVED, MOVING, MOVES to change from one position to another

MOVEABLE *n pl.* -S movable

MOVEABLY *adv* movably

MOVED past tense of move

MOVELESS *adj* incapable of movement

MOVEMENT *n pl.* -S the act of moving

MOVER *n pl.* -S one that moves

MOVIE *n pl.* -S a motion picture

MOVIEDOM *n pl.* -S filmdom

MOVING present participle of move

MOVINGLY	adv so as to affect the emotions
MOW	v MOWED, MOWN, MOWING, MOWS to cut down standing herbage
MOWER	n pl. -S one that mows
MOXA	n pl. -S a Chinese plant
MOXIE	n pl. -S spirit or courage
MOZETTA	n pl. -TAS or -TE mozzetta
MOZO	n pl. -ZOS a manual laborer
MOZZETTA	n pl. -TAS or -TE a hooded cape worn by bishops
MRIDANGA	n pl. -S a drum of India
MU	n pl. -S a Greek letter
MUCH	n pl. -ES a great amount
MUCHNESS	n pl. -ES the quality of being great
MUCID	adj musty
MUCIDITY	n pl. -TIES the state of being mucid
MUCILAGE	n pl. -S an adhesive substance
MUCIN	n pl. -S a protein secreted by the mucous membranes MUCINOID, MUCINOUS adj
MUCK	v -ED, -ING, -S to fertilize with manure
MUCKER	n pl. -S a vulgar person
MUCKIER	comparative of mucky
MUCKIEST	superlative of mucky
MUCKILY	adv in a mucky manner
MUCKLE	n pl. -S a large amount
MUCKLUCK	n pl. -S mukluk
MUCKRAKE	v -RAKED, -RAKING, -RAKES to search for and expose corruption
MUCKWORM	n pl. -S a worm found in manure
MUCKY	adj MUCKIER, MUCKIEST filthy
MUCLUC	n pl. -S mukluk
MUCOID	n pl. -S a complex protein MUCOIDAL adj
MUCOR	n pl. -S a type of fungus
MUCOSA	n pl. -SAE or -SAS a mucous membrane MUCOSAL adj
MUCOSE	adj mucous
MUCOSITY	n pl. -TIES the state of being mucous
MUCOUS	adj secreting or containing mucus
MUCRO	n pl. -CRONES a sharp point at the end of certain plant and animal organs
MUCUS	n pl. -ES a viscid bodily fluid

MUD	v MUDDED, MUDDING, MUDS to cover with mud (soft, wet earth)
MUDCAP	v -CAPPED, -CAPPING, -CAPS to cover an explosive with mud before detonating
MUDDER	n pl. -S a racehorse that runs well on a muddy track
MUDDIED	past tense of muddy
MUDDIER	comparative of muddy
MUDDIES	present 3d person sing. of muddy
MUDDIEST	superlative of muddy
MUDDILY	adv in a muddy manner
MUDDING	present participle of mud
MUDDLE	v -DLED, -DLING, -DLES to mix in a disordered manner
MUDDLER	n pl. -S one that muddles
MUDDY	adj -DIER, -DIEST covered or filled with mud
MUDDY	v -DIED, -DYING, -DIES to make or become muddy
MUDFISH	n pl. -ES a fish found in mud or muddy water
MUDGUARD	n pl. -S a fender
MUDLARK	n pl. -S a street urchin
MUDPUPPY	n pl. -PIES a large salamander
MUDRA	n pl. -S a hand gesture in East Indian classical dancing
MUDROCK	n pl. -S pelite
MUDROOM	n pl. -S a room for shedding muddy clothing or footwear
MUDSILL	n pl. -S the lowest supporting timber of a structure
MUDSTONE	n pl. -S a type of rock
MUEDDIN	n pl. -S muezzin
MUENSTER	n pl. -S a mild cheese
MUEZZIN	n pl. -S a Muslim crier who calls the faithful to prayer
MUFF	v -ED, -ING, -S to bungle
MUFFIN	n pl. -S a small, round bread
MUFFLE	v -FLED, -FLING, -FLES to wrap with something to deaden sound
MUFFLER	n pl. -S a device for deadening sound
MUFTI	n pl. -S a judge who interprets Muslim religious law
MUG	v MUGGED, MUGGING, MUGS to assault with intent to rob
MUGG	v -ED, -ING, -S to make funny faces
MUGGAR	n pl. -S mugger

MUGGED	past tense of mug	**MULTIFID**	adj divided into many parts
MUGGER	n pl. -S a large Asian crocodile	**MULTIJET**	adj having more than two jets
MUGGIER	comparative of muggy	**MULTIPED**	n pl. -S an animal having many feet
MUGGIEST	superlative of muggy	**MULTIPLE**	n pl. -S the product of a quantity by an integer
MUGGILY	adv in a muggy manner		
MUGGING	n pl. -S a street assault or beating	**MULTIPLY**	v -PLIED, -PLYING, -PLIES to increase in number
MUGGINS	n pl. MUGGINS a card game	**MULTURE**	n pl. -S a fee paid to a miller for grinding grain
MUGGUR	n pl. -S mugger		
MUGGY	adj -GIER, -GIEST warm and humid	**MUM**	v MUMMED, MUMMING, MUMS to act in a disguise
MUGWORT	n pl. -S a flowering plant	**MUMBLE**	v -BLED, -BLING, -BLES to speak unclearly
MUGWUMP	n pl. -S a political independent		
MUHLY	n pl. MUHLIES a perennial grass	**MUMBLER**	n pl. -S one that mumbles
		MUMM	v -ED, -ING, -S to mum
MUJIK	n pl. -S muzhik	**MUMMED**	past tense of mum and mumm
MUKLUK	n pl. -S a soft boot worn by Eskimos	**MUMMER**	n pl. -S one that mums
		MUMMERY	n pl. -MERIES a performance by mummers
MULATTO	n pl. -TOES or -TOS the offspring of one white and one black parent	**MUMMIED**	past tense of mummy
		MUMMIES	present 3d person sing. of mummy
MULBERRY	n pl. -RIES a tree bearing an edible, berrylike fruit	**MUMMIFY**	v -FIED, -FYING, -FIES to preserve by embalming
MULCH	v -ED, -ING, -ES to provide with a protective covering for the soil		
		MUMMING	present participle of mum
MULCT	v -ED, -ING, -S to defraud	**MUMMY**	v -MIED, -MYING, -MIES to mummify
MULE	v MULED, MULING, MULES to strike from dies belonging to two different issues, as a coin		
		MUMP	v -ED, -ING, -S to beg
MULETA	n pl. -S a red cloth used by a matador	**MUMPER**	n pl. -S one that mumps
		MUN	n pl. -S man; fellow
MULETEER	n pl. -S one who drives mules (hoofed work animals)	**MUNCH**	v -ED, -ING, -ES to chew with a crackling sound
		MUNCHER	n pl. -S one that munches
MULEY	n pl. -LEYS a hornless cow	**MUNDANE**	adj ordinary
MULING	present participle of mule	**MUNDUNGO**	n pl. -GOS a foul-smelling tobacco
MULISH	adj stubborn MULISHLY adv		
MULL	v -ED, -ING, -S to ponder	**MUNGO**	n pl. -GOS a low-quality wool
MULLA	n pl. -S mullah	**MUNGOOSE**	n pl. -S mongoose
MULLAH	n pl. -S a Muslim religious leader or teacher	**MUNIMENT**	n pl. -S a means of defense
		MUNITION	v -ED, -ING, -S to furnish with war materiel
MULLEIN	n pl. -S a Eurasian herb		
MULLEN	n pl. -S mullein	**MUNNION**	n pl. -S a muntin
MULLER	n pl. -S a grinding implement	**MUNSTER**	n pl. -S muenster
MULLET	n pl. -S an edible fish	**MUNTIN**	n pl. -S a dividing strip for window panes
MULLEY	n pl. -LEYS muley		
MULLIGAN	n pl. -S a stew of various meats and vegetables	**MUNTING**	n pl. -S muntin
		MUNTJAC	n pl. -S a small Asian deer
MULLION	v -ED, -ING, -S to provide with vertical dividing strips	**MUNTJAK**	n pl. -S muntjac
		MUON	n pl. -S an atomic particle MUONIC adj
MULLITE	n pl. -S a mineral		
MULLOCK	n pl. -S waste earth or rock from a mine MULLOCKY adj	**MURA**	n pl. -S a Japanese village

MURAENID *n* pl. -S a moray

MURAL *n* pl. -S a painting applied directly to a wall or ceiling

MURALIST *n* pl. -S a painter of murals

MURDER *v* -ED, -ING, -S to kill unlawfully with premediated malice

MURDEREE *n* pl. -S one that is murdered

MURDERER *n* pl. -S one that murders

MURE *v* MURED, MURING, MURES to immure

MUREIN *n* pl. -S a type of polymer

MUREX *n* pl. -RICES or -REXES a marine mollusk

MURIATE *n* pl. -S chloride

MURIATED *adj* pickled

MURICATE *adj* covered with short, sharp points

MURICES a pl. of murex

MURID *n* pl. -S a murine

MURINE *n* pl. -S any of a family of small rodents

MURING present participle of mure

MURK *adj* MURKER, MURKEST dark **MURKLY** *adv*

MURK *n* pl. -S darkness

MURKY *adj* MURKIER, MURKIEST dark **MURKILY** *adv*

MURMUR *v* -ED, -ING, -S to speak unclearly

MURMURER *n* pl. -S one that murmurs

MURPHY *n* pl. -PHIES a potato

MURR *n* pl. -S murre

MURRA *n* pl. -S a substance used to make fine vases and cups in ancient Rome

MURRAIN *n* pl. -S a disease of cattle

MURRE *n* pl. -S a diving bird

MURRELET *n* pl. -S a small diving bird

MURREY *n* pl. -REYS a dark purple color

MURRHA *n* pl. -S murra **MURRHINE** *adj*

MURRINE *adj* pertaining to murra

MURRY *n* pl. -RIES a moray

MURTHER *v* -ED, -ING, -S to murder

MUSCA *n* pl. -CAE any of a genus of flies

MUSCADEL *n* pl. -S muscatel

MUSCAT *n* pl. -S a sweet, white grape

MUSCATEL *n* pl. -S a wine made from muscat grapes

MUSCID *n* pl. -S musca

MUSCLE *v* -CLED, -CLING, -CLES to proceed by force

MUSCLY *adj* composed of muscle (tissue that produces bodily movement)

MUSCULAR *adj* pertaining to muscle

MUSE *v* MUSED, MUSING, MUSES to ponder

MUSEFUL *adj* pensive

MUSER *n* pl. -S one that muses

MUSETTE *n* pl. -S a small bagpipe

MUSEUM *n* pl. -S a place where objects of lasting interest or value are cared for and exhibited

MUSH *v* -ED, -ING, -ES to travel over snow with a dog sled

MUSHER *n* pl. -S one that mushes

MUSHROOM *v* -ED, -ING, -S to grow or spread rapidly

MUSHY *adj* MUSHIER, MUSHIEST pulpy **MUSHILY** *adv*

MUSIC *n* pl. -S vocal or instrumental sounds organized to produce a unified composition

MUSICAL *n* pl. -S a play in which dialogue is interspersed with songs and dances

MUSICALE *n* pl. -S a program of music performed at a social gathering

MUSICIAN *n* pl. -S one who performs or composes music

MUSING *n* pl. -S contemplation

MUSINGLY *adv* in a pensive manner

MUSJID *n* pl. -S a mosque

MUSK *n* pl. -S a strongly odorous substance secreted by certain animals

MUSKEG *n* pl. -S a marsh

MUSKET *n* pl. -S a type of firearm

MUSKETRY *n* pl. -RIES the technique of firing small arms

MUSKIE *n* pl. -S a freshwater fish

MUSKIER comparative of musky

MUSKIEST superlative of musky

MUSKILY *adv* in a musky manner

MUSKIT *n* pl. -S mesquite

MUSKRAT *n* pl. -S an aquatic rodent

MUSKY *adj* MUSKIER, MUSKIEST resembling musk

MUSLIN *n* pl. -S a cotton fabric

MUSPIKE *n* pl. -S a freshwater fish

MUSQUASH *n* pl. -ES the muskrat

MUSS *v* -ED, -ING, -ES to mess

MUSSEL *n* pl. -S a bivalve mollusk

MUSSY *adj* MUSSIER, MUSSIEST messy **MUSSILY** *adv*

MUST	v -ED, -ING, -S to become musty	**MUTISM**	n pl. -S muteness
		MUTT	n pl. -S a mongrel dog
MUSTACHE	n pl. -S a growth of hair on the upper lip	**MUTTER**	v -ED, -ING, -S to speak unclearly
MUSTANG	n pl. -S a wild horse	**MUTTERER**	n pl. -S one that mutters
MUSTARD	n pl. -S a pungent seasoning	**MUTTON**	n pl. -S the flesh of sheep used as food **MUTTONY** adj
MUSTEE	n pl. -S an octoroon		
MUSTER	v -ED, -ING, -S to summon or assemble	**MUTUAL**	adj shared in common **MUTUALLY** adv
MUSTH	n pl. -S a state of frenzy occurring in male elephants	**MUTUEL**	n pl. -S a system of betting on races
MUSTY	adj MUSTIER, MUSTIEST having a stale odor **MUSTILY** adv	**MUTULE**	n pl. -S an ornamental block used in classical Greek architecture **MUTULAR** adj
MUT	n pl. -S mutt	**MUUMUU**	n pl. -S a long, loose dress
MUTABLE	adj capable of change **MUTABLY** adv	**MUZHIK**	n pl. -S a Russian peasant
		MUZJIK	n pl. -S muzhik
MUTAGEN	n pl. -S a substance that causes biological mutation	**MUZZIER**	comparative of muzzy
		MUZZIEST	superlative of muzzy
MUTANT	n pl. -S something that undergoes mutation	**MUZZILY**	adv in a muzzy manner
MUTASE	n pl. -S an enzyme	**MUZZLE**	v -ZLED, -ZLING, -ZLES to put a covering over the mouth of to prevent biting or eating
MUTATE	v -TATED, -TATING, -TATES to undergo mutation		
MUTATION	n pl. -S the act of changing **MUTATIVE** adj	**MUZZLER**	n pl. -S one that muzzles
		MUZZY	adj -ZIER, -ZIEST confused
MUTCH	n pl. -ES a close-fitting cap	**MY**	pron the possessive form of the pronoun I
MUTCHKIN	n pl. -S a Scottish unit of liquid measure		
		MYALGIA	n pl. -S muscular pain **MYALGIC** adj
MUTE	adj MUTER, MUTEST characterized by an absence of speech **MUTELY** adv	**MYASIS**	n pl. MYASES myiasis
		MYCELE	n pl. -S mycelium
MUTE	v MUTED, MUTING, MUTES to deaden the sound of **MUTEDLY** adv	**MYCELIUM**	n pl. -LIA the vegetative portion of a fungus **MYCELIAL, MYCELIAN, MYCELOID** adj
MUTENESS	n pl. -ES the state of being mute		
		MYCETOMA	n pl. -MAS or -MATA a fungous infection
MUTER	comparative of mute		
MUTEST	superlative of mute	**MYCOLOGY**	n pl. -GIES the branch of botany dealing with fungi
MUTICOUS	adj lacking a point		
MUTILATE	v -LATED, -LATING, -LATES to deprive of a limb or other essential part	**MYCOSIS**	n pl. -COSES a disease caused by a fungus **MYCOTIC** adj
		MYELIN	n pl. -S a fatty substance that encases certain nerve fibers **MYELINIC** adj
MUTINE	v -TINED, -TINING, -TINES to mutiny		
		MYELINE	n pl. -S myelin
MUTINEER	v -ED, -ING, -S to mutiny	**MYELITIS**	n pl. -LITIDES inflammation of the bone marrow
MUTING	present participle of mute		
MUTINIED	past tense of mutiny	**MYELOID**	adj pertaining to bone marrow
MUTINIES	present 3d person sing. of mutiny	**MYELOMA**	n pl. -MAS or -MATA a tumor of the bone marrow
MUTINING	present participle of mutine	**MYIASIS**	n pl. MYIASES infestation of human tissue by fly maggots
MUTINOUS	adj disposed to mutiny		
MUTINY	v -NIED, -NYING, -NIES to revolt against constituted authority	**MYLONITE**	n pl. -S a type of rock
		MYNA	n pl. -S an Asian bird

MYNAH *n pl.* -S myna

MYNHEER *n pl.* -S a Dutch title of courtesy for a man

MYOBLAST *n pl.* -S a cell capable of giving rise to muscle cells

MYOGENIC *adj* originating in muscle tissue

MYOGRAPH *n pl.* -S an instrument for recording muscular contractions

MYOID *adj* resembling muscle

MYOLOGY *n pl.* -GIES the study of muscles **MYOLOGIC** *adj*

MYOMA *n pl.* -MAS or -MATA a tumor composed of muscle tissue

MYOPATHY *n pl.* -THIES a disorder of muscle tissue

MYOPE *n pl.* -S one who is affected with myopia

MYOPIA *n pl.* -S a visual defect **MYOPIC** *adj*

MYOPY *n pl.* -PIES myopia

MYOSCOPE *n pl.* -S an instrument for observing muscular contractions

MYOSIN *n pl.* -S a protein found in muscle tissue

MYOSIS *n pl.* MYOSES miosis

MYOSOTE *n pl.* -S myosotis

MYOSOTIS *n pl.* -TISES a flowering plant

MYOTIC *n pl.* -S miotic

MYOTOME *n pl.* -S a portion of an embryonic somite

MYOTONIA *n pl.* -S temporary muscular rigidity **MYOTONIC** *adj*

MYRIAD *n pl.* -S a very large number

MYRIAPOD *n pl.* -S a multi-legged arthropod

MYRICA *n pl.* -S a medicinal tree bark

MYRIOPOD *n pl.* -S myriapod

MYRMIDON *n pl.* -S a loyal follower

MYRRH *n pl.* -S an aromatic gum resin **MYRRHIC** *adj*

MYRTLE *n pl.* -S an evergreen shrub

MYSELF *pron* a form of the 1st person sing. pronoun

MYSOST *n pl.* -S a mild cheese

MYSTAGOG *n pl.* -S a teacher of religious mysteries

MYSTERY *n pl.* -TERIES something that is not or cannot be known, understood, or explained

MYSTIC *n pl.* -S one who professes to have had mystical experiences

MYSTICAL *adj* spiritually significant or symbolic

MYSTICLY *adv* in a mystical manner

MYSTIFY *v* -FIED, -FYING, -FIES to perplex

MYSTIQUE *n pl.* -S an aura of mystery or mystical power surrounding a particular person or thing

MYTH *n pl.* -S a type of traditional story

MYTHIC *adj* mythical

MYTHICAL *adj* based on or described in a myth

MYTHOS *n pl.* -THOI a myth

MYXEDEMA *n pl.* -S a disease caused by decreased activity of the thyroid gland

MYXOCYTE *n pl.* -S a large cell found in mucous tissue

MYXOID *adj* containing mucus

MYXOMA *n pl.* -MAS or -MATA a tumor composed of mucous tissue

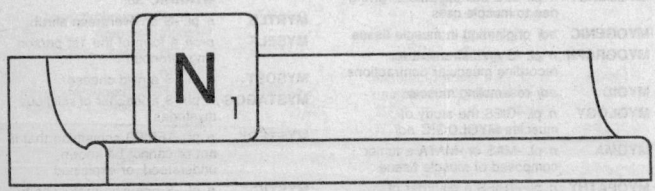

NA *adv* no; not

NAB *v* NABBED, NABBING, NABS to capture or arrest

NABIS *n* pl. NABIS a group of French artists

NABOB *n* pl. -S one who has become rich in India

NABOBERY *n* pl. -ERIES the state of being a nabob

NABOBESS *n* pl. -ES a female nabob

NABOBISM *n* pl. -S great wealth and luxury

NACELLE *n* pl. -S a shelter on an aircraft

NACRE *n* pl. -S the pearly internal layer of certain shells NACRED, NACREOUS *adj*

NADIR *n* pl. -S a point on the celestial sphere NADIRAL *adj*

NAE *adv* no; not

NAETHING *n* pl. -S nothing

NAEVUS *n* pl. -VI nevus NAEVOID *adj*

NAG *v* NAGGED, NAGGING, NAGS to find fault incessantly

NAGANA *n* pl. -S a disease of horses in Africa

NAGGER *n* pl. -S one that nags

NAGGING present participle of nag

NAIAD *n* pl. -S or -ES a water nymph

NAIF *n* pl. -S a naive person

NAIL *v* -ED, -ING, -S to fasten with a nail (a slender piece of metal)

NAILER *n* pl. -S one that nails

NAILFOLD *n* pl. -S a fold of skin around the fingernail

NAILHEAD *n* pl. -S the top of a nail

NAILSET *n* pl. -S a steel rod for driving a nail into something

NAINSOOK *n* pl. -S a cotton fabric

NAIVE *adj* NAIVER, NAIVEST lacking sophistication NAIVELY *adv*

NAIVE *n* pl. -S a naive person

NAIVETE *n* pl. -S the quality of being naive

NAIVETY *n* pl. -TIES naivete

NAKED *adj* -KEDER, -KEDEST being without clothing or covering NAKEDLY *adv*

NALED *n* pl. -S an insecticide

NALOXONE *n* pl. -S a chemical compound

NAME *v* NAMED, NAMING, NAMES to give a title to NAMABLE, NAMEABLE *adj*

NAMELESS *adj* lacking distinction or fame

NAMELY *adv* that is to say

NAMER *n* pl. -S one that names

NAMESAKE *n* pl. -S one who is named after another

NAMING present participle of name

NANA *n* pl. -S a grandmother

NANCE *n* pl. -S an effeminate male

NANDIN *n* pl. -S an evergreen shrub

NANISM *n* pl. -S abnormal smallness

NANKEEN *n* pl. -S a cotton fabric

NANKIN *n* pl. -S nankeen

NANNIE *n* pl. -S nanny

NANNY *n* pl. -NIES a children's nurse

NANOGRAM *n* pl. -S a unit of mass and weight

NANOWATT *n* pl. -S a unit of power

NAOS *n* pl. NAOI an ancient temple

NAP *v* NAPPED, NAPPING, NAPS to sleep briefly

NAPALM *v* -ED, -ING, -S to assault with a type of incendiary bomb

NAPE *n* pl. -S the back of the neck

NAPERY *n pl.* -PERIES table linen

NAPHTHA *n pl.* -S a volatile liquid

NAPHTHOL *n pl.* -S a chemical compound

NAPHTHYL *adj* containing a certain chemical group

NAPHTOL *n pl.* -S naphthol

NAPIFORM *adj* shaped like a turnip

NAPKIN *n pl.* -S a piece of material used to wipe the hands and mouth

NAPLESS *adj* threadbare

NAPOLEON *n pl.* -S a type of pastry

NAPPE *n pl.* -S a type of rock formation

NAPPED past tense of nap

NAPPER *n pl.* -S one that naps

NAPPIE *n pl.* -S a diaper

NAPPING present participle of nap

NAPPY *adj* -PIER, -PIEST kinky

NARC *n pl.* -S an undercover drug agent

NARCEIN *n pl.* -S narceine

NARCEINE *n pl.* -S an opium derivative

NARCISM *n pl.* -S excessive love of oneself

NARCISSI *n/pl* bulbous flowering plants

NARCIST *n pl.* -S one given to narcism

NARCO *n pl.* -COS narc

NARCOSE *adj* characterized by stupor

NARCOSIS *n pl.* -COSES a drug-induced stupor

NARCOTIC *n pl.* -S a drug that dulls the senses

NARD *n pl.* -S a fragrant ointment **NARDINE** *adj*

NARES pl. of naris

NARGHILE *n pl.* -S a hookah

NARGILE *n pl.* -S narghile

NARGILEH *n pl.* -S narghile

NARIS *n pl.* NARES a nostril **NARIAL**, **NARIC**, **NARINE** *adj*

NARK *v* -ED, -ING, -S to spy or inform

NARRATE *v* -RATED, -RATING, -RATES to tell a story

NARRATER *n pl.* -S narrator

NARRATOR *n pl.* -S one that narrates

NARROW *adj* -ROWER, -ROWEST of little width **NARROWLY** *adv*

NARROW *v* -ED, -ING, -S to make narrow

NARTHEX *n pl.* -ES a vestibule in a church

NARWAL *n pl.* -S narwhal

NARWHAL *n pl.* -S an arctic aquatic mammal

NARWHALE *n pl.* -S narwhal

NARY *adj* not one

NASAL *n pl.* -S a sound uttered through the nose

NASALISE *v* -ISED, -ISING, -ISES to nasalize

NASALITY *n pl.* -TIES the quality or an instance of being produced nasally

NASALIZE *v* -IZED, -IZING, -IZES to produce sounds nasally

NASALLY *adv* through the nose

NASCENCE *n pl.* -S nascency

NASCENCY *n pl.* -CIES birth; origin

NASCENT *adj* coming into existence

NASION *n pl.* -S a point in the skull **NASIAL** *adj*

NASTIC *adj* pertaining to an automatic response of plants

NASTY *adj* -TIER, -TIEST offensive to the senses **NASTILY** *adv*

NATAL *adj* pertaining to one's birth

NATALITY *n pl.* -TIES birth rate

NATANT *adj* floating or swimming **NATANTLY** *adv*

NATATION *n pl.* -S the act of swimming

NATATORY *adj* pertaining to swimming

NATES *n/pl* the buttocks

NATHLESS *adv* nevertheless

NATION *n pl.* -S a politically organized people who share a territory, customs, and history

NATIONAL *n pl.* -S a citizen of a nation

NATIVE *n pl.* -S an original inhabitant of an area

NATIVELY *adv* in an inborn manner

NATIVISM *n pl.* -S a policy of favoring the interests of native inhabitants

NATIVIST *n pl.* -S an advocate of nativism

NATIVITY *n pl.* -TIES the process of being born

NATRIUM *n pl.* -S sodium

NATRON *n pl.* -S a chemical compound

NATTER *v* -ED, -ING, -S to chatter

NATTY *adj* -TIER, -TIEST neatly dressed **NATTILY** *adv*

NATURAL *n pl.* -S a type of musical note

NATURE *n pl.* -S the essential qualities of a person or thing **NATURED** *adj*

NAUGHT *n pl.* -S a zero

NAUGHTY *adj* -TIER, -TIEST disobedient

NAUMACHY *n pl.* -CHIES a mock sea battle

NAUPLIUS *n pl.* -PLII a form of certain crustaceans **NAUPLIAL** *adj*

NAUSEA *n pl.* -S a stomach disturbance

NAUSEANT *n pl.* -S an agent that induces nausea

NAUSEATE *v* -ATED, -ATING, -ATES to affect with nausea

NAUSEOUS *adj* affected with nausea

NAUTCH *n pl.* -ES a dancing exhibition in India

NAUTICAL *adj* pertaining to ships

NAUTILUS *n pl.* -LUSES or -LI a spiral-shelled mollusk

NAVAID *n pl.* -S a navigational device

NAVAL *adj* pertaining to ships **NAVALLY** *adv*

NAVAR *n pl.* -S a system of air navigation

NAVE *n pl.* -S the main part of a church

NAVEL *n pl.* -S a depression in the abdomen

NAVETTE *n pl.* -S a gem cut in a pointed oval form

NAVICERT *n pl.* -S a document permitting a vessel passage through a naval blockade

NAVIES *pl.* of navy

NAVIGATE *v* -GATED, -GATING, -GATES to plan and control the course of

NAVVY *n pl.* -VIES a manual laborer

NAVY *n pl.* -VIES a nation's warships

NAWAB *n pl.* -S a nabob

NAY *n pl.* NAYS a negative vote

NAZI *n pl.* -S a type of fascist

NAZIFY *v* -FIED, -FYING, -FIES to cause to be like a nazi

NEAP *n pl.* -S a tide of lowest range

NEAR *adj* NEARER, NEAREST situated within a short distance

NEAR *v* -ED, -ING, -S to approach

NEARBY *adj* near

NEARLY *adv* -LIER, -LIEST with close approximation

NEARNESS *n pl.* -ES the state of being near

NEAT *adj* NEATER, NEATEST being in a state of cleanliness and order

NEAT *n pl.* -S a bovine

NEATEN *v* -ED, -ING, -S to make neat

NEATH *prep* beneath

NEATHERD *n pl.* -S a cowherd

NEATLY *adv* in a neat manner

NEATNESS *n pl.* -ES the state of being neat

NEB *n pl.* -S the beak of a bird

NEBBISH *n pl.* -ES a meek person

NEBULA *n pl.* -LAS or -LAE a cloud-like interstellar mass **NEBULAR** *adj*

NEBULE *adj* composed of successive short curves

NEBULISE *v* -LISED, -LISING, -LISES to nebulize

NEBULIZE *v* -LIZED, -LIZING, -LIZES to reduce to a fine spray

NEBULOSE *adj* nebulous

NEBULOUS *adj* unclear

NEBULY *adj* nebule

NECK *v* -ED, -ING, -S to kiss and caress in lovemaking

NECKBAND *n pl.* -S a band worn around the neck (the part of the body joining the head to the trunk)

NECKING *n pl.* -S a small molding near the top of a column

NECKLACE *n pl.* -S an ornament worn around the neck

NECKLESS *adj* having no neck

NECKLIKE *adj* resembling the neck

NECKLINE *n pl.* -S the line formed by the neck opening of a garment

NECKTIE *n pl.* -S a strip of fabric worn around the neck

NECKWEAR *n pl.* -S something that is worn around the neck

NECROPSY *v* -SIED, -SYING, -SIES to perform an autopsy on

NECROSE *v* -CROSED, -CROSING, -CROSES to affect with necrosis

NECROSIS *n pl.* -CROSES the death of living tissue **NECROTIC** *adj*

NECTAR *n pl.* -S a delicious drink

NECTARY *n pl.* -TARIES a plant gland

NEE *adj* born with the name of

NEED *v* -ED, -ING, -S to have an urgent or essential use for

NEEDER *n pl.* -S one that needs

NEEDFUL *n pl.* -S something that is needed

NEEDIER comparative of needy

NEEDIEST superlative of needy

NEEDILY *adv* in a needy manner

NEEDLE *v* -DLED, -DLING, -DLES to sew with a slender, pointed instrument

NEEDLER *n pl.* -S one that needles

NEEDLESS *adj* not necessary

NEEDLING *n pl.* -S the act of one who needles

NEEDY *adj* NEEDIER, NEEDIEST in a state of poverty

NEEM *n pl.* -S an East Indian tree

NEEP *n pl.* -S a turnip

NEGATE *v* -GATED, -GATING, -GATES to nullify

NEGATER *n pl.* -S one that negates

NEGATION *n pl.* -S the act of negating

NEGATIVE *v* -TIVED, -TIVING, -TIVES to veto

NEGATON *n pl.* -S negatron

NEGATOR *n pl.* -S negater

NEGATRON *n pl.* -S an electron

NEGLECT *v* -ED, -ING, -S to fail to pay attention to

NEGLIGE *n pl.* -S negligee

NEGLIGEE *n pl.* -S a woman's dressing gown

NEGRO *n pl.* -GROES a member of the black race of mankind

NEGROID *n pl.* -S a negro

NEGUS *n pl.* -ES an alcoholic beverage

NEIF *n pl.* -S nieve

NEIGH *v* -ED, -ING, -S to utter the cry of a horse

NEIGHBOR *v* -ED, -ING, -S to live close to

NEIST *adj* next

NEITHER *adj* not one or the other

NEKTON *n pl.* -S free-swimming marine animals NEKTONIC *adj*

NELSON *n pl.* -S a wrestling hold

NELUMBO *n pl.* -BOS an aquatic herb

NEMA *n pl.* -S a nematode

NEMATIC *adj* pertaining to a phase of a liquid crystal

NEMATODE *n pl.* -S a kind of worm

NEMESIS *n pl.* NEMESES an unbeatable opponent

NENE *n pl.* NENE a Hawaiian goose

NEOLITH *n pl.* -S an ancient stone implement

NEOLOGY *n pl.* -GIES a new word or phrase NEOLOGIC *adj*

NEOMORPH *n pl.* -S a type of biological structure

NEOMYCIN *n pl.* -S an antibiotic drug

NEON *n pl.* -S a gaseous element NEONED *adj*

NEONATE *n pl.* -S a newborn child NEONATAL *adj*

NEOPHYTE *n pl.* -S a novice

NEOPLASM *n pl.* -S a tumor

NEOPRENE *n pl.* -S a synthetic rubber

NEOTENY *n pl.* -NIES attainment of sexual maturity in the larval stage NEOTENIC *adj*

NEOTERIC *n pl.* -S a modern author

NEOTYPE *n pl.* -S a specimen of a species

NEPENTHE *n pl.* -S a drug that induces forgetfulness

NEPHEW *n pl.* -S a son of one's brother or sister

NEPHRIC *adj* renal

NEPHRISM *n pl.* -S ill health caused by a kidney disease

NEPHRITE *n pl.* -S a mineral

NEPHRON *n pl.* -S an excretory unit of a kidney

NEPOTISM *n pl.* -S favoritism shown to a relative NEPOTIC *adj*

NEPOTIST *n pl.* -S one who practices nepotism

NEREID *n pl.* -S a sea nymph

NEREIS *n pl.* -REIDES a marine worm

NERITIC *adj* pertaining to shallow water

NEROL *n pl.* -S a fragrant alcohol

NEROLI *n pl.* -S a fragrant oil

NERTS *interj* — used to express defiance or disgust

NERTZ *interj* nerts

NERVATE *adj* having veins

NERVE *v* NERVED, NERVING, NERVES to give courage to

NERVIER comparative of nervy

NERVIEST superlative of nervy

NERVILY *adv* in a nervy manner

NERVINE *n pl.* -S a soothing medicine

NERVING *n pl.* -S a type of veterinary operation

NERVOUS *adj* easily excited

NERVULE *n pl.* -S nervure

NERVURE *n pl.* -S a vascular ridge on a leaf

NERVY *adj* NERVIER, NERVIEST impudent

NESCIENT *n pl.* -S one who is ignorant

NESS *n pl.* -ES a headland

NEST *v* -ED, -ING, -S to build a nest (a structure for holding bird eggs)

NESTER *n pl.* -S one that nests

NESTLE *v* -TLED, -TLING, -TLES to lie snugly

NESTLER *n pl.* -S one that nestles

NESTLIKE *adj* resembling a nest

NESTLING *n pl.* -S a young bird

NESTOR *n pl.* -S a wise old man

NET *v* NETTED, NETTING, NETS to catch in a net (a type of openwork fabric)

NETHER *adj* situated below

NETLESS *adj* having no net

NETLIKE *adj* resembling a net

NETOP *n pl.* -S friend; companion

NETSUKE *n pl.* -S a button-like fixture on Japanese clothing

NETT *v* -ED, -ING, -S to net

NETTABLE *adj* capable of being netted

NETTED past tense of net, nett

NETTER *n pl.* -S one that nets

NETTIER comparative of netty

NETTIEST superlative of netty

NETTING *n pl.* -S a net

NETTLE *v* -TLED, -TLING, -TLES to make angry

NETTLER *n pl.* -S one that nettles

NETTLY *adj* -TLIER, -TLIEST prickly

NETTY *adj* -TIER, -TIEST resembling a net

NETWORK *v* -ED, -ING, -S to cover with or as if with crossing lines

NEUM *n pl.* -S neume

NEUME *n pl.* -S a sign used in musical notation **NEUMATIC, NEUMIC** *adj*

NEURAL *adj* pertaining to the nervous system **NEURALLY** *adv*

NEURAXON *n pl.* -S a part of a neuron

NEURITIC *n pl.* -S one affected with neuritis

NEURITIS *n pl.* -RITIDES or -RITISES inflammation of a nerve

NEUROID *adj* resembling a nerve

NEUROMA *n pl.* -MAS or -MATA a type of tumor

NEURON *n pl.* -S the basic cellular unit of the nervous system **NEURONAL, NEURONIC** *adj*

NEURONE *n pl.* -S neuron

NEUROSIS *n pl.* -ROSES a type of emotional disturbance **NEUROSAL** *adj*

NEUROTIC *n pl.* -S one affected with a neurosis

NEUSTON *n pl.* -S an aggregate of small aquatic organisms

NEUTER *v* -ED, -ING, -S to castrate

NEUTRAL *n pl.* -S one that is impartial

NEUTRINO *n pl.* -NOS an atomic particle

NEUTRON *n pl.* -S an atomic particle

NEVE *n pl.* -S a granular snow

NEVER *adv* at no time

NEVUS *n pl.* -VI a birthmark **NEVOID** *adj*

NEW *adj* NEWER, NEWEST existing only a short time

NEW *n pl.* -S something that is new

NEWBORN *n pl.* -S a recently born infant

NEWCOMER *n pl.* -S one that has recently arrived

NEWEL *n pl.* -S a staircase support

NEWFOUND *adj* newly found

NEWISH *adj* somewhat new

NEWLY *adv* recently

NEWLYWED *n pl.* -S a person recently married

NEWMOWN *adj* recently mown

NEWNESS *n pl.* -ES the state of being new

NEWS *n/pl* a report of recent events

NEWSBOY *n pl.* -BOYS a boy who delivers or sells newspapers

NEWSCAST *n pl.* -S a news broadcast

NEWSIER comparative of newsy

NEWSIES pl. of newsy

NEWSIEST superlative of newsy

NEWSLESS *adj* having no news

NEWSMAN *n pl.* -MEN a news reporter

NEWSPEAK *n pl.* -S a deliberately ambiguous language

NEWSREEL *n pl.* -S a short movie presenting current events

NEWSROOM *n pl.* -S a room where the news is gathered

NEWSY *adj* NEWSIER, NEWSIEST full of news

NEWSY *n pl.* NEWSIES a newsboy

NEWT *n pl.* -S a small salamander

NEWTON *n pl.* -S a unit of force

NEXT *adj* coming immediately after; adjoining

NEXTDOOR *adj* located in the next building or room

NEXUS *n pl.* -ES a connection or link

NGWEE *n pl.* NGWEE a Zambian unit of currency

NIACIN *n pl.* -S a B vitamin

NIB *v* NIBBED, NIBBING, NIBS to provide with a penpoint

NIBBLE *v* -BLED, -BLING, -BLES to eat with small bites

NIBBLER *n pl.* -S one that nibbles

NIBLICK *n pl.* -S a golf club

NIBLIKE *adj* resembling a penpoint

NICE *adj* NICER, NICEST pleasing to the senses NICELY *adv*

NICENESS *n pl.* -ES the quality of being nice

NICETY *n pl.* -TIES a fine point or distinction

NICHE *v* NICHED, NICHING, NICHES to place in a receding space or hollow

NICK *v* -ED, -ING, -S to make a shallow cut in

NICKEL *v* -ELED, -ELING, -ELS or -ELLED, -ELLING, -ELS to plate with nickel (a metallic element)

NICKELIC *adj* pertaining to or containing nickel

NICKER *v* -ED, -ING, -S to neigh

NICKLE *n pl.* -S nickel

NICKNACK *n pl.* -S a trinket

NICKNAME *v* -NAMED, -NAMING, -NAMES to give an alternate name to

NICOL *n pl.* -S a type of prism

NICOTIN *n pl.* -S nicotine

NICOTINE *n pl.* -S a poisonous alkaloid in tobacco

NICTATE *v* -TATED, -TATING, -TATES to wink

NIDAL *adj* pertaining to a nidus

NIDE *v* NIDED, NIDING, NIDES to nest

NIDERING *n pl.* -S a coward

NIDGET *n pl.* -S an idiot

NIDI *a pl.* of nidus

NIDIFY *v* -FIED, -FYING, -FIES to nest

NIDING present participle of nide

NIDUS *n pl.* NIDI or NIDUSES a nest or breeding place

NIECE *n pl.* -S a daughter of one's brother or sister

NIELLIST *n pl.* -S one that niellos

NIELLO *n pl.* -LI or -LOS a black metallic substance

NIELLO *v* -ED, -ING, -S to decorate with niello

NIEVE *n pl.* -S the fist or hand

NIFFER *v* -ED, -ING, -S to barter

NIFTY *adj* -TIER, -TIEST stylish; pleasing

NIFTY *n pl.* -TIES something that is nifty

NIGGARD *v* -ED, -ING, -S to act stingily

NIGGER *n pl.* -S a black person — an offensive term

NIGGLE *v* -GLED, -GLING, -GLES to worry over petty details

NIGGLER *n pl.* -S one that niggles

NIGGLING *n pl.* -S petty or meticulous work

NIGH *adj* NIGHER, NIGHEST near

NIGH *v* -ED, -ING, -S to approach

NIGHNESS *n pl.* -ES the state of being nigh

NIGHT *n pl.* -S the period from sunset to sunrise

NIGHTCAP *n pl.* -S a cap worn to bed

NIGHTIE *n pl.* -S a nightgown

NIGHTIES *pl.* of nighty

NIGHTJAR *n pl.* -S a nocturnal bird

NIGHTLY *adv* every night; at night

NIGHTY *n pl.* NIGHTIES nightie

NIGRIFY *v* -FIED, -FYING, -FIES to make black

NIGROSIN *n pl.* -S a type of dye

NIHIL *n pl.* -S nothing

NIHILISM *n pl.* -S a doctrine that denies traditional values

NIHILIST *n pl.* -S an adherent of nihilism

NIHILITY *n pl.* -TIES the state of being nothing

NIL *n pl.* -S nothing

NILGAI *n pl.* -S a large antelope

NILGAU *n pl.* -S nilgai

NILGHAI *n pl.* -S nilgai

NILGHAU *n pl.* -S nilgai

NILL *v* -ED, -ING, -S to be unwilling

NIM *v* NIMMED, NIMMING, NIMS to steal

NIMBLE *adj* -BLER, -BLEST agile NIMBLY *adv*

NIMBUS *n pl.* -BI or -BUSES a luminous cloud NIMBUSED *adj*

NIMIETY *n pl.* -ETIES excess NIMIOUS *adj*

NIMMED	past tense of nim
NIMMING	present participle of nim
NIMROD	n pl. -S a hunter
NINE	n pl. -S a number
NINEBARK	n pl. -S a flowering shrub
NINEFOLD	adj nine times as great
NINEPIN	n pl. -S a wooden pin used in a bowling game
NINETEEN	n pl. -S a number
NINETY	n pl. -TIES a number
NINNY	n pl. -NIES a fool **NINNYISH** adj
NINON	n pl. -S a sheer fabric
NINTH	n pl. -S one of nine equal parts
NINTHLY	adv in the ninth place
NIOBIUM	n pl. -S a metallic element **NIOBIC, NIOBOUS** adj
NIP	v NIPPED, NIPPING, NIPS to pinch
NIPA	n pl. -S a palm tree
NIPPER	n pl. -S one that nips
NIPPIER	comparative of nippy
NIPPIEST	superlative of nippy
NIPPILY	adv in a nippy manner
NIPPING	present participle of nip
NIPPLE	n pl. -S a protuberance on the breast
NIPPY	adj -PIER, -PIEST sharp or biting
NIRVANA	n pl. -S a blessed state in Buddhism **NIRVANIC** adj
NISEI	n pl. -S one born in America of immigrant Japanese parents
NISI	adj not yet final
NISUS	n pl. NISUS an effort
NIT	n pl. -S the egg of a parasitic insect
NITCHIE	n pl. -S an American Indian — an offensive term
NITER	n pl. -S a chemical salt
NITID	adj bright
NITON	n pl. -S radon
NITPICK	v -ED, -ING, -S to fuss over petty details
NITRATE	v -TRATED, -TRATING, -TRATES to treat with nitric acid
NITRATOR	n pl. -S one that nitrates
NITRE	n pl. -S niter
NITRIC	adj containing nitrogen
NITRID	n pl. -S nitride
NITRIDE	n pl. -S a compound of nitrogen

NITRIFY	v -FIED, -FYING, -FIES to combine with nitrogen
NITRIL	n pl. -S nitrile
NITRILE	n pl. -S a chemical compound
NITRITE	n pl. -S a salt of nitrous acid
NITRO	n pl. -TROS a nitrated product
NITROGEN	n pl. -S a gaseous element
NITROLIC	adj pertaining to a class of acids
NITROSO	adj containing nitrosyl
NITROSYL	n pl. -S a univalent radical
NITROUS	adj containing nitrogen
NITTY	adj -TIER, -TIEST full of nits
NITWIT	n pl. -S a stupid person
NIVAL	adj pertaining to snow
NIVEOUS	adj resembling snow
NIX	v -ED, -ING, -ES to veto
NIXIE	n pl. -S a female water sprite
NIXY	n pl. NIXIES an undeliverable piece of mail
NIZAM	n pl. -S a former sovereign of India
NIZAMATE	n pl. -S the territory of a nizam
NO	n pl. NOS or NOES a negative reply
NOB	n pl. -S a wealthy person
NOBBIER	comparative of nobby
NOBBIEST	superlative of nobby
NOBBILY	adv in a nobby manner
NOBBLE	v -BLED, -BLING, -BLES to disable a racehorse
NOBBLER	n pl. -S one that nobbles
NOBBY	adj -BIER, -BIEST elegant
NOBELIUM	n pl. -S a radioactive element
NOBILITY	n pl. -TIES the social class composed of nobles
NOBLE	adj -BLER, -BLEST possessing qualities of excellence
NOBLE	n pl. -S a person of high birth, rank, or title
NOBLEMAN	n pl. -MEN a noble
NOBLER	comparative of noble
NOBLESSE	n pl. -S the nobility
NOBLEST	superlative of noble
NOBLY	adv in a noble manner
NOBODY	n pl. -BODIES an unimportant person
NOCENT	adj harmful
NOCK	v -ED, -ING, -S to notch a bow or arrow
NOCTUID	n pl. -S a night-flying moth **NOCTUOID** adj

NOCTULE n pl. -S a large bat

NOCTURN n pl. -S a religious service

NOCTURNE n pl. -S a musical composition

NOCUOUS adj harmful

NOD v NODDED, NODDING, NODS to briefly lower the head forward

NODAL adj of the nature of a node **NODALLY** adv

NODALITY n pl. -TIES the state of being nodal

NODDED past tense of nod

NODDER n pl. -S one that nods

NODDIES pl. of noddy

NODDING present participle of nod

NODDLE v -DLED, -DLING, -DLES to nod frequently

NODDY n pl. -DIES a fool

NODE n pl. -S a swollen enlargement

NODI pl. of nodus

NODICAL adj pertaining to an astronomical point

NODOSE adj having nodes

NODOSITY n pl. -TIES the state of being nodose

NODOUS adj nodose

NODULE n pl. -S a small node **NODULAR, NODULOSE, NODULOUS** adj

NODUS n pl. -DI a difficulty

NOEL n pl. -S a Christmas carol

NOESIS n pl. -SISES the process of reason

NOETIC adj pertaining to reason

NOG n pl. -S a strong ale

NOGG n pl. -S nog

NOGGIN n pl. -S a small cup

NOGGING n pl. -S a type of masonry

NOH n pl. NOH the classical drama of Japan

NOHOW adv in no manner

NOIL n pl. -S a kind of short fiber **NOILY** adj

NOIR adj black

NOISE v NOISED, NOISING, NOISES to spread as a rumor or report

NOISOME adj disgusting; harmful

NOISY adj NOISIER, NOISIEST making loud sounds **NOISILY** adv

NOLO n pl. -LOS a type of legal plea

NOM n pl. -S a name

NOMA n pl. -S a severe inflammation of the mouth

NOMAD n pl. -S a wanderer **NOMADIC** adj

NOMADISM n pl. -S the mode of life of a nomad

NOMARCH n pl. -S the head of a nome

NOMARCHY n pl. -ARCHIES a nome

NOMBLES n/pl numbles

NOMBRIL n pl. -S a point on a heraldic shield

NOME n pl. -S a province of modern Greece

NOMEN n pl. -MINA the second name of an ancient Roman

NOMINAL n pl. -S a word functioning as a noun

NOMINATE v -NATED, -NATING, -NATES to name as a candidate

NOMINEE n pl. -S one that is nominated

NOMISM n pl. -S strict adherence to moral law **NOMISTIC** adj

NOMOGRAM n pl. -S a type of graph

NOMOLOGY n pl. -GIES the science of law

NOMOS n pl. NOMOI law

NONA n pl. -S a virus disease

NONACID n pl. -S a substance that is not an acid

NONADULT n pl. -S a person who is not an adult

NONAGE n pl. -S a period of immaturity

NONAGON n pl. -S a nine-sided polygon

NONBANK adj not involving a bank

NONBASIC adj not basic

NONBEING n pl. -S lack of being

NONBOOK n pl. -S a book of little literary merit

NONCASH adj other than cash

NONCE n pl. -S the present occasion

NONCOM n pl. -S a noncommissioned officer

NONDAIRY adj having no milk products

NONE n pl. -S one of seven canonical daily periods for prayer and devotion

NONEGO n pl. -GOS all that is not part of the ego

NONELECT adj not chosen

NONEMPTY adj not empty

NONENTRY n pl. -TRIES the fact of not entering

NONEQUAL n pl. -S one that is not equal

NONESUCH n pl. -ES a person or thing without an equal

NONEVENT *n* pl. -S an expected event that does not occur

NONFARM *adj* not pertaining to the farm

NONFAT *adj* having no fat solids

NONFATAL *adj* not fatal

NONFLUID *n* pl. -S a substance that is not a fluid

NONFOCAL *adj* not focal

NONFOOD *adj* pertaining to something other than food

NONGAME *adj* not hunted for food, sport, or fur

NONGREEN *adj* not green

NONGUILT *n* pl. -S the absence of guilt

NONHARDY *adj* not hardy

NONHERO *n* pl. -ROES an antihero

NONHUMAN *adj* not human

NONIDEAL *adj* not ideal

NONIONIC *adj* not ionic

NONJUROR *n* pl. -S one who refuses to take a required oath

NONLEGAL *adj* not legal

NONLIFE *n* pl. -LIVES the absence of life

NONLOCAL *n* pl. -S one that is not local

NONMAN *n* pl. -MEN a being that is not a man

NONMETAL *n* pl. -S an element that lacks metallic properties

NONMODAL *adj* not modal

NONMONEY *adj* not involving money

NONMORAL *adj* not pertaining to morals

NONNAVAL *adj* not naval

NONOBESE *adj* not obese

NONOWNER *n* pl. -S one who is not the owner

NONPAGAN *n* pl. -S one who is not a pagan

NONPAPAL *adj* not papal

NONPAR *adj* being a stock that has no face value

NONPARTY *adj* not affiliated with any political party

NONPLUS *v* -PLUSED, -PLUSING, -PLUSES or -PLUSSED, -PLUSSING, -PLUSSES to baffle

NONPOLAR *adj* not polar

NONPROS *v* -PROSSED, -PROSSING, -PROSSES to enter a judgment against a plaintiff who fails to prosecute

NONQUOTA *adj* not included in or subject to a quota

NONRATED *adj* not rated

NONRIGID *adj* not rigid

NONRIVAL *n* pl. -S an unimportant rival

NONROYAL *adj* not royal

NONRURAL *adj* not rural

NONSENSE *n* pl. -S behavior or language that is meaningless or absurd

NONSKED *n* pl. -S an airline without scheduled flying times

NONSKID *adj* designed to inhibit skidding

NONSKIER *n* pl. -S one that does not ski

NONSLIP *adj* designed to prevent slipping

NONSOLAR *adj* not solar

NONSOLID *n* pl. -S a substance that is not a solid

NONSTICK *adj* allowing of easy removal of cooked food particles

NONSTOP *adj* making no stops

NONSUCH *n* pl. -ES nonesuch

NONSUGAR *n* pl. -S a substance that is not a sugar

NONSUIT *v* -ED, -ING, -S to dismiss the lawsuit of

NONTAX *n* pl. -ES a tax of little consequence

NONTIDAL *adj* not tidal

NONTITLE *adj* pertaining to an athletic contest in which a title is not at stake

NONTOXIC *adj* not toxic

NONTRUMP *adj* not having a trump

NONTRUTH *n* pl. -S something that is not true

NONUNION *n* pl. -S failure of a broken bone to heal

NONUPLE *n* pl. -S a number nine times as great as another

NONURBAN *adj* not urban

NONUSE *n* pl. -S failure to use

NONUSER *n* pl. -S one that is not a user

NONUSING *adj* not using

NONVIRAL *adj* not viral

NONVOCAL *adj* not vocal

NONVOTER *n* pl. -S one that does not vote

NONWHITE *n* pl. -S a person who is not of the white race

NONWOODY *adj* not woody

NONWOVEN *adj* made without weaving

NONZERO *adj* having a value other than zero

NOO *adv* now

NOODLE *v* -DLED, -DLING, -DLES to play idly on a musical instrument

NOOK *n pl.* -S a corner, as in a room **NOOKLIKE** *adj*

NOOKY *n pl.* NOOKIES sexual intercourse — an offensive term

NOON *n pl.* -S midday

NOONDAY *n pl.* -DAYS noon

NOONING *n pl.* -S a meal eaten at noon

NOONTIDE *n pl.* -S noon

NOONTIME *n pl.* -S noon

NOOSE *v* NOOSED, NOOSING, NOOSES to secure with a type of loop

NOOSER *n pl.* -S one that nooses

NOPAL *n pl.* -S a cactus

NOPE *adv* no

NOR *conj* and not

NORIA *n pl.* -S a type of waterwheel

NORITE *n pl.* -S a granular rock **NORITIC** *adj*

NORLAND *n pl.* -S a region in the north

NORM *n pl.* -S a standard regarded as typical for a specific group

NORMAL *n pl.* -S the usual or expected state or form

NORMALCY *n pl.* -CIES conformity with the norm

NORMALLY *adv* as a rule; usually

NORMED *adj* having a norm

NORMLESS *adj* having no norm

NORTH *n pl.* -S a point of the compass

NORTHER *n pl.* -S a wind or storm from the north

NORTHERN *n pl.* -S a person living in the north

NORTHING *n pl.* -S movement toward the north

NOSE *v* NOSED, NOSING, NOSES to sniff with the nose (the organ of smell)

NOSEBAG *n pl.* -S a feedbag

NOSEBAND *n pl.* -S a part of a horse's bridle

NOSED past tense of nose

NOSEGAY *n pl.* -GAYS a bouquet

NOSELESS *adj* having no nose

NOSELIKE *adj* resembling a nose

NOSEY *adj* NOSIER, NOSIEST nosy

NOSH *v* -ED, -ING, -ES to eat snacks between meals

NOSHER *n pl.* -S one that noshes

NOSIER comparative of nosy, nosey

NOSIEST superlative of nosy, nosey

NOSILY *adv* in a nosy manner

NOSINESS *n pl.* -ES the quality of being nosy

NOSING *n pl.* -S a projecting edge

NOSOLOGY *n pl.* -GIES a classification of diseases

NOSTOC *n pl.* -S a freshwater alga

NOSTRIL *n pl.* -S an external opening of the nose

NOSTRUM *n pl.* -S a medicine of one's own invention

NOSY *adj* NOSIER, NOSIEST unduly curious

NOT *adv* in no way

NOTA *pl.* of notum

NOTABLE *n pl.* -S a person of distinction

NOTABLY *adv* in a distinguished manner

NOTAL *adj* pertaining to a notum

NOTARIAL *adj* pertaining to a notary

NOTARIZE *v* -RIZED, -RIZING, -RIZES to certify through a notary

NOTARY *n pl.* -RIES a public officer who certifies documents

NOTATE *v* -TATED, -TATING, -TATES to put into notation

NOTATION *n pl.* -S a system of symbols

NOTCH *v* -ED, -ING, -ES to make an angular cut in

NOTCHER *n pl.* -S one that notches

NOTE *v* NOTED, NOTING, NOTES to write down

NOTEBOOK *n pl.* -S a book in which to write

NOTECASE *n pl.* -S a billfold

NOTED past tense of note

NOTEDLY *adv* in a famous manner

NOTELESS *adj* undistinguished

NOTER *n pl.* -S one that notes

NOTHING *n pl.* -S the absence of all quantity or magnitude

NOTICE *v* -TICED, -TICING, -TICES to become aware of

NOTIFIER *n pl.* -S one that notifies

NOTIFY *v* -FIED, -FYING, -FIES to inform

NOTING present participle of note

NOTION *n pl.* -S a general idea **NOTIONAL** *adj*

NOTORNIS *n pl.* NOTORNIS a flightless bird

NOTTURNO *n pl.* -NI a nocturne

NOTUM *n pl.* -TA a part of the thorax of an insect

NOUGAT *n pl.* -S a chewy candy

NOUGHT *n pl.* -S naught

NOUMENON *n pl.* -MENA an object of intellectual intuition **NOUMENAL** *adj*

NOUN *n pl.* -S a word used to denote the name of something **NOUNAL, NOUNLESS** *adj* **NOUNALLY** *adv*

NOURISH *v* -ED, -ING, -ES to sustain with food

NOUS *n pl.* -ES mind, reason, or intellect

NOVA *n pl.* -VAS or -VAE a type of star **NOVALIKE** *adj*

NOVATION *n pl.* -S the substitution of a new legal obligation for an old one

NOVEL *n pl.* -S a fictional prose narrative

NOVELISE *v* -ISED, -ISING, -ISES to novelize

NOVELIST *n pl.* -S a writer of novels

NOVELIZE *v* -IZED, -IZING, -IZES to put into the form of a novel

NOVELLA *n pl.* -LAS or -LE a short novel

NOVELLY *adv* in a new or unusual manner

NOVELTY *n pl.* -TIES something new or unusual

NOVENA *n pl.* -NAS or -NAE a religious devotion lasting nine days

NOVERCAL *adj* pertaining to a stepmother

NOVICE *n pl.* -S a person new to any field or activity

NOW *n pl.* -S the present time

NOWADAYS *adv* in these times

NOWAY *adv* in no way

NOWAYS *adv* noway

NOWHERE *n pl.* -S a nonexistent place

NOWISE *adv* not at all

NOWT *n pl.* -S naught

NOXIOUS *adj* harmful to health

NOYADE *n pl.* -S an execution by drowning

NOZZLE *n pl.* -S a projecting spout

NTH *adj* pertaining to an indefinitely large ordinal number

NU *n pl.* -S a Greek letter

NUANCE *n pl.* -S a slight variation **NUANCED** *adj*

NUB *n pl.* -S a protuberance or knob

NUBBIER comparative of nubby

NUBBIEST superlative of nubby

NUBBIN *n pl.* -S an undeveloped fruit

NUBBLE *n pl.* -S a small nub

NUBBLY *adj* -BLIER, -BLIEST having nubbles

NUBBY *adj* -BIER, -BIEST having nubs

NUBIA *n pl.* -S a woman's scarf

NUBILE *adj* suitable for marriage

NUBILITY *n pl.* -TIES the quality of being nubile

NUBILOSE *adj* nubilous

NUBILOUS *adj* cloudy

NUCELLUS *n pl.* -LI the essential part of a plant ovule **NUCELLAR** *adj*

NUCHA *n pl.* -CHAE the nape of the neck

NUCHAL *n pl.* -S an anatomical part lying in the region of the nape

NUCLEAL *adj* nuclear

NUCLEAR *adj* pertaining to a nucleus

NUCLEASE *n pl.* -S an enzyme

NUCLEATE *v* -ATED, -ATING, -ATES to form into a nucleus

NUCLEI a *pl.* of nucleus

NUCLEIN *n pl.* -S a protein found in nuclei

NUCLEOLE *n pl.* -S a part of a nucleus

NUCLEOLI *n/pl* nucleoles

NUCLEON *n pl.* -S an atomic particle

NUCLEUS *n pl.* -CLEI or -CLEUSES an essential part of a cell

NUCLIDE *n pl.* -S a species of atom **NUCLIDIC** *adj*

NUDE *adj* NUDER, NUDEST being without clothing or covering **NUDELY** *adv*

NUDE *n pl.* -S a nude figure

NUDENESS *n pl.* -ES nudity

NUDER comparative of nude

NUDEST superlative of nude

NUDGE *v* NUDGED, NUDGING, NUDGES to push gently

NUDGER *n pl.* -S one that nudges

NUDICAUL *adj* having leafless stems

NUDIE *n pl.* -S a movie featuring nude performers

NUDISM *n pl.* -S the practice of going nude

NUDIST *n pl.* -S an advocate of nudism

NUDITY *n pl.* -TIES the state of being nude

NUDNICK *n pl.* -S nudnik

NUDNIK   *n* pl. -S an annoying person

NUGATORY   *adj* having no power

NUGGET   *n* pl. -S a mass of solid matter **NUGGETY** *adj*

NUISANCE   *n* pl. -S a source of annoyance

NUKE   *n* pl. -S a nuclear weapon or power plant

NULL   *v* -ED, -ING, -S to reduce to nothing

NULLAH   *n* pl. -S a ravine

NULLIFY   *v* -FIED, -FYING, -FIES to make useless or ineffective

NULLITY   *n* pl. -TIES something of no legal force

NUMB   *adj* NUMBER, NUMBEST lacking sensation

NUMB   *v* -ED, -ING, -S to make numb

NUMBER   *v* -ED, -ING, -S to count

NUMBERER   *n* pl. -S one that numbers

NUMBFISH   *n* pl. -ES a fish capable of emitting electric shocks

NUMBLES   *n/pl* animal entrails

NUMBLY   *adv* in a numb manner

NUMBNESS   *n* pl. -ES the state of being numb

NUMEN   *n* pl. -MINA a deity

NUMERAL   *n* pl. -S a symbol that expresses a number

NUMERARY   *adj* pertaining to numbers

NUMERATE   *v* -ATED, -ATING, -ATES to count

NUMERIC   *n* pl. -S a numeral

NUMEROUS   *adj* many

NUMINA   pl. of numen

NUMINOUS   *n* pl. -ES the presence or revelation of the numen

NUMMARY   *adj* pertaining to coins

NUMMULAR   *adj* shaped like a coin

NUMSKULL   *n* pl. -S a dunce

NUN   *n* pl. -S a woman belonging to a religious order

NUNCIO   *n* pl. -CIOS an ambassador from the pope

NUNCLE   *n* pl. -S an uncle

NUNLIKE   *adj* resembling a nun

NUNNERY   *n* pl. -NERIES a religious house for nuns

NUNNISH   *adj* of, pertaining to, or characteristic of a nun

NUPTIAL   *n* pl. -S a wedding

NURL   *n* -ED, -ING, -S to knurl

NURSE   *v* NURSED, NURSING, NURSES to care for the sick or infirm

NURSER   *n* pl. -S a baby's bottle

NURSERY   *n* pl. -ERIES a room for young children

NURSING   *n* pl. -S the profession of one who nurses

NURSLING   *n* pl. -S an infant

NURTURE   *v* -TURED, -TURING, -TURES to nourish

NURTURER   *n* pl. -S one that nurtures

NUT   *v* NUTTED, NUTTING, NUTS to gather nuts (hard-shelled dry fruits)

NUTANT   *adj* drooping

NUTATE   *v* -TATED, -TATING, -TATES to exhibit nutation

NUTATION   *n* pl. -S an oscillatory movement of the axis of a rotating body

NUTBROWN   *adj* of a dark brown

NUTGALL   *n* pl. -S a gallnut

NUTGRASS   *n* pl. -ES a perennial herb

NUTHATCH   *n* pl. -ES a small bird

NUTHOUSE   *n* pl. -S an insane asylum

NUTLET   *n* pl. -S a small nut

NUTLIKE   *adj* resembling a nut

NUTMEAT   *n* pl. -S the edible kernel of a nut

NUTMEG   *n* pl. -S an aromatic seed used as a spice

NUTPICK   *n* pl. -S a device for extracting the kernels from nuts

NUTRIA   *n* pl. -S the coypu

NUTRIENT   *n* pl. -S a nourishing substance

NUTSEDGE   *n* pl. -S nutgrass

NUTSHELL   *n* pl. -S the shell of a nut

NUTTED   past tense of nut

NUTTER   *n* pl. -S one that gathers nuts

NUTTING   present participle of nut

NUTTY   *adj* -TIER, -TIEST abounding in nuts **NUTTILY** *adv*

NUTWOOD   *n* pl. -S a nut-bearing tree

NUZZLE   *v* -ZLED, -ZLING, -ZLES to push with the nose

NYALA   *n* pl. -S an antelope

NYLGHAI   *n* pl. -S nilgai

NYLGHAU   *n* pl. -S nilgai

NYLON   *n* pl. -S a synthetic material

NYMPH   *n* pl. -S a female spirit **NYMPHAL, NYMPHEAN** *adj*

NYMPHA   *n* pl. -PHAE a fold of the vulva

NYMPHET   *n* pl. -S a young nymph

NYMPHO   *n* pl. -PHOS a woman obsessed by sexual desire

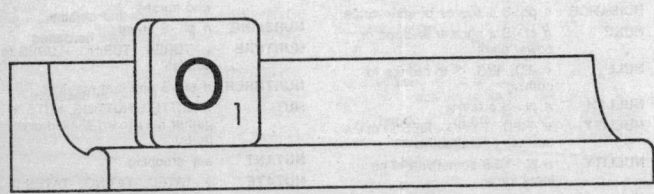

OAF	n pl. OAFS or OAVES a clumsy, stupid person **OAFISH** adj **OAFISHLY** adv		**OBEDIENT**	adj obeying or willing to obey
			OBEISANT	adj showing reverence or respect
OAK	n pl. -S a hardwood tree or shrub **OAKEN, OAKLIKE** adj		**OBELI**	pl. of obelus
			OBELIA	n pl. -S a marine hydroid
OAKMOSS	n pl. -ES a lichen that grows on oak trees		**OBELISE**	v -LISED, -LISING, -LISES to obelize
OAKUM	n pl. -S loosely twisted hemp fiber		**OBELISK**	n pl. -S a four-sided shaft of stone with a pyramidal top
OAR	v -ED, -ING, -S to propel with oars (long, broad-bladed poles)		**OBELISM**	n pl. -S the act of obelizing
			OBELIZE	v -LIZED, -LIZING, -LIZES to mark with an obelus
OARFISH	n pl. -ES a marine fish		
OARLESS	adj having no oars		**OBELUS**	n pl. -LI a symbol used in ancient manuscripts to indicate a doubtful passage
OARLIKE	adj resembling an oar		
OARLOCK	n pl. -S a device for holding an oar in place		
			OBESE	adj very fat **OBESELY** adv
OARSMAN	n pl. -MEN a person who rows a boat		**OBESITY**	n pl. -TIES the state or condition of being obese
OASIS	n pl. OASES a green area in a desert region		**OBEY**	v -ED, -ING, -S to follow the commands or guidance of **OBEYABLE** adj
OAST	n pl. -S a type of kiln		
OAT	n pl. -S a cereal grass		**OBEYER**	n pl. -S one that obeys
OATCAKE	n pl. -S a cake made of oatmeal		**OBI**	n pl. -S obeah
			OBIA	n pl. -S obeah
OATEN	adj pertaining to oats		**OBIISM**	n pl. -S obeahism
OATER	n pl. -S a cowboy movie		**OBIT**	n pl. -S an obituary
OATH	n pl. -S a formal declaration or promise to fulfill a pledge		**OBITUARY**	n pl. -ARIES a published notice of a death
OATLIKE	adj resembling oats		
OATMEAL	n pl. -S meal made from oats		**OBJECT**	v -ED, -ING, -S to argue in opposition
OAVES	a pl. of oaf		
OBDURACY	n pl. -CIES the quality or an instance of being obdurate		**OBJECTOR**	n pl. -S one that objects
			OBLAST	n pl. -LASTS or -LASTI an administrative division of the Soviet Union
OBDURATE	adj stubborn		
OBE	n pl. -S obeah		
OBEAH	n pl. -S a form of sorcery of African origin		**OBLATE**	n pl. -S a layman residing in a monastery
OBEAHISM	n pl. -S the use of obeah		**OBLATELY**	adv elliptically

OBLATION *n pl.* -S the act of making a religious offering **OBLATORY** *adj*

OBLIGATE *v* -GATED, -GATING, -GATES to oblige

OBLIGATO *n pl.* -TI or -TOS an important musical part

OBLIGE *v* OBLIGED, OBLIGING, OBLIGES to put in one's debt by a favor or service

OBLIGEE *n pl.* -S one that is obliged

OBLIGER *n pl.* -S one that obliges

OBLIGING present participle of oblige

OBLIGOR *n pl.* -S one who places himself under a legal obligation

OBLIQUE *v* OBLIQUED, OBLIQUING, OBLIQUES to slant

OBLIVION *n pl.* -S the state of being forgotten; the act of forgetting

OBLONG *n pl.* -S something that is oblong (elongated)

OBLONGLY *adv* in an oblong manner

OBLOQUY *n pl.* -QUIES abusive language

OBOE *n pl.* -S a woodwind instrument

OBOIST *n pl.* -S one who plays the oboe

OBOL *n pl.* -S a coin of ancient Greece

OBOLE *n pl.* -S a coin of medieval France

OBOLUS *n pl.* -LI an obol

OBOVATE *adj* ovate with the narrow end at the base

OBOVOID *adj* ovoid with the narrow end at the base

OBSCENE *adj* -SCENER, -SCENEST indecent

OBSCURE *adj* -SCURER, -SCUREST dark or indistinct

OBSCURE *v* -SCURED, -SCURING, -SCURES to make obscure

OBSEQUY *n pl.* -QUIES a funeral rite

OBSERVE *v* -SERVED, -SERVING, -SERVES to look attentively

OBSERVER *n pl.* -S one that observes

OBSESS *v* -ED, -ING, -ES to dominate the thoughts of

OBSESSOR *n pl.* -S something that obsesses

OBSIDIAN *n pl.* -S a volcanic glass

OBSOLETE *v* -LETED, -LETING, -LETES to make out-of-date

OBSTACLE *n pl.* -S something that obstructs

OBSTRUCT *v* -ED, -ING, -S to get in the way of

OBTAIN *v* -ED, -ING, -S to gain possession of

OBTAINER *n pl.* -S one that obtains

OBTECT *adj* covered by a hardened secretion

OBTECTED *adj* obtect

OBTEST *v* -ED, -ING, -S to beseech

OBTRUDE *v* -TRUDED, -TRUDING, -TRUDES to thrust forward

OBTRUDER *n pl.* -S one that obtrudes

OBTUND *v* -ED, -ING, -S to deaden

OBTURATE *v* -RATED, -RATING, -RATES to close or stop up

OBTUSE *adj* -TUSER, -TUSEST dull **OBTUSELY** *adv*

OBVERSE *n pl.* -S the side of a coin bearing the main design

OBVERT *v* -ED, -ING, -S to turn so as to show a different surface

OBVIATE *v* -ATED, -ATING, -ATES to prevent or eliminate by effective measures **OBVIABLE** *adj*

OBVIATOR *n pl.* -S one that obviates

OBVIOUS *adj* easily perceived or understood

OBVOLUTE *adj* rolled or tuned in

OCA *n pl.* -S a South American herb

OCARINA *n pl.* -S a wind instrument

OCCASION *v* -ED, -ING, -S to cause

OCCIDENT *n pl.* -S the west

OCCIPUT *n pl.* -PITA or -PUTS the back part of the skull

OCCLUDE *v* -CLUDED, -CLUDING, -CLUDES to close or stop up

OCCLUSAL *adj* pertaining to the biting surface of a tooth

OCCULT *v* -ED, -ING, -S to conceal

OCCULTER *n pl* -S one that occults

OCCULTLY *adv* secretly

OCCUPANT *n pl.* -S a resident

OCCUPIER *n pl.* -S one that occupies

OCCUPY *v* -PIED, -PYING, -PIES to engage the attention or energies of

OCCUR *v* -CURRED, -CURRING, -CURS to take place

OCEAN *n pl.* -S the vast body of salt water that covers most of the earth's surface **OCEANIC** *adj*

OCELLAR *adj* pertaining to an ocellus

OCELLATE *adj* having ocelli

OCELLUS *n* pl. -LI a minute simple eye

OCELOT *n* pl. -S an American wildcat
OCELOID *adj*

OCHER *v* -ED, -ING, -S to color with ocher (a red or yellow iron ore used as a pigment)

OCHEROUS *adj* containing or resembling ocher

OCHERY *adj* ocherous

OCHONE *interj* — used to express grief

OCHRE *v* OCHRED, OCHRING, OCHRES to ocher

OCHREA *n* pl. -REAE ocrea

OCHREOUS *adj* ocherous

OCHRING present participle of ochre

OCHROID *adj* ocherous

OCHROUS *adj* ocherous

OCHRY *adj* ochery

OCOTILLO *n* pl. -LOS a Mexican shrub

OCREA *n* pl. -REAE a sheathing plant part

OCREATE *adj* having ocrea

OCTAD *n* pl. -S a group of eight
OCTADIC *adj*

OCTAGON *n* pl. -S an eight-sided polygon

OCTAL *adj* pertaining to a number system with a base of eight

OCTANE *n* pl. -S a liquid hydrocarbon

OCTANGLE *n* pl. -S an octagon

OCTANT *n* pl. -S an eighth of a circle
OCTANTAL *adj*

OCTARCHY *n* pl. -TARCHIES a government by eight persons

OCTAVE *n* pl. -S a type of musical interval **OCTAVAL** *adj*

OCTAVO *n* pl. -VOS a page size

OCTET *n* pl. -S a group of eight

OCTETTE *n* pl. -S octet

OCTONARY *n* pl. -NARIES a stanza of eight lines

OCTOPI a pl. of octopus

OCTOPOD *n* pl. -S any of an order of eight-armed mollusks

OCTOPUS *n* pl. -PUSES, -PI, or -PODES a nocturnal octopod

OCTOROON *n* pl. -S a person of one-eighth black ancestry

OCTROI *n* pl. -S a tax on certain articles brought into a city

OCTUPLE *v* -PLED, -PLING, -PLES to multiply by eight

OCTUPLET *n* pl. -S a group of eight related items

OCTUPLEX *adj* being eight times as great

OCTUPLING present participle of octuple

OCTUPLY *adv* to eight times the degree

OCTYL *n* pl. -S a univalent radical

OCULAR *n* pl. -S an eyepiece

OCULARLY *adv* by means of the eyes or sight

OCULIST *n* pl. -S a physician who treats diseases of the eye

OD *n* pl. -S a hypothetical force of natural power

ODALISK *n* pl. -S a female slave in a harem

ODD *adj* ODDER, ODDEST unusual

ODD *n* pl. -S one that is odd

ODDBALL *n* pl. -S an eccentric person

ODDISH *adj* somewhat odd

ODDITY *n* pl. -TIES one that is odd

ODDLY *adv* in an odd manner

ODDMENT *n* pl. -S a remnant

ODDNESS *n* pl. -ES the state of being odd

ODE *n* pl. -S a lyric poem

ODEON *n* pl. -S odeum

ODEUM *n* pl. ODEA a theater or concert hall

ODIC *adj* pertaining to an ode

ODIOUS *adj* deserving or causing hatred
ODIOUSLY *adv*

ODIUM *n* pl. -S hatred

ODOGRAPH *n* pl. -S an odometer

ODOMETER *n* pl. -S a device for measuring distance traveled

ODOMETRY *n* pl. -TRIES the process of using an odometer

ODONATE *n* pl. -S any of an order of predacious insects

ODONTOID *n* pl. -S a toothlike vertebral projection

ODOR *n* pl. -S the property of a substance that affects the sense of smell ODORED, ODORFUL *adj*

ODORANT *n* pl. -S an odorous substance

ODORIZE *v* -IZED, -IZING, -IZES to make odorous

ODORLESS *adj* having no odor

ODOROUS *adj* having an odor

ODOUR *n* pl. -S odor ODOURFUL *adj*

ODYL *n* pl. -S an od

ODYLE *n* pl. -S odyl

ODYSSEY *n* pl. -SEYS a long, wandering journey

OE *n* pl. -S a whirlwind off the Faeroe islands

OECOLOGY *n* pl. -GIES ecology

OEDEMA *n* pl. -MAS or -MATA edema

OEDIPAL *adj* pertaining to the libidinal feelings in a child toward the parent of the opposite sex

OEDIPEAN *adj* oedipal

OEILLADE *n* pl. -S an amorous look

OENOLOGY *n* pl. -GIES the study of wines

OENOMEL *n* pl. -S an ancient Greek beverage of wine and honey

OERSTED *n* pl. -S a unit of magnetic intensity

OESTRIN *n* pl. -S estrin

OESTRIOL *n* pl. -S estriol

OESTRONE *n* pl. -S estrone

OESTROUS *adj* estrous

OESTRUM *n* pl. -S estrum

OESTRUS *n* pl. -ES estrus

OEUVRE *n* pl. -S a work of art

OF *prep* coming from

OFAY *n* pl. OFAYS a white person — an offensive term

OFF *v* -ED, -ING, -S to go away

OFFAL *n* pl. -S waste material

OFFBEAT *n* pl. -S an unaccented beat in a musical measure

OFFCAST *n* pl. -S a castoff

OFFENCE *n* pl. -S offense

OFFEND *v* -ED, -ING, -S to commit an offense

OFFENDER *n* pl. -S one that offends

OFFENSE *n* pl. -S a violation of a moral or social code

OFFER *v* -ED, -ING, -S to present for acceptance or rejection

OFFERER *n* pl. -S one that offers

OFFERING *n* pl. -S a contribution

OFFEROR *n* pl. -S offeror

OFFHAND *adv* without preparation

OFFICE *n* pl. -S a position of authority

OFFICER *v* -ED, -ING, -S to furnish with officers (persons holding positions of authority)

OFFICIAL *n* pl. -S one that holds a position of authority

OFFING *n* pl. -S the near future

OFFISH *adj* aloof OFFISHLY *adv*

OFFLOAD *v* -ED, -ING, -S to unload

OFFPRINT *v* -ED, -ING, -S to reprint an excerpt

OFFSET *v* -SET, -SETTING, -SETS to compensate for

OFFSHOOT *n* pl. -S a lateral shoot from a main stem

OFFSHORE *adv* away from the shore

OFFSIDE *adj* being illegally in front of the ball in football

OFFSTAGE *adj* being on a part of the stage not visible to the audience

OFT *adv* OFTER, OFTEST often

OFTEN *adv* -ENER, -ENEST frequently

OFTTIMES *adv* often

OGAM *n* pl. -S ogham

OGDOAD *n* pl. -S a group of eight

OGEE *n* pl. -S an S-shaped molding

OGHAM *n* pl. -S an Old Irish alphabet OGHAMIC *adj*

OGHAMIST *n* pl. -S one who writes in ogham

OGIVE *n* pl. -S a pointed arch OGIVAL *adj*

OGLE *v* OGLED, OGLING, OGLES to stare at

OGLER *n* pl. -S one that ogles

OGRE *n* pl. -S a monster

OGREISH *adj* resembling an ogre

OGREISM *n* pl. -S the state of being ogreish

OGRESS *n* pl. -ES a female ogre

OGRISH *adj* ogreish OGRISHLY *adv*

OGRISM *n* pl. -S ogreism

OH *v* -ED, -ING, -S to exclaim in surprise, pain, or desire

OHIA *n* pl. -S lehua

OHM *n* pl. -S a unit of electrical resistance OHMIC *adj*

OHMAGE *n* pl. -S electrical resistance expressed in ohms

OHMMETER *n* pl. -S an instrument for measuring ohmage

OHO *interj* — used to express surprise or exultation

OIDIUM *n* pl. OIDIA a type of fungus

OIL *v* -ED, -ING, -S to supply with oil (a greasy liquid used for lubrication, fuel, or illumination)

OILBIRD *n* pl. -S a tropical bird

OILCAMP *n* pl. -S a living area for workers at an oil well

OILCAN *n* pl. -S a can for applying lubricating oil

OILCLOTH *n* pl. -S a waterproof fabric

OILCUP *n* pl. -S a closed cup for supplying lubricant

OILER *n* pl. -S one that oils

OILHOLE *n* pl. -S a hole through which lubricating oil is injected

OILIER comparative of oily

OILIEST superlative of oily

OILILY *adv* in an oily manner

OILINESS *n* pl. -ES the state of being oily

OILMAN *n* pl. -MEN one who owns or operates oil wells

OILPAPER *n* pl. -S a water-resistant paper

OILPROOF *adj* impervious to oil

OILSEED *n* pl. -S a seed from which oil is pressed out

OILSKIN *n* pl. -S a waterproof fabric

OILSTONE *n* pl. -S a stone for sharpening tools

OILTIGHT *adj* being so tight as to prevent the passage of oil

OILWAY *n* pl. -WAYS a channel for the passage of oil

OILY *adj* OILIER, OILIEST covered or soaked with oil

OINK *v* -ED, -ING, -S to utter the natural grunt of a hog

OINOLOGY *n* pl. -GIES oenology

OINOMEL *n* pl. -S oenomel

OINTMENT *n* pl. -S a viscous preparation applied to the skin as a medicine or cosmetic

OITICICA *n* pl. -S a South American tree

OKA *n* pl. -S a Turkish unit of weight

OKAPI *n* pl. -S an African ruminant mammal

OKAY *v* -ED, -ING, -S to approve

OKE *n* pl. -S oka

OKEH *n* pl. -S approval

OKEYDOKE *adj* perfectly all right

OKRA *n* pl. -S a tall annual herb

OLD *adj* OLDER, OLDEST or ELDER, ELDEST living or existing for a relatively long time

OLD *n* pl. -S an individual of a specified age

OLDEN *adj* pertaining to a bygone era

OLDIE *n* pl. -S a popular song of an earlier day

OLDISH *adj* somewhat old

OLDNESS *n* pl. -ES the state of being old

OLDSTER *n* pl. -S an old person

OLDSTYLE *n* pl. -S a style of printing type

OLDWIFE *n* pl. -WIVES a marine fish

OLE *n* pl. -S a shout of approval

OLEA pl. of oleum

OLEANDER *n* pl. -S a flowering shrub

OLEASTER *n* pl. -S a flowering shrub

OLEATE *n* pl. -S a chemical salt

OLEFIN *n* pl. -S an alkene OLEFINIC *adj*

OLEFINE *n* pl. -S olefin

OLEIC *adj* pertaining to oil

OLEIN *n* pl. -S the liquid portion of a fat

OLEINE *n* pl. -S olein

OLEO *n* pl. OLEOS margarine

OLEUM *n* pl. OLEA oil

OLEUM *n* pl. -S a corrosive liquid

OLIBANUM *n* pl. -S a fragrant resin

OLIGARCH *n* pl. -S a ruler in a government by the few

OLIGOMER *n* pl. -S a type of polymer

OLIO *n* pl. OLIOS a miscellaneous collection

OLIVARY *adj* shaped like an olive

OLIVE *n* pl. -S the small oval fruit of a Mediterranean tree

OLIVINE *n* pl. -S a mineral OLIVINIC *adj*

OLLA *n* pl. -S a wide-mouthed pot or jar

OLOGIST *n* pl. -S an expert in a particular ology

OLOGY *n* pl. -GIES a branch of knowledge

OLYMPIAD *n* pl. -S a celebration of the Olympic Games

OM *n* pl. -S a mantra used in contemplation of ultimate reality

OMASUM *n* pl. -SA the third stomach of a ruminant

OMBER *n* pl. -S ombre

OMBRE *n* pl. -S a card game

OMEGA *n* pl. -S a Greek letter

OMELET *n* pl. -S a dish of beaten eggs cooked and folded around a filling

OMELETTE *n* pl. -S omelet

OMEN *v* -ED, -ING, -S to be an omen (a prophetic sign) of

OMENTUM *n* pl. -TA or -TUMS a fold in an abdominal membrane OMENTAL *adj*

OMER *n* pl. -S a Hebrew unit of dry measure

OMICRON *n* pl. -S a Greek letter

OMIKRON *n pl.* -S omicron

OMINOUS *adj* portending evil

OMISSION *n pl.* -S something left undone

OMISSIVE *adj* marked by omission

OMIT *v* OMITTED, OMITTING, OMITS to leave out

OMNIARCH *n pl.* -S an almighty ruler

OMNIBUS *n pl.* -ES a bus

OMNIFIC *adj* unlimited in creative power

OMNIFORM *adj* of all forms

OMNIMODE *adj* of all modes

OMNIVORA *n/pl* omnivores

OMNIVORE *n pl.* -S an animal that eats all kinds of food

OMOPHAGY *n pl.* -GIES the eating of raw flesh

OMPHALOS *n pl.* -LI a central point

ON *n pl.* -S the side of the wicket where a batsman stands in cricket

ONAGER *n pl.* -GERS or -GRI a wild ass of central Asia

ONANISM *n pl.* -S coitus deliberately interrupted to prevent insemination

ONANIST *n pl.* -S one who practices onanism

ONCE *n pl.* -S one single time

ONCIDIUM *n pl.* -S a tropical orchid

ONCOLOGY *n pl.* -GIES the science of tumors

ONCOMING *n pl.* -S an approach

ONDOGRAM *n pl.* -S a graph of electric wave forms

ONE *n pl.* -S a number

ONEFOLD *adj* constituting a single, undivided whole

ONEIRIC *adj* pertaining to dreams

ONENESS *n pl.* -ES unity

ONEROUS *adj* burdensome or oppressive

ONERY *adj* -ERIER, -ERIEST ornery

ONESELF *pron* a person's self

ONETIME *adj* former

ONGOING *adj* continuing without interruption

ONION *n pl.* -S the edible bulb of a cultivated herb

ONIUM *adj* characterized by a complex cation

ONLOOKER *n pl.* -S a spectator

ONLY *adv* with nothing or no one else

ONRUSH *n pl.* -ES a forward rush or flow

ONSET *n pl.* -S a beginning

ONSHORE *adv* toward the shore

ONSIDE *adj* not offside

ONSTAGE *adj* being on a part of the stage visible to the audience

ONTIC *adj* having real being or existence

ONTO *prep* to a position upon

ONTOGENY *n pl.* -NIES the development of an individual organism

ONTOLOGY *n pl.* -GIES the branch of philosophy that deals with being

ONUS *n pl.* -ES a burden or responsibility

ONWARD *adv* toward a point ahead or in front

ONWARDS *adv* onward

ONYX *n pl.* -ES a variety of quartz

OOCYST *n pl.* -S a zygote

OOCYTE *n pl.* -S an egg before maturation

OODLES *n pl.* OODLES a large amount

OODLINS *n pl.* OODLINS oodles

OOGAMETE *n pl.* -S a female gamete of certain protozoa

OOGAMOUS *adj* having structurally dissimilar gametes

OOGAMY *n pl.* -MIES the state of being oogamous

OOGENY *n pl.* -NIES the development of ova

OOGONIUM *n pl.* -NIA or -NIUMS a female sexual organ in certain algae and fungi OOGONIAL *adj*

OOH *v* -ED, -ING, -S to exclaim in amazement, joy, or surprise

OOLACHAN *n pl.* -S eulachon

OOLITE *n pl.* -S a variety of limestone OOLITIC *adj*

OOLITH *n pl.* -S oolite

OOLOGIST *n pl.* -S an expert in oology

OOLOGY *n pl.* -GIES the study of birds' eggs OOLOGIC *adj*

OOLONG *n pl.* -S a dark Chinese tea

OOMIAC *n pl.* -S umiak

OOMIACK *n pl.* -S umiak

OOMIAK *n pl.* -S umiak

OOMPH *n pl.* -S spirited vigor

OOPHYTE *n pl.* -S a stage of development in certain plants OOPHYTIC *adj*

OOPS *interj* — used to express mild apology, surprise, or dismay

OORALI *n pl.* -S curare

OORIE *adj* ourie

OOSPERM *n pl.* -S a fertilized egg

OOSPHERE *n pl.* -S an unfertilized egg within an oogonium

OOSPORE *n pl.* -S a fertilized egg within an oogonium OOSPORIC *adj*

OOT *n pl.* -S out

OOTHECA *n pl.* -CAE an egg case of certain insects OOTHECAL *adj*

OOTID *n pl.* -S one of the four sections into which a mature ovum divides

OOZE *v* OOZED, OOZING, OOZES to flow or leak out slowly

OOZINESS *n pl.* -ES the state of being oozy

OOZY *adj* OOZIER, OOZIEST containing or resembling soft mud or slime OOZILY *adv*

OP *n pl.* -S a style of abstract art

OPACIFY *v* -FIED, -FYING, -FIES to make opaque

OPACITY *n pl.* -TIES something that is opaque

OPAH *n pl.* -S a marine fish

OPAL *n pl.* -S a mineral

OPALESCE *v* -ESCED, -ESCING, -ESCES to emit an iridescent shimmer of colors

OPALINE *n pl.* -S an opaque white glass

OPAQUE *adj* OPAQUER, OPAQUEST impervious to light OPAQUELY *adv*

OPAQUE *v* OPAQUED, OPAQUING, OPAQUES to make opaque

OPE *v* OPED, OPING, OPES to open

OPEN *adj* OPENER, OPENEST affording unobstructed access, passage, or view

OPEN *v* -ED, -ING, -S to cause to become open OPENABLE *adj*

OPENER *n pl.* -S one that opens

OPENING *n pl.* -S a vacant or unobstructed space

OPENLY *adv* in an open manner

OPENNESS *n pl.* -ES the state of being open

OPENWORK *n pl.* -S ornamental or structural work containing numerous openings

OPERA *n pl.* -S a form of musical drama

OPERABLE *adj* usable OPERABLY *adv*

OPERAND *n pl.* -S a quantity on which a mathematical operation is performed

OPERANT *n pl.* -S one that operates

OPERATE *v* -ATED, -ATING, -ATES to perform a function

OPERATIC *n pl.* -S the technique of staging operas

OPERATOR *n pl.* -S a symbol that represents a mathematical function

OPERCELE *n pl.* -S opercule

OPERCULA *n/pl* opercules

OPERCULE *n pl.* -S an anatomical part that serves as a lid or cover

OPERETTA *n pl.* -S a light musical drama with spoken dialogue

OPERON *n pl.* -S a type of gene cluster

OPEROSE *adj* involving great labor

OPHIDIAN *n pl.* -S a snake

OPHITE *n pl.* -S an igneous rock OPHITIC *adj*

OPIATE *v* -ATED, -ATING, -ATES to treat with opium

OPINE *v* OPINED, OPINING, OPINES to hold or state as an opinion

OPING present participle of ope

OPINION *n pl.* -S a conclusion or judgment one holds to be true

OPIUM *n pl.* -S an addictive narcotic

OPIUMISM *n pl.* -S opium addiction

OPOSSUM *n pl.* -S an arboreal mammal

OPPIDAN *n pl.* -S a townsman

OPPILATE *v* -LATED, -LATING, -LATES to obstruct OPPILANT *adj*

OPPONENT *n pl.* -S one that opposes another

OPPOSE *v* -POSED, -POSING, -POSES to be in contention or conflict with

OPPOSER *n pl.* -S one that opposes

OPPOSITE *n pl.* -S one that is radically different from another in some related way

OPPRESS *v* -ED, -ING, -ES to burden by abuse of power or authority

OPPUGN *v* -ED, -ING, -S to assail with argument

OPPUGNER *n pl.* -S one that oppugns

OPSIN *n pl.* -S a type of protein

OPSONIC *adj* pertaining to opsonin

OPSONIFY *v* -FIED, -FYING, -FIES to opsonize

OPSONIN *n* pl. -S an antibody of blood serum

OPSONIZE *v* -NIZED, -NIZING, -NIZES to form opsonins in

OPT *v* -ED, -ING, -S to choose

OPTATIVE *n* pl. -S a mood of verbs that expresses a wish or desire

OPTIC *n* pl. -S an eye

OPTICAL *adj* pertaining to sight

OPTICIAN *n* pl. -S one who makes or deals in optical goods

OPTICIST *n* pl. -S one engaged in the study of light and vision

OPTIMA *a* pl. of optimum

OPTIMAL *adj* most desirable

OPTIME *n* pl. -S an honor student in mathematics at Cambridge University

OPTIMISE *v* -MISED, -MISING, -MISES to optimize

OPTIMISM *n* pl. -S a disposition to look on the favorable side of things

OPTIMIST *n* pl. -S one who exhibits optimism

OPTIMIZE *v* -MIZED, -MIZING, -MIZES to make as perfect, useful, or effective as possible

OPTIMUM *n* pl. -MA or -MUMS the most favorable condition for obtaining a given result

OPTION *v* -ED, -ING, -S to grant an option (a right to buy or sell something at a specified price within a specified time) on

OPTIONAL *n* pl. -S an elective course of study

OPTIONEE *n* pl. -S one who holds a legal option

OPULENCE *n* pl. -S wealth

OPULENCY *n* pl. -CIES opulence

OPULENT *adj* wealthy

OPUNTIA *n* pl. -S an American cactus

OPUS *n* pl. OPERA or OPUSES a literary or musical work

OPUSCULA *n/pl* opuscules

OPUSCULE *n* pl. -S a minor work

OQUASSA *n* pl. -S a small lake trout

OR *n* pl. -S the heraldic color gold

ORA pl. of os

ORACH *n* pl. -ES a cultivated plant

ORACHE *n* pl. -S orach

ORACLE *n* pl. -S a person through whom a deity is believed to speak **ORACULAR** *adj*

ORAL *n* pl. -S an examination requiring spoken answers

ORALITY *n* pl. -TIES the state of being produced orally

ORALLY *adv* through the mouth

ORANG *n* pl. -S a large ape

ORANGE *n* pl. -S a citrus fruit

ORANGERY *n* pl. -RIES a place where orange trees are cultivated

ORANGEY *adj* -ANGIER, -ANGIEST orangy

ORANGISH *adj* of a somewhat orange color

ORANGY *adj* -ANGIER, -ANGIEST resembling or suggestive of an orange

ORATE *v* ORATED, ORATING, ORATES to speak formally

ORATION *n* pl. -S a formal speech

ORATOR *n* pl. -S one that orates

ORATORIO *n* pl. -RIOS a type of musical composition

ORATORY *n* pl. -RIES the art of public speaking

ORATRESS *n* pl. -ES oratrix

ORATRIX *n* pl. -TRICES a female orator

ORB *v* -ED, -ING, -S to form into a circle or sphere

ORBIT *v* -ED, -ING, -S to move or revolve around

ORBITAL *n* pl. -S a subdivision of a nuclear shell

ORBITER *n* pl. -S one that orbits

ORC *n* pl. -S a marine mammal

ORCA *n* pl. -S orc

ORCEIN *n* pl. -S a reddish brown dye

ORCHARD *n* pl. -S an area for the cultivation of fruit trees

ORCHID *n* pl. -S a flowering plant

ORCHIL *n* pl. -S a purple dye

ORCHIS *n* pl. -CHISES an orchid

ORCHITIS *n* pl. -TISES inflammation of the testicle **ORCHITIC** *adj*

ORCIN *n* pl. -S orcinol

ORCINOL *n* pl. -S a chemical compound

ORDAIN *v* -ED, -ING, -S to invest with holy authority

ORDAINER *n* pl. -S one that ordains

ORDEAL *n* pl. -S a severely difficult or painful experience

ORDER *v* -ED, -ING, -S to give a command or instruction to

ORDERER *n* pl. -S one that orders

ORDERLY *n* pl. -LIES a male attendant

ORDINAL *n* pl. -S a number designating position in a series

ORDINAND *n* pl. -S a person about to be ordained

ORDINARY *adj* -NARIER, -NARIEST of a kind to be expected in the normal order of events

ORDINARY *n* pl. -NARIES something that is ordinary

ORDINATE *n* pl. -S a particular geometric coordinate

ORDINES a pl. of ordo

ORDNANCE *n* pl. -S artillery; a cannon

ORDO *n* pl. -DINES or -DOS a calendar of religious directions

ORDURE *n* pl. -S manure

ORE *n* pl. -S a mineral or rock containing a valuable metal

OREAD *n* pl. -S a mountain nymph in Greek mythology

ORECTIC *adj* pertaining to appetites or desires

ORECTIVE *adj* orectic

OREGANO *n* pl. -NOS an aromatic herb used as a seasoning

OREIDE *n* pl. -S oroide

ORFRAY *n* pl. -FRAYS orphrey

ORGAN *n* pl. -S a differentiated part of an organism performing a specific function

ORGANA a pl. of organon and organum

ORGANDIE *n* pl. -S organdy

ORGANDY *n* pl. -DIES a cotton fabric

ORGANIC *n* pl. -S a substance of animal or vegetable origin

ORGANISE *v* -NISED, -NISING, -NISES to organize

ORGANISM *n* pl. -S any form of animal or plant life

ORGANIST *n* pl. -S one who plays the organ (a keyboard musical instrument)

ORGANIZE *v* -NIZED, -NIZING, -NIZES to form into an orderly whole

ORGANON *n* pl. -GANA or -GANONS a system of rules for scientific investigation

ORGANUM *n* pl. -GANA or -GANUMS organon

ORGANZA *n* pl. -S a sheer fabric

ORGASM *n* pl. -S the climax of sexual excitement **ORGASMIC**, **ORGASTIC** *adj*

ORGEAT *n* pl. -S an almond-flavored syrup

ORGIAC *adj* of the nature of an orgy

ORGIC *adj* orgiac

ORGULOUS *adj* proud

ORGY *n* pl. -GIES a party marked by unrestrained sexual indulgence

ORIBATID *n* pl. -S any of a family of eyeless mites

ORIBI *n* pl. -S an African antelope

ORIEL *n* pl. -S a type of projecting window

ORIENT *v* -ED, -ING, -S to adjust in relation to something else

ORIENTAL *n* pl. -S an inhabitant of an eastern country

ORIFICE *n* pl. -S a mouth or mouthlike opening

ORIGAMI *n* pl. -S the Japanese art of paper folding

ORIGAN *n* pl. -S marjoram

ORIGANUM *n* pl. -S an aromatic herb

ORIGIN *n* pl. -S a coming into being

ORIGINAL *n* pl. -S the first form of something

ORINASAL *n* pl. -S a sound pronounced through both the mouth and nose

ORIOLE *n* pl. -S an American songbird

ORISON *n* pl. -S a prayer

ORLE *n* pl. -S a heraldic border

ORLOP *n* pl. -S the lowest deck of a ship

ORMER *n* pl. -S an abalone

ORMOLU *n* pl. -S an alloy used to imitate gold

ORNAMENT *v* -ED, -ING, -S to decorate

ORNATE *adj* elaborately or excessively ornamented **ORNATELY** *adv*

ORNERY *adj* -NERIER, -NERIEST stubborn and mean-spirited

ORNIS *n* pl. ORNITHES avifauna

ORNITHIC *adj* pertaining to birds

OROGENY *n* pl. -NIES the process of mountain formation **OROGENIC** *adj*

OROIDE *n* pl. -S an alloy used to imitate gold

OROLOGY *n* pl. -GIES the study of mountains

OROMETER *n* pl. -S a type of barometer

OROTUND *adj* full and clear in sound

ORPHAN *v* -ED, -ING, -S to deprive of both parents

ORPHIC *adj* mystical

ORPHICAL *adj* orphic

ORPHREY *n pl.* -PHREYS an ornamental band or border

ORPIMENT *n pl.* -S a yellow dye

ORPIN *n pl.* -S orpine

ORPINE *n pl.* -S a perennial herb

ORRA *adj* occasional

ORRERY *n pl.* -RERIES a mechanical model of the solar system

ORRICE *n pl.* -S orris

ORRIS *n pl.* -RISES a flowering plant

ORT *n pl.* -S a scrap of food

ORTHICON *n pl.* -S a type of television camera tube

ORTHO *adj* pertaining to reproduction in a photograph of the full range of colors in nature

ORTHODOX *n pl.* -ES one holding traditional beliefs

ORTHOEPY *n pl.* -EPIES the study of correct pronunciation

ORTHOTIC *adj* pertaining to the bracing of weak joints or muscles

ORTOLAN *n pl.* -S a European bird

ORYX *n pl.* -ES an African antelope

OS *n pl.* -S an orifice

OS *n pl.* OSSA a bone

OS *n pl.* OSAR an esker

OSCINE *n pl.* -S any of a family of songbirds OSCININE *adj*

OSCITANT *adj* yawning

OSCULA *pl.* of osculum

OSCULANT *adj* adhering closely

OSCULAR *adj* pertaining to the mouth

OSCULATE *v* -LATED, -LATING, -LATES to kiss

OSCULE *n pl.* -S osculum

OSCULUM *n pl.* -LA an opening in a sponge

OSE *n pl.* -S an esker

OSIER *n pl.* -S a European tree

OSMATIC *adj* depending mainly on the sense of smell

OSMIUM *n pl.* -S a metallic element OSMIC, OSMIOUS *adj*

OSMOL *n pl.* -S a unit of osmotic pressure OSMOLAL *adj*

OSMOLAR *adj* osmotic

OSMOSE *v* -MOSED, -MOSING, -MOSES to undergo osmosis

OSMOSIS *n pl.* -MOSES a form of diffusion of a fluid through a membrane

OSMOTIC *adj* pertaining to osmosis

OSMOUS *adj* containing osmium

OSMUND *n pl.* -S any of a genus of large ferns

OSMUNDA *n pl.* -S osmund

OSNABURG *n pl.* -S a cotton fabric

OSPREY *n pl.* -PREYS an American hawk

OSSA *pl.* of os

OSSEIN *n pl.* -S a protein substance in bone

OSSEOUS *adj* resembling bone

OSSIA *conj* or else — used as a musical direction

OSSICLE *n pl.* -S a small bone

OSSIFIC *adj* pertaining to the formation of bone

OSSIFIER *n pl.* -S one that ossifies

OSSIFY *v* -FIED, -FYING, -FIES to convert into bone

OSSUARY *n pl.* -ARIES a receptacle for the bones of the dead

OSTEAL *adj* osseous

OSTEITIS *n pl.* -ITIDES inflammation of bone OSTEITIC *adj*

OSTEOID *n pl.* -S uncalcified bone matrix

OSTEOMA *n pl.* -MAS or -MATA a tumor of bone tissue

OSTIA *pl.* of ostium

OSTIARY *n pl.* -ARIES a doorkeeper at a church

OSTINATO *n pl.* -TOS a constantly recurring musical phrase

OSTIOLE *n pl.* -S a small bodily opening OSTIOLAR *adj*

OSTIUM *n pl.* OSTIA an opening in a bodily organ

OSTLER *n pl.* -S hostler

OSTMARK *n pl.* -S a monetary unit of East Germany

OSTOMY *n pl.* -MIES a type of surgical operation

OSTOSIS *n pl.* -TOSES or -TOSISES the formation of bone

OSTRACOD *n pl.* -S a minute freshwater crustacean

OSTRICH *n pl.* -ES a large, flightless bird

OTALGIA *n pl.* -S pain in the ear OTALGIC *adj*

OTALGY *n pl.* -GIES otalgia

OTHER *n pl.* -S one that remains of two or more

OTIC *adj* pertaining to the ear

OTIOSE — adj lazy OTIOSELY adv

OTIOSITY — n pl. -TIES the state of being otiose

OTITIS — n pl. OTITIDES inflammation of the ear OTITIC adj

OTOCYST — n pl. -S an organ of balance in many invertebrates

OTOLITH — n pl. -S a hard mass that forms in the inner ear

OTOLOGY — n pl. -GIES the science of the ear

OTOSCOPE — n pl. -S an instrument for examining the ear

OTOSCOPY — n pl. -PIES the use of an otoscope

OTTAR — n pl. -S attar

OTTAVA — n pl. -S an octave

OTTER — n pl. -S a carnivorous mammal

OTTO — n pl. -TOS attar

OTTOMAN — n pl. -S a type of sofa

OUABAIN — n pl. -S a cardiac stimulant

OUCH — n pl. -ES a setting for a precious stone

OUD — n pl. -S a stringed instrument of northern Africa

OUGHT — v -ED, -ING, -S to owe

OUISTITI — n pl. -S a South American monkey

OUNCE — n pl. -S a unit of weight

OUPH — n pl. -S an ouphe

OUPHE — n pl. -S an elf

OUR — pron a possessive form of the pronoun we

OURANG — n pl. -S orang

OURARI — n pl. -S curare

OUREBI — n pl. -S oribi

OURIE — adj shivering with cold

OURS — pron a possessive form of the pronoun we

OURSELF — pron myself — used in formal or regal contexts

OUSEL — n pl. -S ouzel

OUST — v -ED, -ING, -S to expel or remove from a position or place

OUSTER — n pl. -S the act of ousting

OUT — v -ED, -ING, -S to be revealed

OUTACT — v -ED, -ING, -S to surpass in acting

OUTADD — v -ED, -ING, -S to surpass in adding

OUTAGE — n pl. -S a failure or interruption in use or functioning

OUTARGUE — v -GUED, -GUING, -GUES to get the better of by arguing

OUTASK — v -ED, -ING, -S to surpass in asking

OUTATE — past tense of outeat

OUTBACK — n pl. -S isolated rural country

OUTBAKE — v -BAKED, -BAKING, -BAKES to surpass in baking

OUTBARK — v -ED, -ING, -S to surpass in barking

OUTBAWL — v -ED, -ING, -S to surpass in bawling

OUTBEAM — v -ED, -ING, -S to surpass in beaming

OUTBEG — v -BEGGED, -BEGGING, -BEGS to surpass in begging

OUTBID — v -BID, -BIDDEN, -BIDDING, -BIDS to bid higher than

OUTBLAZE — v -BLAZED, -BLAZING, -BLAZES to surpass in brilliance of light

OUTBLEAT — v -ED, -ING, -S to surpass in bleating

OUTBLESS — v -ED, -ING, -ES to surpass in blessing

OUTBLOOM — v -ED, -ING, -S to surpass in blooming

OUTBLUFF — v -ED, -ING, -S to surpass in bluffing

OUTBLUSH — v -ED, -ING, -ES to surpass in blushing

OUTBOARD — n pl. -S a type of motor

OUTBOAST — v -ED, -ING, -S to surpass in boasting

OUTBOUND — adj outward bound

OUTBOX — v -ED, -ING, -ES to surpass in boxing

OUTBRAG — v -BRAGGED, -BRAGGING, -BRAGS to surpass in bragging

OUTBRAVE — v -BRAVED, -BRAVING, -BRAVES to surpass in courage

OUTBREAK — n pl. -S a sudden eruption

OUTBREED — v -BRED, -BREEDING, -BREEDS to interbreed relatively unrelated stocks

OUTBRIBE — v -BRIBED, -BRIBING, -BRIBES to surpass in bribing

OUTBUILD — v -BUILT, -BUILDING, -BUILDS to surpass in building

OUTBULLY — v -LIED, -LYING, -LIES to surpass in bullying

OUTBURN — v -BURNED or -BURNT, -BURNING, -BURNS to burn longer than

OUTBURST n pl. -S a sudden and violent outpouring

OUTBY adv outdoors

OUTBYE adv outby

OUTCAPER v -ED, -ING, -S to surpass in capering

OUTCAST n pl. -S one that is cast out

OUTCASTE n pl. -S a Hindu who has been expelled from his caste

OUTCATCH v -CAUGHT, -CATCHING, -CATCHES to surpass in catching

OUTCAVIL v -ILED, -ILING, -ILS or -ILLED, -ILLING, -ILS to surpass in caviling

OUTCHARM v -ED, -ING, -S to surpass in charming

OUTCHEAT v -ED, -ING, -S to surpass in cheating

OUTCHIDE v -CHIDED or -CHID, -CHIDDEN, -CHIDING, -CHIDES to surpass in chiding

OUTCLASS v -ED, -ING, -ES to surpass so decisively as to appear of a higher class

OUTCLIMB v -CLIMBED or -CLOMB, -CLIMBING, -CLIMBS to surpass in climbing

OUTCOME n pl. -S a result

OUTCOOK v -ED, -ING, -S to surpass in cooking

OUTCRAWL v -ED, -ING, -S to surpass in crawling

OUTCRIED past tense of outcry

OUTCRIES present 3d person sing. of outcry

OUTCROP v -CROPPED, -CROPPING, -CROPS to protrude above the soil

OUTCROSS v -ED, -ING, -ES to cross with a relatively unrelated individual

OUTCROW v -ED, -ING, -S to surpass in crowing

OUTCRY v -CRIED, -CRYING, -CRIES to cry louder than

OUTCURSE v -CURSED, -CURSING, -CURSES to surpass in cursing

OUTCURVE n pl. -S a type of pitch in baseball

OUTDANCE v -DANCED, -DANCING, -DANCES to surpass in dancing

OUTDARE v -DARED, -DARING, -DARES to surpass in daring

OUTDATE v -DATED, -DATING, -DATES to make out-of-date

OUTDO v -DID, -DONE, -DOING, -DOES to exceed in performance

OUTDODGE v -DODGED, -DODGING, -DODGES to surpass in dodging

OUTDOER n pl. -S one that outdoes

OUTDONE past participle of outdo

OUTDOOR adj pertaining to the open air

OUTDOORS adv in the open air

OUTDRANK past tense of outdrink

OUTDRAW v -DREW, -DRAWN, -DRAWING, -DRAWS to attract a larger audience than

OUTDREAM v -DREAMED or -DREAMT, -DREAMING, -DREAMS to surpass in dreaming

OUTDRESS v -ED, -ING, -ES to surpass in dressing

OUTDREW past tense of outdraw

OUTDRINK v -DRANK, -DRUNK, -DRINKING, -DRINKS to surpass in drinking

OUTDRIVE v -DROVE, -DRIVEN, -DRIVING, -DRIVES to drive a golf ball farther than

OUTDROP v -DROPPED, -DROPPING, -DROPS to surpass in dropping

OUTDRUNK past participle of outdrink

OUTEAT v -ATE, -EATEN, -EATING, -EATS to surpass in eating

OUTECHO v -ED, -ING, -ES to surpass in echoing

OUTER n pl. -S a part of a target

OUTFABLE v -BLED, -BLING, -BLES to surpass in fabling

OUTFACE v -FACED, -FACING, -FACES to confront unflinchingly

OUTFALL n pl. -S the outlet of a body of water

OUTFAST v -ED, -ING, -S to surpass in fasting

OUTFAWN v -ED, -ING, -S to surpass in fawning

OUTFEAST v -ED, -ING, -S to surpass in feasting

OUTFEEL v -FELT, -FEELING, -FEELS to surpass in feeling

OUTFIELD n pl. -S a part of a baseball field

OUTFIGHT v -FOUGHT, -FIGHTING, -FIGHTS to defeat

OUTFIND v -FOUND, -FINDING, -FINDS to surpass in finding

OUTFIRE v -FIRED, -FIRING, -FIRES to surpass in firing

OUTFIT v -FITTED, -FITTING, -FITS to equip

OUTFLANK v -ED, -ING, -S to gain a tactical advantage over

OUTFLOW v -ED, -ING, -S to flow out

OUTFLY v -FLEW, -FLOWN, -FLYING, -FLIES to surpass in speed of flight

OUTFOOL v -ED, -ING, -S to surpass in fooling

OUTFOOT v -ED, -ING, -S to surpass in speed

OUTFOUGHT past tense of outfight

OUTFOUND past tense of outfind

OUTFOX v -ED, -ING, -ES to outwit

OUTFROWN v -ED, -ING, -S to frown more than

OUTGAIN v -ED, -ING, -S to gain more than

OUTGAS v -GASSED, -GASSING, -GASSES to remove gas from

OUTGIVE v -GAVE, -GIVEN, -GIVING, -GIVES to give more than

OUTGLARE v -GLARED, -GLARING, -GLARES to surpass in glaring

OUTGLOW v -ED, -ING, -S to surpass in glowing

OUTGNAW v -GNAWED, -GNAWN, -GNAWING, -GNAWS to surpass in gnawing

OUTGO v -WENT, -GONE, -GOING, -GOES to go beyond

OUTGOING n pl. -S a departure

OUTGREW past tense of outgrow

OUTGRIN v -GRINNED, -GRINNING, -GRINS to surpass in grinning

OUTGROUP n pl. -S a group of people outside one's own group

OUTGROW v -GREW, -GROWN, -GROWING, -GROWS to grow too large for

OUTGUESS v -ED, -ING, -ES to anticipate the actions of

OUTGUIDE v -GUIDED, -GUIDING, -GUIDES to surpass in guiding

OUTGUN v -GUNNED, -GUNNING, -GUNS to surpass in firepower

OUTGUSH n pl. -ES a gushing out

OUTHAUL n pl. -S a rope for extending a sail along a spar

OUTHEAR v -HEARD, -HEARING, -HEARS to surpass in hearing

OUTHIT v -HIT, -HITTING, -HITS to get more hits than

OUTHOUSE n pl. -S a toilet housed in a small structure

OUTHOWL v -ED, -ING, -S to surpass in howling

OUTHUMOR v -ED, -ING, -S to surpass in humoring

OUTING n pl. -S a short pleasure trip

OUTJINX v -ED, -ING, -ES to surpass in jinxing

OUTJUMP v -ED, -ING, -S to surpass in jumping

OUTJUT v -JUTTED, -JUTTING, -JUTS to stick out

OUTKEEP v -KEPT, -KEEPING, -KEEPS to surpass in keeping

OUTKICK v -ED, -ING, -S to surpass in kicking

OUTKISS v -ED, -ING, -ES to surpass in kissing

OUTLAID past tense of outlay

OUTLAIN past participle of outlie

OUTLAND n pl. -S a foreign land

OUTLAST v -ED, -ING, -S to last longer than

OUTLAUGH v -ED, -ING, -S to surpass in laughing

OUTLAW v -ED, -ING, -S to prohibit

OUTLAWRY n pl. -RIES habitual defiance of the law

OUTLAY n -LAID, -LAYING, -LAYS to pay out

OUTLEAP v -LEAPED or -LEAPT, -LEAPING, -LEAPS to surpass in leaping

OUTLEARN v -LEARNED or -LEARNT, -LEARNING, -LEARNS to surpass in learning

OUTLET n pl. -S a passage for escape or discharge

OUTLIE v -LAY, -LAIN, -LYING, -LIES to lie beyond

OUTLIER n pl. -S an outlying area or portion

OUTLINE v -LINED, -LINING, -LINES to indicate the main features or different parts of

OUTLIVE v -LIVED, -LIVING, -LIVES to live longer than

OUTLIVER n pl. -S one that outlives

OUTLOOK n pl. -S a point of view

OUTLOVE v -LOVED, -LOVING, -LOVES to surpass in loving

OUTLYING present participle of outlie

OUTMAN v -MANNED, -MANNING, -MANS to surpass in manpower

OUTMARCH v -ED, -ING, -ES to surpass in marching

OUTMATCH v -ED, -ING, -ES to outdo

OUTMODE v -MODED, -MODING, -MODES to outdate

OUTMOST adj farthest out

OUTMOVE v -MOVED, -MOVING, -MOVES to move faster or farther than

OUTPACE v -PACED, -PACING, -PACES to surpass in speed

OUTPAINT v -ED, -ING, -S to surpass in painting

OUTPASS v -ED, -ING, -ES to excel in passing a football

OUTPITY v -PITIED, -PITYING, -PITIES to surpass in pitying

OUTPLAN v -PLANNED, -PLANNING, -PLANS to surpass in planning

OUTPLAY v -ED, -ING, -S to excel or defeat in a game

OUTPLOD v -PLODDED, -PLODDING, -PLODS to surpass in plodding

OUTPOINT v -ED, -ING, -S to score more points than

OUTPOLL v -ED, -ING, -S to get more votes than

OUTPORT n pl. -S a port of export or departure

OUTPOST n pl. -S a body of troops stationed at a distance from the main body

OUTPOUR v -ED, -ING, -S to pour out

OUTPRAY v -ED, -ING, -S to surpass in praying

OUTPREEN v -ED, -ING, -S to surpass in preening

OUTPRESS v -ED, -ING, -ES to surpass in pressing

OUTPRICE v -PRICED, -PRICING, -PRICES to surpass in pricing

OUTPULL v -ED, -ING, -S to attract a larger audience or following than

OUTPUSH v -ED, -ING, -ES to surpass in pushing

OUTPUT v -PUTTED, -PUTTING, -PUTS to produce

OUTQUOTE v -QUOTED, -QUOTING, -QUOTES to surpass in quoting

OUTRACE v -RACED, -RACING, -RACES to run faster or farther than

OUTRAGE v -RAGED, -RAGING, -RAGES to arouse anger or resentment in

OUTRAISE v -RAISED, -RAISING, -RAISES to surpass in raising

OUTRAN past tense of outrun

OUTRANCE n pl. -S the last extremity

OUTRANG past tense of outring

OUTRANGE v -RANGED, -RANGING, -RANGES to surpass in range

OUTRANK v -ED, -ING, -S to rank higher than

OUTRAVE v -RAVED, -RAVING, -RAVES to surpass in raving

OUTRE adj deviating from what is usual or proper

OUTREACH v -ED, -ING, -ES to reach beyond

OUTREAD v -READ, -READING, -READS to surpass in reading

OUTRIDE v -RODE, -RIDDEN, -RIDING, -RIDES to ride faster or better than

OUTRIDER n pl. -S a mounted attendant who rides before or beside a carriage

OUTRIGHT adj being without limit or reservation

OUTRING v -RANG, -RUNG, -RINGING, -RINGS to ring louder than

OUTRIVAL v -VALED, -VALING, -VALS or -VALLED, -VALLING, -VALS to outdo in a competition or rivalry

OUTROAR v -ED, -ING, -S to roar louder than

OUTROCK v -ED, -ING, -S to surpass in rocking

OUTRODE past tense of outride

OUTROLL v -ED, -ING, -S to roll out

OUTROOT v -ED, -ING, -S to pull up by the roots

OUTRUN v -RAN, -RUNNING, -RUNS to run faster than

OUTRUNG past participle of outring

OUTRUSH n pl. -ES a rushing out

OUTSAIL v -ED, -ING, -S to sail faster than

OUTSANG past tense of outsing

OUTSAT past tense of outsit

OUTSAVOR v -ED, -ING, -S to surpass in a distinctive taste or smell

OUTSAW past tense of outsee

OUTSCOLD v -ED, -ING, -S to surpass in scolding

OUTSCORE v -SCORED, -SCORING, -SCORES to score more points than

OUTSCORN v -ED, -ING, -S to surpass in scorning

OUTSEE v -SAW, -SEEN, -SEEING, -SEES to see beyond

OUTSELL v -SOLD, -SELLING, -SELLS to sell more than

OUTSERT n pl. -S a folded sheet placed around a folded section of printed matter

OUTSERVE v -SERVED, -SERVING, -SERVES to surpass in serving

OUTSET n pl. -S a beginning

OUTSHAME v -SHAMED, -SHAMING, -SHAMES to surpass in shaming

OUTSHINE v -SHONE or -SHINED, -SHINING, -SHINES to shine brighter than

OUTSHOOT v -SHOT, -SHOOTING, -SHOOTS to shoot better than

OUTSHOUT v -ED, -ING, -S to shout louder than

OUTSIDE n pl. -S the outer side, surface, or part

OUTSIDER n pl. -S one that does not belong to a particular group

OUTSIGHT n pl. -S the power of perceiving external things

OUTSIN v -SINNED, -SINNING, -SINS to surpass in sinning

OUTSING v -SANG, -SUNG, -SINGING, -SINGS to surpass in singing

OUTSIT v -SAT, -SITTING, -SITS to remain sitting or in session longer than

OUTSIZE n pl. -S an unusual size
OUTSIZED adj

OUTSKIRT n pl. -S an outlying area

OUTSLEEP v -SLEPT, -SLEEPING, -SLEEPS to sleep later than

OUTSMART v -ED, -ING, -S to outwit

OUTSMILE v -SMILED, -SMILING, -SMILES to surpass in smiling

OUTSMOKE v -SMOKED, -SMOKING, -SMOKES to surpass in smoking

OUTSNORE v -SNORED, -SNORING, -SNORES to surpass in snoring

OUTSOAR v -ED, -ING, -S to soar beyond

OUTSOLD past tense of outsell

OUTSOLE n pl. -S the outer sole of a boot or shoe

OUTSPAN v -SPANNED, -SPANNING, -SPANS to unharness a draft animal

OUTSPEAK v -SPOKE, -SPOKEN, -SPEAKING, -SPEAKS to outdo in speaking

OUTSPELL v -SPELLED or -SPELT, -SPELLING, -SPELLS to surpass in spelling

OUTSPEND v -SPENT, -SPENDING, -SPENDS to exceed the limits of in spending

OUTSPOKE past tense of outspeak

OUTSPOKEN past participle of outspeak

OUTSTAND v -STOOD, -STANDING, -STANDS to endure beyond

OUTSTARE v -STARED, -STARING, -STARES to outface

OUTSTART v -ED, -ING, -S to get ahead of at the start

OUTSTATE v -STATED, -STATING, -STATES to surpass in stating

OUTSTAY v -ED, -ING, -S to surpass in staying power

OUTSTEER v -ED, -ING, -S to surpass in steering

OUTSTOOD past tense of outstand

OUTSTRIP v -STRIPPED, -STRIPPING, -STRIPS to go faster or farther than

OUTSTUDY v -STUDIED, -STUDYING, -STUDIES to surpass in studying

OUTSTUNT v -ED, -ING, -S to surpass in stunting

OUTSULK v -ED, -ING, -S to surpass in sulking

OUTSUNG past participle of outsing

OUTSWEAR v -SWORE or -SWARE, -SWORN, -SWEARING, -SWEARS to surpass in swearing

OUTSWIM v -SWAM, -SWUM, -SWIMMING, -SWIMS to swim faster or farther than

OUTTAKE n pl. -S a passage outwards

OUTTALK v -ED, -ING, -S to surpass in talking

OUTTASK v -ED, -ING, -S to surpass in tasking

OUTTELL v -TOLD, -TELLING, -TELLS to say openly

OUTTHANK v -ED, -ING, -S to surpass in thanking

OUTTHINK v -THOUGHT, -THINKING, -THINKS to get the better of by thinking

OUTTHROB v -THROBBED, -THROBBING, -THROBS to surpass in throbbing

OUTTHROW v -THREW, -THROWN, -THROWING, -THROWS to throw farther or more accurately than

OUTTOLD past tense of outtell

OUTTOWER v -ED, -ING, -S to tower above

OUTTRADE v -TRADED, -TRADING, -TRADES to get the better of in a trade

OUTTRICK v -ED, -ING, -S to get the better of by trickery

OUTTROT v -TROTTED, -TROTTING, -TROTS to surpass in trotting

OUTTRUMP v -ED, -ING, -S to outplay

OUTTURN n pl. -S a quantity produced

OUTVALUE v -UED, -UING, -UES to be worth more than

OUTVAUNT v -ED, -ING, -S to surpass in vaunting

OUTVOICE v -VOICED, -VOICING, -VOICES to surpass in loudness of voice

OUTVOTE v -VOTED, -VOTING, -VOTES to defeat by a majority of votes

OUTWAIT v -ED, -ING, -S to exceed in patience

OUTWALK v -ED, -ING, -S to surpass in walking

OUTWAR v -WARRED, -WARRING, -WARS to surpass in warring

OUTWARD adv toward the outside

OUTWARDS adv outward

OUTWARRED past tense of outwar

OUTWARRING present participle of outwar

OUTWASH n pl. -ES detritus washed from a glacier

OUTWASTE v -WASTED, -WASTING, -WASTES to surpass in wasting

OUTWATCH v -ED, -ING, -ES to watch longer than

OUTWEAR v -WORE, -WORN, -WEARING, -WEARS to last longer than

OUTWEARY v -RIED, -RYING, -RIES to surpass in wearying

OUTWEEP v -WEPT, -WEEPING, -WEEPS to weep more than

OUTWEIGH v -ED, -ING, -S to weigh more than

OUTWENT past tense of outgo

OUTWEPT past tense of outweep

OUTWHIRL v -ED, -ING, -S to surpass in whirling

OUTWILE v -WILED, -WILING, -WILES to surpass in wiling

OUTWILL v -ED, -ING, -S to surpass in willpower

OUTWIND v -ED, -ING, -S to cause to be out of breath

OUTWISH v -ED, -ING, -ES to surpass in wishing

OUTWIT v -WITTED, -WITTING, -WITS to get the better of by superior cleverness

OUTWORE past tense of outwear

OUTWORK v -WORKED or -WROUGHT, -WORKING, -WORKS to work faster or better than

OUTWORN past participle of outwear

OUTWRITE v -WROTE or -WRIT, -WRITTEN, -WRITING, -WRITES to write better than

OUTWROUGHT a past tense of outwork

OUTYELL v -ED, -ING, -S to yell louder than

OUTYELP v -ED, -ING, -S to surpass in yelping

OUTYIELD v -ED, -ING, -S to surpass in yield

OUZEL n pl. -S a European bird

OUZO n pl. -ZOS a Greek liqueur

OVA pl. of ovum

OVAL n pl. -S an oval (egg-shaped) figure or object

OVALITY n pl. -TIES ovalness

OVALLY adv in the shape of an oval

OVALNESS n pl. -ES the state of being oval

OVARIAL adj ovarian

OVARIAN adj pertaining to an ovary

OVARIES pl. of ovary

OVARIOLE n pl. -S one of the tubes of which the ovaries of most insects are composed

OVARITIS n pl. -RITIDES inflammation of an ovary

OVARY n pl. -RIES a female reproductive gland

OVATE adj egg-shaped **OVATELY** adv

OVATION n pl. -S an expression or demonstration of popular acclaim

OVEN n pl. -S an enclosed compartment in which substances are heated **OVENLIKE** adj

OVENBIRD n pl. -S an American songbird

OVENWARE n pl. -S heat-resistant dishes for baking and serving food

OVER	v -ED, -ING, -S to leap above and to the other side of
OVERABLE	adj excessively able
OVERACT	v -ED, -ING, -S to act with exaggeration
OVERAGE	n pl. -S an amount in excess
OVERALL	n pl. -S a loose outer garment
OVERAPT	adj excessively apt
OVERARCH	v -ED, -ING, -ES to form an arch over
OVERARM	adj done with the arm above the shoulder
OVERATE	past tense of overeat
OVERAWE	v -AWED, -AWING, -AWES to subdue by inspiring awe
OVERBAKE	v -BAKED, -BAKING, -BAKES to bake too long
OVERBEAR	v -BORE, -BORNE or -BORN, -BEARING, -BEARS to bring down by superior weight or force
OVERBET	v -BETTED, -BETTING, -BETS to bet too much
OVERBID	v -BID, -BIDDEN, -BIDDING, -BIDS to bid higher than
OVERBIG	adj too big
OVERBITE	n pl. -S a faulty closure of the teeth
OVERBLOW	v -BLEW, -BLOWN, -BLOWING, -BLOWS to give excessive importance to
OVERBOLD	adj excessively bold or forward
OVERBOOK	v -ED, -ING, -S to issue reservations in excess of the space available
OVERBORE	past tense of overbear
OVERBORN	a past participle of overbear
OVERBORNE	a past participle of overbear
OVERBOUGHT	past tense of overbuy
OVERBRED	adj bred too finely or to excess
OVERBUSY	adj too busy
OVERBUY	v -BOUGHT, -BUYING, -BUYS to buy in quantities exceeding need or demand
OVERCALL	v -ED, -ING, -S to overbid
OVERCAME	past tense of overcome
OVERCAST	v -CAST, -CASTING, -CASTS to become cloudy or dark
OVERCOAT	n pl. -S a warm coat worn over indoor clothing
OVERCOLD	adj too cold

OVERCOME	v -CAME, -COMING, -COMES to get the better of
OVERCOOK	v -ED, -ING, -S to cook too long
OVERCOOL	v -ED, -ING, -S to make too cool
OVERCOY	adj too coy
OVERCRAM	v -CRAMMED, -CRAMMING, -CRAMS to stuff or cram to excess
OVERCROP	v -CROPPED, -CROPPING, -CROPS to exhaust the fertility of by cultivating to excess
OVERDARE	v -DARED, -DARING, -DARES to become too daring
OVERDEAR	adj too dear; too costly
OVERDECK	v -ED, -ING, -S to adorn extravagantly
OVERDO	v -DID, -DONE, -DOING, -DOES to do to excess
OVERDOER	n pl. -S one that overdoes
OVERDOSE	v -DOSED, -DOSING, -DOSES to give an excessive dose to
OVERDRAW	v -DREW, -DRAWN, -DRAWING, -DRAWS to draw checks on in excess of the balance
OVERDRY	adj too dry
OVERDUE	adj not paid when due
OVERDYE	v -DYED, -DYEING, -DYES to dye with too much color
OVEREASY	adj too easy
OVEREAT	v -ATE, -EATEN, -EATING, -EATS to eat to excess
OVERFAR	adj too great in distance, extent, or degree
OVERFAST	adj too fast
OVERFAT	adj too fat
OVERFEAR	v -ED, -ING, -S to fear too much
OVERFEED	v -FED, -FEEDING, -FEEDS to feed too much
OVERFILL	v -ED, -ING, -S to fill to overflowing
OVERFISH	v -ED, -ING, -ES to deplete the supply of fish in an area by fishing to excess
OVERFLOW	v -FLOWED, -FLOWN, -FLOWING, -FLOWS to flow over the top of
OVERFLY	v -FLEW, -FLOWN, -FLYING, -FLIES to fly over
OVERFOND	adj too fond or affectionate
OVERFOUL	adj too foul
OVERFREE	adj too free
OVERFULL	adj too full

OVERGILD v -GILDED or -GILT, -GILDING, -GILDS to gild over

OVERGIRD v -GIRDED or -GIRT, -GIRDING, -GIRDS to gird to excess

OVERGLAD adj too glad

OVERGOAD v -ED, -ING, -S to goad too much

OVERGROW v -GREW, -GROWN, -GROWING, -GROWS to grow over

OVERHAND v -ED, -ING, -S to sew with short, vertical stitches

OVERHANG v -HUNG, -HANGING, -HANGS to hang or project over

OVERHARD adj too hard

OVERHATE v -HATED, -HATING, -HATES to hate to excess

OVERHAUL v -ED, -ING, -S to examine carefully for needed repairs

OVERHEAD n pl. -S the general cost of running a business

OVERHEAP v -ED, -ING, -S to heap up or accumulate to excess

OVERHEAR v -HEARD, -HEARING, -HEARS to hear without the speaker's knowledge or intention

OVERHEAT v -ED, -ING, -S to heat to excess

OVERHIGH adj too high

OVERHOLD v -HELD, -HOLDING, -HOLDS to rate too highly

OVERHOLY adj too holy

OVERHOPE v -HOPED, -HOPING, -HOPES to hope exceedingly

OVERHOT adj too hot

OVERHUNG past tense of overhang

OVERHUNT v -ED, -ING, -S to deplete the supply of game in an area by hunting to excess

OVERIDLE adj too idle

OVERJOY v -ED, -ING, -S to fill with great joy

OVERJUST adj too just

OVERKEEN adj too keen

OVERKILL v -ED, -ING, -S to destroy with more nuclear force than required

OVERKIND adj too kind

OVERLADE v -LADED, -LADEN, -LADING, -LADES to load with too great a burden

OVERLAID past tense of overlay

OVERLAIN past participle of overlie

OVERLAND n pl. -S a train or stagecoach that travels over land

OVERLAP v -LAPPED, -LAPPING, -LAPS to extend over and cover a part of

OVERLATE adj too late

OVERLAX adj too lax

OVERLAY v -LAID, -LAYING, -LAYS to lay over

OVERLEAF adv on the other side of the page

OVERLEAP v -LEAPED or -LEAPT, -LEAPING, -LEAPS to leap over

OVERLET v -LET, -LETTING, -LETS to let to excess

OVERLEWD adj too lewd

OVERLIE v -LAY, -LAIN, -LYING, -LIES to lie over

OVERLIVE v -LIVED, -LIVING, -LIVES to outlive

OVERLOAD v -ED, -ING, -S to load to excess

OVERLONG adj too long

OVERLOOK v -ED, -ING, -S to fail to notice

OVERLORD v -ED, -ING, -S to rule tyrannically

OVERLOUD adj too loud

OVERLOVE v -LOVED, -LOVING, -LOVES to love to excess

OVERLY adv to an excessive degree

OVERLYING present participle of overlie

OVERMAN n pl. -MEN a foreman

OVERMAN v -MANNED, -MANNING, -MANS to provide with more men than are needed

OVERMANY adj too many

OVERMEEK adj excessively meek

OVERMELT v -ED, -ING, -S to melt too much

OVERMEN pl. of overman

OVERMILD adj too mild

OVERMIX v -ED, -ING, -ES to mix too much

OVERMUCH n pl. -ES an excess

OVERNEAR adj too near

OVERNEAT adj too neat

OVERNEW adj too new

OVERNICE adj excessively nice

OVERPASS v -PASSED or -PAST, -PASSING, -PASSES to pass over

OVERPAY v -PAID, -PAYING, -PAYS to pay too much

OVERPERT adj too pert

OVERPLAY v -ED, -ING, -S to exaggerate

OVERPLUS n pl. -ES a surplus

OVERPLY v -PLIED, -PLYING, -PLIES to ply to excess; overwork

OVERRAN past tense of overrun

OVERRANK adj too luxuriant in growth

OVERRASH adj too rash

OVERRATE v -RATED, -RATING, -RATES to rate too highly

OVERRICH adj too rich

OVERRIDE v -RODE, -RIDDEN, -RIDING, -RIDES to ride over

OVERRIFE adj too rife

OVERRIPE adj too ripe

OVERRODE past tense of override

OVERRUDE adj excessively rude

OVERRUFF v -ED, -ING, -S to trump with a higher trump card than has already been played

OVERRULE v -RULED, -RULING, -RULES to disallow the arguments of

OVERRUN v -RAN, -RUNNING, -RUNS to spread or swarm over

OVERSAD adj excessively sad

OVERSALE n pl. -S the act of overselling

OVERSALT v -ED, -ING, -S to salt to excess

OVERSAVE v -SAVED, -SAVING, -SAVES to save too much

OVERSAW past tense of oversee

OVERSEA adv overseas

OVERSEAS adv beyond or across the sea

OVERSEE v -SAW, -SEEN, -SEEING, -SEES to watch over and direct

OVERSEED v -ED, -ING, -S to seed to excess

OVERSEER n pl. -S one that oversees

OVERSELL v -SOLD, -SELLING, -SELLS to sell more of than can be delivered

OVERSET v -SET, -SETTING, -SETS to turn or tip over

OVERSEW v -SEWED, -SEWN, -SEWING, -SEWS to overhand

OVERSHOE n pl. -S a protective outer shoe

OVERSHOT n pl. -S a type of fabric weave

OVERSICK adj too sick

OVERSIDE n pl. -S the other side of a phonograph record

OVERSIZE n pl. -S an unusually large size

OVERSLIP v -SLIPPED or -SLIPT, -SLIPPING, -SLIPS to leave out

OVERSLOW adj too slow

OVERSOAK v -ED, -ING, -S to soak too much

OVERSOFT adj too soft

OVERSOLD past tense of oversell

OVERSOON adv too soon

OVERSOUL n pl. -S a supreme reality or mind in transcendentalism

OVERSPIN n pl. -S a forward spin imparted to a ball

OVERSTAY v -ED, -ING, -S to stay beyond the limits or duration of

OVERSTEP v -STEPPED, -STEPPING, -STEPS to go beyond

OVERSTIR v -STIRRED, -STIRRING, -STIRS to stir too much

OVERSUP v -SUPPED, -SUPPING, -SUPS to sup to excess

OVERSURE adj too sure

OVERT adj open to view OVERTLY adv

OVERTAKE v -TOOK, -TAKEN, -TAKING, -TAKES to catch up with

OVERTAME adj too tame

OVERTART adj too tart

OVERTASK v -ED, -ING, -S to task too severely

OVERTAX v -ED, -ING, -ES to tax too heavily

OVERTHIN adj too thin

OVERTIME v -TIMED, -TIMING, -TIMES to exceed the desired timing for

OVERTIRE v -TIRED, -TIRING, -TIRES to tire excessively

OVERTOIL v -ED, -ING, -S to wear out or exhaust by excessive toil

OVERTONE n pl. -S a higher partial tone

OVERTOOK past tense of overtake

OVERTOP v -TOPPED, -TOPPING, -TOPS to rise above the top of

OVERTRIM v -TRIMMED, -TRIMMING, -TRIMS to trim too much

OVERTURE v -TURED, -TURING, -TURES to propose

OVERTURN v -ED, -ING, -S to turn over

OVERURGE v -URGED, -URGING, -URGES to urge too much

OVERUSE v -USED, -USING, -USES to use too much

OVERVIEW n pl. -S a summary

OVERVOTE v -VOTED, -VOTING, -VOTES to defeat by a majority of votes

OVERWARM v -ED, -ING, -S to warm too much

OVERWARY adj too wary

OVERWEAK adj too weak

OVERWEAR v -WORE, -WORN, -WEARING, -WEARS to wear out

OVERWEEN v -ED, -ING, -S to be arrogant

OVERWET v -WETTED, -WETTING, -WETS to wet too much

OVERWIDE adj too wide

OVERWILY adj too wily

OVERWIND v -WOUND, -WINDING, -WINDS to wind too much, as a watch

OVERWISE adj too wise

OVERWORD n pl. -S a word or phrase repeated at intervals in a song

OVERWORE past tense of overwear

OVERWORK v -WORKED or -WROUGHT, -WORKING, -WORKS to cause to work too hard

OVERWORN past participle of overwear

OVERWOUND past tense of overwind

OVERWROUGHT a past tense of overwork

OVERZEAL n pl. -S excess of zeal

OVIBOS n pl. OVIBOS a wild ox

OVICIDE n pl. -S an agent that kills eggs OVICIDAL adj

OVIDUCT n pl. -S a tube through which ova travel from an ovary OVIDUCAL adj

OVIFORM adj shaped like an egg

OVINE n pl. -S a sheep or a closely related animal

OVIPARA n/pl egg-laying animals

OVIPOSIT v -ED, -ING, -S to lay eggs

OVISAC n pl. -S a sac containing an ovum or ova

OVOID n pl. -S an egg-shaped body OVOIDAL adj

OVOLO n pl. -LI or -LOS a convex molding

OVONIC adj pertaining to a branch of electronics

OVULATE v -LATED, -LATING, -LATES to produce ova

OVULE n pl. -S a rudimentary seed OVULAR, OVULARY adj

OVUM n pl. OVA the female reproductive cell of animals

OW interj — used to express sudden pain

OWE v OWED, OWING, OWES to be under obligation to pay or repay

OWL n pl. -S a nocturnal bird

OWLET n pl. -S a young owl

OWLISH adj resembling an owl OWLISHLY adv

OWLLIKE adj owlish

OWN v -ED, -ING, -S to have as a belonging OWNABLE adj

OWNER n pl. -S one that owns

OWSE n pl. OWSEN ox

OX n pl. OXEN a hoofed mammal

OX n pl. -ES a clumsy person

OXALATE v -LATED, -LATING, -LATES to treat with an oxalate (a chemical salt)

OXALIS n pl. -ALISES a flowering plant OXALIC adj

OXAZINE n pl. -S a chemical compound

OXBLOOD n pl. -S a deep red color

OXBOW n pl. -S a U-shaped piece of wood in an ox yoke

OXCART n pl. -S an ox-drawn cart

OXEN pl. of ox

OXEYE n pl. -S a flowering plant

OXFORD n pl. -S a type of shoe

OXHEART n pl. -S a variety of sweet cherry

OXID n pl. -S oxide

OXIDABLE adj capable of being oxidized

OXIDANT n pl. -S an oxidizing agent

OXIDASE n pl. -S an oxidizing enzyme OXIDASIC adj

OXIDATE v -DATED, -DATING, -DATES to oxidize

OXIDE n pl. -S a binary compound of oxygen with another element or radical OXIDIC adj

OXIDISE v -DISED, -DISING, -DISES to oxidize

OXIDISER n pl. -S oxidizer

OXIDIZE v -DIZED, -DIZING, -DIZES to combine with oxygen

OXIDIZER n pl. -S an oxidant

OXIM n pl. -S oxime

OXIME n pl. -S a chemical compound

OXLIP n pl. -S a flowering plant

OXPECKER n pl. -S an African bird

OXTAIL n pl. -S the tail of an ox

OXTER n pl. -S the armpit

OXTONGUE n pl. -S a European herb

OXY adj containing oxygen

OXYACID n pl. -S an acid that contains oxygen

OXYGEN   *n* pl. -S a gaseous element
   OXYGENIC *adj*

OXYMORON   *n* pl. -MORA a combination of contradictory or incongruous words

OXYPHIL   *n* pl. -S oxyphile

OXYPHILE   *n* pl. -S an organism that thrives in a relatively acid environment

OXYSALT   *n* pl. -S a salt of an oxyacid

OXYSOME   *n* pl. -S a structural unit of cellular cristae

OXYTOCIC   *n* pl. -S a drug that hastens the process of childbirth

OXYTOCIN   *n* pl. -S a pituitary hormone

OXYTONE   *n* pl. -S a word having heavy stress on the last syllable

OY   *interj* — used to express dismay or pain

OYER   *n* pl. -S a type of legal writ

OYES   *n* pl. OYESSES oyez

OYEZ   *n* pl. OYESSES a cry used to introduce the opening of a court of law

OYSTER   *v* -ED, -ING, -S to gather oysters (edible mollusks)

OYSTERER   *n* pl. -S one that gathers or sells oysters

OZONE   *n* pl. -S a form of oxygen
   OZONIC *adj*

OZONIDE   *n* pl. -S a compound of ozone

OZONISE   *v* -ISED, -ISING, -ISES to ozonize

OZONIZE   *v* -IZED, -IZING, -IZES to convert into ozone

OZONIZER   *n* pl. -S a device for converting oxygen into ozone

OZONOUS   *adj* pertaining to ozone

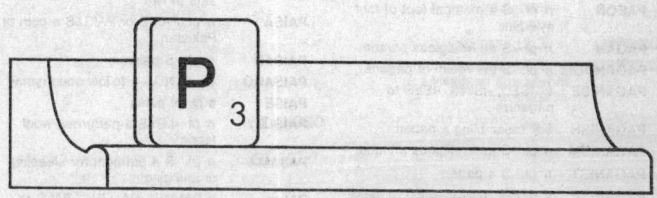

PA	*n* pl. -S a father
PABULUM	*n* pl. -S food **PABULAR** *adj*
PAC	*n* pl. -S a shoe patterned after a moccasin
PACA	*n* pl. -S a large rodent
PACE	*v* PACED, PACING, PACES to walk with a regular step
PACER	*n* pl. -S a horse whose gait is a pace
PACHA	*n* pl. -S pasha
PACHADOM	*n* pl. -S pashadom
PACHALIC	*n* pl. -S pashalik
PACHISI	*n* pl. -S a board game of India
PACHOULI	*n* pl. -S an East Indian herb
PACHUCO	*n* pl. -COS a flashy Mexican-American youth
PACIFIC	*adj* peaceful
PACIFIED	past tense of pacify
PACIFIER	*n* pl. -S one that pacifies
PACIFIES	present 3d person sing. of pacify
PACIFISM	*n* pl. -S opposition to war or violence
PACIFIST	*n* pl. -S an advocate of pacifism
PACIFY	*v* -FIED, -FYING, -FIES to make peaceful
PACING	present participle of pace
PACK	*v* -ED, -ING, -S to put into a receptacle for transportation or storage **PACKABLE** *adj*
PACKAGE	*v* -AGED, -AGING, -AGES to make into a package (a wrapped or boxed object)
PACKAGER	*n* pl. -S one that packages
PACKER	*n* pl. -S one that packs
PACKET	*v* -ED, -ING, -S to make into a small package

PACKING	*n* pl. -S material used to pack
PACKLY	*adv* intimately
PACKMAN	*n* pl. -MEN a peddler
PACKNESS	*n* pl. -ES intimacy
PACKSACK	*n* pl. -S a carrying bag to be worn on the back
PACKWAX	*n* pl. -ES paxwax
PACT	*n* pl. -S an agreement
PACTION	*n* pl. -S a pact
PAD	*v* PADDED, PADDING, PADS to line or stuff with soft material
PADAUK	*n* pl. -S a tropical tree
PADDIES	pl. of paddy
PADDING	*n* pl. -S material with which to pad
PADDLE	*v* -DLED, -DLING, -DLES to propel with a broad-bladed implement
PADDLER	*n* pl. -S one that paddles
PADDLING	*n* pl. -S the act of one who paddles
PADDOCK	*v* -ED, -ING, -S to confine in an enclosure for horses
PADDY	*n* pl. -DIES a rice field
PADISHAH	*n* pl. -S a sovereign
PADLE	*n* pl. -S a hoe
PADLOCK	*v* -ED, -ING, -S to secure with a type of lock
PADNAG	*n* pl. -S a horse that moves along at an easy pace
PADOUK	*n* pl. -S padauk
PADRE	*n* pl. PADRES or PADRI a Christian clergyman
PADRONE	*n* pl. -NES or -NI a master
PADSHAH	*n* pl. -S padishah
PADUASOY	*n* pl. -SOYS a strong silk fabric
PAEAN	*n* pl. -S a song of joy

PAEANISM *n pl.* -S the chanting of a paean

PAELLA *n pl.* -S a saffron-flavored stew

PAEON *n pl.* -S a metrical foot of four syllables

PAGAN *n pl.* -S an irreligious person

PAGANDOM *n pl.* -S the realm of pagans

PAGANISE *v* -ISED, -ISING, -ISES to paganize

PAGANISH *adj* resembling a pagan

PAGANISM *n pl.* -S an irreligious attitude

PAGANIST *n pl.* -S a pagan

PAGANIZE *v* -IZED, -IZING, -IZES to make irreligious

PAGE *v* PAGED, PAGING, PAGES to summon by calling out the name of

PAGEANT *n pl.* -S an elaborate public spectacle

PAGEBOY *n pl.* -BOYS a woman's hairstyle

PAGED past tense of page

PAGINAL *adj* pertaining to the pages of a book

PAGINATE *v* -NATED, -NATING, -NATES to number the pages of

PAGING present participle of page

PAGOD *n pl.* -S pagoda

PAGODA *n pl.* -S a Far Eastern temple

PAGURIAN *n pl.* -S a hermit crab

PAGURID *n pl.* -S a pagurian

PAH *interj* — used as an exclamation of disgust

PAHLAVI *n pl.* -S a coin of Iran

PAID a past tense of pay

PAIK *v* -ED, -ING, -S to beat or strike

PAIL *n pl.* -S a watertight cylindrical container

PAILFUL *n pl.* PAILFULS or PAILSFUL as much as a pail will hold

PAIN *v* -ED, -ING, -S to cause pain (suffering or distress)

PAINCH *n pl.* -ES paunch

PAINFUL *adj* -FULLER, -FULLEST causing pain

PAINLESS *adj* not causing pain

PAINT *v* -ED, -ING, -S to make a representation of with paints (coloring substances)

PAINTER *n pl.* -S one that paints

PAINTING *n pl.* -S a picture made with paints

PAINTY *adj* PAINTIER, PAINTIEST covered with paint

PAIR *v* -ED, -ING, -S to arrange in sets of two

PAISA *n pl.* PAISE or PAISAS a coin of Pakistan

PAISAN *n pl.* -S paisano

PAISANO *n pl.* -NOS a fellow countryman

PAISE a pl. of paisa

PAISLEY *n pl.* -LEYS a patterned wool fabric

PAJAMA *n pl.* -S a garment for sleeping or lounging

PAL *v* PALLED, PALLING, PALS to associate as friends

PALABRA *n pl.* -S a word

PALACE *n pl.* -S a royal residence PALACED *adj*

PALADIN *n pl.* -S a knightly champion

PALAIS *n pl.* PALAIS a palace

PALATAL *n pl.* -S a bone of the palate

PALATE *n pl.* -S the roof of the mouth

PALATIAL *adj* resembling a palace

PALATINE *n pl.* -S a high officer of an empire

PALAVER *v* -ED, -ING, -S to chatter

PALAZZO *n pl.* -ZI an impressive building

PALE *adj* PALER, PALEST lacking intensity of color

PALE *v* PALED, PALING, PALES to make or become pale

PALEA *n pl.* -LEAE a small bract PALEAL *adj*

PALEFACE *n pl.* -S a white person

PALELY *adv* in a pale manner

PALENESS *n pl.* -ES the quality of being pale

PALER comparative of pale

PALEST superlative of pale

PALESTRA *n pl.* -TRAS or -TRAE a school for athletics in ancient Greece

PALET *n pl.* -S a palea

PALETOT *n pl.* -S a loose overcoat

PALETTE *n pl.* -S a board on which an artist mixes colors

PALEWAYS *adv* palewise

PALEWISE *adv* vertically

PALFREY *n pl.* -FREYS a riding horse

PALIER comparative of paly

PALIEST superlative of paly

PALIKAR *n pl.* -S a Greek soldier

PALING *n pl.* -S a picket fence

PALINODE   *n* pl. -S a formal retraction

PALISADE   *v* -SADED, -SADING, -SADES to fortify with a heavy fence

PALISH   *adj* somewhat pale

PALL   *v* -ED, -ING, -S to become insipid

PALLADIA   *n/pl* safeguards

PALLADIC   *adj* pertaining to the metallic element palladium

PALLED   past tense of pal

PALLET   *n* pl. -S a bed or mattress of straw

PALLETTE   *n* pl. -S a piece of armor protecting the armpit

PALLIA   a pl. of pallium

PALLIAL   *adj* pertaining to a part of the brain

PALLIATE   *v* -ATED, -ATING, -ATES to conceal the seriousness of

PALLID   *adj* pale **PALLIDLY** *adv*

PALLIER   comparative of pally

PALLIEST   superlative of pally

PALLING   present participle of pal

PALLIUM   *n* pl. -LIA or -LIUMS a cloak worn in ancient Rome

PALLOR   *n* pl. -S paleness

PALLY   *adj* -LIER, -LIEST marked by close friendship

PALM   *v* -ED, -ING, -S to touch with the palm (inner surface) of the hand

PALMAR   *adj* pertaining to the palm

PALMARY   *adj* worthy of praise

PALMATE   *adj* resembling an open hand

PALMATED   *adj* palmate

PALMER   *n* pl. -S a religious pilgrim

PALMETTE   *n* pl. -S a type of ornament

PALMETTO   *n* pl. -TOS or -TOES a tropical tree

PALMIER   comparative of palmy

PALMIEST   superlative of palmy

PALMIST   *n* pl. -S a fortune-teller

PALMITIN   *n* pl. -S a chemical compound

PALMLIKE   *adj* resembling a palm tree

PALMY   *adj* PALMIER, PALMIEST marked by prosperity

PALMYRA   *n* pl. -S a tropical tree

PALOMINO   *n* pl. -NOS a slender-legged horse

PALOOKA   *n* pl. -S an inferior boxer

PALP   *n* pl. -S a palpus

PALPABLE   *adj* capable of being felt **PALPABLY** *adv*

PALPAL   *adj* pertaining to a palpus

PALPATE   *v* -PATED, -PATING, -PATES to examine by touch

PALPATOR   *n* pl. -S one that palpates

PALPEBRA   *n* pl. -BRAE an eyelid

PALPUS   *n* pl. -PI a sensory organ of an arthropod

PALSY   *v* -SIED, -SYING, -SIES to paralyze

PALTER   *v* -ED, -ING, -S to talk or act insincerely

PALTERER   *n* pl. -S one that palters

PALTRY   *adj* -TRIER, -TRIEST petty **PALTRILY** *adv*

PALUDAL   *adj* pertaining to a marsh

PALUDISM   *n* pl. -S malaria

PALY   *adj* PALIER, PALIEST somewhat pale

PAM   *n* pl. -S the jack of clubs in certain card games

PAMPA   *n* pl. -S a grassland of South America

PAMPEAN   *n* pl. -S a native of the pampas

PAMPER   *v* -ED, -ING, -S to treat with extreme or excessive indulgence

PAMPERER   *n* pl. -S one that pampers

PAMPERO   *n* pl. -ROS a cold, dry wind

PAMPHLET   *n* pl. -S a printed work with a paper cover

PAN   *v* PANNED, PANNING, PANS to criticize harshly

PANACEA   *n* pl. -S a remedy for all diseases or ills **PANACEAN** *adj*

PANACHE   *n* pl. -S an ornamental tuft of feathers

PANADA   *n* pl. -S a thick sauce

PANAMA   *n* pl. -S a lightweight hat

PANATELA   *n* pl. -S a long, slender cigar

PANCAKE   *v* -CAKED, -CAKING, -CAKES to land an airplane in a certain manner

PANCHAX   *n* pl. -ES a tropical fish

PANCREAS   *n* pl. -ES a large gland

PANDA   *n* pl. -S a carnivorous mammal

PANDANUS   *n* pl. -NI or -NUSES a tropical plant

PANDECT   *n* pl. -S a complete body of laws

PANDEMIC   *n* pl. -S a widespread disease

PANDER   *v* -ED, -ING, -S to provide gratification for others' desires

PANDERER n pl. -S one that panders

PANDIED past tense of pandy

PANDIES present 3d person sing. of pandy

PANDIT n pl. -S a wise or learned man in India

PANDOOR n pl. -S pandour

PANDORA n pl. -S bandore

PANDORE n pl. -S bandore

PANDOUR n pl. -S a marauding soldier

PANDOWDY n pl. -DIES an apple dessert

PANDURA n pl. -S bandore

PANDY v -DIED, -DYING, -DIES to punish by striking the hand

PANE n pl. -S a sheet of glass for a window **PANED** adj

PANEL v -ELED, -ELING, -ELS or -ELLED, -ELLING, -ELS to decorate with thin sheets of material

PANELING n pl. -S material with which to panel

PANELIST n pl. -S a member of a discussion or advisory group

PANELLED past tense of panel

PANELLING a present participle of panel

PANETELA n pl. -S panatela

PANFISH n pl. -ES any small fish that can be fried whole

PANFUL n pl. -S as much as a pan will hold

PANG v -ED, -ING, -S to cause to have spasms of pain

PANGA n pl. -S a large knife

PANGEN n pl. -S a hypothetical heredity-controlling particle of proto-plasm

PANGOLIN n pl. -S a toothless mammal

PANHUMAN adj pertaining to all humanity

PANIC v -ICKED, -ICKING, -ICS to be overwhelmed by fear

PANICKY adj -ICKIER, -ICKIEST tending to panic

PANICLE n pl. -S a loosely branched flower cluster **PANICLED** adj

PANICUM n pl. -S a grass

PANIER n pl. -S pannier

PANMIXIA n pl. -S random mating within a breeding population

PANNE n pl. -S a lustrous velvet

PANNED past tense of pan

PANNIER n pl. -S a large basket

PANNIKIN n pl. -S a small saucepan

PANNING present participle of pan

PANOCHA n pl. -S a coarse Mexican sugar

PANOCHE n pl. -S panocha

PANOPLY n pl. -PLIES a suit of armor

PANOPTIC adj including everything visible in one view

PANORAMA n pl. -S a complete view

PANPIPE n pl. -S a musical instrument

PANSOPHY n pl. -PHIES universal knowledge

PANSY n pl. -SIES a flowering plant

PANT v -ED, -ING, -S to breathe quickly and with difficulty

PANTHEON n pl. -S a temple dedicated to all the gods

PANTHER n pl. -S a leopard

PANTIE n pl. -S a woman's or child's undergarment

PANTIES pl. of panty

PANTILE n pl. -S a roofing tile **PANTILED** adj

PANTOFLE n pl. -S a slipper

PANTOUM n pl. -S a verse form

PANTRY n pl. -TRIES a closet or room for storing kitchen utensils

PANTSUIT n pl. -S a type of woman's suit

PANTY n pl. PANTIES pantie

PANZER n pl. -S an armored combat vehicle

PAP n pl. -S a soft food for infants

PAPA n pl. -S a father

PAPACY n pl. -CIES the office of the pope

PAPAIN n pl. -S an enzyme

PAPAL adj pertaining to the pope **PAPALLY** adv

PAPAW n pl. -S a fleshy fruit

PAPAYA n pl. -S a melon-like fruit **PAPAYAN** adj

PAPER v -ED, -ING, -S to cover or wrap with paper (a thin sheet material made of cellulose pulp)

PAPERBOY n pl. -BOYS a newsboy

PAPERER n pl. -S one that papers

PAPERY adj resembling paper

PAPHIAN n pl. -S a prostitute

PAPILLA n pl. -LAE a nipple-like projection **PAPILLAR** adj

PAPILLON n pl. -S a small dog having large ears

PAPIST	*n* pl. -S a Roman Catholic — an offensive term **PAPISTIC** *adj*
PAPISTRY	*n* pl. -TRIES the Roman Catholic religion — an offensive term
PAPOOSE	*n* pl. -S an American Indian baby
PAPPI	a pl. of pappus
PAPPIER	comparative of pappy
PAPPIES	pl. of pappy
PAPPIEST	superlative of pappy
PAPPOOSE	*n* pl. -S papoose
PAPPUS	*n* pl. -PI a tuft of bristles on the achene of certain plants **PAPPOSE, PAPPOUS** *adj*
PAPPY	*adj* -PIER, -PIEST resembling pap
PAPPY	*n* pl. -PIES a father
PAPRICA	*n* pl. -S paprika
PAPRIKA	*n* pl. -S a seasoning made from red peppers
PAPULA	*n* pl. -LAE papule
PAPULE	*n* pl. -S a pimple **PAPULAN, PAPULAR, PAPULOSE** *adj*
PAPYRUS	*n* pl. -RUSES or -RI a tall aquatic plant **PAPYRAL, PAPYRIAN, PAPYRINE** *adj*
PAR	*v* PARRED, PARRING, PARS to shoot in a standard number of strokes in golf
PARA	*n* pl. -S a monetary unit of Yugoslavia
PARABLE	*n* pl. -S a simple story conveying a moral or religious lesson
PARABOLA	*n* pl. -S a conic section
PARACHOR	*n* pl. -S a mathematical constant that relates molecular volume to surface tension
PARADE	*v* -RADED, -RADING, -RADES to march in a public procession
PARADER	*n* pl. -S one that parades
PARADIGM	*n* pl. -S a pattern or example
PARADING	present participle of parade
PARADISE	*n* pl. -S a place of extreme beauty or delight
PARADOS	*n* pl. -ES a protective embankment
PARADOX	*n* pl. -ES a statement seemingly contradictory or absurd yet perhaps true
PARADROP	*v* -DROPPED, -DROPPING, -DROPS to deliver by parachute
PARAFFIN	*v* -ED, -ING, -S to coat with a waxy substance
PARAFORM	*n* pl. -S a substance used as an antiseptic
PARAGOGE	*n* pl. -S the addition of a sound or sounds at the end of a word
PARAGON	*v* -ED, -ING, -S to compare with
PARAKEET	*n* pl. -S a small parrot
PARALLAX	*n* pl. -ES an apparent optical displacement of an object
PARALLEL	*v* -LELED, -LELING, -LELS or -LELLED, -LELLING, -LELS to be similar or analogous to
PARALYSE	*v* -LYSED, -LYSING, -LYSES to paralyze
PARALYZE	*v* -LYZED, -LYZING, -LYZES to render incapable of movement
PARAMENT	*n* pl. -MENTS or -MENTA an ornamental vestment
PARAMO	*n* pl. -MOS a plateau region of South America
PARAMOUR	*n* pl. -S an illicit lover
PARANG	*n* pl. -S a heavy knife
PARANOEA	*n* pl. -S paranoia
PARANOIA	*n* pl. -S a mental disorder
PARANOID	*n* pl. -S one affected with paranoia
PARAPET	*n* pl. -S a protective wall
PARAPH	*n* pl. -S a flourish at the end of a signature
PARAQUAT	*n* pl. -S a weed killer
PARAQUET	*n* pl. -S a parakeet
PARASANG	*n* pl. -S a Persian unit of distance
PARASHAH	*n* pl. -SHOTH or -SHIOTH a passage in Jewish scripture
PARASITE	*n* pl. -S an organism that lives and feeds on or in another organism
PARASOL	*n* pl. -S a small, light umbrella
PARAVANE	*n* pl. -S an underwater device used to cut cables
PARBOIL	*v* -ED, -ING, -S to cook partially by boiling for a short time
PARCEL	*v* -CELED, -CELING, -CELS or -CELLED, -CELLING, -CELS to divide into parts or shares
PARCENER	*n* pl. -S a joint heir
PARCH	*v* -ED, -ING, -ES to make very dry
PARD	*n* pl. -S a leopard
PARDAH	*n* pl. -S purdah
PARDEE	*interj* pardi

PARDI *interj* — used as a mild oath

PARDIE *interj* pardi

PARDINE *adj* pertaining to a leopard

PARDNER *n* pl. -S chum; friend

PARDON *v* -ED, -ING, -S to release from liability for an offense

PARDONER *n* pl. -S one that pardons

PARDY *interj* pardi

PARE *v* PARED, PARING, PARES to cut off the outer covering of

PARECISM *n* pl. -S the state of having the male and female sexual organs beside or near each other

PAREIRA *n* pl. -S a medicinal plant root

PARENT *v* -ED, -ING, -S to exercise the functions of a parent (a father or mother)

PARENTAL *adj* pertaining to a parent

PARER *n* pl. -S one that pares

PARESIS *n* pl. -RESES partial loss of the ability to move

PARETIC *n* pl. -S one affected with paresis

PAREU *n* pl. -S a Polynesian garment

PAREVE *adj* parve

PARFAIT *n* pl. -S a frozen dessert

PARFLESH *n* pl. -ES a rawhide soaked in lye to remove the hair and dried

PARFOCAL *adj* having lenses with the corresponding focal points in the same plane

PARGE *v* PARGED, PARGING, PARGES to parget

PARGET *v* -GETED, -GETING, -GETS or -GETTED, -GETTING, -GETS to cover with plaster

PARGO *n* pl. -GOS a food fish

PARHELIA *n/pl* bright circular spots appearing on a solar halo

PARHELIC *adj* pertaining to parhelia

PARIAH *n* pl. -S a social outcast

PARIAN *n* pl. -S a hard, white porcelain

PARIES *n* pl. PARIETES the wall of an organ

PARIETAL *n* pl. -S a bone of the skull

PARING *n* pl. -S something pared off

PARIS *n* pl. -ISES a European herb

PARISH *n* pl. -ES an ecclesiastical district

PARITY *n* pl. -TIES equality

PARK *v* -ED, -ING, -S to leave a vehicle in a location for a time

PARKA *n* pl. -S a hooded garment

PARKER *n* pl. -S one that parks

PARKING *n* pl. -S an area in which vehicles may be left

PARKLAND *n* pl. -S a grassland region with isolated or grouped trees

PARKLIKE *adj* resembling an outdoor recreational area

PARKWAY *n* pl. -WAYS a wide highway

PARLANCE *n* pl. -S a manner of speaking

PARLANDO *adj* sung in a manner suggestive of speech

PARLANTE *adj* parlando

PARLAY *v* -ED, -ING, -S to bet an original wager and its winnings on a subsequent event

PARLE *v* PARLED, PARLING, PARLES to parley

PARLEY *v* -LEYED, -LEYING, -LEYS to discuss terms with an enemy

PARLEYER *n* pl. -S one that parleys

PARLING present participle of parle

PARLOR *n* pl. -S a room for the entertainment of visitors

PARLOUR *n* pl. -S parlor

PARLOUS *adj* dangerous

PARODIC *adj* comically imitative

PARODIED past tense of parody

PARODIES present 3d person sing. of parody

PARODIST *n* pl. -S one who parodies

PARODOS *n* pl. -DOI an ode sung in ancient Greek drama

PARODY *v* -DIED, -DYING, -DIES to imitate a serious literary work for comic effect

PAROL *n* pl. -S an utterance

PAROLE *v* -ROLED, -ROLING, -ROLES to release from prison before completion of the imposed sentence

PAROLEE *n* pl. -S one who is paroled

PARONYM *n* pl. -S a word having the same root as another

PAROQUET *n* pl. -S a parakeet

PAROTIC *adj* situated near the ear

PAROTID *n* pl. -S a salivary gland

PAROTOID *n* pl. -S a gland of certain toads and frogs

PAROUS *adj* having produced offspring

PAROXYSM *n* pl. -S a sudden fit or attack

PARQUET *v* -ED, -ING, -S to furnish with a floor of inlaid design

PARR *n* pl. -S a young salmon

PARRAL	n pl. -S parrel	**PARTLY**	adv in some measure or degree
PARRED	past tense of par	**PARTNER**	v -ED, -ING, -S to associate with in some activity of common interest
PARREL	n pl. -S a sliding loop of rope or chain used on a ship		
PARRIDGE	n pl. -S porridge	**PARTON**	n pl. -S a hypothetical atomic particle
PARRIED	past tense of parry		
PARRIES	present 3d person sing. of parry	**PARTOOK**	past tense of partake
		PARTWAY	adv to some extent
PARRING	present participle of par	**PARTY**	v -TIED, -TYING, -TIES to attend a social gathering
PARRITCH	n pl. -ES porridge		
PARROKET	n pl. -S parakeet	**PARURA**	n pl. -S parure
PARROT	v -ED, -ING, -S to repeat or imitate without thought or understanding	**PARURE**	n pl. -S a set of matched jewelry
		PARVE	adj made without milk or meat
PARROTER	n pl. -S one that parrots	**PARVENU**	n pl. -S one who has suddenly risen above his class
PARROTY	adj resembling a parrot (a hook-billed tropical bird)		
		PARVENUE	adj characteristic of a parvenu
PARRY	v -RIED, -RYING, -RIES to ward off a blow	**PARVIS**	n pl. -VISES an enclosed area in front of a church
PARSE	v PARSED, PARSING, PARSES to describe and analyze grammatically **PARSABLE** adj	**PARVISE**	n pl. -S parvis
		PARVOLIN	n pl. -S an oily liquid obtained from fish
PARSEC	n pl. -S a unit of astronomical distance	**PAS**	n pl. PAS a dance step
PARSER	n pl. -S one that parses	**PASCHAL**	n pl. -S a candle used in certain religious ceremonies
PARSING	present participle of parse		
PARSLEY	n pl. -LEYS a cultivated herb	**PASE**	n pl. -S a movement of a matador's cape
PARSNIP	n pl. -S a European herb		
PARSON	n pl. -S a clergyman **PARSONIC** adj	**PASEO**	n pl. -SEOS a leisurely stroll
		PASH	v -ED, -ING, -ES to strike violently
PART	v -ED, -ING, -S to divide or break into separate pieces		
		PASHA	n pl. -S a former Turkish high official
PARTAKE	v -TOOK, -TAKEN, -TAKING, -TAKES to participate		
		PASHADOM	n pl. -S the rank of a pasha
PARTAKER	n pl. -S one that partakes	**PASHALIC**	n pl. -S pashalik
PARTAN	n pl. -S an edible crab	**PASHALIK**	n pl. -S the territory of a pasha
PARTERRE	n pl. -S a section of a theater	**PASQUIL**	n pl. -S a satire or lampoon
PARTIAL	n pl. -S a simple component of a complex tone	**PASS**	v -ED, -ING, -ES to go by
		PASSABLE	adj fairly good or acceptable **PASSABLY** adv
PARTIBLE	adj divisible		
PARTICLE	n pl. -S a very small piece or part	**PASSADE**	n pl. -S a turn of a horse backward or forward on the same ground
PARTIED	past tense of party		
PARTIES	present 3d person sing. of party	**PASSADO**	n pl. -DOS or -DOES a forward thrust in fencing
PARTING	n pl. -S a division or separation		
PARTISAN	n pl. -S a firm supporter of a person, party, or cause	**PASSAGE**	v -SAGED, -SAGING, -SAGES to make a voyage
PARTITA	n pl. -S a set of related instrumental pieces	**PASSANT**	adj walking with the farther forepaw raised — used of a heraldic animal
PARTITE	adj divided into parts		
PARTIZAN	n pl. -S partisan	**PASSBAND**	n pl. -S a frequency band that permits transmission with maximum efficiency
PARTLET	n pl. -S a woman's garment		
		PASSBOOK	n pl. -S a bankbook
		PASSE	adj outmoded

PASSEE *adj* passe

PASSEL *n pl.* -S a large quantity or number

PASSER *n pl.* -S one that passes

PASSERBY *n pl.* PASSERSBY one who passes by

PASSIBLE *adj* capable of feeling or suffering

PASSIM *adv* here and there

PASSING *n pl.* -S a death

PASSION *n pl.* -S an intense emotion

PASSIVE *n pl.* -S a verb form

PASSKEY *n pl.* -KEYS a key that opens several different locks

PASSLESS *adj* incapable of being traveled over or through

PASSOVER *n pl.* -S the lamb eaten at the feast of a Jewish holiday

PASSPORT *n pl.* -S a document allowing travel from one country to another

PASSUS *n pl.* -ES a section of a story or poem

PASSWORD *n pl.* -S a secret word that must be spoken to gain admission

PAST *n pl.* -S time gone by

PASTA *n pl.* -S a food made of dough

PASTE *v* PASTED, PASTING, PASTES to fasten with a sticky mixture

PASTEL *n pl.* -S a soft, delicate hue

PASTER *n pl.* -S one that pastes

PASTERN *n pl.* -S a part of a horse's foot

PASTICCI *n/pl* pastiches

PASTICHE *n pl.* -S an artistic work made of fragments from various sources

PASTIER comparative of pasty

PASTIES pl. of pasty

PASTIEST superlative of pasty

PASTIL *n pl.* -S pastille

PASTILLE *n pl.* -S a lozenge

PASTIME *n pl.* -S a recreational activity

PASTINA *n pl.* -S a type of macaroni

PASTING present participle of paste

PASTNESS *n pl.* -ES the state of being past or gone by

PASTOR *v* -ED, -ING, -S to serve as the spiritual overseer of

PASTORAL *n pl.* -S a literary or artistic work that depicts country life

PASTRAMI *n pl.* -S a highly seasoned smoked beef

PASTROMI *n pl.* -S pastrami

PASTRY *n pl.* -TRIES a sweet baked food

PASTURAL *adj* pertaining to a pasture

PASTURE *v* -TURED, -TURING, -TURES to put in a pasture (a grazing area)

PASTURER *n pl.* -S one that pastures livestock

PASTY *adj* PASTIER, PASTIEST pale and unhealthy in appearance

PASTY *n pl.* PASTIES a meat pie

PAT *v* PATTED, PATTING, PATS to touch lightly

PATACA *n pl.* -S a monetary unit of Macao

PATAGIUM *n pl.* -GIA a wing membrane of a bat

PATAMAR *n pl.* -S a sailing vessel

PATCH *v* -ED, -ING, -ES to mend or cover a hole or weak spot in

PATCHER *n pl.* -S one that patches

PATCHY *adj* PATCHIER, PATCHIEST uneven in quality PATCHILY *adv*

PATE *n pl.* -S the top of the head PATED *adj*

PATELLA *n pl.* -LAE or -LAS the flat movable bone at the front of the knee PATELLAR *adj*

PATEN *n pl.* -S a plate

PATENCY *n pl.* -CIES the state of being obvious

PATENT *v* -ED, -ING, -S to obtain a patent (a government grant protecting the rights of an inventor) on

PATENTEE *n pl.* -S one that holds a patent

PATENTLY *adv* obviously

PATENTOR *n pl.* -S one that grants a patent

PATER *n pl.* -S a father

PATERNAL *adj* pertaining to a father

PATH *n pl.* -S a trodden way or track

PATHETIC *adj* arousing pity

PATHLESS *adj* having no path

PATHOGEN *n pl.* -S any disease-producing organism

PATHOS *n pl.* -ES a quality that arouses feelings of pity or compassion

PATHWAY *n pl.* -WAYS a path

PATIENCE *n pl.* -S the quality of being patient

PATIENT *adj* -TIENTER, -TIENTEST able to endure disagreeable circumstances without complaint

PATIENT *n pl.* -S one who is under medical treatment

PATIN *n pl.* -S paten

PATINA *n pl.* -NAE or -NAS a green film that forms on bronze

PATINE *v* -TINED, -TINING, -TINES to cover with a patina

PATIO *n pl.* -TIOS an outdoor paved area adjoining a house

PATLY *adv* suitably

PATNESS *n pl.* -ES suitability

PATOIS *n pl.* PATOIS a dialect

PATRIOT *n pl.* -S one who loves his country

PATROL *v* -TROLLED, -TROLLING, -TROLS to pass through an area for the purposes of observation or security

PATRON *n pl.* -S a regular customer PATRONAL, PATRONLY *adj*

PATROON *n pl.* -S a landowner granted manorial rights under old Dutch law

PATSY *n pl.* -SIES a person who is easily fooled

PATTAMAR *n pl.* -S patamar

PATTED past tense of pat

PATTEE *adj* paty

PATTEN *n pl.* -S a shoe having a thick wooden sole

PATTER *v* -ED, -ING, -S to talk glibly or rapidly

PATTERER *n pl.* -S one that patters

PATTERN *v* -ED, -ING, -S to make according to a prescribed design

PATTIE *n pl.* -S patty

PATTING present participle of pat

PATTY *n pl.* -TIES a small, flat cake of chopped food

PATTYPAN *n pl.* -S a pan in which patties are baked

PATULENT *adj* patulous

PATULOUS *adj* spreading; open

PATY *adj* formee

PAUCITY *n pl.* -TIES smallness of number or quantity

PAUGHTY *adj* arrogant

PAULDRON *n pl.* -S a piece of armor for the shoulder

PAULIN *n pl.* -S a sheet of waterproof material

PAUNCH *n pl.* -ES the belly or abdomen PAUNCHED *adj*

PAUNCHY *adj* PAUNCHIER, PAUNCHIEST having a protruding belly

PAUPER *v* -ED, -ING, -S to reduce to poverty

PAUSAL *adj* pertaining to a break or rest in speaking or writing

PAUSE *v* PAUSED, PAUSING, PAUSES to stop temporarily

PAUSER *n pl.* -S one that pauses

PAVAN *n pl.* -S a slow, stately dance

PAVANE *n pl.* -S pavan

PAVE *v* PAVED, PAVING, PAVES to cover with material that forms a firm, level surface

PAVEMENT *n pl.* -S a paved surface

PAVER *n pl.* -S one that paves

PAVID *adj* timid

PAVILION *v* -ED, -ING, -S to cover with a large tent

PAVIN *n pl.* -S pavan

PAVING *n pl.* -S pavement

PAVIOR *n pl.* -S a paver

PAVIOUR *n pl.* -S a paver

PAVIS *n pl.* -ISES a large medieval shield

PAVISE *n pl.* -S pavis

PAVISER *n pl.* -S a soldier carrying a pavis

PAVONINE *adj* resembling a peacock

PAW *v* -ED, -ING, -S to strike or scrape with a beating motion

PAWER *n pl.* -S one that paws

PAWKY *adj* PAWKIER, PAWKIEST sly PAWKILY *adv*

PAWL *n pl.* -S a hinged mechanical part

PAWN *v* -ED, -ING, -S to give as security for something borrowed PAWNABLE *adj*

PAWNAGE *n pl.* -S an act of pawning

PAWNEE *n pl.* -S one to whom something is pawned

PAWNER *n pl.* -S one that pawns something

PAWNOR *n pl.* -S pawner

PAWNSHOP *n pl.* -S a place where things are pawned

PAWPAW *n pl.* -S papaw

PAX *n* pl. -ES a ceremonial embrace given to signify Christian love and unity

PAXWAX *n* pl. -ES the nuchal ligament of a quadruped

PAY *v* PAID or PAYED, PAYING, PAYS to give money or something of value in exchange for goods or services

PAYABLE *adj* profitable PAYABLY *adv*

PAYCHECK *n* pl. -S a check in payment of wages or salary

PAYDAY *n* pl. -DAYS the day on which wages are paid

PAYEE *n* pl. -S one to whom money is paid

PAYER *n* pl. -S one that pays

PAYLOAD *n* pl. -S the part of a cargo producing income

PAYMENT *n* pl. -S something that is paid

PAYNIM *n* pl. -S a pagan

PAYOFF *n* pl. -S the act of distributing gains

PAYOLA *n* pl. -S a secret payment for favors

PAYOR *n* pl. -S payer

PAYROLL *n* pl. -S a list of employees entitled to payment

PE *n* pl. -S a Hebrew letter

PEA *n* pl. -S the edible seed of an annual herb

PEACE *v* PEACED, PEACING, PEACES to be or become silent

PEACEFUL *adj* -FULLER, -FULLEST undisturbed; calm

PEACH *v* -ED, -ING, -ES to inform against someone

PEACHER *n* pl. -S one that peaches

PEACHY *adj* PEACHIER, PEACHIEST dandy

PEACING present participle of peace

PEACOAT *n* pl. -S a heavy woolen jacket

PEACOCK *v* -ED, -ING, -S to strut vainly

PEACOCKY *adj* -COCKIER, -COCKIEST vain

PEAFOWL *n* pl. -S a large pheasant

PEAG *n* pl. -S wampum

PEAGE *n* pl. -S peag

PEAHEN *n* pl. -S a female peafowl

PEAK *v* -ED, -ING, -S to reach a maximum

PEAKIER comparative of peaky

PEAKIEST superlative of peaky

PEAKISH *adj* somewhat sickly

PEAKLESS *adj* having no peak (a pointed top)

PEAKLIKE *adj* resembling a peak

PEAKY *adj* PEAKIER, PEAKIEST sickly

PEAL *v* -ED, -ING, -S to ring out

PEALIKE *adj* resembling a pea

PEAN *n* pl. -S paean

PEANUT *n* pl. -S the nutlike seed or pod of an annual vine

PEAR *n* pl. -S a fleshy fruit

PEARL *v* -ED, -ING, -S to adorn with pearls (smooth, rounded masses formed in certain mollusks)

PEARLASH *n* pl. -ES an alkaline compound

PEARLER *n* pl. -S one that dives for pearls

PEARLITE *n* pl. -S a cast-iron alloy

PEARLY *adj* PEARLIER, PEARLIEST resembling a pearl

PEARMAIN *n* pl. -S a variety of apple

PEART *adj* PEARTER, PEARTEST lively PEARTLY *adv*

PEASANT *n* pl. -S a person of inferior social rank

PEASCOD *n* pl. -S peasecod

PEASE *n* pl. PEASEN or PEASES a pea

PEASECOD *n* pl. -S a pea pod

PEAT *n* pl. -S a substance composed of partially decayed vegetable matter

PEATY *adj* PEATIER, PEATIEST resembling or containing peat

PEAVEY *n* pl. -VEYS a lever used to move logs

PEAVY *n* pl. -VIES peavey

PEBBLE *v* -BLED, -BLING, -BLES to cover with pebbles (small, rounded stones)

PEBBLY *adj* -BLIER, -BLIEST resembling pebbles

PECAN *n* pl. -S a nut-bearing tree

PECCABLE *adj* liable to sin

PECCANCY *n* pl. -CIES the state of being peccant

PECCANT *adj* sinful

PECCARY *n* pl. -RIES a hoofed mammal

PECCAVI *n* pl. -S a confession of sin

PECH *v* -ED, -ING, -S to pant

PECHAN *n* pl. -S the stomach

PECK *v* -ED, -ING, -S to strike with the beak or something pointed

PECKER *n pl.* -S one that pecks

PECKY *adj* PECKIER, PECKIEST marked by decay caused by fungi

PECTASE *n pl.* -S an enzyme

PECTATE *n pl.* -S a chemical salt

PECTEN *n pl.* -TENS or -TINES a comblike anatomical part

PECTIN *n pl.* -S a carbohydrate derivative **PECTIC** *adj*

PECTIZE *v* -TIZED, -TIZING, -TIZES to change into a jelly

PECTORAL *n pl.* -S something worn on the breast

PECULATE *v* -LATED, -LATING, -LATES to embezzle

PECULIAR *n pl.* -S something belonging exclusively to a person

PECULIUM *n pl.* -LIA private property

PED *n pl.* -S a natural soil aggregate

PEDAGOG *n pl.* -S a teacher

PEDAGOGY *n pl.* -GIES the work of a teacher

PEDAL *v* -ALED, -ALING, -ALS or -ALLED, -ALLING, -ALS to operate by means of foot levers

PEDALFER *n pl.* -S a type of soil

PEDALIER *n pl.* -S the pedal keyboard of an organ

PEDALLED past tense of pedal

PEDALLING present participle of pedal

PEDANT *n pl.* -S one who flaunts his knowledge **PEDANTIC** *adj*

PEDANTRY *n pl.* -RIES ostentatious display of knowledge

PEDATE *adj* resembling a foot **PEDATELY** *adv*

PEDDLE *v* -DLED, -DLING, -DLES to travel about selling wares

PEDDLER *n pl.* -S one that peddles

PEDDLERY *n pl.* -RIES the trade of a peddler

PEDDLING present tense of peddle

PEDERAST *n pl.* -S a man who engages in sexual activities with boys

PEDES *pl.* of pes

PEDESTAL *v* -TALED, -TALING, -TALS or -TALLED, -TALLING, -TALS to provide with an architectural support or base

PEDICAB *n pl.* -S a passenger vehicle that is pedaled

PEDICEL *n pl.* -S a slender basal part of an organism

PEDICLE *n pl.* -S pedicel **PEDICLED** *adj*

PEDICURE *v* -CURED, -CURING, -CURES to administer a cosmetic treatment to the feet and toenails

PEDIFORM *adj* shaped like a foot

PEDIGREE *n pl.* -S a line of ancestors

PEDIMENT *n pl.* -S a triangular architectural part

PEDIPALP *n pl.* -S an appendage of an arachnid

PEDLAR *n pl.* -S peddler

PEDLARY *n pl.* -LARIES peddlery

PEDLER *n pl.* -S peddler

PEDOCAL *n pl.* -S a type of soil

PEDOLOGY *n pl.* -GIES the scientific study of the behavior and development of children

PEDRO *n pl.* -DROS a card game

PEDUNCLE *n pl.* -S a flower stalk

PEE *v* PEED, PEEING, PEES to urinate — an offensive term

PEEBEEN *n pl.* -S a large hardwood evergreen tree

PEEK *v* -ED, -ING, -S to look furtively or quickly

PEEKABOO *n pl.* -BOOS a children's game

PEEL *v* -ED, -ING, -S to strip off an outer covering of **PEELABLE** *adj*

PEELER *n pl.* -S one that peels

PEELING *n pl.* -S a piece or strip that has been peeled off

PEEN *v* -ED, -ING, -S to beat with the non-flat end of a hammerhead

PEEP *v* -ED, -ING, -S to utter a short, shrill cry

PEEPER *n pl.* -S one that peeps

PEEPHOLE *n pl.* -S a small opening through which one may look

PEEPSHOW *n pl.* -S an exhibition viewed through a small opening

PEEPUL *n pl.* -S pipal

PEER *v* -ED, -ING, -S to look narrowly or searchingly

PEERAGE *n pl.* -S the rank of a nobleman

PEERESS *n pl.* -ES a noblewoman

PEERIE *n pl.* -S peery

PEERLESS *adj* having no equal

PEERY *n pl.* PEERIES a child's toy

PEESWEEP *n pl.* -S a lapwing

PEETWEET *n pl.* -S a wading bird

PEEVE v PEEVED, PEEVING, PEEVES to annoy

PEEVISH adj irritable

PEEWEE n pl. -S an unusually small person or thing

PEEWIT n pl. -S pewit

PEG v PEGGED, PEGGING, PEGS to fasten with a peg (a wooden pin)

PEGBOARD n pl. -S a board with holes for pegs

PEGBOX n pl. -ES a part of a stringed instrument

PEGGED past tense of peg

PEGGING present participle of peg

PEGLESS adj lacking a peg

PEGLIKE adj resembling a peg

PEIGNOIR n pl. -S a woman's gown

PEIN v -ED, -ING, -S to peen

PEISE v PEISED, PEISING, PEISES to weigh

PEKAN n pl. -S a carnivorous mammal

PEKE n pl. -S a small, long-haired dog

PEKIN n pl. -S a silk fabric

PEKOE n pl. -S a black tea

PELAGE n pl. -S the coat or covering of a mammal PELAGIAL adj

PELAGIC adj oceanic

PELE n pl. -S a medieval fortified tower

PELERINE n pl. -S a woman's cape

PELF n pl. -S money or wealth

PELICAN n pl. -S a large, web-footed bird

PELISSE n pl. -S a long outer garment

PELITE n pl. -S a rock composed of fine fragments PELITIC adj

PELLAGRA n pl. -S a niacin-deficiency disease

PELLET v -ED, -ING, -S to strike with pellets (small rounded masses)

PELLETAL adj resembling a pellet

PELLICLE n pl. -S a thin skin or film

PELLMELL n pl. -S a jumbled mass

PELLUCID adj transparent

PELON adj hairless

PELORIA n pl. -S abnormal regularity of a flower form PELORIAN, PELORIC adj

PELORUS n pl. -ES a navigational instrument

PELOTA n pl. -S a court game of Spanish origin

PELT v -ED, -ING, -S to strike repeatedly with blows or missiles

PELTAST n pl. -S a soldier of ancient Greece

PELTATE adj shaped like a shield

PELTER n pl. -S one that pelts

PELTRY n pl. -RIES an animal skin

PELVIC n pl. -S a bone of the pelvis

PELVIS n pl. -VES or -VISES a part of the skeleton

PEMBINA n pl. -S a variety of cranberry

PEMICAN n pl. -S pemmican

PEMMICAN n pl. -S a food prepared by North American Indians

PEMOLINE n pl. -S a drug used experimentally to improve memory

PEMPHIX n pl. -ES a skin disease

PEN v PENNED, PENNING, PENS to write with a pen (an instrument for writing with fluid ink)

PENAL adj pertaining to punishment

PENALISE v -ISED, -ISING, -ISES to penalize

PENALITY n pl. -TIES liability to punishment

PENALIZE v -IZED, -IZING, -IZES to subject to a penalty

PENALLY adv in a penal manner

PENALTY n pl. -TIES a punishment imposed for violation of a law, rule, or agreement

PENANCE v -ANCED, -ANCING, -ANCES to impose a type of punishment upon

PENANG n pl. -S a cotton fabric

PENATES n/pl the Roman gods of the household

PENCE a pl. of penny

PENCEL n pl. -S a small flag

PENCHANT n pl. -S a strong liking for something

PENCIL v -CILED, -CILING, -CILS or -CILLED, -CILLING, -CILS to produce by using a pencil (a writing and drawing implement)

PENCILER n pl. -S one that pencils

PEND v -ED, -ING, -S to remain undecided or unsettled

PENDANT n pl. -S a hanging ornament

PENDENCY n pl. -CIES a pending state

PENDENT *n* pl. -S pendant

PENDULUM *n* pl. -S a type of free swinging body **PENDULAR** *adj*

PENES a pl. of penis

PENGO *n* pl. -GOS a former monetary unit of Hungary

PENGUIN *n* pl. -S a flightless, aquatic bird

PENICIL *n* pl. -S a small tuft of hairs

PENIS *n* pl. -NES or -NISES the male organ of copulation **PENIAL, PENILE** *adj*

PENITENT *n* pl. -S a person who repents his sins

PENKNIFE *n* pl. -KNIVES a small pocketknife

PENLIGHT *n* pl. -S a small flashlight

PENLITE *n* pl. -S penlight

PENMAN *n* pl. -MEN an author

PENNA *n* pl. -NAE any of the feathers that determine a bird's shape

PENNAME *n* pl. -S a name used by an author instead of his real name

PENNANT *n* pl. -S a long, narrow flag

PENNATE *adj* having wings or feathers

PENNATED *adj* pennate

PENNED past tense of pen

PENNER *n* pl. -S one that pens

PENNI *n* pl. -NIA or -NIS a Finnish coin

PENNIES a pl. of penny

PENNINE *n* pl. -S a mineral

PENNING present participle of pen

PENNON *n* pl. -S a pennant **PENNONED** *adj*

PENNY *n* pl. PENNIES or PENCE a coin of the United Kingdom

PENOCHE *n* pl. -S penuche

PENOLOGY *n* pl. -GIES the science of the punishment of crime

PENONCEL *n* pl. -S a small pennon

PENPOINT *n* pl. -S the point of a pen

PENSEE *n* pl. -S a thought

PENSIL *n* pl. -S pencil

PENSILE *adj* hanging loosely

PENSION *v* -ED, -ING, -S to grant a retirement allowance to

PENSIONE *n* pl. -S a boarding house

PENSIVE *adj* engaged in deep thought

PENSTER *n* pl. -S a writer

PENSTOCK *n* pl. -S a conduit for conveying water to a waterwheel

PENT *adj* confined

PENTACLE *n* pl. -S a five-pointed star

PENTAD *n* pl. -S a group of five

PENTAGON *n* pl. -S a five-sided polygon

PENTANE *n* pl. -S a volatile liquid

PENTARCH *n* pl. -S one of five joint rulers

PENTOMIC *adj* made up of five battle groups

PENTOSAN *n* pl. -S a complex carbohydrate

PENTOSE *n* pl. -S a sugar having five carbon atoms per molecule

PENTYL *n* pl. -S amyl

PENUCHE *n* pl. -S a fudge-like candy

PENUCHI *n* pl. -S penuche

PENUCHLE *n* pl. -S pinochle

PENUCKLE *n* pl. -S pinochle

PENULT *n* pl. -S the next to last syllable in a word

PENUMBRA *n* pl. -BRAE or -BRAS a partial shadow

PENURY *n* pl. -RIES extreme poverty

PEON *n* pl. -S or -ES an unskilled laborer

PEONAGE *n* pl. -S the condition of being a peon

PEONISM *n* pl. -S peonage

PEONY *n* pl. -NIES a flowering plant

PEOPLE *v* -PLED, -PLING, -PLES to furnish with inhabitants

PEOPLER *n* pl. -S one that peoples

PEP *v* PEPPED, PEPPING, PEPS to fill with energy

PEPERONI *n* pl. -S a highly seasoned sausage

PEPLOS *n* pl. -ES a garment worn by women in ancient Greece

PEPLUM *n* pl. -LUMS or -LA a short section attached to the waistline of a garment **PEPLUMED** *adj*

PEPLUS *n* pl. -ES peplos

PEPO *n* pl. -POS a fruit having a fleshy interior and a hard rind

PEPONIDA *n* pl. -S pepo

PEPONIUM *n* pl. -S pepo

PEPPED past tense of pep

PEPPER *v* -ED, -ING, -S to season with pepper (a pungent condiment)

PEPPERER *n* pl. -S one that peppers

PEPPERY *adj* resembling pepper

PEPPING present participle of pep

PEPPY *adj* -PIER, -PIEST full of energy **PEPPILY** *adv*

PEPSIN *n* pl. -S a digestive enzyme of the stomach

PEPSINE *n* pl. -S pepsin

PEPTIC *n* pl. -S a substance that promotes digestion

PEPTID *n* pl. -S peptide

PEPTIDE *n* pl. -S a combination of amino acids **PEPTIDIC** *adj*

PEPTIZE *v* -TIZED, -TIZING, -TIZES to increase the colloidal dispersion of

PEPTIZER *n* pl. -S one that peptizes

PEPTONE *n* pl. -S a protein compound **PEPTONIC** *adj*

PER *prep* for each

PERACID *n* pl. -S a type of acid

PERCALE *n* pl. -S a cotton fabric

PERCEIVE *v* -CEIVED, -CEIVING, -CEIVES to become aware of through the senses

PERCENT *n* pl. -S one part in a hundred

PERCEPT *n* pl. -S something that is perceived

PERCH *v* -ED, -ING, -ES to sit or rest on an elevated place

PERCHER *n* pl. -S one that perches

PERCOID *n* pl. -S a spiny-finned fish

PERCUSS *v* -ED, -ING, -ES to strike with force

PERDIE *interj* pardi

PERDU *n* pl. -S a soldier sent on a dangerous mission

PERDUE *n* pl. -S perdu

PERDY *interj* pardi

PEREGRIN *n* pl. -S a swift falcon much used in falconry

PERFECT *adj* -FECTER, -FECTEST lacking fault or defect; of an extreme kind

PERFECT *v* -ED, -ING, -S to make perfect

PERFECTA *n* pl. -S a system of betting

PERFECTO *n* pl. -TOS a medium-sized cigar

PERFIDY *n* pl. -DIES deliberate breach of faith or trust

PERFORCE *adv* of necessity

PERFORM *v* -ED, -ING, -S to begin and carry through to completion

PERFUME *v* -FUMED, -FUMING, -FUMES to fill with a fragrant odor

PERFUMER *n* pl. -S one that perfumes

PERFUSE *v* -FUSED, -FUSING, -FUSES to spread over or through something

PERGOLA *n* pl. -S a shaded shelter or passageway

PERHAPS *n* pl. -ES something open to doubt or conjecture

PERI *n* pl. -S a supernatural being of Persian mythology

PERIANTH *n* pl. -S an outer covering of a flower

PERIAPT *n* pl. -S an amulet

PERIBLEM *n* pl. -S a region of plant tissue

PERICARP *n* pl. -S the wall of a ripened plant ovary or fruit

PERICOPE *n* pl. -PES or -PAE a selection from a book

PERIDERM *n* pl. -S an outer layer of plant tissue

PERIDIUM *n* pl. -IA the covering of the spore-bearing organ in many fungi **PERIDIAL** *adj*

PERIDOT *n* pl. -S a mineral

PERIGEE *n* pl. -S the point in the orbit of a celestial body which is nearest to the earth **PERIGEAL**, **PERIGEAN** *adj*

PERIGON *n* pl. -S an angle equal to 360 degrees

PERIGYNY *n* pl. -NIES the state of being situated on a cuplike organ surrounding the pistil

PERIL *v* -ILED, -ILING, -ILS or -ILLED, -ILLING, -ILS to imperil

PERILLA *n* pl. -S an Asian herb

PERILOUS *adj* dangerous

PERILUNE *n* pl. -S the point in the orbit of a celestial body which is nearest to the moon

PERINEUM *n* pl. -NEA a region of the body at the lower end of the trunk **PERINEAL** *adj*

PERIOD *n* pl. -S a portion of time

PERIODIC *adj* recurring at regular intervals

PERIODID *n* pl. -S an iodide

PERIOTIC *adj* surrounding the ear

PERIPETY *n* pl. -TIES a sudden change in a course of events

PERIPTER *n* pl. -S a structure with a row of columns around all sides

PERIQUE *n* pl. -S a dark tobacco

PERISARC *n* pl. -S a protective covering of certain hydrozoans

PERISH *v* -ED, -ING, -ES to die

PERIWIG *n* pl. -S a wig

PERJURE *v* -JURED, -JURING, -JURES to make a perjurer of

PERJURER n pl. -S one guilty of perjury

PERJURY n pl. -RIES the willful giving of false testimony under oath in a judicial proceeding

PERK v -ED, -ING, -S to carry oneself jauntily

PERKISH adj somewhat perky

PERKY adj PERKIER, PERKIEST jaunty PERKILY adv

PERLITE n pl. -S a volcanic glass PERLITIC adj

PERM n pl. -S a long-lasting hair setting

PERMEASE n pl. -S a catalyzing agent

PERMEATE v -ATED, -ATING, -ATES to spread through

PERMIT v -MITTED, -MITTING, -MITS to allow

PERMUTE v -MUTED, -MUTING, -MUTES to change the order of

PERONEAL adj pertaining to the fibula

PERORAL adj occurring through the mouth

PERORATE v -RATED, -RATING, -RATES to make a lengthy speech

PEROXID n pl. -S peroxide

PEROXIDE v -IDED, -IDING, -IDES to treat with peroxide (a bleaching agent)

PERPEND v -ED, -ING, -S to ponder

PERPENT n pl. -S a large building stone

PERPLEX v -ED, -ING, -ES to make mentally uncertain

PERRON n pl. -S an outdoor stairway

PERRY n pl. -RIES a beverage of pear juice often fermented

PERSALT n pl. -S a chemical salt

PERSE n pl. -S a blue color

PERSIST v -ED, -ING, -S to continue resolutely in some activity

PERSON n pl. -S a human being

PERSONA n pl. -NAE a character in a literary work

PERSONA n pl. -S the public role that a person assumes

PERSONAL n pl. -S a brief, private notice in a newspaper

PERSPIRE v -SPIRED, -SPIRING, -SPIRES to give off moisture through the pores of the skin PERSPIRY adj

PERSUADE v -SUADED, -SUADING, -SUADES to cause to do something by means of argument, reasoning, or entreaty

PERT adj PERTER, PERTEST impudent PERTLY adv

PERTAIN v -ED, -ING, -S to have reference or relation

PERTNESS n pl. -ES the quality of being pert

PERTURB v -ED, -ING, -S to disturb greatly

PERUKE n pl. -S a wig

PERUSAL n pl. -S the act of perusing

PERUSE v -RUSED, -RUSING, -RUSES to read

PERUSER n pl. -S one that peruses

PERVADE v -VADED, -VADING, -VADES to spread through every part of

PERVADER n pl. -S one that pervades

PERVERSE adj willfully deviating from desired or expected conduct

PERVERT v -ED, -ING, -S to turn away from the right course of action

PERVIOUS adj capable of being penetrated

PES n pl. PEDES a foot or footlike part

PESADE n pl. -S the position of a horse when rearing

PESETA n pl. -S a monetary unit of Spain

PESEWA n pl. -S a monetary unit of Ghana

PESKY adj -KIER, -KIEST annoying PESKILY adv

PESO n pl. -SOS a monetary unit of various Spanish-speaking countries

PESSARY n pl. -RIES a contraceptive device worn in the vagina

PEST n pl. -S an annoying person or thing

PESTER v -ED, -ING, -S to bother

PESTERER n pl. -S one that pesters

PESTHOLE n pl. -S a place liable to epidemic disease

PESTLE v -TLED, -TLING, -TLES to crush with a club-shaped hand tool

PET v PETTED, PETTING, PETS to caress with the hand

PETAL n pl. -S a leaflike part of a corolla PETALED, PETALLED adj

PETALINE adj resembling a petal

PETALODY n pl. -DIES the metamorphosis of various floral organs into petals

PETALOID adj resembling a petal

PETALOUS	*adj* having petals	**PEWTER**	*n pl.* -S a tin alloy
PETARD	*n pl.* -S an explosive device	**PEWTERER**	*n pl.* -S one that makes articles of pewter
PETASOS	*n pl.* -ES petasus		
PETASUS	*n pl.* -ES a broad-brimmed hat worn in ancient Greece	**PEYOTE**	*n pl.* -S a cactus
		PEYOTL	*n pl.* -S peyote
PETCOCK	*n pl.* -S a small valve or faucet	**PEYTRAL**	*n pl.* -S a piece of armor for the breast of a horse
PETECHIA	*n pl.* -CHIAE a small hemorrhagic spot on a body surface		
		PEYTREL	*n pl.* -S peytral
PETER	*v* -ED, -ING, -S to diminish gradually	**PFENNIG**	*n pl.* -NIGS or -NIGE a bronze coin of Germany
PETIOLAR	*adj* pertaining to a petiole	**PHAETON**	*n pl.* -S a light carriage
PETIOLE	*n pl.* -S the stalk of a leaf **PETIOLED** *adj*	**PHAGE**	*n pl.* -S an organism that destroys bacteria
PETIT	*adj* small; minor	**PHALANGE**	*n pl.* -S any bone of a finger or toe
PETITE	*n pl.* -S a clothing size for short women		
		PHALANX	*n pl.* -ES a formation of infantry in ancient Greece
PETITION	*v* -ED, -ING, -S to make a formal request		
		PHALLI	a pl. of phallus
PETREL	*n pl.* -S a small seabird	**PHALLIC**	*adj* pertaining to a phallus
PETRIFY	*v* -FIED, -FYING, -FIES to convert into stone or a stony substance	**PHALLISM**	*n pl.* -S worship of the phallus as symbolic of nature's creative power
PETROL	*n pl.* -S gasoline		
PETROLIC	*adj* derived from petroleum	**PHALLIST**	*n pl.* -S one who practices phallism
PETRONEL	*n pl.* -S a portable firearm	**PHALLUS**	*n pl.* -LI or -LUSES the penis
PETROSAL	*adj* petrous	**PHANTASIED** past tense of phantasy
PETROUS	*adj* resembling stone in hardness	**PHANTASIES** present 3d person sing. of phantasy
PETTED	past tense of pet		
PETTEDLY	*adv* peevishly	**PHANTASM**	*n pl.* -S a creation of the imagination
PETTER	*n pl.* -S one that pets		
PETTI	pl. of petto	**PHANTAST**	*n pl.* -S fantast
PETTIER	comparative of petty	**PHANTASY**	*v* -SIED, -SYING, -SIES to fantasy
PETTIEST	superlative of petty		
PETTIFOG	*v* -FOGGED, -FOGGING, -FOGS to quibble	**PHANTOM**	*n pl.* -S something existing in appearance only
PETTILY	*adv* in a petty manner	**PHARAOH**	*n pl.* -S a ruler of ancient Egypt
PETTING	present participle of pet	**PHARISEE**	*n pl.* -S a hypocritically self-righteous person
PETTISH	*adj* peevish		
PETTLE	*v* -TLED, -TLING, -TLES to caress	**PHARMACY**	*n pl.* -CIES a drugstore
		PHAROS	*n pl.* -ES a lighthouse or beacon to guide seamen
PETTO	*n pl.* -TI the breast		
PETTY	*adj* -TIER, -TIEST insignificant	**PHARYNX**	*n pl.* -YNGES or -YNXES a section of the digestive tract
PETULANT	*adj* peevish		
PETUNIA	*n pl.* -S a tropical herb	**PHASE**	*v* PHASED, PHASING, PHASES to plan or carry out by phases (distinct stages of development) **PHASEAL, PHASIC** *adj*
PETUNTSE	*n pl.* -S a mineral		
PETUNTZE	*n pl.* -S petuntse		
PEW	*n pl.* -S a bench for seating people in church	**PHASEOUT**	*n pl.* -S a gradual stopping of operations
		PHASIS	*n pl.* PHASES a phase
PEWEE	*n pl.* -S a small bird		
PEWIT	*n pl.* -S the lapwing	**PHASMID**	*n pl.* -S a tropical insect

PHAT	adj susceptible of easy and rapid typesetting	**PHONEME**	n pl. -S a unit of speech PHONEMIC adj
PHATIC	adj sharing feelings rather than ideas	**PHONETIC**	adj pertaining to speech sounds
PHEASANT	n pl. -S a large, long-tailed bird	**PHONEY**	adj -NIER, -NIEST phony
PHELLEM	n pl. -S a layer of plant cells	**PHONEY**	n pl. -NEYS a phony
PHELONIA	n/pl liturgical vestments	**PHONIC**	adj pertaining to the nature of sound
PHENAZIN	n pl. -S a chemical compound	**PHONICS**	n/pl the science of sound
PHENETIC	adj pertaining to a type of classificatory system	**PHONIER**	comparative of phoney and phony
PHENETOL	n pl. -S a volatile liquid	**PHONIES**	pl. of phony
PHENIX	n pl. -ES phoenix	**PHONIEST**	superlative of phoney and phony
PHENOL	n pl. -S a caustic compound	**PHONILY**	adv in a phony manner
PHENOLIC	n pl. -S a synthetic resin	**PHONING**	present participle of phone
PHENOM	n pl. -S a person of extraordinary ability or promise	**PHONO**	n pl. -NOS a record player
PHENYL	n pl. -S a univalent chemical radical PHENYLIC adj	**PHONON**	n pl. -S a quantum of vibrational energy
PHEW	interj — used to express relief, fatigue, or disgust	**PHONY**	adj -NIER, -NIEST not genuine or real
PHI	n pl. -S a Greek letter	**PHONY**	n pl. -NIES one that is phony
PHIAL	n pl. -S a vial	**PHOOEY**	interj — used as an exclamation of disgust or contempt
PHILABEG	n pl. -S filibeg		
PHILIBEG	n pl. -S filibeg		
PHILOMEL	n pl. -S a songbird		
PHILTER	v -ED, -ING, -S to put under the spell of a love potion	**PHORATE**	n pl. -S an insecticide
PHILTRE	v -TRED, -TRING, -TRES to philter	**PHOSGENE**	n pl. -S a poisonous gas
		PHOSPHID	n pl. -S a chemical compound
PHIMOSIS	n pl. -MOSES the abnormal constriction of the opening of the prepuce PHIMOTIC adj	**PHOSPHIN**	n pl. -S a poisonous gas
		PHOSPHOR	n pl. -S a substance that will emit light when exposed to radiation
PHIZ	n pl. -ES a face or facial expression	**PHOT**	n pl. -S a unit of illumination
PHLEGM	n pl. -S a thick mucus secreted in the air passages	**PHOTIC**	adj pertaining to light
PHLEGMY	adj PHLEGMIER, PHLEGMIEST resembling phlegm	**PHOTICS**	n/pl the science of light
		PHOTO	v -ED, -ING, -S to photograph
PHLOEM	n pl. -S a complex plant tissue	**PHOTOG**	n pl. -S one who takes photographs
PHLOX	n pl. -ES a flowering plant	**PHOTOMAP**	v -MAPPED, -MAPPING, -MAPS to map by means of aerial photography
PHOBIA	n pl. -S an obsessive or irrational fear PHOBIC adj		
PHOCINE	adj pertaining to seals	**PHOTON**	n pl. -S a quantum of radiant energy PHOTONIC adj
PHOEBE	n pl. -S a small bird	**PHOTOPIA**	n pl. -S vision in bright light PHOTOPIC adj
PHOENIX	n pl. -ES a mythical bird		
PHON	n pl. -S a unit of loudness	**PHOTOSET**	v -SET, -SETTING, -SETS to prepare for printing by photographic means
PHONAL	adj pertaining to speech sounds		
PHONATE	v -NATED, -NATING, -NATES to produce speech sounds	**PHPHT**	interj pht
		PHRASAL	adj pertaining to a group of two or more associated words
PHONE	v PHONED, PHONING, PHONES to telephone	**PHRASE**	v PHRASED, PHRASING, PHRASES to express in words

PHRASING *n pl.* -S manner or style of verbal expression

PHRATRY *n pl.* -TRIES a tribal unit among primitive peoples PHRATRAL, PHRATRIC *adj*

PHREATIC *adj* pertaining to underground waters

PHRENIC *adj* pertaining to the mind

PHRENSY *v* -SIED, -SYING, -SIES to frenzy

PHT *interj* — used as an expression of mild anger or annoyance

PHTHALIC *adj* pertaining to a certain acid

PHTHALIN *n pl.* -S a chemical compound

PHTHISIC *n pl.* -S phthisis

PHTHISIS *n pl.* PHTHISES a disease of the lungs

PHYLA *pl.* of phylon and phylum

PHYLAE *pl.* of phyle

PHYLAR *adj* pertaining to a phylum

PHYLAXIS *n pl.* -AXISES an inhibiting of infection by the body

PHYLE *n pl.* -LAE a political subdivision in ancient Greece PHYLIC *adj*

PHYLESIS *n pl.* -LESES or -LESISES the course of evolutionary development PHYLETIC *adj*

PHYLLARY *n pl.* -RIES a bract of certain plants

PHYLLITE *n pl.* -S a foliated rock

PHYLLODE *n pl.* -S a flattened petiole that serves as a leaf

PHYLLOID *n pl.* -S a leaflike plant part

PHYLLOME *n pl.* -S a leaf of a plant

PHYLON *n pl.* -LA a genetically related group

PHYLUM *n pl.* -LA a taxonomic division

PHYSES *pl.* of physis

PHYSIC *v* -ICKED, -ICKING, -ICS to treat with medicine

PHYSICAL *n pl.* -S a medical examination of the body

PHYSIQUE *n pl.* -S the form or structure of the body

PHYSIS *n pl.* PHYSES the principle of growth or change in nature

PHYTANE *n pl.* -S a chemical compound

PHYTIN *n pl.* -S a chemical salt

PHYTOID *adj* resembling a plant

PHYTON *n pl.* -S a structural unit of a plant PHYTONIC *adj*

PI *n pl.* -S a Greek letter

PI *v* PIED, PIEING or PIING, PIES to jumble or disorder

PIA *n pl.* -S a membrane of the brain

PIACULAR *adj* atoning

PIAFFE *v* PIAFFED, PIAFFING, PIAFFES to perform a piaffer

PIAFFER *n pl.* -S a movement in horsemanship

PIAL *adj* pertaining to a pia

PIAN *n pl.* -S a tropical disease PIANIC *adj*

PIANISM *n pl.* -S performance on the piano

PIANIST *n pl.* -S one who plays the piano

PIANO *n pl.* -NOS a musical instrument

PIASABA *n pl.* -S piassava

PIASAVA *n pl.* -S piassava

PIASSABA *n pl.* -S piassava

PIASSAVA *n pl.* -S a coarse, stiff fiber

PIASTER *n pl.* -S a monetary unit of several Arab countries

PIASTRE *n pl.* -S piaster

PIAZZA *n pl.* -ZAS or -ZE a public square in an Italian town

PIBROCH *n pl.* -S a musical piece played on the bagpipe

PIC *n pl.* -S a photograph

PICA *n pl.* -S a craving for unnatural food

PICACHO *n pl.* -CHOS an isolated peak of a hill

PICADOR *n pl.* -ES or -S a horseman in a bullfight

PICAL *adj* resembling a pica

PICARA *n pl.* -S a female picaro

PICARO *n pl.* -ROS a vagabond

PICAROON *v* -ED, -ING, -S to act as a pirate

PICAYUNE *n pl.* -S a former Spanish-American coin

PICCOLO *n pl.* -LOS a small flute

PICE *n pl.* PICE a former coin of India and Pakistan

PICEOUS *adj* glossy-black in color

PICK *v* -ED, -ING, -S to select

PICKADIL *n pl.* -S a type of collar

PICKAX *v* -ED, -ING, -ES to use a pickax (a tool for breaking hard surfaces)

PICKAXE *v* -AXED, -AXING, -AXES to pickax

PICKEER v -ED, -ING, -S to skirmish in advance of an army

PICKER n pl. -S one that picks

PICKEREL n pl. -S a freshwater fish

PICKET v -ED, -ING, -S to stand outside of some location, as a business, to publicize one's grievances against it

PICKETER n pl. -S one who pickets

PICKIER comparative of picky

PICKIEST superlative of picky

PICKING n pl. -S the act of one that picks

PICKLE v -LED, -LING, -LES to preserve or flavor in a solution of brine or vinegar

PICKLOCK n pl. -S a tool for opening locks

PICKOFF n pl. -S a play in baseball

PICKUP n pl. -S a small truck

PICKWICK n pl. -S a device for raising wicks in oil lamps

PICKY adj PICKIER, PICKIEST fussy

PICLORAM n pl. -S an herbicide

PICNIC v -NICKED, -NICKING, -NICS to go on a picnic (an outdoor excursion with food)

PICNICKY adj pertaining to a picnic

PICOGRAM n pl. -S one trillionth of a gram

PICOLIN n pl. -S picoline

PICOLINE n pl. -S a chemical compound

PICOT v -ED, -ING, -S to edge with ornamental loops

PICOTEE n pl. -S a variety of carnation

PICQUET n pl. -S piquet

PICRATE n pl. -S a chemical salt
PICRATED adj

PICRIC adj having a very bitter taste

PICRITE n pl. -S an igneous rock

PICTURE v -TURED, -TURING, -TURES to make a visual representation of

PICUL n pl. -S an Asian unit of weight

PIDDLE v -DLED, -DLING, -DLES to waste time

PIDDLER n pl. -S one that piddles

PIDDOCK n pl. -S a bivalve mollusk

PIDGIN n pl. -S a mixed language

PIE v PIED, PIEING, PIES to pi

PIEBALD n pl. -S a spotted animal

PIECE v PIECED, PIECING, PIECES to join into a whole

PIECER n pl. -S one that pieces

PIECING n pl. -S material to be sewn together

PIECRUST n pl. -S the crust of a pie

PIED past tense of pie

PIEDFORT n pl. -S piefort

PIEDMONT n pl. -S an area lying at the foot of a mountain

PIEFORT n pl. -S an unusually thick coin

PIEING a present participle of pi

PIEPLANT n pl. -S a rhubarb

PIER n pl. -S a structure extending from land out over water

PIERCE v PIERCED, PIERCING, PIERCES to cut or pass into or through

PIERCER n pl. -S one that pierces

PIERROT n pl. -S a clown

PIETA n pl. -S a representation of the Virgin Mary mourning over the body of Christ

PIETIES pl. of piety

PIETISM n pl. -S piety

PIETIST n pl. -S a pious person

PIETY n pl. -TIES the quality or state of being pious

PIFFLE v -FLED, -FLING, -FLES to babble

PIG v PIGGED, PIGGING, PIGS to bear pigs (cloven-hoofed mammals)

PIGBOAT n pl. -S a submarine

PIGEON n pl. -S a short-legged bird

PIGFISH n pl. -ES a marine fish

PIGGED past tense of pig

PIGGERY n pl. -GERIES a pigpen

PIGGIE n pl. -S piggy

PIGGIES pl. of piggy

PIGGIN n pl. -S a small wooden pail

PIGGING present participle of pig

PIGGISH adj greedy or dirty

PIGGY n pl. -GIES a small pig

PIGLET n pl. -S a small pig

PIGMENT v -ED, -ING, -S to add a coloring matter to

PIGMY n pl. -MIES pygmy

PIGNUS n pl. -NORA property held as security for a debt

PIGNUT n pl. -S a hickory nut

PIGPEN n pl. -S a place where pigs are kept

PIGSKIN n pl. -S the skin of a pig

PIGSNEY n pl. -NEYS a darling

PIGSTICK v -ED, -ING, -S to hunt for wild boar

PIGSTY   n pl. -STIES a pigpen

PIGTAIL   n pl. -S a tight braid of hair

PIGWEED   n pl. -S a weedy plant

PIKA   n pl. -S a small mammal

PIKAKE   n pl. -S an East Indian vine

PIKE   v PIKED, PIKING, PIKES to pierce with a pike (a long spear)

PIKEMAN   n pl. -MEN a soldier armed with a pike

PIKER   n pl. -S a stingy person

PIKING   present participle of pike

PILAF   n pl. -S a dish made of seasoned rice and often meat

PILAFF   n pl. -S pilaf

PILAR   adj pertaining to hair

PILASTER   n pl. -S a rectangular column

PILAU   n pl. -S pilaf

PILAW   n pl. -S pilaf

PILCHARD   n pl. -S a small marine fish

PILE   v PILED, PILING, PILES to lay one upon the other

PILEA   pl. of pileum

PILEATE   adj having a pileus

PILEATED   adj pileate

PILED   past tense of pile

PILEI   pl. of pileus

PILEOUS   adj pilose

PILEUM   n pl. -LEA the top of a bird's head

PILEUP   n pl. -S a collision involving several motor vehicles

PILEUS   n pl. -LEI the umbrella-shaped portion of a mushroom

PILEWORT   n pl. -S a medicinal plant

PILFER   v -ED, -ING, -S to steal

PILFERER   n pl. -S one that pilfers

PILGRIM   n pl. -S a traveler or wanderer

PILI   n pl. -S a Philippine tree

PILIFORM   adj resembling a hair

PILING   n pl. -S a structure of building supports

PILL   v -ED, -ING, -S to dose with pills (small, rounded masses of medicine)

PILLAGE   v -LAGED, -LAGING, -LAGES to plunder

PILLAGER   n pl. -S one that pillages

PILLAR   v -ED, -ING, -S to provide with vertical building supports

PILLBOX   n pl. -ES a small box for pills

PILLION   n pl. -S a pad or cushion for an extra rider on a horse or motorcycle

PILLORY   v -RIED, -RYING, -RIES to expose to public ridicule or abuse

PILLOW   v -ED, -ING, -S to rest on a pillow (a cushion for the head)

PILLOWY   adj resembling a pillow

PILOSE   adj covered with hair

PILOSITY   n pl. -TIES the state of being pilose

PILOT   v -ED, -ING, -S to control the course of

PILOTAGE   n pl. -S the act of piloting

PILOTING   n pl. -S a branch of navigation

PILOUS   adj pilose

PILSENER   n pl. -S pilsner

PILSNER   n pl. -S a light beer

PILULE   n pl. -S a small pill PILULAR adj

PILUS   n pl. -LI a hair or hairlike structure

PILY   adj divided into a number of wedge-shaped heraldic designs

PIMA   n pl. -S a strong, high-grade cotton

PIMENTO   n pl. -TOS pimiento

PIMIENTO   n pl. -TOS a sweet pepper

PIMP   v -ED, -ING, -S to solicit clients for a prostitute

PIMPLE   n pl. -S an inflamed swelling of the skin PIMPLED adj

PIMPLY   adj -PLIER, -PLIEST covered with pimples

PIN   v PINNED, PINNING, PINS to fasten with a pin (a slender, pointed piece of metal)

PINA   n pl. -S a pineapple

PINAFORE   n pl. -S a child's apron

PINANG   n pl. -S a palm tree

PINASTER   n pl. -S a pine tree

PINATA   n pl. -S a pottery jar used in a Mexican game

PINBALL   n pl. -S an electric game

PINBONE   n pl. -S the hipbone

PINCER   n pl. -S one of the two pivoted parts of a grasping tool

PINCH   v -ED, -ING, -ES to squeeze between two edges or surfaces

PINCHBUG   n pl. -S a large beetle

PINCHECK   n pl. -S a fabric design

PINCHER   n pl. -S one that pinches

PINDER *n* pl. -S an official who formerly impounded stray animals

PINDLING *adj* puny or sickly

PINE *v* PINED, PINING, PINES to yearn intensely

PINEAL *adj* shaped like a pinecone

PINECONE *n* pl. -S a cone-shaped fruit of a pine tree

PINED past tense of pine

PINELIKE *adj* resembling a pine (an evergreen tree)

PINENE *n* pl. -S the main constituent of turpentine

PINERY *n* pl. -ERIES an area where pineapples are grown

PINESAP *n* pl. -S a fragrant herb

PINETUM *n* pl. -TA a plantation of pine trees

PINEWOOD *n* pl. -S the wood of a pine tree

PINEY *adj* PINIER, PINIEST piny

PINFISH *n* pl. -ES a small marine fish

PINFOLD *v* -ED, -ING, -S to confine in an enclosure for stray animals

PING *v* -ED, -ING, -S to produce a brief, high-pitched sound

PINGER *n* pl. -S a device for producing pulses of sound

PINGO *n* pl. -GOS a hill forced up by the effects of frost

PINGRASS *n* pl. -ES a European weed

PINGUID *adj* greasy

PINHEAD *n* pl. -S the head of a pin

PINHOLE *n* pl. -S a small hole made by a pin

PINIER comparative of piney and piny

PINIEST superlative of piney and piny

PINING present participle of pine

PINION *v* -ED, -ING, -S to remove or bind the wing feathers of to prevent flight

PINITE *n* pl. -S a mineral

PINK *adj* PINKER, PINKEST of a pale reddish hue

PINK *v* -ED, -ING, -S to stab with a pointed weapon

PINKEYE *n* pl. -S an inflammation of the eye

PINKIE *n* pl. -S the little finger

PINKIES pl. of pinky

PINKING *n* pl. -S a method of cutting or decorating

PINKISH *adj* somewhat pink

PINKLY *adv* with a pink hue

PINKNESS *n* pl. -ES the state of being pink

PINKO *n* pl. PINKOS or PINKOES a person who holds somewhat radical political views

PINKROOT *n* pl. -S a medicinal plant root

PINKY *n* pl. PINKIES pinkie

PINNA *n* pl. -NAE or -NAS a feather, wing, or winglike part

PINNACE *n* pl. -S a small sailing ship

PINNACLE *v* -CLED, -CLING, -CLES to place on a summit

PINNAE a pl. of pinna

PINNAL *adj* pertaining to a pinna

PINNATE *adj* resembling a feather

PINNATED *adj* pinnate

PINNED past tense of pin

PINNER *n* pl. -S one that pins

PINNING present participle of pin

PINNIPED *n* pl. -S a mammal with limbs modified into flippers

PINNULA *n* pl. -LAE pinnule PINNULAR *adj*

PINNULE *n* pl. -S a pinnate part or organ

PINOCHLE *n* pl. -S a card game

PINOCLE *n* pl. -S pinochle

PINOLE *n* pl. -S a finely ground flour

PINON *n* pl. -S or -ES a pine tree

PINPOINT *v* -ED, -ING, -S to locate precisely

PINPRICK *v* -ED, -ING, -S to puncture with a pin

PINSCHER *n* pl. -S a large, short-haired dog

PINT *n* pl. -S a liquid and dry measure of capacity

PINTA *n* pl. -S a skin disease

PINTADA *n* pl. -S pintado

PINTADO *n* pl. -DOS or -DOES a large food fish

PINTAIL *n* pl. -S a river duck

PINTANO *n* pl. -NOS a tropical fish

PINTLE *n* pl. -S a pin on which something turns

PINTO *n* pl. -TOS or -TOES a spotted horse

PINTSIZE *adj* small

PINUP *n* pl. -S a picture that may be pinned up on a wall

PINWALE *n* pl. -S a type of fabric

PINWEED *n* pl. -S a perennial herb

PINWHEEL *n* pl. -S a child's toy resembling a windmill

PINWORK *n pl.* -S a type of embroidery

PINWORM *n pl.* -S a parasitic worm

PINY *adj* PINIER, PINIEST suggestive of or covered with pine trees

PINYON *n pl.* -S pinon

PIOLET *n pl.* -S an ice ax

PION *n pl.* -S an atomic particle PIONIC *adj*

PIONEER *v* -ED, -ING, -S to take part in the beginnings of

PIOSITY *n pl.* -TIES an excessive show of piety

PIOUS *adj* marked by religious reverence PIOUSLY *adv*

PIP *v* PIPPED, PIPPING, PIPS to break through the shell of an egg

PIPAGE *n pl.* -S a system of pipes

PIPAL *n pl.* -S a fig tree of India

PIPE *v* PIPED, PIPING, PIPES to convey by means of a pipe (a hollow cylinder)

PIPEAGE *n pl.* -S pipage

PIPEFISH *n pl.* -ES a slender fish

PIPEFUL *n pl.* -S a quantity sufficient to fill a tobacco pipe

PIPELESS *adj* having no pipe

PIPELIKE *adj* resembling a pipe

PIPELINE *v* -LINED, -LINING, -LINES to convey by a line of pipe

PIPER *n pl.* -S one that plays on a tubular musical instrument

PIPERINE *n pl.* -S a chemical compound

PIPESTEM *n pl.* -S the stem of a tobacco pipe

PIPET *v* -PETTED, -PETTING, -PETS to pipette

PIPETTE *v* -PETTED, -PETTING, -PETTES to measure liquid with a calibrated tube

PIPIER comparative of pipy

PIPIEST superlative of pipy

PIPING *n pl.* -S a system of pipes

PIPINGLY *adv* shrilly

PIPIT *n pl.* -S a songbird

PIPKIN *n pl.* -S a small pot

PIPPED past tense of pip

PIPPIN *n pl.* -S any of several varieties of apple

PIPPING present participle of pip

PIPY *adj* PIPIER, PIPIEST shrill

PIQUANCY *n pl.* -CIES the quality of being piquant

PIQUANT *adj* having an agreeably sharp taste

PIQUE *v* PIQUED, PIQUING, PIQUES to arouse anger or resentment in

PIQUET *n pl.* -S a card game

PIRACY *n pl.* -CIES robbery on the high seas

PIRAGUA *n pl.* -S a dugout canoe

PIRANA *n pl.* -S piranha

PIRANHA *n pl.* -S a voracious fish

PIRARUCU *n pl.* -S a large food fish

PIRATE *v* -RATED, -RATING, -RATES to commit piracy

PIRATIC *adj* pertaining to piracy

PIRAYA *n pl.* -S piranha

PIRN *n pl.* -S a spinning-wheel bobbin

PIROG *n pl.* -ROGEN, -ROGHI or -ROGI a large Russian pastry

PIROGUE *n pl.* -S piragua

PIROQUE *n pl.* -S piragua

PIROZHOK *n pl.* -ROZHKI, -ROSHKI or -ROJKI a small Russian pastry

PISCARY *n pl.* -RIES a place for fishing

PISCATOR *n pl.* -S a fisherman

PISCINA *n pl.* -NAE or -NAS a basin used in certain church ceremonies PISCINAL *adj*

PISCINE *adj* pertaining to fish

PISH *v* -ED, -ING, -ES to express contempt

PISIFORM *n pl.* -S a small bone of the wrist

PISMIRE *n pl.* -S an ant

PISOLITE *n pl.* -S a limestone

PISS *v* -ED, -ING, -ES to urinate — an offensive term

PISSANT *n pl.* -S an ant

PISSOIR *n pl.* -S a public urinal

PISTACHE *n pl.* -S a shade of green

PISTIL *n pl.* -S the seed-bearing organ of flowering plants

PISTOL *v* -TOLED, -TOLING, -TOLS or -TOLLED, -TOLLING, -TOLS to shoot with a small firearm

PISTOLE *n pl.* -S a former European gold coin

PISTON *n pl.* -S a part of an engine

PIT *v* PITTED, PITTING, PITS to mark with cavities or depressions

PITA *n pl.* -S a strong fiber

PITAPAT	v -PATTED, -PATTING, -PATS to make a repeated tapping sound	**PIXY**	n pl. PIXIES a playfully mischievous fairy or elf PIXYISH adj
PITCH	v -ED, -ING, -ES to throw	**PIZAZZ**	n pl. -ES the quality of being exciting or attractive
PITCHER	n pl. -S a container for holding and pouring liquids	**PIZZA**	n pl. -S an Italian open pie
PITCHIER	comparative of pitchy	**PIZZERIA**	n pl. -S a place where pizzas are made and sold
PITCHIEST	superlative of pitchy	**PIZZLE**	n pl. -S the penis of an animal
PITCHILY	adv in a very dark manner	**PLACABLE**	adj capable of being placated PLACABLY adv
PITCHMAN	n pl. -MEN a salesman of small wares	**PLACARD**	v -ED, -ING, -S to publicize by means of posters
PITCHOUT	n pl. -S a type of pitch in baseball	**PLACATE**	v -CATED, -CATING, -CATES to soothe or mollify
PITCHY	adj PITCHIER, PITCHIEST tarry	**PLACATER**	n pl. -S one that placates
PITEOUS	adj pitiful	**PLACE**	v PLACED, PLACING, PLACES to set in a particular position
PITFALL	n pl. -S a hidden danger or difficulty	**PLACEBO**	n pl. -BOS or -BOES a substance containing no medication that is given for its psychological effect
PITH	v -ED, -ING, -S to sever the spinal cord of		
PITHEAD	n pl. -S a mine entrance	**PLACEMAN**	n pl. -MEN a political appointee to a public office
PITHLESS	adj lacking force		
PITHY	adj PITHIER, PITHIEST concise PITHILY adv	**PLACENTA**	n pl. -TAS or -TAE a vascular organ in most mammals
PITIABLE	adj pitiful PITIABLY adv	**PLACER**	n pl. -S one that places
PITIED	past tense of pity	**PLACET**	n pl. -S a vote of assent
PITIER	n pl. -S one that pities	**PLACID**	adj calm or peaceful PLACIDLY adv
PITIES	present 3d person sing. of pity		
PITIFUL	adj -FULLER, -FULLEST arousing pity	**PLACING**	present participle of place
		PLACK	n pl. -S a former coin of Scotland
PITILESS	adj having no pity		
PITMAN	n pl. -MEN a mine worker	**PLACKET**	n pl. -S a slit in a garment
PITMAN	n pl. -S a connecting rod	**PLACOID**	n pl. -S a fish having platelike scales
PITON	n pl. -S a metal spike used in mountain climbing		
PITSAW	n pl. -S a large saw for cutting logs	**PLAFOND**	n pl. -S an elaborately decorated ceiling
PITTANCE	n pl. -S a small allowance of money	**PLAGAL**	adj designating a medieval musical mode
PITTED	past tense of pit	**PLAGE**	n pl. -S a bright region on the sun
PITTING	n pl. -S an arrangement of cavities or depressions		
PITY	v PITIED, PITYING, PITIES to feel pity (sorrow aroused by another's misfortune)	**PLAGIARY**	n pl. -RIES the act of passing off another's work as one's own
		PLAGUE	v PLAGUED, PLAGUING, PLAGUES to harass or torment
PIU	adv more — used as a musical direction		
		PLAGUER	n pl. -S one that plagues
PIVOT	v -ED, -ING, -S to turn on a shaft or rod	**PLAGUEY**	adj plaguy
		PLAGUING	present participle of plague
PIVOTAL	adj critically important	**PLAGUY**	adj troublesome PLAGUILY adv
PIX	n pl. -ES pyx	**PLAICE**	n pl. -S a European flatfish
PIXIE	n pl. -S pixy PIXIEISH adj	**PLAID**	n pl. -S a woolen scarf of a checkered pattern PLAIDED adj
PIXINESS	n pl. -ES the state of being playfully mischievous		

PLAIN *adj* PLAINER, PLAINEST evident PLAINLY *adv*

PLAIN *v* -ED, -ING, -S to complain

PLAINT *n pl.* -S a complaint

PLAISTER *v* -ED, -ING, -S to plaster

PLAIT *v* -ED, -ING, -S to braid

PLAITER *n pl.* -S one that plaits

PLAITING *n pl.* -S something that is plaited

PLAN *v* PLANNED, PLANNING, PLANS to formulate a plan (a method for achieving an end)

PLANAR *adj* flat

PLANARIA *n pl.* -S an aquatic flatworm

PLANATE *adj* having a flat surface

PLANCH *n pl.* -ES a plank

PLANCHE *n pl.* -S planch

PLANCHET *n pl.* -S a flat piece of metal for stamping into a coin

PLANE *v* PLANED, PLANING, PLANES to make smooth or even

PLANER *n pl.* -S one that planes

PLANET *n pl.* -S a celestial body

PLANFORM *n pl.* -S the contour of an object as viewed from above

PLANGENT *adj* resounding loudly

PLANING present participle of plane

PLANISH *v* -ED, -ING, -ES to toughen and smooth by hammering lightly

PLANK *v* -ED, -ING, -S to cover with planks (long, flat pieces of lumber)

PLANKING *n pl.* -S covering made of planks

PLANKTER *n pl.* -S any organism that is an element of plankton

PLANKTON *n pl.* -S the minute animal and plant life of a body of water

PLANLESS *adj* having no plan

PLANNED past tense of plan

PLANNER *n pl.* -S one that plans

PLANNING *n pl.* -S the establishment of goals or policies

PLANOSOL *n pl.* -S a type of soil

PLANT *v* -ED, -ING, -S to place in the ground for growing

PLANTAIN *n pl.* -S a short-stemmed herb

PLANTAR *adj* pertaining to the sole of the foot

PLANTER *n pl.* -S one that plants

PLANTING *n pl.* -S an area where plants are grown

PLANULA *n pl.* -LAE the free-swimming larva of certain organisms PLANULAR *adj*

PLAQUE *n pl.* -S an ornamental plate or disk

PLASH *v* -ED, -ING, -ES to weave together

PLASHER *n pl.* -S one that plashes

PLASHY *adj* PLASHIER, PLASHIEST marshy

PLASM *n pl.* -S plasma

PLASMA *n pl.* -S the liquid part of blood PLASMIC *adj*

PLASMID *n pl.* -S a hereditary structure of a cell

PLASMIN *n pl.* -S an enzyme

PLASMOID *n pl.* -S a type of high energy particle

PLASMON *n pl.* -S a determinant of inheritance believed to exist in cells

PLASTER *v* -ED, -ING, -S to cover with plaster (a mixture of lime, sand, and water)

PLASTERY *adj* resembling plaster

PLASTIC *n pl.* -S any of a group of synthetic or natural moldable materials

PLASTID *n pl.* -S a structure in plant cells

PLASTRON *n pl.* -S a part of the shell of a turtle PLASTRAL *adj*

PLASTRUM *n pl.* -S plastron

PLAT *v* PLATTED, PLATTING, PLATS to plait

PLATAN *n pl.* -S a large tree

PLATANE *n pl.* -S platan

PLATE *v* PLATED, PLATING, PLATES to coat with a thin layer of metal

PLATEAU *n pl.* -TEAUS or -TEAUX a level stretch of elevated land

PLATEAU *v* -ED, -ING, -S to reach a period or condition of stability

PLATED past tense of plate

PLATEFUL *n pl.* PLATEFULS or PLATESFUL the quantity that fills a plate (a shallow dish)

PLATELET *n pl.* -S a small, flattened body

PLATEN *n pl.* -S the roller of a typewriter

PLATER *n pl.* -S one that plates

PLATESFUL a pl. of plateful

PLATFORM *n pl.* -S a raised floor or flat surface

PLATIER   comparative of platy

PLATIES   a pl. of platy

PLATIEST   superlative of platy

PLATINA   *n* pl. -S platinum

PLATING   *n* pl. -S a thin layer of metal

PLATINIC   *adj* pertaining to platinum

PLATINUM   *n* pl. -S a metallic element

PLATONIC   *adj* purely spiritual and free from sensual desire

PLATOON   *v* -ED, -ING, -S to alternate with another player at the same position

PLATTED   past tense of plat

PLATTER   *n* pl. -S a large, shallow dish

PLATTING   present participle of plat

PLATY   *adj* PLATIER, PLATIEST split into thin, flat pieces

PLATY   *n* pl. PLATYS or PLATIES a small tropical fish

PLATYPUS   *n* pl. -PUSES or -PI an aquatic mammal

PLAUDIT   *n* pl. -S an expression of praise

PLAUSIVE   *adj* expressing praise

PLAY   *v* -ED, -ING, -S to engage in amusement or sport PLAYABLE *adj*

PLAYA   *n* pl. -S the bottom of a desert basin

PLAYACT   *v* -ED, -ING, -S to take part in a theatrical performance

PLAYBACK   *n* pl. -S the act of replaying a newly made recording

PLAYBILL   *n* pl. -S a program for a theatrical performance

PLAYBOOK   *n* pl. -S a book containing one or more literary works for the stage

PLAYBOY   *n* pl. -BOYS a man devoted to pleasurable activities

PLAYDAY   *n* pl. -DAYS a holiday

PLAYDOWN   *n* pl. -S a playoff

PLAYER   *n* pl. -S one that plays

PLAYFUL   *adj* frolicsome

PLAYGIRL   *n* pl. -S a woman devoted to pleasurable activities

PLAYGOER   *n* pl. -S one who attends the theater

PLAYLAND   *n* pl. -S a recreational area

PLAYLESS   *adj* lacking playfulness

PLAYLET   *n* pl. -S a short theatrical performance

PLAYLIKE   *adj* resembling a theatrical performance

PLAYMATE   *n* pl. -S a companion in play

PLAYOFF   *n* pl. -S a series of games played to determine a championship

PLAYPEN   *n* pl. -S an enclosure in which a young child may play

PLAYROOM   *n* pl. -S a recreation room

PLAYSUIT   *n* pl. -S a sports outfit for women and children

PLAYTIME   *n* pl. -S a time for play or amusement

PLAYWEAR   *n* pl. -S clothing worn for leisure activities

PLAZA   *n* pl. -S a public square

PLEA   *n* pl. -S an entreaty

PLEACH   *v* -ED, -ING, -ES to weave together

PLEAD   *v* PLEADED or PLED, PLEADING, PLEADS to ask for earnestly

PLEADER   *n* pl. -S one that pleads

PLEADING   *n* pl. -S an allegation in a legal action

PLEASANT   *adj* -ANTER, -ANTEST pleasing

PLEASE   *v* PLEASED, PLEASING, PLEASES to give enjoyment or satisfaction to

PLEASER   *n* pl. -S one that pleases

PLEASURE   *v* -SURED, -SURING, -SURES to please

PLEAT   *v* -ED, -ING, -S to fold in an even manner

PLEATER   *n* pl. -S one that pleats

PLEB   *n* pl. -S a commoner

PLEBE   *n* pl. -S a freshman at a military or naval academy

PLEBEIAN   *n* pl. -S a commoner

PLECTRON   *n* pl. -TRONS or -TRA plectrum

PLECTRUM   *n* pl. -TRUMS or -TRA an implement used to pluck the strings of a stringed instrument

PLED   a past tense of plead

PLEDGE   *v* PLEDGED, PLEDGING, PLEDGES to give as security for something borrowed

PLEDGEE   *n* pl. -S one to whom something is pledged

PLEDGEOR   *n* pl. -S pledger

PLEDGER   *n* pl. -S one that pledges something

PLEDGET   *n* pl. -S a pad of absorbent cotton

PLEDGING   present participle of pledge

PLEDGOR   *n* pl. -S pledger

PLEIAD n pl. -S or -ES a group of seven illustrious persons

PLENA a pl. of plenum

PLENARY adj complete in every respect

PLENISH v -ED, -ING, -ES to fill up

PLENISM n pl. -S the doctrine that space is fully occupied by matter

PLENIST n pl. -S an advocate of plenism

PLENTY n pl. -TIES a sufficient or abundant amount

PLENUM n pl. -NUMS or -NA space considered as fully occupied by matter

PLEONASM n pl. -S the use of needless words

PLEOPOD n pl. -S an appendage of crustaceans

PLESSOR n pl. -S plexor

PLETHORA n pl. -S an excess

PLEURA n pl. -RAE or -RAS a membrane that envelops the lungs **PLEURAL** adj

PLEURISY n pl. -SIES inflammation of the pleura

PLEURON n pl. -RA a part of a thoracic segment of an insect

PLEUSTON n pl. -S aquatic vegetation

PLEXOR n pl. -S a small, hammer-like medical instrument

PLEXUS n pl. -ES an interlacing of parts

PLIABLE adj easily bent **PLIABLY** adv

PLIANCY n pl. -CIES the quality of being pliant

PLIANT adj easily bent **PLIANTLY** adv

PLICA n pl. -CAE a fold of skin **PLICAL** adj

PLICATE adj pleated

PLICATED adj plicate

PLIE n pl. -S a movement in ballet

PLIED past tense of ply

PLIER n pl. -S one that plies

PLIES present 3d person sing. of ply

PLIGHT v -ED, -ING, -S to promise or bind by a solemn pledge

PLIGHTER n pl. -S one that plights

PLIMSOL n pl. -S plimsoll

PLIMSOLE n pl. -S plimsoll

PLIMSOLL n pl. -S a rubber-soled cloth shoe

PLINK v -ED, -ING, -S to shoot at random targets

PLINKER n pl. -S one that plinks

PLINTH n pl. -S a stone or slab upon which a column or pedestal rests

PLISKIE n pl. -S a practical joke

PLISKY n pl. -KIES pliskie

PLISSE n pl. -S a puckered texture of cloth

PLOD v PLODDED, PLODDING, PLODS to walk heavily

PLODDER n pl. -S one that plods

PLOIDY n pl. -DIES the extent of repetition of the basic number of chromosomes

PLONK v -ED, -ING, -S to plunk

PLOP v PLOPPED, PLOPPING, PLOPS to drop or fall heavily

PLOSION n pl. -S a release of breath after the articulation of certain consonants

PLOSIVE n pl. -S a sound produced by plosion

PLOT v PLOTTED, PLOTTING, PLOTS to plan secretly

PLOTLESS adj planless

PLOTTAGE n pl. -S an area of land

PLOTTED past tense of plot

PLOTTER n pl. -S one that plots

PLOTTIER comparative of plotty

PLOTTIES pl. of plotty

PLOTTING present participle of plot

PLOTTY adj -TIER, -TIEST full of intrigue, as a novel

PLOTTY n pl. -TIES a hot, spiced beverage

PLOUGH v -ED, -ING, -S to plow

PLOUGHER n pl. -S one that ploughs

PLOVER n pl. -S a shore bird

PLOW v -ED, -ING, -S to turn up land with a plow (a farm implement) **PLOWABLE** adj

PLOWBACK n pl. -S a reinvestment of profits in a business

PLOWBOY n pl. -BOYS a boy who leads a plow team

PLOWER n pl. -S one that plows

PLOWHEAD n pl. -S the clevis of a plow

PLOWLAND n pl. -S land suitable for cultivation

PLOWMAN n pl. -MEN a man who plows

PLOY v -ED, -ING, -S to move from a line into column

PLUCK v -ED, -ING, -S to pull out or off

PLUCKER n pl. -S one that plucks

PLUCKY   adj PLUCKIER, PLUCKIEST brave and spirited **PLUCKILY** adv

PLUG   v PLUGGED, PLUGGING, PLUGS to seal or close with a plug (a piece of material used to fill a hole)

PLUGGER   n pl. -S one that plugs

PLUGLESS   adj having no plug

PLUGUGLY   n pl. -LIES a hoodlum

PLUM   n pl. -S a fleshy fruit

PLUMAGE   n pl. -S the feathers of a bird **PLUMAGED** adj

PLUMATE   adj resembling a feather

PLUMB   v -ED, -ING, -S to determine the depth of

PLUMBAGO   n pl. -GOS graphite

PLUMBER   n pl. -S one who installs and repairs plumbing

PLUMBERY   n pl. -ERIES the work of a plumber

PLUMBIC   adj containing lead

PLUMBING   n pl. -S the pipe system of a building

PLUMBISM   n pl. -S lead poisoning

PLUMBOUS   adj containing lead

PLUMBUM   n pl. -S lead

PLUME   v PLUMED, PLUMING, PLUMES to cover with feathers

PLUMELET   n pl. -S a small feather

PLUMIER   comparative of plumy

PLUMIEST   superlative of plumy

PLUMING   present participle of plume

PLUMIPED   n pl. -S a bird having feathered feet

PLUMLIKE   adj resembling a plum

PLUMMET   v -ED, -ING, -S to drop straight down

PLUMMY   adj -MIER, -MIEST full of plums

PLUMOSE   adj having feathers

PLUMP   adj PLUMPER, PLUMPEST well-rounded and full in form

PLUMP   v -ED, -ING, -S to make plump

PLUMPEN   v -ED, -ING, -S to plump

PLUMPER   n pl. -S a heavy fall

PLUMPISH   adj somewhat plump

PLUMPLY   adv in a plump way

PLUMULE   n pl. -S the primary bud of a plant embryo **PLUMULAR** adj

PLUMY   adj PLUMIER, PLUMIEST covered with feathers

PLUNDER   v -ED, -ING, -S to rob of goods by force

PLUNGE   v PLUNGED, PLUNGING, PLUNGES to throw or thrust suddenly or forcibly into something

PLUNGER   n pl. -S one that plunges

PLUNK   v -ED, -ING, -S to fall or drop heavily

PLUNKER   n pl. -S one that plunks

PLURAL   n pl. -S a word that expresses more than one

PLURALLY   adv in a manner or form that expresses more than one

PLUS   n pl. PLUSES or PLUSSES an additional quantity

PLUSH   adj PLUSHER, PLUSHEST luxurious **PLUSHLY** adv

PLUSH   n pl. -ES a fabric with a long pile

PLUSHY   adj PLUSHIER, PLUSHIEST luxurious **PLUSHILY** adv

PLUSSAGE   n pl. -S an amount over and above another

PLUSSES   a pl. of plus

PLUTON   n pl. -S a formation of igneous rock **PLUTONIC** adj

PLUVIAL   n pl. -S a prolonged period of wet climate

PLUVIOSE   adj pluvious

PLUVIOUS   adj pertaining to rain

PLY   v PLIED, PLYING, PLIES to supply with or offer repeatedly **PLYINGLY** adv

PLYER   n pl. -S plier

PLYWOOD   n pl. -S a building material

PNEUMA   n pl. -S the soul or spirit

POACEOUS   adj pertaining to plants of the grass family

POACH   v -ED, -ING, -ES to trespass for the purpose of taking game or fish

POACHER   n pl. -S one that poaches

POACHY   adj POACHIER, POACHIEST swampy

POCHARD   n pl. -S a sea duck

POCK   v -ED, -ING, -S to mark with pocks (pustules caused by an eruptive disease)

POCKET   v -ED, -ING, -S to place in a pouch sewed into a garment

POCKETER   n pl. -S one that pockets

POCKMARK   v -ED, -ING, -S to mark with scars caused by an eruptive disease

POCKY *adj* POCKIER, POCKIEST covered with pocks **POCKILY** *adv*

POCO *adv* a little — used as a musical direction

POCOSIN *n pl.* -S an upland swamp

POD *v* PODDED, PODDING, PODS to produce seed vessels

PODAGRA *n pl.* -S gout in the foot **PODAGRAL, PODAGRIC** *adj*

PODESTA *n pl.* -S an Italian magistrate

PODGY *adj* PODGIER, PODGIEST pudgy **PODGILY** *adv*

PODIA a pl. of podium

PODIATRY *n pl.* -TRIES the study and treatment of the human foot

PODITE *n pl.* -S a limb segment of an arthropod **PODITIC** *adj*

PODIUM *n pl.* -DIUMS or -DIA a small platform

PODOMERE *n pl.* -S a podite

PODSOL *n pl.* -S podzol **PODSOLIC** *adj*

PODZOL *n pl.* -S an infertile soil **PODZOLIC** *adj*

POECHORE *n pl.* -S a semiarid region

POEM *n pl.* -S a composition in verse

POESY *n pl.* -ESIES poetry

POET *n pl.* -S one who writes poems

POETESS *n pl.* -ES a female poet

POETIC *adj* pertaining to poetry

POETICAL *adj* poetic

POETICS *n/pl* poetic theory or practice

POETISE *v* -ISED, -ISING, -ISES to poetize

POETISER *n pl.* -S a poetizer

POETIZE *v* -IZED, -IZING, -IZES to write poetry

POETIZER *n pl.* -S one that poetizes

POETLESS *adj* lacking a poet

POETLIKE *adj* resembling a poet

POETRY *n pl.* -RIES literary work in metrical form

POGEY *n pl.* -GEYS any form of government relief

POGIES pl. of pogy

POGONIA *n pl.* -S a small orchid

POGONIP *n pl.* -S a dense fog of suspended ice particles

POGROM *v* -ED, -ING, -S to massacre systematically

POGY *n pl.* -GIES a marine fish

POH *interj* — used to express disgust

POI *n pl.* -S a Hawaiian food

POIGNANT *adj* emotionally distressing

POILU *n pl.* -S a French soldier

POIND *v* -ED, -ING, -S to seize and sell the property of to satisfy a debt

POINT *v* -ED, -ING, -S to indicate direction with the finger

POINTE *n pl.* -S a ballet position

POINTER *n pl.* -S one that points

POINTMAN *n pl.* -MEN a certain player in hockey

POINTY *adj* POINTIER, POINTIEST coming to a sharp, tapering end

POISE *v* POISED, POISING, POISES to hold in a state of equilibrium

POISER *n pl.* -S one that poises

POISON *v* -ED, -ING, -S to administer a harmful substance to

POISONER *n pl.* -S one that poisons

POITREL *n pl.* -S peytral

POKE *v* POKED, POKING, POKES to push or prod

POKER *n pl.* -S one that pokes

POKEROOT *n pl.* -S pokeweed

POKEWEED *n pl.* -S a perennial herb

POKEY *n pl.* -KEYS poky

POKIER comparative of poky

POKIES pl. of poky

POKIEST superlative of poky

POKILY *adv* in a poky manner

POKINESS *n pl.* -ES the state of being poky

POKING present participle of poke

POKY *n pl.* POKIES a jail

POKY *adj* POKIER, POKIEST slow

POL *n pl.* -S a politician

POLAR *n pl.* -S a straight line related to a point

POLARISE *v* -ISED, -ISING, -ISES to polarize

POLARITY *n pl.* -TIES the possession of two opposite qualities

POLARIZE *v* -IZED, -IZING, -IZES to give polarity to

POLARON *n pl.* -S a type of electron

POLDER *n pl.* -S a tract of low land reclaimed from a body of water

POLE *v* POLED, POLING, POLES to propel with a pole (a long, thin piece of wood or metal)

POLEAX *v* -ED, -ING, -ES to strike with an axlike weapon

POLEAXE   v -AXED, -AXING, -AXES to poleax

POLECAT   n pl. -S a carnivorous mammal

POLED   past tense of pole

POLEIS   pl. of polis

POLELESS   adj having no pole

POLEMIC   n pl. -S a controversial argument

POLEMIST   n pl. -S one who engages in polemics

POLEMIZE   v -MIZED, -MIZING, -MIZES to engage in polemics

POLENTA   n pl. -S a thick mush of cornmeal

POLER   n pl. -S one that poles

POLESTAR   n pl. -S a guiding principle

POLEWARD   adv in the direction of either extremity of the earth's axis

POLEYN   n pl. -S a protective piece of leather for the knee

POLICE   v -LICED, -LICING, -LICES to make clean or orderly

POLICY   n pl. -CIES an action or a procedure considered with reference to prudence or expediency

POLING   present participle of pole

POLIO   n pl. -LIOS an infectious virus disease

POLIS   n pl. -LEIS an ancient Greek city-state

POLISH   v -ED, -ING, -ES to make smooth and lustrous by rubbing

POLISHER   n pl. -S one that polishes

POLITE   adj -LITER, -LITEST showing consideration for others POLITELY adv

POLITIC   adj shrewd

POLITICK   v -ED, -ING, -S to engage in politics

POLITICO   n pl. -COS or -COES one who politicks

POLITICS   n/pl the art or science of government

POLITY   n pl. -TIES a form or system of government

POLKA   v -ED, -ING, -S to perform a lively dance

POLL   v -ED, -ING, -S to question for the purpose of surveying public opinion

POLLACK   n pl. -S a marine food fish

POLLARD   v -ED, -ING, -S to cut the top branches of a tree back to the trunk

POLLEE   n pl. -S one who is polled

POLLEN   v -ED, -ING, -S to convey pollen (the fertilizing element in a seed plant) to

POLLER   n pl. -S one that polls

POLLEX   n pl. -LICES the innermost digit of the forelimb POLLICAL adj

POLLINIA   n/pl masses of pollen grains

POLLINIC   adj pertaining to pollen

POLLIST   n pl. -S a poller

POLLIWOG   n pl. -S a tadpole

POLLOCK   n pl. -S pollack

POLLSTER   n pl. -S a poller

POLLUTE   v -LUTED, -LUTING, -LUTES to make unclean or impure

POLLUTER   n pl. -S one that pollutes

POLLYWOG   n pl. -S polliwog

POLO   n pl. -LOS a game played on horseback

POLOIST   n pl. -S a polo player

POLONIUM   n pl. -S a radioactive element

POLTROON   n pl. -S a base coward

POLY   n pl. POLYS a type of white blood cell

POLYBRID   n pl. -S a type of hybrid plant

POLYCOT   n pl. -S a type of plant

POLYENE   n pl. -S a chemical compound POLYENIC adj

POLYGALA   n pl. -S a flowering plant

POLYGAMY   n pl. -MIES the condition of having more than one spouse at the same time

POLYGENE   n pl. -S a type of gene

POLYGLOT   n pl. -S one that speaks or writes several languages

POLYGON   n pl. -S a closed plane figure bounded by straight lines

POLYGONY   n pl. -NIES an herb

POLYGYNY   n pl. -NIES the condition of having more than one wife at the same time

POLYMATH   n pl. -S a person of great and varied learning

POLYMER   n pl. -S a complex chemical compound

POLYNYA   n pl. -S an area of open water surrounded by sea ice

POLYP   n pl. -S an invertebrate

POLYPARY   n pl. -ARIES the common supporting structure of a polyp colony

POLYPI   a pl. of polypus

POLYPIDE   n pl. -S a polyp

POLYPNEA n pl. -S rapid breathing

POLYPOD n pl. -S a many-footed organism

POLYPODY n pl. -DIES a fern

POLYPOID adj resembling a polyp

POLYPORE n pl. -S a type of fungus

POLYPOUS adj pertaining to a polyp

POLYPUS n pl. -PI or -PUSES a growth protruding from the mucous lining of an organ

POLYSEMY n pl. -MIES diversity of meanings

POLYSOME n pl. -S a cluster of protein particles

POLYTENE adj having chromosomes of a certain type

POLYTENY n pl. -NIES the state of being polytene

POLYTYPE n pl. -S a crystal structure

POLYURIA n pl. -S excessive urination **POLYURIC** adj

POLYZOAN n pl. -S a bryozoan

POLYZOIC adj composed of many zooids

POMACE n pl. -S the pulpy residue of crushed fruits

POMADE v -MADED, -MADING, -MADES to apply a perfumed hair dressing to

POMANDER n pl. -S a mixture of aromatic substances

POMATUM n pl. -S a perfumed hair dressing

POME n pl. -S a fleshy fruit with a core

POMELO n pl. -LOS a grapefruit

POMMEE adj having arms with knoblike ends — used of a heraldic cross

POMMEL v -MELED, -MELING, -MELS or -MELLED, -MELLING, -MELS to strike with the fists

POMOLOGY n pl. -GIES the study of fruits

POMP n pl. -S stately or splendid display

POMPANO n pl. -NOS a marine food fish

POMPOM n pl. -S an antiaircraft cannon

POMPON n pl. -S an ornamental tuft or ball

POMPOUS adj marked by exaggerated self-importance

PONCE n pl. -S a man who solicits clients for a prostitute

PONCHO n pl. -CHOS a type of cloak

POND n pl. -S a body of water smaller than a lake

PONDER v -ED, -ING, -S to consider something deeply and thoroughly

PONDERER n pl. -S one that ponders

PONDWEED n pl. -S an aquatic plant

PONE n pl. -S a corn bread

PONENT adj affirmative

PONGEE n pl. -S a type of silk

PONGID n pl. -S an anthropoid ape

PONIARD v -ED, -ING, -S to stab with a dagger

PONIED past tense of pony

PONIES present 3d person sing. of pony

PONS n pl. PONTES a band of nerve fibers in the brain

PONTIFEX n pl. -FICES an ancient Roman priest

PONTIFF n pl. -S a pope or bishop

PONTIFIC adj pertaining to a pope or bishop

PONTIFICES pl. of pontifex

PONTIL n pl. -S a punty

PONTINE adj pertaining to bridges

PONTON n pl. -S pontoon

PONTOON n pl. -S a flat-bottomed boat

PONY v -NIED, -NYING, -NIES to prepare lessons with the aid of a literal translation

PONYTAIL n pl. -S a hairstyle

POOCH n pl. -ES a dog

POOD n pl. -S a Russian unit of weight

POODLE n pl. -S a heavy-coated dog

POOH v -ED, -ING, -S to express contempt for

POOL v -ED, -ING, -S to combine in a common fund

POOLHALL n pl. -S a poolroom

POOLROOM n pl. -S an establishment for the playing of billiards

POON n pl. -S an East Indian tree

POOP v -ED, -ING, -S to tire out

POOR adj POORER, POOREST lacking the means of support

POORI n pl. -S a light, flat wheat cake

POORISH adj somewhat poor

POORLY adv in a poor manner

POORNESS n pl. -ES the state of being poor

POORTITH *n* pl. -S poverty

POP *v* POPPED, POPPING, POPS to make a sharp, explosive sound

POPCORN *n* pl. -S a variety of corn

POPE *n* pl. -S the head of the Roman Catholic Church **POPELESS**, **POPELIKE** *adj*

POPEDOM *n* pl. -S the office of a pope

POPERY *n* pl. -ERIES Roman Catholicism — an offensive term

POPEYED *adj* having bulging eyes

POPGUN *n* pl. -S a toy gun

POPINJAY *n* pl. -JAYS a vain person

POPISH *adj* pertaining to the Roman Catholic Church — an offensive term **POPISHLY** *adv*

POPLAR *n* pl. -S a fast-growing tree

POPLIN *n* pl. -S a durable fabric

POPLITIC *adj* pertaining to the part of the leg behind the knee

POPOVER *n* pl. -S a very light egg muffin

POPPA *n* pl. -S papa

POPPED past tense of pop

POPPER *n* pl. -S one that pops

POPPET *n* pl. -S a mechanical valve

POPPIED *adj* covered with poppies

POPPIES pl. of poppy

POPPING present participle of pop

POPPLE *v* -PLED, -PLING, -PLES to move in a bubbling or rippling manner

POPPY *n* pl. -PIES a flowering plant

POPULACE *n* pl. -S the common people

POPULAR *adj* liked by many people

POPULATE *v* -LATED, -LATING, -LATES to inhabit

POPULISM *n* pl. -S populists' doctrines

POPULIST *n* pl. -S a member of a party which represents the common people

POPULOUS *adj* containing many inhabitants

PORCH *n* pl. -ES a covered structure at the entrance to a building

PORCINE *adj* pertaining to swine

PORE *v* PORED, PORING, PORES to gaze intently

PORGY *n* pl. -GIES a marine food fish

PORISM *n* pl. -S a type of mathematical proposition

PORK *n* pl. -S the flesh of swine used as food

PORKER *n* pl. -S a pig

PORKIER comparative of porky

PORKIES pl. of porky

PORKIEST superlative of porky

PORKPIE *n* pl. -S a man's hat

PORKWOOD *n* pl. -S a tropical tree

PORKY *adj* PORKIER, PORKIEST resembling pork

PORKY *n* pl. -KIES a porcupine

PORN *n* pl. -S pornography

PORNO *n* pl. -NOS pornography

POROSE *adj* porous

POROSITY *n* pl. -TIES the state of being porous

POROUS *adj* having minute openings **POROUSLY** *adv*

PORPHYRY *n* pl. -RIES an igneous rock

PORPOISE *n* pl. -S an aquatic mammal

PORRECT *adj* extended forward

PORRIDGE *n* pl. -S a soft food

PORT *v* -ED, -ING, -S to shift to the left side

PORTABLE *n* pl. -S something that can be carried

PORTABLY *adv* so as to be capable of being carried

PORTAGE *v* -TAGED, -TAGING, -TAGES to transport from one navigable waterway to another

PORTAL *n* pl. -S a door, gate, or entrance **PORTALED** *adj*

PORTANCE *n* pl. -S demeanor

PORTEND *v* -ED, -ING, -S to serve as an omen of

PORTENT *n* pl. -S an omen

PORTER *n* pl. -S a person employed to carry luggage

PORTHOLE *n* pl. -S a small window in a ship's side

PORTICO *n* pl. -COS or -COES a type of porch

PORTIERE *n* pl. -S a curtain for a doorway

PORTION *v* -ED, -ING, -S to divide into shares for distribution

PORTLESS *adj* having no place for ships to load or unload

PORTLY *adj* -LIER, -LIEST rather heavy or fat

PORTRAIT *n* pl. -S a likeness of a person

PORTRAY *v* -ED, -ING, -S to represent pictorially

PORTRESS *n* pl. -ES a female doorkeeper

POSADA *n* pl. -S an inn

POSE	v POSED, POSING, POSES to assume a fixed position	**POSTFACE**	n pl. -S a brief note placed at the end of a publication
POSER	n pl. -S one that poses	**POSTFIX**	v -ED, -ING, -ES to affix at the end of something
POSEUR	n pl. -S an affected or insincere person	**POSTFORM**	v -ED, -ING, -S to shape subsequently
POSH	adj POSHER, POSHEST stylish or elegant	**POSTHOLE**	n pl. -S a hole dug to secure a fence post
POSIES	pl. of posy		
POSING	present participle of pose	**POSTICHE**	n pl. -S an imitation
POSINGLY	adv in a posing manner	**POSTIN**	n pl. -S posteen
POSIT	v -ED, -ING, -S to place	**POSTING**	n pl. -S the act of transferring to a ledger
POSITION	v -ED, -ING, -S to put in a particular location	**POSTIQUE**	n pl. -S postiche
POSITIVE	adj -TIVER, -TIVEST certain	**POSTLUDE**	n pl. -S a closing musical piece
POSITIVE	n pl. -S a quantity greater than zero	**POSTMAN**	n pl. -MEN a mailman
POSITRON	n pl. -S an atomic particle	**POSTMARK**	v -ED, -ING, -S to stamp mail with an official mark
POSOLOGY	n pl. -GIES a branch of medicine that deals with drug dosages	**POSTORAL**	adj situated behind the mouth
		POSTPAID	adv with the postage prepaid
POSSE	n pl. -S a body of men summoned to aid a peace officer	**POSTPONE**	v -PONED, -PONING, -PONES to put off to a future time
		POSTURAL	adj pertaining to the position of the body
POSSESS	v -ED, -ING, -ES to have as property	**POSTURE**	v -TURED, -TURING, -TURES to assume a particular position
POSSET	n pl. -S a hot, spiced drink	**POSTURER**	n pl. -S one that postures
POSSIBLE	adj -BLER, -BLEST capable of happening or proving true POSSIBLY adv	**POSTWAR**	adj occurring or existing after a war
POSSUM	n pl. -S opossum	**POSY**	n pl. -SIES a flower or bouquet
POST	v -ED, -ING, -S to affix in a public place	**POT**	v POTTED, POTTING, POTS to put in a pot (a round, fairly deep container)
POSTAGE	n pl. -S the charge for mailing an item		
POSTAL	n pl. -S a postcard	**POTABLE**	n pl. -S a liquid suitable for drinking
POSTALLY	adv in a manner pertaining to the mails	**POTAGE**	n pl. -S a thick soup
		POTAMIC	adj pertaining to rivers
POSTANAL	adj situated behind the anus	**POTASH**	n pl. -ES an alkaline compound
POSTBAG	n pl. -S a mailbag	**POTASSIC**	adj pertaining to potassium (a metallic element)
POSTBOX	n pl. -ES a mailbox		
POSTBOY	n pl. -BOYS a boy who carries mail	**POTATION**	n pl. -S the act of drinking
		POTATO	n pl. -TOES the edible tuber of a cultivated plant
POSTCARD	n pl. -S a card for use in the mail		
POSTCAVA	n pl. -VAE a vein in higher vertebrates	**POTATORY**	adj pertaining to drinking
		POTBELLY	n pl. -LIES a protruding abdominal region
POSTDATE	v -DATED, -DATING, -DATES to give a date later than the actual date to	**POTBOIL**	v -ED, -ING, -S to produce a literary or artistic work of poor quality
POSTEEN	n pl. -S an Afghan outer garment	**POTBOY**	n pl. -BOYS a boy who serves customers in a tavern
POSTER	n pl. -S a printed or written notice for posting	**POTEEN**	n pl. -S Irish whiskey that is distilled unlawfully
POSTERN	n pl. -S a rear door or gate	**POTENCE**	n pl. -S potency

POTENCY	n pl. -CIES the quality of being potent
POTENT	adj powerful POTENTLY adv
POTFUL	n pl. -S as much as a pot can hold
POTHEAD	n pl. -S one who smokes marijuana
POTHEEN	n pl. -S poteen
POTHER	v -ED, -ING, -S to trouble
POTHERB	n pl. -S any herb used as a food or seasoning
POTHOLE	n pl. -S a deep hole in a road POTHOLED adj
POTHOOK	n pl. -S a hook for lifting or hanging pots
POTHOUSE	n pl. -S a tavern
POTICHE	n pl. -S a type of vase
POTION	n pl. -S a magical or medicinal drink
POTLACH	n pl. -ES a ceremonial feast
POTLACHE	n pl. -S potlach
POTLATCH	v -ED, -ING, -ES to hold a ceremonial feast for
POTLIKE	adj resembling a pot
POTLUCK	n pl. -S food which is incidentally available
POTMAN	n pl. -MEN a man who serves customers in a tavern
POTPIE	n pl. -S a deep-dish pie containing meat and vegetables
POTSHARD	n pl. -S potsherd
POTSHERD	n pl. -S a fragment of broken pottery
POTSHOT	v -SHOT, -SHOTTING, -SHOTS to shoot randomly at
POTSIE	n pl. -S potsy
POTSTONE	n pl. -S a variety of steatite
POTSY	n pl. -SIES a children's game
POTTAGE	n pl. -S a thick soup
POTTED	past tense of pot
POTTEEN	n pl. -S poteen
POTTER	v -ED, -ING, -S to putter
POTTERER	n pl. -S one that potters
POTTERY	n pl. -TERIES ware molded from clay and hardened by heat
POTTIER	comparative of potty
POTTIES	pl. of potty
POTTIEST	superlative of potty
POTTING	present participle of pot
POTTLE	n pl. -S a drinking vessel
POTTO	n pl. -TOS a lemur of tropical Africa

POTTY	adj -TIER, -TIEST of little importance
POTTY	n pl. -TIES a small toilet seat
POUCH	v -ED, -ING, -ES to put in a pouch (a small, flexible receptacle)
POUCHY	adj POUCHIER, POUCHIEST resembling a pouch
POUF	n pl. -S a loose roll of hair POUFED adj
POUFF	n pl. -S pouf POUFFED adj
POUFFE	n pl. -S pouf
POULARD	n pl. -S a spayed hen
POULARDE	n pl. -S poulard
POULT	n pl. -S a young domestic fowl
POULTICE	v -TICED, -TICING, -TICES to apply a healing substance to
POULTRY	n pl. -TRIES domestic fowls kept for eggs or meat
POUNCE	v POUNCED, POUNCING, POUNCES to make a sudden assault or approach
POUNCER	n pl. -S one that pounces
POUND	v -ED, -ING, -S to strike heavily and repeatedly
POUNDAGE	n pl. -S the act of impounding
POUNDAL	n pl. -S a unit of force
POUNDER	n pl. -S one that pounds
POUR	v -ED, -ING, -S to cause to flow POURABLE adj
POURER	n pl. -S one that pours
POUSSIE	n pl. -S pussy
POUT	v -ED, -ING, -S to protrude the lips in ill humor
POUTER	n pl. -S one that pouts
POUTFUL	adj pouty
POUTY	adj POUTIER, POUTIEST tending to pout
POVERTY	n pl. -TIES the state of being poor
POW	n pl. -S an explosive sound
POWDER	v -ED, -ING, -S to reduce to powder (matter in a finely divided state)
POWDERER	n pl. -S one that powders
POWDERY	adj resembling powder
POWER	v -ED, -ING, -S to provide with means of propulsion
POWERFUL	adj possessing great force
POWTER	n pl. -S a domestic pigeon
POWWOW	v -ED, -ING, -S to hold a conference
POX	v -ED, -ING, -ES to infect with syphilis

POXVIRUS	*n pl.* -ES a type of virus
POYOU	*n pl.* -S an armadillo of Argentina
POZZOLAN	*n pl.* -S a finely divided material used to make cement
PRAAM	*n pl.* -S pram
PRACTIC	*adj* practical
PRACTICE	*v* -TICED, -TICING, -TICES to perform often so as to acquire skill
PRACTISE	*v* -TISED, -TISING, -TISES to practice
PRAECIPE	*n pl.* -S a legal writ
PRAEDIAL	*adj* pertaining to land
PRAEFECT	*n pl.* -S prefect
PRAELECT	*v* -ED, -ING, -S to prelect
PRAETOR	*n pl.* -S an ancient Roman magistrate
PRAHU	*n pl.* -S prau
PRAIRIE	*n pl.* -S a tract of grassland
PRAISE	*v* PRAISED, PRAISING, PRAISES to express approval or admiration of
PRAISER	*n pl.* -S one that praises
PRALINE	*n pl.* -S a confection made of nuts cooked in sugar
PRAM	*n pl.* -S a flat-bottomed boat
PRANCE	*v* PRANCED, PRANCING, PRANCES to spring forward on the hind legs
PRANCER	*n pl.* -S one that prances
PRANDIAL	*adj* pertaining to a meal
PRANG	*v* -ED, -ING, -S to cause to crash
PRANK	*v* -ED, -ING, -S to adorn gaudily
PRANKISH	*adj* mischievous
PRAO	*n pl.* PRAOS prau
PRASE	*n pl.* -S a mineral
PRAT	*n pl.* -S the buttocks
PRATE	*v* PRATED, PRATING, PRATES to chatter
PRATER	*n pl.* -S one that prates
PRATFALL	*n pl.* -S a fall on the buttocks
PRATING	present participle of prate
PRATIQUE	*n pl.* -S clearance given a ship by the health authority of a port
PRATTLE	*v* -TLED, -TLING, -TLES to babble
PRATTLER	*n pl.* -S one that prattles
PRAU	*n pl.* -S a swift Malaysian sailing vessel
PRAWN	*v* -ED, -ING, -S to fish for prawns (edible shellfishes)

PRAWNER	*n pl.* -S one that prawns
PRAXIS	*n pl.* PRAXISES or PRAXES practical use of a branch of learning
PRAY	*v* -ED, -ING, -S to address prayers to
PRAYER	*n pl.* -S a devout petition to a deity
PREACH	*v* -ED, -ING, -ES to advocate or recommend urgently
PREACHER	*n pl.* -S one that preaches
PREACHY	*adj* PREACHIER, PREACHIEST tending to preach
PREACT	*v* -ED, -ING, -S to act beforehand
PREADAPT	*v* -ED, -ING, -S to adapt beforehand
PREADMIT	*v* -MITTED, -MITTING, -MITS to admit beforehand
PREADOPT	*v* -ED, -ING, -S to adopt beforehand
PREADULT	*adj* preceding adulthood
PREAGED	*adj* previously aged
PREALLOT	*v* -LOTTED, -LOTTING, -LOTS to allot beforehand
PREAMBLE	*n pl.* -S an introductory statement
PREAMP	*n pl.* -S an amplifier
PREANAL	*adj* situated in front of the anus
PREARM	*v* -ED, -ING, -S to arm beforehand
PREAVER	*v* -VERRED, -VERRING, -VERS to aver or assert beforehand
PREAXIAL	*adj* situated in front of an axis
PREBASAL	*adj* situated in front of a base
PREBEND	*n pl.* -S a clergyman's stipend
PREBILL	*v* -ED, -ING, -S to bill beforehand
PREBIND	*v* -BOUND, -BINDING, -BINDS to bind in durable materials for library use
PREBLESS	*v* -ED, -ING, -ES to bless beforehand
PREBOIL	*v* -ED, -ING, -S to boil beforehand
PREBOUND	past tense of prebind
PRECAST	*v* -CAST, -CASTING, -CASTS to cast and finish before placing into position
PRECAVA	*n pl.* -VAE a vein in higher vertebrates PRECAVAL *adj*
PRECEDE	*v* -CEDED, -CEDING, -CEDES to go before
PRECENT	*v* -ED, -ING, -S to lead a church choir in singing

PRECEPT n pl. -S a rule of conduct

PRECESS v -ED, -ING, -ES to rotate with a complex motion

PRECHECK v -ED, -ING, -S to check beforehand

PRECHILL v -ED, -ING, -S to chill beforehand

PRECIEUX adj excessively refined

PRECINCT n pl. -S a subdivision of a city or town

PRECIOUS n pl. -ES a darling

PRECIPE n pl. -S praecipe

PRECIS v -ED, -ING, -ES to make a concise summary of

PRECISE adj -CISER, -CISEST sharply and clearly defined or stated

PRECITED adj previously cited

PRECLEAN v -ED, -ING, -S to clean beforehand

PRECLUDE v -CLUDED, -CLUDING, -CLUDES to make impossible by previous action

PRECOOK v -ED, -ING, -S to cook beforehand

PRECOOL v -ED, -ING, -S to cool beforehand

PRECURE v -CURED, -CURING, -CURES to cure beforehand

PREDATE v -DATED, -DATING, -DATES to date before the actual or a specified time

PREDATOR n pl. -S one that plunders

PREDAWN n pl. -S the time just before dawn

PREDIAL adj praedial

PREDICT v -ED, -ING, -S to tell of or about in advance

PREDUSK n pl. -S the time just before dusk

PREE v PREED, PREEING, PREES to test by tasting

PREELECT v -ED, -ING, -S to elect or choose beforehand

PREEMIE n pl. -S an infant born prematurely

PREEMPT v -ED, -ING, -S to acquire by prior right

PREEN v -ED, -ING, -S to smooth or clean with the beak or tongue

PREENACT v -ED, -ING, -S to enact beforehand

PREENER n pl. -S one that preens

PREEXIST v -ED, -ING, -S to exist before

PREFAB v -FABBED, -FABBING, -FABS to construct beforehand

PREFACE v -ACED, -ACING, -ACES to provide with an introductory statement

PREFACER n pl. -S one that prefaces

PREFECT n pl. -S an ancient Roman official

PREFER v -FERRED, -FERRING, -FERS to hold in higher regard or esteem

PREFIX v -ED, -ING, -ES to add as a prefix (a form affixed to the beginning of a root word)

PREFIXAL adj pertaining to or being a prefix

PREFOCUS v -CUSED, -CUSING, -CUSES or -CUSSED, -CUSSING, -CUSSES to focus beforehand

PREFORM v -ED, -ING, -S to form beforehand

PREFRANK v -ED, -ING, -S to frank beforehand

PREGAME adj preceding a game

PREGNANT adj carrying a developing fetus in the uterus

PREHEAT v -ED, -ING, -S to heat beforehand

PREHUMAN n pl. -S a prototype of man

PREJUDGE v -JUDGED, -JUDGING, -JUDGES to judge beforehand

PRELACY n pl. -CIES the office of a prelate

PRELATE n pl. -S a high-ranking clergyman **PRELATIC** adj

PRELECT v -ED, -ING, -S to lecture

PRELEGAL adj occurring before the commencement of studies in law

PRELIM n pl. -S a minor match preceding the main event

PRELIMIT v -ED, -ING, -S to limit beforehand

PRELUDE v -LUDED, -LUDING, -LUDES to play a musical introduction

PRELUDER n pl. -S one that preludes

PREMAN n pl. -MEN a hypothetical ancestor of man

PREMED n pl. -S a student preparing for the study of medicine

PREMEDIC n pl. -S a premed

PREMEN pl. of preman

PREMIE n pl. -S preemie

PREMIER n pl. -S a prime minister

PREMIERE v -MIERED, -MIERING, -MIERES to present publicly for the first time

PREMISE v -MISED, -MISING, -MISES to state in advance

PREMISS n pl. -ES a proposition in logic

PREMIUM n pl. -S an additional payment

PREMIX v -ED, -ING, -ES to mix before use

PREMOLAR n pl. -S a tooth

PREMORSE adj ending abruptly, as if bitten off

PREMUNE adj resistant to a disease

PRENAME n pl. -S a forename

PRENATAL adj prior to birth

PRENOMEN n pl. -MENS or -MINA the first name of an ancient Roman

PRENTICE v -TICED, -TICING, -TICES to place with an employer for instruction in a trade

PREP v PREPPED, PREPPING, PREPS to attend a preparatory school

PREPACK v -ED, -ING, -S to package before retail distribution

PREPAID past tense of prepay

PREPARE v -PARED, -PARING, -PARES to put in proper condition or readiness

PREPARER n pl. -S one that prepares

PREPAY v -PAID, -PAYING, -PAYS to pay in advance

PREPENSE adj planned in advance

PREPLACE v -PLACED, -PLACING, -PLACES to place beforehand

PREPLAN v -PLANNED, -PLANNING, -PLANS to plan in advance

PREPLANT adj occurring before planting

PREPPED past tense of prep

PREPPIE n pl. -S one who preps

PREPPING present participle of prep

PREPRINT v -ED, -ING, -S to print in advance

PREPUCE n pl. -S a fold of skin covering the penis

PREPUNCH v -ED, -ING, -ES to punch in advance

PRERENAL adj situated in front of the kidney

PRESA n pl. -SE a musical symbol

PRESAGE v -SAGED, -SAGING, -SAGES to foretell

PRESAGER n pl. -S one that presages

PRESCIND v -ED, -ING, -S to consider separately

PRESCORE v -SCORED, -SCORING, -SCORES to record the sound of before filming

PRESE pl. of presa

PRESELL v -SOLD, -SELLING, -SELLS to promote a product not yet being sold to the public

PRESENCE n pl. -S close proximity

PRESENT v -ED, -ING, -S to bring into the presence of someone

PRESERVE v -SERVED, -SERVING, -SERVES to keep free from harm or danger

PRESET v -SET, -SETTING, -SETS to set beforehand

PRESHAPE v -SHAPED, -SHAPING, -SHAPES to shape beforehand

PRESHOW v -SHOWED, -SHOWN, -SHOWING, -SHOWS to show beforehand

PRESIDE v -SIDED, -SIDING, -SIDES to occupy the position of authority

PRESIDER n pl. -S one that presides

PRESIDIA n/pl Soviet executive committees

PRESIDIO n pl. -DIOS a Spanish fort

PRESIFT v -ED, -ING, -S to sift beforehand

PRESOAK v -ED, -ING, -S to soak beforehand

PRESOLD past tense of presell

PRESS v -ED, -ING, -ES to act upon with steady force

PRESSER n pl. -S one that presses

PRESSMAN n pl. -MEN a printing press operator

PRESSOR adj causing an increase in blood pressure

PRESSRUN n pl. -S a continuous operation of a printing press

PRESSURE v -SURED, -SURING, -SURES to apply force to

PREST n pl. -S a loan

PRESTAMP v -ED, -ING, -S to stamp beforehand

PRESTER n pl. -S a priest

PRESTIGE n pl. -S distinction or reputation in the eyes of people

PRESTO n pl. -TOS a musical passage played in rapid tempo

PRESUME v -SUMED, -SUMING, -SUMES to take for granted

PRESUMER n pl. -S one that presumes

PRETASTE v -TASTED, -TASTING, -TASTES to taste beforehand

PRETAX adj existing before provision for taxes

PRETEEN   *n* pl. -S a child under the age of thirteen

PRETENCE   *n* pl. -S pretense

PRETEND   *v* -ED, -ING, -S to assume or display a false appearance of

PRETENSE   *n* pl. -S the act of pretending

PRETERIT   *n* pl. -S a past tense in grammar

PRETEST   *v* -ED, -ING, -S to give a preliminary test to

PRETEXT   *v* -ED, -ING, -S to allege as an excuse

PRETOR   *n* pl. -S praetor

PRETREAT   *v* -ED, -ING, -S to treat beforehand

PRETTIED   past tense of pretty

PRETTIER   comparative of pretty

PRETTIES   present 3d person sing. of pretty

PRETTIEST   superlative of pretty

PRETTIFY   *v* -FIED, -FYING, -FIES to make pretty

PRETTY   *v* -TIED, -TYING, -TIES to make pretty

PRETTY   *adj* -TIER, -TIEST pleasing to the eye **PRETTILY** *adv*

PRETZEL   *n* pl. -S a glazed, salted cracker

PREUNION   *n* pl. -S a union beforehand

PREUNITE   *v* -UNITED, -UNITING, -UNITES to unite beforehand

PREVAIL   *v* -ED, -ING, -S to triumph

PREVENT   *v* -ED, -ING, -S to keep from happening

PREVIEW   *v* -ED, -ING, -S to view or exhibit in advance

PREVIOUS   *adj* coming or occurring before in time or order

PREVISE   *v* -VISED, -VISING, -VISES to foresee

PREVISOR   *n* pl. -S one that previses

PREVUE   *v* -VUED, -VUING, -VUES to preview

PREWAR   *adj* occurring or existing before a war

PREWARM   *v* -ED, -ING, -S to warm beforehand

PREWARN   *v* -ED, -ING, -S to warn in advance

PREWASH   *v* -ED, -ING, -ES to wash beforehand

PREWRAP   *v* -WRAPPED, -WRAPPING, -WRAPS to wrap beforehand

PREX   *n* pl. -ES prexy

PREXY   *n* pl. PREXIES a president

PREY   *v* -ED, -ING, -S to seize and devour animals for food

PREYER   *n* pl. -S one that preys

PRIAPEAN   *adj* priapic

PRIAPI   a pl. of priapus

PRIAPIC   *adj* phallic

PRIAPISM   *n* pl. -S a persistent erection of the penis

PRIAPUS   *n* pl. -PUSES or -PI a representation of the phallus

PRICE   *v* PRICED, PRICING, PRICES to set a value on

PRICER   *n* pl. -S one that prices

PRICEY   *adj* PRICIER, PRICIEST expensive

PRICIER   comparative of pricey and pricy

PRICIEST   superlative of pricey and pricy

PRICING   present participle of price

PRICK   *v* -ED, -ING, -S to puncture slightly

PRICKER   *n* pl. -S one that pricks

PRICKET   *n* pl. -S a spike for holding a candle upright

PRICKIER   comparative of pricky

PRICKIEST   superlative of pricky

PRICKLE   *v* -LED, -LING, -LES to prick

PRICKLY   *adj* -LIER, -LIEST having many sharp points

PRICKY   *adj* PRICKIER, PRICKIEST prickly

PRICY   *adj* PRICIER, PRICIEST pricey

PRIDE   *v* PRIDED, PRIDING, PRIDES to feel pride (a feeling of self-esteem)

PRIDEFUL   *adj* full of pride

PRIED   past tense of pry

PRIEDIEU   *n* pl. -DIEUS or -DIEUX a piece of furniture for kneeling on during prayer

PRIER   *n* pl. -S one that pries

PRIES   present 3d person sing. of pry

PRIEST   *v* -ED, -ING, -S to ordain as a priest (one authorized to perform religious rites)

PRIESTLY   *adj* -LIER, -LIEST characteristic of or befitting a priest

PRIG   *v* PRIGGED, PRIGGING, PRIGS to steal

PRIGGERY   *n* pl. -GERIES priggism

PRIGGISH   *adj* marked by priggism

PRIGGISM *n pl.* -S prim adherence to convention

PRILL *v* -ED, -ING, -S to convert into pellets

PRIM *adj* PRIMMER, PRIMMEST formally precise or proper

PRIM *v* PRIMMED, PRIMMING, PRIMS to give a prim expression to

PRIMA *n pl.* -S primo

PRIMACY *n pl.* -CIES the state of being first

PRIMAGE *n pl.* -S an amount paid as an addition to freight charges

PRIMAL *adj* being at the beginning or foundation

PRIMARY *n pl.* -RIES a preliminary election

PRIMATE *n pl.* -S any of an advanced order of mammals PRIMATAL *adj*

PRIME *v* PRIMED, PRIMING, PRIMES to make ready

PRIMELY *adv* excellently

PRIMER *n pl.* -S a book that covers the basics of a subject

PRIMERO *n pl.* -ROS a card game

PRIMEVAL *adj* pertaining to the earliest ages

PRIMI *a pl.* of primo

PRIMINE *n pl.* -S the outer covering of an ovule

PRIMING *n pl.* -S the act of one that primes

PRIMLY *adv* in a prim manner

PRIMMED past tense of prim

PRIMMER comparative of prim

PRIMMEST superlative of prim

PRIMMING present participle of prim

PRIMNESS *n pl.* -ES the state of being prim

PRIMO *n pl.* -MOS or -MI the main part in a musical piece

PRIMP *v* -ED, -ING, -S to dress or adorn carefully

PRIMROSE *n pl.* -S a perennial herb

PRIMSIE *adj* prim

PRIMULA *n pl.* -S primrose

PRIMUS *n pl.* -ES the head bishop of Scotland

PRINCE *n pl.* -S a non-reigning male member of a royal family

PRINCELY *adj* -LIER, -LIEST of or befitting a prince

PRINCESS *n pl.* -ES a non-reigning female member of a royal family

PRINCIPE *n pl.* -PI a prince

PRINCOCK *n pl.* -S a coxcomb

PRINCOX *n pl.* -ES princock

PRINK *v* -ED, -ING, -S to dress or adorn in a showy manner

PRINKER *n pl.* -S one that prinks

PRINT *v* -ED, -ING, -S to produce by pressed type on a surface

PRINTER *n pl.* -S one that prints

PRINTERY *n pl.* -ERIES a place where printing is done

PRINTING *n pl.* -S a reproduction from a printing surface

PRINTOUT *n pl.* -S the printed output of a computer

PRIOR *n pl.* -S an officer in a monastery

PRIORATE *n pl.* -S the office of a prior

PRIORESS *n pl.* -ES a nun corresponding in rank to a prior

PRIORIES *pl.* of priory

PRIORITY *n pl.* -TIES precedence established by importance

PRIORLY *adv* previously

PRIORY *n pl.* -RIES a religious house

PRISE *v* PRISED, PRISING, PRISES to raise or force with a lever

PRISERE *n pl.* -S a succession of vegetational stages

PRISM *n pl.* -S a solid which disperses light into a spectrum

PRISMOID *n pl.* -S a geometric solid

PRISON *v* -ED, -ING, -S to imprison

PRISONER *n pl.* -S one that is imprisoned

PRISS *n pl.* -ES a prissy

PRISSY *adj* -SIER, -SIEST excessively or affectedly proper PRISSILY *adv*

PRISSY *n pl.* -SIES one who is prissy

PRISTANE *n pl.* -S a chemical compound

PRISTINE *adj* pertaining to the earliest time or state

PRITHEE *interj* — used to express a wish or request

PRIVACY *n pl.* -CIES the state of being private

PRIVATE *adj* -VATER, -VATEST secluded from the sight, presence, or intrusion of others

PRIVATE *n pl.* -S a soldier of lower rank

PRIVET *n pl.* -S an ornamental shrub

PRIVIER comparative of privy

PRIVIES pl. of privy

PRIVITY n pl. -TIES private knowledge

PRIVY adj PRIVIER, PRIVIEST private **PRIVILY** adv

PRIVY n pl. PRIVIES an outhouse

PRIZE v PRIZED, PRIZING, PRIZES to value highly

PRIZER n pl. -S one who vies for a reward

PRO n pl. PROS an argument or vote in favor of something

PROA n pl. -S prau

PROBABLE adj likely to occur or prove true **PROBABLY** adv

PROBAND n pl. -S one whose reactions or responses are studied

PROBANG n pl. -S a surgical rod

PROBATE v -BATED, -BATING, -BATES to establish the validity of

PROBE v PROBED, PROBING, PROBES to investigate or examine thoroughly

PROBER n pl. -S one that probes

PROBIT n pl. -S a unit of statistical probability

PROBITY n pl. -TIES complete and confirmed integrity

PROBLEM n pl. -S a perplexing question or situation

PROCAINE n pl. -S a compound used as a local anesthetic

PROCARP n pl. -S a female sexual organ in certain algae

PROCEED v -ED, -ING, -S to go forward or onward

PROCESS v -ED, -ING, -ES to treat or prepare by a special method

PROCHAIN adj prochein

PROCHEIN adj nearest in time, relation, or degree

PROCLAIM v -ED, -ING, -S to make known publicly or officially

PROCTOR v -ED, -ING, -S to supervise

PROCURAL n pl. -S the act of procuring

PROCURE v -CURED, -CURING, -CURES to obtain by effort

PROCURER n pl. -S one that procures

PROD v PRODDED, PRODDING, PRODS to jab with something pointed

PRODDER n pl. -S one that prods

PRODIGAL n pl. -S one who spends lavishly and foolishly

PRODIGY n pl. -GIES a child having exceptional talent or ability

PRODROME n pl. -DROMES or -DROMATA a sign of impending disease

PRODUCE v -DUCED, -DUCING, -DUCES to bring into existence

PRODUCER n pl. -S one that produces

PRODUCT n pl. -S something produced by labor or effort

PROEM n pl. -S an introductory statement **PROEMIAL** adj

PROETTE n pl. -S a female professional athlete

PROF n pl. -S a professor

PROFANE v -FANED, -FANING, -FANES to treat with irreverence or abuse

PROFANER n pl. -S one that profanes

PROFESS v -ED, -ING, -ES to affirm openly

PROFFER v -ED, -ING, -S to present for acceptance

PROFILE v -FILED, -FILING, -FILES to draw an outline of

PROFILER n pl. -S one that profiles

PROFIT v -ED, -ING, -S to gain an advantage or benefit

PROFITER n pl. -S one that profits

PROFOUND adj -FOUNDER, -FOUNDEST intellectually deep and penetrating

PROFOUND n pl. -S something that is very deep

PROFUSE adj pouring forth generously

PROG v PROGGED, PROGGING, PROGS to prowl about for food or plunder

PROGENY n pl. -NIES a descendant or offspring

PROGGER n pl. -S one that progs

PROGGING present participle of prog

PROGNOSE v -NOSED, -NOSING, -NOSES to forecast the probable course of a disease

PROGRADE adj pertaining to the orbital motion of a body

PROGRAM v -GRAMED, -GRAMING, -GRAMS or -GRAMMED, -GRAMMING, -GRAMS to arrange in a plan of proceedings

PROGRESS v -ED, -ING, -ES to move forward or onward

PROHIBIT v -ED, -ING, -S to forbid by authority

PROJECT *v* -ED, -ING, -S to extend outward

PROJET *n pl.* -S a plan or outline

PROLABOR *adj* favoring organized labor

PROLAMIN *n pl.* -S a simple protein

PROLAN *n pl.* -S a sex hormone

PROLAPSE *v* -LAPSED, -LAPSING, -LAPSES to fall or slip out of place

PROLATE *adj* extended lengthwise

PROLE *n pl.* -S a member of the working class

PROLEG *n pl.* -S an abdominal leg of certain insect larvae

PROLIFIC *adj* producing abundantly

PROLINE *n pl.* -S an amino acid

PROLIX *adj* tediously long and wordy **PROLIXLY** *adv*

PROLOG *v* -ED, -ING, -S to prologue

PROLOGUE *v* -LOGUED, -LOGUING, -LOGUES to preface

PROLONG *v* -ED, -ING, -S to lengthen in duration

PROLONGE *n pl.* -S a rope used for pulling a gun carriage

PROM *n pl.* -S a formal dance

PROMISE *v* -ISED, -ISING, -ISES to make a declaration of assurance

PROMISEE *n pl.* -S one who is promised something

PROMISER *n pl.* -S promisor

PROMISING present participle of promise

PROMISOR *n pl.* -S one that promises

PROMOTE *v* -MOTED, -MOTING, -MOTES to contribute to the progress of

PROMOTER *n pl.* -S one that promotes

PROMPT *adj* PROMPTER, PROMPTEST quick to act or respond

PROMPT *v* -ED, -ING, -S to induce to action

PROMPTER *n pl.* -S one that prompts

PROMPTLY *adv* in a prompt manner

PROMULGE *v* -MULGED, -MULGING, -MULGES to proclaim

PRONATE *v* -NATED, -NATING, -NATES to turn the palm downward or backward

PRONATOR *n pl.* -S or -ES a forearm or forelimb muscle

PRONE *adj* lying with the front or face downward **PRONELY** *adv*

PRONG *v* -ED, -ING, -S to pierce with a pointed projection

PRONOTUM *n pl.* -NOTA a hard outer plate of an insect

PRONOUN *n pl.* -S a word that may be used in place of a noun

PRONTO *adv* quickly

PROOF *v* -ED, -ING, -S to examine for errors

PROOFER *n pl.* -S one that proofs

PROP *v* PROPPED, PROPPING, PROPS to keep from falling

PROPANE *n pl.* -S a flammable gas

PROPEL *v* -PELLED, -PELLING, -PELS to cause to move forward or onward

PROPEND *v* -ED, -ING, -S to have a tendency toward

PROPENE *n pl.* -S a flammable gas

PROPENOL *n pl.* -S a flammable liquid

PROPENSE *adj* tending toward

PROPENYL *adj* pertaining to a certain chemical group

PROPER *adj* -ERER, -EREST suitable **PROPERLY** *adv*

PROPER *n pl.* -S a portion of the Mass

PROPERTY *n pl.* -TIES something owned

PROPHAGE *n pl.* -S a form of virus

PROPHASE *n pl.* -S the first stage in mitosis

PROPHECY *n pl.* -CIES a prediction

PROPHESY *v* -SIED, -SYING, -SIES to predict

PROPHET *n pl.* -S one who predicts

PROPINE *v* -PINED, -PINING, -PINES to offer as a gift

PROPJET *n pl.* -S a type of airplane

PROPMAN *n pl.* -MEN a man in charge of stage properties

PROPOLIS *n pl.* -LISES a resinous substance used as a cement by bees

PROPONE *v* -PONED, -PONING, -PONES to propose

PROPOSAL *n pl.* -S something that is proposed

PROPOSE *v* -POSED, -POSING, -POSES to put forward for consideration or acceptance

PROPOSER *n pl.* -S one that proposes

PROPOUND *v* -ED, -ING, -S to propose

PROPPED past tense of prop

PROPPING present participle of prop

PROPYL *n pl.* -S a univalent radical **PROPYLIC** *adj*

PROPYLON *n* pl. -LA an entrance to a temple

PRORATE *v* -RATED, -RATING, -RATES to divide proportionately

PROROGUE *v* -ROGUED, -ROGUING, -ROGUES to discontinue a session of

PROSAIC *adj* pertaining to prose

PROSAISM *n* pl. -S a prosaic style

PROSAIST *n* pl. -S a writer of prose

PROSE *v* PROSED, PROSING, PROSES to write prose (writing without metrical structure)

PROSECT *v* -ED, -ING, -S to dissect

PROSER *n* pl. -S a prosaist

PROSIER comparative of prosy

PROSIEST superlative of prosy

PROSILY *adv* in a prosy manner

PROSING present participle of prose

PROSIT *interj* — used as a drinking toast

PROSO *n* pl. -SOS millet

PROSODY *n* pl. -DIES the study of poetical forms PROSODIC *adj*

PROSOMA *n* pl. -S the front region of the body of an invertebrate PROSOMAL *adj*

PROSPECT *v* -ED, -ING, -S to explore for mineral deposits

PROSPER *v* -ED, -ING, -S to be successful or fortunate

PROST *interj* prosit

PROSTATE *n* pl. -S a gland in male mammals

PROSTYLE *n* pl. -S a building having a row of columns across the front only

PROSY *adj* PROSIER, PROSIEST prosaic

PROTAMIN *n* pl. -S a simple protein

PROTASIS *n* pl. -ASES the introductory part of a classical drama PROTATIC *adj*

PROTEA *n* pl. -S an evergreen shrub

PROTEAN *adj* readily taking on different shapes or forms

PROTEASE *n* pl. -S an enzyme

PROTECT *v* -ED, -ING, -S to keep from harm, attack, or injury

PROTEGE *n* pl. -S one whose career is promoted by an influential person

PROTEGEE *n* pl. -S a female protege

PROTEI pl. of proteus

PROTEID *n* pl. -S protein

PROTEIDE *n* pl. -S proteid

PROTEIN *n* pl. -S a nitrogenous organic compound

PROTEND *v* -ED, -ING, -S to extend

PROTEOSE *n* pl. -S a water-soluble protein

PROTEST *v* -ED, -ING, -S to express strong objection

PROTEUS *n* pl. -TEI any of a genus of aerobic bacteria

PROTIST *n* pl. -S any of a group of unicellular organisms

PROTIUM *n* pl. -S an isotope of hydrogen

PROTOCOL *v* -COLED, -COLING, -COLS or -COLLED, -COLLING, -COLS to form a preliminary draft of an official document

PROTON *n* pl. -S an atomic particle PROTONIC *adj*

PROTOPOD *n* pl. -S a part of a crustacean appendage

PROTOXID *n* pl. -S an oxide

PROTOZOA *n/pl* unicellular microscopic organisms

PROTRACT *v* -ED, -ING, -S to prolong

PROTRUDE *v* -TRUDED, -TRUDING, -TRUDES to extend beyond the main portion

PROTYL *n* pl. -S protyle

PROTYLE *n* pl. -S a hypothetical substance from which all the elements are supposedly derived

PROUD *adj* PROUDER, PROUDEST having or displaying pride PROUDLY *adv*

PROUDFUL *adj* prideful

PROUNION *adj* favoring labor unions

PROVE *v* PROVED, PROVEN, PROVING, PROVES to establish the truth or validity of PROVABLE *adj* PROVABLY *adv*

PROVENLY *adv* without doubt

PROVER *n* pl. -S one that proves

PROVERB *v* -ED, -ING, -S to make a byword of

PROVIDE *v* -VIDED, -VIDING, -VIDES to supply

PROVIDER *n* pl. -S one that provides

PROVINCE *n* pl. -S an administrative division of a country

PROVING present participle of prove

PROVIRUS *n* pl. -ES a form of virus PROVIRAL *adj*

PROVISO *n* pl. -SOS or -SOES a clause in a document introducing a condition or restriction

PROVOKE *v* -VOKED, -VOKING, -VOKES to incite to anger or resentment

PROVOKER *n* pl. -S one that provokes

PROVOST *n* pl. -S a high-ranking university official

PROW *n* pl. -S the forward part of a ship

PROW *adj* PROWER, PROWEST brave

PROWAR *adj* favoring war

PROWESS *n* pl. -ES exceptional ability

PROWL *v* -ED, -ING, -S to move about stealthily

PROWLER *n* pl. -S one that prowls

PROXEMIC *adj* pertaining to a branch of environmental study

PROXIES pl. of proxy

PROXIMAL *adj* located near the point of origin

PROXIMO *adj* of or occurring in the following month

PROXY *n* pl. PROXIES a person authorized to act for another

PRUDE *n* pl. -S a prudish person

PRUDENCE *n* pl. -S the quality of being prudent

PRUDENT *adj* having, showing, or exercising good judgment

PRUDERY *n* pl. -ERIES excessive regard for propriety, modesty, or morality

PRUDISH *adj* marked by prudery

PRUINOSE *adj* having a powdery covering

PRUNE *v* PRUNED, PRUNING, PRUNES to cut off branches or parts from **PRUNABLE** *adj*

PRUNELLA *n* pl. -S a strong woolen fabric

PRUNELLE *n* pl. -S a plum-flavored liqueur

PRUNELLO *n* pl. -LOS prunella

PRUNER *n* pl. -S one that prunes

PRUNING present participle of prune

PRURIENT *adj* having lustful thoughts or desires

PRURIGO *n* pl. -GOS a skin disease

PRURITUS *n* pl. -ES intense itching **PRURITIC** *adj*

PRUSSIC *adj* pertaining to a type of acid

PRUTA *n* pl. PRUTOT prutah

PRUTAH *n* pl. PRUTOTH a monetary unit of Israel

PRY *v* PRIED, PRYING, PRIES to inquire impertinently into private matters **PRYINGLY** *adv*

PRYER *n* pl. -S prier

PRYTHEE *interj* prithee

PSALM *v* -ED, -ING, -S to praise in psalms (sacred songs)

PSALMIC *adj* of or pertaining to a psalm

PSALMIST *n* pl. -S a writer of psalms

PSALMODY *n* pl. -DIES the use of psalms in worship

PSALTER *n* pl. -S a book of psalms

PSALTERY *n* pl. -TERIES an ancient stringed musical instrument

PSALTRY *n* pl. -TRIES psaltery

PSAMMITE *n* pl. -S a fine-grained rock

PSCHENT *n* pl. -S a crown worn by ancient Egyptian kings

PSEPHITE *n* pl. -S a rock composed of small pebbles

PSEUDO *adj* false or counterfeit

PSHAW *v* -ED, -ING, -S to utter an expression of disapproval

PSI *n* pl. -S a Greek letter

PSILOSIS *n* pl. -LOSES a tropical disease **PSILOTIC** *adj*

PSOAS *n* pl. PSOAI or PSOAE a muscle of the loin

PSOCID *n* pl. -S a minute winged insect

PSORALEA *n* pl. -S a plant of the bean family

PSST *interj* — used to attract someone's attention

PSYCH *v* -ED, -ING, -S to put into the proper frame of mind

PSYCHE *n* pl. -S the mental structure of a person

PSYCHIC *n* pl. -S one sensitive to extrasensory phenomena

PSYCHO *n* pl. -CHOS a mentally unstable person

PSYLLA *n* pl. -S any of various plant lice

PSYLLID *n* pl. -S psylla

PTERIN *n* pl. -S a chemical compound

PTEROPOD *n* pl. -S a type of mollusk

PTERYLA *n* pl. -LAE a feathered area on the skin of a bird

PTISAN *n* pl. -S a tea of herbs or barley

PTOMAIN *n* pl. -S ptomaine

PTOMAINE *n* pl. -S a compound produced by the decomposition of protein

PTOSIS — *n pl.* PTOSES a drooping of the upper eyelid PTOTIC *adj*

PTYALIN — *n pl.* -S a salivary enzyme

PTYALISM — *n pl.* -S an excessive flow of saliva

PUB — *n pl.* -S a tavern

PUBERTY — *n pl.* -TIES a period of sexual maturation PUBERAL, PUBERTAL *adj*

PUBES — *n pl.* PUBES the lower part of the abdomen

PUBIC — *adj* pertaining to the pubes or pubis

PUBIS — *n pl.* PUBES the forward portion of either of the hipbones

PUBLIC — *n pl.* -S the community or the people as a whole

PUBLICAN — *n pl.* -S one who owns or manages a pub

PUBLICLY — *adv* by the public

PUBLISH — *v* -ED, -ING, -ES to print and issue to the public

PUCCOON — *n pl.* -S an herb that yields a red dye

PUCE — *n pl.* -S a dark red color

PUCK — *n pl.* -S a rubber disk used in ice hockey

PUCKA — *adj* pukka

PUCKER — *v* -ED, -ING, -S to gather into small wrinkles or folds

PUCKERER — *n pl.* -S one that puckers

PUCKERY — *adj* -ERIER, -ERIEST having a tendency to pucker

PUCKISH — *adj* impish

PUD — *n pl.* -S pudding

PUDDING — *n pl.* -S a thick, soft dessert

PUDDLE — *v* -DLED, -DLING, -DLES to strew with puddles (small pools of water)

PUDDLER — *n pl.* -S one who subjects iron to puddling

PUDDLING — *n pl.* -S the process of converting pig iron to wrought iron

PUDDLY — *adj* -DLIER, -DLIEST full of puddles

PUDENCY — *n pl.* -CIES modesty

PUDENDUM — *n pl.* -DA the external genital organs of a woman PUDENDAL *adj*

PUDGY — *adj* PUDGIER, PUDGIEST short and fat PUDGILY *adv*

PUDIC — *adj* pertaining to the pudendum

PUEBLO — *n pl.* -LOS a communal dwelling of certain Indian tribes

PUERILE — *adj* childish

PUFF — *v* -ED, -ING, -S to blow in short gusts

PUFFBALL — *n pl.* -S any of various globular fungi

PUFFER — *n pl.* -S one that puffs

PUFFERY — *n pl.* -ERIES excessive public praise

PUFFIN — *n pl.* -S a sea bird

PUFFY — *adj* -FIER, -FIEST swollen PUFFILY *adv*

PUG — *v* PUGGED, PUGGING, PUGS to fill in with clay or mortar

PUGAREE — *n pl.* -S pugree

PUGGAREE — *n pl.* -S pugree

PUGGED — past tense of pug

PUGGIER — comparative of puggy

PUGGIEST — superlative of puggy

PUGGING — present participle of pug

PUGGISH — *adj* somewhat stubby

PUGGREE — *n pl.* -S pugree

PUGGRY — *n pl.* -GRIES pugree

PUGGY — *adj* -GIER, -GIEST puggish

PUGH — *interj* — used to express disgust

PUGILISM — *n pl.* -S the art or practice of fighting with the fists

PUGILIST — *n pl.* -S one who fights with his fists

PUGMARK — *n pl.* -S a footprint

PUGREE — *n pl.* -S a cloth band wrapped around a hat

PUISNE — *n pl.* -S one of lesser rank

PUISSANT — *adj* powerful

PUKE — *v* PUKED, PUKING, PUKES to vomit

PUKKA — *adj* genuine

PUL — *n pl.* PULS or PULI a coin of Afghanistan

PULE — *v* PULED, PULING, PULES to whine

PULER — *n pl.* -S one that pules

PULI — *n pl.* -LIK or -LIS a long-haired sheepdog

PULICENE — *adj* pertaining to fleas

PULICIDE — *n pl.* -S an agent used for destroying fleas

PULIK — a *pl.* of puli

PULING — *n pl.* -S a plaintive cry

PULINGLY — *adv* in a whining manner

PULL v -ED, -ING, -S to exert force in order to cause motion toward the force

PULLBACK n pl. -S a restraint or drawback

PULLER n pl. -S one that pulls

PULLET n pl. -S a young hen

PULLEY n pl. -LEYS a device used for lifting weight

PULLMAN n pl. -S a railroad sleeping car

PULLOUT n pl. -S a withdrawal

PULLOVER n pl. -S a garment that is put on by being drawn over the head

PULMONIC adj pertaining to the lungs

PULMOTOR n pl. -S a respiratory device

PULP v -ED, -ING, -S to reduce to pulp (a soft, moist mass of matter)

PULPAL adj pertaining to pulp PULPALLY adv

PULPER n pl. -S one that pulps

PULPIER comparative of pulpy

PULPIEST superlative of pulpy

PULPILY adv in a pulpy manner

PULPIT n pl. -S a platform in a church PULPITAL adj

PULPLESS adj having no pulp

PULPOUS adj pulpy

PULPWOOD n pl. -S soft wood used in making paper

PULPY adj PULPIER, PULPIEST resembling pulp

PULQUE n pl. -S a fermented Mexican beverage

PULSANT adj pulsating

PULSAR n pl. -S a celestial source of radio waves

PULSATE v -SATED, -SATING, -SATES to expand and contract rhythmically

PULSATOR n pl. -S something that pulsates

PULSE v PULSED, PULSING, PULSES to pulsate

PULSEJET n pl. -S a type of engine

PULSER n pl. -S a device that causes pulsations

PULSING present participle of pulse

PULSION n pl. -S propulsion

PULSOJET n pl. -S pulsejet

PULVILLI n/pl pads between the claws of an insect's foot

PULVINUS n pl. -NI a swelling at the base of a leaf PULVINAR adj

PUMA n pl. -S a cougar

PUMELO n pl. -LOS pomelo

PUMICE v -ICED, -ICING, -ICES to polish with a porous volcanic rock

PUMICER n pl. -S one that pumices

PUMICITE n pl. -S a porous volcanic rock

PUMMEL v -MELED, -MELING, -MELS or -MELLED, -MELLING, -MELS to pommel

PUMP v -ED, -ING, -S to cause to flow by means of a pump (a device for moving fluids)

PUMPER n pl. -S one that pumps

PUMPKIN n pl. -S a large, edible fruit

PUMPLESS adj lacking a pump

PUMPLIKE adj resembling a pump

PUN v PUNNED, PUNNING, PUNS to make a pun (a play on words)

PUNA n pl. -S a cold, arid plateau

PUNCH v -ED, -ING, -ES to perforate with a type of tool

PUNCHEON n pl. -S a vertical supporting timber

PUNCHER n pl. -S one that punches

PUNCHY adj PUNCHIER, PUNCHIEST dazed

PUNCTATE adj covered with dots

PUNCTUAL adj being on time

PUNCTURE v -TURED, -TURING, -TURES to pierce with a pointed object

PUNDIT n pl. -S a Hindu scholar PUNDITIC adj

PUNDITRY n pl. -RIES the learning of pundits

PUNG n pl. -S a box-shaped sleigh

PUNGENCY n pl. -CIES the state of being pungent

PUNGENT adj sharply affecting the organs of taste or smell

PUNIER comparative of puny

PUNIEST superlative of puny

PUNILY adv in a puny manner

PUNINESS n pl. -ES the state of being puny

PUNISH v -ED, -ING, -ES to impose a penalty on in requital for wrongdoing

PUNISHER n pl. -S one that punishes

PUNITION n pl. -S the act of punishing; punishment

PUNITIVE adj inflicting punishment

PUNITORY adj punitive

PUNK n pl. -S dry, decayed wood used as tinder

PUNK adj PUNKER, PUNKEST of inferior quality

PUNKA n pl. -S a ceiling fan used in India

PUNKAH n pl. -S punka

PUNKEY n pl. -KEYS punkie

PUNKIE n pl. -S a biting gnat

PUNKIN n pl. -S pumpkin

PUNKY adj PUNKIER, PUNKIEST resembling punk

PUNNED past tense of pun

PUNNER n pl. -S a punster

PUNNING present participle of pun

PUNNY adj -NIER, -NIEST being or involving a pun

PUNSTER n pl. -S one who is given to punning

PUNT v -ED, -ING, -S to propel through water with a pole

PUNTER n pl. -S one that punts

PUNTO n pl. -TOS a hit or thrust in fencing

PUNTY n pl. -TIES an iron rod used in glassmaking

PUNY adj PUNIER, PUNIEST of inferior size, strength, or significance

PUP v PUPPED, PUPPING, PUPS to give birth to puppies

PUPA n pl. -PAS or -PAE an intermediate stage of a metamorphic insect **PUPAL** adj

PUPARIUM n pl. -IA a pupal shell **PUPARIAL** adj

PUPATE v -PATED, -PATING, -PATES to pass through the pupal stage

PUPATION n pl. -S the act of pupating

PUPFISH n pl. -ES a small, freshwater fish

PUPIL n pl. -S a student under the close supervision of a teacher

PUPILAGE n pl. -S the state of being a pupil

PUPILAR adj pertaining to a part of the eye

PUPILARY adj pupilar

PUPPED past tense of pup

PUPPET n pl. -S a small figure, as of a person or animal, manipulated by the hand

PUPPETRY n pl. -RIES the art of making or manipulating puppets

PUPPING present participle of pup

PUPPY n pl. -PIES a young dog **PUPPYISH** adj

PUPPYDOM n pl. -S the world of puppies

PUR v PURRED, PURRING, PURS to purr

PURANA n pl. -S a Hindu scripture **PURANIC** adj

PURBLIND adj partially blind

PURCHASE v -CHASED, -CHASING, -CHASES to acquire by the payment of money

PURDA n pl. -S purdah

PURDAH n pl. -S a curtain used in India to seclude women

PURE adj PURER, PUREST free from anything different, inferior, or contaminating

PUREBRED n pl. -S an animal of unmixed stock

PUREE v -REED, -REEING, -REES to reduce to a thick pulp by cooking and sieving

PURELY adv in a pure manner

PURENESS n pl. -ES the quality of being pure

PURER comparative of pure

PUREST superlative of pure

PURFLE v -FLED, -FLING, -FLES to decorate the border of

PURFLING n pl. -S an ornamental border

PURGE v PURGED, PURGING, PURGES to purify

PURGER n pl. -S one that purges

PURGING n pl. -S the act of purifying

PURI n pl. -S poori

PURIFIER n pl. -S one who purifies

PURIFY v -FIED, -FYING, -FIES to free from impurities

PURIN n pl. -S purine

PURINE n pl. -S a chemical compound

PURISM n pl. -S strict adherence to traditional correctness

PURIST n pl. -S one who practices purism **PURISTIC** adj

PURITAN n pl. -S a rigorously moral or religious person

PURITY n pl. -TIES the quality of being pure

PURL v -ED, -ING, -S to knit with a particular stitch

PURLIEU n pl. -S an outlying or neighboring area

PURLIN n pl. -S a horizontal supporting timber

PURLINE n pl. -S purlin

PURLOIN v -ED, -ING, -S to steal

PURPLE adj -PLER, -PLEST of a color intermediate between red and blue

PURPLE v -PLED, -PLING, -PLES to make purple

PURPLISH adj somewhat purple

PURPLY adj purplish

PURPORT v -ED, -ING, -S to profess or claim

PURPOSE v -POSED, -POSING, -POSES to resolve to perform or accomplish

PURPURA n pl. -S a disease characterized by purple spots on the skin

PURPURE n pl. -S the heraldic color purple

PURPURIC adj pertaining to purpura

PURPURIN n pl. -S a reddish dye

PURR v -ED, -ING, -S to utter a low, vibrant sound

PURRED past tense of pur and purr

PURRING present participle of pur and purr

PURSE v PURSED, PURSING, PURSES to pucker

PURSER n pl. -S an officer in charge of a ship's accounts

PURSIER comparative of pursy

PURSIEST superlative of pursy

PURSILY adv in a pursy manner

PURSING present participle of purse

PURSLANE n pl. -S a common garden herb

PURSUANT adv in accordance

PURSUE v -SUED, -SUING, -SUES to follow in order to overtake or capture

PURSUER n pl. -S one that pursues

PURSUIT n pl. -S the act of pursuing

PURSY adj PURSIER, PURSIEST short of breath

PURULENT adj secreting pus

PURVEY v -ED, -ING, -S to supply

PURVEYOR n pl. -S one that purveys

PURVIEW n pl. -S the extent of operation, authority, or concern

PUS n pl. -ES a viscous fluid formed in infected tissue

PUSH v -ED, -ING, -ES to exert force in order to cause motion away from the force

PUSHBALL n pl. -S a type of ball game

PUSHCART n pl. -S a light cart pushed by hand

PUSHDOWN n pl. -S a store of computer data

PUSHER n pl. -S one that pushes

PUSHFUL adj pushy

PUSHIER comparative of pushy

PUSHIEST superlative of pushy

PUSHILY adv in a pushy manner

PUSHOVER n pl. -S an easily defeated person or team

PUSHPIN n pl. -S a large-headed pin

PUSHUP n pl. -S a type of exercise

PUSHY adj PUSHIER, PUSHIEST offensively aggressive

PUSLEY n pl. -LEYS pussley

PUSLIKE adj resembling pus

PUSS n pl. -ES a cat

PUSSIER comparative of pussy

PUSSIES pl. of pussy

PUSSIEST superlative of pussy

PUSSLEY n pl. -LEYS purslane

PUSSLIKE adj catlike

PUSSLY n pl. -LIES pussley

PUSSY n pl. PUSSIES a cat

PUSSY adj -SIER, -SIEST full of pus

PUSSYCAT n pl. -S a cat

PUSTULE n pl. -S a small elevation of the skin containing pus
PUSTULAR, PUSTULED adj

PUT v PUT, PUTTING, PUTS to place in a particular position

PUTAMEN n pl. -MINA the hard covering of the kernel of certain fruits

PUTATIVE adj generally regarded as such

PUTLOG n pl. -S a horizontal supporting timber

PUTOFF n pl. -S an excuse

PUTON n pl. -S a hoax or deception

PUTOUT n pl. -S an act of causing an out in baseball

PUTREFY v -FIED, -FYING, -FIES to make or become putrid

PUTRID adj being in a decomposed, foul-smelling state **PUTRIDLY** adv

PUTSCH n pl. -ES a suddenly executed attempt to overthrow a government

PUTT v -ED, -ING, -S to hit with a light stroke in golf

PUTTEE   *n pl.* -S a strip of cloth wound around the leg

PUTTER   *v* -ED, -ING, -S to occupy oneself in a leisurely or ineffective manner

PUTTERER   *n pl.* -S one that putters

PUTTIED   past tense of putty

PUTTIER   *n pl.* -S one that putties

PUTTING   present participle of put

PUTTY   *v* -TIED, -TYING, -TIES to fill with a type of cement

PUZZLE   *v* -ZLED, -ZLING, -ZLES to cause uncertainty and indecision in

PUZZLER   *n pl.* -S something that puzzles

PYA   *n pl.* -S a copper coin of Burma

PYAEMIA   *n pl.* -S pyemia PYAEMIC *adj*

PYCNIDIA   *n/pl* spore-bearing organs of certain fungi

PYE   *n pl.* -S a book of ecclesiastical rules in the pre-Reformation English church

PYELITIS   *n pl.* -TISES inflammation of the pelvis or the kidney PYELITIC *adj*

PYEMIA   *n pl.* -S the presence of pus in the blood PYEMIC *adj*

PYGIDIUM   *n pl.* -IA the posterior region of certain invertebrates PYGIDIAL *adj*

PYGMY   *n pl.* -MIES a small person PYGMAEAN, PYGMEAN, PYGMOID, PYGMYISH *adj*

PYGMYISM   *n pl.* -S a stunted or dwarfish condition

PYIC   *adj* pertaining to pus

PYIN   *n pl.* -S a protein compound contained in pus

PYJAMAS   *n pl.* PYJAMAS pajamas

PYKNIC   *n pl.* -S a person having a broad, stocky build

PYLON   *n pl.* -S a tall structure marking an entrance or approach

PYLORUS   *n pl.* -RI or -RUSES the opening between the stomach and the duodenum PYLORIC *adj*

PYODERMA   *n pl.* -S a pus-causing skin disease

PYOGENIC   *adj* producing pus

PYOID   *adj* puslike

PYORRHEA   *n pl.* -S a discharge of pus

PYOSIS   *n pl.* -OSES the formation of pus

PYRALID   *n pl.* -S a long-legged moth

PYRAMID   *v* -ED, -ING, -S to raise or increase by adding amounts gradually

PYRAN   *n pl.* -S a chemical compound PYRANOID *adj*

PYRANOSE   *n pl.* -S a simple sugar

PYRE   *n pl.* -S a pile of combustible material

PYRENE   *n pl.* -S a putamen

PYRENOID   *n pl.* -S a protein body of certain lower organisms

PYRETIC   *adj* pertaining to fever

PYREXIA   *n pl.* -S fever PYREXIAL, PYREXIC *adj*

PYRIC   *adj* pertaining to burning

PYRIDINE   *n pl.* -S a flammable liquid PYRIDIC *adj*

PYRIFORM   *adj* pear-shaped

PYRITE   *n pl.* -S a metallic sulfide PYRITIC, PYRITOUS *adj*

PYROGEN   *n pl.* -S a substance that produces fever

PYROLA   *n pl.* -S a perennial herb

PYROLOGY   *n pl.* -GIES the scientific examination of materials by heat

PYROLYZE   *v* -LYZED, -LYZING, -LYZES to affect compounds by the application of heat

PYRONE   *n pl.* -S a chemical compound

PYRONINE   *n pl.* -S a dye

PYROPE   *n pl.* -S a variety of garnet

PYROSIS   *n pl.* -SISES heartburn

PYROSTAT   *n pl.* -S a thermostat

PYROXENE   *n pl.* -S any of a group of minerals common in igneous rocks

PYRRHIC   *n pl.* -S a type of metrical foot

PYRROL   *n pl.* -S pyrrole

PYRROLE   *n pl.* -S a chemical compound PYRROLIC *adj*

PYRUVATE   *n pl.* -S a chemical salt

PYTHON   *n pl.* -S a large snake PYTHONIC *adj*

PYURIA   *n pl.* -S the presence of pus in the urine

PYX   *n pl.* -ES a container in which the eucharistic bread is kept

PYXIDES   *pl.* of pyxis

PYXIDIUM   *n pl.* -IA a type of seed vessel

PYXIE   *n pl.* -S an evergreen shrub

PYXIS   *n pl.* PYXIDES a pyxidium

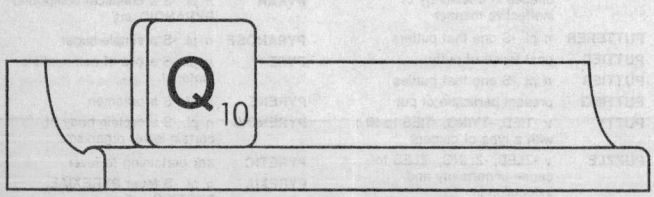

QAID	n pl. -S caid
QINDAR	n pl. -S qintar
QINTAR	n pl. -S a monetary unit of Albania
QIVIUT	n pl. -S the wool of a musk-ox
QOPH	n pl. -S koph
QUA	adv in the capacity of
QUACK	v -ED, -ING, -S to utter the characteristic cry of a duck
QUACKERY	n pl. -ERIES fraudulent practice
QUACKISH	adj fraudulent
QUACKISM	n pl. -S quackery
QUAD	v QUADDED, QUADDING, QUADS to space out by means of quadrats
QUADRANS	n pl. -RANTES an ancient Roman coin
QUADRANT	n pl. -S a quarter section of a circle
QUADRAT	n pl. -S a piece of type metal used for filling spaces
QUADRATE	v -RATED, -RATING, -RATES to correspond or agree
QUADRIC	n pl. -S a type of geometric surface
QUADRIGA	n pl. -GAE a chariot drawn by four horses
QUADROON	n pl. -S a person of one-quarter black ancestry
QUAERE	n pl. -S a question
QUAESTOR	n pl. -S an ancient Roman magistrate
QUAFF	v -ED, -ING, -S to drink deeply
QUAFFER	n pl. -S one that quaffs
QUAG	n pl. -S a quagmire
QUAGGA	n pl. -S an extinct zebralike mammal
QUAGGY	adj -GIER, -GIEST marshy

QUAGMIRE	n pl. -S an area of marshy ground
QUAGMIRY	adj -MIRIER, -MIRIEST marshy
QUAHAUG	n pl. -S quahog
QUAHOG	n pl. -S an edible clam
QUAI	n pl. -S quay
QUAICH	n pl. -ES or -S a small drinking vessel
QUAIGH	n pl. -S quaich
QUAIL	v -ED, -ING, -S to cower
QUAINT	adj QUAINTER, QUAINTEST pleasingly old-fashioned or unfamiliar QUAINTLY adv
QUAKE	v QUAKED, QUAKING, QUAKES to shake or vibrate
QUAKER	n pl. -S one that quakes
QUAKY	adj QUAKIER, QUAKIEST tending to quake QUAKILY adv
QUALE	n pl. -LIA a property considered apart from things having the property
QUALIFY	v -FIED, -FYING, -FIES to make suitable or capable
QUALITY	n pl. -TIES a characteristic or attribute
QUALM	n pl. -S a feeling of doubt or misgiving
QUALMISH	adj having qualms
QUALMY	adj QUALMIER, QUALMIEST qualmish
QUAMASH	n pl. -ES camass
QUANDANG	n pl. -S quandong
QUANDARY	n pl. -RIES a dilemma
QUANDONG	n pl. -S an Australian tree
QUANT	v -ED, -ING, -S to propel through water with a pole
QUANTA	pl. of quantum
QUANTAL	adj pertaining to a quantum

QUANTIC *n pl.* -S a type of mathematical function

QUANTIFY *v* -FIED, -FYING, -FIES to determine the quantity of

QUANTITY *n pl.* -TIES a specified or indefinite amount or number

QUANTIZE *v* -TIZED, -TIZING, -TIZES to limit the possible values of to a discrete set

QUANTONG *n pl.* -S quandong

QUANTUM *n pl.* -TA a fundamental unit of energy

QUARE *adj* queer

QUARK *n pl.* -S a hypothetical atomic particle

QUARREL *v* -RELED, -RELING, -RELS or -RELLED, -RELLING, -RELS to engage in an angry dispute

QUARRIER *n pl.* -S one that quarries

QUARRY *v* -RIED, -RYING, -RIES to dig stone from an excavation

QUART *n pl.* -S a liquid measure of capacity

QUARTAN *n pl.* -S a recurrent malarial fever

QUARTE *n pl.* -S a fencing thrust

QUARTER *v* -ED, -ING, -S to divide into four equal parts

QUARTERN *n pl.* -S one-fourth of something

QUARTET *n pl.* -S a group of four

QUARTIC *n pl.* -S a type of mathematical function

QUARTILE *n pl.* -S a portion of a frequency distribution

QUARTO *n pl.* -TOS the size of a piece of paper cut four from a sheet

QUARTZ *n pl.* -ES a mineral

QUASAR *n pl.* -S a distant celestial object emitting strong radio waves

QUASH *v* -ED, -ING, -ES to suppress completely

QUASI *adj* similar but not exactly the same

QUASS *n pl.* -ES kvass

QUASSIA *n pl.* -S a tropical tree

QUASSIN *n pl.* -S a medicinal compound obtained from the wood of a quassia

QUATE *adj* quiet

QUATORZE *n pl.* -S a set of four cards of the same denomination scoring fourteen points

QUATRAIN *n pl.* -S a stanza of four lines

QUATRE *n pl.* -S the four at cards or dice

QUAVER *v* -ED, -ING, -S to quiver

QUAVERER *n pl.* -S one that quavers

QUAVERY *adj* quivery

QUAY *n pl.* QUAYS a wharf QUAYLIKE *adj*

QUAYAGE *n pl.* -S a charge for the use of a quay

QUAYSIDE *n pl.* -S the area adjacent to a quay

QUEAN *n pl.* -S a harlot

QUEASY *adj* -SIER, -SIEST easily nauseated QUEASILY *adv*

QUEAZY *adj* -ZIER, -ZIEST queasy

QUEEN *v* -ED, -ING, -S to make a queen (a female monarch) of

QUEENLY *adj* -LIER, -LIEST of or befitting a queen

QUEER *adj* QUEERER, QUEEREST deviating from the expected or normal

QUEER *v* -ED, -ING, -S to spoil the effect or success of

QUEERISH *adj* somewhat queer

QUEERLY *adv* in a queer manner

QUELL *v* -ED, -ING, -S to suppress

QUELLER *n pl.* -S one that quells

QUENCH *v* -ED, -ING, -ES to put out or extinguish

QUENCHER *n pl.* -S one that quenches

QUENELLE *n pl.* -S a type of dumpling

QUERCINE *adj* pertaining to oaks

QUERIDA *n pl.* -S a female sweetheart

QUERIED past tense of query

QUERIER *n pl.* -S a querist

QUERIES present 3d person sing. of query

QUERIST *n pl.* -S one who queries

QUERN *n pl.* -S a hand-turned grain mill

QUERY *v* -RIED, -RYING, -RIES to question

QUEST *v* -ED, -ING, -S to make a search

QUESTER *n pl.* -S one that quests

QUESTION *v* -ED, -ING, -S to put a question (an inquiry) to

QUESTOR *n pl.* -S quaestor

QUETZAL *n pl.* -S or -ES a tropical bird

QUEUE *v* QUEUED, QUEUING or QUEUEING, QUEUES to line up

QUEUER *n pl.* -S one that queues

QUEY	*n pl.* QUEYS a young cow	**QUINIC**	*adj* pertaining to quinine
QUEZAL	*n pl.* -S or -ES quetzal	**QUINIELA**	*n pl.* -S quinella
QUIBBLE	*v* -BLED, -BLING, -BLES to argue over trivialities	**QUININ**	*n pl.* -S quinine
		QUININA	*n pl.* -S quinine
QUIBBLER	*n pl.* -S one that quibbles	**QUININE**	*n pl.* -S a medicinal alkaloid
QUICHE	*n pl.* -S a custard-filled pastry	**QUINNAT**	*n pl.* -S a food fish
QUICK	*adj* QUICKER, QUICKEST acting or capable of acting with speed	**QUINOA**	*n pl.* -S a weedy plant
		QUINOID	*n pl.* -S a chemical compound
		QUINOL	*n pl.* -S a chemical compound
QUICK	*n pl.* -S a sensitive area of flesh	**QUINOLIN**	*n pl.* -S a chemical compound
		QUINONE	*n pl.* -S a chemical compound
QUICKEN	*v* -ED, -ING, -S to speed up	**QUINSY**	*n pl.* -SIES an inflammation of the tonsils
QUICKIE	*n pl.* -S something done quickly		
QUICKLY	*adv* in a quick manner	**QUINT**	*n pl.* -S a group of five
QUICKSET	*n pl.* -S a plant suitable for hedges	**QUINTAIN**	*n pl.* -S an object used as a target in a medieval sport
QUID	*n pl.* -S a portion of something to be chewed	**QUINTAL**	*n pl.* -S a unit of weight
		QUINTAN	*n pl.* -S a recurrent fever
QUIDDITY	*n pl.* -TIES the true nature of a thing	**QUINTAR**	*n pl.* -S qintar
		QUINTET	*n pl.* -S a group of five
QUIDNUNC	*n pl.* -S a nosy person	**QUINTIC**	*n pl.* -S a type of mathematical function
QUIET	*adj* -ETER, -ETEST making little or no noise	**QUINTILE**	*n pl.* -S a portion of a frequency distribution
QUIET	*v* -ED, -ING, -S to cause to be quiet		
		QUINTIN	*n pl.* -S a fine linen
QUIETEN	*v* -ED, -ING, -S to quiet	**QUIP**	*v* QUIPPED, QUIPPING, QUIPS to make witty remarks
QUIETER	*n pl.* -S one that quiets		
QUIETISM	*n pl.* -S a form of religious mysticism	**QUIPPISH**	*adj* witty
		QUIPPU	*n pl.* -S quipu
QUIETIST	*n pl.* -S an advocate of quietism	**QUIPSTER**	*n pl.* -S one that quips
		QUIPU	*n pl.* -S an ancient calculating device
QUIETLY	*adv* in a quiet manner		
QUIETUDE	*n pl.* -S a state of tranquillity	**QUIRE**	*v* QUIRED, QUIRING, QUIRES to arrange sheets of paper in sets of twenty-four
QUIETUS	*n pl.* -ES a final settlement		
QUIFF	*n pl.* -S a forelock		
QUILL	*v* -ED, -ING, -S to press small ridges in	**QUIRK**	*v* -ED, -ING, -S to twist
		QUIRKY	*adj* QUIRKIER, QUIRKIEST tricky QUIRKILY *adv*
QUILLAI	*n pl.* -S an evergreen tree		
QUILLET	*n pl.* -S a trivial distinction	**QUIRT**	*v* -ED, -ING, -S to strike with a riding whip
QUILT	*v* -ED, -ING, -S to stitch together with padding in between		
		QUISLING	*n pl.* -S a traitor who aids the invaders of his country
QUILTER	*n pl.* -S one that quilts		
QUILTING	*n pl.* -S material that is used for making quilts	**QUIT**	*v* QUITTED, QUITTING, QUITS to end one's engagement in or occupation with
QUINARY	*n pl.* -RIES a group of five		
QUINATE	*adj* arranged in groups of five	**QUITCH**	*n pl.* -ES a perennial grass
QUINCE	*n pl.* -S an apple-like fruit	**QUITE**	*adv* to the fullest extent
QUINCUNX	*n pl.* -ES an arrangement of five objects	**QUITRENT**	*n pl.* -S a fixed rent due from a socage tenant
		QUITTED	past tense of quit
QUINELLA	*n pl.* -S a type of bet in horse racing	**QUITTER**	*n pl.* -S one that quits
		QUITTING	present participle of quit

QUITTOR *n pl.* -S an inflammation of an animal's hoof

QUIVER *v* -ED, -ING, -S to shake with a slight but rapid motion

QUIVERER *n pl.* -S one that quivers

QUIVERY *adj* marked by quivering

QUIXOTE *n pl.* -S a quixotic person

QUIXOTIC *adj* extremely idealistic

QUIXOTRY *n pl.* -TRIES quixotic action or thought

QUIZ *v* QUIZZED, QUIZZING, QUIZZES to test the knowledge of by asking questions

QUIZZER *n pl.* -S one that quizzes

QUOD *n pl.* -S a prison

QUOIN *v* -ED, -ING, -S to secure with a type of wedge

QUOIT *v* -ED, -ING, -S to play a throwing game similar to ringtoss

QUOMODO *n pl.* -DOS a means or manner

QUONDAM *adj* that once was

QUORUM *n pl.* -S a particularly chosen group

QUOTA *n pl.* -S a proportional part or share

QUOTE *v* QUOTED, QUOTING, QUOTES to repeat the words of **QUOTABLE** *adj* **QUOTABLY** *adv*

QUOTER *n pl.* -S one that quotes

QUOTH *v* said — QUOTH is the only accepted form of this verb; it cannot be conjugated

QUOTHA *interj* — used to express surprise or sarcasm

QUOTIENT *n pl.* -S the number resulting from the division of one number by another

QUOTING present participle of quote

QURSH *n pl.* -ES a monetary unit of Saudi Arabia

QURUSH *n pl.* -ES qursh

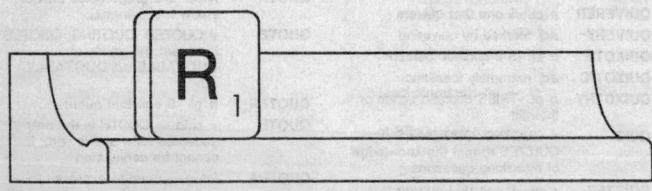

RABATO	n pl. -TOS a wide, lace-edged collar
RABBET	v -ED, -ING, -S to cut a groove in
RABBI	n pl. -S or -ES a Jewish spiritual leader
RABBIN	n pl. -S rabbi
RABBINIC	adj pertaining to rabbis
RABBIT	v -ED, -ING, -S to hunt rabbits (rodent-like mammals)
RABBITER	n pl. -S one that rabbits
RABBITRY	n pl. -RIES a place where rabbits are kept
RABBLE	v -BLED, -BLING, -BLES to mob
RABBLER	n pl. -S an iron bar used in puddling
RABBONI	n pl. -S master; teacher — used as a Jewish title of respect
RABIC	adj pertaining to rabies
RABID	adj affected with rabies RABIDLY adv
RABIDITY	n pl. -TIES the state of being rabid
RABIES	n pl. RABIES an infectious virus disease RABIETIC adj
RACCOON	n pl. -S a carnivorous mammal
RACE	v RACED, RACING, RACES to compete in a contest of speed
RACEMATE	n pl. -S a chemical salt
RACEME	n pl. -S a mode of arrangement of flowers along an axis RACEMED adj
RACEMIC	adj constituting a chemical compound that is optically inactive
RACEMISM	n pl. -S the state of being racemic

RACEMIZE	v -MIZED, -MIZING, -MIZES to convert into a racemic compound
RACEMOID	adj pertaining to a raceme
RACEMOSE	adj having the form of a raceme
RACEMOUS	adj racemose
RACER	n pl. -S one that races
RACEWAY	n pl. -WAYS a channel for conducting water
RACHET	n pl. -S ratchet
RACHIS	n pl. -CHISES or -CHIDES the spinal column RACHIAL adj
RACHITIS	n pl. -TIDES rickets RACHITIC adj
RACIAL	adj pertaining to an ethnic group RACIALLY adv
RACIER	comparative of racy
RACIEST	superlative of racy
RACILY	adv in a racy manner
RACINESS	n pl. -ES the quality of being racy
RACING	n pl. -S the sport of engaging in contests of speed
RACISM	n pl. -S a doctrine of racial superiority
RACIST	n pl. -S an advocate of racism
RACK	v -ED, -ING, -S to place in a type of framework
RACKER	n pl. -S one that racks
RACKET	v -ED, -ING, -S to make a loud noise
RACKETY	adj -ETIER, -ETIEST noisy
RACKLE	adj impetuous; rash
RACKWORK	n pl. -S a type of mechanism
RACLETTE	n pl. -S a cheese dish
RACON	n pl. -S a type of radar transmitter

RACOON n pl. -S raccoon

RACQUET n pl. -S a lightweight implement used in various ball games

RACY adj RACIER, RACIEST bordering on impropriety or indecency

RAD v RADDED, RADDING, RADS to fear

RADAR n pl. -S an electronic locating device

RADDLE v -DLED, -DLING, -DLES to weave together

RADIABLE adj capable of radiating

RADIAL n pl. -S a part diverging from a center

RADIALE n pl. -LIA a bone of the carpus

RADIALLY adv in a diverging manner

RADIAN n pl. -S a unit of angular measure

RADIANCE n pl. -S brightness

RADIANCY n pl. -CIES radiance

RADIANT n pl. -S a point from which rays are emitted

RADIATE v -ATED, -ATING, -ATES to emit rays

RADIATOR n pl. -S a heating device

RADICAL n pl. -S a group of atoms that acts as a unit in chemical compounds

RADICAND n pl. -S a quantity in mathematics

RADICATE v -CATED, -CATING, -CATES to cause to take root

RADICEL n pl. -S a rootlet

RADICES a pl. of radix

RADICLE n pl. -S a part of a plant embryo

RADII a pl. of radius

RADIO v -ED, -ING, -S to transmit by radio (an apparatus for wireless communication)

RADIOMAN n pl. -MEN a radio operator or technician

RADISH n pl. -ES a pungent, edible root

RADIUM n pl. -S a radioactive element

RADIUS n pl. -DII or -DIUSES a straight line from the center of a circle to the circumference

RADIX n pl. -DICES or -DIXES the root of a plant

RADOME n pl. -S a domelike device used to shelter a radar antenna

RADON n pl. -S a radioactive element

RADULA n pl. -LAE or -LAS a tonguelike organ of mollusks RADULAR adj

RAFF n pl. -S riffraff

RAFFIA n pl. -S a palm tree

RAFFISH adj tawdry

RAFFLE v -FLED, -FLING, -FLES to dispose of by a form of lottery

RAFFLER n pl. -S one that raffles

RAFT v -ED, -ING, -S to transport on a raft (a type of buoyant structure)

RAFTER n pl. -S a supporting beam

RAFTSMAN n pl. -MEN one who manages a raft

RAG v RAGGED, RAGGING, RAGS to scold

RAGA n pl. -S a Hindu musical form

RAGBAG n pl. -S a bag for storing scraps of cloth

RAGE v RAGED, RAGING, RAGES to act or speak with violent anger

RAGEE n pl. -S ragi

RAGGED adj -GEDER, -GEDEST tattered RAGGEDLY adv

RAGGEDY adj somewhat ragged

RAGGING present participle of rag

RAGGLE n pl. -S a groove cut in masonry

RAGGY n pl. -GIES ragi

RAGI n pl. -S an East Indian cereal grass

RAGING present participle of rage

RAGINGLY adv in a furious manner

RAGLAN n pl. -S a type of overcoat

RAGMAN n pl. -MEN one who gathers and sells scraps of cloth

RAGOUT v -ED, -ING, -S to make into a highly seasoned stew

RAGTAG n pl. -S riffraff

RAGTIME n pl. -S a style of American dance music

RAGWEED n pl. -S a weedy herb

RAGWORT n pl. -S a flowering plant

RAH interj — used to cheer on a team or player

RAIA n pl. -S rayah

RAID v -ED, -ING, -S to make a sudden assault on

RAIDER n pl. -S one that raids

RAIL v -ED, -ING, -S to scold in abusive or insolent language

RAILBIRD n pl. -S a racing enthusiast

RAILER	n pl. -S one that rails	**RAKING**	present participle of rake
RAILHEAD	n pl. -S the end of a railroad line	**RAKISH**	adj dapper RAKISHLY adv
RAILING	n pl. -S a fence-like barrier	**RALE**	n pl. -S an abnormal respiratory sound
RAILLERY	n pl. -LERIES good-natured teasing	**RALLIED**	past tense of rally
		RALLIER	n pl. -S one that rallies
RAILROAD	v -ED, -ING, -S to transport by railroad (a type of road on which locomotives are run)	**RALLINE**	adj pertaining to a family of marsh birds
RAILWAY	n pl. -WAYS a railroad	**RALLY**	v -LIED, -LYING, -LIES to call together for a common purpose
RAIMENT	n pl. -S clothing	**RALLYE**	n pl. -S a type of automobile race
RAIN	v -ED, -ING, -S to fall like rain (drops of water condensed from atmospheric vapor)	**RALLYING**	n pl. -S the sport of driving in rallyes
RAINBAND	n pl. -S a dark band in the solar spectrum	**RALLYIST**	n pl. -S a participant in a rallye
RAINBIRD	n pl. -S a type of bird	**RAM**	v RAMMED, RAMMING, RAMS to strike with great force
RAINBOW	n pl. -S an arc of spectral colors formed in the sky	**RAMATE**	adj having branches
RAINCOAT	n pl. -S a waterproof coat	**RAMBLE**	v -BLED, -BLING, -BLES to wander
RAINDROP	n pl. -S a drop of rain		
RAINFALL	n pl. -S a fall of rain	**RAMBLER**	n pl. -S one that rambles
RAINIER	comparative of rainy	**RAMBUTAN**	n pl. -S the edible fruit of a Malayan tree
RAINIEST	superlative of rainy	**RAMEE**	n pl. -S ramie
RAINILY	adv in a rainy manner	**RAMEKIN**	n pl. -S a cheese dish
RAINLESS	adj having no rain	**RAMENTUM**	n pl. -TA a scale formed on the surface of leaves
RAINOUT	n pl. -S atomic fallout occurring in precipitation	**RAMEQUIN**	n pl. -S ramekin
RAINWASH	n pl. -ES the washing away of material by rain	**RAMET**	n pl. -S an independent member of a clone
RAINWEAR	n pl. -S waterproof clothing	**RAMI**	pl. of ramus
RAINY	adj RAINIER, RAINIEST marked by rain	**RAMIE**	n pl. -S an Asian shrub
		RAMIFORM	adj shaped like a branch
RAISE	v RAISED, RAISING, RAISES to move to a higher position RAISABLE adj	**RAMIFY**	v -FIED, -FYING, -FIES to divide into branches
RAISER	n pl. -S one that raises	**RAMILIE**	n pl. -S ramillie
RAISIN	n pl. -S a dried grape RAISINY adj	**RAMILLIE**	n pl. -S a type of wig
		RAMJET	n pl. -S a type of engine
RAISING	n pl. -S an elevation	**RAMMED**	past tense of ram
RAISONNE	adj arranged systematically	**RAMMER**	n pl. -S one that rams
RAJ	n pl. -ES dominion; sovereignty	**RAMMIER**	comparative of rammy
RAJA	n pl. -S rajah	**RAMMIEST**	superlative of rammy
RAJAH	n pl. -S a king or prince in India	**RAMMING**	present participle of ram
RAKE	v RAKED, RAKING, RAKES to gather with a toothed implement	**RAMMISH**	adj resembling a ram (a male sheep)
RAKEE	n pl. -S raki	**RAMMY**	adj -MIER, -MIEST rammish
RAKEHELL	n pl. -S a man lacking in moral restraint	**RAMOSE**	adj having many branches RAMOSELY adv
RAKEOFF	n pl. -S a share of profits	**RAMOSITY**	n pl. -TIES the state of being ramose
RAKER	n pl. -S one that rakes		
RAKI	n pl. -S a Turkish liqueur	**RAMOUS**	adj ramose

RAMP   v -ED, -ING, -S to rise or stand on the hind legs

RAMPAGE   v -PAGED, -PAGING, -PAGES to move about wildly or violently

RAMPAGER   n pl. -S one that rampages

RAMPANCY   n pl. -CIES the state of being rampant

RAMPANT   adj unrestrained

RAMPART   v -ED, -ING, -S to furnish with a fortifying embankment

RAMPIKE   n pl. -S a standing dead tree

RAMPION   n pl. -S a European plant

RAMPOLE   n pl. -S rampike

RAMROD   n pl. -S a rod used in loading a firearm

RAMSHORN   n pl. -S a snail used as an aquarium scavenger

RAMSON   n pl. -S a broad-leaved garlic

RAMTIL   n pl. -S a tropical plant

RAMULOSE   adj having many small branches

RAMULOUS   adj ramulose

RAMUS   n pl. -MI a branch-like part of a structure

RAN   past tense of run and rin

RANCE   n pl. -S a variety of marble

RANCH   v -ED, -ING, -ES to work on a ranch (an establishment for raising livestock)

RANCHER   n pl. -S one that owns or works on a ranch

RANCHERO   n pl. -ROS a rancher

RANCHMAN   n pl. -MEN a rancher

RANCHO   n pl. -CHOS a ranch

RANCID   adj having an unpleasant odor or taste

RANCOR   n pl. -S bitter and vindictive enmity RANCORED adj

RANCOUR   n pl. -S rancor

RAND   n pl. -S a strip of leather at the heel of a shoe

RANDAN   n pl. -S a boat rowed by three persons

RANDIES   pl. of randy

RANDOM   n pl. -S a haphazard course

RANDOMLY   adv in a haphazard manner

RANDY   n pl. RANDIES a rude person

RANEE   n pl. -S a rani

RANG   past tense of ring

RANGE   v RANGED, RANGING, RANGES to place in a particular order

RANGER   n pl. -S an officer supervising the care of a forest

RANGY   adj RANGIER, RANGIEST tall and slender

RANI   n pl. -S the wife of a rajah

RANID   n pl. -S any of a large family of frogs

RANK   v -ED, -ING, -S to determine the relative position of

RANK   adj RANKER, RANKEST strong and disagreeable in odor or taste

RANKER   n pl. -S an enlisted soldier

RANKISH   adj somewhat rank

RANKLE   v -KLED, -KLING, -KLES to cause irritation or resentment in

RANKLY   adv in a rank manner

RANKNESS   n pl. -ES the state of being rank

RANPIKE   n pl. -S rampike

RANSACK   v -ED, -ING, -S to search thoroughly

RANSOM   v -ED, -ING, -S to obtain the release of by paying a demanded price

RANSOMER   n pl. -S one that ransoms

RANT   v -ED, -ING, -S to speak in a loud or vehement manner

RANTER   n pl. -S one that rants

RANULA   n pl. -S a cyst formed under the tongue

RAP   v RAPPED, RAPPING, RAPS to strike sharply

RAPACITY   n pl. -TIES the quality of being ravenous

RAPE   v RAPED, RAPING, RAPES to force to submit to sexual intercourse

RAPER   n pl. -S a rapist

RAPESEED   n pl. -S the seed of a European herb

RAPHE   n pl. RAPHAE or RAPHES a seamlike ridge between two halves of an organ or part

RAPHIA   n pl. -S raffia

RAPHIDE   n pl. -S a needle-shaped crystal occurring in plant cells

RAPHIS   n pl. -PHIDES raphide

RAPID   adj -IDER, -IDEST moving or acting with great speed RAPIDLY adv

RAPID   n pl. -S a fast-moving part of a river

RAPIDITY   n pl. -TIES the state of being rapid

RAPIER   n pl. -S a long, slender sword RAPIERED adj

RAPINE n pl. -S the taking of property by force

RAPING present participle of rape

RAPIST n pl. -S one who rapes

RAPPAREE n pl. -S a plunderer

RAPPED past tense of rap

RAPPEE n pl. -S a strong snuff

RAPPEL v -PELLED, -PELLING, -PELS to descend from a steep height by means of a rope

RAPPEN n pl. RAPPEN a Swiss coin

RAPPER n pl. -S one that raps

RAPPING present participle of rap

RAPPINI n/pl immature turnip plants

RAPPORT n pl. -S a harmonious relationship

RAPT adj deeply engrossed RAPTLY adv

RAPTNESS n pl. -ES the state of being rapt

RAPTOR n pl. -S a bird of prey

RAPTURE v -TURED, -TURING, -TURES to fill with great joy

RARE adj RARER, RAREST occurring infrequently

RAREBIT n pl. -S a cheese dish

RAREFIER n pl. -S one that rarefies

RAREFY v -EFIED, -EFYING, -EFIES to make less dense

RARELY adv not often

RARENESS n pl. -ES the quality of being rare

RARER comparative of rare

RARERIPE n pl. -S a fruit that ripens early

RAREST superlative of rare

RARIFY v -FIED, -FYING, -FIES to rarefy

RARING adj full of enthusiasm

RARITY n pl. -TIES rareness

RAS n pl. -ES an Ethiopian prince

RASBORA n pl. -S a tropical fish

RASCAL n pl. -S an unscrupulous or dishonest person

RASCALLY adj characteristic of a rascal

RASE v RASED, RASING, RASES to raze

RASER n pl. -S one that rases

RASH adj RASHER, RASHEST acting without due caution or forethought

RASH n pl. -ES a skin eruption RASHLIKE adj

RASHER n pl. -S a thin slice of meat

RASHLY adv in a rash manner

RASHNESS n pl. -ES the state of being rash

RASING present participle of rase

RASORIAL adj habitually scratching the ground for food

RASP v -ED, -ING, -S to rub with something rough

RASPER n pl. -S one that rasps

RASPISH adj irritable

RASPY adj RASPIER, RASPIEST rough

RASSLE v -SLED, -SLING, -SLES to wrestle

RASTER n pl. -S the area reproducing images on the picture tube of a television set

RASURE n pl. -S erasure

RAT v RATTED, RATTING, RATS to hunt rats (long-tailed rodents)

RATABLE adj capable of being rated RATABLY adv

RATAFEE n pl. -S ratafia

RATAFIA n pl. -S an almond-flavored liqueur

RATAL n pl. -S an amount on which rates are assessed

RATAN n pl. -S rattan

RATANY n pl. -NIES rhatany

RATAPLAN v -PLANNED, -PLANNING, -PLANS to make a rapidly repeating sound

RATATAT n pl. -S a quick, sharp rapping sound

RATCH n pl. -ES a ratchet

RATCHET n pl. -S a mechanism which allows motion in one direction only

RATE v RATED, RATING, RATES to estimate the value of

RATEABLE adj ratable RATEABLY adv

RATEL n pl. -S a carnivorous mammal

RATER n pl. -S one that rates

RATFINK n pl. -S a contemptible person

RATFISH n pl. -ES a marine fish

RATH adj rathe

RATHE adj appearing or ripening early

RATHER adv preferably

RATHOLE n pl. -S a hole made by a rat

RATICIDE n pl. -S a substance for killing rats

RATIFIER n pl. -S one that ratifies

RATIFY v -FIED, -FYING, -FIES to approve and sanction formally

RATINE n pl. -S a heavy fabric

RATING   *n pl.* -S relative estimate or evaluation

RATIO   *n pl.* -TIOS a proportional relationship

RATION   *v* -ED, -ING, -S to distribute in fixed portions

RATIONAL   *n pl.* -S a number that can be expressed as a quotient of integers

RATITE   *n pl.* -S a flightless bird

RATLIKE   *adj* resembling a rat

RATLIN   *n pl.* -S ratline

RATLINE   *n pl.* -S one of the ropes forming the steps of a rope ladder on a ship

RATO   *n pl.* -TOS a rocket-assisted airplane takeoff

RATOON   *v* -ED, -ING, -S to sprout from a root planted the previous year

RATOONER   *n pl.* -S a plant that ratoons

RATSBANE   *n pl.* -S rat poison

RATTAIL   *n pl.* -S a marine fish

RATTAN   *n pl.* -S a palm tree

RATTED   past tense of rat

RATTEEN   *n pl.* -S a coarse woolen fabric

RATTEN   *v* -ED, -ING, -S to harass

RATTENER   *n pl.* -S one that rattens

RATTER   *n pl.* -S an animal used for catching rats

RATTIER   comparative of ratty

RATTIEST   superlative of ratty

RATTING   present participle of rat

RATTISH   *adj* ratlike

RATTLE   *v* -TLED, -TLING, -TLES to make a quick succession of short, sharp sounds

RATTLER   *n pl.* -S one that rattles

RATTLING   *n pl.* -S ratline

RATTLY   *adj* tending to rattle

RATTON   *n pl.* -S a rat

RATTOON   *v* -ED, -ING, -S to ratoon

RATTRAP   *n pl.* -S a trap for catching rats

RATTY   *adj* -TIER, -TIEST infested with rats

RAUCITY   *n pl.* -TIES the state of being raucous

RAUCOUS   *adj* loud and unruly

RAUNCHY   *adj* -CHIER, -CHIEST slovenly

RAVAGE   *v* -AGED, -AGING, -AGES to destroy

RAVAGER   *n pl.* -S one that ravages

RAVE   *v* RAVED, RAVING, RAVES to speak irrationally or incoherently

RAVEL   *v* -ELED, -ELING, -ELS or -ELLED, -ELLING, -ELS to separate the threads of

RAVELER   *n pl.* -S one that ravels

RAVELIN   *n pl.* -S a type of fortification

RAVELING   *n pl.* -S a loose thread

RAVELLED   a past tense of ravel

RAVELLER   *n pl.* -S raveler

RAVELLING   *n pl.* -S raveling

RAVELLY   *adj* tangled

RAVEN   *v* -ED, -ING, -S to eat in a ravenous manner

RAVENER   *n pl.* -S one that ravens

RAVENING   *n pl.* -S rapacity

RAVENOUS   *adj* extremely hungry

RAVER   *n pl.* -S one that raves

RAVIGOTE   *n pl.* -S a spiced vinegar sauce

RAVIN   *v* -ED, -ING, -S to raven

RAVINE   *n pl.* -S a narrow, steep-sided valley

RAVING   *n pl.* -S irrational, incoherent speech

RAVINGLY   *adv* in a delirious manner

RAVIOLI   *n pl.* -S an Italian dish

RAVISH   *v* -ED, -ING, -ES to seize and carry off by force

RAVISHER   *n pl.* -S one that ravishes

RAW   *adj* RAWER, RAWEST uncooked

RAW   *n pl.* -S a sore or irritated spot

RAWBONED   *adj* having little flesh

RAWHIDE   *v* -HIDED, -HIDING, -HIDES to beat with a type of whip

RAWISH   *adj* somewhat raw

RAWLY   *adv* in a raw manner

RAWNESS   *n pl.* -ES the state of being raw

RAX   *v* -ED, -ING, -ES to stretch out

RAY   *v* -ED, -ING, -S to emit rays (narrow beams of light)

RAYA   *n pl.* -S rayah

RAYAH   *n pl.* -S a non-Muslim inhabitant of Turkey

RAYGRASS   *n pl.* -ES ryegrass

RAYLESS   *adj* having no rays

RAYON   *n pl.* -S a synthetic fiber

RAZE   *v* RAZED, RAZING, RAZES to tear down or demolish

RAZEE   *v* -ZEED, -ZEEING, -ZEES to make lower by removing the upper deck, as a ship

RAZER	n pl. -S one that razes	
RAZING	present participle of raze	
RAZOR	v -ED, -ING, -S to shave or cut with a sharp-edged instrument	
RAZZ	v -ED, -ING, -ES to deride	
RE	n pl. -S the second tone of the diatonic musical scale	

R₁ E₁

Following is a list of self-explanatory verbs containing the prefix RE- (again):

REABSORB v -ED, -ING, -S
REACCEDE v -CEDED, -CEDING, -CEDES
REACCENT v -ED, -ING, -S
REACCEPT v -ED, -ING, -S
REACCUSE v -CUSED, -CUSING, -CUSES
READAPT v -ED, -ING, -S
READD v -ED, -ING, -S
READDICT v -ED, -ING, -S
READJUST v -ED, -ING, -S
READMIT v -MITTED, -MITTING, -MITS
READOPT v -ED, -ING, -S
READORN v -ED, -ING, -S
REAFFIRM v -ED, -ING, -S
REAFFIX v -ED, -ING, -ES
REALIGN v -ED, -ING, -S
REALLOT v -LOTTED, -LOTTING, -LOTS
REALTER v -ED, -ING, -S
REANNEX v -ED, -ING, -ES
REANOINT v -ED, -ING, -S
REAPPEAR v -ED, -ING, -S
REAPPLY v -PLIED, -PLYING, -PLIES
REARGUE v -GUED, -GUING, -GUES
REARM v -ED, -ING, -S
REAROUSE v -AROUSED, -AROUSING, -AROUSES
REARREST v -ED, -ING, -S
REASCEND v -ED, -ING, -S
REASSAIL v -ED, -ING, -S
REASSERT v -ED, -ING, -S
REASSESS v -ED, -ING, -ES
REASSIGN v -ED, -ING, -S
REASSORT v -ED, -ING, -S

REASSUME v -SUMED, -SUMING, -SUMES
REASSURE v -SURED, -SURING, -SURES
REATTACH v -ED, -ING, -ES
REATTACK v -ED, -ING, -S
REATTAIN v -ED, -ING, -S
REAVOW v -ED, -ING, -S
REAWAKE v -AWAKED or -AWOKE, -AWOKEN, -AWAKING, -AWAKES
REAWAKEN v -ED, -ING, -S
REBAIT v -ED, -ING, -S
REBID v -BID, -BIDDEN, -BIDDING, -BIDS
REBILL v -ED, -ING, -S
REBIND v -BOUND, -BINDING, -BINDS
REBLOOM v -ED, -ING, -S
REBOARD v -ED, -ING, -S
REBOIL v -ED, -ING, -S
REBOUND past tense of rebind
REBUILD v -BUILT or -BUILDED, -BUILDING, -BUILDS
REBURY v -BURIED, -BURYING, -BURIES
REBUTTON v -ED, -ING, -S
RECANE v -CANED, -CANING, -CANES
RECARRY v -RIED, -RYING, -RIES
RECAST v -CAST, -CASTING, -CASTS
RECHANGE v -CHANGED, -CHANGING, -CHANGES
RECHARGE v -CHARGED, -CHARGING, -CHARGES
RECHART v -ED, -ING, -S
RECHECK v -ED, -ING, -S
RECHOOSE v -CHOSE, -CHOSEN, -CHOOSING, -CHOOSES
RECIRCLE v -CLED, -CLING, -CLES
RECLAD a past tense of reclothe
RECLASP v -ED, -ING, -S
RECLEAN v -ED, -ING, -S
RECLOTHE v -CLOTHED or -CLAD, -CLOTHING, -CLOTHES
RECOAL v -ED, -ING, -S
RECOCK v -ED, -ING, -S
RECODIFY v -FIED, -FYING, -FIES
RECOIN v -ED, -ING, -S
RECOLOR v -ED, -ING, -S

RECOMB	v -ED, -ING, -S		**REEMIT**	v -EMITTED, -EMITTING, -EMITS
RECOMMIT	v -MITTED, -MITTING, -MITS		**REEMPLOY**	v -ED, -ING, -S
RECOOK	v -ED, -ING, -S		**REENACT**	v -ED, -ING, -S
RECOPY	v -COPIED, -COPYING, -COPIES		**REENDOW**	v -ED, -ING, -S
RECOUPLE	v -PLED, -PLING, -PLES		**REENGAGE**	v -GAGED, -GAGING, -GAGES
RECRATE	v -CRATED, -CRATING, -CRATES		**REENJOY**	v -ED, -ING, -S
			REENLIST	v -ED, -ING, -S
RECROSS	v -ED, -ING, -ES		**REENTER**	v -ED, -ING, -S
RECROWN	v -ED, -ING, -S		**REEQUIP**	v -EQUIPPED, -EQUIPPING, -EQUIPS
RECUT	v -CUT, -CUTTING, -CUTS			
REDATE	v -DATED, -DATING, -DATES		**REERECT**	v -ED, -ING, -S
REDEFEAT	v -ED, -ING, -S		**REEVOKE**	v -EVOKED, -EVOKING, -EVOKES
REDEFINE	v -FINED, -FINING, -FINES			
REDEFY	v -FIED, -FYING, -FIES		**REEXPEL**	v -PELLED, -PELLING, -PELS
REDEMAND	v -ED, -ING, -S		**REEXPORT**	v -ED, -ING, -S
REDENY	v -NIED, -NYING, -NIES		**REFALL**	v -FELL, -FALLEN, -FALLING, -FALLS
REDEPLOY	v -ED, -ING, -S			
REDESIGN	v -ED, -ING, -S		**REFASTEN**	v -ED, -ING, -S
REDID	past tense of redo		**REFEED**	v -FED, -FEEDING, -FEEDS
REDIGEST	v -ED, -ING, -S		**REFELL**	past tense of refall
REDIP	v -DIPPED or -DIPT, -DIPPING, -DIPS		**REFIGHT**	v -FOUGHT, -FIGHTING, -FIGHTS
			REFIGURE	v -URED, -URING, -URES
REDIVIDE	v -VIDED, -VIDING, -VIDES		**REFILE**	v -FILED, -FILING, -FILES
REDO	v -DID, -DONE, -DOING, -DOES		**REFILL**	v -ED, -ING, -S
REDOCK	v -ED, -ING, -S		**REFILM**	v -ED, -ING, -S
REDRAW	v -DREW, -DRAWN, -DRAWING, -DRAWS		**REFILTER**	v -ED, -ING, -S
			REFIND	v -FOUND, -FINDING, -FINDS
REDRIED	past tense of redry		**REFIRE**	v -FIRED, -FIRING, -FIRES
REDRIES	present 3d person sing. of redry		**REFIX**	v -ED, -ING, -ES
REDRILL	v -ED, -ING, -S		**REFLEW**	past tense of refly
REDRIVE	v -DROVE, -DRIVEN, -DRIVING, -DRIVES		**REFLIES**	present 3d person sing. of refly
REDRY	v -DRIED, -DRYING, -DRIES		**REFLOAT**	v -ED, -ING, -S
REDYE	v -DYED, -DYEING, -DYES		**REFLOOD**	v -ED, -ING, -S
REEARN	v -ED, -ING, -S		**REFLOW**	v -ED, -ING, -S
REECHO	v -ED, -ING, -ES		**REFLOWER**	v -ED, -ING, -S
REEDIT	v -ED, -ING, -S		**REFLY**	v -FLEW, -FLOWN, -FLYING, -FLIES
REEJECT	v -ED, -ING, -S			
REELECT	v -ED, -ING, -S		**REFOCUS**	v -CUSED, -CUSING, -CUSES or -CUSSED, -CUSSING, -CUSSES
REEMBARK	v -ED, -ING, -S			
REEMBODY	v -BODIED, -BODYING, -BODIES		**REFOLD**	v -ED, -ING, -S
			REFORGE	v -FORGED, -FORGING, -FORGES
REEMERGE	v -EMERGED, -EMERGING, -EMERGES			
			REFORMAT	v -MATTED, -MATTING, -MATS

REFOUGHT past tense of refight

REFOUND v -ED, -ING, -S

REFRAME v -FRAMED, -FRAMING, -FRAMES

REFREEZE v -FROZE, -FROZEN, -FREEZING, -FREEZES

REFRONT v -ED, -ING, -S

REFRY v -FRIED, -FRYING, -FRIES

REFUEL v -ELED, -ELING, -ELS or -ELLED, -ELLING, -ELS

REGAIN v -ED, -ING, -S

REGATHER v -ED, -ING, -S

REGAUGE v -GAUGED, -GAUGING, -GAUGES

REGAVE past tense of regive

REGEAR v -ED, -ING, -S

REGILD v -GILDED or -GILT, -GILDING, -GILDS

REGIVE v -GAVE, -GIVEN, -GIVING, -GIVES

REGLAZE v -GLAZED, -GLAZING, -GLAZES

REGLOSS v -ED, -ING, -ES

REGLOW v -ED, -ING, -S

REGLUE v -GLUED, -GLUING, -GLUES

REGRADE v -GRADED, -GRADING, -GRADES

REGRAFT v -ED, -ING, -S

REGRANT v -ED, -ING, -S

REGREW past tense of regrow

REGRIND v -GROUND, -GRINDING, -GRINDS

REGROOVE v -GROOVED, -GROOVING, -GROOVES

REGROUP v -ED, -ING, -S

REGROW v -GREW, -GROWN, -GROWING, -GROWS

REHAMMER v -ED, -ING, -S

REHANDLE v -DLED, -DLING, -DLES

REHANG v -HUNG or -HANGED, -HANGING, -HANGS

REHARDEN v -ED, -ING, -S

REHASH v -ED, -ING, -ES

REHEAR v -HEARD, -HEARING, -HEARS

REHEAT v -ED, -ING, -S

REHEEL v -ED, -ING, -S

REHEM v -HEMMED, -HEMMING, -HEMS

REHINGE v -HINGED, -HINGING, -HINGES

REHIRE v -HIRED, -HIRING, -HIRES

REHUNG a past tense of rehang

REIGNITE v -NITED, -NITING, -NITES

REIMAGE v -AGED, -AGING, -AGES

REIMPORT v -ED, -ING, -S

REIMPOSE v -POSED, -POSING, -POSES

REINCITE v -CITED, -CITING, -CITES

REINCUR v -CURRED, -CURRING, -CURS

REINDEX v -ED, -ING, -ES

REINDUCE v -DUCED, -DUCING, -DUCES

REINDUCT v -ED, -ING, -S

REINFECT v -ED, -ING, -S

REINFORM v -ED, -ING, -S

REINFUSE v -FUSED, -FUSING, -FUSES

REINJURE v -JURED, -JURING, -JURES

REINSERT v -ED, -ING, -S

REINSURE v -SURED, -SURING, -SURES

REINTER v -TERRED, -TERRING, -TERS

REINVENT v -ED, -ING, -S

REINVEST v -ED, -ING, -S

REINVITE v -VITED, -VITING, -VITES

REINVOKE v -VOKED, -VOKING, -VOKES

REISSUE v -SUED, -SUING, -SUES

REJOIN v -ED, -ING, -S

REJUDGE v -JUDGED, -JUDGING, -JUDGES

REKEY v -ED, -ING, -S

REKINDLE v -DLED, -DLING, -DLES

REKNIT v -KNITTED, -KNITTING, -KNITS

RELABEL v -BELED, -BELING, -BELS or -BELLED, -BELLING, -BELS

RELACE v -LACED, -LACING, -LACES

RELAUNCH v -ED, -ING, -ES

RELAY v -LAID, -LAYING, -LAYS

RELEARN v -LEARNED or -LEARNT, -LEARNING, -LEARNS

RELEND v -LENT, -LENDING, -LENDS

RELET v -LET, -LETTING, -LETS

RELETTER v -ED, -ING, -S

RELIGHT v -LIGHTED or -LIT, -LIGHTING, -LIGHTS

RELINE v -LINED, -LINING, -LINES

RELIST	v -ED, -ING, -S
RELIT	a past tense of relight
RELOAD	v -ED, -ING, -S
RELOAN	v -ED, -ING, -S
REMAIL	v -ED, -ING, -S
REMAKE	v -MADE, -MAKING, -MAKES
REMAP	v -MAPPED, -MAPPING, -MAPS
REMARRY	v -RIED, -RYING, -RIES
REMATCH	v -ED, -ING, -ES
REMEET	v -MET, -MEETING, -MEETS
REMELT	v -ED, -ING, -S
REMEND	v -ED, -ING, -S
REMERGE	v -MERGED, -MERGING, -MERGES
REMET	past tense of remeet
REMIX	v -MIXED or -MIXT, -MIXING, -MIXES
REMODIFY	v -FIED, -FYING, -FIES
REMOLD	v -ED, -ING, -S
REMOUNT	v -ED, -ING, -S
RENAME	v -NAMED, -NAMING, -NAMES
RENOTIFY	v -FIED, -FYING, -FIES
RENUMBER	v -ED, -ING, -S
REOBJECT	v -ED, -ING, -S
REOBTAIN	v -ED, -ING, -S
REOCCUPY	v -PIED, -PYING, -PIES
REOCCUR	v -CURRED, -CURRING, -CURS
REOIL	v -ED, -ING, -S
REOPEN	v -ED, -ING, -S
REOPPOSE	v -POSED, -POSING, -POSES
REORDAIN	v -ED, -ING, -S
REORDER	v -ED, -ING, -S
REORIENT	v -ED, -ING, -S
REPACIFY	v -FIED, -FYING, -FIES
REPACK	v -ED, -ING, -S
REPAINT	v -ED, -ING, -S
REPAPER	v -ED, -ING, -S
REPASS	v -ED, -ING, -ES
REPAVE	v -PAVED, -PAVING, -PAVES
REPEOPLE	v -PLED, -PLING, -PLES
REPERK	v -ED, -ING, -S
REPHRASE	v -PHRASED, -PHRASING, -PHRASES
REPIN	v -PINNED, -PINNING, -PINS

REPLAN	v -PLANNED, -PLANNING, -PLANS
REPLANT	v -ED, -ING, -S
REPLATE	v -PLATED, -PLATING, -PLATES
REPLAY	v -ED, -ING, -S
REPLEDGE	v -PLEDGED, -PLEDGING, -PLEDGES
REPLUNGE	v -PLUNGED, -PLUNGING, -PLUNGES
REPOLISH	v -ED, -ING, -ES
REPOUR	v -ED, -ING, -S
REPOWER	v -ED, -ING, -S
REPRICE	v -PRICED, -PRICING, -PRICES
REPRINT	v -ED, -ING, -S
REPROBE	v -PROBED, -PROBING, -PROBES
REPURIFY	v -FIED, -FYING, -FIES
REPURSUE	v -SUED, -SUING, -SUES
REREAD	v -READ, -READING, -READS
RERECORD	v -ED, -ING, -S
RERISE	v -ROSE, -RISEN, -RISING, -RISES
REROLL	v -ED, -ING, -S
REROUTE	v -ROUTED, -ROUTING, -ROUTES
RESADDLE	v -DLED, -DLING, -DLES
RESAID	past tense of resay
RESAIL	v -ED, -ING, -S
RESALUTE	v -LUTED, -LUTING, -LUTES
RESAMPLE	v -PLED, -PLING, -PLES
RESAW	v -SAWED, -SAWN, -SAWING, -SAWS
RESAY	v -SAID, -SAYING, -SAYS
RESCORE	v -SCORED, -SCORING, -SCORES
RESCREEN	v -ED, -ING, -S
RESEAL	v -ED, -ING, -S
RESEAT	v -ED, -ING, -S
RESEE	v -SAW, -SEEN, -SEEING, -SEES
RESEED	v -ED, -ING, -S
RESEEK	v -SOUGHT, -SEEKING, -SEEKS
RESEEN	past participle of resee
RESEIZE	v -SEIZED, -SEIZING, -SEIZES
RESELL	v -SOLD, -SELLING, -SELLS

RESEND	v -SENT, -SENDING, -SENDS
RESET	v -SET, -SETTING, -SETS
RESETTLE	v -TLED, -TLING, -TLES
RESEW	v -SEWED, -SEWN, -SEWING, -SEWS
RESHAPE	v -SHAPED, -SHAPING, -SHAPES
RESHIP	v -SHIPPED, -SHIPPING, -SHIPS
RESHOE	v -SHOD, -SHOEING, -SHOES
RESHOOT	v -SHOT, -SHOOTING, -SHOOTS
RESHOW	v -SHOWED, -SHOWN, -SHOWING, -SHOWS
RESIFT	v -ED, -ING, -S
RESILVER	v -ED, -ING, -S
RESIZE	v -SIZED, -SIZING, -SIZES
RESMELT	v -ED, -ING, -S
RESMOOTH	v -ED, -ING, -S
RESOLD	past tense of resell
RESOLDER	v -ED, -ING, -S
RESOLE	v -SOLED, -SOLING, -SOLES
RESOUGHT	past tense of reseek
RESOW	v -SOWED, -SOWN, -SOWING, -SOWS
RESPELL	v -SPELLED or -SPELT, -SPELLING, -SPELLS
RESPREAD	v -SPREAD, -SPREADING, -SPREADS
RESPRING	v -SPRANG or -SPRUNG, -SPRINGING, -SPRINGS
RESTACK	v -ED, -ING, -S
RESTAFF	v -ED, -ING, -S
RESTAGE	v -STAGED, -STAGING, -STAGES
RESTAMP	v -ED, -ING, -S
RESTART	v -ED, -ING, -S
RESTATE	v -STATED, -STATING, -STATES
RESTOCK	v -ED, -ING, -S
RESTRIKE	v -STRUCK, -STRICKEN, -STRIKING, -STRIKES
RESTRING	v -STRUNG, -STRINGING, -STRINGS
RESTRIVE	v -STROVE, -STRIVEN, -STRIVING, -STRIVES
RESTRUCK	past tense of restrike
RESTRUNG	past tense of restring
RESTUDY	v -STUDIED, -STUDYING, -STUDIES
RESTUFF	v -ED, -ING, -S
RESTYLE	v -STYLED, -STYLING, -STYLES
RESUBMIT	v -MITTED, -MITTING, -MITS
RESUMMON	v -ED, -ING, -S
RESUPPLY	v -PLIED, -PLYING, -PLIES
RESURVEY	v -ED, -ING, -S
RETAILOR	v -ED, -ING, -S
RETASTE	v -TASTED, -TASTING, -TASTES
RETEACH	v -TAUGHT, -TEACHING, -TEACHES
RETELL	v -TOLD, -TELLING, -TELLS
RETEST	v -ED, -ING, -S
RETHINK	v -THOUGHT, -THINKING, -THINKS
RETHREAD	v -ED, -ING, -S
RETIE	v -TIED, -TYING, -TIES
RETIME	v -TIMED, -TIMING, -TIMES
RETINT	v -ED, -ING, -S
RETITLE	v -TLED, -TLING, -TLES
RETOLD	past tense of retell
RETRACK	v -ED, -ING, -S
RETRAIN	v -ED, -ING, -S
RETRIM	v -TRIMMED, -TRIMMING, -TRIMS
RETRY	v -TRIED, -TRYING, -TRIES
RETUNE	v -TUNED, -TUNING, -TUNES
RETWIST	v -ED, -ING, -S
RETYING	present participle of retie
RETYPE	v -TYPED, -TYPING, -TYPES
REUNIFY	v -FIED, -FYING, -FIES
REUNITE	v -UNITED, -UNITING, -UNITES
REUSE	v -USED, -USING, -USES
REUTTER	v -ED, -ING, -S
REVALUE	v -UED, -UING, -UES
REVERIFY	v -FIED, -FYING, -FIES
REVEST	v -ED, -ING, -S
REVIEW	v -ED, -ING, -S
REVISIT	v -ED, -ING, -S
REVOICE	v -VOICED, -VOICING, -VOICES
REWAKE	v -WAKED or -WOKE, -WOKEN, -WAKING, -WAKES

REWAKEN	v -ED, -ING, -S
REWAN	a past tense of rewin
REWARM	v -ED, -ING, -S
REWASH	v -ED, -ING, -ES
REWAX	v -ED, -ING, -ES
REWEAVE	v -WOVE or -WEAVED, -WOVEN, -WEAVING, -WEAVES
REWEIGH	v -ED, -ING, -S
REWELD	v -ED, -ING, -S
REWIDEN	v -ED, -ING, -S
REWIN	v -WON or -WAN, -WINNING, -WINS
REWIND	v -WOUND or -WINDED, -WINDING, -WINDS
REWIRE	v -WIRED, -WIRING, -WIRES
REWOKE	a past tense of rewake
REWOKEN	past participle of rewake
REWON	a past tense of rewin
REWORK	v -WORKED or -WROUGHT, -WORKING, -WORKS
REWOUND	a past tense of rewind
REWOVE	a past tense of reweave
REWOVEN	past participle of reweave
REWRAP	v -WRAPPED, or -WRAPT, -WRAPPING, -WRAPS
REWRITE	v -WROTE, -WRITTEN, -WRITING, -WRITES
REWROUGHT	a past tense of rework
REZONE	v -ZONED, -ZONING, -ZONES
REACH	v -ED, -ING, -ES to stretch out or put forth
REACHER	n pl. -S one that reaches
REACT	v -ED, -ING, -S to respond to a stimulus
REACTANT	n pl. -S one that reacts
REACTION	n pl. -S the act of reacting
REACTIVE	adj tending to react
REACTOR	n pl. -S one that reacts
READ	v READ, READING, READS to look at so as to take in the meaning of, as something written or printed **READABLE** adj **READABLY** adv
READER	n pl. -S one that reads
READIED	past tense of ready

READIER	comparative of ready
READIES	present 3d person sing. of ready
READIEST	superlative of ready
READILY	adv in a ready manner
READING	n pl. -S material that is read
READOUT	n pl. -S a presentation of computer data
READY	adj READIER, READIEST prepared
READY	v READIED, READYING, READIES to make ready
REAGENT	n pl. -S a substance used in a chemical reaction to ascertain the nature or composition of another
REAGIN	n pl. -S a type of antibody **REAGINIC** adj
REAL	adj REALER, REALEST having actual existence
REAL	n pl. -S or -ES a former monetary unit of Spain
REAL	n pl. REIS a former monetary unit of Portugal and Brazil
REALGAR	n pl. -S a mineral
REALIA	n/pl objects used by a teacher to illustrate everyday living
REALISE	v -ISED, -ISING, -ISES to realize
REALISER	n pl. -S one that realises
REALISM	n pl. -S concern with fact or reality
REALIST	n pl. -S one who is concerned with fact or reality
REALITY	n pl. -TIES something that is real
REALIZE	v -IZED, -IZING, -IZES to understand completely
REALIZER	n pl. -S one that realizes
REALLY	adv actually
REALM	n pl. -S a kingdom
REALNESS	n pl. -ES the state of being real
REALTY	n pl. -TIES property in buildings and land
REAM	v -ED, -ING, -S to enlarge with a reamer
REAMER	n pl. -S a tool used to enlarge holes
REAP	v -ED, -ING, -S to cut for harvest **REAPABLE** adj
REAPER	n pl. -S one that reaps
REAPHOOK	n pl. -S an implement used in reaping
REAR	v -ED, -ING, -S to lift upright

REARER *n pl.* -S one that rears

REARMICE *n/pl* reremice

REARMOST *adj* coming or situated last

REARWARD *n pl.* -S the rearmost division of an army

REASCENT *n pl.* -S a new or second ascent

REASON *v* -ED, -ING, -S to derive inferences or conclusions from known or presumed facts

REASONER *n pl.* -S one that reasons

REATA *n pl.* -S riata

REAVE *v* REAVED or REFT, REAVING, REAVES to plunder

REAVER *n pl.* -S one that reaves

REB *n pl.* -S a Confederate soldier

REBATE *v* -BATED, -BATING, -BATES to deduct or return from a payment or bill

REBATER *n pl.* -S one that rebates

REBATO *n pl.* -TOS rabato

REBBE *n pl.* -S a rabbi

REBEC *n pl.* -S an ancient stringed instrument

REBECK *n pl.* -S rebec

REBEL *v* -BELLED, -BELLING, -BELS to oppose the established government of one's land

REBELDOM *n pl.* -S an area controlled by rebels

REBIRTH *n pl.* -S a new or second birth

REBOANT *adj* resounding loudly

REBOP *n pl.* -S a type of music

REBORN *adj* born again

REBOUND *v* -ED, -ING, -S to spring back

REBOZO *n pl.* -ZOS a long scarf

REBRANCH *v* -ED, -ING, -ES to form secondary branches

REBUFF *v* -ED, -ING, -S to reject or refuse curtly

REBUKE *v* -BUKED, -BUKING, -BUKES to criticize sharply

REBUKER *n pl.* -S one that rebukes

REBURIAL *n pl.* -S a second burial

REBUS *n pl.* -ES a type of puzzle

REBUT *v* -BUTTED, -BUTTING, -BUTS to refute

REBUTTAL *n pl.* -S argument or proof that rebuts

REBUTTER *n pl.* -S one that rebuts

REBUTTING present participle of rebut

REC *n pl.* -S recreation

RECALL *v* -ED, -ING, -S to call back

RECALLER *n pl.* -S one that recalls

RECANT *v* -ED, -ING, -S to make a formal retraction or disavowal of

RECANTER *n pl.* -S one that recants

RECAP *v* -CAPPED, -CAPPING, -CAPS to review by a brief summary

RECEDE *v* -CEDED, -CEDING, -CEDES to move back or away

RECEIPT *v* -ED, -ING, -S to mark as having been paid

RECEIVE *v* -CEIVED, -CEIVING, -CEIVES to come into possession of

RECEIVER *n pl.* -S one that receives

RECENCY *n pl.* -CIES the state of being recent

RECENT *adj* -CENTER, -CENTEST of or pertaining to a time not long past RECENTLY *adv*

RECEPT *n pl.* -S a type of mental image

RECEPTOR *n pl.* -S a nerve ending specialized to receive stimuli

RECESS *v* -ED, -ING, -ES to place in a receding space or hollow

RECHEAT *n pl.* -S a hunting call

RECIPE *n pl.* -S a set of instructions for making something

RECISION *n pl.* -S a cancellation

RECITAL *n pl.* -S a detailed account

RECITE *v* -CITED, -CITING, -CITES to declaim or say from memory

RECITER *n pl.* -S one that recites

RECK *v* -ED, -ING, -S to be concerned about

RECKLESS *adj* foolishly heedless of danger

RECKON *v* -ED, -ING, -S to count or compute

RECKONER *n pl.* -S one that reckons

RECLAIM *v* -ED, -ING, -S to make suitable for cultivation or habitation

RECLAME *n pl.* -S publicity

RECLINE *v* -CLINED, -CLINING, -CLINES to lean or lie back

RECLINER *n pl.* -S one that reclines

RECLUSE *n pl.* -S one who lives in solitude and seclusion

RECOIL *v* -ED, -ING, -S to draw back in fear or disgust

RECOILER *n pl.* -S one that recoils

RECON *n pl.* -S a preliminary survey

RECONVEY *v* -ED, -ING, -S to convey back to a previous position

RECORD v -ED, -ING, -S to set down for preservation

RECORDER n pl. -S one that records

RECOUNT v -ED, -ING, -S to relate in detail

RECOUP v -ED, -ING, -S to get back the equivalent of

RECOUPE adj divided twice

RECOURSE n pl. -S a turning or applying to someone or something for aid

RECOVER v -ED, -ING, -S to obtain again after losing

RECOVERY n pl. -ERIES an economic upturn

RECREANT n pl. -S a coward

RECREATE v -ATED, -ATING, -ATES to refresh mentally or physically

RECRUIT v -ED, -ING, -S to engage for military service

RECTA a pl. of rectum

RECTAL adj pertaining to the rectum RECTALLY adv

RECTI pl. of rectus

RECTIFY v -FIED, -FYING, -FIES to correct

RECTO n pl. -TOS a right-hand page of a book

RECTOR n pl. -S a clergyman in charge of a parish

RECTORY n pl. -RIES a rector's dwelling

RECTRIX n pl. -TRICES a feather of a bird's tail

RECTUM n pl. -TUMS or -TA the terminal portion of the large intestine

RECTUS n pl. -TI a straight muscle

RECUR v -CURRED, -CURRING, -CURS to happen again

RECURVE v -CURVED, -CURVING, -CURVES to curve backward or downward

RECUSANT n pl. -S one who refuses to accept established authority

RECUSE v -CUSED, -CUSING, -CUSES to disqualify or challenge as judge in a particular case

RECYCLE v -CLED, -CLING, -CLES to process in order to extract useful materials

RED adj REDDER, REDDEST of the color of blood

RED v REDDED, REDDING, REDS to redd

REDACT v -ED, -ING, -S to prepare for publication

REDACTOR n pl. -S one that redacts

REDAN n pl. -S a type of fortification

REDARGUE v -GUED, -GUING, -GUES to disprove

REDBAIT v -ED, -ING, -S to denounce as Communist

REDBAY n pl. -BAYS a small tree

REDBIRD n pl. -S a bird with red plummage

REDBONE n pl. -S a hunting dog

REDBRICK adj pertaining to modern British universities

REDBUD n pl. -S a small tree

REDBUG n pl. -S a chigger

REDCAP n pl. -S a porter

REDCOAT n pl. -S a British soldier during the American Revolution

REDD v -ED, -ING, -S to put in order

REDDED past tense of red and redd

REDDEN v -ED, -ING, -S to make or become red

REDDER n pl. -S one that redds

REDDEST superlative of red

REDDING present participle of red and redd

REDDISH adj somewhat red

REDDLE v -DLED, -DLING, -DLES to ruddle

REDE v REDED, REDING, REDES to advise

REDEAR n pl. -S a common sunfish

REDEEM v -ED, -ING, -S to buy back

REDEEMER n pl. -S one that redeems

REDEYE n pl. -S a railroad danger signal

REDFIN n pl. -S a freshwater fish

REDFISH n pl. -ES an edible rockfish

REDHEAD n pl. -S a person with red hair

REDHORSE n pl. -S a freshwater fish

REDIA n pl. -DIAE or -DIAS the larva of certain flatworms REDIAL adj

REDING present participle of rede

REDIRECT v -ED, -ING, -S to change the course or direction of

REDLEG n pl. -S a bird with red legs

REDLY adv with red color

REDNECK n pl. -S a white, rural laborer of the southern United States

REDNESS n pl. -ES the state of being red

REDO n pl. -DOS something that is done again

REDOLENT adj fragrant

REDOUBLE v -BLED, -BLING, -BLES to double

REDOUBT n pl. -S an enclosed fortification

REDOUND v -ED, -ING, -S to have an effect or consequence

REDOUT n pl. -S a condition in which blood is driven to the head

REDOWA n pl. -S a lively dance

REDOX n pl. -ES a type of chemical reaction

REDPOLL n pl. -S a small finch

REDRAFT v -ED, -ING, -S to make a revised copy of

REDRAWER n pl. -S one that redraws

REDRESS v -ED, -ING, -ES to set right

REDROOT n pl. -S a perennial herb

REDSHANK n pl. -S a shore bird

REDSHIRT v -ED, -ING, -S to keep a college athlete out of varsity play in order to extend his eligibility

REDSKIN n pl. -S a North American Indian

REDSTART n pl. -S a small songbird

REDTOP n pl. -S a type of grass

REDUCE v -DUCED, -DUCING, -DUCES to diminish

REDUCER n pl. -S one that reduces

REDUVIID n pl. -S a bloodsucking insect

REDWARE n pl. -S an edible seaweed

REDWING n pl. -S a European thrush

REDWOOD n pl. -S a very tall evergreen tree

REE n pl. -S the female Eurasian sandpiper

REED v -ED, -ING, -S to fasten with reeds (the stalks of tall grasses)

REEDBIRD n pl. -S the bobolink

REEDBUCK n pl. -S an African antelope

REEDIER comparative of reedy

REEDIEST superlative of reedy

REEDIFY v -FIED, -FYING, -FIES to rebuild

REEDING n pl. -S a convex molding

REEDLING n pl. -S a marsh bird

REEDY adj REEDIER, REEDIEST abounding in reeds

REEF v -ED, -ING, -S to reduce the area of a sail

REEFER n pl. -S one that reefs

REEFY adj REEFIER, REEFIEST abounding in ridges of rock

REEK v -ED, -ING, -S to give off a strong, unpleasant odor

REEKER n pl. -S one that reeks

REEKY adj REEKIER, REEKIEST reeking

REEL v -ED, -ING, -S to wind on a type of rotary device REELABLE adj

REELER n pl. -S one that reels

REENTRY n pl. -TRIES a new or second entry

REEST v -ED, -ING, -S to balk

REEVE v REEVED or ROVE, ROVEN, REEVING, REEVES to fasten by passing through or around something

REF v REFFED, REFFING, REFS to referee

REFACE v -FACED, -FACING, -FACES to repair the outer surface of

REFECT v -ED, -ING, -S to refresh with food and drink

REFEL v -FELLED, -FELLING, -FELS to reject

REFER v -FERRED, -FERRING, -FERS to direct to a source for help or information

REFEREE v -EED, -EEING, -EES to supervise the play in certain sports

REFERENT n pl. -S something referred to

REFERRAL n pl. -S one that is referred

REFERRED past tense of refer

REFERRER n pl. -S one that refers

REFERRING present participle of refer

REFFED past tense of ref

REFFING present participle of ref

REFINE v -FINED, -FINING, -FINES to free from impurities

REFINER n pl. -S one that refines

REFINERY n pl. -ERIES a place where crude material is refined

REFINING present participle of refine

REFINISH v -ED, -ING, -ES to give a new surface to

REFIT v -FITTED, -FITTING, -FITS to prepare and equip for additional use

REFLATE v -FLATED, -FLATING, -FLATES to inflate again

REFLECT v -ED, -ING, -S to turn or throw back from a surface

REFLET n pl. -S special brilliance of surface

REFLEX v -ED, -ING, -ES to bend back

REFLEXLY adv in a reflexed manner

REFLUENT *adj* flowing back

REFLUX *v* -ED, -ING, -ES to cause to flow back

REFOREST *v* -ED, -ING, -S to replant with trees

REFORM *v* -ED, -ING, -S to change to a better state

REFORMER *n pl.* -S one that reforms

REFRACT *v* -ED, -ING, -S to deflect in a particular manner, as a ray of light

REFRAIN *v* -ED, -ING, -S to keep oneself back

REFRESH *v* -ED, -ING, -ES to restore the well-being and vigor of

REFT a past tense of reave

REFUGE *v* -UGED, -UGING, -UGES to give or take shelter

REFUGEE *n pl.* -S one who flees for safety

REFUGIUM *n pl.* -GIA a stable area during a period of continental climactic change

REFUND *v* -ED, -ING, -S to give back

REFUNDER *n pl.* -S one that refunds

REFUSAL *n pl.* -S the act of refusing

REFUSE *v* -FUSED, -FUSING, -FUSES to express oneself as unwilling to accept, do, or comply with

REFUSER *n pl.* -S one that refuses

REFUTAL *n pl.* -S the act of refuting

REFUTE *v* -FUTED, -FUTING, -FUTES to prove to be false or erroneous

REFUTER *n pl.* -S one that refutes

REGAINER *n pl.* -S one that regains

REGAL *adj* of or befitting a king

REGALE *v* -GALED, -GALING, -GALES to delight

REGALIA *n/pl* the rights and privileges of a king

REGALITY *n pl.* -TIES regal authority

REGALLY *adv* in a regal manner

REGARD *v* -ED, -ING, -S to look upon with a particular feeling

REGATTA *n pl.* -S a boat race

REGELATE *v* -LATED, -LATING, -LATES to refreeze ice by reducing the pressure

REGENCY *n pl.* -CIES the office of a regent

REGENT *n pl.* -S one who rules in the place of a sovereign **REGENTAL** *adj*

REGES pl. of rex

REGICIDE *n pl.* -S the killing of a king

REGIME *n pl.* -S a system of government

REGIMEN *n pl.* -S a systematic plan

REGIMENT *v* -ED, -ING, -S to form into military units

REGINA *n pl.* -NAE or -NAS queen **REGINAL** *adj*

REGION *n pl.* -S an administrative area or division

REGIONAL *n pl.* -S something that serves as a region

REGISTER *v* -ED, -ING, -S to record officially

REGISTRY *n pl.* -TRIES the act of registering

REGIUS *adj* holding a professorship founded by the sovereign

REGLET *n pl.* -S a flat, narrow molding

REGMA *n pl.* -MATA a type of fruit

REGNA pl. of regnum

REGNAL *adj* pertaining to a king or his reign

REGNANCY *n pl.* -CIES the state of being regnant

REGNANT *adj* reigning

REGNUM *n pl.* -NA dominion

REGOLITH *n pl.* -S a layer of loose rock

REGORGE *v* -GORGED, -GORGING, -GORGES to vomit

REGOSOL *n pl.* -S a type of soil

REGRATE *v* -GRATED, -GRATING, -GRATES to buy up in order to sell for a higher price in the same area

REGREET *v* -ED, -ING, -S to greet in return

REGRESS *v* -ED, -ING, -ES to go back

REGRET *v* -GRETTED, -GRETTING, -GRETS to look back upon with sorrow or remorse

REGROWTH *n pl.* -S a new or second growth

REGULAR *n pl.* -S an habitual customer

REGULATE *v* -LATED, -LATING, -LATES to control according to rule

REGULUS *n pl.* -LI or -LUSES a mass that forms beneath the slag in a furnace **REGULINE** *adj*

REHEARSE *v* -HEARSED, -HEARSING, -HEARSES to practice in preparation for a public appearance

REHEATER *n pl.* -S one that reheats

REHOUSE v -HOUSED, -HOUSING, -HOUSES to establish in a new housing unit

REI n pl. -S an erroneous English form for a former Portuguese coin

REIF n pl. -S robbery

REIFIER n pl. -S one that reifies

REIFY v -IFIED, -IFYING, -IFIES to regard as real or concrete

REIGN v -ED, -ING, -S to exercise sovereign power

REIN v -ED, -ING, -S to restrain

REINDEER n pl. -S a large deer

REINLESS adj unrestrained

REINSMAN n pl. -MEN a skilled rider of horses

REIS pl. of real

REISSUER n pl. -S one that reissues

REITBOK n pl. -S the reedbuck

REIVE v REIVED, REIVING, REIVES to plunder

REIVER n pl. -S one that reives

REJECT v -ED, -ING, -S to refuse to accept, consider, or make use of

REJECTEE n pl. -S one that is rejected

REJECTER n pl. -S one that rejects

REJECTOR n pl. -S rejecter

REJIGGER v -ED, -ING, -S to alter

REJOICE v -JOICED, -JOICING, -JOICES to feel joyful

REJOICER n pl. -S one that rejoices

RELAPSE v -LAPSED, -LAPSING, -LAPSES to fall or slip back into a former state

RELAPSER n pl. -S one that relapses

RELATE v -LATED, -LATING, -LATES to give an account of

RELATER n pl. -S one that relates

RELATION n pl. -S a significant association between two or more things

RELATIVE n pl. -S one who is connected with another by blood or marriage

RELATOR n pl. -S relater

RELAX v -ED, -ING, -ES to make less tense or rigid

RELAXANT n pl. -S a drug that relieves muscular tension

RELAXER n pl. -S one that relaxes

RELAXIN n pl. -S a female hormone

RELAY v -ED, -ING, -S to send along by using fresh sets to replace tired ones

RELEASE v -LEASED, -LEASING, -LEASES to set free

RELEASER n pl. -S one that releases

RELEGATE v -GATED, -GATING, -GATES to assign

RELENT v -ED, -ING, -S to become less severe

RELEVANT adj pertaining to the matter at hand

RELIABLE adj suitable to be relied on RELIABLY adv

RELIANCE n pl. -S confident or trustful dependence

RELIANT adj showing reliance

RELIC n pl. -S a surviving memorial of something past

RELICT n pl. -S an organism surviving in a changed environment

RELIED past tense of rely

RELIEF n pl. -S aid in the form of money or necessities

RELIER n pl. -S one that relies

RELIES present 3d person sing. of rely

RELIEVE v -LIEVED, -LIEVING, -LIEVES to lessen or free from pain or discomfort

RELIEVER n pl. -S one that relieves

RELIEVO n pl. -VOS the projection of figures or forms from a flat background

RELIGION n pl. -S the worship of a god or the supernatural

RELIQUE n pl. -S relic

RELISH v -ED, -ING, -ES to enjoy

RELIVE v -LIVED, -LIVING, -LIVES to experience again

RELOADER n pl. -S one that reloads

RELOCATE v -CATED, -CATING, -CATES to establish in a new place

RELUCENT adj reflecting light

RELUCT v -ED, -ING, -S to show opposition

RELUME v -LUMED, -LUMING, -LUMES to light again

RELUMINE v -MINED, -MINING, -MINES to relume

RELY v -LIED, -LYING, -LIES to place trust or confidence

REM n pl. -S a quantity of ionizing radiation

REMAIN v -ED, -ING, -S to continue in the same state

REMAN   v -MANNED, -MANNING, -MANS to furnish with a fresh supply of men

REMAND   v -ED, -ING, -S to send back

REMANENT   adj remaining

REMANNED past tense of reman

REMANNING present participle of reman

REMARK   v -ED, -ING, -S to say or write briefly or casually

REMARKER   n pl. -S one that remarks

REMARQUE   n pl. -S a mark made in the margin of an engraved plate

REMEDIAL   adj intended to correct something

REMEDY   v -DIED, -DYING, -DIES to relieve or cure

REMEMBER   v -ED, -ING, -S to bring to mind again

REMEX   n pl. REMIGES a flight feather of a bird's wing **REMIGIAL** adj

REMIND   v -ED, -ING, -S to cause to remember

REMINDER   n pl. -S one that reminds

REMINT   v -ED, -ING, -S to melt down and make into new coin

REMISE   v -MISED, -MISING, -MISES to give up a claim to

REMISS   adj careless **REMISSLY** adv

REMIT   v -MITTED, -MITTING, -MITS to send money in payment

REMITTAL   n pl. -S the act of remitting

REMITTER   n pl. -S one that remits

REMITTING present participle of remit

REMITTOR   n pl. -S remitter

REMNANT   n pl. -S something remaining

REMODEL   v -ELED, -ELING, -ELS or -ELLED, -ELLING, -ELS to make over

REMOLADE   n pl. -S a piquant sauce

REMORA   n pl. -S a type of marine fish **REMORID** adj

REMORSE   n pl. -S deep anguish caused by a sense of guilt

REMOTE   adj -MOTER, -MOTEST situated far away **REMOTELY** adv

REMOTION   n pl. -S the act of removing

REMOVAL   n pl. -S the act of removing

REMOVE   v -MOVED, -MOVING, -MOVES to take or move away

REMOVER   n pl. -S one that removes

REMUDA   n pl. -S a herd of horses

RENAL   adj pertaining to the kidneys

RENATURE   v -TURED, -TURING, -TURES to restore natural qualities

REND   v RENT or RENDED, RENDING, RENDS to tear apart forcibly

RENDER   v -ED, -ING, -S to cause to be or become

RENDERER   n pl. -S one that renders

RENDIBLE   adj capable of being rent

RENDZINA   n pl. -S a type of soil

RENEGADE   v -GADED, -GADING, -GADES to become a traitor

RENEGADO   n pl. -DOS or -DOES a traitor

RENEGE   v -NEGED, -NEGING, -NEGES to fail to carry out a promise or commitment

RENEGER   n pl. -S one that reneges

RENEW   v -ED, -ING, -S to make new or as if new again

RENEWAL   n pl. -S the act of renewing

RENEWER   n pl. -S one that renews

RENIFORM   adj kidney-shaped

RENIG   v -NIGGED, -NIGGING, -NIGS to renege

RENIN   n pl. -S an enzyme

RENITENT   adj resisting physical pressure

RENNASE   n pl. -S rennin

RENNET   n pl. -S a lining membrane in the stomach of certain young animals

RENNIN   n pl. -S an enzyme

RENOGRAM   n pl. -S a photographic depiction of the course of renal excretion

RENOUNCE   v -NOUNCED, -NOUNCING, -NOUNCES to disown

RENOVATE   v -VATED, -VATING, -VATES to make like new

RENOWN   v -ED, -ING, -S to make famous

RENT   v -ED, -ING, -S to obtain temporary use of in return for compensation **RENTABLE** adj

RENTAL   n pl. -S an amount paid or collected as rent

RENTE   n pl. -S annual income under French law

RENTER   n pl. -S one that rents

RENTIER   n pl. -S one that receives a fixed income

RENVOI   n pl. -S the expulsion by a government of an alien

REOFFER   v -ED, -ING, -S to offer for public sale

REOVIRUS   n pl. -ES a type of virus

REP   n pl. -S a cross-ribbed fabric

REPAID past tense of repay

REPAIR v -ED, -ING, -S to restore to good condition

REPAIRER n pl. -S one that repairs

REPAND adj having a wavy margin REPANDLY adv

REPARTEE n pl. -S a quick, witty reply

REPAST v -ED, -ING, -S to eat or feast

REPAY v -PAID, -PAYING, -PAYS to pay back

REPEAL v -ED, -ING, -S to revoke

REPEALER n pl. -S one that repeals

REPEAT v -ED, -ING, -S to say or do again

REPEATER n pl. -S one that repeats

REPEL v -PELLED, -PELLING, -PELS to drive away

REPELLER n pl. -S one that repels

REPENT v -ED, -ING, -S to feel remorse or self-reproach for a past action

REPENTER n pl. -S one that repents

REPETEND n pl. -S a phrase or sound that is repeated

REPINE v -PINED, -PINING, -PINES to express discontent

REPINER n pl. -S one that repines

REPLACE v -PLACED, -PLACING, -PLACES to take the place of

REPLACER n pl. -S one that replaces

REPLETE adj abundantly supplied

REPLEVIN v -ED, -ING, -S to replevy

REPLEVY v -PLEVIED, -PLEVYING, -PLEVIES to regain possession of by legal action

REPLICA n pl. -S a close copy or reproduction

REPLIER n pl. -S one that replies

REPLY v -PLIED, -PLYING, -PLIES to answer

REPORT v -ED, -ING, -S to give an account of

REPORTER n pl. -S one that reports

REPOSAL n pl. -S the act of reposing

REPOSE v -POSED, -POSING, -POSES to lie at rest

REPOSER n pl. -S one that reposes

REPOSIT v -ED, -ING, -S to put away

REPOUSSE n pl. -S a raised design hammered in metal

REPP n pl. -S rep

REPPED adj resembling rep

REPRESS v -ED, -ING, -ES to keep under control

REPRIEVE v -PRIEVED, -PRIEVING, -PRIEVES to postpone the punishment of

REPRISAL n pl. -S an act of retaliation

REPRISE v -PRISED, -PRISING, -PRISES to take back by force

REPRO n pl. -PROS a trial sheet of printed material suitable for photographic reproduction

REPROACH v -ED, -ING, -ES to find fault with

REPROOF n pl. -S criticism for a fault

REPROVAL n pl. -S reproof

REPROVE v -PROVED, -PROVING, -PROVES to rebuke

REPROVER n pl. -S one that reproves

REPTANT adj creeping or crawling

REPTILE n pl. -S any of a class of cold-blooded, air-breathing verte-brates

REPUBLIC n pl. -S a constitutional form of government

REPUGN v -ED, -ING, -S to oppose

REPULSE v -PULSED, -PULSING, -PULSES to drive back

REPULSER n pl. -S one that repulses

REPUTE v -PUTED, -PUTING, -PUTES to consider to be as specified

REQUEST v -ED, -ING, -S to express a desire for

REQUIEM n pl. -S a musical composition for the dead

REQUIN n pl. -S a voracious shark

REQUIRE v -QUIRED, -QUIRING, -QUIRES to have need of

REQUIRER n pl. -S one that requires

REQUITAL n pl. -S something given in return, compensation, or retaliation

REQUITE v -QUITED, -QUITING, -QUITES to make equivalent return for

REQUITER n pl. -S one that requites

RERAN past tense of rerun

REREDOS n pl. -ES an ornamental screen behind an altar

REREMICE n/pl bats (flying mammals)

REREWARD n pl. -S rearward

REROLLER n pl. -S one that rerolls

RERUN v -RAN, -RUNNING, -RUNS to present a repetition of a recorded performance

RES   *n* pl. RES a particular thing or matter

RESALE   *n* pl. -S the act of selling again

RESCALE   *v* -SCALED, -SCALING, -SCALES to plan on a new scale

RESCIND   *v* -ED, -ING, -S to annul

RESCRIPT   *n* pl. -S something rewritten

RESCUE   *v* -CUED, -CUING, -CUES to free from danger

RESCUER   *n* pl. -S one that rescues

RESEARCH   *v* -ED, -ING, -ES to investigate thoroughly

RESEAU   *n* pl. -SEAUS or -SEAUX a filter screen for making color films

RESECT   *v* -ED, -ING, -S to excise part of an organ or structure surgically

RESEDA   *n* pl. -S a flowering plant

RESELLER   *n* pl. -S one that resells

RESEMBLE   *v* -BLED, -BLING, -BLES to be similar to

RESENT   *v* -ED, -ING, -S to feel or express annoyance or ill will at

RESERVE   *v* -SERVED, -SERVING, -SERVES to keep back for future use

RESERVER   *n* pl. -S one that reserves

RESETTER   *n* pl. -S one that resets

RESH   *n* pl. -ES a Hebrew letter

RESHAPER   *n* pl. -S one that reshapes something

RESID   *n* pl. -S a type of fuel oil

RESIDE   *v* -SIDED, -SIDING, -SIDES to dwell permanently or continuously

RESIDENT   *n* pl. -S one who resides

RESIDER   *n* pl. -S a resident

RESIDUA   a pl. of residuum

RESIDUAL   *n* pl. -S something left over

RESIDUE   *n* pl. -S something remaining after the removal of a part

RESIDUUM   *n* pl. -SIDUA or -SIDUUMS residue

RESIGN   *v* -ED, -ING, -S to give up one's office or position

RESIGNER   *n* pl. -S one that resigns

RESILE   *v* -SILED, -SILING, -SILES to spring back

RESIN   *v* -ED, -ING, -S to treat with resin (a viscous substance obtained from certain plants)

RESINATE   *v* -ATED, -ATING, -ATES to resin

RESINIFY   *v* -FIED, -FYING, -FIES to convert into resin

RESINOID   *n* pl. -S a resinous substance

RESINOUS   *adj* resembling resin

RESINY   *adj* resinous

RESIST   *v* -ED, -ING, -S to strive against

RESISTER   *n* pl. -S one that resists

RESISTOR   *n* pl. -S a device in an electric circuit

RESOJET   *n* pl. -S a pulsejet

RESOLUTE   *adj* -LUTER, -LUTEST characterized by firmness or determination

RESOLUTE   *n* pl. -S one who is resolute

RESOLVE   *v* -SOLVED, -SOLVING, -SOLVES to make a firm decision about

RESOLVER   *n* pl. -S one that resolves

RESONANT   *n* pl. -S a resounding sound

RESONATE   *v* -NATED, -NATING, -NATES to resound

RESORB   *v* -ED, -ING, -S to absorb again

RESORCIN   *n* pl. -S a chemical compound

RESORT   *v* -ED, -ING, -S to go frequently or habitually

RESORTER   *n* pl. -S one that resorts

RESOUND   *v* -ED, -ING, -S to make a loud, long, or echoing sound

RESOURCE   *n* pl. -S an available supply

RESPECT   *v* -ED, -ING, -S to have a high regard for

RESPIRE   *v* -SPIRED, -SPIRING, -SPIRES to breathe

RESPITE   *v* -SPITED, -SPITING, -SPITES to relieve temporarily

RESPOND   *v* -ED, -ING, -S to say or act in return

RESPONSA   *n/pl* written rabbinic decisions

RESPONSE   *n* pl. -S a reply or reaction

REST   *v* -ED, -ING, -S to refresh oneself by ceasing work or activity

RESTER   *n* pl. -S one that rests

RESTFUL   *adj* -FULLER, -FULLEST tranquil

RESTIVE   *adj* difficult to control

RESTLESS   *adj* unable or disinclined to remain at rest

RESTORAL   *n* pl. -S the act of restoring

RESTORE   *v* -STORED, -STORING, -STORES to bring back to a former or original condition

RESTORER   *n* pl. -S one that restores

RESTRAIN v -ED, -ING, -S to hold back from action

RESTRICT v -ED, -ING, -S to keep within certain boundaries

RESULT v -ED, -ING, -S to occur as a consequence

RESUME v -SUMED, -SUMING, -SUMES to take up again after interruption

RESUMER n pl. -S one that resumes

RESUPINE adj lying on the back

RESURGE v -SURGED, -SURGING, -SURGES to rise again

RET v RETTED, RETTING, RETS to soak in order to loosen the fiber from the woody tissue

RETABLE n pl. -S a raised shelf above an altar

RETAIL v -ED, -ING, -S to sell in small quantities

RETAILER n pl. -S one that retails

RETAIN v -ED, -ING, -S to keep possession of

RETAINER n pl. -S one that retains

RETAKE v -TOOK, -TAKEN, -TAKING, -TAKES to take back

RETAKER n pl. -S one that retakes

RETARD v -ED, -ING, -S to slow the progress of

RETARDER n pl. -S one that retards

RETCH v -ED, -ING, -ES to make an effort to vomit

RETE n pl. -TIA an anatomical mesh or network

RETEM n pl. -S a desert shrub

RETENE n pl. -S a chemical compound

RETIA pl. of rete

RETIAL adj pertaining to a rete

RETIARII n/pl ancient Roman gladiators

RETIARY adj resembling a net

RETICENT adj tending to be silent

RETICLE n pl. -S a network of lines in the eyepiece of an optical instrument

RETICULA n/pl netlike structures

RETICULE n pl. -S a woman's handbag

RETIFORM adj arranged like a net

RETINA n pl. -NAS or -NAE a membrane of the eye

RETINAL n pl. -S retinene

RETINENE n pl. -S a pigment in the retina

RETINITE n pl. -S a fossil resin

RETINOL n pl. -S a liquid hydrocarbon

RETINUE n pl. -S a group of attendants
RETINUED adj

RETINULA n pl. -LAE or -LAS a neural receptor of an arthropod's eye

RETIRANT n pl. -S a retiree

RETIRE v -TIRED, -TIRING, -TIRES to go away or withdraw

RETIREE n pl. -S one who has retired from his vocation

RETIRER n pl. -S one that retires

RETIRING adj shy

RETOOK past tense of retake

RETOOL v -ED, -ING, -S to reequip with tools

RETORT v -ED, -ING, -S to answer back sharply

RETORTER n pl. -S one that retorts

RETOUCH v -ED, -ING, -ES to add new details or touches to

RETRACE v -TRACED, -TRACING, -TRACES to go back over

RETRACT v -ED, -ING, -S to take back

RETRAL adj situated toward the back
RETRALLY adv

RETREAD v -ED, -ING, -S to furnish with a new tread

RETREAT v -ED, -ING, -S to go back or backward

RETRENCH v -ED, -ING, -ES to curtail

RETRIAL n pl. -S a second trial

RETRIEVE v -TRIEVED, -TRIEVING, -TRIEVES to get back

RETROACT v -ED, -ING, -S to act in return

RETROFIT v -FITTED, -FITTING, -FITS to furnish with new parts not originally available

RETRORSE adj bent backward

RETSINA n pl. -S a resin-flavored Greek wine

RETTED past tense of ret

RETTING present participle of ret

RETURN v -ED, -ING, -S to come or go back

RETURNEE n pl. -S one that has returned

RETURNER n pl. -S one that returns

RETUSE adj having a rounded apex with a shallow notch — used of leaves

REUNION n pl. -S a reuniting of persons after separation

REUNITER n pl. -S one that reunites

REUSABLE adj capable of being used again

REV *v* REVVED, REVVING, REVS to increase the speed of

REVAMP *v* -ED, -ING, -S to make over

REVAMPER *n pl.* -S one that revamps

REVANCHE *n pl.* -S a political policy designed to regain lost territory

REVEAL *v* -ED, -ING, -S to make known

REVEALER *n pl.* -S one that reveals

REVEHENT *adj* carrying back

REVEILLE *n pl.* -S a morning bugle call

REVEL *v* -ELED, -ELING, -ELS or -ELLED, -ELLING, -ELS to engage in revelry

REVELER *n pl.* -S one that revels

REVELLER *n pl.* -S reveler

REVELRY *n pl.* -RIES noisy merrymaking

REVENANT *n pl.* -S one that returns

REVENGE *v* -VENGED, -VENGING, -VENGES to inflict injury in return for

REVENGER *n pl.* -S one that revenges

REVENUE *n pl.* -S the income of a government **REVENUAL, REVENUED** *adj*

REVENUER *n pl.* -S a revenue officer

REVERB *n pl.* -S an echo effect in recorded music

REVERE *v* -VERED, -VERING, -VERES to regard with great respect

REVEREND *n pl.* -S a clergyman

REVERENT *adj* deeply respectful

REVERER *n pl.* -S one that reveres

REVERIE *n pl.* -S a daydream

REVERIES *pl.* of revery

REVERING present participle of revere

REVERS *n pl.* REVERS a part of a garment turned back to show the inside

REVERSAL *n pl.* -S the act of reversing

REVERSE *v* -VERSED, -VERSING, -VERSES to turn or move in the opposite direction

REVERSER *n pl.* -S one that reverses

REVERSO *n pl.* -VERSOS verso

REVERT *v* -ED, -ING, -S to return to a former state

REVERTER *n pl.* -S one that reverts

REVERY *n pl.* -ERIES reverie

REVET *v* -VETTED, -VETTING, -VETS to face with masonry

REVIEWAL *n pl.* -S the act of reviewing

REVIEWER *n pl.* -S one that reviews

REVILE *v* -VILED, -VILING, -VILES to denounce with abusive language

REVILER *n pl.* -S one that reviles

REVISAL *n pl.* -S a revision

REVISE *v* -VISED, -VISING, -VISES to make a new or improved version of

REVISER *n pl.* -S one that revises

REVISION *n pl.* -S a revised version

REVISOR *n pl.* -S reviser

REVISORY *adj* pertaining to revision

REVIVAL *n pl.* -S renewed attention to or interest in something

REVIVE *v* -VIVED, -VIVING, -VIVES to bring back to life or consciousness

REVIVER *n pl.* -S one that revives

REVIVIFY *v* -FIED, -FYING, -FIES to give new life to

REVIVING present participle of revive

REVOKE *v* -VOKED, -VOKING, -VOKES to annul by taking back

REVOKER *n pl.* -S one that revokes

REVOLT *v* -ED, -ING, -S to rise up against authority

REVOLTER *n pl.* -S one that revolts

REVOLUTE *adj* rolled backward or downward

REVOLVE *v* -VOLVED, -VOLVING, -VOLVES to turn about an axis

REVOLVER *n pl.* -S a type of handgun

REVUE *n pl.* -S a type of musical show

REVUIST *n pl.* -S a writer of revues

REVULSED *adj* affected with revulsion

REVVED past tense of rev

REVVING present participle of rev

REWARD *v* -ED, -ING, -S to give recompense to for worthy behavior

REWARDER *n pl.* -S one that rewards

REWINDER *n pl.* -S one that rewinds

REWORD *v* -ED, -ING, -S to state again in other words

REWRITER *n pl.* -S one that rewrites

REX *n pl.* REGES king

REX *n pl.* -ES an animal with a single wavy layer of hair

REYNARD *n pl.* -S a fox

RHABDOM *n pl.* -S a rodlike structure in the retinula

RHABDOME *n pl.* -S rhabdom

RHACHIS n pl. -CHISES or -CHIDES rachis

RHAMNOSE n pl. -S a sugar found in plants

RHAMNUS n pl. -ES a thorny tree or shrub

RHAPHE n pl. -PHAE or -PHES raphe

RHAPSODE n pl. -S a reciter of epic poetry in ancient Greece

RHAPSODY n pl. -DIES an exalted expression of feeling

RHATANY n pl. -NIES a South American shrub

RHEA n pl. -S a flightless bird

RHEBOK n pl. -S a large antelope

RHEMATIC adj pertaining to a verb

RHENIUM n pl. -S a metallic element

RHEOBASE n pl. -S the smallest amount of electricity required to stimulate a nerve

RHEOLOGY n pl. -GIES the study of matter in the fluid state

RHEOPHIL adj living in flowing water

RHEOSTAT n pl. -S a resistor used to control electric current

RHESUS n pl. -ES an Asian monkey

RHETOR n pl. -S a teacher of rhetoric

RHETORIC n pl. -S the study of effective speech and writing

RHEUM n pl. -S a watery discharge from the eyes or nose RHEUMIC adj

RHEUMY adj RHEUMIER, RHEUMIEST marked by rheum

RHINAL adj pertaining to the nose

RHINITIS n pl. RHINITIDES inflammation of the mucous membranes of the nose

RHINO n pl. -NOS a rhinoceros

RHIZOBIA n/pl rod-shaped bacteria

RHIZOID n pl. -S a rootlike structure

RHIZOMA n pl. -MATA rhizome

RHIZOME n pl. -S a rootlike, underground stem RHIZOMIC adj

RHIZOPOD n pl. -S any of a class of protozoans

RHIZOPUS n pl. -PI or -PUSES any of a genus of mold fungi

RHO n pl. RHOS a Greek letter

RHODAMIN n pl. -S a red dye

RHODIUM n pl. -S a metallic element RHODIC adj

RHODORA n pl. -S a flowering shrub

RHOMB n pl. -S a rhombus

RHOMBI a pl. of rhombus

RHOMBIC adj having the shape of a rhombus

RHOMBOID n pl. -S a type of geometric figure

RHOMBUS n pl. -BUSES or -BI a type of geometric figure

RHONCHUS n pl. -CHI a rattling respiratory sound RHONCHAL adj

RHUBARB n pl. -S a perennial herb

RHUMB n pl. -S a point of the mariner's compass

RHUMBA v -ED, -ING, -S to rumba

RHUS n pl. -ES any of a genus of shrubs and trees

RHYME v RHYMED, RHYMING, RHYMES to compose verse with corresponding terminal sounds

RHYMER n pl. -S one that rhymes

RHYOLITE n pl. -S a volcanic rock

RHYTA pl. of rhyton

RHYTHM n pl. -S movement or procedure with uniform recurrence of strong and weak elements

RHYTHMIC n pl. -S the science of rhythm

RHYTON n pl. -TA an ancient Greek drinking horn

RIAL n pl. -S a monetary unit of Iran

RIALTO n pl. -TOS a marketplace

RIANT adj cheerful RIANTLY adv

RIATA n pl. -S a lasso

RIB v RIBBED, RIBBING, RIBS to poke fun at

RIBALD n pl. -S one who uses crude language

RIBALDLY adv crudely

RIBALDRY n pl. -RIES crude language

RIBAND n pl. -S a ribbon

RIBBAND n pl. -S a long, narrow strip used in shipbuilding

RIBBED past tense of rib

RIBBER n pl. -S one that ribs

RIBBIER comparative of ribby

RIBBIEST superlative of ribby

RIBBING n pl. -S the act of one that ribs

RIBBON v -ED, -ING, -S to decorate with ribbons (narrow strips of fine fabric)

RIBBONY adj resembling ribbon

RIBBY adj -BIER, -BIEST marked by prominent ribs (curved bony rods in the body)

RIBES n pl. RIBES a flowering shrub

RIBGRASS n pl. -ES a weedy plant

RIBLESS	adj having no ribs	**RIDDED**	past tense of rid
RIBLET	n pl. -S the rib end in a breast of lamb or veal	**RIDDEN**	past participle of ride
		RIDDER	n pl. -S one that rids
RIBLIKE	adj resembling a rib	**RIDDING**	present participle of rid
RIBOSE	n pl. -S a pentose sugar	**RIDDLE**	v -DLED, -DLING, -DLES to pierce with many holes
RIBOSOME	n pl. -S a particle composed of protein and ribonucleic acid	**RIDDLER**	n pl. -S one that riddles
RIBWORT	n pl. -S ribgrass	**RIDE**	v RODE, RIDDEN, RIDING, RIDES to sit on, control, and be conveyed by an animal or machine
RICE	v RICED, RICING, RICES to press through a ricer		
RICEBIRD	n pl. -S the bobolink	**RIDEABLE**	adj ridable
RICER	n pl. -S a kitchen utensil consisting of a container perforated with small holes	**RIDENT**	adj laughing
		RIDER	n pl. -S one that rides
RICERCAR	n pl. -S an instrumental composition	**RIDGE**	v RIDGED, RIDGING, RIDGES to form into ridges (long, narrow elevations)
RICH	adj RICHER, RICHEST having wealth		
		RIDGEL	n pl. -S a ridgling
RICHEN	v -ED, -ING, -S to make rich	**RIDGIER**	comparative of ridgy
RICHES	n/pl wealth	**RIDGIEST**	superlative of ridgy
RICHLY	adv in a rich manner	**RIDGIL**	n pl. -S a ridgling
RICHNESS	n pl. -ES the state of being rich	**RIDGING**	present participle of ridge
RICHWEED	n pl. -S a flowering plant	**RIDGLING**	n pl. -S a male animal with undescended testicles
RICIN	n pl. -S a poisonous protein		
RICING	present participle of rice	**RIDGY**	adj RIDGIER, RIDGIEST having ridges
RICINUS	n pl. -ES a large-leaved plant		
RICK	v -ED, -ING, -S to pile hay in stacks	**RIDICULE**	v -CULED, -CULING, -CULES to make fun of
RICKETS	n/pl a disease resulting from vitamin D deficiency	**RIDING**	n pl. -S the act of one that rides
RICKETY	adj -ETIER, -ETIEST likely to fall or collapse	**RIDLEY**	n pl. -LEYS a sea turtle
		RIDOTTO	n pl. -TOS a public musical entertainment in 18th century England
RICKEY	n pl. -EYS an alcoholic beverage containing lime juice, sugar, and soda water		
		RIEL	n pl. -S a monetary unit of Cambodia
RICKRACK	n pl. -S a flat braid used as a trimming		
		RIEVER	n pl. -S reaver
RICKSHA	n pl. -S rickshaw	**RIFE**	adj RIFER, RIFEST abundant RIFELY adv
RICKSHAW	n pl. -S a small, two-wheeled passenger vehicle		
		RIFENESS	n pl. -ES the state of being rife
RICOCHET	v -CHETED, -CHETING, -CHETS or -CHETTED, -CHETTING, -CHETS to rebound from a surface	**RIFF**	v -ED, -ING, -S to riffle
		RIFFLE	v -FLED, -FLING, -FLES to flip through hastily
RICOTTA	n pl. -S an Italian cheese	**RIFFLER**	n pl. -S a filing and scraping tool
RICRAC	n pl. -S rickrack		
RICTUS	n pl. -ES the expanse of the open mouth **RICTAL** adj	**RIFFRAFF**	n pl. -S the disreputable element of society
RID	v RID or RIDDED, RIDDING, RIDS to free from something objectionable	**RIFLE**	v -FLED, -FLING, -FLES to search through and rob
		RIFLEMAN	n pl. -MEN a soldier armed with a rifle (a type of firearm)
RIDABLE	adj capable of being ridden	**RIFLER**	n pl. -S one that rifles
RIDDANCE	n pl. -S deliverance	**RIFLERY**	n pl. -RIES the practice of shooting at targets with a rifle

RIFLING	*n* pl. -S the system of grooves in a gun barrel
RIFT	*v* -ED, -ING, -S to form rifts (clefts)
RIFTLESS	*adj* having no rift
RIG	*v* RIGGED, RIGGING, RIGS to put in proper condition for use
RIGADOON	*n* pl. -S a lively dance
RIGATONI	*n* pl. -S a tubular pasta
RIGAUDON	*n* pl. -S rigadoon
RIGGED	past tense of rig
RIGGER	*n* pl. -S one that rigs
RIGGING	*n* pl. -S the system of lines, chains, and tackle used aboard a ship
RIGHT	*adj* RIGHTER, RIGHTEST being in accordance with what is good, proper, or just
RIGHT	*v* -ED, -ING, -S to put in proper order or condition
RIGHTER	*n* pl. -S one that rights
RIGHTFUL	*adj* just or proper
RIGHTIES	pl. of righty
RIGHTISM	*n* pl. -S a conservative political philosophy
RIGHTIST	*n* pl. -S an advocate of rightism
RIGHTLY	*adv* in a right manner
RIGHTO	*interj* — used to express cheerful consent
RIGHTY	*n* pl. RIGHTIES a right-handed person
RIGID	*adj* not flexible
RIGIDIFY	*v* -FIED, -FYING, -FIES to make rigid
RIGIDITY	*n* pl. -TIES the state of being rigid
RIGIDLY	*adv* in a rigid manner
RIGOR	*n* pl. -S strictness or severity
RIGORISM	*n* pl. -S strictness or severity in conduct or attitude
RIGORIST	*n* pl. -S one that professes rigorism
RIGOROUS	*adj* characterized by rigor
RIGOUR	*n* pl. -S rigor
RIKISHA	*n* pl. -S rickshaw
RIKSHAW	*n* pl. -S rickshaw
RILE	*v* RILED, RILING, RILES to anger
RILEY	*adj* angry
RILIEVO	*n* pl. -VI relievo
RILING	present participle of rile
RILL	*v* -ED, -ING, -S to flow like a rill (a small brook)

RILLE	*n* pl. -S a valley on the moon's surface
RILLET	*n* pl. -S a small rill
RIM	*v* RIMMED, RIMMING, RIMS to provide with a rim (an outer edge)
RIME	*v* RIMED, RIMING, RIMES to rhyme
RIMER	*n* pl. -S one that rimes
RIMESTER	*n* pl. -S a rimer
RIMFIRE	*adj* designed for the use of certain cartridges
RIMIER	comparative of rimy
RIMIEST	superlative of rimy
RIMING	present participle of rime
RIMLAND	*n* pl. -S an outlying area
RIMLESS	*adj* having no rim
RIMMED	past tense of rim
RIMMER	*n* pl. -S a reamer
RIMMING	present participle of rim
RIMOSE	*adj* marked by cracks RIMOSELY *adv*
RIMOSITY	*n* pl. -TIES the state of being rimose
RIMOUS	*adj* rimose
RIMPLE	*v* -PLED, -PLING, -PLES to wrinkle
RIMROCK	*n* pl. -S a type of rock formation
RIMY	*adj* RIMIER, RIMIEST frosty
RIN	*v* RAN, RINNING, RINS to run or melt
RIND	*n* pl. -S a thick and firm outer covering RINDED *adj*
RING	*v* -ED, -ING, -S to form a ring (a circular band) around
RING	*v* RANG, RUNG, RINGING, RINGS to give forth a clear, resonant sound
RINGBARK	*v* -ED, -ING, -S to make an encircling cut through the bark of
RINGBOLT	*n* pl. -S a type of eyebolt
RINGBONE	*n* pl. -S a bony growth on a horse's foot
RINGDOVE	*n* pl. -S a European pigeon
RINGENT	*adj* having open liplike parts
RINGER	*n* pl. -S one that rings
RINGHALS	*n* pl. -ES a venomous snake
RINGLET	*n* pl. -S a small ring
RINGLIKE	*adj* resembling a ring
RINGNECK	*n* pl. -S a bird having a ring of color around the neck

RINGSIDE   n pl. -S the area just outside a boxing or wrestling ring (a square enclosure)

RINGTAIL   n pl. -S an animal having a tail with ringlike markings

RINGTAW   n pl. -S a game of marbles

RINGTOSS   n pl. -ES a game in which the object is to toss a ring onto an upright stick

RINGWORM   n pl. -S a skin disease

RINK   n pl. -S a surface of ice for skating

RINNING   present participle of rin

RINSE   v RINSED, RINSING, RINSES to cleanse with clear water RINSABLE, RINSIBLE adj

RINSER   n pl. -S one that rinses

RINSING   n pl. -S the act of one that rinses

RIOT   v -ED, -ING, -S to take part in a violent public disturbance

RIOTER   n pl. -S one that riots

RIOTOUS   adj characterized by rioting

RIP   v RIPPED, RIPPING, RIPS to tear or cut apart roughly

RIPARIAN   adj pertaining to the bank of a river

RIPCORD   n pl. -S a cord pulled to release a parachute

RIPE   adj RIPER, RIPEST fully developed RIPELY adv

RIPE   v RIPED, RIPING, RIPES to cleanse

RIPEN   v -ED, -ING, -S to become ripe

RIPENER   n pl. -S one that ripens

RIPENESS   n pl. -ES the state of being ripe

RIPER   comparative of ripe

RIPEST   superlative of ripe

RIPIENO   n pl. -NI or -NOS tutti

RIPING   present participle of ripe

RIPOST   v -ED, -ING, -S to riposte

RIPOSTE   v -POSTED, -POSTING, -POSTES to make a return thrust in fencing

RIPPABLE   adj capable of being ripped

RIPPED   past tense of rip

RIPPER   n pl. -S one that rips

RIPPING   adj excellent

RIPPLE   v -PLED, -PLING, -PLES to form ripples (small waves)

RIPPLER   n pl. -S a toothed tool for cleaning flax fiber

RIPPLET   n pl. -S a small ripple

RIPPLING   present participle of ripple

RIPPLY   adj -PLIER, -PLIEST marked by ripples

RIPRAP   v -RAPPED, -RAPPING, -RAPS to strengthen with a foundation of broken stones

RIPSAW   n pl. -S a type of saw

RIPTIDE   n pl. -S a tide that opposes other tides

RISE   v ROSE, RISEN, RISING, RISES to move upward

RISER   n pl. -S one that rises

RISHI   n pl. -S a Hindu sage

RISIBLE   adj inclined to laugh RISIBLY adv

RISIBLES   n/pl a sense of the ridiculous

RISING   n pl. -S the act of one that rises

RISK   v -ED, -ING, -S to expose to a chance of injury or loss

RISKER   n pl. -S one that risks

RISKY   adj RISKIER, RISKIEST dangerous RISKILY adv

RISOTTO   n pl. -TOS a rice dish

RISQUE   adj bordering on impropriety or indecency

RISSOLE   n pl. -S a small roll filled with meat or fish

RISUS   n pl. -ES a grin or laugh

RITARD   n pl. -S a musical passage with a gradual slackening in tempo

RITE   n pl. -S a ceremonial act or procedure

RITTER   n pl. -S a knight

RITUAL   n pl. -S a system of rites

RITUALLY   adv ceremonially

RITZ   n pl. -ES pretentious display

RITZY   adj RITZIER, RITZIEST elegant RITZILY adv

RIVAGE   n pl. -S a coast, shore, or bank

RIVAL   v -VALED, -VALING, -VALS or -VALLED, -VALLING, -VALS to strive to equal or surpass

RIVALRY   n pl. -RIES competition

RIVE   v RIVED, RIVEN, RIVING, RIVES to tear apart

RIVER   n pl. -S a large, natural stream of water

RIVERBED   n pl. -S the area covered or once covered by a river

RIVERINE   adj pertaining to a river

RIVET   v -ETED, -ETING, -ETS or -ETTED, -ETTING, -ETS to fasten with a type of metal bolt

RIVETER n pl. -S one that rivets

RIVIERA n pl. -S a coastal resort area

RIVIERE n pl. -S a necklace of precious stones

RIVING present participle of rive

RIVULET n pl. -S a small stream

RIYAL n pl. -S a monetary unit of Saudi Arabia

ROACH v -ED, -ING, -ES to cause to arch

ROAD n pl. -S an open way for public passage

ROADBED n pl. -S the foundation for a railroad track

ROADLESS adj having no roads

ROADSIDE n pl. -S the area along the side of a road

ROADSTER n pl. -S a light, open automobile

ROADWAY n pl. -WAYS a road

ROADWORK n pl. -S outdoor running as a form of physical conditioning

ROAM v -ED, -ING, -S to move about without purpose or plan

ROAMER n pl. -S one that roams

ROAN n pl. -S an animal having a coat sprinkled with white or gray

ROAR v -ED, -ING, -S to utter a loud, deep sound

ROARER n pl. -S one that roars

ROARING n pl. -S a loud, deep sound

ROAST v -ED, -ING, -S to cook with dry heat

ROASTER n pl. -S one that roasts

ROB v ROBBED, ROBBING, ROBS to take property from illegally

ROBALO n pl. -LOS a marine food fish

ROBAND n pl. -S a piece of yarn used to fasten a sail

ROBBED past tense of rob

ROBBER n pl. -S one that robs

ROBBERY n pl. -BERIES the act of one who robs

ROBBIN n pl. -S a roband

ROBBING present participle of rob

ROBE v ROBED, ROBING, ROBES to cover with a robe (a long, loose outer garment)

ROBIN n pl. -S a songbird

ROBLE n pl. -S an oak tree

ROBORANT n pl. -S an invigorating drug

ROBOT n pl. -S a humanlike machine that performs various functions

ROBOTICS n/pl a field of interest concerned with robots

ROBOTISM n pl. -S the state of being a robot

ROBOTIZE v -IZED, -IZING, -IZES to make automatic

ROBOTRY n pl. -RIES the science of robots

ROBUST adj -BUSTER, -BUSTEST strong and healthy **ROBUSTLY** adv

ROC n pl. -S a lengendary bird of prey

ROCHET n pl. -S a linen vestment

ROCK v -ED, -ING, -S to move back and forth

ROCKABY n pl. -BIES a song used to lull a child to sleep

ROCKABYE n pl. -S rockaby

ROCKAWAY n pl. -WAYS a light carriage

ROCKER n pl. -S a rocking chair

ROCKERY n pl. -ERIES a rock garden

ROCKET v -ED, -ING, -S to convey by means of a rocket (a device propelled by the reaction of escaping gases)

ROCKETER n pl. -S one that designs or launches rockets

ROCKETRY n pl. -RIES the science of rockets

ROCKFALL n pl. -S a mass of fallen rocks

ROCKFISH n pl. -ES a fish living around rocks

ROCKIER comparative of rocky

ROCKIEST superlative of rocky

ROCKLESS adj having no rocks

ROCKLIKE adj resembling a rock (a large mass of stone)

ROCKLING n pl. -S a marine fish

ROCKOON n pl. -S a small rocket

ROCKROSE n pl. -S a flowering plant

ROCKWEED n pl. -S a brown seaweed

ROCKWORK n pl. -S a natural mass of rocks

ROCKY adj ROCKIER, ROCKIEST unsteady

ROCOCO n pl. -COS a style of architecture and decoration

ROD v RODDED, RODDING, RODS to provide with a rod (a straight, slender piece of wood, metal, or other material)

RODE past tense of ride

RODENT n pl. -S a gnawing mammal

RODEO n pl. -DEOS a public exhibition of cowboy skills

RODLESS *adj* having no rod

RODLIKE *adj* resembling a rod

RODMAN *n pl.* -MEN a surveyor's assistant

RODSMAN *n pl.* -MEN rodman

ROE *n pl.* -S the mass of eggs within a female fish

ROEBUCK *n pl.* -S the male of a small Eurasian deer

ROENTGEN *n pl.* -S a unit of radiation dosage

ROGATION *n pl.* -S the proposal of a law in ancient Rome

ROGATORY *adj* requesting information

ROGER *n pl.* -S the pirate flag bearing the skull and crossbones

ROGUE *v* ROGUED, ROGUEING or ROGUING, ROGUES to defraud

ROGUERY *n pl.* -ERIES roguish conduct

ROGUISH *adj* dishonest

ROIL *v* -ED, -ING, -S to make muddy

ROILY *adj* ROILIER, ROILIEST muddy

ROISTER *v* -ED, -ING, -S to revel

ROLAMITE *n pl.* -S a nearly frictionless mechanical device

ROLE *n pl.* -S a part played by an actor

ROLL *v* -ED, -ING, -S to move along by repeatedly turning over

ROLLAWAY *adj* mounted on rollers for easy movement

ROLLBACK *n pl.* -S a return to a lower level of prices or wages

ROLLER *n pl.* -S a cylindrical device that rolls or rotates

ROLLICK *v* -ED, -ING, -S to frolic

ROLLICKY *adj* given to rollicking

ROLLING *n pl.* -S the act of one that rolls

ROLLMOP *n pl.* -S a fillet of herring

ROLLOUT *n pl.* -S a type of play in football

ROLLOVER *n pl.* -S a motor vehicle accident in which the vehicle overturns

ROLLTOP *adj* having a flexible, sliding cover

ROLLWAY *n pl.* -WAYS an incline for rolling logs

ROMAINE *n pl.* -S a variety of lettuce

ROMAN *n pl.* -S a metrical narrative of medieval France

ROMANCE *v* -MANCED, -MANCING, -MANCES to woo

ROMANCER *n pl.* -S one that romances

ROMANIZE *v* -IZED, -IZING, -IZES to write in the Roman alphabet

ROMANO *n pl.* -NOS an Italian cheese

ROMANTIC *n pl.* -S a fanciful person

ROMAUNT *n pl.* -S a long, medieval narrative

ROMP *v* -ED, -ING, -S to play boisterously

ROMPER *n pl.* -S one that romps

ROMPISH *adj* inclined to romp

RONDEAU *n pl.* -DEAUX a short poem of fixed form

RONDEL *n pl.* -S a rondeau of 14 lines

RONDELET *n pl.* -S a rondeau of 5 or 7 lines

RONDELLE *n pl.* -S rondel

RONDO *n pl.* -DOS a type of musical composition

RONDURE *n pl.* -S a circle or sphere

RONION *n pl.* -S a mangy animal or person

RONNEL *n pl.* -S an insecticide

RONTGEN *n pl.* -S roentgen

RONYON *n pl.* -S ronion

ROOD *n pl.* -S a crucifix

ROOF *v* -ED, -ING, -S to provide with a roof (the external upper covering of a building)

ROOFER *n pl.* -S one that builds or repairs roofs

ROOFING *n pl.* -S material for a roof

ROOFLESS *adj* having no roof

ROOFLIKE *adj* resembling a roof

ROOFLINE *n pl.* -S the profile of a roof

ROOFTOP *n pl.* -S a roof

ROOFTREE *n pl.* -S a horizontal timber in a roof

ROOK *v* -ED, -ING, -S to swindle

ROOKERY *n pl.* -ERIES a colony of rooks (European crows)

ROOKIE *n pl.* -S a novice

ROOKY *adj* ROOKIER, ROOKIEST abounding in rooks

ROOM *v* -ED, -ING, -S to occupy a room (a walled space within a building)

ROOMER *n pl.* -S a lodger

ROOMETTE *n pl.* -S a small room

ROOMFUL *n pl.* -S as much as a room will hold

ROOMMATE *n pl.* -S one with whom a room is shared

ROOMY	*adj* ROOMIER, ROOMIEST spacious **ROOMILY** *adv*
ROORBACK	*n pl.* -S a false story used for political advantage
ROOSE	*v* ROOSED, ROOSING, ROOSES to praise
ROOSER	*n pl.* -S one that rooses
ROOST	*v* -ED, -ING, -S to settle down for rest or sleep
ROOSTER	*n pl.* -S a male chicken
ROOT	*v* -ED, -ING, -S to put forth a root (an underground portion of a plant)
ROOTAGE	*n pl.* -S a system of roots
ROOTER	*n pl.* -S one that gives encouragement or support
ROOTHOLD	*n pl.* -S the embedding of a plant to soil through the growing of roots
ROOTIER	comparative of rooty
ROOTIEST	superlative of rooty
ROOTLESS	*adj* having no roots
ROOTLET	*n pl.* -S a small root
ROOTLIKE	*adj* resembling a root
ROOTY	*adj* ROOTIER, ROOTIEST full of roots
ROPE	*v* ROPED, ROPING, ROPES to bind with a rope (a thick line of twisted fibers) **ROPABLE** *adj*
ROPER	*n pl.* -S one that ropes
ROPERY	*n pl.* -ERIES a place where ropes are made
ROPEWALK	*n pl.* -S a long path where ropes are made
ROPEWAY	*n pl.* -WAYS an aerial cable used to transport freight
ROPIER	comparative of ropy
ROPIEST	superlative of ropy
ROPILY	*adv* in a ropy manner
ROPINESS	*n pl.* -ES the quality of being ropy
ROPING	present participle of rope
ROPY	*adj* ROPIER, ROPIEST resembling a rope or ropes
ROQUE	*n pl.* -S a form of croquet
ROQUET	*v* -ED, -ING, -S to cause one's own ball to hit another in croquet
RORQUAL	*n pl.* -S a large whale
ROSARIA	a *pl.* of rosarium
ROSARIAN	*n pl.* -S a cultivator of roses
ROSARIUM	*n pl.* -IA or -IUMS a rose garden
ROSARY	*n pl.* -RIES a series of prayers in the Roman Catholic Church
ROSCOE	*n pl.* -S a pistol
ROSE	*v* ROSED, ROSING, ROSES to make the color of a rose (a reddish flower)
ROSEATE	*adj* rose-colored
ROSEBAY	*n pl.* -BAYS an evergreen shrub
ROSEBUD	*n pl.* -S the bud of a rose
ROSEBUSH	*n pl.* -ES a shrub that bears roses
ROSED	past tense of rose
ROSEFISH	*n pl.* -ES a marine food fish
ROSELIKE	*adj* resembling a rose
ROSELLE	*n pl.* -S a tropical plant
ROSEMARY	*n pl.* -MARIES an evergreen shrub
ROSEOLA	*n pl.* -S a rose-colored skin rash **ROSEOLAR** *adj*
ROSEROOT	*n pl.* -S a perennial herb
ROSERY	*n pl.* -ERIES a place where roses are grown
ROSET	*n pl.* -S resin
ROSETTE	*n pl.* -S an ornament resembling a rose
ROSEWOOD	*n pl.* -S a tropical tree
ROSIER	comparative of rosy
ROSIEST	superlative of rosy
ROSILY	*adv* in a rosy manner
ROSIN	*v* -ED, -ING, -S to treat with rosin (a brittle resin)
ROSINESS	*n pl.* -ES the state of being rosy
ROSING	present participle of rose
ROSINOUS	*adj* resembling rosin
ROSINY	*adj* rosinous
ROSOLIO	*n pl.* -LIOS a liqueur made from raisins and brandy
ROSTELLA	*n/pl* small, beaklike structures
ROSTER	*n pl.* -S a list of names
ROSTRA	a *pl.* of rostrum
ROSTRAL	*adj* pertaining to a rostrum
ROSTRATE	*adj* having a rostrum
ROSTRUM	*n pl.* -TRA or -TRUMS a beaklike process or part
ROSULATE	*adj* arranged in the form of a rosette
ROSY	*adj* ROSIER, ROSIEST rose-colored
ROT	*v* ROTTED, ROTTING, ROTS to decompose
ROTA	*n pl.* -S a roster

ROTARY *n* pl. -RIES a rotating part or device

ROTATE *v* -TATED, -TATING, -TATES to turn about an axis

ROTATION *n* pl. -S the act or an instance of rotating **ROTATIVE** *adj*

ROTATOR *n* pl. -S one that rotates

ROTATOR *n* pl. -ES a muscle serving to rotate a part of the body

ROTATORY *adj* pertaining to rotation

ROTCH *n* pl. -ES rotche

ROTCHE *n* pl. -S a seabird

ROTE *n* pl. -S mechanical routine

ROTENONE *n* pl. -S an insecticide

ROTGUT *n* pl. -S inferior liquor

ROTIFER *n* pl. -S a microscopic aquatic organism

ROTIFORM *adj* shaped like a wheel

ROTL *n* pl. ROTLS or ARTAL a unit of weight in Muslim countries

ROTO *n* pl. -TOS a type of printing process

ROTOR *n* pl. -S a rotating part of a machine

ROTOTILL *v* -ED, -ING, -S to till soil with a type of farming implement

ROTTED past tense of rot

ROTTEN *adj* -TENER, -TENEST being in a state of decay **ROTTENLY** *adv*

ROTTER *n* pl. -S a scoundrel

ROTTING present participle of rot

ROTUND *adj* marked by roundness **ROTUNDLY** *adv*

ROTUNDA *n* pl. -S a round building

ROTURIER *n* pl. -S a commoner

ROUBLE *n* pl. -S ruble

ROUCHE *n* pl. -S ruche

ROUE *n* pl. -S a lecherous man

ROUEN *n* pl. -S any of a breed of domestic ducks

ROUGE *v* ROUGED, ROUGING, ROUGES to color with a red cosmetic

ROUGH *adj* ROUGHER, ROUGHEST having an uneven surface

ROUGH *v* -ED, -ING, -S to make rough

ROUGHAGE *n* pl. -S coarse, bulky food

ROUGHDRY *v* -DRIED, -DRYING, -DRIES to dry without ironing, as washed clothes

ROUGHEN *v* -ED, -ING, -S to make rough

ROUGHER *n* pl. -S one that roughs

ROUGHHEW *v* -HEWED, -HEWN, -HEWING, -HEWS to shape roughly

ROUGHISH *adj* somewhat rough

ROUGHLEG *n* pl. -S a large hawk

ROUGHLY *adv* in a rough manner

ROUGING present participle of rouge

ROULADE *n* pl. -S a musical embellishment

ROULEAU *n* pl. -LEAUX or -LEAUS a roll of coins wrapped in paper

ROULETTE *v* -LETTED, -LETTING, -LETTES to make tiny slits in

ROUND *adj* ROUNDER, ROUNDEST shaped like a sphere

ROUND *v* -ED, -ING, -S to make round

ROUNDEL *n* pl. -S a round figure or object

ROUNDER *n* pl. -S a tool for rounding

ROUNDISH *adj* somewhat round

ROUNDLET *n* pl. -S a small circle

ROUNDLY *adv* in a round manner

ROUNDUP *n* pl. -S the driving together of cattle scattered over a range

ROUP *v* -ED, -ING, -S to auction

ROUPET *adj* roupy

ROUPY *adj* ROUPIER, ROUPIEST hoarse ROUPILY *adv*

ROUSE *v* ROUSED, ROUSING, ROUSES to bring out of a state of sleep or inactivity

ROUSER *n* pl. -S one that rouses

ROUSSEAU *n* pl. -S fried pemmican

ROUST *v* -ED, -ING, -S to arouse and drive out

ROUSTER *n* pl. -S a wharf laborer and deckhand

ROUT *v* -ED, -ING, -S to defeat overwhelmingly

ROUTE *v* ROUTED, ROUTING, ROUTES to send on a particular course

ROUTEMAN *n* pl. -MEN one who conducts business on a customary course

ROUTER *n* pl. -S a scooping tool

ROUTEWAY *n* pl. -WAYS an established course of travel

ROUTH *n* pl. -S an abundance

ROUTINE *n* pl. -S a regular course of procedure

ROUTING present participle of route

ROUX *n* pl. ROUX a mixture of butter and flour

ROVE *v* ROVED, ROVING, ROVES to roam

ROVEN   a past participle of reeve

ROVER   *n pl.* -S one that roves

ROVING   *n pl.* -S a roll of textile fibers

ROVINGLY   *adv* in a roving manner

ROW   *v* -ED, -ING, -S to propel by means of oars ROWABLE *adj*

ROWAN   *n pl.* -S a Eurasian tree

ROWBOAT   *n pl.* -S a small boat designed to be rowed

ROWDY   *adj* -DIER, -DIEST disorderly in behavior ROWDILY *adv*

ROWDY   *n* -DIES a rowdy person

ROWDYISH   *adj* tending to be rowdy

ROWDYISM   *n pl.* -S disorderly behavior

ROWEL   *v* -ELED, -ELING, -ELS or -ELLED, -ELLING, -ELS to prick with a spiked wheel in order to urge forward

ROWEN   *n pl.* -S a second growth of grass

ROWER   *n pl.* -S one that rows

ROWING   *n pl.* -S the sport of racing in light, long, and narrow rowboats

ROWLOCK   *n pl.* -S an oarlock

ROWTH   *n pl.* -S routh

ROYAL   *n pl.* -S a size of printing paper

ROYALISM   *n pl.* -S support of a monarch or monarchy

ROYALIST   *n pl.* -S a supporter of a monarch or monarchy

ROYALLY   *adv* in a kingly manner

ROYALTY   *n pl.* -TIES the status or power of a monarch

ROYSTER   *v* -ED, -ING, -S to roister

ROZZER   *n pl.* -S a policeman

RUB   *v* RUBBED, RUBBING, RUBS to move along the surface of a body with pressure

RUBABOO   *n pl.* -BOOS a type of soup

RUBACE   *n pl.* -S rubasse

RUBAIYAT   *n pl.* RUBAIYAT four-lined stanzas in Persian poetry

RUBASSE   *n pl.* -S a variety of quartz

RUBATO   *n pl.* -TOS a fluctuation of speed within a musical phrase

RUBBABOO   *n pl.* -BOOS rubaboo

RUBBED   past tense of rub

RUBBER   *n pl.* -S an elastic substance RUBBERY *adj*

RUBBING   *n pl.* -S an image produced by rubbing

RUBBISH   *n pl.* -ES worthless, unwanted matter RUBBISHY *adj*

RUBBLE   *v* -BLED, -BLING, -BLES to reduce to rubble (broken pieces)

RUBBLY   *adj* -BLIER, -BLIEST abounding in rubble

RUBDOWN   *n pl.* -S a brisk rubbing of the body

RUBE   *n pl.* -S a rustic

RUBELLA   *n pl.* -S a virus disease

RUBEOLA   *n pl.* -S a virus disease RUBEOLAR *adj*

RUBICUND   *adj* ruddy

RUBIDIUM   *n pl.* -S a metallic element RUBIDIC *adj*

RUBIED   past tense of ruby

RUBIER   comparative of ruby

RUBIES   present 3d person sing. of ruby

RUBIEST   superlative of ruby

RUBIGO   *n pl.* -GOS red iron oxide

RUBIOUS   *adj* ruby-colored

RUBLE   *n pl.* -S a monetary unit of the Soviet Union

RUBRIC   *n pl.* -S a part of a manuscript or book that appears in red RUBRICAL *adj*

RUBUS   *n pl.* RUBUS a plant of the rose family

RUBY   *v* -BIED, -BYING, -BIES to tint with the color of a ruby (a deep-red precious stone)

RUBY   *adj* -BIER, -BIEST of a deep-red color

RUBYLIKE   *adj* resembling a ruby

RUCHE   *n pl.* -S a pleated strip of fine fabric

RUCHING   *n pl.* -S a ruche

RUCK   *v* -ED, -ING, -S to wrinkle or crease

RUCKSACK   *n pl.* -S a knapsack

RUCKUS   *n pl.* -ES a noisy disturbance

RUCTION   *n pl.* -S a ruckus

RUCTIOUS   *adj* quarrelsome

RUDD   *n pl.* -S a freshwater fish

RUDDER   *n pl.* -S a vertical blade used to direct the course of a vessel

RUDDIER   comparative of ruddy

RUDDIEST   superlative of ruddy

RUDDILY   *adv* in a ruddy manner

RUDDLE   *v* -DLED, -DLING, -DLES to color with a red dye

RUDDOCK   *n pl.* -S a European bird

RUDDY *adj* -DIER, -DIEST having a healthy, reddish color

RUDE *adj* RUDER, RUDEST discourteous or impolite **RUDELY** *adv*

RUDENESS *n pl.* -ES the quality of being rude

RUDERAL *n pl.* -S a plant growing in poor land

RUDESBY *n pl.* -BIES a rude person

RUDEST superlative of rude

RUDIMENT *n pl.* -S a basic principle or element

RUE *v* RUED, RUING, RUES to feel sorrow or remorse for

RUEFUL *adj* feeling sorrow or remorse **RUEFULLY** *adv*

RUER *n pl.* -S one that rues

RUFF *v* -ED, -ING, -S to trump

RUFFE *n pl.* -S a freshwater fish

RUFFIAN *n pl.* -S a tough, lawless person

RUFFLE *v* -FLED, -FLING, -FLES to destroy the smoothness of

RUFFLER *n pl.* -S one that ruffles

RUFFLIKE *adj* resembling a ruff (a pleated collar)

RUFFLING present participle of ruffle

RUFFLY *adj* not smooth

RUFOUS *adj* reddish

RUG *v* RUGGED, RUGGING, RUGS to tear roughly

RUGA *n pl.* -GAE an anatomical fold or wrinkle **RUGAL, RUGATE** *adj*

RUGBY *n pl.* -BIES a form of football

RUGGED *adj* -GEDER, -GEDEST having an uneven surface **RUGGEDLY** *adv*

RUGGER *n pl.* -S rugby

RUGGING present participle of rug

RUGLIKE *adj* resembling a rug (a thick fabric used as a floor covering)

RUGOSE *adj* full of wrinkles **RUGOSELY** *adv*

RUGOSITY *n pl.* -TIES the state of being rugose

RUGOUS *adj* rugose

RUGULOSE *adj* having small wrinkles

RUIN *v* -ED, -ING, -S to destroy **RUINABLE** *adj*

RUINATE *v* -ATED, -ATING, -ATES to ruin

RUINER *n pl.* -S one that ruins

RUING present participle of rue

RUINOUS *adj* destructive

RULE *v* RULED, RULING, RULES to exercise control over **RULABLE** *adj*

RULELESS *adj* not restrained or regulated by law

RULER *n pl.* -S one that rules

RULING *n pl.* -S an authoritative decision

RUM *n pl.* -S an alcoholic liquor

RUM *adj* RUMMER, RUMMEST odd

RUMBA *v* -ED, -ING, -S to perform a ballroom dance

RUMBLE *v* -BLED, -BLING, -BLES to make a deep, thunderous sound

RUMBLER *n pl.* -S one that rumbles

RUMBLING *n pl.* -S a deep, thunderous sound

RUMBLY *adj* tending to rumble

RUMEN *n pl.* -MINA or -MENS a part of the stomach of a ruminant **RUMINAL** *adj*

RUMINANT *n pl.* -S a hoofed, even-toed mammal

RUMINATE *v* -NATED, -NATING, -NATES to chew again

RUMMAGE *v* -MAGED, -MAGING, -MAGES to search thoroughly through

RUMMAGER *n pl.* -S one that rummages

RUMMER *n pl.* -S a large drinking glass

RUMMEST superlative of rum

RUMMY *n pl.* -MIES a card game

RUMMY *adj* -MIER, -MIEST odd

RUMOR *v* -ED, -ING, -S to spread by hearsay

RUMOUR *v* -ED, -ING, -S to rumor

RUMP *n pl.* -S the lower and back part of the trunk **RUMPLESS** *adj*

RUMPLE *v* -PLED, -PLING, -PLES to wrinkle

RUMPLY *adj* -PLIER, -PLIEST rumpled

RUMPUS *n pl.* -ES a noisy disturbance

RUN *v* RAN, RUNNING, RUNS to move by rapid steps

RUNABOUT *n pl.* -S a small, open auto

RUNAGATE *n pl.* -S a deserter

RUNAWAY *n pl.* -AWAYS one that runs away

RUNBACK *n pl.* -S a type of run in football

RUNDLE *n pl.* -S a rung

RUNDLET *n pl.* -S a small barrel

RUNDOWN *n pl.* -S a summary

RUNE *n pl.* -S a letter of an ancient alphabet **RUNELIKE** *adj*

RUNG n pl. -S a crosspiece forming a step of a ladder **RUNGLESS** adj

RUNIC adj pertaining to a rune

RUNKLE v -KLED, -KLING, -KLES to wrinkle

RUNLESS adj scoring no runs in baseball

RUNLET n pl. -S a small stream

RUNNEL n pl. -S a small stream

RUNNER n pl. -S one that runs

RUNNING n pl. -S a race

RUNNY adj -NIER, -NIEST tending to drip

RUNOFF n pl. -S rainfall that is not absorbed by the soil

RUNOUT n pl. -S the end of a film strip

RUNOVER n pl. -S matter for publication that exceeds the allotted space

RUNROUND n pl. -S evasive action

RUNT n pl. -S a small person or animal **RUNTISH** adj

RUNTY adj RUNTIER, RUNTIEST small

RUNWAY n pl. -WAYS a landing and takeoff strip for aircraft

RUPEE n pl. -S a monetary unit of India

RUPIAH n pl. -S a monetary unit of Indonesia

RUPTURE v -TURED, -TURING, -TURES to burst

RURAL adj pertaining to the country

RURALISE v -ISED, -ISING, -ISES to ruralize

RURALISM n pl. -S the state of being rural

RURALIST n pl. -S one who lives in the country

RURALITE n pl. -S a ruralist

RURALITY n pl. -TIES the state of being rural

RURALIZE v -IZED, -IZING, -IZES to make rural

RURALLY adv in a rural manner

RURBAN adj partially rural and urban

RUSE n pl. -S a deception

RUSH v -ED, -ING, -ES to move swiftly

RUSHEE n pl. -S a college student seeking admission to a fraternity or sorority

RUSHER n pl. -S one that rushes

RUSHIER comparative of rushy

RUSHIEST superlative of rushy

RUSHING n pl. -S yardage gained in football by running plays

RUSHLIKE adj resembling a rush (a grasslike marsh plant)

RUSHY adj RUSHIER, RUSHIEST abounding in rushes

RUSINE adj pertaining to a genus of deer

RUSK n pl. -S a sweetened biscuit

RUSSET n pl. -S a reddish or yellowish brown color **RUSSETY** adj

RUSSIFY v -FIED, -FYING, -FIES to make Russian

RUST v -ED, -ING, -S to form rust (a reddish coating that forms on iron) **RUSTABLE** adj

RUSTIC n pl. -S one who lives in the country **RUSTICAL** adj

RUSTICLY adv in a rural manner

RUSTIER comparative of rusty

RUSTIEST superlative of rusty

RUSTILY adv in a rusty manner

RUSTLE v -TLED, -TLING, -TLES to make a succession of slight, soft sounds

RUSTLER n pl. -S one that rustles

RUSTLESS adj free from rust

RUSTLING present participle of rustle

RUSTY adj RUSTIER, RUSTIEST covered with rust

RUT v RUTTED, RUTTING, RUTS to make ruts (grooves) in

RUTABAGA n pl. -S a plant having a thick, edible root

RUTH n pl. -S compassion

RUTHENIC adj pertaining to a rare, metallic element

RUTHFUL adj full of compassion

RUTHLESS adj having no compassion

RUTILANT adj having a reddish glow

RUTILE n pl. -S a mineral

RUTTED past tense of rut

RUTTIER comparative of rutty

RUTTIEST superlative of rutty

RUTTILY adv in a rutty manner

RUTTING present participle of rut

RUTTISH adj lustful

RUTTY adj -TIER, -TIEST marked by ruts

RYA n pl. -S a Scandinavian handwoven rug

RYE n pl. -S a cereal grass

RYEGRASS n pl. -ES a European grass

RYKE v RYKED, RYKING, RYKES to reach

RYND n pl. -S an iron support

RYOT n pl. -S a tenant farmer in India

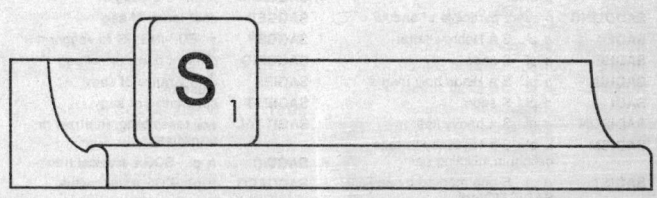

SAB	v SABBED, SABBING, SABS to sob	**SACCULE**	n pl. -S a small sac
		SACCULUS	n pl. -LI saccule
SABATON	n pl. -S a piece of armor for the foot	**SACHEM**	n pl. -S a North American Indian chief **SACHEMIC** adj
SABBAT	n pl. -S an assembly of demons and witches	**SACHET**	n pl. -S a small bag containing perfumed powder **SACHETED** adj
SABBATH	n pl. -S sabbat		
SABBATIC	adj bringing a period of rest	**SACK**	v -ED, -ING, -S to put into a sack (a large bag)
SABBED	past tense of sab	**SACKBUT**	n pl. -S a medieval trombone
SABBING	present participle of sab	**SACKER**	n pl. -S one that sacks
SABE	v SABED, SABEING, SABES to savvy	**SACKFUL**	n pl. SACKFULS or SACKSFUL as much as a sack will hold
SABER	v -ED, -ING, -S to strike with a saber (a type of sword)	**SACKING**	n pl. -S material for making sacks
SABIN	n pl. -S a unit of sound absorption	**SACKLIKE**	adj resembling a sack
		SACKSFUL	a pl. of sackful
SABINE	n pl. -S savin	**SACLIKE**	adj resembling a sac
SABIR	n pl. -S a French-based pidgin language	**SACQUE**	n pl. -S a loose-fitting dress
		SACRA	pl. of sacrum
SABLE	n pl. -S a carnivorous mammal	**SACRAL**	n pl. -S a vertebra or nerve situated near the sacrum
SABOT	n pl. -S a wooden shoe		
SABOTAGE	v -TAGED, -TAGING, -TAGES to destroy maliciously	**SACRARIA**	n/pl ancient Roman shrines
		SACRED	adj dedicated to or set apart for the worship of a deity **SACREDLY** adv
SABOTEUR	n pl. -S one who sabotages		
SABRA	n pl. -S a native Israeli		
SABRE	v -BRED, -BRING, -BRES to sabre	**SACRIST**	n pl. -S a person in charge of a sacristy
		SACRISTY	n pl. -TIES a room in which sacred vessels and vestments are kept
SABULOSE	adj sabulous		
SABULOUS	adj sandy		
SAC	n pl. -S a pouchlike structure in an animal or plant	**SACRUM**	n pl. -CRA a bone of the pelvis
		SAD	adj SADDER, SADDEST unhappy
SACATON	n pl. -S a perennial grass		
SACBUT	n pl. -S sackbut	**SADDEN**	v -ED, -ING, -S to make sad
SACCADE	n pl. -S a rapid, jerky movement of the eye **SACCADIC** adj	**SADDHU**	n pl. -S sadhu
		SADDLE	v -DLED, -DLING, -DLES to put a saddle (a leather seat for a rider) on
SACCATE	adj having a sac		
SACCULAR	adj resembling a sac		

SADDLER *n pl.* -S one that makes, repairs, or sells saddles

SADDLERY *n pl.* -DLERIES the shop of a saddler

SADDLING present participle of saddle

SADE *n pl.* -S a Hebrew letter

SADHE *n pl.* -S sade

SADHU *n pl.* -S a Hindu holy man

SADI *n pl.* -S sade

SADIRON *n pl.* -S a heavy flatiron

SADISM *n pl.* -S a tendency to take delight in inflicting pain

SADIST *n pl.* -S one marked by sadism **SADISTIC** *adj*

SADLY *adv* in a sad manner

SADNESS *n pl.* -ES the state of being sad

SAE *adv* so

SAFARI *v* -ED, -ING, -S to go on a hunting expedition

SAFE *adj* SAFER, SAFEST free from danger **SAFELY** *adv*

SAFE *n pl.* -S a metal receptacle for storing valuables

SAFENESS *n pl.* -ES the quality of being safe

SAFER comparative of safe

SAFEST superlative of safe

SAFETY *v* -TIED, -TYING, -TIES to protect against failure, breakage, or accident

SAFFRON *n pl.* -S a flowering plant

SAFRANIN *n pl.* -S a red dye

SAFROL *n pl.* -S safrole

SAFROLE *n pl.* -S a poisonous liquid

SAG *v* SAGGED, SAGGING, SAGS to bend or sink downward from weight or pressure

SAGA *n pl.* -S a medieval Scandinavian narrative

SAGACITY *n pl.* -TIES wisdom

SAGAMAN *n pl.* -MEN a writer of sagas

SAGAMORE *n pl.* -S an Algonquian Indian chief

SAGANASH *n pl.* -ES a white man — an Algonquian Indian term

SAGBUT *n pl.* -S sackbut

SAGE *adj* SAGER, SAGEST wise **SAGELY** *adv*

SAGE *n pl.* -S an aromatic herb used as seasoning

SAGENESS *n pl.* -ES wisdom

SAGER comparative of sage

SAGEST superlative of sage

SAGGAR *v* -ED, -ING, -S to bake in a saggar (a protective clay casing)

SAGGARD *n pl.* -S a saggar

SAGGED past tense of sag

SAGGER *v* -ED, -ING, -S to saggar

SAGGING present participle of sag

SAGIER comparative of sagy

SAGIEST superlative of sagy

SAGITTAL *adj* resembling an arrow or arrowhead

SAGO *n pl.* -GOS a tropical tree

SAGUARO *n pl.* -ROS a tall cactus

SAGUM *n pl.* -GA a cloak worn by ancient Roman soldiers

SAGY *adj* SAGIER, SAGIEST flavored with sage

SAHIB *n pl.* -S sir; master — used as a term of respect in colonial India

SAHIWAL *n pl.* -S any of a breed of humped dairy cattle

SAHUARO *n pl.* -ROS saguaro

SAICE *n pl.* -S syce

SAID *n pl.* -S sayyid

SAIGA *n pl.* -S a small antelope

SAIL *v* -ED, -ING, -S to move across the surface of water by the action of wind **SAILABLE** *adj*

SAILBOAT *n pl.* -S a boat that sails

SAILER *n pl.* -S a vessel that sails

SAILFISH *n pl.* -ES a large marine fish

SAILING *n pl.* -S the act of one that sails

SAILOR *n pl.* -S a member of a ship's crew **SAILORLY** *adj*

SAIN *v* -ED, -ING, -S to make the sign of the cross on

SAINFOIN *n pl.* -S a perennial herb

SAINT *v* -ED, -ING, -S to declare to be a saint (a person of exceptional holiness)

SAINTDOM *n pl.* -S the condition of being a saint

SAINTLY *adj* -LIER, -LIEST of or befitting a saint

SAITH a present 3d person sing. of say

SAITHE *n pl.* SAITHE a marine food fish

SAIYID *n pl.* -S sayyid

SAJOU *n pl.* -S a capuchin

SAKE *n pl.* -S benefit, interest, or advantage

SAKER n pl. -S a Eurasian falcon

SAKI n pl. -S a Japanese liquor

SAL n pl. -S salt

SALAAM v -ED, -ING, -S to greet with a low bow

SALABLE adj capable of being or fit to be sold **SALABLY** adv

SALACITY n pl. -TIES lewdness

SALAD n pl. -S a dish of green, raw vegetables

SALADANG n pl. -S a wild ox

SALAMI n pl. -S a seasoned sausage

SALARIAT n pl. -S the class of salaried persons

SALARY v -RIED, -RYING, -RIES to pay a periodic, fixed compensation to

SALE n pl. -S the act or an instance of selling

SALEABLE adj salable **SALEABLY** adv

SALEP n pl. -S a starchy meal ground from the roots of certain orchids

SALEROOM n pl. -S a room in which goods are displayed for sale

SALESMAN n pl. -MEN a man who sells merchandise

SALIC adj pertaining to a group of igneous rocks

SALICIN n pl. -S a chemical compound

SALICINE n pl. -S salicin

SALIENCE n pl. -S a projecting feature or detail

SALIENCY n pl. -CIES salience

SALIENT n pl. -S the part of a fortification projecting closest to the enemy

SALIFY v -FIED, -FYING, -FIES to combine with a salt

SALINA n pl. -S a pond, marsh, or lake containing salt water

SALINE n pl. -S a salt solution

SALINITY n pl. -TIES a concentration of salt

SALINIZE v -NIZED, -NIZING, -NIZES to treat with salt

SALIVA n pl. -S a fluid secreted by the glands of the mouth **SALIVARY** adj

SALIVATE v -VATED, -VATING, -VATES to secrete saliva

SALL v shall — SALL is the only form of this verb; it cannot be conjugated

SALLET n pl. -S a light medieval helmet

SALLIED past tense of sally

SALLIER n pl. -S one that sallies

SALLIES present 3d person sing. of sally

SALLOW adj -LOWER, -LOWEST of a sickly yellowish color **SALLOWLY** adv

SALLOW v -ED, -ING, -S to make sallow

SALLOWY adj abounding in willow trees

SALLY v -LIED, -LYING, -LIES to rush out suddenly

SALMI n pl. -S a dish of roasted game birds

SALMON n pl. -S a food fish

SALMONID n pl. -S a fish of the salmon family

SALOL n pl. -S a chemical compound

SALON n pl. -S a large room in which guests are received

SALOON n pl. -S a tavern

SALOOP n pl. -S a hot drink made from an infusion of aromatic herbs

SALP n pl. -S salpa

SALPA n pl. -PAE or -PAS a free-swimming tunicate

SALPIAN n pl. -S salpa

SALPID n pl. -S salpa

SALPINX n pl. -PINGES an anatomical tube

SALSIFY n pl. -FIES a European herb

SALSILLA n pl. -S a tropical plant

SALT v -ED, -ING, -S to treat with salt (a crystalline compound used as a seasoning and preservative)

SALT adj SALTER, SALTEST salty

SALTANT adj jumping or dancing

SALTBOX n pl. -ES a type of house

SALTBUSH n pl. -ES a salt-tolerant plant

SALTER n pl. -S one that salts

SALTERN n pl. -S a place where salt is produced

SALTIE n pl. -S a deep-sea vessel sailing the Great Lakes

SALTIER n pl. -S saltire

SALTIEST superlative of salty

SALTILY adv in a salty manner

SALTINE n pl. -S a salted cracker

SALTIRE n pl. -S a heraldic design

SALTISH adj somewhat salty

SALTLESS adj having no salt

SALTLIKE adj resembling salt

SALTNESS *n* pl. -ES the state of being salty

SALTPAN *n* pl. -S a large pan for making salt by evaporation

SALTWORK *n* pl. -S a saltern

SALTWORT *n* pl. -S a seaside herb

SALTY *adj* SALTIER, SALTIEST tasting of or containing salt

SALUKI *n* pl. -S a tall, slender dog

SALUTARY *adj* producing a beneficial effect

SALUTE *v* -LUTED, -LUTING, -LUTES to greet with a sign of welcome or respect

SALUTER *n* pl. -S one that salutes

SALVABLE *adj* capable of being saved SALVABLY *adv*

SALVAGE *v* -VAGED, -VAGING, -VAGES to save from loss or destruction

SALVAGEE *n* pl. -S one in whose favor salvage has been effected

SALVAGER *n* pl. -S one that salvages

SALVAGING present participle of salvage

SALVE *v* SALVED, SALVING, SALVES to soothe

SALVER *n* pl. -S a tray or serving platter

SALVIA *n* pl. -S a flowering plant

SALVIFIC *adj* having the power to save

SALVING present participle of salve

SALVO *v* -ED, -ING, -S or -ES to discharge firearms simultaneously

SALVOR *n* pl. -S a salvager

SAMARA *n* pl. -S a dry, one-seeded fruit

SAMARIUM *n* pl. -S a metallic element

SAMBA *v* -ED, -ING, -S to perform a Brazilian dance

SAMBAR *n.* pl. -S a large Asian deer

SAMBHAR *n* pl. -S sambar

SAMBHUR *n* pl. -S sambar

SAMBO *n* pl. -BOS a Latin American of mixed black and Indian ancestry

SAMBUCA *n* pl. -S an ancient stringed instrument

SAMBUKE *n* pl. -S sambuca

SAMBUR *n* pl. -S sambar

SAME *adj* resembling in every relevant respect

SAMECH *n* pl. -S samek

SAMEK *n* pl. -S a Hebrew letter

SAMEKH *n* pl. -S samek

SAMENESS *n* pl. -ES lack of change or variety

SAMIEL *n* pl. -S the simoom

SAMISEN *n* pl. -S a Japanese stringed instrument

SAMITE *n* pl. -S a silk fabric

SAMLET *n* pl. -S a young salmon

SAMOVAR *n* pl. -S a metal urn for heating water

SAMP *n* pl. -S coarsely ground corn

SAMPAN *n* pl. -S a flat-bottomed Chinese skiff

SAMPHIRE *n* pl. -S a European herb

SAMPLE *v* -PLED, -PLING, -PLES to test a representative portion of a whole

SAMPLER *n* pl. -S one that samples

SAMPLING *n* pl. -S a small part selected for analysis

SAMSARA *n* pl. -S the cycle of birth, death, and rebirth in Buddhism

SAMSHU *n* pl. -S a Chinese liquor

SAMURAI *n* pl. -S a Japanese warrior

SANATIVE *adj* having the power to cure or heal

SANCTA a pl. of sanctum

SANCTIFY *v* -FIED, -FYING, -FIES to make holy

SANCTION *v* -ED, -ING, -S to authorize

SANCTITY *n* pl. -TIES holiness

SANCTUM *n* pl. -TUMS or -TA a sacred place

SAND *v* -ED, -ING, -S to cover with sand (a loose, granular rock material)

SANDAL *v* -DALED, -DALING, -DALS or -DALLED, -DALLING, -DALS to provide with sandals (light, open shoes)

SANDARAC *n* pl. -S an aromatic resin

SANDBAG *v* -BAGGED, -BAGGING, -BAGS to surround with bags of sand

SANDBANK *n* pl. -S a large mass of sand

SANDBAR *n* pl. -S a ridge of sand formed in a river or sea

SANDBOX *n* pl. -ES a box containing sand for children to play in

SANDBUR *n* pl. -S an annual herb

SANDBURR *n* pl. -S sandbur

SANDER *n* pl. -S one that sands

SANDFISH *n* pl. -ES a marine fish

SANDFLY *n* pl. -FLIES a biting fly

SANDHI *n* pl. -S a process of phonetic modification

SANDHOG *n* pl. -S a worker who digs or works in sand

SANDIER comparative of sandy

SANDIEST superlative of sandy

SANDLIKE adj resembling sand

SANDLING n pl. -S a marine fish

SANDLOT n pl. -S a vacant lot

SANDMAN n pl. -MEN a mythical person who makes children sleepy by sprinkling sand in their eyes

SANDPEEP n pl. -S a wading bird

SANDPILE n pl. -S a pile of sand

SANDPIT n pl. -S a pit dug in sandy soil

SANDSOAP n pl. -S a type of soap

SANDWICH v -ED, -ING, -ES to place between two layers or objects

SANDWORM n pl. -S a sand-dwelling worm

SANDWORT n pl. -S a flowering plant

SANDY adj SANDIER, SANDIEST containing or covered with sand

SANE adj SANER, SANEST mentally sound **SANELY** adv

SANE v SANED, SANING, SANES to sain

SANENESS n pl. -ES sanity

SANER comparative of sane

SANEST superlative of sane

SANG past tense of sing

SANGA n pl. -S sangar

SANGAR n pl. -S a temporary fortification for two or three men

SANGAREE n pl. -S an alcoholic beverage

SANGER n pl. -S sangar

SANGH n pl. -S an association promoting unity between the different groups in Hinduism

SANGRIA n pl. -S an alcoholic beverage

SANGUINE n pl. -S a red color

SANICLE n pl. -S a medicinal herb

SANIES n pl. SANIES a fluid discharged from wounds **SANIOUS** adj

SANING present participle of sane

SANITARY n pl. -TARIES a public urinal

SANITATE v -TATED, -TATING, -TATES to sanitize

SANITIES pl. of sanity

SANITISE v -TISED, -TISING, -TISES to sanitize

SANITIZE v -TIZED, -TIZING, -TIZES to guard against infection or disease by cleaning or sterilizing

SANITY n pl. -TIES the state of being sane

SANJAK n pl. -S an administrative district of Turkey

SANK past tense of sink

SANNOP n pl. -S sannup

SANNUP n pl. -S a married male American Indian

SANNYASI n pl. -S a Hindu monk

SANS prep without

SANSAR n pl. -S sarsar

SANSEI n pl. -S a grandchild of Japanese immigrants to the United States

SANSERIF n pl. -S a typeface without serifs

SANTALIC adj pertaining to sandalwood

SANTIMS n pl. -TIMI a former coin of Latvia

SANTIR n pl. -S a Persian dulcimer

SANTOL n pl. -S a tropical tree

SANTONIN n pl. -S a chemical compound

SANTOUR n pl. -S santir

SAP v SAPPED, SAPPING, SAPS to deplete or weaken gradually

SAPAJOU n pl. -S a capuchin

SAPHEAD n pl. -S a foolish, stupid, or gullible person

SAPHENA n pl. -NAE a vein of the leg

SAPID adj pleasant to the taste

SAPIDITY n pl. -TIES the state of being sapid

SAPIENCE n pl. -S wisdom

SAPIENCY n pl. -CIES sapience

SAPIENS adj pertaining to recent man

SAPIENT adj wise

SAPLESS adj lacking vitality

SAPLING n pl. -S a young tree

SAPONIFY v -FIED, -FYING, -FIES to convert into soap

SAPONIN n pl. -S a soapy substance obtained from plants

SAPONINE n pl. -S saponin

SAPONITE n pl. -S a mineral found in veins and cavities of rocks

SAPOR n pl. -S flavor **SAPOROUS** adj

SAPOTA n pl. -S an evergreen tree

SAPOUR n pl. -S sapor

SAPPED past tense of sap

SAPPER n pl. -S a military engineer

SAPPHIC n pl. -S a type of verse form

SAPPHIRE n pl. -S a blue gem

SAPPHISM n pl. -S lesbianism

SAPPHIST *n* pl. -S a lesbian

SAPPING present participle of sap

SAPPY *adj* -PIER, -PIEST silly **SAPPILY** *adv*

SAPREMIA *n* pl. -S a form of blood poisoning **SAPREMIC** *adj*

SAPROBE *n* pl. -S an organism that derives its nourishment from decaying organic matter **SAPROBIC** *adj*

SAPROPEL *n* pl. -S mud consisting chiefly of decaying organic matter

SAPSAGO *n* pl. -GOS a hard green cheese

SAPWOOD *n* pl. -S the newly formed outer wood of a tree

SARABAND *n* pl. -S a stately Spanish dance

SARAPE *n* pl. -S serape

SARCASM *n* pl. -S a sharply mocking or contemptuous remark

SARCENET *n* pl. -S a silk fabric

SARCOID *n* pl. -S a disease of horses

SARCOMA *n* pl. -MAS or -MATA a type of tumor

SARCOUS *adj* composed of flesh or muscle

SARD *n* pl. -S a variety of quartz

SARDAR *n* pl. -S sirdar

SARDINE *n* pl. -S a small food fish

SARDIUS *n* pl. -ES sard

SARDONIC *adj* mocking

SARDONYX *n* pl. -ES a variety of quartz

SAREE *n* pl. -S sari

SARGASSO *n* pl. -GASSOS a brownish seaweed

SARGE *n* pl. -S sergeant

SARI *n* pl. -S an outer garment worn by Hindu women

SARIN *n* pl. -S a toxic gas

SARK *n* pl. -S a shirt

SARMENT *n* pl. -S a type of plant stem

SARMENTA *n/pl* sarments

SAROD *n* pl. -S a lute of northern India

SARODE *n* pl. -S sarod

SARODIST *n* pl. -S one who plays the sarod

SARONG *n* pl. -S an outer garment worn in the Pacific islands

SARSAR *n* pl. -S a cold, whistling wind

SARSEN *n* pl. -S a large sandstone block

SARSENET *n* pl. -S sarcenet

SARTOR *n* pl. -S a tailor

SARTORII *n/pl* flat, narrow thigh muscles

SASH *v* -ED, -ING, -ES to furnish with a frame in which glass is set

SASHAY *v* -ED, -ING, -S to flounce

SASHIMI *n* pl. -S a Japanese dish of sliced raw fish

SASIN *n* pl. -S an antelope of India

SASS *v* -ED, -ING, -ES to talk impudently to

SASSABY *n* pl. -BIES an African antelope

SASSIER comparative of sassy

SASSIEST superlative of sassy

SASSILY *adv* in a sassy manner

SASSWOOD *n* pl. -S an African tree

SASSY *n* pl. -SIES sasswood

SASSY *adj* SASSIER, SASSIEST impudent

SASTRUGA *n* pl. -GI a ridge of snow formed by the wind in polar regions

SAT past tense of sit

SATANG *n* pl. -S a monetary unit of Thailand

SATANIC *adj* extremely evil

SATANISM *n* pl. -S worship of the powers of evil

SATANIST *n* pl. -S one who practices satanism

SATARA *n* pl. -S a woolen fabric

SATCHEL *n* pl. -S a small carrying bag

SATE *v* SATED, SATING, SATES to satiate

SATEEN *n* pl. -S a cotton fabric

SATEM *adj* pertaining to a group of Indo-European languages

SATI *n* pl. -S suttee

SATIABLE *adj* capable of being satiated **SATIABLY** *adv*

SATIATE *v* -ATED, -ATING, -ATES to satisfy to or beyond capacity

SATIETY *n* pl. -ETIES the state of being satiated

SATIN *n* pl. -S a smooth fabric

SATINET *n* pl. -S a thin satin

SATING present participle of sate

SATINPOD *n* pl. -S a flowering plant

SATINY *adj* resembling satin

SATIRE *n* pl. -S the use of derisive wit to attack folly or wickedness **SATIRIC** *adj*

SATIRISE *v* -RISED, -RISING, -RISES to satirize

SATIRIST *n pl.* -S one who satirizes

SATIRIZE *v* -RIZED, -RIZING, -RIZES to subject to satire

SATISFY *v* -FIED, -FYING, -FIES to provide fully with what is desired, expected, or needed

SATORI *n pl.* -S the illumination of spirit sought by Zen Buddhists

SATRAP *n pl.* -S a governor of a province in ancient Persia

SATRAPY *n pl.* -PIES the territory of a satrap

SATURANT *n pl.* -S a substance used to saturate

SATURATE *v* -RATED, -RATING, -RATES to fill completely with something that permeates

SATYR *n pl.* -S a woodland deity of Greek mythology **SATYRIC** *adj*

SATYRID *n pl.* -S a brownish butterfly

SAU *n pl.* SAU xu

SAUCE *v* SAUCED, SAUCING, SAUCES to season with sauce (a flavorful liquid dressing)

SAUCEBOX *n pl.* -ES a saucy person

SAUCEPAN *n pl.* -S a cooking utensil

SAUCER *n pl.* -S a small, shallow dish

SAUCH *n pl.* -S saugh

SAUCING present participle of sauce

SAUCY *adj* SAUCIER, SAUCIEST impudent **SAUCILY** *adv*

SAUGER *n pl.* -S a freshwater fish

SAUGH *n pl.* -S a willow tree **SAUGHY** *adj*

SAUL *n pl.* -S soul

SAULT *n pl.* -S a waterfall

SAUNA *n pl.* -S a Finnish steam bath

SAUNTER *v* -ED, -ING, -S to walk in a leisurely manner

SAUREL *n pl.* -S a marine fish

SAURIAN *n pl.* -S any of a suborder of reptiles

SAUROPOD *n pl.* -S any of a suborder of large dinosaurs

SAURY *n pl.* -RIES a marine fish

SAUSAGE *n pl.* -S finely chopped and seasoned meat stuffed into a casing

SAUTE *v* -TEED or -TED, -TEING, -TES to fry in a small amount of fat

SAUTERNE *n pl.* -S a sweet white wine

SAUTOIR *n pl.* -S a saltire

SAUTOIRE *n pl.* -S sautoir

SAVABLE *adj* capable of being saved

SAVAGE *adj* -AGER, -AGEST fierce **SAVAGELY** *adv*

SAVAGE *v* -AGED, -AGING, -AGES to attack or treat brutally

SAVAGERY *n pl.* -RIES the quality of being savage

SAVAGEST superlative of savage

SAVAGING present participle of savage

SAVAGISM *n pl.* -S savagery

SAVANNA *n pl.* -S a flat, treeless grassland

SAVANNAH *n pl.* -S savanna

SAVANT *n pl.* -S a man of profound learning

SAVATE *n pl.* -S a pugilistic sport

SAVE *v* SAVED, SAVING, SAVES to rescue from danger, injury, or loss **SAVEABLE** *adj*

SAVELOY *n pl.* -LOYS a highly seasoned sausage

SAVER *n pl.* -S one that saves

SAVIN *n pl.* -S an evergreen shrub

SAVINE *n pl.* -S savin

SAVING *n pl.* -S the act or an instance of saving

SAVINGLY *adv* in a thrifty manner

SAVIOR *n pl.* -S one that saves

SAVIOUR *n pl.* -S savior

SAVOR *v* -ED, -ING, -S to taste or smell with pleasure

SAVORER *n pl.* -S one that savors

SAVORIER comparative of savory

SAVORIES pl. of savory

SAVOROUS *adj* savory

SAVORY *adj* -VORIER, -VORIEST pleasant to the taste or smell **SAVORILY** *adv*

SAVORY *n pl.* -VORIES a savory dish served before or after a meal

SAVOUR *v* -ED, -ING, -S to savor

SAVOURER *n pl.* -S savorer

SAVOURY *adj* -VOURIER, -VOURIEST savory

SAVOURY *n pl.* -VOURIES a savory

SAVOY *n pl.* -VOYS a variety of cabbage

SAVVY *v* -VIED, -VYING, -VIES to understand

SAW *v* SAWED, SAWN, SAWING, SAWS to cut or divide with a saw (a type of cutting tool)

SAWBILL *n pl.* -S a tropical bird

SAWBONES *n pl.* -BONESES a surgeon

SAWBUCK *n pl.* -S a sawhorse

SAWDUST *n pl.* -S small particles of wood produced in sawing

SAWER *n pl.* -S one that saws

SAWFISH *n pl.* -ES a marine fish

SAWFLY *n pl.* -FLIES a winged insect

SAWHORSE *n pl.* -S a rack used to support a piece of wood being sawed

SAWLIKE *adj* resembling a saw

SAWLOG *n pl.* -S a log large enough to saw into boards

SAWMILL *n pl.* -S a place where logs are sawed

SAWN a past participle of saw

SAWNEY *n pl.* -NEYS a foolish person

SAWTOOTH *n pl.* -TEETH a cutting edge on a saw

SAWYER *n pl.* -S one that saws wood for a living

SAX *n pl.* -ES a saxophone

SAXATILE *adj* living or growing among rocks

SAXHORN *n pl.* -S a brass wind instrument

SAXONY *n pl.* -NIES a woolen fabric

SAXTUBA *n pl.* -S a bass saxhorn

SAY *v* SAID, SAYING, present sing. 2d person SAY, SAYEST, or SAYST, 3d person SAYS or SAITH to utter **SAYABLE** *adj*

SAYER *n pl.* -S one that says

SAYID *n pl.* -S sayyid

SAYING *n pl.* -S a maxim

SAYONARA *n pl.* -S goodby

SAYST a present 2d person sing. of say

SAYYID *n pl.* -S lord; sir — used as a title of respect for a Muslim dignitary

SCAB *v* SCABBED, SCABBING, SCABS to become covered with a scab (a crust that forms over a healing wound)

SCABBARD *v* -ED, -ING, -S to put into a sheath, as a sword

SCABBLE *v* -BLED, -BLING, -BLES to shape roughly

SCABBY *adj* -BIER, -BIEST covered with scabs **SCABBILY** *adv*

SCABIES *n pl.* SCABIES a skin disease

SCABIOSA *n pl.* -S scabious

SCABIOUS *n pl.* -ES a flowering plant

SCABLIKE *adj* resembling a scab

SCABROUS *adj* roughened with small projections

SCAD *n pl.* -S a marine fish

SCAFFOLD *v* -ED, -ING, -S to provide with a scaffold (a temporary platform for workmen)

SCAG *n pl.* -S heroin

SCALABLE *adj* capable of being scaled **SCALABLY** *adv*

SCALADE *n pl.* -S an act of scaling the walls of a fortification

SCALADO *n pl.* -DOS scalade

SCALAGE *n pl.* -S a percentage deduction to compensate for shrinkage

SCALAR *n pl.* -S a mathematical quantity possessing only magnitude

SCALARE *n pl.* -S a tropical fish

SCALAWAG *n pl.* -S a rascal

SCALD *v* -ED, -ING, -S to burn with hot liquid or steam

SCALDIC *adj* skaldic

SCALE *v* SCALED, SCALING, SCALES to climb up or over

SCALENE *adj* designating a triangle having no two sides equal

SCALENUS *n pl.* -NI a muscle of the neck

SCALEPAN *n pl.* -S a pan on a weighing scale

SCALER *n pl.* -S one that scales

SCALIER comparative of scaly

SCALIEST superlative of scaly

SCALING present participle of scale

SCALL *n pl.* -S a scaly eruption of the skin

SCALLION *n pl.* -S an onion-like plant

SCALLOP *v* -ED, -ING, -S to bake in a sauce topped with bread crumbs

SCALP *v* -ED, -ING, -S to remove an upper part from

SCALPEL *n pl.* -S a small surgical knife

SCALPER *n pl.* -S one that scalps

SCALY *adj* SCALIER, SCALIEST peeling off in flakes

SCAM *n pl.* -S a swindle

SCAMMONY *n pl.* -NIES a climbing plant

SCAMP *v* -ED, -ING, -S to perform in a hasty or careless manner

SCAMPER *v* -ED, -ING, -S to run playfully about

SCAMPI *n pl.* SCAMPI large shrimp used in Italian cooking

SCAMPISH adj rascally

SCAN v SCANNED, SCANNING, SCANS to examine closely

SCANDAL v -DALED, -DALING, -DALS or -DALLED, -DALLING, -DALS to defame

SCANDENT adj climbing, as a plant

SCANDIA n pl. -S an oxide of scandium

SCANDIUM n pl. -S a metallic element SCANDIC adj

SCANNED past tense of scan

SCANNER n pl. -S one that scans

SCANNING n pl. -S close examination

SCANSION n pl. -S the analysis of verse into metrical feet and rhythm patterns

SCANT adj SCANTER, SCANTEST meager

SCANT v -ED, -ING, -S to provide with a meager portion

SCANTIER comparative of scanty

SCANTIES n/pl brief panties for women

SCANTLY adv in a scant manner

SCANTY adj SCANTIER, SCANTIEST meager SCANTILY adv

SCAPE v SCAPED, SCAPING, SCAPES to escape

SCAPHOID n pl. -S a bone of the wrist

SCAPOSE adj bearing a leafless stalk

SCAPULA n pl. -LAE or -LAS a bone of the shoulder

SCAPULAR n pl. -S a sleeveless outer garment worn by monks

SCAR v SCARRED, SCARRING, SCARS to form a scar (a mark left by the healing of injured tissue)

SCARAB n pl. -S a large, black beetle

SCARCE adj SCARCER, SCARCEST infrequently seen or found

SCARCELY adv by a narrow margin

SCARCITY n pl. -TIES the quality of being scarce

SCARE v SCARED, SCARING, SCARES to frighten

SCARER n pl. -S one that scares

SCAREY adj SCARIER, SCARIEST scary

SCARF n pl. SCARFS or SCARVES a piece of cloth worn for warmth or protection

SCARF v -ED, -ING, -S to cover with a scarf

SCARFPIN n pl. -S a tiepin

SCARIER comparative of scarey and scary

SCARIEST superlative of scarey and scary

SCARIFY v -FIED, -FYING, -FIES to make superficial cuts in

SCARING present participle of scare

SCARIOSE adj scarious

SCARIOUS adj thin, dry, and membranous

SCARLESS adj having no scars

SCARLET n pl. -S a red color

SCARP v -ED, -ING, -S to cut or make into a steep slope

SCARPER v -ED, -ING, -S to flee

SCARPH v -ED, -ING, -S to unite by means of a type of joint

SCARRED past tense of scar

SCARRING present participle of scar

SCARRY adj -RIER, -RIEST marked with scars

SCART v -ED, -ING, -S to scratch

SCARVES a pl. of scarf

SCARY adj SCARIER, SCARIEST frightening

SCAT v SCATTED, SCATTING, SCATS to leave hastily

SCATBACK n pl. -S a type of player in football

SCATHE v SCATHED, SCATHING, SCATHES to criticize severely

SCATT n pl. -S a tax

SCATTED past tense of scat

SCATTER v -ED, -ING, -S to go or send in various directions

SCATTING present participle of scat

SCATTY adj -TIER, -TIEST crazy

SCAUP n pl. -S a sea duck

SCAUPER n pl. -S an engraving tool

SCAUR n pl. -S a protruding, isolated rock

SCAVENGE v -ENGED, -ENGING, -ENGES to search through rubbish for usable items

SCENA n pl. -S an elaborate composition for a single voice

SCENARIO n pl. -IOS a summary of the plot of a dramatic work

SCEND v -ED, -ING, -S to rise upward, as a ship on a wave

SCENE n pl. -S the place where some action or event occurs

SCENERY n pl. -ERIES a picturesque landscape or view

SCENIC *adj* pertaining to scenery

SCENICAL *adj* scenic

SCENT *v* -ED, -ING, -S to fill with an odor

SCEPTER *v* -ED, -ING, -S to invest with royal authority

SCEPTIC *n pl.* -S skeptic

SCEPTRAL *adj* pertaining to royal authority

SCEPTRE *v* -TRED, -TRING, -TRES to scepter

SCHAPPE *n pl.* -S a silk fabric

SCHAV *n pl.* -S a chilled soup

SCHEDULE *v* -ULED, -ULING, -ULES to assign to a certain date or time

SCHEMA *n pl.* -MATA a generalized diagram or plan

SCHEME *v* SCHEMED, SCHEMING, SCHEMES to plan or plot

SCHEMER *n pl.* -S one that schemes

SCHERZO *n pl.* -ZOS or -ZI a lively musical movement

SCHILLER *n pl.* -S a brownish luster occurring on certain minerals

SCHISM *n pl.* -S a division into opposing parties

SCHIST *n pl.* -S a rock that readily splits into parallel layers

SCHIZO *n pl.* SCHIZOS a schizoid

SCHIZOID *n pl.* -S a person affected with a type of psychotic disorder

SCHIZONT *n pl.* -S an organism that reproduces by a form of asexual reproduction

SCHLEP *v* SCHLEPPED, SCHLEPPING, SCHLEPS to lug or drag

SCHLEPP *v* -ED, -ING, -S to schlep

SCHLOCK *n pl.* -S inferior merchandise

SCHMALTZ *n pl.* -ES excessive sentimentality

SCHMALZ *n pl.* -ES schmaltz

SCHMALZY *adj* SCHMALZIER, SCHMALZIEST characterized by schmaltz

SCHMEER *v* -ED, -ING, -S to bribe

SCHMELZE *n pl.* -S a type of decorative glass

SCHMO *n pl.* SCHMOES a stupid person

SCHMOE *n pl.* -S schmo

SCHMOOS *v* -ED, -ING, -ES to schmooze

SCHMOOSE *v* SCHMOOSED, SCHMOOSING, SCHMOOSES to schmooze

SCHMOOZE *v* SCHMOOZED, SCHMOOZING, SCHMOOZES to gossip

SCHMUCK *n pl.* -S a foolish or clumsy person

SCHNAPPS *n pl.* SCHNAPPS a strong liquor

SCHNAPS *n pl.* SCHNAPS schnapps

SCHNECKE *n pl.* -KEN a sweet roll

SCHNOOK *n pl.* -S an easily deceived person

SCHOLAR *n pl.* -S a learned person

SCHOLIUM *n pl.* -LIA or -LIUMS an explanatory marginal note

SCHOOL *v* -ED, -ING, -S to educate in an institution of learning

SCHOONER *n pl.* -S a sailing vessel

SCHORL *n pl.* -S a mineral

SCHRIK *n pl.* -S sudden fright

SCHTICK *n pl.* -S shtick

SCHUIT *n pl.* -S a Dutch sailing vessel

SCHUL *n pl.* SCHULN shul

SCHUSS *v* -ED, -ING, -ES to make a fast, straight run in skiing

SCHWA *n pl.* -S a type of vowel sound

SCIAENID *n pl.* -S a carnivorous fish

SCIATIC *n pl.* -S a nerve, vein, or artery situated near the hip

SCIATICA *n pl.* -S a painful disorder of the hip and adjoining areas

SCIENCE *n pl.* -S a department of systematized knowledge

SCILICET *adv* namely

SCILLA *n pl.* -S a flowering plant

SCIMETAR *n pl.* -S a scimitar

SCIMITAR *n pl.* -S a curved Oriental sword

SCIMITER *n pl.* -S a scimitar

SCINCOID *n pl.* -S one of a family of smooth, short-limbed lizards

SCIOLISM *n pl.* -S superficial knowledge

SCIOLIST *n pl.* -S one whose knowledge is superficial

SCION *n pl.* -S a child or descendant

SCIROCCO *n pl.* -COS sirocco

SCIRRHUS *n pl.* -RHI or -RHUSES a hard tumor

SCISSILE *adj* capable of being cut or split easily

SCISSION *n pl.* -S the act of cutting or splitting

SCISSOR *v* -ED, -ING, -S to cut with a two-bladed cutting implement

SCISSURE n pl. -S a lengthwise cut

SCIURINE n pl. -S a rodent of the squirrel family

SCIUROID adj resembling a squirrel

SCLAFF v -ED, -ING, -S to strike the ground with the club before hitting the ball in golf

SCLAFFER n pl. -S one that sclaffs

SCLERA n pl. -RAS or -RAE the white, fibrous outer coat of the eyeball SCLERAL adj

SCLEREID n pl. -S a type of plant cell

SCLERITE n pl. -S one of the hard plates forming the outer covering of an arthropod

SCLEROID adj sclerous

SCLEROMA n pl. -MATA a hardened patch of cellular tissue

SCLEROSE v -ROSED, -ROSING, -ROSES to become hard, as tissue

SCLEROUS adj hardened

SCOFF v -ED, -ING, -S to express rude doubt or derision

SCOFFER n pl. -S one that scoffs

SCOFFLAW n pl. -S an habitual law violator

SCOLD v -ED, -ING, -S to rebuke harshly

SCOLDER n pl. -S one that scolds

SCOLDING n pl. -S a harsh reproof

SCOLEX n pl. -LECES or -LICES the knoblike head of a tapeworm

SCOLIOMA n pl. -S abnormal curvature of the spine

SCOLLOP v -ED, -ING, -S to scallop

SCONCE v SCONCED, SCONCING, SCONCES to fine

SCONE n pl. -S a flat, round cake

SCOOP v -ED, -ING, -S to take up with a scoop (a spoonlike utensil)

SCOOPER n pl. -S one that scoops

SCOOPFUL n pl. SCOOPFULS or SCOOPSFUL as much as a scoop will hold

SCOOT v -ED, -ING, -S to go quickly

SCOOTER n pl. -S a two-wheeled vehicle

SCOP n pl. -S an Old English poet

SCOPE n pl. -S extent

SCOPULA n pl. -LAE or -LAS a dense tuft of hairs

SCORCH v -ED, -ING, -ES to burn slightly so as to alter the color or taste

SCORCHER n pl. -S one that scorches

SCORE v SCORED, SCORING, SCORES to make a point in a game or contest

SCOREPAD n pl. -S a pad on which scored points are recorded

SCORER n pl. -S one that scores

SCORIA n pl. -RIAE the refuse of a smelted metal or ore

SCORIFY v -FIED, -FYING, -FIES to reduce to scoria

SCORING present participle of score

SCORN v -ED, -ING, -S to treat or regard with contempt

SCORNER n pl. -S one that scorns

SCORNFUL adj feeling or expressing contempt

SCORPION n pl. -S a stinging arachnid

SCOT n pl. -S a tax

SCOTCH v -ED, -ING, -ES to put a definite end to

SCOTER n pl. -S a sea duck

SCOTIA n pl. -S a concave molding

SCOTOMA n pl. -MAS or -MATA a blind spot in the field of vision

SCOTOPIA n pl. -S vision in dim light SCOTOPIC adj

SCOTTIE n pl. -S a short-legged terrier

SCOUR v -ED, -ING, -S to cleanse or polish by hard rubbing

SCOURER n pl. -S one that scours

SCOURGE v SCOURGED, SCOURGING, SCOURGES to punish severely

SCOURGER n pl. -S one that scourges

SCOURING n pl. -S material removed by scouring

SCOUSE n pl. -S a type of meat stew

SCOUT v -ED, -ING, -S to observe for the purpose of obtaining information

SCOUTER n pl. -S one that scouts

SCOUTH n pl. -S plenty

SCOUTHER v -ED, -ING, -S to scorch

SCOUTING n pl. -S the act of one that scouts

SCOW v -ED, -ING, -S to transport by scow (a flat-bottomed boat)

SCOWDER v -ED, -ING, -S to scouther

SCOWL v -ED, -ING, -S to frown angrily

SCOWLER n pl. -S one that scowls

SCRABBLE v -BLED, -BLING, -BLES to claw or grope about frantically

SCRABBLY adj raspy

SCRAG v SCRAGGED, SCRAGGING, SCRAGS to wring the neck of

SCRAGGLY adj -GLIER, -GLIEST uneven

SCRAGGY adj -GIER, -GIEST scrawny

SCRAICH v -ED, -ING, -S to utter a shrill cry

SCRAIGH v -ED, -ING, -S to scraich

SCRAM v SCRAMMED, SCRAMMING, SCRAMS to leave quickly

SCRAMBLE v -BLED, -BLING, -BLES to move or climb hurriedly

SCRANNEL n pl. -S a thin person

SCRAP v SCRAPPED, SCRAPPING, SCRAPS to discard

SCRAPE v SCRAPED, SCRAPING, SCRAPES to rub so as to remove an outer layer

SCRAPER n pl. -S one that scrapes

SCRAPIE n pl. -S a disease of sheep

SCRAPING n pl. -S something scraped off

SCRAPPED past tense of scrap

SCRAPPER n pl. -S a fighter

SCRAPPIER comparative of scrappy

SCRAPPIEST superlative of scrappy

SCRAPPING present participle of scrap

SCRAPPLE n pl. -S a seasoned mixture of ground meat and cornmeal

SCRAPPY adj -PIER, -PIEST marked by fighting spirit

SCRATCH v -ED, -ING, -ES to make a thin, shallow cut or mark on

SCRATCHY adj SCRATCHIER, SCRATCHIEST uneven in quality

SCRAWL v -ED, -ING, -S to write hastily or illegibly

SCRAWLER n pl. -S one that scrawls

SCRAWLY adj SCRAWLIER, SCRAWLIEST written hastily or illegibly

SCRAWNY adj -NIER, -NIEST extremely thin

SCREAK v -ED, -ING, -S to screech

SCREAKY adj screechy

SCREAM v -ED, -ING, -S to utter a prolonged, piercing cry

SCREAMER n pl. -S one that screams

SCREE n pl. -S a mass of rocks at the foot of a slope

SCREECH v -ED, -ING, -ES to utter a harsh, shrill cry

SCREECHY adj SCREECHIER, SCREECHIEST screeching

SCREED v -ED, -ING, -S to shred

SCREEN v -ED, -ING, -S to provide with a screen (a device designed to divide, conceal, or protect)

SCREENER n pl. -S one that screens

SCREW v -ED, -ING, -S to attach with a screw (a type of metal fastener)

SCREWER n pl. -S one that screws

SCREWY adj SCREWIER, SCREWIEST crazy

SCRIBAL adj pertaining to a public clerk or secretary

SCRIBBLE v -BLED, -BLING, -BLES to write hastily or carelessly

SCRIBE v SCRIBED, SCRIBING, SCRIBES to mark with a scriber

SCRIBER n pl. -S a pointed instrument used for marking off material to be cut

SCRIEVE v SCRIEVED, SCRIEVING, SCRIEVES to move along swiftly and smoothly

SCRIM n pl. -S a cotton fabric

SCRIMP v -ED, -ING, -S to be very or overly thrifty

SCRIMPIT adj meager

SCRIMPY adj SCRIMPIER, SCRIMPIEST meager

SCRIP n pl. -S a small piece of paper

SCRIPT v -ED, -ING, -S to prepare a written text for, as a play or motion picture

SCRIVE v SCRIVED, SCRIVING, SCRIVES to engrave

SCROD n pl. -S a young cod

SCROFULA n pl. -S a disease of the lymph glands

SCROGGY adj -GIER, -GIEST of stunted growth

SCROLL n pl. -S a roll of parchment or paper with writing on it

SCROOGE n pl. -S a miserly person

SCROOP v -ED, -ING, -S to make a harsh, grating sound

SCROTUM n pl. -TA or -TUMS the pouch of skin that contains the testes **SCROTAL** adj

SCROUGE v SCROUGED, SCROUGING, SCROUGES to crowd

SCROUNGE v SCROUNGED, SCROUNGING, SCROUNGES to gather by foraging

SCROUNGY adj SCROUNGIER, SCROUNGIEST dirty

SCRUB v SCRUBBED, SCRUBBING, SCRUBS to rub hard in order to clean

SCRUBBER n pl. -S one that scrubs

SCRUBBY adj -BIER, -BIEST inferior in size or quality

SCRUFF n pl. -S the back of the neck

SCRUFFY adj -FIER, -FIEST shabby

SCRUM n pl. -S a formation around the ball in rugby

SCRUNCH v -ED, -ING, -ES to crush

SCRUPLE v -PLED, -PLING, -PLES to hesitate because of ethical considerations

SCRUTINY n pl. -NIES a close examination

SCUBA n pl. -S an underwater breathing device

SCUD v SCUDDED, SCUDDING, SCUDS to run or move swiftly

SCUDO n pl. -DI a former Italian coin

SCUFF v -ED, -ING, -S to walk without lifting the feet

SCUFFLE v -FLED, -FLING, -FLES to struggle in a rough, confused manner

SCUFFLER n pl. -S one that scuffles

SCULK v -ED, -ING, -S to skulk

SCULKER n pl. -S skulker

SCULL v -ED, -ING, -S to propel with a type of oar

SCULLER n pl. -S one that sculls

SCULLERY n pl. -LERIES a room in which kitchen utensils are cleaned and stored

SCULLION n pl. -S a kitchen servant who does menial work

SCULP v -ED, -ING, -S to sculpt

SCULPIN n pl. -S a freshwater fish

SCULPT v -ED, -ING, -S to form an image or representation of from solid material

SCULPTOR n pl. -S one that sculpts

SCUM v SCUMMED, SCUMMING, SCUMS to remove the scum (impure or extraneous matter) from

SCUMBLE v -BLED, -BLING, -BLES to soften the outlines or colors of by rubbing lightly

SCUMLIKE adj resembling scum

SCUMMED past tense of scum

SCUMMER n pl. -S one that scums

SCUMMING present participle of scum

SCUMMY adj -MIER, -MIEST covered with scum

SCUNNER v -ED, -ING, -S to feel loathing or disgust

SCUP n pl. -S a marine food fish

SCUPPAUG n pl. -S scup

SCUPPER v -ED, -ING, -S to ambush

SCURF n pl. -S scaly or shredded dry skin

SCURFY adj SCURFIER, SCURFIEST covered with scurf

SCURRIED past tense of scurry

SCURRIES present 3d person sing. of scurry

SCURRIL adj scurrile

SCURRILE adj expressed in coarse and abusive language

SCURRY v -RIED, -RYING, -RIES to move hurriedly

SCURVY adj -VIER, -VIEST base or contemptible SCURVILY adv

SCURVY n pl. -VIES a disease resulting from vitamin C deficiency

SCUT n pl. -S a short tail, as of a rabbit

SCUTA pl. of scutum

SCUTAGE n pl. -S a tax exacted by a feudal lord in lieu of military service

SCUTATE adj shaped like a shield

SCUTCH v -ED, -ING, -ES to separate the woody fiber from by beating

SCUTCHER n pl. -S one that scutches

SCUTE n pl. -S a horny plate or scale

SCUTELLA n/pl small, scutate organs or parts

SCUTTER v -ED, -ING, -S to scurry

SCUTTLE v -TLED, -TLING, -TLES to scurry

SCUTUM n pl. -TA scute

SCYPHATE adj shaped like a cup

SCYTHE v SCYTHED, SCYTHING, SCYTHES to cut with a scythe (a single-bladed cutting implement)

SEA n pl. -S the ocean

SEABAG n pl. -S a bag used by a sailor

SEABEACH n pl. -ES a beach lying along the sea

SEABED n pl. -S a seafloor

SEABIRD n pl. -S a bird frequenting the ocean or seacoast

SEABOARD n pl. -S the seacoast

SEABOOT n pl. -S a waterproof boot

SEABORNE adj carried on or over the sea

SEACOAST n pl. -S land bordering on the sea

SEACOCK *n pl.* -S a valve in a ship's hull

SEACRAFT *n pl.* -S skill in sea navigation

SEADOG *n pl.* -S a fogbow

SEADROME *n pl.* -S an airport in the sea

SEAFARER *n pl.* -S a sailor

SEAFLOOR *n pl.* -S the bottom of a sea

SEAFOOD *n pl.* -S edible fish or shellfish from the sea

SEAFOWL *n pl.* -S a seabird

SEAFRONT *n pl.* -S an area along the edge of the sea

SEAGIRT *adj* surrounded by the sea

SEAGOING *adj* designed for use on the sea

SEAL *v* -ED, -ING, -S to close or make secure against access, leakage, or passage **SEALABLE** *adj*

SEALANT *n pl.* -S a sealing agent

SEALER *n pl.* -S one that seals

SEALERY *n pl.* -ERIES the occupation of hunting seals

SEALLIKE *adj* resembling a seal (an aquatic mammal)

SEALSKIN *n pl.* -S the skin of a seal

SEAM *v* -ED, -ING, -S to join with a seam (a line formed by sewing two pieces of fabric together)

SEAMAN *n pl.* -MEN a sailor **SEAMANLY** *adj*

SEAMARK *n pl.* -S a landmark serving as a navigational guide to mariners

SEAMER *n pl.* -S one that seams

SEAMIER comparative of seamy

SEAMIEST superlative of seamy

SEAMLESS *adj* having no seam

SEAMLIKE *adj* resembling a seam

SEAMOUNT *n pl.* -S an undersea mountain

SEAMSTER *n pl.* -S a person whose occupation is sewing

SEAMY *adj* SEAMIER, SEAMIEST unpleasant

SEANCE *n pl.* -S a meeting of persons seeking spiritualistic messages

SEAPIECE *n pl.* -S a seascape

SEAPLANE *n pl.* -S an airplane designed to take off from or land on the water

SEAPORT *n pl.* -S a harbor or town accessible to seagoing ships

SEAQUAKE *n pl.* -S an undersea earthquake

SEAR *adj* SEARER, SEAREST sere

SEAR *v* -ED, -ING, -S to burn the surface of

SEARCH *v* -ED, -ING, -ES to look through or over carefully in order to find something

SEARCHER *n pl.* -S one that searches

SEARER comparative of sear

SEAREST superlative of sear

SEASCAPE *n pl.* -S a picture of the sea

SEASCOUT *n pl.* -S a boy scout trained in water activities

SEASHELL *n pl.* -S the shell of a marine mollusk

SEASHORE *n pl.* -S land bordering on the sea

SEASICK *adj* affected with nausea caused by the motion of a vessel at sea

SEASIDE *n pl.* -S the seashore

SEASON *v* -ED, -ING, -S to heighten or improve the flavor of by adding savory ingredients

SEASONAL *adj* occurring at a certain time of the year

SEASONER *n pl.* -S one that seasons

SEAT *v* -ED, -ING, -S to place on a seat (something on which one sits)

SEATER *n pl.* -S one that seats

SEATING *n pl.* -S material for covering seats

SEATLESS *adj* having no seat

SEATMATE *n pl.* -S one with whom one shares a seat

SEATRAIN *n pl.* -S a ship equipped to carry railroad cars

SEATWORK *n pl.* -S work done at one's seat

SEAWALL *n pl.* -S a wall to protect a shoreline from erosion

SEAWAN *n pl.* -S wampum

SEAWANT *n pl.* -S seawan

SEAWARD *n pl.* -S the direction toward the open sea

SEAWARE *n pl.* -S seaweed used as fertilizer

SEAWATER *n pl.* -S water from the sea

SEAWAY *n pl.* -WAYS the headway made by a ship

SEAWEED *n pl.* -S a plant growing in the sea

SEBACIC *adj* derived from a certain acid

SEBASIC *adj* sebacic

SEBUM *n pl.* -S a fatty matter secreted by certain glands of the skin

SEC *n pl.* -S secant

SECANT *n pl.* -S a trigonometric function of an angle

SECANTLY *adv* in an intersecting manner

SECATEUR *n pl.* -S a pruning tool

SECCO *n pl.* -COS the art of painting on dry plaster

SECEDE *v* -CEDED, -CEDING, -CEDES to withdraw formally from an alliance or association

SECEDER *n pl.* -S one that secedes

SECERN *v* -ED, -ING, -S to discern as separate

SECLUDE *v* -CLUDED, -CLUDING, -CLUDES to remove or set apart from others

SECOND *v* -ED, -ING, -S to give support or encouragement to

SECONDE *n pl.* -S a position in fencing

SECONDER *n pl.* -S one that seconds

SECONDLY *adv* in the next place after the first

SECONDO *n pl.* -DI the lower part in a piano duet

SECPAR *n pl.* -S a parsec

SECRECY *n pl.* -CIES the condition of being secret

SECRET *adj* -CRETER, -CRETEST kept from knowledge or view

SECRET *n pl.* -S something kept from the knowledge of others

SECRETE *v* -CRETED, -CRETING, -CRETES to generate and separate out from cells or bodily fluids

SECRETIN *n pl.* -S a hormone

SECRETLY *adv* in a secret manner

SECRETOR *n pl.* -S one that secretes

SECT *n pl.* -S a group of people united by common beliefs or interests

SECTARY *n pl.* -RIES a member of a sect

SECTILE *adj* capable of being cut smoothly

SECTION *v* -ED, -ING, -S to divide into sections (distinct parts)

SECTOR *v* -ED, -ING, -S to divide into sectors (sections)

SECTORAL *adj* of or pertaining to a sector

SECULAR *n pl.* -S a layman

SECUND *adj* having the parts or organs arranged on one side only **SECUNDLY** *adv*

SECUNDUM *adv* according to

SECURE *adj* -CURER, -CUREST free from danger **SECURELY** *adv*

SECURE *v* -CURED, -CURING, -CURES to make firm or tight

SECURER *n pl.* -S one that secures

SECUREST superlative of secure

SECURING present participle of secure

SECURITY *n pl.* -TIES the state of being secure

SEDAN *n pl.* -S a type of automobile

SEDARIM a pl. of seder

SEDATE *adj* -DATER, -DATEST calm **SEDATELY** *adv*

SEDATE *v* -DATED, -DATING, -DATES to administer a sedative to

SEDATION *n pl.* -S the reduction of stress or excitement by the use of sedatives

SEDATIVE *n pl.* -S a drug that induces a calm state

SEDER *n pl.* -DARIM or -DERS a Jewish ceremonial dinner

SEDERUNT *n pl.* -S a prolonged sitting

SEDGE *n pl.* -S a marsh plant

SEDGY *adj* SEDGIER, SEDGIEST abounding in sedge

SEDILE *n pl.* -LIA one of the seats in a church for the use of the officiating clergy

SEDILIUM *n pl.* -LIA sedile

SEDIMENT *v* -ED, -ING, -S to settle to the bottom of a liquid

SEDITION *n pl.* -S incitement of rebellion against a government

SEDUCE *v* -DUCED, -DUCING, -DUCES to lead astray **SEDUCIVE** *adj*

SEDUCER *n pl.* -S one that seduces

SEDULITY *n pl.* -TIES the state of being sedulous

SEDULOUS *adj* diligent

SEDUM *n pl.* -S a flowering plant

SEE *v* SAW, SEEN, SEEING, SEES to perceive with the eyes **SEEABLE** *adj*

SEECATCH *n pl.* -CATCHIE an adult male fur seal

SEED *v* -ED, -ING, -S to plant seeds (propagative plant structures) in

SEEDBED *n pl.* -S land prepared for seeding

SEEDCAKE *n pl.* -S a sweet cake containing aromatic seeds

SEEDCASE *n pl.* -S a pericarp

SEEDER n pl. -S one that seeds

SEEDIER comparative of seedy

SEEDIEST superlative of seedy

SEEDILY adv in a seedy manner

SEEDLESS adj having no seeds

SEEDLIKE adj resembling a seed

SEEDLING n pl. -S a young plant

SEEDMAN n pl. -MEN seedsman

SEEDPOD n pl. -S a type of seed vessel

SEEDSMAN n pl. -MEN a dealer in seeds

SEEDTIME n pl. -S the season for sowing seeds

SEEDY adj SEEDIER, SEEDIEST containing seeds; inferior in condition or quality

SEEING n pl. -S the act of one that sees

SEEK v SOUGHT, SEEKING, SEEKS to go in search of

SEEKER n pl. -S one that seeks

SEEL v -ED, -ING, -S to stitch closed the eyes of, as a falcon during training

SEELY adj frail

SEEM v -ED, -ING, -S to give the impression of being

SEEMER n pl. -S one that seems

SEEMING n pl. -S outward appearance

SEEMLY adj -LIER, -LIEST of pleasing appearance

SEEN past participle of see

SEEP v -ED, -ING, -S to pass slowly through small openings

SEEPAGE n pl. -S the quantity of fluid that has seeped

SEEPY adj SEEPIER, SEEPIEST soaked or oozing with water

SEER n pl. -S a prophet

SEERESS n pl. -ES a female seer

SEESAW v -ED, -ING, -S to move up and down or back and forth

SEETHE v SEETHED, SEETHING, SEETHES to surge or foam as if boiling

SEGETAL adj growing in fields of grain

SEGGAR n pl. -S a saggar

SEGMENT v -ED, -ING, -S to divide into sections

SEGNO n pl. -GNI or -GNOS a musical sign

SEGO n pl. -GOS a perennial herb

SEGUE v -GUED, -GUEING, -GUES to proceed without pause from one musical theme to another

SEI n pl. -S a rorqual

SEICENTO n pl. -TOS the seventeenth century

SEICHE n pl. -S an oscillation of the surface of a lake or landlocked sea

SEIDEL n pl. -S a large beer glass

SEIGNEUR n pl. -S seignior

SEIGNIOR n pl. -S a feudal lord

SEIGNORY n pl. -GNORIES the power of a seignior

SEINE v SEINED, SEINING, SEINES to catch fish with a large, vertically hanging net

SEINER n pl. -S one that seines

SEISE v SEISED, SEISING, SEISES to seize SEISABLE adj

SEISER n pl. -S seizer

SEISIN n pl. -S seizin

SEISING n pl. -S seizing

SEISM n pl. -S an earthquake SEISMAL, SEISMIC adj

SEISMISM n pl. -S the natural activity involved in earthquakes

SEISOR n pl. -S seizor

SEISURE n pl. -S seizure

SEIZE v SEIZED, SEIZING, SEIZES to take hold of suddenly and forcibly SEIZABLE adj

SEIZER n pl. -S one that seizes

SEIZIN n pl. -S legal possession of land

SEIZING n pl. -S the act of one that seizes

SEIZOR n pl. -S one that takes seizin

SEIZURE n pl. -S the act of seizing

SEJANT adj represented in a sitting postion — used of a heraldic animal

SEJEANT adj sejant

SEL n pl. -S self

SELADANG n pl. -S saladang

SELAH n pl. -S a word of unknown meaning often marking the end of a verse in the Psalms

SELAMLIK n pl. -S the portion of a Turkish house reserved for men

SELCOUTH adj unusual

SELDOM adj infrequent SELDOMLY adv

SELECT v -ED, -ING, -S to choose

SELECTEE n pl. -S one that is selected

SELECTLY adv by selection

SELECTOR n pl. -S one that selects

SELENATE n pl. -S a chemical salt

SELENIC adj pertaining to selenium

SELENIDE n pl. -S a compound of selenium

SELENITE n pl. -S a variety of gypsum

SELENIUM n pl. -S a nonmetallic element **SELENOUS** adj

SELF n pl. SELVES the total, essential, or particular being of one person

SELF v -ED, -ING, -S to inbreed

SELFDOM n pl. -S selfhood

SELFHEAL n pl. -S a perennial herb

SELFHOOD n pl. -S the state of being an individual person

SELFISH adj concerned chiefly or only with oneself

SELFLESS adj unselfish

SELFNESS n pl. -ES selfhood

SELFSAME adj identical

SELFWARD adv toward oneself

SELL v SOLD, SELLING, SELLS to give up to another for money or other valuable consideration **SELLABLE** adj

SELLE n pl. -S a saddle

SELLER n pl. -S one that sells

SELLOUT n pl. -S a performance for which all seats have been sold

SELSYN n pl. -S a type of remote-control device

SELTZER n pl. -S carbonated mineral water

SELVAGE n pl. -S the edge of a woven fabric finished to prevent raveling **SELVAGED** adj

SELVEDGE n pl. -S selvage

SELVES pl. of self

SEMANTIC adj pertaining to meaning

SEMATIC adj serving as a warning

SEME n pl. -S a type of ornamental pattern

SEMEME n pl. -S the meaning of a morpheme

SEMEN n pl. -MINA or -MENS a fluid produced in the male reproductive organs

SEMESTER n pl. -S a period constituting half of an academic year

SEMI n pl. -S a freight trailer

SEMIARID adj characterized by light rainfall

SEMIBALD adj partly bald

SEMICOMA n pl. -S a coma from which a person can be aroused

SEMIDEAF adj partly deaf

SEMIDOME n pl. -S a half dome

SEMIDRY adj moderately dry

SEMIFIT adj conforming somewhat to the lines of the body

SEMIGALA adj somewhat gala

SEMIHARD adj moderately hard

SEMIHIGH adj moderately high

SEMIHOBO n pl. -BOS or -BOES a person having some of the characteristics of a hobo

SEMILOG adj having one scale logarithmic and the other arithmetic

SEMIMAT adj having a slight luster

SEMIMATT adj semimat

SEMIMUTE adj having partially lost the faculty of speech

SEMINA a pl. of semen

SEMINAL adj pertaining to semen

SEMINAR n pl. -S an advanced study group at a college or university

SEMINARY n pl. -NARIES a school for the training of priests, ministers, or rabbis

SEMINUDE adj partly nude

SEMIOSIS n pl. -OSES a process in which something functions as a sign to an organism

SEMIOTIC n pl. -S a general theory of signs and symbolism

SEMIPRO n pl. -PROS one who is engaged in some field or sport for pay on a part-time basis

SEMIRAW adj somewhat raw

SEMIS n pl. -MISES a coin of ancient Rome

SEMISOFT adj moderately soft

SEMITIST n pl. -S one who favors Jewish interests

SEMITONE n pl. -S a type of musical tone

SEMIWILD adj somewhat wild

SEMOLINA n pl. -S a granular product of wheat used for pasta

SEMPLE adj of humble birth

SEMPLICE adj simple — used as a musical direction

SEMPRE adv in the same manner throughout — used as a musical direction

SEN n pl. SEN a monetary unit of Japan

SENARIUS *n pl.* -NARII a Greek or Latin verse consisting of six metrical feet

SENARY *adj* pertaining to the number six

SENATE *n pl.* -S an assembly having high deliberative and legislative functions

SENATOR *n pl.* -S a member of a senate

SEND *v* SENT, SENDING, SENDS to cause to go SENDABLE *adj*

SENDAL *n pl.* -S a silk fabric

SENDER *n pl.* -S one that sends

SENDOFF *n pl.* -S a farewell celebration

SENECA *n pl.* -S senega

SENECIO *n pl.* -CIOS a flowering plant

SENEGA *n pl.* -S a medicinal plant root

SENGI *n pl.* SENGI a monetary unit of Zaire

SENHOR *n pl.* -S or -ES a Portuguese or Brazilian gentleman

SENHORA *n pl.* -S a married Portuguese or Brazilian woman

SENILE *n pl.* -S one who exhibits senility

SENILELY *adv* in a senile manner

SENILITY *n pl.* -TIES mental and physical infirmity due to old age

SENIOR *n pl.* -S a person who is older than another

SENITI *n pl.* SENITI a monetary unit of Tonga

SENNA *n pl.* -S a medicinal plant

SENNET *n pl.* -S a call sounded on a trumpet signaling the entrance or exit of actors

SENNIGHT *n pl.* -S a week

SENNIT *n pl.* -S braided straw used in making hats

SENOPIA *n pl.* -S an improvement of near vision

SENOR *n pl.* -S or -ES a Spanish gentleman

SENORA *n pl.* -S a married Spanish woman

SENORITA *n pl.* -S an unmarried Spanish girl or woman

SENSA pl. of sensum

SENSATE *v* -SATED, -SATING, -SATES to sense

SENSE *v* SENSED, SENSING, SENSES to perceive by the senses (any of certain agencies through which an individual receives impressions of the external world)

SENSEFUL *adj* sensible

SENSIBLE *adj* -BLER, -BLEST having or showing good judgment SENSIBLY *adv*

SENSIBLE *n pl.* -S something that can be sensed

SENSILLA *n/pl* simple sense organs

SENSING present participle of sense

SENSOR *n pl.* -S a device that receives and responds to a stimulus

SENSORIA *n/pl* the parts of the brain concerned with the reception and interpretation of sensory stimuli

SENSORY *adj* pertaining to the senses or sensation

SENSUAL *adj* pertaining to the physical senses

SENSUM *n pl.* -SA an object of perception or sensation

SENSUOUS *adj* pertaining to or derived from the senses

SENT past tense of send

SENTENCE *v* -TENCED, -TENCING, -TENCES to declare judicially the extent of punishment to be imposed

SENTI *n pl.* SENTI a monetary unit of Tanzania

SENTIENT *n pl.* -S a person or thing capable of sensation

SENTINEL *v* -NELED, -NELING, -NELS or -NELLED, -NELLING, -NELS to stand guard

SENTRY *n pl.* -TRIES one who stands guard

SEPAL *n pl.* -S one of the individual leaves of a calyx SEPALED, SEPALINE, SEPALLED, SEPALOID, SEPALOUS *adj*

SEPARATE *v* -RATED, -RATING, -RATES to set or keep apart

SEPIA *n pl.* -S a brown pigment SEPIC *adj*

SEPOY *n pl.* -POYS a native of India serving in the British army

SEPPUKU *n pl.* -S a Japanese form of suicide

SEPSIS *n pl.* SEPSES bacterial invasion of the body

SEPT *n pl.* -S a clan

SEPTA pl. of septum

SEPTAL *adj* pertaining to a septum

SEPTARIA *n/pl* limestone nodules

SEPTATE *adj* having a septum

SEPTET   *n* pl. -S a group of seven

SEPTETTE   *n* pl. -S septet

SEPTIC   *n* pl. -S an agent producing sepsis **SEPTICAL** *adj*

SEPTIME   *n* pl. -S a position in fencing

SEPTUM   *n* pl. -TA a dividing membrane or partition

SEPTUPLE   *v* -PLED, -PLING, -PLES to make seven times as great

SEQUEL   *n* pl. -S something that follows and serves as a continuation

SEQUELA   *n* pl. -QUELAE an abnormal condition resulting from a preceding disease

SEQUENCE   *v* -QUENCED, -QUENCING, -QUENCES to arrange in consecutive order

SEQUENCY   *n* pl. -CIES the following of one thing after another

SEQUENT   *n* pl. -S something that follows

SEQUIN   *n* pl. -S a shiny ornamental disk **SEQUINED** *adj*

SEQUITUR   *n* pl. -S the conclusion of an inference

SEQUOIA   *n* pl. -S a large evergreen tree

SER   *n* pl. -S a unit of weight of India

SERA   a pl. of serum

SERAC   *n* pl. -S a large mass of ice broken off of a glacier

SERAGLIO   *n* pl. -GLIOS a harem

SERAI   *n* pl. -S a Turkish palace

SERAIL   *n* pl. -S a seraglio

SERAL   *adj* pertaining to a series of ecological changes

SERAPE   *n* pl. -S a colorful woolen shawl

SERAPH   *n* pl. -APHS, -APHIM, or -APHIN a winged celestial being **SERAPHIC** *adj*

SERAPHIM   *n* pl. -S seraph

SERDAB   *n* pl. -S a chamber within an ancient Egyptian tomb

SERE   *adj* SERER, SEREST withered; dry

SERE   *v* SERED, SERING, SERES to sear

SEREIN   *n* pl. -S a fine rain falling from an apparently clear sky

SERENADE   *v* -NADED, -NADING, -NADES to perform an honorific evening song for

SERENATA   *n* pl. -TAS or -TE a dramatic cantata

SERENE   *adj* SERENER, SERENEST calm; tranquil **SERENELY** *adv*

SERENE   *n* pl. -S a serene condition or expanse

SERENITY   *n* pl. -TIES the state of being serene

SERER   comparative of sere

SEREST   superlative of sere

SERF   *n* pl. -S a feudal slave

SERFAGE   *n* pl. -S serfdom

SERFDOM   *n* pl. -S the state of being a serf

SERFHOOD   *n* pl. -S serfdom

SERFISH   *adj* characteristic of a serf

SERFLIKE   *adj* serfish

SERGE   *n* pl. -S a twilled fabric

SERGEANT   *n* pl. -S a noncommissioned military officer

SERGING   *n* pl. -S a process of finishing the raw edges of a fabric

SERIAL   *n* pl. -S a literary or dramatic work presented in successive installments

SERIALLY   *adv* in the manner or form of a serial

SERIATE   *v* -ATED, -ATING, -ATES to put into a series

SERIATIM   *adv* serially

SERICIN   *n* pl. -S a kind of protein

SERIEMA   *n* pl. -S a Brazilian bird

SERIES   *n* pl. SERIES an arrangement of one after another

SERIF   *n* pl. -S a fine line used to finish off the main stroke of a letter

SERIN   *n* pl. -S a European finch

SERINE   *n* pl. -S an amino acid

SERING   present participle of sere

SERINGA   *n* pl. -S a Brazilian tree

SERIOUS   *adj* thoughtful or subdued in appearance or manner

SERJEANT   *n* pl. -S sergeant

SERMON   *n* pl. -S a religious discourse **SERMONIC** *adj*

SEROLOGY   *n* pl. -GIES the science of serums

SEROSA   *n* pl. -SAS or -SAE a thin membrane lining certain bodily cavities **SEROSAL** *adj*

SEROSITY   *n* pl. -TIES the quality or state of being serous

SEROTINE   *n* pl. -S a European bat

SEROTYPE   *n* pl. -S a group of closely related organisms distinguished by a common set of antigens

SEROUS *adj* of or resembling serum

SEROW *n pl.* -S an Asian antelope

SERPENT *n pl.* -S a snake

SERPIGO *n pl.* -GOES or -GINES a spreading skin eruption

SERRANID *n pl.* -S a marine fish

SERRATE *v* -RATED, -RATING, -RATES to furnish with toothlike projections

SERRY *v* -RIED, -RYING, -RIES to crowd together

SERUM *n pl.* -RUMS or -RA the watery portion of whole blood **SERUMAL** *adj*

SERVABLE *adj* capable of serving or being served

SERVAL *n pl.* -S an African wildcat

SERVANT *n pl.* -S one that serves others

SERVE *v* SERVED, SERVING, SERVES to work for

SERVER *n pl.* -S one that serves another

SERVICE *v* -VICED, -VICING, -VICES to repair

SERVICER *n pl.* -S one that services

SERVILE *adj* slavishly submissive

SERVING *n pl.* -S a portion of food

SERVITOR *n pl.* -S a male servant

SERVO *n pl.* -VOS an automatic device used to control another mechanism

SESAME *n pl.* -S an East Indian plant

SESAMOID *n pl.* -S a nodular mass of bone or cartilage

SESSILE *adj* permanently attached

SESSION *n pl.* -S a meeting of a legislative or judicial body for the transaction of business

SESSPOOL *n pl.* -S cesspool

SESTERCE *n pl.* -S a coin of ancient Rome

SESTET *n pl.* -S a stanza of six lines

SESTINA *n pl.* -S a type of verse form

SESTINE *n pl.* -S sestina

SET *v* SET, SETTING, SETS to put in a particular position

SETA *n pl.* -TAE a coarse, stiff hair **SETAL** *adj*

SETBACK *n pl.* -S a defeat

SETIFORM *adj* having the form of a seta

SETLINE *n pl.* -S a strong fishing line

SETOFF *n pl.* -S something that offsets something else

SETON *n pl.* -S a type of surgical thread

SETOSE *adj* covered with setae

SETOUS *adj* setose

SETOUT *n pl.* -S a display

SETSCREW *n pl.* -S a type of screw

SETTEE *n pl.* -S a long seat with a high back

SETTER *n pl.* -S one that sets

SETTING *n pl.* -S the scenery used in a dramatic production

SETTLE *v* -TLED, -TLING, -TLES to place in a desired state or order

SETTLER *n pl.* -S one that settles

SETTLING *n pl.* -S sediment

SETTLOR *n pl.* -S one that makes a legal settlement

SETULOSE *adj* covered with seta

SETULOUS *adj* setulose

SETUP *n pl.* -S the way something is arranged

SEVEN *n pl.* -S a number

SEVENTH *n pl.* -S one of seven equal parts

SEVENTY *n pl.* -TIES a number

SEVER *v* -ED, -ING, -S to divide or cut into parts

SEVERAL *n pl.* -S a few persons or things

SEVERE *adj* -VERER, -VEREST unsparing in the treatment of others **SEVERELY** *adv*

SEVERITY *n pl.* -TIES the quality or state of being severe

SEW *v* SEWED, SEWN, SEWING, SEWS to mend or fasten with a needle and thread

SEWAGE *n pl.* -S the waste matter carried off by sewers

SEWAN *n pl.* -S seawan

SEWAR *n pl.* -S a medieval servant

SEWER *n pl.* -S an underground conduit for carrying off liquid and solid waste

SEWERAGE *n pl.* -S sewage

SEWING *n pl.* -S material that has been or is to be sewed

SEWN *a* past participle of sew

SEX *v* -ED, -ING, -ES to determine the sex (the property by which organisms are classified according to reproductive functions) of

SEXIER comparative of sexy

SEXIEST superlative of sexy

SEXILY *adv* in a sexy manner

SEXINESS n pl. -ES the quality or state of being sexy

SEXISM n pl. -S prejudice or discrimination against women

SEXIST n pl. -S one that practices sexism

SEXLESS adj lacking sexual characteristics

SEXOLOGY n pl. -GIES the study of human sexual behavior

SEXPOT n pl. -S a sexually attractive woman

SEXT n pl. -S one of seven canonical daily periods for prayer and devotion

SEXTAIN n pl. -S a stanza of six lines

SEXTAN n pl. -S a recurrent malarial fever

SEXTANT n pl. -S an instrument for measuring angular distances

SEXTARII n/pl ancient Roman units of liquid measure

SEXTET n pl. -S a group of six

SEXTETTE n pl. -S sextet

SEXTILE n pl. -S the position of two celestial bodies when they are sixty degrees apart

SEXTO n pl. -TOS sixmo

SEXTON n pl. -S a maintenance worker of a church

SEXTUPLE v -PLED, -PLING, -PLES to make six times as great

SEXTUPLY adv to six times as much or as many

SEXUAL adj pertaining to sex SEXUALLY adv

SEXY adj SEXIER, SEXIEST arousing sexual desire

SFERICS n/pl an electronic detector of storms

SFORZATO n pl. -TOS the playing of a tone or chord with sudden force

SFUMATO n pl. -TOS a technique used in painting

SH interj — used to urge silence

SHABBY adj -BIER, -BIEST ragged SHABBILY adv

SHACK n pl. -S a shanty

SHACKLE v -LED, -LING, -LES to confine with metal fastenings placed around the wrists or ankles

SHACKLER n pl. -S one that shackles

SHACKO n pl. -KOS or -KOES shako

SHAD n pl. -S a food fish

SHADBLOW n pl. -S a shadbush

SHADBUSH n pl. -ES a flowering tree or shrub

SHADCHAN n pl. -CHANIM or -CHANS a Jewish marriage broker

SHADDOCK n pl. -S a citrus fruit

SHADE v SHADED, SHADING, SHADES to screen from light or heat

SHADER n pl. -S one that shades

SHADFLY n pl. -FLIES a winged insect

SHADIER comparative of shady

SHADIEST superlative of shady

SHADILY adv in a shady manner

SHADING n pl. -S protection against light or heat

SHADOOF n pl. -S a device used in Egypt for raising water for irrigation

SHADOW v -ED, -ING, -S to make dark or gloomy

SHADOWER n pl. -S one that shadows

SHADOWY adj -OWIER, -OWIEST dark

SHADRACH n pl. -S a mass of unfused material in the hearth of a blast furnace

SHADUF n pl. -S shadoof

SHADY adj SHADIER, SHADIEST shaded

SHAFT v -ED, -ING, -S to push or propel with a pole

SHAFTING n pl. -S a system of rods for transmitting motion or power

SHAG v SHAGGED, SHAGGING, SHAGS to make shaggy

SHAGBARK n pl. -S a hardwood tree

SHAGGY adj -GIER, -GIEST covered with long, coarse hair SHAGGILY adv

SHAGREEN n pl. -S the rough skin of certain sharks

SHAH n pl. -S an Iranian ruler

SHAHDOM n pl. -S the territory ruled by a shah

SHAIRD n pl. -S shard

SHAIRN n pl. -S sharn

SHAITAN n pl. -S an evil spirit

SHAKE v SHOOK, SHAKEN, SHAKING, SHAKES to move to and fro with short, rapid movements SHAKABLE adj

SHAKEOUT n pl. -S a minor economic recession

SHAKER n pl. -S one that shakes

SHAKEUP n pl. -S a total reorganization

SHAKIER comparative of shaky

SHAKIEST	superlative of shaky
SHAKILY	adv in a shaky manner
SHAKING	present participle of shake
SHAKO	n pl. -KOS or -KOES a type of military hat
SHAKY	adj SHAKIER, SHAKIEST shaking
SHALE	n pl. -S a fissile rock
SHALED	adj having a shell or husk
SHALIER	comparative of shaly
SHALIEST	superlative of shaly
SHALL	v present sing. 2d person SHALL or SHALT, past sing. 2d person SHOULD, SHOULDST, or SHOULDEST — used as an auxiliary to express futurity, inevitability, or command
SHALLOON	n pl. -S a woolen fabric
SHALLOP	n pl. -S a small, open boat
SHALLOT	n pl. -S a plant resembling an onion
SHALLOW	adj -LOWER, -LOWEST having little depth
SHALLOW	v -ED, -ING, -S to make shallow
SHALOM	interj peace — used as a Jewish greeting and farewell
SHALT	a present 2d person sing. of shall
SHALY	adj SHALIER, SHALIEST resembling shale
SHAM	v SHAMMED, SHAMMING, SHAMS to feign
SHAMABLE	adj capable of being shamed
SHAMAN	n pl. -S a medicine man among certain North American Indians SHAMANIC adj
SHAMBLE	v -BLED, -BLING, -BLES to walk awkwardly
SHAME	v SHAMED, SHAMING, SHAMES to cause to feel a painful sense of guilt or degradation
SHAMEFUL	adj disgraceful
SHAMES	n pl. -MOSIM shammes
SHAMING	present participle of shame
SHAMMAS	n pl. -MASIM shammes
SHAMMASH	n pl. -MASHIM shammes
SHAMMED	past tense of sham
SHAMMER	n pl. -S one that shams
SHAMMES	n pl. -MOSIM a minor official of a synagogue
SHAMMIED	past tense of shammy
SHAMMIES	present 3d person sing. of shammy
SHAMMING	present participle of sham
SHAMMOS	n pl. -MOSIM shammes
SHAMMOSIM	pl. of shammes
SHAMMY	v -MIED, -MYING, -MIES to chamois
SHAMOIS	n pl. SHAMOIS chamois
SHAMOSIM	pl. of shames
SHAMOY	v -ED, -ING, -S to chamois
SHAMPOO	v -ED, -ING, -S to cleanse with a special preparation
SHAMROCK	n pl. -S a three-leaved plant
SHAMUS	n pl. -ES a private detective
SHANDY	n pl. -DIES an alcoholic drink
SHANGHAI	v -ED, -ING, -S to kidnap for service aboard a ship
SHANK	v -ED, -ING, -S to hit sharply to the right, as a golf ball
SHANTEY	n pl. -TEYS chantey
SHANTI	n pl. -S peace
SHANTIES	pl. of shanty
SHANTIH	n pl. -S shanti
SHANTUNG	n pl. -S a silk fabric
SHANTY	n pl. -TIES a small, crudely built dwelling
SHAPE	v SHAPED, SHAPEN, SHAPING, SHAPES to give shape (outward form) to SHAPABLE adj
SHAPELY	adj -LIER, -LIEST having a pleasing shape
SHAPER	n pl. -S one that shapes
SHAPEUP	n pl. -S a system of hiring a work crew
SHAPING	present participle of shape
SHARD	n pl. -S a fragment of broken pottery
SHARE	v SHARED, SHARING, SHARES to have, get, or use in common with another or others SHARABLE adj
SHARER	n pl. -S one that shares
SHARIF	n pl. -S sherif
SHARING	present participle of share
SHARK	v -ED, -ING, -S to live by trickery
SHARKER	n pl. -S one that sharks
SHARN	n pl. -S cow dung SHARNY adj
SHARP	adj SHARPER, SHARPEST suitable for or capable of cutting or piercing
SHARP	v -ED, -ING, -S to raise in pitch, as a musical tone
SHARPEN	v -ED, -ING, -S to make sharp

SHARPER	n pl. -S a swindler
SHARPIE	n pl. -S a very alert person
SHARPLY	adv in a sharp manner
SHARPY	n pl. SHARPIES sharpie
SHASHLIK	n pl. -S kabob
SHASLIK	n pl. -S shashlik
SHAT	a past tense of shit — an offensive term
SHATTER	v -ED, -ING, -S to break into pieces
SHAUGH	n pl. -S a thicket
SHAUL	v -ED, -ING, -S to shoal
SHAVE	v SHAVED, SHAVEN, SHAVING, SHAVES to sever the hair close to the roots SHAVABLE adj
SHAVER	n pl. -S one that shaves
SHAVIE	n pl. -S a trick or prank
SHAVING	n pl. -S something shaved off
SHAW	v SHAWED, SHAWN, SHAWING, SHAWS to show
SHAWL	v -ED, -ING, -S to wrap in a shawl (a piece of cloth worn as a covering)
SHAWM	n pl. -S an early woodwind instrument
SHAWN	past participle of shaw
SHAY	n pl. SHAYS a chaise
SHE	n pl. -S a female person
SHEA	n pl. -S an African tree
SHEAF	v -ED, -ING, -S to sheave
SHEAL	n pl. -S shealing
SHEALING	n pl. -S a shepherd's hut
SHEAR	v SHEARED or SHORE, SHORN, SHEARING, SHEARS to cut the hair from
SHEARER	n pl. -S one that shears
SHEATH	v -ED, -ING, -S to sheathe
SHEATHE	v SHEATHED, SHEATHING, SHEATHES to put into a protective case
SHEATHER	n pl. -S one that sheathes
SHEAVE	v SHEAVED, SHEAVING, SHEAVES to gather into a bundle
SHEBANG	n pl. -S a situation, organization, or matter
SHEBEAN	n pl. -S shebeen
SHEBEEN	n pl. -S a place where liquor is sold illegally
SHED	v SHEDDED, SHEDDING, SHEDS to house in a shed (a small, low structure)

SHEDABLE	adj capable of being cast off
SHEDDER	n pl. -S one that casts off something
SHEDDING	present participle of shed
SHEEN	v -ED, -ING, -S to shine
SHEENEY	n pl. -NEYS sheenie — an offensive term
SHEENFUL	adj shining
SHEENIE	n pl. -S a Jew — an offensive term
SHEENY	adj SHEENIER, SHEENIEST shining
SHEEP	n pl. SHEEP a ruminant mammal
SHEEPDOG	n pl. -S a dog trained to guard and herd sheep
SHEEPISH	adj embarrassed
SHEEPMAN	n pl. -MEN a person who raises sheep
SHEER	v -ED, -ING, -S to swerve
SHEER	adj SHEERER, SHEEREST of very thin texture SHEERLY adv
SHEET	v -ED, -ING, -S to cover with a sheet (a thin, rectangular piece of material)
SHEETER	n pl. -S one that sheets
SHEETFED	adj pertaining to a type of printing press
SHEETING	n pl. -S material in the form of sheets
SHEEVE	n pl. -S a grooved pulley wheel
SHEGETZ	n pl. SHKOTZIM a non-Jewish boy or young man
SHEIK	n pl. -S an Arab chief
SHEIKDOM	n pl. -S the area ruled by a sheik
SHEIKH	n pl. -S sheik
SHEITAN	n pl. -S shaitan
SHEKEL	n pl. -S an ancient unit of weight and money
SHELDUCK	n pl. -S a European duck
SHELF	n pl. SHELVES a flat rigid structure used to support articles
SHELFFUL	n pl. -S as much as a shelf can hold
SHELL	v -ED, -ING, -S to divest of a shell (a hard outer covering)
SHELLAC	v -LACKED, -LACKING, -LACS to cover with a thin varnish
SHELLACK	v -ED, -ING, -S to shellac
SHELLER	n pl. -S one that shells
SHELLY	adj SHELLIER, SHELLIEST abounding in seashells

SHELTER v -ED, -ING, -S to provide cover or protection for

SHELTIE n pl. -S a small, shaggy pony

SHELTY n pl. -TIES sheltie

SHELVE v SHELVED, SHELVING, SHELVES to place on a shelf

SHELVER n pl. -S one that shelves

SHELVES pl. of shelf

SHELVING n pl. -S material for shelves

SHELVY adj SHELVIER, SHELVIEST inclining gradually

SHEND v SHENT, SHENDING, SHENDS to disgrace

SHEOL n pl. -S hell

SHEPHERD v -ED, -ING, -S to watch over carefully

SHERBERT n pl. -S sherbet

SHERBET n pl. -S a frozen fruit-flavored mixture

SHERD n pl. -S shard

SHEREEF n pl. -S sherif

SHERIF n pl. -S an Arab ruler

SHERIFF n pl. -S a law-enforcement officer of a county

SHERLOCK n pl. -S a detective

SHEROOT n pl. -S cheroot

SHERRIS n pl. -RISES sherry

SHERRY n pl. -RIES a type of wine

SHETLAND n pl. -S a wool yarn

SHEUCH n pl. -S sheugh

SHEUGH n pl. -S a ditch

SHEW v SHEWED, SHEWN, SHEWING, SHEWS to show

SHEWER n pl. -S one that shews

SHH interj sh

SHIBAH n pl. -S shiva

SHICKSA n pl. -S shiksa

SHIED past tense of shy

SHIEL n pl. -S shieling

SHIELD v -ED, -ING, -S to provide with a protective cover or shelter

SHIELDER n pl. -S one that shields

SHIELING n pl. -S shealing

SHIER n pl. -S a horse having a tendency to shy

SHIES present 3d person sing. of shy

SHIEST a superlative of shy

SHIFT v -ED, -ING, -S to move from one position to another

SHIFTER n pl. -S one that shifts

SHIFTY adj SHIFTIER, SHIFTIEST tricky SHIFTILY adv

SHIGELLA n pl. -LAE or -LAS any of a genus of aerobic bacteria

SHIKAR v -KARRED, -KARRING, -KARS to hunt

SHIKAREE n pl. -S a big game hunter

SHIKARI n pl. -S shikaree

SHIKARRED past tense of shikar

SHIKARRING present participle of shikar

SHIKSA n pl. -S a non-Jewish girl or young woman

SHIKSE n pl. -S shiksa

SHILINGI n pl. SHILINGI a monetary unit of Tanzania

SHILL v -ED, -ING, -S to act as a decoy

SHILLALA n pl. -S a short, thick club

SHILLING n pl. -S a former monetary unit of Great Britain

SHILPIT adj sickly

SHILY adv in a shy manner

SHIM v SHIMMED, SHIMMING, SHIMS to fill out or level by inserting a thin wedge

SHIMMER v -ED, -ING, -S to glimmer

SHIMMERY adj shimmering

SHIMMING present participle of shim

SHIMMY v -MIED, -MYING, -MIES to vibrate or wobble

SHIN v SHINNED, SHINNING, SHINS to climb by gripping and pulling alternately with the hands and legs

SHINBONE n pl. -S the tibia

SHINDIG n pl. -S an elaborate dance or party

SHINDY n pl. -DYS or -DIES a shindig

SHINE v SHONE or SHINED, SHINING, SHINES to emit light

SHINER n pl. -S one that shines

SHINGLE v -GLED, -GLING, -GLES to cover with shingles (thin, oblong pieces of building material)

SHINGLER n pl. -S one that shingles

SHINGLY adj covered with small, loose stones

SHINIER comparative of shiny

SHINIEST superlative of shiny

SHINILY adv in a shiny manner

SHINING adj emitting or reflecting light

SHINLEAF n pl. -LEAFS or -LEAVES a perennial herb

SHINNED past of shin

SHINNERY n pl. -NERIES a dense growth of small trees

SHINNEY	n pl. -NEYS a form of hockey
SHINNING	present participle of shin
SHINNY	v -NIED, -NYING, -NIES to shin
SHINY	adj SHINIER, SHINIEST filled with light
SHIP	v SHIPPED, SHIPPING, SHIPS to transport by ship (a vessel suitable for navigation in deep water)
SHIPLAP	n pl. -S an overlapping joint used in carpentry
SHIPLOAD	n pl. -S as much as a ship can carry
SHIPMAN	n pl. -MEN a sailor
SHIPMATE	n pl. -S a fellow sailor
SHIPMENT	n pl. -S something that is shipped
SHIPPED	past tense of ship
SHIPPEN	n pl. -S a cowshed
SHIPPER	n pl. -S one that ships
SHIPPING	n pl. -S the business of one that ships
SHIPPON	n pl. -S shippen
SHIPSIDE	n pl. -S the area alongside a ship
SHIPWAY	n pl. -WAYS a canal deep enough to serve ships
SHIPWORM	n pl. -S a wormlike mollusk
SHIPYARD	n pl. -S a place where ships are built or repaired
SHIRE	n pl. -S a territorial division of Great Britain
SHIRK	v -ED, -ING, -S to avoid work or duty
SHIRKER	n pl. -S one that shirks
SHIRR	v -ED, -ING, -S to draw into three or more parallel rows, as cloth
SHIRRING	n pl. -S a shirred arrangement of cloth
SHIRT	n pl. -S a garment for the upper part of the body
SHIRTING	n pl. -S fabric used for making shirts
SHIRTY	adj SHIRTIER, SHIRTIEST angry
SHIST	n pl. -S schist
SHIT	v SHITTED or SHAT, SHITTING, SHITS to defecate — an offensive term
SHITTAH	n pl. -S a hardwood tree
SHITTIM	n pl. -S the wood of the shittah
SHITTING	present participle of shit — an offensive term
SHIV	n pl. -S a knife

SHIVA	n pl. -S a period of mourning
SHIVAH	n pl. -S shiva
SHIVAREE	v -REED, -REEING, -REES to chivaree
SHIVE	n pl. -S a thin fragment
SHIVER	v -ED, -ING, -S to tremble with fear or cold
SHIVERER	n pl. -S one that shivers
SHIVERY	adj shivering
SHKOTZIM	pl. of shegetz
SHLEMIEL	n pl. -S an unlucky bungler
SHLOCK	n pl. -S schlock
SHMO	n pl. SHMOES schmo
SHNAPS	n pl. SHNAPS schnapps
SHOAL	adj SHOALER, SHOALEST shallow
SHOAL	v -ED, -ING, -S to become shallow
SHOALY	adj SHOALIER, SHOALIEST full of shallow areas
SHOAT	n pl. -S a young hog
SHOCK	v -ED, -ING, -S to strike with great surprise, horror, or disgust
SHOCKER	n pl. -S one that shocks
SHOD	a past tense of shoe
SHODDEN	a past participle of shoe
SHODDY	adj -DIER, -DIEST of inferior quality SHODDILY adv
SHODDY	n pl. -DIES a low-quality wool
SHOE	n pl. SHOES or SHOON a covering for the foot
SHOE	v SHOD or SHOED, SHODDEN, SHOEING, SHOES to provide with shoes
SHOEBILL	n pl. -S a wading bird
SHOEHORN	v -ED, -ING, -S to force into a small space
SHOELACE	n pl. -S a lace for fastening a shoe
SHOEPAC	n pl. -S a waterproof boot
SHOEPACK	n pl. -S shoepac
SHOER	n pl. -S one that shoes horses
SHOETREE	n pl. -S a device shaped like a foot that is inserted into a shoe to preserve its shape
SHOFAR	n pl. SHOFARS or SHOFROTH a ram's-horn trumpet blown in certain Jewish rituals
SHOG	v SHOGGED, SHOGGING, SHOGS to move along
SHOGUN	n pl. -S a former military leader of Japan SHOGUNAL adj

SHOJI *n pl.* -S a paper screen used as a partition or door in a Japanese house

SHOLOM *interj* shalom

SHONE a past tense of shine

SHOO *v* -ED, -ING, -S to drive away

SHOOFLY *n pl.* -FLIES a child's rocker

SHOOK *n pl.* -S a set of parts for assembling a barrel or packing

SHOOL *v* -ED, -ING, -S to shovel

SHOON a pl. of shoe

SHOOT *v* SHOT, SHOOTING, SHOOTS to hit, wound, or kill with a missile discharged from a weapon

SHOOTER *n pl.* -S one that shoots

SHOOTING *n pl.* -S the act of one that shoots

SHOP *v* SHOPPED, SHOPPING, SHOPS to examine goods with intent to buy

SHOPBOY *n pl.* -BOYS a salesclerk

SHOPGIRL *n pl.* -S a salesgirl

SHOPHAR *n pl.* -PHARS or -PHROTH shofar

SHOPLIFT *v* -ED, -ING, -S to steal goods from a store

SHOPMAN *n pl.* -MEN one who owns or operates a small store

SHOPPE *n pl.* -S a small store

SHOPPED past tense of shop

SHOPPER *n pl.* -S one that shops

SHOPPING *n pl.* -S the act of one that shops

SHOPTALK *n pl.* -S conversation concerning one's business or occupation

SHOPWORN *adj* worn out from being on display in a store

SHORAN *n pl.* -S a type of navigational system

SHORE *v* SHORED, SHORING, SHORES to prop with a supporting timber

SHORING *n pl.* -S a system of supporting timbers

SHORL *n pl.* -S schorl

SHORN a past participle of shear

SHORT *adj* SHORTER, SHORTEST having little length

SHORT *v* -ED, -ING, -S to cause a type of electrical malfunction in

SHORTAGE *n pl.* -S an insufficient supply or amount

SHORTCUT *n pl.* -S a shorter or quicker way

SHORTEN *v* -ED, -ING, -S to make or become shorter

SHORTIA *n pl.* -S a perennial herb

SHORTIE *n pl.* -S shorty

SHORTIES pl. of shorty

SHORTISH *adj* somewhat short

SHORTLY *adv* in a short time

SHORTY *n pl.* SHORTIES one that is short

SHOT *v* SHOTTED, SHOTTING, SHOTS to load with shot (small lead or steel pellets)

SHOTE *n pl.* -S shoat

SHOTGUN *v* -GUNNED, -GUNNING, -GUNS to shoot with a type of gun

SHOTT *n pl.* -S chott

SHOTTED past tense of shot

SHOTTEN *adj* having spawned — used of a fish

SHOTTING present participle of shot

SHOULD past tense of shall

SHOULDER *v* -ED, -ING, -S to assume the burden or responsibility of

SHOULDEST a 2d person sing. past tense of shall

SHOULDST a 2d person sing. past tense of shall

SHOUT *v* -ED, -ING, -S to utter loudly

SHOUTER *n pl.* -S one that shouts

SHOVE *v* SHOVED, SHOVING, SHOVES to push roughly

SHOVEL *v* -ELED, -ELING, -ELS or -ELLED, -ELLING, -ELS to take up with a shovel (a digging implement)

SHOVELER *n pl.* -S one that shovels

SHOVER *n pl.* -S one that shoves

SHOVING present participle of shove

SHOW *v* SHOWED, SHOWN, SHOWING, SHOWS to cause or permit to be seen

SHOWBOAT *n pl.* -S a boat on which theatrical performances are given

SHOWCASE *v* -CASED, -CASING, -CASES to exhibit

SHOWDOWN *n pl.* -S an event that forces the conclusion of an issue

SHOWER *v* -ED, -ING, -S to fall in a brief, heavy rain

SHOWERY *adj* showering

SHOWGIRL *n pl.* -S a chorus girl

SHOWIER	comparative of showy
SHOWIEST	superlative of showy
SHOWILY	*adv* in a showy manner
SHOWING	*n pl.* -S an exhibition or display
SHOWMAN	*n pl.* -MEN a theatrical producer
SHOWN	past participle of show
SHOWOFF	*n pl.* -S one given to pretentious display
SHOWROOM	*n pl.* -S a room used for the display of merchandise
SHOWY	*adj* SHOWIER, SHOWIEST making a great or brilliant display
SHRANK	past tense of shrink
SHRAPNEL	*n pl.* SHRAPNEL fragments from an exploding bomb, mine, or shell
SHRED	*v* SHREDDED, SHREDDING, SHREDS to tear into small strips
SHREDDER	*n pl.* -S one that shreds
SHREW	*v* -ED, -ING, -S to curse
SHREWD	*adj* SHREWDER, SHREWDEST having keen insight **SHREWDLY** *adv*
SHREWISH	*adj* ill-tempered
SHRI	*n pl.* -S sri
SHRIEK	*v* -ED, -ING, -S to utter a shrill cry
SHRIEKER	*n pl.* -S one that shrieks
SHRIEKY	*adj* SHRIEKIER, SHRIEKIEST shrill
SHRIEVAL	*adj* pertaining to a sheriff
SHRIEVE	*v* SHRIEVED, SHRIEVING, SHRIEVES to shrive
SHRIFT	*n pl.* -S the act of shriving
SHRIKE	*n pl.* -S a predatory bird
SHRILL	*adj* SHRILLER, SHRILLEST having a high-pitched and piercing quality **SHRILLY** *adv*
SHRILL	*v* -ED, -ING, -S to utter a shrill sound
SHRIMP	*v* -ED, -ING, -S to catch shrimps (small marine decapods)
SHRIMPER	*n pl.* -S a shrimp fisher
SHRIMPY	*adj* SHRIMPIER, SHRIMPIEST abounding in shrimp
SHRINE	*v* SHRINED, SHRINING, SHRINES to place in a shrine (a receptacle for sacred relics)

SHRINK	*v* SHRANK, SHRUNK or SHRUNKEN, SHRINKING, SHRINKS to contract or draw back
SHRINKER	*n pl.* -S one that shrinks
SHRIVE	*v* SHROVE or SHRIVED, SHRIVEN, SHRIVING, SHRIVES to hear the confession of and grant absolution to
SHRIVEL	*v* -ELED, -ELING, -ELS or -ELLED, -ELLING, -ELS to contract into wrinkles
SHRIVER	*n pl.* -S one that shrives
SHRIVING	present participle of shrive
SHROFF	*v* -ED, -ING, -S to test the genuineness of, as a coin
SHROUD	*v* -ED, -ING, -S to wrap in burial clothing
SHROVE	a past tense of shrive
SHRUB	*n pl.* -S a low, woody plant
SHRUBBY	*adj* -BIER, -BIEST covered with shrubs
SHRUG	*v* SHRUGGED, SHRUGGING, SHRUGS to raise and contract the shoulders
SHRUNK	a past tense of shrink
SHRUNKEN	a past participle of shrink
SHTETEL	*n pl.* SHTETLACH a Jewish village
SHTETL	*n* SHTETLACH shtetel
SHTICK	*n pl.* -S an entertainment routine
SHUCK	*v* -ED, -ING, -S to remove the husk or shell from
SHUCKER	*n pl.* -S one that shucks
SHUCKING	*n pl.* -S the act of one that shucks
SHUDDER	*v* -ED, -ING, -S to tremble
SHUDDERY	*adj* shuddering
SHUFFLE	*v* -FLED, -FLING, -FLES to walk without lifting the feet
SHUFFLER	*n pl.* -S one that shuffles
SHUL	*n pl.* SHULN or SHULS a synagogue
SHUN	*v* SHUNNED, SHUNNING, SHUNS to avoid
SHUNNER	*n pl.* -S one that shuns
SHUNPIKE	*n pl.* -S a side road taken to avoid paying tolls
SHUNT	*v* -ED, -ING, -S to turn aside
SHUNTER	*n pl.* -S one that shunts
SHUSH	*v* -ED, -ING, -ES to silence
SHUT	*v* SHUT, SHUTTING, SHUTS to close

SHUTDOWN *n* pl. -S a temporary closing of an industrial plant

SHUTE *v* SHUTED, SHUTING, SHUTES to chute

SHUTEYE *n* pl. -S sleep

SHUTOFF *n* pl. -S a device that shuts something off

SHUTOUT *n* pl. -S a game in which one team fails to score

SHUTTER *v* -ED, -ING, -S to provide with shutters (hinged window covers)

SHUTTING present participle of shut

SHUTTLE *v* -TLED, -TLING, -TLES to move or travel back and forth

SHWANPAN *n* pl. -S swanpan

SHY *adj* SHIER, SHIEST or SHYER, SHYEST timid

SHY *v* SHIED, SHYING, SHIES to move suddenly back or aside, as in fear

SHYER *n* pl. -S shier

SHYLOCK *v* -ED, -ING, -S to lend money at high interest rates

SHYLY *adv* in a shy manner

SHYNESS *n* pl. -ES the state of being shy

SHYSTER *n* pl. -S an unscrupulous lawyer or politician

SI *n* pl. -S ti

SIAL *n* pl. -S a type of rock formation SIALIC *adj*

SIALOID *adj* resembling saliva

SIAMANG *n* pl. -S a large, black gibbon

SIAMESE *n* pl. -S a water pipe with a connection for two hoses

SIB *n* pl. -S a sibling

SIBB *n* pl. -S sib

SIBILANT *n* pl. -S a speech sound produced by the fricative passage of breath through a narrow orifice

SIBILATE *v* -LATED, -LATING, -LATES to hiss

SIBLING *n* pl. -S one having the same parents as another

SIBYL *n* pl. -S a female prophet SIBYLIC, SIBYLLIC *adj*

SIC *v* SICCED, SICCING, SICS to urge to attack

SICCAN *adj* such

SICE *n* pl. -S syce

SICK *adj* SICKER, SICKEST affected with disease or ill health

SICK *v* -ED, -ING, -S to sic

SICKBAY *n* pl. -BAYS a ship's hospital

SICKBED *n* pl. -S a sick person's bed

SICKEN *v* -ED, -ING, -S to make sick

SICKENER *n* pl. -S one that sickens

SICKERLY *adv* securely

SICKISH *adj* somewhat sick

SICKLE *v* -LED, -LING, -LES to cut with an agricultural implement having a single blade

SICKLY *adj* -LIER, -LIEST appearing as if sick SICKLILY *adv*

SICKLY *v* -LIED, -LYING, -LIES to make sickly

SICKNESS *n* pl. -ES the state of being sick

SICKROOM *n* pl. -S a room occupied by a sick person

SIDDUR *n* pl. -DURIM or -DURS a Jewish prayer book

SIDE *v* SIDED, SIDING, SIDES to agree with or support

SIDEARM *adj* thrown with a sideways sweep of the arm

SIDEBAND *n* pl. -S a band of radio frequencies

SIDECAR *n* pl. -S a passenger car attached to a motorcycle

SIDED past tense of side

SIDEHILL *n* pl. -S a hillside

SIDEKICK *n* pl. -S a close friend

SIDELINE *v* -LINED, -LINING, -LINES to put out of action

SIDELING *adj* sloping

SIDELONG *adj* directed to one side

SIDEMAN *n* pl. -MEN a member of a jazz band

SIDEREAL *adj* pertaining to the stars

SIDERITE *n* pl. -S a mineral

SIDESHOW *n* pl. -S a small show offered in addition to a main attraction

SIDESLIP *v* -SLIPPED, -SLIPPING, -SLIPS to slip to one side

SIDESPIN *n* pl. -S a type of spin imparted to a ball

SIDESTEP *v* -STEPPED, -STEPPING, -STEPS to step to one side

SIDEWALK *n* pl. -S a paved walk for pedestrians

SIDEWALL *n* pl. -S a side surface of a tire

SIDEWARD *adv* toward one side

SIDEWAY *adv* sideways

SIDEWAYS *adv* toward or from one side

SIDEWISE *adv* sideways

SIDING *n* pl. -S material used for surfacing a frame building

SIDLE v -DLED, -DLING, -DLES to move sideways

SIDLER n pl. -S one that sidles

SIEGE v SIEGED, SIEGING, SIEGES to attempt to capture or gain

SIEMENS n pl. SIEMENS a unit of electrical conductance

SIENITE n pl. -S syenite

SIENNA n pl. -S a brown pigment

SIEROZEM n pl. -S a type of soil

SIERRA n pl. -S a mountain range **SIERRAN** adj

SIESTA n pl. -S an afternoon nap or rest

SIEUR n pl. -S an old French title of respect for a man

SIEVE v SIEVED, SIEVING, SIEVES to pass through a sieve (a utensil for separating the coarse parts from the fine parts of loose matter)

SIFFLEUR n pl. -S an animal that makes a whistling noise

SIFT v -ED, -ING, -S to sieve

SIFTER n pl. -S one that sifts

SIFTING n pl. -S the work of a sifter

SIGANID n pl. -S any of a family of fishes

SIGH v -ED, -ING, -S to let out a sigh (a deep, audible breath)

SIGHER n pl. -S one that sighs

SIGHLESS adj uttering no sigh

SIGHLIKE adj resembling a sigh

SIGHT v -ED, -ING, -S to observe or notice

SIGHTER n pl. -S one that sights

SIGHTLY adj -LIER, -LIEST pleasing to look at

SIGHTSEE v -SAW, -SEEN, -SEEING, -SEES to visit and view places of interest

SIGIL n pl. -S an official seal

SIGLOS n pl. -LOI an ancient Persian coin

SIGMA n pl. -S a Greek letter **SIGMATE** adj

SIGMOID n pl. -S an S-shaped curve in a bodily part

SIGN v -ED, -ING, -S to write one's name on

SIGNAL v -NALED, -NALING, -NALS or -NALLED, -NALLING, -NALS to notify by a means of communication

SIGNALER n pl. -S one that signals

SIGNALLY adv notably

SIGNER n pl. -S one that signs

SIGNET v -ED, -ING, -S to mark with an official seal

SIGNIFY v -FIED, -FYING, -FIES to make known

SIGNIOR n pl. -GNIORI or -GNIORS signor

SIGNIORY n pl. -GNIORIES signory

SIGNOR n pl. -GNORI or -GNORS an Italian title of courtesy for a man

SIGNORA n pl. -GNORE or -GNORAS an Italian title of courtesy for a married woman

SIGNORE n pl. -GNORI signor

SIGNORY n pl. -GNORIES seignory

SIGNPOST v -ED, -ING, -S to provide with signposts (posts bearing signs)

SIKE n pl. -S syke

SIKER adj secure

SILAGE n pl. -S fodder that has been preserved in a silo

SILANE n pl. -S a chemical compound

SILD n pl. -S a young herring

SILENCE v -LENCED, -LENCING, -LENCES to make silent

SILENCER n pl. -S one that silences

SILENI pl. of silenus

SILENT adj -LENTER, -LENTEST making no sound or noise **SILENTLY** adv

SILENTS n/pl silent movies

SILENUS n pl. -NI a woodland deity of Greek mythology

SILESIA n pl. -S a cotton fabric

SILEX n pl. -ES silica

SILICA n pl. -S a form of silicon

SILICATE n pl. -S a chemical salt

SILICIC adj pertaining to silicon

SILICIDE n pl. -S a silicon compound

SILICIFY v -FIED, -FYING, -FIES to convert into silica

SILICIUM n pl. -S silicon

SILICLE n pl. -S a short, flat silique

SILICON n pl. -S a nonmetallic element

SILICONE n pl. -S a silicon compound

SILIQUA n pl. -QUAE silique

SILIQUE n pl. -LIQUES a type of seed vessel

SILK v -ED, -ING, -S to cover with silk (a soft, lustrous fabric)

SILKEN	adj made of silk	**SIMITAR**	n pl. -S scimitar
SILKIER	comparative of silky	**SIMLIN**	n pl. -S cymling
SILKIEST	superlative of silky	**SIMMER**	v -ED, -ING, -S to cook below or just at the boiling point
SILKILY	adv in a silky manner		
SILKLIKE	adj resembling silk	**SIMNEL**	n pl. -S a crisp bread
SILKWEED	n pl. -S milkweed	**SIMOLEON**	n pl. -S a dollar
SILKWORM	n pl. -S a caterpillar that spins a cocoon of silk fibers	**SIMONIAC**	n pl. -S one who practices simony
SILKY	adj SILKIER, SILKIEST resembling silk	**SIMONIES**	pl. of simony
		SIMONIST	n pl. -S a simoniac
SILL	n pl. -S the horizontal piece that bears the upright portion of a frame	**SIMONIZE**	v -NIZED, -NIZING, -NIZES to polish with wax
		SIMONY	n pl. -NIES the buying or selling of a church office
SILLABUB	n pl. -S an alcoholic beverage or dessert	**SIMOOM**	n pl. -S a hot, dry desert wind
SILLER	n pl. -S silver	**SIMOON**	n pl. -S simoom
SILLIBUB	n pl. -S sillabub	**SIMP**	n pl. -S a foolish person
SILLY	adj -LIER, -LIEST showing a lack of good sense SILLILY adv	**SIMPER**	v -ED, -ING, -S to smile in a silly manner
SILLY	n pl. -LIES a silly person	**SIMPERER**	n pl. -S one that simpers
SILO	v -ED, -ING, -S to store in a silo (a tall, cylindrical structure)	**SIMPLE**	adj SIMPLER, SIMPLEST not complex or complicated
SILOXANE	n pl. -S a chemical compound	**SIMPLE**	n pl. -S something that is simple
SILT	v -ED, -ING, -S to fill with silt (a sedimentary material)	**SIMPLEX**	n pl. -PLEXES, -PLICES, or -PLICIA a simple word
SILTY	adj SILTIER, SILTIEST full of silt	**SIMPLIFY**	v -FIED, -FYING, -FIES to make simple
SILURID	n pl. -S any of a family of catfishes	**SIMPLISM**	n pl. -S the tendency to oversimplify an issue or problem
SILUROID	n pl. -S a silurid		
SILVA	n pl. -VAS or -VAE sylva	**SIMPLY**	adv in a simple manner
SILVAN	n pl. -S sylvan	**SIMULANT**	n pl. -S one that simulates
SILVER	v -ED, -ING, -S to cover with silver (a metallic element)	**SIMULAR**	n pl. -S a simulant
		SIMULATE	v -LATED, -LATING, -LATES to take on the appearance of
SILVERER	n pl. -S one that silvers		
SILVERLY	adv with a silvery appearance	**SIN**	v SINNED, SINNING, SINS to commit a sin (an offense against religious or moral law)
SILVERN	adj resembling silver		
SILVERY	adj silvery		
SILVICAL	adj pertaining to silvics	**SINAPISM**	n pl. -S a pasty mixture applied to an irritated part of the body
SILVICS	n/pl the study of forest trees		
SIM	n pl. -S simulation	**SINCE**	adv from then until now
SIMA	n pl. -S an igneous rock	**SINCERE**	adj -CERER, -CEREST free from hypocrisy or falseness
SIMAR	n pl. -S a woman's light jacket or robe		
		SINCIPUT	n pl. -CIPUTS or -CIPITA the forehead
SIMARUBA	n pl. -S a tropical tree		
SIMAZINE	n pl. -S an herbicide	**SINE**	n pl. -S a trigonometric function of an angle
SIMIAN	n pl. -S an ape or monkey		
SIMILAR	adj being like but not completely identical to	**SINECURE**	n pl. -S an office or position requiring little or no work
SIMILE	n pl. -S a figure of speech	**SINEW**	v -ED, -ING, -S to strengthen
SIMIOID	adj simious	**SINEWY**	adj lean and muscular
SIMIOUS	adj pertaining to simians	**SINFONIA**	n pl. -NIE a symphony

SINFUL *adj* marked by sin **SINFULLY** *adv*

SING *v* SANG, SUNG, SINGING, SINGS to utter with musical inflections of the voice **SINGABLE** *adj*

SINGE *v* SINGED, SINGEING, SINGES to burn slightly

SINGER *n* pl. -S one that sings

SINGLE *v* -GLED, -GLING, -GLES to select from a group

SINGLET *n* pl. -S a man's undershirt or jersey

SINGLY *adv* without the company of others

SINGSONG *n* pl. -S monotonous cadence in speaking or reading

SINGULAR *n* pl. -S a word form that denotes one person or thing

SINH *n* pl. -S a hyperbolic function of an angle

SINICIZE *v* -CIZED, -CIZING, -CIZES to modify by Chinese influence

SINISTER *adj* threatening or portending evil

SINK *v* SANK, SUNK or SUNKEN, SINKING, SINKS to move to a lower level **SINKABLE** *adj*

SINKAGE *n* pl. -S the act, process, or degree of sinking

SINKER *n* pl. -S one that sinks

SINKHOLE *n* pl. -S a natural depression in a land surface

SINLESS *adj* free from sin

SINNED past tense of sin

SINNER *n* pl. -S one that sins

SINNING present participle of sin

SINOLOGY *n* pl. -GIES the study of the Chinese

SINOPIA *n* pl. -PIAS or -PIE a red pigment

SINSYNE *adv* since

SINTER *v* -ED, -ING, -S to make cohesive by the combined action of heat and pressure

SINUATE *v* -ATED, -ATING, -ATES to curve in and out

SINUOUS *adj* characterized by curves, bends, or turns

SINUS *n* pl. -ES a cranial cavity

SINUSOID *n* pl. -S a mathematical curve

SIP *v* SIPPED, SIPPING, SIPS to drink in small quantities

SIPE *v* SIPED, SIPING, SIPES to seep

SIPHON *v* -ED, -ING, -S to draw off through a siphon (a type of tube)

SIPHONAL *adj* of or pertaining to a siphon

SIPHONIC *adj* siphonal

SIPING present participle of sipe

SIPPED past tense of sip

SIPPER *n* pl. -S one that sips

SIPPET *n* pl. -S a small piece of bread soaked in gravy

SIPPING present participle of sip

SIR *n* pl. -S a respectful form of address used to a man

SIRDAR *n* pl. -S a person of rank in India

SIRE *v* SIRED, SIRING, SIRES to beget

SIREE *n* pl. -S sirree

SIREN *n* pl. -S a device that produces a penetrating warning sound

SIRENIAN *n* pl. -S any of an order of aquatic mammals

SIRING present participle of sire

SIRLOIN *n* pl. -S a cut of beef

SIROCCO *n* pl. -COS a hot, dry wind

SIRRA *n* pl. -S sirrah

SIRRAH *n* pl. -S a form of address used to inferiors

SIRREE *n* pl. -S sir

SIRUP *n* pl. -S syrup **SIRUPY** *adj*

SIRVENTE *n* pl. -S a satirical medieval song or poem

SIS *n* pl. SISES sister

SISAL *n* pl. -S a strong fiber used for rope

SISKIN *n* pl. -S a Eurasian finch

SISSY *n* pl. -SIES an effeminate man or boy

SISSY *adj* SISSIER, SISSIEST sissyish

SISSYISH *adj* resembling a sissy

SISTER *v* -ED, -ING, -S to treat like a sister (a female sibling)

SISTERLY *adj* of or resembling a sister

SISTRA a pl. of sistrum

SISTROID *adj* included between the convex sides of two intersecting curves

SISTRUM *n* pl. -TRUMS or -TRA an ancient Egyptian percussion instrument

SIT *v* SAT, SITTEN, SITTING, SITS to rest on the buttocks

SITAR *n* pl. -S a lute of India

SITARIST *n* pl. -S one who plays the sitar

SITE *v* SITED, SITING, SITES to place in position for operation

SITH *adv* since

SITHENCE *adv* since

SITHENS *adv* since

SITI a pl. of situs

SITING present participle of site

SITOLOGY *n* pl. -GIES the science of nutrition and diet

SITTEN a past participle of sit

SITTER *n* pl. -S one that sits

SITTING *n* pl. -S a meeting or session

SITUATE *v* -ATED, -ATING, -ATES to place in a certain position

SITUS *n* pl. -TI or -TUSES a position or location

SITZMARK *n* pl. -S a mark left in the snow by a skier who has fallen backward

SIVER *n* pl. -S a sewer

SIX *n* pl. -ES a number

SIXFOLD *adj* being six times as great as

SIXMO *n* pl. -MOS a paper size

SIXPENCE *n* pl. -S a British coin worth six pennies

SIXPENNY *adj* worth sixpence

SIXTE *n* pl. -S a fencing parry

SIXTEEN *n* pl. -S a number

SIXTH *n* pl. -S one of six equal parts

SIXTHLY *adv* in the sixth place

SIXTIETH *n* pl. -S one of sixty equal parts

SIXTY *n* pl. -TIES a number

SIZABLE *adj* of considerable size SIZABLY *adv*

SIZAR *n* pl. -S a British student who receives financial assistance from his college

SIZE *v* SIZED, SIZING, SIZES to arrange according to size (physical proportions)

SIZEABLE *adj* sizable SIZEABLY *adv*

SIZER *n* pl. -S sizar

SIZIER comparative of sizy

SIZIEST superlative of sizy

SIZINESS *n* pl. -ES the quality or state of being sizy

SIZING *n* pl. -S a substance used as a glaze or filler for porous materials

SIZY *adj* SIZIER, SIZIEST viscid

SIZZLE *v* -ZLED, -ZLING, -ZLES to burn or fry with a hissing sound

SIZZLER *n* pl. -S a very hot day

SKAG *n* pl. -S heroin

SKALD *n* pl. -S an ancient Scandinavian poet SKALDIC *adj*

SKAT *n* pl. -S a card game

SKATE *v* SKATED, SKATING, SKATES to glide over ice or the ground on skates (shoes fitted with runners or wheels)

SKATER *n* pl. -S one that skates

SKATING *n* pl. -S the sport of gliding on skates

SKATOL *n* pl. -S skatole

SKATOLE *n* pl. -S a chemical compound

SKEAN *n* pl. -S a type of dagger

SKEANE *n* pl. -S a length of yarn wound in a loose coil

SKEE *v* SKEED, SKEEING, SKEES to ski

SKEEN *n* pl. -S skean

SKEET *n* pl. -S the sport of shooting at clay pigeons hurled in the air by spring traps

SKEETER *n* pl. -S a skeet shooter

SKEG *n* pl. -S a timber that connects the keel and sternpost of a ship

SKEIGH *adj* proud

SKEIN *v* -ED, -ING, -S to wind into long, loose coils

SKELETON *n* pl. -S the supporting or protective framework of a human or animal body SKELETAL *adj*

SKELLUM *n* pl. -S a rascal

SKELP *v* SKELPED or SKELPIT, SKELPING, SKELPS to slap

SKELTER *v* -ED, -ING, -S to scurry

SKENE *n* pl. -S skean

SKEP *n* pl. -S a beehive

SKEPSIS *n* pl. -SISES the attitude or outlook of a skeptic

SKEPTIC *n* pl. -S a person who doubts generally accepted ideas

SKERRY *n* pl. -RIES a small, rocky island

SKETCH *v* -ED, -ING, -ES to make a rough, hasty drawing of

SKETCHER *n* pl. -S one that sketches

SKETCHY *adj* SKETCHIER, SKETCHIEST lacking in completeness or clearness

SKEW v -ED, -ING, -S to turn aside

SKEWBACK n pl. -S a sloping surface against which the end of an arch rests

SKEWBALD n pl. -S a horse having patches of brown and white

SKEWER v -ED, -ING, -S to pierce with a long pin, as meat

SKEWNESS n pl. -ES lack of symmetry

SKI v -ED, -ING, -S to travel on skis (long, narrow strips of wood or metal)

SKIABLE adj capable of being skied over

SKIAGRAM n pl. -S a picture made up of shadows or outlines

SKIBOB n pl. -S a vehicle used for traveling over snow

SKID v SKIDDED, SKIDDING, SKIDS to slide sideways as a result of a loss of traction

SKIDDER n pl. -S one that skids

SKIDDOO v -ED, -ING, -S to go away

SKIDDY adj -DIER, -DIEST likely to cause skidding

SKIDOO v -ED, -ING, -S to skiddoo

SKIDWAY n pl. -WAYS a platform on which logs are piled for loading or sawing

SKIED past tense of ski and sky

SKIER n pl. -S one that skis

SKIES present 3d person sing. of sky

SKIEY adj skyey

SKIFF n pl. -S a small, open boat

SKIFFLE v -FLED, -FLING, -FLES to play a particular style of music

SKIING n pl. -S the sport of traveling on skis

SKIJORER n pl. -S a skier who is drawn over snow by a horse or vehicle

SKILFUL adj skillful

SKILL n pl. -S the ability to do something well SKILLED adj

SKILLESS adj having no skill

SKILLET n pl. -S a frying pan

SKILLFUL adj having skill

SKILLING n pl. -S a former coin of Scandinavian countries

SKIM v SKIMMED, SKIMMING, SKIMS to remove floating matter from the surface of

SKIMMER n pl. -S one that skims

SKIMMING n pl. -S something that is skimmed from a liquid

SKIMO n pl. -MOS an Eskimo

SKIMP v -ED, -ING, -S to scrimp

SKIMPY adj SKIMPIER, SKIMPIEST scanty SKIMPILY adv

SKIN v SKINNED, SKINNING, SKINS to strip or deprive of skin (the membranous tissue covering the body of an animal)

SKINFUL n pl. -S as much as a skin container can hold

SKINHEAD n pl. -S one whose hair is cut very short

SKINK v -ED, -ING, -S to pour out or serve, as liquor

SKINKER n pl. -S one that skinks

SKINLESS adj having no skin

SKINLIKE adj resembling skin

SKINNED past tense of skin

SKINNER n pl. -S one that skins

SKINNING present participle of skin

SKINNY adj -NIER, -NIEST very thin

SKINT adj having no money

SKIORING n pl. -S a form of skiing

SKIP v SKIPPED, SKIPPING, SKIPS to move with light springing steps

SKIPJACK n pl. -S a marine fish

SKIPLANE n pl. -S an airplane designed to take off from or land on snow

SKIPPED past tense of skip

SKIPPER v -ED, -ING, -S to act as master or captain of

SKIPPET n pl. -S a small box for protecting an official seal

SKIPPING present participle of skip

SKIRL v -ED, -ING, -S to produce a shrill sound

SKIRMISH v -ED, -ING, -ES to engage in a minor battle

SKIRR v -ED, -ING, -S to move rapidly

SKIRRET n pl. -S an Asian herb

SKIRT v -ED, -ING, -S to go or pass around

SKIRTER n pl. -S one that skirts

SKIRTING n pl. -S a board at the base of a wall

SKIT n pl. -S a short dramatic scene

SKITE v SKITED, SKITING, SKITES to move away quickly

SKITTER v -ED, -ING, -S to move lightly or rapidly along a surface

SKITTERY adj -TERIER, -TERIEST skittish

SKITTISH adj easily frightened

SKITTLE   *n* pl. -S a wooden pin used in a bowling game

SKIVE   *v* SKIVED, SKIVING, SKIVES to pare

SKIVER   *n* pl. -S one that skives

SKIVVY   *n* pl. -VIES a female servant

SKIWEAR   *n* pl. -S clothing suitable for wear while skiing

SKLENT   *v* -ED, -ING, -S to slant

SKOAL   *v* -ED, -ING, -S to drink to the health of

SKOOKUM   *adj* excellent

SKREEGH   *v* -ED, -ING, -S to screech

SKREIGH   *v* -ED, -ING, -S to screech

SKUA   *n* pl. -S a predatory seabird

SKULK   *v* -ED, -ING, -S to move about stealthily

SKULKER   *n* pl. -S one that skulks

SKULL   *n* pl. -S the framework of the head **SKULLED** *adj*

SKULLCAP   *n* pl. -S a close-fitting cap

SKUNK   *v* -ED, -ING, -S to defeat overwhelmingly

SKY   *v* SKIED or SKYED, SKYING, SKIES to hit or throw toward the sky (the upper atmosphere)

SKYBORNE   *adj* airborne

SKYCAP   *n* pl. -S a porter at an airport

SKYDIVE   *v* -DIVED or -DOVE, -DIVING, -DIVES to parachute from an airplane for sport

SKYDIVER   *n* pl. -S one that skydives

SKYEY   *adj* resembling the sky

SKYHOOK   *n* pl. -S a hook conceived as being suspended from the sky

SKYJACK   *v* -ED, -ING, -S to hijack an airplane

SKYLARK   *v* -ED, -ING, -S to frolic

SKYLIGHT   *n* pl. -S a window in a roof or ceiling

SKYLINE   *n* pl. -S the horizon

SKYMAN   *n* pl. -MEN an aviator

SKYPHOS   *n* pl. -PHOI a drinking vessel used in ancient Greece

SKYSAIL   *n* pl. -S a type of sail

SKYWARD   *adv* toward the sky

SKYWARDS   *adv* skyward

SKYWAY   *n* pl. -WAYS an elevated highway

SKYWRITE   *v* -WROTE, -WRITTEN, -WRITING, -WRITES to write in the sky by releasing a visible vapor from an airplane

SLAB   *v* SLABBED, SLABBING, SLABS to cover with slabs (broad, flat pieces of solid material)

SLABBER   *v* -ED, -ING, -S to slobber

SLABBERY   *adj* slobbery

SLABBING   present participle of slab

SLACK   *adj* SLACKER, SLACKEST not tight or taut

SLACK   *v* -ED, -ING, -S to slacken

SLACKEN   *v* -ED, -ING, -S to make less tight or taut

SLACKER   *n* pl. -S a shirker

SLACKLY   *adv* in a slack manner

SLAG   *v* SLAGGED, SLAGGING, SLAGS to convert into slag (the fused residue of a smelted ore)

SLAGGY   *adj* -GIER, -GIEST resembling slag

SLAIN   past participle of slay

SLAKE   *v* SLAKED, SLAKING, SLAKES to quench **SLAKABLE** *adj*

SLAKER   *n* pl. -S one that slakes

SLALOM   *v* -ED, -ING, -S to ski in a zigzag course

SLAM   *v* SLAMMED, SLAMMING, SLAMS to shut forcibly and noisily

SLANDER   *v* -ED, -ING, -S to defame

SLANG   *v* -ED, -ING, -S to assail with harsh or coarse language

SLANGY   *adj* SLANGIER, SLANGIEST given to vulgarity **SLANGILY** *adv*

SLANK   a past tense of slink

SLANT   *v* -ED, -ING, -S to deviate from the horizontal or vertical

SLAP   *v* SLAPPED, SLAPPING, SLAPS to strike with the open hand

SLAPDASH   *n* pl. -ES careless work

SLAPJACK   *n* pl. -S a pancake

SLAPPED   past tense of slap

SLAPPER   *n* pl. -S one that slaps

SLAPPING   present participle of slap

SLASH   *v* -ED, -ING, -ES to cut with violent sweeping strokes

SLASHER   *n* pl. -S one that slashes

SLASHING   *n* pl. -S the act of one that slashes

SLAT   *v* SLATTED, SLATTING, SLATS to provide with slats (narrow strips of wood or metal)

SLATCH   *n* pl. -ES a calm between breaking waves

SLATE   v SLATED, SLATING, SLATES to cover with slate (a roofing material)

SLATER   n pl. -S one that slates

SLATHER   v -ED, -ING, -S to spread thickly

SLATIER   comparative of slaty

SLATIEST   superlative of slaty

SLATING   n pl. -S the act of one that slates

SLATTED   past tense of slat

SLATTERN   n pl. -S a slovenly woman

SLATTING   present participle of slat

SLATY   adj SLATIER, SLATIEST resembling slate

SLAVE   v SLAVED, SLAVING, SLAVES to work like a slave (one who is owned by another)

SLAVER   v -ED, -ING, -S to drool

SLAVERER   n pl. -S one that slavers

SLAVERY   n pl. -ERIES ownership of one person by another

SLAVEY   n pl. -EYS a female servant

SLAVING   present participle of slave

SLAVISH   adj pertaining to or characteristic of a slave

SLAW   n pl. -S coleslaw

SLAY   v SLEW, SLAIN, SLAYING, SLAYS to kill violently

SLAYER   n pl. -S one that slays

SLEAVE   v SLEAVED, SLEAVING, SLEAVES to separate into filaments

SLEAZY   adj SLEAZIER, SLEAZIEST shoddy **SLEAZILY** adv

SLED   v SLEDDED, SLEDDING, SLEDS to convey on a sled (a vehicle for carrying people or loads over snow or ice)

SLEDDER   n pl. -S one that sleds

SLEDDING   n pl. -S the act of one that sleds

SLEDGE   v SLEDGED, SLEDGING, SLEDGES to convey on a type of sled

SLEEK   adj SLEEKER, SLEEKEST smooth and glossy

SLEEK   v -ED, -ING, -S to make sleek

SLEEKEN   v -ED, -ING, -S to sleek

SLEEKIER   comparative of sleeky

SLEEKIEST   superlative of sleeky

SLEEKIT   adj sleek

SLEEKLY   adv in a sleek manner

SLEEKY   adj SLEEKIER, SLEEKIEST sleek

SLEEP   v SLEPT, SLEEPING, SLEEPS to be in a natural, periodic state of rest

SLEEPER   n pl. -S one that sleeps

SLEEPING   n pl. -S the act of one that sleeps

SLEEPY   adj SLEEPIER, SLEEPIEST ready or inclined to sleep **SLEEPILY** adv

SLEET   v -ED, -ING, -S to shower sleet (frozen rain)

SLEETY   adj SLEETIER, SLEETIEST resembling sleet

SLEEVE   v SLEEVED, SLEEVING, SLEEVES to furnish with a sleeve (the part of a garment covering the arm)

SLEIGH   v -ED, -ING, -S to ride in a sled

SLEIGHER   n pl. -S one that sleighs

SLEIGHT   n pl. -S deftness

SLENDER   adj -DERER, -DEREST thin

SLEPT   past tense of sleep

SLEUTH   v -ED, -ING, -S to act as a detective

SLEW   v -ED, -ING, -S to slue

SLICE   v SLICED, SLICING, SLICES to cut into thin, flat pieces

SLICER   n pl. -S one that slices

SLICK   adj SLICKER, SLICKEST smooth and slippery

SLICK   v -ED, -ING, -S to make slick

SLICKER   n pl. -S an oilskin raincoat

SLICKLY   adv in a slick manner

SLIDE   v SLID, SLIDDEN, SLIDING, SLIDES to move smoothly along a surface **SLIDABLE** adj

SLIDER   n pl. -S one that slides

SLIDEWAY   n pl. -WAYS a route along which something slides

SLIDING   present participle of slide

SLIER   a comparative of sly

SLIEST   a superlative of sly

SLIGHT   adj SLIGHTER, SLIGHTEST small in size or amount **SLIGHTLY** adv

SLIGHT   v -ED, -ING, -S to treat with disregard

SLILY   adv in a sly manner

SLIM   adj SLIMMER, SLIMMEST slender

SLIM   v SLIMMED, SLIMMING, SLIMS to make slim

SLIME	v SLIMED, SLIMING, SLIMES to cover with slime (viscous mud)	**SLIPWAY**	n pl. -WAYS an area sloping toward the water in a shipyard
SLIMIER	comparative of slimy	**SLIT**	v SLITTED, SLITTING, SLITS to make a slit (a long, narrow cut) in
SLIMIEST	superlative of slimy		
SLIMILY	adv in a slimy manner	**SLITHER**	v -ED, -ING, -S to slide from side to side
SLIMING	present participle of slime		
SLIMLY	adv in a slim manner	**SLITHERY**	adj slippery
SLIMMED	past tense of slim	**SLITLESS**	adj having no slits
SLIMMER	comparative of slim	**SLITTED**	past tense of slit
SLIMMEST	superlative of slim	**SLITTER**	n pl. -S one that slits
SLIMMING	present participle of slim	**SLITTING**	present participle of slit
SLIMNESS	n pl. -ES the state of being slim	**SLIVER**	v -ED, -ING, -S to cut into long, thin pieces
SLIMPSY	adj -SIER, -SIEST slimsy		
SLIMSY	adj -SIER, -SIEST flimsy	**SLIVERER**	n pl. -S one that slivers
SLIMY	adj SLIMIER, SLIMIEST resembling slime	**SLIVOVIC**	n pl. -ES a plum brandy
		SLOB	n pl. -S a slovenly or boorish person
SLING	v SLUNG, SLINGING, SLINGS to throw with a sudden motion		
		SLOBBER	v -ED, -ING, -S to drool
SLINGER	n pl. -S one that slings	**SLOBBERY**	adj slobbering
SLINK	v SLUNK or SLANK, SLINKING, SLINKS to move stealthily	**SLOBBISH**	adj resembling a slob
		SLOE	n pl. -S a plumlike fruit
SLINKY	adj SLINKIER, SLINKIEST stealthy SLINKILY adv	**SLOG**	v SLOGGED, SLOGGING, SLOGS to plod
SLIP	v SLIPPED or SLIPT, SLIPPING, SLIPS to slide suddenly and accidentally	**SLOGAN**	n pl. -S a motto adopted by a group
		SLOGGER	n pl. -S one that slogs
SLIPCASE	n pl. -S a protective box for a book	**SLOGGING**	present participle of slog
		SLOID	n pl. -S sloyd
SLIPE	v SLIPED, SLIPING, SLIPES to peel	**SLOJD**	n pl. -S sloyd
		SLOOP	n pl. -S a type of sailing vessel
SLIPFORM	v -ED, -ING, -S to construct with the use of a mold in which concrete is placed to set	**SLOP**	v SLOPPED, SLOPPING, SLOPS to spill or splash
		SLOPE	v SLOPED, SLOPING, SLOPES to slant
SLIPKNOT	n pl. -S a type of knot		
SLIPLESS	adj free from errors	**SLOPER**	n pl. -S one that slopes
SLIPOUT	n pl. -S an insert in a newspaper	**SLOPPED**	past tense of slop
		SLOPPING	present participle of slop
SLIPOVER	n pl. -S a pullover	**SLOPPY**	adj -PIER, -PIEST messy SLOPPILY adv
SLIPPAGE	n pl. -S a falling off from a standard or level		
		SLOPWORK	n pl. -S the manufacture of cheap clothing
SLIPPED	a past tense of slip		
SLIPPER	n pl. -S a light, low shoe	**SLOSH**	v -ED, -ING, -ES to move with a splashing motion
SLIPPERY	adj -PERIER, -PERIEST causing or tending to cause slipping		
		SLOSHY	adj SLOSHIER, SLOSHIEST slushy
SLIPPING	present participle of slip		
SLIPPY	adj -PIER, -PIEST slippery	**SLOT**	v SLOTTED, SLOTTING, SLOTS to cut a long, narrow opening in
SLIPSHOD	adj carelessly done or made		
SLIPSLOP	n pl. -S watery food	**SLOTBACK**	n pl. -S a type of football player
SLIPSOLE	n pl. -S a thin insole	**SLOTH**	n pl. -S a slow-moving arboreal mammal
SLIPT	a past tense of slip		
SLIPUP	n pl. -S a mistake	**SLOTHFUL**	adj sluggish
SLIPWARE	n pl. -S a type of pottery		

SLOTTED past tense of slot

SLOTTING present participle of slot

SLOUCH v -ED, -ING, -ES to sit, stand, or move with a drooping posture

SLOUCHER n pl. -S one that slouches

SLOUCHY adj SLOUCHIER, SLOUCHIEST slouching

SLOUGH v -ED, -ING, -S to cast off

SLOUGHY adj SLOUGHIER, SLOUGHIEST miry

SLOVEN n pl. -S a slovenly person

SLOVENLY adj -LIER, -LIEST habitually untidy or unclean

SLOW adj SLOWER, SLOWEST moving with little speed

SLOW v -ED, -ING, -S to lessen the speed of

SLOWDOWN n pl. -S a lessening of pace

SLOWISH adj somewhat slow

SLOWLY adv in a slow manner

SLOWNESS n pl. -ES the state of being slow

SLOWPOKE n pl. -S a slow individual

SLOWWORM n pl. -S a European lizard having no legs

SLOYD n pl. -S a Swedish system of manual training

SLUB v SLUBBED, SLUBBING, SLUBS to draw out and twist slightly

SLUBBER v -ED, -ING, -S to stain or dirty

SLUBBING n pl. -S a slightly twisted roll of textile fibers

SLUDGE n pl. -S a muddy deposit

SLUDGY adj SLUDGIER, SLUDGIEST covered with sludge

SLUE v SLUED, SLUING, SLUES to cause to move sideways

SLUFF v -ED, -ING, -S to discard a card or cards

SLUG v SLUGGED, SLUGGING, SLUGS to strike heavily

SLUGABED n pl. -S one inclined to stay in bed out of laziness

SLUGFEST n pl. -S a vigorous fight

SLUGGARD n pl. -S an habitually lazy person

SLUGGED past tense of slug

SLUGGER n pl. -S one that slugs

SLUGGING present participle of slug

SLUGGISH adj displaying little movement or activity

SLUICE v SLUICED, SLUICING, SLUICES to wash with a sudden flow of water

SLUICY adj falling in streams

SLUING present participle of slue

SLUM v SLUMMED, SLUMMING, SLUMS to visit slums (squalid urban areas)

SLUMBER v -ED, -ING, -S to sleep

SLUMBERY adj sleepy

SLUMGUM n pl. -S the residue remaining after honey is extracted from a honeycomb

SLUMLORD n pl. -S a landlord of slum property

SLUMMED past tense of slum

SLUMMER n pl. -S one that slums

SLUMMING present participle of slum

SLUMMY adj -MIER, -MIEST resembling a slum

SLUMP v -ED, -ING, -S to fall or sink suddenly

SLUNG past tense of sling

SLUNK a past tense of slink

SLUR v SLURRED, SLURRING, SLURS to pass over lightly or carelessly

SLURB n pl. -S a poorly planned suburban area **SLURBAN** adj

SLURP v -ED, -ING, -S to eat or drink noisily

SLURRED past tense of slur

SLURRING present participle of slur

SLURRY v -RIED, -RYING, -RIES to convert into a type of watery mixture

SLUSH v -ED, -ING, -ES to splash with slush (partly melted snow)

SLUSHY adj SLUSHIER, SLUSHIEST resembling slush **SLUSHILY** adv

SLUT n pl. -S a slovenly woman **SLUTTISH** adj

SLY adj SLIER, SLIEST or SLYER, SLYEST crafty **SLYLY** adv

SLYBOOTS n pl. SLYBOOTS a sly person

SLYNESS n pl. -ES the quality or state of being sly

SLYPE n pl. -S a narrow passage in an English cathedral

SMACK v -ED, -ING, -S to strike sharply

SMACKER n pl. -S one that smacks

SMALL adj SMALLER, SMALLEST of limited size or quantity

SMALL   n pl. -S a small part

SMALLAGE   n pl. -S a wild celery

SMALLISH   adj somewhat small

SMALLPOX   n pl. -ES a virus disease

SMALT   n pl. -S a blue pigment

SMALTI   a pl. of smalto

SMALTINE   n pl. -S smaltite

SMALTITE   n pl. -S a mineral

SMALTO   n pl. -TOS or -TI colored glass used in mosaics

SMARAGD   n pl. -S an emerald

SMARAGDE   n pl. -S smaragd

SMARM   n pl. -S trite sentimentality

SMARMY   adj SMARMIER, SMARMIEST marked by excessive flattery

SMART   v -ED, -ING, -S to cause a sharp, stinging pain

SMART   adj SMARTER, SMARTEST characterized by mental acuity

SMARTEN   v -ED, -ING, -S to improve in appearance

SMARTIE   n pl. -S smarty

SMARTLY   adv in a smart manner

SMARTY   n pl. SMARTIES an obnoxiously conceited person

SMASH   v -ED, -ING, -ES to shatter violently

SMASHER   n pl. -S one that smashes

SMASHUP   n pl. -S a collision of motor vehicles

SMATTER   v -ED, -ING, -S to speak with little knowledge

SMAZE   n pl. -S an atmospheric mixture of smoke and haze

SMEAR   v -ED, -ING, -S to spread with a sticky, greasy, or dirty substance

SMEARER   n pl. -S one that smears

SMEARY   adj SMEARIER, SMEARIEST smeared

SMECTIC   adj pertaining to a phase of a liquid crystal

SMEDDUM   n pl. -S ground malt powder

SMEEK   v -ED, -ING, -S to smoke

SMEGMA   n pl. -S sebum

SMELL   v SMELLED or SMELT, SMELLING, SMELLS to perceive by means of the olfactory nerves

SMELLER   n pl. -S one that smells

SMELLY   adj SMELLIER, SMELLIEST having an unpleasant odor

SMELT   v -ED, -ING, -S to melt or fuse, as ores

SMELTER   n pl. -S one that smelts

SMELTERY   n pl. -ERIES a place for smelting

SMERK   v -ED, -ING, -S to smirk

SMEW   n pl. -S a Eurasian duck

SMIDGEN   n pl. -S a very small amount

SMIDGEON   n pl. -S smidgen

SMIDGIN   n pl. -S smidgen

SMILAX   n pl. -ES a twining plant

SMILE   v SMILED, SMILING, SMILES to upturn the corners of the mouth in pleasure

SMILER   n pl. -S one that smiles

SMIRCH   v -ED, -ING, -ES to soil

SMIRK   v -ED, -ING, -S to smile in an affected or smug manner

SMIRKER   n pl. -S one that smirks

SMIRKY   adj SMIRKIER, SMIRKIEST smirking

SMITE   v SMOTE, SMIT or SMITTEN, SMITING, SMITES to strike heavily

SMITER   n pl. -S one that smites

SMITH   n pl. -S a worker in metals

SMITHERY   n pl. -ERIES the trade of a smith

SMITHY   n pl. SMITHIES the workshop of a smith

SMITING   present participle of smite

SMITTEN   a past participle of smite

SMOCK   v -ED, -ING, -S to furnish with a smock (a loose outer garment)

SMOCKING   n pl. -S a type of embroidery

SMOG   n pl. -S an atmospheric mixture of smoke and fog **SMOGLESS** adj

SMOGGY   adj -GIER, -GIEST filled with smog

SMOKE   v SMOKED, SMOKING, SMOKES to emit smoke (the gaseous product of burning materials) **SMOKABLE** adj

SMOKEPOT   n pl. -S a container for giving off smoke

SMOKER   n pl. -S one that smokes

SMOKEY   adj SMOKIER, SMOKIEST smoky

SMOKING   present participle of smoke

SMOKY   adj SMOKIER, SMOKIEST filled with smoke **SMOKILY** adv

SMOLDER   v -ED, -ING, -S to burn with no flame

SMOLT   *n* pl. -S a young salmon

SMOOCH   *v* -ED, -ING, -ES to kiss

SMOOCHY   *adj* smudgy

SMOOTH   *adj* SMOOTHER, SMOOTHEST having a surface that is free from irregularities

SMOOTH   *v* -ED, -ING, -S to make smooth

SMOOTHEN   *v* -ED, -ING, -S to smooth

SMOOTHER   *n* pl. -S one that smooths

SMOOTHIE   *n* pl. -S a person with polished manners

SMOOTHLY   *adv* in a smooth manner

SMOOTHY   *n* pl. SMOOTHIES smoothie

SMOTE   past tense of smite

SMOTHER   *v* -ED, -ING, -S to prevent from breathing

SMOTHERY   *adj* tending to smother

SMOULDER   *v* -ED, -ING, -S to smolder

SMUDGE   *v* SMUDGED, SMUDGING, SMUDGES to smear or dirty

SMUDGY   *adj* SMUDGIER, SMUDGIEST smudged SMUDGILY *adv*

SMUG   *adj* SMUGGER, SMUGGEST highly self-satisfied

SMUGGLE   *v* -GLED, -GLING, -GLES to import or export illicitly

SMUGGLER   *n* pl. -S one that smuggles

SMUGLY   *adv* in a smug manner

SMUGNESS   *n* pl. -ES the quality or state of being smug

SMUT   *v* SMUTTED, SMUTTING, SMUTS to soil

SMUTCH   *v* -ED, -ING, -ES to smudge

SMUTCHY   *adj* SMUTCHIER, SMUTCHIEST smudgy

SMUTTED   past tense of smut

SMUTTING   present participle of smut

SMUTTY   *adj* -TIER, -TIEST obscene SMUTTILY *adv*

SNACK   *v* -ED, -ING, -S to eat a light meal

SNAFFLE   *v* -FLED, -FLING, -FLES to obtain by devious means

SNAFU   *v* -ED, -ING, -S to bring into a state of confusion

SNAG   *v* SNAGGED, SNAGGING, SNAGS to catch on a snag (a jagged protuberance)

SNAGGY   *adj* -GIER, -GIEST full of snags

SNAGLIKE   *adj* resembling a snag

SNAIL   *v* -ED, -ING, -S to move slowly

SNAKE   *v* SNAKED, SNAKING, SNAKES to move like a snake (a limbless reptile)

SNAKY   *adj* SNAKIER, SNAKIEST resembling a snake SNAKILY *adv*

SNAP   *v* SNAPPED, SNAPPING, SNAPS to make a sharp cracking sound

SNAPBACK   *n* pl. -S a sudden rebound or recovery

SNAPLESS   *adj* lacking a snap (a type of fastening device)

SNAPPED   past tense of snap

SNAPPER   *n* pl. -S one that snaps

SNAPPIER   comparative of snappy

SNAPPIEST   superlative of snappy

SNAPPILY   *adv* in a snappy manner

SNAPPING   present participle of snap

SNAPPISH   *adj* tending to speak in an impatient or irritable manner

SNAPPY   *adj* -PIER, -PIEST snappish

SNAPSHOT   *v* -SHOTTED, -SHOTTING, -SHOTS to photograph informally and quickly

SNAPWEED   *n* pl. -S a flowering plant

SNARE   *v* SNARED, SNARING, SNARES to trap

SNARER   *n* pl. -S one that snares

SNARK   *n* pl. -S an imaginary animal

SNARL   *v* -ED, -ING, -S to growl viciously

SNARLER   *n* pl. -S one that snarls

SNARLY   *adj* SNARLIER, SNARLIEST tangled

SNASH   *n* pl. -ES abusive language

SNATCH   *v* -ED, -ING, -ES to seize suddenly

SNATCHER   *n* pl. -S one that snatches

SNATCHY   *adj* SNATCHIER, SNATCHIEST occurring irregularly

SNATH   *n* pl. -S the handle of a scythe

SNATHE   *n* pl. -S snath

SNAW   *v* -ED, -ING, -S to snow

SNAZZY   *adj* -ZIER, -ZIEST very stylish

SNEAK   *v* SNEAKED or SNUCK, SNEAKING, SNEAKS to move stealthily

SNEAKER   *n* pl. -S one that sneaks

SNEAKY   *adj* SNEAKIER, SNEAKIEST deceitful SNEAKILY *adv*

SNEAP   *v* -ED, -ING, -S to chide

SNECK   *n* pl. -S a latch

SNED   *v* SNEDDED, SNEDDING, SNEDS to prune

SNEER	v -ED, -ING, -S to curl the lip in contempt	**SNIPPY**	adj -PIER, -PIEST snappish SNIPPILY adv
SNEERER	n pl. -S one that sneers	**SNIT**	n pl. -S a state of agitation
SNEERFUL	adj given to sneering	**SNITCH**	v -ED, -ING, -ES to tattle
SNEESH	n pl. -ES snuff	**SNITCHER**	n pl. -S one that snitches
SNEEZE	v SNEEZED, SNEEZING, SNEEZES to make a sudden, involuntary expiration of breath	**SNIVEL**	v -ELED, -ELING, -ELS or -ELLED, -ELLING, -ELS to cry or whine with sniffling
SNEEZER	n pl. -S one that sneezes	**SNIVELER**	n pl. -S one that snivels
SNEEZY	adj SNEEZIER, SNEEZIEST tending to sneeze	**SNOB**	n pl. -S one who tends to avoid or rebuff those regarded as inferior
SNELL	n pl. -S a short line by which a fishhook is attached to a longer line	**SNOBBERY**	n pl. -BERIES snobbish behavior
SNELL	adj SNELLER, SNELLEST keen	**SNOBBIER**	comparative of snobby
SNIB	v SNIBBED, SNIBBING, SNIBS to latch	**SNOBBIEST**	superlative of snobby
		SNOBBILY	adv in a snobby manner
SNICK	v -ED, -ING, -S to nick	**SNOBBISH**	adj characteristic of a snob
SNICKER	v -ED, -ING, -S to utter a partly stifled laugh	**SNOBBISM**	n pl. -S snobbery
SNICKERY	adj tending to snicker	**SNOBBY**	adj -BIER, -BIEST snobbish
SNIDE	adj SNIDER, SNIDEST maliciously derogatory SNIDELY adv	**SNOOD**	v -ED, -ING, -S to secure with a snood (a net or fabric cap for the hair)
SNIFF	v -ED, -ING, -S to inhale audibly through the nose	**SNOOK**	v -ED, -ING, -S to sniff
SNIFFER	n pl. -S one that sniffs	**SNOOKER**	n pl. -S a pocket billiards game
SNIFFIER	comparative of sniffy	**SNOOL**	v -ED, -ING, -S to yield meekly
SNIFFIEST	superlative of sniffy	**SNOOP**	v -ED, -ING, -S to pry about
SNIFFILY	adv in a sniffy manner	**SNOOPER**	n pl. -S one that snoops
SNIFFISH	adj haughty	**SNOOPY**	adj SNOOPIER, SNOOPIEST given to snooping SNOOPILY adv
SNIFFLE	v -FLED, -FLING, -FLES to sniff repeatedly		
SNIFFLER	n pl. -S one that sniffles	**SNOOT**	v -ED, -ING, -S to treat with disdain
SNIFFY	adj -FIER, -FIEST sniffish	**SNOOTY**	adj SNOOTIER, SNOOTIEST snobbish SNOOTILY adv
SNIFTER	n pl. -S a pear-shaped liquor glass		
SNIGGER	v -ED, -ING, -S to snicker	**SNOOZE**	v SNOOZED, SNOOZING, SNOOZES to sleep lightly
SNIGGLE	v -GLED, -GLING, -GLES to fish for eels	**SNOOZER**	n pl. -S one that snoozes
SNIGGLER	n pl. -S one that sniggles	**SNOOZLE**	v -ZLED, -ZLING, -ZLES to nuzzle
SNIP	v SNIPPED, SNIPPING, SNIPS to cut with a short, quick stroke	**SNOOZY**	adj SNOOZIER, SNOOZIEST drowsy
SNIPE	v SNIPED, SNIPING, SNIPES to shoot at individuals from a concealed place	**SNORE**	v SNORED, SNORING, SNORES to breathe loudly while sleeping
SNIPER	n pl. -S one that snipes	**SNORER**	n pl. -S one that snores
SNIPPED	past tense of snip	**SNORKEL**	v -ED, -ING, -S to swim underwater with a type of breathing device
SNIPPER	n pl. -S one that snips		
SNIPPET	n pl. -S a small piece snipped off	**SNORT**	v -ED, -ING, -S to exhale noisily through the nostrils
SNIPPETY	adj -PETIER, -PETIEST snippy	**SNORTER**	n pl. -S one that snorts
SNIPPING	present participle of snip	**SNOT**	n pl. -S nasal mucus

SNOTTY *adj* -TIER, -TIEST arrogant **SNOTTILY** *adv*

SNOUT *v* -ED, -ING, -S to provide with a nozzle

SNOUTISH *adj* snouty

SNOUTY *adj* SNOUTIER, SNOUTIEST resembling a long, projecting nose

SNOW *v* -ED, -ING, -S to fall as snow (precipitation in the form of ice crystals)

SNOWBALL *v* -ED, -ING, -S to increase at a rapidly accelerating rate

SNOWBANK *n pl.* -S a mound of snow

SNOWBELL *n pl.* -S a flowering shrub

SNOWBIRD *n pl.* -S a small bird

SNOWBUSH *n pl.* -ES a flowering shrub

SNOWCAP *n pl.* -S a covering of snow

SNOWDROP *n pl.* -S a European herb

SNOWFALL *n pl.* -S a fall of snow

SNOWIER comparative of snowy

SNOWIEST superlative of snowy

SNOWILY *adv* in a snowy manner

SNOWLAND *n pl.* -S an area marked by a great amount of snow

SNOWLESS *adj* having no snow

SNOWLIKE *adj* resembling snow

SNOWMAN *n pl.* -MEN a figure of a person that is made of snow

SNOWMELT *n pl.* -S water produced by the melting of snow

SNOWPACK *n pl.* -S an accumulation of packed snow

SNOWPLOW *v* -ED, -ING, -S to execute a type of skiing maneuver

SNOWSHED *n pl.* -S a structure built to provide protection against snow

SNOWSHOE *v* -SHOED, -SHOEING, -SHOES to walk on snowshoes (oval frames that allow a person to walk on deep snow)

SNOWSUIT *n pl.* -S a child's garment for winter wear

SNOWY *adj* SNOWIER, SNOWIEST abounding in snow

SNUB *v* SNUBBED, SNUBBING, SNUBS to treat with contempt or neglect

SNUBBER *n pl.* -S one that snubs

SNUBBY *adj* -BIER, -BIEST blunt

SNUBNESS *n pl.* -ES bluntness

SNUCK a past tense of sneak

SNUFF *v* -ED, -ING, -S to use or inhale snuff (powdered tobacco)

SNUFFBOX *n pl.* -ES a box for holding snuff

SNUFFER *n pl.* -S one that snuffs

SNUFFIER comparative of snuffy

SNUFFIEST superlative of snuffy

SNUFFILY *adv* in a snuffy manner

SNUFFLE *v* -FLED, -FLING, -FLES to sniffle

SNUFFLER *n pl.* -S one that snuffles

SNUFFLY *adj* -FLIER, -FLIEST tending to snuffle

SNUFFY *adj* SNUFFIER, SNUFFIEST dingy

SNUG *adj* SNUGGER, SNUGGEST warmly comfortable

SNUG *v* SNUGGED, SNUGGING, SNUGS to make snug

SNUGGERY *n pl.* -GERIES a snug place

SNUGGEST superlative of snug

SNUGGING present participle of snug

SNUGGLE *v* -GLED, -GLING, -GLES to lie or press closely

SNUGLY *adv* in a snug manner

SNUGNESS *n pl.* -ES the quality or state of being snug

SNYE *n pl.* -S a side channel in a river or creek

SO *n pl.* SOS sol

SOAK *v* -ED, -ING, -S to saturate thoroughly in liquid

SOAKAGE *n pl.* -S the act of soaking

SOAKER *n pl.* -S one that soaks

SOAP *v* -ED, -ING, -S to treat with soap (a cleansing agent)

SOAPBARK *n pl.* -S a tropical tree

SOAPBOX *n pl.* -ES a box for soap

SOAPIER comparative of soapy

SOAPIEST superlative of soapy

SOAPILY *adv* in a soapy manner

SOAPLESS *adj* having no soap

SOAPLIKE *adj* resembling soap

SOAPSUDS *n/pl* suds (soapy water)

SOAPWORT *n pl.* -S a perennial herb

SOAPY *adj* SOAPIER, SOAPIEST containing or resembling soap

SOAR *v* -ED, -ING, -S to fly at a great height

SOARER *n pl.* -S one that soars

SOARING *n pl.* -S the sport of flying in a heavier-than-air craft without power

SOAVE *n pl.* -S an Italian wine

SOB	*v* SOBBED, SOBBING, SOBS to cry with a convulsive catching of the breath
SOBBER	*n pl.* -S one that sobs
SOBEIT	*conj* provided that
SOBER	*adj* SOBERER, SOBEREST having control of one's faculties
SOBER	*v* -ED, -ING, -S to make sober
SOBERIZE	*v* -IZED, -IZING, -IZES to sober
SOBERLY	*adv* in a sober manner
SOBFUL	*adj* given to sobbing
SOBRIETY	*n pl.* -ETIES the quality or state of being sober
SOCAGE	*n pl.* -S a form of feudal land tenure
SOCAGER	*n pl.* -S a tenant by socage
SOCCAGE	*n pl.* -S socage
SOCCER	*n pl.* -S a type of ball game
SOCIABLE	*n pl.* -S a social
SOCIABLY	*adv* in a friendly manner
SOCIAL	*n pl.* -S a friendly gathering
SOCIALLY	*adv* with respect to society
SOCIETY	*n pl.* -ETIES an organized group of persons **SOCIETAL** *adj*
SOCK	*n pl.* SOCKS or SOX a knitted or woven covering for the foot
SOCK	*v* -ED, -ING, -S to strike forcefully
SOCKET	*v* -ED, -ING, -S to furnish with a socket (an opening for receiving something)
SOCKEYE	*n pl.* -S a food fish
SOCKMAN	*n pl.* -MEN socman
SOCLE	*n pl.* -S a block used as a base for a column or pedestal
SOCMAN	*n pl.* -MEN a socager
SOD	*v* SODDED, SODDING, SODS to cover with sod (turf)
SODA	*n pl.* -S a type of chemical compound **SODALESS** *adj*
SODALIST	*n pl.* -S a member of a sodality
SODALITE	*n pl.* -S a mineral
SODALITY	*n pl.* -TIES a society
SODAMIDE	*n pl.* -S a chemical compound
SODDED	past tense of sod
SODDEN	*v* -ED, -ING, -S to make soggy
SODDENLY	*adv* in a soggy manner
SODDING	present participle of sod
SODDY	*n pl.* -DIES a house built of sod
SODIUM	*n pl.* -S a metallic element **SODIC** *adj*
SODOMITE	*n pl.* -S one who practices sodomy
SODOMY	*n pl.* -OMIES unnatural copulation
SOEVER	*adv* at all
SOFA	*n pl.* -S a long, upholstered seat
SOFAR	*n pl.* -S a system for locating underwater explosions
SOFFIT	*n pl.* -S the underside of an architectural structure
SOFT	*adj* SOFTER, SOFTEST yielding readily to pressure
SOFT	*n pl.* -S a soft object or part
SOFTA	*n pl.* -S a Muslim theological student
SOFTBACK	*n pl.* -S a book bound in a flexible paper cover
SOFTBALL	*n pl.* -S a type of ball
SOFTEN	*v* -ED, -ING, -S to make soft
SOFTENER	*n pl.* -S one that softens
SOFTHEAD	*n pl.* -S a foolish person
SOFTIE	*n pl.* -S softy
SOFTIES	pl. of softy
SOFTLY	*adv* in a soft manner
SOFTNESS	*n pl.* -ES the quality or state of being soft
SOFTWARE	*n pl.* -S written or printed data used in computer operations
SOFTWOOD	*n pl.* -S the soft wood of various trees
SOFTY	*n pl.* SOFTIES a sentimental person
SOGGED	*adj* soggy
SOGGY	*adj* -GIER, -GIEST heavy with moisture **SOGGILY** *adv*
SOIGNE	*adj* carefully done
SOIGNEE	*adj* soigne
SOIL	*v* -ED, -ING, -S to make dirty
SOILAGE	*n pl.* -S green crops for feeding animals
SOILLESS	*adj* carried on without soil (finely divided rock mixed with organic matter)
SOILURE	*n pl.* -S a stain or smudge
SOIREE	*n pl.* -S an evening party
SOJA	*n pl.* -S the soybean
SOJOURN	*v* -ED, -ING, -S to stay temporarily
SOKE	*n pl.* -S a feudal right to administer justice within a certain territory
SOKEMAN	*n pl.* -MEN socman

SOL n pl. -S the fifth tone of the diatonic musical scale

SOLA a pl. of solum

SOLACE v -LACED, -LACING, -LACES to console

SOLACER n pl. -S one that solaces

SOLAN n pl. -S a gannet

SOLAND n pl. -S solan

SOLANDER n pl. -S a protective box for library materials

SOLANIN n pl. -S solanine

SOLANINE n pl. -S a poisonous alkaloid

SOLANO n pl. -NOS a strong, hot wind

SOLANUM n pl. -S any of a genus of herbs and shrubs

SOLAR adj pertaining to the sun

SOLARIA a pl. of solarium

SOLARISE v -ISED, -ISING, -ISES to solarize

SOLARISM n pl. -S an interpretation of folk tales as concepts of the nature of the sun

SOLARIUM n pl. -IA or -IUMS a room exposed to the sun

SOLARIZE v -IZED, -IZING, -IZES to expose to sunlight

SOLATE v -ATED, -ATING, -ATES to change to a fluid colloidal system

SOLATIA pl. of solatium

SOLATION n pl. -S the act of solating

SOLATIUM n pl. -TIA a compensation given for damage to the feelings

SOLD past tense of sell

SOLDAN n pl. -S a Muslim ruler

SOLDER v -ED, -ING, -S to join closely together

SOLDERER n pl. -S one that solders

SOLDI pl. of soldo

SOLDIER v -ED, -ING, -S to perform military service

SOLDIERY n pl. -DIERIES the military profession

SOLDO n pl. -DI a former coin of Italy

SOLE v SOLED, SOLING, SOLES to furnish with a sole (the bottom surface of a shoe or boot)

SOLECISE v -CISED, -CISING, -CISES to solecize

SOLECISM n pl. -S an ungrammatical combination of words in a sentence

SOLECIST n pl. -S one who solecizes

SOLECIZE v -CIZED, -CIZING, -CIZES to use solecisms

SOLED past tense of sole

SOLELESS adj having no sole

SOLELY adv singly

SOLEMN adj -EMNER, -EMNEST serious

SOLEMNLY adv

SOLENESS n pl. -ES the state of being the only one

SOLENOID n pl. -S a type of electric coil

SOLERET n pl. -S solleret

SOLFEGE n pl. -S a type of singing exercise

SOLFEGGI n/pl solfeges

SOLGEL adj involving some changes in the state of a colloidal system

SOLI a pl. of solo

SOLICIT v -ED, -ING, -S to ask for earnestly

SOLID adj -IDER, -IDEST having definite shape and volume

SOLID n pl. -S a solid substance

SOLIDAGO n pl. -GOS a flowering plant

SOLIDARY adj united

SOLIDI pl. of solidus

SOLIDIFY v -FIED, -FYING, -FIES to make solid

SOLIDITY n pl. -TIES the quality or state of being solid

SOLIDLY adv in a solid manner

SOLIDUS n pl. -DI a coin of ancient Rome

SOLING present participle of sole

SOLION n pl. -S an electronic detecting and amplifying device

SOLIQUID n pl. -S a fluid colloidal system

SOLITARY n pl. -TARIES one who lives alone

SOLITUDE n pl. -S the state of being alone

SOLLERET n pl. -S a sabaton

SOLO n pl. -LOS or -LI a musical composition for a single voice or instrument

SOLO v -ED, -ING, -S to perform alone

SOLOIST n pl. -S one that performs a solo

SOLON n pl. -S a wise lawgiver

SOLONETS n pl. -ES solonetz

SOLONETZ n pl. -ES a type of soil

SOLSTICE n pl. -S the time of the year when the sun is at its greatest distance from the celestial equator

SOLUBLE *n pl.* -S something that is soluble (capable of being dissolved)

SOLUBLY *adv* in a soluble manner

SOLUM *n pl.* -LA or -LUMS a soil layer

SOLUS *adj* alone

SOLUTE *n pl.* -S a dissolved substance

SOLUTION *n pl.* -S a homogenous liquid mixture

SOLVABLE *adj* capable of being solved

SOLVATE *v* -VATED, -VATING, -VATES to convert into a type of ion

SOLVE *v* SOLVED, SOLVING, SOLVES to find the answer or explanation for

SOLVENCY *n pl.* -CIES the ability to pay all debts

SOLVENT *n pl.* -S a substance capable of dissolving others

SOLVER *n pl.* -S one that solves

SOLVING present participle of solve

SOMA *n pl.* -MATA or -MAS the body of an organism **SOMATIC** *adj*

SOMBER *adj* gloomy **SOMBERLY** *adv*

SOMBRE *adj* somber **SOMBRELY** *adv*

SOMBRERO *n pl.* -ROS a broad-brimmed hat

SOMBROUS *adj* somber

SOME *adj* being an unspecified number or part

SOMEBODY *n pl.* -BODIES an important person

SOMEDAY *adv* at some future time

SOMEDEAL *adv* to some degree

SOMEHOW *adv* by some means

SOMEONE *n pl.* -S a somebody

SOMERSET *v* -SETED, -SETING, -SETS or -SETTED, -SETTING, -SETS to roll the body in a complete circle, head over heels

SOMETIME *adv* at some future time

SOMEWAY *adv* somehow

SOMEWAYS *adv* someway

SOMEWHAT *n pl.* -S an unspecified number or part

SOMEWHEN *adv* sometime

SOMEWISE *adv* somehow

SOMITE *n pl.* -S a longitudinal segment of the body of some animals **SOMITAL, SOMITIC** *adj*

SON *n pl.* -S a male child

SONANCE *n pl.* -S sound

SONANT *n pl.* -S a sound uttered with vibration of the vocal cords **SONANTAL, SONANTIC** *adj*

SONAR *n pl.* -S an underwater locating device

SONARMAN *n pl.* -MEN a person who operates sonar equipment

SONATA *n pl.* -S a type of musical composition

SONATINA *n pl.* -TINAS or -TINE a short sonata

SONDE *n pl.* -S a device for observing atmospheric phenomena

SONDER *n pl.* -S a class of small yachts

SONE *n pl.* -S a unit of loudness

SONG *n pl.* -S a musical composition written or adapted for singing

SONGBIRD *n pl.* -S a bird that utters a musical call

SONGBOOK *n pl.* -S a book of songs

SONGFEST *n pl.* -S an informal gathering for group singing

SONGFUL *adj* melodious

SONGLESS *adj* incapable of singing

SONGLIKE *adj* resembling a song

SONGSTER *n pl.* -S a singer

SONIC *adj* pertaining to sound

SONICATE *v* -CATED, -CATING, -CATES to disrupt with sound waves

SONICS *n/pl* the science dealing with the practical applications of sound

SONLESS *adj* having no son

SONLIKE *adj* resembling a son

SONLY *adj* pertaining to a son

SONNET *v* -NETED, -NETING, -NETS or -NETTED, -NETTING, -NETS to compose a sonnet (a type of poem)

SONNY *n pl.* -NIES a small boy

SONORANT *n pl.* -S a type of voiced sound

SONORITY *n pl.* -TIES the quality or state of being sonorous

SONOROUS *adj* characterized by a full and loud sound

SONOVOX *n pl.* -ES a sound effects device

SONSHIP *n pl.* -S the state of being a son

SONSIE *adj* -SIER, -SIEST sonsy

SONSY *adj* -SIER, -SIEST comely

SOOCHONG *n pl.* -S souchong

SOOEY *interj* — used in calling pigs

SOON adv SOONER, SOONEST in the near future

SOONER n pl. -S one who settles on government land before it is officially opened for settlement

SOOT v -ED, -ING, -S to cover with soot (a black substance produced by combustion)

SOOTH adj SOOTHER, SOOTHEST true

SOOTH n pl. -S truth

SOOTHE v SOOTHED, SOOTHING, SOOTHES to restore to a quiet or normal state

SOOTHER n pl. -S one that soothes

SOOTHEST superlative of sooth

SOOTHING present participle of soothe

SOOTHLY adv in truth

SOOTHSAY v -SAID, -SAYING, -SAYS to predict

SOOTY adj SOOTIER, SOOTIEST covered with soot SOOTILY adv

SOP v SOPPED, SOPPING, SOPS to dip or soak in a liquid

SOPH n pl. -S a sophomore

SOPHIES pl. of sophy

SOPHISM n pl. -S a plausible but fallacious argument

SOPHIST n pl. -S one that uses sophisms

SOPHY n pl. -PHIES a ruler of Persia

SOPITE v -PITED, -PITING, -PITES to put to sleep

SOPOR n pl. -S an abnormally deep sleep

SOPPED past tense of sop

SOPPING adj very wet

SOPPY adj -PIER, -PIEST very wet

SOPRANO n pl. -NOS or -NI the highest singing voice

SORA n pl. -S a marsh bird

SORB v -ED, -ING, -S to take up and hold by absorption or adsorption SORBABLE adj

SORBATE n pl. -S a sorbed substance

SORBENT n pl. -S a substance that sorbs

SORBET n pl. -S sherbet

SORBIC adj pertaining to a type of fruit

SORBITOL n pl. -S a chemical compound

SORBOSE n pl. -S a type of sugar

SORCERER n pl. -S one who practices sorcery

SORCERY n pl. -CERIES alleged use of supernatural powers

SORD n pl. -S a flight of mallards

SORDID adj filthy SORDIDLY adv

SORDINE n pl. -S a device used to muffle the tone of a musical instrument

SORDINO n pl. -NI sordine

SORE adj SORER, SOREST painfully sensitive to the touch

SORE n pl. -S a sore area on the body

SOREHEAD n pl. -S a person who is easily angered or offended

SOREL n pl. -S sorrel

SORELY adv in a sore manner

SORENESS n pl. -ES the quality or state of being sore

SORER comparative of sore

SOREST superlative of sore

SORGHO n pl. -GHOS sorgo

SORGHUM n pl. -S a cereal grass

SORGO n pl. -GOS a variety of sorghum

SORI pl. of sorus

SORICINE adj belonging to the shrew family of mammals

SORITES n pl. SORITES a type of argument used in logic SORITIC adj

SORN v -ED, -ING, -S to force oneself on others for food and lodging

SORNER n pl. -S one that sorns

SOROCHE n pl. -S mountain sickness

SORORAL adj sisterly

SORORATE n pl. -S the marriage of a man usually with his deceased wife's sister

SORORITY n pl. -TIES a social club for women

SOROSIS n pl. -ROSES or -ROSISES a women's club or society

SORPTION n pl. -S the act or process of sorbing SORPTIVE adj

SORREL n pl. -S a reddish brown color

SORRIER comparative of sorry

SORRIEST superlative of sorry

SORRILY adv in a sorry manner

SORROW v -ED, -ING, -S to grieve

SORROWER n pl. -S one that sorrows

SORRY adj -RIER, -RIEST feeling grief or penitence

SORT v -ED, -ING, -S to arrange according to kind, class, or size SORTABLE adj SORTABLY adv

SORTER n pl. -S one that sorts

SORTIE *v* -TIED, -TIEING, -TIES to attack suddenly from a defensive position

SORUS *n* pl. -RI a cluster of plant reproductive bodies

SOT *n* pl. -S an habitual drunkard

SOTH *n* pl. -S sooth

SOTOL *n* pl. -S a flowering plant

SOTTISH *adj* resembling a sot

SOU *n* pl. -S a former French coin

SOUARI *n* pl. -S a tropical tree

SOUBISE *n* pl. -S a sauce of onions and butter

SOUCAR *n* pl. -S a Hindu banker

SOUCHONG *n* pl. -S a Chinese tea

SOUDAN *n* pl. -S soldan

SOUFFLE *n* pl. -S a light, baked dish

SOUGH *v* -ED, -ING, -S to make a moaning or sighing sound

SOUGHT past tense of seek

SOUL *n* pl. -S the spiritual aspect of human beings SOULED, SOULLESS, SOULLIKE *adj*

SOULFUL *adj* full of emotion

SOUND *adj* SOUNDER, SOUNDEST being in good health or condition

SOUND *v* -ED, -ING, -S to make a sound (something that stimulates the auditory receptors)

SOUNDBOX *n* pl. -ES a resonant cavity in a musical instrument

SOUNDER *n* pl. -S one that sounds

SOUNDING *n* pl. -S a sampling or test of opinions

SOUNDLY *adv* in a sound manner

SOUP *v* -ED, -ING, -S to increase the power or efficiency of

SOUPCON *n* pl. -S a minute amount

SOUPY *adj* SOUPIER, SOUPIEST foggy

SOUR *adj* SOURER, SOUREST sharp or biting to the taste

SOUR *v* -ED, -ING, -S to make or become sour

SOURBALL *n* pl. -S a sour candy

SOURCE *n* pl. -S a point of origin

SOURDINE *n* pl. -S a sordine

SOURISH *adj* somewhat sour

SOURLY *adv* in a sour manner

SOURNESS *n* pl. -ES the quality or state of being sour

SOURPUSS *n* pl. -ES a grouchy person

SOURSOP *n* pl. -S a tropical tree

SOURWOOD *n* pl. -S a flowering tree

SOUSE *v* SOUSED, SOUSING, SOUSES to immerse

SOUTACHE *n* pl. -S a flat, narrow braid

SOUTANE *n* pl. -S a cassock

SOUTER *n* pl. -S a shoemaker

SOUTH *v* -ED, -ING, -S to move toward the south (a cardinal point of the compass)

SOUTHER *n* pl. -S a wind or storm from the south

SOUTHERN *n* pl. -S a person living in the south

SOUTHING *n* pl. -S movement toward the south

SOUTHPAW *n* pl. -S a left-handed person

SOUTHRON *n* pl. -S a southern

SOUVENIR *n* pl. -S a memento

SOVIET *n* pl. -S a legislative body in a Communist country

SOVKHOZ *n* pl. -KHOZES or -KHOZY a state-owned farm in the Soviet Union

SOVRAN *n* pl. -S a monarch

SOVRANLY *adv* supremely

SOVRANTY *n* pl. -TIES a monarchy

SOW *v* SOWED, SOWN, SOWING, SOWS to scatter over land for growth, as seed SOWABLE *adj*

SOWANS *n* pl. SOWANS sowens

SOWAR *n* pl. -S a mounted native soldier in India

SOWBELLY *n* pl. -LIES pork cured in salt

SOWBREAD *n* pl. -S a flowering plant

SOWCAR *n* pl. -S soucar

SOWENS *n* pl. SOWENS porridge made from oat husks

SOWER *n* pl. -S one that sows

SOWN past participle of sow

SOX a pl. of sock

SOY *n* pl. SOYS the soybean

SOYA *n* pl. -S soy

SOYBEAN *n* pl. -S the seed of a cultivated Asian herb

SOZIN *n* pl. -S a type of protein

SOZINE *n* pl. -S sozin

SPA *n* pl. -S a mineral spring

SPACE *v* SPACED, SPACING, SPACES to set some distance apart

SPACEMAN *n* pl. -MEN an astronaut

SPACER *n* pl. -S one that spaces

SPACIAL	*adj* spatial
SPACING	*n* pl. -S the distance between any two objects
SPACIOUS	*adj* vast or ample in extent
SPADE	*v* SPADED, SPADING, SPADES to take up with a spade (a digging implement)
SPADEFUL	*n* pl. -S as much as a spade can hold
SPADER	*n* pl. -S one that spades
SPADICES	pl. of spadix
SPADILLE	*n* pl. -S the highest trump in certain card games
SPADING	present participle of spade
SPADIX	*n* pl. -DICES a flower cluster
SPADO	*n* pl. -DONES a castrated man or animal
SPAE	*v* SPAED, SPAEING, SPAES to foretell
SPAEING	*n* pl. -S the act of foretelling
SPAGYRIC	*n* pl. -S a person skilled in alchemy
SPAHEE	*n* pl. -S spahi
SPAHI	*n* pl. -S a Turkish cavalryman
SPAIL	*n* pl. -S spale
SPAIT	*n* pl. -S spate
SPAKE	a past tense of speak
SPALE	*n* pl. -S a splinter or chip
SPALL	*v* -ED, -ING, -S to break up into fragments
SPALLER	*n* pl. -S one that spalls
SPALPEEN	*n* pl. -S a rascal
SPAN	*v* SPANNED, SPANNING, SPANS to extend over or across
SPANCEL	*v* -CELED, -CELING, -CELS or -CELLED, -CELLING, -CELS to bind or fetter with a rope
SPANDREL	*n* pl. -S a space between two adjoining arches
SPANDRIL	*n* pl. -S spandrel
SPANG	*adv* directly
SPANGLE	*v* -GLED, -GLING, -GLES to adorn with spangles (bits of sparkling metal)
SPANGLY	*adj* -GLIER, -GLIEST covered with spangles
SPANIEL	*n* pl. -S a dog with silky hair
SPANK	*v* -ED, -ING, -S to slap on the buttocks
SPANKER	*n* pl. -S one that spanks
SPANKING	*n* pl. -S the act of one that spanks

SPANLESS	*adj* having no extent
SPANNED	past tense of span
SPANNER	*n* pl. -S one that spans
SPANNING	present participle of span
SPANWORM	*n* pl. -S an inchworm
SPAR	*v* SPARRED, SPARRING, SPARS to provide with spars (stout poles used to support rigging)
SPARABLE	*n* pl. -S a type of nail
SPARE	*v* SPARED, SPARING, SPARES to refrain from punishing, harming, or destroying
SPARE	*adj* SPARER, SPAREST meager SPARELY *adv*
SPARER	*n* pl. -S one that spares
SPARERIB	*n* pl. -S a cut of pork
SPAREST	*adj* superlative of spare
SPARGE	*v* SPARGED, SPARGING, SPARGES to sprinkle
SPARGER	*n* pl. -S one that sparges
SPARID	*n* pl. -S any of a family of marine fishes
SPARING	present participle of spare
SPARK	*v* -ED, -ING, -S to give off sparks (small fiery particles)
SPARKER	*n* pl. -S something that sparks
SPARKIER	comparative of sparky
SPARKIEST	superlative of sparky
SPARKILY	*adv* in a lively manner
SPARKISH	*adj* jaunty
SPARKLE	*v* -KLED, -KLING, -KLES to give off or reflect flashes of light
SPARKLER	*n* pl. -S something that sparkles
SPARKY	*adj* SPARKIER, SPARKIEST lively
SPARLIKE	*adj* resembling a spar
SPARLING	*n* pl. -S a young herring
SPAROID	*n* pl. -S a sparid
SPARRED	past tense of spar
SPARRIER	comparative of sparry
SPARRIEST	superlative of sparry
SPARRING	present participle of spar
SPARROW	*n* pl. -S a small bird
SPARRY	*adj* -RIER, -RIEST resembling spar (a lustrous mineral)
SPARSE	*adj* SPARSER, SPARSEST thinly distributed SPARSELY *adv*
SPARSITY	*n* pl. -TIES the quality or state of being sparse

SPASM n pl. -S an abnormal, involuntary muscular contraction

SPASTIC n pl. -S one suffering from spastic paralysis (a paralysis with muscle spasms)

SPAT v SPATTED, SPATTING, SPATS to strike lightly

SPATE n pl. -S a freshet

SPATHE n pl. -S a leaflike organ of certain plants SPATHAL, SPATHED, SPATHOSE adj

SPATHIC adj sparry

SPATIAL adj of or pertaining to space

SPATTED past tense of spat

SPATTER v -ED, -ING, -S to scatter in drops

SPATTING present participle of spat

SPATULA n pl. -S a mixing implement SPATULAR adj

SPAVIE n pl. -S spavin SPAVIET adj

SPAVIN n pl. -S a disease of horses SPAVINED adj

SPAWN v -ED, -ING, -S to deposit eggs

SPAWNER n pl. -S one that spawns

SPAY v -ED, -ING, -S to remove the ovaries of

SPEAK v SPOKE or SPAKE, SPOKEN, SPEAKING, SPEAKS to utter words

SPEAKER n pl. -S one that speaks

SPEAKING n pl. -S a speech or discourse

SPEAN v -ED, -ING, -S to wean

SPEAR v -ED, -ING, -S to pierce with a spear (a long, pointed weapon)

SPEARER n pl. -S one that spears

SPEARMAN n pl. -MEN a person armed with a spear

SPECIAL adj -CIALER, -CIALEST of a distinct or particular kind or character

SPECIAL n pl. -S a special person or thing

SPECIATE v -ATED, -ATING, -ATES to undergo a type of evolutionary process

SPECIE n pl. -S coined money

SPECIFIC n pl. -S a remedy intended for a particular disease

SPECIFY v -FIED, -FYING, -FIES to state in detail

SPECIMEN n pl. -S a part or individual representative of a group or whole

SPECIOUS adj having a false look of truth or authenticity

SPECK v -ED, -ING, -S to mark with small spots

SPECKLE v -LED, -LING, -LES to speck

SPECS n/pl eyeglasses

SPECTATE v -TATED, -TATING, -TATES to attend and view

SPECTER n pl. -S a visible disembodied spirit

SPECTRA a pl. of spectrum

SPECTRAL adj resembling a specter

SPECTRE n pl. -S specter

SPECTRUM n pl. -TRA or -TRUMS an array of the components of a light wave

SPECULUM n pl. -LA or -LUMS a medical instrument SPECULAR adj

SPED a past tense of speed

SPEECH n pl. -ES the faculty or act of speaking

SPEED v SPED or SPEEDED, SPEEDING, SPEEDS to move swiftly

SPEEDER n pl. -S one that speeds

SPEEDIER comparative of speedy

SPEEDIEST superlative of speedy

SPEEDILY adv in a speedy manner

SPEEDING n pl. -S the act of driving faster than the law allows

SPEEDUP n pl. -S an acceleration of production without an increase in pay

SPEEDWAY n pl. -WAYS a road designed for rapid travel

SPEEDY adj SPEEDIER, SPEEDIEST swift

SPEEL v -ED, -ING, -S to climb

SPEER v -ED, -ING, -S to inquire

SPEERING n pl. -S inquiry

SPEIL v -ED, -ING, -S to speel

SPEIR v -ED, -ING, -S to speer

SPEISE n pl. -S speiss

SPEISS n pl. -ES a metallic mixture obtained in smelting certain ores

SPELAEAN adj spelean

SPELEAN adj living in caves

SPELL v SPELLED or SPELT, SPELLING, SPELLS to name or write the letters of in order

SPELLER n pl. -S one that spells words

SPELLING n pl. -S a sequence of letters composing a word

SPELT n pl. -S a variety of wheat

SPELTER   *n pl.* -S zinc in the form of ingots

SPELTZ   *n pl.* -ES spelt

SPELUNK   *v* -ED, -ING, -S to explore caves

SPENCE   *n pl.* -S a pantry

SPENCER   *n pl.* -S a trysail

SPEND   *v* SPENT, SPENDING, SPENDS to pay out

SPENDER   *n pl.* -S one that spends

SPENT   past tense of spend

SPERM   *n pl.* -S a male gamete **SPERMIC** *adj*

SPERMARY   *n pl.* -RIES an organ in which sperms are formed

SPERMINE   *n pl.* -S a chemical compound

SPERMOUS   *adj* resembling or made up of sperms

SPEW   *v* -ED, -ING, -S to vomit

SPEWER   *n pl.* -S one that spews

SPHAGNUM   *n pl.* -S a grayish moss

SPHENE   *n pl.* -S a mineral

SPHENIC   *adj* shaped like a wedge

SPHENOID   *n pl.* -S a bone of the skull

SPHERAL   *adj* of, pertaining to, or having the form of a sphere

SPHERE   *v* SPHERED, SPHERING, SPHERES to form into a sphere (a type of geometric solid)

SPHERIC   *adj* spheral

SPHERICS   *n/pl* the geometry of figures on the surface of a sphere

SPHERIER   comparative of sphery

SPHERIEST   superlative of sphery

SPHERING   present participle of sphere

SPHEROID   *n pl.* -S a type of geometric solid

SPHERULE   *n pl.* -S a small sphere

SPHERY   *adj* SPHERIER, SPHERIEST resembling a sphere

SPHINGES   a pl. of sphinx

SPHINGID   *n pl.* -S the hawkmoth

SPHINX   *n pl.* SPHINXES or SPHINGES a monster in Egyptian mythology

SPHYGMUS   *n pl.* -ES the pulse **SPHYGMIC** *adj*

SPIC   *n pl.* -S a Spanish-American person — an offensive term

SPICA   *n pl.* -CAE or -CAS an ear of grain **SPICATE, SPICATED** *adj*

SPICCATO   *n pl.* -TOS a method of playing a stringed instrument

SPICE   *v* SPICED, SPICING, SPICES to season with a spice (an aromatic vegetable substance)

SPICER   *n pl.* -S one that spices

SPICERY   *n pl.* -ERIES a spicy quality

SPICEY   *adj* SPICIER, SPICIEST spicy

SPICIER   comparative of spicy

SPICIEST   superlative of spicy

SPICILY   *adv* in a spicy manner

SPICING   present participle of spice

SPICK   *n pl.* -S spic — an offensive term

SPICULA   *n pl.* -LAE spicule **SPICULAR** *adj*

SPICULE   *n pl.* -S a needlelike structure

SPICULUM   *n pl.* -LA spicule

SPICY   *adj* SPICIER, SPICIEST containing spices

SPIDER   *n pl.* -S a type of arachnid

SPIDERY   *adj* -DERIER, -DERIEST resembling a spider

SPIED   past tense of spy

SPIEGEL   *n pl.* -S a type of cast iron

SPIEL   *v* -ED, -ING, -S to talk at length

SPIELER   *n pl.* -S one that spiels

SPIER   *v* -ED, -ING, -S to speer

SPIES   present 3d person sing. of spy

SPIFFING   *adj* spiffy

SPIFFY   *adj* -FIER, -FIEST stylish **SPIFFILY** *adv*

SPIGOT   *n pl.* -S a faucet

SPIK   *n pl.* -S spic — an offensive term

SPIKE   *v* SPIKED, SPIKING, SPIKES to fasten with a spike (a long, thick nail)

SPIKELET   *n pl.* -S a type of flower cluster

SPIKER   *n pl.* -S one that spikes

SPIKING   present participle of spike

SPIKY   *adj* SPIKIER, SPIKIEST resembling a spike **SPIKILY** *adv*

SPILE   *v* SPILED, SPILING, SPILES to stop up with a wooden plug

SPILIKIN   *n pl.* -S a strip of wood used in a game

SPILING   *n pl.* -S a piling

SPILL   *v* SPILLED or SPILT, SPILLING, SPILLS to cause to run out of a container

SPILLAGE   *n pl.* -S something that is spilled

SPILLER   *n pl.* -S one that spills

SPILLWAY	*n pl.* -WAYS a channel for surplus water in a reservoir
SPILT	a past tense of spill
SPILTH	*n pl.* -S spillage
SPIN	*v* SPUN, SPINNING, SPINS to draw out and twist into threads
SPINACH	*n pl.* -ES a cultivated herb
SPINAGE	*n pl.* -S spinach
SPINAL	*n pl.* -S an injection of an anesthetic into the spinal cord
SPINALLY	*adv* with respect to the spine
SPINATE	*adj* bearing thorns
SPINDLE	*v* -DLED, -DLING, -DLES to impale on a slender rod
SPINDLER	*n pl.* -S one that spindles
SPINDLY	*adj* -DLIER, -DLIEST long and slender
SPINE	*n pl.* -S the vertebral column SPINED *adj*
SPINEL	*n pl.* -S a mineral
SPINELLE	*n pl.* -S spinel
SPINET	*n pl.* -S a small piano
SPINIER	comparative of spiny
SPINIEST	superlative of spiny
SPINIFEX	*n pl.* -ES an Australian grass
SPINLESS	*adj* having no rotation
SPINNER	*n pl.* -S one that spins
SPINNERY	*n pl.* -NERIES a spinning mill
SPINNEY	*n pl.* -NEYS a thicket
SPINNING	*n pl.* -S the act of one that spins
SPINNY	*n pl.* -NIES spinney
SPINOFF	*n pl.* -S a new application or incidental result
SPINOR	*n pl.* -S a type of mathematical vector
SPINOSE	*adj* spiny
SPINOUS	*adj* spiny
SPINOUT	*n pl.* -S a rotational skid by an automobile
SPINSTER	*n pl.* -S an unmarried woman who is past the usual age for marrying
SPINULA	*n pl.* -LAE spinule
SPINULE	*n pl.* -S a small thorn
SPINY	*adj* SPINIER, SPINIEST bearing or covered with thorns
SPIRACLE	*n pl.* -S an orifice through which breathing occurs
SPIRAEA	*n pl.* -S spirea

SPIRAL	*v* -RALED, -RALING, -RALS or -RALLED, -RALLING, -RALS to move like a spiral (a type of plane curve)
SPIRALLY	*adv* in a spiral manner
SPIRANT	*n pl.* -S a speech sound produced by the forcing of breath through a narrow passage
SPIRE	*v* SPIRED, SPIRING, SPIRES to rise in a tapering manner
SPIREA	*n pl.* -S a flowering shrub
SPIREM	*n pl.* -S spireme
SPIREME	*n pl.* -S a filament forming part of a cell nucleus during mitosis
SPIRILLA	*n/pl* spirally twisted, aerobic bacteria
SPIRING	present participle of spire
SPIRIT	*v* -ED, -ING, -S to carry off secretly
SPIROID	*adj* resembling a spiral
SPIRT	*v* -ED, -ING, -S to spurt
SPIRULA	*n pl.* -LAE or -LAS a spiral-shelled mollusk
SPIRY	*adj* tall, slender, and tapering
SPIT	*v* SPITTED, SPITTING, SPITS to impale on a spit (a pointed rod on which meat is turned)
SPITAL	*n pl.* -S a hospital
SPITBALL	*n pl.* -S a type of pitch in baseball
SPITE	*v* SPITED, SPITING, SPITES to treat with malice
SPITEFUL	*adj* -FULLER, -FULLEST malicious
SPITFIRE	*n pl.* -S a quick-tempered person
SPITING	present participle of spite
SPITTED	past tense of spit
SPITTER	*n pl.* -S a spitball
SPITTING	present participle of spit
SPITTLE	*n pl.* -S saliva
SPITTOON	*n pl.* -S a receptacle for saliva
SPITZ	*n pl.* -ES a dog having a heavy coat
SPIV	*n pl.* -S a petty criminal
SPLAKE	*n pl.* -S a freshwater fish
SPLASH	*v* -ED, -ING, -ES to scatter a liquid about
SPLASHER	*n pl.* -S one that splashes
SPLASHY	*adj* SPLASHIER, SPLASHIEST showy

SPLAT *n* pl. -S a piece of wood forming the middle of a chair back

SPLATTER *v* -ED, -ING, -S to spatter

SPLAY *v* -ED, -ING, -S to spread out

SPLEEN *n* pl. -S a ductless organ of the body

SPLEENY *adj* SPLEENIER, SPLEENIEST peevish

SPLENDID *adj* -DIDER, -DIDEST magnificent

SPLENDOR *n* pl. -S magnificence

SPLENIA pl. of splenium

SPLENIAL *adj* pertaining to the splenius

SPLENIC *adj* pertaining to the spleen

SPLENIUM *n* pl. -NIA a surgical bandage

SPLENIUS *n* pl. -NII a muscle of the neck

SPLENT *n* pl. -S a splint

SPLICE *v* SPLICED, SPLICING, SPLICES to join at the ends

SPLICER *n* pl. -S one that splices

SPLINE *v* SPLINED, SPLINING, SPLINES to provide with a spline (a key that connects two rotating mechanical parts)

SPLINT *v* -ED, -ING, -S to brace with a splint (a thin piece of wood)

SPLINTER *v* -ED, -ING, -S to split into sharp, slender pieces

SPLIT *v* SPLIT, SPLITTING, SPLITS to separate lengthwise

SPLITTER *n* pl. -S one that splits

SPLORE *n* pl. -S a carousal

SPLOSH *v* -ED, -ING, -ES to splash

SPLOTCH *v* -ED, -ING, -ES to mark with large, irregular spots

SPLOTCHY *adj* SPLOTCHIER, SPLOTCHIEST splotched

SPLURGE *v* SPLURGED, SPLURGING, SPLURGES to spend money lavishly

SPLURGY *adj* SPLURGIER, SPLURGIEST tending to splurge

SPLUTTER *v* -ED, -ING, -S to speak rapidly and confusedly

SPODE *n* pl. -S a fine china

SPOIL *v* SPOILED or SPOILT, SPOILING, SPOILS to impair the value or quality of

SPOILAGE *n* pl. -S something that is spoiled or wasted

SPOILER *n* pl. -S one that spoils

SPOILT a past tense of spoil

SPOKE *v* SPOKED, SPOKING, SPOKES to provide with spokes (rods that support the rim of a wheel)

SPOKEN past participle of speak

SPOLIATE *v* -ATED, -ATING, -ATES to plunder

SPONDAIC *n* pl. -S a spondee

SPONDEE *n* pl. -S a type of metrical foot

SPONGE *v* SPONGED, SPONGING, SPONGES to wipe with a sponge (a mass of absorbent material)

SPONGER *n* pl. -S one that sponges

SPONGIER comparative of spongy

SPONGIEST superlative of spongy

SPONGILY *adv* in a spongy manner

SPONGIN *n* pl. -S a fibrous material

SPONGING present participle of sponge

SPONGY *adj* SPONGIER, SPONGIEST resembling a sponge

SPONSAL *adj* pertaining to marriage

SPONSION *n* pl. -S the act of sponsoring

SPONSON *n* pl. -S a projection from the side of a ship

SPONSOR *v* -ED, -ING, -S to make oneself responsible for

SPONTOON *n* pl. -S a spear-like weapon

SPOOF *v* -ED, -ING, -S to hoax

SPOOK *v* -ED, -ING, -S to scare

SPOOKISH *adj* spooky

SPOOKY *adj* SPOOKIER, SPOOKIEST scary **SPOOKILY** *adv*

SPOOL *v* -ED, -ING, -S to wind on a small cylinder

SPOON *v* -ED, -ING, -S to take up with a spoon (a type of eating utensil)

SPOONEY *adj* SPOONIER, SPOONIEST spoony

SPOONEY *n* pl. -EYS a spoony

SPOONFUL *n* pl. SPOONFULS or SPOONSFUL as much as a spoon will hold

SPOONIER comparative of spooney

SPOONIES pl. of spoony

SPOONIEST superlative of spooney

SPOONING present participle of spoon

SPOONY *adj* SPOONIER, SPOONIEST overly sentimental **SPOONILY** *adv*

SPOONY *n* pl. SPOONIES a spoony person

SPOOR *v* -ED, -ING, -S to track

SPORADIC *adj* occurring at irregular intervals

SPORAL *adj* of, pertaining to, or resembling a spore

SPORE *v* SPORED, SPORING, SPORES to produce spores (asexual, usually single-celled reproductive bodies)

SPOROID *adj* resembling a spore

SPORRAN *n pl.* -S a large purse worn by Scottish Highlanders

SPORT *v* -ED, -ING, -S to frolic

SPORTER *n pl.* -S one that sports

SPORTFUL *adj* sportive

SPORTIVE *adj* playful

SPORTY *adj* SPORTIER, SPORTIEST showy **SPORTILY** *adv*

SPORULE *n pl.* -S a small spore **SPORULAR** *adj*

SPOT *v* SPOTTED, SPOTTING, SPOTS to mark with spots (small, roundish discolorations)

SPOTLESS *adj* perfectly clean

SPOTTER *n pl.* -S one that spots

SPOTTING present participle of spot

SPOTTY *adj* -TIER, -TIEST marked with spots **SPOTTILY** *adv*

SPOUSAL *n pl.* -S marriage

SPOUSE *v* SPOUSED, SPOUSING, SPOUSES to marry

SPOUT *v* -ED, -ING, -S to eject in a rapid stream

SPOUTER *n pl.* -S one that spouts

SPRADDLE *v* -DLED, -DLING, -DLES to straddle

SPRAG *n pl.* -S a device used to prevent a vehicle from rolling backward

SPRAIN *v* -ED, -ING, -S to weaken by a sudden and violent twisting or wrenching

SPRANG a past tense of spring

SPRAT *n pl.* -S a small herring

SPRATTLE *v* -TLED, -TLING, -TLES to struggle

SPRAWL *v* -ED, -ING, -S to stretch out ungracefully

SPRAWLER *n pl.* -S one that sprawls

SPRAWLY *adj* SPRAWLIER, SPRAWLIEST tending to sprawl

SPRAY *v* -ED, -ING, -S to disperse in fine particles

SPRAYER *n pl.* -S one that sprays

SPREAD *v* SPREAD, SPREADING, SPREADS to open or expand over a larger area

SPREADER *n pl.* -S one that spreads

SPREE *n pl.* -S an unrestrained indulgence in an activity

SPRENT *adj* sprinkled over

SPRIER a comparative of spry

SPRIEST a superlative of spry

SPRIG *v* SPRIGGED, SPRIGGING, SPRIGS to fasten with small, thin nails

SPRIGGER *n pl.* -S one that sprigs

SPRIGGY *adj* -GIER, -GIEST having small branches

SPRIGHT *n pl.* -S sprite

SPRING *v* SPRANG or SPRUNG, SPRINGING, SPRINGS to move upward suddenly and swiftly

SPRINGAL *n pl.* -S a young man

SPRINGE *v* SPRINGED, SPRINGEING, SPRINGES to catch with a type of snare

SPRINGER *n pl.* -S one that springs

SPRINGY *adj* SPRINGIER, SPRINGIEST resilient

SPRINKLE *v* -KLED, -KLING, -KLES to scatter drops or particles on

SPRINT *v* -ED, -ING, -S to run at top speed

SPRINTER *n pl.* -S one that sprints

SPRIT *n pl.* -S a ship's spar

SPRITE *n pl.* -S an elf or fairy

SPROCKET *n pl.* -S a toothlike projection that engages with the links of a chain

SPROUT *v* -ED, -ING, -S to begin to grow

SPRUCE *adj* SPRUCER, SPRUCEST neat and trim in appearance **SPRUCELY** *adv*

SPRUCE *v* SPRUCED, SPRUCING, SPRUCES to make spruce

SPRUCY *adj* SPRUCIER, SPRUCIEST spruce

SPRUE *n pl.* -S a tropical disease

SPRUG *n pl.* -S a sparrow

SPRUNG a past tense of spring

SPRY *adj* SPRYER, SPRYEST or SPRIER, SPRIEST nimble **SPRYLY** *adv*

SPRYNESS *n pl.* -ES the quality or state of being spry

SPUD *v* SPUDDED, SPUDDING, SPUDS to remove with a spade-like tool

SPUDDER — n pl. -S a tool for removing bark from trees

SPUE — v SPUED, SPUING, SPUES to spew

SPUME — v SPUMED, SPUMING, SPUMES to foam

SPUMIER — comparative of spumy

SPUMIEST — superlative of spumy

SPUMING — present participle of spume

SPUMONE — n pl. -S an Italian ice cream

SPUMONI — n pl. -S spumone

SPUMOUS — adj spumy

SPUMY — adj SPUMIER, SPUMIEST foamy

SPUN — past tense of spin

SPUNK — v -ED, -ING, -S to begin to burn

SPUNKIE — n pl. -S a light caused by the combustion of marsh gas

SPUNKY — adj SPUNKIER, SPUNKIEST plucky SPUNKILY adv

SPUR — v SPURRED, SPURRING, SPURS to urge on with a spur (a horseman's goad)

SPURGALL — v -ED, -ING, -S to injure with a spur

SPURGE — n pl. -S a tropical plant

SPURIOUS — adj not genuine

SPURN — v -ED, -ING, -S to reject with contempt

SPURNER — n pl. -S one that spurns

SPURRED — past tense of spur

SPURRER — n pl. -S one that spurs

SPURREY — n pl. -REYS spurry

SPURRIER — n pl. -S one that makes spurs

SPURRING — present participle of spur

SPURRY — n pl. -RIES a European weed

SPURT — v -ED, -ING, -S to gush forth

SPURTLE — n pl. -S a stick for stirring porridge

SPUTA — pl. of sputum

SPUTNIK — n pl. -S a Soviet artificial earth satellite

SPUTTER — v -ED, -ING, -S to eject particles in short bursts

SPUTUM — n pl. -TA saliva

SPY — v SPIED, SPYING, SPIES to watch secretly

SPYGLASS — n pl. -ES a small telescope

SQUAB — n pl. -S a young pigeon

SQUABBLE — v -BLED, -BLING, -BLES to quarrel

SQUABBY — adj -BIER, -BIEST short and fat

SQUAD — v SQUADDED, SQUADDING, SQUADS to form into squads (small, organized groups)

SQUADRON — v -ED, -ING, -S to arrange in squadrons (units of military organization)

SQUALENE — n pl. -S a chemical compound

SQUALID — adj -IDER, -IDEST marked by filthiness caused by neglect or poverty

SQUALL — v -ED, -ING, -S to cry or scream loudly

SQUALLER — n pl. -S one that squalls

SQUALLY — adj SQUALLIER, SQUALLIEST gusty

SQUALOR — n pl. -S the quality or state of being squalid

SQUAMA — n pl. -MAE a scale SQUAMATE, SQUAMOSE, SQUAMOUS adj

SQUANDER — v -ED, -ING, -S to spend wastefully

SQUARE — adj SQUARER, SQUAREST having four equal sides and four right angles

SQUARE — v SQUARED, SQUARING, SQUARES to make square

SQUARELY — adv in a direct manner

SQUARER — n pl. -S one that squares

SQUAREST — superlative of square

SQUARING — present participle of square

SQUARISH — adj somewhat square

SQUASH — v -ED, -ING, -ES to press into a pulp or flat mass

SQUASHER — n pl. -S one that squashes

SQUASHY — adj SQUASHIER, SQUASHIEST soft and moist

SQUAT — v SQUATTED, SQUATTING, SQUATS to sit on one's heels

SQUAT — adj SQUATTER, SQUATTEST short and thick SQUATLY adv

SQUATTER — v -ED, -ING, -S to move through water

SQUATTING — present participle of squat

SQUATTY — adj -TIER, -TIEST squat

SQUAW — n pl. -S an American Indian woman

SQUAWK — v -ED, -ING, -S to utter a loud, harsh cry

SQUAWKER — n pl. -S one that squawks

SQUEAK — v -ED, -ING, -S to make a sharp, high-pitched sound

SQUEAKER n pl. -S one that squeaks

SQUEAKY adj SQUEAKIER, SQUEAKIEST tending to squeak

SQUEAL v -ED, -ING, -S to utter a sharp, shrill cry

SQUEALER n pl. -S one that squeals

SQUEEGEE v -GEED, -GEEING, -GEES to wipe with a squeegee (an implement for removing water from a surface)

SQUEEZE v SQUEEZED, SQUEEZING, SQUEEZES to press hard upon

SQUEEZER n pl. -S one that squeezes

SQUEG v SQUEGGED, SQUEGGING, SQUEGS to oscillate in an irregular manner

SQUELCH v -ED, -ING, -ES to squash

SQUELCHY adj SQUELCHIER, SQUELCHIEST squashy

SQUIB v SQUIBBED, SQUIBBING, SQUIBS to lampoon

SQUID v SQUIDDED, SQUIDDING, SQUIDS to fish for squid (ten-armed marine mollusks)

SQUIFFED adj drunk

SQUIFFY adj squiffed

SQUIGGLE v -GLED, -GLING, -GLES to wriggle

SQUIGGLY adj -GLIER, -GLIEST wriggly

SQUILGEE v -GEED, -GEEING, -GEES to squeegee

SQUILL n pl. -S a Eurasian herb

SQUILLA n pl. -LAS or -LAE a burrowing crustacean

SQUINCH v -ED, -ING, -ES to squint

SQUINNY v -NIED, -NYING, -NIES to squint

SQUINNY adj -NIER, -NIEST squinty

SQUINT adj SQUINTER, SQUINTEST cross-eyed

SQUINT v -ED, -ING, -S to look with the eyes partly closed

SQUINTER n pl. -S one that squints

SQUINTY adj SQUINTIER, SQUINTIEST marked by squinting

SQUIRE v SQUIRED, SQUIRING, SQUIRES to serve as a squire (an escort)

SQUIREEN n pl. -S an owner of a small estate

SQUIRISH adj of, resembling, or befitting a squire

SQUIRM v -ED, -ING, -S to wriggle

SQUIRMER n pl. -S one that squirms

SQUIRMY adj SQUIRMIER, SQUIRMIEST wriggly

SQUIRREL v -RELED, -RELING, -RELS or -RELLED, -RELLING, -RELS to store up for future use

SQUIRT v -ED, -ING, -S to eject in a thin, swift stream

SQUIRTER n pl. -S one that squirts

SQUISH v -ED, -ING, -ES to squash

SQUISHY adj SQUISHIER, SQUISHIEST squashy

SQUOOSH v -ED, -ING, -ES to squash

SQUUSH v -ED, -ING, -ES to squash

SRADDHA n pl. -S sradha

SRADHA n pl. -S a Hindu ceremonial offering

SRI n pl. -S mister; sir — used as a Hindu title of respect

STAB v STABBED, STABBING, STABS to pierce with a pointed weapon

STABBER n pl. -S one that stabs

STABILE n pl. -S a stationary abstract sculpture

STABLE adj -BLER, -BLEST resistant to sudden change or position or condition

STABLE v -BLED, -BLING, -BLES to put in a stable (a shelter for domestic animals)

STABLER n pl. -S one that keeps a stable

STABLEST superlative of stable

STABLING n pl. -S accommodation for animals in a stable

STABLISH v -ED, -ING, -ES to establish

STABLY adv in a stable manner

STACCATO n pl. -TOS or -TI a musical passage marked by the short, clear-cut playing of tones

STACK v -ED, -ING, -S to pile

STACKER n pl. -S one that stacks

STACTE n pl. -S a spice used by the ancient Jews in making incense

STADDLE n pl. -S a platform on which hay is stacked

STADE n pl. -S an ancient Greek unit of length

STADIA n pl. -S a method of surveying distances

STADIUM n pl. -S a structure in which athletic events are held

STAFF v -ED, -ING, -S to provide with a staff (a body of assistants)

STAFFER n pl. -S a member of a staff

STAG — v STAGGED, STAGGING, STAGS to attend a social function without a female companion

STAGE — v STAGED, STAGING, STAGES to produce for public view

STAGER — n pl. -S an experienced person

STAGEY — adj STAGIER, STAGIEST stagy

STAGGARD — n pl. -S a full-grown male red deer

STAGGART — n pl. -S staggard

STAGGED — past tense of stag

STAGGER — v -ED, -ING, -S to walk or stand unsteadily

STAGGERY — adj unsteady

STAGGIE — n pl. -S a colt

STAGGING — present participle of stag

STAGGY — adj -GIER, -GIEST having the appearance of a mature male

STAGIER — comparative of stagey and stagy

STAGIEST — superlative of stagey and stagy

STAGILY — adv in a stagy manner

STAGING — n pl. -S a temporary platform

STAGNANT — adj not moving or flowing

STAGNATE — v -NATED, -NATING, -NATES to become stagnant

STAGY — adj STAGIER, STAGIEST having a theatrical quality

STAID — adj STAIDER, STAIDEST sober and sedate STAIDLY adv

STAIG — n pl. -S a colt

STAIN — v -ED, -ING, -S to discolor or dirty

STAINER — n pl. -S one that stains

STAIR — n pl. -S a rest for the foot used in going from one level to another

STAIRWAY — n pl. -WAYS a flight of stairs

STAKE — v STAKED, STAKING, STAKES to fasten with a stake (a pointed piece of wood or metal)

STAKEOUT — n pl. -S a surveillance of an area especially by the police

STALAG — n pl. -S a German prisoner-of-war camp

STALE — adj STALER, STALEST not fresh STALELY adv

STALE — v STALED, STALING, STALES to become stale

STALK — v -ED, -ING, -S to pursue stealthily

STALKER — n pl. -S one that stalks

STALKY — adj STALKIER, STALKIEST long and slender STALKILY adv

STALL — v -ED, -ING, -S to stop the progress of

STALLION — n pl. -S an uncastrated male horse

STALWART — n pl. -S an unwavering partisan

STAMEN — n pl. -S the pollen-bearing organ of flowering plants

STAMINA — n pl. -S endurance STAMINAL adj

STAMMEL — n pl. -S a red color

STAMMER — v -ED, -ING, -S to speak with involuntary breaks and pauses

STAMP — v -ED, -ING, -S to bring the foot down heavily

STAMPEDE — v -PEDED, -PEDING, -PEDES to cause to run away in headlong panic

STAMPER — n pl. -S one that stamps

STANCE — n pl. -S a manner of standing

STANCH — adj STANCHER, STANCHEST staunch

STANCH — v -ED, -ING, -ES to stop the flow of blood from

STANCHER — n pl. -S one that stanches

STANCHLY — adv in a stanch manner

STAND — v STOOD, STANDING, STANDS to assume or maintain an upright position

STANDARD — n pl. -S an established measure of comparison

STANDBY — n pl. -BYS one that can be relied on

STANDEE — n pl. -S one who stands because of the lack of seats

STANDER — n pl. -S one that stands

STANDING — n pl. -S a position or condition in society

STANDISH — n pl. -ES a receptacle for pens and ink

STANDOFF — n pl. -S a tie or draw, as in a game

STANDOUT — n pl. -S one that shows marked superiority

STANDPAT — adj resisting or opposing change

STANDUP — adj having an upright position

STANE — v STANED, STANING, STANES to stone

STANG — v -ED, -ING, -S to sting

STANHOPE — n pl. -S a light, open carriage

STANING — present participle of stane

STANK — n pl. -S a pond

STANNARY n pl. -RIES a tin-mining region

STANNIC adj pertaining to tin

STANNITE n pl. -S an ore of tin

STANNOUS adj pertaining to tin

STANNUM n pl. -S tin

STANZA n pl. -S a division of a poem STANZAED, STANZAIC adj

STAPEDES pl. of stapes

STAPELIA n pl. -S an African plant

STAPES n pl. -PEDES a bone of the middle ear

STAPH n pl. -S any of various spherical bacteria

STAPLE v -PLED, -PLING, -PLES to fasten by means of a U-shaped metal loop

STAPLER n pl. -S a stapling device

STAR v STARRED, STARRING, STARS to shine as a star (a natural luminous body visible in the sky)

STARCH v -ED, -ING, -ES to treat with starch (a solid carbohydrate)

STARCHY adj STARCHIER, STARCHIEST containing starch

STARDOM n pl. -S the status of a preeminent performer

STARDUST n pl. -S a romantic quality

STARE v STARED, STARING, STARES to gaze fixedly

STARER n pl. -S one that stares

STARETS n pl. STARTSY a spiritual adviser in the Eastern Orthodox Church

STARFISH n pl. -ES a star-shaped marine animal

STARGAZE v -GAZED, -GAZING, -GAZES to gaze at the stars

STARING present participle of stare

STARK adj STARKER, STARKEST harsh in appearance STARKLY adv

STARLESS adj having no stars

STARLET n pl. -S a small star

STARLIKE adj resembling a star

STARLING n pl. -S a European bird

STARLIT adj lighted by the stars

STARNOSE n pl. -S a burrowing mammal

STARRED past tense of star

STARRING present participle of star

STARRY adj -RIER, -RIEST abounding with stars

START v -ED, -ING, -S to set out

STARTER n pl. -S one that starts

STARTLE v -TLED, -TLING, -TLES to frighten or surprise suddenly

STARTLER n pl. -S one that startles

STARTSY pl. of starets

STARVE v STARVED, STARVING, STARVES to die from lack of food

STARVER n pl. -S one that starves

STARWORT n pl. -S a flowering plant

STASES pl. of stasis

STASH v -ED, -ING, -ES to store in a secret place

STASIMON n pl. -MA a choral ode in ancient Greek drama

STASIS n pl. STASES a stoppage of the normal flow of bodily fluids

STATABLE adj capable of being stated

STATAL adj pertaining to a national government

STATANT adj standing with all feet on the ground — used of a heraldic animal

STATE v STATED, STATING, STATES to set forth in words

STATEDLY adv regularly

STATELY adj -LIER, -LIEST dignified

STATER n pl. -S one that states

STATIC n pl. -S random noise produced in a radio or television receiver STATICAL adj

STATICE n pl. -S a flowering plant

STATING present participle of state

STATION v -ED, -ING, -S to assign to a position

STATISM n pl. -S a theory of government

STATIST n pl. -S an adherent of statism

STATIVE n pl. -S a verb that expresses a condition

STATOR n pl. -S the part of a machine about which the rotor revolves

STATUARY n pl. -ARIES a group of statues

STATUE n pl. -S a three-dimensional work of art STATUED adj

STATURE n pl. -S the natural height of a human or animal body

STATUS n pl. -ES relative position

STATUTE n pl. -S a law enacted by the legislative branch of a government

STAUMREL n pl. -S a dolt

STAUNCH adj STAUNCHER, STAUNCHEST firm and dependable

STAUNCH	v -ED, -ING, -ES to stanch
STAVE	v STAVED or STOVE, STAVING, STAVES to drive or thrust away
STAW	a past tense of steal
STAY	v STAYED or STAID, STAYING, STAYS to continue in a place or condition
STAYER	n pl. -S one that stays
STAYSAIL	n pl. -S a type of sail
STEAD	v -ED, -ING, -S to be of advantage to
STEADIED	past tense of steady
STEADIER	n pl. -S one that steadies
STEADIES	present 3d person sing. of steady
STEADING	n pl. -S a small farm
STEADY	adj STEADIER, STEADIEST firm in position STEADILY adv
STEADY	v STEADIED, STEADYING, STEADIES to make steady
STEAK	n pl. -S a slice of meat
STEAL	v STOLE or STAW, STOLEN, STEALING, STEALS to take without right or permission
STEALAGE	n pl. -S theft
STEALER	n pl. -S one that steals
STEALING	n pl. -S the act of one that steals
STEALTH	n pl. -S stealthy procedure
STEALTHY	adj STEALTHIER, STEALTHIEST intended to escape observation
STEAM	v -ED, -ING, -S to expose to steam (water in the form of vapor)
STEAMER	v -ED, -ING, -S to travel by steamship
STEAMY	adj STEAMIER, STEAMIEST marked by steam STEAMILY adv
STEAPSIN	n pl. -S an enzyme
STEARATE	n pl. -S a chemical salt
STEARIN	n pl. -S the solid portion of a fat STEARIC adj
STEARINE	n pl. -S stearin
STEATITE	n pl. -S a variety of talc
STEDFAST	adj staunch
STEED	n pl. -S a horse
STEEK	v -ED, -ING, -S to shut
STEEL	v -ED, -ING, -S to cover with steel (a tough iron alloy)
STEELIE	n pl. -S a steel playing marble

STEELY	adj STEELIER, STEELIEST resembling steel
STEENBOK	n pl. -S an African antelope
STEEP	adj STEEPER, STEEPEST inclined sharply
STEEP	v -ED, -ING, -S to soak in a liquid
STEEPEN	v -ED, -ING, -S to make steep
STEEPER	n pl. -S one that steeps
STEEPLE	n pl. -S a tapering structure on a church tower STEEPLED adj
STEEPLY	adv in a steep manner
STEER	v -ED, -ING, -S to direct the course of
STEERAGE	n pl. -S the act of steering
STEERER	n pl. -S one that steers
STEEVE	v STEEVED, STEEVING, STEEVES to stow in the hold of a ship
STEEVING	n pl. -S the angular elevation of a bowsprit from a ship's keel
STEGODON	n pl. -S an extinct elephant-like mammal
STEIN	n pl. -S a beer mug
STEINBOK	n pl. -S steenbok
STELA	n pl. -LAE or -LAI an inscribed slab used as a monument STELAR, STELENE adj
STELE	n pl. -S the central portion of vascular tissue in a plant stem STELIC adj
STELLA	n pl. -S a former coin of the United States
STELLAR	adj pertaining to the stars
STELLATE	adj shaped like a star
STELLIFY	v -FIED, -FYING, -FIES to convert into a star
STEM	v STEMMED, STEMMING, STEMS to remove stems (ascending axes of a plant) from
STEMLESS	adj having no stem
STEMLIKE	adj resembling a stem
STEMMA	n pl. -MAS or -MATA a scroll recording the genealogy of a family in ancient Rome
STEMMED	past tense of stem
STEMMER	n pl. -S one that removes stems
STEMMERY	n pl. -MERIES a place where tobacco leaves are stripped
STEMMING	present participle of stem
STEMMY	adj -MIER, -MIEST abounding in stems

STEMSON *n* pl. -S a supporting timber of a ship

STEMWARE *n* pl. -S a type of glassware

STENCH *n* pl. -ES a foul odor

STENCHY *adj* STENCHIER, STENCHIEST having a stench

STENCIL *v* -CILED, -CILING, -CILS or -CILLED, -CILLING, -CILS to mark by means of a perforated sheet of material

STENGAH *n* pl. -S a mixed drink

STENO *n* pl. STENOS a stenographer

STENOSED *adj* affected with stenosis

STENOSIS *n* pl. -NOSES a narrowing of a bodily passage STENOTIC *adj*

STENTOR *n* pl. -S a person having a very loud voice

STEP *v* STEPPED, STEPPING, STEPS to move by lifting the foot and setting it down in another place

STEPDAME *n* pl. -S a stepmother

STEPLIKE *adj* resembling a stair

STEPPE *n* pl. -S a vast treeless plain

STEPPED past tense of step

STEPPER *n* pl. -S one that steps

STEPPING present participle of step

STEPSON *n* pl. -S a son of one's spouse by a former marriage

STEPWISE *adj* marked by a gradual progression

STERE *n* pl. -S a unit of volume

STEREO *v* -ED, -ING, -S to make a type of printing plate

STERIC *adj* pertaining to the spatial relationships of atoms in a molecule

STERICAL *adj* steric

STERIGMA *n* pl. -MAS or -MATA a spore-bearing stalk of certain fungi

STERILE *adj* incapable of producing offspring

STERLET *n* pl. -S a small sturgeon

STERLING *n* pl. -S British money

STERN *adj* STERNER, STERNEST unyielding

STERN *n* pl. -S the rear part of a ship

STERNA a pl. of sternum

STERNAL *adj* pertaining to the sternum

STERNITE *n* pl. -S a somitic sclerite

STERNLY *adv* in a stern manner

STERNSON *n* pl. -S a reinforcing post of a ship

STERNUM *n* pl. -NA or -NUMS a long, flat supporting bone of most vertebrates

STERNWAY *n* pl. -WAYS the backward movement of a vessel

STEROID *n* pl. -S a type of chemical compound

STEROL *n* pl. -S a type of solid alcohol

STERTOR *n* pl. -S a deep snoring sound

STET *v* STETTED, STETTING, STETS to cancel a previously made printing correction

STETSON *n* pl. -S a broad-brimmed hat

STEW *v* -ED, -ING, -S to cook by boiling slowly

STEWARD *v* -ED, -ING, -S to manage

STEWBUM *n* pl. -S a drunken bum

STEWPAN *n* pl. -S a pan used for stewing

STEY *adj* steep

STHENIA *n* pl. -S excessive energy STHENIC *adj*

STIBIAL *adj* pertaining to stibium

STIBINE *n* pl. -S a poisonous gas

STIBIUM *n* pl. -S antimony

STIBNITE *n* pl. -S an ore of antimony

STICH *n* pl. -S a line of poetry STICHIC *adj*

STICK *v* -ED, -ING, -S to support with slender pieces of wood

STICK *v* STUCK, STICKING, STICKS to pierce with a pointed object

STICKER *n* pl. -S an adhesive label

STICKFUL *n* pl. -S an amount of set type

STICKIER comparative of sticky

STICKIEST superlative of sticky

STICKILY *adv* in a sticky manner

STICKIT *adj* unsuccessful

STICKLE *v* -LED, -LING, -LES to argue stubbornly

STICKLER *n* pl. -S one that stickles

STICKMAN *n* pl. -MEN one who supervises the play at a dice table

STICKOUT *n* pl. -S one that is conspicuous

STICKPIN *n* pl. -S a decorative tiepin

STICKUM *n* pl. -S a substance that causes adhesion

STICKUP *n* pl. -S a robbery at gunpoint

STICKY *adj* STICKIER, STICKIEST tending to adhere

STIED a past tense of sty

STIES present 3d person sing. of sty

STIFF *adj* STIFFER, STIFFEST difficult to bend or stretch

STIFF	n pl. -S a corpse
STIFFEN	v -ED, -ING, -S to make stiff
STIFFISH	adj somewhat stiff
STIFFLY	adv in a stiff manner
STIFLE	v -FLED, -FLING, -FLES to smother
STIFLER	n pl. -S one that stifles
STIGMA	n pl. -MAS or -MATA a mark of disgrace STIGMAL adj
STILBENE	n pl. -S a chemical compound
STILBITE	n pl. -S a mineral
STILE	n pl. -S a series of steps for passing over a fence or wall
STILETTO	v -ED, -ING, -S or -ES to stab with a short dagger
STILL	adj STILLER, STILLEST free from sound or motion
STILL	v -ED, -ING, -S to make still
STILLMAN	n pl. -MEN one who operates a distillery
STILLY	adj STILLIER, STILLIEST still
STILT	v -ED, -ING, -S to raise on stilts (long, slender poles)
STIME	n pl. -S a glimpse
STIMULUS	n pl. -LI something that causes a response
STIMY	v -MIED, -MYING, -MIES to stymie
STING	v STUNG, STINGING, STINGS to prick painfully
STINGER	n pl. -S one that stings
STINGIER	comparative of stingy
STINGIEST	superlative of stingy
STINGILY	adv in a stingy manner
STINGO	n pl. -GOS a strong ale or beer
STINGRAY	n pl. -RAYS a flat-bodied marine fish
STINGY	adj -GIER, -GIEST unwilling to spend or give
STINK	v STANK or STUNK, STINKING, STINKS to emit a foul odor
STINKARD	n pl. -S a despicable person
STINKBUG	n pl. -S an insect that emits a foul odor
STINKER	n pl. -S one that stinks
STINKIER	comparative of stinky
STINKIEST	superlative of stinky
STINKO	adj drunk
STINKPOT	n pl. -S a jar containing foul-smelling combustibles formerly used in warfare
STINKY	adj STINKIER, STINKIEST emitting a foul odor

STINT	v -ED, -ING, -S to limit
STINTER	n pl. -S one that stints
STIPE	n pl. -S a slender supporting part of a plant STIPED adj
STIPEL	n pl. -S a small stipule
STIPEND	n pl. -S a fixed sum of money paid periodically
STIPES	n pl. STIPITES a stipe
STIPPLE	v -PLED, -PLING, -PLES to draw, paint, or engrave by means of dots or short touches
STIPPLER	n pl. -S one that stipples
STIPULE	n pl. -S an appendage at the base of a leaf in certain plants STIPULAR, STIPULED adj
STIR	v STIRRED, STIRRING, STIRS to pass an implement through in circular motions
STIRK	n pl. -S a young cow
STIRP	n pl. -S lineage
STIRPS	n pl. STIRPES a family or branch of a family
STIRRED	past tense of stir
STIRRER	n pl. -S one that stirs
STIRRING	present participle of stir
STIRRUP	n pl. -S a support for the foot of a horseman
STITCH	v -ED, -ING, -ES to join by making in-and-out movements with a threaded needle
STITCHER	n pl. -S one that stitches
STITHY	v STITHIED, STITHYING, STITHIES to forge on an anvil
STIVER	n pl. -S a former Dutch coin
STOA	n pl. STOAE, STOAI, or STOAS an ancient Greek covered walkway
STOAT	n pl. -S a weasel with a black-tipped tail
STOB	v STOBBED, STOBBING, STOBS to stab
STOCCADO	n pl. -DOS a thrust with a rapier
STOCCATA	n pl. -S stoccado
STOCK	v -ED, -ING, -S to keep for future sale or use
STOCKADE	v -ADED, -ADING, -ADES to build a type of protective fence around
STOCKCAR	n pl. -S a boxcar for carrying livestock
STOCKER	n pl. -S a young animal suitable for being fattened for market
STOCKIER	comparative of stocky

STOCKIEST superlative of stocky

STOCKILY adv in a stocky manner

STOCKING n pl. -S a knitted or woven covering for the foot and leg

STOCKISH adj stupid

STOCKIST n pl. -S one who stocks goods

STOCKMAN n pl. -MEN one who owns or raises livestock

STOCKPOT n pl. -S a pot in which broth is prepared

STOCKY adj STOCKIER, STOCKIEST having a short, thick body

STODGE v STODGED, STODGING, STODGES to stuff full with food

STODGY adj STODGIER, STODGIEST boring STODGILY adv

STOGEY n pl. -GEYS stogy

STOGIE n pl. -S stogy

STOGY n pl. -GIES a long, slender cigar

STOIC n pl. -S one who is indifferent to pleasure or pain STOICAL adj

STOICISM n pl. -S indifference to pleasure or pain

STOKE v STOKED, STOKING, STOKES to supply a furnace with fuel

STOKER n pl. -S one that stokes

STOKESIA n pl. -S a perennial herb

STOKING present participle of stoke

STOLE n pl. -S a long-wide scarf STOLED adj

STOLEN past participle of steal

STOLID adj -IDER, -IDEST showing little or no emotion STOLIDLY adv

STOLLEN n pl. -S a sweet bread

STOLON n pl. -S a type of plant stem STOLONIC adj

STOMA n pl. -MAS or -MATA a minute opening in the epidermis of a plant organ

STOMACH v -ED, -ING, -ES to tolerate

STOMACHY adj paunchy

STOMAL adj stomatal

STOMATA a pl. of stoma

STOMATAL adj pertaining to a stoma

STOMATE n pl. -S a stoma

STOMATIC adj pertaining to the mouth

STOMODEA n/pl embryonic oral cavities

STOMP v -ED, -ING, -S to tread heavily

STOMPER n pl. -S one that stomps

STONE v STONED, STONING, STONES to pelt with stones (pieces of concreted earthy or mineral matter) STONABLE adj

STONEFLY n pl. -FLIES a winged insect

STONER n pl. -S one that stones

STONEY adj STONIER, STONIEST stony

STONIER comparative of stony

STONIEST superlative of stony

STONILY adv in a stony manner

STONING present participle of stone

STONISH v -ED, -ING, -ES to astonish

STONY adj STONIER, STONIEST abounding in stones

STOOD past tense of stand

STOOGE v STOOGED, STOOGING, STOOGES to act as a comedian's straight man

STOOK v -ED, -ING, -S to stack upright in a field for drying, as bundles of grain

STOOKER n pl. -S one that stooks

STOOL v -ED, -ING, -S to defecate

STOOLIE n pl. -S an informer

STOOP v -ED, -ING, -S to bend the body forward and down

STOOPER n pl. -S one that stoops

STOP v STOPPED or STOPT, STOPPING, STOPS to discontinue the progress or motion of

STOPCOCK n pl. -S a type of faucet

STOPE v STOPED, STOPING, STOPES to excavate in layers, as ore

STOPER n pl. -S one that stopes

STOPGAP n pl. -S a temporary substitute

STOPING present participle of stope

STOPOVER n pl. -S a brief stop in the course of a journey

STOPPAGE n pl. -S the act of stopping

STOPPED a past tense of stop

STOPPER v -ED, -ING, -S to plug

STOPPING present participle of stop

STOPPLE v -PLED, -PLING, -PLES to stopper

STOPT a past tense of stop

STORABLE n pl. -S something that can be stored

STORAGE n pl. -S a place for storing

STORAX n pl. -ES a fragrant resin

STORE v STORED, STORING, STORES to put away for future use

STOREY	n pl. -REYS a horizontal division of a building **STOREYED** adj
STORIED	past tense of story
STORIES	present 3d person sing. of story
STORING	present participle of store
STORK	n pl. -S a wading bird
STORM	v -ED, -ING, -S to blow violently
STORMY	adj STORMIER, STORMIEST storming **STORMILY** adv
STORY	v -RIED, -RYING, -RIES to relate as a story (an account of an event or series of events)
STOSS	adj facing the direction from which a glacier moves
STOTINKA	n pl. -KI a monetary unit of Bulgaria
STOUND	v -ED, -ING, -S to ache
STOUP	n pl. -S a basin for holy water
STOUR	n pl. -S dust
STOURE	n pl. -S stour
STOURIE	adj stoury
STOURY	adj dusty
STOUT	adj STOUTER, STOUTEST fat
STOUT	n pl. -S a strong, dark ale
STOUTEN	v -ED, -ING, -S to make stout
STOUTISH	adj somewhat stout
STOUTLY	adv in a stout manner
STOVE	n pl. -S a heating apparatus
STOVER	n pl. -S coarse food for cattle
STOW	v -ED, -ING, -S to pack **STOWABLE** adj
STOWAGE	n pl. -S goods in storage
STOWAWAY	n pl. -AWAYS one who hides aboard a conveyance to obtain free passage
STOWP	n pl. -S stoup
STRADDLE	v -DLED, -DLING, -DLES to sit, stand, or walk with the legs wide apart
STRAFE	v STRAFED, STRAFING, STRAFES to attack with machine-gun fire from an airplane
STRAFER	n pl. -S one that strafes
STRAGGLE	v -GLED, -GLING, -GLES to stray
STRAGGLY	adj -GLIER, -GLIEST irregularly spread out
STRAIGHT	adj STRAIGHTER, STRAIGHTEST extending uniformly in one direction without bends or irregularities
STRAIGHT	v -ED, -ING, -S to make straight
STRAIN	v -ED, -ING, -S to exert to the utmost
STRAINER	n pl. -S a utensil used to separate liquids from solids
STRAIT	n pl. -S a narrow waterway connecting two larger bodies of water
STRAIT	adj STRAITER, STRAITEST narrow **STRAITLY** adv
STRAITEN	v -ED, -ING, -S to make strait
STRAKE	n pl. -S a line of planking extending along a ship's hull **STRAKED** adj
STRAMASH	n pl. -ES an uproar
STRAMONY	n pl. -NIES a poisonous weed
STRAND	v -ED, -ING, -S to leave in an unfavorable situation
STRANDER	n pl. -S a machine that twists fibers into rope
STRANG	adj strong
STRANGE	adj STRANGER, STRANGEST unusual or unfamiliar
STRANGER	v -ED, -ING, -S to estrange
STRANGLE	v -GLED, -GLING, -GLES to choke to death
STRAP	v STRAPPED, STRAPPING, STRAPS to fasten with a strap (a narrow strip of flexible material)
STRAPPER	n pl. -S one that straps
STRASS	n pl. -ES a brilliant glass used in making imitation gems
STRATA	n pl. -S a stratum
STRATAL	adj pertaining to a stratum
STRATEGY	n pl. -GIES a plan for obtaining a specific goal
STRATH	n pl. -S a wide river valley
STRATI	pl. of stratus
STRATIFY	v -FIED, -FYING, -FIES to form or arrange in layers
STRATOUS	adj stratal
STRATUM	n pl. -TA or -TUMS a layer of material
STRATUS	n pl. -TI a type of cloud
STRAVAGE	v -VAGED, -VAGING, -VAGES to stroll
STRAVAIG	v -ED, -ING, -S to stravage
STRAW	v -ED, -ING, -S to cover with straw (stalks of threshed grain)
STRAWHAT	adj pertaining to a summer theater situated in a resort area
STRAWY	adj STRAWIER, STRAWIEST resembling straw

STRAY   v -ED, -ING, -S to wander from the proper area or course

STRAYER   n pl. -S one that strays

STREAK   v -ED, -ING, -S to cover with streaks (long, narrow marks)

STREAKER   n pl. -S one that streaks

STREAKY   adj STREAKIER, STREAKIEST covered with streaks

STREAM   v -ED, -ING, -S to flow in a steady current

STREAMER   n pl. -S a long, narrow flag

STREAMY   adj STREAMIER, STREAMIEST streaming

STREEK   v -ED, -ING, -S to stretch

STREEKER   n pl. -S one that streeks

STREET   n pl. -S a public thoroughfare

STRENGTH   n pl. -S capacity for exertion or endurance

STREP   n pl. -S any of various spherical or oval bacteria

STRESS   v -ED, -ING, -ES to place emphasis on

STRESSOR   n pl. -S a type of stimulus

STRETCH   v -ED, -ING, -ES to draw out or open to full length

STRETCHY   adj STRETCHIER, STRETCHIEST having a tendency to stretch

STRETTA   n pl. -TE or -TAS stretto

STRETTO   n pl. -TI or -TOS a concluding musical passage played at a faster tempo

STREUSEL   n pl. -S a topping for coffee cakes

STREW   v STREWED, STREWN, STREWING, STREWS to scatter about

STREWER   n pl. -S one that strews

STRIA   n pl. STRIAE a thin groove, stripe, or streak

STRIATE   v -ATED, -ATING, -ATES to mark with striae

STRICK   n pl. -S a bunch of flax fibers

STRICKEN   adj strongly affected or afflicted

STRICKLE   v -LED, -LING, -LES to shape or smooth with a strickle (an instrument for leveling off grain)

STRICT   adj STRICTER, STRICTEST kept within narrow and specific limits STRICTLY adv

STRIDE   v STRODE or STRID, STRIDDEN, STRIDING, STRIDES to walk with long steps

STRIDENT   adj shrill

STRIDER   n pl. -S one that strides

STRIDING   present participle of stride

STRIDOR   n pl. -S a strident sound

STRIFE   n pl. -S bitter conflict or dissension

STRIGIL   n pl. -S a scraping instrument

STRIGOSE   adj covered with short, stiff hairs

STRIKE   v STRUCK or STROOK, STRICKEN or STRUCKEN, STRIKING, STRIKES to come or cause to come into contact with

STRIKER   n pl. -S one that strikes

STRING   v STRUNG or STRINGED, STRINGING, STRINGS to provide with strings (slender cords)

STRINGER   n pl. -S one that strings

STRINGY   adj STRINGIER, STRINGIEST resembling a string or strings

STRIP   v STRIPPED or STRIPT, STRIPPING, STRIPS to remove the outer covering from

STRIPE   v STRIPED, STRIPING, STRIPES to mark with stripes (long, distinct bands)

STRIPER   n pl. -S a food and game fish

STRIPIER   comparative of stripy

STRIPIEST   superlative of stripy

STRIPING   n pl. -S the stripes marked or painted on something

STRIPPED   a past tense of strip

STRIPPER   n pl. -S one that strips

STRIPPING   present participle of strip

STRIPT   a past tense of strip

STRIPY   adj STRIPIER, STRIPIEST marked with stripes

STRIVE   v STROVE or STRIVED, STRIVEN, STRIVING, STRIVES to exert much effort or energy

STRIVER   n pl. -S one that strives

STROBE   n pl. -S a device that produces brief, high-intensity flashes of light

STROBIC   adj spinning

STROBIL   n pl. -S strobile

STROBILA   n pl. -LAE the entire body of a tapeworm

STROBILE   n pl. -S the conical, multiple fruit of certain trees

STROBILI   n/pl strobiles

STRODE   a past tense of stride

STROKE   v STROKED, STROKING, STROKES to rub gently

STROKER n pl. -S one that strokes

STROLL v -ED, -ING, -S to walk in a leisurely manner

STROLLER n pl. -S one that strolls

STROMA n pl. -MATA the substance that forms the framework of an organ or cell **STROMAL** adj

STRONG adj STRONGER, STRONGEST having great strength **STRONGLY** adv

STRONGYL n pl. -S a parasitic worm

STRONTIA n pl. -S a chemical compound **STRONTIC** adj

STROOK a past tense of strike

STROP v STROPPED, STROPPING, STROPS to sharpen on a strip of leather

STROPHE n pl. -S a part of an ancient Greek choral ode **STROPHIC** adj

STROUD n pl. -S a coarse woolen blanket

STROVE a past tense of strive

STROW v STROWED, STROWN, STROWING, STROWS to strew

STROY v -ED, -ING, -S to destroy

STROYER n pl. -S one that stroys

STRUCK a past tense of strike

STRUCKEN a past participle of strike

STRUDEL n pl. -S a type of pastry

STRUGGLE v -GLED, -GLING, -GLES to make strenuous efforts against opposition

STRUM v STRUMMED, STRUMMING, STRUMS to play a stringed instrument by running the fingers lightly across the strings

STRUMA n pl. -MAE or -MAS scrofula

STRUMMER n pl. -S one that strums

STRUMMING present participle of strum

STRUMOSE adj having a struma

STRUMOUS adj having or pertaining to a struma

STRUMPET n pl. -S a prostitute

STRUNG a past tense of string

STRUNT v -ED, -ING, -S to strut

STRUT v STRUTTED, STRUTTING, STRUTS to walk with a pompous air

STRUTTER n pl. -S one that struts

STUB v STUBBED, STUBBING, STUBS to strike accidentally against a projecting object

STUBBIER comparative of stubby

STUBBIEST superlative of stubby

STUBBILY adv in a stubby manner

STUBBING present participle of stub

STUBBLE n pl. -S a short, rough growth of beard **STUBBLED** adj

STUBBLY adj -BLIER, -BLIEST covered with stubble

STUBBORN adj unyielding

STUBBY adj -BIER, -BIEST short and thick

STUCCO v -ED, -ING, -ES or -S to coat with a type of plaster

STUCCOER n pl. -S one that stuccoes

STUCK past tense of stick

STUD v STUDDED, STUDDING, STUDS to set thickly with small projections

STUDBOOK n pl. -S a record of the pedigree of purebred animals

STUDDIE n pl. -S an anvil

STUDDING n pl. -S the framework of a wall

STUDENT n pl. -S a person formally engaged in learning

STUDFISH n pl. -ES a freshwater fish

STUDIED past tense of study

STUDIER n pl. -S one that studies

STUDIES present 3d person sing. of study

STUDIO n pl. -DIOS an artist's workroom

STUDIOUS adj given to study

STUDWORK n pl. -S studding

STUDY v STUDIED, STUDYING, STUDIES to apply the mind to the acquisition of knowledge

STUFF v -ED, -ING, -S to fill or pack tightly

STUFFER n pl. -S one that stuffs

STUFFING n pl. -S material with which something is stuffed

STUFFY adj STUFFIER, STUFFIEST poorly ventilated **STUFFILY** adv

STUIVER n pl. -S stiver

STULL n pl. -S a supporting timber in a mine

STULTIFY v -FIED, -FYING, -FIES to cause to appear absurd

STUM v STUMMED, STUMMING, STUMS to increase the fermentation of by adding grape juice

STUMBLE v -BLED, -BLING, -BLES to miss one's step in walking or running

STUMBLER n pl. -S one that stumbles

STUMMED past tense of stum

STUMMING present participle of stum

STUMP v -ED, -ING, -S to baffle

STUMPAGE n pl. -S uncut marketable timber

STUMPER n pl. -S a baffling question

STUMPY adj STUMPIER, STUMPIEST short and thick

STUN v STUNNED, STUNNING, STUNS to render senseless or incapable of action

STUNG past tense of sting

STUNK a past tense of stink

STUNNED past tense of stun

STUNNER n pl. -S one that stuns

STUNNING adj strikingly beautiful or attractive

STUNSAIL n pl. -S a type of sail

STUNT v -ED, -ING, -S to hinder the normal growth of

STUPA n pl. -S a Buddhist shrine

STUPE n pl. -S a medicated cloth to be applied to a wound

STUPEFY v -FIED, -FYING, -FIES to dull the senses of

STUPID adj -PIDER, -PIDEST mentally slow STUPIDLY adv

STUPID n pl. -S a stupid person

STUPOR n pl. -S a state of reduced sensibility

STURDY adj -DIER, -DIEST strong and durable STURDILY adv

STURDY n pl. -DIES a disease of sheep STURDIED adj

STURGEON n pl. -S an edible fish

STURT n pl. -S contention

STUTTER v -ED, -ING, -S to speak with spasmodic repetition

STY v STIED or STYED, STYING, STIES to keep in a pigpen

STYE n pl. -S an inflamed swelling of the eyelid

STYGIAN adj gloomy

STYLAR adj pertaining to a stylus

STYLATE adj bearing a stylet

STYLE v STYLED, STYLING, STYLES to name

STYLER n pl. -S one that styles

STYLET n pl. -S a small, stiff organ or appendage of certain animals

STYLI a pl. of stylus

STYLING n pl. -S the way in which something is styled

STYLISE v -ISED, -ISING, -ISES to stylize

STYLISER n pl. -S one that stylises

STYLISH adj fashionable

STYLISING present participle of stylise

STYLIST n pl. -S one who is a master of a literary or rhetorical style

STYLITE n pl. -S an early Christian ascetic STYLITIC adj

STYLIZE v -IZED, -IZING, -IZES to make conventional

STYLIZER n pl. -S one that stylizes

STYLOID adj slender and pointed

STYLUS n pl. -LI or -LUSES a pointed instrument for writing, marking, or engraving

STYMIE v -MIED, -MIEING, -MIES to thwart

STYMY v -MIED, -MYING, -MIES to stymie

STYPSIS n pl. -SISES the use of a styptic

STYPTIC n pl. -S a substance used to check bleeding

STYRAX n pl. -ES storax

STYRENE n pl. -S a liquid hydrocarbon

SUABLE adj capable of being sued SUABLY adv

SUASION n pl. -S persuasion SUASIVE, SUASORY adj

SUAVE adj SUAVER, SUAVEST smoothly affable and polite SUAVELY adv

SUAVITY n pl. -TIES the state of being suave

SUB v SUBBED, SUBBING, SUBS to act as a substitute

SUBA n pl. -S subah

SUBABBOT n pl. -S a subordinate abbot

SUBACID adj slightly sour

SUBACRID adj somewhat acrid

SUBACUTE adj somewhat acute

SUBADAR n pl. -S subahdar

SUBADULT n pl. -S an individual approaching adulthood

SUBAGENT n pl. -S a subordinate agent

SUBAH n pl. -S a province of India

SUBAHDAR n pl. -S a governor of a subah

SUBALAR adj somewhat alar

SUBAREA n pl. -S a subdivision of an area

SUBARID adj somewhat arid

SUBATOM n pl. -S a component of an atom

SUBAXIAL *adj* somewhat axial

SUBBASE *n* pl. -S the lowest part of a base

SUBBASS *n* pl. -ES a pedal stop producing the lowest tones of an organ

SUBBED past tense of sub

SUBBING *n* pl. -S a thin coating on the support of a photographic film

SUBBREED *n* pl. -S a distinguishable strain within a breed

SUBCAUSE *n* pl. -S a subordinate cause

SUBCELL *n* pl. -S a subdivision of a cell

SUBCHIEF *n* pl. -S a subordinate chief

SUBCLAN *n* pl. -S a subdivision of a clan

SUBCLASS *v* -ED, -ING, -ES to place in a subdivision of a class

SUBCLERK *n* pl. -S a subordinate clerk

SUBCOOL *v* -ED, -ING, -S to cool below the freezing point without solidification

SUBCUTIS *n* pl. -CUTES or -CUTISES the deeper part of the dermis

SUBDEAN *n* pl. -S a subordinate dean

SUBDEB *n* pl. -S a girl the year before she becomes a debutante

SUBDEPOT *n* pl. -S a military depot that operates under the jurisdiction of another depot

SUBDUAL *n* pl. -S the act of subduing

SUBDUCE *v* -DUCED, -DUCING, -DUCES to take away

SUBDUCT *v* -ED, -ING, -S to subduce

SUBDUE *v* -DUED, -DUING, -DUES to bring under control

SUBDUER *n* pl. -S one that subdues

SUBECHO *n* pl. -ECHOES an inferior echo

SUBEDIT *v* -ED, -ING, -S to act as the assistant editor of

SUBENTRY *n* pl. -TRIES an entry made under a more general entry

SUBEPOCH *n* pl. -S a subdivision of an epoch

SUBER *n* pl. -S phellem

SUBERECT *adj* nearly erect

SUBERIC *adj* pertaining to cork

SUBERIN *n* pl. -S a substance found in cork cells

SUBERISE *v* -ISED, -ISING, -ISES to suberize

SUBERIZE *v* -IZED, -IZING, -IZES to convert into cork tissue

SUBEROSE *adj* corky

SUBEROUS *adj* suberose

SUBFIELD *n* pl. -S a subset of a mathematical field that is itself a field

SUBFIX *n* pl. -ES a distinguishing symbol or letter written below another character

SUBFLOOR *n* pl. -S a rough floor laid as a base for a finished floor

SUBFLUID *adj* somewhat fluid

SUBFUSC *adj* dark in color

SUBGENUS *n* pl. -GENERA or -GENUSES a subdivision of a genus

SUBGRADE *n* pl. -S a surface on which a pavement is placed

SUBGROUP *n* pl. -S a distinct group within a group

SUBGUM *adj* prepared with mixed vegetables

SUBHEAD *n* pl. -S the heading of a subdivision

SUBHUMAN *n* pl. -S one that is less than human

SUBHUMID *adj* somewhat humid

SUBIDEA *n* pl. -S an inferior idea

SUBINDEX *n* pl. -DEXES or -DICES a subfix

SUBITEM *n* pl. -S an item that forms a subdivision of a larger topic

SUBITO *adv* quickly — used as a musical direction

SUBJECT *v* -ED, -ING, -S to cause to experience

SUBJOIN *v* -ED, -ING, -S to add at the end

SUBLATE *v* -LATED, -LATING, -LATES to cancel

SUBLEASE *v* -LEASED, -LEASING, -LEASES to sublet

SUBLET *v* -LET, -LETTING, -LETS to rent leased property to another

SUBLEVEL *n* pl. -S a lower level

SUBLIME *adj* -LIMER, -LIMEST of elevated or noble quality

SUBLIME *v* -LIMED, -LIMING, -LIMES to make sublime

SUBLIMER *n* pl. -S one that sublimes

SUBLIMEST superlative of sublime

SUBLIMING present participle of sublime

SUBMERGE *v* -MERGED, -MERGING, -MERGES to place below the surface of a liquid

SUBMERSE *v* -MERSED, -MERSING, -MERSES to submerge

SUBMISS *adj* inclined to submit

SUBMIT *v* -MITTED, -MITTING, -MITS to yield to the power of another

SUBNASAL *adj* situated under the nose

SUBNODAL *adj* situated under a node

SUBOPTIC *adj* situated under the eyes

SUBORAL *adj* situated under the mouth

SUBORDER *n pl.* -S a category of related families within an order

SUBORN *v* -ED, -ING, -S to induce to commit perjury

SUBORNER *n pl.* -S one that suborns

SUBOVAL *adj* nearly oval

SUBOVATE *adj* nearly ovate

SUBOXIDE *n pl.* -S an oxide containing relatively little oxygen

SUBPAR *adj* below par

SUBPART *n pl.* -S a subdivision of a part

SUBPENA *v* -ED, -ING, -S to subpoena

SUBPHYLA *n/pl* divisions within a phylum

SUBPLOT *n pl.* -S a secondary literary plot

SUBPOENA *v* -ED, -ING, -S to summon with a type of judicial writ

SUBPOLAR *adj* situated just outside the polar circles

SUBPUBIC *adj* situated under the pubis

SUBRACE *n pl.* -S a subdivision of a race

SUBRENT *n pl.* -S rent from a subtenant

SUBRING *n pl.* -S a subset of a mathematical ring that is itself a ring

SUBRULE *n pl.* -S a subordinate rule

SUBSALE *n pl.* -S a resale of purchased goods

SUBSECT *n pl.* -S a sect directly derived from another

SUBSERE *n pl.* -S a type of ecological succession

SUBSERVE *v* -SERVED, -SERVING, -SERVES to serve to promote

SUBSET *n pl.* -S a mathematical set contained within a larger set

SUBSHAFT *n pl.* -S a shaft that is beneath another shaft

SUBSHRUB *n pl.* -S a low shrub

SUBSIDE *v* -SIDED, -SIDING, -SIDES to sink to a lower or normal level

SUBSIDER *n pl.* -S one that subsides

SUBSIDY *n pl.* -DIES a grant or contribution of money

SUBSIST *v* -ED, -ING, -S to continue to exist

SUBSOIL *v* -ED, -ING, -S to plow so as to turn up the subsoil (the layer of earth beneath the surface soil)

SUBSOLAR *adj* situated directly beneath the sun

SUBSONIC *adj* moving at a speed less than that of sound

SUBSPACE *n pl.* -S a subset of a mathematical space

SUBSTAGE *n pl.* -S a part of a microscope for supporting accessories

SUBSUME *v* -SUMED, -SUMING, -SUMES to classify within a larger category

SUBTEEN *n pl.* -S a person approaching the teenage years

SUBTEND *v* -ED, -ING, -S to extend under or opposite to

SUBTEXT *n pl.* -S written or printed matter under a more general text

SUBTILE *adj* -TILER, -TILEST subtle

SUBTILTY *n pl.* -TIES subtlety

SUBTITLE *v* -TLED, -TLING, -TLES to give a secondary title to

SUBTLE *adj* -TLER, -TLEST so slight as to be difficult to detect **SUBTLY** *adv*

SUBTLETY *n pl.* -TIES the state of being subtle

SUBTONE *n pl.* -S a low or subdued tone

SUBTONIC *n pl.* -S a type of musical tone

SUBTOPIC *n pl.* -S a secondary topic

SUBTOTAL *v* -TALED, -TALING, -TALS or -TALLED, -TALLING, -TALS to total a portion of

SUBTRACT *v* -ED, -ING, -S to take away

SUBTRIBE *n pl.* -S a subdivision of a tribe

SUBTUNIC *n pl.* -S a tunic worn under another tunic

SUBTYPE *n pl.* -S a type that is subordinate to or included in another type

SUBULATE *adj* slender and tapering to a point

SUBUNIT *n pl.* -S a unit that is a part of a larger unit

SUBURB *n pl.* -S a residential area adjacent to a city **SUBURBED** *adj*

SUBURBAN *n pl.* -S one who lives in a suburb

SUBURBIA *n pl.* -S the suburbs of a city

SUBVENE *v* -VENED, -VENING, -VENES to arrive or occur as a support or relief

SUBVERT *v* -ED, -ING, -S to destroy completely

SUBVICAR *n pl.* -S a subordinate vicar

SUBVIRAL *adj* pertaining to a part of a virus

SUBVOCAL *adj* mentally formulated as words

SUBWAY *n pl.* -WAYS an underground railroad

SUBZONE *n pl.* -S a subdivision of a zone

SUCCAH *n pl.* -CAHS or -COTH sukkah

SUCCEED *v* -ED, -ING, -S to accomplish something desired or intended

SUCCESS *n pl.* -ES the attainment of something desired or intended

SUCCINCT *adj* -CINCTER, -CINCTEST clearly expressed in few words

SUCCINIC *adj* pertaining to amber

SUCCINYL *n pl.* -S a univalent radical

SUCCOR *v* -ED, -ING, -S to go to the aid of

SUCCORER *n pl.* -S one that succors

SUCCORY *n pl.* -RIES chicory

SUCCOTH *a pl.* of succah

SUCCOUR *v* -ED, -ING, -S to succor

SUCCUBA *n pl.* -BAE a succubus

SUCCUBUS *n pl.* -BI or -BUSES a female demon

SUCCUMB *v* -ED, -ING, -S to yield to superior force

SUCCUSS *v* -ED, -ING, -ES to shake violently

SUCH *adj* of that kind

SUCHLIKE *adj* of a similar kind

SUCHNESS *n pl.* -ES essential or characteristic quality

SUCK *v* -ED, -ING, -S to draw in by establishing a partial vacuum

SUCKER *v* -ED, -ING, -S to strip of lower shoots or branches

SUCKFISH *n pl.* -ES a remora

SUCKLE *v* -LED, -LING, -LES to give milk to from the breast

SUCKLER *n pl.* -S one that suckles

SUCKLESS *adj* having no juice

SUCKLING *n pl.* -S a young mammal that has not been weaned

SUCRASE *n pl.* -S an enzyme

SUCRE *n pl.* -S a monetary unit of Ecuador

SUCROSE *n pl.* -S a type of sugar

SUCTION *n pl.* -S the act of sucking

SUDARIUM *n pl.* -IA a cloth for wiping the face

SUDARY *n pl.* -RIES sudarium

SUDATION *n pl.* -S excessive sweating

SUDATORY *n pl.* -RIES a hot-air bath for inducing sweating

SUDD *n pl.* -S a floating mass of vegetation

SUDDEN *adj* happening quickly and without warning **SUDDENLY** *adv*

SUDDEN *n pl.* -S a sudden occurrence

SUDOR *n pl.* -S sweat **SUDORAL** *adj*

SUDS *v* -ED, -ING, -ES to wash in soapy water

SUDSER *n pl.* -S one that sudses

SUDSLESS *adj* having no suds

SUDSY *adj* SUDSIER, SUDSIEST foamy

SUE *v* SUED, SUING, SUES to institute legal proceedings against

SUEDE *v* SUEDED, SUEDING, SUEDES to finish leather with a soft, napped surface

SUER *n pl.* -S one that sues

SUET *n pl.* -S the hard, fatty tissue around the kidneys of cattle and sheep **SUETY** *adj*

SUFFARI *n pl.* -S a safari

SUFFER *v* -ED, -ING, -S to feel pain or distress

SUFFERER *n pl.* -S one that suffers

SUFFICE *v* -FICED, -FICING, -FICES to be adequate

SUFFICER *n pl.* -S one that suffices

SUFFIX *v* -ED, -ING, -ES to add as a suffix (a form affixed to the end of a root word)

SUFFIXAL *adj* pertaining to or being a suffix

SUFFLATE *v* -FLATED, -FLATING, -FLATES to inflate

SUFFRAGE *n pl.* -S the right to vote

SUFFUSE *v* -FUSED, -FUSING, -FUSES to spread through or over

SUGAR *v* -ED, -ING, -S to cover with sugar (a sweet carbohydrate)

SUGARY *adj* -ARIER, -ARIEST containing or resembling sugar

SUGGEST *v* -ED, -ING, -S to bring or put forward for consideration

SUGH *v* -ED, -ING, -S to sough

SUICIDAL *adj* self-destructive

SUICIDE *v* -CIDED, -CIDING, -CIDES to kill oneself intentionally

SUING present participle of sue

SUINT *n pl.* -S a natural grease found in the wool of sheep

SUIT v -ED, -ING, -S to be appropriate to

SUITABLE adj appropriate **SUITABLY** adv

SUITCASE n pl. -S a flat, rectangular piece of luggage

SUITE n pl. -S a series of things forming a unit

SUITING n pl. -S fabric for making suits

SUITLIKE adj resembling a suit (a set of garments)

SUITOR n pl. -S one that is courting a woman

SUKIYAKI n pl. -S a Japanese dish

SUKKAH n pl. -KAHS or -KOTH a temporary shelter in which meals are eaten during a Jewish festival

SULCATE adj having long, narrow furrows

SULCATED adj sulcate

SULCUS n pl. -CI furrow

SULDAN n pl. -S soldan

SULFA n pl. -S a bacteria-inhibiting drug

SULFATE v -FATED, -FATING, -FATES to treat with sulfuric acid

SULFID n pl. -S sulfide

SULFIDE n pl. -S a sulfur compound

SULFINYL n pl. -S a bivalent radical

SULFITE n pl. -S a chemical salt **SULFITIC** adj

SULFO adj sulfonic

SULFONAL n pl. -S a sulfone used as a sedative

SULFONE n pl. -S a sulfur compound

SULFONIC adj containing a certain univalent radical

SULFONYL n pl. -S a bivalent radical

SULFUR v -ED, -ING, -S to treat with sulfur (a nonmetallic element)

SULFURET v -RETED, -RETING, -RETS or -RETTED, -RETTING, -RETS to treat with sulfur

SULFURIC adj pertaining to sulfur

SULFURY adj resembling sulfur

SULFURYL n pl. -S sulfonyl

SULK v -ED, -ING, -S to be sulky

SULKER n pl. -S one that sulks

SULKY adj SULKIER, SULKIEST sullenly aloof or withdrawn **SULKILY** adv

SULKY n pl. SULKIES a light horse-drawn vehicle

SULLAGE n pl. -S sewage

SULLEN adj -LENER, -LENEST showing a brooding ill humor or resentment **SULLENLY** adv

SULLY v -LIED, -LYING, -LIES to soil

SULPHA n pl. -S sulfa

SULPHATE v -PHATED, -PHATING, -PHATES to sulfate

SULPHID n pl. -S sulfide

SULPHIDE n pl. -S sulfide

SULPHITE n pl. -S sulfite

SULPHONE n pl. -S sulfone

SULPHUR v -ED, -ING, -S to sulfur

SULPHURY adj sulfury

SULTAN n pl. -S the ruler of a Muslim country **SULTANIC** adj

SULTANA n pl. -S a sultan's wife

SULTRY adj -TRIER, -TRIEST very hot and humid **SULTRILY** adv

SUM v SUMMED, SUMMING, SUMS to add into one total

SUMAC n pl. -S a flowering tree or shrub

SUMACH n pl. -S sumac

SUMLESS adj too large for calculation

SUMMA n pl. -MAE or -MAS a comprehensive work covering a specific subject

SUMMABLE adj capable of being summed

SUMMAND n pl. -S an addend

SUMMARY n pl. -RIES a condensation of the substance of a larger work

SUMMATE v -MATED, -MATING, -MATES to sum

SUMMED past tense of sum

SUMMER v -ED, -ING, -S to pass the summer (the warmest season of the year)

SUMMERLY adj summery

SUMMERY adj -MERIER, -MERIEST characteristic of summer

SUMMING present participle of sum

SUMMIT n pl. -S the highest point **SUMMITAL** adj

SUMMITRY n pl. -RIES the use of conferences between chiefs of state for international negotiation

SUMMON v -ED, -ING, -S to order to appear

SUMMONER n pl. -S one that summons

SUMMONS v -ED, -ING, -ES to summon with a court order

SUMO n pl. -MOS a Japanese form of wrestling

SUMP *n pl.* -S a low area serving as a drain or receptacle for liquids

SUMPTER *n pl.* -S a pack animal

SUMPWEED *n pl.* -S a marsh plant

SUN *v* SUNNED, SUNNING, SUNS to expose to the sun (the star around which the earth revolves)

SUNBACK *adj* cut low to expose the back to sunlight

SUNBAKED *adj* baked by the sun

SUNBATH *n pl.* -S an exposure to sunlight

SUNBATHE *v* -BATHED, -BATHING, -BATHES to take a sunbath

SUNBEAM *n pl.* -S a beam of sunlight

SUNBIRD *n pl.* -S a tropical bird

SUNBOW *n pl.* -S an arc of spectral colors formed by the sun shining through a mist

SUNBURN *v* -BURNED or -BURNT, -BURNING, -BURNS to burn or discolor from exposure to the sun

SUNBURST *n pl.* -S a burst of sunlight

SUNDAE *n pl.* -S a dish of ice cream served with a topping

SUNDER *v* -ED, -ING, -S to break apart

SUNDERER *n pl.* -S one that sunders

SUNDEW *n pl.* -S a marsh plant

SUNDIAL *n pl.* -S a type of time-telling device

SUNDOG *n pl.* -S a small rainbow

SUNDOWN *n pl.* -S sunset

SUNDRIES *n/pl* miscellaneous items

SUNDROPS *n pl.* SUNDROPS a flowering plant

SUNDRY *adj* miscellaneous

SUNFAST *adj* resistant to fading by the sun

SUNFISH *n pl.* -ES a marine fish

SUNG past participle of sing

SUNGLASS *n pl.* -ES a lens for concentrating the sun's rays in order to produce heat

SUNGLOW *n pl.* -S a glow in the sky caused by the sun

SUNK a past participle of sink

SUNKEN a past participle of sink

SUNKET *n pl.* -S a tidbit

SUNLAMP *n pl.* -S a lamp that radiates ultraviolet rays

SUNLAND *n pl.* -S an area marked by a great amount of sunshine

SUNLESS *adj* having no sunlight

SUNLIGHT *n pl.* -S the light of the sun

SUNLIKE *adj* resembling the sun

SUNLIT *adj* lighted by the sun

SUNN *n pl.* -S an East Indian shrub

SUNNA *n pl.* -S the body of traditional Muslim law

SUNNED past tense of sun

SUNNING present participle of sun

SUNNY *adj* -NIER, -NIEST filled with sunlight SUNNILY *adv*

SUNRISE *n pl.* -S the ascent of the sun above the horizon in the morning

SUNROOF *n pl.* -S an automobile roof having an openable panel

SUNROOM *n pl.* -S a room built to admit a great amount of sunlight

SUNSCALD *n pl.* -S an injury of woody plants caused by the sun

SUNSET *n pl.* -S the descent of the sun below the horizon in the evening

SUNSHADE *n pl.* -S something used as a protection from the sun

SUNSHINE *n pl.* -S the light of the sun SUNSHINY *adj*

SUNSPOT *n pl.* -S a dark spot on the surface of the sun

SUNSTONE *n pl.* -S a variety of quartz

SUNSUIT *n pl.* -S an outfit worn for sunbathing

SUNTAN *n pl.* -S a brown color on the skin produced by exposure to the sun

SUNUP *n pl.* -S sunrise

SUNWARD *adv* toward the sun

SUNWARDS *adv* sunward

SUNWISE *adv* from left to right

SUP *v* SUPPED, SUPPING, SUPS to eat supper

SUPE *n pl.* -S an actor without a speaking part

SUPER *v* -ED, -ING, -S to reinforce with a thin cotton mesh, as a book

SUPERADD *v* -ED, -ING, -S to add further

SUPERB *adj* -PERBER, -PERBEST of excellent quality SUPERBLY *adv*

SUPEREGO *n pl.* -EGOS a part of the psyche

SUPERFIX *n pl.* -ES a recurrent pattern of stress in speech

SUPERIOR *n pl.* -S one of higher rank, quality, or authority than another

SUPERJET n pl. -S a type of jet airplane

SUPERLIE v -LAY, -LAIN, -LYING, -LIES to lie above

SUPERMAN n pl. -MEN a hypothetical superior man

SUPERNAL adj pertaining to the sky

SUPERSEX n pl. -ES a type of sterile organism

SUPERTAX n pl. -ES an additional tax

SUPINATE v -NATED, -NATING, -NATES to turn so that the palm is facing upward

SUPINE n pl. -S a Latin verbal noun

SUPINELY adv in an inactive manner

SUPPED past tense of sup

SUPPER n pl. -S an evening meal

SUPPING present participle of sup

SUPPLANT v -ED, -ING, -S to take the place of

SUPPLE adj -PLER, -PLEST pliant SUPPLELY adv

SUPPLE v -PLED, -PLING, -PLES to make supple

SUPPLIER n pl. -S one that supplies

SUPPLY v -PLIED, -PLYING, -PLIES to furnish with what is needed

SUPPORT v -ED, -ING, -S to hold up or add strength to

SUPPOSAL n pl. -S something supposed

SUPPOSE v -POSED, -POSING, -POSES to assume to be true

SUPPOSER n pl. -S one that supposes

SUPPRESS v -ED, -ING, -ES to put an end to forcibly

SUPRA adv above

SUPREME adj -PREMER, -PREMEST highest in power or authority

SURA n pl. -S a chapter of the Koran

SURAH n pl. -S a silk fabric

SURAL adj pertaining to the calf of the leg

SURBASE n pl. -S a molding or border above the base of a structure SURBASED adj

SURCEASE v -CEASED, -CEASING, -CEASES to cease

SURCOAT n pl. -S an outer coat or cloak

SURD n pl. -S a voiceless speech sound

SURE adj SURER, SUREST free from doubt

SUREFIRE adj sure to meet expectations

SURELY adv certainly

SURENESS n pl. -ES the state of being sure

SURER comparative of sure

SUREST superlative of sure

SURETY n pl. -TIES sureness

SURF v -ED, -ING, -S to ride breaking waves on a long, narrow board SURFABLE adj

SURFACE v -FACED, -FACING, -FACES to apply an outer layer to

SURFACER n pl. -S one that surfaces

SURFBIRD n pl. -S a shore bird

SURFBOAT n pl. -S a strong rowboat

SURFEIT v -ED, -ING, -S to supply to excess

SURFER n pl. -S one that surfs

SURFFISH n pl. -ES a marine fish

SURFIER comparative of surfy

SURFIEST superlative of surfy

SURFING n pl. -S the act or sport of riding the surf (breaking waves)

SURFLIKE adj resembling breaking waves

SURFY adj SURFIER, SURFIEST abounding in breaking waves

SURGE v SURGED, SURGING, SURGES to move in a swelling manner

SURGEON n pl. -S one who practices surgery

SURGER n pl. -S one that surges

SURGERY n pl. -GERIES the treatment of medical problems by operation

SURGICAL adj pertaining to surgery

SURGING present participle of surge

SURGY adj surging

SURICATE n pl. -S a burrowing mammal

SURLY adj -LIER, -LIEST sullenly rude SURLILY adv

SURMISE v -MISED, -MISING, -MISES to infer with little evidence

SURMISER n pl. -S one that surmises

SURMOUNT v -ED, -ING, -S to get over or across

SURNAME v -NAMED, -NAMING, -NAMES to give a family name to

SURNAMER n pl. -S one that surnames

SURPASS v -ED, -ING, -ES to go beyond

SURPLICE n pl. -S a loose-fitting vestment

SURPLUS n pl. -ES an excess

SURPRINT v -ED, -ING, -S to print over something already printed

SURPRISE v -PRISED, -PRISING, -PRISES to come upon unexpectedly

SURPRIZE   v -PRIZED, -PRIZING, -PRIZES to surprise

SURRA   n pl. -S a disease of domestic animals

SURREAL   adj having dreamlike qualities

SURREY   n pl. -REYS a light carriage

SURROUND   v -ED, -ING, -S to extend completely around

SURROYAL   n pl. -S the topmost prong of a stag's antler

SURTAX   v -ED, -ING, -ES to assess with an extra tax

SURTOUT   n pl. -S a close-fitting overcoat

SURVEIL   v -VEILLED, -VEILLING, -VEILS to watch closely

SURVEY   v -ED, -ING, -S to determine the boundaries, area, or elevations of by measuring angles and distances

SURVEYOR   n pl. -S one that surveys land

SURVIVAL   n pl. -S a living or continuing longer than another person or thing

SURVIVE   v -VIVED, -VIVING, -VIVES to remain in existence

SURVIVER   n pl. -S survivor

SURVIVOR   n pl. -S one that survives

SUSLIK   n pl. -S a Eurasian rodent

SUSPECT   v -ED, -ING, -S to think guilty on slight evidence

SUSPEND   v -ED, -ING, -S to cause to stop for a period

SUSPENSE   n pl. -S a state of mental uncertainty or excitement

SUSPIRE   v -PIRED, -PIRING, -PIRES to sigh

SUSTAIN   v -ED, -ING, -S to maintain by providing with food and drink

SUSURRUS   n pl. -ES a soft rustling sound

SUTLER   n pl. -S one who peddles goods to soldiers

SUTRA   n pl. -S a Hindu aphorism

SUTTA   n pl. -S sutra

SUTTEE   n pl. -S a Hindu widow cremated on her husband's funeral pile to show her devotion to him

SUTURAL   adj pertaining to the line of junction between two bones

SUTURE   v -TURED, -TURING, -TURES to unite by sewing

SUZERAIN   n pl. -S a feudal lord

SVARAJ   n pl. -ES swaraj

SVEDBERG   n pl. -S a unit of time

SVELTE   adj SVELTER, SVELTEST gracefully slender **SVELTELY** adv

SWAB   v SWABBED, SWABBING, SWABS to clean with a large mop

SWABBER   n pl. -S one that swabs

SWABBIE   n pl. -S a sailor

SWABBING   present participle of swab

SWABBY   n pl. -BIES swabbie

SWADDLE   v -DLED, -DLING, -DLES to wrap in bandages

SWAG   v SWAGGED, SWAGGING, SWAGS to sway

SWAGE   v SWAGED, SWAGING, SWAGES to shape with a hammering tool

SWAGER   n pl. -S one that swages

SWAGGED   past tense of swag

SWAGGER   v -ED, -ING, -S to walk with a pompous air

SWAGGING   present participle of swag

SWAGING   present participle of swage

SWAGMAN   n pl. -MEN a hobo

SWAIL   n pl. -S swale

SWAIN   n pl. -S a country boy **SWAINISH** adj

SWALE   n pl. -S a tract of low, marshy ground

SWALLOW   v -ED, -ING, -S to take through the mouth and esophagus into the stomach

SWAM   past tense of swim

SWAMI   n pl. -S a Hindu religious teacher

SWAMIES   pl. of swamy

SWAMP   v -ED, -ING, -S to inundate

SWAMPER   n pl. -S one that lives in a swampy area

SWAMPISH   adj swampy

SWAMPY   adj SWAMPIER, SWAMPIEST marshy

SWAMY   n pl. -MIES swami

SWAN   v SWANNED, SWANNING, SWANS to swear

SWANG   a past tense of swing

SWANHERD   n pl. -S one who tends swans (large aquatic birds)

SWANK   adj SWANKER, SWANKEST imposingly elegant

SWANK   v -ED, -ING, -S to swagger

SWANKY   adj SWANKIER, SWANKIEST swank **SWANKILY** adv

SWANLIKE *adj* resembling a swan

SWANNED past tense of swan

SWANNERY *n pl.* -NERIES a place where swans are raised

SWANNING present participle of swan

SWANPAN *n pl.* -S a Chinese abacus

SWANSKIN *n pl.* -S the skin of a swan

SWAP *v* SWAPPED, SWAPPING, SWAPS to trade

SWAPPER *n pl.* -S one that swaps

SWARAJ *n pl.* -ES self-government in British India

SWARD *v* -ED, -ING, -S to cover with turf

SWARE a past tense of swear

SWARF *n pl.* -S material removed by a cutting tool

SWARM *v* -ED, -ING, -S to move in a large group

SWARMER *n pl.* -S one that swarms

SWART *adj* swarthy

SWARTH *n pl.* -S turf

SWARTHY *adj* -THIER, -THIEST having a dark complexion

SWARTY *adj* swarthy

SWASH *v* -ED, -ING, -ES to swagger

SWASHER *n pl.* -S one that swashes

SWASTICA *n pl.* -S swastika

SWASTIKA *n pl.* -S a geometrical figure used as a symbol or ornament

SWAT *v* SWATTED, SWATTING, SWATS to hit sharply

SWATCH *n pl.* -ES a sample piece of cloth

SWATH *n pl.* -S a row of cut grass or grain

SWATHE *v* SWATHED, SWATHING, SWATHES to wrap in bandages

SWATHER *n pl.* -S one that swathes

SWATTED past tense of swat

SWATTER *n pl.* -S one that swats

SWATTING present participle of swat

SWAY *v* -ED, -ING, -S to move slowly back and forth SWAYABLE *adj*

SWAYBACK *n pl.* -S an abnormal sagging of the back

SWAYER *n pl.* -S one that sways

SWAYFUL *adj* capable of influencing

SWEAR *v* SWORE or SWARE, SWORN, SWEARING, SWEARS to utter a solemn oath

SWEARER *n pl.* -S one that swears

SWEAT *v* -ED, -ING, -S to perspire

SWEATBOX *n pl.* -ES a small enclosure in which one is made to sweat

SWEATER *n pl.* -S a knitted outer garment

SWEATY *adj* SWEATIER, SWEATIEST covered with perspiration SWEATILY *adv*

SWEDE *n pl.* -S a rutabaga

SWEENY *n pl.* -NIES atrophy of the shoulder muscles in horses

SWEEP *v* SWEPT, SWEEPING, SWEEPS to clear or clean with a brush or broom

SWEEPER *n pl.* -S one that sweeps

SWEEPING *n pl.* -S the act of one that sweeps

SWEEPY *adj* SWEEPIER, SWEEPIEST of wide range or scope

SWEER *adj* lazy

SWEET *adj* SWEETER, SWEETEST pleasing to the taste

SWEET *n pl.* -S something that is sweet

SWEETEN *v* -ED, -ING, -S to make sweet

SWEETIE *n pl.* -S darling

SWEETING *n pl.* -S a sweet apple

SWEETISH *adj* somewhat sweet

SWEETLY *adv* in a sweet manner

SWEETSOP *n pl.* -S a tropical tree

SWELL *v* SWELLED, SWOLLEN, SWELLING, SWELLS to increase in size or volume

SWELL *adj* SWELLER, SWELLEST stylish

SWELLING *n pl.* -S something that is swollen

SWELTER *v* -ED, -ING, -S to suffer from oppressive heat

SWELTRY *adj* -TRIER, -TRIEST oppressively hot

SWEPT past tense of sweep

SWERVE *v* SWERVED, SWERVING, SWERVES to turn aside suddenly from a straight course

SWERVER *n pl.* -S one that swerves

SWEVEN *n pl.* -S a dream or vision

SWIFT *adj* SWIFTER, SWIFTEST moving with a great rate of motion

SWIFT *n pl.* -S a fast-flying bird

SWIFTER *n pl.* -S a rope on a ship

SWIFTLY *adv* in a swift manner

SWIG *v* SWIGGED, SWIGGING, SWIGS to drink deeply or rapidly

SWIGGER n pl. -S one that swigs

SWILL v -ED, -ING, -S to swig

SWILLER n pl. -S one that swills

SWIM v SWAM, SWUM, SWIMMING, SWIMS to propel oneself in water by natural means

SWIMMER n pl. -S one that swims

SWIMMING n pl. -S the act of one that swims

SWIMMY adj -MIER, -MIEST dizzy **SWIMMILY** adv

SWIMSUIT n pl. -S a bathing suit

SWINDLE v -DLED, -DLING, -DLES to take money or property from by fraudulent means

SWINDLER n pl. -S one that swindles

SWINE n pl. SWINE a domestic pig

SWINEPOX n pl. -ES a disease of swine

SWING v SWINGED or SWANG, SWINGING, SWINGS to move freely back and forth

SWINGE v SWINGED, SWINGEING, SWINGES to flog

SWINGER n pl. -S one that swings

SWINGLE v -GLED, -GLING, -GLES to scutch

SWINGY adj SWINGIER, SWINGIEST marked by swinging

SWINISH adj resembling or befitting swine

SWINK v -ED, -ING, -S to toil

SWINNEY n pl. -NEYS sweeny

SWIPE v SWIPED, SWIPING, SWIPES to strike with a sweeping blow

SWIPLE n pl. -S a part of a threshing device

SWIPPLE n pl. -S swiple

SWIRL v -ED, -ING, -S to move with a whirling motion

SWIRLY adj SWIRLIER, SWIRLIEST swirling

SWISH v -ED, -ING, -ES to move with a prolonged hissing sound

SWISHER n pl. -S one that swishes

SWISHY adj SWISHIER, SWISHIEST swishing

SWISS n pl. -ES a cotton fabric

SWITCH v -ED, -ING, -ES to beat with a flexible rod

SWITCHER n pl. -S one that switches

SWITH adv quickly

SWITHE adv swith

SWITHER v -ED, -ING, -S to doubt

SWITHLY adv swith

SWIVE v SWIVED, SWIVING, SWIVES to copulate with

SWIVEL v -ELED, -ELING, -ELS or -ELLED, -ELLING, -ELS to turn on a pivoted support

SWIVET n pl. -S a state of nervous excitement

SWIVING present participle of swive

SWIZZLE v -ZLED, -ZLING, -ZLES to drink excessively

SWIZZLER n pl. -S one that swizzles

SWOB v SWOBBED, SWOBBING, SWOBS to swab

SWOBBER n pl. -S swabber

SWOLLEN past participle of swell

SWOON v -ED, -ING, -S to faint

SWOONER n pl. -S one that swoons

SWOOP v -ED, -ING, -S to make a sudden descent

SWOOPER n pl. -S one that swoops

SWOOSH v -ED, -ING, -ES to move with a rustling sound

SWOP v SWOPPED, SWOPPING, SWOPS to swap

SWORD n pl. -S a weapon having a long blade for cutting or thrusting

SWORDMAN n pl. -MEN one skilled in the use of a sword

SWORE a past tense of swear

SWORN past participle of swear

SWOT v SWOTTED, SWOTTING, SWOTS to swat

SWOTTER n pl. -S one that swots

SWOUN v -ED, -ING, -S to swoon

SWOUND v -ED, -ING, -S to swoon

SWUM past participle of swim

SWUNG a past tense of swing

SYBARITE n pl. -S a person devoted to pleasure and luxury

SYBO n pl. -BOES the cibol

SYCAMINE n pl. -S the mulberry tree

SYCAMORE n pl. -S a North American tree

SYCE n pl. -S a male servant in India

SYCEE n pl. -S fine uncoined silver formerly used in China as money

SYCOMORE n pl. -S sycamore

SYCONIUM n pl. -NIA a fleshy multiple fruit

SYCOSIS n pl. -COSES an inflammatory disease of the hair follicles

SYENITE n pl. -S an igneous rock SYENITIC adj

SYKE n pl. -S a small stream

SYLLABI a pl. of syllabus

SYLLABIC n pl. -S a speech sound of high sonority

SYLLABLE v -BLED, -BLING, -BLES to pronounce syllables (units of spoken language)

SYLLABUB n pl. -S sillabub

SYLLABUS n pl. -BI or -BUSES an outline of a course of study

SYLPH n pl. -S a slender, graceful girl or woman SYLPHIC, SYLPHISH, SYLPHY adj

SYLPHID n pl. -S a young sylph

SYLVA n pl. -VAS or -VAE the forest trees of an area

SYLVAN n pl. -S one that lives in a forest

SYLVATIC adj pertaining to a forest

SYLVIN n pl. -S sylvite

SYLVINE n pl. -S sylvite

SYLVITE n pl. -S an ore of potassium

SYMBION n pl. -S symbiont

SYMBIONT n pl. -S an organism living in close association with another

SYMBIOT n pl. -S symbiont

SYMBIOTE n pl. -S symbiont

SYMBOL v -BOLED, -BOLING, -BOLS or -BOLLED, -BOLLING, -BOLS to serve as a symbol (a representation) of

SYMBOLIC adj pertaining to a symbol

SYMMETRY n pl. -TRIES an exact correspondence between the opposite halves of a figure

SYMPATHY n pl. -THIES a feeling of compassion for another's suffering

SYMPATRY n pl. -RIES the state of occupying the same area without loss of identity from interbreeding

SYMPHONY n pl. -NIES an orchestral composition

SYMPODIA n/pl plant stems made up of a series of superposed branches

SYMPOSIA n/pl conferences for the purpose of discussion

SYMPTOM n pl. -S an indication of something

SYN adv syne

SYNAGOG n pl. -S a building for Jewish worship

SYNAPSE v -APSED, -APSING, -APSES to come together in synapsis

SYNAPSIS n pl. -APSES the point at which a nervous impulse passes from one neuron to another SYNAPTIC adj

SYNC v -ED, -ING, -S to cause to operate in unison

SYNCARP n pl. -S a fleshy multiple fruit

SYNCARPY n pl. -PIES the state of being a syncarp

SYNCH v -ED, -ING, -S to sync

SYNCHRO n pl. -CHROS a selsyn

SYNCLINE n pl. -S a type of rock formation

SYNCOM n pl. -S a type of communications satellite

SYNCOPE n pl. -S the contraction of a word by omitting one or more sounds from the middle SYNCOPAL, SYNCOPIC adj

SYNCYTIA n/pl masses of protoplasm resulting from cell fusion

SYNDESIS n pl. -DESES or -DESISES synapsis

SYNDET n pl. -S a synthetic detergent

SYNDETIC adj serving to connect

SYNDIC n pl. -S a business agent SYNDICAL adj

SYNDROME n pl. -S a group of symptoms that characterize a particular disorder

SYNE adv since

SYNECTIC adj pertaining to a system of problem solving

SYNERGIA n pl. -S synergy

SYNERGID n pl. -S a cell found in the embryo sac of a seed plant

SYNERGY n pl. -GIES combined action SYNERGIC adj

SYNESIS n pl. -SISES a type of grammatical construction

SYNGAMY n pl. -MIES the union of two gametes SYNGAMIC adj

SYNOD n pl. -S a church council SYNODAL, SYNODIC adj

SYNONYM n pl. -S a word having the same meaning as another

SYNONYME n pl. -S synonym

SYNONYMY n pl. -MIES equivalence of meaning

SYNOPSIS n pl. -OPSES a summary SYNOPTIC adj

SYNOVIA n pl. -S a lubricating fluid secreted by certain membranes SYNOVIAL adj

SYNTAX   *n* pl. -ES the way in which words are put together to form phrases and sentences

SYNTONY   *n* pl. -NIES the tuning of transmitters and receivers with each other **SYNTONIC** *adj*

SYNURA   *n* pl. -RAE any of a genus of protozoa

SYPHER   *v* -ED, -ING, -S to overlap so as to make an even surface, as beveled plank edges

SYPHILIS   *n* pl. -LISES a venereal disease

SYPHON   *v* -ED, -ING, -S to siphon

SYREN   *n* pl. -S siren

SYRINGA   *n* pl. -S an ornamental shrub

SYRINGE   *v* -RINGED, -RINGING, -RINGES to cleanse or treat with injected fluid

SYRINX   *n* pl. -INGES or -INXES the vocal organ of a bird

SYRPHIAN   *n* pl. -S syrphid

SYRPHID   *n* pl. -S a winged insect

SYRUP   *n* pl. -S a thick, sweet liquid **SYRUPY** *adj*

SYSTEM   *n* pl. -S a group of interacting elements forming a unified whole

SYSTEMIC   *n* pl. -S a type of pesticide

SYSTOLE   *n* pl. -S the normal rhythmic contraction of the heart **SYSTOLIC** *adj*

SYZYGY   *n* pl. -GIES the configuration of the earth, moon, and sun lying in a straight line **SYZYGAL**, **SYZYGIAL** *adj*

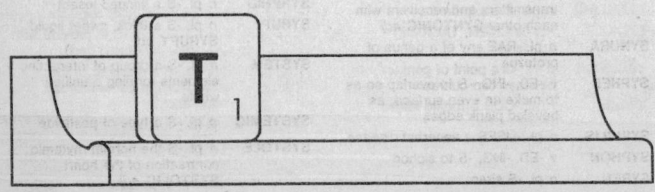

TA	n pl. -S an expression of gratitude
TAB	v TABBED, TABBING, TABS to name or designate
TABANID	n pl. -S a bloodsucking insect
TABARD	n pl. -S a sleeveless outer garment **TABARDED** adj
TABARET	n pl. -S a silk fabric
TABBED	past tense of tab
TABBIED	past tense of tabby
TABBIES	present 3d person sing. of tabby
TABBING	present participle of tab
TABBIS	n pl. -BISES a silk fabric
TABBY	v -BIED, -BYING, -BIES to give a wavy appearance to
TABER	v -ED, -ING, -S to tabor
TABES	n pl. TABES a syphilitic disease
TABETIC	n pl. -S one affected with tabes
TABID	adj affected with tabes
TABLA	n pl. -S a small drum
TABLE	v -BLED, -BLING, -BLES to place on a table (a piece of furniture having a flat upper surface)
TABLEAU	n pl. -LEAUX or -LEAUS a picture
TABLEFUL	n pl. TABLEFULS or TABLESFUL as much as a table can hold
TABLET	v -LETED, -LETING, -LETS or -LETTED, -LETTING, -LETS to inscribe on a small, flat surface
TABLETOP	n pl. -S the top of a table
TABLING	present participle of table
TABLOID	n pl. -S a small newspaper
TABOO	v -ED, -ING, -S to exclude from use, approach, or mention

TABOR	v -ED, -ING, -S to beat on a small drum
TABORER	n pl. -S one that tabors
TABORET	n pl. -S a small drum
TABORIN	n pl. -S taborine
TABORINE	n pl. -S a taboret
TABOUR	v -ED, -ING, -S to tabor
TABOURER	n pl. -S taborer
TABOURET	n pl. -S taboret
TABU	v -ED, -ING, -S to taboo
TABULAR	adj of or pertaining to a list
TABULATE	v -LATED, -LATING, -LATES to arrange in a list
TACE	n pl. -S tasse
TACET	interj be silent — used as a musical direction
TACH	n pl. -S a device for indicating speed of rotation
TACHE	n pl. -S a clasp or buckle
TACHINID	n pl. -S a grayish fly
TACHISM	n pl. -S action painting
TACHIST	n pl. -S an action painter
TACHISTE	n pl. -S tachist
TACIT	adj unspoken **TACITLY** adv
TACITURN	adj habitually silent
TACK	v -ED, -ING, -S to fasten with tacks (short, sharp-pointed nails)
TACKER	n pl. -S one that tacks
TACKET	n pl. -S a hobnail
TACKEY	adj TACKIER, TACKIEST tacky
TACKIER	comparative of tacky
TACKIEST	superlative of tacky
TACKIFY	v -FIED, -FYING, -FIES to make tacky
TACKILY	adv in a tacky manner

TACKLE	v -LED, -LING, -LES to seize and throw to the ground
TACKLER	n pl. -S one that tackles
TACKLESS	adj having no tacks
TACKLING	n pl. -S equipment
TACKY	adj TACKIER, TACKIEST adhesive
TACNODE	n pl. -S a point of contact between two curves
TACO	n pl. -COS a tortilla folded around a filling
TACONITE	n pl. -S a low-grade iron ore
TACT	n pl. -S skill in dealing with delicate situations
TACTFUL	adj having tact
TACTIC	n pl. -S a maneuver for gaining an objective TACTICAL adj
TACTILE	adj pertaining to the sense of touch
TACTION	n pl. -S the act of touching
TACTLESS	adj lacking tact
TACTUAL	adj tactile
TAD	n pl. -S a small boy
TADPOLE	n pl. -S the aquatic larva of an amphibian
TAE	prep to
TAEL	n pl. -S a Chinese unit of weight
TAENIA	n pl. -NIAE or -NIAS a headband worn in ancient Greece
TAFFAREL	n pl. -S taffrail
TAFFEREL	n pl. -S taffrail
TAFFETA	n pl. -S a lustrous fabric
TAFFIA	n pl. -S a tafia
TAFFRAIL	n pl. -S a rail around the stern of a ship
TAFFY	n pl. -FIES a chewy candy
TAFIA	n pl. -S an inferior rum
TAG	v TAGGED, TAGGING, TAGS to provide with a tag (an identifying marker)
TAGALONG	n pl. -S one that follows another
TAGBOARD	n pl. -S a material for making shipping tags
TAGGED	past tense of tag
TAGGER	n pl. -S one that tags
TAGGING	present participle of tag
TAGLIKE	adj resembling a tag
TAGMEME	n pl. -S the smallest unit of meaningful grammatical relation
TAGRAG	n pl. -S riffraff

TAHR	n pl. -S a goatlike mammal
TAHSIL	n pl. -S a district in India
TAIGA	n pl. -S a subarctic evergreen forest
TAIGLACH	n pl. TAIGLACH teiglach
TAIL	v -ED, -ING, -S to provide with a tail (a hindmost part)
TAILBACK	n pl. -S a member of the backfield in some football formations
TAILBONE	n pl. -S the coccyx
TAILCOAT	n pl. -S a man's coat
TAILER	n pl. -S one that secretly follows another
TAILGATE	v -GATED, -GATING, -GATES to drive dangerously close behind another vehicle
TAILING	n pl. -S the part of a projecting stone or brick that is inserted into a wall
TAILLE	n pl. -S a former French tax
TAILLESS	adj having no tail
TAILLIKE	adj resembling a tail
TAILOR	v -ED, -ING, -S to fit with clothes
TAILPIPE	n pl. -S an exhaust pipe
TAILRACE	n pl. -S a part of a millrace
TAILSKID	n pl. -S a support on which the tail of an airplane rests
TAILSPIN	n pl. -S the spiral descent of a stalled airplane
TAILWIND	n pl. -S a wind coming from behind a moving vehicle
TAIN	n pl. -S a thin plate
TAINT	v -ED, -ING, -S to touch or affect slightly with something bad
TAIPAN	n pl. -S a venomous snake
TAJ	n pl. -ES a tall, conical cap worn in Muslim countries
TAKAHE	n pl. -S a flightless bird
TAKE	v TOOK, TAKEN, TAKING, TAKES to get possession of TAKABLE, TAKEABLE adj
TAKEDOWN	n pl. -S an article that can be taken apart easily
TAKEOFF	n pl. -S the act of rising in flight
TAKEOUT	n pl. -S the act of removing
TAKEOVER	n pl. -S the act of assuming control
TAKER	n pl. -S one that takes
TAKIN	n pl. -S a goatlike mammal
TAKING	n pl. -S a seizure

TAKINGLY *adv* in an attractive manner

TALA *n* pl. -S a traditional rhythmic pattern of music in India

TALAPOIN *n* pl. -S a small African monkey

TALAR *n* pl. -S a long cloak

TALARIA *n/pl* winged sandals worn by various figures of classical mythology

TALC *v* TALCKED, TALCKING, TALCS or TALCED, TALCING, TALCS to treat with talc (a soft mineral with a soapy texture) TALCKY, TALCOSE, TALCOUS *adj*

TALCUM *n* pl. -S a powder made from talc

TALE *n* pl. -S a story

TALENT *n* pl. -S a special natural ability TALENTED *adj*

TALER *n* pl. -S a former German coin

TALESMAN *n* pl. -MEN a person summoned to fill a vacancy on a jury

TALEYSIM a pl. of tallith

TALI pl. of talus

TALION *n* pl. -S a retaliation for a crime

TALIPED *n* pl. -S a person afflicted with clubfoot

TALIPES *n* pl. TALIPES clubfoot

TALIPOT *n* pl. -S a tall palm tree

TALISMAN *n* pl. -S an object believed to possess magical powers

TALK *v* -ED, -ING, -S to communicate by speaking

TALKABLE *adj* able to be talked about

TALKER *n* pl. -S one that talks

TALKIE *n* pl. -S a moving picture with synchronized sound

TALKING *n* pl. -S conversation

TALKY *adj* TALKIER, TALKIEST tending to talk a great deal

TALL *adj* TALLER, TALLEST having great height

TALLAGE *v* -LAGED, -LAGING, -LAGES to tax

TALLAISIM a pl. of tallith

TALLBOY *n* pl. -BOYS a highboy

TALLIED past tense of tally

TALLIER *n* pl. -S one that tallies

TALLIES present 3d person sing. of tally

TALLISH *adj* somewhat tall

TALLITH *n* pl. TALLITHES, TALLITHIM, TALLITOTH, TALEYSIM, or TALLAISIM a Jewish prayer shawl

TALLNESS *n* pl. -ES the state of being tall

TALLOL *n* pl. -S a resinous liquid

TALLOW *v* -ED, -ING, -S to smear with tallow (a mixture of animal fats)

TALLOWY *adj* resembling tallow

TALLY *v* -LIED, -LYING, -LIES to count

TALLYHO *v* -ED, -ING, -S to make an encouraging shout to hunting hounds

TALLYMAN *n* pl. -MEN a person who tallies

TALMUDIC *adj* pertaining to the body of Jewish civil and religious law

TALON *n* pl. -S a claw of a bird of prey TALONED *adj*

TALOOKA *n* pl. -S taluk

TALUK *n* pl. -S an estate in India

TALUKA *n* pl. -S taluk

TALUS *n* pl. -LI a bone of the foot

TALUS *n* pl. -ES a slope formed by an accumulation of rock debris

TAM *n* pl. -S a tight-fitting Scottish cap

TAMABLE *adj* capable of being tamed

TAMAL *n* pl. -S tamale

TAMALE *n* pl. -S a Mexican dish

TAMANDU *n* pl. -S tamandua

TAMANDUA *n* pl. -S an arboreal anteater

TAMARACK *n* pl. -S a timber tree

TAMARAO *n* pl. -RAOS tamarau

TAMARAU *n* pl. -S a small buffalo of the Philippines

TAMARIN *n* pl. -S a South American monkey

TAMARIND *n* pl. -S a tropical tree

TAMARISK *n* pl. -S an evergreen shrub

TAMASHA *n* pl. -S a public entertainment in India

TAMBAC *n* pl. -S tombac

TAMBALA *n* pl. -S a monetary unit of Malawi

TAMBOUR *v* -ED, -ING, -S to embroider on a round wooden frame

TAMBOURA *n* pl. -S tambura

TAMBUR *n* pl. -S tambura

TAMBURA *n* pl. -S a stringed instrument

TAME *adj* TAMER, TAMEST gentle or docile

TAME *v* TAMED, TAMING, TAMES to make tame

TAMEABLE *adj* tamable

TAMEIN *n* pl. -S a garment worn by Burmese women

TAMELESS *adj* not capable of being tamed

TAMELY *adv* in a tame manner

TAMENESS *n* pl. -ES the state of being tame

TAMER *n* pl. -S one that tames

TAMEST superlative of tame

TAMING present participle of tame

TAMIS *n* pl. -ISES a strainer made of cloth mesh

TAMMIE *n* pl. -S tammy

TAMMY *n* pl. -MIES a fabric of mixed fibers

TAMP *v* -ED, -ING, -S to pack down by tapping

TAMPALA *n* pl. -S an annual herb

TAMPAN *n* pl. -S a biting insect

TAMPER *v* -ED, -ING, -S to interfere in a harmful manner

TAMPERER *n* pl. -S one that tampers

TAMPION *n* pl. -S a plug for the muzzle of a cannon

TAMPON *v* -ED, -ING, -S to plug with a cotton pad

TAN *v* TANNED, TANNING, TANS to convert hide into leather by soaking in chemicals

TAN *adj* TANNER, TANNEST brown from the sun's rays

TANAGER *n* pl. -S a brightly colored bird

TANBARK *n* pl. -S a tree bark used as a source of tannin

TANDEM *n* pl. -S a bicycle built for two

TANG *v* -ED, -ING, -S to provide with a pungent flavor

TANGELO *n* pl. -LOS a citrus fruit

TANGENCE *n* pl. -S tangency

TANGENCY *n* pl. -CIES the state of being in immediate physical contact

TANGENT *n* pl. -S a straight line in contact with a curve at one point

TANGIBLE *n* pl. -S something palpable

TANGIBLY *adv* palpably

TANGIER comparative of tangy

TANGIEST superlative of tangy

TANGLE *v* -GLED, -GLING, -GLES to bring together in intricate confusion

TANGLER *n* pl. -S one that tangles

TANGLY *adj* -GLIER, -GLIEST tangled

TANGO *v* -ED, -ING, -S to perform a Latin-American dance

TANGRAM *n* pl. -S a Chinese puzzle

TANGY *adj* TANGIER, TANGIEST pungent

TANIST *n* pl. -S the heir apparent to a Celtic chief

TANISTRY *n* pl. -RIES the system of electing a tanist

TANK *v* -ED, -ING, -S to store in a tank (a container usually for liquids)

TANKA *n* pl. -S a Japanese verse form

TANKAGE *n* pl. -S the capacity of a tank

TANKARD *n* pl. -S a tall drinking vessel

TANKER *n* pl. -S a ship designed to transport liquids

TANKFUL *n* pl. -S the amount a tank can hold

TANKSHIP *n* pl. -S a tanker

TANNABLE *adj* capable of being tanned

TANNAGE *n* pl. -S the process of tanning

TANNATE *n* pl. -S a chemical salt

TANNED past tense of tan

TANNER *n* pl. -S one that tans

TANNERY *n* pl. -NERIES a place where hides are tanned

TANNEST superlative of tan

TANNIC *adj* pertaining to tannin

TANNIN *n* pl. -S a chemical compound used in tanning

TANNING *n* pl. -S the process of converting hides into leather

TANNISH *adj* somewhat tan

TANREC *n* pl. -S tenrec

TANSY *n* pl. -SIES a perennial herb

TANTALUM *n* pl. -S a metallic element **TANTALIC** *adj*

TANTALUS *n* pl. -ES a case for wine bottles

TANTARA *n* pl. -S the sound of a trumpet or horn

TANTIVY *n* pl. -TIVIES a hunting cry

TANTO *adv* so much — used as a musical direction

TANTRA *n* pl. -S one of a class of Hindu religious writings **TANTRIC** *adj*

TANTRUM *n* pl. -S a fit of rage

TANYARD *n* pl. -S the section of a tannery containing the vats

TAO *n* pl. -S the path of virtuous conduct according to a Chinese philosophy

TAP *v* TAPPED, TAPPING, TAPS to strike gently

TAPA *n* pl. -S a cloth made from tree bark

TAPADERA n pl. -S a part of a saddle

TAPADERO n pl. -ROS tapadera

TAPALO n pl. -LOS a scarf worn in Latin-American countries

TAPE v TAPED, TAPING, TAPES to fasten with tape (a long, narrow strip or band)

TAPELESS adj being without tape

TAPELIKE adj resembling tape

TAPELINE n pl. -S a tape for measuring distances

TAPER v -ED, -ING, -S to become gradually narrower toward one end

TAPERER n pl. -S one that carries a candle in a religious procession

TAPESTRY v -TRIED, -TRYING, -TRIES to decorate with woven wall hangings

TAPETUM n pl. -TA a layer of cells in some plants **TAPETAL** adj

TAPEWORM n pl. -S a parasitic worm

TAPHOLE n pl. -S a hole in a blast furnace

TAPHOUSE n pl. -S a tavern

TAPING present participle of tape

TAPIOCA n pl. -S a starchy food

TAPIR n pl. -S a hoofed mammal

TAPIS n pl. -PISES material used for wall hangings and floor coverings

TAPPED past tense of tap

TAPPER n pl. -S one that taps

TAPPET n pl. -S a sliding rod that causes another part of a mechanism to move

TAPPING n pl. -S the process or means by which something is tapped

TAPROOM n pl. -S a barroom

TAPROOT n pl. -S the main root of a plant

TAPSTER n pl. -S one that dispenses liquor in a barroom

TAR v TARRED, TARRING, TARS to cover with tar (a black viscous liquid)

TARANTAS n pl. -ES a Russian carriage

TARBOOSH n pl. -ES a cap worn by Muslim men

TARBUSH n pl. -ES tarboosh

TARDIER comparative of tardy

TARDIES pl. of tardy

TARDO adj slow — used as a musical direction

TARDY adj TARDIER, TARDIEST late **TARDILY** adv

TARDY n pl. -DIES an instance of being late

TARE v TARED, TARING, TARES to determine the weight of a container holding goods

TARGE n pl. -S a small, round shield

TARGET v -ED, -ING, -S to make a goal of

TARIFF v -ED, -ING, -S to tax imported or exported goods

TARING present participle of tare

TARLATAN n pl. -S a cotton fabric

TARLETAN n pl. -S tarlatan

TARMAC n pl. -S an asphalt road

TARN n pl. -S a small mountain lake

TARNAL adj damned **TARNALLY** adv

TARNISH v -ED, -ING, -ES to dull the luster of

TARO n pl. -ROS a tropical plant

TAROC n pl. -S tarok

TAROK n pl. -S a card game

TAROT n pl. -S any of a set of playing cards used for fortune-telling

TARP n pl. -S a protective canvas covering

TARPAN n pl. -S an Asian wild horse

TARPAPER n pl. -S a heavy paper coated with tar

TARPON n pl. -S a marine game fish

TARRAGON n pl. -S a perennial herb

TARRE v TARRED, TARRING, TARRES to urge to action

TARRED past tense of tar

TARRIED past tense of tarry

TARRIER n pl. -S one that tarries

TARRIES present 3d person sing. of tarry

TARRIEST superlative of tarry

TARRING present participle of tar and tarre

TARRY v -RIED, -RYING, -RIES to delay or be slow in acting or doing

TARRY adj -RIER, -RIEST resembling tar

TARSAL n pl. -S a bone of the foot

TARSI pl. of tarsus

TARSIA n pl. -S intarsia

TARSIER n pl. -S a nocturnal primate

TARSUS n pl. TARSI a part of the foot

TART adj TARTER, TARTEST having a sharp, sour taste

TART	v -ED, -ING, -S to dress up	**TATTLE**	v -TLED, -TLING, -TLES to reveal the activities of another
TARTAN	n pl. -S a patterned woolen fabric	**TATTLER**	n pl. -S one that tattles
TARTANA	n pl. -S a Mediterranean sailing vessel	**TATTOO**	v -ED, -ING, -S to mark the skin with indelible pigments
TARTAR	n pl. -S a crust on the teeth **TARTARIC** adj	**TATTOOER**	n pl. -S one that tattoos
TARTISH	adj somewhat tart	**TATTY**	adj -TIER, -TIEST shabby
TARTLET	n pl. -S a small pie	**TAU**	n pl. -S a Greek letter
TARTLY	adv in a tart manner	**TAUGHT**	past tense of teach
TARTNESS	n pl. -ES the state of being tart	**TAUNT**	v -ED, -ING, -S to challenge or reproach sarcastically
TARTRATE	n pl. -S a chemical salt	**TAUNTER**	n pl. -S one that taunts
TARTUFE	n pl. -S tartuffe	**TAUPE**	n pl. -S a dark gray color
TARTUFFE	n pl. -S a hypocrite	**TAURINE**	n pl. -S a chemical compound
TARWEED	n pl. -S a flowering plant	**TAUT**	adj TAUTER, TAUTEST fully stretched, so as not to be slack
TARZAN	n pl. -S a person of superior strength and agility	**TAUT**	v -ED, -ING, -S to tangle
TASK	v -ED, -ING, -S to assign a job to	**TAUTAUG**	n pl. -S tautog
		TAUTEN	v -ED, -ING, -S to make taut
TASKWORK	n pl. -S hard work	**TAUTLY**	adv in a taut manner
TASS	n pl. -ES a drinking cup	**TAUTNESS**	n pl. -ES the state of being taut
TASSE	n pl. -S tasset	**TAUTOG**	n pl. -S a marine fish
TASSEL	v -SELED, -SELING, -SELS or -SELLED, -SELLING, -SELS to adorn with dangling ornaments	**TAUTOMER**	n pl. -S a type of chemical compound
		TAUTONYM	n pl. -S a type of taxonomic designation
TASSET	n pl. -S a piece of plate armor for the upper thigh	**TAV**	n pl. -S a Hebrew letter
TASSIE	n pl. -S tass	**TAVERN**	n pl. -S a place where liquor is sold to be drunk on the premises
TASTE	v TASTED, TASTING, TASTES to perceive the flavor of by taking into the mouth **TASTABLE** adj	**TAVERNER**	n pl. -S one that runs a tavern
TASTEFUL	adj tasty	**TAW**	v -ED, -ING, -S to convert into white leather by the application of minerals
TASTER	n pl. -S one that tastes	**TAWDRY**	adj -DRIER, -DRIEST gaudy **TAWDRILY** adv
TASTING	present participle of taste		
TASTY	adj TASTIER, TASTIEST pleasant to the taste **TASTILY** adv	**TAWDRY**	n pl. -DRIES gaudy finery
		TAWER	n pl. -S one that taws
TAT	v TATTED, TATTING, TATS to make tatting	**TAWIE**	adj docile
		TAWNEY	n pl. -NEYS tawny
TATAMI	n pl. -S straw matting used as a floor covering	**TAWNY**	adj -NIER, -NIEST light brown **TAWNILY** adv
TATE	n pl. -S a tuft of hair	**TAWNY**	n pl. -NIES a light brown color
TATER	n pl. -S a potato	**TAWPIE**	n pl. -S a foolish young person
TATOUAY	n pl. -AYS a South American armadillo	**TAWSE**	v TAWSED, TAWSING, TAWSES to flog
TATTED	past tense of tat	**TAX**	v -ED, -ING, -ES to place a tax (a charge imposed by authority for public purposes) on
TATTER	v -ED, -ING, -S to become torn and worn		
TATTIER	comparative of tatty	**TAXA**	a pl. of taxon
TATTIEST	superlative of tatty	**TAXABLE**	adj subject to tax **TAXABLY** adv
TATTING	n pl. -S delicate handmade lace		

TAXABLE *n* pl. -S a taxable item

TAXATION *n* pl. -S the process of taxing

TAXEME *n* pl. -S a minimum grammatical feature of selection **TAXEMIC** *adj*

TAXER *n* pl. -S one that taxes

TAXI *v* TAXIED, TAXIING or TAXYING, TAXIS or TAXIES to travel in a taxicab

TAXICAB *n* pl. -S an automobile for hire

TAXIMAN *n* pl. -MEN the operator of a taxicab

TAXINGLY *adv* in an onerous manner

TAXITE *n* pl. -S a volcanic rock **TAXITIC** *adj*

TAXIWAY *n* pl. -WAYS a paved strip at an airport

TAXLESS *adj* free from taxation

TAXMAN *n* pl. -MEN one who collects taxes

TAXON *n* pl. TAXA or TAXONS a unit of scientific classification

TAXONOMY *n* pl. -MIES the study of scientific classification

TAXPAID *adj* paid for by taxes

TAXPAYER *n* pl. -S one that pays taxes

TAXUS *n* pl. TAXUS an evergreen tree or shrub

TAXWISE *adj* pertaining to taxes

TAXYING a present participle of taxi

TAZZA *n* pl. -ZAS or -ZE an ornamental bowl

TEA *n* pl. -S a beverage made by infusing dried leaves in boiling water

TEABERRY *n* pl. -RIES a North American shrub

TEABOARD *n* pl. -S a tray for serving tea

TEABOWL *n* pl. -S a teacup having no handle

TEABOX *n* pl. -ES a box for tea leaves

TEACAKE *n* pl. -S a small cake served with tea

TEACART *n* pl. -S a wheeled table used in serving tea

TEACH *v* TAUGHT, TEACHING, TEACHES to impart knowledge or skill to

TEACHER *n* pl. -S one that teaches

TEACHING *n* pl. -S a doctrine

TEACUP *n* pl. -S a cup in which tea is served

TEAHOUSE *n* pl. -S a public establishment serving tea

TEAK *n* pl. -S an East Indian tree

TEAKWOOD *n* pl. -S the wood of the teak

TEAL *n* pl. -S a river duck

TEAM *v* -ED, -ING, -S to form a team (a group of persons associated in a joint action)

TEAMAKER *n* pl. -S one that makes tea

TEAMMATE *n* pl. -S a member of the same team

TEAMSTER *n* pl. -S a truck driver

TEAMWORK *n* pl. -S cooperative effort to achieve a common goal

TEAPOT *n* pl. -S a vessel used in making and serving tea

TEAPOY *n* pl. -POYS a small table used in serving tea

TEAR *v* -ED, -ING, -S to emit tears (drops of saline liquid secreted by a gland of the eye)

TEAR *v* TORE, TORN, TEARING, TEARS to pull apart or into pieces **TEARABLE** *adj*

TEARDOWN *n* pl. -S the process of disassembling

TEARDROP *n* pl. -S a tear

TEARER *n* pl. -S one that tears or rips

TEARFUL *adj* full of tears

TEARGAS *v* -GASSED, -GASSING, -GASES or -GASSES to subject to a gas that irritates the eyes

TEARIER comparative of teary

TEARIEST superlative of teary

TEARILY *adv* in a teary manner

TEARLESS *adj* being without tears

TEAROOM *n* pl. -S a restaurant serving tea

TEARY *adj* TEARIER, TEARIEST tearful

TEASE *v* TEASED, TEASING, TEASES to make fun of

TEASEL *v* -SELED, -SELING, -SELS or -SELLED, -SELLING, -SELS to raise a soft surface on fabric with a bristly flower head

TEASELER *n* pl. -S one that teasels

TEASER *n* pl. -S one that teases

TEASHOP *n* pl. -S a tearoom

TEASING present participle of tease

TEASPOON *n* pl. -S a small spoon

TEAT *n* pl. -S a mammary gland **TEATED** *adj*

TEATIME *n* pl. -S the customary time for tea

TEAWARE *n* pl. -S a tea service

TEAZEL   v -ZELED, -ZELING, -ZELS or -ZELLED, -ZELLING, -ZELS to teasel

TEAZLE   v -ZLED, -ZLING, -ZLES to teasel

TECHED   adj crazy

TECHNIC   n pl. -S technique

TECHY   adj TECHIER, TECHIEST tetchy TECHILY adv

TECTA   pl. of tectum

TECTAL   adj pertaining to a tectum

TECTONIC   adj pertaining to construction

TECTRIX   n pl. -TRICES a small feather of a bird's wing

TECTUM   n pl. -TA a bodily structure resembling or serving as a roof

TED   v TEDDED, TEDDING, TEDS to spread for drying

TEDDER   n pl. -S one that teds

TEDDY   n pl. -DIES a woman's undergarment

TEDIOUS   adj causing weariness

TEDIUM   n pl. -S the state of being tedious

TEE   v TEED, TEEING, TEES to place a golf ball on a small peg

TEEM   v -ED, -ING, -S to be full to overflowing

TEEMER   n pl. -S one that teems

TEEN   n pl. -S a teenager

TEENAGE   adj pertaining to teenagers

TEENAGED   adj teenage

TEENAGER   n pl. -S a person between the ages of thirteen and nineteen

TEENER   n pl. -S a teenager

TEENFUL   adj filled with grief

TEENSY   adj -SIER, -SIEST tiny

TEENTSY   adj -SIER, -SIEST tiny

TEENY   adj -NIER, -NIEST tiny

TEEPEE   n pl. -S tepee

TEETER   v -ED, -ING, -S to move unsteadily

TEETH   pl. of tooth

TEETHE   v TEETHED, TEETHING, TEETHES to cut teeth

TEETHER   n pl. -S an object for a baby to bite on during teething

TEETHING   n pl. -S the first growth of teeth

TEETOTAL   v -TALED, -TALING, -TALS or -TALLED, -TALLING, -TALS to abstain completely from alcoholic beverages

TEETOTUM   n pl. -S a spinning toy

TEFF   n pl. -S a cereal grass

TEG   n pl. -S a yearling sheep

TEGMEN   n pl. -MINA a covering

TEGMENTA   n/pl anatomical coverings

TEGMINAL   adj pertaining to a tegmen

TEGUA   n pl. -S a type of moccasin

TEGULAR   adj resembling a tile

TEGUMEN   n pl. -MINA tegmen

TEGUMENT   n pl. -S a covering

TEIGLACH   n pl. TEIGLACH a confection consisting of balls of dough boiled in honey

TEIID   n pl. -S a tropical American lizard

TEIND   n pl. -S a tithe

TEKTITE   n pl. -S a glassy body believed to be of meteoritic origin TEKTITIC adj

TELA   n pl. -LAE an anatomical tissue

TELAMON   n pl. -ES a male figure used as a supporting column

TELE   n pl. -S a television set

TELECAST   v -ED, -ING, -S to broadcast by television

TELEDU   n pl. -S a carnivorous mammal

TELEFILM   n pl. -S a motion picture made for television

TELEGA   n pl. -S a Russian wagon

TELEGONY   n pl. -NIES the supposed influence of a previous sire on the offspring of later matings of the mother with other males

TELEGRAM   v -GRAMMED, -GRAMMING, -GRAMS to send a message by telegraph

TELEMAN   n pl. -MEN a naval officer

TELEMARK   n pl. -S a type of turn in skiing

TELEOST   n pl. -S a bony fish

TELEPLAY   n pl. -PLAYS a play written for television

TELEPORT   v -ED, -ING, -S to transport by a process that involves no physical means

TELERAN   n pl. -S a system of air navigation

TELESIS   n pl. TELESES planned progress

TELETHON   n pl. -S a fund-raising television program

TELEVIEW   v -ED, -ING, -S to observe by means of television

TELEVISE   v -VISED, -VISING, -VISES to broadcast by television (an electronic system of transmitting images and sound)

TELEX v -ED, -ING, -ES to send a message by a type of telegraphic system

TELFER v -ED, -ING, -S to telpher

TELFORD n pl. -S a road made of stones

TELIA pl. of telium

TELIAL adj pertaining to a telium

TELIC adj directed toward a goal

TELIUM n pl. -LIA a sorus on the host plant of a rust fungus

TELL v TOLD, TELLING, TELLS to give a detailed account of TELLABLE adj

TELLER n pl. -S a bank employee who receives and pays out money

TELLIES pl. of telly

TELLTALE n pl. -S a tattler

TELLURIC adj pertaining to the earth

TELLY n pl. -LIES a television set

TELOME n pl. -S a structural unit of a vascular plant TELOMIC adj

TELOS n pl. TELOI an ultimate end

TELPHER v -ED, -ING, -S to transport by a system of aerial cable cars

TELSON n pl. -S the terminal segment of an arthropod TELSONIC adj

TEMBLOR n pl. -S or -ES an earthquake

TEMERITY n pl. -TIES foolish boldness

TEMPEH n pl. -S an Asian food

TEMPER v -ED, -ING, -S to moderate by adding a counterbalancing agent

TEMPERA n pl. -S a technique of painting

TEMPERER n pl. -S one that tempers

TEMPEST v -ED, -ING, -S to agitate violently

TEMPI a pl. of tempo

TEMPLAR n pl. -S a lawyer or student of law in London

TEMPLATE n pl. -S a pattern used as a guide in making something

TEMPLE n pl. -S a house of worship TEMPLED adj

TEMPLET n pl. -S template

TEMPO n pl. -PI or -POS the rate of speed of a musical piece

TEMPORAL n pl. -S a bone of the skull

TEMPT v -ED, -ING, -S to entice to commit an unwise or immoral act

TEMPTER n pl. -S one that tempts

TEMPURA n pl. -S a Japanese dish

TEN n pl. -S a number

TENABLE adj capable of being held TENABLY adv

TENACE n pl. -S a combination of two high cards in some card games

TENACITY n pl. -TIES perseverance or persistence

TENACULA n/pl hooked surgical instruments

TENAIL n pl. -S tenaille

TENAILLE n pl. -S an outer defense

TENANCY n pl. -CIES the temporary occupancy of something that belongs to another

TENANT v -ED, -ING, -S to inhabit

TENANTRY n pl. -RIES tenancy

TENCH n pl. -ES a freshwater fish

TEND v -ED, -ING, -S to be disposed or inclined

TENDANCE n pl. -S watchful care

TENDENCE n pl. -S tendance

TENDENCY n pl. -CIES an inclination to act or think in a particular way

TENDER adj -DERER, -DEREST soft or delicate

TENDER v -ED, -ING, -S to present for acceptance

TENDERER n pl. -S one that tenders

TENDERLY adv in a tender manner

TENDON n pl. -S a band of tough, fibrous tissue

TENDRIL n pl. -S a leafless organ of climbing plants

TENEBRAE n/pl a religious service

TENEMENT n pl. -S an apartment house

TENESMUS n pl. -ES an urgent but ineffectual effort to defecate or urinate TENESMIC adj

TENET n pl. -S a principle, belief, or doctrine held to be true

TENFOLD n pl. -S an amount ten times as great as a given unit

TENIA n pl. -NIAE or -NIAS a tapeworm

TENIASIS n pl. -SISES infestation with tapeworms

TENNER n pl. -S a ten-dollar bill

TENNIS n pl. -NISES an outdoor ball game

TENNIST n pl. -S a tennis player

TENON v -ED, -ING, -S to unite by means of a tenon (a projection on the end of a piece of wood)

TENONER n pl. -S one that tenons

TENOR *n* pl. -S a high male singing voice

TENORITE *n* pl. -S a mineral

TENOTOMY *n* pl. -MIES the surgical division of a tendon

TENOUR *n* pl. -S tenor

TENPENCE *n* pl. -S the sum of ten pennies

TENPENNY *adj* worth tenpence

TENPIN *n* pl. -S a bowling pin

TENREC *n* pl. -S a mammal that feeds on insects

TENSE *adj* TENSER, TENSEST taut **TENSELY** *adv*

TENSE *v* TENSED, TENSING, TENSES to make tense

TENSIBLE *adj* capable of being stretched **TENSIBLY** *adv*

TENSILE *adj* tensible

TENSING present participle of tense

TENSION *v* -ED, -ING, -S to make tense

TENSITY *n* pl. -TIES the state of being tense

TENSIVE *adj* causing tensity

TENSOR *n* pl. -S a muscle that stretches a body part

TENT *v* -ED, -ING, -S to live in a tent (a type of portable shelter)

TENTACLE *n* pl. -S an elongated, flexible appendage of some animals

TENTAGE *n* pl. -S a supply of tents

TENTER *v* -ED, -ING, -S to stretch on a type of frame

TENTH *n* pl. -S one of ten equal parts

TENTHLY *adv* in the tenth place

TENTIE *adj* TENTIER, TENTIEST tenty

TENTIER comparative of tenty

TENTIEST superlative of tenty

TENTLESS *adj* having no tent

TENTLIKE *adj* resembling a tent

TENTY *adj* TENTIER, TENTIEST watchful

TENUIS *n* pl. -UES a voiceless phonetic stop

TENUITY *n* pl. -ITIES lack of substance or strength

TENUOUS *adj* having little substance or strength

TENURE *n* pl. -S the holding of something **TENURED, TENURIAL** *adj*

TENUTO *n* pl. -TI or -TOS a musical note or chord held longer than its normal duration

TEOCALLI *n* pl. -S an Aztec temple

TEOPAN *n* pl. -S a teocalli

TEOSINTE *n* pl. -S an annual grass

TEPA *n* pl. -S a chemical compound

TEPAL *n* pl. -S a division of a perianth

TEPEE *n* pl. -S a conical tent of some North American Indians

TEPEFY *v* -FIED, -FYING, -FIES to make tepid

TEPHRA *n* pl. -S solid material ejected from a volcano

TEPHRITE *n* pl. -S a volcanic rock

TEPID *adj* moderately warm **TEPIDLY** *adv*

TEPIDITY *n* pl. -TIES the state of being tepid

TEQUILA *n* pl. -S a Mexican liquor

TERAI *n* pl. -S a sun hat with a wide brim

TERAOHM *n* pl. -S one trillion ohms

TERAPH *n* pl. -APHIM an image of a Semitic household god

TERATISM *n* pl. -S a malformed fetus **TERATOID** *adj*

TERATOMA *n* pl. -MAS or -MATA a type of tumor

TERBIA *n* pl. -S an oxide of terbium

TERBIUM *n* pl. -S a metallic element **TERBIC** *adj*

TERCE *n* pl. -S tierce

TERCEL *n* pl. -S a male falcon

TERCELET *n* pl. -S tercel

TERCET *n* pl. -S a group of three lines of verse

TEREBENE *n* pl. -S a mixture of terpenes

TEREBIC *adj* pertaining to an acid derived from oil of turpentine

TEREDO *n* pl. -DOS or -DINES a bivalve mollusk

TEREFAH *adj* tref

TERETE *adj* cylindrical and slightly tapering

TERGA pl. of tergum

TERGAL *adj* pertaining to a tergum

TERGITE *n* pl. -S a tergum

TERGUM *n* pl. -GA a back part of a segment of an arthropod

TERIYAKI *n* pl. -S a Japanese food

TERM *v* -ED, -ING, -S to give a name to

TERMER *n* pl. -S a prisoner serving a specified sentence

TERMINAL *n pl.* -S an end or extremity

TERMINUS *n pl.* -NI or -NUSES a terminal

TERMITE *n pl.* -S an insect resembling an ant **TERMITIC** *adj*

TERMLESS *adj* having no limits

TERMLY *adv* periodically

TERMOR *n pl.* -S one that holds land for a certain number of years

TERMTIME *n pl.* -S the time when a school or court is in session

TERN *n pl.* -S a seabird

TERNARY *n pl.* -RIES a group of three

TERNATE *adj* arranged in groups of three

TERNE *n pl.* -S an alloy of lead and tin

TERNION *n pl.* -S a group of three

TERPENE *n pl.* -S a chemical compound **TERPENIC** *adj*

TERPINOL *n pl.* -S a fragrant liquid

TERRA *n pl.* -RAE earth; land

TERRACE *v* -RACED, -RACING, -RACES to provide with a terrace (a raised embankment)

TERRAIN *n pl.* -S a tract of land

TERRANE *n pl.* -S a rock formation

TERRAPIN *n pl.* -S a North American tortoise

TERRARIA *n/pl* glass enclosures for plants or small animals

TERRAS *n pl.* -ES trass

TERRAZZO *n pl.* -ZOS a mosaic flooring

TERREEN *n pl.* -S terrine

TERRELLA *n pl.* -S a spherical magnet

TERRENE *n pl.* -S a land area

TERRET *n pl.* -S a metal ring on a harness

TERRIBLE *adj* very bad **TERRIBLY** *adv*

TERRIER *n pl.* -S a small, active dog

TERRIES *pl.* of terry

TERRIFIC *adj* very good; fine

TERRIFY *v* -FIED, -FYING, -FIES to fill with terror

TERRINE *n pl.* -S an earthenware jar

TERRIT *n pl.* -S terret

TERROR *n pl.* -S intense fear

TERRY *n pl.* -RIES an absorbent fabric

TERSE *adj* TERSER, TERSEST succinct **TERSELY** *adv*

TERTIAL *n pl.* -S a flight feather of a bird's wing

TERTIAN *n pl.* -S a recurrent fever

TERTIARY *n pl.* -ARIES a tertial

TESLA *n pl.* -S a unit of magnetic induction

TESSERA *n pl.* -SERAE a small square used in mosaic work

TEST *v* -ED, -ING, -S to subject to an examination **TESTABLE** *adj*

TESTA *n pl.* -TAE the hard outer coating of a seed

TESTACY *n pl.* -CIES the state of being testate

TESTATE *adj* having made a valid will before death

TESTATOR *n pl.* -S one that makes a will

TESTEE *n pl.* -S one that is tested

TESTER *n pl.* -S one that tests

TESTES *pl.* of testis

TESTICLE *n pl.* -S a testis

TESTIER comparative of testy

TESTIEST superlative of testy

TESTIFY *v* -FIED, -FYING, -FIES to make a declaration of truth under oath

TESTILY *adv* in a testy manner

TESTING present participle of test

TESTIS *n pl.* TESTES a male reproductive gland

TESTON *n pl.* -S a former French coin

TESTOON *n pl.* -S teston

TESTUDO *n pl.* -DINES or -DOS a portable screen used as a shield by the ancient Romans

TESTY *adj* TESTIER, TESTIEST irritable

TETANAL *adj* pertaining to tetanus

TETANIC *n pl.* -S a drug capable of causing convulsions

TETANIES *pl.* of tetany

TETANISE *v* -NISED, -NISING, -NISES to tetanize

TETANIZE *v* -NIZED, -NIZING, -NIZES to affect with convulsions

TETANUS *n pl.* -ES an infectious disease **TETANOID** *adj*

TETANY *n pl.* -NIES a condition marked by painful muscular spasms

TETCHED *adj* crazy

TETCHY *adj* TETCHIER, TETCHIEST irritable **TETCHILY** *adv*

TETH *n pl.* -S a Hebrew letter

TETHER *v* -ED, -ING, -S to fasten to a fixed object with a rope

TETOTUM *n pl.* -S teetotum

TETRA *n pl.* -S a tropical fish

TETRACID *n pl.* -S a type of acid

TETRAD *n pl.* -S a group of four TETRADIC *adj*

TETRAGON *n pl.* -S a four-sided polygon

TETRAMER *n pl.* -S a type of polymer

TETRAPOD *n pl.* -S a four-footed animal

TETRARCH *n pl.* -S one of four joint rulers

TETRODE *n pl.* -S a type of electron tube

TETROXID *n pl.* -S a type of oxide

TETRYL *n pl.* -S a chemical compound

TETTER *n pl.* -S a skin disease

TEUCH *adj* teugh

TEUGH *adj* tough TEUGHLY *adv*

TEW *v* -ED, -ING, -S to work hard

TEXAS *n pl.* -ES the uppermost structure on a steamboat

TEXT *n pl.* -S the main body of a written or printed work

TEXTBOOK *n pl.* -S a book used in the study of a subject

TEXTILE *n pl.* -S a woven fabric

TEXTLESS *adj* having no text

TEXTUAL *adj* pertaining to a text

TEXTUARY *n pl.* -ARIES a specialist in the study of the Scriptures

TEXTURAL *adj* pertaining to the surface characteristics of something

TEXTURE *v* -TURED, -TURING, -TURES to make by weaving

THACK *v* -ED, -ING, -S to thatch

THAE *adj* these; those

THAIRM *n pl.* -S tharm

THALAMUS *n pl.* -MI a part of the brain THALAMIC *adj*

THALER *n pl.* -S taler

THALLIUM *n pl.* -S a metallic element THALLIC, THALLOUS *adj*

THALLUS *n pl.* -LI or -LUSES a plant body without true root, stem, or leaf THALLOID *adj*

THAN *conj* — used to introduce the second element of a comparison

THANAGE *n pl.* -S the land held by a thane

THANATOS *n pl.* -ES an instinctual desire for death

THANE *n pl.* -S a man holding land by military service in Anglo-Saxon England

THANK *v* -ED, -ING, -S to express gratitude to

THANKER *n pl.* -S one that thanks

THANKFUL *adj* -FULLER, -FULLEST feeling gratitude

THARM *n pl.* -S the belly

THAT *pron pl.* THOSE the one indicated

THATAWAY *adv* in that direction

THATCH *v* -ED, -ING, -ES to cover with thatch (plant stalks by a god)

THATCHER *n pl.* -S one that thatches

THATCHY *adj* resembling thatch

THAW *v* -ED, -ING, -S to melt

THAWER *n pl.* -S one that thaws

THAWLESS *adj* never thawing

THE *definite article* — used to specify or make particular

THEARCHY *n pl.* -CHIES rule by a god

THEATER *n pl.* -S a building for dramatic presentations THEATRIC *adj*

THEATRE *n pl.* -S theater

THEBAINE *n pl.* -S a poisonous alkaloid

THECA *n pl.* -CAE a protective anatomical covering THECAL, THECATE *adj*

THEE *pron* the objective case of the pronoun thou

THEELIN *n pl.* -S estrone

THEELOL *n pl.* -S estriol

THEFT *n pl.* -S the act of stealing

THEGN *n pl.* -S thane THEGNLY *adj*

THEIN *n pl.* -S theine

THEINE *n pl.* -S caffeine

THEIR *pron* a possessive form of the pronoun they

THEIRS *pron* a possessive form of the pronoun they

THEISM *n pl.* -S belief in the existence of a god

THEIST *n pl.* -S one who believes in the existence of a god THEISTIC *adj*

THELITIS *n pl.* -TISES inflammation of the nipple

THEM *pron* the objective case of the pronoun they

THEMATIC *adj* pertaining to a theme

THEME *n pl.* -S a subject discussed in speech or writing

THEN *n pl.* -S that time

THENAGE *n pl.* -S thanage

THENAL *adj* pertaining to the palm of the hand

THENAR *n pl.* -S the palm of the hand

THENCE *adv* from that place

THEOCRAT *n pl.* -S a person who rules as a representative of a god

THEODICY *n pl.* -CIES a defense of God's goodness in respect to the existence of evil

THEOGONY *n pl.* -NIES an account of the origin of the gods

THEOLOG *n pl.* -S a student of theology

THEOLOGY *n pl.* -GIES the study of religion

THEONOMY *n pl.* -MIES rule by a god

THEORBO *n pl.* -BOS an ancient lute

THEOREM *n pl.* -S a proposition that is demonstrably true or is assumed to be so

THEORIES ·pl. of theory

THEORISE *v* -RISED, -RISING, -RISES to theorize

THEORIST *n pl.* -S one that theorizes

THEORIZE *v* -RIZED, -RIZING, -RIZES to form theories

THEORY *n pl.* -RIES a group of propositions used to explain a class of phenomena

THERAPY *n pl.* -PIES the treatment of illness or disability

THERE *n pl.* -S that place

THEREAT *adv* at that place or time

THEREBY *adv* by that means

THEREFOR *adv* for that

THEREIN *adv* in that place

THEREMIN *n pl.* -S a musical instrument

THEREOF *adv* of that

THEREON *adv* on that

THERETO *adv* to that

THERIAC *n pl.* -S molasses

THERIACA *n pl.* -S theriac

THERM *n pl.* -S a unit of quantity of heat

THERMAE *n/pl* hot springs

THERMAL *n pl.* -S a rising mass of warm air

THERME *n pl.* -S therm

THERMEL *n pl.* -S a device for temperature measurement

THERMIC *adj* pertaining to heat

THERMION *n pl.* -S an ion emitted by a heated body

THERMIT *n pl.* -S thermite

THERMITE *n pl.* -S a metallic mixture that produces intense heat when ignited

THERMOS *n pl.* -ES a container used to keep liquids either hot or cold

THEROID *adj* resembling a beast

THEROPOD *n pl.* -S a carnivorous dinosaur

THESAURI *n/pl* dictionaries of synonyms and antonyms

THESE pl. of this

THESIS *n pl.* THESES a proposition put forward for discussion

THESPIAN *n pl.* -S an actor or actress

THETA *n pl.* -S a Greek letter

THETIC *adj* arbitrary

THETICAL *adj* thetic

THEURGY *n pl.* -GIES divine intervention in human affairs **THEURGIC** *adj*

THEW *n pl.* -S a well-developed muscle **THEWY** *adj*

THEWLESS *adj* weak

THEY *pron* the 3d person pl. pronoun in the nominative case

THIAMIN *n pl.* -S thiamine

THIAMINE *n pl.* -S a B vitamin

THIAZIDE *n pl.* -S a drug used to treat high blood pressure

THIAZIN *n pl.* -S thiazine

THIAZINE *n pl.* -S a chemical compound

THIAZOL *n pl.* -S thiazole

THIAZOLE *n pl.* -S a chemical compound

THICK *adj* THICKER, THICKEST having relatively great extent from one surface to its opposite

THICK *n pl.* -S the thickest part

THICKEN *v* -ED, -ING, -S to make thick

THICKET *n pl.* -S a dense growth of shrubs or small trees **THICKETY** *adj*

THICKISH *adj* somewhat thick

THICKLY *adv* in a thick manner

THICKSET *n pl.* -S a thicket

THIEF *n pl.* THIEVES one that steals

THIEVE *v* THIEVED, THIEVING, THIEVES to steal

THIEVERY *n pl.* -ERIES the act or practice of stealing

THIEVES pl. of thief

THIEVING present participle of thieve

THIEVISH *adj* given to stealing

THIGH *n pl.* -S a part of the leg **THIGHED** *adj*

THILL *n pl.* -S a shaft of a vehicle

THIMBLE *n pl.* -S a cap used to protect the fingertip during sewing

THIN *adj* THINNER, THINNEST having relatively little density or thickness

THIN   *v* THINNED, THINNING, THINS to make thin

THINCLAD   *n pl.* -S a runner on a track team

THINDOWN   *n pl.* -S a lessening in the number of atomic particles and cosmic rays passing through the earth's atmosphere

THINE   *pron* a possessive form of the pronoun thou

THING   *n pl.* -S an inanimate object

THINK   *v* THOUGHT, THINKING, THINKS to formulate in the mind

THINKER   *n pl.* -S one that thinks

THINKING   *n pl.* -S an opinion or judgment

THINLY   *adv* in a thin manner

THINNED   past tense of thin

THINNER   *n pl.* -S one that thins

THINNESS   *n pl.* -ES the quality or state of being thin

THINNEST   superlative of thin

THINNING   present participle of thin

THINNISH   *adj* somewhat thin

THIO   *adj* containing sulfur

THIOL   *n pl.* -S a sulfur compound THIOLIC *adj*

THIONATE   *n pl.* -S a chemical salt

THIONIC   *adj* pertaining to sulfur

THIONIN   *n pl.* -S a violet dye

THIONINE   *n pl.* -S thionin

THIONYL   *n pl.* -S sulfinyl

THIOPHEN   *n pl.* -S a chemical compound

THIOTEPA   *n pl.* -S a chemical compound

THIOUREA   *n pl.* -S a chemical compound

THIR   *pron* these

THIRAM   *n pl.* -S a chemical compound

THIRD   *n pl.* -S one of three equal parts

THIRDLY   *adv* in the third place

THIRL   *v* -ED, -ING, -S to thrill

THIRLAGE   *n pl.* -S an obligation requiring feudal tenants to grind grain at a certain mill

THIRST   *v* -ED, -ING, -S to feel a desire or need to drink

THIRSTER   *n pl.* -S one that thirsts

THIRSTY   *adj* THIRSTIER, THIRSTIEST feeling a desire or need to drink

THIRTEEN   *n pl.* -S a number

THIRTY   *n pl.* -TIES a number

THIS   *pron pl.* THESE the person or thing just mentioned

THISTLE   *n pl.* -S a prickly plant THISTLY *adj*

THITHER   *adv* in that direction

THO   *conj* though

THOLE   *v* THOLED, THOLING, THOLES to endure

THOLEPIN   *n pl.* -S a pin that serves as an oarlock

THOLOS   *n pl.* -LOI a circular, underground tomb

THONG   *n pl.* -S a narrow strip of leather used for binding THONGED *adj*

THORAX   *n pl.* -RACES or -RAXES the part of the body between the neck and the abdomen THORACAL, THORACIC *adj*

THORIA   *n pl.* -S an oxide of thorium

THORIC   *adj* pertaining to thorium

THORITE   *n pl.* -S a thorium ore

THORIUM   *n pl.* -S a metallic element

THORN   *v* -ED, -ING, -S to prick with a thorn (a sharp, rigid projection on a plant)

THORNY   *adj* THORNIER, THORNIEST full of thorns THORNILY *adv*

THORO   *adj* thorough

THORON   *n pl.* -S a radioactive isotope of radon

THOROUGH   *adj* -OUGHER, -OUGHEST complete in all respects

THORP   *n pl.* -S a small village

THORPE   *n pl.* -S thorp

THOSE   *pl.* of that

THOU   *v* -ED, -ING, -S to address as "thou" (the 2d person sing. pronoun in the nominative case)

THOUGH   *conj* despite the fact that

THOUGHT   *n pl.* -S a product of thinking

THOUSAND   *n pl.* -S a number

THOWLESS   *adj* listless

THRALDOM   *n pl.* -S servitude

THRALL   -ED, -ING, -S to enslave

THRASH   *v* -ED, -ING, -ES to beat

THRASHER   *n pl.* -S one that thrashes

THRAVE   *n pl.* -S a unit of measure for grain

THRAW   *v* -ED, -ING, -S to twist

THRAWART   *adj* stubborn

THRAWN   *adj* twisted THRAWNLY *adv*

THREAD   *v* -ED, -ING, -S to pass a thread (a very slender cord) through

THREADER *n pl.* -S one that threads

THREADY *adj* THREADIER, THREADIEST resembling a thread

THREAP *v* -ED, -ING, -S to dispute

THREAPER *n pl.* -S one that threaps

THREAT *v* -ED, -ING, -S to threaten

THREATEN *v* -ED, -ING, -S to be a source of danger to

THREE *n pl.* -S a number

THREEP *v* -ED, -ING, -S to threap

THRENODE *n pl.* -S a threnody

THRENODY *n pl.* -DIES a song of lamentation

THRESH *v* -ED, -ING, -ES to separate the grain or seeds from a plant mechanically

THRESHER *n pl.* -S one that threshes

THREW past tense of throw

THRICE *adv* three times

THRIFT *n pl.* -S care and wisdom in the management of one's resources

THRIFTY *adj* THRIFTIER, THRIFTIEST displaying thrift

THRILL *v* -ED, -ING, -S to excite greatly

THRILLER *n pl.* -S one that thrills

THRIP *n pl.* -S a British coin

THRIVE *v* THROVE or THRIVED, THRIVEN, THRIVING, THRIVES to grow vigorously

THRIVER *n pl.* -S one that thrives

THRO *prep* through

THROAT *v* -ED, -ING, -S to utter in a hoarse voice

THROATY *adj* THROATIER, THROATIEST hoarse

THROB *v* THROBBED, THROBBING, THROBS to pulsate

THROBBER *n pl.* -S one that throbs

THROE *n pl.* -S a violent spasm of pain

THROMBIN *n pl.* -S an enzyme

THROMBUS *n pl.* -BI a clot occluding a blood vessel

THRONE *v* THRONED, THRONING, THRONES to place on a throne (a royal chair)

THRONG *v* -ED, -ING, -S to crowd into

THROSTLE *n pl.* -S a songbird

THROTTLE *v* -TLED, -TLING, -TLES to strangle

THROUGH *prep* by way of

THROVE a past tense of thrive

THROW *v* THREW, THROWN, THROWING, THROWS to propel through the air with a movement of the arm

THROWER *n pl.* -S one that throws

THRU *prep* through

THRUM *v* THRUMMED, THRUMMING, THRUMS to play a stringed instrument idly or monotonously

THRUMMER *n pl.* -S one that thrums

THRUMMY *adj* -MIER, -MIEST shaggy

THRUPUT *n pl.* -S the amount of raw material processed within a given time

THRUSH *n pl.* -ES a songbird

THRUST *v* -ED, -ING, -S to push forcibly

THRUSTER *n pl.* -S one that thrusts

THRUSTOR *n pl.* -S thruster

THRUWAY *n pl.* -WAYS an express highway

THUD *v* THUDDED, THUDDING, THUDS to make a dull, heavy sound

THUG *n pl.* -S a brutal ruffian or assassin

THUGGEE *n pl.* -S thuggery in India

THUGGERY *n pl.* -GERIES thuggish behavior

THUGGISH *adj* characteristic of a thug

THUJA *n pl.* -S an evergreen tree or shrub

THULIA *n pl.* -S an oxide of thulium

THULIUM *n pl.* -S a metallic element

THUMB *v* -ED, -ING, -S to leaf through with the thumb (the short, thick digit of the human hand)

THUMBKIN *n pl.* -S a screw that is turned by the thumb and fingers

THUMBNUT *n pl.* -S a nut that is turned by the thumb and fingers

THUMP *v* -ED, -ING, -S to strike so as to make a dull, heavy sound

THUMPER *n pl.* -S one that thumps

THUNDER *v* -ED, -ING, -S to produce a loud, resounding sound

THUNDERY *adj* accompanied with thunder

THURIBLE *n pl.* -S a censer

THURIFER *n pl.* -S one who carries a thurible in a religious ceremony

THURL *n pl.* -S the hip joint in cattle

THUS *adv* in this manner

THUSLY *adv* thus

THUYA *n pl.* -S thuja

THWACK	v -ED, -ING, -S to strike with something flat
THWACKER	n pl. -S one that thwacks
THWART	v -ED, -ING, -S to prevent the accomplishment of
THWARTER	n pl. -S one that thwarts
THWARTLY	adv athwart
THY	pron a possessive form of the pronoun thou
THYME	n pl. -S an aromatic herb
THYMEY	adj THYMIER, THYMIEST thymy
THYMI	a pl. of thymus
THYMIC	adj pertaining to thyme
THYMIER	comparative of thymey and thymy
THYMIEST	superlative of thymey and thymy
THYMINE	n pl. -S a chemical compound
THYMOL	n pl. -S a chemical compound
THYMUS	n pl. -MI or -MUSES a glandular structure in the body
THYMY	adj THYMIER, THYMIEST abounding in thyme
THYREOID	adj pertaining to the thyroid
THYROID	n pl. -S an endocrine gland
THYROXIN	n pl. -S an amino acid
THYRSE	n pl. -S thyrsus
THYRSUS	n pl. -SI a type of flower cluster THYRSOID adj
THYSELF	pron yourself
TI	n pl. -S the seventh tone of the diatonic musical scale
TIARA	n pl. -S a jeweled headpiece worn by women TIARAED adj
TIBIA	n pl. -IAE or -IAS a bone of the leg TIBIAL adj
TIC	n pl. -S an involuntary muscular contraction
TICAL	n pl. -S a former Thai unit of weight
TICK	v -ED, -ING, -S to make a recurrent clicking sound
TICKER	n pl. -S one that ticks
TICKET	v -ED, -ING, -S to attach a tag to
TICKING	n pl. -S a strong cotton fabric
TICKLE	v -LED, -LING, -LES to touch lightly so as to produce a tingling sensation
TICKLER	n pl. -S one that tickles
TICKLISH	adj sensitive to tickling
TICKSEED	n pl. -S a flowering plant
TICKTACK	v -ED, -ING, -S to ticktock

TICKTOCK	v -ED, -ING, -S to make the ticking sound of a clock
TICTAC	v -TACKED, -TACKING, -TACS to ticktack
TICTOC	v -TOCKED, -TOCKING, -TOCS to ticktock
TIDAL	adj pertaining to the tides TIDALLY adv
TIDBIT	n pl. -S a choice bit of food
TIDDLY	adj slightly drunk
TIDE	v TIDED, TIDING, TIDES to flow like the tide (the rise and fall of the ocean's waters)
TIDELAND	n pl. -S land alternately covered and uncovered by the tide
TIDELESS	adj lacking a tide
TIDELIKE	adj resembling a tide
TIDEMARK	n pl. -S a mark showing the highest or lowest point of a tide
TIDERIP	n pl. -S a riptide
TIDEWAY	n pl. -WAYS a tidal channel
TIDIED	past tense of tidy
TIDIER	comparative of tidy
TIDIES	present 3d person sing. of tidy
TIDIEST	superlative of tidy
TIDILY	adv in a tidy manner
TIDINESS	n pl. -ES the state of being tidy
TIDING	n pl. -S a piece of news
TIDY	adj -DIER, -DIEST neat and orderly
TIDY	v -DIED, -DYING, -DIES to make tidy
TIDYTIPS	n pl. TIDYTIPS an annual herb
TIE	v TIED, TYING or TIEING, TIES to fasten with a cord or rope
TIEBACK	n pl. -S a loop for holding a curtain back to one side
TIECLASP	n pl. -S a clasp for securing a necktie
TIED	past tense of tie
TIEPIN	n pl. -S a pin for securing a necktie
TIER	v -ED, -ING, -S to arrange in tiers (rows placed one above another)
TIERCE	n pl. -S one of seven canonical daily periods for prayer and devotion
TIERCED	adj divided into three equal parts
TIERCEL	n pl. -S tercel
TIFF	v -ED, -ING, -S to have a petty quarrel

TIFFANY	*n* pl. -NIES a thin, mesh fabric	**TIMBREL**	*n* pl. -S a percussion instrument
TIFFIN	*v* -ED, -ING, -S to lunch	**TIME**	*v* TIMED, TIMING, TIMES to determine the speed or duration of
TIGER	*n* pl. -S a large feline mammal		
TIGEREYE	*n* pl. -S a gemstone		
TIGERISH	*adj* resembling a tiger	**TIMECARD**	*n* pl. -S a card for recording an employee's times of arrival and departure
TIGHT	*adj* TIGHTER, TIGHTEST firmly or closely fixed in place **TIGHTLY** *adv*		
		TIMELESS	*adj* having no beginning or end
TIGHTEN	*v* -ED, -ING, -S to make tight	**TIMELY**	*adj* -LIER, -LIEST occurring at the right moment
TIGHTS	*n/pl* a close-fitting garment		
TIGHTWAD	*n* pl. -S a miser	**TIMEOUS**	*adj* timely
TIGLON	*n* pl. -S the offspring of a male tiger and a female lion	**TIMEOUT**	*n* pl. -S a brief suspension of activity
TIGON	*n* pl. -S tiglon	**TIMER**	*n* pl. -S one that times
TIGRESS	*n* pl. -ES a female tiger	**TIMEWORK**	*n* pl. -S work paid for by the hour or by the day
TIGRISH	*adj* tigerish		
TIKE	*n* pl. -S tyke	**TIMEWORN**	*adj* showing the effects of long use or wear
TIKI	*n* pl. -S a wood or stone image of a Polynesian god		
		TIMID	*adj* -IDER, -IDEST lacking courage or self-confidence **TIMIDLY** *adv*
TIL	*n* pl. -S the sesame plant		
TILAPIA	*n* pl. -S an African fish		
TILBURY	*n* pl. -BURIES a carriage having two wheels	**TIMIDITY**	*n* pl. -TIES the quality of being timid
TILDE	*n* pl. -S a mark placed over a letter to indicate its sound	**TIMING**	*n* pl. -S the selection of the proper moment for doing something
TILE	*v* TILED, TILING, TILES to cover with tiles (thin slabs of baked clay)		
		TIMOROUS	*adj* fearful
		TIMOTHY	*n* pl. -THIES a European grass
TILEFISH	*n* pl. -ES a marine food fish	**TIMPANO**	*n* pl. -NI a kettledrum
TILELIKE	*adj* resembling a tile	**TIMPANUM**	*n* pl. -NA or -NUMS tympanum
TILER	*n* pl. -S one that tiles	**TIN**	*v* TINNED, TINNING, TINS to coat with tin (a metallic element)
TILING	*n* pl. -S a surface of tiles		
TILL	*v* -ED, -ING, -S to prepare land for crops by plowing **TILLABLE** *adj*		
		TINAMOU	*n* pl. -S a South American game bird
TILLAGE	*n* pl. -S cultivated land		
TILLER	*v* -ED, -ING, -S to put forth stems from a root	**TINCAL**	*n* pl. -S crude borax
		TINCT	*v* -ED, -ING, -S to tinge
TILT	*v* -ED, -ING, -S to cause to slant **TILTABLE** *adj*	**TINCTURE**	*v* -TURED, -TURING, -TURES to tinge
TILTER	*n* pl. -S one that tilts	**TINDER**	*n* pl. -S readily combustible material **TINDERY** *adj*
TILTH	*n* pl. -S tillage		
TILTYARD	*n* pl. -S an area for jousting contests	**TINE**	*v* TINED, TINING, TINES to lose
		TINEA	*n* pl. -S a fungous skin disease **TINEAL** *adj*
TIMARAU	*n* pl. -S tamarau		
TIMBAL	*n* pl. -S a large drum	**TINEID**	*n* pl. -S one of a family of moths
TIMBALE	*n* pl. -S a pastry shell shaped like a drum		
		TINFOIL	*n* pl. -S a thin metal sheeting
TIMBER	*v* -ED, -ING, -S to furnish with timber (wood used as a building material)	**TINFUL**	*n* pl. -S as much as a tin container can hold
		TING	*v* -ED, -ING, -S to emit a high-pitched metallic sound
TIMBRE	*n* pl. -S the quality given to a sound by its overtones	**TINGE**	*v* TINGED, TINGEING or TINGING, TINGES to apply a trace of color to

TINGLE   v -GLED, -GLING, -GLES to cause a prickly, stinging sensation

TINGLER   n pl. -S one that tingles

TINGLY   adj -GLIER, -GLIEST tingling

TINHORN   n pl. -S a showily pretentious person

TINIER   comparative of tiny

TINIEST   superlative of tiny

TINILY   adv in a tiny manner

TININESS   n pl. -ES the quality of being tiny

TINING   present participle of tine

TINKER   v -ED, -ING, -S to repair in an unskilled or experimental manner

TINKERER   n pl. -S one that tinkers

TINKLE   v -KLED, -KLING, -KLES to make slight, sharp, metallic sounds

TINKLING   n pl. -S the sound made by something that tinkles

TINKLY   adj -KLIER, -KLIEST producing a tinkling sound

TINLIKE   adj resembling tin

TINMAN   n pl. -MEN a tinsmith

TINNED   past tense of tin

TINNER   n pl. -S a tin miner

TINNIER   comparative of tinny

TINNIEST   superlative of tinny

TINNILY   adv in a tinny manner

TINNING   present participle of tin

TINNITUS   n pl. -ES a ringing sound in the ears

TINNY   adj -NIER, -NIEST of or resembling tin

TINPLATE   n pl. -S thin sheet iron coated with tin

TINSEL   v -SELED, -SELING, -SELS or -SELLED, -SELLING, -SELS to give a showy or gaudy appearance to

TINSELLY   adj cheaply gaudy

TINSMITH   n pl. -S one who works with tin

TINSTONE   n pl. -S a tin ore

TINT   v -ED, -ING, -S to color slightly or delicately

TINTER   n pl. -S one that tints

TINTING   n pl. -S the process of one that tints

TINTLESS   adj lacking color

TINTYPE   n pl. -S a kind of photograph

TINWARE   n pl. -S articles made of tinplate

TINWORK   n pl. -S something made of tin

TINY   adj TINIER, TINIEST very small

TIP   v TIPPED, TIPPING, TIPS to tilt

TIPCART   n pl. -S a type of cart

TIPCAT   n pl. -S a game resembling baseball

TIPI   n pl. -S tepee

TIPLESS   adj having no point or extremity

TIPOFF   n pl. -S a hint or warning

TIPPABLE   adj capable of being tipped

TIPPED   past tense of tip

TIPPER   n pl. -S one that tips

TIPPET   n pl. -S a covering for the shoulders

TIPPIER   comparative of tippy

TIPPIEST   superlative of tippy

TIPPING   present participle of tip

TIPPLE   v -PLED, -PLING, -PLES to drink alcoholic beverages

TIPPLER   n pl. -S one that tipples

TIPPY   adj -PIER, -PIEST unsteady

TIPSIER   comparative of tipsy

TIPSIEST   superlative of tipsy

TIPSILY   adv in a tipsy manner

TIPSTAFF   n pl. -STAFFS or -STAVES an attendant in a court of law

TIPSTER   n pl. -S one that sells information to gamblers

TIPSTOCK   n pl. -S a part of a gun

TIPSY   adj -SIER, -SIEST slightly drunk

TIPTOE   v -TOED, -TOEING, -TOES to walk on the tips of one's toes

TIPTOP   n pl. -S the highest point

TIRADE   n pl. -S a long, vehement speech

TIRE   v TIRED, TIRING, TIRES to grow tired

TIRED   adj TIREDER, TIREDEST sapped of strength **TIREDLY** adv

TIRELESS   adj seemingly incapable of tiring

TIRESOME   adj tedious

TIRING   present participle of tire

TIRL   v -ED, -ING, -S to make a vibrating sound

TIRO   n pl. -ROS tyro

TIRRIVEE   n pl. -S a tantrum

TISANE   n pl. -S a ptisan

TISSUAL   adj pertaining to tissue

TISSUE   v -SUED, -SUING, -SUES to weave into tissue (a fine sheer fabric)

TISSUEY *adj* resembling tissue

TIT *n pl.* -S a small bird

TITAN *n pl.* -S a person of great size

TITANATE *n pl.* -S a chemical salt

TITANESS *n pl.* -ES a female titan

TITANIA *n pl.* -S a mineral

TITANIC *adj* of great size

TITANISM *n pl.* -S revolt against social conventions

TITANITE *n pl.* -S a mineral

TITANIUM *n pl.* -S a metallic element

TITANOUS *adj* pertaining to titanium

TITBIT *n pl.* -S tidbit

TITER *n pl.* -S the strength of a chemical solution

TITHABLE *adj* subject to the payment of tithes

TITHE *v* TITHED, TITHING, TITHES to pay a tithe (a small tax)

TITHER *n pl.* -S one that tithes

TITHING *n pl.* -S the act of levying tithes

TITHONIA *n pl.* -S a tall herb

TITI *n pl.* -S an evergreen shrub or tree

TITIAN *n pl.* -S a reddish brown color

TITIVATE *v* -VATED, -VATING, -VATES to dress smartly

TITLARK *n pl.* -S a songbird

TITLE *v* -TLED, -TLING, -TLES to furnish with a title (a distinctive appellation)

TITLIST *n pl.* -S a sports champion

TITMAN *n pl.* -MEN the smallest of a litter of pigs

TITMOUSE *n pl.* -MICE a small bird

TITRABLE *adj* capable of being titrated

TITRANT *n pl.* -S the reagent used in titration

TITRATE *v* -TRATED, -TRATING, -TRATES to determine the strength of a solution by adding a reagent until a desired reaction occurs

TITRATOR *n pl.* -S one that titrates

TITRE *n pl.* -S titer

TITTER *v* -ED, -ING, -S to utter a restrained, nervous laugh

TITTERER *n pl.* -S one that titters

TITTIE *n pl.* -S a sister

TITTIES pl. of titty

TITTLE *n pl.* -S a very small mark in writing or printing

TITTUP *v* -TUPED, -TUPING, -TUPS or -TUPPED, -TUPPING, -TUPS to move in a lively manner

TITTUPPY *adj* shaky; unsteady

TITTY *n pl.* -TIES a teat

TITULAR *n pl.* -S one who holds a title

TITULARY *n pl.* -LARIES a titular

TIVY *adv* with great speed

TIZZY *n pl.* -ZIES a state of nervous confusion

TMESIS *n pl.* TMESES the separation of the parts of a compound word by an intervening word or words

TO *prep* in the direction of

TOAD *n pl.* -S a tailless, jumping amphibian

TOADFISH *n pl.* -ES a marine fish

TOADFLAX *n pl.* -ES a perennial herb

TOADIED past tense of toady

TOADIES present 3d person sing. of toady

TOADISH *adj* resembling a toad

TOADLESS *adj* having no toads

TOADLIKE *adj* resembling a toad

TOADY *v* TOADIED, TOADYING, TOADIES to engage in servile flattering

TOADYISH *adj* characteristic of one that toadies

TOADYISM *n pl.* -S toadyish behavior

TOAST *v* -ED, -ING, -S to brown by exposure to heat

TOASTER *n pl.* -S a device for toasting

TOASTY *adj* TOASTIER, TOASTIEST comfortably warm

TOBACCO *n pl.* -COS or -COES an annual herb cultivated for its leaves

TOBOGGAN *v* -ED, -ING, -S to ride on a long, narrow sled

TOBY *n pl.* -BIES a type of drinking mug

TOCCATA *n pl.* -TAS or -TE a musical composition usually for an organ

TOCHER *v* -ED, -ING, -S to give a dowry to

TOCOLOGY *n pl.* -GIES the branch of medicine dealing with childbirth

TOCSIN *n pl.* -S an alarm sounded on a bell

TOD *n pl.* -S a British unit of weight

TODAY *n pl.* -DAYS the present day

TODDIES pl. of toddy

TODDLE v -DLED, -DLING, -DLES to walk unsteadily

TODDLER n pl. -S one that toddles

TODDY n pl. -DIES an alcoholic beverage

TODY n pl. -DIES a West Indian bird

TOE v TOED, TOEING, TOES to touch with the toe (one of the terminal members of the foot)

TOECAP n pl. -S a covering for the tip of a shoe or boot

TOEHOLD n pl. -S a space that supports the toes in climbing

TOELESS adj having no toes

TOELIKE adj resembling a toe

TOENAIL v -ED, -ING, -S to fasten with obliquely driven nails

TOEPIECE n pl. -S a piece of a shoe designed to cover the toes

TOEPLATE n pl. -S a metal tab attached to the tip of a shoe

TOESHOE n pl. -S a dance slipper without a heel

TOFF n pl. -S a dandy

TOFFEE n pl. -S a chewy candy

TOFFY n pl. -FIES a chewy candy

TOFFY n pl. -FIES toffee

TOFT n pl. -S a hillock

TOFU n pl. -S a soft Oriental cheese made from soybean milk

TOG v TOGGED, TOGGING, TOGS to clothe

TOGA n pl. -GAS or -GAE an outer garment worn in ancient Rome TOGAED adj

TOGATE adj pertaining to ancient Rome

TOGATED adj wearing a toga

TOGETHER adv into a union or relationship

TOGGED past tense of tog

TOGGERY n pl. -GERIES clothing

TOGGING present participle of tog

TOGGLE v -GLED, -GLING, -GLES to fasten with a type of pin or short rod

TOGGLER n pl. -S one that toggles

TOGUE n pl. -S a freshwater fish

TOIL v -ED, -ING, -S to work strenuously

TOILE n pl. -S a sheer linen fabric

TOILER n pl. -S one that toils

TOILET v -ED, -ING, -S to dress and groom oneself

TOILETRY n pl. -TRIES an article used in dressing and grooming oneself

TOILETTE n pl. -S the act of dressing and grooming oneself

TOILFUL adj toilsome

TOILSOME adj demanding much exertion

TOILWORN adj worn by toil

TOIT v -ED, -ING, -S to saunter

TOKAY n pl. -KAYS a Malaysian gecko

TOKE n pl. -S a puff on a marijuana cigarette

TOKEN v -ED, -ING, -S to serve as a sign of

TOKENISM n pl. -S the policy of making only a superficial effort

TOKOLOGY n pl. -GIES tocology

TOKONOMA n pl. -S a small alcove in a Japanese house

TOLA n pl. -S a unit of weight used in India

TOLAN n pl. -S a chemical compound

TOLANE n pl. -S tolan

TOLBOOTH n pl. -S a prison

TOLD past tense of tell

TOLE v TOLED, TOLING, TOLES to allure

TOLEDO n pl. -DOS a finely tempered sword

TOLERANT adj inclined to tolerate

TOLERATE v -ATED, -ATING, -ATES to allow without active opposition

TOLIDIN n pl. -S tolidine

TOLIDINE n pl. -S a chemical compound

TOLING present participle of tole

TOLL v -ED, -ING, -S to collect or impose a toll (a fixed charge for a service or privilege)

TOLLAGE n pl. -S a toll

TOLLBAR n pl. -S a tollgate

TOLLER n pl. -S a collector of tolls

TOLLGATE n pl. -S a gate where a toll is collected

TOLLMAN n pl. -MEN a toller

TOLLWAY n pl. -WAYS a road on which tolls are collected

TOLU n pl. -S a fragrant resin

TOLUATE n pl. -S a chemical salt

TOLUENE n pl. -S a flammable liquid

TOLUIC adj pertaining to any of four isomeric acids derived from toluene

TOLUID n pl. -S toluide

TOLUIDE n pl. -S an amide

TOLUIDIN n pl. -S an amine

TOLUOL n pl. -S toluene

TOLUOLE n pl. -S toluol

TOLUYL n pl. -S a univalent chemical radical

TOLYL n pl. -S a univalent chemical radical

TOM n pl. -S the male of various animals

TOMAHAWK v -ED, -ING, -S to strike with a light ax

TOMALLEY n pl. -LEYS the liver of a lobster

TOMAN n pl. -S a coin of Iran

TOMATO n pl. -TOES the fleshy, edible fruit of a perennial plant

TOMB v -ED, -ING, -S to place in a tomb (a burial vault or chamber)

TOMBAC n pl. -S an alloy of copper and zinc

TOMBACK n pl. -S tombac

TOMBAK n pl. -S tombac

TOMBAL adj pertaining to a tomb

TOMBLESS adj having no tomb

TOMBLIKE adj resembling a tomb

TOMBOLO n pl. -LOS a sandbar connecting an island to the mainland

TOMBOY n pl. -BOYS a girl who prefers boyish activities

TOMCAT n pl. -S a male cat

TOMCOD n pl. -S a marine fish

TOME n pl. -S a large book

TOMENTUM n pl. -TA a network of small blood vessels

TOMFOOL n pl. -S a foolish person

TOMMY n pl. -MIES a loaf of bread

TOMMYROT n pl. -S nonsense

TOMOGRAM n pl. -S a photograph made with X rays

TOMORROW n pl. -S the day following today

TOMPION n pl. -S tampion

TOMTIT n pl. -S a small bird

TON n pl. -S a unit of weight

TONAL adj pertaining to tone **TONALLY** adv

TONALITY n pl. -TIES a system of tones

TONDO n pl. -DI a circular painting

TONE v TONED, TONING, TONES to give a particular tone (a sound of definite pitch and vibration) to

TONELESS adj lacking in tone

TONEME n pl. -S a tonal unit of speech **TONEMIC** adj

TONER n pl. -S one that tones

TONETICS n/pl the phonetic study of tone in language **TONETIC** adj

TONETTE n pl. -S a simple flute

TONG v -ED, -ING, -S to lift with a type of grasping device

TONGA n pl. -S a light cart used in India

TONGER n pl. -S one that tongs

TONGMAN n pl. -MEN a member of a Chinese secret society

TONGUE v TONGUED, TONGUING, TONGUES to touch with the tongue (an organ of the mouth)

TONGUING n pl. -S the use of the tongue in articulating notes on a wind instrument

TONIC n pl. -S something that invigorates or refreshes

TONICITY n pl. -TIES normal, healthy bodily condition

TONIER comparative of tony

TONIEST superlative of tony

TONIGHT n pl. -S the present night

TONING present participle of tone

TONISH adj stylish **TONISHLY** adv

TONLET n pl. -S a skirt of plate armor

TONNAGE n pl. -S total weight in tons

TONNE n pl. -S a unit of weight

TONNEAU n pl. -NEAUS or -NEAUX the rear seating compartment of an automobile

TONNER n pl. -S an object having a specified tonnage

TONNISH adj tonish

TONSIL n pl. -S a lymphoid organ **TONSILAR** adj

TONSURE v -SURED, -SURING, -SURES to shave the head of

TONTINE n pl. -S a form of collective life insurance

TONUS n pl. -ES a normal state of tension in muscle tissue

TONY adj TONIER, TONIEST stylish

TOO adv in addition

TOOK past tense of take

TOOL v -ED, -ING, -S to form or finish with a tool (an implement used in manual work)

TOOLBOX n pl. -ES a box for tools

TOOLER n pl. -S one that tools

TOOLHEAD n pl. -S a part of a machine

TOOLING n pl. -S ornamentation done with tools

TOOLLESS *adj* having no tools

TOOLROOM *n pl.* -S a room where tools are stored

TOOLSHED *n pl.* -S a building where tools are stored

TOOM *adj* empty

TOON *n pl.* -S an East Indian tree

TOOT *v* -ED, -ING, -S to sound a horn or whistle in short blasts

TOOTER *n pl.* -S one that toots

TOOTH *n pl.* TEETH one of the hard structures attached in a row to each jaw

TOOTH *v* -ED, -ING, -S to furnish with toothlike projections

TOOTHY *adj* TOOTHIER, TOOTHIEST having or showing prominent teeth **TOOTHILY** *adv*

TOOTLE *v* -TLED, -TLING, -TLES to toot softly or repeatedly

TOOTLER *n pl.* -S one that tootles

TOOTS *n pl.* -ES a woman or girl — usually used as a form of address

TOOTSIE *n pl.* -S tootsy

TOOTSY *n pl.* -SIES a foot

TOP *v* TOPPED, TOPPING, TOPS to cut off the top (the highest part, point, or surface) of

TOPAZ *n pl.* -ES a mineral **TOPAZINE** *adj*

TOPCOAT *n pl.* -S a lightweight overcoat

TOPCROSS *n pl.* -ES a cross between a purebred male and inferior female stock

TOPE *v* TOPED, TOPING, TOPES to drink liquor to excess

TOPEE *n pl.* -S topi

TOPER *n pl.* -S one that topes

TOPFUL *adj* topfull

TOPFULL *adj* full to the top

TOPH *n pl.* -S tufa

TOPHE *n pl.* -S tufa

TOPHUS *n pl.* -PHI a deposit of urates in the tissue around a joint

TOPI *n pl.* -S a sun helmet

TOPIARY *n pl.* -ARIES the art of trimming shrubs into shapes

TOPIC *n pl.* -S a subject of discourse **TOPICAL** *adj*

TOPING present participle of tope

TOPKICK *n pl.* -S a first sergeant

TOPKNOT *n pl.* -S an ornament for the hair

TOPLESS *adj* having no top

TOPLOFTY *adj* -LOFTIER, -LOFTIEST haughty

TOPMAST *n pl.* -S a mast of a ship

TOPMOST *adj* highest

TOPNOTCH *adj* excellent

TOPOI pl. of topos

TOPOLOGY *n pl.* -GIES a branch of mathematics

TOPONYM *n pl.* -S the name of a place

TOPONYMY *n pl.* -MIES the study of toponyms

TOPOS *n pl.* -POI a stock rhetorical theme

TOPOTYPE *n pl.* -S a specimen selected from a locality typical of a species

TOPPED past tense of top

TOPPER *n pl.* -S one that tops

TOPPING *n pl.* -S something that forms a top

TOPPLE *v* -PLED, -PLING, -PLES to fall forward

TOPSAIL *n pl.* -S a sail of a ship

TOPSIDE *n pl.* -S the upper portion of a ship

TOPSOIL *v* -ED, -ING, -S to remove the surface layer of soil from

TOPSTONE *n pl.* -S the stone at the top of a structure

TOPWORK *v* -ED, -ING, -S to graft scions of another variety of plant on the main branches of

TOQUE *n pl.* -S a close-fitting woman's hat

TOQUET *n pl.* -S toque

TOR *n pl.* -S a high, craggy hill

TORA *n pl.* -S torah

TORAH *n pl.* -S the body of Jewish law

TORC *n pl.* -S a metal collar or necklace

TORCH *v* -ED, -ING, -ES to set on fire

TORCHERE *n pl.* -S a type of electric lamp

TORCHIER *n pl.* -S torchere

TORCHON *n pl.* -S a coarse lace

TORE *n pl.* -S a torus

TOREADOR *n pl.* -S a bullfighter

TORERO *n pl.* -ROS a bullfighter

TOREUTIC *adj* pertaining to a type of metalwork

TORI pl. of torus

TORIC *adj* pertaining to a torus

TORIES	pl. of tory	**TORTILLA**	n pl. -S a round, flat cake of unleavened cornmeal
TORII	n pl. TORII the gateway of a Japanese temple	**TORTIOUS**	adj of the nature of a tort
TORMENT	v -ED, -ING, -S to inflict with great bodily or mental suffering	**TORTOISE**	n pl. -S any of an order of reptiles having the body enclosed in a bony shell
TORN	past participle of tear		
TORNADO	n pl. -DOES or -DOS a violent windstorm **TORNADIC** adj	**TORTONI**	n pl. -S a type of ice cream
		TORTRIX	n pl. -ES a small moth
TORNILLO	n pl. -LOS a flowering shrub	**TORTUOUS**	adj marked by repeated turns or bends
TORO	n pl. -ROS a bull		
TOROID	n pl. -S a type of geometric surface **TOROIDAL** adj	**TORTURE**	v -TURED, -TURING, -TURES to subject to severe physical pain
TOROSE	adj cylindrical and swollen at intervals	**TORTURER**	n pl. -S one that tortures
		TORULA	n pl. -LAE or -LAS a type of fungus
TOROSITY	n pl. -TIES the quality or state of being torose		
		TORUS	n pl. -RI a large convex molding
TOROUS	adj torose	**TORY**	n pl. -RIES a political conservative
TORPEDO	v -ED, -ING, -ES or -S to damage or sink with an underwater missile		
		TOSH	n pl. -ES nonsense
TORPID	n pl. -S a racing boat	**TOSS**	v TOSSED or TOST, TOSSING, TOSSES to throw lightly
TORPIDLY	adv in a sluggish manner		
TORPOR	n pl. -S mental or physical inactivity	**TOSSER**	n pl. -S one that tosses
		TOSSPOT	n pl. -S a drunkard
TORQUATE	adj having a torques	**TOSSUP**	n pl. -S an even choice or chance
TORQUE	v TORQUED, TORQUING, TORQUES to cause to twist		
		TOST	a past tense of toss
TORQUER	n pl. -S one that torques	**TOT**	v TOTTED, TOTTING, TOTS to total
TORQUES	n pl. -QUESES a band of feathers, hair, or coloration around the neck		
		TOTABLE	adj capable of being toted
TORQUING	present participle of torque	**TOTAL**	v -TALED, -TALING, -TALS or -TALLED, -TALLING, -TALS to ascertain the entire amount of
TORR	n pl. TORR a unit of pressure		
TORREFY	v -FIED, -FYING, -FIES to subject to intense heat	**TOTALISE**	v -ISED, -ISING, -ISES to totalize
TORRENT	n pl. -S a rapid stream of water	**TOTALISM**	n pl. -S centralized control by an autocratic authority
TORRID	adj -RIDER, -RIDEST extremely hot **TORRIDLY** adv		
		TOTALITY	n pl. -TIES the quality or state of being complete
TORRIFY	v -FIED, -FYING, -FIES to torrefy	**TOTALIZE**	v -IZED, -IZING, -IZES to make complete
TORSADE	n pl. -S a twisted cord		
TORSE	n pl. -S a wreath of twisted silks	**TOTALLED**	a past tense of total
		TOTALLING	a present participle of total
TORSI	a pl. of torso	**TOTALLY**	adv completely
TORSION	n pl. -S the act of twisting	**TOTE**	v TOTED, TOTING, TOTES to carry by hand
TORSK	n pl. -S a marine food fish		
TORSO	n pl. -SI or -SOS the trunk of the human body	**TOTEM**	n pl. -S a natural object serving as the emblem of a family or clan **TOTEMIC** adj
TORT	n pl. -S a civil wrong		
TORTE	n pl. TORTEN or TORTES a rich cake	**TOTEMISM**	n pl. -S a system of tribal division according to totems
		TOTEMIST	n pl. -S a specialist in totemism
TORTILE	adj twisted; coiled	**TOTEMITE**	n pl. -S a totemist
		TOTER	n pl. -S one that totes

TOTHER *pron* the other

TOTING present participle of tote

TOTTED past tense of tot

TOTTER *v* -ED, -ING, -S to walk unsteadily

TOTTERER *n pl.* -S one that totters

TOTTERY *adj* shaky

TOTTING present participle of tot

TOUCAN *n pl.* -S a tropical bird

TOUCH *v* -ED, -ING, -ES to be in or come into contact with

TOUCHE *interj* — used to acknowledge a hit in fencing

TOUCHER *n pl.* -S one that touches

TOUCHUP *n pl.* -S an act of finishing by adding minor improvements

TOUCHY *adj* TOUCHIER, TOUCHIEST overly sensitive **TOUCHILY** *adv*

TOUGH *adj* TOUGHER, TOUGHEST strong and resilient

TOUGH *n pl.* -S a rowdy

TOUGHEN *v* -ED, -ING, -S to make tough

TOUGHIE *n pl.* -S a tough

TOUGHIES pl. of toughy

TOUGHISH *adj* somewhat tough

TOUGHLY *adv* in a tough manner

TOUGHY *n pl.* TOUGHIES toughie

TOUPEE *n pl.* -S a wig worn to cover a bald spot

TOUR *v* -ED, -ING, -S to travel from place to place

TOURACO *n pl.* -COS an African bird

TOURER *n pl.* -S a large, open automobile

TOURING *n pl.* -S cross-country skiing for pleasure

TOURISM *n pl.* -S the practice of touring for pleasure

TOURIST *n pl.* -S one who tours for pleasure **TOURISTY** *adj*

TOURNEY *v* -ED, -ING, -S to compete in a tournament

TOUSE *v* TOUSED, TOUSING, TOUSES to tousle

TOUSLE *v* -SLED, -SLING, -SLES to dishevel

TOUT *v* -ED, -ING, -S to solicit brazenly

TOUTER *n pl.* -S one that touts

TOUZLE *v* -ZLED, -ZLING, -ZLES to tousle

TOVARICH *n pl.* -ES comrade

TOVARISH *n pl.* -ES tovarich

TOW *v* -ED, -ING, -S to pull by means of a rope or chain

TOWAGE *n pl.* -S the price paid for towing

TOWARD *prep* in the direction of

TOWARDLY *adj* favorable

TOWARDS *prep* toward

TOWAWAY *n pl.* -AWAYS the act of towing away a vehicle

TOWBOAT *n pl.* -S a tugboat

TOWEL *v* -ELED, -ELING, -ELS or -ELLED, -ELLING, -ELS to wipe with a towel (an absorbent cloth)

TOWELING *n pl.* -S material used for towels

TOWER *v* -ED, -ING, -S to rise to a great height

TOWERY *adj* -ERIER, -ERIEST very tall

TOWHEAD *n pl.* -S a head of light blond hair

TOWHEE *n pl.* -S a common finch

TOWIE *n pl.* -S a form of contract bridge for three players

TOWLINE *n pl.* -S a line used in towing

TOWMOND *n pl.* -S a year

TOWMONT *n pl.* -S towmond

TOWN *n pl.* -S a center of population smaller than a city

TOWNEE *n pl.* -S a townsman

TOWNFOLK *n/pl* the inhabitants of a town

TOWNIE *n pl.* -S a nonstudent who lives in a college town

TOWNIES pl. of towny

TOWNISH *adj* characteristic of a town

TOWNLESS *adj* having no towns

TOWNLET *n pl.* -S a small town

TOWNSHIP *n pl.* -S an administrative division of a county

TOWNSMAN *n pl.* -MEN a resident of a town

TOWNWEAR *n pl.* -S apparel that is suitable for wear in the city

TOWNY *n pl.* TOWNIES townie

TOWPATH *n pl.* -S a path along a river that is used by animals towing boats

TOWROPE *n pl.* -S a rope used in towing

TOWY *adj* resembling coarse hemp or flax fiber

TOXAEMIA *n pl.* -S toxemia **TOXAEMIC** *adj*

TOXEMIA *n pl.* -S the condition of having toxins in the blood **TOXEMIC** *adj*

TOXIC	*adj* pertaining to a toxin	**TRACTOR**	*n* pl. -S a motor vehicle used in farming
TOXICAL	*adj* toxic		
TOXICANT	*n* pl. -S a poisonous substance	**TRAD**	*adj* traditional
TOXICITY	*n* pl. -TIES the quality of being poisonous	**TRADE**	*v* TRADED, TRADING, TRADES to give in exchange for another commodity **TRADABLE** *adj*
TOXIN	*n* pl. -S a poisonous substance		
TOXINE	*n* pl. -S toxin	**TRADER**	*n* pl. -S one that trades
TOXOID	*n* pl. -S a type of toxin	**TRADITOR**	*n* pl. -ES a traitor among the early Christians
TOY	*v* -ED, -ING, -S to amuse oneself as if with a toy (a child's plaything)	**TRADUCE**	*v* -DUCED, -DUCING, -DUCES to defame
TOYER	*n* pl. -S one that toys	**TRADUCER**	*n* pl. -S one that traduces
TOYISH	*adj* frivolous	**TRAFFIC**	*v* -FICKED, -FICKING, -FICS to engage in buying and selling
TOYLESS	*adj* having no toy		
TOYLIKE	*adj* resembling a toy	**TRAGEDY**	*n* pl. -DIES a disastrous event
TOYO	*n* pl. -YOS a smooth straw used in making hats	**TRAGI**	pl. of tragus
		TRAGIC	*adj* of the nature of a tragedy
TOYON	*n* pl. -S an ornamental evergreen shrub	**TRAGICAL**	*adj* tragic
		TRAGOPAN	*n* pl. -S an Asian pheasant
TRABEATE	*adj* constructed with horizontal beams	**TRAGUS**	*n* pl. -GI a part of the external opening of the ear
TRACE	*v* TRACED, TRACING, TRACES to follow the course of	**TRAIK**	*v* -ED, -ING, -S to trudge
		TRAIL	*v* -ED, -ING, -S to drag along a surface
TRACER	*n* pl. -S one that traces		
TRACERY	*n* pl. -ERIES ornamental work of interlaced lines	**TRAILER**	*v* -ED, -ING, -S to transport by means of a trailer (a vehicle drawn by another)
TRACHEA	*n* pl. -CHEAE or -CHEAS the passage for conveying air to the lungs **TRACHEAL** *adj*	**TRAIN**	*v* -ED, -ING, -S to instruct systematically
TRACHEID	*n* pl. -S a long, tubular plant cell	**TRAINEE**	*n* pl. -S a person receiving training
TRACHLE	*v* -LED, -LING, -LES to draggle	**TRAINER**	*n* pl. -S one that trains
TRACHOMA	*n* pl. -S a disease of the eye	**TRAINFUL**	*n* pl. -S as much as a railroad train will hold
TRACHYTE	*n* pl. -S a light-colored igneous rock	**TRAINING**	*n* pl. -S systematic instruction
TRACING	*n* pl. -S something that is traced	**TRAINMAN**	*n* pl. -MEN a railroad employee
		TRAINWAY	*n* pl. -WAYS a railway
TRACK	*v* -ED, -ING, -S to follow the marks left by an animal, a person, or a vehicle	**TRAIPSE**	*v* TRAIPSED, TRAIPSING, TRAIPSES to walk about in an idle or aimless manner
TRACKAGE	*n* pl. -S the track system of a railroad	**TRAIT**	*n* pl. -S a distinguishing characteristic
TRACKER	*n* pl. -S one that tracks	**TRAITOR**	*n* pl. -S one who betrays another
TRACKING	*n* pl. -S the placement of students within a curriculum	**TRAJECT**	*v* -ED, -ING, -S to transmit
TRACKMAN	*n* pl. -MEN a railroad worker	**TRAM**	*v* TRAMMED, TRAMMING, TRAMS to convey in a tramcar
TRACT	*n* pl. -S an expanse of land		
TRACTATE	*n* pl. -S a treatise	**TRAMCAR**	*n* pl. -S a streetcar
TRACTILE	*adj* capable of being drawn out in length	**TRAMEL**	*v* -ELED, -ELING, -ELS or -ELLED, -ELLING, -ELS to trammel
TRACTION	*n* pl. -S the act of pulling or drawing over a surface **TRACTIVE** *adj*	**TRAMELL**	*v* -ED, -ING, -S to trammel
		TRAMLESS	*adj* having no tramcar

TRAMLINE *n* pl. -S a streetcar line

TRAMMED past tense of tram

TRAMMEL *v* -MELED, -MELING, -MELS or -MELLED, -MELLING, -MELS to hinder

TRAMMING present participle of tram

TRAMP *v* -ED, -ING, -S to walk with a firm, heavy step

TRAMPER *n* pl. -S one that tramps

TRAMPISH *adj* resembling a vagabond

TRAMPLE *v* -PLED, -PLING, -PLES to tread on heavily

TRAMPLER *n* pl. -S one that tramples

TRAMROAD *n* pl. -S a railway in a mine

TRAMWAY *n* pl. -WAYS a tramline

TRANCE *v* TRANCED, TRANCING, TRANCES to put into a trance (a semiconscious state)

TRANGAM *n* pl. -S a gewgaw

TRANQUIL *adj* -QUILER, -QUILEST or -QUILLER, -QUILLEST free from disturbance

TRANS *adj* characterized by the arrangement of different atoms on opposite sides of the molecule

TRANSACT *v* -ED, -ING, -S to carry out

TRANSECT *v* -ED, -ING, -S to cut across

TRANSEPT *n* pl. -S a major transverse part of the body of a church

TRANSFER *v* -FERRED, -FERRING, -FERS to convey from one source to another

TRANSFIX *v* -FIXED or -FIXT, -FIXING, -FIXES to impale

TRANSHIP *v* -SHIPPED, -SHIPPING, -SHIPS to transfer from one conveyance to another

TRANSIT *v* -ED, -ING, -S to pass across or through

TRANSMIT *v* -MITTED, -MITTING, -MITS to send from one place or person to another

TRANSOM *n* pl. -S a small window above a door or another window

TRANSUDE *v* -SUDED, -SUDING, -SUDES to pass through a membrane

TRAP *v* TRAPPED or TRAPT, TRAPPING, TRAPS to catch in a trap (a device for capturing and holding animals)

TRAPAN *v* -PANNED, -PANNING, -PANS to trepan

TRAPBALL *n* pl. -S a type of ball game

TRAPDOOR *n* pl. -S a lifting or sliding door covering an opening

TRAPES *v* -ED, -ING, -ES to traipse

TRAPEZE *n* pl. -S a gymnastic apparatus

TRAPEZIA *n/pl* four-sided polygons having no parallel sides

TRAPLIKE *adj* resembling a trap

TRAPNEST *v* -ED, -ING, -S to determine the productivity of hens with a type of nest

TRAPPEAN *adj* pertaining to traprock

TRAPPED a past tense of trap

TRAPPER *n* pl. -S one that traps

TRAPPING *n* pl. -S a covering for a horse

TRAPPOSE *adj* trappean

TRAPPOUS *adj* trappean

TRAPROCK *n* pl. -S an igneous rock

TRAPT a past tense of trap

TRAPUNTO *n* pl. -TOS a decorative quilted design

TRASH *v* -ED, -ING, -ES to free from trash (worthless or waste matter)

TRASHMAN *n* pl. -MEN a person who removes trash

TRASHY *adj* TRASHIER, TRASHIEST resembling trash TRASHILY *adv*

TRASS *n* pl. -ES a volcanic rock

TRAUCHLE *v* -LED, -LING, -LES to trachle

TRAUMA *n* pl. -MAS or -MATA a severe emotional shock

TRAVAIL *v* -ED, -ING, -S to toil

TRAVE *n* pl. -S a frame for confining a horse

TRAVEL *v* -ELED, -ELING, -ELS or -ELLED, -ELLING, -ELS to go from one place to another

TRAVELER *n* pl. -S one that travels

TRAVELOG *n* pl. -S a lecture or film on traveling

TRAVERSE *v* -VERSED, -VERSING, -VERSES to pass across or through

TRAVESTY *v* -TIED, -TYING, -TIES to parody

TRAVOIS *n* pl. -ES a type of sled

TRAVOISE *n* pl. -S travois

TRAWL *v* -ED, -ING, -S to fish by dragging a net along the sea bottom

TRAWLER *n* pl. -S a boat used for trawling

TRAWLEY *n* pl. -LEYS a small truck or car for conveying material

TRAY *n pl.* TRAYS a flat, shallow receptacle

TRAYFUL *n pl.* -S as much as a tray will hold

TREACLE *n pl.* -S molasses TREACLY *adj*

TREAD *v* TROD, TRODE, or TREADED, TRODDEN, TREADING, TREADS to walk on, over, or along

TREADER *n pl.* -S one that treads

TREADLE *v* -LED, -LING, -LES to work a foot lever

TREADLER *n pl.* -S one that treadles

TREASON *n pl.* -S violation of allegiance toward one's country

TREASURE *v* -URED, -URING, -URES to value highly

TREASURY *n pl.* -URIES a place where funds are received, kept, and disbursed

TREAT *v* -ED, -ING, -S to behave in a particular way toward

TREATER *n pl.* -S one that treats

TREATISE *n pl.* -S a formal and systematic written account of a subject

TREATY *n pl.* -TIES a formal agreement between two or more nations

TREBLE *v* -BLED, -BLING, -BLES to triple

TREBLY *adv* triply

TRECENTO *n pl.* -TOS the fourteenth century

TREDDLE *v* -DLED, -DLING, -DLES to treadle

TREE *v* TREED, TREEING, TREES to drive up a tree (a tall, woody plant)

TREELESS *adj* having no tree

TREELIKE *adj* resembling a tree

TREENAIL *n pl.* -S a wooden peg used for fastening timbers

TREETOP *n pl.* -S the top of a tree

TREF *adj* unfit for use according to Jewish law

TREFAH *adj* tref

TREFOIL *n pl.* -S a plant having ternate leaves

TREHALA *n pl.* -S a sweet, edible substance forming the pupal case of certain weevils

TREK *v* TREKKED, TREKKING, TREKS to make a slow or arduous journey

TREKKER *n pl.* -S one that treks

TRELLIS *v* -ED, -ING, -ES to provide with a trellis (a frame used as a support for climbing plants)

TREMBLE *v* -BLED, -BLING, -BLES to shake involuntarily

TREMBLER *n pl.* -S one that trembles

TREMBLY *adj* -BLIER, -BLIEST marked by trembling

TREMOLO *n pl.* -LOS a vibrating musical effect

TREMOR *n pl.* -S a shaking movement

TRENAIL *n pl.* -S treenail

TRENCH *v* -ED, -ING, -ES to dig a long, narrow excavation in the ground

TRENCHER *n pl.* -S a wooden platter for serving food

TREND *v* -ED, -ING, -S to take a particular course

TRENDY *adj* TRENDIER, TRENDIEST very fashionable TRENDILY *adv*

TREPAN *v* -PANNED, -PANNING, -PANS to trephine

TREPANG *n pl.* -S a marine animal

TREPHINE *v* -PHINED, -PHINING, -PHINES to operate on with a surgical saw

TREPID *adj* timorous

TRESPASS *v* -ED, -ING, -ES to enter upon the land of another unlawfully

TRESS *n pl.* -ES a long lock of hair TRESSED *adj*

TRESSEL *n pl.* -S trestle

TRESSIER comparative of tressy

TRESSIEST superlative of tressy

TRESSOUR *n pl.* -S tressure

TRESSURE *n pl.* -S a type of heraldic design

TRESSY *adj* TRESSIER, TRESSIEST abounding in tresses

TRESTLE *n pl.* -S a framework for supporting a bridge

TRET *n pl.* -S an allowance formerly paid to purchasers for waste incurred in transit

TREVET *n pl.* -S trivet

TREWS *n/pl* close-fitting tartan trousers

TREY *n pl.* TREYS a three in cards, dice, or dominoes

TRIABLE *adj* subject to judicial examination

TRIACID *n pl.* -S a type of acid

TRIAD *n pl.* -S a group of three

TRIADIC *n pl.* -S a member of a triad

TRIADISM n pl. -S the quality or state of being a triad

TRIAGE n pl. -S a system of treating disaster victims

TRIAL n pl. -S a judicial examination

TRIANGLE n pl. -S a polygon having three sides

TRIARCHY n pl. -CHIES government by three persons

TRIAXIAL adj having three axes

TRIAZIN n pl. -S triazine

TRIAZINE n pl. -S a chemical compound

TRIAZOLE n pl. -S a chemical compound

TRIBADE n pl. -S a lesbian **TRIBADIC** adj

TRIBAL adj pertaining to a tribe **TRIBALLY** adv

TRIBASIC adj having three replaceable hydrogen atoms

TRIBE n pl. -S a group of people sharing a common ancestry, language, and culture

TRIBRACH n pl. -S a type of metrical foot

TRIBUNAL n pl. -S a court of justice

TRIBUNE n pl. -S a defender of the rights of the people

TRIBUTE n pl. -S something given to show respect, gratitude, or admiration

TRICE v TRICED, TRICING, TRICES to haul up with a rope

TRICEPS n pl. -ES an arm muscle

TRICHINA n pl. -NAE or -NAS a parasitic worm

TRICHITE n pl. -S a minute mineral body found in volcanic rocks

TRICHOID adj hairlike

TRICHOME n pl. -S a hairlike outgrowth

TRICING present participle of trice

TRICK v -ED, -ING, -S to deceive

TRICKER n pl. -S one that tricks

TRICKERY n pl. -ERIES deception

TRICKIE adj TRICKIER, TRICKIEST tricky

TRICKIER comparative of tricky

TRICKIEST superlative of tricky

TRICKILY adv in a tricky manner

TRICKISH adj tricky

TRICKLE v -LED, -LING, -LES to flow or fall in drops

TRICKLY adj -LIER, -LIEST marked by trickling

TRICKSY adj -SIER, -SIEST mischievous

TRICKY adj TRICKIER, TRICKIEST characterized by deception

TRICLAD n pl. -S an aquatic flatworm

TRICOLOR n pl. -S a flag having three colors

TRICORN n pl. -S a hat with the brim turned up on three sides

TRICORNE n pl. -S tricorn

TRICOT n pl. -S a knitted fabric

TRICTRAC n pl. -S a form of backgammon

TRICYCLE n pl. -S a vehicle having three wheels

TRIDENT n pl. -S a spear having three prongs

TRIDUUM n pl. -S a period of three days of prayer

TRIED past tense of try

TRIENE n pl. -S a type of chemical compound

TRIENNIA n/pl periods of three years

TRIENS n pl. -ENTES a coin of ancient Rome

TRIER n pl. -S one that tries

TRIES present 3d person sing. of try

TRIETHYL adj containing three ethyl groups

TRIFID adj divided into three parts

TRIFLE v -FLED, -FLING, -FLES to waste time

TRIFLER n pl. -S one that trifles

TRIFLING n pl. -S a waste of time

TRIFOCAL n pl. -S a type of lens

TRIFOLD adj having three parts

TRIFORIA n/pl galleries in a church

TRIFORM adj having three forms

TRIG adj TRIGGER, TRIGGEST neat

TRIG v TRIGGED, TRIGGING, TRIGS to make trig

TRIGGER v -ED, -ING, -S to actuate

TRIGGEST superlative of trig

TRIGGING present participle of trig

TRIGLY adv in a trig manner

TRIGLYPH n pl. -S an architectural ornament

TRIGNESS n pl. -ES the quality or state of being trig

TRIGO n pl. -GOS wheat

TRIGON n pl. -S an ancient stringed instrument

TRIGONAL adj shaped like a triangle

TRIGRAPH n pl. -S a group of three letters representing one sound

TRIHEDRA *n/pl* figures having three plane surfaces meeting at a point

TRIJET *n* pl. -S an airplane powered by three jet engines

TRILBY *n* pl. -BIES a soft felt hat

TRILL *v* -ED, -ING, -S to sing or play with a vibrating effect

TRILLER *n* pl. -S one that trills

TRILLION *n* pl. -S a number

TRILLIUM *n* pl. -S a flowering plant

TRILOBAL *adj* trilobed

TRILOBED *adj* having three lobes

TRILOGY *n* pl. -GIES a group of three related literary works

TRIM *adj* TRIMMER, TRIMMEST neat and orderly

TRIM *v* TRIMMED, TRIMMING, TRIMS to make trim by cutting

TRIMARAN *n* pl. -S a sailing vessel

TRIMER *n* pl. -S a type of chemical compound

TRIMETER *n* pl. -S a verse of three metrical feet

TRIMLY *adv* in a trim manner

TRIMMED past tense of trim

TRIMMER *n* pl. -S one that trims

TRIMMEST superlative of trim

TRIMMING *n* pl. -S something added as a decoration

TRIMNESS *n* pl. -ES the state of being trim

TRIMORPH *n* pl. -S a substance existing in three forms

TRIMOTOR *n* pl. -S an airplane powered by three engines

TRINAL *adj* having three parts

TRINARY *adj* consisting of three parts

TRINDLE *v* -DLED, -DLING, -DLES to trundle

TRINE *v* TRINED, TRINING, TRINES to place in a particular astrological position

TRINITY *n* pl. -TIES a group of three

TRINKET *v* -ED, -ING, -S to deal secretly

TRINKUMS *n/pl* small ornaments

TRINODAL *adj* having three nodes

TRIO *n* pl. TRIOS a group of three

TRIODE *n* pl. -S a type of electron tube

TRIOL *n* pl. -S a type of chemical compound

TRIOLET *n* pl. -S a short poem of fixed form

TRIOSE *n* pl. -S a simple sugar

TRIOXID *n* pl. -S trioxide

TRIOXIDE *n* pl. -S a type of oxide

TRIP *v* TRIPPED, TRIPPING, TRIPS to stumble

TRIPACK *n* pl. -S a type of film pack

TRIPART *adj* divided into three parts

TRIPE *n* pl. -S a part of the stomach of a ruminant that is used as food

TRIPEDAL *adj* having three feet

TRIPHASE *adj* having three phases

TRIPLANE *n* pl. -S a type of airplane

TRIPLE *v* -PLED, -PLING, -PLES to make three times as great

TRIPLET *n* pl. -S a group of three of one kind

TRIPLEX *n* pl. -ES an apartment having three floors

TRIPLING present participle of triple

TRIPLITE *n* pl. -S a mineral

TRIPLOID *n* pl. -S a cell having a chromosome number that is three times the basic number

TRIPLY *adv* in a triple degree, manner, or number

TRIPOD *n* pl. -S a stand having three legs TRIPODAL, TRIPODIC *adj*

TRIPODY *n* pl. -DIES a verse of three metrical feet

TRIPOLI *n* pl. -S a soft, friable rock

TRIPOS *n* pl. -ES a tripod

TRIPPED past tense of trip

TRIPPER *n* pl. -S one that trips

TRIPPET *n* pl. -S a part of a mechanism designed to strike another part

TRIPPING *n* pl. -S the act of one that trips

TRIPTANE *n* pl. -S a chemical compound

TRIPTYCA *n* pl. -S a triptych

TRIPTYCH *n* pl. -S an ancient writing tablet

TRIREME *n* pl. -S an ancient Greek or Roman warship

TRISCELE *n* pl. -S triskele

TRISECT *v* -ED, -ING, -S to divide into three equal parts

TRISEME *n* pl. -S a type of metrical foot TRISEMIC *adj*

TRISKELE *n* pl. -S a figure consisting of three branches radiating from a center

TRISMUS *n* pl. -ES lockjaw TRISMIC *adj*

TRISOME *n* pl. -S an organism having one chromosome in addition to the usual diploid number

TRISOMIC *n* pl. -S a trisome

TRISOMY *n* pl. -MIES the condition of being a trisome

TRISTATE *adj* pertaining to an area made up of three adjoining states

TRISTE *adj* sad

TRISTEZA *n* pl. -S a disease of citrus trees

TRISTFUL *adj* sad

TRISTICH *n* pl. -S a stanza of three lines

TRITE *adj* TRITER, TRITEST used so often as to be made commonplace **TRITELY** *adv*

TRITHING *n* pl. -S an administrative division in England

TRITICUM *n* pl. -S a cereal grass

TRITIUM *n* pl. -S an isotope of hydrogen

TRITOMA *n* pl. -S an African herb

TRITON *n* pl. -S a marine mollusk

TRITONE *n* pl. -S a musical interval of three whole tones

TRIUMPH *v* -ED, -ING, -S to be victorious

TRIUMVIR *n* pl. -VIRS or -VIRI one of a ruling body of three in ancient Rome

TRIUNE *n* pl. -S a trinity

TRIUNITY *n* pl. -TIES a trinity

TRIVALVE *n* pl. -S a type of shell

TRIVET *n* pl. -S a small stand having three legs

TRIVIA *n/pl* insignificant matters

TRIVIAL *adj* insignificant

TRIVIUM *n* pl. -IA a group of studies in medieval schools

TROAK *v* -ED, -ING, -S to troke

TROCAR *n* pl. -S a surgical instrument

TROCHAIC *n* pl. -S a trochee

TROCHAL *adj* shaped like a wheel

TROCHAR *n* pl. -S trocar

TROCHE *n* pl. -S a medicated lozenge

TROCHEE *n* pl. -S a type of metrical foot

TROCHIL *n* pl. -S an African bird

TROCHILI *n/pl* trochils

TROCHLEA *n* pl. -LEAE or -LEAS an anatomical structure resembling a pulley

TROCHOID *n* pl. -S a type of geometric curve

TROCK *v* -ED, -ING, -S to troke

TROD a past tense of tread

TRODDEN past participle of tread

TRODE a past tense of tread

TROFFER *n* pl. -S a fixture for fluorescent lighting

TROGON *n* pl. -S a tropical bird

TROIKA *n* pl. -S a Russian carriage

TROILITE *n* pl. -S a mineral

TROILUS *n* pl. -ES a large butterfly

TROIS *n* pl. TROIS the number three

TROKE *v* TROKED, TROKING, TROKES to exchange

TROLAND *n* pl. -S a unit of measurement of retinal response to light

TROLL *n* pl. -S a dwarf or giant of Teutonic folklore

TROLL *v* -ED, -ING, -S to fish with a slowly trailing line

TROLLER *n* pl. -S one that trolls

TROLLEY *v* -ED, -ING, -S to convey by streetcar

TROLLIED past tense of trolly

TROLLIES present 3d person sing. of trolly

TROLLING *n* pl. -S the act of one that trolls

TROLLOP *n* pl. -S a prostitute **TROLLOPY** *adj*

TROLLY *v* -LIED, -LYING, -LIES to trolley

TROMBONE *n* pl. -S a brass wind instrument

TROMMEL *n* pl. -S a screen used for sifting rock, ore, or coal

TROMP *v* -ED, -ING, -S to tramp

TROMPE *n* pl. -S a device used for supplying air to a furnace

TRONA *n* pl. -S a mineral

TRONE *n* pl. -S a weighing device

TROOP *v* -ED, -ING, -S to move or gather in crowds

TROOPER *n* pl. -S a cavalryman

TROOPIAL *n* pl. -S a troupial

TROOZ *n/pl* trews

TROP *adv* too much

TROPE *n* pl. -S the figurative use of a word

TROPHIC *adj* pertaining to nutrition

TROPHY *v* -PHIED, -PHYING, -PHIES to honor with a trophy (a symbol of victory)

TROPIC *n* pl. -S either of two circles of the celestial sphere on each side of the equator **TROPICAL** *adj*

TROPIN *n* pl. -S tropine

TROPINE *n* pl. -S a poisonous alkaloid

TROPISM *n* pl. -S the involuntary response of an organism to an external stimulus

TROT *v* TROTTED, TROTTING, TROTS to go at a gait between a walk and a run

TROTH *v* -ED, -ING, -S to betroth

TROTLINE *n* pl. -S a strong fishing line

TROTTED past tense of trot

TROTTER *n* pl. -S a horse that trots

TROTTING present participle of trot

TROTYL *n* pl. -S an explosive

TROUBLE *v* -BLED, -BLING, -BLES to distress

TROUBLER *n* pl. -S one that troubles

TROUGH *n* pl. -S a long, narrow receptacle

TROUNCE *v* TROUNCED, TROUNCING, TROUNCES to beat severely

TROUPE *v* TROUPED, TROUPING, TROUPES to tour with a theatrical company

TROUPER *n* pl. -S a member of a theatrical company

TROUPIAL *n* pl. -S a tropical bird

TROUPING present participle of troupe

TROUSER *adj* pertaining to trousers

TROUSERS *n/pl* a garment for the lower part of the body

TROUT *n* pl. -S a freshwater fish

TROUTY *adj* TROUTIER, TROUTIEST abounding in trout

TROUVERE *n* pl. -S a medieval poet

TROUVEUR *n* pl. -S trouvere

TROVE *n* pl. -S a valuable discovery

TROVER *n* pl. -S a type of legal action

TROW *v* -ED, -ING, -S to suppose

TROWEL *v* -ELED, -ELING, -ELS or -ELLED, -ELLING, -ELS to smooth with a trowel (a hand tool having a flat blade)

TROWELER *n* pl. -S one that trowels

TROWSERS *n/pl* trousers

TROWTH *n* pl. -S truth

TROY *n* pl. TROYS a system of weights

TRUANCY *n* pl. -CIES an act of truanting

TRUANT *v* -ED, -ING, -S to stay out of school without permission

TRUANTRY *n* pl. -RIES truancy

TRUCE *v* TRUCED, TRUCING, TRUCES to suspend hostilities by mutual agreement

TRUCK *v* -ED, -ING, -S to transport by truck (an automotive vehicle designed to carry loads)

TRUCKAGE *n* pl. -S transportation of goods by trucks

TRUCKER *n* pl. -S a truck driver

TRUCKING *n* pl. -S truckage

TRUCKLE *v* -LED, -LING, -LES to yield weakly

TRUCKLER *n* pl. -S one that truckles

TRUCKMAN *n* pl. -MEN a trucker

TRUDGE *v* TRUDGED, TRUDGING, TRUDGES to walk tiredly

TRUDGEN *n* pl. -S a swimming stroke

TRUDGEON *n* pl. -S trudgen

TRUDGER *n* pl. -S one that trudges

TRUDGING present participle of trudge

TRUE *adj* TRUER, TRUEST consistent with fact or reality

TRUE *v* TRUED, TRUING or TRUEING, TRUES to bring to conformity with a standard or requirement

TRUEBLUE *n* pl. -S a person of unwavering loyalty

TRUEBORN *adj* genuinely such by birth

TRUED past tense of true

TRUELOVE *n* pl. -S a sweetheart

TRUENESS *n* pl. -ES the quality or state of being true

TRUER comparative of true

TRUEST superlative of true

TRUFFE *n* pl. -S truffle

TRUFFLE *n* pl. -S an edible fungus TRUFFLED *adj*

TRUING a present participle of true

TRUISM *n* pl. -S an obvious truth TRUISTIC *adj*

TRULL *n* pl. -S a prostitute

TRULY *adv* in conformity with fact or reality

TRUMEAU *n* pl. -MEAUX a column supporting part of a doorway

TRUMP *v* -ED, -ING, -S to outdo

TRUMPERY *n* pl. -ERIES worthless finery

TRUMPET *v* -ED, -ING, -S to sound on a trumpet (a brass wind instrument)

TRUNCATE *v* -CATED, -CATING, -CATES to shorten by cutting off a part

TRUNDLE *v* -DLED, -DLING, -DLES to propel by causing to rotate

TRUNDLER *n* pl. -S one that trundles

TRUNK n pl. -S the main stem of a tree **TRUNKED** adj

TRUNNEL n pl. -S treenail

TRUNNION n pl. -S a pin or pivot on which something can be rotated

TRUSS v -ED, -ING, -ES to secure tightly

TRUSSER n pl. -S one that trusses

TRUSSING n pl. -S the framework of a structure

TRUST v -ED, -ING, -S to place confidence in

TRUSTEE v -TEED, -TEEING, -TEES to commit to the care of an administrator

TRUSTER n pl. -S one that trusts

TRUSTFUL adj inclined to trust

TRUSTY adj TRUSTIER, TRUSTIEST worthy of trust **TRUSTILY** adv

TRUSTY n pl. TRUSTIES one worthy of trust

TRUTH n pl. -S conformity to fact or reality

TRUTHFUL adj telling the truth

TRY v TRIED, TRYING, TRIES to attempt

TRYINGLY adv in a distressing manner

TRYMA n pl. -MATA a type of nut

TRYOUT n pl. -S a test of ability

TRYPSIN n pl. -S an enzyme **TRYPTIC** adj

TRYSAIL n pl. -S a type of sail

TRYST v -ED, -ING, -S to agree to meet

TRYSTE n pl. -S a market

TRYSTER n pl. -S one that trysts

TRYWORKS n/pl a type of furnace

TSADE n pl. -S sade

TSADI n pl. -S sade

TSAR n pl. -S czar

TSARDOM n pl. -S czardom

TSAREVNA n pl. -S czarevna

TSARINA n pl. -S czarina

TSARISM n pl. -S czarism

TSARIST n pl. -S czarist

TSARITZA n pl. -S czaritza

TSETSE n pl. -S an African fly

TSIMMES n pl. TSIMMES tzimmes

TSK v -ED, -ING, -S to utter an exclamation of annoyance

TSKTSK v -ED, -ING, -S to tsk

TSUBA n pl. TSUBA a part of a Japanese sword

TSUNAMI n pl. -S a very large ocean wave **TSUNAMIC** adj

TSURIS n pl. TSURIS a series of misfortunes

TUATARA n pl. -S a large reptile

TUATERA n pl. -S tuatara

TUB v TUBBED, TUBBING, TUBS to wash in a tub (a round, open vessel)

TUBA n pl. -BAS or -BAE a brass wind instrument

TUBAL adj pertaining to a tube

TUBATE adj tubular

TUBBABLE adj suitable for washing in a tub

TUBBED past tense of tub

TUBBER n pl. -S one that tubs

TUBBING present participle of tub

TUBBY adj -BIER, -BIEST short and fat

TUBE v TUBED, TUBING, TUBES to provide with a tube (a long, hollow cylinder)

TUBELESS adj having no tube

TUBELIKE adj resembling a tube

TUBER n pl. -S a thick underground stem

TUBERCLE n pl. -S a small, rounded swelling

TUBEROID adj pertaining to a tuber

TUBEROSE n pl. -S a Mexican herb

TUBEROUS adj pertaining to a tuber

TUBEWORK n pl. -S tubing

TUBFUL n pl. -S as much as a tub will hold

TUBIFEX n pl. -ES an aquatic worm

TUBIFORM adj tubular

TUBING n pl. -S material in the form of a tube

TUBLIKE adj resembling a tub

TUBULAR adj shaped like a tube

TUBULATE v -LATED, -LATING, -LATES to form into a tube

TUBULE n pl. -S a small tube

TUBULOSE adj tubular

TUBULOUS adj tubular

TUBULURE n pl. -S a short tubular opening

TUCHUN n pl. -S a Chinese military governor

TUCK v -ED, -ING, -S to fold under

TUCKAHOE	n pl. -S the edible root of certain arums	**TUMULOUS**	adj tumulose
TUCKER	v -ED, -ING, -S to weary	**TUMULT**	n pl. -S a great din and commotion
TUCKET	n pl. -S a trumpet fanfare	**TUMULUS**	n pl. -LI or -LUSES a mound over a grave
TUFA	n pl. -S a porous limestone		
TUFF	n pl. -S a volcanic rock	**TUN**	v TUNNED, TUNNING, TUNS to store in a large cask
TUFFET	n pl. -S a clump of grass		
TUFT	v -ED, -ING, -S to form into tufts (clusters of flexible outgrowths attached at the base)	**TUNA**	n pl. -S a marine food fish
		TUNABLE	adj capable of being tuned TUNABLY adv
		TUNDISH	n pl. -ES a receptacle for molten metal
TUFTER	n pl. -S one that tufts		
TUFTY	adj TUFTIER, TUFTIEST abounding in tufts TUFTILY adv	**TUNDRA**	n pl. -S a level, treeless expanse of arctic land
TUG	v TUGGED, TUGGING, TUGS to pull with force	**TUNE**	v TUNED, TUNING, TUNES to put into the proper pitch
TUGBOAT	n pl. -S a boat built for towing	**TUNEABLE**	adj tunable TUNEABLY adv
TUGGER	n pl. -S one that tugs	**TUNEFUL**	adj melodious
TUGGING	present participle of tug	**TUNELESS**	adj not tuneful
TUGLESS	adj being without a rope or chain with which to pull	**TUNER**	n pl. -S one that tunes
		TUNG	n pl. -S a Chinese tree
TUGRIK	n pl. -S a Mongolian unit of currency	**TUNGSTEN**	n pl. -S a metallic element TUNGSTIC adj
TUI	n pl. -S a bird of New Zealand	**TUNIC**	n pl. -S a loose-fitting garment
TUILLE	n pl. -S a tasset	**TUNICA**	n pl. -CAE an enveloping membrane or layer of body tissue
TUITION	n pl. -S a fee for instruction		
TULADI	n pl. -S a freshwater fish		
TULE	n pl. -S a tall marsh plant	**TUNICATE**	n pl. -S a small marine animal
TULIP	n pl. -S a flowering plant	**TUNICLE**	n pl. -S a type of vestment
TULLE	n pl. -S a silk material	**TUNING**	present participle of tune
TULLIBEE	n pl. -S a freshwater fish	**TUNNAGE**	n pl. -S tonnage
TUMBLE	v -BLED, -BLING, -BLES to fall or roll end over end	**TUNNED**	past tense of tun
		TUNNEL	v -NELED, -NELING, -NELS or -NELLED, -NELLING, -NELS to dig a tunnel (an underground passageway)
TUMBLER	n pl. -S one that tumbles		
TUMBLING	n pl. -S the sport of gymnastics		
TUMBREL	n pl. -S a type of cart	**TUNNELER**	n pl. -S one that tunnels
TUMBRIL	n pl. -S tumbrel	**TUNNING**	present participle of tun
TUMEFY	v -FIED, -FYING, -FIES to swell	**TUNNY**	n pl. -NIES a tuna
TUMID	adj swollen TUMIDLY adv	**TUP**	v TUPPED, TUPPING, TUPS to copulate with a ewe
TUMIDITY	n pl. -TIES the quality or state of being tumid		
		TUPELO	n pl. -LOS a softwood tree
TUMMY	n pl. -MIES the stomach	**TUPIK**	n pl. -S an Eskimo tent
TUMOR	n pl. -S an abnormal swelling TUMORAL, TUMOROUS adj	**TUPPED**	past tense of tup
		TUPPENCE	n pl. -S twopence
TUMOUR	n pl. -S tumor	**TUPPING**	present participle of tup
TUMP	n pl. -S tumpline	**TUPPENNY**	adj twopenny
TUMPLINE	n pl. -S a strap for supporting a load on the back	**TUQUE**	n pl. -S a knitted woolen cap
		TURACO	n pl. -COS touraco
TUMULAR	adj having the form of a mound	**TURACOU**	n pl. -S touraco
TUMULI	a pl. of tumulus	**TURBAN**	n pl. -S a head covering worn by Muslims TURBANED adj
TUMULOSE	adj full of mounds		

TURBARY n pl. -RIES a place where peat can be dug

TURBETH n pl. -S turpeth

TURBID adj thick or opaque with roiled sediment **TURBIDLY** adv

TURBINAL n pl. -S a bone of the nasal passage

TURBINE n pl. -S a type of engine

TURBIT n pl. -S a domestic pigeon

TURBITH n pl. -S turpeth

TURBO n pl. -BOS a turbine

TURBOCAR n pl. -S an auto powered by a gas turbine

TURBOFAN n pl. -S a type of jet engine

TURBOJET n pl. -S a type of jet engine

TURBOT n pl. -S a European flatfish

TURD n pl. -S a piece of dung

TURDINE adj belonging to a large family of singing birds

TUREEN n pl. -S a large, deep bowl

TURF n pl. TURFS or TURVES a surface layer of earth containing a dense growth of grass and its roots

TURF v -ED, -ING, -S to cover with turf

TURFIER comparative of turfy

TURFIEST superlative of turfy

TURFLESS adj having no turf

TURFLIKE adj resembling turf

TURFMAN n pl. -MEN a person who is devoted to horse racing

TURFSKI n pl. -S a type of ski

TURFY adj TURFIER, TURFIEST covered with turf

TURGENCY n pl. -CIES turgor

TURGENT adj turgid

TURGID adj swollen **TURGIDLY** adv

TURGITE n pl. -S an iron ore

TURGOR n pl. -S the quality or state of being turgid

TURKEY n pl. -KEYS a large American bird

TURKOIS n pl. -ES turquois

TURMERIC n pl. -S an East Indian herb

TURMOIL v -ED, -ING, -S to throw into an uproar

TURN v -ED, -ING, -S to move around a central point **TURNABLE** adj

TURNCOAT n pl. -S a traitor

TURNDOWN n pl. -S a rejection

TURNER n pl. -S one that turns

TURNERY n pl. -ERIES the process of shaping articles on a lathe

TURNHALL n pl. -S a building where gymnasts practice

TURNING n pl. -S a rotation about an axis

TURNIP n pl. -S an edible plant root

TURNKEY n pl. -KEYS a person who has charge of a prison's keys

TURNOFF n pl. -S a road that branches off from a larger one

TURNOUT n pl. -S an assemblage of people

TURNOVER n pl. -S an upset or overthrow

TURNPIKE n pl. -S a highway on which tolls are collected

TURNSOLE n pl. -S a plant that turns with the sun

TURNSPIT n pl. -S one that turns a roasting spit

TURNUP n pl. -S a part of a garment that is turned up

TURPETH n pl. -S a medicinal plant root

TURPS n pl. TURPS turpentine

TURQUOIS n pl. -ES a greenish blue gem

TURRET n pl. -S a small tower **TURRETED** adj

TURRICAL adj resembling a turret

TURTLE v -TLED, -TLING, -TLES to catch turtles (tortoises)

TURTLER n pl. -S one that turtles

TURTLING n pl. -S the act of one that turtles

TURVES a pl. of turf

TUSCHE n pl. -S a liquid used in lithography

TUSH v -ED, -ING, -ES to tusk

TUSK v -ED, -ING, -S to gore with a tusk (a long, pointed tooth extending outside of the mouth)

TUSKER n pl. -S an animal with tusks

TUSKLESS adj having no tusk

TUSKLIKE adj resembling a tusk

TUSSAH n pl. -S an Asian silkworm

TUSSAL adj pertaining to a cough

TUSSAR n pl. -S tussah

TUSSEH n pl. -S tussah

TUSSER n pl. -S tussah

TUSSIS n pl. -SISES a cough **TUSSIVE** adj

TUSSLE v -SLED, -SLING, -SLES to struggle

TUSSOCK *n pl.* -S a clump of grass
TUSSOCKY *adj*

TUSSOR *n pl.* -S tussah

TUSSORE *n pl.* -S tussah

TUSSUCK *n pl.* -S tussock

TUSSUR *n pl.* -S tussah

TUT *v* TUTTED, TUTTING, TUTS to utter an exclamation of impatience

TUTEE *n pl.* -S one who is being tutored

TUTELAGE *n pl.* -S the act of tutoring

TUTELAR *n pl.* -S a tutelary

TUTELARY *n pl.* -LARIES one who has the power to protect

TUTOR *v* -ED, -ING, -S to instruct privately

TUTORAGE *n pl.* -S tutelage

TUTORESS *n pl.* -ES a female who tutors

TUTORIAL *n pl.* -S a session of tutoring

TUTOYER *v* -TOYERED or -TOYED, -TOYERING, -TOYERS to address familiarly

TUTTED past tense of tut

TUTTI *n pl.* -S a musical passage performed by all the performers

TUTTING present participle of tut

TUTTY *n pl.* -TIES an impure zinc oxide

TUTU *n pl.* -S a short ballet skirt

TUX *n pl.* -ES a tuxedo

TUXEDO *n pl.* -DOES or -DOS a man's semiformal dinner coat

TUYER *n pl.* -S tuyere

TUYERE *n pl.* -S a pipe through which air is forced into a blast furnace

TWA *n pl.* -S two

TWADDLE *v* -DLED, -DLING, -DLES to talk foolishly

TWADDLER *n pl.* -S one that twaddles

TWAE *n pl.* -S two

TWAIN *n pl.* -S a set of two

TWANG *v* -ED, -ING, -S to make a sharp, vibrating sound

TWANGIER comparative of twangy

TWANGIEST superlative of twangy

TWANGLE *v* -GLED, -GLING, -GLES to twang

TWANGLER *n pl.* -S one that twangles

TWANGY *adj* TWANGIER, TWANGIEST twanging

TWANKY *n pl.* -KIES a variety of green tea

TWASOME *n pl.* -S twosome

TWAT *n pl.* -S the vulva — an offensive term

TWATTLE *v* -TLED, -TLING, -TLES to twaddle

TWEAK *v* -ED, -ING, -S to pinch and twist sharply

TWEAKY *adj* TWEAKIER, TWEAKIEST twitchy

TWEED *n pl.* -S a coarse woolen fabric

TWEEDLE *v* -DLED, -DLING, -DLES to perform casually on a musical instrument

TWEEDY *adj* TWEEDIER, TWEEDIEST resembling tweed

TWEEN *prep* between

TWEET *v* -ED, -ING, -S to chirp

TWEETER *n pl.* -S a loudspeaker designed to reproduce high-pitched sounds

TWEEZE *v* TWEEZED, TWEEZING, TWEEZES to pluck with a tweezer

TWEEZER *n pl.* -S a pincerlike tool

TWELFTH *n pl.* -S the number twelve in a series

TWELVE *n pl.* -S a number

TWELVEMO *n pl.* -MOS a page size

TWENTY *n pl.* -TIES a number

TWERP *n pl.* -S a small, impudent person

TWIBIL *n pl.* -S a battle-ax with two cutting edges

TWIBILL *n pl.* -S twibil

TWICE *adv* two times

TWIDDLE *v* -DLED, -DLING, -DLES to play idly with something

TWIDDLER *n pl.* -S one that twiddles

TWIER *n pl.* -S tuyere

TWIG *v* TWIGGED, TWIGGING, TWIGS to observe

TWIGGEN *adj* made of twigs (small branches)

TWIGGY *adj* -GIER, -GIEST twiglike

TWIGLESS *adj* having no twigs

TWIGLIKE *adj* resembling a twig

TWILIGHT *n pl.* -S the early evening light

TWILIT *adj* lighted by twilight

TWILL *v* -ED, -ING, -S to weave so as to produce a diagonal pattern

TWILLING *n pl.* -S a twilled fabric

TWIN *v* TWINNED, TWINNING, TWINS to bring together in close association

TWINBORN *adj* born at the same birth

TWINE *v* TWINED, TWINING, TWINES to twist together

TWINER *n pl.* -S one that twines

TWINGE *v* TWINGED, TWINGING, TWINGES to affect with a sharp pain

TWINIER comparative of twiny

TWINIEST superlative of twiny

TWINIGHT *adj* pertaining to a baseball doubleheader that begins in the late afternoon

TWINING present participle of twine

TWINKLE *v* -KLED, -KLING, -KLES to shine with a flickering or sparkling light

TWINKLER *n pl.* -S one that twinkles

TWINKLY *adj* twinkling

TWINNED past tense of twin

TWINNING *n pl.* -S the bearing of two children at the same birth

TWINSHIP *n pl.* -S close similarity or association

TWINY *adj* TWINIER, TWINIEST resembling twine (a strong string)

TWIRL *v* -ED, -ING, -S to rotate rapidly

TWIRLER *n pl.* -S one that twirls

TWIRLY *adj* TWIRLIER, TWIRLIEST curved

TWIRP *n pl.* -S twerp

TWIST *v* -ED, -ING, -S to combine by winding together

TWISTER *n pl.* -S one that twists

TWISTING *n pl.* -S a form of trickery used in selling life insurance

TWIT *v* TWITTED, TWITTING, TWITS to ridicule

TWITCH *v* -ED, -ING, -ES to move or pull with a sudden motion

TWITCHER *n pl.* -S one that twitches

TWITCHY *adj* TWITCHIER, TWITCHIEST fidgety

TWITTED past tense of twit

TWITTER *v* -ED, -ING, -S to utter a succession of chirping sounds

TWITTERY *adj* nervously agitated

TWITTING present participle of twit

TWIXT *prep* between

TWO *n pl.* TWOS a number

TWOFER *n pl.* -S something sold at the rate of two for the price of one

TWOFOLD *n pl.* -S an amount twice as great as a given unit

TWOPENCE *n pl.* -S a British coin worth two pennies

TWOPENNY *adj* worth twopence

TWOSOME *n pl.* -S a group of two

TWYER *n pl.* -S tuyere

TYCOON *n pl.* -S a wealthy and powerful business person

TYE *n pl.* -S a chain on a ship

TYEE *n pl.* -S a food fish

TYING a present participle of tie

TYKE *n pl.* -S a small child

TYMBAL *n pl.* -S timbal

TYMPAN *n pl.* -S a drum

TYMPANA a pl. of tympanum

TYMPANAL *adj* tympanic

TYMPANI *n/pl* kettledrums

TYMPANIC *adj* pertaining to the tympanum

TYMPANUM *n pl.* -NA or -NUMS the middle ear

TYMPANY *n pl.* -NIES a swelling of the abdomen

TYNE *v* TYNED, TYNING, TYNES to tine

TYPAL *adj* typical

TYPE *v* TYPED, TYPING, TYPES to write with a typewriter TYPEABLE *adj*

TYPEBAR *n pl.* -S a part of a typewriter

TYPECASE *n pl.* -S a tray for holding printing type

TYPECAST *v* -CAST, -CASTING, -CASTS to cast in an acting role befitting one's own nature

TYPED past tense of type

TYPEFACE *n pl.* -S the face of printing type

TYPESET *v* -SET, -SETTING, -SETS to set in type

TYPEY *adj* TYPIER, TYPIEST typy

TYPHOID *n pl.* -S an infectious disease

TYPHON *n pl.* -S a type of signal horn

TYPHOON *n pl.* -S a tropical hurricane TYPHONIC *adj*

TYPHOSE *adj* pertaining to typhoid

TYPHUS *n pl.* -ES an infectious disease TYPHOUS *adj*

TYPIC *adj* typical

TYPICAL *adj* having the nature of a representative specimen

TYPIER comparative of typey and typy

TYPIEST superlative of typey and typy

TYPIFIER *n* pl. -S one that typifies

TYPIFY *v* -FIED, -FYING, -FIES to serve as a typical example of

TYPING present participle of type

TYPIST *n* pl. -S one who types

TYPO *n* pl. -POS a typographical error

TYPOLOGY *n* pl. -GIES the study of classification according to common characteristics

TYPP *n* pl. -S a unit of yarn size

TYPY *adj* TYPIER, TYPIEST characterized by strict conformance to the characteristics of a group

TYRAMINE *n* pl. -S a chemical compound

TYRANNIC *adj* characteristic of a tyrant

TYRANNY *n* pl. -NIES the rule of a tyrant

TYRANT *n* pl. -S an absolute ruler

TYRE *v* TYRED, TYRING, TYRES to furnish with a covering for a wheel

TYRO *n* pl. -ROS a beginner
TYRONIC *adj*

TYROSINE *n* pl. -S an amino acid

TYTHE *v* TYTHED, TYTHING, TYTHES to tithe

TZADDIK *n* pl. -DIKIM zaddik

TZAR *n* pl. -S czar

TZARDOM *n* pl. -S czardom

TZAREVNA *n* pl. -S czarevna

TZARINA *n* pl. -S czarina

TZARISM *n* pl. -S czarism

TZARIST *n* pl. -S czarist

TZARITZA *n* pl. -S czaritza

TZETZE *n* pl. -S tsetse

TZIGANE *n* pl. -S a gypsy

TZIMMES *n* pl. TZIMMES a vegetable stew

TZITZIS *n* pl. TZITZIS zizith

TZITZITH *n* pl. TZITZITH zizith

TZURIS *n* pl. TZURIS tsuris

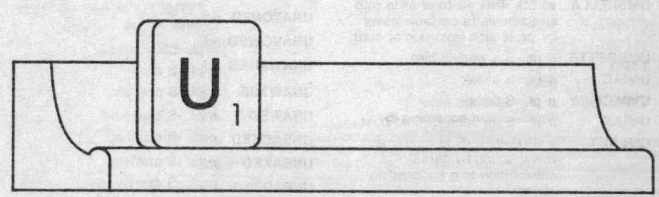

UBIETY	n pl. -ETIES the state of having a definite location
UBIQUE	adv everywhere
UBIQUITY	n pl. -TIES the state of being everywhere at the same time
UDDER	n pl. -S a mammary gland
UDO	n pl. UDOS a Japanese herb
UDOMETER	n pl. -S a rain gauge
UDOMETRY	n pl. -TRIES the measurement of rain
UGH	n pl. -S the sound of a cough or grunt
UGLIER	comparative of ugly
UGLIEST	superlative of ugly
UGLIFIER	n pl. -S one that uglifies
UGLIFY	v -FIED, -FYING, -FIES to make ugly
UGLINESS	n pl. -ES the state of being ugly
UGLY	adj -LIER, -LIEST displeasing to the sight UGLILY adv
UGSOME	adj disgusting
UHLAN	n pl. -S one of a body of Prussian cavalry
UINTAITE	n pl. -S a variety of asphalt
UIT	prep out of
UKASE	n pl. -S an edict
UKE	n pl. -S ukelele
UKELELE	n pl. -S ukulele
UKULELE	n pl. -S a small guitar-like instrument
ULAMA	n pl. -S ulema
ULAN	n pl. -S uhlan
ULCER	v -ED, -ING, -S to affect with an ulcer (a type of lesion)
ULCERATE	v -ATED, -ATING, -ATES to ulcer
ULCEROUS	adj being or affected with an ulcer

ULEMA	n pl. -S a Muslim scholar
ULEXITE	n pl. -S a mineral
ULLAGE	n pl. -S the amount that a container lacks of being full ULLAGED adj
ULNA	n pl. -NAE or -NAS a bone of the forearm ULNAR adj
ULSTER	n pl. -S a long, loose overcoat
ULTERIOR	adj more remote
ULTIMA	n pl. -S the last syllable of a word
ULTIMACY	n pl. -CIES an ultimate
ULTIMATA	n/pl final proposals
ULTIMATE	n pl. -S something final or fundamental
ULTIMO	adj of or occurring in the preceding month
ULTRA	n pl. -S an ultraist
ULTRAISM	n pl. -S advocacy of extreme measures
ULTRAIST	n pl. -S an advocate of extreme measures
ULTRARED	n pl. -S infrared
ULULANT	adj howling
ULULATE	v -LATED, -LATING, -LATES to howl
ULVA	n pl. -S an edible seaweed
UMBEL	n pl. -S a type of flower cluster UMBELED, UMBELLAR, UMBELLED adj
UMBELLET	n pl. -S a small umbel
UMBER	v -ED, -ING, -S to color with a brown pigment
UMBILICI	n/pl navels
UMBLES	n/pl the entrails of a deer
UMBO	n pl. -BONES or -BOS the rounded elevation at the center of a shield UMBONAL, UMBONATE, UMBONIC adj

UMBRA *n* pl. -BRAE or -BRAS a dark area UMBRAL *adj*

UMBRAGE *n* pl. -S resentment

UMBRELLA *v* -ED, -ING, -S to provide with an umbrella (a portable cover for protection from rain or sun)

UMBRETTE *n* pl. -S a wading bird

UMIAC *n* pl. -S umiak

UMIACK *n* pl. -S umiak

UMIAK *n* pl. -S an open Eskimo boat

UMLAUT *v* -ED, -ING, -S to modify a vowel sound by partial assimilation to a succeeding sound

UMP *v* -ED, -ING, -S to umpire

UMPIRAGE *n* pl. -S the function of an umpire

UMPIRE *v* -PIRED, -PIRING, -PIRES to act as umpire (a person appointed to rule on the plays in a game)

UMPTEEN *adj* indefinitely numerous

UMTEENTH *adj* being the last in an indefinitely numerous series

UN *pron* pl. -S one

[U₁] [N₁]

Following is a list of self-explanatory adjectives and adverbs containing the prefix UN- (not):

UNABATED *adj*

UNABLE *adj*

UNABUSED *adj*

UNACTED *adj*

UNAFRAID *adj*

UNAGED *adj*

UNAGEING *adj*

UNAGILE *adj*

UNAGING *adj*

UNAIDED *adj*

UNAIMED *adj*

UNAIRED *adj*

UNALIKE *adj*

UNALLIED *adj*

UNAMUSED *adj*

UNANELED *adj*

UNAPT *adj*

UNAPTLY *adv*

UNARGUED *adj*

UNARTFUL *adj*

UNASKED *adj*

UNATONED *adj*

UNAVOWED *adj*

UNAWAKED *adj*

UNAWARE *adj*

UNAWED *adj*

UNBACKED *adj*

UNBAKED *adj*

UNBARBED *adj*

UNBASED *adj*

UNBEATEN *adj*

UNBENIGN *adj*

UNBIASED *adj*

UNBITTED *adj*

UNBLAMED *adj*

UNBLEST *adj*

UNBLOODY *adj*

UNBONED *adj*

UNBORN *adj*

UNBOUGHT *adj*

UNBOWED *adj*

UNBRED *adj*

UNBROKE *adj*

UNBROKEN *adj*

UNBURIED *adj*

UNBURNED *adj*

UNBURNT *adj*

UNCALLED *adj*

UNCANDID *adj*

UNCARING *adj*

UNCASHED *adj*

UNCAUGHT *adj*

UNCAUSED *adj*

UNCHARY *adj*

UNCHASTE *adj*

UNCHEWED *adj*

UNCHIC *adj*

UNCHOSEN *adj*

UNCIVIL *adj*

UNCLEAN *adj* -CLEANER, -CLEANEST

UNCLEAR *adj* -CLEARER, -CLEAREST

UNCLOYED	adj	UNFALLEN	adj
UNCOATED	adj	UNFANCY	adj
UNCOINED	adj	UNFAZED	adj
UNCOMBED	adj	UNFEARED	adj
UNCOMELY	adj	UNFED	adj
UNCOMIC	adj	UNFELT	adj
UNCOMMON	adj -MONER, -MONEST	UNFILIAL	adj
UNCOOKED	adj	UNFILLED	adj
UNCOOL	adj	UNFILMED	adj
UNCOUTH	adj	UNFIRED	adj
UNCURED	adj	UNFISHED	adj
UNCURSED	adj	UNFLEXED	adj
UNCUT	adj	UNFOILED	adj
UNDAMPED	adj	UNFOND	adj
UNDARING	adj	UNFORCED	adj
UNDATED	adj	UNFORGED	adj
UNDECKED	adj	UNFORKED	adj
UNDENIED	adj	UNFORMED	adj
UNDEVOUT	adj	UNFOUGHT	adj
UNDIMMED	adj	UNFOUND	adj
UNDREAMT	adj	UNFRAMED	adj
UNDRIED	adj	UNFUNDED	adj
UNDULLED	adj	UNFUNNY	adj
UNDYED	adj	UNFUSED	adj
UNEAGER	adj	UNFUSSY	adj
UNEARNED	adj	UNGALLED	adj
UNEATEN	adj	UNGENIAL	adj
UNEDIBLE	adj	UNGENTLE	adj
UNEDITED	adj	UNGENTLY	adv
UNENDED	adj	UNGIFTED	adj
UNENDING	adj	UNGLAZED	adj
UNENVIED	adj	UNGOWNED	adj
UNERASED	adj	UNGRACED	adj
UNERRING	adj	UNGRADED	adj
UNEVADED	adj	UNGREEDY	adj
UNEVEN	adj -EVENER, -EVENEST	UNGUIDED	adj
UNEVENLY	adv	UNHAILED	adj
UNEXOTIC	adj	UNHALVED	adj
UNEXPERT	adj	UNHAPPY	adj -PIER, -PIEST
UNFADED	adj	UNHARMED	adj
UNFADING	adj	UNHASTY	adj
UNFAIR	adj -FAIRER, -FAIREST	UNHEALED	adj
UNFAIRLY	adv	UNHEARD	adj

UNHEATED	adj	
UNHEEDED	adj	
UNHELPED	adj	
UNHEROIC	adj	
UNHEWN	adj	
UNHIP	adj	
UNHIRED	adj	
UNHOLILY	adv	
UNHOLY	adj	-LIER, -LIEST
UNHUMAN	adj	
UNHUNG	adj	
UNHURT	adj	
UNIDEAL	adj	
UNIMBUED	adj	
UNIRONED	adj	
UNISSUED	adj	
UNJADED	adj	
UNJOINED	adj	
UNJOYFUL	adj	
UNJUDGED	adj	
UNJUST	adj	
UNJUSTLY	adv	
UNKEPT	adj	
UNKIND	adj	-KINDER, -KINDEST
UNKINDLY	adv	-LIER, -LIEST
UNKINGLY	adj	
UNKISSED	adj	
UNKOSHER	adj	
UNLAWFUL	adj	
UNLEASED	adj	
UNLED	adj	
UNLETHAL	adj	
UNLETTED	adj	
UNLEVIED	adj	
UNLICKED	adj	
UNLIKE	adj	
UNLIKELY	adj	-LIER, -LIEST
UNLINED	adj	
UNLISTED	adj	
UNLIT	adj	
UNLIVELY	adj	
UNLOBED	adj	
UNLOVED	adj	

UNLOVELY	adj	-LIER, -LIEST
UNLOVING	adj	
UNLUCKY	adj	-LUCKIER, -LUCKIEST
UNMANFUL	adj	
UNMANLY	adj	
UNMAPPED	adj	
UNMARKED	adj	
UNMARRED	adj	
UNMATED	adj	
UNMATTED	adj	
UNMEANT	adj	
UNMELLOW	adj	
UNMELTED	adj	
UNMENDED	adj	
UNMET	adj	
UNMILLED	adj	
UNMIXED	adj	
UNMIXT	adj	
UNMODISH	adj	
UNMOLTEN	adj	
UNMOVED	adj	
UNMOVING	adj	
UNMOWN	adj	
UNNAMED	adj	
UNNEEDED	adj	
UNNOISY	adj	
UNNOTED	adj	
UNOILED	adj	
UNOPEN	adj	
UNOPENED	adj	
UNORNATE	adj	
UNOWNED	adj	
UNPAID	adj	
UNPAIRED	adj	
UNPARTED	adj	
UNPAVED	adj	
UNPAYING	adj	
UNPITIED	adj	
UNPLACED	adj	
UNPLAYED	adj	
UNPLIANT	adj	
UNPLOWED	adj	
UNPOETIC	adj	

UNPOISED	adj	UNSAWN	adj
UNPOLITE	adj	UNSCALED	adj
UNPOLLED	adj	UNSEARED	adj
UNPOSED	adj	UNSEEDED	adj
UNPOSTED	adj	UNSEEING	adj
UNPRETTY	adj	UNSEEMLY	adj -LIER, -LIEST
UNPRICED	adj	UNSEEN	adj
UNPRIMED	adj	UNSEIZED	adj
UNPRIZED	adj	UNSENT	adj
UNPROBED	adj	UNSERVED	adj
UNPROVED	adj	UNSEXUAL	adj
UNPROVEN	adj	UNSHADED	adj
UNPRUNED	adj	UNSHAKEN	adj
UNPURE	adj	UNSHAMED	adj
UNPURGED	adj	UNSHAPED	adj
UNQUIET	adj -ETER, -ETEST	UNSHAPEN	adj
UNRAISED	adj	UNSHARED	adj
UNRAKED	adj	UNSHARP	adj
UNRANKED	adj	UNSHAVED	adj
UNRATED	adj	UNSHAVEN	adj
UNRAZED	adj	UNSHED	adj
UNREAD	adj	UNSHOD	adj
UNREADY	adj -READIER, -READIEST	UNSHORN	adj
UNREAL	adj	UNSHRUNK	adj
UNREALLY	adv	UNSHUT	adj
UNRENTED	adj	UNSIFTED	adj
UNREPAID	adj	UNSIGNED	adj
UNRESTED	adj	UNSILENT	adj
UNRHYMED	adj	UNSINFUL	adj
UNRIFLED	adj	UNSIZED	adj
UNRIMED	adj	UNSLAKED	adj
UNRINSED	adj	UNSMOKED	adj
UNRISEN	adj	UNSOAKED	adj
UNROUGH	adj	UNSOBER	adj
UNRULED	adj	UNSOCIAL	adj
UNRUSHED	adj	UNSOILED	adj
UNSAFE	adj	UNSOLD	adj
UNSAFELY	adv	UNSOLID	adj
UNSALTED	adj	UNSOLVED	adj
UNSATED	adj	UNSORTED	adj
UNSAVED	adj	UNSOUGHT	adj
UNSAVORY	adj	UNSOUND	adj -SOUNDER, -SOUNDEST
UNSAWED	adj	UNSOURED	adj

UNSOWED	adj	UNTRUE	adj -TRUER, -TRUEST
UNSOWN	adj	UNTRULY	adv
UNSPENT	adj	UNTRUSTY	adj
UNSPILT	adj	UNTUFTED	adj
UNSPLIT	adj	UNTURNED	adj
UNSPOILT	adj	UNUNITED	adj
UNSPRUNG	adj	UNURGED	adj
UNSPUN	adj	UNUSABLE	adj
UNSTABLE	adj -BLER, -BLEST	UNUSED	adj
UNSTABLY	adv	UNUSUAL	adj
UNSTEADY	adj -STEADIER, -STEADIEST	UNVALUED	adj
UNSTUNG	adj	UNVARIED	adj
UNSUBTLE	adj	UNVEINED	adj
UNSUITED	adj	UNVERSED	adj
UNSUNG	adj	UNVEXED	adj
UNSUNK	adj	UNVEXT	adj
UNSURE	adj	UNVIABLE	adj
UNSURELY	adv	UNVOCAL	adj
UNSWAYED	adj	UNWALLED	adj
UNSWEPT	adj	UNWANTED	adj
UNTAGGED	adj	UNWARIER	comparative of unwary
UNTAKEN	adj	UNWARIEST	superlative of unwary
UNTAME	adj	UNWARILY	adv
UNTAMED	adj	UNWARMED	adj
UNTANNED	adj	UNWARNED	adj
UNTAPPED	adj	UNWARPED	adj
UNTASTED	adj	UNWARY	adj -WARIER, -WARIEST
UNTAXED	adj	UNWASTED	adj
UNTENDED	adj	UNWAXED	adj
UNTESTED	adj	UNWEANED	adj
UNTHAWED	adj	UNWEARY	adj
UNTIDILY	adv	UNWED	adj
UNTIDY	adj -DIER, -DIEST	UNWEDDED	adj
UNTILLED	adj	UNWEEDED	adj
UNTILTED	adj	UNWELDED	adj
UNTIMELY	adj -LIER, -LIEST	UNWELL	adj
UNTINGED	adj	UNWEPT	adj
UNTIRED	adj	UNWETTED	adj
UNTIRING	adj	UNWIELDY	adj -WIELDIER, -WIELDIEST
UNTITLED	adj	UNWIFELY	adj
UNTOLD	adj	UNWILLED	adj
UNTRACED	adj	UNWISE	adj -WISER, -WISEST
UNTRIED	adj	UNWISELY	adv

UNWON *adj*

UNWOODED *adj*

UNWOOED *adj*

UNWORKED *adj*

UNWORN *adj*

UNWORTHY *adj* -THIER, -THIEST

UNWRUNG *adj*

UNZONED *adj*

UNAI *n pl.* -S unau

UNANCHOR *v* -ED, -ING, -S to loosen from an anchor

UNARM *v* -ED, -ING, -S to disarm

UNARY *adj* consisting of a single element

UNAU *n pl.* -S a two-toed sloth

UNAWARES *adv* without warning

UNBAR *v* -BARRED, -BARRING, -BARS to remove a bar from

UNBATED *adj* unabated

UNBE *v* to cease to have being — UNBE is the only accepted form of this verb; it cannot be conjugated

UNBEAR *v* -BEARED, -BEARING, -BEARS to free from the pressure of a rein

UNBELIEF *n pl.* -S lack of belief

UNBELT *v* -ED, -ING, -S to remove the belt of

UNBEND *v* -BENT or -BENDED, -BENDING, -BENDS to make or allow to become straight

UNBID *adj* unbidden

UNBIDDEN *adj* not invited

UNBIND *v* -BOUND, -BINDING, -BINDS to free from bindings

UNBLOCK *v* -ED, -ING, -S to free from being blocked

UNBODIED *adj* having no body

UNBOLT *v* -ED, -ING, -S to open by withdrawing a bolt (a metal bar)

UNBONNET *v* -ED, -ING, -S to uncover the head

UNBOSOM *v* -ED, -ING, -S to reveal

UNBOUND past tense of unbind

UNBOX *v* -ED, -ING, -ES to remove from a box

UNBRACE *v* -BRACED, -BRACING, -BRACES to free from braces

UNBRAID *v* -ED, -ING, -S to separate the strands of

UNBREECH *v* -ED, -ING, -ES to remove the breeches of

UNBRIDLE *v* -DLED, -DLING, -DLES to set loose

UNBUCKLE *v* -LED, -LING, -LES to loosen a buckle

UNBUILD *v* -BUILT, -BUILDING, -BUILDS to demolish

UNBUNDLE *v* -DLED, -DLING, -DLES to price separately

UNBURDEN *v* -ED, -ING, -S to free from a burden

UNBUTTON *v* -ED, -ING, -S to unfasten the buttons of

UNCAGE *v* -CAGED, -CAGING, -CAGES to release from a cage

UNCAKE *v* -CAKED, -CAKING, -CAKES to break up a cake (a block of compacted matter)

UNCANNY *adj* -NIER, -NIEST strange and inexplicable

UNCAP *v* -CAPPED, -CAPPING, -CAPS to remove the cap from

UNCASE *v* -CASED, -CASING, -CASES to remove from a case

UNCHAIN *v* -ED, -ING, -S to free by removing a chain

UNCHANCY *adj* unlucky

UNCHARGE *v* -CHARGED, -CHARGING, -CHARGES to acquit

UNCHOKE *v* -CHOKED, -CHOKING, -CHOKES to free from obstruction

UNCHURCH *v* -ED, -ING, -ES to expel from a church

UNCI *pl.* of uncus

UNCIA *n pl.* -CIAE a coin of ancient Rome

UNCIAL *n pl.* -S a style of writing

UNCIALLY *adv* in the uncial style

UNCIFORM *n pl.* -S a bone of the wrist

UNCINAL *adj* uncinate

UNCINATE *adj* bent at the end like a hook

UNCINUS *n pl.* -NI an uncinate structure

UNCLAD a past tense of unclothe

UNCLAMP *v* -ED, -ING, -S to free from a clamp

UNCLASP *v* -ED, -ING, -S to free from a clasp

UNCLE *n pl.* -S the brother of one's father or mother

UNCLENCH *v* -ED, -ING, -ES to open from a clenched position

UNCLINCH *v* -ED, -ING, -ES to unclench

UNCLOAK   v -ED, -ING, -S to remove a cloak from

UNCLOG   v -CLOGGED, -CLOGGING, -CLOGS to free from a difficulty or obstruction

UNCLOSE   v -CLOSED, -CLOSING, -CLOSES to open

UNCLOTHE   v -CLOTHED or -CLAD, -CLOTHING, -CLOTHES to divest of clothing

UNCLOUD   v -ED, -ING, -S to free from clouds

UNCO   n pl. -COS a stranger

UNCOCK   v -ED, -ING, -S to remove from a cocked position

UNCOFFIN   v -ED, -ING, -S to remove from a coffin

UNCOIL   v -ED, -ING, -S to release from a coiled position

UNCORK   v -ED, -ING, -S to draw the cork from

UNCOUPLE   v -PLED, -PLING, -PLES to disconnect

UNCOVER   v -ED, -ING, -S to remove the covering from

UNCRATE   v -CRATED, -CRATING, -CRATES to remove from a crate

UNCREATE   v -ATED, -ATING, -ATES to deprive of existence

UNCROSS   v -ED, -ING, -ES to change from a crossed position

UNCROWN   v -ED, -ING, -S to deprive of a crown

UNCTION   n pl. -S the act of anointing

UNCTUOUS   adj greasy

UNCURB   v -ED, -ING, -S to remove restraints from

UNCURL   v -ED, -ING, -S to straighten the curls of

UNCUS   n pl. -CI a hook-shaped anatomical part

UNDE   adj wavy

UNDEE   adj unde

UNDER   prep in a lower position than

UNDERACT   v -ED, -ING, -S to act subtly and with restraint

UNDERAGE   n pl. -S a shortage

UNDERARM   n pl. -S the armpit

UNDERATE   past tense of undereat

UNDERBID   v -BID, -BIDDING, -BIDS to bid lower than

UNDERBUD   v -BUDDED, -BUDDING, -BUDS to bud from beneath

UNDERBUY   v -BOUGHT, -BUYING, -BUYS to buy at a lower price than

UNDERCUT   v -CUT, -CUTTING, -CUTS to cut under

UNDERDO   v -DID, -DONE, -DOING, -DOES to do insufficiently

UNDERDOG   n pl. -S one who is expected to lose

UNDEREAT   v -ATE, -EATEN, -EATING, -EATS to eat an insufficient amount

UNDERFED   adj fed an insufficient amount

UNDERFUR   n pl. -S the thick, soft fur beneath the outer coat of certain mammals

UNDERGO   v -WENT, -GONE, -GOING, -GOES to be subjected to

UNDERGOD   n pl. -S a lesser god

UNDERJAW   n pl. -S the lower jaw

UNDERLAIN   past participle of underlie

UNDERLAP   v -LAPPED, -LAPPING, -LAPS to extend partly under

UNDERLAY   v -LAID, -LAYING, -LAYS to place under

UNDERLET   v -LET, -LETTING, -LETS to lease at less than the usual value

UNDERLIE   v -LAY, -LAIN, -LYING, -LIES to lie under

UNDERLIP   n pl. -S the lower lip

UNDERLIT   adj lacking adequate light

UNDERLYING   present participle of underlie

UNDERPAY   v -PAID, -PAYING, -PAYS to pay less than is deserved

UNDERPIN   v -PINNED, -PINNING, -PINS to support from below

UNDERRUN   v -RAN, -RUNNING, -RUNS to pass or extend under

UNDERSEA   adv beneath the surface of the sea

UNDERSET   n pl. -S a current below the surface of the ocean

UNDERTAX   v -ED, -ING, -ES to tax less than the usual amount

UNDERTOW   n pl. -S the seaward pull of receding waves breaking on a shore

UNDERWAY   adv in progress

UNDERWENT   past tense of undergo

UNDID   past tense of undo

UNDIES   n/pl underwear

UNDINE   n pl. -S a female water spirit

UNDO	v -DID, -DONE, -DOING, -DOES to bring to ruin
UNDOCK	v -ED, -ING, -S to move away from a dock
UNDOER	n pl. -S one that undoes
UNDOING	n pl. -S a cause of ruin
UNDONE	past participle of undo
UNDOUBLE	v -BLED, -BLING, -BLES to unfold
UNDRAPE	v -DRAPED, -DRAPING, -DRAPES to strip of drapery
UNDRAW	v -DREW, -DRAWN, -DRAWING, -DRAWS to draw open
UNDRESS	v -DRESSED or -DREST, -DRESSING, -DRESSES to remove one's clothing
UNDRUNK	adj not swallowed
UNDUE	adj exceeding what is appropriate or normal
UNDULANT	adj undulating
UNDULATE	v -LATED, -LATING, -LATES to move with a wavelike motion
UNDULY	adv in an undue manner
UNDY	adj unde
UNDYING	adj not subject to death
UNEARTH	v -ED, -ING, -S to dig up
UNEASE	n pl. -S mental or physical discomfort
UNEASY	adj -EASIER, -EASIEST marked by mental or physical discomfort **UNEASILY** adv
UNEQUAL	n pl. -S one that is not equal to another
UNFAITH	n pl. -S lack of faith
UNFASTEN	v -ED, -ING, -S to release from fastenings
UNFENCE	v -FENCED, -FENCING, -FENCES to remove a fence from
UNFETTER	v -ED, -ING, -S to free from fetters
UNFIT	v -FITTED, -FITTING, -FITS to make unsuitable
UNFITLY	adv in an unsuitable manner
UNFIX	v -FIXED or -FIXT, -FIXING, -FIXES to unfasten
UNFOLD	v -ED, -ING, -S to open something that is folded
UNFOLDER	n pl. -S one that unfolds
UNFORGOT	adj not forgotten
UNFREE	v -FREED, -FREEING, -FREES to deprive of freedom
UNFREEZE	v -FROZE, -FROZEN, -FREEZING, -FREEZES to cause to thaw

UNFROCK	v -ED, -ING, -S to divest of ecclesiastical authority
UNFURL	v -ED, -ING, -S to unroll
UNGAINLY	adj -LIER, -LIEST awkward
UNGIRD	v -GIRDED or -GIRT, -GIRDING, -GIRDS to remove a belt from
UNGLOVE	v -GLOVED, -GLOVING, -GLOVES to uncover by removing a glove
UNGLUE	v -GLUED, -GLUING, -GLUES to disjoin
UNGODLY	adj -LIER, -LIEST impious
UNGOT	adj ungotten
UNGOTTEN	adj not obtained
UNGUAL	adj pertaining to an unguis
UNGUARD	v -ED, -ING, -S to leave unprotected
UNGUENT	n pl. -S an ointment
UNGUIS	n pl. -GUES a nail, claw, or hoof
UNGULA	n pl. -LAE an unguis **UNGULAR** adj
UNGULATE	n pl. -S a hoofed mammal
UNHAIR	v -ED, -ING, -S to remove the hair from
UNHALLOW	v -ED, -ING, -S to profane
UNHAND	v -ED, -ING, -S to remove the hand from
UNHANDY	adj -HANDIER, -HANDIEST difficult to handle
UNHANG	v -HUNG or -HANGED, -HANGING, -HANGS to detach from a hanging support
UNHAT	v -HATTED, -HATTING, -HATS to remove one's hat
UNHELM	v -ED, -ING, -S to remove the helmet of
UNHINGE	v -HINGED, -HINGING, -HINGES to remove from hinges
UNHITCH	v -ED, -ING, -ES to free from being hitched
UNHOOD	v -ED, -ING, -S to remove a hood from
UNHOOK	v -ED, -ING, -S to remove from a hook
UNHOPED	adj not hoped for or expected
UNHORSE	v -HORSED, -HORSING, -HORSES to cause to fall from a horse
UNHOUSE	v -HOUSED, -HOUSING, -HOUSES to deprive of a protective shelter
UNHUSK	v -ED, -ING, -S to remove the husk from

UNIALGAL	*adj* pertaining to a single algal cell
UNIAXIAL	*adj* having one axis
UNICOLOR	*adj* of one color
UNICORN	*n pl.* -S a mythical horselike creature
UNICYCLE	*n pl.* -S a one-wheeled vehicle
UNIDEAED	*adj* lacking ideas
UNIFACE	*n pl.* -S a coin having a design on only one side
UNIFIC	*adj* unifying
UNIFIED	past tense of unify
UNIFIER	*n pl.* -S one that unifies
UNIFIES	present 3d person sing. of unify
UNIFILAR	*adj* having only one thread, wire, or fiber
UNIFORM	*adj* -FORMER, -FORMEST unchanging
UNIFORM	*v* -ED, -ING, -S to make uniform
UNIFY	*v* -FIED, -FYING, -FIES to make into a coherent whole
UNILOBED	*adj* having one lobe
UNION	*n pl.* -S a number of persons, parties, or political entities united for a common purpose
UNIONISE	*v* -ISED, -ISING, -ISES to unionize
UNIONISM	*n pl.* -S the principle of forming a union
UNIONIST	*n pl.* -S an advocate of unionism
UNIONIZE	*v* -IZED, -IZING, -IZES to form into a union
UNIPOD	*n pl.* -S a one-legged support
UNIPOLAR	*adj* showing only one kind of polarity
UNIQUE	*adj* UNIQUER, UNIQUEST existing as the only one of its kind; very unusual **UNIQUELY** *adv*
UNIQUE	*n pl.* -S something that is unique
UNISEX	*n pl.* -ES the condition of not being distinguishable as to sex
UNISON	*n pl.* -S complete agreement **UNISONAL** *adj*
UNIT	*n pl.* -S a specific quantity used as a standard of measurement
UNITAGE	*n pl.* -S amount in units
UNITARY	*adj* pertaining to a unit
UNITE	*v* UNITED, UNITING, UNITES to bring together so as to form a whole **UNITEDLY** *adv*
UNITER	*n pl.* -S one that unites
UNITIES	pl. of unity
UNITIVE	*adj* serving to unite
UNITIZE	*v* -IZED, -IZING, -IZES to divide into units
UNITY	*n pl.* -TIES the state of being one single entity
UNIVALVE	*n pl.* -S a mollusk having a single shell
UNIVERSE	*n pl.* -S the totality of all existing things
UNIVOCAL	*n pl.* -S a word having only one meaning
UNKEMPT	*adj* untidy
UNKEND	*adj* unkenned
UNKENNED	*adj* not known or recognized
UNKENNEL	*v* -NELED, -NELING, -NELS or -NELLED, -NELLING, -NELS to release from a kennel
UNKENT	*adj* unkenned
UNKNIT	*v* -KNITTED, -KNITTING, -KNITS to unravel
UNKNOT	*v* -KNOTTED, -KNOTTING, -KNOTS to undo a knot in
UNKNOWN	*n pl.* -S one that is not known
UNLACE	*v* -LACED, -LACING, -LACES to unfasten the laces of
UNLADE	*v* -LADED, -LADEN, -LADING, -LADES to unload
UNLAID	past tense of unlay
UNLASH	*v* -ED, -ING, -ES to untie the lashing (a type of binding) of
UNLATCH	*v* -ED, -ING, -ES to open by lifting the latch (a fastening device)
UNLAY	*v* -LAID, -LAYING, -LAYS to untwist
UNLEAD	*v* -ED, -ING, -S to remove the lead from
UNLEARN	*v* -LEARNED or -LEARNT, -LEARNING, -LEARNS to put out of one's knowledge or memory
UNLEASH	*v* -ED, -ING, -ES to free from a leash
UNLESS	*conj* except on the condition that
UNLET	*adj* not rented
UNLEVEL	*v* -ELED, -ELING, -ELS or -ELLED, -ELLING, -ELS to make uneven
UNLIMBER	*v* -ED, -ING, -S to prepare for action
UNLINK	*v* -ED, -ING, -S to unfasten the links (connecting devices) of

UNLIVE   v -LIVED, -LIVING, -LIVES to live so as to make amends for

UNLOAD   v -ED, -ING, -S to remove the load or cargo from

UNLOADER   n pl. -S one that unloads

UNLOCK   v -ED, -ING, -S to unfasten the lock of

UNLOOSE   v -LOOSED, -LOOSING, -LOOSES to set free

UNLOOSEN   v -ED, -ING, -S to unloose

UNMAKE   v -MADE, -MAKING, -MAKES to destroy

UNMAKER   n pl. -S one that unmakes

UNMAN   v -MANNED, -MANNING, -MANS to deprive of courage

UNMASK   v -ED, -ING, -S to remove a mask from

UNMASKER   n pl. -S one that unmasks

UNMEET   adj improper **UNMEETLY** adv

UNMEW   v -ED, -ING, -S to set free

UNMINGLE   v -GLED, -GLING, -GLES to separate things that are mixed

UNMITER   v -ED, -ING, -S to depose from the rank of bishop

UNMITRE   v -TRED, -TRING, -TRES to unmiter

UNMOLD   v -ED, -ING, -S to remove from a mold

UNMOOR   v -ED, -ING, -S to release from moorings

UNMORAL   adj amoral

UNMUFFLE   v -FLED, -FLING, -FLES to free from something that muffles

UNMUZZLE   v -ZLED, -ZLING, -ZLES to remove a muzzle from

UNNAIL   v -ED, -ING, -S to remove the nails from

UNNERVE   v -NERVED, -NERVING, -NERVES to deprive of courage

UNPACK   v -ED, -ING, -S to remove the contents of

UNPACKER   n pl. -S one that unpacks

UNPAGED   adj having no page numbers

UNPEG   v -PEGGED, -PEGGING, -PEGS to remove the pegs from

UNPEN   v -PENNED or -PENT, -PENNING, -PENS to release from confinement

UNPEOPLE   v -PLED, -PLING, -PLES to remove people from

UNPERSON   n pl. -S one who is removed completely from recognition

UNPICK   v -ED, -ING, -S to remove the stitches from

UNPILE   v -PILED, -PILING, -PILES to take or disentangle from a pile

UNPIN   v -PINNED, -PINNING, -PINS to remove the pins from

UNPLAIT   v -ED, -ING, -S to undo the plaits of

UNPLUG   v -PLUGGED, -PLUGGING, -PLUGS to take a plug out of

UNPUCKER   v -ED, -ING, -S to remove the wrinkles from

UNPUZZLE   v -ZLED, -ZLING, -ZLES to work out the obscured meaning of

UNQUIET   n pl. -S a state of unrest

UNQUOTE   v -QUOTED, -QUOTING, -QUOTES to close a quotation

UNRAVEL   v -ELED, -ELING, -ELS or -ELLED, -ELLING, -ELS to separate the threads of

UNREASON   v -ED, -ING, -S to disrupt the sanity of

UNREEL   v -ED, -ING, -S to unwind from a reel

UNREELER   n pl. -S one that unreels

UNREEVE   v -REEVED or -ROVE, -ROVEN, -REEVING, -REEVES to withdraw a rope from an opening

UNRENT   adj not torn

UNREPAIR   n pl. -S lack of repair

UNREST   n pl. -S a disturbed or uneasy state

UNRIDDLE   v -DLED, -DLING, -DLES to solve

UNRIG   v -RIGGED, -RIGGING, -RIGS to divest of rigging

UNRIP   v -RIPPED, -RIPPING, -RIPS to rip open

UNRIPE   adj -RIPER, -RIPEST not ripe **UNRIPELY** adv

UNROBE   v -ROBED, -ROBING, -ROBES to undress

UNROLL   v -ED, -ING, -S to open something that is rolled up

UNROOF   v -ED, -ING, -S to strip off the roof of

UNROOT   v -ED, -ING, -S to uproot

UNROUND   v -ED, -ING, -S to articulate without rounding the lips

UNROVE   a past tense of unreeve

UNROVEN   a past participle of unreeve

UNRULY   adj -LIER, -LIEST difficult to control

UNSADDLE   v -DLED, -DLING, -DLES to remove the saddle from

UNSAFETY   n pl. -TIES lack of safety

UNSAY   *v* -SAID, -SAYING, -SAYS to retract something said

UNSCREW   *v* -ED, -ING, -S to remove the screws from

UNSEAL   *v* -ED, -ING, -S to remove the seal of

UNSEAM   *v* -ED, -ING, -S to open the seams of

UNSEAT   *v* -ED, -ING, -S to remove from a seat

UNSET   *v* -SET, -SETTING, -SETS to unsettle

UNSETTLE   *v* -TLED, -TLING, -TLES to make unstable

UNSEW   *v* -SEWED, -SEWN, -SEWING, -SEWS to undo the sewing of

UNSEX   *v* -ED, -ING, -ES to deprive of sexual power

UNSHELL   *v* -ED, -ING, -S to remove the shell from

UNSHIFT   *v* -ED, -ING, -S to release the shift key on a typewriter

UNSHIP   *v* -SHIPPED, -SHIPPING, -SHIPS to unload from a ship

UNSICKER   *adj* unreliable

UNSIGHT   *v* -ED, -ING, -S to prevent from seeing

UNSLING   *v* -SLUNG, -SLINGING, -SLINGS to remove from a slung position

UNSNAP   *v* -SNAPPED, -SNAPPING, -SNAPS to undo the snaps of

UNSNARL   *v* -ED, -ING, -S to untangle

UNSOLDER   *v* -ED, -ING, -S to separate

UNSONCY   *adj* unsonsie

UNSONSIE   *adj* unlucky

UNSONSY   *adj* unsonsie

UNSPEAK   *v* -SPOKE, -SPOKEN, -SPEAKING, -SPEAKS to unsay

UNSPHERE   *v* -SPHERED, -SPHERING, -SPHERES to remove from a sphere

UNSTACK   *v* -ED, -ING, -S to remove from a stack

UNSTATE   *v* -STATED, -STATING, -STATES to deprive of status

UNSTEADY   *v* -STEADIED, -STEADYING, -STEADIES to make unsteady

UNSTEEL   *v* -ED, -ING, -S to make soft

UNSTEP   *v* -STEPPED, -STEPPING, -STEPS to remove from a socket

UNSTICK   *v* -STUCK, -STICKING, -STICKS to disjoin

UNSTOP   *v* -STOPPED, -STOPPING, -STOPS to remove a stopper from

UNSTRAP   *v* -STRAPPED, -STRAPPING, -STRAPS to remove a strap from

UNSTRESS   *n* pl. -ES a syllable having relatively weak stress

UNSTRING   *v* -STRUNG, -STRINGING, -STRINGS to remove from a string

UNSWATHE   *v* -SWATHED, -SWATHING, -SWATHES to unbind

UNSWEAR   *v* -SWORE, -SWORN, -SWEARING, -SWEARS to retract something sworn

UNTACK   *v* -ED, -ING, -S to remove a tack from

UNTANGLE   *v* -GLED, -GLING, -GLES to free from tangles

UNTEACH   *v* -TAUGHT, -TEACHING, -TEACHES to cause to unlearn something

UNTETHER   *v* -ED, -ING, -S to free from a tether

UNTHINK   *v* -THOUGHT, -THINKING, -THINKS to dismiss from the mind

UNTHREAD   *v* -ED, -ING, -S to remove the thread from

UNTHRONE   *v* -THRONED, -THRONING, -THRONES to remove from a throne

UNTIDY   *v* -DIED, -DYING, -DIES to make untidy

UNTIE   *v* -TIED, -TYING, -TIES to free from something that ties

UNTIL   *prep* up to the time of

UNTO   *prep* to

UNTOWARD   *adj* unruly

UNTREAD   *v* -TROD, -TRODDEN, -TREADING, -TREADS to retrace

UNTRIM   *v* -TRIMMED, -TRIMMING, -TRIMS to strip of trimming

UNTRUSS   *v* -ED, -ING, -ES to free from a truss

UNTRUTH   *n* pl. -S something that is untrue

UNTUCK   *v* -ED, -ING, -S to release from being tucked up

UNTUNE   *v* -TUNED, -TUNING, -TUNES to put out of tune

UNTWINE   *v* -TWINED, -TWINING, -TWINES to separate the twisted or tangled parts of

UNTWIST   *v* -ED, -ING, -S to untwine

UNTYING	present participle of untie	UPBYE	adv a little farther on
UNVEIL	v -ED, -ING, -S to remove a covering from	UPCAST	v -CAST, -CASTING, -CASTS to cast up
UNVOICE	v -VOICED, -VOICING, -VOICES to deprive of voice or vocal quality	UPCHUCK	v -ED, -ING, -S to vomit
		UPCLIMB	v -ED, -ING, -S to climb up
UNWASHED	n pl. -S an ignorant or underprivileged group	UPCOIL	v -ED, -ING, -S to coil up
		UPCOMING	adj about to happen or appear
UNWEAVE	v -WOVE, -WOVEN, -WEAVING, -WEAVES to undo something woven	UPCURL	v -ED, -ING, -S to curl up
		UPCURVE	v -CURVED, -CURVING, -CURVES to curve upward
UNWEIGHT	v -ED, -ING, -S to reduce the weight of	UPDART	v -ED, -ING, -S to dart up
UNWIND	v -WOUND, -WINDING, -WINDS to reverse the winding of	UPDATE	v -DATED, -DATING, -DATES to bring up to date
UNWINDER	n pl. -S one that unwinds	UPDATER	n pl. -S one that updates
UNWISDOM	n pl. -S lack of wisdom	UPDIVE	v -DIVED or -DOVE, -DIVING, -DIVES to spring upward
UNWISH	v -ED, -ING, -ES to cease to wish for		
UNWIT	v -WITTED, -WITTING, -WITS to make insane	UPDO	n pl. -DOS an upswept hairdo
		UPDRAFT	n pl. -S an upward movement of air
UNWONTED	adj unusual	UPDRY	v -DRIED, -DRYING, -DRIES to dry completely
UNWORTHY	n pl. -THIES an unworthy person		
		UPEND	v -ED, -ING, -S to set or stand on end
UNWOUND	past tense of unwind		
UNWOVE	past tense of unweave	UPFIELD	adv into the part of the field toward which the offensive team is going
UNWOVEN	past participle of unweave		
UNWRAP	v -WRAPPED, -WRAPPING, -WRAPS to remove the wrapping from	UPFLING	v -FLUNG, -FLINGING, -FLINGS to fling up
		UPFLOW	v -ED, -ING, -S to flow up
UNYEANED	adj unborn	UPFOLD	v -ED, -ING, -S to fold up
UNYOKE	v -YOKED, -YOKING, -YOKES to free from a yoke	UPGATHER	v -ED, -ING, -S to gather up
		UPGAZE	v -GAZED, -GAZING, -GAZES to gaze up
UNZIP	v -ZIPPED, -ZIPPING, -ZIPS to open the zipper of		
UP	v UPPED, UPPING, UPS to raise	UPGIRD	v -GIRDED or -GIRT, -GIRDING, -GIRDS to gird completely
UPAS	n pl. -ES an Asian tree	UPGOING	adj going up
UPBEAR	v -BORE, -BORNE, -BEARING, -BEARS to raise aloft	UPGRADE	v -GRADED, -GRADING, -GRADES to raise to a higher grade or standard
UPBEARER	n pl. -S one that upbears		
UPBEAT	n pl. -S an unaccented beat in a musical measure	UPGROW	v -GREW, -GROWN, -GROWING, -GROWS to grow up
UPBIND	v -BOUND, -BINDING, -BINDS to bind completely	UPGROWTH	n pl. -S the process of growing
UPBOIL	v -ED, -ING, -S to boil up	UPHEAP	v -ED, -ING, -S to heap up
UPBORE	past tense of upbear	UPHEAVAL	n pl. -S the act of upheaving
UPBORNE	past participle of upbear	UPHEAVE	v -HEAVED or -HOVE, -HEAVING, -HEAVES to heave up
UPBOUND	past tense of upbind		
UPBRAID	v -ED, -ING, -S to reproach severely	UPHEAVER	n pl. -S one that upheaves
		UPHELD	past tense of uphold
UPBUILD	v -BUILT, -BUILDING, -BUILDS to build up	UPHILL	n pl. -S an upward slope
UPBY	adv upbye	UPHOARD	v -ED, -ING, -S to hoard up

UPHOLD v -HELD, -HOLDING, -HOLDS to hold aloft

UPHOLDER n pl. -S one that upholds

UPHOVE a past tense of upheave

UPHROE n pl. -S euphroe

UPKEEP n pl. -S the cost of maintaining something in good condition

UPLAND n pl. -S the higher land of a region

UPLANDER n pl. -S an inhabitant of an upland

UPLEAP v -LEAPED or -LEAPT, -LEAPING, -LEAPS to leap up

UPLIFT v -ED, -ING, -S to lift up

UPLIFTER n pl. -S one that uplifts

UPLIGHT v -LIGHTED or -LIT, -LIGHTING, -LIGHTS to light to a higher degree

UPMOST adj highest

UPO prep upon

UPON prep on

UPPED past tense of up

UPPER n pl. -S the part of a boot or shoe above the sole

UPPERCUT v -CUT, -CUTTING, -CUTS to strike an upward blow

UPPILE v -PILED, -PILING, -PILES to pile up

UPPING n pl. -S the process of marking young swans for identification purposes

UPPISH adj uppity **UPPISHLY** adv

UPPITY adj tending to be snobbish and arrogant

UPPROP v -PROPPED, -PROPPING, -PROPS to prop up

UPRAISE v -RAISED, -RAISING, -RAISES to raise up

UPRAISER n pl. -S one that upraises

UPREACH v -ED, -ING, -ES to reach up

UPREAR v -ED, -ING, -S to upraise

UPRIGHT v -ED, -ING, -S to make vertical

UPRISE v -ROSE, -RISEN, -RISING, -RISES to rise up

UPRISER n pl. -S one that uprises

UPRISING n pl. -S a revolt

UPRIVER n pl. -S an area lying toward the source of a river

UPROAR n pl. -S a state of noisy excitement and confusion

UPROOT v -ED, -ING, -S to pull up by the roots

UPROOTAL n pl. -S the act of uprooting

UPROOTER n pl. -S one that uproots

UPROSE past tense of uprise

UPROUSE v -ROUSED, -ROUSING, -ROUSES to rouse up

UPRUSH v -ED, -ING, -ES to rush up

UPSEND v -SENT, -SENDING, -SENDS to send upward

UPSET v -SET, -SETTING, -SETS to overturn

UPSETTER n pl. -S one that upsets

UPSHIFT v -ED, -ING, -S to shift an automotive vehicle into a higher gear

UPSHOOT v -SHOT, -SHOOTING, -SHOOTS to shoot upward

UPSHOT n pl. -S the final result

UPSIDE n pl. -S the upper side

UPSILON n pl. -S a Greek letter

UPSOAR v -ED, -ING, -S to soar upward

UPSPRING v -SPRANG or -SPRUNG, -SPRINGING, -SPRINGS to spring up

UPSTAGE v -STAGED, -STAGING, -STAGES to outdo theatrically

UPSTAIR adj pertaining to an upper floor

UPSTAIRS adv up the stairs

UPSTAND v -STOOD, -STANDING, -STANDS to stand up on one's feet

UPSTARE v -STARED, -STARING, -STARES to stare upward

UPSTART v -ED, -ING, -S to spring up suddenly

UPSTATE n pl. -S the northern region of a state

UPSTATER n pl. -S an inhabitant of an upstate region

UPSTEP v -STEPPED, -STEPPING, -STEPS to step up

UPSTIR v -STIRRED, -STIRRING, -STIRS to stir up

UPSTOOD past tense of upstand

UPSTREAM adv toward the source of a stream

UPSTROKE n pl. -S an upward stroke

UPSURGE v -SURGED, -SURGING, -SURGES to surge up

UPSWEEP v -SWEPT, -SWEEPING, -SWEEPS to sweep upward

UPSWELL v -SWELLED, -SWOLLEN, -SWELLING, -SWELLS, to swell up

UPSWING v -SWUNG, -SWINGING, -SWINGS to swing upward

UPTAKE n pl. -S an upward ventilating shaft

UPTEAR v -TORE, -TORN, -TEARING, -TEARS to tear out by the roots

UPTHROW v -THREW, -THROWN, -THROWING, -THROWS to throw upward

UPTHRUST v -THRUST, -THRUSTING, -THRUSTS to thrust up

UPTIGHT adj nervous

UPTILT v -ED, -ING, -S to tilt upward

UPTIME n pl. -S the time during which machinery is functioning

UPTORE past tense of uptear

UPTORN past participle of uptear

UPTOSS v -ED, -ING, -ES to toss upward

UPTOWN n pl. -S the upper part of a city

UPTOWNER n pl. -S one that lives uptown

UPTREND n pl. -S a tendency upward or toward growth

UPTURN v -ED, -ING, -S to turn up or over

UPWAFT v -ED, -ING, -S to waft upward

UPWARD adv toward a higher place or position **UPWARDLY** adv

UPWARDS adv upward

UPWELL v -ED, -ING, -S to well up

UPWIND n pl. -S a wind that blows against one's course

URACIL n pl. -S a chemical compound

URAEI a pl. of uraeus

URAEMIA n pl. -S uremia **URAEMIC** adj

URAEUS n pl. URAEI or URAEUSES the figure of the sacred serpent on the headdress of ancient Egyptian rulers

URALITE n pl. -S a mineral **URALITIC** adj

URANIC adj pertaining to uranium

URANIDE n pl. -S uranium

URANISM n pl. -S homosexuality

URANITE n pl. -S a mineral **URANITIC** adj

URANIUM n pl. -S a radioactive element

URANOUS adj pertaining to uranium

URANYL n pl. -S a bivalent radical **URANYLIC** adj

URARE n pl. -S curare

URARI n pl. -S curare

URASE n pl. -S urease

URATE n pl. -S a chemical salt **URATIC** adj

URBAN adj pertaining to a city

URBANE adj -BANER, -BANEST refined and elegant **URBANELY** adv

URBANISE v -ISED, -ISING, -ISES to urbanize

URBANISM n pl. -S the life-style of city dwellers

URBANIST n pl. -S a specialist in city planning

URBANITE n pl. -S one who lives in a city

URBANITY n pl. -TIES the quality of being urbane

URBANIZE v -IZED, -IZING, -IZES to cause to take on urban characteristics

URCHIN n pl. -S a mischievous boy

URD n pl. -S an annual bean grown in India

UREA n pl. -S a chemical compound **UREAL** adj

UREASE n pl. -S an enzyme

UREDIA pl. of uredium

UREDIAL adj pertaining to a uredium

UREDINIA n/pl uredia

UREDIUM n pl. -DIA a spore-producing organ of certain fungi

UREDO n pl. -DOS a skin irritation

UREIC adj pertaining to urea

UREIDE n pl. -S a chemical compound

UREMIA n pl. -S an abnormal condition of the blood **UREMIC** adj

URETER n pl. -S the duct that conveys urine from the kidney to the bladder **URETERAL, URETERIC** adj

URETHAN n pl. -S urethane

URETHANE n pl. -S a chemical compound

URETHRA n pl. -THRAE or -THRAS the duct through which urine is discharged from the bladder **URETHRAL** adj

URETIC adj pertaining to urine

URGE v URGED, URGING, URGES to force forward

URGENCY n pl. -CIES the quality of being urgent

URGENT adj requiring immediate attention **URGENTLY** adv

URGER n pl. -S one that urges

URGING present participle of urge

URGINGLY adv in an urging manner

URIC adj pertaining to urine

URIDINE n pl. -S a chemical compound

URINAL n pl. -S a fixture used for urinating

URINARY n pl. -NARIES a urinal

URINATE v -NATED, -NATING, -NATES to discharge urine

URINE n pl. -S a liquid containing body wastes

URINEMIA n pl. -S uremia **URINEMIC** adj

URINOSE adj pertaining to urine

URINOUS adj pertaining to urine

URN n pl. -S a type of vase **URNLIKE** adj

UROCHORD n pl. -S a rodlike structure in certain lower vertebrates

URODELE n pl. -S a type of amphibian

UROLITH n pl. -S a concretion in the urinary tract

UROLOGY n pl. -GIES the branch of medicine dealing with the urinary tract **UROLOGIC** adj

UROPOD n pl. -S an abdominal limb of an arthropod **UROPODAL** adj

UROSCOPY n pl. -PIES analysis of the urine as a means of diagnosis

UROSTYLE n pl. -S a part of the vertebral column of frogs and toads

URSA n pl. -SAE a female bear

URSIFORM adj having the form of a bear

URSINE adj pertaining to a bear

URTICANT n pl. -S an urticating substance

URTICATE v -CATED, -CATING, -CATES to cause itching or stinging

URUS n pl. -ES an extinct European ox

URUSHIOL n pl. -S a toxic liquid

US pron the objective case of the pronoun we

USABLE adj capable of being used **USABLY** adv

USAGE n pl. -S a firmly established and generally accepted practice or procedure

USANCE n pl. -S usage

USAUNCE n pl. -S usance

USE v USED, USING, USES to put into service

USEABLE adj usable **USEABLY** adv

USEFUL adj serving a purpose **USEFULLY** adv

USELESS adj serving no purpose

USER n pl. -S one that uses

USHER v -ED, -ING, -S to conduct to a place

USING present participle of use

USNEA n pl. -S any of a genus of lichens

USQUABAE n pl. -S usquebae

USQUE n pl. -S usquebae

USQUEBAE n pl. -S whiskey

USTULATE adj scorched

USUAL n pl. -S something that is usual (ordinary)

USUALLY adv ordinarily

USUFRUCT n pl. -S the legal right to use another's property so long as it is not damaged or altered

USURER n pl. -S one that practices usury

USURIES pl. of usury

USURIOUS adj practicing usury

USURP v -ED, -ING, -S to seize and hold without legal authority

USURPER n pl. -S one that usurps

USURY n pl. -RIES the lending of money at an exorbitant interest rate

UT n pl. -S the musical tone C in the French solmization system now replaced by do

UTA n pl. -S any of a genus of large lizards

UTENSIL n pl. -S a useful implement

UTERUS n pl. UTERI or UTERUSES an organ of female mammals **UTERINE** adj

UTILE adj useful

UTILIDOR n pl. -S an insulated system of pipes for use in arctic regions

UTILISE v -LISED, -LISING, -LISES to utilize

UTILISER n pl. -S utilizer

UTILITY n pl. -TIES the quality of being useful

UTILIZE v -LIZED, -LIZING, -LIZES to make use of

UTILIZER n pl. -S one that utilizes

UTMOST n pl. -S the greatest degree or amount

UTOPIA n pl. -S a place of ideal perfection

UTOPIAN n pl. -S one who believes in the perfectibility of human society

UTOPISM n pl. -S the body of ideals or principles of a utopian

UTOPIST n pl. -S a utopian

UTRICLE n pl. -S a saclike cavity in the inner ear

UTRICULI n/pl utricles

UTTER v -ED, -ING, -S to give audible expression to

UTTERER	*n* pl. -S one that utters	**UVULAR**	*n* pl. -S a uvularly produced sound
UTTERLY	*adv* totally		
UVEA	*n* pl. -S a layer of the eye **UVEAL** *adj*	**UVULARLY**	*adv* with the use of the uvula
UVEITIS	*n* pl. -ITISES inflammation of the uvea **UVEITIC** *adj*	**UVULITIS**	*n* pl. -TISES inflammation of the uvula
UVEOUS	*adj* pertaining to the uvea	**UXORIAL**	*adj* pertaining to a wife
UVULA	*n* pl. -LAE or -LAS the pendent, fleshy portion of the soft palate	**UXORIOUS**	*adj* excessively submissive or devoted to one's wife

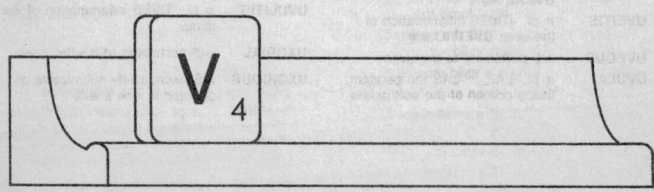

VACANCY	n pl. -CIES the quality or state of being vacant	**VAGRANCY**	n pl. -CIES the state of being a vagrant
VACANT	adj empty **VACANTLY** adv	**VAGRANT**	n pl. -S a wanderer with no apparent means of support
VACATE	v -CATED, -CATING, -CATES to make vacant	**VAGROM**	adj wandering
VACATION	v -ED, -ING, -S to take a vacation (a period of time devoted to rest and relaxation)	**VAGUE**	adj VAGUER, VAGUEST not clearly expressed or understood **VAGUELY** adv
VACCINA	n pl. -S vaccinia	**VAGUS**	n pl. -GI a cranial nerve
VACCINE	n pl. -S a preparation given to produce immunity to a specific disease **VACCINAL** adj	**VAHINE**	n pl. -S wahine
		VAIL	v -ED, -ING, -S to lower
VACCINIA	n pl. -S cowpox	**VAIN**	adj VAINER, VAINEST filled with undue admiration for oneself **VAINLY** adv
VACUA	a pl. of vacuum		
VACUITY	n pl. -ITIES an empty space	**VAINNESS**	n pl. -ES the quality or state of being vain
VACUOLE	n pl. -S a small cavity in organic tissue **VACUOLAR** adj	**VAIR**	n pl. -S a fur used for lining and trimming medieval garments
VACUOUS	adj empty		
VACUUM	n pl. VACUUMS or VACUA a space entirely devoid of matter	**VAKEEL**	n pl. -S a native lawyer in India
		VAKIL	n pl. -S vakeel
VACUUM	v -ED, -ING, -S to use a device that cleans by suction	**VALANCE**	v -LANCED, -LANCING, -LANCES to furnish with a short drapery
VADOSE	adj located above the permanent groundwater level		
		VALE	n pl. -S a valley
VAGABOND	v -ED, -ING, -S to live like a vagabond (a vagrant)	**VALENCE**	n pl. -S the degree of combining power of an element or radical
VAGAL	adj pertaining to the vagus nerve **VAGALLY** adv		
		VALENCIA	n pl. -S a woven fabric
VAGARY	n pl. -RIES a whim	**VALENCY**	n pl. -CIES valence
VAGI	pl. of vagus	**VALERATE**	n pl. -S a chemical salt
VAGILE	adj free to move about	**VALERIAN**	n pl. -S a perennial herb **VALERIC** adj
VAGILITY	n pl. -TIES freedom of movement		
		VALET	v -ED, -ING, -S to act as a personal servant to
VAGINA	n pl. -NAE or -NAS the passage leading from the uterus to the vulva **VAGINAL** adj	**VALGUS**	n pl. -ES the position of a joint that is abnormally turned outward **VALGOID** adj
VAGINATE	adj enclosed in a sheath		
VAGOTOMY	n pl. -MIES surgical division of the vagus nerve	**VALIANCE**	n pl. -S valor
		VALIANCY	n pl. -CIES valor

VALIANT   *n pl.* -S a courageous person

VALID   *adj* based on evidence that can be supported

VALIDATE   *v* -DATED, -DATING, -DATES to give legal force to

VALIDITY   *n pl.* -TIES the quality or state of being valid

VALIDLY   *adv* in a valid manner

VALINE   *n pl.* -S an amino acid

VALISE   *n pl.* -S a small piece of hand luggage

VALKYR   *n pl.* -S valkyrie

VALKYRIE   *n pl.* -S a maiden in Norse mythology

VALLATE   *adj* bordered by a raised edge

VALLEY   *n pl.* -LEYS a depression of the earth's surface

VALONIA   *n pl.* -S a substance obtained from dried acorn cups and used in tanning and dyeing

VALOR   *n pl.* -S courage

VALORISE   *v* -ISED, -ISING, -ISES to valorize

VALORIZE   *v* -IZED, -IZING, -IZES to establish and maintain the price of by governmental action

VALOROUS   *adj* courageous

VALOUR   *n pl.* -S valor

VALSE   *n pl.* -S a concert waltz

VALUABLE   *n pl.* -S a possession of value

VALUABLY   *adv* with value

VALUATE   *v* -ATED, -ATING, -ATES to appraise

VALUATOR   *n pl.* -S one that valuates

VALUE   *v* -UED, -UING, -UES to estimate the value (the quality that renders a thing useful or desirable) of

VALUER   *n pl.* -S one that values

VALUTA   *n pl.* -S the agreed or exchange value of a currency

VALVAL   *adj* resembling or pertaining to a valve

VALVAR   *adj* valval

VALVATE   *adj* having valves or parts resembling valves

VALVE   *v* VALVED, VALVING, VALVES to provide with a valve (a device for controlling the flow of a liquid or gas)

VALVELET   *n pl.* -S a small valve

VALVULA   *n pl.* -LAE valvule

VALVULAR   *adj* pertaining to a valve

VALVULE   *n pl.* -S a small valve

VAMBRACE   *n pl.* -S a piece of armor for the forearm

VAMOOSE   *v* -MOOSED, -MOOSING, -MOOSES to leave quickly

VAMOSE   *v* -MOSED, -MOSING, -MOSES to vamoose

VAMP   *v* -ED, -ING, -S to repair or patch

VAMPER   *n pl.* -S one that vamps

VAMPIRE   *n pl.* -S a reanimated corpse believed to feed on sleeping persons' blood **VAMPIRIC** *adj*

VAMPISH   *adj* seductive

VAN   *n pl.* -S a large motor vehicle

VANADATE   *n pl.* -S a chemical salt

VANADIUM   *n pl.* -S a metallic element **VANADIC, VANADOUS** *adj*

VANDA   *n pl.* -S a tropical orchid

VANDAL   *n pl.* -S one who willfully destroys or defaces property **VANDALIC** *adj*

VANDYKE   *n pl.* -S a short, pointed beard **VANDYKED** *adj*

VANE   *n pl.* -S a device for showing the direction of the wind **VANED** *adj*

VANG   *n pl.* -S a rope on a ship

VANGUARD   *n pl.* -S the forefront of a movement

VANILLA   *n pl.* -S a flavoring extract **VANILLIC** *adj*

VANILLIN   *n pl.* -S a chemical compound used in flavoring

VANISH   *v* -ED, -ING, -ES to disappear

VANISHER   *n pl.* -S one that vanishes

VANITY   *n pl.* -TIES inflated pride in oneself **VANITIED** *adj*

VANMAN   *n pl.* -MEN a person who drives a van

VANQUISH   *v* -ED, -ING, -ES to defeat in battle

VANTAGE   *n pl.* -S superiority over a competitor

VANWARD   *adv* toward the front

VAPID   *adj* insipid **VAPIDLY** *adv*

VAPIDITY   *n pl.* -TIES the quality or state of being vapid

VAPOR   *v* -ED, -ING, -S to emit vapor (visible floating moisture)

VAPORER   *n pl.* -S one that vapors

VAPORING   *n pl.* -S boastful talk

VAPORISE   *v* -ISED, -ISING, -ISES to vaporize

VAPORISH   *adj* resembling vapor

VAPORIZE *v* -IZED, -IZING, -IZES to convert into vapor

VAPOROUS *adj* vaporish

VAPORY *adj* vaporish

VAPOUR *v* -ED, -ING, -S to vapor

VAPOURER *n pl.* -S vaporer

VAPOURY *adj* vapory

VAQUERO *n pl.* -ROS a cowboy

VARA *n pl.* -S a Spanish unit of length

VARIA *n/pl* a collection of various literary works

VARIABLE *n pl.* -S something that varies

VARIABLY *adv* in a varying manner

VARIANCE *n pl.* -S a license to perform an act contrary to the usual rule

VARIANT *n pl.* -S a variable

VARIATE *v* -ATED, -ATING, -ATES to vary

VARICES pl. of varix

VARICOSE *adj* abnormally swollen or dilated

VARIED past tense of vary

VARIEDLY *adv* in a varied manner

VARIER *n pl.* -S one that varies

VARIES present 3d person sing. of vary

VARIETY *n pl.* -ETIES something differing from others of the same general kind **VARIETAL** *adj*

VARIFORM *adj* having various forms

VARIOLA *n pl.* -S smallpox **VARIOLAR** *adj*

VARIOLE *n pl.* -S a foveola

VARIORUM *n pl.* -S an edition containing various versions of a text

VARIOUS *adj* of diverse kinds

VARISTOR *n pl.* -S a type of electrical resistor

VARIX *n pl.* VARICES a varicose vein

VARLET *n pl.* -S a knave

VARLETRY *n pl.* -RIES a group of common people

VARMENT *n pl.* -S varmint

VARMINT *n pl.* -S an animal considered to be a pest

VARNA *n pl.* -S any of the four main Hindu social classes

VARNISH *v* -ED, -ING, -ES to give a glossy appearance to

VARNISHY *adj* glossy

VARSITY *n pl.* -TIES the principal team representing a university, college, or school in any activity

VARUS *n pl.* -ES a malformation of a bone or joint

VARVE *n pl.* -S a deposit of sedimentary material **VARVED** *adj*

VARY *v* VARIED, VARYING, VARIES to become or make different

VAS *n pl.* VASA an anatomical duct **VASAL** *adj*

VASCULAR *adj* pertaining to ducts that convey body liquids

VASCULUM *n pl.* -LA or -LUMS a box used to hold plant specimens

VASE *n pl.* -S a rounded, decorative container **VASELIKE** *adj*

VASIFORM *adj* having the form of a vase

VASSAL *n pl.* -S a person granted the use of land by a feudal lord in return for homage and allegiance

VAST *adj* VASTER, VASTEST of great extent or size

VAST *n pl.* -S a vast space

VASTIER comparative of vasty

VASTIEST superlative of vasty

VASTITY *n pl.* -TIES vastness

VASTLY *adv* to a vast extent or degree

VASTNESS *n pl.* -ES the quality or state of being vast

VASTY *adj* VASTIER, VASTIEST vast

VAT *v* VATTED, VATTING, VATS to put into a vat (a large container for holding liquids)

VATFUL *n pl.* -S as much as a vat will hold

VATIC *adj* pertaining to a prophet

VATICAL *adj* vatic

VATICIDE *n pl.* -S the killing of a prophet

VATTED past tense of vat

VATTING present participle of vat

VAU *n pl.* -S vav

VAULT *v* -ED, -ING, -S to provide with a vault (an arched ceiling)

VAULTER *n pl.* -S one that leaps

VAULTING *n pl.* -S the structure forming a vault

VAULTY *adj* VAULTIER, VAULTIEST resembling a vault

VAUNT *v* -ED, -ING, -S to brag

VAUNTER *n pl.* -S one that vaunts

VAUNTFUL *adj* boastful

VAUNTIE *adj* boastful

VAUNTY *adj* vauntie

VAV *n pl.* -S a Hebrew letter

VAVASOR *n pl.* -S a high-ranking vassal

VAVASOUR *n pl.* -S vavasor

VAVASSOR *n pl.* -S vavasor

VAW *n pl.* -S vav

VAWARD *n pl.* -S the foremost part

VAWNTIE *adj* vaunty

VEAL *v* -ED, -ING, -S to kill and prepare a calf for food

VEALER *n pl.* -S a calf raised for food

VEALY *adj* VEALIER, VEALIEST immature

VECTOR *v* -ED, -ING, -S to guide in flight by means of radioed directions

VEDALIA *n pl.* -S an Australian ladybug

VEDETTE *n pl.* -S a small boat used for scouting

VEE *n pl.* -S the letter V

VEENA *n pl.* -S vina

VEEP *n pl.* -S a vice-president

VEEPEE *n pl.* -S veep

VEER *v* -ED, -ING, -S to change direction

VEERY *n pl.* -RIES a songbird

VEG *n pl.* VEG a vegetable

VEGAN *n pl.* -S one that eats only plant products

VEGANISM *n pl.* -S the practice of eating only plant products

VEGETAL *adj* pertaining to plants

VEGETANT *adj* characteristic of plant life

VEGETATE *v* -TATED, -TATING, -TATES to grow in the manner of a plant

VEGETE *adj* healthy

VEGETIST *n pl.* -S one that eats only plant products

VEGETIVE *adj* growing or capable of growing

VEHEMENT *adj* ardent

VEHICLE *n pl.* -S a device used as a means of conveyance

VEIL *v* -ED, -ING, -S to provide with a veil (a piece of sheer fabric worn over the face)

VEILEDLY *adv* in a disguised manner

VEILER *n pl.* -S one that veils

VEILING *n pl.* -S a veil

VEILLIKE *adj* resembling a veil

VEIN *v* -ED, -ING, -S to fill with veins (tubular blood vessels)

VEINAL *adj* of or pertaining to the veins

VEINER *n pl.* -S a tool used in wood carving

VEINIER comparative of veiny

VEINIEST superlative of veiny

VEINING *n pl.* -S a network of veins

VEINLESS *adj* having no veins

VEINLET *n pl.* -S a small vein

VEINLIKE *adj* resembling a vein

VEINULE *n pl.* -S venule

VEINULET *n pl.* -S venule

VEINY *adj* VEINIER, VEINIEST full of veins

VELA pl. of velum

VELAMEN *n pl.* -MINA a velum

VELAR *n pl.* -S a kind of speech sound

VELARIUM *n pl.* -IA an awning over an ancient Roman theater

VELARIZE *v* -IZED, -IZING, -IZES to pronounce with the back of the tongue touching the soft palate

VELATE *adj* having a velum

VELD *n pl.* -S veldt

VELDT *n pl.* -S a grassland of southern Africa

VELIGER *n pl.* -S a larval stage of certain mollusks

VELITES *n/pl* foot soldiers of ancient Rome

VELLEITY *n pl.* -ITIES a very low degree of desire

VELLUM *n pl.* -S a fine parchment

VELOCE *adv* rapidly — used as a musical direction

VELOCITY *n pl.* -TIES rapidity of motion

VELOUR *n pl.* -S a fabric resembling velvet

VELOUTE *n pl.* -S a type of sauce

VELUM *n pl.* -LA a thin membranous covering or partition

VELURE *v* -LURED, -LURING, -LURES to smooth with a velvet or silk pad, as a hat

VELVERET *n pl.* -S a fabric resembling velvet

VELVET *n pl.* -S a soft, smooth fabric VELVETED, VELVETY *adj*

VENA *n pl.* -NAE a vein

VENAL *adj* open to bribery VENALLY *adv*

VENALITY *n pl.* -TIES the quality or state of being venal

VENATIC *adj* pertaining to hunting

VENATION *n* pl. -S an arrangement of veins

VEND *v* -ED, -ING, -S to sell
VENDABLE *adj*

VENDACE *n* pl. -S a European fish

VENDEE *n* pl. -S a buyer

VENDER *n* pl. -S vendor

VENDETTA *n* pl. -S a feud between two families

VENDIBLE *n* pl. -S a salable article

VENDIBLY *adv* salably

VENDOR *n* pl. -S a seller

VENDUE *n* pl. -S a public sale

VENEER *v* -ED, -ING, -S to overlay with thin layers of material

VENEERER *n* pl. -S one that veneers

VENENATE *v* -NATED, -NATING, -NATES to poison

VENENOSE *adj* poisonous

VENERATE *v* -ATED, -ATING, -ATES to revere

VENEREAL *adj* involving the genital organs

VENERY *n* pl. -ERIES sexual intercourse

VENETIAN *n* pl. -S a flexible window screen

VENGE *v* VENGED, VENGING, VENGES to avenge

VENGEFUL *adj* seeking to avenge

VENIAL *adj* easily excused or forgiven
VENIALLY *adv*

VENIN *n* pl. -S a toxin found in snake venom

VENINE *n* pl. -S venin

VENIRE *n* pl. -S a type of judicial writ

VENISON *n* pl. -S the edible flesh of a deer

VENOM *v* -ED, -ING, -S to inject with venom (a poisonous secretion of certain animals)

VENOMER *n* pl. -S one that venoms

VENOMOUS *adj* poisonous

VENOSE *adj* venous

VENOSITY *n* pl. -TIES the quality of state of being venous

VENOUS *adj* full of veins **VENOUSLY** *adv*

VENT *v* -ED, -ING, -S to provide with a vent (an opening for the escape of gas or liquid)

VENTAGE *n* pl. -S a small opening

VENTAIL *n* pl. -S the adjustable front of a medieval helmet

VENTER *n* pl. -S the abdomen

VENTLESS *adj* having no vent

VENTRAL *n* pl. -S a fin located on the underside of a fish

VENTURE *v* -TURED, -TURING, -TURES to risk

VENTURER *n* pl. -S one that ventures

VENTURI *n* pl. -S a device for measuring the flow of a fluid

VENTURING present participle of venture

VENUE *n* pl. -S the locale of an event

VENULE *n* pl. -S a small vein **VENULAR**, **VENULOSE**, **VENULOUS** *adj*

VERA *adj* very

VERACITY *n* pl. -TIES conformity to truth

VERANDA *n* pl. -S a type of porch

VERANDAH *n* pl. -S veranda

VERATRIA *n* pl. -S veratrin

VERATRIN *n* pl. -S a poisonous mixture of alkaloids

VERATRUM *n* pl. -S a poisonous herb

VERB *n* pl. -S a word used to express an act, occurrence, or mode of being

VERBAL *n* pl. -S a word derived from a verb

VERBALLY *adv* in a spoken manner

VERBATIM *adv* word for word

VERBENA *n* pl. -S a flowering plant

VERBIAGE *n* pl. -S an excess of words

VERBID *n* pl. -S a verbal

VERBIFY *v* -FIED, -FYING, -FIES to use as a verb

VERBILE *n* pl. -S one whose mental imagery consists of words

VERBLESS *adj* lacking a verb

VERBOSE *adj* wordy

VERBOTEN *adj* forbidden

VERDANCY *n* pl. -CIES the quality or state of being verdant

VERDANT *adj* green with vegetation

VERDERER *n* pl. -S an officer in charge of the royal forests of England

VERDEROR *n* pl. -S verderer

VERDICT *n* pl. -S the decision of a jury at the end of a legal proceeding

VERDIN *n* pl. -S a small bird

VERDITER *n* pl. -S a blue or green pigment

VERDURE *n* pl. -S green vegetation **VERDURED** *adj*

VERECUND *adj* shy

VERGE *v* VERGED, VERGING, VERGES to come near

VERGENCE *n pl.* -S a movement of one eye in relation to the other

VERGER *n pl.* -S a church official

VERGING present participle of verge

VERGLAS *n pl.* -ES a thin coating of ice on rock

VERIDIC *adj* truthful

VERIER comparative of very

VERIEST superlative of very

VERIFIER *n pl.* -S one that verifies

VERIFY *v* -FIED, -FYING, -FIES to prove to be true

VERILY *adv* in truth

VERISM *n pl.* -S realism in art or literature

VERISMO *n pl.* -MOS verism

VERIST *n pl.* -S one who practices verism **VERISTIC** *adj*

VERITAS *n pl.* -TATES truth

VERITY *n pl.* -TIES truth

VERJUICE *n pl.* -S the juice of sour or unripe fruit

VERMEIL *n pl.* -S a red color

VERMES *pl.* of vermis

VERMIAN *adj* pertaining to worms

VERMIN *n pl.* VERMIN small, common, harmful, or objectionable animals

VERMIS *n pl.* -MES a part of the brain

VERMOULU *adj* eaten by worms

VERMOUTH *n pl.* -S a liqueur

VERMUTH *n pl.* -S vermouth

VERNACLE *n pl.* -S vernicle

VERNAL *adj* pertaining to spring **VERNALLY** *adv*

VERNICLE *n pl.* -S veronica

VERNIER *n pl.* -S an auxiliary scale used with a main scale to obtain fine measurements

VERNIX *n pl.* -ES a fatty substance covering the skin of a fetus

VERONICA *n pl.* -S a handkerchief bearing the image of Christ's face

VERRUCA *n pl.* -CAE a wart

VERSAL *adj* entire

VERSANT *n pl.* -S the slope of a mountain or mountain chain

VERSE *v* VERSED, VERSING, VERSES to versify

VERSEMAN *n pl.* -MEN one who versifies

VERSER *n pl.* -S a verseman

VERSET *n pl.* -S a versicle

VERSICLE *n pl.* -S a short line of metrical writing

VERSIFY *v* -FIED, -FYING, -FIES to change from prose into metrical form

VERSINE *n pl.* -S a trigonometric function of an angle

VERSING present participle of verse

VERSION *n pl.* -S an account or description from a particular point of view

VERSO *n pl.* -SOS a left-hand page of a book

VERST *n pl.* -S a Russian measure of distance

VERSTE *n pl.* -S verst

VERSUS *prep* against

VERT *n pl.* -S the heraldic color green

VERTEBRA *n pl.* -BRAE or -BRAS any of the bones or segments forming the spinal column

VERTEX *n pl.* -TEXES or -TICES the highest point of something

VERTICAL *n pl.* -S something that is vertical (extending up and down)

VERTICIL *n pl.* -S a circular arrangement, as of flowers or leaves, about a point on an axis

VERTIGO *n pl.* -GOES, -GOS, or -GINES a disordered state in which the individual or his surroundings seem to whirl dizzily

VERTU *n pl.* -S virtu

VERVAIN *n pl.* -S a flowering plant

VERVE *n pl.* -S vivacity

VERVET *n pl.* -S an African monkey

VERY *adj* VERIER, VERIEST absolute

VESICA *n pl.* -CAE a bladder **VESICAL** *adj*

VESICANT *n pl.* -S a chemical warfare agent that induces blistering

VESICATE *v* -CATED, -CATING, -CATES to blister

VESICLE *n pl.* -S a small bladder

VESICULA *n pl.* -LAE a vesicle

VESPER *n pl.* -S an evening service, prayer, or song

VESPERAL *n pl.* -S a covering for an altar cloth

VESPIARY *n pl.* -ARIES a nest of wasps

VESPID *n pl.* -S a wasp

VESPINE *adj* pertaining to wasps

VESSEL *n pl.* -S a craft for traveling on water **VESSELED** *adj*

VEST   v -ED, -ING, -S to place in the control of

VESTA   n pl. -S a short friction match

VESTAL   n pl. -S a chaste woman

VESTALLY   adv chastely

VESTEE   n pl. -S a garment worn under a woman's jacket or blouse

VESTIARY   n pl. -ARIES a dressing room

VESTIGE   n pl. -S a visible sign of something that is no longer in existence

VESTIGIA   n/pl vestiges

VESTING   n pl. -S the right of an employee to share in and withdraw from a pension fund without penalty

VESTLESS   adj being without a vest

VESTLIKE   adj resembling a vest (a short, sleeveless garment)

VESTMENT   n pl. -S one of the ceremonial garments of the clergy

VESTRY   n pl. -TRIES a room in which vestments are kept **VESTRAL** adj

VESTURAL   adj pertaining to clothing

VESTURE   v -TURED, -TURING, -TURES to clothe

VESUVIAN   n pl. -S a mineral

VET   v VETTED, VETTING, VETS to treat animals medically

VETCH   n pl. -ES a climbing plant

VETERAN   n pl. -S a former member of the armed forces

VETIVER   n pl. -S an Asian grass

VETO   v -ED, -ING, -ES to forbid or prevent authoritatively

VETOER   n pl. -S one that vetoes

VETTED   past tense of vet

VETTING   present participle of vet

VEX   v VEXED or VEXT, VEXING, VEXES to annoy

VEXATION   n pl. -S a cause of trouble

VEXEDLY   adv in a vexed manner

VEXER   n pl. -S one that vexes

VEXIL   n pl. -S vexillum

VEXILLUM   n pl. -LA the web or vane of a feather **VEXILLAR** adj

VEXINGLY   adv in a vexing manner

VEXT   a past tense of vex

VIA   prep by way of

VIABLE   adj capable of living **VIABLY** adv

VIADUCT   n pl. -S a type of bridge

VIAL   v VIALED, VIALING, VIALS or VIALLED, VIALLING, VIALS to put in a vial (a small container for liquids)

VIAND   n pl. -S an article of food

VIATIC   adj pertaining to traveling

VIATICAL   adj viatic

VIATICUM   n pl. -CA or -CUMS an allowance for traveling expenses

VIATOR   n pl. -ES or -S a traveler

VIBES   n/pl a percussion instrument

VIBIST   n pl. -S one who plays the vibes

VIBRANCE   n pl. -S vibrancy

VIBRANCY   n pl. -CIES the quality or state of being vibrant

VIBRANT   n pl. -S a sonant

VIBRATE   v -BRATED, -BRATING, -BRATES to move back and forth rapidly

VIBRATO   n pl. -TOS a tremulous or pulsating musical effect

VIBRATOR   n pl. -S something that vibrates

VIBRIO   n pl. -RIOS any of a genus of bacteria shaped like a comma **VIBRIOID** adj

VIBRION   n pl. -S vibrio

VIBRISSA   n pl. -SAE one of the stiff hairs growing about the mouth of certain mammals

VIBURNUM   n pl. -S a flowering shrub

VICAR   n pl. -S a church official

VICARAGE   n pl. -S the office of a vicar

VICARATE   n pl. -S vicarage

VICARIAL   adj pertaining to a vicar

VICARLY   adj vicarial

VICE   v VICED, VICING, VICES to vise

VICELESS   adj having no immoral habits

VICENARY   adj pertaining to the number twenty

VICEROY   n pl. -ROYS one who rules as the representative of a sovereign

VICHY   n pl. -CHIES a type of mineral water

VICINAGE   n pl. -S vicinity

VICINAL   adj nearby

VICING   present participle of vice

VICINITY   n pl. -TIES the region near or about a place

VICIOUS   adj dangerously aggressive

VICOMTE   n pl. -S a French nobleman

VICTIM n pl. -S one who suffers from a destructive or injurious action

VICTOR n pl. -S one who defeats an adversary

VICTORIA n pl. -S a light carriage

VICTORY n pl. -RIES a successful outcome in a contest or struggle

VICTRESS n pl. -ES a female victor

VICTUAL v -UALED, -UALING, -UALS or -UALLED, -UALLING, -UALS to provide with food

VICUGNA n pl. -S vicuna

VICUNA n pl. -S a ruminant mammal

VIDE v see — used to direct a reader to another item; VIDE is the only form of this verb; it cannot be conjugated

VIDEO n pl. -EOS television

VIDETTE n pl. -S vedette

VIDICON n pl. -S a type of television camera tube

VIDUITY n pl. -ITIES the quality or state of being a widow

VIE v VIED, VYING, VIES to strive for superiority

VIER n pl. -S one that vies

VIEW v -ED, -ING, -S to look at VIEWABLE adj

VIEWER n pl. -S one that views

VIEWIER comparative of viewy

VIEWIEST superlative of viewy

VIEWING n pl. -S an act of seeing, watching, or looking

VIEWLESS adj having no opinions

VIEWY adj VIEWIER, VIEWIEST showy

VIGIL n pl. -S a period of watchfulness maintained during normal sleeping hours

VIGILANT adj watchful

VIGNETTE v -GNETTED, -GNETTING, -GNETTES to describe briefly

VIGOR n pl. -S active strength or force

VIGORISH n pl. -ES a charge paid to a bookie on a bet

VIGOROSO adv with emphasis and spirit — used as a musical direction

VIGOROUS adj full of vigor

VIGOUR n pl. -S vigor

VIKING n pl. -S a Scandinavian pirate

VILAYET n pl. -S an administrative division of Turkey

VILE adj VILER, VILEST physically repulsive VILELY adv

VILENESS n pl. -ES the state of being vile

VILIFIER n pl. -S one that vilifies

VILIFY v -FIED, -FYING, -FIES to defame

VILIPEND v -ED, -ING, -S to vilify

VILL n pl. -S a village

VILLA n pl. -LAE or -LAS an agricultural estate of ancient Rome

VILLADOM n pl. -S the world constituted by suburban residences and their occupants

VILLAGE n pl. -S a small community in a rural area

VILLAGER n pl. -S one who lives in a village

VILLAIN n pl. -S a cruelly malicious person

VILLAINY n pl. -LAINIES conduct characteristic of a villain

VILLATIC adj rural

VILLEIN n pl. -S a type of serf

VILLUS n pl. -LI one of the hairlike projections found on certain membranes VILLOSE, VILLOUS adj

VIM n pl. -S energy

VIMEN n pl. -MINA a long, flexible branch of a plant VIMINAL adj

VIN n pl. -S wine

VINA n pl. -S a stringed instrument of India

VINAL n pl. -S a synthetic textile fiber

VINASSE n pl. -S a residue left after the distillation of liquor

VINCA n pl. -S a flowering plant

VINCIBLE adj capable of being conquered

VINCULUM n pl. -LA or -LUMS a unifying bond

VINE v VINED, VINING, VINES to grow like a vine (a climbing plant)

VINEAL adj vinous

VINEGAR n pl. -S a sour liquid used as a condiment or preservative VINEGARY adj

VINERY n pl. -ERIES a place in which grapevines are grown

VINEYARD n pl. -S an area planted with grapevines

VINIC adj derived from wine

VINIER comparative of viny

VINIEST superlative of viny

VINIFERA n pl. -S a European grape

VINING present participle of vine

VINO n pl. -NOS wine

VINOSITY n pl. -TIES the character of a wine

VINOUS adj pertaining to wine **VINOUSLY** adv

VINTAGE n pl. -S a season's yield of wine from a vineyard

VINTAGER n pl. -S one that harvests wine grapes

VINTNER n pl. -S a wine merchant

VINY adj VINIER, VINIEST covered with vines

VINYL n pl. -S a type of plastic **VINYLIC** adj

VIOL n pl. -S a stringed instrument

VIOLA n pl. -S a stringed instrument

VIOLABLE adj capable of being violated **VIOLABLY** adv

VIOLATE v -LATED, -LATING, -LATES to break or disregard the terms or requirements of

VIOLATER n pl. -S violator

VIOLATOR n pl. -S one that violates

VIOLENCE n pl. -S violent action

VIOLENT adj marked by intense physical force or roughness

VIOLET n pl. -S a flowering plant

VIOLIN n pl. -S a stringed instrument

VIOLIST n pl. -S one who plays the viol or viola

VIOLONE n pl. -S a stringed instrument

VIOMYCIN n pl. -S an antibiotic

VIPER n pl. -S a venomous snake **VIPERINE, VIPERISH, VIPEROUS** adj

VIRAGO n pl. -GOES or -GOS a noisy, domineering woman

VIRAL adj pertaining to or caused by a virus **VIRALLY** adv

VIRELAI n pl. -S virelay

VIRELAY n pl. -LAYS a medieval French verse form

VIREMIA n pl. -S the presence of a virus in the blood **VIREMIC** adj

VIREO n pl. -EOS a small bird

VIRES pl. of vis

VIRGA n pl. -S wisps of precipitation evaporating before reaching ground

VIRGATE n pl. -S an early English measure of land area

VIRGIN n pl. -S a person who has never had sexual intercourse

VIRGINAL n pl. -S a musical instrument

VIRGULE n pl. -S a diagonal printing mark used to separate alternatives

VIRICIDE n pl. -S a substance that destroys viruses

VIRID adj verdant

VIRIDIAN n pl. -S a bluish-green pigment

VIRIDITY n pl. -TIES verdancy

VIRILE adj having masculine vigor

VIRILISM n pl. -S the development of male secondary sex characteristics in a female

VIRILITY n pl. -TIES the quality or state of being virile

VIRION n pl. -S a virus particle

VIRL n pl. -S a metal ring or cap put around a shaft to prevent splitting

VIROLOGY n pl. -GIES the study of viruses

VIROSIS n pl. -ROSES infection with a virus

VIRTU n pl. -S a love or taste for the fine arts

VIRTUAL adj having the effect but not the actual form of what is specified

VIRTUE n pl. -S moral excellence

VIRTUOSA n pl. -SAS or -SE a female virtuoso

VIRTUOSO n pl. -SOS or -SI a highly skilled artistic performer

VIRTUOUS adj characterized by virtue

VIRUCIDE n pl. -S viricide

VIRULENT adj extremely poisonous

VIRUS n pl. -ES any of a class of submicroscopic pathogens

VIS n pl. VIRES force or power

VISA v -ED, -ING, -S to put an official endorsement on, as a passport

VISAGE n pl. -S the face or facial expression of a person **VISAGED** adj

VISARD n pl. -S vizard

VISCACHA n pl. -S a burrowing rodent

VISCERA pl. of viscus

VISCERAL adj pertaining to the internal organs

VISCID adj thick and adhesive **VISCIDLY** adv

VISCOID adj somewhat viscid

VISCOSE n pl. -S a viscous solution

VISCOUNT n pl. -S a British nobleman

VISCOUS	*adj* having relatively high resistance to flow
VISCUS	*n pl.* -CERA an internal organ
VISE	*v* VISED, VISING, VISES to hold in a vise (a clamping device)
VISE	*v* VISEED, VISEING, VISES to visa
VISELIKE	*adj* resembling a vice
VISIBLE	*adj* capable of being seen VISIBLY *adv*
VISING	present participle of vise
VISION	*v* -ED, -ING, -S to imagine
VISIONAL	*adj* imaginary
VISIT	*v* -ED, -ING, -S to go or come to see someone or something
VISITANT	*n pl.* -S a visitor
VISITER	*n pl.* -S visitor
VISITOR	*n pl.* -S one that visits
VISIVE	*adj* visible
VISOR	*v* -ED, -ING, -S to provide with a visor (a projecting brim)
VISTA	*n pl.* -S a distant view VISTAED *adj*
VISUAL	*adj* pertaining to the sense of sight VISUALLY *adv*
VITA	*n pl.* -TAE a brief, autobiographical sketch
VITAL	*adj* necessary to life
VITALISE	*v* -ISED, -ISING, -ISES to vitalize
VITALISM	*n pl.* -S a philosophical doctrine
VITALIST	*n pl.* -S an advocate of vitalism
VITALITY	*n pl.* -TIES exuberant physical strength or mental vigor
VITALIZE	*v* -IZED, -IZING, -IZES to give life to
VITALLY	*adv* in a vital manner
VITALS	*n/pl* vital organs
VITAMER	*n pl.* -S a type of chemical compound
VITAMIN	*n pl.* -S any of various organic substances essential to proper nutrition
VITAMINE	*n pl.* -S vitamin
VITELLIN	*n pl.* -S a protein found in egg yolk
VITELLUS	*n pl.* -ES the yolk of an egg
VITESSE	*n pl.* -S speed
VITIATE	*v* -ATED, -ATING, ATES to impair the value or quality of VITIABLE *adj*
VITIATOR	*n pl.* -S one that vitiates
VITILIGO	*n pl.* -GOS a skin disease

VITREOUS	*adj* resembling glass
VITRIC	*adj* pertaining to glass
VITRIFY	*v* -FIED, -FYING, -FIES to convert into glass
VITRINE	*n pl.* -S a glass showcase for art objects
VITRIOL	*v* -OLED, -OLING, -OLS or -OLLED, -OLLING, -OLS to treat with sulfuric acid
VITTA	*n pl.* -TAE a streak or band of color VITTATE *adj*
VITTLE	*v* -TLED, -TLING, -TLES to victual
VITULINE	*adj* pertaining to a calf
VIVA	*n pl.* -S a shout or cry used to express approval
VIVACE	*adj* lively — used as a musical direction
VIVACITY	*n pl.* -TIES the quality or state of being lively
VIVARIUM	*n pl.* -IA or -IUMS a place for raising and keeping live animals
VIVARY	*n pl.* -RIES vivarium
VIVE	*interj* — used as an exclamation of approval
VIVERRID	*n pl.* -S any of a family of small carnivorous mammals
VIVERS	*n/pl* food
VIVID	*adj* -IDER, -IDEST strikingly bright or intense VIVIDLY *adv*
VIVIFIC	*adj* vivifying
VIVIFIER	*n pl.* -S one that vivifies
VIVIFY	*v* -FIED, -FYING, -FIES to give life to
VIVIPARA	*n/pl* animals that bring forth living young
VIVISECT	*v* -ED, -ING, -S to dissect the living body of
VIXEN	*n pl.* -S a shrewish woman VIXENISH, VIXENLY *adj*
VIZARD	*n pl.* -S a mask VIZARDED *adj*
VIZCACHA	*n pl.* -S viscacha
VIZIER	*n pl.* -S a high official in some Muslim countries
VIZIR	*n pl.* -S vizier VIZIRIAL *adj*
VIZIRATE	*n pl.* -S the office of a vizir
VIZOR	*v* -ED, -ING, -S to visor
VIZSLA	*n pl.* -S a Hungarian breed of dog
VOCABLE	*n pl.* -S a word
VOCABLY	*adv* in a manner that may be voiced aloud
VOCAL	*n pl.* -S a sound produced with the voice

VOCALIC *n* pl. -S a vowel sound

VOCALISE *v* -ISED, -ISING, -ISES to vocalize

VOCALISM *n* pl. -S the act of vocalizing

VOCALIST *n* pl. -S a singer

VOCALITY *n* pl. -TIES possession or exercise of vocal powers

VOCALIZE *v* -IZED, -IZING, -IZES to produce with the voice

VOCALLY *adv* with the voice

VOCATION *n* pl. -S the work in which a person is regularly employed

VOCATIVE *n* pl. -S a grammatical case used in some languages

VOCES pl. of vox

VOCODER *n* pl. -S an electronic device used in transmitting speech signals

VODKA *n* pl. -S a liquor

VODUN *n* pl. -S a primitive religion of the West Indies

VOE *n* pl. -S a small bay, creek, or inlet

VOGIE *adj* vain

VOGUE *n* pl. -S the current trend or style **VOGUISH** *adj*

VOICE *v* VOICED, VOICING, VOICES to express or utter

VOICEFUL *adj* sonorous

VOICER *n* pl. -S one that voices

VOICING present participle of voice

VOID *v* -ED, -ING, -S to make void (of no legal force or effect) **VOIDABLE** *adj*

VOIDANCE *n* pl. -S the act or process of voiding

VOIDER *n* pl. -S one that voids

VOIDNESS *n* pl. -ES the quality or state of being void

VOILE *n* pl. -S a sheer fabric

VOLANT *adj* flying or capable of flying

VOLANTE *adj* moving with light rapidity — used as a musical direction

VOLAR *adj* pertaining to flight

VOLATILE *n* pl. -S a winged creature

VOLCANIC *n* pl. -S a rock produced by a volcano

VOLCANO *n* pl. -NOES or -NOS an opening in the earth's crust through which molten rock and gases are ejected

VOLE *v* VOLED, VOLING, VOLES to win all the tricks in a card game

VOLERY *n* pl. -ERIES a large birdcage

VOLITANT *adj* volant

VOLITION *n* pl. -S the power of choosing or determining

VOLITIVE *adj* pertaining to volition

VOLLEY *v* -ED, -ING, -S to return a tennis ball before it touches the ground

VOLLEYER *n* pl. -S one that volleys

VOLOST *n* pl. -S an administrative district in Russia

VOLPLANE *v* -PLANED, -PLANING, -PLANES to glide in an airplane

VOLT *n* pl. -S a unit of electromotive force

VOLTA *n* pl. -TE a turning

VOLTAGE *n* pl. -S electromotive force expressed in volts

VOLTAISM *n* pl. -S electricity produced by chemical action **VOLTAIC** *adj*

VOLTE *n* pl. -S a fencing movement

VOLTI *interj* — used to direct musicians to turn the page

VOLUBLE *adj* talkative **VOLUBLY** *adv*

VOLUME *v* -UMED, -UMING, -UMES to send or give out in large quantities

VOLUTE *n* pl. -S a spiral architectural ornament **VOLUTED** *adj*

VOLUTIN *n* pl. -S a granular substance that is common in microorganisms

VOLUTION *n* pl. -S a spiral

VOLVA *n* pl. -S a membranous sac that encloses certain immature mushrooms **VOLVATE** *adj*

VOLVOX *n* pl. -ES any of a genus of freshwater protozoa

VOLVULUS *n* pl. -LI or -LUSES a twisting of the intestine that causes obstruction

VOMER *n* pl. -S a bone of the skull **VOMERINE** *adj*

VOMICA *n* pl. -CAE a cavity in the body containing pus

VOMIT *v* -ED, -ING, -S to eject the contents of the stomach through the mouth

VOMITER *n* pl. -S one that vomits

VOMITIVE *n* pl. -S an emetic

VOMITO *n* pl. -TOS the black vomit of yellow fever

VOMITORY *n* pl. -RIES an emetic

VOMITOUS *adj* pertaining to vomiting

VOMITUS *n* pl. -ES vomited matter

VON *prep* of; from — used in some surnames

VOODOO *v* -ED, -ING, -S to hex

VORACITY *n* pl. -TIES the quality or state of being ravenous

VORLAGE *n* pl. -S a position in skiing

VORTEX *n* pl. -TEXES or -TICES a whirling mass of fluid **VORTICAL** *adj*

VOTABLE *adj* capable of being voted on

VOTARESS *n* pl. -ES a female votary

VOTARIST *n* pl. -S a votary

VOTARY *n* pl. -RIES a person who is bound by religious vows

VOTE *v* VOTED, VOTING, VOTES to cast a vote (a formal expression of will or opinion)

VOTEABLE *adj* votable

VOTELESS *adj* having no vote

VOTER *n* pl. -S one that votes

VOTING present participle of vote

VOTIVE *adj* performed in fulfillment of a vow **VOTIVELY** *adv*

VOTRESS *n* pl. -ES votaress

VOUCH *v* -ED, -ING, -ES to give one's personal assurance or guarantee

VOUCHEE *n* pl. -S one for whom another vouches

VOUCHER *v* -ED, -ING, -S to establish the authenticity of

VOUSSOIR *n* pl. -S a wedge-shaped building stone

VOW *v* -ED, -ING, -S to make a vow (a solemn promise)

VOWEL *n* pl. -S a type of speech sound

VOWELIZE *v* -IZED, -IZING, -IZES to provide with symbols used to indicate vowels

VOWER *n* pl. -S one that vows

VOWLESS *adj* having made no vow

VOX *n* pl. VOCES voice

VOYAGE *v* -AGED, -AGING, -AGES to travel

VOYAGER *n* pl. -S one that voyages

VOYAGEUR *n* pl. -S a person employed by a fur company to transport goods between distant stations

VOYEUR *n* pl. -S one who is sexually gratified by looking at sexual objects or acts

VROOM *v* -ED, -ING, -S to run an engine at high speed

VROUW *n* pl. -S a Dutch woman

VROW *n* pl. -S vrouw

VUG *n* pl. -S a small cavity in a rock or lode **VUGGY** *adj*

VUGG *n* pl. -S vug

VUGH *n* pl. -S vug

VULCANIC *adj* pertaining to a volcano

VULGAR *adj* -GARER, -GAREST crude **VULGARLY** *adv*

VULGAR *n* pl. -S a common person

VULGATE *n* pl. -S the common speech of a people

VULGO *adv* commonly

VULGUS *n* pl. -ES an exercise in Latin formerly required of pupils in some English public schools

VULPINE *adj* pertaining to a fox

VULTURE *n* pl. -S a bird of prey

VULVA *n* pl. -VAE or -VAS the external genital organs of a female **VULVAL, VULVAR, VULVATE** *adj*

VULVITIS *n* pl. -TISES inflammation of the vulva

VYING present participle of vie

VYINGLY *adv* in a vying manner

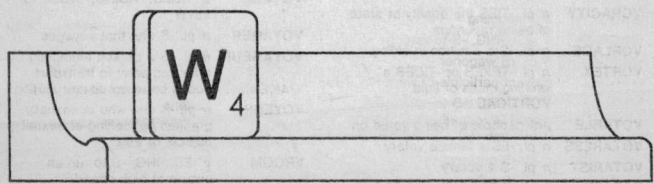

WAB	*n* pl. -S a web
WABBLE	*v* -BLED, -BLING, -BLES to wobble
WABBLER	*n* pl. -S one that wabbles
WABBLY	*adj* -BLIER, -BLIEST wobbly
WACK	*n* pl. -S a wacky person
WACKE	*n* pl. -S a type of basaltic rock
WACKY	*adj* WACKIER, WACKIEST very irrational **WACKILY** *adv*
WAD	*v* -DDED, -DDING, -WADS to form into a wad (a small mass of soft material)
WADABLE	*adj* wadeable
WADDER	*n* pl. -S one that wads
WADDIE	*n* pl. -S a cowboy
WADDIED	past tense of waddy
WADDIES	present 3d person sing. of waddy
WADDING	*n* pl. -S a wad
WADDLE	*v* -DLED, -DLING, -DLES to walk with short, swaying steps
WADDLER	*n* pl. -S one that waddles
WADDLY	*adj* having or being a waddling gait
WADDY	*v* -DIED, -DYING, -DIES to strike with a thick club
WADE	*v* WADED, WADING, WADES to walk through water
WADEABLE	*adj* capable of being passed through by wading
WADER	*n* pl. -S one that wades
WADI	*n* pl. -S the bed of a usually dry watercourse
WADIES	pl. of wady
WADING	present participle of wade
WADMAAL	*n* pl. -S wadmal
WADMAL	*n* pl. -S a thick woolen fabric
WADMEL	*n* pl. -S wadmal
WADMOL	*n* pl. -S wadmal
WADMOLL	*n* pl. -S wadmal
WADSET	*v* -SETTED, -SETTING, -SETS to mortgage
WADY	*n* pl. -DIES wadi
WAE	*n* pl. -S woe
WAEFU	*adj* waeful
WAEFUL	*adj* woeful
WAENESS	*n* pl. -ES woeness
WAESUCK	*interj* waesucks
WAESUCKS	*interj* — used to express pity
WAFER	*v* -ED, -ING, -S to seal with an adhesive disk
WAFERY	*adj* resembling a wafer (a thin, crisp biscuit)
WAFF	*v* -ED, -ING, -S to wave
WAFFIE	*n* pl. -S a vagabond
WAFFLE	*v* -FLED, -FLING, -FLES to talk foolishly
WAFT	*v* -ED, -ING, -S to carry lightly over air or water
WAFTAGE	*n* pl. -S the act of wafting
WAFTER	*n* pl. -S one that wafts
WAFTURE	*n* pl. -S waftage
WAG	*v* WAGGED, WAGGING, WAGS to move briskly up and down or to and fro
WAGE	*v* WAGED, WAGING, WAGES to engage in or carry on
WAGELESS	*adj* unpaid
WAGER	*v* -ED, -ING, -S to risk on an uncertain outcome
WAGERER	*n* pl. -S one that wagers
WAGGED	past tense of wag
WAGGER	*n* pl. -S one that wags
WAGGERY	*n* pl. -GERIES waggish behavior

WAGGING present participle of wag

WAGGISH *adj* playfully humorous

WAGGLE *v* -GLED, -GLING, -GLES to wag

WAGGLY *adj* waggling

WAGGON *v* -ED, -ING, -S to wagon

WAGGONER *n* pl. -S wagoner

WAGING present participle of wage

WAGON *v* -ED, -ING, -S to convey by wagon (a four-wheeled, horse-drawn vehicle)

WAGONAGE *n* pl. -S conveyance by wagon

WAGONER *n* pl. -S one who drives a wagon

WAGSOME *adj* waggish

WAGTAIL *n* pl. -S a songbird

WAHCONDA *n* pl. -S wakanda

WAHINE *n* pl. -S a Hawaiian woman

WAHOO *n* pl. -HOOS a flowering shrub

WAIF *v* -ED, -ING, -S to throw away

WAIL *v* -ED, -ING, -S to utter a long, mournful cry

WAILER *n* pl. -S one that wails

WAILFUL *adj* mournful

WAILSOME *adj* wailful

WAIN *n* pl. -S a large, open wagon

WAINSCOT *v* -SCOTED, -SCOTING, -SCOTS or -SCOTTED, -SCOTTING, -SCOTS to line the walls of rooms with wooden paneling

WAIR *v* -ED, -ING, -S to spend

WAIST *n* pl. -S the part of the body between the ribs and the hips **WAISTED** *adj*

WAISTER *n* pl. -S a seaman stationed in the middle section of a ship

WAISTING *n* pl. -S a type of dressmaking material

WAIT *v* -ED, -ING, -S to stay in expectation of

WAITER *n* pl. -S one who serves food in a restaurant

WAITING *n* pl. -S the act of one who waits

WAITRESS *n* pl. -ES a woman who serves food in a restaurant

WAIVE *v* WAIVED, WAIVING, WAIVES to give up intentionally

WAIVER *n* pl. -S the act of waiving something

WAKANDA *n* pl. -S a supernatural force in Sioux beliefs

WAKE *v* WAKED or WOKE, WOKEN, WAKING, WAKES to rouse from sleep

WAKEFUL *adj* not sleeping or able to sleep

WAKELESS *adj* unbroken — used of sleep

WAKEN *v* -ED, -ING, -S to wake

WAKENER *n* pl. -S one that wakens

WAKENING *n* pl. -S the act of one that wakens

WAKER *n* pl. -S one that wakes

WAKERIFE *adj* wakeful

WAKIKI *n* pl. -S shell money of the South Sea Islands

WAKING present participle of wake

WALE *v* WALED, WALING, WALES to mark with welts

WALER *n* pl. -S an Australian-bred saddle horse

WALIES pl. of waly

WALING present participle of wale

WALK *v* -ED, -ING, -S to advance on foot **WALKABLE** *adj*

WALKAWAY *n* pl. -AWAYS an easy victory

WALKER *n* pl. -S one that walks

WALKING *n* pl. -S the act of one that walks

WALKOUT *n* pl. -S a strike by workers

WALKOVER *n* pl. -S a walkaway

WALKUP *n* pl. -S an apartment house having no elevator

WALKWAY *n* pl. -WAYS a passage for walking

WALKYRIE *n* pl. -S valkyrie

WALL *v* -ED, -ING, -S to provide with a wall (an upright structure built to enclose an area)

WALLA *n* pl. -S wallah

WALLABY *n* pl. -BIES a small kangaroo

WALLAH *n* pl. -S a person engaged in a particular occupation or activity

WALLAROO *n* pl. -ROOS a large kangaroo

WALLET *n* pl. -S a flat folding case

WALLEYE *n* pl. -S an eye having a white cornea **WALLEYED** *adj*

WALLIE *n* pl. -S a valet

WALLIES pl. of wally

WALLOP *v* -ED, -ING, -S to beat soundly

WALLOPER *n* pl. -S one that wallops

WALLOW *v* -ED, -ING, -S to roll about

WALLOWER *n* pl. -S one that wallows

WALLY *n* pl. -LIES waly

WALNUT n pl. -S an edible nut

WALRUS n pl. -ES a marine mammal

WALTZ v -ED, -ING, -ES to perform a ballroom dance

WALTZER n pl. -S one that waltzes

WALY n pl. WALIES something visually pleasing

WAMBLE v -BLED, -BLING, -BLES to move unsteadily

WAMBLY adj -BLIER, -BLIEST unsteady

WAME n pl. -S the belly

WAMEFOU n pl. -S a bellyful

WAMEFUL n pl. -S wamefou

WAMMUS n pl. -ES wamus

WAMPISH v -ED, -ING, -ES to throw about

WAMPUM n pl. -S a form of currency formerly used by North American Indians

WAMPUS n pl. -ES wamus

WAMUS n pl. -ES a heavy outer jacket

WAN adj WANNER, WANNEST unnaturally pale

WAN v WANNED, WANNING, WANS to become wan

WAND n pl. -S a slender rod

WANDER v -ED, -ING, -S to move about with no destination or purpose

WANDERER n pl. -S one that wanders

WANDEROO n pl. -ROOS an Asian monkey

WANDLE adj supple

WANE v WANED, WANING, WANES to decrease in size or extent

WANEY adj WANIER, WANIEST wany

WANGAN n pl. -S wanigan

WANGLE v -GLED, -GLING, -GLES to obtain or accomplish by contrivance

WANGLER n pl. -S one that wangles

WANGUN n pl. -S wanigan

WANIER comparative of waney and wany

WANIEST superlative of waney and wany

WANIGAN n pl. -S a supply chest used in a logging camp

WANING present participle of wane

WANION n pl. -S vengeance

WANLY adv in a wan manner

WANNED past tense of wan

WANNER comparative of wan

WANNESS n pl. -ES the quality of being wan

WANNEST superlative of wan

WANNIGAN n pl. -S wanigan

WANNING present participle of wan

WANT v -ED, -ING, -S to have a desire for

WANTAGE n pl. -S something that is lacking

WANTER n pl. -S one that wants

WANTON v -ED, -ING, -S to behave immorally

WANTONER n pl. -S one that wantons

WANTONLY adv immorally

WANY adj WANIER, WANIEST waning in some parts

WAP v WAPPED, WAPPING, WAPS to wrap

WAPITI n pl. -S a large deer

WAR v WARRED, WARRING, WARS to engage in war (a state of open, armed conflict)

WARBLE v -BLED, -BLING, -BLES to sing with melodic embellishments

WARBLER n pl. -S one that warbles

WARCRAFT n pl. -S the art of war

WARD v -ED, -ING, -S to turn aside

WARDEN n pl. -S the chief officer of a prison

WARDENRY n pl. -RIES the office of a warden

WARDER n pl. -S a person who guards something

WARDRESS n pl. -ES a female warden

WARDROBE n pl. -S a collection of garments

WARDROOM n pl. -S a recreation area on a warship

WARDSHIP n pl. -S the state of being under a guardian

WARE v WARED, WARING, WARES to beware of

WAREROOM n pl. -S a room in which goods are displayed for sale

WARFARE n pl. -S the act of engaging in war

WARFARIN n pl. -S a chemical compound

WARHEAD n pl. -S the front part of a missile containing the explosive

WARIER comparative of wary

WARIEST superlative of wary

WARILY adv in a wary manner

WARINESS n pl. -ES the state of being wary

WARING present participle of ware

WARISON n pl. -S a call to attack

WARK   v -ED, -ING, -S to endure pain

WARLESS   adj free from war

WARLIKE   adj disposed to engage in war

WARLOCK   n pl. -S a sorcerer

WARLORD   n pl. -S a military leader of a warlike nation

WARM   adj WARMER, WARMEST moderately hot

WARM   v -ED, -ING, -S to make warm

WARMAKER   n pl. -S one that wars

WARMER   n pl. -S one that warms

WARMISH   adj somewhat warm

WARMLY   adv in a warm manner

WARMNESS   n pl. -ES the state of being warm

WARMOUTH   n -S a freshwater fish

WARMTH   n pl. -S warmness

WARMUP   n pl. -S a preparatory exercise or procedure

WARN   v -ED, -ING, -S to make aware of impending or possible danger

WARNER   n pl. -S one that warns

WARNING   n pl. -S something that warns

WARP   v -ED, -ING, -S to turn or twist out of shape

WARPAGE   n pl. -S the act of warping

WARPATH   n pl. -S the route taken by attacking American Indians

WARPER   n pl. -S one that warps

WARPLANE   n pl. -S an airplane armed for combat

WARPOWER   n pl. -S the power to make war

WARPWISE   adv in a vertical direction

WARRAGAL   n pl. -S warrigal

WARRANT   v -ED, -ING, -S to give authority to

WARRANTY   n pl. -TIES the act of warranting

WARRED   past tense of war

WARREN   n pl. -S a place where rabbits live and breed

WARRENER   n pl. -S the keeper of a warren

WARRIGAL   n pl. -S a dingo

WARRING   present participle of war

WARRIOR   n pl. -S one engaged or experienced in warfare

WARSAW   n pl. -S a marine fish

WARSHIP   n pl. -S a ship armed for combat

WARSLE   v -SLED, -SLING, -SLES to wrestle

WARSLER   n pl. -S a wrestler

WARSTLE   v -TLED, -TLING, -TLES to wrestle

WARSTLER   n pl. -S a wrestler

WART   n pl. -S a protuberance on the skin WARTED adj

WARTHOG   n pl. -S an African wild hog

WARTIER   comparative of warty

WARTIEST   superlative of warty

WARTIME   n pl. -S a time of war

WARTLIKE   adj resembling a wart

WARTY   adj WARTIER, WARTIEST covered with warts

WARWORK   n pl. -S work done during a war

WARWORN   adj showing the effects of war

WARY   adj WARIER, WARIEST watchful

WAS   1st and 3d person sing. past indicative of be

WASH   v -ED, -ING, -ES to cleanse by immersing in or applying a liquid

WASHABLE   adj capable of being washed without damage

WASHBOWL   n pl. -S a bowl used for washing oneself

WASHDAY   n pl. -DAYS a day set aside for washing clothes

WASHER   n pl. -S one that washes

WASHIER   comparative of washy

WASHIEST   superlative of washy

WASHING   n pl. -S articles washed or to be washed

WASHOUT   n pl. -S an erosion of earth by the action of water

WASHRAG   n pl. -S a small cloth used for washing oneself

WASHROOM   n pl. -S a lavatory

WASHTUB   n pl. -S a tub used for washing clothes

WASHY   adj WASHIER, WASHIEST overly diluted

WASP   n pl. -S a stinging insect WASPISH, WASPLIKE adj

WASPY   adj WASPIER, WASPIEST resembling a wasp WASPILY adv

WASSAIL   v -ED, -ING, -S to drink to the health of

WAST   n pl. -S west

WASTABLE   adj capable of being wasted

WASTAGE   n pl. -S something that is wasted

WASTE   v WASTED, WASTING, WASTES to use thoughtlessly

WASTEFUL   adj tending to waste

WASTELOT n pl. -S a vacant lot

WASTER n pl. -S one that wastes

WASTERIE n pl. -S wastry

WASTERY n pl. -RIES wastry

WASTEWAY n pl. -WAYS a channel for excess water

WASTING present participle of waste

WASTREL n pl. -S one that wastes

WASTRIE n pl. -S wastry

WASTRY n pl. -RIES reckless extravagance

WAT adj WATTER, WATTEST wet

WAT n pl. -S a hare

WATAP n pl. -S a thread made from the roots of various trees

WATAPE n pl. -S watap

WATCH v -ED, -ING, -ES to observe carefully

WATCHCRY n pl. -CRIES a password

WATCHDOG v -DOGGED, -DOGGING, -DOGS to act as a guardian for

WATCHER n pl. -S one that watches

WATCHEYE n pl. -S a walleye

WATCHFUL adj closely observant or alert

WATCHMAN n pl. -MEN a man employed to stand guard

WATCHOUT n pl. -S the act of looking out for something

WATER v -ED, -ING, -S to sprinkle with water (a transparent, odorless, tasteless liquid)

WATERAGE n pl. -S the conveyance of goods by water

WATERBED n pl. -S a bed whose mattress is a plastic bag filled with water

WATERDOG n pl. -S a large salamander

WATERER n pl. -S one that waters

WATERIER comparative of watery

WATERIEST superlative of watery

WATERILY adv in a watery manner

WATERING n pl. -S the act of one that waters

WATERISH adj watery

WATERLOG v -LOGGED, -LOGGING, -LOGS to soak with water

WATERLOO n pl. -LOOS a decisive defeat

WATERMAN n pl. -MEN a boatman

WATERWAY n pl. -WAYS a navigable body of water

WATERY adj -TERIER, -TERIEST containing water

WATT n pl. -S a unit of power

WATTAGE n pl. -S an amount of power in terms of watts

WATTAPE n pl. -S watap

WATTER comparative of wat

WATTEST superlative of wat

WATTHOUR n pl. -S a unit of energy

WATTLE v -TLED, -TLING, -TLES to weave into a network

WATTLESS adj denoting a type of electric current

WAUCHT v -ED, -ING, -S to waught

WAUGH adj damp

WAUGHT v -ED, -ING, -S to drink deeply

WAUK v -ED, -ING, -S to wake

WAUL v -ED, -ING, -S to cry like a cat

WAUR adj worse

WAVE v WAVED, WAVING, WAVES to move freely back and forth or up and down

WAVEBAND n pl. -S a range of radio frequencies

WAVEFORM n pl. -S a type of mathematical graph

WAVELESS adj having no waves (moving ridges on the surface of a liquid)

WAVELET n pl. -S a small wave

WAVELIKE adj resembling a wave

WAVEOFF n pl. -S the act of denying landing permission to an approaching aircraft

WAVER v -ED, -ING, -S to move back and forth

WAVERER n pl. -S one that wavers

WAVERY adj wavering

WAVEY n pl. -VEYS the snow goose

WAVIER comparative of wavy

WAVIES pl. of wavy

WAVIEST superlative of wavy

WAVILY adv in a wavy manner

WAVINESS n pl. -ES the state of being wavy

WAVING present participle of wave

WAVY adj WAVIER, WAVIEST having waves

WAVY n pl. -VIES wavey

WAW n pl. -S vav

WAWL v -ED, -ING, -S to waul

WAX v -ED, -ING, -ES to coat with wax (a natural, heat-sensitive substance)

WAXBERRY n pl. -RIES a berry with a waxy coating

WAXBILL   *n* pl. -S a tropical bird

WAXEN   *adj* covered with wax

WAXER   *n* pl. -S one that waxes

WAXIER   comparative of waxy

WAXIEST   superlative of waxy

WAXILY   *adv* in a waxy manner

WAXINESS   *n* pl. -ES the quality of being waxy

WAXING   *n* pl. -S the act of one that waxes

WAXLIKE   *adj* resembling wax

WAXPLANT   *n* pl. -S a tropical plant

WAXWEED   *n* pl. -S an annual herb

WAXWING   *n* pl. -S a type of passerine bird

WAXWORK   *n* pl. -S an effigy made of wax

WAXWORM   *n* pl. -S a moth that infests beehives

WAXY   *adj* WAXIER, WAXIEST resembling wax

WAY   *n* pl. WAYS a method of doing something

WAYBILL   *n* pl. -S a list of goods relative to a shipment

WAYFARER   *n* pl. -S a traveler

WAYGOING   *n* pl. -S the act of leaving

WAYLAY   *v* -LAID, -LAYING, -LAYS to ambush

WAYLAYER   *n* pl. -S one that waylays

WAYLESS   *adj* having no road or path

WAYSIDE   *n* pl. -S the side of a road

WAYWARD   *adj* willful

WAYWORN   *adj* fatigued by travel

WE   *pron* 1st person pl. pronoun in the nominative case

WEAK   *adj* WEAKER, WEAKEST lacking strength

WEAKEN   *v* -ED, -ING, -S to make weak

WEAKENER   *n* pl. -S one that weakens

WEAKFISH   *n* pl. -ES a marine fish

WEAKISH   *adj* somewhat weak

WEAKLING   *n* pl. -S a weak person

WEAKLY   *adj* -LIER, -LIEST weak and sickly

WEAKNESS   *n* pl. -ES the state of being weak

WEAL   *n* pl. -S a welt

WEALD   *n* pl. -S a woodland

WEALTH   *n* pl. -S a great quantity of valuable material

WEALTHY   *adj* WEALTHIER, WEALTHIEST having wealth

WEAN   *v* -ED, -ING, -S to withhold mother's milk from and substitute other nourishment

WEANER   *n* pl. -S one that weans

WEANLING   *n* pl. -S a recently weaned child or animal

WEAPON   *v* -ED, -ING, -S to supply with a weapon (an instrument used in combat)

WEAPONRY   *n* pl. -RIES an aggregate of weapons

WEAR   *v* WORE, WORN, WEARING, WEARS to have on one's person

WEARABLE   *n* pl. -S a garment

WEARER   *n* pl. -S one that wears something

WEARIED   past tense of weary

WEARIER   comparative of weary

WEARIES   present 3d person sing. of weary

WEARIEST   superlative of weary

WEARIFUL   *adj* tiresome

WEARISH   *adj* tasteless

WEARY   *adj* -RIER, -RIEST tired WEARILY *adv*

WEARY   *v* -RIED, -RYING, -RIES to make or become weary

WEASAND   *n* pl. -S the throat

WEASEL   *v* -ED, -ING, -S to act evasively

WEASON   *n* pl. -S weasand

WEATHER   *v* -ED, -ING, -S to expose to atmospheric conditions

WEAVE   *v* WOVE or WEAVED, WOVEN, WEAVING, WEAVES to form by interlacing threads

WEAVER   *n* pl. -S one that weaves

WEAZAND   *n* pl. -S weasand

WEB   *v* WEBBED, WEBBING, WEBS to provide with a web (an interlaced fabric or structure)

WEBBING   *n* pl. -S a woven strip of fiber

WEBBY   *adj* -BIER, -BIEST weblike

WEBER   *n* pl. -S a unit of magnetic flux

WEBFED   *adj* pertaining to a type of printing press

WEBFOOT   *n* pl. -FEET a foot having the toes joined by a membrane

WEBLESS   *adj* having no webs

WEBLIKE   *adj* resembling a web

WEBSTER   *n* pl. -S a weaver

WEBWORM   *n* pl. -S a web-spinning caterpillar

WECHT n pl. -S weight

WED v WEDDED, WEDDING, WEDS to marry

WEDDER n pl. -S one that weds

WEDDING n pl. -S a marriage ceremony

WEDEL v -ED, -ING, -S to perform a wedeln

WEDELN h pl. -S a skiing technique

WEDGE v WEDGED, WEDGING, WEDGES to force apart with a wedge (a tapering piece of wood or metal)

WEDGIE n pl. -S a type of woman's shoe

WEDGY adj WEDGIER, WEDGIEST resembling a wedge

WEDLOCK n pl. -S the state of being married

WEE adj WEER, WEEST very small

WEE n pl. -S a short time

WEED v -ED, -ING, -S to remove weeds (undesirable plants)

WEEDER n pl. -S one that weeds

WEEDIER comparative of weedy

WEEDIEST superlative of weedy

WEEDILY adv in a weedy manner

WEEDLESS adj having no weeds

WEEDLIKE adj resembling a weed

WEEDY adj WEEDIER, WEEDIEST resembling a weed

WEEK n pl. -S a period of seven days

WEEKDAY n pl. -DAYS any day of the week except Sunday

WEEKEND v -ED, -ING, -S to spend the weekend (the end of the week)

WEEKLONG adj continuing for a week

WEEKLY n pl. -LIES a publication issued once a week

WEEL adj well

WEEN v -ED, -ING, -S to suppose

WEENIE n pl. -S a wiener

WEENSY adj -SIER, -SIEST tiny

WEENY adj -NIER, -NIEST tiny

WEEP v WEPT, WEEPING, WEEPS to express sorrow by shedding tears

WEEPER n pl. -S one that weeps

WEEPY adj WEEPIER, WEEPIEST tending to weep

WEER comparative of wee

WEEST superlative of wee

WEET v -ED, -ING, -S to know

WEEVER n pl. -S a marine fish

WEEVIL n pl. -S a small beetle WEEVILED, WEEVILLY, WEEVILY adj

WEEWEE v -WEED, -WEEING, -WEES to urinate

WEFT n pl. -S a woven fabric or garment

WEFTWISE adv in a horizontal direction

WEIGELA n pl. -S a flowering shrub

WEIGELIA n pl. -S weigela

WEIGH v -ED, -ING, -S to determine the weight of

WEIGHER n pl. -S one that weighs

WEIGHMAN n pl. -MEN one whose occupation is weighing goods

WEIGHT v -ED, -ING, -S to add weight (heaviness) to

WEIGHTER n pl. -S one that weights

WEIGHTY adj WEIGHTIER, WEIGHTIEST having great weight

WEINER n pl. -S wiener

WEIR n pl. -S a fence placed in a stream to catch fish

WEIRD adj WEIRDER, WEIRDEST mysteriously strange

WEIRD n pl. -S destiny

WEIRDIE n pl. -S a very strange person

WEIRDIES pl. of weirdy

WEIRDLY adv in a weird manner

WEIRDO n pl. WEIRDOES or WEIRDOS weirdie

WEIRDY n pl. WEIRDIES weirdie

WEKA n pl. -S a flightless bird

WELCH v -ED, -ING, -ES to welsh

WELCHER n pl. -S one that welshes

WELCOME v -COMED, -COMING, -COMES to greet cordially

WELCOMER n pl. -S one that welcomes

WELD v -ED, -ING, -S to join by applying heat WELDABLE adj

WELDER n pl. -S one that welds

WELDLESS adj having no welded joints

WELDMENT n pl. -S a unit composed of welded pieces

WELDOR n pl. -S welder

WELFARE n pl. -S general well-being

WELKIN n pl. -S the sky

WELL v -ED, -ING, -S to rise to the surface and flow forth

WELLADAY n pl. -DAYS wellaway

WELLAWAY n pl. -WAYS an expression of sorrow

WELLBORN *adj* of good birth or ancestry

WELLCURB *n pl.* -S the stone ring around a well (a hole dug in the ground to obtain water)

WELLDOER *n pl.* -S a doer of good deeds

WELLHEAD *n pl.* -S the source of a spring or stream

WELLHOLE *n pl.* -S the shaft of a well

WELLNESS *n pl.* -ES the state of being healthy

WELLSITE *n pl.* -S a mineral

WELSH *v* -ED, -ING, -ES to fail to pay a debt

WELSHER *n pl.* -S one that welshes

WELT *v* -ED, -ING, -S to mark with welts (ridges or lumps raised on the skin)

WELTER *v* -ED, -ING, -S to roll about

WELTING *n pl.* -S a cord or strip used to reinforce a seam

WEN *n pl.* -S a benign tumor of the skin

WENCH *v* -ED, -ING, -ES to consort with prostitutes

WENCHER *n pl.* -S one that wenches

WEND *v* -ED, -ING, -S to proceed along

WENDIGO *n pl.* -GOS windigo

WENNISH *adj* wenny

WENNY *adj* -NIER, -NIEST resembling a wen

WENT past tense of go

WEPT past tense of weep

WERE a *pl.* and 2d person *sing.* past indicative, and past subjunctive of be

WEREGILD *n pl.* -S wergeld

WEREWOLF *n pl.* -WOLVES a person capable of assuming the form of a wolf

WERGELD *n pl.* -S a price paid for the taking of a man's life in Anglo-Saxon law

WERGELT *n pl.* -S wergeld

WERGILD *n pl.* -S wergeld

WERT a 2d person *sing.* past tense of be

WERWOLF *n pl.* -WOLVES werwolf

WESKIT *n pl.* -S a vest

WESSAND *n pl.* -S weasand

WEST *n pl.* -S a cardinal point of the compass

WESTER *v* -ED, -ING, -S to move toward the west

WESTERLY *n pl.* -LIES a wind from the west

WESTERN *n pl.* -S one who lives in the west

WESTING *n pl.* -S a shifting west

WESTMOST *adj* farthest west

WESTWARD *n pl.* -S a direction toward the west

WET *adj* WETTER, WETTEST covered or saturated with a liquid

WET *v* WETTED, WETTING, WETS to make wet

WETBACK *n pl.* -S a Mexican who enters the United States illegally — an offensive term

WETHER *n pl.* -S a gelded male sheep

WETLAND *n pl.* -S land containing much soil moisture

WETLY *adv* in a wet manner

WETNESS *n pl.* -ES the state of being wet

WETPROOF *adj* waterproof

WETTABLE *adj* capable of being wetted

WETTED past tense of wet

WETTER *n pl.* -S one that wets

WETTEST superlative of wet

WETTING *n pl.* -S a liquid used in moistening something

WETTISH *adj* somewhat wet

WHA *pron* who

WHACK *v* -ED, -ING, -S to strike sharply

WHACKER *n pl.* -S one that whacks

WHACKY *adj* WHACKIER, WHACKIEST wacky

WHALE *v* WHALED, WHALING, WHALES to engage in the hunting of whales (large marine mammals)

WHALEMAN *n pl.* -MEN a whaler

WHALER *n pl.* -S a person engaged in whaling

WHALING *n pl.* -S the industry of hunting and processing whales

WHAM *v* WHAMMED, WHAMMING, WHAMS to hit with a loud impact

WHAMMY *n pl.* -MIES a supernatural spell bringing bad luck

WHANG *v* -ED, -ING, -S to beat with a whip

WHANGEE *n pl.* -S an Asian grass

WHAP *v* WHAPPED, WHAPPING, WHAPS to whop

WHAPPER *n pl.* -S whopper

WHARF *v* -ED, -ING, -S to moor to a wharf (a landing place for vessels)

WHARFAGE *n pl.* -S the use of a wharf

WHARVE *n pl.* -S a round piece of wood used in spinning thread

WHAT *n pl.* -S the true nature of something

WHATEVER *adj* being what or who it may be

WHATNOT *n pl.* -S an ornamental set of shelves

WHAUP *n pl.* -S a European bird

WHEAL *n pl.* -S a welt

WHEAT *n pl.* -S a cereal grass

WHEATEAR *n pl.* -S a small bird of northern regions

WHEATEN *adj* pertaining to wheat

WHEE *interj* — used to express delight

WHEEDLE *v* -DLED, -DLING, -DLES to attempt to persuade by flattery

WHEEDLER *n pl.* -S one that wheedles

WHEEL *v* -ED, -ING, -S to convey on wheels (circular frames designed to turn on an axis)

WHEELER *n pl.* -S one that wheels

WHEELIE *n pl.* -S a maneuver made on a wheeled vehicle

WHEELING *n pl.* -S the condition of a road for vehicles

WHEELMAN *n pl.* -MEN a helmsman

WHEEN *n pl.* -S a fairly large amount

WHEEP *v* -ED, -ING, -S to wheeple

WHEEPLE *v* -PLED, -PLING, -PLES to give forth a prolonged whistle

WHEEZE *v* WHEEZED, WHEEZING, WHEEZES to breathe with a whistling sound

WHEEZER *n pl.* -S one that wheezes

WHEEZY *adj* WHEEZIER, WHEEZIEST characterized by wheezing WHEEZILY *adv*

WHELK *n pl.* -S a pustule

WHELKY *adj* WHELKIER, WHELKIEST marked with whelks

WHELM *v* -ED, -ING, -S to cover with water

WHELP *v* -ED, -ING, -S to give birth to

WHEN *n pl.* -S the time in which something is done or occurs

WHENAS *conj* at which time

WHENCE *adv* from what place

WHENEVER *adv* at whatever time

WHERE *n pl.* -S the place at or in which something is located or occurs

WHEREAS *n pl.* -ES an introductory statement of a formal document

WHEREAT *adv* at what

WHEREBY *adv* by what

WHEREIN *adv* in what

WHEREOF *adv* of what

WHEREON *adv* on what

WHERETO *adv* to what

WHEREVER *adv* in or to whatever place

WHERRY *v* -RIED, -RYING, -RIES to transport in a light rowboat

WHERVE *n pl.* -S wharve

WHET *v* WHETTED, WHETTING, WHETS to sharpen by friction

WHETHER *conj* if it be the case that

WHETTER *n pl.* -S one that whets

WHETTING present participle of whet

WHEW *n pl.* -S a whistling sound

WHEY *n pl.* WHEYS the watery part of milk WHEYEY, WHEYISH *adj*

WHEYFACE *n pl.* -S a pale, sallow face

WHICH *pron* what particular one or ones

WHICKER *v* -ED, -ING, -S to whinny

WHID *v* WHIDDED, WHIDDING, WHIDS to move rapidly and quietly

WHIDAH *n pl.* -S whydah

WHIFF *v* -ED, -ING, -S to blow or convey with slight gusts of air

WHIFFER *n pl.* -S one that whiffs

WHIFFET *n pl.* -S an insignificant person

WHIFFLE *v* -FLED, -FLING, -FLES to move or think erratically

WHIFFLER *n pl.* -S one that whiffles

WHILE *v* WHILED, WHILING, WHILES to cause to pass pleasantly

WHILOM *adv* formerly

WHILST *conj* during the time that

WHIM *n pl.* -S an impulsive idea

WHIMBREL *n pl.* -S a shore bird

WHIMPER *v* -ED, -ING, -S to cry with plaintive, broken sounds

WHIMSEY *n pl.* -SEYS whimsy

WHIMSY *n pl.* -SIES a whim WHIMSIED *adj*

WHIN *n pl.* -S furze

WHINCHAT *n pl.* -S a songbird

WHINE *v* WHINED, WHINING, WHINES to utter a plaintive, high-pitched sound

WHINER   *n* pl. -S one that whines

WHINEY   *adj* WHINIER, WHINIEST whiny

WHINIER   comparative of whiny

WHINIEST   superlative of whiny

WHINING   present participle of whine

WHINNY   *v* -NIED, -NYING, -NIES to neigh in a low or gentle manner

WHINNY   *adj* -NIER, -NIEST abounding in whin

WHINY   *adj* WHINIER, WHINIEST tending to whine

WHIP   *v* WHIPPED or WHIPT, WHIPPING, WHIPS to strike with a whip (an instrument for administering corporal punishment)

WHIPCORD   *n* pl. -S a strong, twisted cord

WHIPLASH   *n* pl. -ES the lash of a whip

WHIPLIKE   *adj* resembling a whip

WHIPPED   a past tense of whip

WHIPPER   *n* pl. -S one that whips

WHIPPET   *n* pl. -S a small, swift dog

WHIPPIER   comparative of whippy

WHIPPIEST   superlative of whippy

WHIPPING   *n* pl. -S material used to whip

WHIPPY   *adj* -PIER, -PIEST pertaining to or resembling a whip

WHIPRAY   *n* pl. -RAYS a stingray

WHIPSAW   *v* -SAWED, -SAWN, -SAWING, -SAWS to cut with a narrow, tapering saw

WHIPT   a past tense of whip

WHIPTAIL   *n* pl. -S a lizard having a long, slender tail

WHIPWORM   *n* pl. -S a parasitic worm

WHIR   *v* WHIRRED, WHIRRING, WHIRS to move with a buzzing sound

WHIRL   *v* -ED, -ING, -S to revolve rapidly

WHIRLER   *n* pl. -S one that whirls

WHIRLY   *adj* WHIRLIER, WHIRLIEST marked by a whirling motion

WHIRLY   *n* pl. WHIRLIES a small tornado

WHIRR   *v* -ED, -ING, -S to whir

WHIRRED   past tense of whir

WHIRRING   present participle of whir

WHIRRY   *v* -RIED, -RYING, -RIES to hurry

WHISH   *v* -ED, -ING, -ES to move with a hissing sound

WHISHT   *v* -ED, -ING, -S to hush

WHISK   *v* -ED, -ING, -S to move briskly

WHISKER   *n* pl. -S a hair on a man's face WHISKERY *adj*

WHISKEY   *n* pl. -KEYS a liquor

WHISKY   *n* pl. -KIES whiskey

WHISPER   *v* -ED, -ING, -S to speak softly

WHISPERY   *adj* resembling a whisper

WHIST   *v* -ED, -ING, -S to hush

WHISTLE   *v* -TLED, -TLING, -TLES to make a shrill, clear musical sound

WHISTLER   *n* pl. -S one that whistles

WHIT   *n* pl. -S a particle

WHITE   *adj* WHITER, WHITEST of the color of pure snow

WHITE   *v* WHITED, WHITING, WHITES to whiten

WHITECAP   *n* pl. -S a wave with a crest of foam

WHITEFLY   *n* pl. -FLIES a small whitish insect

WHITELY   *adv* in a white manner

WHITEN   *v* -ED, -ING, -S to make white

WHITENER   *n* pl. -S one that whitens

WHITEOUT   *n* pl. -S an arctic weather condition

WHITER   comparative of white

WHITEST   superlative of white

WHITEY   *n* pl. -EYS a white man — an offensive term

WHITHER   *adv* to what place

WHITIES   pl. of whity — an offensive term

WHITING   *n* pl. -S a marine food fish

WHITISH   *adj* somewhat white

WHITLOW   *n* pl. -S an inflammation of the finger or toe

WHITRACK   *n* pl. -S a weasel

WHITTER   *n* pl. -S a large draft of liquor

WHITTLE   *v* -TLED, -TLING, -TLES to cut or shave bits from

WHITTLER   *n* pl. -S one that whittles

WHITTRET   *n* pl. -S a weasel

WHITY   *n* pl. WHITIES whitey — an offensive term

WHIZ   *v* WHIZZED, WHIZZING, WHIZZES to move with a buzzing or hissing sound

WHIZBANG   *n* pl. -S a type of explosive shell

WHIZZ   *v* -ED, -ING, -ES to whiz

WHIZZED   past tense of whiz

WHIZZER   *n* pl. -S one that whizzes

WHIZZES present 3d person sing. of whiz

WHIZZING present participle of whiz

WHO *pron* what or which person or persons

WHOA *interj* — used to command an animal to stop

WHODUNIT *n* pl. -S a mystery story

WHOEVER *pron* whatever person

WHOLE *n* pl. -S all the parts or elements entering into and making up a thing

WHOLISM *n* pl. -S holism

WHOLLY *adv* totally

WHOM *pron* the objective case of who

WHOMEVER *pron* the objective case of whoever

WHOMP *v* -ED, -ING, -S to defeat decisively

WHOMSO *pron* the objective case of whoso

WHOOP *v* -ED, -ING, -S to utter loud cries

WHOOPEE *n* pl. -S boisterous fun

WHOOPER *n* pl. -S one that whoops

WHOOPLA *n* pl. -S a noisy commotion

WHOOSH *v* -ED, -ING, -ES to move with a hissing sound

WHOOSIS *n* pl. -SISES an object or person whose name is not known

WHOP *v* WHOPPED, WHOPPING, WHOPS to strike forcibly

WHOPPER *n* pl. -S something unusually large

WHORE *v* WHORED, WHORING, WHORES to consort with prostitutes

WHOREDOM *n* pl. -S prostitution

WHORESON *n* pl. -S a bastard

WHORING present participle of whore

WHORISH *adj* lewd

WHORL *n* pl. -S a circular arrangement of similar parts WHORLED *adj*

WHORT *n* pl. -S an edible berry

WHORTLE *n* pl. -S whort

WHOSE *pron* the possessive case of who

WHOSEVER *pron* the possessive case of whoever

WHOSIS *n* pl. -SISES whoosis

WHOSO *pron* whoever

WHUMP *v* -ED, -ING, -S to thump

WHY *n* pl. WHYS the reason or cause of something

WHYDAH *n* pl. -S an African bird

WICH *n* pl. -ES wych

WICK *n* pl. -S a bundle of loosely twisted fibers in a candle or oil lamp

WICKAPE *n* pl. -S wicopy

WICKED *adj* -EDER, -EDEST evil WICKEDLY *adv*

WICKER *n* pl. -S a slender, pliant twig or branch

WICKET *n* pl. -S a small door or gate

WICKING *n* pl. -S material for wicks

WICKIUP *n* pl. -S an American Indian hut

WICKYUP *n* pl. -S wickiup

WICOPY *n* pl. -PIES a flowering shrub

WIDDER *n* pl. -S a widow

WIDDIE *n* pl. -S widdy

WIDDLE *v* -DLED, -DLING, -DLES to wriggle

WIDDY *n* pl. -DIES a hangman's noose

WIDE *adj* WIDER, WIDEST having great extent from side to side WIDELY *adv*

WIDE *n* pl. -S a type of bowled ball in cricket

WIDEN *v* -ED, -ING, -S to make wide or wider

WIDENER *n* pl. -S one that widens

WIDENESS *n* pl. -ES the state of being wide

WIDER comparative of wide

WIDEST superlative of wide

WIDGEON *n* pl. -S a river duck

WIDGET *n* pl. -S a gadget

WIDISH *adj* somewhat wide

WIDOW *v* -ED, -ING, -S to deprive of a husband

WIDOWER *n* pl. -S a man whose wife has died and who has not remarried

WIDTH *n* pl. -S extent from side to side

WIDTHWAY *adv* from side to side

WIELD *v* -ED, -ING, -S to handle or use effectively

WIELDER *n* pl. -S one that wields

WIELDY *adj* WIELDIER, WIELDIEST easily wielded

WIENER *n* pl. -S a frankfurter

WIENIE *n* pl. -S a wiener

WIFE *n* pl. WIVES a woman married to a man

WIFE   v WIFED, WIFING, WIFES to wive

WIFEDOM   n pl. -S the status or function of a wife

WIFEHOOD   n pl. -S the state of being a wife

WIFELESS   adj having no wife

WIFELIKE   adj wifely

WIFELY   adj -LIER, -LIEST of or befitting a wife

WIFING   present participle of wife

WIG   v WIGGED, WIGGING, WIGS to provide with a wig (an artificial covering of hair for the head)

WIGAN   n pl. -S a stiff fabric

WIGEON   n pl. -S widgeon

WIGGED   past tense of wig

WIGGERY   n pl. -GERIES a wig

WIGGING   n pl. -S a scolding

WIGGLE   v -GLED, -GLING, -GLES to move with short, quick movements from side to side

WIGGLER   n pl. -S one that wiggles

WIGGLY   adj -GLIER, -GLIEST tending to wiggle

WIGHT   n pl. -S a living being

WIGLESS   adj having no wig

WIGLET   n pl. -S a small wig

WIGLIKE   adj resembling a wig

WIGMAKER   n pl. -S one that makes wigs

WIGWAG   v -WAGGED, -WAGGING, -WAGS to move back and forth

WIGWAM   n pl. -S an American Indian dwelling

WIKIUP   n pl. -S wickiup

WILCO   interj — used to indicate that a message received will be complied with

WILD   adj WILDER, WILDEST living in a natural state

WILD   n pl. -S an uninhabited or uncultivated area

WILDCAT   v -CATTED, -CATTING, -CATS to search for oil in an area of doubtful productivity

WILDER   v -ED, -ING, -S to bewilder

WILDFIRE   n pl. -S a raging, destructive fire

WILDFOWL   n pl. -S a wild game bird

WILDING   n pl. -S a wild plant or animal

WILDISH   adj somewhat wild

WILDLIFE   n pl. WILDLIFE wild animals and vegetation

WILDLING   n pl. -S a wilding

WILDLY   adv in a wild manner

WILDNESS   n pl. -ES the state of being wild

WILDWOOD   n pl. -S natural forest land

WILE   v WILED, WILING, WILES to entice

WILFUL   adj willful WILFULLY adv

WILIER   comparative of wily

WILIEST   superlative of wily

WILILY   adv in a wily manner

WILINESS   n pl. -ES the quality of being wily

WILING   present participle of wile

WILL   v -ED, -ING, -S to decide upon WILLABLE adj

WILL   v past sing. 2d person WOULD, WOULDEST, or WOULDST — used as an auxiliary followed by a simple infinitive to express futurity, inclination, likelihood, or requirement

WILLER   n pl. -S one that wills

WILLET   n pl. -S a shore bird

WILLFUL   adj bent on having one's own way

WILLIED   past tense of willy

WILLIES   present 3d person sing. of willy

WILLING   adj -INGER, -INGEST inclined or favorably disposed in mind

WILLIWAU   n pl. -S williwaw

WILLIWAW   n pl. -S a violent gust of cold wind

WILLOW   v -ED, -ING, -S to clean textile fibers with a certain machine

WILLOWER   n pl. -S one that willows

WILLOWY   adj -LOWIER, -LOWIEST pliant

WILLY   v -LIED, -LYING, -LIES to willow

WILLYARD   adj willful

WILLYART   adj willyard

WILLYWAW   n pl. -S williwaw

WILT   v -ED, -ING, -S to become limp

WILY   adj WILIER, WILIEST crafty

WIMBLE   v -BLED, -BLING, -BLES to bore with a hand tool

WIMPLE   v -PLED, -PLING, -PLES to pleat

WIN   v WON or WAN, WINNING, WINS to be victorious

WIN   v WINNED, WINNING, WINS to winnow

WINCE   v WINCED, WINCING, WINCES to flinch

WINCER	*n pl.* -S one that winces	**WINE**	*v* WINED, WINING, WINES to provide with wine (the fermented juice of the grape)
WINCEY	*n pl.* -CEYS a type of fabric		
WINCH	*v* -ED, -ING, -ES to raise with a winch (a hoisting machine)	**WINELESS**	*adj* having no wine
		WINERY	*n pl.* -ERIES an establishment for making wine
WINCHER	*n pl.* -S one that winches		
WINCING	present participle of wince	**WINESHOP**	*n pl.* -S a shop where wine is sold
WIND	*v* WOUND or WINDED, WINDING, WINDS to pass around an object or fixed center WINDABLE *adj*	**WINESKIN**	*n pl.* -S a goatskin bag for holding wine
		WINESOP	*n pl.* -S a food sopped in wine
WINDAGE	*n pl.* -S the effect of the wind (air in natural motion) on a projectile	**WINEY**	*adj* WINIER, WINIEST winy
		WING	*v* -ED, -ING, -S to travel by means of wings (organs of flight)
WINDBAG	*n pl.* -S a talkative person		
WINDBURN	*v* -BURNED or -BURNT, -BURNING, -BURNS to be affected with skin irritation caused by exposure to the wind	**WINGBACK**	*n pl.* -S a certain player in football
		WINGBOW	*n pl.* -S a mark on the wing of a domestic fowl
WINDER	*n pl.* -S one that winds		
WINDFALL	*n pl.* -S a sudden and unexpected gain	**WINGDING**	*n pl.* -S a lively party
		WINGEDLY	*adv* swiftly
WINDFLAW	*n pl.* -S a gust of wind	**WINGER**	*n pl.* -S a certain player in soccer
WINDGALL	*n pl.* -S a swelling on a horse's leg		
		WINGIER	comparative of wingy
WINDIER	comparative of windy	**WINGIEST**	superlative of wingy
WINDIEST	superlative of windy	**WINGLESS**	*adj* having no wings
WINDIGO	*n pl.* -GOS an evil demon in Algonquian mythology	**WINGLET**	*n pl.* -S a small wing
		WINGLIKE	*adj* resembling a wing
WINDILY	*adv* in a windy manner	**WINGMAN**	*n pl.* -MEN a pilot behind the leader of a flying formation
WINDING	*n pl.* -S material wound about an object		
		WINGOVER	*n pl.* -S a flight maneuver
WINDLASS	*v* -ED, -ING, -ES to raise with a windlass (a hoisting machine)	**WINGSPAN**	*n pl.* -S the distance from the tip of one of a pair of wings to that of the other
WINDLE	*v* -DLED, -DLING, -DLES to wind		
		WINGY	*adj* WINGIER, WINGIEST swift
WINDLESS	*adj* being without wind	**WINIER**	comparative of winey and winy
WINDLING	*n pl.* -S a bundle of straw	**WINIEST**	superlative of winey and winy
WINDMILL	*v* -ED, -ING, -S to rotate solely under the force of a passing airstream	**WINING**	present participle of wine
		WINISH	*adj* winy
		WINK	*v* -ED, -ING, -S to close and open one eye quickly
WINDOW	*v* -ED, -ING, -S to provide with a window (an opening in a wall to admit light and air)		
		WINKER	*n pl.* -S one that winks
WINDPIPE	*n pl.* -S the trachea	**WINKLE**	*v* -KLED, -KLING, -KLES to displace, extract, or evict from a position
WINDROW	*v* -ED, -ING, -S to arrange in long rows, as hay or grain		
		WINNABLE	*adj* able to be won
WINDSOCK	*n pl.* -S a device used to indicate wind direction	**WINNED**	past tense of win (to winnow)
		WINNER	*n pl.* -S one that wins
WINDUP	*n pl.* -S a conclusion	**WINNING**	*n pl.* -S money won in a game or competition
WINDWARD	*n pl.* -S the direction from which the wind blows		
		WINNOCK	*n pl.* -S a window
WINDWAY	*n pl.* -WAYS a passage for air	**WINNOW**	*v* -ED, -ING, -S to free grain from impurities
WINDY	*adj* WINDIER, WINDIEST marked by strong wind		

WINNOWER n pl. -S one that winnows

WINO n pl. WINOES or WINOS one who is habitually drunk on wine

WINSOME adj -SOMER, -SOMEST charming

WINTER v -ED, -ING, -S to pass the winter (the coldest season of the year)

WINTERER n pl. -S one that winters

WINTERLY adj wintry

WINTERY adj -TERIER, -TERIEST wintry

WINTLE v -TLED, -TLING, -TLES to stagger

WINTRY adj -TRIER, -TRIEST characteristic of winter **WINTRILY** adv

WINY adj WINIER, WINIEST having the taste or qualities of wine

WINZE n pl. -S a steeply inclined mine shaft

WIPE v WIPED, WIPING, WIPES to rub lightly in order to clean or dry

WIPEOUT n pl. -S a fall from a surfboard

WIPER n pl. -S one that wipes

WIPING present participle of wipe

WIRE v WIRED, WIRING, WIRES to fasten with wire (a slender rod, strand, or thread of ductile metal) **WIRABLE** adj

WIREDRAW v -DREW, -DRAWN, -DRAWING, -DRAWS to draw into wire

WIREHAIR n pl. -S a dog having a wiry coat

WIRELESS v -ED, -ING, -ES to radio

WIRELIKE adj resembling wire

WIREMAN n pl. -MEN one who makes or works with wire

WIRER n pl. -S one that wires

WIRETAP v -TAPPED, -TAPPING, -TAPS to intercept messages by means of a concealed monitoring device

WIREWAY n pl. -WAYS a tube for protecting electric wires

WIREWORK n pl. -S an article made of wire

WIREWORM n pl. -S a wirelike worm

WIRIER comparative of wiry

WIRIEST superlative of wiry

WIRILY adv in a wiry manner

WIRINESS n pl. -ES the quality of being wiry

WIRING n pl. -S a system of electric wires

WIRRA interj — used to express sorrow

WIRY adj WIRIER, WIRIEST resembling wire

WIS v past tense WIST to know — WIS and WIST are the only accepted forms of this verb; it cannot be conjugated further

WISDOM n pl. -S the power of true and right discernment

WISE v WISED, WISING, WISES to become aware or informed

WISE adj WISER, WISEST having wisdom

WISEACRE n pl. -S a pretentiously wise person

WISED past tense of wise

WISELY adv -LIER, -LIEST in a wise manner

WISENESS n pl. -ES wisdom

WISENT n pl. -S a European bison

WISER comparative of wise

WISEST superlative of wise

WISH v -ED, -ING, -ES to feel an impulse toward attainment or possession of something

WISHA interj — used to express surprise

WISHBONE n pl. -S a forked bone in front of a bird's breastbone

WISHER n pl. -S one that wishes

WISHFUL adj desirous

WISHLESS adj not wishful

WISING present participle of wise

WISP v -ED, -ING, -S to twist into a wisp (a small bunch or bundle)

WISPIER comparative of wispy

WISPIEST superlative of wispy

WISPILY adv in a wispy manner

WISPISH adj wispy

WISPLIKE adj wispy

WISPY adj WISPIER, WISPIEST resembling a wisp

WISS v -ED, -ING, -ES to wish

WIST v -ED, -ING, -S to know

WISTARIA n pl. -S wisteria

WISTERIA n pl. -S a flowering shrub

WISTFUL adj yearning

WIT n pl. -S intelligence

WIT v WIST, WITING or WITTING, present sing. 1st person WOT, 2d WOST or WOSTTETH, 3d WOT or WOTTETH, present pl. WITE or WITEN to know

WITAN	n/pl the members of a national council in Anglo-Saxon England
WITCH	v -ED, -ING, -ES to bewitch
WITCHERY	n pl. -ERIES sorcery
WITCHING	n pl. -S sorcery
WITCHY	adj WITCHIER, WITCHIEST malicious
WITE	v WITED, WITING, WITES to blame
WITEN	a present pl. of wit
WITH	prep in the company of
WITHAL	adv in addition
WITHDRAW	v -DREW, -DRAWN, -DRAWING, -DRAWS to move back or away
WITHE	v WITHED, WITHING, WITHES to bind with flexible twigs
WITHER	v -ED, -ING, -S to dry up and wilt
WITHERER	n pl. -S one that withers
WITHHOLD	v -HELD, -HOLDING, -HOLDS to hold back
WITHIER	comparative of withy
WITHIES	pl. of withy
WITHIEST	superlative of withy
WITHIN	n pl. -S an interior place or area
WITHING	present participle of withe
WITHOUT	n pl. -S an exterior place or area
WITHY	n pl. WITHIES a flexible twig
WITHY	adj WITHIER, WITHIEST flexible and tough
WITING	present participle of wit and wite
WITLESS	adj lacking intelligence
WITLING	n pl. -S one who considers himself witty
WITLOOF	n pl. -S chicory
WITNESS	v -ED, -ING, -ES to see or know by personal experience
WITNEY	n pl. -NEYS a heavy woolen fabric
WITTED	adj having intelligence
WITTIER	comparative of witty
WITTIEST	superlative of witty
WITTILY	adv in a witty manner
WITTING	n pl. -S knowledge
WITTOL	n pl. -S a man who tolerates his wife's infidelity
WITTY	adj -TIER, -TIEST humorously clever
WIVE	v WIVED, WIVING, WIVES to marry a woman

WIVER	n pl. -S wivern
WIVERN	n pl. -S a two-legged dragon
WIVES	pl. of wife
WIVING	present participle of wive
WIZ	n pl. -ES a very clever or skillful person
WIZARD	n pl. -S a sorcerer **WIZARDLY** adj
WIZARDRY	n pl. -RIES sorcery
WIZEN	v -ED, -ING, -S to shrivel
WIZZEN	n pl. -S weasand
WO	n pl. WOS woe
WOAD	n pl. -S a blue dye **WOADED** adj
WOADWAX	n pl. -ES an ornamental shrub
WOALD	n pl. -S a yellow pigment
WOBBLE	v -BLED, -BLING, -BLES to move unsteadily
WOBBLER	n pl. -S one that wobbles
WOBBLY	adj -BLIER, -BLIEST unsteady
WOBBLY	n pl. -BLIES a member of the Industrial Workers of the World
WOBEGONE	adj affected with woe
WOE	n pl. -S tremendous grief
WOEFUL	adj -FULLER, -FULLEST full of woe **WOEFULLY** adv
WOENESS	n pl. -ES sadness
WOESOME	adj woeful
WOFUL	adj woeful **WOFULLY** adv
WOK	n pl. -S a cooking utensil
WOKE	a past tense of wake
WOKEN	a past participle of wake
WOLD	n pl. -S an elevated tract of open land
WOLF	n pl. WOLVES a carnivorous mammal
WOLF	v -ED, -ING, -S to devour voraciously
WOLFER	n pl. -S one who hunts wolves
WOLFFISH	n pl. -ES a marine fish
WOLFISH	adj wolflike
WOLFLIKE	adj resembling a wolf
WOLFRAM	n pl. -S tungsten
WOLVER	n pl. -S wolfer
WOLVES	pl. of wolf
WOMAN	n pl. WOMEN an adult human female
WOMAN	v -ED, -ING, -S to play the part of a woman
WOMANISE	v -ISED, -ISING, -ISES to womanize

WOMANISH *adj* characteristic of a woman

WOMANIZE *v* -IZED, -IZING, -IZES to make effeminate

WOMANLY *adj* -LIER, -LIEST having the qualities of a woman

WOMB *n* pl. -S the uterus **WOMBED** *adj*

WOMBAT *n* pl. -S a nocturnal mammal

WOMBY *adj* WOMBIER, WOMBIEST hollow

WOMEN pl. of woman

WOMERA *n* pl. -S a device used to propel spears

WOMMERA *n* pl. -S womera

WON *v* WONNED, WONNING, WONS to dwell

WONDER *v* -ED, -ING, -S to have a feeling of curiosity or doubt

WONDERER *n* pl. -S one that wonders

WONDROUS *adj* marvelous

WONKY *adj* -KIER, -KIEST unsteady

WONNED past tense of won

WONNER *n* pl. -S a prodigy

WONNING present participle of won

WONT *v* -ED, -ING, -S to make accustomed to

WONTEDLY *adv* in a usual manner

WONTON *n* pl. -S a pork-filled dumpling used in Chinese cooking

WOO *v* -ED, -ING, -S to seek the affection of

WOOD *v* -ED, -ING, -S to furnish with wood (the hard, fibrous substance beneath the bark of a tree or shrub)

WOODBIN *n* pl. -S a bin for holding firewood

WOODBIND *n* pl. -S woodbine

WOODBINE *n* pl. -S a European shrub

WOODBOX *n* pl. -ES a woodbin

WOODCHAT *n* pl. -S a European shrike

WOODCOCK *n* pl. -S a game bird

WOODCUT *n* pl. -S an engraved block of wood

WOODEN *adj* -ENER, -ENEST resembling wood in stiffness **WOODENLY** *adv*

WOODHEN *n* pl. -S the weka

WOODIER comparative of woody

WOODIEST superlative of woody

WOODLAND *n* pl. -S land covered with trees

WOODLARK *n* pl. -S a songbird

WOODLESS *adj* having no wood

WOODLORE *n* pl. -S knowledge of the forest

WOODLOT *n* pl. -S an area restricted to the growing of forest trees

WOODMAN *n* pl. -MEN woodsman

WOODNOTE *n* pl. -S a song or call of a forest bird

WOODPILE *n* pl. -S a pile of wood

WOODRUFF *n* pl. -S an aromatic herb

WOODSHED *v* -SHEDDED, -SHEDDING, -SHEDS to practice on a musical instrument

WOODSIA *n* pl. -S a small fern

WOODSMAN *n* pl. -MEN one who works or lives in the forest

WOODSY *adj* WOODSIER, WOODSIEST suggestive of a forest

WOODWAX *n* pl. -ES woadwax

WOODWIND *n* pl. -S a musical wind instrument

WOODWORK *n* pl. -S work made of wood

WOODWORM *n* pl. -S a wood-boring worm

WOODY *adj* WOODIER, WOODIEST containing or resembling wood

WOOER *n* pl. -S one that woos

WOOF *v* -ED, -ING, -S to utter a gruff barking sound

WOOFER *n* pl. -S a loudspeaker designed to reproduce low-pitched sounds

WOOINGLY *adv* attractively

WOOL *n* pl. -S the dense, soft hair forming the coat of certain mammals **WOOLED** *adj*

WOOLEN *n* pl. -S a fabric made of wool

WOOLER *n* pl. -S a domestic animal raised for its wool

WOOLFELL *n* pl. -S woolskin

WOOLIE *n* pl. -S a woolly

WOOLIER comparative of wooly

WOOLIES pl. of wooly

WOOLIEST superlative of wooly

WOOLLEN *n* pl. -S woolen

WOOLLIER comparative of woolly

WOOLLIES pl. of woolly

WOOLLIEST superlative of woolly

WOOLLIKE *adj* resembling wool

WOOLLY *adj* -LIER, -LIEST consisting of or resembling wool

WOOLLY *n* pl. -LIES a garment made of wool

WOOLMAN *n* pl. -MEN a dealer in wool

WOOLPACK *n* pl. -S a bag for packing a bale of wool

WOOLSACK *n* pl. -S a sack of wool

WOOLSHED *n* pl. -S a building in which sheep are sheared

WOOLSKIN *n* pl. -S a sheepskin with the wool still on it

WOOLY *adj* WOOLIER, WOOLIEST woolly

WOOLY *n* pl. WOOLIES a woolly

WOOMERA *n* pl. -S womera

WOOPS *interj* oops

WOORALI *n* pl. -S curare

WOORARI *n* pl. -S curare

WOOSH *v* -ED, -ING, -ES to whoosh

WOOZY *adj* -ZIER, -ZIEST dazed WOOZILY *adv*

WOP *n* pl. -S an Italian — an offensive term

WORD *v* -ED, -ING, -S to express in words (speech sounds that communicate meaning)

WORDAGE *n* pl. -S the number of words used

WORDBOOK *n* pl. -S a dictionary

WORDIER comparative of wordy

WORDIEST superlative of wordy

WORDILY *adv* in a wordy manner

WORDING *n* pl. -S the act or style of expressing in words

WORDLESS *adj* being without words

WORDPLAY *n* pl. -PLAYS a witty exchange of words

WORDY *adj* WORDIER, WORDIEST using many or too many words

WORE past tense of wear

WORK *v* WORKED or WROUGHT, WORKING, WORKS to exert one's powers of body or mind for some purpose

WORKABLE *adj* capable of being done

WORKADAY *adj* everyday

WORKBAG *n* pl. -S a bag for holding work instuments and materials

WORKBOAT *n* pl. -S a boat used for commercial purposes

WORKBOOK *n* pl. -S an exercise book for a student

WORKBOX *n* pl. -ES a box for holding work instruments and materials

WORKDAY *n* pl. -DAYS a day on which work is done

WORKER *n* pl. -S one that works

WORKFOLK *n/pl* manual laborers

WORKING *n* pl. -S a mining excavation

WORKLESS *adj* unemployed

WORKLOAD *n* pl. -S the amount of work assigned to an employee

WORKMAN *n* pl. -MEN a male worker

WORKOUT *n* pl. -S a period of physical exercise

WORKROOM *n* pl. -S a room in which work is done

WORKSHOP *n* pl. -S a workroom

WORKUP *n* pl. -S an intensive diagnostic study

WORKWEEK *n* pl. -S the number of hours worked in a week

WORLD *n* pl. -S the earth and all its inhabitants

WORLDLY *adj* -LIER, -LIEST pertaining to the world

WORM *v* -ED, -ING, -S to rid of worms (small, limbless invertebrates)

WORMER *n* pl. -S one that worms

WORMHOLE *n* pl. -S a hole made by a burrowing worm

WORMIER comparative of wormy

WORMIEST superlative of wormy

WORMIL *n* pl. -S a lump in the skin of an animal's back

WORMISH *adj* wormlike

WORMLIKE *adj* resembling a worm

WORMROOT *n* pl. -S pinkroot

WORMSEED *n* pl. -S a tropical plant

WORMWOOD *n* pl. -S a European herb

WORMY *adj* WORMIER, WORMIEST infested with worms

WORN *adj* affected by wear or use

WORNNESS *n* pl. -ES the state of being worn

WORRIED past tense of worry

WORRIER *n* pl. -S one that worries

WORRIT *v* -ED, -ING, -S to worry

WORRY *v* -RIED, -RYING, -RIES to feel anxious and uneasy about something

WORSE *n* pl. -S something that is worse (bad in a greater degree)

WORSEN *v* -ED, -ING, -S to make or become worse

WORSER *adj* worse

WORSET *n* pl. -S worsted

WORSHIP — *v* -SHIPED, -SHIPING, -SHIPS or -SHIPPED, -SHIPPING, -SHIPS to honor and love as a divine being

WORST — *v* -ED, -ING, -S to defeat

WORSTED — *n* pl. -S a woolen yarn

WORT — *n* pl. -S a plant, herb, or vegetable

WORTH — *v* -ED, -ING, -S to befall

WORTHFUL — *adj* worthy

WORTHY — *adj* -THIER, -THIEST having value or merit **WORTHILY** *adv*

WORTHY — *n* pl. -THIES a worthy person

WOST — a present 2d person sing. of wit

WOSTTETH — a present 2d person sing. of wit

WOT — *v* WOTTED, WOTTING, WOTS to know

WOTTETH — a present 3d person sing. of wit

WOULD — past tense of will

WOULDEST — a 2d person sing. past tense of will

WOULDST — a 2d person sing. past tense of will

WOUND — *v* -ED, -ING, -S to inflict an injury upon

WOVE — a past tense of weave

WOVEN — past participle of weave

WOW — *v* -ED, -ING, -S to excite to enthusiastic approval

WOWSER — *n* pl. -S a puritanical person

WRACK — *v* -ED, -ING, -S to wreck

WRACKFUL — *adj* destructive

WRAITH — *n* pl. -S a ghost

WRANG — *n* pl. -S a wrong

WRANGLE — *v* -GLED, -GLING, -GLES to argue noisily

WRANGLER — *n* pl. -S one that wrangles

WRAP — *v* WRAPPED or WRAPT, WRAPPING, WRAPS to enclose in something wound or folded about

WRAPPER — *n* pl. -S one that wraps

WRAPPING — *n* pl. -S the material in which something is wrapped

WRAPT — a past tense of wrap

WRASSE — *n* pl. -S a marine fish

WRASTLE — *v* -TLED, -TLING, -TLES to wrestle

WRATH — *v* -ED, -ING, -S to make wrathful

WRATHFUL — *adj* extremely angry

WRATHY — *adj* WRATHIER, WRATHIEST wrathful **WRATHILY** *adv*

WREAK — *v* -ED, -ING, -S to inflict

WREAKER — *n* pl. -S one that wreaks

WREATH — *n* pl. -S a band of flowers **WREATHY** *adj*

WREATHE — *v* WREATHED, WREATHEN, WREATHING, WREATHES to shape into a wreath

WRECK — *v* -ED, -ING, -S to cause the ruin of

WRECKAGE — *n* pl. -S the act of wrecking

WRECKER — *n* pl. -S one that wrecks

WRECKFUL — *adj* destructive

WRECKING — *n* pl. -S the occupation of salvaging wrecked objects

WREN — *n* pl. -S a small songbird

WRENCH — *v* -ED, -ING, -ES to twist suddenly and forcibly

WREST — *v* -ED, -ING, -S to take away by force

WRESTER — *n* pl. -S one that wrests

WRESTLE — *v* -TLED, -TLING, -TLES to engage in a type of hand-to-hand contest

WRESTLER — *n* pl. -S one that wrestles

WRETCH — *n* pl. -ES a wretched person

WRETCHED — *adj* -EDER, -EDEST extremely unhappy

WRIED — past tense of wry

WRIER — a comparative of wry

WRIES — present 3d person sing. of wry

WRIEST — a superlative of wry

WRIGGLE — *v* -GLED, -GLING, -GLES to turn or twist in a sinuous manner

WRIGGLER — *n* pl. -S one that wriggles

WRIGGLY — *adj* -GLIER, -GLIEST wriggling

WRIGHT — *n* pl. -S one who constructs or creates

WRING — *v* WRUNG or WRINGED, WRINGING, WRINGS to twist so as to compress

WRINGER — *n* pl. -S one that wrings

WRINKLE — *v* -KLED, -KLING, -KLES to make wrinkles (small ridges or furrows) in

WRINKLY — *adj* -KLIER, -KLIEST having wrinkles

WRIST — *n* pl. -S the junction between the hand and forearm

WRISTLET — *n* pl. -S a band worn around the wrist

WRISTY	*adj* WRISTIER, WRISTIEST using much wrist action
WRIT	*n* pl. -S a written legal order
WRITE	*v* WROTE, WRITTEN, WRITING, WRITES to form characters or symbols on a surface with an instrument **WRITABLE** *adj*
WRITER	*n* pl. -S one that writes
WRITHE	*v* WRITHED, WRITHING, WRITHES to squirm or twist in pain
WRITHEN	*adj* twisted
WRITHER	*n* pl. -S one that writhes
WRITHING	present participle of writhe
WRITING	*n* pl. -S a written composition
WRITTEN	past participle of write
WRONG	*adj* WRONGER, WRONGEST not according to what is right, proper, or correct
WRONG	*v* -ED, -ING, -S to treat injuriously or unjustly
WRONGER	*n* pl. -S one that wrongs
WRONGFUL	*adj* wrong
WRONGLY	*adv* in a wrong manner
WROTE	past tense of write

WROTH	*adj* very angry
WROTHFUL	*adj* wroth
WROUGHT	a past tense of work
WRUNG	a past tense of wring
WRY	*adj* WRIER, WRIEST or WRYER, WRYEST contorted **WRYLY** *adv*
WRY	*v* WRIED, WRYING, WRIES to contort
WRYNECK	*n* pl. -S a European bird
WRYNESS	*n* pl. -ES the state of being wry
WUD	*adj* insane
WURST	*n* pl. -S sausage
WURZEL	*n* pl. -S a variety of beet
WYCH	*n* pl. -ES a European elm
WYE	*n* pl. -S the letter Y
WYLE	*v* WYLED, WYLING, WYLES to beguile
WYND	*n* pl. -S a narrow street
WYNN	*n* pl. -S the rune for W
WYTE	*v* WYTED, WYTING, WYTES to wite
WYVERN	*n* pl. -S wivern

XANTHATE *n* pl. -S a chemical salt

XANTHEIN *n* pl. -S the water-soluble part of the coloring matter in yellow flowers

XANTHENE *n* pl. -S a chemical compound

XANTHIC *adj* tending to have a yellow color

XANTHIN *n* pl. -S a yellow pigment

XANTHINE *n* pl. -S a chemical compound

XANTHOMA *n* pl. -MAS or -MATA a skin disease

XANTHONE *n* pl. -S a chemical compound

XANTHOUS *adj* yellow

XEBEC *n* pl. -S a Mediterranean sailing vessel

XENIA *n* pl. -S the effect of pollen on certain plant structures **XENIAL** *adj*

XENIC *adj* pertaining to a type of culture medium

XENOGAMY *n* pl. -MIES the transfer of pollen from one plant to another

XENOGENY *n* pl. -NIES the supposed production of offspring totally different from the parent

XENOLITH *n* pl. -S a rock fragment included in another rock

XENON *n* pl. -S a gaseous element

XERARCH *adj* developing in a dry area

XERIC *adj* requiring only a small amount of moisture

XEROSERE *n* pl. -S a dry-land sere

XEROSIS *n* pl. -ROSES abnormal dryness of a body part or tissue **XEROTIC** *adj*

XERUS *n* pl. -ES an African ground squirrel

XI *n* pl. -S a Greek letter

XIPHOID *n* pl. -S a part of the sternum

XU *n* pl. XU a monetary unit of Vietnam

XYLAN *n* pl. -S a substance found in cell walls of plants

XYLEM *n* pl. -S a complex plant tissue

XYLENE *n* pl. -S a flammable hydrocarbon

XYLIDIN *n* pl. -S xylidine

XYLIDINE *n* pl. -S a chemical compound

XYLOCARP *n* pl. -S a hard, woody fruit

XYLOID *adj* resembling wood

XYLOL *n* pl. -S xylene

XYLOSE *n* pl. -S a type of sugar

XYLOTOMY *n* pl. -MIES the preparation of sections of wood for microscopic examination

XYLYL *n* pl. -S a univalent radical

XYST *n* pl. -S xystus

XYSTER *n* pl. -S a surgical instrument for scraping bones

XYSTOS *n* pl. -TOI xystus

XYSTUS *n* pl. -TI a roofed area where athletes trained in ancient Greece

YA	*pron* you
YABBER	*v* -ED, -ING, -S to jabber
YACHT	*v* -ED, -ING, -S to sail in a yacht (a vessel used for pleasure cruising or racing)
YACHTER	*n pl.* -S one who sails a yacht
YACHTING	*n pl.* -S the sport of sailing in yachts
YACHTMAN	*n pl.* -MEN a yachter
YACK	*v* -ED, -ING, -S to yak
YAFF	*v* -ED, -ING, -S to bark
YAGER	*n pl.* -S jaeger
YAGI	*n pl.* -S a type of shortwave antenna
YAH	*interj* — used as an exclamation of disgust
YAHOO	*n pl.* -HOOS a coarse, uncouth person
YAHOOISM	*n pl.* -S coarse, uncouth behavior
YAIRD	*n pl.* -S a garden
YAK	*v* YAKKED, YAKKING, YAKS to chatter
YALD	*adj* yauld
YAM	*n pl.* -S a plant having an edible root
YAMEN	*n pl.* -S the residence of a Chinese public official
YAMMER	*v* -ED, -ING, -S to whine or complain peevishly
YAMMERER	*n pl.* -S one that yammers
YAMUN	*n pl.* -S yamen
YANG	*n pl.* -S the masculine active principle in Chinese cosmology
YANK	*v* -ED, -ING, -S to pull suddenly
YANQUI	*n pl.* -S a United States citizen
YAP	*v* YAPPED, YAPPING, YAPS to bark shrilly
YAPOCK	*n pl.* -S an aquatic mammal
YAPOK	*n pl.* -S yapock
YAPON	*n pl.* -S yaupon
YAPPED	past tense of yap
YAPPER	*n pl.* -S one that yaps
YAPPING	present participle of yap
YAR	*adj* yare
YARD	*v* -ED, -ING, -S to put in a yard (a tract of ground adjacent to a building)
YARDAGE	*n pl.* -S the use of an enclosure for livestock at a railroad station
YARDARM	*n pl.* -S either end of a ship's spar
YARDBIRD	*n pl.* -S an army recruit
YARDMAN	*n pl.* -MEN a man employed to do outdoor work
YARDWAND	*n pl.* -S a measuring stick
YARE	*adj* YARER, YAREST nimble **YARELY** *adv*
YARMELKE	*n pl.* -S yarmulke
YARMULKE	*n pl.* -S a skullcap worn by Jewish males
YARN	*v* -ED, -ING, -S to tell a long story
YARROW	*n pl.* -S a perennial herb
YASHMAC	*n pl.* -S yashmak
YASHMAK	*n pl.* -S a veil worn by Muslim women
YASMAK	*n pl.* -S yashmak
YATAGAN	*n pl.* -S yataghan
YATAGHAN	*n pl.* -S a Turkish sword
YAUD	*n pl.* -S an old mare
YAULD	*adj* vigorous
YAUP	*v* -ED, -ING, -S to yawp
YAUPER	*n pl.* -S one that yaups
YAUPON	*n pl.* -S an evergreen shrub

YAW	v -ED, -ING, -S to deviate from an intended course
YAWL	v -ED, -ING, -S to yowl
YAWMETER	n pl. -S an instrument in an aircraft
YAWN	v -ED, -ING, -S to open the mouth wide with a deep inhalation of air
YAWNER	n pl. -S one that yawns
YAWP	v -ED, -ING, -S to utter a loud, harsh cry
YAWPER	n pl. -S one that yawps
YAWPING	n pl. -S a loud, harsh cry
YAY	adv to this extent
YCLEPED	adj yclept
YCLEPT	adj called; named
YE	pron you
YEA	n pl. -S an affirmative vote
YEAH	adv yes
YEALING	n pl. -S a person of the same age
YEAN	v -ED, -ING, -S to bear young
YEANLING	n pl. -S the young of a sheep or goat
YEAR	n pl. -S a period of time consisting of 365 or 366 days
YEARBOOK	n pl. -S a book published each year by a graduating class
YEARLIES	pl. of yearly
YEARLING	n pl. -S an animal past its first year and not yet two years old
YEARLONG	adj lasting through a year
YEARLY	n pl. -LIES a publication appearing once a year
YEARN	v -ED, -ING, -S to have a stong or deep desire
YEARNER	n pl. -S one that yearns
YEARNING	n pl. -S a strong or deep desire
YEAST	v -ED, -ING, -S to foam
YEASTY	adj YEASTIER, YEASTIEST foamy YEASTILY adv
YEELIN	n pl. -S yealing
YEGG	n pl. -S a burglar
YEGGMAN	n pl. -MEN a yegg
YEH	adv yeah
YELD	adj not giving milk
YELK	n pl. -S yolk
YELL	v -ED, -ING, -S to cry out loudly
YELLER	n pl. -S one that yells
YELLOW	adj -LOWER, -LOWEST of a bright color like that of ripe lemons YELLOWLY adv
YELLOW	v -ED, -ING, -S to make or become yellow
YELLOWY	adj somewhat yellow
YELP	v -ED, -ING, -S to utter a sharp, shrill cry
YELPER	n pl. -S one that yelps
YEN	v YENNED, YENNING, YENS to yearn
YENTA	n pl. -S a gossipy woman
YEOMAN	n pl. -MEN an independent farmer YEOMANLY adj
YEOMANRY	n pl. -RIES the collective body of yeomen
YEP	adv yes
YERBA	n pl. -S a South American beverage resembling tea
YERK	v -ED, -ING, -S to beat vigorously
YES	v YESSED, YESSING, YESSES or YESES to give an affirmative reply to
YESHIVA	n pl. -VAS or -VOTH an orthodox Jewish school
YESHIVAH	n pl. -S yeshiva
YESSED	past tense of yes
YESSES	a 3d person sing. of yes
YESSING	present participle of yes
YESTER	adj pertaining to yesterday
YESTERN	adj yester
YESTREEN	n pl. -S the previous evening
YET	adv up to now
YETI	n pl. -S the abominable snowman
YETT	n pl. -S a gate
YEUK	v -ED, -ING, -S to itch
YEUKY	adj itchy
YEW	n pl. -S an evergreen tree or shrub
YID	n pl. -S a Jew — an offensive term
YIELD	v -ED, -ING, -S to give up
YIELDER	n pl. -S one that yields
YILL	n pl. -S ale
YIN	n pl. -S the feminine passive principle in Chinese cosmology
YINCE	adv once
YIP	v YIPPED, YIPPING, YIPS to yelp
YIPE	interj — used to express fear or surprise
YIPES	interj yipe
YIPPED	past tense of yip

YIPPEE	*interj* — used to express joy
YIPPIE	*n* pl. -S a politically radical hippie
YIPPING	present participle of yip
YIRD	*n* pl. -S earth
YIRR	*v* -ED, -ING, -S to snarl
YIRTH	*n* pl. -S yird
YOD	*n* pl. -S a Hebrew letter
YODEL	*v* -DELED, -DELING, -DELS or -DELLED, -DELLING, -DELS to sing with a fluctuating voice
YODELER	*n* pl. -S one that yodels
YODELLER	*n* pl. -S yodeler
YODH	*n* pl. -S yod
YODLE	*v* -DLED, -DLING, -DLES to yodel
YODLER	*n* pl. -S yodeler
YOGA	*n* pl. -S a Hindu philosophy involving physical and mental disciplines
YOGEE	*n* pl. -S yogi
YOGH	*n* pl. -S a Middle English letter
YOGHOURT	*n* pl. -S yogurt
YOGHURT	*n* pl. -S yogurt
YOGI	*n* pl. -S a person who practices yoga
YOGIC	*adj* pertaining to yoga
YOGIN	*n* pl. -S yogi
YOGINI	*n* pl. -S a female yogi
YOGURT	*n* pl. -S a food made from milk
YOICKS	*interj* — used to encourage hunting hounds
YOKE	*v* -YOKED, YOKING, YOKES to fit with a yoke (a wooden frame for joining together draft animals)
YOKEL	*n* pl. -S a naive or gullible rustic
YOKELESS	*adj* having no yoke
YOKELISH	*adj* resembling a yokel
YOKEMATE	*n* pl. -S a companion in work
YOKING	present participle of yoke
YOLK	*n* pl. -S the yellow portion of an egg **YOLKED** *adj*
YOLKY	*adj* YOLKIER, YOLKIEST resembling a yolk
YOM	*n* pl. YOMIM day
YON	*adv* yonder
YOND	*adv* yonder
YONDER	*adv* over there
YONI	*n* pl. -S a symbol for the vulva in Hindu religion
YONKER	*n* pl. -S younker

YORE	*n* pl. -S time past
YOU	*pron* the 2d person sing. or pl. pronoun
YOUNG	*adj* YOUNGER, YOUNGEST being in the early period of life or growth
YOUNG	*n* pl. -S offspring
YOUNGER	*n* pl. -S an inferior in age
YOUNGISH	*adj* somewhat young
YOUNKER	*n* pl. -S a young gentleman
YOUPON	*n* pl. -S yaupon
YOUR	*adj* a possessive form of the pronoun you
YOURN	*pron* yours
YOURS	*pron* a possessive form of the pronoun you
YOURSELF	*pron* pl. -SELVES a form of the 2d person pronoun
YOUSE	*pron* you
YOUTH	*n* pl. -S a young person
YOUTHEN	*v* -ED, -ING, -S to make youthful
YOUTHFUL	*adj* young
YOW	*v* -ED, -ING, -S to yowl
YOWE	*n* pl. -S a ewe
YOWIE	*n* pl. -S a small ewe
YOWL	*v* -ED, -ING, -S to utter a loud, long, mournful cry
YOWLER	*n* pl. -S one that yowls
YPERITE	*n* pl. -S a poisonous gas
YTTERBIA	*n* pl. -S a chemical compound. **YTTERBIC** *adj*
YTTRIA	*n* pl. -S a chemical compound
YTTRIUM	*n* pl. -S a metallic element **YTTRIC** *adj*
YUAN	*n* pl. -S a monetary unit of China
YUCCA	*n* pl. -S a tropical plant
YUGA	*n* pl. -S an age of time in Hinduism
YUK	*v* YUKKED, YUKKING, YUKS to laugh loudly
YULAN	*n* pl. -S a Chinese tree
YULE	*n* pl. -S Christmas time
YULETIDE	*n* pl. -S yule
YUMMY	*adj* -MIER, -MIEST delicious
YUMMY	*n* pl. -MIES something delicious
YUP	*adv* yep
YUPON	*n* pl. -S yaupon
YURT	*n* pl. YURTA or YURTS a portable tent
YWIS	*adv* iwis

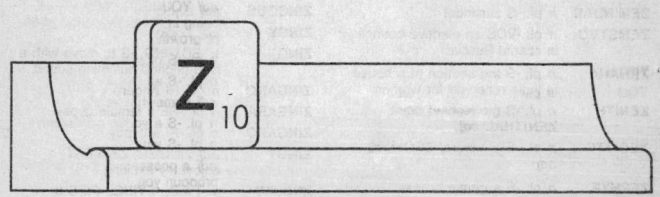

ZABAIONE n pl. -S a dessert resembling custard

ZABAJONE n pl. -S zabaione

ZACATON n pl. -S a Mexican grass

ZADDIK n pl. -DIKIM a virtuous person by Jewish religious standards

ZAFFAR n pl. -S zaffer

ZAFFER n pl. -S a blue ceramic coloring

ZAFFIR n pl. -S zaffer

ZAFFRE n pl. -S zaffer

ZAFTIG adj full-bosomed

ZAG v ZAGGED, ZAGGING, ZAGS to turn sharply

ZAIBATSU n pl. ZAIBATSU a powerful family combine in Japan

ZAIRE n pl. -S a monetary unit of Zaire

ZAMARRA n pl. -S a sheepskin coat

ZAMARRO n pl. -ROS zamarra

ZAMIA n pl. -S a tropical plant

ZAMINDAR n pl. -S a tax collector in precolonial India

ZANANA n pl. -S zenana

ZANDER n pl. -S a freshwater fish

ZANIER comparative of zany

ZANIES pl. of zany

ZANINESS n pl. -ES the quality or state of being zany

ZANY adj ZANIER, ZANIEST ludicrously comical ZANILY adv

ZANY n pl. -NIES a zany person

ZANYISH adj somewhat zany

ZANZA n pl. -S an African musical instrument

ZAP v ZAPPED, ZAPPING, ZAPS to kill or destroy

ZAPATEO n pl. -TEOS a Spanish dance

ZAPTIAH n pl. -S a Turkish policeman

ZAPTIEH n pl. -S zaptiah

ZARATITE n pl. -S a chemical compound

ZAREBA n pl. -S an improvised stockade

ZAREEBA n pl. -S zareba

ZARF n pl. -S a metal holder for a coffee cup

ZARIBA n pl. -S zareba

ZARZUELA n pl. -S a Spanish operetta

ZASTRUGA n pl. -GI sastruga

ZAX n pl. -ES a tool for cutting roof slates

ZAYIN n pl. -S a Hebrew letter

ZEAL n pl. -S enthusiastic devotion

ZEALOT n pl. -S one who is zealous

ZEALOTRY n pl. -RIES excessive zeal

ZEALOUS adj filled with zeal

ZEATIN n pl. -S a chemical compound found in maize

ZEBEC n pl. -S xebec

ZEBECK n pl. -S xebec

ZEBRA n pl. -S an African mammal that is related to the horse ZEBRAIC adj

ZEBRASS n pl. -ES the offspring of a zebra and an ass

ZEBRINE adj pertaining to a zebra

ZEBROID adj zebrine

ZEBU n pl. -S an Asian ox

ZECCHIN n pl. -S zecchino

ZECCHINO n pl. -NI or -NOS a former gold coin of Italy

ZECHIN n pl. -S zecchino

ZED n pl. -S the letter Z

ZEDOARY n pl. -ARIES the medicinal root of a tropical plant

ZEE   n pl. -S the letter Z

ZEIN   n pl. -S a simple protein

ZELKOVA   n pl. -S a Japanese tree

ZEMINDAR   n pl. -S zamindar

ZEMSTVO   n pl. -VOS an elective council in czarist Russia

ZENANA   n pl. -S the section of a house in India reserved for women

ZENITH   n pl. -S the highest point ZENITHAL adj

ZEOLITE   n pl. -S a mineral ZEOLITIC adj

ZEPHYR   n pl. -S a gentle breeze

ZEPPELIN   n pl. -S a long, rigid airship

ZERO   v -ED, -ING, -ES or -S to aim at the exact center of a target

ZEST   v -ED, -ING, -S to fill with zest (invigorating excitement)

ZESTFUL   adj full of zest

ZESTY   adj ZESTIER, ZESTIEST marked by zest

ZETA   n pl. -S a Greek letter

ZEUGMA   n pl. -S the use of a word to modify or govern two or more words, while applying to each in a different sense

ZIBELINE   n pl. -S a soft fabric

ZIBET   n pl. -S an Asian civet

ZIBETH   n pl. -S zibet

ZIG   v ZIGGED, ZIGGING, ZIGS to turn sharply

ZIGGURAT   n pl. -S an ancient Babylonian temple tower

ZIGZAG   v -ZAGGED, -ZAGGING, -ZAGS to proceed on a course marked by sharp turns

ZIKKURAT   n pl. -S ziggurat

ZIKURAT   n pl. -S ziggurat

ZILCH   n pl. -ES nothing

ZILLAH   n pl. -S an administrative district in India

ZILLION   n pl. -S an indeterminately large number

ZINC   v ZINCED, ZINCING, ZINCS or ZINCKED, ZINCKING, ZINCS to coat with zinc (a metallic element)

ZINCATE   n pl. -S a chemical salt

ZINCIC   adj pertaining to zinc

ZINCIFY   v -FIED, -FYING, -FIES to coat with zinc

ZINCITE   n pl. -S an ore of zinc

ZINCKED   a past tense of zinc

ZINCKING   a present participle of zinc

ZINCKY   adj resembling zinc

ZINCOID   adj zincic

ZINCOUS   adj zincic

ZINCY   adj zincky

ZING   v -ED, -ING, -S to move with a high-pitched humming sound

ZINGANO   n pl. -NI zingaro

ZINGARA   n pl. -RE a female gypsy

ZINGARO   n pl. -RI a gypsy

ZINGY   adj ZINGIER, ZINGIEST enjoyably exciting

ZINKIFY   v -FIED, -FYING, -FIES to zincify

ZINKY   adj zincky

ZINNIA   n pl. -S a tropical plant

ZIP   v ZIPPED, ZIPPING, ZIPS to move with speed and vigor

ZIPPER   v -ED, -ING, -S to fasten with a zipper (a fastener consisting of two rows of interlocking teeth)

ZIPPY   adj -PIER, -PIEST full of energy

ZIRAM   n pl. -S a chemical salt

ZIRCON   n pl. -S a mineral

ZIRCONIA   n pl. -S a chemical compound

ZIRCONIC   adj pertaining to a certain metallic element

ZITHER   n pl. -S a stringed instrument

ZITHERN   n pl. -S zither

ZITI   n pl. -S a tubular pasta

ZIZITH   n/pl the tassels on the four corners of a Jewish prayer shawl

ZIZZLE   v -ZLED, -ZLING, -ZLES to sizzle

ZLOTY   n pl. ZLOTYS a monetary unit of Poland

ZOA   a pl. of zoon

ZOARIUM   n pl. -IA a colony of bryozoans ZOARIAL adj

ZODIAC   n pl. -S an imaginary belt encircling the celestial sphere ZODIACAL adj

ZOEA   n pl. ZOEAE or ZOEAS a larval form of certain crustaceans ZOEAL adj

ZOFTIG   adj zaftig

ZOIC   adj pertaining to animals or animal life

ZOISITE   n pl. -S a mineral

ZOMBI   n pl. -S a snake god of voodoo cults in West Africa

ZOMBIE   n pl. -S zombi

ZOMBIISM n pl. -S the system of beliefs connected with zombis

ZONAL adj pertaining to a zone **ZONALLY** adv

ZONARY adj zonal

ZONATE adj arranged in zones

ZONATED adj zonate

ZONATION n pl. -S arrangement in zones

ZONE v ZONED, ZONING, ZONES to arrange in zones (areas distinguished from other adjacent areas)

ZONELESS adj having no zone or belt

ZONER n pl. -S one that zones

ZONETIME n pl. -S standard time used at sea

ZONING present participle of zone

ZONKED adj under the influence of alcohol or a drug

ZONULA n pl. -LAE or -LAS zonule

ZONULE n pl. -S a small zone **ZONULAR** adj

ZOO n pl. ZOOS a place where animals are kept for public exhibition

ZOOCHORE n pl. -S a plant dispersed by animals

ZOOGENIC adj caused by animals or their activities

ZOOGLEA n pl. -GLEAE or -GLEAS a jellylike mass of bacteria **ZOOGLEAL** adj

ZOOGLOEA n pl. -GLOEAE or -GLOEAS zooglea

ZOOID n pl. -S an organic cell or body capable of independent movement **ZOOIDAL** adj

ZOOKS interj — used as a mild oath

ZOOLATER n pl. -S one that worships animals

ZOOLATRY n pl. -TRIES the worship of animals

ZOOLOGY n pl. -GIES the science that deals with animals **ZOOLOGIC** adj

ZOOM v -ED, -ING, -S to move with a loud humming sound

ZOOMANIA n pl. -S an excessive interest in animals

ZOOMETRY n pl. -TRIES the measurement of animals or animal parts

ZOOMORPH n pl. -S something in the form of an animal

ZOON n pl. ZOA or ZOONS the whole product of one fertilized egg **ZOONAL** adj

ZOONOSIS n pl. -NOSES a disease that can be transmitted from animals to man **ZOONOTIC** adj

ZOOPHILE n pl. -S a lover of animals

ZOOPHYTE n pl. -S an invertebrate animal

ZOOSPERM n pl. -S the male fertilizing element of an animal

ZOOSPORE n pl. -S a type of spore

ZOOTOMY n pl. -MIES the dissection of animals **ZOOTOMIC** adj

ZORI n pl. ZORI a type of sandal

ZORIL n pl. -S a small African mammal

ZORILLA n pl. -S zoril

ZORILLE n pl. -S zoril

ZORILLO n pl. -LOS zoril

ZOSTER n pl. -S a virus disease

ZOUAVE n pl. -S a French infantryman

ZOUNDS interj — used as a mild oath

ZOWIE interj — used to express surprise or pleasure

ZOYSIA n pl. -S a perennial grass

ZUCCHINI n pl. -S a vegetable

ZWIEBACK n pl. -S a sweetened bread

ZYGOMA n pl. -MAS or -MATA the cheekbone

ZYGOSIS n pl. -GOSES the union of two gametes **ZYGOSE** adj

ZYGOSITY n pl. -TIES the makeup of a particular zygote

ZYGOTE n pl. -S a cell formed by the union of two gametes **ZYGOTIC** adj

ZYGOTENE n pl. -S a stage in meiosis

ZYMASE n pl. -S an enzyme

ZYME n pl. -S an enzyme

ZYMOGEN n pl. -S a substance that develops into an enzyme when suitably activated

ZYMOGENE n pl. -S zymogen

ZYMOLOGY n pl. -GIES the science of fermentation

ZYMOSIS n pl. -MOSES fermentation **ZYMOTIC** adj

ZYMURGY n pl. -GIES a branch of chemistry dealing with fermentation

ZYZZYVA n pl. -S a tropical weevil